ORCADIA.

THE

Saint-Clairs of the Isles.

A HISTORY

> " Resistless seas
> Surge round the storm-swept Orcades
> Where erst Saint-Clair bore princely sway
> O'er isle and islet, strait and bay,
> Still nods their palace to its fall,
> Thy pride and sorrow, fair Kirkwall "
>
> SCOTT

The Saint-Clairs of the Isles

BEING

A HISTORY OF

THE SEA-KINGS OF ORKNEY

AND

THEIR SCOTTISH SUCCESSORS OF THE SIRNAME OF SINCLAIR.

ARRANGED AND ANNOTATED

BY

ROLAND WILLIAM SAINT-CLAIR.

ILLUSTRATED THROUGHOUT.

Auckland, N.Z. :
H. BRETT, GENERAL PRINTER AND PUBLISHER, SHORTLAND AND FORT STREETS.
1898.
[ALL RIGHTS RESERVED.]

1212715

TO

THE MEMORY OF

HENRY DE ST. CLAIR, JARL, "THE HOLY,"

RULER OF ORKNEY,

PREMIER MAGNATE OF NORWAY, BARON OF ROSLIN,

LORD HIGH ADMIRAL OF SCOTLAND,

WHO FELL DEFENDING HIS REALM, THIS HISTORY OF

HIS DOMINIONS AND DESCENDANTS IS

PIOUSLY DEDICATED

BY

THE AUTHOR

PREFACE

"THE SAINT CLAIRS OF THE ISLES" herein submitted to the readers is intended to be a comprehensive work upon the *gens de Sancto Claro* in the Orcades, Scotland, and elsewhere, arranged in chronological sequence and, as far as possible, in narrative style

It has been thought desirable to strictly adhere to the text of those eminent authorities who have already treated upon various parts of the subject-matter of this work, and with that object permission has been solicited and conceded to utilise freely and fully the works enumerated below *

I cannot too clearly express my sense of obligation for various copyright concessions, and hope that my efforts with the book will in part justify the consideration accorded.

To Mr Henry Brett, of Auckland, publisher of this book, my especial acknowledgments are manifestly due I have also to thank the Hon Norman Sinclair, Master of Caithness, for contributing matter relating to the 52nd and subsequent Earls of Caithness, Sir John Rose George Sinclair, Bart, of Dunbeath, for many useful notes and genealogical tables; Mrs A Stuart, 19 Regent Terrace, Edinburgh, for notes on the Dreux and de Coucy connection with Scotland, the Right Hon Lord Sinclair for memoranda relating to the Master of Sinclair, etc, the H Herr Count Sinclair for notices of the chivalrous Swedes, the H Herr Count James Henry Sinclair, of Lambahof, for a copy of the "Genealogical Descendance," on which Chapter XIII is based, C F Bricka, Royal Archivist of Denmark C T Odhner, Royal Archivist of Sweden, and H. Huitfeld Kaas, Royal Archivist of Norway, for courteous replies to important queries; the Hon Chas H St Clair, of Morgan City, La, for topographical notes and other valuable assistance, E G Sinckler, J P., Barbados, for notes supplied; Henry A Rye, of Stretton, Burton-on-Trent, for abstracts from interesting documents, His Grace the Duke of Sutherland for supplying certified copy of Appendix I. Douglas and Foulis, Edinburgh, for the prompt supply of text-books ordered from time to time I have further to express my consciousness of obligation to the Hon Sir Robert Stout, K C.M G, and Messrs Gilbert Goudie, Francis J Grant, Alfred W. Johnston (Imperial Institute, London), Edward Shillington (Librarian Free Public Library, Auckland), and Thomas Sinclair, M A (Torquay, England), for authority to publish the expression of their favourable opinions of the MS of this work

ROLAND WM. ST CLAIR.

Auckland, New Zealand,
St Magnus' Day,
16th April, 1898.

---

*These are the works for which permission to utilise has been obtained —"Orkneyinga Saga " and "Caithness Family History," from Mr David Douglas, Edinburgh, ' Normans in Europe," from Messrs Longmans, Green & Co, "Zetland County Families," from Francis J Grant, W S, Carrick Pursuivant of Arms, Notes, from Gilbert Goudie, Calder's "History of Caithness," from Alexander Rae, of Wick, " Sinclairs of England," "Caithness Events," and Translations, from Thomas Sinclair, M A, of Belgrave Lodge, Torquay, "The History of the Sinclair Family in Europe and America," from the Hon Leonard Allison Morrison, A M, Canobie Lake, Windham, New Hampshire, United States, and Colonel the Hon Chas A Sinclair of Portsmouth, N H, "The Voyages of the Zeni," from the Hakluyt Society. "The St Clair Papers " from Robert Clarke & Co, Cincinnati U S A, "The Scottish Expedition to Norway in 1612, from Thomas Nelson & Sons, Edinburgh

CONTENTS

(i) Short Title—(ii) Title—(iii) Inscription—(iv) Preface—(v) Contents

BOOK I

CHAP				PAGE.
	INTRODUCTION			1
I	THE HOUSE OF ODIN —			
	1 Chaos—Odinic Myths			3
	2 Dawn—Rögnvald of Moeri, Jarl		fl 850—912	6
II	DUKES OF NORMANDY		912—1017	10
III	SEA-KINGS OF ORKNEY —			
	1 The Norse Line	(28)	871—1156	20
	2 The Athol Line	(3)	1139—1231	64
	3 The Angus Line	(7)	1231—1321	82
	4 The Stratherne Line	(2)	1321—1357	86
	5 The Earldom in Contested Succession		1357—1379	93
	6 The Saint-Clair Line	(3)	1379—1471	96
IV	THE SAINT-CLAIRS OF THE ISLES —			
	Period of Post-Comitial Rule		1471—1567	127
	Orcadian Scions—The Sinclairs of Warsetter, of Tohop and Saba, of Ethay, of Essenquoy, of Greenwall, Flottay and Gyre, of Clumlie, Towquoy, and Hammer, of Gorne and Burwick, of Overbrugh, of Craya, of Rapness, of Estaquoy, of Nethergarth, of Campston, of Damsay, and of Conyar			138
	Zetland Scions—The Sinclairs of Strom and Brugh, of House, Aith, and Scalloway, of Havera and Brew, of Quendale, of Goat, of Bullister and Swining, of Sandwick and Mousa, and of Toft, &c			163
V	EARLS OF CAITHNESS	(55)	871—1896	179
VI	CADETS OF CAITHNESS —			
	The Sinclairs of Stemster and Dunbeath; of Murkle, of Broynach, Sarclet, &c, of Assery, of Lybster, of Scotscalder, of Geise, of Greenland and Rattar, of Freswick, of Mey, of Durran, of Olrig, of Latheron, of Brabster-Myre, of Barrock, of Risgill or Swinzie, of Bridgend, of Dun, of Southdun, of Brabsterdorran, of Forss, of Stirkoke, of Ulbster, of Kirk and Myrelandhorn, of Lybster (Reay), of Achingale and Newton, of Hoy and Oldfield, of Borlum, Toftkemp, and Thura			220
VII	BARONETICAL BRANCHES —			
	Of Mey, of Dunbeath and Barrock, and of Ulbster			254
VIII	THE LONGFORMACUS LINE —			
	Lords of Longformacus, Baronets of Longformacus, and of Stevenson			260
IX	THE LORDS OF ROSSLIN —			
	Feudal Period			266
	Feudal-Transition Period			286
	The Sinclairs of Pitcairn and Whitekirk, of Dryden, Spottis, Woodhouselee, &c			294
X	BARONS OF RAVENSCRAIG —			
	Branches of Balgreggie, and of Saintclerholme			297
XI	THE LORDS SINCLAIR (Herdmanston Line)			307
XII	THE LORDS OF HERDMANSTON —			
	Feudal and Transition Periods			311
XIII	NOBLES IN SWEDEN AND ALSACE			317
XIV	IRISH SCIONS —			
	The Sinclairs of Holyhill, the Sinclaires of Belfast, and of Ballymena, Vestiges			322
XV	THE ST CLARES OF ENGLAND —			
	Norman Notices, Castellans of Colchester, the Aeslingham Group, the Bradfield St Clares, the St Clares of Aldham, Igtham, Burstow, &c, the Somerset St Clares, the Devonshire House; Incidental Notices, the St Clairs of Staverton Court			326

XVI THE ST CLAIRS AND SINCLAIRS OF NORTH AMERICA — New Hampshire Scions, the Sinclairs of Columbia, Me, Incidental Notices, the Sinclairs of Virginia, the Sinclairs of Northumberland County, Penn, the Sinclairs from Pennycuick, Scotland, the Sinclairs from Tiree, Argyleshire, General St Clair and his descendants, Scions from France, Various, the Sincklers of the Barbados, West Indies, &c, &c	342
XVII GUILLERMUS, GODFATHER OF THE GENS	418
XVIII ORCADIAN FAMILIES—An Outline — Baikie, Balfour, Beattoun, Bellenden, Borwick, Clouston, Corrigall,* Craigie, Cromarty, Cursiter,* Dischington, Fea, Flett, Fotheringhame, Foubister,* Garriock, Gordon, Græme, Groat, Halcro,* Harcus, Heddle,* Hourston, Irving, Isbister,* Johnston, Kirkness,* Knarston,* Laing, Leask,* Linklater,* Loutitt, Moncrieff, Moodie, Mowat, Muir, Redland,* Rendall,* Sinclair, Stewart, Sutherland, Traill, Tulloch, Yule, Various *Of that Ilk	420

BOOK II

HISTORIETTES.

THE EARLS OF ATHOL (ROYAL CELTIC LINE, 1115—1215) —	431
Maormors of Angus (900-1243)	433
Earls Palatine of Stratherne (1115-1344)	435
The Orcadian Episcopate	440
The Caithness Episcopate	442
Orcadian Argonauts, or Voyages of the Zeni (1374—1404)	445
Told of Zetland, Chamberlain of Ross	453
Hereditary Protectorate of the Scottish Masonic Craft	454
The First Grand Master—William St Clair, Last of Rosslyn (1778)	456
The King's Bishop (1312-32), the Great Minion (1523-85), Henry, Bishop of Ross (1565), John, Bishop of Brechin (1566)	460
Scottish Courtiers —The Queen's Knight (1490—1513), Queen Margaret's "Pet" (1520-28, The Keeper of the Privy Seal (1567)	463
Councillor of the Danish Realm (1625)	464
Academical Celebrities —David St Clair, Professor Paris Univ (1603-22), John Sinclair, A M, Regent St Andrews (1646-87), George Sinclair, Glasgow Univ (1654-96), Andrew St Clair, Edinburgh Univ (1720-47)	465
The Master of Sinclair (1750), A Distinguished Diplomatist (1762)	466
An Unfortunate Envoy (1691—1739)	467
Senators of the College of Justice —Lord Murkle (1755), Lord Woodhall (1761-65)	467
The Pastor of Keiss (1767), Comrade of Washington (1736—1818)	468
The Able Ulbsters—Scotland's Proto-Statistician (1754—1835)	470
Swedish Soldiers of Fortune —Military Tactician (1803), Knight of the Legion of Honour (1820)	471
Eminent Antipodeans —The Hon Andrew Sinclair, M D (1861), Founders of Blenheim, N Z, John Sinclair, Mayor of Invercargill, N Z	473

BOOK III.

CAMEOS AND SAGAS *

St Clair,* Orcadia*	476
The Sword Chant of Thorstein the Red*	477
The Visit of Earl Thorfinn*	478
The Royal Hunt of Roslin	479
Help and Hold—A Legend of the House of St Clair*	480
The Heart of Bruce*	481
The Death of Haco	482
The Hero of Bridgenorth	484

CONTENTS

Roslin Chapel*	485
Harald, Bard of Brave St Clair,* The Dirge of Rosabelle*	489
The Drum-head Charter (a Tale of Flodden Field), The House of St. Clair*	486
Traditions of Summerdale	488
A Merrie Jest, A Legend of Stroma	490
Roslin Castle,* Fair Isle*—An Incident of the Spanish Armada	491
The Kringelen Ambush	492
The Massacre of Kringellen,* Malcolm Sinclair's Visa*	494
Sinclair's Chains, Roslin's Daughter, or Captain Wedderburn's Courtship*	496
The Standing Stones of Stennis	498
The Legend of Louisa St Clair, Legend of the Polwarth Thorn	499
The Orcadian Homeland*	500

Book IV

APPENDICES

A —Charters of Herdmanston —I The Original Grant of Carfræ (1160), II Charter of Confirmation (1196), III Instrument in Renewal (1434)	502
B.—Grant of Innerleith (1280)	503
C —Charter of Roskelyn (1280)	504
D —Diploma of the Orcadian Succession (870 to 1420)	504
E —Installation Documents of Earl Henry I (1379)	508
F —Amends of Malise Sparre (1387)	511
G —Charges of the Orcadian Commons (1425)	511
H —Testament of Sir David Sinclar of Swynbrocht, Knycht (1506)	514
I —Special Destination of Caithness (1344)	515
J —Act in Recognition of Henry, Lord St Clair (1489)	526
K —Respite in favour of Edward Sinclare and others for the Slaughter of the Earl of Caithness	516
L —Deed of Resignation of the Hereditary Protectorate of the Scottish Masonic Craft	517
M —Calendar of Documents relating to the Earlier History of Orcadia	517
N —Chartulary of Rosslyn	519
O —Variants of the Name of St Clair	521
P —Earlier Scottish Earldoms	522
Q —Scottish Historical Families	522
R —The St Clair Armoury	523
Genealogical Tables —	
Normans, Danes, Anglo-Saxons	527
Jarls of Orkney	528
The Lines of Earl Paul and Earl Erlend	529
Descendants of Paul the First (amplified), of Hrolf, and of Moddan	530
The Angus and Stratherne Lines	531
The St Clair Line	532
The Lords Sinclair	533
The St Clairs of Roslin	534
Earls of Caithness (St Clair Line)	535
Seize Quartiers,—John V, xlixth Earl of Caithness, John Sinclair of Tolhuip	536
Topography	537
Bibliography	537
Glossary	539
Notes and Queries	543
Registers	552
Authorities and Aids	554
Conclusion	556
List of Subscribers	557

ILLUSTRATIONS

No		PAGE
1	Map of Orcadia	*(Frontispiece)*
2	Thor's Hammer	6
3	Fac-simile of Orkneyinger's Saga	22
4	St Magnus' Cathedral	63
5	Norse War Galley (Viking Age)	75
6	Burghal Seal of Kirkwall	95
7	Kirkwall—Winter View	99
8	Rosslyn Castle (Restored)	105
9	Rosslyn Chapel—The Nave	119
10	Noltland Castle	131
11	Porch, St Magnus' Cathedral	135
12	William Sinclair, Harbourmaster of Kirkwall	157
13	James Leask Sinclair	159
14	Mary Mowat Sinclair	159
15	Roland William St Clair, "the Author"	162
16	Mousa Tower	177
17	Castles Sinclair and Girnigo	188
18	The Caithness Arms	194
19	John VI, 55th Earl of Caithness	219
20	Thomas Sinclair, M A	226
21	Seal of Sir William de St Clair, A D 1292	279
22	Ravenscraig Castle (Ruins)	300
23	Lord Sinclair, The Right Hon	310
24	Fredrik Carl, Count Sinclair	319
25	The present Count Sinclair	320
26	The present Countess Sinclair	320
27	The Hon John Grandison Sinclair	386
28	The Hon Chas H St Clair	393
29	Colonel the Hon Chas A Sinclair	398
30	His Excellency Major-General Arthur St Clair	417
31	William St Clair, "The Last Rosslyn"	459
32	Sir John Sinclair of Ulbster, Bart	470
33	Charles Gideon Sinclair, Swedish Baron	471
34	The Hon Andrew Sinclair, Surgeon, R N	472
35	Christina Sutherland Sinclair	473
36	The Hon James Sinclair, M P C, New Zealand	473
37	His Worship the Mayor of Invercargill, N Z	475
38	Effigy of Sir William St Clair	480
39	The Nave, St Magnus' Cathedral	483
40	The Under Chapel, Rosslinn	485
41	Fair Isle	491
42	The Sinclair Monument at Kringellen	493
43	Malcolm Sinclair, Swedish Baron	495
44	Sinclair's Chains	496
45	The Standing Stones of Stennis	498
46	Roslin Chapel—Exterior View	501

THE SAINT-CLAIRS OF THE ISLES.

BOOK I

INTRODUCTION

"THE Saint-Clairs figure prominently in history, song and story. In Normandy they controlled lands, castles and troops of men, and were closely allied to royal blood. At Hastings their prowess was conspicuous, and materially helped to decide the fate of that eventful day. They appear in the Battle Abbey Roll Early in the eleventh century, William 'le Blond' (the Seemly), second son of Waleran, Lord of Saint Clair, and Helena, daughter of Richard, Duke of Normandy, settled in Scotland, soon his name appears on the roll of the nobles of King Malcolm Canmore, and thenceforward for generations his descendants are found in loyal support of the Scottish monarchs, who trusted them implicitly through good and ill. Honoured with the confidence of the ancient Celtic line; entrusted with the royal fortress of Edinburgh during the war of the Scottish Succession, companions-in-arms of the patriot Bruce, in later times, the St Clairs shared in the triumphs and humiliations of the House of Stuart, receiving honours on the one hand, and on the other privation and exile. Reconciled to the union of Scotland with England, and to the Protestant Succession, they continued devotedly attached to royalty without exception, until the signal gun in the American War of Independence was fired, when the American hero supported the cause of Freedom, while those at Home sided with the motherland, but whether as Catholic or Protestant, monarchist or republican, always displaying a martial spirit, and ever true to the cause espoused."*

Considering the revival of interest in family records in these learned latter years, it seems strange to have to admit that the history of so renowned a *gens* should still be unwritten Such is nevertheless the case, and the present work is but an epitome of extracts taken from the most readily accessible sources, to be the pioneer for some future historian to present in an amplified form.

Although it was when rulers of the Orcades that the St. Clairs attained the zenith of their splendour, yet they are seldom mentioned in association with those Isles—the acquisition of which raised them to 'pride of place' in the nobility of Scotland and of the three Scandinavian kingdoms

The history of the St. Clairs and that of the Orcades being so inextricably interwoven, it has been thought well to begin this work with an account of the puissant House of Odin (eventually heired by the St Clairs), the noblest and most heroic of the ruling dynasties of the North, and in the person of Rolf the Founder, originator of that

---
* The St Clair Papers

INTRODUCTORY.

dynasty on whose empire 'the sun never sets.' While it is incontestably established that the St. Clairs are representatives of Einar the Earl, brother of Rolf,* it is contended by a modern writer† that as legitimate heirs-male of Malger, Count of Mortain and Corbeil, the eventual heir-male of Richard the Good, Duke of the Normans, they also represent Rolf himself; and it is further stated‡ that they are heirs-of-line of Richard III. of Normandy.

Having premised this much, it only remains to add that a work on the St. Clairs would be *regrettably* incomplete did it not contain an account of the notable deeds of their warlike predecessors, those 'stout battellers' the ancient Scandinavian Jarls of Orkney, of Odinic descent, who will be described at some length, that readers not familiar with the history of those parts may the better understand the dominions and traditions heired by the St. Clairs.

In perusing the various works on the St. Clairs and on Orkney, it appears that those on the former, while ample in their notice of the name in the Scottish mainland, have but scanty, insufficient, and erroneous references to the St. Clairs of the Isles, and the works on Orkney are similarly defective in their notices of the St. Clairs, whether Orcadian or Scottish. This volume will, therefore, attempt to in part remedy the defect, and it is as a tribute to the memory of the long-forgotten Orcadian descendants of the Earls—in historic interest, heroic achievement, and manly endeavour, the peers of their Scottish collaterals—that the present title has been chosen.

The chapters being arranged in chronological sequence, the plan of the work will unfold as read.

* Orkn. Saga.   † Au. of Sinclairs of England.   ‡ Genealogie of the St. Clairs.

CHAPTER I

THE HOUSE OF ODIN.*

CHAOS. ODINIC MYTHS

For the ancestral home of the Orcadian Jarls we must voyage to the Norwegian Uplands, fitting cradle for this primeval line, noble even beyond the breath of tradition It was in those lofty regions that we learn from the pre-historic Eddas, our Scandinavian forefathers attributed not only the creation of their race, but the origin of mankind For when we refer to the mythology preserved in the Eddas we are told —*

In the beginning of time when yet there was nought, two regions lay on each side of chaos To the north Niflheim, the abode of mist and snow, and cloud and cold To the south, Muspell, where it is so hot and bright that it burns, and none may tread save those who have an heritage there. The king of that country is Surtr, who guards the land with a flaming sword When the hot blasts from Muspell met the cold rime and frost that came out of Niflheim, the frost melted by the might of Surtr, and became a great giant, Ymir, the sire of all the frost giants But besides the giant, the ice-drops as they melted formed a cow, on whose milk Ymir fed, and as she licked the rime-covered stones, a man named Buri arose, who was the father of Odin and his brethren These are the Æsir, or good gods, and between these and the frost giants war arose, till at last Ymir was slain and all his race but one From this one sprang the later race of frost giants

With the body of the giant Odin made the world The sea and waters are his blood; earth his flesh; the rocks his bones, pebbles his teeth and jaws; his skull was raised aloft and the heavens were made of it, the clouds are his brains. But the sun, moon, and stars are formed of the fires which came out of Muspell These Odin fixed in the heavens, and ordered their goings Odin, the father of all (*Allfadır*) next made man, and gave him a soul which shall never perish, though the body decay

Odin was the greatest of the gods Next to him comes Frigga, his wife, who knows the fate of all men, though she never reveals it. Then Thor, his first-born son—the Thunderer —the chiefest of gods for strength, the sworn foe of the old frost giants, the tamer and queller of all unholy things. Next Baldr, of fairest face and hair, the mildest spoken of the gods, type of purity and innocence These, with Freyr, who rules over rain and sunshine and the fruitfulness of the earth; and Freyia, the goddess of love; and many others, live in Midgard, the centre of the earth Here they have built themselves a castle, Asgard, high above the earth, whence they can see all that goes on among mortals Here shall the good live with Odin after death, while the wicked shall go to Niflheim (hell), the place of darkness and of cold. But these simple myths were mingled with those of a more savage and sterner character

---

The Normans in Europe

THE HOUSE OF ODIN.

Odin is not the All-father alone, but the God of Battle *(Valfadir)* as well, and as such is worshipped by bloody sacrifices Instead of the peaceful after-life in Midgard, men look forward to Valhalla—the Hall of the Slain—where those who die in battle, shall feast with Odin. There, their pastime shall be to fight with each other from dawn till mealtime, when they ride back to Valhalla and sit down to drink Those who die of sickness or old age shall go to hell ; the murderers and the foresworn to Ná, a region formed of adders' backs wattled together, whose heads spit venom and form streams in which these shall wade for ever

Meanwhile among the gods there is strife and woe. Of the children of the old frost giants, one Loki had been fostered by Odin, and brought up among his children, to their ruin Fair of face is he, but a traitor, ill-tempered, deceitful, and of fickle mood

With the rise of the traitor the golden age of the Æsir, or the good gods, is at an end, and the old quarrels between them and the frost giants are resumed Yet so long as Baldr lived, sin and wickedness could not prevail on earth, nor could the ancient race triumph over the Æsir To kill Baldr, therefore, was was Loki's constant aim, and by treachery he succeeded The gods, warned by the soothsayers that Baldr was doomed to die, made him free from death by sickness, or stones or trees, or beast or bird , and rejoicing in their triumph, found harmless pastime in shooting at Baldr and smiting him with stones, while he remained unharmed One tree, the mistletoe, they had not named, and Loki, making arrows of it gave them into the hands of Hodr, the blind god Armed with these weapons he joined his brethren in the sport and shooting, slew fair Baldr, who went to hell Loki indeed fell before the vengeance of Thor, but the doom of the gods was sealed ; and, heralded by three winters with no summer in between, 'the twilight of the gods' drew on Then Surtr, the primeval god, should at last come forth, and hurling fire over the world, destroy the gods, both good and bad Then should arise another heaven, where the worthy dead should dwell with Surtr, and Balder the Beautiful should thither return from hell

From Odin and his sons most royal families in the North lands loved to derive their descent The elder sons seemed to have remained for generations in the home-land, but the younger branches issued forth in search of empire, and we presently find several scions of the deified hero of Scandinavia leading the Saxon invaders of Britain and establishing themselves permanently there. Of these the line of Cerdic of Wessex, ninth in descent from Bældæg,[*] son of Odin, finally survived the rest, only to surrender to William of Normandy, a descendant, though a bastard, of the senior and more puissant line of Thor The course of descent receives illustration in "Fundinn Noregr,"[†] from which the following is a citation :—

"Now shall be told the proofs how Norway was first inhabited, how kingly stocks began there, and why they are called Skjoldings, Budlings, Bragnings, Odlings, Volsungs, or Niflungs, from which the royal races have come.

"There was a giant, King Fornjot,[‡] who ruled over the regions called Finland and Kvenland, lying to the east of the Helsingbight (Gulf of Bothnia), which goes northward to meet the White Sea He had three sons named Hler, or Ægir, who ruled over the seas, another Logi, ruler of fires, and the third Kari, who presided over the winds, and he was father of Jokull, father of King Snæs the Old, whose children were these—Thorri,

---
[*] Lappenberg   [†] Orkneyingers' Saga (Rolls' trans)
[‡] One of the numerous alternative names for Thor

Fonn, Drifa, and Mjoll. Thorri had two sons, Norr and Gorr, and a daughter Goi. He was a noble king, ruling over Kvenland and Finland, observing sacrifices annually at mid-winter, whence called Thorri's sacrifice, and from that the month took its name. The Kvens sacrificed to him to ensure snow and good travelling on the shoes. That was their harvest. One winter, Goi, his daughter, was missed, and when the month had passed Thorri enjoined sacrifice to divine her location, but without success. Thus originated the month Goi. Four winters after her brothers made vow to search for her, Norr on the land, and Gorr to search the outscars and islands with vessels, each having many men.

"Gorr held on with his ships out along the sea-bight, and so into the Allans-haf, and after that he searched the Swedish skerries far and wide, and the isles in the East sea, and then the Gothland scars, and thence to Denmark, where he viewed the isles, and found those of his kinsmen who were come from Hler the Old, out of Hler's isle (Laesso in the Cattegat), and he then still held on his voyage, but hearing nothing of his sister.

"Norr had bided till the snow was on the heath and suitable for shoes, after which he issued forth from Kvenland and inside the sea-bight, when he met a party of Lapps from the hinder-land of Finmark, who wished to stop his passage, so a battle ensued, which ended in the flight of the Lapps, for might and magic were with Norr, and his foes became panic-stricken as swine when they heard the war-cry and saw weapons flash. Norr and his party now went west on the Kjol, and were a long time foraging in and traversing unpeopled parts, proceeding till they came to where the water turns westward from the fells. It directed them to a sea where was a firth as large as a sea-bight. There were there great tilths, and great dales came down to the firth. Norr and his men gave battle to the people, whom they overcame as weeds over cornfields—all fell or fled, and Norr became king, remaining there all summer until it snowed on the heaths, when he shaped his course up along the dale which goes south from Drontheim firth. Sending a detachment coastwise round Maeren, he reduced all to subjection. He continued his course over the fell to the south of the dale-bight, then still south along the dales till he reached great water, called Mjosen, when he received advice of a defeat to his men by King Sokni, which caused him to turn west again towards the fell, and he arrived in the Valders district, whence he passed seawards, entering the Sogn, a long and narrow firth, where he engaged Sokni in battle. It was hard fought, because their witchcraft had no hold on Sokni. Norr pressing hard forward, came to hand strokes with Sokni, who fell with many of his men. Norr then fared on into the firth that goes north from Sogn, where the vanquished leader had ruled. It is now called Sokni's Dale. Norr stayed there a long time, and now it is known as Norafirth. He had great battles west of the Kjol, and these kings fell before him. Vee and Vei, Hunding and Heming, and he laid under him that land all to the sea.

"The brothers met in Norafirth. Nori went up the Kjol to Ulfa-moar, thence to Estridale into Vermeland, and along the lake Vaener, and so to the sea, and laid under him all land west of those bounds, and it is now called Norway. At midwinter they came into Heidmark, meeting Hrolf of Berg, son of the giant Svadi, from north of Dofrafell, by Ashilda, daughter of King Eystein, who had long ruled over Heidmark. Hrolf had abducted Goi from Kvenland, and on hearing of his approach, they advanced together to meet Norr, to whom Hrolf offered single combat. They fought long without wounding each other, and at length Hrolf became Norr's man, and banqueted him and gave him to wife his sister Hodda, Svadi's daughter. After that Norr returned west to the sea, meeting in Norafirth, Gorr, just back from the Dumbs-haf (Frozen Sea), who had seized as his own all the isles on that way. Then these brothers shared the realm between them, so that Norr should have all the mainland from Jotunheim in the north to Alfheim in the south, which is now called Norway. He ruled that realm while he lived, and his sons after him, and they shared the land amongst them, and so the realms began to get smaller and smaller as the kings got more and more numerous, and so they were divided into provinces. (A list of his descendants is given.)

"Gorr, on the other hand, was to have all those isles which lay on the larboard of his warship as he shaped north, between which and the mainland he could pass in a ship with a fixed rudder. Gorr having the isles was for that called a sea-king. His sons were Heiti and Beiti, Meitir and Geitir; they were mighty sea-kings and overbearing men. They made many inroads on the realm of Norr's sons, and had numberless battles, in which now one, now the other, won the day. Beiti ran his war-galley into Drontheim and fought there, lying where it is now called Beit-sea and Beitstede. He placed a ship-sledge under the galley, and had also deep snow and good sledging. He then took the helm, hoisted sail, and had the ship dragged from the innermost bight of Beitstede over the Ellida-eid, or Galley-neck to Naumdale, and claimed for his own all the land lying to larboard, which is many tilths and much land. Beiti, the sea-king, was father of Heiti, the sea-king, father of Svadi, and Geitir was the father of Glammi and Gylfi, Meiti, the sea-king, was father of Maevil and Myndill, which latter was father of Ekkill and Skekkill.

"Heiti, Gorr's son, was father of Sveidi, the sea-king, the father of Halfdan the Old, the father of Ivar, Jarl of the Uplands, the father of Eystein *Glumra* the father of Rognvald Jarl, who was called the mighty and wise in council, and men say both were true names."

THOR'S HAMMER—THE SVASTIKA SYMBOL.

DAWN —ROGNVALD OF MOERI, JARL

WHEN the 'twilight of the gods' ended in dawn, many ruling families claiming Odinic origin are found firmly established in Norway. Of these the principal were the Ynglings, the Skjoldings, the ancestors of Hakon Jarl, and those of Rognvald of Moeri. The Ynglingatal, a genealogical poem composed for Rognvald Heidumhoeri, or 'the Heaven-high' (the uncle of Harald Fairhair) traces the family of Rognvald through thirty generations up to Odin. Ari, in Iceland, traces his ancestry through thirty-seven degrees up to Yngvi Tyrkja-King from Olaf the White, King of Dublin, who was thirtieth in descent. From "Fundinn Noregr," or "Norway Found," we obtain the semi-mythical descent of Hrolf, the founder of Normandy. In it he is derived from

Fornjot, or Thor, the heir of Odin according to the principle of primogeniture and so the representatives of Rollo must depose those of Cerdic from the heirship of Odin, unless we are to allow postremogeniture to supersede primogeniture.

Passing from chaos to dawn, it is found that Halfdan the Old was father of Ivar, Jarl of the Uplands, who was sire to Eystein (*Glumra*) the Orator. Eystein had two sons, Rognvald, hereafter Jarl of Moeri, and Sigurd the Sea-king, to whom Rognvald transferred the sovereignty of the Orkneys, which the ambitious Sigurd aimed at making the centre of a naval empire, stretching from the Archipelago of Zetland to the Isle of Man. Forming an alliance with Thorstein the Red, he in part succeeded in his object, and together they wrested Caithness and Sutherland from the Scottish sovereign. But death ensuing immediately thereafter, all projects of further conquest were arrested. The Earldom of Caithness is, however, to this day enjoyed by his representative, and thus presents the singular and extraordinary instance of the transmission of a British dignity for over a millennium. Other writers* ascribe to Eystein the Orator a third son, Eric the Bad, who appears in Norman annals as Malahulc (Mal-Eric), uncle of Hrolf, but in the absence of any reference to him in the Norse Sagas, it seems more probable that he would have been an uncle of Hrolf on the spindle side—a son of Hrolf *Nefia*. From the solicitude shown by Ragnhilda, the Lady of Moeri, regarding her wayward son, it seems reasonable to suppose she may have urged her brother Eric to accompany Hrolf in his career of conquest.

Of Earl Rognvald we learn much from the Sagas. When Harald Fairhair started upon his career of subjugating all Norway, Rognvald was his staunchest supporter and most trusted adviser. After the naval victory of Hafursfiord all Norway submitted to Harald, and the first whom that monarch rewarded was Rognvald, to whom he assigned the revenues of both the Moeri (*i.e.*, North and South Moeri, which are divided the one from the other by the Romsdale Firth. They stretch eastward along the coast from Stadt to Naumdale). Harald, in accordance with a vow, had allowed his magnificent head of hair to remain unshorn until Norway was subdued. The sublime function of removing it was now performed by Rognvald, Norway's only earl. Rognvald was of the very highest consequence, and is variously termed the Stout, the Strong, the Rich, the Robust, the Mighty, the Potent, the Wise, etc., etc. He was married to Ragnhild, a daughter of Hrolf *Nefia*, by whom he had three sons, Ivar, Hrolf, and Thorir. After Hafursfiord an exodus took place from Norway, and the exiles used the Scottish Isles as viking stations from whence to harass the Norwegian coasts, to the great irritation of King Harald, who set forth with firm intent to purge those parts. Rognvald of Moeri, his son Ivar, and his brother Sigurd accompanied Harald. The expedition was completely successful, but in one of the skirmishes in the Hebudes, Ivar met his fate. As some compensation to Rognvald for the death of his heir, King Harald assigned to him the Orcadian and Zetlandic Archipelagoes. Rognvald, however, having great estates in Norway, transferred them to his brother Sigurd, who had been flag-captain to King Harald.

When Sigurd fell in Caithness, his son Guttorm succeeded him, but dying within a year from his accession, the dominions reverted to Earl Rognvald, who re-granted them first to Hallad, who presently abdicated, and thereafter to Einar. Returning to Norway,

---

* Burke, Lives of the Lindseys, &c. Orkn. Saga, Rolls (trans) edn.

Rognvald seems to have been chiefly occupied in the administration of his earldoms, which were no doubt enlivened by the many stirring events incidental to the age in which he lived. Hrolf, his second son, was exiled for an act of vikingry, and thereon steered first for the Western Isles, and thence to Gaul, where he waged war till pacified by the cession of Neustria. Rognvald was too eminent to remain long unenvied, and the sons of Harald, who were now attaining man's estate, began to cast longing glances at his possessions. At last the two most turbulent, Halfdan and Gudrod, assailed him in Moeri, and setting fire to his house, the noble Jarl perished in the flames, full of honours. His sons have left a permanent record in European history. Ivar, as has already been seen, was slain in the Hebrides; Hrolf conquered Neustria and settled there, his companions being the ancestors of most of the British nobility; while Thorir the Silent succeeded his father as Jarl of Moeri, and espoused Alof *Arbot*, the daughter of King Harald Fairhair, by whom he had issue Berghot, who was mother of Hakon Jarl, the Great, thereafter sovereign of Norway. His other sons were by different wives, of whom the noble earl, like his sovereign King Harald, probably had a plurality. Those whose names have been transmitted to us are Hrollaug, Hallad and Einar. Hallad was created fourth Earl of the Orkneys, but finding himself too much occupied in repelling the incessant attacks of vikings, abdicated and retired to his odal possessions in Norway. Rognvald then summoned his remaining sons to attend a family council at which to select a more warlike successor to the peaceable Hallad. It was attended by Thorir, Hrolf, Hrollaug and Einar. The Jarl asked which of them would go and rule the Islesmen. First came Thorir, who bade his father prepare him ships; but Thorir was the favourite son, and Rognvald said, though he was well qualified for the work, he must stay at Moeri, and succeed him. Then Hrolf,* the tall champion, stepped forth, so tall, that no horse could carry him—he was ready to go. 'Just the man,' said his father, 'so far as strength and daring go, but too untamed in spirit as yet to settle down quietly.' Then came Hrollaug. 'Do you wish me to go?' Rognvald replied he would never do for an Earl. 'You have a temper quite unfit for strife, your path lies to Iceland; in that land you will be famous, rich in family and friends, but in this quarter your fate does not lie.' Then Einar advanced and said, 'Let me go to Orkney, and I promise you shall never set eyes on me again, which you will think the best thing that can happen.' The Earl decided in favour of Einar, who thus became fifth Jarl of the Orkneys. As for Hrollaug, he took himself off to King Harald, with whom he stayed awhile, for father and son never hit it off in temper after that day. Some time after he sailed for Iceland, by the king's advice, and having followed Ingolf's example, and thrown his pillars overboard, found them in the West, and dwelt there. He was a great chief, and kept up his friendship with King Harald, though he never went back to Norway. King Harald sent him a sword and drinking horn, and ring of gold, five ounces in weight, and these precious things were long famous.† From him was descended the great family of the Sturlungs, of which Snorro Sturleson, the historian, was a member. His father, Sturla Thordarson, was a man of consequence, and held by hereditary right (being of Odinic origin through Hrollaug) the dignity of a Godar, which in the times of Odin worship was hereditary in certain families descended from the twelve Diars, Drottars, or Godars, who accompanied Odin from Asgard. The office of Godar combined the functions of priest and judge ‡

---
* Another acct., *vide infra*, states Hrolf was absent from this conference
† Article "Norsemen in Iceland." See Oxford Essays, 1858, by G. W. Dasent
‡ Laing's "Heimskringla," p. 188

It was while Einar ruled Orcadia that Rögnvald met his death, and the Norwegian prince Halfdan hastened to the Isles, hoping to similarly serve Einar. But the agile Earl was too alert to be surprised. Crossing to Caithness, he suddenly returned to effect the capture of the too-confident Halfdan, upon whom he exacted the barbaric vengeance of carving a blood-eagle on his back. From Einar the Earl we date the permanence of the Orcadian dynasty, which continued in his line till the death of Erlend III., the twenty-sixth Earl. An account of his descendants will appear at greater length in another chapter, headed the Sea-Kings of Orkney; and meantime we will pass on to follow the career of Hrolf and his successors, Dukes of the Normans.

CHAPTER II.

DUKES OF NORMANDY.

ROLF, THE FOUNDER *

912—927

M.—1 Popa, d of Count Berenger of Bayeux
2 Gisela, d of K Charles *the Simple*

CONTEMPORARY PRINCES

FRANCE	896, Charles IV, *the Simple*	922, Robert I.	923, Rudolf
NORWAY	863, Harald *Fairhair*, to 934		
ENGLAND	901, Edward *the Elder*.	924, Athelstan	

ROLF, son of Rognvald, Earl of Moeri, by his lady Ragnhilda, daughter of Rolf *Nefia*, was a renowned sea-king Named after his maternal grandfather, he further obtained from the restless activity of his movements the soubriquet of 'Ganger,' or 'Walker' He made much warfare in the East One summer when he returned from 'Vikingry,' or a raiding expedition in the East, he committed acts of depredation in Viken King Harald Fairhair, who was then in that district, was very angry when he heard of this, for he had strictly forbidden robbery within his land He therefore announced at a Thing that he made Rolf an outlaw from Norway. When Rolf's mother heard this she went to Harald to ask for pardon for Rolf, but the king was so angry that her prayers were of no avail. Then she sang —

> "Thinkst thou, King Harald, in thine anger
> To drive away my brave Rolf Ganger,
> Like a mad wolf, from out the land ?
> Why, Harald, raise thy mighty hand ?
> Why banish Næfia's gallant name-son,
> The brother of brave udal-men ?
> Why is thy cruelty so fell ?
> Bethink thee, monarch, is it well
> With such a wolf at wolf to play ?
> Who, driven to the wild woods away,
> May make the king's best deer his prey " †

Rolf then went westward across the sea to the Hebudes (the Sudreyar), and is described as following the calling of a viking in Gaul and England for nearly forty years before his final settlement at Rouen He is said to have joined Guthrum in his wars against Alfred, but to have been persuaded by the Saxon King to leave England and seek

---

* The Normans in Europe   † Laing's Heimskringla

richer spoil in France In 876 he entered the Seine, and from then till 912 ravaged the unfortunate country. In 888, the fatal year which saw the final dismemberment of the Empire of Charles the Great, began the famous siege of Paris by Rolf. The town was, however, successfully defended by its Count, Eudes, who in reward was for a time chosen King of France Contemporary chroniclers are silent from 900 to 911, and when they speak again Rolf is found in possession of Rouen, and Gaul in a pitiable state. In spite of his repulse by the Count of Paris, Rolf continued his devastations, until at last Charles of France granted him by treaty the territories which were already his own, and thus, as Alfred the Great had done for England, gained a respite for his distracted kingdom. By this treaty of ST CLAIR sur-Epte (912) Rolf secured the country from the Epte to the sea, and the overlordship of Brittany, with the hand of Gisela, the daughter of Charles the Simple; and with a nominal acceptance of Christianity as the price of the treaty, was led to the font by Robert, Count of Paris, who consented to be his godfather. To the demand of Charles that Rolf should do homage to him, and kiss the royal foot, the independent Northman answered indignantly, 'Ne si, by Got' (Not so, by God) When at last he consented that it should be done by proxy, it is said that King Charles was thrown backwards by the rudeness of the Norse soldier as he raised the foot to perform the prescribed salute The tale probably points to an act of nominal homage done by Rolf, but the Normans of later date appealed to it to show that they held their country of no higher sovereign-in-chief, but of God alone, and were proud of an insult offered with impunity to a descendant of the great Emperor of the West In 922, when Robert of Paris broke out in rebellion, Rolf and the Northmen who had settled in the Loire, aided Charles at the battle of Soissons, where Robert paid the penalty with his life. The following year, however, Charles unwisely trusted himself to the plighted troth of Herbert of Vermandois, who faithlessly seized him and kept him prisoner, with one short interval, until his death. In revenge Rolf ravaged the country of the Duke of Paris, and a long war of four years ensued, generally to the advantage of the Norman Duke This, though not successful in opening the prison of his royal father-in-law, resulted in two important acquisitions to the Norman territory The Bessin, the district around Bayeux, was granted to Rolf, as well as the land of Maine The annexation of the Bessin was his last exploit Shortly afterwards (927), at the demand of his people, he abdicated unwillingly in favour of his son Five more years, it is said, he lived, and then the old man of four-score and odd years—years teeming with deeds of strange contrast, of stranger import to future times—disappears from history. As we stand over his tomb in the chapel of St. Romanus, at Rouen, strange are the thoughts which flit across our mind. Here lies the once dread sea-king, the pillager of France; then one of the most powerful of her sons, a Duke, a legislator, the father of his people, the progenitor of a long line of dukes and kings. When all is told, we know but little of him. Many of the rolls which would have recorded his fame were probably burnt by his own hand. To recall all the events of his varied life is now beyond the power of man, but the best proof of his power and his genius is, that it was his life that inspired a Canon of his own town, Bayeux, to write one of the earliest romances of modern Europe, and that while all other settlements of the race in France and Germany rapidly disappeared, his alone has lasted on and deeply affected future ages

By his second wife, Gisela of France, he was issueless, but by his first wife, Popa, daughter of Count Berenger, of Bayeux he had one son, his successor William.

WILLIAM LONGSWORD.*

927—943

M —1 Espriota, *a Breton*
  2 Leutgarda d of Herbert II of Vermandois

CONTEMPORARY PRINCES

FRANCE	923, Rudolf	936, Louis IV, *d'Outremer*
ENGLAND	924, Athelstan	940, Edmund I

The occasion of Rolf's abdication was seized by the Bretons as a fitting opportunity to free themselves from the Norman domination When Charles the Simple granted Brittany to Rolf at ST CLAIR-sur-Epte, he made cession of a territory over which he had no real control So now, the Bretons, roused by the change of rulers at Rouen, rose under two of their princes, Berenger and Alan, massacred the Northmen in their country and invaded the Norman duchy (930—932) William, however, completely crushed the revolt Berenger submitted, Alan fled to the court of Athelstan, and, when restored on the intercession of the latter, was forced to accept the terms imposed by the conqueror at the first suppression of the rebellion The result was an important increase of the Norman territory by the acquisition of the Côtentin and the Channel Islands, and the formal acknowledgment of the Norman supremacy over the rest of Brittany

His next difficulty was the disaffection in Bayeux, where the Northmen witnessed with strong dislike the gradual conversion of the rest of Normandy to the language, manners, and customs of the Franks William, encouraged by the bravery of his father's trusted adviser, Bernard the Dane, decided to deal firmly with the rebels and (932—3) pouncing on them suddenly, utterly routed them After the insurrection he strove to crush out the Norse element, and became more thoroughly French than ever Hence, perhaps, his adhesion given to Rudolf at this date, and his repudiation of the lovely Espriota, his first wife—whom he had married by Norse rite, that is, without religious ties—for Leutgarda, sister of Herbert of Vermandois, and his neglect of Richard, Espriota's son Towards the end of his life he changed his policy. He welcomed a fresh arrival of Danes, and allowed them to settle peaceably in the newly acquired district of Cotentin His son Richard, suddenly emerging from obscurity, became the darling of his father, was entrusted to William's old tutor, Botho, the Danish-born, and Bernard the Dane, and sent to Bayeux to be instructed in the Northern tongue

Arnulf of Flanders viewed William's partiality to the new arrivals of Northmen with great apprehension, and formed a coalition against him In December, 942, William was treacherously invited by Arnulf to a negotiation with him on the Somme at Pecquigny, separated from his adherents, and basely murdered on the Flemish side of the river. William who is generally called *Longsword* by historians, was thus snatched away in the midst of a changeable, aimless life ; and the existence of his race and issue in France was endangered by the long rule of a minor.

RICHARD THE FEARLESS.*

942—996.

M —1 Emma, d of Hugh the Great
  2 Guenora

CONTEMPORARY PRINCES

FRANCE	936, Louis IV.	954, Lothaire	986, Louis V	987, Hugh *Capet*
ENGLAND	940, Edmund I	946, Edred	955, Edwy	959, Edgar
		975, Edward II	978, Ethelred II	

On the accession of young Richard he was surrounded by great dangers. The old Northern non-observance of religious marriage rites between his parents laid him open to the imputation of bastardy. The ambiguous position was undoubtedly an element of difficulty There were enemies enough who gladly seized the opportunity of disputing Richard's inheritance, and Leutgarda, who had married Theobald of Blois, pursued her stepson all her life with the hostility traditional of a stepmother Fortunately for Richard, he was amongst the faithful friends of his father, Bernard the Dane, Ivo de Bellesme, and Osmund de Centville Louis of France and Hugh of Paris united to reduce Normandy Accordingly, the duchy was invaded, the Danish party overthrown, Rouen seized, and Louis gained possession of young Richard, while Hugh secured Evreux Richard was sent prisoner to Laon, from which, aided by his trusty companion, Osmund, he escaped hidden in a truss of hay, and the standard of revolt was raised—945. Fortunately for Richard, in his hour of peril, Harald *Bluetooth*, King of Denmark, grandfather of Knut the Great, appeared on the coast, rallied the Normans round his standard (945), and meeting Louis on the Dive, utterly routed his forces Louis, made prisoner in personal combat with Harald, succeeded in escaping, only to fall in the hands of other enemies Harald, after passing through the land confirming the authority of the young Duke, returned to his northern home

The next year (946) Hugh of Paris, anxious to secure the alliance of Richard, betrothed to him his young daughter Emma, and Richard thereon commended himself to Hugh, whose influence in France now became supreme In 956 Hugh died, leaving by will, his son Hugh Capet, a boy of 13, hereafter King of France, under the guardianship of Richard, and the alliance was cemented in 960 by the consummation of the marriage between Emma and Richard

The rest of Richard's reign was comparatively quiet, if we except a short war with England in 991. This is said to have been caused by the shelter offered by Richard to the Danes who, under Sweyn of Denmark, son of Harald *Bluetooth*, were again beginning to trouble England, and entering on that political conquest which culminated in the establishment of Knut upon the English throne. The war was soon put an end to by the mediation of the Pope, and is important only as forming the first instance in which the Norman dukes were brought into direct connection with the English kings.

Richard had no children by Emma, but by Guenora, to whom he had been united in

---

* The Normans in Europe

the Northern way, he had a numerous progeny. He eventually married her according to Christian rites, and by the doctrine of the Church, his children became legitimatised Of these, RICHARD succeeded him, ROBERT was Count of Evreux, and Archbishop of Rouen, MALGER was Count of Mortain, in the Côtentin, and acquired the Earldom of Corbeil by marriage with the heiress of that lordship Amongst his daughters were EMMA, married first to Ethelred the Unready, and secondly to Knut the Great, both these sovereigns being anxious to strengthen their houses by alliance with the line of Thor; HADUISA, married to Geoffrey, Count of Brittany; MATILDA, married to Eudes II, Count of Blois.

RICHARD II, THE GOOD *

996—1026

M — Judith of Brittany

CONTEMPORARY PRINCES

FRANCE   996, Robert II
ENGLAND   978, Ethelred II   1016 {Edmund II, *Ironsides*
                                     {Knut *the Great*

Richard the Second succeeded his father at a somewhat early age, and amongst the first things requiring his attention was a revolt of the peasants Richard getting word of it in time, crushed it out with merciless severity In all the wars of King Robert of France we find Richard lending valuable assistance, while the King of Paris acts as mediator in some of Richard's quarrels

Richard connected himself with the rising House of Blois, and married his sister Maude to Eudes, her dower being the County of Dreux, over which a brief quarrel ensued. With Brittany he allied himself by a double marriage He married Judith, sister of Geoffrey, Count of Rennes, who had established his supremacy over the country and gained the title of Duke, and Haduisa, his sister, became Geoffrey's wife. When Geoffrey died, his sons, Alan and Odo, fell under the guardianship of their uncle and suzerain

When Ethelred of England fled from the Danes in 1013, he sought refuge with Richard, bringing with him the Æthelings—Alfred and Edward In Normandy, Edward, afterwards the Confessor, imbibed those Norman tastes which led him to introduce Normans into England when he regained his ancestral throne, and here he contracted that friendship with William the Bastard which hurried on the downfall of his line

During Richard's reign the Normans began to seek for enterprise beyond his dominions Spain first attracted them, and thither Roger de Toesny sailed in 1018 to war against the Moors, and to found, if possible, a dominion for himself. This, however, had no lasting results Far more important is the settlement of the Normans at Aversa, in Italy, where the sons of Tancred of Hauteville won first the dukedom of Apulia, and

* The Normans in Europe

then the kingdom of Sicily. William, Drogo, and Humfrey of Hanteville ruled Apulia in succession, and then their brother Robert Guiscard, the Wise, succeeded them. He completed the conquest of Apulia and Calabria, and wrested the ducal title from Pope Nicholas. He and his son Bohemond, Prince of Antioch, began a series of invasions against Constantinople. To Roger, his youngest brother, the twelfth son of Tancred, he entrusted the conquest of Sicily.

Richard II. died without a dream of the great destiny awaiting his race in the south. Three years before the settlement at Aversa he had passed peacefully away, leaving his son RICHARD, the third of his name, as his successor to the dukedom. His other children were ROBERT, afterwards duke, WILLIAM of Arques, Count of Talou, MALGER Archbishop of Rouen, ALICE, married Renaud, Count of Burgundy, ELEANOR, married Baldwin IV, *the Bearded*, of Flanders, and ADELISA, married Stephen II, of Blois.

RICHARD III *
1026—1028

SYNCHRONISMS :
FRANCE 996, Robert II. ENGLAND 1016, Knut *the Great*

Richard III. only enjoyed his dukedom two years, and these were clouded by domestic quarrels with his brother Robert. A dispute arose between the brothers as to Robert's share, and as to the possession of the important castle of Falaise. The reconciliation was speedily followed by Richard's death from poison, administered, many said, by Robert.

"The History of the Saint-Clairs" † states that Helena, daughter of Richard, was married to Waleran, Lord of Saint-Clair. The age of this Duke is variously stated, but there can be little doubt that he was of full age in 1025, when Renaud of Burgundy had been confined in prison by Hugues, Bishop of Auxerre, and Count of Chalons, for Richard II. thereupon sent his sons, Richard and Robert, with an army to relieve their brother-in-law, and Count Hugues was compelled to present himself with a saddle on his back (the usual custom at that period), and crave mercy at the hands of the sons of the Duke of Normandy. Richard left a natural son named Nicholas, who in 1042 was Abbot of St Ouen ‡

ROBERT, THE MAGNIFICENT *
1028—1035

M.—Estrith, d. of K. Sweyn of Denmark

SYNCHRONISMS
FRANCE 996, Robert II., 1031, Henry I. ENGLAND 1016, Knut

Among contemporaries Robert of Normandy was called the Magnificent, which best accords with the reckless, extravagant liberality of his character, although he is also called 'the Devil' and 'the Saint.'

---

* The Normans in Europe   † Van Bassan   ‡ The Conq. and his Companions

Alan of Brittany attempted to throw off his allegiance, but was reduced to submission. Robert assumed the position of a protector of exiled princes and a king-maker. Baldwin IV. of Flanders, driven forth by his rebellious son, was restored by the Norman Duke. He assisted Henry of France to regain his throne (1031—1033), for which service he received the over-lordship of the Vexin. He revived the pretensions of the Æthelings to the English throne, and claimed the cession of England. Upon Knut's refusal, he attempted to invade England, but the Dane was too firmly seated, and the expedition failed.

His life closed with a strange pilgrimage to the Holy Land, the stories of which surround him with the romance of a knight errant. With ostentatious liberality his mules were shod with shoes of silver gilt, and carelessly attached by one nail alone, that they might be lost and speak of the riches of him who had passed that way. Arrived at the Court of Constantinople, he treated the Emperor with a rudeness and contempt which were best answered by the studied courtesy of the more refined monarch of the East. When he reached the gates of Jerusalem, we are told of the contest of liberality between him and the Emir, Robert paying all the tolls of those pilgrims who waited outside the gates, too poor to pay their fee for entrance; which the Emir, not to be outdone, returned on his departure. On his way home Robert's pilgrimage and life were suddenly cut short in Bithynia, where he died, some said by poison. It is related that he met with Fulk Nerra, Count of Anjou, at Constantinople, in 1035, and they travelled thence together to the Holy Land, escorted by some merchants of Antioch, who had offered to be their guides. Robert becoming fatigued, was carried in a litter by four Moors. A Norman pilgrim returning from Jerusalem, meeting his sovereign with this equipage, asked if he had any message to send his friends. "Tell them," said the Duke, "that thou sawest me borne to Paradise by four devils."*

By Estrith, sister of Knut, Robert had no issue. Before setting out for Jerusalem he assembled his baronage, and declaring his natural son William (by one Herleve, daughter of a furrier of Falaise) his heir, those present did homage and took the oath of allegiance to William, then between seven and eight years of age.

WILLIAM THE CONQUEROR †

1035—1087

M.—Matilda of Flanders

CONTEMPORARY PRINCES

FRANCE	1031, Henry I	1060, Philip I	
ENGLAND	1035, Harald I	1039, Horda-Knut	1042, Edward *the Confessor*
		1066, Harald II, *Infelix*	

William, though born a bastard, soon justified the pride of his father by his excellence in all knightly feats of strength, and probably Robert would have most willingly married Herleve, and thus legitimatised him, if Estrith were not still alive and presenting an

---

* The Conq. and his Companions, p. 79 † Freeman and Planché

insuperable obstacle Before departing for the East he committed William to the care of his cousin, Alan of Brittany, who fulfilled the position of regent with honour and fidelity While Robert lived the nobles submitted in sullen silence, but the news of his death was the signal for general anarchy In his very cradle William had been cursed by William Talvas de Belesme, the descendant of Ivo de Belesme, the trusty friend of Richard *Sans Peur* "Shame, shame, thrice shame," cried he, "for by thee and thine shall I and mine be brought to loss and dishonour " The curse of de Belesme found echo throughout the dukedom Alan of Brittany met his fate by poison before the stronghold of the Montgomeries Other friends of William were assassinated, and he himself narrowly escaped the same fate

In sketching the history of William, the three decisive epochs of ducal domination are marked by the battles of Val-es-dunes, Varaville, and Hastings His first trouble was a conspiracy of Guy, Count of Burgundy, his cousin, who claimed the duchy as his by right of birth. Guy won to his side many of the leading Norman nobles, amongst others Nigel of St. Saviour, Viscount of the Coutances, Randolf, Viscount of Bayeux, and Hamon, Lord of Thorigny, whom Benoit de St More distinguishes with the remarkable soubriquet of Anti-Christ, but who is more generally known as Hamo *Dentatus*, or *aux Dents** To these we may add Grimbald of Plessis William was at Valognes. One night in 1047 he was roused from sleep by his court jester and urged to fly without delay. Mounting his steed in haste he rode in the direction of Falaise He forded the estuary formed by the Ouse and Dive, with an ebbing tide, and landed safely on the other side in the Bayeux district Pressing on at sunrise he drew near the church and castle of Rye, and found Hubert the lord thereof standing in front of the chateau Hubert recognised the Duke, gave him a fresh mount, and bade his three sons ride by his side and never leave him till he was safely lodged in his own castle of Falaise The loyal sons faithfully executed their father's command, and we are not surprised, writes Freeman, to find that the House of Rye rose high in the favour of William, and we can hardly grudge them their share in the lands of England, when we find that Eudo, the son of Hubert, the King's *Dapifer*, and Sheriff of Essex, was not only the founder of the great House of St John at Colchester, but won a purer fame as one of the very few Normans in high authority who knew how to win the love and confidence of the conquered Angles At this critical juncture William had recourse to the assistance of his suzerain, Henry of France, by whom he was favourably received. A French army, with the King at its head, was soon ready to march to the Duke's support. The French and the loyal Normans joining their forces some miles to the east of Caen, engaged the rebel host in the neighbourhood of the memorable Val-es-dunes Before the battle, William was strengthened by the defection of Ralph of Tesson, Lord of the Forest of Cingueleiz, who deserted the rebels and crossed over to the ducal army All fought with valour. William slew with his own hand Hardrez, the choicest warrior of Bayeux, and the King of France was twice unhorsed—once by a knight of the Cotentin, and again by Hamon, Lord of Thorigny, who paid for the distinction with his life By the express order of King Henry, Hamon was buried with all fitting splendour before the Church of Our Lady at Esquai, on the Orne After William slew Hardrez, Randolf began to falter and presently fled, leaving Neil fighting on The valiant Neil was the last to flee He was exiled to Brittany, but was soon restored to ducal favour Guy of Burgundy returned to his native

---

* Hence anti-Deus in error

land, the Burgundian palatinate. Grimbald died in fetters in prison. Thus ended in favour of William the battle of Val-es-dunes, which marks the first decisive epoch of ducal domination, the other two being Varaville and Hastings.

About 1051 the County of Mortain,—Moritolium, in the diocese of Avranches—was held by William, surnamed the Warling, son of Mauger, a lawful son of Richard the Fearless and Guenora. He was therefore a first cousin of the late Duke Robert, and if the succession had been limited to heirs-male, would have ranked next after William of Arques, Count of Talou, and Malger, Archbishop of Rouen, sons of Richard II.; and after Richard, Count of Evreux, only son of Robert, Count of Evreux, Archbishop of Rouen, a son of Richard the Fearless. His name has not occurred in the accounts of former disturbances, but it is clear that he might, like so many others, have felt himself aggrieved by the accession of the bastard. Among the knights in the service of William, Count of Mortain, was one hitherto unknown to history, but to become famous. Robert le Bigod, patriarch of the future powerful House of Bigod, was now a knight so poor that he craved leave of his Lord to depart from his service and to seek his fortune among his countrymen, who were carving out for themselves lordships and principalities in Apulia. The Count bade him stay where he was; within eighty days he, Robert le Bigod, would be able there in Normandy to lay his hands on whatever good things it pleased him. In such a speech treason plainly lurked, and Robert, whether from duty to his sovereign or in the hope of winning favour with a more powerful master, determined that the matter should come to the ear of the Duke. The Bigod was a kinsman of Richard d'Avranches, now high in favour at the court of William. By his means Robert obtained an introduction to the Duke, and told him of the treasonable words of the Count of Mortain. William accordingly sent for his cousin and charged him with plotting against the State. He had, the Duke told him, determined again to disturb the peace of the country, and again to bring about the reign of license. But while he, Duke William, lived, the peace which Normandy so much needed should, by God's help, never be disturbed again. Count William must at once leave the country, and not return to it during the life-time of his namesake the Duke. The proud Lord of Mortain was thus driven to doing what his poor knight had thought of doing. He went to the wars in Apulia in humble guise enough, attended by a single esquire. The Duke at once bestowed the vacant County of Mortain upon his half-brother Robert, the son of Herluin and Herleve. Thus, says our informant, did William pluck down the proud kindred of his father and lift up the lowly kindred of his mother [*]. Historians agree that William the Warling was banished on the mere suspicion of treason. Orderic Vital, when referring to the circumstance, narrates "The Duke disinherited and drove out of Normandy William the Warling, Count of Mortain, for a single word."

The many other notable incidents during the rule of William the Conqueror belong more to English history, and are therefore omitted as foreign to the scope of this work.

Hamon aux Dents, who perished at Val-es-dunes, is stated to have been Earl of Corbeil, and a son of Malger, Count of Mortain, and a modern writer[†] endeavours to establish Walter, Lord of St Clair in Normandy, as brother to Hamo Fitz-Hamo *Dentatus*, and also in near relationship to Hubert, Lord of Rye, which latter was sent as ambassador to Edward the Confessor by the Norman Duke. The other legitimate scions of the

---

[*] Planche. [†] An of the Sinclairs of England

WILLIAM THE CONQUEROR.

Norman Dukes were the sons of Richard II.—Malger, Archbishop of Rouen, whom Duke William banished to the Channel Islands, where he died without lawful issue; and William of Arques, Count of Talou, who also died issueless. Richard, Count of Evreux, only son of Robert, Archbishop of Rouen (second son of Richard I.), left one son, William, Count of Evreux, who had no issue. Malger, Earl of Corbeil and Mortain (third son of Richard I.), had issue William the Warling, exiled to Apulia, of whose issue there is no account. The male line of Rollo in lawful descent is thus presumably extinct, and the representation would therefore devolve on the heir-general. "The History of the St. Clairs" states that Waleran, Lord of St. Clair, married the daughter of Duke Richard of Normandy. The sire de St. Clair accompanied Duke William at Hastings, where he fought with distinction, and his name is enumerated on the Roll of Battle Abbey. Wace records: "Hue de Mortemer with three other knights, the sires of Anvilliers, Onebec, and St. Cler, charged a body of the Angles who had fallen back on a rising ground, and overthrew many."

THE EARLDOM OF ORKNEY.

DYNASTIES SINCE THE NORWEGIAN CONQUEST,

871—1471

Order	Earls	Title to Earldom	Regnal Years Accession	Regnal Years Demission	Remarks
		THE HOUSE OF ODIN, OR NORSE LINE			
1	Rognvald, *Earl of Moer*	Inv by K. Har Fairhair	871	890	Burnt in Moeri
* 2	Sigurd *the Sea-king*	Brother of Rognvald	871	882	Slain in Caithness
* 3	Guttorm	Son of Sigurd	882	883	Died childless
4	Hallad	Son of Rognvald	885	885	Abdicated
5	Einar, *Torf-Finar*	,,	885	910	Natural death
6	Arnkell	Son of Torf-Einar	910	950	Fell in England
7	Erlend	,,	910	950	
* 8	Thorfinn *Cleaver or Helmets*	,,	910	963	Natural death
* 9	Arnfinn	Son of Thorfinn	963	967	Murdered at Murkle
* 10	Havard *the Blessed*	,,	963	970	Slain at Stenness
* 11	Ljot	,,	963	976	Slain in Caithness
* 12	Skuli	,,	963	974	Fell in Caithness
* 13	Hlodver	,,	963	980	Natural death
* 14	Sigurd II, *the Stout*	Son of Hlodver	980	1014	Fell at Clontarf
15	Somerled	Son of Sigurd II	1014	1015	Died issueless
16	Einar II	,,	1014	1026	Slain in Deerness
17	Brusi	,,	1014	1031	Natural death
* 18	Thorfinn II *the Great*	,,	1014	1064	,,
19	Rognvald II	Son of Brusi	1035	1046	Slain in Papa Stronsay
* 20	Paul	Son of Thorfinn II	1064	1103	D in exile at Bergen
* 21	Erlend II	,,	1064	1103	,, Nidaros
	(Sigurd *Crown Prince of Norway*,	Viceroy of the Isles	1098	1103	*Succeeds to Norway*)
* 22	Hakon *the Imperious*	Son of Paul	1103	1122	Natural death
23	St Magnus *the Martyr*	Son of Erlend II	1103	1115	Executed by Haco
* 24	Harald *the Orator*	Son of Hakon	1122	1127	Poisoned
* 25	Paul II, *the Silent*	,,	1122	1136	Deposed
26	Erlend III, *the Younger*	Son of Harald	1127	1156	Slain in Damsay
27	St Rognvald III, *the Rhymer*	Son of Gunhild, d. of 21	1136	1158	Slain in Caithness
* 29	Harald III, *the Younger*	Son of Ingigerd, d. of 27	1176	1198	Fell at Clairdon
		THE HOUSE OF ATHOL, OR ROYAL SCOTTISH LINE			
* 28	Harald II *the Wicked*	Son of Margaret d. of 22	1139	1206	Natural death
* 30	David	Son of Harald II	1206	1214	,,
* 31	John	,,	1206	1231	Murdered at Thurso

ORCADIAN DYNASTIES.—Continued.

Order	Earls	Title to Earldom	Regnal Years Accession	Regnal Years Demission	Remarks
	THE ANGUS LINE				
*32	Magnus II., *of Angus*	Kinsman of John	1231	1239	
*33	Gilbert	Brother of Magnus II	1239		
*34	Gilbert II	Son of Gilbert I		1256	Period of peace
*35	Magnus III	Son of Gilbert II	1256	1273	
*36	Magnus IV	Son of Magnus III	1273	1284	
*37	John II	,, ,,	1284	1310	
*38	Magnus V.	Son of John II	1310	1321	
	THE STRATHERNE LINE.				
**39	Malise, *Earl of Stratherne*	Heir-at-law to Magn V	1321	1333	[Fell at Halidon Hill]
**40	Malise II, *Earl of Stratherne*	Son of Malise I	1333	1344	Died *s p* male
41	Erengisle Suneson-Jonsson	Son-in-law of Malise II	1353	1357	Died *s p*, 1392
	INTERVAL OF DISPUTED SUCCESSION				
	Thomas de St Clair	Ballivus		1364	Dead 1371
	Hakon Jonsson	Prefect	1369	1379	App by Norwgn Crown
*	Alex de la Ard	Governor & Commissnr	1375	1376	Living 1379
	THE SAINT-CLAIR LINE				
*	Wm de St Clair, *Lord of Roslin*	Mar Isab, d of No 40		1363	Anc of St Clairs of the I
*42	Henry I, *the Holy*	Son of Isab de Strath	1379	1404	Slain by English *v m*
*43	Henry II, Lord St Clair (1st)	Son of Henry I	1404	1420	
*44	William ,, (2nd)	Son of Henry II	1420	1471	Surrendered the dignity
	Wm *the Waster* ,, (3rd)	Eldest son of 2nd Lord		1497	Anc Wars'ter, Saba, &c.
	Henry ,, (4th)	Son of 3rd Lord	1485	1514	Gov and Capt -Genl
	Margaret, Lady Sinclair	Baroness Regent	1514	1539	
	Sir James Sinclair of Sanday	Grandson of 3rd Lord	1515	1535	Gov Kirk'll Castle
	Oliver Sinclair, of 'Solway Moss'	Grandson of 2nd Lord	1540	1548	Governor, &c
	William, 5th Lord Sinclair	Son of 4th Lord	1543		Last 'Lord of the Isles' [Scots
	DUKE OF ORKNEY				
	James Hepburn, E of Bothwell	Grandson of 4th Lord	1567	1567	Pr -Con of Mary, Q of

NOTE —The earlier years are approximated from the Orkneyinga Saga The ancestors of the Earl of Moeri were Norwegian grandees *ab initio* by virtue of their descent from Odin, the great Pagan-Pontiff, 'God, father, and warrior-priest of all the Dacians' The autonomous maritime principality known as the Jarldom of Orkney, and the Earldom of Caithness, are the most ancient in geographical Britain, both of these dignities being in existence coeval with the reign of Alfred the Great, and centuries antecedent to the authentic mention of others The Earldoms of Athol, Angus, and Stratherne occur in the earliest Scottish records

* Also Earls of Caithness (inclusive of Sutherland till after the 31st Earl)

** Also Earls Palatine of Stratherne.

FAC-SIMILE PAGE OF MS. OF ORKNEYINGERS' SAGA.

CHAPTER III

SEA-KINGS OF ORKNEY.*

THE NORSE LINE.

1 Rognvald *of Moeri, Jarl*	871
2 Sigurd *the Powerful*	871—882
3 Guttorm	882—883
4 Hallad	883—885
5 Einar, *Torf Einar*	885—910
6 Arnkell ⎱	
7 Erlend ⎰	910—941

CONTEMPORARY PRINCES

NORWAY	863, Harald *Fairhair*.	934, Eric *Bloodaxe*	940, Hakon *the Good*
NORMANDY	912, Rolf *the Sea King*	927, William, *Longsword*	943, Richard, *the Fearless*
SCOTLAND	862, Constantine II	879, Aodh , Eocha , Grig	892, Donald IV
	904, Constantine III	944, Malcolm I	
ENGLAND	871, Alfred *the Great*	901, Edward *the Elder*	924, Athelstan
	940, Edmund	946, Edred	

ROGNVALD THE MIGHTY, 1st EARL.

By the naval victory of Hafursfiord in 870 Harald Fairhair *(Harfagri)* became sole monarch in Norway. Large numbers of the wealthy and powerful odallers, whom he had dispossessed of their territorial possessions, fled to the Isles of Orkney (anciently known as Inistore) and Zetland, which for a full century previous to this time had been well known as the viking station of the western *haf*—the rendezvous of the Northern rovers, who swept the coasts of the Hebudes and swarmed in the Irish Seas. Fugitives from their fatherland, and outlaws of the new kingdom which Harald had succeeded in establishing in Norway, they settled themselves permanently in the islands. Then they turned their haven of refuge into a base of operations for retaliatory warfare, harrying the Norwegian coasts during the summer, and living at leisure in winter, secure in the islands with their plunder. At length King Harald, irritated by their incessant ravages, collected a powerful fleet, and, visiting Zetland, Orkney, and the Hebudes in succession, he swept their coasts clear of the plunderers, subduing the whole of the Northern and Western Islands as far south as Man. In this expedition he was accompanied by his favourite comrade-in-arms and most trusted counsellor, Rognvald, Jarl of Moeri and Raumsdahl, whose eldest son Ivar and brother Sigurd were also with the fleet. Ivar was slain in one of the numerous fights during the purgation of the Isles, and it is thought he was buried in Sanday, where there is a cairn known as Ivar's Knowe. In order to recompense Rognvald for the loss of his heir to Moeri, King Harald offered him the lordship of the

---
* Authorities—Ork Saga, Torfæus, Barry, Pope, etc.

twin archipelagoes with the title of Jarl of the Orkneys. But as Rognvald had extensive possessions in his own country, together with many dependents and friends—as he was a favourite at the court of his sovereign, from whom he had received many, and expected perhaps still more favours—he preferred a residence at home to one in a distant country with all the wealth and honour it promised to bestow. Averse, however, to offend this prince by rejecting the benefits which his bounty had conferred on him, and, reluctant to let them go past his house, with the consent of his sovereign he transferred the royal gift to his brother Sigurd, who had been Harald's flag captain, and Harald gave him the title of Jarl before leaving the west, where Sigurd remained.

SIGURD THE POWERFUL, 2ND EARL

Earl Sigurd was a mighty warrior, and his conduct evinced that he was not only actuated by the spirit of the times, but had all the distinctive features of his line. His brother's influence had raised him to an elevated rank. His bounty had conferred on him both power and opulence, which, instead of rendering him contented with his lot, only served to augment his ambition, to gratify which he resolved to extend his territories far beyond those limits which the ocean had prescribed.* To effect this purpose he formed an alliance with Thorstein the Red, a warrior of intrepid valour and royal descent, son of Olaf the White, King of Dublin, and the Lady Aude, the Wealthy † In conjunction with Thorstein, Sigurd levied troops and fitted out a squadron, when they crossed to the Scottish mainland and conquered Caithness, Sutherland, and the rich shores of East Ross and fertile plains of Moray ‡ While he remained in this last province he built a fort on the southern side of Moray, which is taken to be the large fort called Eccialsbacka at the Burghead in the parish of Duffus. It was very extensive and strong, having been founded chiefly on rock § His death befell in a most remarkable way. Having a difference with a certain Scottish earl, Melbrigd Tonn (buck-tooth), an appointment was made for a conference to adjust the matters at issue, each earl to be attended by a retinue of 40 men. On the appointed day Sigurd was suspicious of treachery on the part of the Scots. He therefore caused 80 men to be mounted on 40 horses. When Earl Melbrigd saw this, he said to his men "Now have we been treacherously dealt with by Earl Sigurd, for I see two feet at each horse's side, and the men, I believe, are thus twice as many as the steeds. But let us be brave and kill each his man before we die." Then they made themselves ready. When Sigurd saw it he also decided on his plan, and said to his men "Now, let one half of our number dismount, and attack them in flank when the troops meet, while we shall ride at them with all our speed to break their battle array." There was hard fighting immediately, and it was not long till Earl Melbrigd fell, and all his men with him. Earl Sigurd and his men, in bravado, fastened the heads of the slain to their saddle straps, and so they rode home triumphing in their victory. It happened, however, on the homeward ride, that, as Sigurd was spurring his horse, he struck his leg against a projecting tooth of the fallen Scottish earl, which made a slight incision that soon became swollen and painful, eventually resulting in his death. Sigurd the Powerful was hoy-laid (buried in a mound or cairn) on the estuary of the Oykel, and his grave mound, which is still visible, is locally known as Siward's hoch. He was succeeded by his only son

---

Barry *Orkn Saga ' Barry § Pope

GUTTORM, 3RD EARL,

who only enjoyed the earldom for one winter, when, dying childless, it reverted to his uncle, Rognvald, the Founder, and the Isles, for want of a spirited governor, were again infested with the incursions of freebooters, of whom, amongst others, the celebrated Hastings is noted as having passed his life in sailing from Denmark to the Orcades, from the Orcades to Gaul, from Gaul to Ireland, from Ireland to England * In this situation of things Rognvald, either unacquainted with the real state of the country, or blinded by parental affection, appointed to that station his son Hallad, who, as the events but too plainly showed, was altogether unqualified for the dignity †

HALLAD, 4TH EARL

King Harald gave Hallad the title of Jarl, and he came out to the West and took up his residence in Hrossey (Pomona), where he lived in retirement, while piratical hordes of Vikings went prowling about the islands and outlying headlands slaying and plundering The Boendr complained to him of their losses and his supineness in redeeming their wrongs Hallad grew tired of the dignity, resigned the Earldom, and returned to Norway, where he took up his odal rights and afterwards lived a retired life. His rulership was considered very ignominious Some say he was slain in battle in that part of the parish of Reay which lies in Sutherland and is called Strathhalladale It is a valley ten miles in length, divided into two sides by a river called the river of Halladale, running from the south to the north, and falling into the North Sea at Tor. About the middle of this strath, and near a place called Dal Halladha, the country people show a spot where they say a bloody battle was fought between the Scots and the Norwegians. It was on the side of a hill, on the east side of a river, now covered with small cairns, or heaps of stones, where the slain are supposed to be buried, and there they say Halladr, the King of Lochlin's son, was slain They also show the place of his sepulchre on the opposite side of the river, where they assert Halladha and his sword were laid It is a deep circular trench, 12 feet in diameter, and there is a large stone erected in the midst of it ‡

Upon the abdication of Hallad, the Isles became a station for two Danish vikings, Thorir Treskegg and Kalf Skurfa When Jarl Rognvald heard of this he became very angry, and called together his sons, Thorir, Hrollaug, and Einar Hrolf (hereafter conqueror of Neustria) was at that time absent on a war expedition. The details of the conference have been already set forth It was finally resolved that Einar should undertake the office, so Rognvald gave him a fully equipped vessel, and he received from King Harald the title of Earl.

EINAR, 5TH EARL

Einar thereon sailed to Hjaltaland, and there many men gathered round him Then he went on to the Orkneys and met Kalf and Thorir in a great battle, in which the vikings were defeated and both slain This was said about it

| "Hann gaf Treskegg trollum, | Tre-skegg gave he to the Trows |
| Torf-Einarr, drap Skurfu"§ | Skurfa fell before Torf-Einar |

---

* Thierry   † Barry   ‡ Pope   § Orkn Saga, Rolls' text edn

Then Einar took possession of the lands, and soon became a great chief. He was the man who first cut turf (peat) from the ground for fuel, at Torfness in Scotland, for fuel was scarce in the Isles. Einar was a tall man, ugly, and with one eye, yet he was very keen sighted.

When the sons of King Harald grew up, they become envious of the honours and possessions of Rognvald, Earl of Moeri, and two of them, Halfdan and Gudrod, surrounded his residence, fired it, and he was burnt to death with sixty of his retainers. King Harald was justly angry at this, and Halfdan fled, in three large ships, over seas to the west but Gudrod effected a reconciliation with his father. King Harald put Thorer *Tacitus* in his father's estate, and to compensate for his loss gave him his own daughter Alof in marriage. When Halfdan arrived in the Orkneys, Earl Einar crossed over to Caithness, and Halfdan became king over the Islands. Einar returned the same year, and gave battle to Halfdan. The victory was to Einar, and Halfdan fled from his vengeance. Einar then sang this song

Sèkatek Hrolf's or hendi	"Why are not the spear-shafts flying,
ne Hrollaugi fljúga	From the hands of Hrolf and Hrollaug,
'dorr a dolga mengi,	Thickly 'gainst the press of warriors?
dugir oss fodur hefna	Now, my father! I avenge thee
"en i kveld thar er knyjum	While we here are closed in battle,
of kerstraumi romn	Sits Earl Thorir all the evening,
"thegjandi sitr thetta	Silent o'er his cheerless glass"
Thorir jarl a Mæri."	

Next morning Halfdan was found on Rinar's Hill. The Earl made a blood-eagle be cut on his back with the sword, and had his ribs severed from the backbone, and his lungs pulled out. Thus he gave him to Odin as an offering for victory, and then raised a cairn over his remains. When the news of Halfdan's end reached Norway his brothers were greatly enraged, and threatened an expedition to the Isles to avenge them, but King Harald delayed their journey. Einar despised their threats of vengeance. Harald himself took the matter in hand, set out for the Western seas, and came to the Isles, whereupon Einar fled to Caithness. Ambassadors went between them, and peace was made, Harald imposing a fine upon the Isles, adjudging them to pay 60 marks of gold. Earl Einar offered the Boendr to pay the money himself on condition that he should become proprietor of all their freeholds. The Boendr accepted this, because the wealthy ones thought they could at their convenience redeem their freeholds, and the poorer ones had no money. Einar paid the whole sum, and for a long time afterwards the Earls held all the allodial lands until Sigurd the Stout gave back their odal possessions to the Orcadians. King Harald went back to Norway, but Einar ruled over the Orkneys a long time, and died in old age, leaving three sons, Arnkell, Erlend, and Thorfinn the Skull-splitter. In the parish of Latheron, in Caithness, is an old ruin called Knock Einar, probably his Caithness seat.†

ARNKELL AND ERLEND, 6TH AND 7TH EARLS

In their time Athelstan of England ravaged as far as Caithness (934). ‡ By way of reprisal these two Earls joined the forces of Eric Bloodaxe, to assist that king to recover his kingdom of Northumbria. Sailing first to the Western Isles, they obtained reinforce-

ARNKELL AND ERLEND.

ments there, and then cruised along the coasts of Ireland, Cornwall, and the South of England, plundering as they went. Eventually they were brought to a decisive engagement, and Eric and the two Earls fell in battle (anno 941), being the first year of King Edmund's reign.

Gunnhild, Eric's queen, deemed it unsafe to continue longer in England, so gathering all the coin and valuables within reach, she, with her household guards, steered for the Orkneys, of which forcible possession was taken, until later on they elected to depart for Denmark.

THE NORSE LINE.—Continued

8 Thorfinn, *Cleaver of Helmets*		950—963
9 Arnfinn		963—967
10 Havard, *the Happy*		970
11 Ljot	. .	976
12 Skuli	.	974
13 Hlodver *(Ludovic)*		980

Contemporary Princes

NORWAY	940, Hakon *the Good*	963, Harald *Greyskin*	977, Hakon *Jarl*
NORMANDY	943, Richard *the Fearless*		
SCOTLAND	944, Malcolm I	953, Indulf	961, Duff
	965, Culen	970, Kenneth III	

THORFINN 8TH EARL

UPON the death of his brothers Arnkell and Erlend, Thorfinn became sole Earl of the Orkneys, but had to submit for some time to the usurpation of Gunnhild, the Dowager ex-Queen of Northumbria and of Norway, who, with her sons, made conquest of the country, collecting rents and imposing taxes at their pleasure. During the winter they held court in Orkney, and in summer plundered Scotland and Ireland. But on the occasion of war breaking out between Norway and Denmark, Gunnhild resolved to instantly set sail for the latter kingdom. Before embarking she restored Orkney and Hjaltland to Thorfinn, and gave her daughter Ragnhild in marriage to his son, the doomed Arnfinn. Thorfinn was a great warrior, and his fame is transmitted as such to posterity. He espoused Grelod, daughter of Earl Duncan in Caithness by his lady Groa, daughter of Thorstein the Red, and thus by this alliance re-united Caithness to the Orcadian earldom. By Grelod Thorfinn was father of five sons. One was named Havard, Arsœli (blessed with good seasons), the second Hlodver, the third Ljot, the fourth Skuli, and the fifth Arnfinn. The foregoing is the order given in King Olaf Triggveson's Saga*, but in the Orkneyinga Saga they are otherwise ranged as follows—Arnfinn, Havard, Hlodver, Ljot, and Skuli.† Thorfinn died a natural death, and was buried in a mound on Hauga Heath, now Hoxa, a peninsula on the north-west side of South Ronaldsa.

ARNFINN, 9TH EARL.

Arnfinn had, as already mentioned, married the Princess Ragnhilda, daughter of Eric Bloodaxe, ex-King of Norway and of Northumbria, and in a short time by means of her intrigues he was killed in the town of Murkle in Caithness. He was succeeded by his brother

HAVARD, 10TH EARL,

who ruled the Isles with the strictest justice, and in his time the country so abounded in cereals and the other necessaries of life that hence he got the surname of Arsœli, the Happy, or Blessed with good seasons. This honourable soubriquet he might have retained to the end of his days but for an act fatal in its consequences. This was his marriage with the ambitious Ragnhilda, whose hands (though perhaps he was ignorant of the circumstance) were freshly stained with the blood of Arnfinn. Soon tiring of Havard, under promise of marriage, she induced his sister's son Einar *Klining*, to slay him. Einar was warned by a spaeman to postpone the matter, but pretended not to hear, and upon meeting Havard at Steinsness a hard fight ensued, when the Earl was mortally wounded. The place of his fall is called Havard's teigr or lot. Ragnhild disowned having promised Einar any reward or having counselled the Earl's death, and incited Einar *Hardkiopt*, son of another sister of Havard, to avenge his uncle's death. Einar *Hardkiopt* treated the suggestion with circumspection, but forthwith slew his cousin Einar *Klining*.

LJOT AND SKULI, 11TH AND 12TH EARLS.

Havard was succeeded by Ljot, and incredible as it may seem, this Earl was daring enough to marry Ragnhilda, who had compassed the death of both his brothers. Einar *Hardkiopt* having avenged his uncle and slain his cousin, found himself no nearer the Earldom than before. Highly dissatisfied, he wished to collect men and subdue the islands by force, but had great difficulty in getting men, for the Orcadians wished to serve the sons of Thorfinn. Some time afterwards Earl Ljot had Einar slain. Near the boundary line of the parishes of Harra and Firth are two places known as the Cups of Liod and the Chair of Liod, which are understood to be named from an incident in connection with this Earl.

Ljot did not obtain undisputed possession on Havard's death, for Skuli promptly claimed his share of the Earldoms. He was resisted by Ljot, who desired all. So Skuli went to Scotland and had an Earl's title given him by the King of Scots. He then went to Caithness and collected forces, and from thence passed to the Islands and fought with his brother for the dominion of them. Ljot also gathered a numerous army and offered to treat with his brother, but Skuli rejected all proposals. So they fought an obstinate battle, in which Skuli was defeated and took flight to Caithness. The victorious Ljot pursued him and continued in Caithness. Skuli presently returned with another army, being assisted by the Scottish King, and met Ljot at Easterdale, where another great battle ensued, Skuli relying greatly on his auxiliaries from the King of Scotland and the Scottish earl, Magbiod. Skuli at last was slain where the enemy stood thickest, and the Scots army retired in a disorderly panic. In the parish of Loth in Sutherland there is a vestige of an ancient road cut for the passage of an army. This pass or cut road is still

LJOT AND SKULI

called Ca Scuill, or the road of Skuli * Ljot now took possession of Caithness as a conquest, and he was long at war with the Scots, who were greatly vexed at their defeat At length Earl Magbiod came down from Scotland with a large army and engaged Ljot in battle at Scitten or Skidmoor in Caithness. Though the Scottish Earl was far superior in numbers, Ljot had such confidence in his own valour and in the bravery of his troops, that, attacking the Scots with great ardour he put them to flight, slaying and wounding great numbers of them Though victorious, yet he was mortally wounded, dying within a few days of the battle, when the earldom devolved on his surviving brother,

HLODVER, 13TH EARL,

of whom little is recorded, but that he was a great Earl and married Audna, daughter of Kiarval O'Ivar, King of Dublin. Their son was Sigurd the Stout, and their daughter was Hvarflod (also named Nereide and Gormlath and Svanlauga), whom Sigurd gave in marriage to Earl Gilli of the Suderies when that warrior accompanied the sons of Njal to Orkney to meet the valiant Sigurd After the marriage Gilli returned to the Suderies † Hlodver, we are informed, died a natural death soon after his accession, and was buried at Hofn in Caithness

THE NORSE LINE —CONTINUED

14 Sigurd *the Stout* ‡	980—1014
15 Somerled	1014—1015
16 Einar II	1026
17 Brusi	1031

CONTEMPORARY PRINCES

NORWAY	995, Hakon *Jarl*	1000, Olaf Trygveson	1030, St Olaf
SCOTLAND	970, Kenneth III	994, Constantine IV	995, Kenneth IV
	1003, Malcolm II		
NORMANDY	943, Richard *the Fearless*	996, Richard II, *the Good*.	1026, Richard III
	1028, Robert *the Magnificent*		

SIGURD II, 14TH EARL

This Earl was a valorous warrior, and in some of the most expressive traits of his character greatly resembled his predecessor, Sigurd I. He was very successful in extending his boundaries. Caithness and Sutherland he kept from the Scots by main force, and brought Ross, Moray, and Argyle within the sphere of his influence He rendered the Hebrides tributary to his power, and collected his revenues annually in those parts, from which he took occasion to harass and plunder the Irish and the Scottish coasts

Soon after his accession Sigurd was challenged by Finnleik, a Scottish thane, to meet him in battle at Skidamire, on a certain day As yet, being inexperienced in warfare

---
* Pope   † Saga of Sons of Njal
‡ In his time the efete Ethelred of England styled himself 'Basileus of England, &c', and the Orkneys '''' Freeman, Palgrave

and generalship, he hesitated to commit the fate of his earldom to a trial by battle, and took council of his mother, the Princess Audna, a lady greatly celebrated for the qualities most admired in that age, and especially for her skill in divination and sorcery, then styled the 'science of magic.' She wrought for him an enchanted standard, on which was woven with the most elaborate art the image of a black raven, a bird sacred to Odin, the Scandinavian god of war. The raven was represented with wings expanded, soaring on the wind, and directing its flight to heaven. The Lady Audna presented the magical banner to Sigurd, and assured him that whomsoever it preceded would be victorious, but that the standard-bearer himself would fall. She further exhorted him to conduct himself valiantly, for it was more honourable to have a short life of glory and renown than a lengthened one of ignominy and contempt. Sigurd accepted the challenge forthwith, but before proceeding to battle gave those Orcadians who would join his forces, the lands which their ancestors had surrendered to Torf-Einar. This wise step greatly augmented his forces, and meeting Finnleik he gained a decisive victory, but his enchanted colours were fatal to no less than three standard-bearers.

This victory gained him much credit, and we find distinguished men from distant parts hastening to enter his service. Kari Solmund, an Icelander, was admitted into his life-guards and honoured with a commission, and presently was appointed treasurer to the Earl, who employed him to collect the revenues in the Hebudes and bring them to the Orkneys. Next to him were Grim and Helgi, the sons of Njal, who were also received into the guards. After them the Earl's kinsman, Thorstein, the son of Hall, Lord of Sida ; and last of all, Flosi, sister's son to Thorstein, and a man of great bravery.†

The sons of Njal had been storm-driven into a bay on the Scottish coast, and had scarcely dropped anchor when their vessel was attacked by Snækolf and Grjotgard (the sons of Earl Maddan of Dungalsby), kinsmen of Malcolm, the Scots king, in two long vessels. Fortunately for the Icelanders, an Orcadian fleet of ten ships, commanded by their compatriot Kari, put in an appearance, and Kari, though unaware of the nationality of the contending parties, gallantly resolved to support the weaker side. Therefore, the engagement was short, for both Snækolf and Grjotgard were soon slain, the one by Kari and the other by Helgi, and the two ships struck their colours. The victorious Kari then directed his course for the Orkneys, with the sons of Njal, whom he introduced to the Earl, recommending them for the valour they had displayed in the fight, and they stayed the winter with him. Towards the end of winter Helgi grew very dejected, and being asked the cause, inquired of the Earl if he had any Scottish lands which paid him tribute. The Earl replied that he had. Helgi then assured the Earl that the Scots had killed his agents, and secured the harbours to prevent information reaching him. The Earl rejoined that if what he said was true he would highly honour and esteem him, but if otherwise would make a public example of him, and order his head to be struck off. Kari assured the Earl that Helgi was a very prudent man, and son of a man famous for getting information from remote parts, so that he was deserving of credit. The Earl thereon sent an express to Arnliot, his deputy in Stroma, to be informed of what was doing in the Scottish mainland. Arnliot instantly procured intelligence by spies, and acquainted Earl Sigurd that two Scottish earls, Hundi and Melsnati (the latter was nearly related to King Malcolm of Scotland), had killed Havard of Threswick, the Earl's depute in that country, as well as his cousin. The Earl at once transported an army to Caithness,

† Pope.

and receiving reinforcements from other parts of Scotland which belonged to him, attacked the two earls near Dungsbey Head. The Scots earls placed several parties of their army in ambush at some distance from the main body, and, after fighting for some time, sallied out on the Orcadian army and did great execution. All this while Grim and Helgi, the sons of Njal, fought gallantly near the Earl of Orkney's standard. Kari happened to be opposite to Melsnat, and the latter having hurled a spear at him, Kari grasped it, and darting it back, thrust him through the breast. Hundi, the other Scots earl, was so confounded at the death of Melsnat, that he immediately took to flight, followed by his whole army. Earl Sigurd pursued the fugitives, but presently halted upon being informed that Earl Melkolf, with another army, was at hand, and resolved to attack him if he approached Dungsbey. Upon this a council of war was called, and the Earl decided that it would be unwise, after their losses, to meet a fresh army, and therefore, collecting all their spoil, divided it in the Isle of Stroma, and then sailed for the mainland of Orkney, where the Earl had a splendid entertainment, at the conclusion of which he made valuable presents to Grim and Helgi, and gave them commissions as officers in his guard. Kari he complimented with a sword and a gilded spear. These three warriors continued for full three years thereafter at the Earl of Orkney's court, spending the summer in war expeditions, and acquired by their behaviour great riches and renown. From Helgi is derived the name of the Scottish county of Elgin *

The most memorable event in the life of Earl Sigurd was that which befell him as he lay in the harbour of Osmundwall, shortly after his accession to the earldom, about the year 995. Olaf Trygveson, King of Norway, returning from a western cruise, happened to run his vessel into the same harbour, as the Pentland Firth was not to be passed that day. Sigurd was just starting on an expedition with three well-equipped ships. The King sent for him, and requested him to forthwith be baptised, and make all his people profess the Christian faith. In preferring this command, the King reminded Sigurd of the Norwegian supremacy over the Isles, and made recital of those instances where the Earls had admitted the same—to Harald Fairhair, and Eirik Bloodaxe and his family, of whom Ragnhild still survived—and warned him that in case of refusal the islands would be destroyed by fire and sword. Sigurd boldly answered the King that he could not all at once quit the religion of his ancestors, or abrogate the worship of their gods through fear. The King, seeing he was resolutely determined to continue in his idolatry, adopted a more effective means of conviction. Seizing his son Hundi, he held a drawn sword over him, and warned the Earl if he persisted in his refusal that Hundi would be at once killed. The Earl then through necessity obeyed the King, and he and his son received baptism, and further, he performed homage for Orkney, and yielded up Hundi as hostage for his fidelity. King Olaf then ordered the Islesmen to be baptised, and left several divines and other learned men to instruct this infant flock in the religion they had so lately embraced. Having thus settled affairs in Orkney, he took his leave of the Earl in the most friendly manner, and proceeded on his voyage to Norway, carrying with him Hundi, the Orcadian heir-apparent, who on baptism was re-named Ludovic. Ludovic did not long survive his forced exile from Orkney, and when Earl Sigurd was apprised of his death he immediately renounced his allegiance to the king of Norway, and entered into an alliance with King Malcolm of Scotland, whose daughter (Plantula,† Anleta,‡ or Dovada*ǁ) he espoused in second marriage, and by whom he had Thorfinn, hereafter Earl of Orkney

---

* Pope † Balfour ǁ Bp. Tulloch ‘ Burke.

About the year 1011, Thorstein the Icelander came to the Orkneys. He was of good stock, and kin to the Earl, for Thorey, mother of his father Hall of the Side, was a daughter of Ozur, son of Hrollaug, the son of Rognvald of Mæren, from whom the Earl was also descended. Thorstein, who was then seventeen years of age, took post as an archer on Earl Sigurd's flagship, and went with him in the summer about Scotland, when the Earl harried far and wide, and no man challenged Thorstein's dash and daring. Both his kinship and sturdiness pleaded his cause. The Earl slew many kernes, but some fled to the woods, and he continued to carry fire and sword throughout the whole reach of the western lands, returning late in the autumn to Orkney, where he rested for three months and bestowed gifts upon his supporters. Addressing Thorstein he said: "Good manly following have you shown me, so now I ask you to take from me this battle-axe inlaid with gold, which it beseems me you should bear." Thorstein thanked the Earl, and counted it the greatest treasure.*

That autumn came Brennu-Flosi and his men to the Orkneys. Setting sail from Hornfirth in Iceland with all the men of his Thring, they encountered hard weather and lost their reckoning, and at last, on reaching a strange land, got wrecked, losing the ship and cargo, but all lives were saved. On looking at the country two of the crew said: "We are come to Hrossey in the Orkneys." "Then might we have made a better landfall,' said Flosi, "for Grim and Helgi, whom I slew, were in Earl Sigurd's body-guard." As there was naught else for it they decided to submit themselves to the Earl's pleasure, and were directed to his quarters. Upon Flosi announcing himself, the Earl asked: "What have you to say about Helgi, my henchman?" "This," said Flosi, "that I hewed off his head." The Earl ordered them all to be taken into custody, which was done. At that moment entered Thorstein Hall's son, whose sister Steinvora was married to Flosi. Thorstein was in the Earl's body-guard, and on his intercession the Earl took an atonement, and put Flosi in the place which Helgi had filled, and he soon won the attachment of the Earl.*

The last expedition Earl Sigurd made was to Ireland, and it proved fatal to him. This he was importuned to make by many fair promises from King Sigtrygg *Silk-beard* of Dublin. King Sitric came from Dublin to Orkney, to solicit Sigurd's aid against his step-father King Brian. The cause of the war was this: Brian had divorced his Queen Kormlod, whose first husband was Olaf *Quaran*, King of Dublin and the adjacent territories, a very excellent prince. (He was brother to the King of Norway.) Kormlod thereon induced her son Sitric to take her part in a war against Brian. To that end Sitric visited Sigurd, promising in the event of a successful issue that Sigurd should receive Kormlod in marriage and the dominions of Brian. Sigurd accepted the invitation, and engaged to have his army landed in Ireland on Palm Sunday following. Sitric in the meantime was entertained at the Yule feast in Sigurd's hall in the Orcadian mainland, and was set on the high seat, having Earl Sigurd on the one side, and Earl Gilli who had come with him on the other. Gunnar Lambi's son was relating the story of the burning of Njal and his comrades, but giving an unfair version of it, and every now and then laughing out loud. It so happened that, as in answer to an inquiry of King Sitric's how they bore the burning, he was saying that one of them had given way to tears, some of Njal's friends—Kari, Kolbein, and David by name—who had just arrived in Hrossay, chanced to come in the hall. Hearing what was said Kari drew his sword and smote Gunnar on the

---
Orkn Saga Rolls' trans

neck with such a sharp blow that his head spun off on to the board before the King and the Earls, so that the board was all one gore of blood and the Earls' clothing too. Earl Sigurd called out to seize Kari and kill him, but no one stirred, and some spoke up for him, saying he had only done what he had a right to do, and so Kari, who had been one of Earl Sigurd's guard, and was most beloved of his friends, walked away and there was no hue and cry after him *

The two comrades, Kari Solmundson and Kolbein the Black, had sailed from Eyrar a fortnight later than did the party of Flosi from Hornfirth. They reached the Fair Isle that lies between Orkney and Hjaltland, where David the White entertained them, and related all he had heard about the burning David was one of Kari's greatest friends, and gave him guest-quarters for the winter. After slaying Gunnar, Kari and his party sailed for Thraswick, in Caithness, where a worthy man named Skeggi hospitised them for a very long while Flosi now undertook to tell the story, and as he was fair to all, that which he said was believed.

The battle of Clontarf, 1014, in which Earl Sigurd fell, is the most celebrated conflict in which the Norsemen were engaged on this side of the North Sea " It was at Clontarf," says Dasent, "that the old and new faiths met in the lists face to face for their last struggle," and we find Earl Sigurd arrayed on the side of the old faith, notwithstanding his enforced conversion by King Olaf. In the earlier part of the battle the Irish annals describe Sigurd as dealing out wounds and slaughter all round, "no edged weapon could harm him, and there was no strength that yielded not, and no thickness that became not thin before him." From the "Njal Saga" we are informed that his raven banner, which was borne before him, was fulfilling the destiny announced by Audna when bestowing it at Skida Myre, "that it would always bring victory to those before whom it was borne, but death to him who bore it " Twice had the banner-bearer fallen, and Earl Sigurd called on Thorstein, son of Hall of the Side, next to bear the banner. Thorstein was about to lift it, when Asmund the White called out, "Don't bear the banner, for all they who bear it get their death ' " Hrafn the Red," cried Earl Sigurd, " bear thou the banner " " Bear thine own devil thyself," said Hrafn Then said the earl, " 'Tis fittest that the beggar should bear the bag," and with that upraised the banner, and was immediately pierced through with a spear Then flight broke out through all the hosts.†

Fifteen men of the Burners fell in Brian's battle, and there, too, fell Erling of Straumey, and Halldor, son of Gudmund the Powerful.

Portents and omens all through the Northern Seas announced to the Norsemen that the day had gone against them. Dorrud, a man in Caithness, saw twelve witches weaving the woof of war, of which human entrails were the warp and weft, men's heads the weights, a sword the shuttle, and arrows the reels As they wrought, they sang in the Norse language a dreadful song, "How hapless had been the fate of the Earl of Orkney " After completing their ghastly work, they each tore away a portion and rode off, six south and six north The weird song of the witches has been paraphrased by Gray in his *Fatal Sisters* The original Norse version under the title of *The Enchantress* was preserved in North Ronaldsa till past the middle of the eighteenth century, and was at times recited by the natives, some of whom, on Gray's *Ode* being read to them by a minister, reminded him they had often sung it to him in the Norse.

Pope ' Orkn Saga *Introd.*

An event like to Dörrud's befell Brand Gneisti's son in the Faroes. At Swinefell, in Iceland, blood came on the priest's stole on Good Friday, so that he had to put it off. At Thvattwater the priest thought he saw on Good Friday a depth of the sea hard by the altar, and there he saw many awful sights, and it was long ere he could sing the hours.*

The following prodigy happened in Orkney :—Harek, an Orcadian noble, had been anxious to accompany the earl, but Sigurd desired him to remain, and said he should be the first to whom he would communicate the result. Much about the time of the battle, Harek, with several others, saw plainly, as he imagined, the earl, at no great distance, riding towards him at the head of a troop of horse, upon which Harek mounted his own horse on purpose to meet him. They were seen to approach each other, to meet, to embrace, and afterwards, riding up to a rising ground, they disappeared, and no vestige of either of them was ever again seen.†

Earl Gilli, in the Hebudes, dreamt a man came to him saying his name was Hostfinn, and that he was from Ireland. The earl asked tidings thence, and Hostfinn made recital in song, of the great battle in Ireland, of Sigurd's fall, and Brian's victorious death. Flosi and the earl talked much of this dream. A week later Hrafn the Red put in an appearance, and told them of all those slain, and that Thorstein Hall's son took peace from Kerthialfad, remaining with him. Flosi then made preparation for his pilgrimage, and the earl gave him much silver and a ship well equipped, with which he made first for Wales, where he stayed a while. Of this Kari got word, and instructed Skeggi to get him a long ship, fully trimmed and manned, and with Kolbein, David, and others sailed south to Wales, *via* the Scottish firths, where he lay concealed in an inlet. One morning Kol Thorstein's son went up town to buy silver, and he of all the burners had used the bitterest words. Kol had talked much that morning with a mighty dame, and it was practically arranged he was to marry her and settle down there. That same morning Kari went also into the town, and came up when Kol was telling the silver. Kari knew him, and ran at him with drawn sword, and struck him on the neck. But he still went on telling the silver, and his head counted "ten" just as it spun off the body. Kari said, "Go and tell Flosi that I have done this deed." Then he and his ship's company headed north for Beruwick, where they laid up the ship, and went to Whitherne in Scotland, and were with Earl Melkolf that year. Flosi took the incident quietly, and after giving Kol's remains suitable burial, continued his pilgrimage to Rome, and obtained the Papal absolution, for which he gave a great sum. He returned by the east route, staying long in towns, and meeting mighty men, by whom he was highly honoured. The next winter he was in Norway, and had a ship from Earl Eric, with which he made passage to the Hornfirth, and thence made his way to Swinefell. Kari went down to his ship in the summer following, and began his pilgrimage in Normandy, whence he went south and got absolution, returning again by the western way to his ship in Normandy ; and then sailed to Dover, round Wales, north through Scotland's firths to Thraswick, in Caithness, to Master Skeggi's house, where he transferred the vessel to Kolbein and David, in which the former steered for Norway, landing David at the Fair Isle. Kari wintered in Caithness, and hearing that his wife in Iceland had died, got a ship from Skeggi the next summer, and with a company of eighteen made for his home. Starting rather late, they had a long passage, and at last made Ingolf's head, only to have their ship smashed there, but the men's lives were all saved. Then, too, a snow-

---
* Orkn. Saga, Rolls' trans.   † Barry and Pope.

SIGURD II, 14TH EARL.

storm gathered on them, and they were forced to seek shelter from Flosi, who generously gave them winter quarters, and there came about an adjustment of the feud by Kari marrying Hildigunna, daughter of Flosi's brother, and whom Hauskuld, the priest of Whiteness, had had to wife. By Helga, Njal's daughter, Kari had Thorgerda, Ragneida, Valgerda, and Thord, who was burnt in Njal's house; and by Hildigunna, with whom he dwelt first at Broadwater, he had Starkad, Thord, and Flosi. Men say that Flosi, when he had grown old, went abroad for timber to build a hall, and was in Norway one winter, and the following summer was late in embarking. Though warned that his ship was unseaworthy, Flosi, saying she was fully good enough for an old and "fey" man, bore his goods on shipboard and put out to sea, and has never been heard of since *

Before embarking for Ireland, Sigurd had the prudence to put his affairs in order by committing the charge of his earldom to Somerled, Brusi, and Einar, the sons of his first marriage; the young Thorfinn, his only son by the Scottish princess, being put under the guardianship of his royal grandfather. The earl's fate was no sooner known than his three eldest sons divided equally among them the countries of Orkney and Hjaltaland, leaving to their youngest brother Thorfinn—who, on account of his youth, had been put under guardians—the provinces of Caithness and Sutherland, which were confirmed to him by his grandfather, the king of Scotland, who at the same time conferred on him the title and dignity of an earl †

SOMERLED, 15TH EARL,

the eldest of Sigurd's sons, was, we are told, of a mild and peaceable disposition, fair in complexion, and of an obliging manner to all about him. He did not long remain in possession of the dignity. Dying without issue soon after his accession, his share of the earldom was annexed by Einar ‡ In the collection of Scottish coins, one of the most ancient is the *Coin of Somerled*, a silver penny. It has been attributed to one Somerled, a Hebudean lord, but is more probably an Orcadian coin, struck in the time of the 15th Earl, to whose father and brother, Thorfinn II, the Great, the Hebudes are known to have been tributary.

EINAR, 16TH EARL,

seized Somerled's share, and maintained possession by force of arms. Thorfinn immediately laid claim to Somerled's possessions as his right, but the claim, though conceded by Brusi, was disregarded by Einar. Einar is described as constantly aspiring after vast objects, stern in countenance, harsh in speech, unrelenting in nature, and ever ready to undertake the most perilous deeds. His numerous warring expeditions were not always successful, so the heritable odallers suffered severely from his exactions, and, contrasting their condition with that of those under the government of Earl Brusi, whose disposition was similar to that of Somerled, they at last resolved to seek the interposition of Amundi, a noble in high esteem with the Earl. Amundi listened to their solicitations with attention, and would gladly have acted as mediator between the oppressed Orcadians and their Lord, but, knowing the disposition of the Earl, he felt that he would only become a target for his vengeance, nor was there any likelihood of a

* Orkn Saga, Rolls' tr in.

petition resulting in the mitigation of their distress. He therefore declined the dangerous office. The odallers then transferred their solicitations to Amundi's son, Thorkell, who was the most accomplished person in the Isles. Their importunings were so continuous that he at last undertook to approach the Earl on their behalf. So, at the next Thing meeting, Thorkell begged the Earl to spare the people, and told him of their distress. Einar answered blandly, and said he would give great weight to Thorkell's words, but warned him not to again address him on such a matter. "I had intended," he said, "to take out six ships, but shall now not take more than three; but thou, Thorkell, do not ask me this a second time."

The following spring, Earl Einar resolved to make up for his disadvantage of the past year, by an increased naval armament, much to the dismay of his people, who, taking heart from Thorkell's former success, implored him to again act as mediator for them, and he, yielding to their entreaties, undertook to do so. On this occasion, however, the Earl would not listen to him, and became very wroth. Amundi advised his son to avoid the impending storm, and go abroad. Thorkell accordingly crossed the Petland Firth, and took refuge in Caithness with Earl Thorfinn. He stayed there a long while, and became foster-father to the latter Earl, who was still young. From that time he was called Thorkell the Foster, and became a man of great repute.

When Thorfinn attained his majority he re-demanded the third of the Islands, being his share, but Einar, disinclined to divide his possessions, prepared to resist the claim. Thorfinn thereon called his people to arms, and set sail for Orkney. Einar at once collected an army to defend the Isles, and Earl Brusi also gathered his forces and went to meet them, in the hope of effecting a reconciliation, and peace was made on condition that Thorfinn should receive his third. Thorfinn appointed deputies to manage his possessions in the Isles, and lived for the most part in Caithness.

Brusi and Einar now entered into a compact, joining their portions, which Einar was to rule and defend for both, and he who survived the other should inherit his portion. This compact was generally viewed as unfair, for Brusi had a son, Rögnvald, while Einar had no son.

In the summer Einar went on expeditions to Ireland, Scotland, and Wales. One summer when ravaging Ireland, he fought in Lough Larne (Ulreksfiord) with O'Connor (Conchobbar), an Irish king, and was defeated with a heavy loss of men. He attributed this loss chiefly to the Norwegian troops that fought under O'Connor, and were commanded by Eyvind *Urarhorn*, an officer in the life-guards of King Olaf Haraldson, surnamed the Holy. The next summer Eyvind, when sailing from Ireland for Norway, being overtaken by a gale, sought shelter in Osmundwall, now known as Longhope. This coming to the knowledge of Earl Einar, he mustered his men, went thither and executed Eyvind, but gave quarter to most of his followers, whom he allowed to continue on their voyage to Norway. When they related the circumstance to King Olaf, he said very little at the time, but it turned out afterwards he was highly offended.

About this time Earl Thorfinn sent Thorkell to Orkney to collect his rents. While in the Isles, Thorkell received word that Einar resented his presence, and was compassing his death, alleging that it was owing to his instigation that Thorfinn had obtained the third part of Orkney. Thorkell therefore hastily concluded his affairs and re-crossed the Firth, on his return acquainting Thorfinn of what he had heard. He further stated his intention of going over-sea to some remote country, where though an exile he would be free from danger. Thorfinn approved of his resolution, and, assuring him of his regard, suggested Norway as a place equally convenient and honourable for that purpose So in the autumn Thorkell went to Norway, where he was presented to King Olaf, with whom he became such a favourite that he was made one of the Privy Council, and spent the winter in great friendship with the king. Early in the spring King Olaf sent a ship for Earl Thorfinn, inviting him in the most friendly manner to come to Norway Thorfinn promptly accepted the invitation, and went east at once, where he spent most of the summer season. At his departure King Olaf presented him with a stately war-galley, fully equipped; while Thorfinn transferred his own to Thorkell Foster, who was determined to return with him Landing in Orkney in the autumn, they found that Einar had gathered his forces to oppose them Brusi again came to the rescue, and effected a second reconciliation, and the peace was confirmed by oaths Thorkell should be pardoned and restored to favour with Earl Einar, and the friendship was to be sealed by mutual entertainments. Thorkell banqueted the Earl in his hall at Sandwick in Deerness, but it was observed that although Einar and his men were most sumptuously treated, he continued sullen throughout When the feast was over it became Thorkell's turn to accompany the Earl to be similarly treated in return, but from the Earl's manner Thorkell thought it prudent to delay the event as long as possible Meantime it was discovered that along the intended route there were three divisions of armed men in ambush Certain that foul play was intended, he took the initiative and slew the Earl Einar was sitting down, and asked Thorkell if he were ready for the journey Thorkell answered, "I am ready now," and, drawing his sword, dealt the Earl a fatal blow on the head, and then with Hallvard, an Eastfirth Icelander, and the rest of his party, made for their ships, in which they sailed directly for Norway, where he was well received by King Olaf, with whom he spent the winter Earl Einar's men were stupefied by the suddenness of the deed, which they had not expected from Thorkell, and many of them being unarmed, and others his friends, enabled him to get away without opposition

BRUSI, 17TH EARL.

After the death of Einar, Brusi took possession of his share by virtue of their agreement of joint survivorship Thorfinn thought they should each have one-half, but Brusi would not yield Seeing, however, that he could not contend with Thorfinn, who had great estates in Scotland and the support of his grandfather, the Scottish King, Brusi decided to go to King Olaf, taking with him his son Rognvald, then ten years old Thorfinn hearing of this, and recalling his former favourable reception from that sovereign, also hastened to Norway, where their disputes were settled by the arbitrament of Olaf, who adjudged one-third to himself as the forfeited share of Earl Einar for slaying Eyvind Urarhorn, and one-third each to Brusi and Thorfinn. The forfeited share he afterwards gave to Brusi, and further conditioned that the Earls should be reconciled to Thorkell Foster Thorfinn then sailed west, accompanied by Thorkell, while Brusi did not leave till the autumn next, and his heir, Rognvald, remained with King Olaf When the brothers Thorfinn and Brusi came to the Islands, Brusi took possession of two-thirds of the domain, and Thorfinn of one, but he was all the time in Caithness, and placed deputies over the Islands The Isles were in those times very much exposed to the ravages of the Norwegians and Danes, who called there on their viking expeditions to the west and plundered the outlying isles. The defence fell on Brusi alone, who made complaint to Thorfinn about his not contributing to the defence of Orkney and Hjaltaland, although he received his full share of all the land dues and revenues. Then Thorfinn proposed to take two-thirds and defend the whole, leaving Brusi one-third. Although this division did not immediately take place, yet it is said in the History of the Earls that it happened, and that when Knut the Great conquered Norway, after the flight of King Olaf, Thorfinn had two-thirds and Brusi the one-third. After the treaty between the brothers, King Olaf received no homage from Earl Thorfinn. Brusi now disappears from Orcadian history, and his brother comes prominently to the fore.

THE NORSE LINE — CONTINUED

18 Thorfinn II, *the Great*	1031-1064
19 Rognvald II	1035-1046

CONTEMPORARY PRINCES

NORWAY	1030, St Olaf	1035, Swein	1047, Magnus* *the Good.*
NORMANDY	1028, Robert *the Devil*	1035, William *the Conqueror*	
SCOTLAND	1003, Malcolm II	1033, Duncan I	1039, Macbeth
	1056, Malcolm III, *Canmore*		
ENGLAND	1016, Knut	1035, Harald *Harefoot*	1039, Horda-Knut
	1042, Edward *the Confessor*		
	GERMANY	1039, Henry III *the Black*	
	ROME	1049, Leo IX	

THORFINN II., THE GREAT, 18TH EARL

THORFINN now had supreme sway throughout Orcadia, and became a powerful ruler. Of large stature, his visage was stern and forbidding and his features sharp and uncomely. Yet he was a most martial-looking man, and of great energy, emulous of wealth and renown, bold and successful, and a great strategist. He was five years of age when his maternal grandfather, King Malcolm II., assigned to him the comitial dignity and revenues of Caithness; at fourteen he issued from his own territories on maritime expeditions against neighbouring chiefs, and having the assistance of the King of Scots tended to increase his power in the Orkneys.

Soon after the reconciliation of the Earl brothers the King of Scotland died, and the Sagas tell us that Karl Hundason succeeded him. This, however, is in conflict with Scottish history, from which we learn that Malcolm II. was peaceably succeeded by Duncan Crinanson, his grandson. The Saga continues:—King Karl demanded tribute for Caithness, which Thorfinn refused, and war broke out between them. Karl created earl his sister's son Moddan, and appointed him over Caithness. Moddan collected forces in Sutherland, Thorfinn in Caithness, and the latter was re-inforced by an Orcadian

---

* First appearance of the name Magnus in Norse history, stated to be after and in admiration of Charlemagne.

contingent brought over by Thorkell Foster. The Scots being outnumbered retreated, and Thorfinn advancing subdued Sutherland and Ross, and ravaged in Scotland far and wide. Moddan reported his failure to the Scottish King, who was vastly displeased, and started north immediately with eleven warships and a numerous army to punish the defiant Thorfinn. Despatching Moddan landwards for Caithness, he sailed north, hoping to engage Thorfinn between the two forces. The Earl had just embarked for the Isles, when King Karl's navy hove in sight at nightfall. Continuing his course Thorfinn moored his five vessels off Deerness, and immediately sent word to Thorkell to summon the Islesmen. Brusi had the northernmost lot of the isles, and was then there. At daylight next morning King Karl with his eleven ships came suddenly on the scene, and the Earl decided to accept battle. The victory was with the Earl, and the King fled to the Moray Firth, where Thorfinn followed in pursuit as soon as Thorkell had arrived with more men. Hearing that Moddan was at Thurso with a large army, and had sent for men to Ireland, where he had many relatives and friends, it was thought advisable to divide the Orcadian army, Thorkell proceeding to Caithness with one division, while Thorfinn plundered in Scotland with the other. Thorkell surprised Moddan in Thurso by night, setting his house on fire, and while that general attempted to escape, hewed off his head. His men then surrendered, but some got away. Many were slain, others admitted to quarter. Thorkell then hastened with all the troops he could collect in Caithness, Sutherland and Ross, and effected a junction with the Earl in Moray, receiving hearty thanks for his success.

King Karl having levied a fresh army, and the Irish auxiliaries expected by Moddan having arrived, he advanced to renew the war with Thorfinn. The contending parties met at Torfness, south of Baefiord, that of the King outnumbering the Earl's. Thorfinn fought valiantly, foremost of all his men. He had a gold-plated helmet on his head, a sword at his belt, a spear in his hand, and he cut and thrust with both hands. First attacking the Irish wing, it was immediately routed and never regained position. Then King Karl advanced his standard against the Earl, and round it the fiercest struggle ensued, but it ended in the flight of the King, and some say he was slain. Thorfinn drove the fugitives before him through Scotland, subduing the country wherever he went—all the way south to Fife—returning with great booty to Caithness, where he spent the winter.

Every summer Thorfinn went ravaging foreign lands, and in winter made himself famous in the Isles by the immense host he entertained, not only at Yule, as Kings and Earls of other countries did, but throughout the entire winter. In his time one Hrafn Limiricepeta, so called from his frequent voyages to Limerick in Ireland—a Limerick trader—related to Earl Thorfinn some accounts of a Great Ireland in the Western Ocean.[*] It was about this time that Earl Brusi died and Thorfinn took possession of all the Isles, but as Brusi left issue we will here refer to his son, whose many notable deeds and transactions with Thorfinn need illustration.

RÖGNVALD II., 19TH EARL.

Of Rögnvald, it is said, he was in the battle of Stiklestad, where King Olaf the Holy met his death, A. D. 1030. Escaping with other fugitives, Rögnvald bore from the field

---

[*] Heimskringla, p. 60.

of battle the youthful Harald Sigurdson, the Hardrada of later times (half-brother to Olaf), who was wounded dangerously, and placed him with a husbandman, with whom he stayed till cured. Harald, when leaving for Sweden, sang thus:—

> "Who knows," said he, "the day shall come,
> My name shall yet be great at home?"

After placing Harald in comparative safety, Rögnvald crossed the Kjolen range and proceeded through Jamtaland to the Swedish court, where King Onund received him favourably. He was soon joined by Harald, and they went on to Russia, meeting in Novgorod, King Jarisleif, who gave them a hearty reception for the sake of King Olaf the Holy. Harald, Rögnvald, and Erling, the son of Jarl Rögnvald Ulfsson, then entered the service of Jarisleif, as defenders of his country. Harald, however, did not long remain in Russia, but passed on to Constantinople, where he joined the Varangian guard. Rögnvald remained in Russia, spending the winters in Novgorod, and in summer defending the frontiers, where he fought ten battles. Rögnvald was a man of large stature and great strength, and one of the handsomest of men in appearance, and his accomplishments were such that his equal was hardly to be found. The King, as well as the people, highly esteemed him. When Ingigerd, the daughter of the Swedish king Olaf, was married to Jarisleif, she stipulated that Rögnvald should accompany her to Russia, and he received the town and earldom of Ladoga. Presently, Einar Tambarskelmr and Kalf Arnason visited Russia, with the object of inducing Magnus to recover his father's throne. They met Rögnvald in Ladoga, and he had nearly attacked them before they informed him of their object. Einar said that the regicide Kalf repented of having been a party to the dethronement and death of King Olaf the Holy, and now wished to make amends to his son Magnus by restoring him to the Norwegian sovereignty, and supporting him against the Vikings in pay of the Knuts. For this purpose they sought Rögnvald's intercession with the Russian King, and Rögnvald, being softened by these representations, Einar now asked him to go with them to Novgorod, and introduce them and their business to King Jarisleif. When they reached Novgorod, Rögnvald, Queen Ingigerd, and many of the noblemen, pleaded their cause. Jarisleif hesitated to entrust Magnus to the former enemies of his father, but at last, on receiving the oaths of twelve of the noblest Norwegians that their intentions were sincere, he consented. He confided so much in Rögnvald, however, that he did not require him to swear. The Norwegians thereon accepted Magnus as their king, and swore fealty to him.

Einar and Kalf stayed in Novgorod till after Yule, and then went down to Ladoga and procured ships. As soon as the sea was open in the spring, Rögnvald made ready to convey Magnus to his dominions. They went first to Sweden, then to Jamtaland, crossed the Kjol, and came to Veradal. On arriving at Drontheim all the people submitted to him. There Rögnvald heard of his father's death and Thorfinn's annexation of his possessions, so he asked the permission of King Magnus to visit his island home. This was readily granted, and Magnus gave him at the same time the title of Earl and three warships, well equipped, as also the third part of the Islands formerly possessed by Earl Einar.

Rögnvald landed first in those parts which had belonged to his father, whence he sent word to his uncle, Earl Thorfinn, informing him of the position, and demanding the two-thirds of the Isles. Thorfinn at that time was constantly warring with the Hebudeans and the Irish, and felt himself greatly in want of assistance. He therefore gave the following spirited reply to Rögnvald's embassy: "Rögnvald may take possession of the third which rightly belongs to him. As for the third which King Magnus calls his own, we surrendered that to King Olaf the Holy because we were then in his power, not because we thought it just. I and my kinsman Rognvald will agree all the better the less we talk of that third which has been long enough a cause of dispute. But, if Rognvald wishes to be my faithful friend, I consider those possessions in good hands which he has for his pleasure and for the good of us both. His assistance will soon be of greater value to me than the revenues which I derive from them." This answer was satisfactory to Rognvald, who then entered into possession of the two-thirds, and became the ally of Thorfinn.

Early in the ensuing spring Thorfinn gave Rognvald a call for an expedition, to which the latter promptly responded, and in the summer they ravaged in the Hebudes, in Ireland, and in Scotland's Firth conquering wherever they went. At Loch Vatten they had a great victory, celebrated in verse by Arnor, the skald of Thorfinn. After this they returned to winter in the Orkneys. Thus Rognvald passed eight winters, without Thorfinn demurring. Every summer they went on a corsair cruise—sometimes jointly, sometimes severally, as Arnor says:—

> "The chief beloved did many deeds
> Everywhere there fell before him
> Irishmen or British people,
> Fire devoured the Scottish kingdom."

The kinsmen agreed well whenever they met, but when evil men came between them dissensions often arose. Thorfinn dwelt chiefly in Caithness. One summer Thorfinn made war in the Hebudes and in Scotland. Lying at Galloway, where Scotland and England meet, he sent forces to foray in England, and there they collected a lot of spoil, but the English rallied and recaptured it, slaying many of the Orcadians. Some they spared to convey the news to the Earl. Thorfinn was greatly annoyed, and determined to make reprisals as soon as possible. At that time Horda-Knut was King of England and Denmark. The Earl wintered in the Orkneys, but early in the spring he called out a levy from all his domain, and sent word to Rognvald to co-operate. Rognvald assenting, called out his men, and uniting with those Thorfinn had collected from the Isles, Caithness, the Hebudes, Ireland and Scotland, the host set sail for England. Horda-Knut was then in Denmark, but Thorfinn and Rognvald, besides many casual encounters, had two pitched battles with the royal army, defeating it with great slaughter. Thorfinn, in fulfilment of his vow, stayed in England throughout the summer, and returned in autumn to his isleted throne.

About this time King Magnus banished Kalf Arnason, who sought refuge with his nephew-in-law Thorfinn. Between them there was great friendship, for Thorfinn had married Ingibiorg, daughter of Earl Finn Arnason. Through the increased demand upon his hospitality, Thorfinn began to wish for the third of Orkney he had formerly allowed to Rognvald, and send an embassy to demand its restoration. Rognvald convened his supporters in council, but found them dubious as to his chances of success with troops from two-thirds of the Islands, against those Thorfinn could muster from one-third of the Isles, Caithness, the Hebudes, and that vast part of Scotland of which he was over-lord. Being thoroughly determined to resist the claim, he announced his intention of going to Norway, to solicit the assistance of his foster-brother King Magnus. So thither he went, and Magnus supplied him with a large and well equipped army, sending word also to

Kalf Arnason that if he sided with Rögnvald against Thorfinn, his sentence of banishment should be cancelled and his Norwegian estates restored.

Rögnvald first landed in Hjaltland, where he collected men, and went thence to the Orkneys, where he drew more to his flag. Thorfinn was in Caithness when the news reached him, but at once summoned men from Caithness, Scotland, and the Hebudes. Rögnvald sent the royal message to Kalf, who apparently received it well, and followed up his communication by steering for Caithness with a fleet of thirty large ships. He met Earl Thorfinn in the Petland Firth, off Raudabiorg (red cliff), and both sides prepared for battle, Kalf Arnason remaining neutral with his six large ships. The battle was fiercely fought between these veteran warriors. Thorfinn's smaller vessels placed him at a disadvantage, and the day was going against him, when he successfully appealed to Kalf to join his squadron, and their united forces won the day. Rögnvald retreated, and darkness coming on, stood to sea, making for Norway, where he was welcomed by King Magnus. Thorfinn, meantime, subdued the Isles, took up his residence in them, and compelled all the Islesmen to renounce their allegiance to Earl Rögnvald. He kept a great number of men about him, he imported provisions from Caithness, and sent Kalf to the Hebudes to maintain his authority there.

This time Rögnvald resolved to try and regain the Isles by coming on Thorfinn by surprise, so, early in the winter, he sailed for Orkney with a picked crew. At Hjaltaland he heard that Thorfinn was in the Orkneys with a few men, relying on the season for freedom from attack, so Rögnvald pushed on for the Orcadian mainland, and, ascertaining where he was, stole secretly to the place under cover of darkness, and fired the house. The night was pitch dark, favouring the surprise; but it also helped Thorfinn, who managed to elude his assailants by breaking down part of the woodwork of the house, and with Ingibiorg, his consort, in his arms, got away unperceived in the smoke, and during the night rowed unattended in a boat to Caithness. All thought he had perished in the flames. After this Rögnvald took possession of all the Isles, and sent word to Caithness and the Hebudes that he intended to have all the dominions of Thorfinn. Thorfinn, all the while, remained in hiding in Caithness. Rögnvald now established his court at Kirkwall, entertaining liberally. A little before Yule he went to Papa Stronsa, and one evening when warming themselves round the fire, an attendant said they were running short of fuel. The Earl said, "We shall be old enough when these fires are burnt out," intending to have said they would be warm enough. Noticing his blunder, he continued, "I made a slip of the tongue in speaking just now; I do not remember that I ever did so before, and now I recollect what my foster-father, king Olaf, said at Stiklastad* when I noticed one which he made, namely, that if it ever so happened that I should make a slip in my speech, I should not expect to live long after it. It may be that my kinsman Thorfinn is still alive." At that moment the house was surrounded by Thorfinn and his men. Heaping a large pile before the door, they fired it immediately. Rögnvald nevertheless effected his exit, and placing his hands upon a wall, by his great strength vaulted over it, disappearing immediately in the darkness of the night. Thorfinn recog-

---

* King Olaf and Rögnvald were standing on a mound where there were berries, of which the king took some, and squeezed them in his palm. Then, seeing where the banner of the freemen was set up, "Wretched berries," said he, to which Rögnvald remarked, "You made a slip of speech just now, king, you must have meant to say 'people.'" "You are right, earl," said the king, "when you have but a short time to live you will make a slip of speech no less than mine."

† Orkn. Saga, Rolls' trans.

nised him, saying, "There went the earl, for that is his feat and no other man's." Search parties patrolled the beach, and Rognvald was presently traced by the baying of his favourite hound. Thorkell Foster had him seized, and offered a reward to the man who would kill him, but all refused. So Thorkell, the Earl-killer, did it himself. Thorfinn and his men then occupied Rognvald's barge and rowed for the capital, where they surprised, seized, and slew thirty of Rognvald's followers, mostly henchmen and friends of king Magnus. To one Thorfinn gave quarter, sending him east to Norway to tell king Magnus the tidings. The remains of Rognvald were interred in Papa Westra. Men said he was one of the most accomplished and best beloved of all the Orcadian earls, and his death was greatly lamented throughout the Isles. Thorfinn now took possession of the whole islands, and none withstood him. The news reached king Magnus in early spring, and he was much affected. He regarded the death of Rognvald, his foster-brother, as a great loss, which he would by-and-bye avenge, but just then he was at war with King Sweyn of Denmark.

About this time Harald Hardradi arrived in Norway, and king Magnus gave him half the kingdom. One winter, when the two kings' vessels were in Seley, off Lindesness, two war-ships came into the harbour, and rowed up to king Magnus' ship. They were those of Thorfinn, who, having thought it probable that the Norwegian fleet might be diverted from the Danish expedition to the Orkneys, came to offer his assistance, thus hoping to disarm the resentment of King Magnus. He was succeeding in his purpose, when the Norwegian whom he had spared in Kirkwall and sent to Norway with word of the death of Rognvald, put in an appearance, and demanded compensation for his brother, who had been slain by Thorfinn. The Earl reminded the claimant that he should be thankful his own life was spared, and told him he should know that he was not in the habit of paying money for those whom he had caused to be killed, as he had always good reason for such actions. This incident disturbed the relations between Magnus and Thorfinn, the king thinking the earl displayed too little compunction over the matter, and the king turned blood-red with anger. Thorfinn was ostensibly sailing to Jutland with Magnus and the Norwegian fleet, but after this incident judiciously steered further out to sea, and made for the Isles over which he was now sole ruler. Kalf Arnason was frequently with him. Sometimes he made viking trips to the west and plundered in Scotland and Ireland. He was also in England, *and at one time was President of the Orcadian Thingmen.*

On the death of Magnus, Thorfinn sent a friendly message to king Harald Hardradi, which was favourably received, and Harald, the renowned warrior-king, promised Thorfinn his friendship. So the earl went to Norway with two ships of twenty benches each, and more than one hundred men, all fine troops. He found Harald in Hordaland, and on parting received handsome presents from him. Thence Thorfinn went to Denmark, meeting king Sweyn at Aalborg. He invited the earl to stay, and made a splendid feast for him. Then Thorfinn announced he was going to Rome. He called on Henry III., Emperor of Germany, who received him exceedingly well, and gave him many valuable presents, as also many horses; and the earl rode on south to Rome and saw Pope Leo IX, from whom he obtained absolution for all his sins.

Thorfinn's pilgrimage is assigned to the year 1050, the same in which 'the peerless Macbeth' visited Rome (the only Scottish sovereign who ever did so), and as these two potentates were close friends and allies it is assumed they went together. Returning safely, he ceased his corsair career, and turned his attention to the government of his people and his dominions, and the making of laws. He resided frequently in Birsa, and built there Christ's Kirk, a splendid church, and there was the first bishop's see in the Orkneys.

Thorfinn's wife was Ingibiorg, called 'the mother of the earls.' They had two sons who arrived at manhood. One was called Paul and the other Erlend. They were men of large stature, fine looking, wise and gentle, more resembling their mother's relations. They were much loved by the earl and all the people. Thorfinn retained all the dominions of the Orcadian realm till his dying day, and it is truly said he was the most powerful of the Earls. He obtained possession of or rendered tributary nine earldoms in Scotland, all the Hebudes, and a large territory in Ireland. So says Arnor:

"Hrafn's faedi vard hlyda	"Unto Thorfinn ravens'-feeder
sökkr frá Thussa-skerjum—	Armies had to yield obedience,
"rètt segig thjod hve thótti	From Tuscar Rocks right on to Dublin
Thorfinnr—til Dyflinnar."*	Truth I tell, as is recorded."

Thorfinn was five winters old when his grandfather, Malcolm II., gave him the title of earl, and was earl after that for seventy winters, dying towards the end of Harald Hardradi's reign. He was buried at Birsa, in Christ's Kirk, his own erection, and was much lamented in his hereditary dominions; but in those parts which he had conquered by force of arms, many considered it hard to be under his rule, and after his demise many provinces transferred their allegiance to the native chieftains. It then soon became apparent how great a loss Thorfinn's death was to Orcadia.

"Björt verdr sól at sortna,	"The bright sun swarthy shall become,
sökkr fold í mar dökkvan,	In the black sea the earth shall sink,
"brestr erfidi Austra,	Austri's labour shall be ended,
allr brunar sjár med fjöllum.	And the wild sea hide the mountains,
"Adr at Eyjum fridri,	Ere there be, in those fair Islands—
(inndróttar Thorfinni)	Born a chief to rule the people,
"(theim hjálpi gud geymi)	(May our God both help and keep them)
gædingr muni fædast."*	Greater than the lost Earl Thorfinn."

His dowager subsequently married Malcolm Canmore, and their son was Duncan I.,  father of William Fitz-Duncan, who was father of William the Ætheling, known as the 'Boy of Egremont,' whom all the Scots wished to take for their prince.

* Orkn. Saga, Rolls' text.

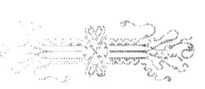

THE NORSE LINE.—Continued *

20 Paul *the Earle*		1064—1103
21 Erlend II , *the Earle*		1064—1103
(*Vice-Royalty of Sigurd, Crown Prince of Norway*		1098—1103)
22 Hakon *the Imperious*		1103—1122
23 St. Magnus *the Martyr*		1103—1115
24 Harald *the Orator*		1122—1127
25 Paul II , *the Silent*		1122—1136
26 Erlend III , *the Younger*		1127—1156

CONTEMPORARY PRINCES

NORWAY	1047, Harald *Hardradi*	1066, Magnus II.	1069, Olaf III., *the Quiet.*
	1093, Magnus *Barefoot*	1103, Olaf IV	1116, Eystein
	1122, Sigurd I.	1130, Magnus IV	1134, Harald *Gille*
SCOTLAND	1056, Malcolm III , *Canmore*	1093, Donaldbane	1098, Edgar
	1107, Alexander I	1124, David I	
ENGLAND	1042, Edward *the Confessor*	1066, Harald *Infelix*	1066, William *the Conqueror.*
	1087, William *Rufus*	1099, Henry I	
ROME ·	1099, Pascal II	1118, Gelasius II	1119, Calixtus II
	1124, Honorius II	1130, Innocent II	

PRELATES †

ORKNEY   William *the Old*   1102—1168

PAUL AND ERLEND, 20TH AND 21ST EARLS

Now the sons of Thorfinn succeeded him. Paul was the elder of the two, and he ruled for both Erlend and himself. Though they did not divide their possessions, they almost always agreed in their dealings. When the brothers had succeeded to the government of the Isles, King Harald Siguidsson came from Norway with a large army. He first touched at Hjaltaland, and thence went to the Orkneys, where he left his queen, Ellisif, and their daughters, Maria and Ingigerd. From the Orkneys he received substantial reinforcements, and both the earls went with him to invade and conquer England. They first landed at Cleveland, and took Scarborough. Then they touched at Holderness, and had a battle there, in which Harald was victorious. On Wednesday, the 26th September, 1066, he was victor in a battle at York, and the following Sunday the borg at Stamfordbridge surrendered to him, so he went on shore to arrange the government of the town, leaving his son Olaf, the Earls Paul and Erlend, and his brother-in-law Eystein *Orri* in charge of the fleet. While on shore he was met by Harald Godwinsson at the head of a numerous army, and fell in the engagement that ensued. After his death Eystein and the Orcadian earls arrived from the ships, and made a stout but ineffectual resistance, for Eystein also fell, and nearly the whole army of the Northmen with him ‡. After the battle Harald Godwinsson generously permitted the Crown Prince Olaf and the Orcadian

---

* Authorities: Orkn Saga, Burcy Popa.   See Historic ties
‡ This encounter was known as "Orri's Storm."

earls to leave England with all the troops that had not fled. So, in the autumn, Olaf set sail from Ravensere to the Orkneys. Maria, daughter of King Harald, died on the same day and at the same hour he fell, and it is said of them that they had but one life. Olaf spent the winter in the Orkneys, and was very friendly to the earls, his kinsmen. Thora, the mother of King Olaf, and Ingibiorg, the mother of the earls, were daughters of two brothers. In the spring Olaf crossed to Norway, and was crowned king along with his brother Magnus.

Earl Paul had married a daughter of Earl Hakon Ivarsson, and they had several children. Beside Hakon, who succeeded him, there were four daughters, of whom THORA was married in Norway to Haldor, son of Brynjulf *Ulfaldi*, INGIRID, married to Einar *Vorsakrak*, HERBIORG, mother of Ingibiorg *Tigna*, married to Sigurd of Westness—they had issue Hakon *Pik* and Brynjolf, and Sigrid (mother of Hakon *Barn* and Herborg, married to Kolbein *Hruga*), and RAGNHILD, who was the mother of Benedikt, the father of Ingibiorg, the mother of Erling the Archdeacon, and Ragnhild had also a daughter Berghot, married to Havard Gunnarsson, and their sons were Magnus, Hakon *Klo*, Dufmal and Thorstein. All these were the families of earls and chiefs in the Orkneys, and all of them will be hereafter mentioned.

The wife of Earl Erlend was Thora, the daughter of Somerled, the son of Ospac by his wife Thordis, daughter of Hall of Side in Iceland. Their sons were Erling and Magnus, and their daughters were Gunnhild and Cecilia. The latter was married to Isak, and their sons were Endridi and Kol. Erling had a natural daughter called Jatvor, whose son was Berg.

While the brother earls ruled Orkney they agreed extremely well, but on their sons attaining manhood Erling and Hakon became very violent. Magnus was the quietest of them all. They were all men of large stature, strong and accomplished in everything. Hakon, Paul's son, wished to take the lead over his cousins. He held himself of higher birth than the sons of Erlend, as his mother was the daughter of Earl Hakon Ivarsson by the Princess Ragnhild, daughter of King Magnus the Good. Hakon wished his friends to have the lion's share of everything before those who leant to the sons of Erlend, but Erlend did not like his sons to be inferior to any in the Isles. A meeting was appointed to adjust these differences, but it soon became apparent that each of the earls was inclined to side with his own son, and therefore no agreement was arrived at and dissensions arose. After this well-disposed men interposed, and a meeting for reconciliation was appointed in the Orcadian mainland, when peace was secured by dividing the islands into two shares, as in the days of Thorfinn and Brusi. Hakon, when he became of age, was very violent, and continually away on war trips. He greatly molested those who adhered to Erlend and his sons, till at last they came to open war. So Havard Gunnarsson and others once more endeavoured to restore tranquility, but Erlend and his sons refused to make peace while Hakon stayed in the Isles. Hakon's friends induced him not to let that condition stand in the way. Hakon now left the Isles and first went to Norway, and there saw King Olaf the Quiet, with whom he remained for a while. This was towards the end of Olaf's reign. After that he went east to Sweden to King Ingi Steinkelsson, who received him well. There he found friends and kinsmen, and was highly honoured on account of the esteem in which Hakon, his mother's sire, was held. This elder Hakon had possessions from Steinkel, the king of the Swedes, ever since he was banished by King Harald Sigurdsson, and became greatly beloved both by king and people. A son of the second daughter of Hakon Ivarsson was Hakon, called the Norwegian, and he was the father of King Eric the Wise, who was King of Denmark after King Eric the Ever-remembered. In Sweden Hakon of Orkney was well treated by King Ingi, but after a time he felt home-sick, and wanted to go west again to the Isles.

Christianity was then newly-planted in Sweden. Many men still dabbled in ancient lore, and were persuaded that by such means they were enabled to foretell future events. Hakon, happening to hear of a man who practised sorcery and spae-craft, became curious to know what he could about his future, and, finding the spaeman, asked if he should succeed in regaining his dominions, or what other fortune awaited him. He was told that he would eventually become sole ruler of the Orkneys, and his sons should rule there after him. Also, that he would commit a great crime.

After this Hakon went to see King Ingi, with whom he stayed a short while, and then obtained leave from the king to depart. He went first to Norway to see his kinsman, King Magnus, who received him very well. There he heard that the government of the Orkneys was almost exclusively in the hands of Earl Erlend and his sons, and that they were greatly loved, but that his father, Paul, took little part in the government. He also perceived that the Orcadians were satisfied with the condition of affairs, and had no desire for his return. Revolving this in his mind, he thought his kinsmen might try to deprive him of his possessions, and that it would be dangerous for him to go west without a numerous retinue. Therefore he devised a scheme to induce King Magnus to put him into his Orkney possessions. This was after Magnus had put Steiga-Thorir and Egil to death, and suppressed all opposition to his rule. Hakon was a sagacious man, and, aware of Magnus' ambition, began to tell him it would be a princely feat to go west and subdue the Isles as Harald the Fairhaired had done, and that if he established his power in the Hebudes he might easily make forays into Ireland and Scotland from them. Then, having subdued the western countries, he might, with the help of the Northmen, attack the English, and thus take revenge for his grandfather, Harald Hardrade. It was evident the king was pleased with this proposal, saying it was spoken like a nobleman and quite according to his mind. "But I wish you not to be surprised, Hakon," said the king, "in case I shall be persuaded by your words to carry an army into the west, if I put forward a strong claim to the possessions there without regard to the claims of any man." Hearing this suggestion, Hakon no longer urged the expedition, nor was it necessary, for Magnus was resolved to undertake it, and gathered together forces throughout his realm. So, when the brothers Paul and Erlend ruled the Orkneys, King Magnus came from Norway with a large army, having with him his son Sigurd, the Crown Prince, then eight years of age. On arriving at the Orkneys he seized the earls, Paul and Erlend, and sent them east to Norway, placing over the Isles his son Sigurd, for whom he appointed counsellors. He then passed on to the Hebudes, accompanied by Magnus and Erling, the sons of Erlend, and by Hakon, the son of Paul. He subdued all the Hebudes, and seized Logman, the son of Gudrod, King of the Western Isles. Thence he went on to Wales, and fought a great battle in Anglesea Sound with Hugh the Stout, Earl of Chester, and Hugh of Montgomery, surnamed the Bold, Earl of Shrewsbury. The latter was killed by an arrow from the bow of King Magnus, and the Normans then fled. Throughout the battle Magnus of Orkney did not take up arms, having no just cause; nor did he shelter himself from the weapons, but sat on the fore-deck. Magnus of Orkney h.......... the n......... waiting at the royal table, and he performed continually the duties of that office. But after the battle in Anglesea Sound he could see he had incurred the king's displeasure, so during the night Magnus stole away. Hiding himself in the woods till the search was over, he afterwards made his way to the court of Edgar, the Scottish king, and stayed there for a while. For some time he was with a certain bishop in Wales. The writer of the "Life of St. Magnus" says he also went to England to wait on King Henry I., son of William the Conqueror, and that he was assisted by King Henry, continuing a year in England with his retinue at the king's charges, and when he came away receiving many costly presents. He did not return to the Orkneys during the life of King Magnus.

King Magnus held northwards along the Scottish coast, and received word from the Scottish sovereign that he was willing to give him all such islands lying west, between which and the mainland he could pass in a vessel with the rudder shipped. By a strategic expedient Magnus added Kintyre to the others, by having his boat drawn across the isthmus, he himself holding the helm. He wintered in the Hebudes, at which the men were discontented. His favourite courtier, Kali Sæbiornsson, of Agdir, advised him to hold a wapinschaw, to ascertain the number of his army. This the king did, and missed many men, after which a watch was kept to prevent desertion. Whilst in the Hebudes, Magnus obtained for his son Sigurd, then nine years of age, the hand of Biadmonia, then five years old, the daughter of Muirceartach, the son of Thialbi, royalet of the Connaught Irish, and son of Brian Boroimhe, King of Munster. This winter Kali of Agdir died from his wounds.

Early in the spring King Magnus left the Hebudes and went first to the Orkneys, where he heard of the death of the Earls. Paul died in Bergen, and Erlend in Drontheim, where he was buried. In order to compensate Kol for the loss of his father, King Magnus married him to Gunnhild, daughter of Earl Erlend. Gunnhild's dowry consisted of Orcadian lands, including a farm at Papul. At his wedding Kol became the vassal of King Magnus. Afterwards he went to Norway with the king, and home to Agdir with his wife, and resided on his estate there. Kol and Gunnhild had two children. Their son was called Kali and their daughter Ingirid. They were both very promising children, and were brought up with affectionate care. After Earl Erlend's death, his wife Thora married a man called Sigurd. Their son was Hakon *Karl*. They had estates in Papul. Of Erling, son of Erlend, some say he fell in Anglesea Sound, but Snorri Sturlusson says he fell in Ulster with King Magnus.

When Magnus had been nine winters king, he went to the west and made war in Ireland, spending the winter in Connaught. The next summer, on St. Bartholomew's Day, 1103, he fell in Ulster. When Sigurd heard of this, he left the Orkneys for Norway, and was made king conjointly with his brothers Eystein and Olaf. He left Biadmonia in the west. One or two winters after King Magnus' death, Hakon of Orkney came from the west, and the kings gave him an earl's title and possessions befitting his birth. He then returned and took possession of the Orkneys. He had always accompanied King Magnus when alive. He was with him in his expedition to Gautland, which is mentioned in the song made about Hakon Paulsson.

HAKON AND MAGNUS, 22ND AND 23RD EARLS.

When Earl Hakon had ruled the Orkneys for some time, Magnus, the son of Earl Erlend, came from Scotland, and wished to have his patrimony, at which all the Orcadians were pleased; but Hakon collected men and refused to surrender any portion of the realm. He, however, at last consented to yield half, if the Norse monarchs approved of it. So Magnus passed to Norway and saw King Eystein, for King Sigurd had then gone to Jerusalem (1107). Eystein received him exceedingly well, and gave him his patrimony—one-half of the Orcades with the title of earl. Thereupon Magnus sailed west to his dominions, every one being glad to see him back. Through the kind offices of mutual friends, Magnus and Hakon agreed very well, and while their friendship continued there were good times and peace reigned in the Orkneys.

The holy Magnus, Earl of the Isles, was a most excellent man, of large stature, noble presence, and intellectual countenance. He was of blameless life, victorious in battles, wise, eloquent, strong-minded, liberal, and magnanimous, sagacious in counsels, and more beloved than any other man. Many other glorious virtues he exhibited to God Himself, but concealed from man.

Magnus and Hakon governed their lands and defended them for some time, the two agreeing well. In a song composed about them, it is said they fought with a chief called Dufniall, their second cousin, who fell before them. They also slew a famous man, Thorbiorn, in Burra Firth, Hjaltland; and other deeds are set forth in song, though not specially narrated here. But presently Hakon became jealous of the popularity and greatness of his cousin, being stirred thereto by men who were evilly-disposed, chief amongst whom were Sigurd and Sighvat *Sock*. The enmity advanced so far that the earls, coming to meet each other in Hrossey, where the Thingstead was, drew up their troops in battle array and prepared to fight, but their mutual friends managed to avert hostilities for the moment, and a reconciliation was confirmed with oaths and shaking of hands. A little later Hakon appointed a day of meeting with the blessed Earl Magnus, to further ratify their friendship: the meeting to take place in the Pasch week in Egilsa, each to be attended with two ships and have an equal number of men. Immediately after Easter, Earl Magnus with his two ships and the stipulated number of men got ready for their voyage to Egilsa. As they were rowing in calm and smooth water, a great wave rose under the ship which was steered by the Earl, and broke over it where he sat. The mariners marvelled greatly at such an occurrence—that a breaker should rise in smooth water where no man could remember one to have arisen, and where the water was so deep. This event was taken to presage Magnus' impending doom. Earl Hakon, on the other hand, came to the meeting place with a numerous army and many ships, equipped as if for battle; and after starting for the destination, announced to his followers that the meeting should finally decide between Magnus and himself, so that both should not rule the Orcadian nation. Many approved of this determination, even adding wicked suggestions, but Sigurd and Sighvat ever counselled the worst things. They then rowed more quickly. Havard Gunnarsson (who was married to Bergliot, daughter of Hakon's sister Ragnhild), the friend and counsellor of the Earls, and equally faithful to them both, was on board Earl Hakon's flag-ship. Hakon had concealed from him this evil plan, in which he would by no means have had any part; and, indeed, when Havard knew Hakon was so resolute in the design, he plunged overboard and swam to a certain uninhabited islet. Magnus, who had first arrived at Egil's Isle, descried Hakon approaching with eight war-ships, and then knew that treachery was intended. His men offered to defend him, but the noble earl declined to imperil their lives, and decided to yield himself to the questionable mercy of Hakon. So, upon being surrounded by his cousin's soldiers, Earl Magnus made these propositions : to go on pilgrimage to Rome or Jerusalem, never returning to the land of his fathers ; to be exiled to Scotland, safe provision being made for his custody in that kingdom ; or, thirdly, to be maimed or blinded and imprisoned. Hakon accepted the last, but the Orcadian nobles said, "One of you we will kill now, and from this day you shall not both rule the lands of the Orkneys." Earl Hakon replied, " Slay him then, for I will rather have earldom and lands than instant death." Their conversation was related by Holdbodi, a truthful bondi in the Hebudes, who was with Earl Magnus when the latter was arrested by his cousin's soldiers. Magnus met his fate with equanimity. Hakon ordered Ofeig, his banner-bearer, to do the deed, but Ofeig indignantly refused. So then Hakon forced Lifolf, his cook, to be executioner. Lifolf wept aloud at having to undertake the office, but Earl Magnus said to him, "Stand before me and hew me a mighty stroke on the head, for it is not fitting that high-born lords should be slain like robbers." After that he made the sign of the cross, stooped under the blow, and his spirit passed into heaven. This was two days after Tiburtiusmas (14th April), 1091. He had been seven winters Earl of the Orkneys along with Earl Hakon. Seventy-four winters had passed since the death of King Olaf, and the kings of Norway at this time were Sigurd, Eystein, and Olaf. The place where the blessed Earl was slain had been previously covered with moss and stones, but shortly afterwards his merits before God became manifest in this wise, that where he was beheaded it became green sward. Thus God showed that he had suffered for righteousness sake, and had obtained the beauty and verdure of Paradise, which is called the Land of the Living. Earl Hakon did not permit his body to be brought to the church for burial.

Thora, the mother of Earl Magnus, had invited both the earls to a banquet after their meeting, and thither Earl Hakon went fresh from the murder of the holy Earl Magnus. Thora herself served at the banquet, and brought the drink to the Earl and his men, who had been present at the murder of her son. And when the drink began to have effect upon the Earl, Thora went before him and pleaded for Christian burial for her son's remains. The Earl became silent and considered her case, as she prayed so meekly, and with tears, that Magnus' body might be brought to church. Looking at his aunt, he saw the tears fall and had compassion, saying, " Bury your son where it pleases you." Then was the Earl's body brought to Hrossey and buried in Christ's Kirk in Birsa, the cathedral church erected by Earl Thorfinn.

Soon after this a heavenly light was seen above his burial place. Men in peril began to pray to him, and their prayers were heard. A celestial odour was frequently observed above his holy grave, from which those suffering from illness received health. Then sufferers made pilgrimages thither, both from the Orkneys and Hjaltaland, and, keeping vigils at his tomb, were cured of all their ills. But people dared not make this known while Hakon was alive. It is said of the men who were most guilty in the death of the sainted Earl, that most of them met with a miserable end. William the Old, first bishop by Romish consecration, occupied the see at this time, and had his seat at Christ's Kirk, Birsa. He was bishop for six winters of the seventh decade. He long disbelieved in the sanctity of Earl Magnus, until his merits became manifest to such a degree that God made his holiness grow the more conspicuous the more it was tried, as is told in the book of his miracles.

Earl Hakon now took possession of all the Orkneys, and exacted an oath of fealty from the Islesmen, receiving also the submission of the supporters of Earl Magnus, whom he heavily fined. Some winters after he prepared to visit Rome. From there he travelled on to Jerusalem, where, according to the custom of the palmers, he sought out the halidoms, bathed in the river Jordan, and brought away several relics from Palestine. Returning to his island realm, he resumed the government, made new laws, which the landowners preferred to the former ones, and became so popular that the Orcadians desired no other lords than Hakon and his issue. When, in advancing years, he died a natural death, it was thought a great loss, for in the latter days of his reign there was unbroken peace. Contemporary with Earl Hakon was Moddan, a wealthy noble who resided at Dale, in Caithness. Moddan had two sons, Eugus *inn ovi* and Ottarr jarl in Thurso, and three daughters, Helga, Frakach (Frakokk), and Thorleif. Helga was mother to Hakon of three children. Their son was Harald the Orator, and their eldest daughter Ingibiorg was married to Olaf, King of the Hebudes; while their second daughter Margaret afterwards married Maddad, Earl of Athole. Frakach was married to Ljot the Miscreant in Sutherland, and their daughter was Steinvor the Stout, married to Thorliot at Rackwick. The sons of the latter were Olvir Rosta (*the Quarreller*), Magnus, Orm, and Moddan, and Einridi, and their daughter Audhild. A second daughter of Frakach was Gudrun, married to Thorstein *Hold* and their son was Thorbiorn *Klerk*. Thorleif Moddan's daughter had a daughter Gunnhild, or Audhild. Hakon the Earl had another son named Paul the Silent, a reserved but popular man. After the death of Hakon he was succeeded by

HARALD AND PAUL, 24TH AND 25TH EARLS.

These brothers soon disagreed, and divided the Orcadian dominions, and then discord arose between the great vassals of each, who were divided into factions. Earl Harald held Caithness from the King of Scots, and he resided frequently there · but sometimes also in Scotland, where he had many friends and kinsmen. When Harald was staying in Sutherland there came to him Sigurd *Slembidjakn*, reputed to be the son of Adalbrekt, a priest. Sigurd came from the court of the Scottish King David, who had held him in high esteem. Earl Harald received him extremely well. Sigurd went into the Islands with Harald and with Frakach, whose husband Ljot was now dead. Frakach and her sister took a large share in the government with Earl Harald. Sigurd was a great favourite with all of them. At this time Audhild, the daughter of Thorleif, was his mistress, and their daughter was Ingigerd, afterwards mother to Hakon Klo. She had before then been married to Eric *Streita*, by whom she was mother of Eirek *Stagbrellu*.

When Sigurd and Frakach came to the Islands great dissensions arose between the brother Earls, and both called together as many of their partisans as they could muster. The most attached to Earl Paul were Sigurd at Westness, who had married Ingibiorg the Noble, a kinswomen of the Earls, and Thorkell, son of Somerled, who was always with

NOTE.—In Halkirk parish Caithness there is a field called Achtin Hacon, or Hacon's field, and in the parish of Tongue a loch called Lochan Haco, which is possibly Loch of Haco.

Paul, and was called his foster-father, Thorkell was of kin to the sainted Earl Magnus, and a most popular man. The friends of the Earls thought no man would more deplore their discord than Thorkell, because of the injury done him by their father Hakon. At last Harald and Sigurd the Slim went to Thorkell the Foster and slew him. This roused the ire of Paul, who only consented to peace upon the banishment from the Orcades of Sigurd and all those incriminated with him. Sigurd the Slim then left the Isles and went to Scotland, staying for a while with Malcolm, King of Scots, by whom he was well entertained. Sigurd was thought a great man in all manly exercises. He remained for a time in Scotland, until he went to Jerusalem. Later on he claimed the Norwegian throne, and established his paternity by ordeal of hot iron, just as King Harald *Gille*, the reigning monarch, had done. Harald declined to recognise the result, and arraigned Sigurd for the slaying of Thorkell. Sigurd effected his escape by plunging overboard with two of his guards in his arms, and presently returning, surprised and slew King Harald. Sigurd then tried, with Danish assistance, to restore King Magnus the Blind, but his forces were totally defeated by the sons of King Harald on the south coast of Norway. Magnus fell in battle, and Sigurd was made captive, to be put to death with almost incredible tortures. The Orcadian Earls in confirming the peace, arranged for Christmas and the chief festivals to be spent together.

Once the brothers were to be entertained at Orphir, one of Earl Harald's estates, and he was to bear the expense of the entertainment for both of them that Christmas, so he was very busy and made great preparations. The sisters Frakach and Helga were there with the Earl, and sat sewing in the stofa, an enclosed portion of the hall at the upper end, where was the pall or dais. Harald happened to enter the apartment where the sisters were, and found them seated on a cross-bench, a newly-made linen garment, spotless as snow, lying between them. The Earl raised it, and, noticing it was embroidered with gold, asked, "To whom does this splendid thing belong?" Frakach replied, "It is intended for your brother Paul." "Why do you make so fine a garment for him? Such pains are not shown in the making of my clothing," said the Earl. Harald had just come out of bed, and was dressed in a shirt and linen drawers with a mantle thrown over the shoulder. Discarding the mantle, he spread out the dress. His mother Helga grasped it, and besought him not to envy his brother his fine clothing, but the Earl pulled it from her and began to put it on. Frakach then snatched at her headgear, and tore her hair, saying his life was endangered if he wore it, and both women wept grievously. Nevertheless Harald put it on, but as soon as it touched his skin a fit of shivering seized him, accompanied by pain so great that he had to take to his bed. He never left it alive, dying in a few days. His friends considered his death a severe loss.

With the consent of the Orcadian estates, Paul immediately entered into possession of his brother's dominions. Considering that the splendid tunic so fatal to Harald had been prepared for himself, Paul preferred that the sisters should not stay in the Isles. Accordingly, with all their attendants—a numerous train—they passed to Caithness, and thence to Frakach's estate in Scotland. This estate became a nursery for many characters prominent in Orcadian history. There

ERLEND III., 26TH EARL,

the son of Harald the Orator, passed his youth, and was brought up under her baneful influence. With Erlend, usually called *the Younger*, to distinguish him from Erlend *the Exile*, the male line of Rögnvald, Earl of Orkney, came to an end, but as most of his doings occur later on, he will not be further referred to here. Of others gathered round Frakach were Olvir the Quarreller, the son of Thorliot, and Steinvor, her daughter, Thorbiorn Klerk, the son of Gudrun and Thorstein Hold; Margaret, daughter of Earl Hakon and Helga, and Eric Stagbrellir was also brought up by her. All these were of great families, and thought they had claims on the Orkneys. Frakach's brothers were Engus the Liberal and Earl Ottar in Thurso, a man of birth and rank.

Earl Paul then ruled the Orkneys, and was very popular. He was somewhat taciturn, spoke little at the Things, and gave others a large share in the government with himself. He was a modest man, gentle to his people, liberal with his money, and spared nothing to his friends. He was not warlike, and kept himself very quiet. At that time there were many noble men descended from earls in the Orkneys. There lived at Westness, in Rousa (Hrolfsey) a noble man named Sigurd, who had married Ingibiorg the Noble. Their sons were Brynjolf and Hakon *Peak*. All these were vassals of Earl Paul; so also were the sons of Havard Gunnarsson, Magnus, and Hakon *Claw*, Thorstein and Dufniall. Their mother was Bergliot, and her mother was Ragnhild, daughter of Earl Paul the Exile. At Tankerness lived one Erling, who had four sons, all of whom were accomplished men. In Gairsay lived Olaf, Hrolf's son, who had another estate in Duncansby, in Caithness. Olaf was a great man, highly honoured by Earl Paul. His wife was named Ashef, a wise woman, accomplished, and of great family. Their sons, Valthiof, Sweyn, and Gunni, were all accomplished men, their sister was named Ingigerd. Sigurd of Paplay had married Thora, the mother of Earl Magnus, and their son was Hakon *Karl*. Both Sigurd and his son were great chiefs. In North Ronaldsay there lived a woman by name Ragna, her son Thorstein was a man of great strength. In Westray there lived at a hamlet a farmer named Helgi, and at Hreppisness a wise and wealthy farmer named Kugi. Thorkell Flettir, a violent and powerful man, also lived in that isle, his sons Thorstein and Haflidi were unpopular men. At Swona, in the Petland Firth, lived a poor man, Grim, who had two sturdy sons, Asbiorn and Margad. In Fair Isle lived Dagfinn. At Flydiuness, in Hrossey, lived Thorstein, who had two wild sons, Asbjorn *the Cross-eyed*, and Bljan. Jaddvor, daughter of Earl Erlend, lived with her son Borgar at Knarstad, they were both rather unpopular. John *Wing* lived at Upland, in Hoey. Rikard, his brother, lived at Brekkur in Strjonsey. They were grand men, and related to Olaf Hrolfson. A man named Grimkell lived at Glettuness. All these men will be mentioned hereafter.

All this time Kol of Agdir in Norway had resided on his estates, and attended to the education of his son Kali, and the latter was now grown up into a most promising man. His hair was of a light auburn colour, and he was of middle size, well and handsomely proportioned, affable, popular, and very highly accomplished, being proficient in the nine arts then held highest in estimation. This we learn from his own verses:—

"Tafl em ek orr at efla,
idróttir kann ek niu,
"tyni ek traudla rúnum,
tid er mer bók ok smithir.
"Skrida kann ek, a skidum,
skyt ek ok ræ'k sva at nytir,
"hvárt-tveggja kann ek hyggja
harp-látt ok bragg-tháttu."

"At the game-board I am skilful,
Knowing in no less than nine arts,
Runic lore I well remember,
Books I like, with tools I'm handy,
Expert am I on the snow-shoes,
With the bow, and pull an oar well,
And, besides, I am an adept
At the harp and making verses."

Kali was frequently with his kinsmen, Solmund, the son of Sigurd Sneis, who was Treasurer at Tunsberg, and had estates at Austr-Agdir. He was a great chief and had a numerous retinue. When Kali was fifteen he accompanied some merchants to England, taking with him a good cargo of merchandise. They went to a trading place called Grimsby where there was a great number of people from Norway, as well as from the Orkneys, Scotland, and the Hebudes. While there he met one Gillichrist, who asked him many things about Norway, and they became great companions. Gillichrist then confided to Kali that his name was Harald, that he was a son of King Magnus Barelegs, and that his mother was in the Hebudes. He further asked how he might be received if he went to Norway. Kali answered he thought King Sigurd would be friendly if not set against him by others. At parting Gillichrist and Kali exchanged presents, and promised each other mutual friendship wherever they might meet. Kali then sailed homewards for Agdir, and held on to Bergen. He was then a dressy man, and being newly come from England had many braveries. In a hostelry there, kept by a worthy housewife named Unna, he met a young man of rank named John, son of Peter Sarksson, of Sogn, one of the king's liegemen. His mother was Helga, daughter of Harek of Saeter. John was also smart in matters of dress, and great fellowship arose between him and Kali, and they parted staunch comrades. John went north to Sogn, and Kali east to Agdir. Kali passed some years occupied in trading trips during the summer, spending the winters either at Agdir or with Solmund.

One summer, on his way to Drontheim, he was weather-bound at an island called Dolls, in which there was an enchanted cavern called the Doll's cave, and report stated that there was much treasure hidden there. A sheet of water stretched across the entrance, and no one dared cross it, save the hardy Kali and Havard, a domestic. They swam over the tiny lake, Kali carrying firewood on his shoulders; but after making a thorough search they failed to find any treasure. Kali raised a pile of stones as a remembrance of their entry, and with his usual facility commemorated the circumstance in verse. The company proceeded to Bergen. Arrived there Kali put up at an inn, where John Petrsson was also staying, and they became very friendly. One evening, after John and Kali had retired, the guests began comparing men, a favourite Norse custom, and Brynjulf, a retainer of John's, ventured to say his master was the best man and of the noblest family south of the Stad. Havard, the companion of Kali, immediately challenged the statement, asserting Solmund was in no way inferior to John, and would be more esteemed by the men of Vik. A quarrel ensued, and Havard, seizing a piece of wood, struck Brynjulf so severe a blow on the head that he fainted. Kali then sent Havard into retirement, but John, divining his destination, despatched Brynjulf after him with ten men, who overtook and slew him. This raised a blood feud between John and Brynjulf on the one part, and Solmund and Hallvard, brother to Havard, on the other, resulting in the assassination of Brynjulf by Hallvard. This was followed by reprisals from John, who unsuccessfully endeavoured to surprise Solmund and Kol, but was wounded and defeated. The next summer, however, he contrived to kill Gunnar and Aslak, two of Kol's kinsmen. These differences were eventually submitted to King Sigurd for adjudication, when a reconciliation was arranged. Wounds and deaths were balanced against each other, and John was to marry Ingirid, daughter of Kol, and they who were enemies before parted good friends. At the same time King Sigurd gave Kali the half of the Orkneys which had belonged to his uncle St Magnus and created him an earl, re-naming him Rögnvald, because his mother, the Lady Gunnhild, said that Rognvald Brusisson was the most accomplished of all the Orcadian earls, and thought the name would bring good fortune

This winter King Sigurd died at Opslo (Christiania), the ancient Norwegian capital. His son Magnus succeeded him, and took possession of all the royal treasures. Harald Gillichrist was at Tunsberg when the news reached him, and he at once convened meetings with his friends, and sent for Rognvald and his father, because since they met in England they had always been friends. Rognvald and Kol had also done most to help Harald to prove his paternity to Sigurd. In this they were assisted by many barons—Ingimar, Thiostolf, and others. So Harald and his partisans held a Hauga-Thing at Tunsberg, and there Harald was accepted as King of one-half of Norway. A nominal peace was effected, Magnus and Harald dividing Norway, but the fourth summer they declared war and fought at Fyrileif (1134), where Magnus with 6,000 men defeated Harald, who had only 1,500. Harald's chief warriors were his brother Kristrod, Earl Rognvald, Ingimar, Thiostolf, and Solmund. Kristrod and Ingimar fell in the battle, and Harald fled to King Eric in Denmark, where he was presently joined by Thiostolf. At Yule, Harald returned to Bergen, seized King Magnus on board his flagship, and had him maimed. Harald then took possession of the whole kingdom, and the next spring he renewed the gift of the Islands and the title of earl to Rognvald.

Kol now resolved to send men to the Orkneys to ask Earl Paul to surrender the half of the Islands bestowed on Rognvald by King Harald, and they should be friends and good kinsmen. But if Paul refused, the embassy should proceed to Frakach and Olvir Rosta, offering them one-half of the Isles jointly with Rognvald if they were willing to acquire it by force of arms. On receiving the message Paul declined to entertain the proposal, and said, "With the assistance of my friends and kinsmen I shall defend the Orkneys as long as God grants me life." The embassy then crossed the Petland Firth, and made the alternative offer to Frakach and Olvir. Frakach received the message favourably, remarking that it was wise of Kol to seek their assistance, as their relatives and connections were both numerous and powerful. "I have now," said she, "married Margaret, Hakon's daughter, to Moddan, Earl of Athole, who is of the noblest family of all the Scottish chiefs. His father, Melmari, is the uncle of King Malcolm, the father of David, who is now King of the Scots. We have many and just claims on the Orkneys, and have ourselves some power. We have the reputation of being far-seeing, and during hostilities all things do not come on us unawares; yet we will be glad to entertain an alliance with Kol and his son for many reasons. Tell them I and Olvir shall bring an army to the Orkneys in midsummer. Let Rognvald meet us then, and have a decisive battle with Earl Paul. During the winter I will collect forces from my kinsmen, friends, and connections in Scotland and the Hebudes." Returning to Norway, these matters were related to Rognvald.

Next summer he sailed west, accompanied by Solmund and John, with a fine body of troops and five or six ships. Adverse winds compelled them to put into Yell Sound, where they stayed feasting, being well received by the boendr. They heard nothing of Frakach, but of her it is to be told that in the spring she went to the Hebudes, where she and Olvir mustered troops and ships. They had in all twelve ships, all of them small and ill-manned. Olvir was the commander, and if they gained a victory he was to have an earldom in the Orkneys. Frakach was also there with many of her retainers. About midsummer they directed their course to the Orkneys to join Rognvald. Earl Paul was then at a feast with Sigurd of Westness in Rousa, when he heard that Earl Rögnvald had arrived in Hjaltland, and that an army was gathering in the Hebudes. So he sent word to Kugi in Westray, and Thorkell Flett, who were wise men; and many other of his chief men he called together. After consultation, it was resolved to summon the Islemen to resist the invaders, and to first advance to meet Rögnvald and decide matters before the arrival of the Hebudeans. The Earl had with him Sweyn Briostreip (*of the Breastrope*), whom he highly esteemed. Sweyn was of large stature and great strength, swarthy and ill-favoured. He was greatly skilled in ancient lore, and had frequently been engaged in out-sittings. In the summer he was always on viking raids, but in the winter stayed with the Earl. He was stationed in the forecastle of the Earl's flagship. During the night the following warriors came to Earl Paul: Eyvind, son of Melbrigd, in a ship fully manned; Olaf, son of Rolf, from Gairsay, had another; Thorkel Flettir, the third; Sigurd, the fourth; and the Earl himself had the fifth. With these five vessels they went to Hrossey, and arrived there in the evening about sunset. Troops gathered to him during the night, but no more ships were to be had. The next day they were to sail to Hjaltland to meet Earl Rögnvald, but in the morning, shortly after sunrise, some men came to Earl Paul reporting that ten or twelve long ships were sighted approaching from the Petland Firth.

Convinced that this was Frakach's party, Paul ordered his men to row against them as fast as possible. Olaf and Sigurd, however, in hourly expectation of further reinforcements, advised them to go leisurely. When Paul's fleet was off Tankerness the long ships, twelve together, sailed to the west from the Moul Head of Dourness. Earl Paul and his men fastened their ships together. The bondi Erling, from Tankerness, and his sons came to him offering their assistance, and then Paul's ships were so crowded that they could not use more men. The Earl asked Erling and his men to bring them stones, which Erling did till prevented by the fighting. When they had prepared themselves Olvir came up and made the attack with a superior force, but his ships were smaller. Olvir himself had a large ship, which he placed beside the Earl's, and there the fighting was the most severe. Olaf attacked the smaller ships of Olvir, and cleared three of them in a short time. Olvir attacked the Earl's ship so fiercely that all the forecastle men were driven abaft the mast. Then Olvir urged his men strongly to board, and set the example by himself jumping from the quarter-deck to the fore part of the ship, being the first to board. Sweyn Briostreip was the foremost of all the Earl's men, and fought bravely. When Paul saw that Olvir had boarded his ship, he urged his men forward and jumped from the quarter-deck to the fore part of the ship. Olvir perceiving this, grasped a spear and hurled it at the Earl, who received it on his shield, but fell down on the deck. Then there was a great shout, but in the same moment Sweyn seized a huge stone and threw it at Olvir. It struck him on the chest with such force that he was thrown overboard and sank; but his men were able to drag him into one of their ships, and it was not known whether he was dead or alive. Then some cut the cables and wanted to flee. All Olvir's men were also driven off the Earl's ship, and began to withdraw. At that moment Olvir recovered, and begged them not to flee; but all pretended not to hear what he said. The Earl pursued the fugitives along the east of Hrossey and Ronaldsey, and into the Petland Firth, where they parted. Then he returned, and five of Olvir's ships remained where they had fought. These the Earl captured and manned. The battle took place on Friday, but in the night the Earl had ships made ready, and many men and two long ships came to him, so that in the morning he had twelve ships all well manned

On Saturday he sailed for Hjaltland and surprised those in charge of Rognvald's ships He slew the men and seized the ships with all their contents In the morning when Rognvald had news of this he mustered his men on the beach, and challenged Paul to come on shore and fight Paul had little faith in the Hjaltlanders, and would not land, but retorted that they should get ships and fight. Rognvald, however, saw he could get no ships in Hjaltland which would equalise his chance, and they parted as matters stood, Paul returning to the Orkneys, while Rognvald passed the summer in Hjaltland, and in the autumn returned to Norway with some merchants It was thought his expedition had come to a ridiculous end. When Rognvald got east he saw his father Kol, and they discussed the failure of his attempt to wrest the Isles from Paul, and how to ensure success on the next occasion Paul, after gaining the two-fold victory, feasted all his friends and vassals. He now resolved to take precautions against being surprised, and arranged to have beacons lit on the various islands if enemies were seen approaching from Hjaltland. There was to be one in the Fair Isle, one also in North Ronaldsa, of which Thorstein, the son of Havard Gunnaisson, had the care, his brother Magnus had charge of one in Sanday, Kugi, of that in Westray, and Sigurd of Westness, of the one in Hrolfsey. Olaf Hrolfsson, crossed to Dungalsbæ, in Caithness, and was to have the emoluments of that place His son Valthiof was at that time in Stronsa.

Earl Paul gave presents to his men, and all promised him their unfailing friendship. He had many men about him in the autumn, until he heard that Rognvald and his men had left Hjaltland Nothing happened in the Islands till Yule. Paul had a grand Yule feast, which he prepared at his estate at Orphir, and invited many guests Valthiof from Stronsa was invited. He went with his men in a ten-oared boat, and they perished, all of them, in the West Firth on Yule Eve That was thought bad news, as Valthiof was a most accomplished man His father Olaf had a large party in Caithness. There were his sons Sweyn and Gunni, and the sons of Grim of Swiney, Asbiorn and Margad, brave-looking fellows, who always followed Sweyn Three nights before Yule, Sweyn, Asbiorn, and Margad had put out to sea to fish, and Asleif and her son Gunni had gone a short distance to meet their friends The night after that Olvir Rosta arrived at Dungalsbae with the party that had been out with him on a viking cruise during the summer. He surprised Olaf in the house, and immediately fired it There Olaf was burnt with five others, but the rest were permitted to escape Olvir and his men took all the moveable property, and then re-embarked After this event Sweyn was called Asleifsson He came home on Yule Eve, and went immediately out north on the Petland Firth. At midnight they came to Grim in Swona, the father of Asbiorn and Margad, he went into the boat to them, and he brought Sweyn to Knarstane in Scapa, where there lived a man named Arnkell, whose sons were Hanef and Sigurd Grim and his sons returned to Swona, and at parting Sweyn gave him a finger-ring of gold Hanef and Sigurd accompanied Sweyn to Orphir Here he was well received, and conducted to his kinsman Eyvind, son of Melbrigd Eyvind presented him to Earl Paul, who received him favourably and asked his news Sweyn told him of his father's death, at which the Earl was much grieved, and said it had in a great measure happened through him He invited Sweyn to stay with him, and the hospitable invitation was accepted with thanks Then they went to evensong.

At Orphir there was a large homestead standing on the hillside, and behind the house was a height From the top of the hill may be seen the Bay of Firth, and in it lies Damsa In this island was a castle, the castellan being Blan, the son of Thorstein of Flydruness In Orphir there was a large wassail hall, the door being near the east gable on the southern wall, and a noble church was in front of the door, and one had to descend steps from the hall to the church. On entering the hall there was a large flagstone on the left, farther in were many large ale vessels, but opposite the outer door was the stofa When the guests came from evensong they were placed in their seats, Sweyn Asleifsson sitting next the Earl on one side, and on the other side next to the Earl was Swein Briostreip, and then John his kinsmen. When the tables were removed there entered men with the tidings of Valthiof's death by drowning This the Earl considered sad news. He ordered that no one should tell it to Sweyn while the Yule feast lasted, adding that he had cares enough already. In the evening when the wassail was over the Earl and most of his guests retired, but Swein Briostreip went and sat out all night, as was his wont At midnight the guests arose and heard mass, and after high mass they sat down to the table. Eyvind shared the management of the feast with the Earl and did not sit down Table-boys and light-bearers stood before the Earl's table, but Eyvind handed goblets to each of the Sweyns. There had long been a coldness between Swein Briostreip and Olaf Hrolfsson and his son Sweyn Asleifsson since he grew up When they came in again memorial toasts were proposed, and they drank out of horns. Then Swein Briostreip wished to exchange with his namesake, saying his was a small one. Eyvind, however, put a big horn into Sweyn Asleifsson's hand, and this he offered to his namesake, who became very angry, and was overheard by the Earl and some of his men muttering to himself, "Sweyn will be the death of Swein, and Swein shall be the death of Sweyn," but nothing was said about it, and the wassailing went on till evensong, when the Earl went out preceded by Sweyn Asleifsson, but the other Swein remained behind drinking. Eyvind apprehending danger to his kinsman, advised him to take the initiative, so, standing in the shadow of the flagstone, Sweyn Asleifsson struck at his namesake, who staggered, but recovering himself, drew his sword and struck at the person whom he thought was his assailant, but it was his kinsman John, and they both fell there.

Eyvind led Sweyn Asleifsson into the stofa, opposite the door, and he was dragged out through a window There Magnus, Eyvind's son, had a horse ready, and accompanied him away behind the house and into the Orrida Firth (Bay of Firth) There he took a boat and brought Sweyn to the castle in Damsay, and the next morning Blan, the castellan, went with him to Bishop William in Egilsay When they arrived there the Bishop was at mass, after which Sweyn was conducted to him secretly. Sweyn told the Bishop the news—the deaths of his father Olaf and brother Valthiof, and the slaughter of Swein and John Then he besought the assistance of the Bishop. That prelate thanked him for slaying Swein, and said it was a good riddance. He kept Sweyn during the Yule-tide, and then sent him to Holdbodi, the son of Hundi, in Tiree in the Hebudes. Holdbodi was a great chief. He received Sweyn well, and there he spent the winter, highly esteemed of all the people.

All concluded that Sweyn Asleifsson had slain his namesake, and the Earl was confirmed in this by Sweyn's absence It was thought that Sweyn had gone to Hakon Karl in Papla, the brother-uterine of St Magnus As the Earl did not hear of Sweyn that winter, he outlawed him, and meantime gave to Thorkell Flett the farm in Stronsa which Valthiof had owned. From Stronsa the Earl went to Rinansay, and was entertained there by Ragna and her son Thorstein. Ragna was accounted a wise woman. They had another farm in Papa, where the Earl spent three nights, as he was prevented by weather from going to Kugi in Westray.

When the spring advanced Earl Paul had the beacons kept up in Fair Isle, North Ronaldsa, and the other islands. Dagfinn, son of Hlodver, had charge of the one in Fair Isle. All this while Rognvald was spending the winter at home at Agdir, in Norway, but not forgetting to make arrangements for his next attempt. During February and March Kol despatched two transport vessels, one west to England to buy provisions and arms, and the other under Solmund south to Denmark to buy such things as Kol told him, because he had all the management of their equipment. When these vessels returned it was arranged to start the week after Easter. Kol, Rognvald, and Solmund had each a warship, they had also a transport ship filled with provisions. When they came to Bergen, King Harald was there, and he gave Rognvald a warship fully manned. John Fot had also a warship. Aslak, son of Erlend, from Hern, and son of the daughter of Steigar-Thorir, had the sixth, he had also a barge filled with provisions. Thus they had six large ships, five cutters, and three transports. Whilst lying at Hern waiting a favourable wind, Rognvald made a long and eloquent speech, the conclusion of which was that he meant either to gain the Orkneys or die there. Kol then arose and suggested that he should seek the help of the holy St. Magnus, and vow if he gained those dominions to erect a stone minster at Kirkwall more magnificent than any other in the Isles, and dedicate it to St Magnus, endowing it suitably that his relics and the Bishop's See may be brought there. All thought this good advice, and the vow was made and confirmed. They then stood out to sea, and with a fair wind soon reached Hjaltland. Kol's first plan was to mislead those in charge of the beacon in the Fair Isle. This he succeeded in doing by a well-executed stratagem. He had a flotilla of small boats brought just in sight of the island, and, gradually hoisting the sail, gave the impression of a large fleet nearing the place. Dagfinn immediately lit the Fair Isle beacon. Thorstein followed with that on North Ronaldsa, and presently the islands were all illuminated with signal fires. As soon as Kol saw the Fair Isle beacon burning he returned to Hjaltland, and then Uni, who had been an accomplice in the slaughter of Brynjulf, appeared on the scene. Taking some provisions and fishing tackle, he sailed in a sixareen for the Fair Isle, accompanied by three Hjaltlanders. He made out that he had been ill-treated by Rognvald's men, and, making himself agreeable, was soon generally liked.

All the Islesmen had rallied round Earl Paul, and the soldiery were kept together for three days. But as no enemies appeared, they began to murmur at the absurdity of lighting beacons upon sighting a few fishers. Thorstein, son of Ragna, was blamed for having lit the beacon on North Ronaldsa. He replied that he could do nothing but light it, and blamed Dagfinn. This resulted in a fray. Sigurd of Westness, with his sons Hakon and Brynjulf, took part with Hlodver, father of Dagfinn, but Thorstein was aided by his kinsmen. Kugi of Westra shrewdly suspected the cause of the sails sighted from Fair Isle and said, "Now may we expect them any day." One Eric was now appointed to the Fair Isle beacon, and Uni's opportunity arrived. Eric allowed him to attend to it, and Uni did so in his own way, pouring water over it, making it so wet that it would not light. Rögnvald set sail for Westra, and came one Friday evening to Pierowall, where dwelt Helgi. When Eric sighted the sails he prepared to go to Earl Paul, and sent a man to tell Uni to fire the beacon; but Uni was absent, and the man, discovering his treachery, reported it to Eric, who informed Earl Paul.

When Rögnvald arrived at Westra, Helgi, Kugi, and the rest of the Westra folk submitted to him, and swore fealty. On Sunday Rögnvald had mass celebrated in Pierowall. Paul now held council with his nobles, and they were for fighting Rögnvald. The latter, hearing of the result, sent men to see, and secure the intervention of the Bishop, and also to Thorstein, son of Ragna, and Thorstein Havardsson in Sanda with the like object. The Bishop procured a fortnight's truce in order that they might endeavour to establish a more lasting peace. Then the islands were allocated that should maintain each of them in the meantime. Earl Rögnvald went to the Mainland and Earl Paul to Rousa.

At this time it happened that the kinsmen, Sweyn Asleifsson, John *Vang* of Upland in Hoy, and Richard of Brekkur in Stronsay, attacked Thorkell Flett on the estate which had belonged to Valthiof, and burnt him in the house with nine others. After that they went to Earl Rögnvald, and told him they would go to Earl Paul with the whole body of their kinsmen if he would not receive them; but he did not turn them away. As soon as Haflidi, son of Thorkell, heard of his father's burning, he went to Earl Paul, who received him well. After this John and his men bound themselves to serve Earl Rögnvald, who had now many followers in the islands, and had become popular. Rögnvald now gave leave to John *Fot*, Solmund, Aslac, and others to go home to Norway.

Early in the spring Sweyn left the Hebudes and went to Scotland to see his friends. He stayed for a long time at Athole with Earl Maddad and Margaret, the daughter of Earl Hakon, and had many secret consultations with them. Hearing there were disturbances in the Orkneys, he became desirous of seeing his kinsmen. He went first to Thurso accompanied by Liotolf, a nobleman with whom he had stayed a long time in the spring. At Thurso they came to Ottar, the brother of Frakach. Liotolf tried to make them compose the matters done by her order, and Earl Ottar made compensation for his part. He promised friendship to Sweyn, who, in return, promised to help Erlend, the son and heir of Earl Harald, to obtain his patrimony in the Orkneys when he should wish to claim it. Sweyn changed ships there and took a barge manned by thirty men. He crossed the Petland Firth with a north-westerly wind, and so along the west side of Hrossay, on to Evie Sound, and along the sound to Rousay. Earl Paul had spent the night at a feast with Sigurd of Westness, and was then hunting otters. Sweyn managed to surprise him with a slight retinue, and in the conflict that ensued took him prisoner, with a loss of six men, having slain about nineteen of Paul's party. The place is now known as Swendroog. They hurried Paul on board and stood to sea, making first for the Moray Firth, and thence to Earl Maddad and Margaret, at Athole, by whom they were well received. Maddad placed Paul in his high seat, and when they were seated Margaret entered with a long train of ladies and advanced to her brother. Then men were procured to amuse them, but Paul was moody—and it was no wonder, for he had many cares. One day Margaret announced that Sweyn should go to the Orkneys, see Earl Rögnvald, and ask him with whom he would prefer to share the dominions of the Orkneys—Earl Paul or Harald, her son, then three winters old. When Paul heard this, he asked permission to retire into a monastery, and that Sweyn might give out to the Islesmen that he had been blinded or slain. Sweyn then went to the Orkneys, but Paul remained behind in Scotland This is how Sweyn related these matters But some say Margaret induced Sweyn to blind Paul, and then threw him into a dungeon, and subsequently induced another man to put him to death. Which of these statements is correct is not known, but it is certain that Earl Paul came never again to the Orkneys, and that he had no dominions in Scotland

It happened at Westness when the Earl did not return that Sigurd sent men to search for him, who reported twenty-five men slain near the stone-heap, where the conflict occurred Sigurd recognised nineteen as the Earl's men, but did not know the other six He then sent to Bishop William, at Egilsey, and stated he thought it was some of Rognvald's work

Borgar, the son of Jatvor, who lived at Gatnip, had seen the barge coming from the South and returning When this was heard it was believed to have been done at the instigation of Frakach and Olvir When the news spread through the Isles that Earl Paul had disappeared, the Islesmen mostly swore fealty to Earl Rognvald; but Sigurd of Westness and his sons, Brynjulf and Hakon, refused to do so till they heard of the fate of the Earl, and others also refused, though some agreed to do so if Paul's fate were not known by a given hour and day. Rognvald did not press them, as many were powerful men, and it was only a matter of time.

One day, at a Thing meeting *in Kirkwall*, it happened that nine armed men were seen walking from Scapa to the meeting When they came near Sweyn was recognised and asked for news by his friends and kinsmen. He said very little, but retired with the Bishop to ask his advice. After consultation the Bishop came to the meeting, and pleaded for Sweyn, explaining for what reason he had left the Orkneys, and the penalties Earl Paul had imposed on him for slaying Swein Briostreip, a most wicked man The Bishop concluded by asking Earl Rognvald and all the people to grant security to Sweyn.

Earl Rognvald granted him security for three nights, and made the Bishop responsible for his custody The next day Rognvald, his father Kol, the Bishop, and Sweyn had a private interview, at which Sweyn related all that had occurred between him and Earl Paul, and they came to the conclusion to send away the bulk of the people at the meeting The Earl arose next morning and gave the people permission to go home; but when the multitude had gone away, he called together all those that remained and made them all renew their promise of security to Sweyn while he told the news. In the morning Hakon *Karl*, the uterine brother of the holy Earl Magnus, was persuaded to tell Sigurd of Westness and his sons of Earl Paul's abduction, that he was not to be expected back to his dominions, and that he had been maimed Said Sigurd, "Great news do I think this about the carrying away of the Earl, yet to me the saddest of all is that he should have been maimed, for he would not be anywhere where I would not go to him." He afterwards told his friends Hakon would not have left him unharmed if he had had a sufficient force with him when he told him these tidings, so greatly was he moved by them

When the news became generally known, all the Orcadians submitted to Earl Rognvald, and he became the sole ruler of Earl Paul's dominions.

THE NORSE LINE.—Continued.

27 St. Rögnvald III., *the Crusader* .. .. .. 1136—1158
29 Harald III., *the Younger* .. .. .. 1176—1198

The Royal Scottish Line.

28 Harald II., *the Wicked* .. .. 1139—1206
30 David .. .. 1206—1214
31 John .. .. 1206—1231

Contemporary Princes:

Norway:	1136, Sigurd.	1155, Eystein II.	1157, Inge I.
	1161, Hakon III.	1162, Magnus V.	1186, Sverre.
	1202, Hakon IV.	1204, Guttorm.	1205, Inge II.
	1207, Hakon V., to 1263		
Scotland:	1124, David I.	1153, Malcolm IV.	1165, William *the Lion*.
	1213, Alexander II., to 1248		
England:	1135, Stephen.	1154, Henry II.	1189, Richard.
	1199, John.	1216, Henry III. to 1272.	
Rome:	1130, Innocent II.	1143, Celestin II.	1144, Lucius II.
	1145, Eugenius III.	1153, Anastasius IV.	1154, Adrian IV.
	1159, Alexander III.	1181, Lucius III.	1185, Urban III.
	1187, Gregory VIII.	Clement III.	1191, Celestin III.
	1198, Innocent III.	1216, Honorius III.	1227, Gregory IX.

Prelates.*

Orkney:	1102, William I., *the Old*.	1168, William II.	1185, Bjarni.
	1223, Jofreyr to 1247.		
Caithness:	1153, Andrew to 1185.	1213, John.	1221, Adam.
	1223, St. Gilbert to 1244.		

ST. ROGNVALD III., 27TH EARL.

Rognvald now—1136—having undisputed sway proceeded, in fulfilment of his vow, to erect the stone minster to St. Magnus, and entrusted the superintendence of the work to his father, who is also credited with having been the architect. The work was proceeded with till 1137, when the Earl's resources became strained and he had recourse to the heritable Odallers for assistance. The Cathedral of St. Magnus is incontestably the most glorious monument of the time of the Norwegian dominion in Scotland. It is one of the two cathedral churches in Scotland remaining entire, and is therefore a national monument, interesting from its antiquity, its beauty, and the rarity of such relics in that part of the empire. Nothing conveys to the mind of the stranger visiting Kirkwall a more vivid impression of the ancient importance of this quaint little town which has been the capital of Orcadia for a millennium, than the grandeur of its cathedral and the imposing aspect of the ruins of the palaces of the Bishops and Earls of Orkney.

* See Historiettes.

ST. ROGNVALD III.

Some two years after Rögnvald's accession, Bishop John of Athol was commissioned by Earl Maddad to go to Orkney and negotiate as to the interests of Harald of Athol. When the bishop and his party arrived none of the Orcadians were able to tell who they were, but one Hrolf, the Earl's chaplain, alone knew him, and told the Earl that it was Bishop John from Athol. The matter was discussed by the Earl and the Bishops of Orkney and Athol, and it was arranged that Harald was entitled to half the Isles, but that Rögnvald should have supreme rule even after Harald reached his majority.

ST. MAGNUS' CATHEDRAL, KIRKWALL.

HARALD II., 28TH EARL.

This was confirmed by the principal Orcadians and Scotsmen, and Harald was taken to Orkney by his foster-father, Thorbiorn Klerk and Gudrun, and though only five years of age, received investiture as Earl. Thorbiorn then married Ingirid, sister to Sweyn Asleifsson.

This period is so fully recorded as to form subject matter sufficient for a special book, and will therefore only be cursorily dealt with. The most remarkable incidents are the exploits of Sweyn and the pilgrimage of Rögnvald to the Holy Land.

As for Sweyn, it is told how, with the approval of the Countess of Athole, he exacted vengeance for his father's death by burning Frakach, and causing Olvir Rosta to fly from the North of Scotland; nor is he again mentioned. After that Sweyn made an alliance with Holdbodi, the Hebudean, and plundered in the Isle of Man and Wales. One Eric, an Icelander, celebrates his little game in song :

" Bæir eru brendir, en buendr rændir,	Half-a-dozen homesteads burning,
(svá hefir Sveinn hagat), sex i morgin :	Half-a-dozen households plundered :
Gjördi hann einum ærinn theirra,	This was Sweyn's work of a morning—
leigir thar kol leigu-manni."*	This his vengeance ; coals he lent them.

Swyen married Ingirid, relict of a Manx nobleman named Andrew, by whom she had a son, Sigmund. She made marriage conditional upon his revenging the death of her former husband. Holdbodi broke faith with Sweyn and endeavoured to surprise him, but unsuccessfully. While Sweyn was in the Hebudes, Earl Rögnvald was in Caithness, being entertained at Wick by one Hroald, whose wife's name was Arnljot. His son was Sweyn, an active fellow. While there Thorbiorn Klerk appeared on the scene, and complained that his father, Thorstein Hold, had been killed by a certain Scottish earl named Valthiof. Rögnvald and Thorbiorn became very intimate, and Sweyn Hroaldsson became Rögnvald's table page. While in Scotland, Thorbiorn slew two men who had assisted at the cremation of Frakach. On Sweyn Asleifsson's return from the Hebudes there was a coolness between the brothers-in-law, but Earl Rögnvald reconciled them.

At this time an Icelandic vessel arrived in the Orkneys, in which was Hall, the son of Thorarinn. He stayed in North Ronaldsa with Thorstein Ragnasson. Presently he thought of seeing the Earl, but Rögnvald would not receive him, so Ragna made a personal application to procure Hall a place at the Earl's Court, and was successful. Hall remained a long time with Earl Rögnvald. They jointly made " The Old Metrekey," with five verses for each different metre. Afterwards that was thought too much, and now only two verses are made for each different metre. (*Clavis Rhythmica*, apparently a kind of rhyming dictionary or reportory of versification.) Torfæus states that this joint production is still extant in the library at Upsala.

Sweyn Asleifsson heard that Holdbodi had returned to the Hebudes, and asked Earl Rögnvald for an armament with which to avenge himself. He was given five ships, one commanded by himself, and the others, by Thorbiorn Klerk, Haflidi, son of Thorkell Flett, Dufnial Havardsson, and Richard Thorleifsson. Holdbodi did not wait for Sweyn's arrival, but fled, leaving Sweyn to ravage the Hebudes far and wide. A dispute arose over the spoil as Sweyn wanted the lion's share, much to the chagrin of Thorbiorn, who

---
Orkn. Saga Rolls' Text.

thought they should share it equally, and, on his return to Caithness, in pursuance of a policy of revenge, divorced Ingirid, his wife, the sister of Sweyn. While in the Hebudes Sweyn had placed Margad Grimsson over his affairs at Dungalsbae and transferred to him the office of deputy, which he held from Earl Rognvald. Margad became overbearing and violent and killed Hroald at Wick, with several others, after which he went to Sweyn at Dungalsbae, and they both returned to Lambaborg (Balquholly Castle), which they fortified. Sweyn Hroaldsson asked Earl Rognvald to assist him in obtaining redress, and many supported his request. So Rognvald crossed to Caithness with Thorbiorn, Haflidi, Dufniai, and Richard, and besieged the fortress, calling on Sweyn to surrender unconditionally. When their provisions were nearly exhausted, Sweyn and Margad got lowered to the sea from the castle cliff, swam to the end of it, and escaped to Sutherland, whence they made their way to Moray. At Duffus they met with an Orcadian trader commanded by Hallvard and Thorkel, with whom they sailed south and plundered the monastery on the Isle of Mey, the head of which was an abbot named Baldvini. Leaving Mey, they made for the Firth of Forth, and found David, King of Scotland, to whom Sweyn related all he had done including the sacrilegious attack at Mey. King David, we are told, made good the losses to those Sweyn had robbed, and wanted him to bring Ingirid to Scotland and enter his service, but Sweyn was too much attached to "the old Rock," and recommended Margad to the King. David sent men to the Orkneys with presents and a message requesting the Earl to restore Sweyn to favour. So Sweyn went north and his estates were restored to him, but Margad remained with King David.

After Sweyn and Margad escaped from Lambaborg the rest surrendered at discretion, and the Earl gave them quarter. Thorbiorn Klerk was despatched south to the Moray Firth in a war-galley of forty men to search for Sweyn, but did not hear of him. So he bethought him of a kindred quest, and went to take revenge on Earl Valthiof who had slain his father. He surprised him banqueting and set fire to the place, and Earl Valthiof, being denied quarter, perished in the flames with thirty of his retainers.

At this time a young man lived in Weir called Kolbein *Hruga*, a very overbearing man, where he built a fine stone castle, which was a strong defence. Kolbein's wife was Herbiorg, the sister of Hakon *Bairn*; but their mother was Sigrid, a daughter of Herborg, Paul's daughter. Their children were Kolbein *Karl*, Bjarni *Skald*, Sumarlid, Aslac, and Frida. They were all well mannered.

The sons of Harald Gille now ruled over Norway. Eystein was the eldest, but Ingi was a legitimate son and most honoured by the Barons, of whom Ogmund and Erling, the son of Kyrpinga *Orm*, assisted him in the government. These counsellors advised King Inge to cultivate the friendship of Earl Rognvald and send him an honourable invitation to the Norwegian court, saying truly he had been so great a friend of King Harald, and, in case of conflict with King Eystein, would prove an invaluable ally. The Earl duly received the invitation and decided to revisit his native land. Earl Harald, who was then fourteen or fifteen years of age, wanted to go with him, so they started together, and found King Inge in Bergen, and Rognvald was well received. Eindridi, *the Young*, then arrived from Constantinople, where he had long been in service in the Varangian Guard. His tales of wonder about those parts suggested a pilgrimage to Palestine, and many seemed eager for the journey. When Rognvald was leaving in the autumn King Inge presented him with two long-ships, small, but very beautiful, and

E

specially built for rowing. Earl Rögnvald gave Harald one of them, called the Fifa; the other was called Hjalp. In these ships the Earls went to sea, holding westward, and Rögnvald received large presents from his friends. On the home voyage a storm arose, and they had to beach the ships near Gulberwick, in Hjaltland. Rögnvald stayed some time in Hjaltland, entertained by Einar in Gulberwick, and in the autumn went to the Orkneys and resided in his dominions. That autumn two Icelanders came to him. One was named Armod, a poet; the other was Oddi, *the Little*, son of Glum, who also made verses well. Both entered his service. At Yule the Earl entertained Bishop William and many nobles, and then it was that he announced his intention of visiting Jerusalem. As the Bishop was a good Parisian scholar, he was requested to accompany the Pilgrims as interpreter. The following went with him—Magnus, son of Havard Gunnarsson; Sweyn Hroaldsson; and others of lesser note; Thorgeir Skotakoll; Oddi the Little; Thorbjorn the Black; Armod the Skald; Thorkel the Crosseyed; Grimkell of Glettuness and Bjarni, son of Thorstein of Flydruness. Two winters were spent in preparation, and then Rögnvald passed to Norway to see how the Barons had progressed.

At Bergen he found Erling, his brother-in-law John, and Aslac, Guttorm arriving later on, as also Eindridi, who put in an appearance in a very ornamentally finished vessel, although it had been understood that none should outvie the Earl. The Earl and his ships had a favourable passage to the Orkneys, but the pride of Eindridi received a curb, as his larger ship became a total loss on the Hjaltlands. He wintered in the Northern Archipelago, and sent men to Norway to rebuild a ship for the Eastern voyage. While waiting for Eindridi disturbances frequently took place. In one of these Sweyn Asleifsson mortally wounded Arni *Stickleg*, a follower of Eindridi, and then escaped to Caithness, leaving the matter to be adjusted by the Earl.

At last everything was ready and Rögnvald called a Thing meeting, which was attended by all the Orcadian nobles. He then transferred the government to his kinsman Harald, who was at that time nearly twenty years of age, and asked them to be faithful during his absence. Immediately on the arrival of Eindridi's ship, which was rather late in the summer, Earl Rögnvald set sail with a squadron of fifteen vessels. The following were commanders:—Earl Rögnvald, Erling *Skakki*, Bishop William, Aslac Erlendsson, Guttorm, Magnus Havardsson, Sweyn Hroaldsson, John Petrsson, Eindridi, and six others of Eindridi's men who are not named.

They sailed first to Scotland, then they passed England and Gaul, landing at Narbonne, where the Count Germanus had recently died, leaving a young and beautiful heiress, Ermingerd, who was under ward of her noblest kinsmen. By the Princess Ermingerd they were royally banqueted, and verses were composed in her honour by Rögnvald, Armod and Oddi. They reached Galicia (Spain) five nights before Yule, and were asked to assist the inhabitants of a certain town against the lord of the castle, one Gudifrey, a foreigner, who greatly oppressed them. They stormed and took the castle, but, through the connivance of Eindridi, Gudifrey managed to escape. Proceeding, they plundered in Moorish Spain, and entered the Straits of Gibraltar. When they had cleared the Sound, Eindridi parted company and with six ships sailed for Marseilles, which action was thought to be a further proof of his allowing Gudifrey to escape. Continuing the voyage, they sailed along the Barbary coast and presently found themselves near Sardinia, where they fell in with a dromund, or Saracen corsair, which they attacked and captured. They anchored in Crete during a strong gale and, leaving it, had a fair wind on to Palestine, arriving at Acre early one Friday morning They went on shore with great pomp and splendour, such as had seldom been seen there. At Acre illness broke out among the crews, and many succumbed to it, amongst others Thorbiorn *the Black*. The Earl and his men, departing from Acre, visited all the holiest places in Palestine, and all bathed in the Jordan They left Palestine in the summer, *en route* through Syria for Constantinople John Petrsson was assassinated in a Syrian city Burying him honourably, they went north to Ægos, and there waited some nights for a fair wind with which to enter Constantinople in the same magnificent manner as King Sigurd the Jorsala-farer had done This they effected, and were well received by the Emperor, Manuel I , and his Varangians. They spent most of the winter at Manuel's court, where Eindridi also arrived, and was highly honoured. Manuel wanted them to enter his service, but before the winter was over the Orcadian pilgrims commenced their homeward trip They first reached Durazzo, and then sailed westwards to Apulia, where the Earl, Bishop William, Erling, and others left their ships and took horse for Rome, whence they made for Denmark, and finally Norway, where all were glad to see them.

While Erling was away in Palestine his brother Ogmund died. Erling was married to Kristin, daughter of King Sigurd Jorsala-farer, and after the death of King Inge their son Magnus was made King, Erling being Regent. Valdemar, King of the Danes, gave him the title of Earl Eindridi came from the South some winters after Earl Rognvald, and attached himself to King Eystein, because he would have nothing to do with Erling On Eystein's death, with Sigurd of Reyr, Eindridi nominated Hakon Haraldsson as king, and slew Gregorius Dagsson and King Inge, but meeting with Erling received a decisive defeat, Hakon being mortally wounded and Eindridi put to flight. Later on he was killed in Viken.

Earl Rognvald spent the summer in Hordaland, in Norway, and heard many tidings from the Isles, where there were great disturbances, most of the nobles having divided themselves into two factions, at the head of one being Earl Harald, and of the other Earl Erlend and Sweyn Asleifsson Many things had happened while Rognvald was in the East. The very summer Rognvald had set out on his journey King Eystein, of Norway, landed in the Isles at Rinansey, and, crossing the Petland Firth in a warship of twenty benches with eighty men, surprised Earl Harald at Thurso The Earl was admitted to ransom on payment of a fine of three marks of gold, and upon surrendering his dominions to be held in future from King Eystein The latter then went ravaging in Scotland and England, as some revenge for King Harald Hardrade When Eystein returned to Norway Harald remained in his Orcadian dominions, and most of the Islesmen were satisfied with his rule. At this time his father, Earl Maddad of Athol, was dead, and his mother, Margaret, had gone to reside in Orkney. She was a handsome woman, but very imperious Now also David, King of Scotland, died, and was succeeded by his grandson, Malcolm the Maiden, who was but a child

Erlend, the heir of Harald the Orator, was now grown up, and spent most of his time in Thorsa After the death of Earl Ottar he was sometimes in the Hebudes on war expeditions He was a very promising man, and accomplished in most things, liberal in money, gentle, open to advice, and greatly loved by his men. He had a large following. He was fostered by a hardy South Isle noble named Anakol, who was his right-hand man, and to whose counsels he chiefly listened. While Rögnvald was away in Palestine Erlend went to the Scottish Court and obtained from King Malcolm the Maiden the title of earl, and that part of Caithness which his father, Earl Harald, had, to be held jointly with his cousin, Earl Harald *the Wicked*. Returning to Caithness, Erlend collected forces and passed to the Orkneys, to obtain possession of the half which he considered his patrimonial inheritance. Harald declined to surrender any part of the Isles; but a year's truce was agreed to, and Erlend was to go to Norway and ask the King for the half which belonged to Rögnvald, and which Harald would then surrender. So Erlend went east to Norway, but Anakol stayed behind with some of his party.

Gunni Olafsson, brother of Sweyn Asleifsson, had children by Margaret, the Dowager Countess of Athol, and Earl Harald banished him from the Isles, so enmity arose between Sweyn and Harald. Sweyn sent Gunni south to Lewis to stay with his friend Liotolf, whose son Fugl was then with Earl Harald. While Erlend was in Norway, Harald spent the winter in Caithness, residing at Wick. Sweyn was then at Freswick, taking care of the estate which his stepsons had there, for his former wife was Ragnhild, daughter of Ogmund, though they lived together but a short time. Their son was Olaf. After that he married Ingirid, daughter of Thorkell; their son was Andreas. On Wednesday, in Passion Week, Sweyn, while going to Lambaborg, saw a transport vessel crossing the Firth, and concluding the barge contained Harald's revenues from Hjaltland, attacked it and seized the cargo. When Harald heard this he said, "Sweyn and I shall have our turns."

During Easter Harald remained in guest quarters. After Easter-week Sweyn passed to the Orkneys in a barge, and at Scapa seized a ship belonging to Fugl, who was on his way from Lewis to visit Earl Harald. Sweyn also took twelve ounces of gold from the house of Sigurd *Klaufi*, a house-carl of the Earl's, he, Sigurd, being absent in Kirkwall. Returning to Caithness, Sweyn passed on to Aberdeen, where he spent a month at the court of King Malcolm, by whom he was well entertained. King Malcolm insisted upon his enjoying all those emoluments of Caithness which he had before becoming Earl Harald's enemy. Sweyn and Malcolm parted excellent friends, and the former sailed north to Orkney. By appointment, arranged by Gauti of Skeggbjornstead, he met Anakol at Sanday, and they adjusted matters relating to Sweyn's seizure of Fugl's ship, Fugl being of kin to Anakol, and it was agreed that the latter should make peace between Sweyn and Erlend on his return from the East, for they were bitter enemies on account of the incineration of Frakach. Sweyn and Anakol then went to Stronsay, and lay off Huipness for some nights.

At this time Thorfinn Brusisson lived at Stronsa; his wife was Ingigerd, who had been deserted by Thorbiorn Klerk. While lying off Huipness, Earl Erlend arrived from Norway, and through the representation of Anakol and Thorfinn reluctantly made peace with Sweyn. Erlend then told of the message from King Eystein, that he should have that part of the Orkneys formerly held by his father, Earl Harald the Orator. Sweyn advised Erlend to go at once to Earl Harald before he heard this from others, and ask him to surrender the dominions. The advice was acted upon. They found Harald in his ship off Corness, but Harald, suspecting hostile intentions, left his ship and entered the castle, to which Erlend and Sweyn laid siege. Eventually peace was secured upon Harald consenting to let Erlend have his part of the Isles, and not to redemand it from him, and this Harald confirmed by oath in the presence of the leading Orcadians. Harald then went over to Caithness, and Erlend and Sweyn convened a Thing meeting of the Islesmen at Kirkwall, when Erlend was accepted as sole ruler, but conditionally upon his allowing Earl Rognvald to have his half whensoever he returned. Sweyn spent the following Yule at his estate in Gairsay.

During this Yule, Harald made a voyage to the Orkneys with four ships and one hundred men. He lay two nights under Grimsa. They landed in the Orcadian mainland, and on the thirteenth day of Yule-tide walked to Firth, and spent the Yule-holiday at Orcahaug (Maeshowe), where two of their men were seized with madness, thus retarding their journey. It was near day when they reached Firth. There they learned that Erlend was aboard his ship, but had been ashore during the day. At Firth Harald killed one Ketil and another, and took prisoner Arnfinn, brother to Anakol, Liotolf, and two others. Harald and Thorbiorn Klerk then returned to Thurso, while the brothers Benedict and Eric went to Freswick Castle with Arnfinn in custody. They now sent word that Arnfinn would not be admitted to ransom until Erlend restored their ship, the one seized off Corness. The Earl was willing to make the exchange, but Anakol dissuaded him from it, saying that Arnfinn should be recovered without such a sacrifice. So, on the Wednesday before Lent, Anakol and Thorstein Ragnasson crossed the Firth by night and stalked Eric, whom they took prisoner to the islands, and Earl Harald liberated Arnfinn and his comrades in exchange for Eric.

In the spring Earl Harald made preparations to go from Caithness north to Hjaltland, his intention being to take the life of Erlend the Young (not Earl Erlend, who would hardly have fallen in love with his aunt), who had wooed his mother, the Countess Dowager of Athol, in defiance of his disapproval. Erlend had carried her off from the Orkneys, and taken up his residence in the Tower of Mousa, in the island of that name. Harald besieged the tower, but it was so difficult to take by assault, that he listened to favourable overtures from Erlend, resulting in the marriage of Erlend and Margaret, and an alliance between him and the Earl, and the summer following they went off east to Norway in company.

Earl Erlend, on the other hand, next went with Sweyn and Anakol on a plundering cruise. They steered first for the Moray Firth, and then made inroads on the east of Scotland, and cruised as far south as North Berwick, in the Firth of Forth, where they captured a large and fine vessel belonging to a Berwick merchant, named Knut the Wealthy. On board was a valuable cargo and Knut's wife. When Knut heard of the seizure he sent fourteen ships in pursuit. The Orcadian squadron lay under the Fern Islands, and, as a gale was blowing, erected awnings, except on Sweyn's boat, as that worthy was too careful to be surprised, notwithstanding that he was rallied about it by one of his company named Einar *Skeif*. Sweyn was first to sight the enemy, and the Orcadians made for the North. They put in under the Isle of May, and Sweyn sent men to Edinburgh to tell the King of Scots of his plunder, but before they came to the town they met twelve men on horseback, who had saddle-bags filled with silver, and when they met they inquired after Sweyn. Sweyn's men told where he was, and asked what was wanted with him. The Scots said they had been told that Sweyn was taken prisoner, and the King of Scots had sent them to ransom him. They thus told their errand. The King did not make much of Knut's loss, but sent a costly shield to Sweyn, and other presents besides. Earl Erlend and Sweyn arrived in the Orkneys rather late in the autumn This summer Earl Harald went east to Norway At the same time Earl Rognvald and Erling Skakki came to Norway from Constantinople, and Rognvald arrived in the Orkneys shortly before Yule, and immediately messengers passed between him and Erlend relative to a settlement of the islands They had an interview at Kirkwall, when they agreed that each should have half of the islands, and they concluded a defensive alliance against Earl Harald should he lay claim to any of them. Rognvald was without ships till his should arrive from the east in the summer. The winter passed in quietness, but in the spring the Earls prepared for a visit from Harald, and Rognvald crossed over to Thurso, while Erlend and Sweyn passed to Hjaltland, hoping to intercept Harald on his return. In the summer Harald left Norway with seven ships, three of which were storm-driven to Hjaltland, and promptly seized by Erlend and Sweyn, but Harald reached the Orkneys with the rest and landed there. He then heard of the alliance between Rognvald and Erlend excluding him from any territory in the islands, and he resolved to cross at once to Caithness and see Rognvald before Erlend could arrive from Hjaltland Erlend and Sweyn had started after Harald, but met with adverse weather off Sumburgh Roost, and Sweyn was driven back to Fair Isle with twelve ships, and all thought the Earl had perished From Fair Isle he sailed to Sanday, where, to his great joy, he found Erlend with three ships. They then went to the Orcadian mainland to enquire about Earl Harald's movements.

When Harald reached Thurso, Rognvald was in Sutherland celebrating the wedding of his heiress Ingirid with Eric Stagbrellir Hearing of Harald's arrival, he rode from Berriedale to Thurso with a large retinue, and through the mediation of Eric Stagbrellir and others an alliance was made at a conference in Thurso Castle, which was nearly upset by the arrival of Thorbiorn Klerk, who attacked Rognvald's men and slew thirteen before the conflict could be stopped by Harald. The two Earls now set out for the Isles to give battle to Erlend They anchored their thirteen ships in Widewall, in S Ronaldsa, and landed

Erlend was lying with his ships at Burswick, in the same island On being made aware of the reconciliation of Rognvald and Harald, and their near presence, Erlend and Sweyn held a consultation, and decided to cross to Caithness at once and winter in the Hebudes So, on Michaelmas Eve, they sailed for Caithness, where they held a great strand-hewing, and early in the winter left Thurso in six long-ships, all well manned and steering west ostensibly bound for the Hebudes When off Ru Stoer, in Assynt, they put about ship and made for the Isles, having a rattling breeze behind them They soon reached Walls, where they were told that the Earls were lying off Knarston, at Scapa, with thirteen ships, and that Erlend the Young, Eric Stagbrellir, and many other men of note were with them Thorbiorn Klerk had gone to Papley on a visit to his brother-in-law, Hakon *Karl* Sweyn resolved to attack them at once, so, four nights before St Simon's mass, an attack was made on Earl Harald and his men, who were completely surprised and routed, many being slain, amongst others a noble, Bjarni, brother of Erlend *Ungi*, and a hundred with him Few of Erlend's men were killed Erlend took fourteen ships and many valuables. Rognvald was on his way to Orphir that evening, but had stopped at Knarston, at the house of an Icelander named Botolf Begla, an excellent skald Erlend's men heard that Rognvald had gone towards Knarston, and enquiring of Botolf, were misled by him, and Rognvald promptly hurried off to Orphir, where he found Harald in hiding, and both crossed at once to Caithness.

Sweyn took Earl Rognvald's ship and treasures as his share of the booty, and these he restored to that Earl. He (Sweyn) advised Erlend to station his ships at Walls, where he could command the Firth, but Erlend yielded to the persuasion of his men and went north to Damsay, St. Adamnan's Isle, carousing in the daytime in a large castle there, and at night sleeping on board the ships, which were fastened together. Thus time passed on till the Yule feast. Five nights before Christmas Sweyn went east to Sandwick, in Deerness, to make peace between his kinswoman Sigrid and her neighbour Bjorn, and spent one night at her place. A friendly neighbour of Sigrid's named Gisl wanted Sweyn to stay with him. When they came to Gisl they heard Erlend was not stopping on board ship at night, so Sweyn sent Margad Grimsson to warn Erlend to heed his advice, adding, "I suspect I shall not have long to provide for this Earl." Margad and the others conveyed Sweyn's message to Erlend, who slept on board that night, but was surprised by the Earls, none perceiving them until they were climbing on board. Orm and Ufi were on the fore part of Erlend's ship. Ufi tried to rouse the Earl, but he was not sober enough, so Ufi jumped overboard with him into a boat, and Orm plunged from the other side and escaped on shore. Margad and his men heard the battle-cry and rowed away round the headland. It was clear moonlight. They saw the Earls go away, and they felt fate had decided between them. Two nights before Yule a spear was seen standing in a heap of seawood, and that spear was found to be fast in Earl Erlend's body.

With him the male line of the Norse Earls of Orkney ended. All Erlend's men took refuge in St. Magnus' Cathedral, and the Earls admitted them to peace. John Vœng, son of a sister of John Wing, previously referred to, was amongst the number. He had been with Hakon Karl, and had a child by his sister. Then he ran away, and was with Anakol on piratical expeditions, but now he was with Erlend, though not in the battle. The Earls would not pardon him till he married Hakon's sister. He afterwards became steward to Earl Harald.

After Erlend's death Sweyn went to Rendale, where he met Margad, who told him of what had happened in Damsey. They then went to Rousay and distributed themselves amongst the farm steadings. In the evening, at a homestead, Sweyn overheard some talk about the death of Erlend amongst Thorfinn, his son Ogmund, and his brother-in-law Erlend. Erlend was boasting of having given the Earl his death blow, and all were declaring they had done right well. Sweyn rushed in and killed Erlend, and Thorfinn was taken prisoner, and Ogmund wounded. Sweyn then went to Tyngvale to his father's brother Helgi, and spent the first few days in hiding. Rognvald was staying in Damsey, and Harald at Kirkwall during Yule-tide. Rognvald sent word to Helgi to tell Sweyn he wanted him to spend the Yule with him and make peace between him and Earl Harald. Sweyn went accordingly.

After Christmas the Earls considered Sweyn's case, and it was adjudged that he should pay a mark of gold to each of the Earls and retain one-half of his estates and a good long-ship. When Sweyn heard of the award he remarked, "Our agreement will only be good in case I am not oppressed." Rognvald, on his part, waived the fine, but Harald presently went to Gairsay and used Sweyn's corn and other property wastefully. Sweyn complained of this to Rognvald, but he only suggested peaceful overtures to Harald. Sweyn, however, was determined to have satisfaction, and with ten men took boat for Gairsay and wished to fire the hall and homestead with the Earl in it. He was dissuaded from doing so by the representations of Sweyn Blakarisson, who said the Earl might not be in the homestead, and, if he were, would not permit Sweyn's wife and daughter to leave it. Sweyn surrounded it and asked his wife, Ingirid, where the Earl was, but as Ingirid was of kin to Earl Harald she would not reveal anything. He had gone out to a certain island (Hoy?) to hunt hares. Sweyn made for the Eller Holm and soon had Harald after him in pursuit. Sweyn took refuge in a cave, the entrance to which was hidden by the rising tide, and baffled his pursuers, who circumnavigated the isle, but without finding him. Leaving his own boat in the cave, he took one from the monks and went to Sanday, where, on landing, they pushed off the small boat, which drifted about till it was wrecked. They came to a homestead at Voluness where lived Bard, kinsman to Sweyn. Bard dared not openly house them, but gave them shelter in a secret apartment. The same evening John *Wing*, Earl Harald's steward, arrived with six men, and Bard welcomed them. The conversation turned on Sweyn and Erlend, John speaking adversely of both. At this, Sweyn could not restrain himself, and emerged from his retreat. John heard him coming, and rushed out from the house and ran till he came to another farm. His feet were very much frost-bitten, and some of his toes fell off.

Through the intercession of Bard, Sweyn gave peace to John's companions. In the morning Bard gave him a boat, and he and his men went south to Burswick, where they stayed in a cave. One morning Sweyn and his men saw a large long-ship coming from Hrolfsey to Ronaldsa, and Sweyn recognised it immediately as Earl Rognvald's, and the one he himself used to command. When they rowed past the Earl's ship, which stuck fast on the beach, Sweyn was standing up with a spear in his hand. When Earl Rognvald saw it he held a shield before him; but Sweyn did not cast the spear, and the Earl, seeing they would get away, ordered a truce-shield to be held aloft. Thereon, Sweyn landed, and came to an understanding with the Earl. While they were talking, Earl Harald's ship was seen steering from Caithness to Walls, so Rognvald advised Sweyn to cross at once to Caithness. This was during Lent. The two left at the same time, the Earl for the Orcadian mainland, and Sweyn for Stroma. Earl Harald recognised Sweyn's boat, and turned into the Firth in pursuit, but on reaching Stroma was too suspicious to land. However, the two were made friends by the mediation of Amundi Huefisson, paternal uncle to Sweyn's stepchildren, and a gale arising, both had to remain there during the night, many sleeping in the same house, and Amundi (doubtless to their mutual satisfaction) put Earl Harald and Sweyn in the same bed. After this Sweyn went to Caithness and Harald to the Orkneys. Then Sweyn went on south to the Dales, spending the Easter with his friend Somerled; but Harald went north to Hjaltland, and was there a long time during the spring. After Easter Sweyn, coming north, seized Bunu-Petr and Blan, brothers of John *Wing*, and confiscated their goods. A gallows was erected, but Sweyn changed his mind, saying they would disgrace John more alive than dead, so he turned them out on the hills, and they were very much frost-bitten before reaching a habitation. Thence Sweyn passed to Lewis, in the Hebudes, where he stayed some time. When John *Wing* heard of his brothers' capture, in retaliation, he seized Olaf Sweynsson, foster-son to Kolbein Hruga, and brought him to Earl Rognvald at Rapness, in Westray. Rognvald ordered his immediate release, telling John it was very foolish of him to seek to incur the enmity of Sweyn or Kolbein, whatever the fate of his brothers.

When Easter had passed, Sweyn started for the Hebudes with a company of sixty men. He first went to Rousay, where he seized Hakon *Karl*, who had assisted Earl Harald when Earl Erlend was slain. Hakon was admitted to ransom for three marks of gold. There Sweyn found his ship, with two of the planks sawn asunder. This had been done by Earl Rognvald's order as Sweyn refused to buy it or accept it as a gift from the Earls. From Rousay Sweyn went to the mainland, and met Rognvald at Birsa, where Sweyn spent the spring with him. Rognvald said he had cut the planks to prevent Sweyn from rowing rashly among the Islands on his return from the Hebudes. Earl Harald returned from Hjaltland at Whitsuntide, and Rognvald arranged a peace-meeting in St Magnus' Church on the Friday during holy week. Rognvald carried a broad-axe to the meeting, and Sweyn went with him. At it the compact of the winter was confirmed. Everything was restored to Sweyn but his ship, which Rognvald gave Harald. Rognvald and Sweyn were standing at the church door while the sail, which had been lying in St Magnus' Church, was being carried out, and Sweyn looked rather gloomy. The following Saturday, after noon-tide service, Earl Harald's men came to Sweyn and said the Earl wished to speak with him. Sweyn consulted Rognvald, who seemed dubious as to the advisability of going. Sweyn went, nevertheless, with five men, and found Harald sitting on a cross-bench with Thorbiorn Klerk beside him, and a few other retainers near by. Thorbiorn presently left the room, to the discomfiture of Sweyn, but soon returned, and presented him with a scarlet tunic and a coat, saying he could hardly call it a gift as it had been taken from Sweyn in the winter. The gifts were accepted. Earl Harald then restored to him his long-ship, and the forfeited half of his property and estates, asking him to stay with him, and their friendship should never be dissolved. Sweyn accepted all this gladly, and forthwith reported matters to Earl Rognvald, who was well pleased at the issue of the interview.

Soon after this Sweyn, Thorbiorn, and Eric sailed on a plundering expedition, first visiting the Hebudes, and then all along the west to the Scilly Isles, where they gained a great victory in St Mary's on Columba's Mass (9th June) and returned to the Orkneys with much booty. Thorbiorn now became counsellor to Earl Harald, and Sweyn went to his Gairsay estate, where he usually wintered, but every summer he went marauding. Thorkell, a follower of Thorbiorn, and Thorarinn *Killinef*, a retainer of Earl Rognvald, quarrelled over their drink at Kirkwall. Thorkell wounded Thorarinn, and, being pursued by Thorarinn's companions, fled to Thorbiorn, who defended them. When Thorarinn recovered, he slew Thorkell as he was going to church, and then ran into church with Thorbiorn close behind. Thorbiorn was going to break the church door open, but Rognvald would not permit the sacrilege, and Thorbiorn crossed to Caithness, where he was frequently guilty of violence to women and man-slaying. He presently returned secretly to the Orkneys, and, coming suddenly on Thorarinn in an inn, wounded him mortally, and fled under cover of darkness. For this the Earl made him an outlaw in every part of his dominions. Thorbiorn, recrossing to Caithness, stayed in hiding with his brother-in-law, Hosvir *the Strong*, who had married Ragnhild, sister to Thorbiorn, and their son was Stephen *the Counsellor*, a follower of Thorbiorn. From there Thorbiorn went to Malcolm, King of Scots, where he remained for a while in high favour with the king. At the Scottish court was a noble called Gillaodran, of great family, but a very violent man. For his numerous violent acts he had incurred the royal displeasure, and fled to the Orkneys, where the Earls received him and appointed him steward of Caithness. But he soon became embroiled in a dispute about the stewardship with a noble named Helgi, a friend of Earl Rögnvald's, whom he attacked and killed, and then went west to the Hebudes, where he was received by Somerled of Argyle, who had married Ragnhild, the daughter of Olaf *Bitling*, King of the Hebudes. Their sons were King Dugald, Reginald, and Angus, and they were called the Dalverja family. Rögnvald sent for Sweyn, and asked him when on his next cruise to keep an eye on Gillaodran, if a chance occurred.

Sweyn started out with five long-ships and brought Somerled to an engagement with his seven ships. The battle was very fierce and doubtful for a long time, but the victory was to Sweyn. Some accounts state Somerled was slain, but from other sources we learn he was killed at Renfrew on 1st January, 1164, having landed there with a fleet of one hundred and sixty galleys to attempt the conquest of Scotland. Later on Sweyn overtook Gillaodran in the Dark Firth (Loch Glean Dubh?) and slew him and fifty of his men. Returning in the autumn, Earl Rögnvald was much pleased with Sweyn's success.

Every summer the Earls were wont to go over to Caithness and up into the forests to hunt the red deer or the reindeer. Thorbiorn Klerk was sometimes at the Scottish court and sometimes in Caithness hiding with his friends. The three whom he most trusted were his brother-in-law Hosvir; Lifolf, who lived in Thorsdal; and Hallvard, son of Dufa, who dwelt at Force, in Caldale, which goes off from Thorsdal. When Rögnvald had been Earl twenty-two winters from the time of "the passing of Paul," the Earls went over to Caithness during the latter end of summer as usual, and on coming to Thurso heard a rumour to the effect that Thorbiorn was in hiding, and intended to attack them if an opportunity arose. In the day-time Earl Rögnvald always rode ahead of his men, and with him were Asolf and his kinsman Jomar. Reaching Calder, they came to a farm when Hallvard the farmer was piling up a stack of corn. Thorbiorn and his men were in the homestead, and Hallvard spoke loudly that they might be warned. Thorbiorn ran out and aimed at the Earl, but Asolf warded off the blow with his hand, which was cut off. The Earl then prepared to dismount, but his foot held fast in the stirrup, and Stephen arriving, thrust him with a spear, while Thorbiorn wounded him again. Jomar requited Thorbiorn with a thrust in the thigh, the spear entering his bowels, and then Thorbiorn and his men made for an adjacent morass. Earl Harald now arrived, and meeting Thorbiorn recognised him. Some of Harald's men wanted to pursue Thorbiorn, but Harald said, as he was closely related to him, he preferred to wait for Earl Rögnvald's opinion. It was some little while before Harald knew what had happened to Earl Rögnvald. His followers then gave chase to Thorbiorn, who appealed to his kinsman for protection, and Harald would have liked to aid him, but Magnus Havard-Gunnisson, a noble and a kinsman of the Earl, and the noblest born of Harald's followers, said if quarter was given Thorbiorn, Harald would be covered with everlasting shame and dishonour, as all would consider he had been guilty of complicity. For his own part he, Magnus, would never give him quarter, but would follow him to the death. His brother Thorstein, Hakon, and Sweyn Hroaldsson spoke to the same effect, and gave chase. Thorbiorn, seeing what had been decided, advised his followers to save themselves by flight, while he asked mercy of Earl Harald, but the Earl said, "Save yourself, Thorbiorn; I have not the heart to kill you; nor will I fight for you against my men." Thorbiorn and his men then sought refuge in a deserted shieling called Asgrim's ærgin, which was fired by Magnus and his party, who slew them, all nine, after a valorous

HARALD II., 28TH EARL.

defence. Earl Harald led his men down the valley of Calder, but those with Magnus went to Fors, wrapped up Earl Rögnvald's body, and brought it down to Thorsa. The death of the Earl occurred five nights after the summer's Marysmas. (The feast of the Assumption of St. Mary, or the 15th August, and the Iceland Annals give 1158 as the year.) Earl Harald brought the body with a splendid following to the Orkneys, and it was buried in St. Magnus' Kirk, and there it rested until God manifested Rögnvald's merits by many and great miracles. Then Bishop Bjarni had his holy remains exhumed, with the permission of the Pope, and he was canonised thirty-four years after his death. Where the blood of the Earl fell on the stones when he died, it may be seen to this day as fresh as if it had just come from the wounds. His death was much lamented, because he was very popular in the Islands and in many other parts. He had been helpful to many, was liberal with his money, gentle, and a true friend, highly accomplished, and a good skald. He left one only child, a daughter, Ingigerd, married to Eric Stagbrellir. Their children were Harald *the Younger*, Magnus *Mangi*, Rögnvald, Ingibiorg, Elin, and Ragnhild.

Earl Harald now assumed possession of all the Islands and became their sole ruler. He was a mighty chief and a man of large stature and great strength. His wife was Afrecca, daughter of the Earl of Fife, and their children were Henry, Hakon, Helena and Margaret. When Hakon was only a few years old Sweyn Asleifsson offered to foster him, so, as soon as he was old enough, he accompanied Sweyn in all his expeditions.

NORSE WAR-GALLEY OF THE VIKING AGE.

Sweyn's occupation was divided according to the seasons. In the winter he resided at home in Gairsay, where he kept eighty men at his own expense, and had such a large wassail-hall that none in the Isles could equal it. In the spring, after he had sowed seed, he went marauding in the Hebudes and Ireland, returning after midsummer. This he called spring-viking. Then he stayed home till the fields were reaped and the corn brought in, when he again sallied forth, and did not return till one month of winter had passed. This was his autumn-viking.

One spring Sweyn sallied forth, taking Hakon of Orkney with him, with a fleet of five large rowing ships to plunder in the Hebudes; but Sweyn was too well known in those parts, and the Hebudeans hid all their moveable property, so he sailed on to the Isle of Man, but got very little booty. He then made for Ireland, and on approaching Dublin fell in with two English merchantmen, laden with English cloth and other merchandise, and bound for Dublin. Sweyn annexed everything of any value and proceeded to the Hebudes, where the cargo was shared. They sailed thence with great pomp. When lying in harbour they covered their ships with the English cloth for display, and on steering home they sewed the cloth on the sails, which gave the sails the appearance of being made entirely of fine stuffs. This was named "the scarlet cruise." Sweyn had also taken a quantity of wine and English mead, and on returning to Gairsay entertained Earl Harald to a splendid feast. Harald cautioned Sweyn that it was well to drive home with a full wain; but Sweyn was resolved to go once more on an autumn-viking before retiring from the then honourable profession of piracy, so he and Hakon of Orkney started with seven long-ships, making the Hebudes, as usual, their first port of call. There they found very little to take, having no doubt already carried away everything worth gathering from that group, so they plundered promiscuously in Ireland, and worked their way south to Dublin, which they surprised and took possession of. The citizens had agreed to surrender the town; but Sweyn was known to be the most exacting man in the west, and they determined to play him false. So, in the morning, when Sweyn advanced to take possession and quarter his men on the town, he was ambushed, and fell with several of his followers in one of the pitfalls dug to ensnare the invaders. Sweyn was the last to fall and, before doing so, he spake these words: "Know all men, whether I die to-day or not, that I am the holy Earl Rögnvald's henchman, and my confidence is where he is with God." His surviving followers made for their ships and put to sea, and nothing is said of their voyage until they arrived in the Orkneys. It has been said that Sweyn was the greatest man in the Western lands, either in old times or at the present day, of those who had not a higher title than he. After his death his sons Olaf and Andrew divided their patrimony, and the next summer they erected a party-wall to the large wassail-hall which he had in Gairsay. Andrew married Frida, the daughter of Kolbein Hruga, and sister to Bishop Bjarni.

After he had divorced himself from Afrecca of Fife, Harald espoused Gormlath (Hvarflod), the daughter of Earl Malcolm of Moray, by whom he had Thorfinn, David, and John, Gunnhild, Herborga and Langlif. When Bishop William the Second died, Biorn, the son of Kolbein Hruga, succeeded him. He was of great consequence, and a dear friend of Earl Harald. Bishop Biorn had a large party of kinsmen in the Isles. The sons of Eric Stagbrellir were Harald the Younger, Magnus *Magni*, and Rögnvald. The brothers went east to Norway to see King Magnus (son of Erling Skakki), and he gave young Harald the title of Earl and that one-half of the Islands which had belonged to the holy Earl Rögnvald, his mother's father.

HARALD III., 29TH EARL

Earl Harald *the Younger* then went west, and with him was Sigurd *Murt*, the son of Ivar *Galli*, who fell at Acre when with Earl Rognvald. Ivar's mother was a daughter of Havard Gunnisson. Sigurd *Murt* was young, handsome, and a great dandy. Magnus *Mangi* remained with the King, and fell with him in Sogn.

It has been seen that Earl Harald the Wicked had by his second marriage allied himself with Hvarflod, daughter of Malcolm MacHeth, the soi-disant Earl of Moray, ex-Bishop Wimund, and pretender to the Scottish throne, and consequently there could be no pacific relations between him and King William the Lion. The events of this period are somewhat confusedly told in the chronicles, but it seems probable that Harald was one of the six earls who rebelled against King Malcolm in 1160, in order to place William of Egremont, grandson of Duncan, on the throne, and that he also supported Donaldbane, the son of William, who aspired to the throne, and from 1180 maintained himself in Moray and Ross, till he was slain at the battle of Macgarvey (1187). Thereafter Harald, presumably in right of his wife, laid claim to that region, for we are informed by Roger de Hoveden, chaplain to Henry II., a contemporary chronicler —
"In 1196, William King of Scots, having gathered a great army, entered Moray to drive out Harald MacMadit, who had occupied that district. But before the king could enter Caithness, Harald fled to his ships, not wishing to risk a battle with the king. Then the King of Scots sent his army to Thurso, the town of the aforesaid Harald, and destroyed his castle there. But Harald, seeing that the king would completely devastate the country, came to the king's feet and placed himself at his mercy, chiefly because of a raging tempest in the sea and the wind being contrary so that he could not go to the Orkneys; and he promised the king that he would bring to him all his enemies when the king should again return to Moray. On that condition the king permitted him to retain a half of Caithness, and the other half he gave to Harald the Younger, grandson of Reginald, a former Earl of Orkney and Caithness. Then the king returned to his own land and Harald to the Orkneys. The king returned in the autumn to Moray, as far as Invernairn, in order to receive the king's enemies from Harald. But, though Harald had brought them as far as the port of Lochloy, near Invernairn, he allowed them to escape, and when the king returned late from hunting, Harald came to him, bringing with him two boys, his grandchildren, to deliver them to the king as hostages. Being asked by the king where were the king's enemies he had promised to deliver up, and where was Thorfinn, his son, whom he had also promised as a hostage, he replied: 'I allowed them to escape, knowing that if I delivered them up to you they would not escape out of your hands. My son I could not bring, for there is no other heir to my lands.' So, because he had not kept the agreement which he had made with the king, he was adjudged to remain in the king's custody until his son should arrive and become a hostage for him. And, because he had permitted the king's enemies to escape, he was also adjudged to have forfeited those lands which he held of the king. The king took Harald with him to Edinburgh Castle, and laid him in chains until his men brought his son Thorfinn from the Orkneys, and on their delivering him up as a hostage to the king, Harald was liberated."

So Harald returned to Orkney, and there remained in peace and quiet until Harald the younger, having received a grant of half of the Orkneys from Magnus Erlingsson, the King of Norway, joined himself to Sigurd *Muri* and many other warriors, and touching at Hjaltland and Caithness, invaded Orkney. Harald the elder, being unwilling to engage with him in battle, left the Orkneys and fled to the Isle of Man. He was followed by the younger Harald, but Harald the elder had left Man before his arrival there, and gone by another way to the Orkneys with his fleet, and there he killed all the adherents of the younger Harald whom he found in the Islands. The latter passed to the Scottish court, and King William the Lion readily embraced his interests, granting him the half of Caithness which had been held by his sainted grandfather. He then hastened on to Caithness, where he had many noble kinsmen, to collect an army. Lifolf *Skalli* commanded his troops. Lifolf had married his sister Ragnhild. Young Harald first preferred a request to the elder Earl Harald, asking the cession of half the Isles, but he refused absolutely to divide his dominions on any condition, and upbraided Lifolf. Both then prepared for war, and the two forces met in Caithness at Wick,—or as some say at Clairdon—where the elder Harald obtained a decisive victory. When ranged in battle array Sigurd and Lifolf each led one wing of the army of the young Harald, and performed prodigies of valour before falling. Lifolf behaved most valiantly of all. The Caithness men say he broke three times through the ranks of the Islesmen before being slain, after having gained great fame. Young Harald's soldiers then fled, and he himself was wounded to the death.

> "Thus fell young Harald, as of old fell his sires,
> And the bright hall of heroes bade hail to his spirit."

He fell near some turf-pits, and that very night a bright light illuminated the place where his blood stained the soil. People said he was truly a saint, and a church was erected on the spot. He was buried in Caithness. Innumerable miracles are by God granted through his merits, which testify that he wished to go to the Orkneys to his kinsmen, Earl Magnus and Earl Rögnvald. The elder Harald subdued all Caithness, and passed in triumph to the Orkneys, but presently went to King William, under safe conduct of Roger and Reginald, the Bishops of St. Andrew's and Rosemarkie, and took to the king a large sum in gold and silver for the redemption of his lands in Caithness. The king said he would restore him Caithness if he would divorce Gormlath, his wife, the daughter of Malcolm MacHeth, and take back his first wife, Afreka, the sister of Duncan, Earl of Fife, and deliver up to him as hostages Laurentius, his priest, and Honaver, the son of Ingemund. But this Harald was unwilling to do. Therefore King William allowed Reginald, royalet of the Hebudes, to purchase from him Caithness, saving the king's annual tribute. Rögnvald's grandmother was the daughter of Earl Hakon the Imperious. Rögnvald was the greatest warrior then in the western lands, and for three years had slept in no other habitation than a warship. He at once collected men from Kintyre and the Hebudes, and being supplied with auxiliaries from Ireland by his brother-in-law, John de Courcy, Lord of Ulster, overran Caithness, but on the approach of winter returned to the Hebudes, leaving the conquered earldom in charge of three deputies—Mani Olafsson, Hrafn the Lawman, and Hlifolf Alli. Harald all this time remained in the Orkneys, but presently sent a partisan across, who slew Hlifolf. Harald followed up the murder by crossing himself. Landing at Scrabster he was met by the Bishop, who endeavoured to mollify him, but Harald had a special grudge against Bishop John, which added to his rage at what he considered the defection of his Caithness subjects. The Bishop had refused to collect from the people of Caithness a tax of one penny annually from each inhabited house, which Earl Harald had some years previously granted to the papal revenues   Accordingly he stormed the "borg" at Scrabster, in which the Bishop and the principal men of the district had taken refuge, and in this evil mood slew almost all who were in it, torturing the recalcitrant Bishop, whom he caused to be blinded and have his tongue removed   As Bishop John recovered both sight and speech by invoking the aid of the holy virgin St. Tredwell, it is presumed the torture was more nominal than real.   Fordun says the use of his tongue and of one eye was in some measure left him   The letter of Pope Innocent, addressed to the Bishop of Orkney, prescribing the penance to be performed by Lomberd, the mutilator of the Bishop, only mentions the cutting out of the tongue.   The two remaining deputies of King Reginald fled to the King of Scots, whose first act was to take revenge on Harald's son Thorfinn   He was blinded and castrated after the barbarous manner of the times, and died miserably in the dungeon of Roxburgh Castle.   Thorfinn appears on record as early as about 1165.   In the Chartulary of Scone there is a document by "Harald, Earl of Orkney, Hetland, and Cataness," granting to the monks of Scone a mark of silver, to be paid annually by himself, his son Turphin, and their heirs   Rognvald's stewards stayed with King William during Advent, and were able to give particular intelligence of everything that happened in Caithness during Earl Harald's stay there   The king was highly enraged at hearing the news, but he said he would pay back double to those who had lost their own.   The first day they stayed with the king twenty-five ells of cloth and an English mark in ready money was given to each of them.   They spent the Yule-tide with the king, and were well treated.

After Yule the king sent word to all the chiefs in his kingdom, and collected a large army throughout the country, and with all these troops he went down to Caithness against Earl Harald.   With this great army he pursued his journey till he came to Eysteindal, where Caithness and Sutherland meet.   The camp of the King of Scots stretched far along the valleys

Earl Harald was in Caithness when he heard the news, and he drew troops together immediately.   It is said he obtained six thousand men, and yet he had no chance to withstand the King of Scots   Then he sent men to him to sue for peace   When this request was brought before King William, he said it was no use asking for peace unless he had every fourth penny that was to be found in all the land of Caithness.   When the Earl received this message he called together the inhabitants and chiefs, and consulted with them   As they, however, had no means of resisting, it was agreed that the Caithnessmen should pay one-fourth of all their property to the King of Scots, except those men who had gone to see the King in winter   Earl Harald went out to the Orkneys, and was to have Caithness, as he held it before King William bestowed the half on Earl Harald the Younger   The Caithness toll of one fourth penny amounted to two thousand marks.   King William then returned to Scotland

Harald had no sooner settled matters with his Scottish suzerain than he found himself similarly situated with his other suzerain, the reigning King of Norway, which kingdom had been for some time in a state of civil war over the succession, contended for by two factions—the one supporting the pretensions of King Sverre, who was ultimately successful, and the other, the claims of Sigurd, son of King Magnus Erlingsson   Many men of noble birth in the Orkneys joined the latter party, and it was very strong.   They were for a while called the Islanders or Goldenlegs.   They met in battle in Flóruvogar, when Sigurd was slain, as also Harald's son-in-law Olaf, and John Hallkelsson. On account of Harald's complicity with the enlisting of the Orcadian legion he was in great disfavour with King Sverre, and was obliged to present himself before that monarch in Bergen. He went from Orkney accompanied by Bishop Bjarni. In presence of a great assembly in Christ's Kirk-garth, the Earl confessed his fault, saying that he was now an old man, as his beard bore witness; that he had bent the knee before many kings, sometimes in closest friendship, but oftener in circumstances of misfortune; that he had not been unfaithful to his allegiance, although some of his people might have done that which was contrary to the king's interests; that he had not been able to rule the Orkneys entirely according to his own will, and that he now came to yield up himself and all his possessions into the king's power. So saying, he advanced, and casting himself to the earth, he laid his head at King Sverre's feet. The king granted him pardon, but took from him the whole of Hjaltland, which was disunited from Orkney until re-granted to Earl Henry St. Clair in 1379. It was also resolved that all the land-tax and fines from Orkney and Hjaltland were to fall to the king in Norway; and the king set his bailiff, by name Arne Löria, with the Earl in Orkney, and Earl Harald durst not act adversely during King Sverre's lifetime, but straightway after his death he caused Arne Löria to be slain, and laid Orkney and Hjaltland under him again, with all scatts and dues as before.*

Harald's chequered career was now drawing to a close. He died in 1206 at the advanced age of seventy-three, having been Earl for twenty years jointly with Earl Rögnvald and forty-eight years after his death. Of his sons, Henry had the earldom of Ross, in Scotland; Hakon is surmised to have fallen with Sweyn Asleifsson in the Dublin ambush; Thorfinn died in captivity in Roxburgh Castle after being mutilated by King William the Lion, to whom he had been surrendered as a hostage; another son, Roderic, is mentioned in Balfour's Annals as being mortally wounded in the first passage-at-arms, in 1196, between Harald and King William; and the other two,

DAVID AND JOHN, 30TH AND 31ST EARLS,

succeeded to the Earldoms of Orkney and Caithness, which were governed jointly for seven years. They held the land like their father as long as there was anarchy in Norway; but when advised that the kings were reconciled, they sent Bishop Bjorn to Norway. He found King Ingi and Earl Hakon in Bergen, to whom he disclosed the nature of his mission, and undertook that the earls should visit Norway the summer following to adjust matters. Some of the king's officers accompanied the Bishop on his homeward trip to the Orkneys, and he returned to Norway with the earls next summer, and the whole business was left by them to the goodwill of the king and the earl. It resulted in the Orcadian earls being doomed to pay a large sum of money; and they had also to give pledges and hostages, and swear to their faithfulness and obedience; but at last King Ingi made them his earls over Orkney and Hjaltland with such conditions as were afterwards kept until their deathday.* Seven years after his accession Earl David died a natural death, and John became sole earl. He usually resided in the Castle of Brathwell, or Brawl, in Caithness.

---

* Orkn. Saga, Rolls' trans.

The Earls and the Bishops of Orcadia seem to have frequently been at variance with each other. We find John becoming embroiled with the Bishop of Caithness, one Adam, a foundling, who had been so exacting to the inhabitants of his diocese that they rose *en masse* and proceeded to Halkirk, where he resided, demanding an abatement of his unjust impositions, but without success. The earl was in the neighbourhood, but remained neutral, so the exasperated populace first killed the episcopal adviser, one Serlo, a monk of Newbottle, and then, notwithstanding the friendly assurances of Hrafn the Lawman, burnt the Bishop himself. This was in 1222. In the quaint language of Wynton, it is related thus :—

> "Hymself bwndyn and wowndyt syne,
> Thai pwt hym in hys awyn kychyne,
> In thair felny and tharc ire,
> Thare thai brynt hym in a fyre"

King Alexander took a terrible vengeance for this crime. The perpetrators were mangled in limb and tortured, and those who were present, to the number of eighty, had their hands and feet hewn off, many dying in consequence. The earl was also heavily fined and deprived of Sutherland, but in a subsequent interview with the King at Forfar he bought back his lands. Fordun tells us that King William, in 1214 [Alex., in 1224 '], made a treaty of peace with him and took his daughter as a hostage.

In the summer of 1224 he was summoned to Norway by King Hakon, having fallen under suspicion of a desire to aid the designs of Earl Skule against Hakon's power in Norway, and, after a conference with the king at Bergen, he returned to Orkney, leaving his only son, Harald, behind him as a hostage. In 1226 Harald, 'the hope of Orkney,' perished at sea, presumably on the homeward voyage to the Isles. In 1231 Olaf, King of Man, touched at Orkney, and Earl John presented him with a large vessel called the "Bison." The same year John became involved with Hanef Ungi, a commissioner whom Hakon had set over the Orkneys, Snækoll Gunnasson, grandson of Earl Rognvald, and Aulver Illteit, who suddenly attacked him in an inn at Thurso, which they fired, and slew him in the cellar before he had time to conceal himself. His assailants then fled for refuge to the castle in Weir built by Kolbein Hruga, where they were promptly besieged by the earl's friends, principal of whom was Sigvald Skralgi, who was allied to the earl. Sigvald commenced a process against all concerned in the deed, and King Hakon summoned all the accessories to Norway. Aulver, Thorkel, and Hrafn were imprisoned, while Hanef, his two brothers Andrew and Kolbein, Snækoll, Somerled, and Andrew, the son of Rolf Keitling, were all imprisoned in the Castle of Bergen. Having brought the perpetrators to justice, Sigvald, with his retinue, which consisted of the best gentlemen in Orkney, sailed homewards, but the ship was lost, and all on board perished, and Orkney sustained such loss thereby as was not recovered for a long time thereafter. Hanef wintered at Dyniarness, in Norway, with Paul Vagashalm, and next spring obtained leave from King Hakon to return home, but being driven by a storm into the Fair Isle, died there. His brother Kolbein died in Trondheim, but Snækoll, son of Gunni, continued a long time with Earl Skule at his court, and thereafter at King Hakon's.

Upon the failure of heirs-male of the Athol line of Earls, the Earldom seems to have been transmitted to the Scottish Earls of Angus.

Ork Saga Roll's trans

THE ANGUS LINE *

32 Magnus II	1231—1239
33 Gilbride	1239—
34 Gilbride II	—1256
35 Magnus III.	1256—1273
36 Magnus IV.	1273—1284
37 John II.	1284—1310
38 Magnus V.	1310—1321

CONTEMPORARY PRINCES ·

NORWAY	1207, Hakon V	1263, Magnus VI	1280, Eric II
	1299, Hakon VI	1319, Magnus VII (II of Sweden)	
SCOTLAND	1213, Alexander II	1249, Alexander III	1286, Margaret
	1292, John	1295, *Interregnum*	1306, Robert Bruce
ENGLAND	1216, Henry III	1272, Edward I	1306, Edward II.
ROME	1227, Gregory IX	1241, Celestin IV	1243, Innocent IV.
	1254, Alex IV	1261, Urban IV.	1265, Clement IV.
	1271, Gregory X	1276, Innocent V	1277, Nicholas III
	1281, Martin IV	Adrian V. Honorius IV, 1285 John XXI	1288, Nicholas IV
	1294, Celestin V	1294, Boniface XIII	1303, Benedict XI
	1305, Clement V	1316, John XXII	

PRELATES †

ORKNEY	1223, Jofreyr	1247, Henry	1270, Peter
	1284, Dolgfinn	1310, William III	
CAITHNESS	1223, St Gilbert	1244, William	1263, Walter
	1274, Archibald	1279, Alan.	1291, Adam.
	ante 1310, Andrew	1310, Ferquhard, to 1328	

MAGNUS II., 32ND EARL

MAGNUS, [second] son of the Earl of Angus, appears among those present at the perambulation of the boundaries of the lands of the Abbey of Aberbrothock on the 16th January, 1222, while on the 2nd October, 1232, he appears amongst the witnesses to a charter of King Alexander II to the chapel of St. Nicholas at Spey as M Earl of Angus and Kataness. The Kataness would be North Caithness only, as about this time King Alexander II, of Scotland, erected Sutherland, or the southern land of Caithness, into a separate earldom in favour of William, son of Hugh Freskin, who was thus first of the Earls of Sutherland. It is not clear how Magnus of Angus inherited the Orkneys, as, on the death of his predecessor, there seem to have been many who had prior claims to the earldom Fordun credits Earl John with a daughter, and from the "Orkneyinga Saga" we gather that he had five sisters, Helena, Margaret,

---

* Ork Saga, Barry, Pope   † See Historiettes

MAGNUS II, 32ND EARL.

Gunnhild, Herborg and Langlif. There was his brother, Earl Henry of Ross, and Sigvald Skralgi was also (of kin) allied to the Earl. Of the descendants of Ingigerd, heiress of St. Rognvald, young Earl Harald had fallen in battle at Clairdon, and his brother Magnus at Sogn, in Norway, with King Magnus, while of the third son of Ingigerd, Rognvald, we have no further account than that he accompanied Harald to Norway to receive investiture. The daughters of Ingigerd and Eric were Ingibiorg, Elin, and Ragnhild. The last was married first to Lifolf Skalli, who fell so gloriously at Clairdon, and afterwards to Gunni Andresson, by whom she had issue Snækoll, who, by the claims preferred against Earl John, seems to have been the *sole* representative of his grandmother, the Lady Ingigerd. As, after the death of Earl John, in 1231, Snækoll stayed some time at the Norwegian court, and Magnus was Earl of Caithness in 1232, it is in the highest degree improbable that Magnus acquired any rights to Orkney through Snækoll or Ingigerd. He must, therefore, have heired John through a daughter or sister. It is thought Earl John left two co-heiresses, one of whom transmitted her rights to Magnus of Angus, who thus acquired one-half of Caithness, and the other, Johanna, who possessed Strathnaver in her own right, and died before 1269, leaving by her husband Freskin, Lord of Duffus, two co-heiresses, Mary, married to Sir Reginald Cheyne, and Christian, married to Sir William de Federith, and each of these had a fourth part of Caithness, for Sir William de Federith resigns his fourth part to Sir Reginald Cheyne, who then appears in possession of one-half of Caithness, the other half being held by Magnus of Angus, Earl of Caithness and Orkney. In the time of Magnus the Second a Jewish ship was lost in the Orkneys. The Iceland Annals record the death of Earl Magnus as occurring in 1239. From the Diploma of the succession of the Earls of Orkney we learn that he was succeeded by

GILBRIDE, 33RD EARL,

who sent ambassadors to King Hakon regarding the commotions in the Isles. He was succeeded by his son

GILBRIDE II, 34TH EARL,

who held both the earldoms of Orkney and that of Caithness, in Scotland. The Iceland Annals, however, only notice one Gilbride, whom they call Gibbon, Earl of Orkney. His death is placed in the year 1256. According to the Diploma, Gilbride II had a daughter, Matilda, and one son, his successor

MAGNUS III, 35TH EARL.

This earl is mentioned in the Saga of King Hakon as accompanying the ill-fated expedition of that monarch against Scotland in 1263. " With King Hakon from Bergen went Magnus, Earl of Orkney, and the king gave him a good long-ship." The full account of Hakon's disastrous expedition and the pathetic circumstances of his death are dealt with further on.

It is mentioned that Earl Magnus III. entered into a contract of privileges with King Magnus VI. of Norway. He died in 1273, leaving two sons who successively succeeded him.

MAGNUS IV., 36TH EARL,

was the eldest of these, who, after he had enjoyed his father's fortune for the space of two years, was, on the festival of St. Olaf, formally created an earl by King Magnus of Norway. The Icelandic Anuals have the entry under the year 1276: "Magnus, King of Norway, gave to Magnus, son of Earl Magnus of Orkney, the title of earl at Tunsberg." He also appears as Earl of Orkney in the document dated 5th of February, 1283, declaring Margaret, the Maiden of Norway, the nearest heir to the Scottish throne. The Annals record this earl as dying in 1284 along with Bishop Peter of Orkney and Sturla the Lawman. The Diploma states that he died without issue, and was succeeded by his brother John in the earldoms of Orkney and Caithness.

JOHN II., 37TH EARL.

As Earl of Caithness, he appears in 1289 as one of the signatories to the letter addressed by the Scottish nobles to King Edward of England, proposing that the young Prince Edward of Wales should marry Margaret, the Maid of Norway. She died at sea off the Orcadian coast on her way to Scotland in 1290.

> "The north wind sobs where Margaret sleeps,
> And still in tears of blood her memory Scotland steeps."*

Her remains were returned to Norway in charge of Bishop Audfinn and Herr Thore Hakonsson, whose wife, Ingibiorg, daughter of Erling, was lady-in-waiting to Margaret. On 1st September, 1290, a payment appears in the Wardrobe Rolls of King Edward I. to Wm. Playfair, messenger to the Earl of Orkney, who brought letters to our Lord the King on the part of Lord John Comyn concerning the reported arrival of the Scottish princess in Orkney—by gift of the king xiii. sh. 4d. Two messengers were thereon sent to Wick, which they reached on the 4th October of that year. On the 13th May of the following year, 1291, Earl John of Orkney had a safe conduct to come to King Edward till the 24th June, when the earl would doubtless communicate to the king all that he knew of the princess' death. The earl's name appears in the list of those summoned to attend the first Parliament of Baliol, and he swore fealty to King Edward at Murkle, in Caithness, in 1297. The seal which is affixed to the writ bears the earl's coat of arms, which was a ship with a tressure of flower-de-luce around it. In 1293 King Erick of Norway had married Isabel, daughter of Robert Bruce, Earl of Carrick, who, in 1297, bore him a daughter, Ingibiorg, to whom Earl John was betrothed in 1299, and from which we assume he had gone to Norway about that time. Although Ingibiorg was only two years old, it was not unusual in those times to have such a disparity of ages at the time of the betrothal, for we find King Hakon a few years later contracting his daughter—an infant of one year—to a full-grown nobleman.

In 1311 Ingibiorg of Norway was betrothed anew, and Earl John must have died before 1312, when his successor appears on record.

MAGNUS V., 38TH EARL.

It was in Earl Magnus' time, and presumably in his favour, that the King of Norway restricted the title of earl to the king's sons and the Earl of Orkney. King

---

* Miss Holford.

Hakon V had appropriated the revenue in 1309, during Magnus' minority, and a new treaty was entered into (1312) between Robert the Bruce and Hakon V to restore peace, when Scottish pirates seized and held to ransom Sir Berner Pess, the Norwegian Governor of the Islands during the earl's nonage, and Orkney had retaliated by a similar outrage upon Patrick of Mowat, a Scot—perhaps the first introduction of two names now common in the Islands.*

Magnus V. appears at Inverness on the 28th October, 1312, with Ferquhard, Bishop of Caithness, witnessing the confirmation by King Robert I and Hakon V. of the prior treaty executed at Perth, 6th July, 1266 between Alex III. and Magnus IV., the son of the unfortunate Hakon, by which the kings of Norway ceded forever the Isle of Man and all the other islands of the Sudreys, and all the islands in the west and south of the great Haf, except the Isles of Orkney and Hjaltland, which were specially reserved to Norway. In consideration of this the King of Scotland became bound to pay to the King of Norway and his heirs for ever an annual sum of 100 merks, within St Magnus' Church, in addition to a payment of 4,000 merks to be paid within the space of four years

The Earl of Orkney was not present at the Battle of Bannockburn, fought on St John's Day, 1314, but it is stated that Halcro of that Ilk, of an ancient and brave family still extant, commanded three hundred men and fought like a hero. He afterwards returned to Orkney with great honour, in commemoration of which there is yearly, on St John the Baptist's Day, a bonfire at every farm-steading in Orkney, when all the Islands and mainland appear as if in a cloud of smoke.†

It is reported that the night before the victory two men came to *Glassumber* (Glastonbury), and desired lodging of the abbot that night, for they intended on the morrow, said they, to goe help the Scots. The abbot entertained them kindly, and rising in the morning next day to visit the guests, and finding none in the cloister, but the beds remaining untouched, he merveiled greatly, and who they should be he could not imagine, except they were angels. It is also reported that the same day the victory was obtained, a knight in glittering armour came riding through Aberdeen, signifying the great victory of the Scots, and one on horseback crossed Petland Firth—which divideth Orkney from the rest of the land—whom they supposed to be St Magnus of Orkney, sometime prince ‡ In recognition of the saintly support, King Robert endowed the church of Orkney with five pounds annually, out of the customs of Aberdeen, to purchase bread, wine, and wax for the use of the abbey.§ In 1320, he, Earl Magnus, subscribed the famous letter to the Pope, asserting the independence of Scotland. Next year Earl Magnus must have been dead, for Caithness is governed by Henry St. Clair as "ballivus" for the King of Scotland, and Orkney by a "ballivus" representing the Norwegian king In 1329 his relict Katherine executes two charters *in viduitate* by which she, as Countess of Orkney and Caithness, purchases from Herr Erling Vidkunnsson, the Lord High Steward, certain lands in Rognvaldsey, including the Petland Skerries. In one of these documents she speaks of Earl John, as he from whom her husband had inherited his possessions, which he left to her, thus corroborating the statement of the Diploma that Magnus was the son of John

---

* Balfour's Memorial † Pope ‡ Hay § White s Bannockburn

THE STRATHERNE LINE *

MALISE I, 39TH EARL

1321—1333.

BORN C 1272 —M [The Heiress of Orkney]
Johanna, d of Sir John de Menteith

PRINCES CONTEMPORANEOUS

NORWAY	SCOTLAND	ROME
1319, Magnus VII	1306, Robert I	1316, John XXII
	1330, DAVID II	

PRELATES †

ORKNEY	1310, William III	1326, William IV
CAITHNESS	1310, Ferquhard	1332, Nicholas

UPON the death of Magnus V., without male issue, the Orcadian succession opened up to heirs female, and although Simon Fraser (who fell at Halidon Hill, 1333) and Margaret, his spouse, are named in 1330 as having inherited half of Magnus' Caithness possessions, the other half and the earldoms of Orkney and Caithness passed by lineal succession undisputed to the House of Stratherne—Scottish Earls Palatine of an ancient Celtic stock.

In the absence of explicit information from contemporary sources, the way in which the Stratherne Line acquired the right to Orkney is at present matter of conjecture According to the Diploma of the succession of the Earls of Orkney, Gilbride II had issue besides his son and successor, a daughter *Matilda*, contemporary with Malise III of Stratherne, and she may have been his first Countess In 1292 Maria, Queen-Dowager of Man, appears as *Comitissa de Stratherne* in the presence of Malise III.,‡ and in 1293 he enters into a marriage contract of his daughter *Matilda* (then not yet in her 20th year) with Robert de Thony. Thus Malise III may have married first the Lady Matilda of Orkney, and by her had issue the daughter *Matilda* and his successor Malise IV. of Stratherne, and on her decease married Maria, relict of Reginald, King of Man, he having died in 1260

Malise I of Orkney and Caithness, and IV of Stratherne, fought under the banners of Bruce in 1310, and took prisoner his father Malise III From a charter of confirmation by King Robert Bruce (1306-1329) of the lands of Kingkell, Brechin to Maria (Marjorie?) de Stratherne, wife of Malise de Stratherne, as the title is not accorded to either of them,

---

* Ork Saga Bars   † See Historiettes   ‡ Nisbet, Ragman Roll

it appears that Malise I of Orkney was then in apparency only to Stratherne, yet (*semble*) the same Maria figures as *Countess of Stratherne* when involved in the Brechin-Soulis conspiracy of 1320, thus Malise III of Stratherne must have died before that date.

Soon after 1319 Malise IV of Stratherne confirms the grant of his father, Earl Malise, to Sir John Murray and Mary, daughter of Malise III *. In 1320 he is one of the Scottish patriot nobles who sign the letter to Pope John

In all probability Malise IV. of Stratherne married a sister of Magnus V, and enjoyed the Orcadian Earldom *jure uxoris* without question, as no formal investiture seems either to have been sought for or obtained. A claim, however, was made for this purpose by one Malise—probably the Master of Orkney—and a caveat entered to secure the revenues in the country till he had time to take the steps that were necessary for obtaining what he considered his right †. In Dean Gule's translation of the Diploma it is recited "Heirfor the said Lord and Erile (Wilzem of Sanct Clare) supponit that it was well knawin till us how oure supreme Lord Mawnis, maist illustre King of Norwege, hed derectit till wmquhill our predecessors his patent letters for his progenitor Earle Malisius, exhortand thame and chargand them to deliver to the said Malisius Erile, all charters, evidens, and letters of previledge pertinent to hyme concernent the Erildome of Orchadie"

The preceding Earl of Orkney and Caithness, Magnus V, was alive in 1320, for on the 6th April of that year he subscribed the letter to Pope John. It seems as if he had been dead in 1321, for in a document addressed by King Robert Bruce to the "ballivi" of the King of Norway in Orkney, dated at Cullen 4th August, 1321, he complains that Alexander Brun, "the king's enemy," convicted of *lese majestatis*, had been received into Orkney, and had been refused to be given up, though instantly demanded "by our ballivus in Caithness, HENRY ST CLAIR" He was certainly dead in 1329, for in that year his dowager Katherine executes two charters as Countess of Orkney and Caithness *in viduitate*.

William III., the Orcadian bishop, was in conflict with his metropolitan about this time. He was suspended by the Archbishop in 1321, but was evidently soon restored to favour, for in 1324 we find him assisting at the consecration of Laurentius, Bishop of Hole. By a deed dated at Bergen 9th September, 1327, he mortgages his dues of Hjaltland to his metropolitan, Eilif, Archbishop of Nidaros, for the payment of 186 marks, which he should have paid the Archbishop for six years teinds. By another document of the same year, Bishop Audfinn requests Bishop William of Orkney to assist his priest Ivar in the collection of *sunnive miel*, a contribution which the inhabitants of Hjaltland had paid from old time to the shrine of St. Sunniva at Bergen. The exact date of this prelate's death has not been ascertained, but William IV, the ninth bishop, succeeded him soon after the year 1328.

In 1331 Earl Malise possessed the fourth part of Caithness, as appears from an entry in the Chamberlain Rolls in that year, another fourth part being in the possession of Simon Fraser and Margaret, his spouse, thus accounting for the half of Caithness which had belonged to Magnus V, and showing that on his death his possessions devolved upon two heirs-female. Simon Fraser and his brother-in-law Malise, Earl of Orkney, Caithness and Stratherne, both perished at the battle of Halidon Hill, 11th July, 1333, in which battle the earl was one of the three leaders of the third division of the Scottish army.

* Nisbet † Burt

Considerable confusion exists as to the dates of succession and mariages of the four last Earls of Stratherne, who were all of the name of Malise. There is record of a Charter of Confirmation by Bruce of a charter [in 1323], by Malise, Earl of Stratherne, to Johanna, daughter of the late Sir J. de Menteith, knt, spouse of the same earl, of the lands of Cortachie, in the shire of Forfar, of Glenlitherner, Dalkeith, and half of Urkwell, in the earldom of Stratherne. From this notice it is to be inferred that Malise was not as yet Earl of Orkney and Caithness Sir John Menteith signed the letter to the Pope in 1320, and is then described as 'guardian' of the earldom of Menteith He last appears in 1329 during the minority of David Bruce, one of whose charters he attested. He had been created Earl of Lennox by Edward I of England, which he abandoned in 1306, it is also stated that the same monarch created him Earl of Athol, and it is thus probable that his daughter succeeded to that dignity in her own right. She is the Johanna de Stratherne noted as having married (1) Malise IV of Stratherne, I of Orkney and Caithness, (2) John Campbell, Earl of Athol [*jure uxoris*], who fell at Halidon Hill in 1333, (3) John de Warrenne, Earl of Warren and Surrey, born 1286, married first to Joan, daughter of the Count de Bar, by whom he had no issue, and from whom in 1315 he obtained a divorce on the ground of a pre-contract of marriage with one Maud de Nereford, whom, however, he did not marry *

When Malise, next Earl of Stratherne and Orkney, was forfeited by the English party for supporting Edward Balliol, King Edward III of England created [the Earl's stepfather], John de Warrenne, Earl of Stratherne anterior to the 2nd March, 1334, from which we infer that the Earl of Surrey married Johanna de Stratherne almost immediately after the death of her second husband, the Earl of Athol There must have been an annulment before July, 1339, when Benedict II granted the Papal dispensation for the marriage of Maurice de Moravia with Johanna, widow of John, Earl of Athole, styling her therein Countess of Stratherne. Maurice de Moravia was related in the third degree to the said John, Earl of Athol, hence the dispensation. He was created Earl of Stratherne on the 31st October, 1345, and fell at the Battle of Durham in 1346. The Earl of Surrey died *s p l* in 1347 at the age of 61 It will be observed that the marriages of Johanna with (2) John, Earl of Athol, and (4) Maurice de Moray were during the Earl of Surrey's life, the latter marriage at least serving to establish the fact of a divorce having been procured from John, Earl de Warrenne, Surrey and Stratherne About 1330 she executed a charter of the lands of Gellow in Cortachy, in which she refers to her father as deceased In the Athol charter-room is a charter granted by her nephew John de Menteith, sheriff of Clackmannanshire, by which it is ascertained that some time before 1352 she wedded (5) William, Earl of Sutherland

She executed a charter during one of her terms of widowhood in favour of Robert of Erskine and his wife, Christian of Keith, her cousin, which is confirmed in 1361 by Robert, Steward of Scotland, and Earl of Stratherne. Christian of Keith was the only daughter of Sir John Menteith, by Elyne, daughter of Gratney, Earl of Mar. Christian Menteith married first Sir Edward Keith, by whom she had Janet Keith, and second Sir Robert Erskine, by whom she had no issue, but a marriage was arranged between Thomas, the eldest son of a previous marriage of Sir Robert, and Janet Keith, the representatives of which marriage now enjoy the Earldom of Mar as heirs of Elyne, wife of Sir John Menteith. The Countess of Stratherne in the foregoing charter could not have

---

History of Westminster

been the daughter of Sir John Menteith, who married the Earl of Stratherne, as in that case she would have been in the relationship of sister to Christian of Keith. It is therefore more likely that she was the daughter of the *Earl* of Menteith mentioned in the Diploma as married to the last Earl of Stratherne, whom she predeceased.

There are several notices in Scottish record publications of Countesses of Stratherne, but it is almost impossible to identify the particular individual meant. Thus notices between 1339–61 may refer to the much-married Johanna de Menteith, to Marjory of Ross, or to Euphemia of Ross, afterwards Queen of Scotland.

THE STRATHERNE LINE —Continued *

MALISE II, 40TH EARL

1333—1345

BORN c. 1300 —M 1 D of the Earl of Menteith
              2 Marjory, d of Hugh, Earl of Ross

PRINCES CONTEMPORANEOUS

NORWAY	SWEDEN	SCOTLAND	ENGLAND
1319 Magnus VII	1319, Magnus II	1330, David II	1330, Edward III.

ROME 1334, Benedict XII   1342, Clement VI

PRELATES.†

ORKNEY   1328, William IV to 1382
CAITHNESS 1332, Nicholas   1340, David   1341, Alan   1342, Thomas de Fingask

AT a time when the highest Scottish dignity was that of earl, and limited to some ten earldoms, this earl united in his person the three ancient dignities of Orkney, Caithness, and Stratherne, and we have seen that in the lifetime of his father when in apparency only he had lodged a caveat to secure the Orcadian revenues.

Upon the death of Andrew Murray at Duplin in 1332, his son Sir William Murray of Tullibardine had a charter from his superior Malise, then Earl of Stratherne, of his estate of Tullibardine on the resignation of Adda, grandmother of Sir William To this deed Sir William de Montefixo, *justicarius Scotiae ex parte borealis aquae de Forth*, is a witness; he executed that office in 1335.‡

There is in the Scottish Chamberlain Rolls of 1340 an entry in regard to a payment by John More for the lands of Berridale in Caithness, which, he says, he acquired from the Earl of Stratherne, and had confirmed by the king There is no record of the movements of Malise, but we learn incidentally that he had betaken himself to his northern possessions upon the forfeiture of the Earldom of Stratherne by his father, which was thereon given by Edward III to John de Warrenne, Earl of Warrenne and Surrey, [stepfather to Malise]. He appears to have made an effort in 1334 to recover the Earldom of Stratherne In that year Edward III, by a letter dated the 2nd March, directed Henry de Beaumont, Earl of Buchan, not to allow any process to be made before him respecting the earldom forfeited for treason by Earl Malise He also wrote a letter of the same date to Edward Balliol, stating that he had heard that Malise, Earl of Stratherne, claimed the county of Stratherne which he had granted to John de Warrenne, Earl of Surrey, and requesting him to act with deliberation

---

       Orku Saga and Barry   † See Historiettes   ‡ Nisbet

MALISE II, 40TH EARL.

The next appearance of Malise the Second is at Inverness, when by document dated 28th May, 1344, he grants to William, Earl of Ross, the marriage of his daughter Isabella, securing to her the Earldom of Caithness on failure of heirs-male to himself and his wife Marjory, sister of the said William. William succeeded his father Hugh, who was slain at Halidon Hill in 1333, but it is stated that he was not confirmed in the earldom for three years on account of his absence in Norway. Thus it seems that Earl Malise must have passed over to Norway about the same period, in all likelihood to obtain investiture of the Earldom of Orkney from Magnus the Norwegian king, and William, Earl of Ross, may have accompanied his brother-in-law.

The Diploma states that Malise was first married to Joanna, daughter of the Earl of Menteith, and that by her he had a daughter Matilda, married to Weyland de Ard. The Diploma further states that Malise was married a second time to a daughter of Hugh, Earl of Ross. From the deed of 1344 we find the name of Malise' then wife was Marjory. In a deed of 1350, William, Earl of Ross, styles his sister Marjory, Countess of Caithness and Orkney, and with her consent appoints his brother Hugh his heir in the event of his own death without male issue. From this it would appear that Malise was then dead. It is likely he died before 31st October, 1345, when his cousin Sir Maurice Moray was created Earl of Stratherne. He must have been dead before 1353, when his son-in-law Erengisle Sunesson obtained the title of Earl of Orkney from the King of Norway, and he is mentioned as dead in 1357 and 1358, and the Earl of Ross is then said to have entered to his lands in Caithness. While Malise was in Norway and Sweden two of his daughters had been married to Swedish noblemen, and from the Diploma we ascertain he had issue by his first wife, the Menteith, one daughter, and by his second wife Marjory four daughters —

1. MATILDA, married Weyland de Arde, and had issue
    Alex de la Ard, Governor and Commissioner of Orkney, 1375, died *s p*
2. ISABELLA, married William St Clair, Lord of Roslin Issue
    Henry, 42nd Earl of Orkney, fl 1379—1404
    David St Clair, of Newburgh, mentioned in 1391
3. ANNOT, or MERETTA, married Erengisle *j u*, 41st Earl of Orkney, 1353
4. A daughter married Gothorm Sperra Issue
    Sir Malise Sper, Lord of Skuldale, slain 1389, *s p*
5. [EUPHEMIA], a daughter died unmarried

ERENGISLE, 41ST EARL *

1353—1357.

Born c 1310—M 1 Meretta
2 Lady Annot of Orkney

PRINCES CONTEMPORANEOUS

NORWAY	SWEDEN	ROMI
1343, Hakon VI	1350, Eric IV	1352, Innocent VI

PRELATES †

ORKNEY 1328, William IV   CAITHNESS 1342, Thomas

The 41st Earl of Orkney was a Swedish noble, the son of Sune Jonsson, grandson of Brynjolf, a Norwegian baron who had accompanied King Hakon on his disastrous trip to the West. As early as 1337 we find Erengisle entrusted with the important duties of Lawman of Tisherad, in his native realm

While his predecessor, the 40th earl, Malise the Second, was in Norway and Sweden [1333-1336], he had effected the marriage of two of his daughters, Erengisle espousing the Lady Annot de Stratherne, and Guttorm Sperra (whose son Malise hereafter figures as *Dominus de Skuldale*‡) espousing her sister

On the death of Malise the Second, or shortly thereafter, Erengisle claimed his wife's share of the earldom In the year 1353 we find him executing a deed on the 10th April as plain Erengisle Sunesson, and on the 6th May following his signature appears to a document drawn up at Vagahuus concerning the Queen's dowry, occupying the foremost place among the nobles of Norway, and with the title of the Earl of Orkney The Diploma informs us that he resided in Orkney, and although it states that he only held his wife's share of the earldom, it is plain from the Vagahuus document that he must have received the title of Earl of the Orcades from the King of Norway

He soon became involved with the Swedish party in favour of King Eric of Pomern, and in 1357 King Magnus of Sweden, as Regent of Norway, sequestrated all his Norwegian estates and declared his title to be forfeited

His right to the earldom would have lapsed with the death of his countess, who died childless before 1360. In that year Erengisle grants certain lands to the monastery of Calmar for the souls of his deceased wives, Meretta and Annot or Agneta, the latter being most probably the daughter and co-heiress of Earl Malise the Second, as the name Annot is not a common one in Sweden Nevertheless he continued to style himself Earl of Orkney during his lifetime, as appears by a deed bearing date 4th March, 1388, in which he is "*Comes Orchadensis.*" He died in 1392.

After his forfeiture in 1357 there ensued an interval of disputed succession.

---

* Orkn Saga and Barry   † See Historiettes   ‡ Roslyn Chartulary

CONTESTED SUCCESSION.*

1357—1379.

1364 Thomas de St Clair,	Ballivus
1369 Hakon Jonsson	Prefect
1375 Alex de la Ard	Governor and Commissioner

SYNCHRONISMS

NORWAY	1343, Hakon VI		
SWEDEN	1350, Eric IV	1359, Magnus II restored	1364, Albert
DENMARK	1340, Waldemar III	1376, Olaf IV	
SCOTLAND	1330, David II	1371, Robert II	
ROME	1352, Innocent VI	1362, Urban V	1370, Gregory XI

PRELATES †

ORKNEY	1328, William IV	
CAITHNESS	1342, Thomas.	1369, Malcolm

DURING this period while the succession to the earldom was disputed by the several heirs and representatives of Malise the Second, the historical notices are few, and the matter preserved at best but fragmentary.

The Archdeacon of Hjaltland—one William Johnsson—appears in a Norse deed dated at Sandwick 4th March, 1360 He is supposed by Munch to be the tenth Bishop of Orkney, William V, who is otherwise only referred to in a record of the time of Robert III of Scotland

In 1363 HENRY SAINT-CLAIR, Lord of Roslin, was sent as ambassador to Copenhagen, where a marriage was in course of celebration between Hakon VI, King of Norway, and Margaret, the future "Semiramis of the North," daughter of Waldemar III. of Denmark. As Henry St. Clair was at that time sick, his procurators got from those princes a confirmation of the lands of Orkney, and it is stated that at the same time a marriage was concluded between himself and King Hakon's sister, a daughter of Magnus II of Sweden ‡

The following year, on the 20th January, 1364, we find a THOMAS DE ST. CLAIR installed at Kirkwall as "ballivus" of the Norwegian king, an ALEXANDER ST. CLAIR, and Euphemia de Stratherne styling herself one of the heirs of the late Malise, Earl of Stratherne These three attest a deed executed at Kirkwall on the date aforesaid, by which Bernard de Rowle resigns to Hugh de Ross (brother of William, Earl of Ross) the whole lands of Fouleroule in Aberdeenshire, the witnesses being John de Gamery and Simon de Othyrles, canons of Caithness, Euphemia de Stratherne, one of the heirs of the late Malise, Earl of Caithness, Thomas de St Clair. ' *ballivus regis Norvagiae*", and Alexander de St Clair Alex. de Sco-Claro, son of the quondam Thos. de St. Clair,

---

† Orkn Saga   † See Historiettes   ‡ Hay or Van Bassan

received in the 41st David II., *i.e.*, 1371, confirmation of a charter from Hugh Ross of Philorth of the lands of Estirtyry, Aberdeen; and of another from William, Earl of Ross, of the lands of Bray with pertinents in the maresium de ffornewyr. in vic. de Inverness.

Euphemia de Stratherne, if not the daughter of Earl Malise, mentioned in the Diploma as having died unmarried, must surely be Euphemia, daughter of Hugh, Earl of Ross, and wife of Robert Stuart, created Earl of Stratherne cr. 1346-53. Earl Malise had espoused her sister Marjory, and she was sister to the Hugh de Ross and William, Earl of Ross, mentioned in the deed. To William, Earl of Ross was entrusted the marriage of the Lady Isabella, daughter of Malise, Earl of Stratherne, Caithness, and Orkney, as is shown by a document dated at Inverness 28th May, 1344, granting her also the Earldom of Caithness failing heirs-male of himself and his wife Marjorie. Euphemia de Stratherne became Queen of Scotland on the accession of Robert Stuart in 1370, and was crowned with great solemnity at Scone, being anointed by the Bishop of Aberdeen.* Thomas de St. Clair, "ballivus," was most probably acting in that capacity for his kinsman [nephew] *durante absentia* at the Danish court.

About 1367 (Skene has *in* 1357) one Duncan Anderson, who appears to have been Scottish, and probably agent for ALEXANDER DE ARD, issues a manifesto to the Islesmen, notifying them that he has under his guardianship the true and legitimate heir of Earl Malise, the former Earl of Orkney; that this heir has now the full and undeniable right to the earldom; and that as he has heard that the King of Norway has recently sequestrated the revenues of the earldom, he warns the inhabitants not to allow those revenues to be taken furth of the land, till the true heir be presented to them, which will be ere very long, if the Lord will. It would seem that a representation must have been made by the Court of Norway to the Scottish King regarding the troubling of the Islands by the claimants or their friends in Scotland, for an edict was issued from Scone in 1367 by King David, forbidding any of his subjects, of whatever rank or condition, to pass into Orkney or frequent its harbours on any other errand than that of lawful commerce.

William IV., the ninth bishop, occupied the Orcadian see at that period. We find an agreement entered into at Kirkiuvaghe (Kirkwall) dated the 25th May, 1369, between him and Hakon Jonsson, negotiated by twenty-three clergy and laymen of the Islands respecting what the bishop ought to pay Hakon on the king's account: mutual friendship to be for the future, and men born in the Islands to be appointed to offices there henceforth. The other persons appearing in the record are "sira Willialmr af Bucchan, erkindiakin j Orkneyum. sira Valter af Bucchan, kanngkr j samastadh. sira Jon proktur. sira Richard af Rollisey. sira Cristen af Teyn. sira Cristen af Sanday. sira Willialmr wod. Thomas arland. Fergus af Rosce. Henri Willialms. Jon of Orkneyum. Willialmr Stormr. Jon. af Boduel. Jon Robertson. Adam af Mekre. Gudbrand Andrsson. Sighurdr af Pappley. Jon sincler. Patrik kaldar. Dunkan af Karmkors. Bube Skinner. Willialmr eruin. Jon af Dunray." Of thirteen seals Nos. 4, 8, 10 and 11 remain on the parchment original. The title "sir" is equivalent to the modern word reverend.

About the year 1374 four Orcadian fishing boats were tossed in a gale towards land far out in the West, since ascertained to be in North America. The survivor returned twenty-six years later, and related his experiences to the 42nd Earl, Henry I.†

In 1375 King Hakon VI. of Norway granted the Earldom of Orkney, for a single year till next St. John's Day, to ALEXANDER DE ARD, naming him in the document,

---

* Balfour's Annals. † Voyages of the Zeni.

CONTESTED SUCCESSION.

however, not as Earl, but simply as GOVERNOR and COMMISSIONER for the King, and declaring in the document addressed to the Islesmen that this grant is given provisionally until the said Alexander shall establish his claim to the earldom. He seems not to have been regarded with much favour by the King, for the grant was not renewed. Alexander de Ard had succeeded to the Earldom of Caithness in right of his mother as heir to Earl Malise. In 1375 he resigned the Castle of Brathwell (Brawl) and all the lands in Caithness, or any part of Scotland, which he had inherited in right of his mother, Matilda de Stratherne, to King Robert II., who bestowed them on his own son David, who appears in 1377-1378 as Earl Palatine of Caithness and Stratherne.

The abeyancy of the earldom was terminated in 1379 in favour of HENRY SAINT-CLAIR, Lord of Roslin, eldest son of Isabella de Stratherne.

SEAL OF THE ROYAL BURGH OF KIRKWALL.

THE SAINT-CLAIR LINE.*

HENRY I, THE HOLY, 42ND EARL.

1379—1404

Born c 1346—M [Florentia, Princess of Denmark]
Jean, d of the Lord of Dirleton.

PRINCES CONTEMPORANEOUS

NORWAY	1343, Hakon VI	1380, Olaf.	1389, Margaret.
SWEDEN	1364, Albert		1389, Margaret
DENMARK		1376, Olaf IV	1387, Margaret
SCOTLAND	1371, Robert II	1390, Robert III	
ROME	} Popes {	1378, Urban VI	1389, Boniface XI
AVIGNON		1378, Clement VII	1394, Benedict XIII

BISHOPS OF ORKNEY.†

1328, William IV   1382, William V   1394, Henry   1397, John

SINCE the termination of the administration of Alexander de Ard as Governor and Commissioner of the Isles on St John's Day, 1376, the earldom remained for three years in commission But in the summer of 1379 Alexander de Ard, titular Earl of Caithness, Henry Saint-Clair, Lord of Roslin, and Malise Sperra, Lord of Skaldale,‡ the three cousins, competitors for the earldom, passed over to Norway to prefer their respective claims to the Norwegian king, and the result was that at Marstrand, on the 2nd August of that year, Henry Saint-Clair received from King Hakon formal investiture of the Earldom of Orkney, and also of the Lordship of Hjaltland, which appanage, since the time of its forfeiture to King Sverre by Earl Harald—first of the Athol line—had been in possession of the crown of Norway

The conditions on which Earl Henry accepted the earldom are set forth in the Deed of Investiture, and, contrasting them with the semi-independence of the ancient earls, it would at first sight appear as if little more were left him than the lands of his fathers. For, although the Earls of Orkney had precedence over all the titled nobility of Norway, and their signatures to the national documents stand always next after the archbishop's, and before the bishops' and nobles'; though the title was the only hereditary one permitted in Norway to a subject not of the blood-royal, yet it was now declared to be subject to the royal option of *investiture*. The Earl was to govern the Isles and enjoy their revenues during the king's pleasure, but he was taken bound to serve the king beyond the confines of the earldom with a hundred men fully equipped, when called

---
* Ork Saga Barry, etc   † See Historiettes   ‡ Skelda in Birsra

upon by the king's message, he was to build no castle or place of strength in the Islands, nor make war, enter into any agreement with the bishop, sell or impignorate any of his rights without the king's express consent, and, moreover, he was to be answerable for his whole administration to the king's court at Bergen. At his death the Earldom and all the Isles were to revert to the King of Norway or his heirs, and if the Earl left sons, they could not succeed to their father's dignity and possessions without the royal investiture.

The reversal concerning Orkney not being found sufficient by King Hakon, the ambassadors were allowed to stay in the city of Tunsberg, in Norway, till His Majesty was satisfied. In the meantime there was a marriage concluded, as is said, betwixt John Saint-Clair, brother to the Earl, and Ingeberg, natural daughter of Waldemar, King of Denmark, by Jova Little, who was a daughter of Sir John Little, Commissioner of Rugen.*

At the following Martinmas Earl Henry was taken bound to pay to the King 1,000 English nobles (about £333 sterling). It was also part of the compact that Malise Sperra, son of Guttorm Sperra, should depart from all his claims to the Earldom in right of his mother; and the Earl left with King Hakon as hostages for the due fulfilment of his share of the contract the following from among his friends and retinue :—William Dalziel, knight, Malise Sperra, and David Crichton.

King Hakon died the next year, 1380, the year following the investiture of the Earl and the events that took place in the Orkneys during the reign of his successor, King Olaf, are entirely unknown to the Norwegian chroniclers.

The Earl seems neither to have courted the favour of his suzerain, nor to have stood in awe of his interference. Without waiting for the royal consent, and in defiance of the prohibition contained in the Deed of Investiture, he forthwith built the Castle of Kirkwall, from which he seems to have thought himself sufficiently independent to regally rule his sea-girt earldom according to his own will and pleasure. This fortress, in later times called "the King's Castle," was constructed with such strength and skill that the witch-haunted mind of the 17th century believed that only the Arch-fiend himself could have been its engineer and architect.†‡

From the fact that King Hakon's investiture of Earl Henry took him bound not to enter into any league with the bishop, nor to establish any friendship with him without the king's consent, we infer that the bishop—William IV.—was then acting in opposition to the king and to the representatives of civil power. The likelihood is that Earl Henry found this episcopal opposition favourable to his own design of making himself practically independent, and represented it as the excuse for the erection of the Castle of Kirkwall, contrary to the terms of his agreement with the Crown. Munch attributes the discord to the growing dislike of the Norwegian inhabitants of the Isles to the Scotsmen, whose numbers, through the influence of the family connections of the later earls, had long been increasing. Whatever may have been the origin, the end of it was that, in some popular commotions of which we have no account, the bishop was slain in the year of grace, 1382.

Earl Henry, after establishing himself in the Isles, turned his attention towards rewarding the cadets of his House, as appears from an evident, whereby he obliges

---

* Hay.
† Balfour. ‡ See letter Earl of Caithness from Kirkwall 7th October, 1614 (Caithness Events).

himself to infeft his beloved cousin, Sir James St. Clair, Baron of Longformacus, in a twenty merkland. The words of the obligation run : "*Universis patent, etc. Nos Henricum de Sancto Claro, Comitem Orcadiæ et Dominum de Roslyn teneri firmiter, et fideliter obligari carissimo consanguineo nostro, Jacobo de Sancto Claro, Domino de Longfurdmakhuse, etc.,*" which evident is dated at Roslin, the 22nd June, 1384. The witnesses are Thomas Erskine of Dun, George Abernethy of Soulis, Walter Halyburton of that Ilk, and John Halyburton of Dirleton.*

At Edinburgh, on the 8th November, 1387, Malise Sper, *Dominus de Skuldale*, agrees with the Earl anent the harm that had been done to him and his tenants as is evidenced by instrument of that date.†

The next year, 1388, is memorable as being the date of Otterburn. The Earl was not present himself, but his kin took a prominent part in it. Tytler has: " At Otterburn, along with the Earl of Douglas, were the Earls of March and Moray, Sir James Lindsay, Sir Alex. Ramsay, and Sir John St. Clair, three soldiers of great experience, and others." Froissart narrates:—" Upon James, Earl of Douglas, being struck down, he continued with his latest breath to encourage his comrades. Sir John St. Clair, his cousin, having asked him 'how he did,' 'Rycht well,' quoth the erle, 'but thanked be god there hath been but a few of my ancestors that hath dyed in their beddes. Bot cosyn, I require you thinke to revenge me, for I reckon myself bot deed, for my herte feinteth oftentymes. My cosyn Walter and you, I praye you raise up again my banner which lyeth on the ground, and my Squyre Davye slain ; but, sirs, show neither to friend nor foe what case ye see me in, for if myne enemyes knew it they wolde rejoyse, and our frendes be discomfited." The two Saint Clairs and Sir James Lyndsay, who was with them, did as they were desired, raised up his banner, and shouted his war-cry of " Douglas. The remainder of the battle was beyond the life of Douglas, for he was dead before it ended, and what was a prophecy in the dying man's mouth became a saying that " the victory was won by a dead man;" and Sir John Sinclair bore the banner.

While these stirring events were occurring in Scotland the Earl was attending to his high offices in Norway, for in 1388 he is present as a Councillor of State, and signs next after the Archbishop Vinoldus in acknowledging Eric of Pomerania as true heir to the realm of Norway. Again, in September, 1389, both Earl Henry and his cousin, Sir Malise Spar, are among those present on the occasion of the accession of King Eric of Pomern.

The "Iceland Annals," under date 1389, have the following entry:—" Malise Sperra, with seven others, slain in Hjaltland by the Earl of Orkney. He had previously been taken prisoner by him. From that conflict there escaped a man servant who, with six men, got safely away to Norway in a sixareen."

Malise appears to have endeavoured to establish himself in Hjaltland in opposition to the Earl. He had seized, it is not stated on what grounds, the possession in Hjaltland which had belonged to Herdis Thorvaldsdatter, and of which John and Sigurd Hafthorsson were the lawful heirs. It seems as if the Earl was about to hold a court to settle the legal rights of the parties concerned. The court would be held at the old Thingstead near Scalloway, but a conflict taking place, the dispute was terminated by the strong hand, and Malise Sperra was slain. The monolith of grey granite close to the roadside between the Lochs of Tingwall and Asta probably marks the spot where he fell.

* Nisbet. † Hay.

HENRY I., 42ND EARL.

In the "Scottish Chamberlain Rolls" of 1438 there is an entry of a receipt of £9 from James Mcfersane for the land formerly belonging to Malise Speir, knight, in the sheriffdom of Banff, remaining in the king's hands. A number of his men having been slain with him, it is probable he was the aggressor, and as both he and the Earl attended at King Eric's coronation in 1389, it is likely the Earl landed in Hjaltland on his way home from Norway for the express purpose of seeing justice done in the cause of the heirs of Herdis.

Early in 1390 Nicolo Zeno, a Venetian nobleman, was wrecked in a storm on the Faroes, and he and his companions were rescued from the wreckers by the Orcadian Earl, Henry St. Clair, who happened to be in the vicinity with an armed retinue. Accosting the Venetians in Latin, he assured them of his protection, and took Nicolo into his service. The Earl had presumably given chase as far as the Faroes to the adherents of his cousin, Sir Malise Speir of Skuldale, and the first exploit in which Nicolo participated was the reduction of that archipelago. This was accomplished with a fleet of thirteen vessels, whereof two only were rowed with oars—the rest were small barks and one ship. As Nicolo greatly contributed towards the skilful navigation of the fleet through the dangerous channels of the various islands, the Earl, in recognition of his services, administered the accolade conferring on him the honour of knighthood, and he thereafter appears designated in the annals of his country as *Sir Nicolo the Chevalier*.*

KIRKWALL, THE ORCADIAN CAPITAL.—WINTER VIEW.

Sir Nicolo now wrote to his brother Antonio at Venice, relating his adventurous experiences, and asking him to join him and bring a vessel. Antonio did as desired, and both brothers won much favour with the Earl.

King Richard II. of England gave a safe conduct, or passport, to Henry, Earl of Orkney and Lord of Roslin, from 10th March, 1391-2 to Michaelmas, with permission to be accompanied by twenty-four persons, the necessary persons, etc., with proviso that no

---
* Voyages of the Zeni.

one fugitive from the English laws should be of the company. The king signed it at Leeds Castle, Kent.

By deed executed at Kirkwall on the 23rd April, 1391 (and subsequently confirmed by King Robert III.), the Earl dispones the lands of Newburgh and Auchdale, in Aberdeenshire, to his brother *David de Sancto Claro* for his services rendered and in exchange for any rights he may have to lands in Orkney and Hjaltland, derived from his mother Isabella St. Clair. Witnesses: Lord Walter de Bochane, Archdeacon of Zetland; dnō Simon de Papay; dnō Thomas de Kirknes; dnō Jno. Punkyne; dnō Michael de Westray; duō hauqno, militibus; Richard de St. Clair; Thomas de Laysk; Alex. de Claphame; Thomas de Leth, etc.

The Earl, to gratify Sir Nicolo Zeno, and also because he knew full well his value, made him commander of his navy (armada). In that capacity Sir Nicolo with his brother Antonio accompanied the Earl to the Hjaltlands, and established order in that group; after which the Earl built a fort in Bressay, where he left Sir Nicolo with some small vessels, and men, and stores, and thinking he had done enough for the present, returned with the rest of the squadron to the capital of his archipelagic dominions.

Being left behind in Bressay, Sir Nicolo determined the next season to make an excursion with the view of discovering land. Accordingly, in the month of July, 1394, he fitted out three small barks, and sailing towards the North, arrived in Greenland, where he stayed some little while observing the manners and customs in those parts. At length, not being accustomed to such severe cold, he fell ill, and a little while after he returned to the Orcades, where he died, a victim to the rigorous climate of the northern regions.*

The next appearance of the Earl is at Roslin on the 13th May, 1396, when Sir John de Drummond of Cargyll (brother of Annabella, queen of Robert III. of Scotland) and his wife Elizabeth make renunciation by deed for them and their heirs in favour of Henry, Earl of Orkney, Lord Roslyn, "patri nostro," and his issue male in respect of claims to the Earl's lands "infra regnum Norvagie."

By charter at Edinburgh on the 24th January, 1404, King Robert the Third of Scotland freed the Earl of the Castle Guard due for his Baronies of Rosline, Pentland, Pentland Moor, Colsland, Merton, and Mertonehall, all in the viscounty or sheriffship of Edinburgh. In this charter the Earl is described only as Earl of Orkney, no other title being specified.†

On the death of Sir Nicolo Zeno, his brother Antonio succeeded him in his wealth and honours, but although he strove hard in various ways, and begged and prayed most earnestly, he could never obtain permission to return to Venice, for the Earl, being a man of great enterprise and daring, had determined to make himself supreme in the Northern seas. The Islesmen were then greatly excited by the strange tales of an Orcadian castaway who had returned from the far West after an absence of twenty-six years, and the Earl was inspired with the project of bringing under his sway the rich and populous lands reported in those distant parts. For that purpose he resolved to equip a fleet on a voyage of discovery and conquest. Setting sail with a considerable number of barks and rowboats, and men, he disappointed Antonio Zeno of the chief command. At the start adverse weather was experienced, and they were unwillingly compelled to circumnavigate Ireland before proceeding on their course, and they eventually reached

* Voyages of the Zeni. † Roslyn Chartulary.

Greenland, but as the voyage had occupied so long a time their stay was of brief duration. Antonio, in writing to his brother, the famous Carlo—'Saviour of Venice'—refers to the exploits of St Clair, "a prince as worthy of immortal memory as any that ever lived, and to the discovery of Greenland on both sides and the city that he founded."* Antonio Zeno returned to Venice in 1404, for it is stated that he remained ten years in the service of the Earl after the death of Sir Nicolo, which happened late in 1394, or early in 1395. It is known that Antonio died in Venice before 1406, and Michaud dates his death as in 1405. It will be observed that the date of Antonio's return coincides with that assigned for the death of the Earl, viz., 1404, the latter event operating to release Antonio, who immediately availed himself of the position.

The panegyrist† of the St Clairs of Roslin writes of Earl Henry as follows — "After the death of Sir William Sinclair, succeeded to him his eldest sone, Henry, Prince of Orknay, Lord Shetland, Lord Saintclair, Lord Chief-Justice of Scotland, Admirall of the Seas, Baron of Roslin, Baron of Pentland Moore (in free forestrie), Baron of Cousland, Baron of Cardain Saintclair, and Great Protector, Keeper, and Defender of the Prince of Scotland, who married Elisabeth, daughter to Malesius, Prince of Orknay, Earl of Kaithness and Stratherne, through which marriage he became Prince of Orknay, and was more honoured than any of his ancestres, for he had power to cause stamp coine within his dominions, to make laws, to remitt crimes, he had his sword of honour carried before him wheresoever he went, he had a crowne in his armes, bore a crowne on his head when he constituted laws, and, in a word, was subject to none, save only he held his lands of the King of Noraway, Sweden, and Danemarke, and entred with them, to whom also it did belong to crown any of those three kings, so that in all those parts he was esteemed a second person next to the king. He builded the Castle of Kirkwell, in Orknay, and proved valiant in all his doeings . . . When Robert II, the first of the Stewarts, succeeded to the Scottish crowne, he no less intirely loved the Prince of Orknay than did his unckle, King David, and in testimony of his love to him, he made him Protector and Keeper of the Prince, his sone, Johne Stewart, Earle of Carrick, because he was both the most noble and trustiest in his realme, as writting yet records, and in the 19th year of his reign he died (1389). Henry Sainclaire, haveing the Prince in his keeping, was advertised of ane armie of Southrons that came to invade the Orcade Isles, who, resisting them with his forces, through his too great negligence and contempt of his oundfriendly forces, he was left breathless by blows battered so fast upon him that no man was able to resist, and left two sones, Henry, his successor, and John (hereafter Foud of the Orcadian secundogeniture of Hjaltland, and nine daughters, who were married thus —The eldest (Beatrix) upon the Earle of Dowglass (James the Gross, Lord Balveny, 1409, Earl of Avondale, 1437, 7th Earl of Douglas, 1440), the second upon the Laird of Dalhousie, the third on the Laird of Calder, named Sandilands, the fourth (Jean) upon the Laird of Corstorphine, named (Sir John) Forrester (ancestor to Lord Forrester), the fifth upon the Earle of Errol, named Hay, the sixth upon the Laird of Drummelzier, named Tweedie; the seventh upon the Laird of Stirling, named Cockburne; the eighth upon the Laird of Maretone, named Heron, and the ninth (Mary) upon the Lord Sommervaill, so named (Thomas Somerville, of Carnwath, ancestor to Lord Somerville)."

* Voyages of the Zeni.   † A m hassan, a fabulous genealogist.

In the Diploma Earl Henry is stated to have married Janet, daughter of Walter Halyburton of Dirleton, by whom he had Henry II., his successor. In an attestation dated 1422, by the Lawman and Canons of Orknay, of the descent and good name of James of Cragy, Laird of Hupe, it is expressly certified that Henry St. Clair was himself married to a daughter of the younger Malise, styled "ELIZABETH de Stratherne, daughter of the late reverend and venerable Malise, Earl of Orkney," and that by her he had a daughter, Margaret, who was married to James of Cragy. Patrick, 13th Bishop of Orknay, appears in this attestation. The Earl had also a daughter, Elisabeth*, married to Sir John de Drummond (*vide supra*). It is stated in several works that he was first married to Florentina, daughter of the King of Denmark, by whom he had no issue. The only Danish sovereign to whom this could apply would be Waldemar III., fl. 1340—75. It is further stated by one historian† that in 1363 there was a marriage concluded between the Earl of Orkney and a daughter of Magnus II., King of Sweden, being sister to Hakon VI. of Norway, suzerain to the Earl.

In addition to the issue enumerated previously, this Earl had a daughter, Marjory‡, wife of Sir David Menzies of Wemyss, to whom the administration of the Isles was entrusted during the minority of his nephew, William, the 44th Earl. Another son, William, obtained, on the 19th August, 1407, a safe conduct to England for six weeks therefrom, and Thomas Sinclair, mandatory in Orkney, 1426, was evidently also a son of this earl.

It will be observed that Hay's account of the manner of the Earl's death agrees with the Diploma, both stating that he was slain in the Orkneys while resisting an invasion from the South, and elsewhere is found *anno* 1404: "A squadron, under Sir Robert Logan, attacked an English fleet of fishers off Aberdeen. Some good ships of Lynn happened to come up in time to aid their countrymen, and Logan himself, with the rest of his company, was taken. The English then landed on some of the Orkneys and spoiled them."§

---

* She is also stated to have been married to Sir John Edmondston (Grant). † Hay. ‡ Nisbet.
§ Holinshed.

NOTE, from Peterkin's Rentals, 1503: "Hoy.—Brabuster beneth the hill wes ane uris terre. Of the quhilk the first erle heurie gaif to the vicar iij. d. terre for the uphauld of ane mess in hoy a day ilk oulk for evir."

THE ST CLAIR LINE

HENRY II, 43RD EARL.

1404—1420

BORN C 1375 —M Egidia Douglas, Lady of Nithsdale

PRINCES CONTEMPORANEOUS

SCOTLAND	1390, Robert III	1406, James I	
ENGLAND	1399, Henry IV	1413, Henry V	
FRANCE	1380, Charles VI		
DENMARK	1387 ⎫	⎧ VII	
NORWAY	1389 ⎬ Margaret	1412, Eric ⎨ III	
SWEDEN	1389 ⎭	⎩ XIII	
ROME	1404, Boniface IX	1404, Innocent I	1406, Gregory XII.
	(1410, Alexander V	1410, John XXIII to 1415)	1417, Martin V
AVIGNON	1404, Benedict XIII to 1424		

PRELATES

ORKNEY 1397, John Patrick 1418 Thos de Tulloch

"NEXT to Prince Henry Saint Clair succeeded his eldest sone Henry, second of the name He was in nothing inferior to his predecessors He married Giles Dowglass, daughter to the most valiant Sir William Dowglass, sone to Archibald, Earle of Dowglass and Lord of Galloway, who for his valour at Carlisle . . got in marriage the fair Algidia, excelling all in her time, grand-daughter to King Robert the Second, surnamed Stewart, of whose beauty it is reported that it did so dazzle the eyes of the beholders that they became presently astonished, but revived in admiring the same. The Earl of Orkney's Lady, Giles Dowglass, was of a family no less famous abroad for their love of noble acts than at home for their eminent nobility and generosity She added the rayes of vertue and holyness to a noble extraction, to the glory of ancestors, and the splendour of her family. Her sweetest delights were retreate, solitude, and reading of good books. She was noways taken with the deceitful appearances of the goods of this world, with pleasures that delight the senses, and with honours that bewitch the most part of mankind. In a word, she listened only to the voice of God. Among the flatteries, applauses and bad examples that often infest the palaces of princes, nature did endow her with all qualities requisit to a comely person, and with so much advantage that nothing could be added to make up a perfect beauty that was not concentered in her. She was of stature somewhat above ordinarie, but the excellency of her minde, the candour of her soule, and the holyness of her life made her incomparably more pleasant. 'Commendebatur excellentis formae bonitate, et maturescentis ævi vigore, et ingenii elegantia, quam vel auxerat, vel certe non falsis virtutem coloribus, gratiorem fecerat aulica educatio, ad honesti quidem similitudinem adumbrata ' ''*

In further reference to her parentage Tytler has "Sir William Douglas, Lord of Nithsdale · This young knight appears to have been the Scottish Paladin of those days of chivalry. His form and strength were almost gigantic, and what gave a peculiar charm to his warlike prowess was the extreme gentleness of his manners, sweet, brave, and generous, he was as faithful to his friends as he was terrible to his enemies. These qualities had gained him the hand of the king's daughter Egidia, a lady of such beauty that the King of France is said to have fallen in love with her from the description of his courtiers, and to have privately despatched a painter into Scotland to buy him her picture, when he found to his disappointment that the princess had already disposed of her hand in her own country ''† The Lord of Nithsdale was known as "The Black Douglas," and on the borders English nurses would hush their children by saying, "The Black Douglas comes," "The Black Douglas will get thee." He married the Lady Algidia in 1387, and immediately set out for Dantzig to assist Waldenrodt, Grand Master of the Teutonic Knights, against the then pagan Prussians under Udislaus Jagello For his conspicuous services he was made Prince of Danesvick, Duke of Spruce,‡ and Admiral of the Fleet, while the Scots were made for ever free citizens of that town In 1390 Sir William was foully murdered on the ancient bridge of Dantzig by a band of assassins employed by Lord Clifford, who had insulted him, and yet dreaded to meet him in mortal combat By his wife he left a daughter known in the encomiastic language of the age as "The Fair Maid of Nithsdale "§ . Through this marriadge the Prince of Orknay obtained great lands and authority, as all the Lordship of Nithsdale, the Wardonrie of the Three Marches betwixt Berwick and Whithorne, with the Baronies of Hectfoord, Harbertshire, Grameshaw, Kirktone, Cavers, Roxborough, and the Sherriship of Nithsdale, with the town of Dumfries He was a valiant Prince, well proportioned, of midle stature, broad bodied, fair in face, yellow haired, hasty and sterne He had the greater part of the Nobility in the Countrey, his Fialls, and their bonds of Manrent, as the Lord Salton named Abernethy, for a hundred pounds a year, the Lord Crighton, so named, the Lord Seton, so named, the Lord Dirleton, named Halyburton; the Lord Halifexburne (sic), the Lord Levingstone of Kalendar, so named, who holds lands in Herbertshire, as Castelough and Akinloch ; the Lord Fleming of Cumbernald, so named, who was his bailiff of Herbertshire, and held lands therof, as his house, the Castle of Rankens, Easter and Wester Summers, Easter and Wester Thomastones, Banknocks, Bangkerne, Brackinlies and Dapes, for the which he was bound to pay yearly one pair of gold spurres, and one conrse of hunting, with a banquet att the Pentecoste, the Lord Borthwick, who hath as yet the liberties of the Earn Craig yearly, pertaining to the Barony of Pentland Hills, and the Lord of Dalkeith with these barons, the Laird of Westendrie named Foster, who got the lands of Tavensmock, Easter and Wester, the lands of Carne, altogither with twenty-four merks yearly of the Barony of Roslin, the Laird of Craigmiller, named Prestone ; the Laird of Gilmertone, named Heron ; the

---

* Van Bassan † Fordun

‡ These titles are given Sir William Douglas in Hume of Godscroft's book, but the authority he cites is " The Monuments of the Sinclairs " § Scottish Soldiers of Fortune

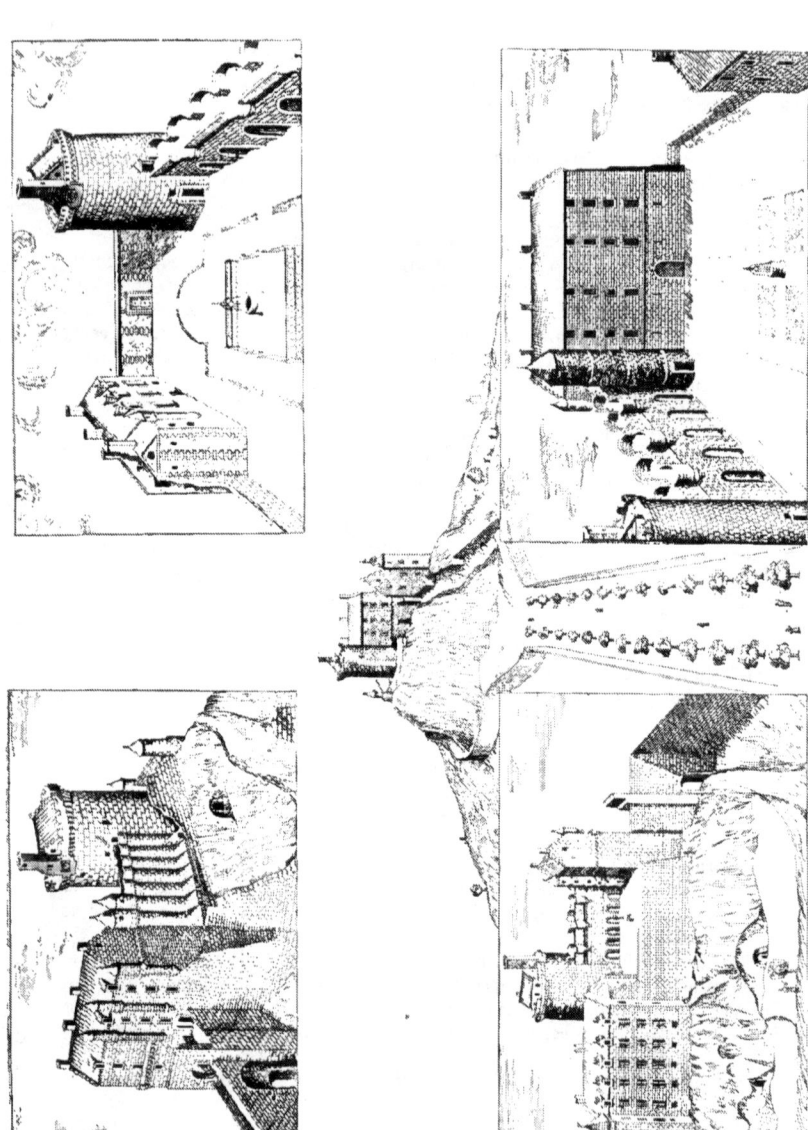

ROSSLYN CASTLE (*Restored*): CRADLE OF THE ST. CLAIR LINEAGE.

Laird of Hermistone, named Saintclaire (his cousin) ; the Laird of Niddrie, named Wachope ; the Laird of Edmistone, so named ; the Laird of Penniecooke, so named ; the Laird of Henderleith, and the Laird of Pompharstane, named Douglas, who got the lands of Mertone, holden of the Barony of Pentland, with sundry other noblemen and gentlemen which to recite were impertinent and tedious ; for one part of the countrey were his allies, ane other held lands of him, the other were his Fialls, so that there were very few except Dowglass and the Earle of Marche, two also of the peers of the land, but were some way bound to him, whom also he used to entertain into his house, att sundrie times of the year, with their Ladies, and servants, as att Easter, Christmess, and other solemne feasts.

He had continually in his house three hundred Riding Gentlemen, and his Princess, fifty-five Gentlewomen, wherof thirty-five were Ladies. He had his dainties tasted before him ; he had meeting him, when he went to Orknay, three hundred men with red scarlet gownes, and coats of black velvet. He builded the great dungeon of Roslin, and other walls therabout, togither with parks for fallow and red deer, and he was mutch esteemed of by King Robert the Third, surnamed Stewart, and therfor he got the Prince James, the first of that name, in keeping, lest he should be taken away by the treason of Robert, Duke of Albanie and Earle of Fife and Monteith, who had the whole government of the kingdome, the King being now deceased, and aimed at the crowne after the King's death, for by treason he had slaine the King's eldest sone, and thought to doe the same by Prince James if he could catch him. But the King fearing the term of his life to draw near, and considering the trouble that might befall the Prince of Orknay after his death, by the deceit of him that was to be Governor ; therfor writting letters both to the Kings of France and England, he caused the Prince of Orknay to committ himself, togither with his sone, Prince James, and young Percie, nephew to the Earle of Northumberland, to the sea's mercie ; but when they had sailed a little space, Prince James not being able to abide the smell of the waters, desired to be att land, where, when they were come, for they landed att his request (30th March, 1405, upon the coast of England at Flamborough) upon their journay to the King, they were taken and imprisoned till afterwards, by the King's command, they were brought to him, to whom they delivered the letters ; who, when he had perused them, and consulted with his Nobles what to doe, att length he resolved to keep them as prisoners, yet so that he caused instructors to teach Prince James, wherthrough he became so learned and expert in all things that he had no equal. The rumour of this imprisonment (1405) comeing to the ears of the King of Scotland, through displeasure he died, and Robert, his brother, Duke of Albanie, was made Governor.*

The prince was long kept in England, but Earl Henry was soon liberated, or rather obtained leave of His Majesty to return to Scotland, upon leaving his brother John as hostage for his returning as prisoner into England by the following Christmas. Van Bassan has a different version of his release, and narrates :—" About this time one John Robinsone, indweller att Pentland, and tenent to the Prince of Orknay, came to England, where his master was imprisoned, and there he played the fool so cunningly, that without any suspition what he was, he had entrance to the prison att his pleasure ; and so, watching his time, one evening he convoyed the Prince of Orknay without the gates in disguised apparell, which he had prepared for the same purpose, where they stayed all the next day, and afterwards made them for journey next evening, for they travelled in the night

---

* Hay.

and rested in the daytime, lest they should be taken by those who were appointed for that purpose by the King They travelled to the borders, where there was great inquiry made for them, when, behold, two sowtherns, not knowing what they were, made them hold their horses, which the Prince perceaving, and catching hold of one of their necks, struck him to the ground, and so bereft him of his life, and then followed the other, who fled with shreeks and lamentable cries, whom he made partake of his companion's reward, so he with his servant prepared themselves, and in short time, being well mounted, arrived in Scotland; where when he was come he desired this Robisone to ask his reward, who desired nothing but that he might goe to Pentland, before he went to Rosline, and pass three times about the Linstone therof, which he did. He was no sooner come to Rosline, but the noble Douglasse, and the Earl of Marche, togither with all the nobles, his servants and fialls, came to welcome his returne, enquiring of his wellfare, where these three Princes, Henry Saintclair, Archibald Dowglass, and George Dumbar, consulted about their affairs, and then departed to their severall dwellings. Robert, Duke of Albanie and Governor, being a malitious tyrant, was mightily commoved heratt, and carrieing hatred in his heart att the Prince of Orknay for keeping Prince James from his terrible treason, therfor he forges a cause whereby he might be revenged upon him, to witt, the treasonable delivering of the Prince of Scotland into the hands of the English, and therupon caused summonds against him, appointing a day for his forfeiture, against which day he had prepared a company of men to resist the Prince's friends who would be most against his pretence; and sent Heralds through all the countrey, discharging all under pain of treason to assist him, but that he should compear that day himself, with a few number of his servants to defend his cause The Prince, considering how unjustly he was accused, in great rage warning his friends and servants, who promised their aid and assistance, and bringing great forces from Zetland and the Orcade Isles sent the Governor this answer, that att the day he should compear, but so that one towne should not contain them both, and in derision desires him to prepare lodgeing for himself and stabling for his horses, for he thought the city not sufficiently furnished Wherat the Governor was mightily offended, and vowed to contain him in less bounds, but the day of forfeiture appointed being come, Duke Robert came to Edinburgh with (10,000) men. The Prince hearing this, haveing with him in company (40,000), resolved to meet him there, where, when he was come, the Duke, mightily afraid, fled with 3 more besides himself to Falkland, where he remained, wherof the Prince haveing knowledge, after great search made, sent one of his company, and he, togither with the other two Princes of the Land, Douglas and Dumbar, constitute a Parliament, in which they appointed to forfeitt Duke Robert, with all his favourers, for his tyrannie and treason used against David, eldest sone to King Robert, which cruelty consisted in this, that after he was licensed by the King, he imprisoned him for his licentious life denieing him all nourishment, and any that pitied him he punished with death as he did a poore woman that gave him meale in att a hole, and ane other that gave him the milk of her breast Att the news of this new Parliament Duke Robert was sore afraid and becam penitent, wherfor he sent his friends to the three Princes to make sure for him, promiseing to amend his life in time to come, who excused all he had done, imputing it to bad counsell Att this excuse they being content, and accepting his promise of amendment, receaved him into favour and restored him to office " *

* Van Bassan, fabulist

It is stated that the year following 30th January, 1405-6, the Earl, with a son of the Duke of Albany and eleven other Scottish magnates, obtained letters of safe conduct for coming into England with a company of fifty persons, in order to be received as hostages for the Earl of Douglas.* But in the list of hostages preserved in an indenture of 14th March, 1407, for the release of Archibald II., fourth Earl of Douglas, the only St. Clair mentioned is Sir William of Hermiston, nor is it likely that a noble of equal importance to Douglas would have been proposed or consented to be exchanged for him.

At Edinburgh on the 17th November, 1407, Archibald II., fourth Earl of Douglas, Lord of Galloway, grants the barony of Herbertshire to Earl Henry and his Countess, the Lady Algidia, and their heirs. This was confirmed by the Regent Albany on 20th November, 1407. Amongst the witnesses in the instrument of infeftment to Egidia, Countess of Orkney, are *Willielmus de Sancto Claro* and *Edwardo de Sancto Claro, Armigeri*. The date of the infeftment in Hay's Genealogie is 1447.† The Barony of Herbertshire was probably granted on the occasion of the Earl's nuptials with the 'Fair Maid of Nithsdale,' who was born in 1390. These two events enable us to arrive approximately at the age of their son, Earl William, who was a minor at the death of his father in 1420, and in 1426 was evidently of age, taking his place as Earl of Orkney in the assize on Murdoch, Duke of Albany.

On the 20th November, 1411, Earl Henry authorised his brother John to redeem in his name from Sir Walter de Lindsay the lands of Johnston and Brumiston in the shire of Mearns, which were woodset to Sir Walter.† The same John received from Henry V. a passport into England, in order to treat of the redemption of the King of Scots; and Earl Henry himself another from the same prince for coming into England with a retinue of twenty persons of whatever degree to remain until the August following.* In the spring of 1412 Earl Henry went to France with Archibald Douglas to assist the French against the English. Bower relates : " The Earl of Douglas was thrice driven back by hostile winds, and having, on the advice of Henry St. Clair, Earl of Orkney, landed at Inchcolme in the Forth, and made offering to St. Columba, the saint sent him with a prosperous wind to Flanders, and brought him safely home again.

" Att this time the Prince of Orkney had all his victualls brought by sea from the north in great abundance, for his house was free for all men, so that there was no indigent that were his friends but receaved food and rayment, no tennents sore oppressed but had sufficient to maintain them, and, in a word, he was a pattern of piety to all his posterity, for his zeal was so great that before all things he preferred God's service, which appeared in this, that he gifted the Abbay of Holyroodhouse so ritchly, with the back and fore Spittles, with the Midle, and Lochrids and Skipperfields, together with the tithes of St. Katherine's Church in the Hopes, which lands were estimate able to feed 7,000 sheep. He gave also to his brother John Saintclair the Kirktone, the Loganhouse, the Earn Craig, the Easter and Wester Summerhopes, with the pertinents therunto upon this condition, that if he had no heirs-male they should return again to the House of Roslin."† Henry, Earl of Orkney, Lord St. Clair and Nithsdale, granted to James St. Clair of Longformacus a charter of twenty merks yearly, to be uplifted out of the lands of Leny, 20th February, 1418.‡

In 1418 John St. Clair swears fealty to King Eric at Helsingborg for the king's lands of Hjaltland, having been specially commissioned by Earl Henry to that effect, and

---

* Barry.   † Roslyn Chartulary.   ‡ Nisbet.

becomes bound to administer the Norse laws according to the ancient usage, and it is stipulated that at his death Hjaltland should again revert to the crown of Norway.*

The Earl executed an indenture at Roslyn the 23rd November, 1419, with Adam of Dalkell of the Buthagh. In the instrument the Earl is described as "a noble lord and a mighty Prince, Henry Earl of Orkney, Lord Sinclair and Niddisdale."† Adam was married to Sabey Menzies, perhaps niece of the Earl. It is stated‡ that in 1418 the Countess of Orkney received papal dispensation to re-marry, but this is inconsistent with the execution of the deed with Adam of Dalkell, and as Bower in his continuation of Fordun assigns 1420 as the date of the Earl's death, the latter date and that of the deed seem to support each other.

Van Bassan continues "As for the ritch ventures that he gave for the service of God att that time, I minde not to insert particularly; only they were of gold and silver and silkes. Here is to be admonished that the affectionat zeale and love to God's glory and service, which was tenderly cherished in the hearts of these our worthy ancestres, should serve as a spurre to pricke us forward in the way of devotione and vertue to imitate their pious example, otherways God will make their zeale to accuse us at the last day."

But to our purpose. Not long after this died Prince Henry Saintclaire. He was "vir militiæ terrestris ac navalis scientia plurimum valens, qui ab adolescentia, magnis rebus, summa fortitudine et felicitate, gestio, apud omnes, gloriam et authoritatem comparavit." He was a man of sharp wit, and projected great matters, when he breathed out his life. I find in the Martyrologe, or obituarium Santæ Mariæ de Newbottle what follows:— 'Obiit Kalendis Februarii, Henricus Comes Orchadiae, qui super ceteros, "ecclesiam nostram diligens multa nobis contulit beneficia. habuimus de bonis ejus, "multa pecora, unam crucem argenteam valentem L lib. vel circiter, in cujus lateribus "Maria et Johannes assistunt, libros et alia, unde ei in perpetuum obnoxii esse debemus; "statuimus pro inde, ut singulis annis, redeunte die obitus sui, fiat pro eo commemoratis "mortuorum, et commendatio ante missam, et habeant die illa fratres xii. solidos ad 'refectionem."

Prince Henry Saintclaire left behind one sone named William, his successor, and one daughter. The daughter was Beatrix, who married Sir James Douglas, brother to Archibald II., 3rd Earl of Douglas, and who appears as of Balveny (1409), Earl of Avondale, 1437. On the murder of William, 6th Earl of Douglas, in 1440, the Earl of Avondale became 7th Earl of Douglas. Beatrix may well have been termed the "Mother of Earls." She had issue William and James, 8th and 9th Earls of Douglas; Archibald, Earl of Moray, Hugh, Earl of Ormond, John, Lord Balveny, and Henry, Bishop of Dunkeld. During the life-time of William, 8th Earl of Douglas, a singular question was raised, whether James, afterwards 9th Earl, or his brother Archibald, Earl of Moray, was the elder twin of the marriage between James the Gross and Beatrix Sinclair, daughter of Henry, Earl of Orkney. After an enquiry before the official of Lothian, who took the evidence of their mother, the Countess-Dowager, and other worthy women, the priority of James was declared, and ratified by a writ under the Great Seal on 9th January, 1450.§ Beatrix, Countess-Dowager of Douglas, was buried in St. Bride's at Douglas, and on a monumental wall-tomb are the arms of Douglas impaling Sinclair, with the following inscription "Hic jacet Domina Beatrix de Sinclaire, filia Domini Henrici, Comitis

---

* Orkn Saga. - Roslyn Chartulary. , Douglas Peerage. ⁶ Dict. Nat. Biog., *Article* Douglas

Orcadum, Domini de Saintclaire, Comitissa de Douglas et Aveniae, Domina Gallovidiae."*

Egidia, relict of Sir Henry Sinclair, is stated to have received the Papal dispensation to marry Alex. Stuart in 1418, but from the indenture of Earl Henry with Adam of Dalkell, we know he was alive on the 3rd November, 1419, and from the entry in the obituarium of St. Mary of Newbottle—which can hardly refer to the death of Earl Henry I., or it would surely have recited the fact of his being mortally wounded in battle with the English invaders—we ascertain he died on the 1st February, 1420. It is said that she married secondly Alexander, third son of Murdoch Stuart, Duke of Albany, who was beheaded along with his father at Stirling, 25th May, 1425; yet when she next appears, † confirming the charter of 10th September, 1425, by John de Blare, dominus de Adamtoun, of the lands of Catsclench to Alexander de Levingstone de Calentare, she is simply Egidia, Comitissa Orcadie, Domina Vallis de Nith et Baronie de Harbartshire. Her seal appended to this confirmation displays her arms impaling those of her husband on the right. As daughter and heiress of Sir William Douglas of Nithsdale, she bears the Douglas arms on the right, and in the fourth quarter the Lion of Galloway, which it will be observed is turned to the left. The Saintclairs subsequently bore the Lion, which has been mistaken by Heralds for the arms of Spar, the Norse Lords in Orkney. Again,* when complaining of the spoliation of her Nithsdale dominions in 1438, she is similarly described, and there is no indication of a second marriage. She was certainly young enough to re-marry at the time of Earl Henry's death, as she was only born in 1390.

There are many references to this Earl Henry in addition to the foregoing. On the 24th March, 1405, he receives a payment for Sir John Drummond, and on the 28th May following witnesses the grant of a cocket to the Bishop of St. Andrew's. On the 15th March, 1406, Henry IV. from Westminster, gave a safe conduct to Henry, Earl of Orkney, and Walter, Lord Haliburton, to come into England with forty persons, to remain till the feast of St. John the Baptist. His seal is appended to a charter he gave to Forrester of Corstorphine, of date 26th November, 1407. At Westminster, 8th April, 1407, Henry IV. signed a passport to Patrick Thomson and Henry Shipman, the masters of a ship from Scotland; and to Alex. Johnson and Robert Black, of Scotland, with twelve persons accompanying them, to London by ship with goods and merchandise coming with Henry, Earl of Orkney. On the supplication of Henry, Earl of Orkney, Alexander Ledale and Robert Williamson, armorials-bearing gentlemen and followers of that earl, had a safe conduct with eight persons by sea and land within England, dated by private seal at Westminster 4th January, 1407-8, from Henry IV., their permission to last till Pentecost. On 20th July, 1408, he attests the Regent's charter of Strathbolgie to Sir Alex. of Seton. Henry, Earl of Orkney, and a Lord William St. Clair signed a charter of Gogar at Dirleton 8th June, 1409, and in the same year he is noted to receive payment from the customs of Linlithgow if so entitled, and in May, 1409, £20 was paid to him for travelling to England on affairs of the Scottish King. In 1410 there is a similar entry about the customs of Linlithgow, and also the Edinburgh customs, while on the 15th May, 1409, and 14th July, 1410, this is noted at Aberdeen: "Et memorandum quod non onerant se de quatuor dacris et quatuor coriis que venerunt de Orcadia per coketam comitis Orcadie."

On 12th September, 1410, the Earl, at Roslin, gave to "our brother-german John and his heirs" a charter of the lands of Sunellis, Hope, and Loganhouse in Pentland Moor, near

---

Hay. † Hay Introd.

HENRY II., 43RD EARL.

Edinburgh, ratified twelve days later by the Regent; and about the same time Sir John Forrester of Corstorphine, Edinburgh, to whom the Earl's sister Jean was married, had the confirmation of a loan of 300 nobles, receiving 12 merks yearly from Dysart and coals till repayment. In 1415 the Earl of Orkney took £42 6s. 8d. from Edinburgh customs; and Henry V., at Westminster, of date 14th April, 1416, gave his protection in England till 15th August to Henry, Earl of Orkney, with 20 persons coming from and returning to Scotland. Hen. Com. de Orcadia is printed as a witness in the Exch. Rolls during the years 1424-5-9; but this must surely be a mistake. On the 10th July, 1424, there is confirmation to Sir John Forrester of Corstorphine, and Margaret his quondam spouse, of a charter from Sir John Drummond de Cargill, of Uchtertire in Perth, *quas Hen. de S. Claro*, Earl of Orkney [had] resigned; and also a confirmation of an impiguoration by Henry St. Clair, Earl of Orkney, to Sir John Forrester de Corstorphine, knight, *fratri suo*.

THE ST. CLAIR LINE.

WILLIAM, 44TH EARL.

1420—1471.

BORN C. 1408.—M. 1. Elizabeth Douglas, Countess-Dowager of Buchan and of the Garioch.
2. Marjory Sutherland of Dunbeath.

PRINCES CONTEMPORANEOUS:

NORWAY: DENMARK:	1412, Eric VII. of Pomern.	1440, Christopher III.	1448, Christian I.
SCOTLAND:	1406, James I.	1436, James II.	1460, James III.
ENGLAND:	1413, Henry V.	1422, Henry VI.	1461, Edward IV.
FRANCE:	1380, Charles VI.	1423, Charles VII.	1461, Louis XI.
ROME:	1417, Martin V.	1431, Eugenius IV.	1447, Nicholas V.
	1455, Calixtus III.	1458, Pius II.	1464, Paul II.
	1471, Sixtus IV.		

PRELATES:

ORKNEY: 1418, Thomas de Tulloch. 1461, William VI. de Tulloch.

"AFTER the death of Prince Henry Saintclaire, succeeded his sone William Sauutclair, Prince of Orknay [Duke of Holdenbourg], Earle of Cathness [and Stratherne], Lord Shetland, Lord Saintclair, Lord Nithsdale, Shirieff of Dumfriese, Lord Admirall of the Scots Seas, Lord Chief Justice of Scotland, Lord Wardin and Justiciar of the three Marches betwixt Berwick and Whithorne, Baron of Rosline, Baron of Pentland and Pentland Moore in free forestrie, Baron of Couslande, Baron of Cardain Saintclair, Baron of Herbertshire, Baron of Hectford, Baron of Grahamshaw, Baron of Kirktone, Baron of Cavers, Baron of Newborough in Buchan, Baron of Roxburgh, Dysart, Polmese, Kenrusi, etc., Knight of the Cockle after the ordre of France [and Knight of the Garter after the order of England, Knight of the Golden Fleece], Great Chancellour, Chamberlain, and Livetenant of Scotland, etc.—titles to wearie a Spaniard.'"*

A curious instrument, which throws some light on the state of the Highlands in 1420, and gives an example of the mixture of Celtic and Norman names, is to be found in a MS. in the Adv. Lib., Jac. V. 4, 22, entitled "Diplomatum Collectio." † As it perhaps refers to Earl William's uncle, it is here inserted in part, as follows :—John Touch, be the Grace of God, Bishop of Rosse ; Dame Mary of ye Ile, Lady of the Yles, and of Rosse ; Hucheon Fraser, Lord of Lovat; John Macloyde, Lorde of Glenelg ; Angus Guthredson of the Ylis ; Schyr Wm. Farquhar, Dean of Rosse ; Walter of Douglas, Scheraff of Elgin ; Walter of Innes, Lord of that Ilke ; John Syncler, Lord of Deskford ;

---
* Van Bassan, tabulist. † Tytler.

John ye Ross, Lord of Kilravache, John McEan of Ardnamurchan, with many othyr, etc. Sir Walter Ogilvie married in 1437 Margaret, heiress of John Syncler, Lord of Deskford, and was ancestor to the Earls of Deskford, Findlater, Seafield, and Banff, who all quarter the Roslin arms.

When James I. returned to Scotland in 1423, he was met at Durham by the Earls of Lennox, Wigtown, Moray, Crawford, March, Orkney, Angus and Stratherne, with the Constable and Marischal of Scotland and a train of the highest barons and gentry of his dominions, amounting altogether to about 300 persons; from whom was selected a band of 28 hostages, comprehending some of the most noble and opulent persons in the country. In the schedule containing their names, the annual rent of their estates is also set down, which renders it a document of much interest as illustrating the wealth and comparative influence of the Scottish aristocracy (Rymer's Fœd, vol. x., pp. 307-9).*

On succeeding to the Earldom, Earl William had scarcely been in possession a year when he was one of the five earls enumerated in the twenty hostages proposed 31st May, 1421, for the redemption of James the First; and when that redemption could not be obtained, he was soon afterwards placed in the list of nobles who received a passport to visit James, King of Scots, then a prisoner in England, for which purpose the Earl received a safe-conduct for himself and twenty-four persons. His father, Henry II, almost during his whole life had been employed in business of the utmost importance, and for this reason found little leisure to cultivate the acquaintance of that sovereign for whom he held the Earldom, or to renew the obligations to which his father had become bound on receiving investiture. Earl William had begun the same active and honourable course, and was likely to be guilty of the same neglect, and perhaps the Danish monarch was not much displeased to see such a powerful subject of another prince fail to perform the conditions stipulated on obtaining the grant, so that he might have a plausible pretext for depriving him of the possession †

Thomas de Tulloch, who became Bishop of Orkney about 1422, was of far more celebrity than his immediate predecessors. Letters of safe-conduct were granted to him and eight persons in his retinue for a whole year by Henry the Sixth, King of England. He seems to have been held in much esteem by his own sovereign for when neither Earl William nor his father had acknowledged his supremacy, King Eric committed the Earldom to him, not as a pledge or in security for debt, but as a solemn trust, to be executed with fidelity, and recalled at the pleasure of the King, or that of any of his lawful successors. This appears evident from the tenor of his letters on receipt of the commission, which expressly declare that he will govern the people with equity and according to law, maintain peace among them to the utmost of his ability, and whenever it should please His Majesty, from whom he received the trust, or any of his successors, to demand restitution, he would readily deliver into their hands not only the citadel of Kirkwall, but the whole Earldom †

The Bishop swore fealty to King Eric in 1420, in the church of Vestenskov in Laland, undertaking the administration of the Islands according to the Norsk law-book and the ancient usages. The document is endorsed "Biscop Thomes breff af Orknoy, at han skal halde Orknoy til myn herres konnungens hand, oc hans efter kommende, oc lade han mit Noren lagh" On the 10th July, 1422, he received as a fief from the King "the

---
* Tytler   † Barry

palace of Kirkwall and pertinents, lying in Orknoy, in Norway, together with the lands of Orknoy and the government thereof." The document is endorsed "Item biscop Thomes aff Orknoy breff um Kirkwaw slot i Orknoy, oc um landet oc greves-chapet ther samestads."* Though this prelate seems to have been well qualified for the trust inasmuch as he had the confidence of the Prince, as well as the affection of the people, his administration was only of one year's duration.†

A Scottish gentleman, David Menzies, of Wemyss, Chief of the Clan Menzies, and uncle‡ to Earl William, was in 1423 entrusted by King Eric with the administration of the Isles; and the Bishop himself and Walter Fraser subscribed his obligation as sureties. This precaution was, however, of no effect, as it could not supply the defect of principle, nor restrain within due bounds a man who seems to have been naturally addicted to arbitrary sway and rapine. Within four years his depravity displayed itself in such various acts of wickedness that the Islesmen, groaning under his power, in 1426 preferred a complaint against him to King Eric containing no less than thirty-five articles of accusation,† setting forth that they had been subjected to oppression and wholesale spoliation during the period of his administration. Among the charges preferred against him, it was asserted that he diminished the value of money by one-half, that he threw the Law-man of the Islands unjustly into prison, and illegally possessed himself of the public seal and law-book of the Isles, which the Law-man's wife had deposited on the altar of the Church of St. Magnus for their security; that he exacted fines and services illegally and with personal violence, and was guilty of many other acts of tyrannical oppression.* Amongst others enumerated in this document is one Thomas Sincler, who seems to have taken a foremost part in bringing about some limitation to the excessive power assumed by Sir David Menzies. Thomas Sincler proceeded to Denmark and obtained authority to correct Sir David's irregularities, but the latter was little inclined to tolerate any power in supersession of his own, and he exiled Thomas to Scotland. In Article XI. a reference is made to "Johannes Craigie, filiusque sororis," etc.§ If this can be construed to mean that John Craigie was Thomas Sincler's sister's son, we can conclude that Thomas was a son of Earl Henry I. and brother to Margaret St. Clair, daughter of Earl Henry by *Elisabeth* de Stratherne, whom we have seen was married to James of Cragy, which fact is recited in the attestation of 1422 by the Law-man and Canons of Orkney.*

To rectify the disorders which such an administration must have produced, and restore among the people contentment and tranquility, Bishop Thomas, whose character was firmly established, was in 1427 re-instated in the government of the Earldom, the functions relating to which he performed with honour for the seven years intervening until the young Earl received his formal investiture.†

That about this period the Orcadians were becoming Scotticised is evidenced by a deed of gift in English or Scottish made on the 6th day of June, in 1433, by one "Duncan off Law" of a house in Kirkwall to one "Donald Clerke" as a marriage portion with Jonet Law, sister of the donor.||

Earl William had taken the title before receiving investiture, for on 10th July, 1424, he is so styled, and in 1426 he appears as Earl of Orkney on the assize at Stirling for the trial of Murdoch, Duke of Albany,* and on the 30th May, 1428, he is described as Earl of Orkney in an enumeration of those present at Edinburgh dealing with a complaint preferred by his mother Egidia, the Lady of Nithsdale and Countess Dowager of Orkney,

* Orkn. Saga Introd.   † Barry.   ‡ Nisbet.   § Balfour App. || Tudor.

with regard to the spoliation of her Nithsdale possessions. His brother-in-law, James Douglas, Earl of Avondale, afterwards seventh Earl of Douglas, was also present on that occasion *

If we had not known the extensive properties that Earl William possessed in Scotland, the high dignity to which he had been raised, and the important duties which he had been called on to perform, we should have been at a loss to assign reasons for the time he had suffered to elapse previously to the application for the investiture of his Earldom. An opportunity, however, now occurred which he embraced for that purpose, and his attempts were crowned with final success. But even before this period his interest does not seem to have been altogether neglected, since one of the articles of charge against Menzies was that he had appropriated to himself rents which belonged to his nephew, the Earl, and had refused to set the public seal to the evidence which he had brought to prove his right.†

Between his father's death and his preference of claim, doubts had arisen respecting Earl William's rights, and other claimants had, it is probable, appeared to avail themselves of that doubt. To clear up this matter, and to free himself from applications from other quarters, as well as to do justice to this celebrated personage, Eric, King of Norway, issued an order to Thomas, Bishop of Orkney, and others, to search the archives, records, and all other evidences, in order to ascertain the point in dispute. That venerable prelate joined those that were named with him to form a jury for executing the business, and after having in the most solemn manner traced his pedigree from the very first of the earls, ascertained his, Earl William's, right beyond the possibility of contradiction (1434).† One of the witnesses to this memorable document, which was executed at Kirkwall, is an Alexander Sinclair, who appends his seal thereto.† The Earl crossed over to Denmark, and King Eric having before him the report of his Royal Commissioners, granted investiture on the 12th August, 1434, on terms nearly similar to those imposed on Earl Henry I in 1379. Moreover, he was to hold for the king and his successors the castle of Kirkwall, which his grandfather Earl Henry I. had erected without royal consent. Amongst his sureties‡ were some of Scotland's most puissant nobles, viz., Archibald III, 5th Earl of Douglas, William, 2nd Earl of Angus, Henry, Bishop of Aberdeen, Robert, Bishop of Caithness; also Sir Alex Ramsay and John de St Clair, and Andrew Crichton, *Armigeri*, a Thomas Sincler, *Armiger*, also appears affixing his seal as a party to the Deed of Investiture.

Not long after this there arose a great discord betwixt the Earl of Orkney and Archibald III, 5th Earle of Douglas, the third of that name, for the sherrifship of Nithsdale, and the Baronie of Hectford, Grahamshawe, Kirktone, Roxburgh and Cavers, togither with the Wardenry of the three Marches betwixt Berwick and Whithorne, so that the Prince would not suffer the Earle of Douglas to pass to Edinburgh through his ground.§

The Dauphin of France, who had been betrothed to Margaret, the daughter of the Scottish King, had now (1434) attained his thirteenth year, and the Princess herself was ten years old. It was accordingly resolved to complete the marriage, and with this view two ambassadors, the Duc de Longueville and the Marquis de Saluses, were sent by King Charles VII. of France to the Scottish Court to escort Princess Margaret back to France, and to renew the ancient amity existing betwixt the two crowns. Immediately the King

---

* Roslyn Chartulare † Barry App ‡ Hay's Geneal § Van Bassan

commanded all to be in readiness, so that by the 20th of June, William St Claire, Earl of Orkney, Lord Admirall of Scotland, had 46 guid ships in readiness to transport the Lady Margaret and her train * The fleet which carried her to her future kingdom, where her lot was singularly wretched, was commanded by the Earl of Orkney.† The Bishop of Brechin, Sir Walter Ogilvie, the Treasurer, Sir Herbert Harris (?), Sir John Maxwell of Calderwood, Sir John Campbell of Loudoun, Sir John Wishart, and many other barons, attended in her suite They were waited on by 140 youthful squires and a guard of 1,000 men-at-arms, and the fleet consisted of three large ships and six barges. They took shipping at Dumbarton, and arrived on the 20th of June, and had a very prosperous voyage to France,* notwithstanding the hostile designs of the English Court In defiance of the truce which then subsisted between the two kingdoms, the English government determined if possible to intercept the Princess upon her passage to France, and for this purpose fitted out a large fleet, which anchored off the coast of Bretagne. The project was, however, unsuccessful. The English were drawn away from their watch by the appearance of a company of Flemish merchantmen, laden with wine from Rochelle, which they pursued and captured, but the triumph was of short duration, for almost immediately after a Spanish fleet appeared in sight, and an engagement took place, in which the English were beaten, their Flemish prizes wrested from their hands, and they themselves compelled to take to flight In the midst of these transactions the little Scottish squadron with the Dauphiness-elect and her suite safely entered the port of Rochelle and disembarked at Neville Priory, where she was received by the Archbishop of Rheims and the Bishop of Poictiers and Xaintonge The marriage was celebrated on the 6th July, 1435,* in the Cathedral church of Tours with great solemnity and much magnificence, in the presence of the King and Queen of France, the Queen of Sicily, and the nobility of both kingdoms † Van Bassan writes:—"Earl William was much esteemed of by the King, and was therfor desired to goe to France with the Lady Margaret, the King's sister, who was desired in marriage by the French King's sone, which he did with great triumph, for he was accompanied with ane hundred brave gentlemen, wherof twinty were well cloathed with cloth of gold, and had chains of gold, and black velvet foot-mantles, twinty in red cramosine velvet, with chaines of gold, and black velvet foot-mantles, twinty in white and black velvet, signifieing his armes, which is a ragged cross in a silver field; twinty cloathed with gold and blew coloured velvet, which signified the armes of Orknay, which is a ship of gold with a double tressure, and flower de luces goeing round about it, in a blew field, and twinty diversely coloured, signifieing the divers armes he had; who, when he was arrived in France, he was honoured of all men, and loved of the King, who made him Knight of the Cockle, after the ordre of France. And after the nuptial rites were celebrated, he tooke his leave of the King and the Court of France, and returned home to his own countrey, but they were all sore displeased att his departure. But when he was returned (from) same, home into Scotland, he was welcomed of the King and all his friends, and with gladness accepted of them all "

At the Christmas festival, 1436, James the First was at Perth, residing in the Dominican monastery. The Queen and her ladies were also resident therein, and James, unconscious of his fate, moved among them with his usual gallantry. One of his attendant knights, remarkable for his personal accomplishments, received from him the soubriquet of *King of Love* James was one evening playing with him at some amusing

---

Balfour's Annals † Tytler

game, when he indulged in a sportive satire on his new title "Sir King of Love," said he, "it is not long since I read a prophecy spoken some time ago, which set forth that this year a king should be slain in this land, and well ye wot, Sir Alexander, there are no kings in this realm but you and I. Let me therefore counsel you to be wary, for I let you know that under God I shall take care of my own safety sufficiently, being under your kingship, and in the service of Love."*

Shortly after the above circumstance the King was in his own apartment, conversing with some ladies and several of his friends on various subjects. A favourite squire drew near and whispered to the King, "In sooth, my Liege, I verily dreamt last night that Sir Robert Graham had slain your Majesty." It is not improbable that this was intended as a timely hint to James, but the squire was sharply reproved by the Earl of Orkney, the same nobleman who founded the chapel at Roslin, who commanded him to be silent, and to tell no such tales in the royal presence. It made some impression on James, however, who had latterly been troubled with dreams of similarly fateful import. He was put to death on the 20th February, 1437-8, notwithstanding all the efforts to further his escape resorted to by the ladies of his court. Lady Katherine Douglas thrust her arm into the bolt of the door, but the delicate arm-bone was in a moment broken by the violence of the assassins, who burst open the door and scrupled not to trample down and wound several of the fair defenders. Elisabeth Douglas having fallen into the cellar whilst attempting to extricate the King, had to remain a powerless witness to his heroic defence. The regicides all suffered the extreme punishment permitted, and the memory of the leader, Sir Robert Graham, was long remembered with abhorrence in the current rhyme :—*

> "Sir Robert Graeme,
> Who slew our King,
> God gave him shame."

The two ladies mentioned would have been nearly related to Earl William.

About the time of these events the Earl married his cousin, Elizabeth Douglas, daughter of Archibald II., Earl of Douglas, Duke of Touraine, and Marshal of France. She had previously been twice married, first to John Stewart, Earl of Buchan and Constable of France (son of the Regent Albany), who perished so gloriously at Verneuil, 16th August, 1424, in company with his father-in-law. By him she had a daughter Margaret, who married George, 2nd Lord Seton, and became progenitrix of the great families of Seton, Earl of Winton and Montgomerie, Earl of Eglinton.† The Countess Dowager of Buchan married secondly Thomas Stewart,§ styled Earl of the Garioch, a natural son of Alexander, Earl of Mar, who in 1426 obtained a charter securing the Mar succession to Sir Thomas, but the latter predeceased the Earl of Mar, who died in 1435, and on the 6th May, 1437, James the Second granted the Earldom of the Garioch to his "well-beloved cousin Elizabeth, spouse of . cousin William, Earle of Orkney and Lord Sinclere."‡

Continuing Hay "Shortly after Earl William returned from his embassy to France he married ane honourable Lady, Dame Elisabeth Douglas, Countess of Buchan, etc., spouse to the Right Hon. John Stewart, Earl of Buchan and Constable of France, who togither with the father and brother was slain in France, at the battle of Verneuil, which was the cause of her returne to Scotland ; but they stayed not long togithir, for they were separated because of consanguinity and affinity, for both this dame Elisabeth Dowglass and Giles Dowglass, mother to this William, the Orcade Prince, were the daughters of two germain brothers, and also Giles, Princess of Orknay, and Robert, the Duke of Albany, and father to this John Stewart, was nearer related ; for Egidia, mother to this Dame Gyles, was Duke Robert his sister ; yet for all this the Prince, not contented with this seperation, sent to the Pope, who dispensed therwith, and so he married her anew again into St. Mathieus, the church where they were seperated. After the which time she was holden in great reverence, both for her birth and for the estate she was in ; for she had serving her 75 gentlewomen, wherof 53 were daughters to noblemen, all cloathed in velvets and silks, with their chains of gold and other pertinents ; togither with 200 rideing gentlemen, who accompanied her in all her journeys. She had carried before her when she went to Edinburgh, if it was darke, 80 lighted torches. Her lodgeing was att the foot of the Blackfryer Wynde ; so that, in a worde, none matched her in all the countrey, save the Queen's Majesty. After the marriage of these noble persons, Prince William made all the bonds of Manred his father had, to be renued and signed, paying to every one of his Fialls according to their estate, as to Lords he gave two hundred pounds, to Barons one hundred. In his house he was royally served in gold and silver vessels, in most princely manner, for the Lord Dirltone was his Master Household, the Lord Borthwick was his Cup-bearer, and the Lord Fleming his Carver, under whom, in time of their absence, was the Laird of Drumlanrig, surnamed Stewart, the Laird of Drumelzier, surnamed Tweedie, and the Laird of Calder, surnamed Sandilands. He had his halls and his chambers richly hung with embroidered hangings ; he builded the church walls of Rosline, haveing rounds with faire chambers, and galleries theron. He builded also the fore-worke that looks to the north-east ; he builded the bridge under the castle, and sundrie office houses. In the south-east side therof, over against the chapell wall, he made plaine the rock on which the castle is builded, for the more strength therof, and he planted a very fair fruit orchard. . . . "

In 1441 Thomas, Bishop of Orkney, repaired to Flanders, in all probability for the purpose of confirming the amicable correspondence existing between Scotland and that country, and congratulating them on the cessation of foreign war and domestic dissension, but the precise object of his mission is not discoverable.* The same year died Earl James 'the Gross' of Douglas, and the ability, pride, and power of that House was revived with appalling strength and vigour in William, his son and successor, who became 8th Earl. His mother, the Lady Beatrix Sinclair, was descended from the sister of King Robert the Third, and was a daughter of the House of Sinclair, Earl of Orkney, which gave him the alliance of this northern Baron.*

Hay continues : " But Earl William's adge creeping on him made him consider how he had spent his time past, and how to spend that which was to come. Therfor, to the end he might not seem unthankful to God for the benefices he receaved from him, it came in his minde to build a house for God's service, of most curious worke, the which that it might be done with greater glory and splendor, he caused artificers to be brought from other regions and forrayne kingdomes, and caused dayly to be abundance of all kinde of workemen present, as masons, carpenters, smiths, barrow-men, and quarriers, with

* Tytler.

Reproduced by permission of J. Valentine & Sons, Dundee.

THE NAVE, ROSSLYN CHAPEL.

others; for it is remembred that for the space of thirty-four years before he never wanted great numbers of such workmen. The foundation of this rare worke he caused to be laid in the yeare of our Lord, 1446, and to the end the worke might be the more rare; first, he caused the draughts to be drawn upon Eastland boords, and made the carpenters to carve them according to the draughts theron, and then gave them for patterns to the massons that they might therby cut the like in stone; and because he thought the massones had not a convenient place to lodge in near the place where he builded this curious colledge, for the towne then stood half a mile from the place where it now stands, towitt, at Bilsdone burne, therfor he made them to build the town of Rosline, that now is extant, and gave every one of them a house, and lands answerable therunto; so that this towne, att that time, by reason of the great concourse of people that had recourse unto the Prince (for it is remembered of him that he entertained all his tenuants that were any way impoverished, and made serve all the poore that came to his gates, so that he spent yearly upon such as came to beg att his gates 120 quarters of meale), became very populous, and had in it abundance of victualls, so that it was thought to be the chiefest towne in all Lothian, except Edinburgh and Hadingtone. He rewarded the massones according to their degree, as to the master massone he gave 40 pounds yearly, and to every one of the rest 10 pounds, and accordingly did he reward the others, as the smiths and the carpenters with others. About this time Edward Saintclair of Draidon comeing with foure grayhounds and some ratches to hunt with the Prince, mett a great company of ratts, and among the rest one old blind lyard one, with a straw in his mouth led by the rest, whereat he greatly merveilled, not thinking what should follow; but within fower days after, towitt, upon the feast day of Saint Leonard, in the year of our Lord, 1447, the Princess, who tooke great delight in little dogs, caused one of the gentlewomen to goe under a bed with a lighted candle to bring forth one of them, that had young whelps, which she doeing, and not being very attentive, set fire on the bed, wherat the fire rose and burnt the bed, and then passed to the ceeling of the great chambre in which the Princess was, wherat she, with all that were in the dungeon, were compelled to fly. The Prince's Chaplain, seeing this, and remembring of all his Master's writtings, passed to the head of the dungeon where they were, and threw out fower great trunks where they were. The news of this fire comeing to the Prince his ears, through the lamentable cries of the ladys and gentlewomen, and the sight therof comeing to his view in the place where he stood, to witt, upon the Colledge Hill, he was sorry for nothing but the loss of his Charters and other writtings; but when the Chaplain, who had saved himself by comeing down the bell-rope tyed to a beam, declared how his Charters and writts were all saved, he became chearful, and went to re-comfort his Princess and the Ladys, desireing them to put away all sorrow, and rewarded his Chaplaine very richly. Yet all this stayed him not from the building of the Colledge, nether his liberality to the poor; but was more liberall to them than before,—applying the safety of his Charters and writings to God's particular Providence. Not long after this dyed the Lady Elisabeth Dowglasse, his Princess, after she had borne to the Prince one sone named William, and a daughter, to witt, Katherine, who was married to Alexander Stewart, Duke of Albany, Earle of Marche, and brother to King James the Thirde."

In 1446 Earl William was summoned by the Norwegian Rigsraad to appear at Bergen on next St. John's Day, to take the oath of allegiance to King Christopher, the successor of King Eric of Pomern,* and on the 25th April, 1448, he appears obtaining from Thomas de Tulloch, Bishop of Orkney, the patronage of St. Duthac's chapel in Kirkwall.†

In "Balfour's Annals," under date 1451, we read : William St. Clair, Earle of Orkuay, is sent this zeire to uplift the Earle of Douglas rents in Galloway and Anandaill; and although he was Lord Chanceller of Scotland, and had a reasonable armey, zet he returned without effectuating his deseing, being oppossed by the Earle of Douglass frinds and followers (the Earle himselve beinge in Italey). . . . Although the Earl of Douglas was in Italy, through the agency of his mother, Lady Beatrix, who at this time (1452) repaired to England, he continued that secret correspondence with the party of the Yorkists, which appears to have been begun by the late Earl.‡ In 1454-5 the castle of Abercorn was besieged by the Earls of Orkney and Angus, at the head of 6,000 men, as Lord Hamilton was in league with the rebellious Earl of Douglas. Upon the representation of friends Lord Hamilton passed over to the royal camp, and was committed to the custody of the Earl of Orkney, who kept him in honourable captivity in Roslyne Castle for a few days, after which he was restored to his dignity and lands. His defection was fatal to the House of Douglas.§

On the 28th August, 1455, King James the Second grants Earl William the Earldom of Caithness, nominally in compensation for his rights to the Lordship of Nithsdale and the various offices appurtenant thereto, but really in recognition of his undoubted hereditary right to that county as the heir male of Malise II. of Caithness and Orkney, by which fact his father had succeeded to Orkney in right of Isabella de Stratherne, ultimate sole heiress of Malise. In the deed he is described as "William, Earl of Orkney, Lord de Saint Clair, our Chancellor and . . . cousin."† On the 13th June, 1456, Roslin is erected into a Burgh of Barony by charter under the Privy Seal. The recital sets forth : "James, be the grace of God, King of Scottis, etc., . . . Forasmekill as we have for the zele, singular lufe, and affection, that we have till our weill bilovitt cousin and chancelar William, Earl of Orkney and of Cathness, Lord Sincler, infeft his town of Roslin, a Burgh in Barony, with Crosse and Merkat, etc." . . .‡

The same year, 1456, on the 15th November, his father-in-law, Alexander Sutherland of Dunbeath, makes his will in the presence of the Earl at Roslin Castle, and from the inventory of property attached to this testament, both of which are still extant, he was a person of great consequence.† The Earl of Orkney had married his daughter Marjory, by his wife Mariota, daughter of Donald, Lord of the Isles and Earl of Ross. As a curious instance of the customs of those times, it is recorded that when Alexander, Lord of the Isles and Earl of Ross, was dining in Edinburgh with the Earl of Orkney, the latter asked, "What light was wont to be burned in his presence?" McDonald turned about, and seeing Lauchlan MacLean behind him, desired the Earl to enquire at the man standing. MacLean said, "There was no other light but wax burned before MacDonald."‖

An incident now (1456) occurred which drew the attention of the Norwegian suzerain to the Orkneys. Biorn, son of Thorleif,¶ the Lieutenant of Iceland, having been driven by a storm into a harbour in the Orkneys, had been seized by the Scottish

---

* Orkn. Saga.　† Hay.　‡ Tytler.　§ Scottish Wars.

Hist. of the MacDonalds, MS. Gregory Collection, Col. Rob. All. 306.

¶ Thorleif's father (or grandfather) Biorn, also Govr. of Iceland, was slain by the English in 1467.

authorities, contrary to the faith of treaties, and cast with his wife and attendants into prison. Christian, the Danish King of Norway, remonstrated thereupon, and also on account of the Annual of Norway due for the Western Isles and the Kingdom of Man by virtue of the treaty concluded between James the First and Eric, King of Norway.*

King James the Second dying in 1460, the estaits elected 6 Governours for the government of the realme during the young king's minority (James the Third), viz., the Bis. of Glasgow and Dunkelden, Lord Chanceler, the Earle of Orknay, with the Lords Grhame and Boyde.† This year also—1460—the king's commissioners in Kirkwall certify to King Christian I. that John of Ross, Lord of the Isles, has for a long time most cruelly endeavoured to depopulate the Islands of Orkney and Shetland by burning the dwellings and slaying the inhabitants, and that in these circumstances Lord William St. Clair, the Earl of Orkney and Caithness, had been prevented from coming to the king.‡ On the 28th June, 1461, Bishop William of Orkney writes to the king from Kirkwall excusing the earl for not having come to take the oath of allegiance, because in the month of June of that year he had been appointed one of the regents of the Kingdom of Scotland on account of the tender years of the Prince (King James III.), and therefore was personally resident in Scotland. The Bishop also repeats the complaint against John of Ross, Lord of the Isles, and the bands of his Islesmen, Irish, and Scots from the woods "who came in great multitudes in the month of June with their ships and fleets in battle array, wasting the lands, plundering the farms, destroying habitations and putting the inhabitants to the sword, without regard to age or sex." Tradition still points in several parts of the Islands to "the Lewismen's graves," probably those of the invaders who were killed in their plundering expeditions through the Isles.‡

There is a record preserved at Kirkwall of the set of the threepenny lands of Stanbuster, in the parish of St. Andrew's, executed by Bishop Thomas on the 12th July, 1455, and confirmed by his successor in 1465. Bishop Thomas must have died before 28th June, 1461, as from the foregoing letter we find his successor in office on that date. William (VI.) de Tulloch was the last bishop during the overlordship of Norway, and tendered his oath of allegiance in 1462.‡ His conduct, we learn, was the initial cause of those circumstances which resulted in the transference of Orkney from Norway to Scotland.

Quoting Tytler, under date 1466 : An event which soon after occurred in Orkney had the effect of renewing the intercourse between the Courts of Scotland and Denmark, although the auspices under which it was resumed were at first rather hostile than friendly. Tulloch, Bishop of Orkney, a Scotsman, and a prelate of high accomplishments and great suavity of manner, enjoyed the esteem of Christiern of Norway and Denmark, and appears to have been entrusted by this northern potentate with a considerable share in the government of those islands, at that time the property of the Norwegian Crown. In some contention or feud between the Bishop and the Earl of Orkney, a baron [of a violent character and] great power, the prelate had been seized and shut up in prison by a son§ of Orkney, who showed no disposition to interfere for his liberation. Upon this Christiern directed letters to the King of Scotland, in which, whilst professing his earnest wishes that the two kingdoms should continue to preserve the most friendly relations to each other, he remonstrated against the treatment of the

---

* Tytler.   † Balfour.   ‡ Orkn. Saga.
§ The Master of Orkney thus occasioning the loss of Orkney, hence his disinherison.

Bishop, requested the King's interference to procure his liberty, and intimated his resolution not to permit the Earl of Orkney to oppress the liege subjects of Norway.

So intent was Christiern upon this matter that additional letters were soon after transmitted to the Scottish King, in which, with the design of expediting his deliberations, a demand was made for the payment of all arrears due by Scotland to Norway, and reiterating his request not only for the liberation of the Bishop, but for the restoration to the royal favour of Sir John Ross of Halkett, the same who had distinguished himself in the famous combat between three warriors of Burgundy and three champions of Scotland. These representations had the desired effect. The Bishop of Orkney appears to have been restored to liberty, and Ross was recalled from banishment and admitted to favour. . . . On the failure of the Norse jarls in the middle of the fourteenth century the Earldom of Orkney had passed by marriage into the ancient and noble House of St. Clair, who received their investiture from the monarch of Norway, and rendered oath of allegiance to that Crown.

On the 8th September, 1468, a contract of marriage was signed between James III. of Scotland and Margaret, daughter of King Christian of Norway, Sweden, and Denmark, by which after discharging the arrears of tribute, styled the Annual of Norway, due by Scotland for Man and the Hebudes, King Christian engaged to pay a dowry of 60,000 florins with his daughter, stipulating for certain jointure lands (including the palace of Linlithgow and the castle of Doune) and her terce of the royal possessions in Scotland, if left a widow. Of the dowry 10,000 florins were to be paid before the departure of the Princess, and the Islands of Orkney were pledged for the balance of 50,000 florins, to be held by the Crown of Scotland until Christian or his successors, Kings of Norway, should redeem them by payment of that sum. Only 2,000 of the 10,000 florins were paid, and Zetland was impignorated for the balance of 8,000 florins under the same conditions (20th May, 1469), and both groups were thus mortgaged *sub firma hypotheca et pignore* for 58,000 florins of the Rhine of 100 pence each, or about £24,166 13s. 4d. sterling. Such was the important transaction on which Britain founds her possession of the Isles, or, as they were generally styled, the Countries of Orkney and Zetland. The transaction was only an Impignoration such as Danish necessities had been frequently forced to make of possessions and territories of which no permanent cession could have been intended, such as Funen, Slesvig, and, more than once, the City and Castle of Copenhagen. Even while creating a new and temporary right for Scotland, it did not extinguish the reversionary claims or present interest of Norway; for that power is found making valid grants and decrees—1485-1500—and the Scots Parliament expressly recognised the ancient native laws in the Islands (1567) a century after the Impignoration. The Plenipotentiaries of Europe assembled at Breda in 1668 attested that the Right of Redemption was unprescribed and imprescribable. Whether this right be still vested in Denmark, or transferred to Sweden with the Norwegian Crown, are questions of the Law of Nations, decided for the present by British preponderancy of metal.*

William Saint Clair, the last of the Orkneyan Jarls, had many objects to gain in the transfer of the Sovereignty of the Islands. More refined and less ignorant than the contemporary herd of nobles, who suspected his studies of subjects unearthly and unholy, he could appreciate, even with some pride, the cloudy romance of his ancestral sagas; but a foreigner by descent if not by birth, he had few sympathies with the Islanders. He

* Balfour's Memorial.

was the most liberal patron of Scottish literature and art in his day. His efforts to consolidate his power and increase his estates had offended the King, estranged the Odallers, and embroiled him with the Bishop and the Lawman, his family partialities had awakened bitter feud between him and his eldest son, and as the vassal and high dignitary of two kings, ruling a province of the one, dangerously near the coast of the other, he might easily become an object of suspicion or umbrage to either or both. Indeed, clouds had already arisen between the Scottish Earl and his Norwegian suzerain, and the substantial splendour of the dignities, titles, lands, and pensions of his Scottish connection outshone the shadowy jurisdictions and waning revenues of his ancient Jarldom. The Impignoration released him from an irksome and unsafe position, enabled him to enhance his Scottish influence, to aggrandize a favourite son by disinheriting an unloved heir of his Odal birthright, and to gratify at once his ambition, affection, and hatred. With the same worldly wisdom which led him to recover at the first favourable opportunity possession of Caithness, in quittance of his claims on Nithsdale, he accepted in 1471, on the 12th May as evidenced by grant of James III, and with the full consent of the King of Norway, the castle and lands of Ravenscraig in Fife, in exchange for his rights to the Earldom of Orkney. On the 20th September following he received a discharge or quittance from the same monarch, James, in respect of any obligations existing with regard to Orkney *

William Tulloch, the Bishop of Orkney, was a Norwegian prelate, but a Scottish priest, and if he had any doubts of transferring the spiritual allegiance of his diocese from Drontheim to St Andrew's, they were speedily relieved by his appointment as Confessor to the Queen, and removed by a favourable Tack (27th August, 1472) of the newly acquired demesne of the Scottish Crown. Indeed, the change was almost essential to his safety, for his frauds and rapacity had provoked the Earl to seize and imprison him, and he owed his liberty only to the express solicitation of the Kings of Denmark and Scotland, with both of whom he had the address to make a merit of his sufferings as a martyrdom for his devotion to their incompatible interests. The warm commendations of Christian were so ably seconded by the Bishop's services to James that the Queen's Confessor became successively Lord Privy Seal, Ambassador to England, and Bishop of Moray *

King Christian addressed a letter to the Communities of Orknay and Zetland on the 28th May, 1469, desiring them to pay obedience and skatt to the King of Scots till redeemed by the King of Norway,† in sequence to which a bull of Pope Sixtus IV, dated at the Vatican 17th August, 1472, placed the See of the Orkneys under the metropolitan Bishop of St Andrew's †

On the 9th September, 1476, Earl William assigns to Sir Oliver Sinclere, knight, his son by his spouse Lady Marjory of Sutherland, and his heirs male, the Baronies of Roslin and Herbertshire, remainder to his brother-german William and his heirs male, remainder to the heirs male of the Earl and Marjory Sutherland ; to which charter are appended the seals of "our lovitt cousings, Sir James of Ledale of Halkerstone, Knight, and Mastre George Carmichael, Thresaurer of Glasgw for the mair sekurnes." In the same year Earl William resigned the Earldom of Caithness, and thereupon a charter was issued by James the Third to his son William of the second marriage ‡

Balfour's Memorial   Orkn Saga   , Hay

In 1478, by order of Parliament, William, Earle of Cathnes, is decerned to refound to the brugh of Innerkeithen, the pettie customis of the brugh of Dysart, intromitted with by him for 17 years. This order was made by Parliament in 1478, so it is clear he only intromitted with those customs 7 years. Yet this requires examen, for though he gets Ravensheugh near unto Dysart in 1471, it is not known when he got Dysart itself.*

Earl William of Orkney died before 3rd July, 1480, when he is referred to as the quondam "per pestiferum morbum, qui a vulgaribus le quhew discebatur. He was a man of rare parts, haveing in him a minde of most noble composition, a perceing witt, fitt for managing great affairs, he was famous not only for moral vertue and piety, but also for military discipline, in high favour with his Prince, and raised to the greatest dignities that in those times a subject had. He was averse from putting criminals to the rack, the tortures wherof make many ane innocent person confess himself guilty, and then with seeming justice be executed, or if he prove so stoute as in torment to deny the facts, yet he comes off with disjoynted bones and such weakness as renders himself and his life a burthen ever after."* It is said he was a knight of the Cockle. Hay narrates "I have seen at his mantle, on his tombe, a medale which appeared to represent Saint Michael, yet being a little defaced I can't positively certifie the business. It is certain he was in great favour with Lewis XI. of France, who established those Knights of Saint Michael att Amboise in 1469." Sir James Balfour in his Peerage tells us Earl William was Knight of the several orders of the Thistle, St. Michael, and of the Golden Fleece, as he has seen the same set forth in a charter.

He frequently appears in Scottish record works. At Dundee in 1435 he becomes responsible for one Nicholas Ayncroft, and the same year there is remission of fines of his men of Dysart for forestalling the burgh of Inverkeithing. In 1448 William, Earl of Orkney, and others, made reprisals on the English in two raids, burning Alnwick and Warkworth, and in 1449 he receives remission of customs on his hides. His first wife died in or before 1452, when the lands of Coule and lands in the Earldom of Moray fall in the king's hands by reason of the death of the Countess of Buchan, and in 1456 the Earl of Orkney's terce of Mar is let to Sir Alex. Seton of Gordon for an agreed price, in consequence of the non-payment of which—40 demys of gold—it was forcibly taken from William Seton of Echt, brother-german of Sir Alex., by William Sinclare on behalf of the Earl of Orkney by reason of rights of his quondam spouse. On the 16th April, 1452, he gets Dysart relieved of duty on salt. On the 1st July, 1454, 7th July and 28th August, 1455, entries are noted, "Coram magnifico et prepotente domino Willelmo comite Orcadie domino de Sancto-claro et cancellario Scocie"; in 1455 "white spurs" are "the reddendo of Herbertshire," while in 1456 the castleward of his baronies of Roslin, Cousland, and Pentland is assessed at £4, and he is entered as having transported the "great bombard" to Threave and back. In 1460 there is reference to his expenses when the king went to Aberdeen; and in 1468 and on 20th November, 1469, the Erle of Orknay is one of the Barons of Parliament. In 1468 Earl William grants to Sir James Creighton of Carnes a charter of Cairniehill, to be holden blench for a penny †

By his first wife, Elizabeth Douglas, Countess-Dowager of Buchan and of the Garioch (dead in 1452) the Earl had

I. WILLIAM *Prodigus*, 'the Waster,' Master of Orkney and Caithness, to whom during his life

---

* W. de Scō Claro dno. de Dyserth is a witness in 34 David II. 1364   H. iv.

he had given the Barony of Newburgh in Aberdeenshire. This William of Newburgh was ancestor to the Lords Sinclair and they of Warsetter, Saba, &c , &c , whom see.

1 KATHERINE, married to Alex , Earl of March, Duke of Albany, second son of King James II , but sentence annulling the marriage between the parties was pronounced by the official of Lothian (2nd March, 1477-8) on account of propinquity of blood. They had one son Alex., who married Margaret, daughter of the Lord Crichton, and had a daughter Margaret, married to David, Lord Drummond * In a parliament held in presence of his younger brother John, the Governor, Alex of Albany, affirmed his claim to the succession failing James V , yet notwithstanding his challenge, being more fit for a cowl, gave over all title he had in his brother's favor, whereupon to deprive him ever hereafter of lawful succession, they turned him into a priest He had first the priory of Whitherne in Galloway , afterwards the abbey of Inchaffray , then that of Scone , was consecrated bishop of Murray 1527, and dying in 1534 was buried at Scone

By his second wife, Marjory Sutherland, Earl William had several sons and daughters

2 ELEANOR, m John Stewart, Earl of Athole, half-brother of James III (mentioned 1480)
3 ELISABETH, wife of Sir John Houston, of Houston
4. MARGARET, m Sir David Boswell of Balmuto, styled of Glasmouth in a record 16th February, 1492-3 (Ex Rolls)
5 EUPHEMIA.
6 MARJORIE, m Andrew Leslie, Master of Rothes
7 MARIETTA
II SIR OLIVER, founder of the cadet branch of the St Clairs of Roslyn
III WILLIAM II , founder of the cadet line of Sinclairs, Earls of Caithness
IV. JOHN, Canon of Glasgow, 3rd July, 1480 , Bishop-nominate of Caithness for 24 years John Sutherland, slain at Wick, 1569, was grandson to his daughter Katherine †
V. SIR DAVID of Swynbrocht, knight, Foud of Shetland, &c , who left issue.
VI ALEXANDER, mentioned 1498 and 1506
VII GEORGE, mentioned 1498
VIII. ROBERT, mentioned 1498 and 1504 On the 27th February, 1506-7, he receives a royal grant of house and land in Edinburgh with annuity
IX ARTHUR, mentioned 1498 and 1504

The seniority of the sons of the second marriage though undetermined, is probably in accordance with the order here given

---

* Nisbet † Hist of Caithness , notes

CHAPTER IV.

PERIOD OF POST-COMITIAL RULE

1471—1567.

LEADING DATES

1485	Henry St Clair obtains tack
1486	First Burghal Charter of Kirkwall
1488-9	Henry St Clair recogn as Lord Saint Clair and "Chieff of yat blude"
	Henry St Clair receives renewal of lease for 13 years
1490	Bishopric Charter of Regality
[1491]	Sir David Synclar, Foud of Zetland
1501	Lord St Clair obtains 19 years' tack, rentals compiled.
1502	Edward Sinclair defeats English raiders.
1513	Lord Sinclair falls at Flodden, Lady Margaret becomes Baroness-Regent.
	Sir Wm Sinclair of Warsetter storms Noltland Castle
1515	James Sinclair elected Governor of Kirkwall Castle
1520	Lady Sinclair secures renewal for 19 years
1528	Battle of Summerdale, defeat of Caithness Invaders.
1536	King James the Fifth visits Kirkwall
1536	Eduerd Synclar of Stroym, Fold of Zetland
1539	Respite to leading Islesmen
1540	Oliver Sinclair obtains tack till 1548
1544	Erection of Cathedral Chapter.
1546	Olave Sinclayr, Heyd Fold of Zetland
1560	The Sinclairs oppose reforms by Bishop Bothwell
1567	James Hepburn, Earl of Bothwell, Duke of Orkney.

WHEN Earl Wm. St Clair, the last of the Orcadian Jarls, surrendered in 1471 all his rights to and jurisdiction within the Earldom of Orkney, he received in exchange from James III. the castle and lands of Ravenscraig in Fife, and a Scottish Act of Parliament was passed on the 20th February of the same year annexing to the Scottish Crown "the Erldome of Orkney and Lordship of Schetland, nocht to be gevin away in time to come to na persain or persainis excep alenarily to ane of the King's sonnis of lauchful bed" This was followed by a bull of Pope Sixtus IV., dated at the Vatican, 17th August, 1472, placing the See of the Orkneys under the metropolitan of St. Andrew's.*

The revenues of the Islands were then farmed out—first to the Bishops of Orkney, and afterwards to Henry, Lord St Clair, and various members of his house The first known grant by the King of Scotland was in 1474—a lease for two years to Wm Tulloch, Bishop of Orkney—the Crown rent consisting of £120 money, 50 chalders of bear at 8 merks per chalder, and 120 salt marts at a mark each, the total £466 13s 4d. Scots. The lease was renewed for three years more, with an abatement on the bear, viz., at only five merks the chalder, the total amount being £366 13s. 4d.† On the translation of Bishop Tulloch to

* Orkn Saga Introd † Peterkin's Notes

the See of Moray in 1478, a new lease issued to his Orcadian successor Andrew—the presentee of John of Denmark to the Bishopric*—the keeping of the castle of Kirkwall being included in the lease, and the same rent being stipulated, *ut in rentali nostro continetur*.† The Exch. Rolls, 1480, note Andrew, Bp. of Orkney, and Robert Yorkstoun, his factor; and again on 21st June, 1484, Andrew, Bp. of Orkney, arrendatarii dominorum Orchadie et Schetland per his factors John Sinclare and Wm. Leslie. The entry also refers to Henry Sinclare and to Peter Hakket and Alex. Lesk *re* the ferms of Sanday. Bishop Andrew received in 1484 an annuity from John Sinclair, and another in 1485 from Henry Sinclair,‡ in which latter year the Archbishop of St. Andrew's is delegated Ambassador to "Or. haly fadr. ye Paip," with instructions that he shall among other things, "impetrait and desir of or. haly fadr. a confirmacoun of ye convencons confederaconus and bands made betwixt or. Sovrne Lord and ye King of Denmark that last decessit of ye donacoun and impignoracoun of ye landes of Orknay and Scheteland and of ppetuale exonacoun Reunussacoun and discharge of ye contribucoun of ye Ilis after ye forme of ye said convencouns."§ Following the Impetration the Scottish Crown proceeded to extend over the lands of the Bishop and Odallers a new claim—that of Superiority, the first advance to which bore the harmless form of a courteous recognition of the Bishop's rights by his new Sovereign, in a Charter of Regality, 10th October, 1490. One of the rights conveyed by this instrument is the *merchetis mulierum!* The assumption of a concurrent sanction of the Norwegian presentee of the Kirklands (1491-2) was followed by the sole presentation—under Papal Sanction—of a Commendator and Successor to the Bishop (8th April, 1498), and shortly afterward by the defiant appointment of an Archdean of Zetland, with a protest against "the temerity and presumption" of the Danish presentee (8th January, 1501-2). The Charter of Regality was confirmed in 1501, and in the civil feuds which long shook the Norwegian throne, the Scottish Patronage of the See of Orkney was thenceforth undisputed.* The same protecting care was accorded to the ancient capital of the Jarldom, which in 1486 was made a royal burgh.‖

Although Earl William surrendered the comitial title and jurisdictions, he still retained large estates throughout all the Isles, and his immediate descendants and collateral members of the Sinclair family are found figuring in the most important events in the insular annals for two centuries thereafter, during the first seventy-five years of which the government of the Isles was almost solely in their hands. In fact, summing up the history of the period, it may be said to be a record of the doings of the Sinclairs, and of transactions connected with the Bishopric. Earl William had died before the 9th February, 1481, when there is an agreement entered into between his disinherited heir, Wm. St. Clair, *Prodigus* 'the Waster,' Master of Orkney, and Sir Oliver St. Clair of Roslin, which refers to their father, the Earl, as being dead:¶ and from the Rentals of 1502-3 it appears that in that year Sir Robert Sutherland, Sir John Sinclair, and others entered into use and adverse occupation of lands in Orkney to the prejudice of the heir-of-line male Henry Sinclair—elder son of the disinherited Master—who obtained a tack of the Isles in 1485,* and the same year granted an annuity to the Bishop.‡

On the 26th January, 1488-9, the Scottish Parliament passed an Act recognising Henry Lord Saintclair, as "Chieff of yat blude," and willing "yarfor that he be callit

---

* Balfour's Memorial. † Peterkin's Notes. ‡ Reg. Privy Seal. § Mackenzie's Grievances.
‖ Kirkwall Records. ¶ Hay Introd.

Lord Saintclair in tyme to cum." Soon after the accession of James IV., a lease of the ancient Earldom of Orkney and Hjaltland was granted 28th May, 1489, to Henry Lord Sinclair. The rent was continued at the same rate as in the Bishop's leases, viz., £366 13s. 4d. Scots, as some atonement, perhaps, for the ill-requited devotedness of his grandfather to the former King.* The tack was granted for 13 years "terris et Dominiis Orchadiæ et Shetland, cum suis pertinentiis," etc.; and besides a lease of the castle of Kirkwall and fortalices, there is also a grant of *jurisdiction* for the same period, "Officiis Justiciariæ Folderiæ et Baliatus dictarum terrarum et dominiorum." On the same date there is an assedation and grant consisting of three instruments in precisely similar terms to his brother-in-law Patrick, Earl of Bothwell. After the irresponsible episcopal rule, the appointment of Henry Lord Sinclair as Captain-General and Governor of the Islands, and the recognition of Sir David Sinclair as the Norse representative and Foud of Hjaltland (1491), gave hope of better times, for after the tyranny of strangers the Orkneyans were prepared to rejoice in the return of kindred rulers, and Sir David was the son and Lord Henry the grandson of their last Earl William. With the tastes and accomplishments, and some of the vices of their time, the Sinclairs were popular in the Islands and favourites in the Courts of Denmark and Scotland. They were in the main just, humane, and generous; they exposed unsparingly the rapacity and frauds of their episcopal predecessors, relaxed their intolerable imposts upon some of the districts, redressed much individual injustice, and liberally relieved the impoverished population.†

There are still a few instances of the connection with Norway. In 1485 the Lawman of Bergen reverses a sale of lands in Hieltland as being contrary to law. His decree is made in convention with the Law-man, Council-men, and Lagrett-man in Hieltland.‡ Sir David Sinclair, Fond of Hjaltland, was Captain of the Palace Guard at Bergen. In 1498 he acquired from his brothers and sisters a charter of their interests in the estate of Swynbrocht, and the pertinents, etc.* As all their seals are stated to be appended entire, if extant this charter will be of value in determining the seniority of the sons of Earl William.

On the first May, 1501, the lease to Lord Sinclair, with the keeping of the castle of Kirkwall, and the jurisdictions of justiciarie, fouderie, and bailliary, was renewed for 19 years, an addition being made of hams "for the King's use" to the rental, which was thereby extended to £433 6s. 8d.* On the 4th June, 1498, by Royal instrument, St. Magnus' Cathedral secured a grant of the Isle of Burray; and the Bishopric Charter of Regality was confirmed in 1501; and a letter directed by James IV. to Lord Sinclair, then Captain-General and Governor of the Isles, charged him "to stop no Law-man in the supplying of the said reverend father, his servants and officers, in the ministration of justice."‡ And the next year after there is another letter to the same effect, directed "to the Lawman of Orknay."‡

After confirmation of his lease, Lord Sinclair had Rentals prepared in 1502–4 showing the charges payable by all occupiers and owners of land. In this census many Sinclairs appear enumerated as in possession of estates. They are probably not of descent from the last Earl, but from his predecessors, collaterals to whom appear in Orkney at an early date, *e.g.:* In 1364 Thos. de St. Clair, *ballivus* for the King of Norway, and Alexander de St. Clair, his son, attest an instrument at Kirkwall; in 1391 Richard de St. Clair is a witness; in 1418 John St. Clair, brother of Earl Henry II., is

---

* Peterkin's Notes. † Balfour's Memorial ‡ Mackenzie's Grievances.

Foud of Hjaltland ; in 1426 Thomas Sincler is opposed to the malpractices of Sir David Menzies ; in 1434 John and Thos St Clair, *armigeri*, are in Denmark with Earl William, and append their seals to his document of Installation ; [in 1446] Alex. Sinclare sets his seal to the Diploma, while in 1437 William and Edwd. de Sco Claro, *armigeri*, attest a precept of infeftment. The last William is perhaps to be identified as the son of John St Clair, Foud of Hjaltland, who served the Emperor Henry in the Holy Wars. This digression may help to account for the number of Sinclairs presently passing under review other than the direct descendants of Earl William David Sinclair, a prudent and discreet man, resident at Kirkwall, on account of the cordial affection he bears to her, conveys his land and dwelling-house to his wife Sonneta and their children, reserving, however, the life use of same to himself. Dated at the said residence in Kirkwall 11th September, 1491 In Lord Sinclair's rental his brother Sir William holds nearly all Sanday and Westray ; a Sir John Sinclair (perhaps either Sir John of Dryden—'the Queen's knicht '—or the Bishop-nominate of Caithness) has lands in North and South Sandvik ; Gilbert and Richeart Sinclair in South Ronaldsa ; while in Stromness, Magnus Sinclair has the Bu of Karstane, Alex Sinclair has Stanagar in Innerstromness, David Sinclair has Mydhous there, and his son William has also a property in Innerstromness while James Sinclair has land in Utterstromness * In the "Skat of Zetland," a contemporaneous compilation, Henrie Sincler is entered for the lands of Skatnes and Burrowland, and Sande Sincler for Schevsbrocht

Orkney was then in capable hands, with Lord Henry as Capt.-General and Governor of the Isles, Sir David, Foud of Hjaltland and Captain of the Palace Guard of Bergen, and Edward Sinclair defeating the English raiders at Papdale, St Ola's, slaying their leader Sir John Elder, 13th August, 1502.† It was probably by the family influence that an act of the Scottish parliament in 1503 to annul all foreign laws within the realm was so altered as to spare the native laws of Orkney and Hjaltland The act "as originally proponit and red" stands as it is here copied · "Item yt all our Sovrane Lords lieges "beand undr. his obesance & i spe'ale all ye Ilis [bat wt in Orknay, Scheteland & ye "Ilis & oyr places]§ be reulit be or Sovrane Lords awne lawis & ye common lawis of ye "Realme & be nai oyr lawis "—Fol Stat ii 244 Among the acts "advisit and concludit," it appears in these terms · "Item It is statute and ordanit that all or. "Sovrane Lorde's lieges beand undr his obeysance and in speciale ye Ilis be Reulit be "or. Sovrane Lorde's awne lawis and ye comon lawis of ye Realme And be nai oyr. "lawis "—Fol. Stat ii p 252 Thus, as originally framed, the bill had reference to Orkney, Shetland, and the Isles, but was passed in an amended form having application to the last only The Isles here meant are the Hebudes ‡

Sir David Sinclair of Swynbrocht being "seik in bodye, nevir the less hail in mynd," executed his Testament at Tingwall, Shetland, on the 9th of July, 1506. Directing his body to be buried in St Magnus' Kirk at Tyngwall, and praying James IV. to protect his testamentary disposition, he proceeds to make numerous bequests which afford an insight into the conditions of the time He leaves to each of his sons 100 merks of land, and to each daughter 50 merks , to my Lorde Sincler the Zetland pension for the current year, and such lands as the testator possessed there after the death of his father the Earl, also his best silver stope (tankard) and his ship 'callit the "Carvel" wyth hir

---

* Peterkin's Rentals   † Jo Ben   ‡ Mackenzie's Grievances
§ These bracketed words are ruled out in the original copy

pertinentis,' etc. There are bequests to Ladye Sincler ; to the son and heir of Henre Lord Synclar ; to Sir William Sincler, Earle of Caithtness, he demises his innes in Edinbrucht ; to Sir William Sincler the Knycht [of Warsettir], valuable portions of his wardrobe ; to "Sande Sincler my brother, some 6 ells of green cloth ; to my sister dwelling in Orknay, all my gudis that ar in Pappay and Housbe ; to Magnus Sincler, my blew doublet set with precious stones and my golden chain which I wear daily ; to James Sincler, capitane for the tym in Dingvell, al my geir that is in Ross ; to Sir Magnus Harrode, twa nobillis, and the Buk of Gud Maneris ; to the Provest of Byrrone ' my signet' ; to the puir folk that come out of Orkney wyth me I leif thame thar awne land or ellis also gude''; his golden chain or collar which the King of Denmark gave him was left to St. George's altar at Roeskilde, the ancient Danish capital. Bequests are also made to the Cathedral Kyrk of Orknaye ; to Sanct Magnus Kyrk in Tyngvell ; and to the Corss Kyrk in Dynrossness ; with ships, lands, cattle, &c., &c., to various persons of names now well known in both archipelagoes. Magnus Sincler, Jhone Mude, &c., attest the execution. Sir David Sinclair died in July or August, 1507. A notarial transcript was made in 1525, at which time the Will doubtless came into effect. His vessel, called the "Carvel," is no doubt the "Yellow Carvel" of Scottish records, and would have proved useful to Lord Henry, who in 1512 was apparently Lord High Admiral, having command of the "Great Michael," the Scottish flagship. Lord Sinclair fell at Flodden the following year (9th September, 1513), and as his son was in minority, Lady Margaret became Baroness-Regent and ruler of the Isles, in which capacity she soon came into conflict with her brother-in-law, Sir William Sinclair of Warsetter, his family and near kinsmen.

NOLTLAND CASTLE.

From a notarial protocol in the possession of Lord Sinclair, there is preserved to us a Decree of the Lawman of Orkney and Shetland and his Council, affirming a sale of land as being according to Insular law. The Decree is dated at Kirkwall in June, 1514, and to this 'Matter of Heritage' Sir Wm. Sinclair of Warsetter is a party to the record—ane nobill and potent man—who notwithstanding has to submit to the law of the land.* Also in another decree *anno* 1519, the High Foud or Lagman—for so the chief judge was called—in order to give a sacred and venerable authority to his sentence, confirms it "be the fayth of the law-buik," as now-a-days men confirm their testimony by the faith of the Holy Gospels * It was about this time that Sir Wm Sinclair of Warsetter took Noltland Castle by storm, but restored it to Dr Edward Stewart, the Bishop who had succeeded to the prelacy in 1511 In "Theiner's Vetera Monumenta" this appears under date 13th December, 1523, "Dux Albaniæ regni Scotiæ gubernator a pontifice petit, ut Joannem Beynstoun, Eduardo epo Orchadensi eius fratri in coadiutorem concedat." Bishop Stewart was not only of illustrious birth, but of an excellent character † He enlarged the cathedral by adding the three first pointed piers and arches at the east end, and the fine east window, which is early middle pointed, of four unfoliated lights, in two divisions, its head filled with a rose of twelve leaves ‡ His arms are amongst the heraldic decorations on the ceiling of the Cathedral Church of St Machar, Aberdeen, and also ornament St Magnus' Cathedral—Or, a fess checky azure and argent within a double tressure flowered counter flowered § He had for a successor in the episcopal dignity Thomas, Bishop of Orkney, whose only action of note was the donation which he made for maintaining the choristers in the Cathedral †

As early as 1515 ‖ the Islanders elected as their leader and virtual Governor, James Sinclair, a natural son of Sir Wm. Sinclair of Warsetter, Lord Henry's brother, and for a few years all went well. The Baroness-Regent in 1520 got the lease extended for 19 more years at the same rent,¶ but now fell in troublous times. The Rents were withheld for three years (1523-5) on the plea of a general devastation by the English fleet in Orkney and Zetland , her son, Lord William, was forced to surrender her castle of Kirkwall, and fled to Caithness, 1528 The year following, Lord William, in alliance with his cousin John Sinclair, Earl of Caithness, and supported by the sanction of the King's Letter of Four Forms,‖ mustered a very considerable military force and embarked for the Isles, sanguine of victory However, James Sinclair, the Governor, rallying the Islesmen for a patriotic effort, encountered the invaders on the confines of the parish of Stennis, routed them completely in the Vale of Summerdale, slew the Earl with 500 of his followers, took prisoner Lord Sinclair, beheaded Nicol Hall the Lawman, and took forcible possession of the Islands.‖ There existed a very bitter feeling of animosity between the Islanders and the Scottish invaders, which receives illustration from a complaint of William Lord Sinclair that Sir James had been guilty of excessive cruelty. Previous to the fight at Summerdale he slew several of his lordship's friends and attendants in the castle of Kirkwall , and a week or two after the battle, among other atrocities, he put to death in cold blood thirty men who had fled for sanctuary to the Cathedral of St Magnus and other places of worship in the country. It is stated in the complaint that he dragged them by force out of the church, stript them naked, and then killed them, "in his contemption of God and halikirk, and breaking of the privilege of the Girth "[1] It is difficult to reconcile the royal policy with reference to this transaction. King James had sanctioned the invasion, and on the defeat of the Scottish Sinclairs he continued to assert his dignity by renewing Lady Sinclair's rights, and by signing

---

* Mackenzie's Grievances   † Barry   ‡ Clouston's Guide   § Catalogue Heraldic Exhbn., Edin
‖ Balfour's Memorial   ¶ Peterkin's Notes.   [1] Calder

an ineffective Few Charter to his illegitimate brother James, Earl of Moray (1530-1); yet he next proceeds to give but one more feudal Grant, and that was to the victorious Governor (1535), whom he knighted and rewarded with lands and legitimation.* Sir James had powerful influence at Court. By his marriage to Lady Barbara Stewart, sister of Henry, Lord Methven (who had married Margaret Tudor, the King's mother), he became connected closely with the royal families of Scotland and England. Relying on these influences, he solicited and secured a grant of the islands of Sanday and Eday, representing them, it is said, as being infertile holms or trivial islets, fit only for domestic pasturing. His grant of the Islands contained every feudal right, and was the first infraction of Odal succession by a clause of single primogeniture.* In 1536 or 1537 this valorous knight fell by accident into the sea and was drowned, leaving behind him the reputation of a brave man, emulous of nothing so much as the freedom and independence of his country.‡ It is otherwise stated that being threatened with the royal displeasure on the discovery of his imposture, he cast himself over a precipitous rock in Deerness, called the Gloup of Linkness, and perished. Jo Ben's account confirms the parochial locality, and adds that he had lost his reason. At Stirling, on the 18th April, 1539, a letter issued under the Privy Seal to "Barbara Stewart, relict of umquhile James Sinclair, of Sanday, knight, her airis and assignees, of the gift of all guides, moveable and immoveable, etc., which pertained to the said umquhile James, and now pertain to our sovereign lord be reason of escheat, because the said umquhile James wilfully slew himself."§ Lady Barbara afterwards married McLeod, the Breve of Lewis; and Margaret, her daughter by Sir James, married Magnus Halcro.

An interesting incident in the Isles was the visitation of Sir John Clare, Admiral of the English fleet, who landed a body of soldiery to destroy the places of strength, but a hurricane suddenly arising divided his forces, and the Orcadians put nearly all to the sword. This happened on the 31st August, 1538.

A memorable event occurred about this time—the visit of James V. to the Isles. In 1536 he embarked from the Forth in a fleet consisting of five gallant vessels, attended by Lindsay, then the most skilful navigator in the Scottish seas. Having reached Orkney, the royal squadron moored in the Bay of Kirkwall; and although the House of Stuart and the family now on the throne of Great Britain derive their claims by descent from Rögnvald the Mighty, Jarl of Orkney, King James V. is the only monarch, Scottish or British, who has ever touched the soil of these Islands since the Scottish impignoration.|| During his visit he confirmed the Burghal Charter of Kirkwall, 8th February, 1536, and is said to have held a Thing in the very ancient tenement still dignified as the Parliament Close.* While in the burgh he was hospitably entertained by Bishop Maxwell in the modern episcopal palace. Robert Maxwell had succeeded Dr. Stewart in 1525. He ornamented the cathedral interior with stalls in the quire, which had curious carvings of arms of former bishops and other devices. He also furnished the tower with a set of finely toned bells, which are still rung daily in a particular chime.¶ The bells carry inscriptions that they were "maid be maister robert maxvel, byschop of Orknay," and display the Maxwell arms: *Argent*, saltier *sable*, with annulet *or* in the centre, maternal difference for Eglintoun.¹ Returning to Scotland, King James granted in 1539 (19th September), a 19 years' Respites to Edward Sinclare of Stroholm, Magnus Sinclare of

---

* Balfour.   + Calder.   ‡ Mackenzie's MS. Notes.   ¿ Barry's Hist.   Peterkin's Notes.
¶ Clouston; Peterkin's Notes.   Anderson's Guide.

Warsettir, John Sinclare of Tohop, William Sinclare of House, Olave Sinclare of Halvera, Magnus Sinclare, Lawrence Sinclare, James Sinclare, etc., for being art and part in the slaughter of the Earl of Caithness at Summerdale. Sir James of Sanday, the leader, had already passed beyond the need of an earthly pardon. From the names enumerated it is evident the Islesmen were very unanimous in their resistance. Eduerd Synclar of Stroym, Fold of Zetland, appears 24th June, 1536, granting a charter, to which he appended his proper seal; and Olave Sinclayr of Havoray, heyd Fold of Zetland, is so noted in a decree dated 10th December, 1546.

The favourable leases to Margaret Lady Sinclair terminated soon after the king's visit to Orkney, by a general Act of Revocation and Annexation, 10th December, 1540.* "The landis and lordship of Orkney and Zetland, and ye illis pertaining thereto, and their pertinentis" were resumed to the crown amongst other gratuities, which are enumerated and annexed in very anxious and pointed terms. "And the saidis landis being annext to remane perpetuallie with the crown, may nowther be given away in fee nor frank-tenement to any personis, quhatevir estate or degree thai be of, without awise decrete and deliverance of ye hale Parliament, *and for the grett reasonable causes concerning the welefair of the realme, first to be avisit and digestlie consideril be the hale estatis*. And albeit it sall happin our souirane Lord that now is, or any his successouris kingis of Scotland, to analie and dispone the saidis lordschipis, landis, etc., that the alienation and disposition sal be of nane avale. But it sal be leful to the king for the tyme to ressaif tha landis to his awin use quhenevir it likes his grace, but (*i.e.*, without) any process of law."* The last lessee of the Sinclair family was Oliver Sinclair, of Pitcairns, who obtained two successive leases, extending to eight years, of the Crown rights, rents, scatts, and admiralty jurisdiction of Orkney and Zetland (which had of old belonged to the Earldom ere it was annexed to Scotland), for which he paid the advanced rent of £2,000 per annum. The first lease was dated 20th April, 1541, and was continued notwithstanding the protest of Lady Margaret Sinclair, of 10th September following. Oliver's right expired in 1548.* The name of Oliver Sinclair is associated in the recollections of every reader of Scottish history with one of the most humiliating transactions recorded in its pages—the disloyalty of the Scottish nobles, the dishonour of the Scottish arms at Solway Moss, and the miserable captivity of the army which ensued. The premature death of James V. and the extinction of the House of St. Clair as rulers in Orkney may be reckoned cotemporary; and nothing now remains to remind the visitor of the scenes of their former greatness at their ancient "home" except the *débris* of their castle.* Oliver Sinclair did not enjoy undisturbed possession of his tack, for on the 10th December, 1543, a litigation betwixt him and the Queen Dowager was agitated in Parliament before the Lords of the Articles and Secret Council. Thereon, McGill, an advocate, made protestation that whatever their lordships might do "anent the mater perseuit be the Quenis Grace agains Oliver Sinclair touching the delivering of the castell of Kirkwall, in Orknay, should turn him to na prejudice anent his ryt, takk, and assedation quhilk he has of the samyn," and objected to the competency of the Court; but they repelled the objection, "because the action concernis the Quenis Grace, quha has the samen privilege as our soverane lady, her dochter, has in that behalf." The cause was resumed the day after, and the record bears, "That quhare hir Grace optenit ane decret of the Lordis of Counsale decerning and ordaining hir Grace to be answerit and obeyit of the males,

Peterkin's Notes.

fermes, profettis, and dewities of all lands and lordschippis, and siclik of all castellis and houses gevin and grantit to hir in dowrie be umqhuelle our Souerane Lord,"—"not the less the said Oliver hes and withaldis fra hir Grace hir castell of Kirkwall, lyand within the lordship of Orknay, and will not deliver the samyn to hir without he be compellit;" "the Quenis Grace being personalie present, and the said Oliver Sinkler compearand by Maister James M'Gill," who denied that Oliver or his servant had refused to give up the castle, a term was allowed the Queen-Dowager to prove the fact. At a subsequent sederunt, the Queen being present, and neither Oliver nor his lawyer appearing, he was ordained to "deliver to the Queen's Grace or hir factors, hir said place and castell of Kirkwall," as he had not appeared to shew cause why he should not have previously done so, having denied that he retained it, "howbeit the said Oliver and his factors hes and wt. haldis the samyn as yit, as was cleerlie preivit befor the saids Lordis."* These are the only notices of Oliver Sinclair as Governor of the Isles, unless he is the person referred to by Bishop Bothwell in a letter dated 5th February, 1560, stating that he was opposed in some of his church reforms by the Sinclairs "instigat be the Justice Clerk." Henry Sinclair, his brother Robert, and their father [Oliver] opposed any change. "Henry's fader said he wald on na sort consent. . . ."†

Robert Reid, prior of Beauly *in commendam*, became Bishop of Orkney in 1540. He was eminent for his enlightened views and conspicuous ability. A foundation Senator of the College of Justice, he afterwards held the Presidency till his death. He was also

PORCH, ST. MAGNUS' CATHEDRAL.

President of the Scottish Parliament; auditor of Exchequer; commissioner for a treaty of peace between Scotland and England; and one of the embassy to France to arrange the marriage of Mary, Queen of Scots, with the Dauphin.‡ Whilst executing the last mission, he was wrecked near Boulogne, and, being seized with a disorder, ended his days at Dieppe in 1558. He added three Romanesque pillars to the west end of St. Magnus' Cathedral (as also the magnificent porch which serves it for entry), the interior arches above which seem never to have been finished,§ and not only rebuilt the old parish church of St. Ola,¶ but restored the ancient Bishop's Palace, adding to it a circular and a square tower called the Mense or Mass Tower. The circular tower is square within, and embellished with well-executed engravings. The walls are of red freestone interspersed with white, and on the north side is a well-preserved statue of Bishop Reid.§ On the 28th October, 1544, by a new erection he remodelled the ecclesiastical foundation of his cathedral, a chapter being established, consisting of seven dignitaries, seven prebendaries, thirteen chaplains, a sacristan, and six choristers. These were as follow:—

* Peterkin's Notes.   † Craven.   ‡ Barry.   § Clouston.   ¶ Tudor.

Dignitaries.—1. The provost or dean, prebendary of Holy Trinity and rector of South Ronaldsa and Burra (Mr. Malm. Halcro). 2. The archdeacon, chaplain, of St. Ola, with the tithes of Birsa and Harra (Mr. John Tyrie). 3. The precentor, prebendary of Orphir, with tithes of Stenness (*sir* Nicholas Hawcro). 4. The chancellor, preb. of St. Mary in Sanda (Mr. Alex. Scott). 5. The treasurer, rector of S. Nicolas in Stronsa (*sir* Stephen Culross). 6. The sub-dean, also the bishop's butler, rector of Hoy and Walls (Mr. Peter Houston). 7. The sub-chantor, prebendary of St. Colme (*sir* Magnus Strang).

Prebendaries.—1. Of St. Cross, in Sanda, who attended to the bells and saw that the floor was kept clean (*sir* Thomas Richartsoun). 2. Of St. Mary, in Evie, who attended to the roof and windows. 3. Of St. Magnus, who acted as confessor to the households of the chapter (*sir* Hugh Halcro). 4. Of *St. John* (Mr. Henry Bartoun). 5. Of St. Laurence (John Maxwell). 6. Of St. Catherine. 7. Of S. Duthac's.

The sacristan was also rector of the parish of St. Columba in Sanda, now known as Burness parish.* The deed, which is still extant, was signed by the bishop and the other members of the chapter "*apud ecclesiam nostram cathedralem*, coram his testibus nobilibus honestis ac discretis viris Patricio Chene de Essilmonth milite, Patricio Mowate de Boquhelly, Alexandro Banerman de Watertoun, Edwardo Sinclair de Strome, Alexandro Innes constabulario Orchaden., Thoma Tulloch de Fluris, Jacobo Cragy de Burgh, Johanne Randaile de eodem, Gilberto Sclater de Burnes, Jacobo Cummvng, Henrico Frenche, magistro Roberto Glen, Henrico Reid, et magistro Petro Galbrath notario publico, cum diversis aliis."† This foundation was confirmed by a Bull under the seal of David Bethune, Archbishop of St. Andrew's, Cardinal and Papal Legate, on the 30th June, 1545. Bishop Reid is the true founder of the University of Edinburgh, for by his will he left 8,000 merks for the purpose of founding a college there, to consist of three schools—one for grammar, one for poetry and oratory, and one for civil and common law. For the said sum a decree was obtained by the King's advocate.‡ He also conceived the design of building a college in the immediate vicinity of the Cathedral for the instruction of youth in grammar and philosophy; and both granted ground and built some part of a square, which he intended should serve for that purpose.‡ His only writings were a geographical description of the Isles of Orkney, and a genealogical and historical account of the family of Sinclair, both of which were written at the desire of the King of Denmark, and were extant in manuscript in the last century.‡ His arms show on an old building in Victoria Street, Kirkwall, viz., Azure, a roebuck's head erased proper.

In 1554 one Bontot, a Frenchman, is made Governor of the Orcade Isles; while the same year Huntly, the Regent, is deprived of *inter alia* the government of Orkney and Zetland which he had.§ The appointment of Bontot is stated to have been very unpopular. It would appear that the revenues of the Isles formed part of the dowry of Queen Mary of Guise, and that she retained them till her death on the 10th June, 1560. On the 26th May, 1564, Lord Robert Stuart acquired a charter of the Isles, with pertinents, fortresses, jurisdictions, etc.; but this grant was soon destined to fall before the gifts conferred on a greater favourite. When Queen Mary espoused James Hepburn, Earl of Bothwell (grandson of the fourth Lord Sinclair)—14th May, 1567—she created him Duke of Orkney, and the Isles, jurisdictions, etc., were all "erectit in ane haill and free dukry,

---
* Tudor. † Peterkin's Rentals. ‡ Barry. § Balf. Annals.

to be callit the dukry of Orknay *for ever.*" However, after his flight from Carberry Hill, his dukedom instead of continuing *dissolved* for ever. In 1581 Lord Robert Stuart acquired the Isles and became Earl of Orkney and Lord of Zetland,* but with the execution of his son and successor Earl Patrick, in 1614, the brief career of the Stewart line came to an end.

Orkney has been an honourable title from the remotest ages, and we are told how Belus was King of the Orkneys before the birth of Christ; how Ganus their king was taken prisoner by Claudius Cæsar, centuries before even the Norse occupation; but the honourable title has now passed to Irish titulados, on which circumstance a modern writer descants:—"It is most singular to find a repetition of the venerable and historic title first bestowed by King Harald Harfagri at the Norwegian conquest of the Orkneys, soon after A.D. 872, upon Rögnvald, Earl of Moeri—gloriously borne by these Princes for nearly four centuries—hallowed by the martyrdom of St. Magnus and the devotion of St. Rögnvald—handed on through the lines of Athol, Angus, Stratherne and St. Clair—resigned to the Crown of Scotland by the still living family of St. Clair, with the Orkneys themselves in 1469—conferred as a duchy upon Bothwell by Queen Mary in view of their marriage—now held, along with a Viscounty of Kirkwall, by a family of origin totally alien to Orkney, and connected only with Tipperary. It is no want of respect either for the great House of Hamilton or for the noble family of which we are speaking, to suspect that the intense hatred of William II. for Scotland—that hatred which found two of its sweetest moments in arranging the massacres of Glencoe and of Darien—sought and found a childish indulgence in the invention of this later peerage."†

* Peterkin's Notes.   † Article—Scottish Review, Jan., 1886.

THE ST. CLAIRS OF THE ISLES.

ORCADIAN SCIONS.*

THE SINCLAIRS OF WARSETTER,
SANDAY.

I. SIR WILLIAM SINCLAIR, KNIGHT, FIRST OF WARSETTER, was a son of 'William the Waster,' the disinherited Master of Orkney (ancestor of all subsequent Lords Sinclair of Ravenscraig). In the 1497 'Rental of my Lord Sinclair that deit at Flodden,' William Sinclair, my Lordis brother, is recorded as holding many lands in Westray, while in 1502 he appears a large owner of lands in Sanday, and is styled SIR William Sinclair. Sir David Sinclair, the Foud of Zetland, in 1506 bequeathed to Sir William Sincler, the Knycht, his "doublet of kletht of gold and my gray satein gowne with thre ostreche fedderis." He acquired the lands of Tohop from Nicol Fraser, and the purchase was confirmed in 1514 by an adjudication of the Orcadian Lawting. The decree refers to him as "ane nobill and potent man Schir William Sinclair of Warsetter, knycht." About the same time he took by storm Noltland Castle in Westray, to which he probably had a possessive right, but was required to restore it to Dr. Stewart, the then episcopal owner. He married Helene, daughter of George, second Earl of Huntly, by Annabella, Princess of Scotland. In the Reg. Great Seal there is on the 13th May, 1527, entry of a charter to Lady Helene Gordone, relict of quondam Sir Wm. Sinclair of Wersister, knight, now spouse of David Hepburn—lands in Newburgh. Sir William was presumably father of

    1. MAGNUS, next of Warsetter, and
    2. JOHN, next of Tohop; and had also natural issue—

Sir James Sinclair (perhaps the legatee in Sir David's will), elected Governor of Kirkwall Castle [in 1515], who having in 1529 defeated the invasion of his Scottish kindred, was knighted by King James V., received Letters of Legitimation,† and in 1535 obtained from the Scottish king a feudal grant of Sanday and Eday upon, it is said, misrepresenting those islands as infertile holms. Hearing of King James' intended visit to Orkney, Sir James, anticipating exposure, sought refuge in death by self-precipitation from the Gloup of Linkness. The previous instances of royal favour which Sir James had received are to be attributed to his powerful connections at court. On the 18th April, 1539, a Royal letter passed the Privy Seal at Stirling, vesting his lands, etc., in his widow, who married secondly McLeod, Breve of the Lewis. He married Lady Barbara Stewart, daughter of Lord Avondale, the Lord Chancellor, and sister-in-law to Margaret Tudor, the Queen-dowager, by whom he had issue an only child,

    MARGARET, who married Magnus Halcro.

II. MAGNUS SINCLAIR OF WARSETTER fought under the leadership of Sir James at Summerdale in 1529, for which he obtained a nineteen years' respite on the 19th

---

* Peterkin's Notes and Rentals: Articles in *Orcadian*, 1895-96; Barry.

† Letters of Legitimation do not confer legitimacy on the grantee. The object of their issue is to confer a status upon persons born out of wedlock, enabling them to devise and bequeath property personally acquired.

September, 1539. He may be the Magnus Sinclair of the Bu of Karstane, Stromness, in 1503, and who attests execution of Sir David Synclar's will in 1506, in which he is left "my blew doublet, the brest set wyth precious staneis, and my hude set with precious staneis, and my goldin chenze the quhilk I weair daılly." Next to him is

III HENRIE SINCLAIR OF WIRSITTER, who on 23rd December, 1597, is one amongst others preferring complaint against the Balfours of Montquhany, Stratherne, and Garth. His successor is

IV WILLIAM SINCLAIR OF WARSETTER, who frequently appears in connection with civil suits from 1615 to 1622. On the 5th May, 1615, Wm Sinclair of Marsetter (sic) appeared before the Court ; on the 30th idem. he is cited at the instance of Wm Sinclair of Ethay; on the 12th June he is inhibited at the Canongate by (Ethay?), and also by James Stewart He is enumerated in the list of gentlemen Suitors before the Earldom Court 1617-1622, and is mentioned in a legal document of 1620 He evidently died between January and April, 1622, for on the 8th April of that year Harie Stewart, Sheriff-Depute of Orkney, produces a charter to him of lands in Sanda maid be Jonet, ane of the twa daughters and airs of umqle Wm Sinclair of Warsetter, with consent of Alex Stewart of Clet now hir spous.

V. HARIE SINCLAIR OF WARSETTER is mentioned in a case 3rd October, 1627, Sinclair of W *als* of one Brown,—as father of

VI WILLIAM SINCLAIR OF WARSETTER, who was his only son This Warsetter subscribed a deed of procuratorie at Kirkwall, 13th January, 1623, protesting that the service of Janet Sinclair aforesaid should be "nowayis preiudiciall to the said William anent his ryt of landis, and @ rentis (annual rents) to him or Agnes Sinclair, his mother, as ane of the airis portioneirs of the said Wm Sinclair of Warsetter " On the 4th October, 1621, compt. on the lands of Holland and Bea ane discreit young man Geo. Gardyne as Pror for Alesoune Sinclair to William Sinclair of Warsetter—Charter be the said William in favour of said Alesone for her lyffrent only—lands in Sanday. On the 4th September, 1623, Mr Harie Aitken institutes process against Wm. Sinclair of (Warsetter) and Alesone Sinclair his spouse On 28th July, 1623, Warsetter institutes process against Wm Sinclair of Ethay and his brother John. Warsetter is enumerated in the Suitors of Court 1623-1631, and is described as only son of Harie Sinclair of Warsetter.

In the Rental of 1595 Thos. Sinclair, prebendar of St. Augustine, holds Lopness, etc , Sanday, in tack, and may be of this family, and from the frequent litigation between the Warsetters and the Edays it is probable the two families were nearly related. Sir James Sinclair, the Governor, had held both Sanday and Eday, and it is stated that at his death in 1536-7 his widow got his lands On her re-marriage she probably leased them or parted with her interest to his relatives.

THE SINCLAIRS OF TOHOP AND SABA,
ST ANDREW'S.

I " SCHIR WILLIAM SINCLAIR OF WARSETTER, Knycht, ane nobill and potent man," acquired the lands of Tolhope or Toob, in the parish of St. Andrew's, from Nicoll Fraser This transfer to Sir William and his heirs was affirmed on appeal by the Orcadian Lawting in 1514.

II. JOHNE SINCLAIR OF TOLLAP fought at the battle of Summerdale in 1529, for which in 1539 a 19 years' amnesty was proclaimed to him and others. The leader of the victorious Islesmen was Sir James Sinclair, natural son of Sir William of Warsetter, and in the enumeration of those respited the order reads thus:—Edward Sinclair of Stroholm in Shetland, Magnus Sinclair of Warsetter, John Sinclair of Tollap, and then several of the Shetland Sinclairs.

III. MANSIE SINCLAIR OF TOHOP is mentioned 10th May, 1619, in the suit of Edward Sinclair of Essinquoy against William Sinclair oy and air of umqle. Mansie Sinclair of Tohop, and Johne Sinclair, merchant in Kirkwall.

IV. JOHN SINCLAIR OF TOBE petitioned Parliament in 1592 against Earl Robert Stewart, and is mentioned on 28th May, 1600, as an indweller of Edinburgh.

V. JAMES SINCLAIR OF TOHOP beneath the yardis is noted in the Bishopric rental of 1595, and is no doubt the link intermediate between umqle. Mansie and his oy and air

VI. WILLIAM SINCLAIR, NEXT OF TOHOP, whose appearances are frequent in Earldom records of every description.

He is on an assise 15th January, 1615; on 1st November, 1616, sues William Irving of Sabay; on 4th November, 1617, yielding the *pas* to Edward Sinclair of Essinquoy, he is ranked second out of the 30 suitors present at the Orcadian Court. In 1618 he and Jean Gordon, his spouse, are noticed, and on 14th December of the same he has a transfer from John Beattoun of Cluik Quoy callit Busquoy in Utter Stromness. 9th November, 1619, finds " Dittays Sinclairis Kirknes et Isbisteris "—at the instance of Robt. Coltart pror. fiscal against William Sinclair of Tolhop, etc., for pursewing with swirds Durks and Quhingers of intention to have bereft of Lyff, etc. He, in turn, obtained from Henry Smythe, 16th October, 1620, caution and lawborrowis that he (Tolhoip), his wyff and bairnis, etc., etc., shall harmless be. On 16th March, 1621, he produced charter to him maid be William Irving of Sava or Saba of the lands of Ovir and Nether Messagris and the lands of Sava or Saba, with all the houses, buildings, etc. The conveyance of Saba was reproduced 23rd April, 1622. On the 21st January, 1623, he is one of the inquisition for jury service of Jonet Sinclair of Warsetter, and on the 5th August idem. appears *ats* of Magnus Sinclair in Gorne. From henceforward he is more usually designed of Sabay. On 9th November, 1627, William Sinclair of Saba finds caution for William Craigie of Papdaill. On 16th February, 1635, he is one of the gentlemen of Orkney subscribing to the Relation of Famine. On 19th November, 1636, William Sinclair of Tohop institutes process against James Colville of Huip, William Henrysone, fiar of Holland, etc. On 26th May, 1637, he compeirit and becam caution for John Cromartie, youngar sone to Skae, ffor the corns Imbarkit be him in the bark callit the " Gift of God," qroff Magnus Flett is skippar, etc. On 6th August, 1639, Saba appears *ats* of James Bakie of Tankerness, his (Tulhope's) sons Robert and Edward being also made parties to the action, while William Sinclair of Tulhope sues Finlayson and Bakie 14th July, 1640. From 1616 to 1643 he is enumerated as a suitor of Court. Saba is last noticed on 7th September, 1651, *ats* of Edward Sinclair of Gyre. In the time of Bishop Law he held the lands of Smewgro, Cowbister and Orokirk in Holme for payments conforme to the rental. He married Jean Gordon, and had issue—

1. ROBERT, his successor; 2. EDWARD; and
3. JAMES of Grottsetter, brother-german to Robert.

VII. ROBERT SINCLAIR OF SABA appears on the valuation of 1653.

On 20th September, 1664, he sued James Bakie of Tankerness, and on 16th March, 1665, Jas. King of Warbuster. On 30th September, 1661, Saba and Beatrix King, his spous, granted Grottsetter with houses to his brother-german James Sinclair now in Grottstetter. On the 20th September, 1661, he gave a Charter of Alienation of his udal land in town of Tronston to Andro Moir there, Sandwick parish, and on 13th October, 1661, he obtained lands in Foubister from Malcolm Foubister of that Ilk. Saba protested against "covenanting," March, 1666. On 10th October, 1676, the Proc. Phiscall proceeded against him for intromitting with the gear of umqle. Beatrice King, his spouse. She was probably a daughter of David King of Warbuster, Hoy, by his spouse Mary, d. of Adam Stewart, brother of Earl Robert. David King was father of James, Lord

Eythin, who commanded the Royalist centre at Marston Moor. Queen Christina created him a peer of Sweden, as Baron Sanshult. A letter addressed to James Sinclair, younger of Saba, by James King, dated at Melgund 6th May, 1668, refers to the "10,000 merks they (of Saba) borrowed of my uncle," and the fact that they had also taken possession of the Hoy property.* On the 6th December, 1676, William Davidsone, wreatter in Kirkwall, and Walter Fairnie, litstar (dyer), thair, lay information against Robert Sinclair of Sabay; James, Edward, and Charles, his sones; and Andro Sinclair, his natural sone—all of whom having conceived ane great and deadlie hatred, rancour, and malice against the complainants, are bound over under Lawborrowis. David Craigie of Oversanda took action 13th April, 1676, against Saba and his eldest son James. On 9th April, 1677, Robert Sinclair of Tulhope, elder sone to umqle. William Sinclair of Tulhope, Isobell Sinclair, spous to Gilbert Irving, etc., are noticed, and on the 4th July, 1678, Robert Sinclair of Saba appears as a witness. By Beatrix King he left issue—

1. JAMES, fiar of Saba; 2. EDWARD; 3 CHARLES. He had also a natural son ANDREW.

VIII. JAMES SINCLAIR, FIAR and LAST OF SABA, succeeded his father.

On 17th April, 1669, compt. Wm. Sinclair, pror. for James Sinclair of Saba, halding ane Charter of Alienation, etc., maid be David Sinclair, only sone and air to umqle. John Sinclair of Hamer, in Griennie to the said James of Saba of the said house of Hammer. On the 29th November, 1673, he granted a Charter of Alienation of heritable lands in Birsa to George Liddell of Hammer, brother-uterine of the aforesaid David; and on the 14th July, 1674, James of Saba is a witness to the instrument of induction in favour of the Rev. John Heggen.* John Gaudie, Archdeacon of Tingwall, Zetland, was on very friendly terms with Saba. Addressing his "very much respected friend, James Sinclair of Saba," he subscribes "To your assured friend and Brother." Saba had desired the present of a Shetland pony, which the Archdeacon sent him in September, 1678. "You'll find it both good and sharp, and in any other thing wherein I can serve you, you may assure yourself of my inclination. Yor (i.e., my) old Mrs. presents her respects to you and your kind bedfellow, to Mr. John Gibson [parson of Holm] and his discreet consort, and to all at Campstone."* [Gaudie had married Margaret, d. of John Sinclair of Quendale, in Shetland.] Gaudie's mother was a Mary Stewart of Campstone,† which accounts for his interest in that part of Orkney. In 1708 the lands of Saba passed to David Traill under reversion be the heirs of the umqle. Edward Sinclair of Campston.

The family of Sinclair of Saba was one of the most ancient in Orkney, having descent through the Knight of Warsetter from the first of the Sinclair Earls and Sir Wm. Sinclair, founder of the Roslins. The heirs of this family (if any) are senior representatives of the House of Sinclair. It may be that the noble Swedish Sinclairs are scions of the Saba stock, as in their "Genealogical Descendance" they cite as an ancestor a William Sinclair, Master of *Seba* and Brobster, who m. Barbe, d. of Sir Hugh Halcro; and the connection of the Saba family with that of King would suggest that the noble Swedes were cadets of Saba who passed to Sweden as protegés of their kinsman John King, Baron Sansbult.

THE SINCLAIRS OF ETHAY.

I. EDWARD SINCLAIR OF ETHAY was the youngest of the eight sons of Sir Wm. Sinclair of Roslin, enumerated in the entail of 1542, and has several appearances in the Roslyn Chartulary, where he is desigued 'of Dryden,' *e.g.*, in Lord Borthwick's retour of 1543 and Seasine thereon 1545. On the 4th July, 1554, he is a witness to the retour of Roslin his brother; and at Roslin on the 1st November, 1582, he witnesses a citation by his brother, Sir Wm. Sinclar of Rosling, knight, for service upon James Lord Borthwick. On the 22nd December, 1582, Mr. John Henryson is of Dryden, and again on 15th April, 1584; while in the Bishopric Rental of 1595 it is noted that "The Vle of Ethay, set in feu by Adam, Bishop of Orkney (1562-1580), to Edward Sinclair, payis 5 lasts flesche and 16 pounds money." On 5th December, 1561, Edward Sinclair [then at Kirkwall]

* Craven. † Grant.

bruder to the Laird of Roslyn, had to find caution underly the law. Edw. Sinclair of Ethay was brother-german of Sir Wm. Sinclair of Roslin. (Charter 28th October, 1583.) In the charge to landlords in Orkney and Zetland for good rule, 30th June, 1597, he is assessed at 2,000 merks.

Patrick, Earl of Orkney, makes answer to complaint of Wm. Sinclair, fiar of Ethay, as follows, in September, 1604 :—(1) The first head of the complaint, bearing that Henrie Blaik, captain of the Castle of Kirkwall, and others in the Earl's name, besieged Wm. Sinclair in his dwelling-house, is not relevant ; and even if it were, the Earl in this mtre. did no wrong, because the said William has often sought to take the life of his father, Edward Sinclair of Ethay, who is 100 years old or thereby, by shooting of hagbuts with bullets at him, and "niping him in the craig as he had bene ane dog, thinking to haif wirreit him." Farther, the said "auld decrepit man having desired the Earl to direct his precepts charging his said son to find lawburrows to him, the said Earl had given orders for his apprehension because he refused to find the said ltres. It was quite competent to the Earl to act in the mtre. as he did, in respect he is sheriff of the shire, justice of the county, and lord of the regality. Again, the Earl did no wrong in seeking for the said William in his house and throughout the country, because the said William had been put to the horn at the instance of Thos. Black for not paying him certain sums of money, and the Earl had been charged as sheriff-principal of Orknay to apprehend him." (2) As to the second head of the complaint, accusing the Earl of ejecting the said William and his family in September last furth of the lands of Holland, the same is civil, and the Lords of Secret Council are no judges therein ; and as to the Earl imprisoning the complainer's wife, and Johnne Pattoun, messenger in Kirk'll, they had liberty to leave at their pleasure ; besides the complainer had no interest to pursue for Pattoun. (3) As to the Earl's deforcing the said messenger, that part of the complaint is not relevant either ; and if it were, the Lords of Secret Council are not judges to the deforcement. (4) The complaint that in Sept. last the Earl demolished the said William's house of Holland, spuilyied his plenishing furth thereof, and ejected him out of the lands of Holland and Skaill, is also civil, and should be remitted to the ordinary judges, viz., the Lords of Session. At that time the Earl was in Halie Island (Restalrig), in England. (5) The complaint that the said William, when he had come to visit his father, had been stayed from landing by six or seven boats sent furth by the Earl, is not relevant. If it were, it could be proven that the complainer, accompanied by three or four score vagabonds—broken Highland men of Caithness, all armed 'werilie,' to have seized the lands of Ethay occupied by his father, and to have slain the father, or else caused him to render to him all he had. The father, fearing their invasion, had sent to the gentleman of the country desiring them to help in resisting the "wickit furie and barbarous interpryis" of the said William and his complices ; "for of the cuntrie men of Caithness thair barbarous interpryissis lang of befoir agains the contrey of Orknay thair remaneis yit experience." (6) Lastly, the complaint that the Earl caused the said William to subscribe an unlawful band, is not relevant, and if it were, is civil, and should be remitted to the judge ordinary.

In June, 1605, Edw. Sinclair of Ethay got letters against the Earl of Orkney that he should be put to liberty. He had issue—

1. WILLIAM, fiar of Ethay, his successor. 2. OLIVER ; 3. GILBERT ; 4. JOHN—brothers to Wm. Sinclair of Ethay.

II. WM. SINCLAIR, SECOND OF ETHAY, is first noticed as fiar of Ethie, on 30th June, 1597, as one of the landlords in Orkney and Zetland cautioned for good rule. He is assessed at £1,000.

On the 13th June, 1600, he obtained caution from Arch. Logan of Coitfield ; and in June, 1605, got ltres. against Patrick, Earl of Orkney, for oppression ; and again on 6th September same got the latter put under caution of 5,000 merks not to harm him, Ethay, Janet Halcro his spous, nor Aliesonn and Elspeth Sinclaris his daughters. On the 11th July, 1606, caution was taken that Oliver Sinclair, brother of Wm. Sinclair, fiar of Ethay, shall not harm his father, Edw. Sinclair. The Earl of Orkney inhibits Sinclair of Eday, 10th June, 1611 ; whom Sir John Arnot also inhibits on the 14th idem.; while on 26th November Earl Patrick makes process against Wm. Sinclair of Ethay ; and on the same day David Heart pursues Oliver Sinclair, his brother. On 30th May, 1615, this Wm. Sinclair of Ethay has a suit against William Sinclair of Warsetter ; and on 12th June of the same he inhibits the latter. On

25th November, 1612, Ethay sues Thomas Sinclair in Lopness, Sanda. In 1616 he and Jonet Halcro his spous are mentioned; and on 10th April, 1622, Wm. Sinclair of Ethay, with his brother Gilbert and his [Wm.'s] sonne Gilbert. On 18th July, 1623, Robert Elphingstoun of Hammigar makes cause against Wm. Sinclair of Ethay and Jonet Halcrow his spous; while on the 28th idem. Wm. Sinclair of Warsetter sues Wm. Sinclair of Ethay and Jone Sinclair his brother, etc. From this time he ceases to be enumerated as a gentleman suitor of the Earldom Court, nor are there any more notices of Sinclairs as of Ethay. He was married to Jonet Halcro, and had issue—

1. GILBERT.   2. ALIESOUN.   3. ELSPETH.

THE SINCLAIRS OF ESSENQUOY,
St. Andrew's.

I. OLIVER SINCLAIR OF ESSENQUOY is the first on record of this family, which was one of the most important of the Orcadian branches.

He was probably a son of Edw. Sinclair of Ethay, and is first noted in the rentals of 1595 in connection with lands in various mainland parishes, viz., Sandwick (Deirness), "ten d. ane fding terre, p. Epo. Set of auld for xx. mks. money to Oliver Sinclair with Grymsquoy in St. Ollawi's parochine ; and now augmentit be my Lord ten mkis. money more ; extendin in the haill to xx. lb. Nota, Oliver Sinclair takes the scatt and teynd of Sandilend and Stoiff. Stambuster (Sanct Androis) 3d. terræ, p. Epo. payis one barrel butter, and of teynd conform to the rentals of auld, 4 meils cost, now sett in assedation to Oliver Sinclair for 2 m. 4s. cost, 9 poultry. Grymsquoy, Quoyland (Sanct Olawis) p. Epo. but scat, pays 5s. argent, 2 poultry, which is contained in Oliver Sinclair's assedation."

On 30th June, 1597, he is one of the landlords in Orkney and Zetland assessed at £1,000 for good rule.

In the Sheriff-Court book of Orkney and Zetland, under date 3rd October, 1612, there is an appearance of Hew, sone to Oliver Sinclair of Essinquoy, in connection with a case of Lawborrowis in Zetland. Oliver, first of Essenquoy, was succeeded by his son

II. EDWARD SINCLAIR, SECOND OF ESSENQUOY, who first occurs on an assise in 1613, and thence continuously to 1641.

The rental of 1614 notes the bishopric lands of North Widfirth (St. Ola's) as in the hands of Sinclair of Essenquoy, feuit to Robert Chalmer. He was M.P. for Orkney and Zetland in the Scottish Parliament of 1617, on 4th November, in which year he heads the list of suitors before the Earldom Court. On 15th August, 1615, James, sone of Johne Louttit (by Helene Sinclair his spous), receives from Essinquoy a discharge for money lent to his people. On 25th November, 1616, he appears for Robert Sinclair of Campston against Francis Mudie of Breckness; and on 10th May, 1619, sues Wm. Sinclair of Tolhoip and Johne Sinclair, merchant in Kirkwall. He granted charter to Alex. Flet in How, Harra, of the houses and lands of Ramsgar in Ovirtoun in Harra, which was produced 23rd November, 1621. Edward Sinclair of Æstenquoy is Sheriff-Depute of Orkney 1st July, 1623. He was conjoined with Robert Sinclair of Campstoun for the purpose of reporting upon the King's lands in the isle of Rousay, of which they were taksmen, and was sworn thereto at Kirkwall, 12th June, 1627 ; and again in the Report of the Paroch of St. Androis, "At St. Ringans Schepell the twentie-ane day of Junii anno 1627 the Commissioners elected thereto viz. Robert Sinclair off Campstoun, David Kinked off Veinsta judicialie suorne in that respect off thair knawledge and insight in that bussiness; and for thair better proceeding did schois the most anchenest men within the paroche to helpe tham be thair informatione, viz., Edward Sinclair of Essinquay etc., quho can testefie their diligence. . . . As for prebendries thair is a part off St. Jon's prebendries in this paroche off St. Androis sett be Mr. Patrike Inglis, minister at Kirk, and prebender off the said stowke, wt. consent of ane reverant father in God, Geo. Bishop of Orkney and the heall chapter, to Campston and Essinquoy for the payment of £20 money to the sd. prebendr as it hes bein to his predecessors off auld." In the parish report at our Leddie Kirk in Deirnes, 25th June, 1627, "The worthe off the Rowms of this Paroche contains allusion to the ten d. half d. land in Sandwike bischops land off auld, and sett to vmquhill Olefer Sinclair of Essinquay for the payment of 20 merks mony, and now in the hands off Edward Sincleir off Essinquay his sone for the payment of £20 to his Majesty's chalmerlens, conforme to the rentell." On the 2nd April, 1630, he was Sheriff-Depute, and commissioned as such by the Lords of Session to take the Aiths of Veritie of

Geo. Bishop of Orkney and Patrick Smyth of Braco, in the case of Mr. Alex. Bruce of Cultmalindie, etc. He was Sheriff-Depute 6th November, 1632; and on 26th May, 1637, when Wm. Sinclair of Saba compeiret re security for John Cromartie for the corns Imbarkit be him in the "Gift of God," Essinquoy again fills that honourable office.

On 16th August, 1635, he was judge of assise on the Dittay of witchcraft against Helene Isbuster On 26th December, 1636, he and his son Gilbert are *ats* of James Baikie of Tankerness for 1,000 merks Scots, etc. In 1640 he is a bailie ordained for St. Ola's, and is a suitor present at the *Curia Capitalis* 24th May, 1641.

He married Ursilla Fulzie, second daughter of Gilbert Fulzie, Archdeacon of Orknay (sasine 1641), and was succeeded by his son

III. GILBERT SINCLAIR, FIAR OF ESSENQUOY, who has a few notices, mostly of a litigious description.

On 24th October, 1620, Gilbert Sinclair appeirand Air of Essinquoy became cautioner for Robert Sinclair, merchant in Kirkwall. On 26th December, 1636, Edwd. Cok, merchant, burgess of Kirkwall, and Margaret Baikie his spous, sue Gilbert Sinclair, Fear of Essinquoy, and Annis Ballendene his spous, for £1000 Scots (pundis usuall mondy of yis our realm.): Inhibited. On the same date he and his father were similarly sued by James Baikie of Tankerness. On the 8th March, 1637, John Grahame, Tailzeor in Kirkwall, and Cristane Carmichell his spous, sue him for 200 merks Scots, and on the 20th October following William Spence, merchant there, also sues him. On 16th May, 1637, Gilbert Sinclair, in Tankerness, sues David Fowbister, in Fowbister, and William his brether, for money due. July 2nd, 1641, Compt. Gilbert Sinclair, Fear of Essinquoy, and became Caution for Barbara Sclaitter, servant to Edward Sinclair of Essinquoy, that she sall satisfie the Kirk. . . . .

During July, 1626, the Kirk Session resolved and passed the following Act :—" Ordanis intimation to be made to the Laird of Græmsay, and to THE NAME OF SINCLAIR, that if their two seates be not compleitly builded betwix this and pasche day nixt to cum, the Session heirafter will dispose upon them, and outred them upon their charges as they shall find to be expedient, both for easing of their awne congregation and likewise for strangers." On the 16th June, 1673, Patrick Trail and William Mudie got an act of session giving them a seat which formerly belonged to Sinclair of Essinquoy, Provest of Kirkwall.

Arms: See Armoury. Taken from an oak pew in St. Magnus' Cathedral.

THE SINCLAIRS OF GREENWALL, FLOTTAY, AND GYRE, HOLM AND ORPHIR.

The Rental of 1614 records Hangaback, Skobister, Gyre, Gossaquoy, and Crowill, "all sett in nyntin yeiris takis to umqule. Henrie Sinclair of Cuikquoy and his airis." The Report on Sanday in 1627 notes lands perteining to Sainct Katharine's prebendarie sett in few be Archbald Balfour, and be him to umquhill Hendrie Sinclaire of Cowquoy, and left be him to his sonne Williame Sinclaire, by and as followis. In Our Ladie parochinne two pennie land, within the toune of How fyive pennie land, and in the parochin of Saint Colme four pennie land and ane half; thir land payis no dewtie to his Majestie, bott all dewties to the fewars, Reserweand tenn pounds payit to the prebendar in name of few dewtie. Henry Sinclair of Cowquoy may have been father of

I. WILLIAM SINCLAIR OF GREENWALL, whose descendants appear in occupation of Cowquoy's lands of Gyre, etc. He figures in a case of Lawborrows 3rd October, 1612; is Chancellor of the Assize of Fifteen 15th January, 1613; and is again on the assize of the 21st idem.

He held the tack of Holme and Paplay, the account of which he rendered to Bishop Law the 11th July, 1614. On 7th January, 1617, he and other Sinclairs make suit against James Stewart of Gramsay, etc., while on the 24th February next thereafter Donald Stewart of Brugh makes cause against

ORCADIAN SCIONS.

Greenwall, &c. The Bishopric Report of 1627 has this: "ITEM William Sinclair holds his lands of Greenwall in the paroch of Ham for payment off twelff ponds," and again, "Greinwall jxd. land fewit be William Sinclair for ane silver dewtie, comforme to the rentall."

(Sd.)   W. Sinclaire of Gremshall,
His Majestie's Comn. ansd. be the parochine of Holme.

On the 15th November, 1629, Greenwall compeared and becam lawborrowis for Thomas Sinclair, eldest lau'll sone to Campston—That Wm. Sinclair of Saba, his wyff, bairnis, &c., sall hairmless and skaithless be; on the 26th May, 1637, he costs to Jon Cromartie, yr., sone to Skae ffiiij. meles beir in the bark callit the "Gift of God." On 30th June, 1640, he and other Sinclairs, &c., including Edmond, his eldest sone, are sued by David Heart of Rusland; and in the November following he is bailie for Holm. In 1641 he is a suitor of the Earldom Court. Greenwall entered into an agreement with Patrik Smyth of Braco, 8th April, 1629, for value received to pay Braco nine meills Malt, but since 1638 had made default. Braco sued him on the 26th March, 1639, and obtained a decree on 1st November, 1642. He had issue—

1. EDMOND, eldest son.   2. ANDREW, m. 1643 Margaret, d. of Robert Sinclair of Campston.

II. EDMOND SINCLAIR identical *(semble)* with Edmond Sinclair of FLOTTAY. The Bishopric Rental of 1595 has a marginal note against Greenwall recording it as "all set again to Edmund Sinclair for £8 money yearly"; and in the rental of 1614, "Grinwall 9d. *terre, pro Rege*, sett to Edmond Sinclair of Flotta, for the yeirlie payment of £8." Flottay died before 9th October, 1639, when Edward and Annas Sinclairs lawfull bairnis to umqle. Edward (sic) Sinclair of Flottay and Magnus Cromartie of Skae spous to said Annas, claim birthright property. In the rental of 1642, Flottay is referred to as umquhile, and as having held in few Larquoy, Ingamyre, Aikers, Garay, Midhous, Sowlie, Skettedbuster, Brek, Swambuster, Hangabak, Skobuster, Gyre, Gossaquoy, Crowall, Windbrek, Inksetter, Quoyclarkis, Nathermyre, Crega, etc., all in Ophir. Ingamyre and Swanbuster (in part) had previously been escheated from certain Sinclairs, and it will be observed that many of these lands had been in Cowquoy's tack.

III. EDWARD SINCLAIR OF GYRE was son of Flottay. In the report of bishopric fews in Orphir for 1642 it is noted, "Thair is fewed yairof be ye said Bischop Law to umquhile Edmond Sinclare of Flotta, the lands of Gayr, Swainbuster, and severall oyr lands, payand conforme to ye rentall, qlk. ar now in ye possession of Edward Sinclare of Gayir his sone." Again, "Item—Edward Sinclair off Gyer holds his lands within the paroch off Orpher for payment, four merkes per meil, conforme to the Rentall"; and "Edward Synclair of Gyr, whose teynds are conteined in my Lord Carrick's tak, hes procured a general commission." Early in 1641 he is a suitor of Court, and described as of 'Geyr and Swainbuster.' Gyre is mentioned in an instrument 30th December, 1650; sues various Orcadians 7th September, 1651; is *ats* of Rev. James Douglas 8th August, 1654, whom he in turn sues on the 23rd December following. He is in the 1653 valuation for his Orphir lands as enumerated in 1642. He is again sued by the Rev. James Douglas, 23rd April, 1657, for 300 merks Scots. He would seem to have died before 25th February, 1662, when Robt. Jack, merchand, burgess of Edinburgh, sues *inter alia* Margaret Sinclair relict of umqle. Edward Sinclair of Gyre, now spous of Mr. James Mowatt of Oliberrie in Zetland, for 200 merks Scots. She was a daughter of George Sinclair of Rapness and Trenabie. He was succeeded in Gyre by his son

IV. GEORGE SINCLAIR OF GYRE, whose first figure in Orcadian history is in a conflict [1664] between himself, Wm. Mudy, yr. of Melsetter, and Alex. Douglas, yr. of Spynie. Gyre and Spynie were both bound over to keep the peace. On the 13th May, 1665, David McClellan of Wodwik proceeds against Geo. Sinclair of Gyre, with consent of Edward Sinclair his father. (The consent here referred to doubtless relates back to the cause of action, perhaps some few years previous, as Edward of Gyre was evidently dead *ante* 1662.) Geo. Rich of Winksetter and Wm. Douglas of Egilsha are before him 15th January, 1669; and on 16th December, 1672, in connection with lands in Rusland in Harra, Gyre is noted as Baillie in that part.

In the Cropt Acct. for Orphir in 1739 Wm. Halcro of Coubister compts. for his lands in Orphir, which formerly pertained to umquild Geo. Sinclair of Gyer.

ADAM SINCLAIR OF GYRE is one amongst others *ats* of Patrik Craigie, lait Provost of Kirkwall, 19th May, 1667.

THE SINCLAIRS OF CLUMLIE, TOWQUOY AND HAMMER.
SANDWICK, WESTRAY, AND BIRSAY.

Clumlie—St. Columb's lie—lies in South Sandwick, and in the Rental of 1503 is described as vjd. terre, conqueist *per comitem Willielmum*. Earl William died *circiter* 1481, when Sir John Sinclair took possession of various lands in Sandwick, and held them in 1503. He may have been ancestor of the subsequent Sinclairs in Sandwick of Tenston (which he had held), of Clumlie, and of Hestwall. Early in the next century there are notices of two Sinclairs designed as of Clumlie, viz., Henry Sinclair of Clumlie, ancestor of those of Towquoy and Hammer, and

I. JAMES SINCLAIR OF CLUMLIE, referred to in the report on the parochin of Sandwick, 1642: "Thair is fewed yrof be ye Erle of Orknay to umquhile James Sincler the lands of Clumlie, payand yrfor conforme to ye rentall, qlk ar now in ye possession of his sone

II. EDWARD SINCLER." In 1640 he was appointed bailie for Sandwick. On 19th January, 1641, he is a suitor of Court, and again on the 24th May next thereafter. He is a witness 4th June, 1646, to the claim of Katherine, Margaret, and Mariorie, dachteris to Magnus Sinclair in Burwick, claiming their shares of patrimony, &c. In the valuation of 1653 he is assessed for his lands of Clumbly. Clumlie died before 22nd August, 1666, on which date Jonet Beinstoun, relict of umqle. Edward Sinclair of Clumlie, is infeft in said Clumlie, which had been settled upon her by marriage contract. An Edward Sinclair, bailie of Sandwick, Mans Sinclair of Burwik, and others, are sworn in to report on Sandwick 5th June, 1627. In the report which was given in on the 19th idem he is described as Edvard Sinclair, appeirand of Clumlie. It is found that "Thair are few heritors amangst us, and thair heritadge is so little that it is not worthie to be called heritadge. Sum off thame hes thair teinds sett to tham selffis, bot payis deire thairfoir, bot the teinds of sum arr ledd."

I. HENRY SINCLAIR OF TOWQUOY was one of the Orcadian gentlemen who in 1592 made supplication to Parliament against an attempt of Earl Robert Stewart to compel them to feudalise their holdings by taking out charters from him.* He is doubtless identical with Henry Sinclair of Clumlie mentioned soon after. On 20th November, 1613, the tackman of Sandwik enumerates 'the guidwyfe of Clumlie.' On 19th July, 1621,

---
* Zetland County Families.

there appear Katharine, eldest daughter of umqle. Henrie Sinclair of Towquoy, and Robert Colthart, merchant in Kirkwall, hir spous; while on the 5th June, 1622, the procurator for Robert Sinclair in Towquoy compeared halding charter maid be Margaret Craigie, relict of umqle. Henrie Sinclair of Clumlie to the said

II. ROBERT SINCLAIR hir sone, of lands in Yle of Rousa, etc. Margaret Craigie is evidently the 'guidwyfe' of 1613, and in the Rental of 1642 Clumlie is noted as 'fewit' to her.

III. WALTER SINCLAIR IN TWQUY is referred to as ordained a bailie for Westray in 1640, and again on 8th March, 1641, when compeared Linklatter, merchand in Kirkwall, and becam cautioner for Jon Sinclair and Harie Sinclair his brother, sonnes law'll to Walter Sinclair, Twquy, "That Magnus Sinclair in Burrik his bairnies, etc., shall be safe and skaithless."

IV. JOHN SINCLAIR OF HAMMAR, son of the preceding, soon adjusted this family feud by marrying Isobel, daughter of the aforesaid Magnus Sinclair of Gorne, and afterwards of Burwick in Sandwick, for on the 16th March, 1641, Jas. Cobbane in Rannibuster became caution and lawborrowis for Issobell Sinclair, relict of umqle. Mr. Francis Liddell, minister at Birsa, and Jon Sinclair *now* hir spous for his entres, "That John Twatt portioner of Twatt his wyiff, bairnis, &c., sall be hairmless kept &c., under paine of ane hundred merkis money," and John was caution for his wyiff also. This Isobel was a freice masterfull woman. She had bought these lands from the Twatts 14th February, 1634. On the 19th May, 1642, Isobel Sinclair, relict of umqle. Mr. Francis Liddell, Archdean of Orkney, and John Sinclair hir now spous, compeirit, gave state and seisin and sold to Alex. Philip the house and lands of Hammer in Greinnie, Birsa, sauld to hir be Hew, sone of Wm. Craigie of Gairsay. The same day compeirit ane provident and discreit young gentilman John Sinclair sone to Walter Sinclair of Towquoy and Isobel Sinclair now his spous, and Alex. Philip resells to them the above house and lands of Hammar. On 6th May, 1647, John and Isobel sold Hammar to David Heart of Russland writer in Kirkwall, the sale being witnessed by John Sinclair in Huntiskarth. On 28th January, 1656, he appears as a witness, with Thos. Liddell his stepson and Halcro his brother-in-law. Hammar is mentioned in 1663, and on 18th April, 1665, he and his spous are *als* of John Graham of Brekness; and on the 18th August following, Kathrine, Margaret, Issobell, and Marjorie Sinclairs, Bairnes of umqle. Magnus Sinclair of Gorne, Jon Sinclair of Hamer, spous to said Issobell, and Wm. Prestone spous to said Marjorie, institute a cross-action against John Graham of Brekness. Hammar had issue

V. DAVID SINCLAIR OF HAMMER, his only sone and air, who alienated Hammer to James Sinclair of Saba, the conveyance being produced by Saba's procurator, one Wm. Sinclair, on 17th April, 1669; and on the 1st March, 1671, a similar conveyance to his eldest brother-uterine George Liddell was produced. Liddell got lands, houses, etc., in Birsa from Jas. Sinclair of Saba, for which charter was produced 29th November, 1673.

SINCLAIR OF GORNE AND BURWICK.
SANDWICK.

MAGNUS SINCLAIR OF GORNE took an active part in the local affairs of his time. His being so much mixed up with the Clumlies and the Tuquoys would indicate a close relationship to them. Hew Spens and Magnus Aith sought Lawborrows against him, the

7th November, 1612, and on the 7th December following David Kirkness of Kirkness becam cautioner for his peacable behaviour. Gorne was Chancellor of Assise 25th February, 1613, in Colville v. Thos. Sinclair; and on the 13th March same, Oliver Isbuster, the Fletts, &c., proceed against Magnus Sinclair of Gorne in Harra. On the 15th October, 1615, Gorne being then baillie in that pairt, bought udal land in Netherbrugh, Harra, from Andro Flett of Redland, Firth; to this transaction Magnus Sinclair in Ovirbrugh, Harra, is a witness. On the 20th January, 1619, there was trial of a cause between Stewart of Graemsay and Magnus Sinclair in Gorne. On 15th March, 1620, he and his spous Merion Irwin are mentioned. On 9th April, 1621, comp. Gorne, Magnus Louttit, in Lyking, and Patrick Millar of Hestwall, as proc. for Elizabeth Sinclair, spous to said Louttit, *re* lands in Wosbuster, &c. In presence of Edward Sinclair, baillie of Sandwick, the same day compear Louttit and Elisabeth Sinclair, his spous, with Mareoun Irving, spous to Gorne, *re* lands from Bishop Graham. On 27th July same, Gorne and his wife sold Beaw and Husgar, in Sandwick, to Andro Linkletter of that Ilk. On 29th April, 1622, comp. Gorne, with Robert Sinclair of Skaill, baillie in that pairt,— To said Magnus for money lent, &c., an annual rent of £40 from William Irving, apparand air of Saba, who on 10th September next thereafter for 400 merks to Gorne and his wife (sister to Saba) the lands of Burwick—pertaining aforetime to the said Magnus— and the Newgar Quoy, near Clumlie. On 5th August, 1623, Gorne sued Tohop, Sabay, &c. Gorne died before 1646, on 4th June in which year, when his daughters claim their shares of his property before Edward Sinclair of Clumlie, &c.; on 19th July, 1656, they make cause against William Irving of Saba, their uncle; on 18th April, 1666, they are *ats* of John Grahame of Brekness, whom they in turn sue the 18th August following. Gorne's daughters by Marion Irving. daughter of Saba, were:

1. KATHARINE.
2. MARGARET.
3. ISSOBELL, m. 1st, the Rev. Francis Liddell. 2nd, John Sinclair of Hammar.
4. MARJORIE, m. Wm. Preston.

THE SINCLAIRS OF OVERBROUGH,
HARRA.

I. MAGNUS SINCLAIR IN OVIRBRUGH witnesses the purchase of Netherbrugh in Harra by Magnus Sinclair of Gorne 15th October, 1617, and on the 13th July preceding a Magnus Sinclair in Brugh obtained security from Alex. Flett in How and William Flett in Netherbrugh, all in Harra.

II. ROBERT SINCLAIR in Ovirbrugh is a witness 8th May, 1634, to a charter of Netleter, Harra, by John Sinclair in Huntskarth, and Katharine Flett, his wife.

III. JOHN SINCLAIR of Ovirbrough is down in the 1653 valuation of Harra. On the 4th March, 1662, compeirit ane famous man John Sinclair, elder in Ovirbrugh in Harra, John Sinclair younger thair his son, and John Sinclair his oy, and John the elder made over Ovirbrugh to John, his son, and John, his grandson—Saufing always his liferent and that of his spous Margaret Lina. This Ovirbrugh was succeeded by his son

IV. JOHN SINCLAIR of Ovirbrough, who amongst many others is *ats* of Captain Robert Irving 7th August, 1673. The next year, 1st December, 1674, he acquired lands in Ovirbrugh and Bimbuster from Robert Burwick. John Sinclair is referred to as in occupation of Ovirbrough 17th May, 1679. His son

V. JOHN SINCLAIR OF OVIRBROUGH witnessed a transaction *re* lands in Rusland 1st December, 1674, and is perhaps the John in Harra horned and inhibited in 1697, when there are also Magnus and James Sinclair in Harra, and Harie Sinclair in Costa for Harra lands, etc. His successor was

VI. JAMES SINCLAIR IN OVIRBROUGH, who comp. 11th June, 1706, with his spous Katharein Wilson (relict of Andro Flett), to whom he gave his house and lands of Ovirbrough in lyferent. On the 25th September following the Chamberlain-Depute obtained a decree against *inter alia* James Sinclair in Ovirbrugh in Harra, John Sinclair thair, John Sinclair in Grimistone thair, etc., while on 16th February, 1719, the Earl of Morton's chamberlain sues *inter alia* James Sinclair in Ovirbrugh, John Sinclair in Gremistone, Margaret Sinclair in Huntscarth, Elspeth Spence (relict of George Sinclair) in Rusland, Katharine Sinclair (relict of Jas. Louttit the elder), etc., all in Harra.

VII. WILLIAM SINCLAIR IN OVIRBRUGH, and Katharine Spence, his spous, obtained from Dr. Hugh Sutherland of Kirkwall a disposition of udal lands in the town of Ovirbrugh with houses, etc.,—as the same have been tenanted by the said Wm. Sinclair till now, 19th June, 1739.

THE SINCLAIRS OF CRAYA,
STROMNESS.

I. JAMES SINCLAIR IN CREYA, near Stromness, and THOMAS SINCLAIR, his brother thair, are witnesses, 6th October, 1634.

II. JOHN SINCLAIR IN CREYA, in the toun of Utterstromness, acquired from William Spens in Quhom, son to umqle. John Spence thair, on 15th February, 1645, stait and seisin of the said hous and lands of Crya. Witnesses: Adam Beattoun in Brekness, Jas. Beattoun in Creya, etc. In succession to him after a long interval is

III. JAMES SINCLAIR, elder of CRAYA, who compeared 16th February, 1727, with Ann Beattoun, his spous, and Jas. Sinclair, their eldest sone, who got "stait" of Craya and of his mother's share of her father's estate, she being one of the heirs portioners of David Beattoun of Glouck, near Stromness.

IV. JAMES SINCLAIR the younger, next of CRAYA, who is noted in the Cropt Acct. of 1739, married Isobel Clouston, and dying without issue, was succeeded by his brother

V. JOHN SINCLAIR OF CRAYA, farmer and tenant of Lidfea in Stromness, who was also married to an Isobel Clouston. His only son

VI. JOHN SINCLAIR OF CRAYA, compd. 25th February, 1769, holding disposition from his parents of Creiya, Manniquoys, etc., with houses, etc., with reservation of liferent to Isobel Clouston, his mother, and Isobel Clouston, his aunt.

THE SINCLAIRS OF RAPNESS,
WESTRAY.

James Saintclair of Stive [Brew] is stated by Van Bassan the Dane to have been the father of

I. MALCOLME SAINTCLAIR OF QUENDALE, in Shetland. In the report of the commissioners on the Estate of the Isle of Sanday, ". . . There is within the said parochin and Ile lands belonging of old to the archdaine of Zetland, sett in few be him to the laird of Asilmountt, and sett be him in wodsett to Malcum Sinclaire of Quandill, and left be him to his sonne George Sinclaire, quho hes the saidis landis in present possessioune, and lyis within the said Ile and parochine, as followis :—In Langtas, in Our Ladie parochine, saxpennie land, in Arstas ane pennie land, in Cleatt ane pennie land, in Sellibister ane half pennie land, ane pennie land in the town of How, within the Croce parochine, and in the parochinne of Sainct Colme fowr pennie land; thir landis payis all their dewties to the said George Sinclair." Malm. Sinclair is a suitor of the Orcadian Court on 4th November, 1617, for his lands of Rapness, and died on the 6th January, 1618, leaving by his wife Margaret, daughter of Hugh Sinclair of Brugh, in Shetland, a large family, of whom his third son

    II. GEORGE SINCLAIR became of CRAIGENDS and RAPNESS. He was present as a suitor of Court 18th February, 1618 On the 21st March, 1619, George Sinclair of Rapness, Malcolm Sinclair of Quendale, and James Sinclair, Fear of Quendale, his sone, appear in *re* The Bu of Ropness. On 29th April, 1622, he attests a transfer of lands of Innertoun of Stromness from James, Hew, Johne and George Sinclairis, brothers-german, indwellers in Tenstone and heritable udallers. He was sworn at Kirkwall 9th June, 1627, to repoirt conforme to the commissioun of the Ile of Westray 29th May, 1633, The Qlk. Day, George Sinclair of Rapness being electit and chosen a Commissioner to the approtching Parliament. . . protestit that ane stent be maid for his maintenance This was resolved and persons appointed to collect same in the various parishes. He sued David Cogill, merchand in Stronsa, the 4th August, 1638, and on 30th July, 1639, he obtained a Decree against WALTER SINCLAIR IN WOSBUSTER for breach of his contract of date 23rd January, 1629. On the 8th August, 1642, a charter of disposition was produced granted be Jas Tulloch of Langskaill, with consent of Helen Henrysone, his spous, of lands in the Yle of Rowsa, etc , to George Sinclair of Rapness He is an absent suitor 19th January, 1641, and styled of Ropnes and Trenabie, and on the 28th March, 1651, Robert Tulloch of Aikeris, in Westra, makes suit against the umqle. Geo Sinclair of Rapness He married Martha, daughter of James Stewart of Gramsay (by his wife Helen Monteith of Egilsay), and had issue

    1 MALCOLM, next of Rapness   2. JAMES
    1 KATHERINE, m 1646, Laurence Stewart of Bigton.
    2 MARGARET, m 1st , Edward Sinclair of Gyre
                    2nd, James Mowat of Ollaberry, fiar of Garth, Shetland
    3 JEAN, m James Rutherford

    III MALCOLM SINCLAIR, THIRD OF RAPNESS, is down in the valuation of 1653 as owner of lands in Sanda Isle Lady Parish—his lands of Clett, Airsta, Sellibuster, etc.; and in Burness Parish—Malcolm Sinclair, sometime of Rapness, for his lands, grassums, etc , there On 17th August, 1654, Patrick Smyth of Braco proceeds against Malcolm Sinclair, eldest sone and air to umqle. Geo Sinclair of Rapnes. His daughter

    MARTHA m 1672, Jas. Sinclair of Goat, in Shetland

    IV. HENRY SINCLAIR OF WOSBUSTER

    V. THOMAS SINCLAIR OF RAPNESS, eldest sone of the preceding, obtained a decree on 8th February, 1711, against Thos Traill of Holland for £333 6s. 8d. scots. Traill was put to the Horn on the 4th July thereafter, and sought suspension of the same 9th August

VI. WILLIAM SINCLAIR, eldest sone to deceast Thomas Sinclair, now tenant in the Bu of Rapness, and Barbara Traill, his spouse—lands in Kirkness, etc., in Sandwick, 24th October, 1751.

In the kirk-yard at Westray there is a tombstone bearing date 1676 which commemorates the members of this family.

ARMS, see Armoury.

THE SINCLAIRS OF ESTAQUOY,
HARRA.

I. JAMES SINCLAIR is noted as tenant of Newclett (now Nettleter) and Estaquoy, in a charter produced 9th June, 1620, by Bishop Graham to Hew Halcro and Jean Stewart his spous.

II. ALEXANDER SINCLAIR IN ESTAQUOY compeared 29th April, 1665, holding Charter of Feu ferme in Estaquoy in Netleter in Harra, to which John Sinclair in Oback, there, is one of the witnesses. May 7th. 1666, How is tenanted by John and Alex. Sinclair thair. 28th February, 1667, Alex. Sinclair in How acquires from Wm. Corrigill his udal lands there. In the valuation on 19th April, 1671, the Commissioners note Alex. Sinclair for his lands of Netcletter; he compeared 29th December same with Charter of Alienation of lands in How, in the same parish; and suffered inhibition 29th August, 1677. On the 28th May, 1680, he gave to his eldest son John, and his youngest son Magnus, stait, etc., of land in Netletter with houses, etc. He had issue

1. JOHN, his successor; 2. JAMES; and 3. THOMAS, witnesses to the charter to their brothers. 4. MAGNUS, afterwards of Estaquoy.

III. JOHN SINCLAIR and his brother Magnus, sones of Alex. Sinclair of Estaquoy, are witnesses 29th December, 1680. John of Estaquoy died before 5th August, 1707, and was succeeded by his eldest son

IV. ALEXANDER SINCLAIR IN NORTHBREK, in Bingaquoy, ffirth, who gave Ltres. of Disposition of some land in How (tenanted by Magnus Sinclair) to the Rev. Thos. Baikie, produced 1st August, 1717. "My grandfather was infeft therein on 28th February, 1667, now 50 years ago, and the property came from the Corrigills of Corrigill or that Ilk." His uncle

V. MAGNUS SINCLAIR, compeared 5th August, 1707, holding disposition from his late brother, John of Estaquoy, of half of Estaquoy and part of How. His eldest son

VI. JAMES SINCLAIR, is mentioned 23rd February, 1710; and on the 8th March, 1717, compeared as of Estoquoy, and with him Margaret Louttit his spous, to whom he gave life-rent in the House and lands of Estoquoy. He witnessed a Harra conveyance 15th September, 1740; and on 25th February, 1749, granted Ltres. of Disposition to Wm. Smith, merchand in Stromness, of lands in Estaquoy with houses, etc., near the lands there possessed by Magnus Flett in Conzier. Wm. Smith produced the same March 10th, 1752.

THE SINCLAIRS OF NETHERGARTH,
HARRA.

I. ROBERT SINCLAIR IN NETHERGARTH, in Harra, acquired on the 15th July, 1626, from Alex. Kirkness in Duther Hous (now Doe Hous), in Sandwick, lands in Skorwall in Quoyloo—in Quoynores—my meadow in Bloomire with houses, etc., thereon, all in Sandwick. On the 14th March, 1643, a Charter of Alienation was produced from Robert Sinclair of Nethergersan in Sandwick of the lands and houses of Ovirtoun in How to Thos. Corrigill in Winksetter in Harra. In 1643 he sold a claim upon Corrigill to umqle. Jas. Spence. His spous was Helen Sinclair.

II. WILLIAM SINCLAIR, son to the umqle. Robert Sinclair in Nethergarsand in Sandwick, has an appearance on 21st April, 1652.

THE SINCLAIRS OF CAMPSTON.

I. ROBERT SINCLAIR, FIRST OF CAMPSTON, is mentioned as dead 15th April, 1614, when a marriage contract is entered into by Hew Sinclair of Damsay, "son of the *late* Robert Sinclair of Campston."* He is probably the Robert Sinclair mentioned by Bishop Bothwell in a letter dated 5th February, 1560, as with his brother Henry and their father opposing any change from the old form of worship, being instigated thereto by Bellenden, the Justice Clerk.* Bishop Bothwell was stepson and Sir John Bellenden nephew to Oliver Sinclair of Solway Moss celebrity, who held the Isles in Tack 1540-48, and to whom the Sinclairs above mentioned are doubtless in near relation. He is noted in the Rental of 1595, "Sanday (St. Androi's Parochin *pro rege*) Adhuc ane Quoy, payis 2 meils cost. Intromettit with the Robert Sinclair. . . ." He had issue

1. ROBERT, next of Campston. 2. HEW of Damsay. 3. EDWARD of Ness.

In the attestation to the signature of Magnus Luttet, takman of Sandwik, 20th November, 1613, Edward of Ness, third son of Robert Sinclair, is referred to as brother of Campston, also a witness on that occasion. In the Rental of 1614 he is rated for Ness, Stromness; and in 1627 reports to His Majestie's Commission as to the state of that parish. On 17th June, 1618, he is *ats* of Malislane Sinclair, spouse of James Stewart, first of Gramsay. 21st November, 1619, Compt. for Edward Sinclair of Ness and Adame Smyth of Stoiff, as pror. for Jonet Redland, relict of umqle. Robert Sinclair of Larquoy, and Magnus Sinclair sone to said Jonet, and Jas. Brown sone to Alex. Brown in Brekness, as pror. for Edward Sinclair, brother to said Magnus—lands in Uttertoun of Stromness in liferent, and to Magnus and Edward in fee, etc. On 2nd November idem—Edward Sinclair of Ness, James Sinclair of Grott, Nicoll Sinclair, merchant in Kirkwall, Marjorie Sinclair in Larquoy, and Alex. Sinclair in Fealquoy—Skelberries, lands in Outertoune of Stromness, etc. On 28th February, 1622, he is a witness to moneys payit be Alex. Broun of Brekness, etc. In 1640 he is ordained a bailie; in 1641 is in the enumeration of Earldom suitors, and is rated in the 1653 valuation. He was apparently succeeded in Ness by his nephew, David of Ryssay.

II. ROBERT SINCLAIR, SECOND OF CAMPSTON, occupies an important position in Orcadian records. In 1611 he is *ats* of Patrick, Earl of Orkney; in 1613 he attests the signature of Magnus Luttet, Takman of Sandvik; in 1615 is *ats* of Sir Jas. Stewart; and in 1616 sues Francis Mudie of Breckness. In 1617 he is an absent suitor of the Earldom Court, of which when present he is invariably first of his name to be enumerated; and he and his son Thomas make suit against Jas. Stewart of Gramsay. In 1618 he is *ats* of Harie Stewart, Fear of Gramsay; in 1618 mentioned with John Sinclair, merchant in Kirkwall, and Wm. Sinclair of Tohoip; on 9th November idem. is mentioned with Hew Sinclair, brother-german, and Wm. Sinclair of Greinwall; on 4th December Robert Sinclair of Campston and Helen Achesoune his spous. On 1st July, 1623, he was Sheriff-Depute, acting in conjunction with Edward Sinclair of Æstenquoy. In 1627 his brother-german, Hugh Sinclair of Damsay, became security for him for offence against Bishop

---

* Craven.

Graham. In 1627 Campstane and Essenquoy have the haill prebendarie in tack, and the same year they were sworn to report upon the parish of Rousay and Egilsay; and they are again associated to report on St. Andrew's. In 1633 Campston entered protest against the service of Jonet Sinclair as nearest and lau'll air of umqle. Wm. Sinclair of Holland, his son Edward compeiring for him on that occasion. In 1635 he subscribed the Relation of Famine. In 1640 David Heart of Rusland sues Robert Sinclair of Campston. Issue :

 1. THOMAS SINCLAIR, fear of Campston, his eldest sone ; and
 2. EDWARD SINCLAIR, his second sone. There were also daughters—
 1. ELIZABETH, who in 1649 sued her brother Thomas for her rights.
 2. MARGARET, m. 1643 Andrew, son of Wm. Sinclair of Greinwall.

Robert Sinclair of Campston is present amongst the gentlemen suitors of the Earldom Court, 26th October, 1641 ; and dying about 1645-9, was succeeded by his eldest son

 III. THOMAS SINCLAIR, THIRD OF CAMPSTON, for whom when fiar in 1629 Wm. Sinclair of Greinwall became lawborrowis in security for Wm. Sinclair of Saba and his family. In 1638 he is *ats* of John Craigie of Sandis. In 1645, as fear, he alienates various lands in Rousa and Firth to James Traill in Westness (Rousa). His sister Elizabeth sues him for her rights in 1649, which implies the death of his father. In 1651 he is *ats* of Edward Sinclair of Gyre, and is down in the valuation of 1653 for various lands in St. Andrew's and Firth. On the 30th September, 1662, he and his spous Marie Stewart are mentioned. He had issue

 1. EDWARD, next of Campston. 2. JOHN, second son (sasine 1643).

 IV. EDWARD SINCLAIR, FOURTH OF CAMPSTANE, was proceeded against 10th October, 1676, by Thos. Stewart, Proc. Fiscal for Orkney and Zetland, for intromitting with the gear of umqle. Thos. Sinclair his father. Edward Sinclair was succeeded by his only son

 V. EDWARD SINCLAIR, FIFTH AND LAST OF CAMPSTON. On the 21st September, 1708, David Traill assigns lands in Sabay to his son Patrick under reversion be the heirs of umqle. Edward Sinclair of Campston ; and on 18th December, 1725, compt. David Traill of Sabay holding disposition by Edward Sinclair only sone to deceast Edward Sinclair of Campston and Eliz. Wilson his spous—and air to the also deceast Thos. Sinclair of Campston his grandfather—lands in St. Andrew's and lands of Campstane. Witnesses Jerome Sinclair in Stromness and Jas. Allan his servitor. This notice is followed by another on 19th June, 1729, when Patrick Traill of Sabay sues Edward Sinclair "onlie lawfull sone on life to the deceast Edwd. Sinclair sometyme residenter in Campstone in Parish of St. Andrew's in the County of Orknay and Elizabeth Wilson his spous daughter to deceased Thos. Wilson of Hunclet sometyme merchant in Kirkwall," for 10,000 merks scots, etc. This Edward Sinclair of Campston is stated to have been father of

 VI. EDWARD SINCLAIR, who by Kirstane or Christane Sinclair was father of a daughter

  ISOBEL, m. to Peter Sinclair, and had issue
   JOHN SINCLAIR, married in 1789. Issue
    JAMES SINCLAIR, father of
     JAMES SINCLAIR, resident at Upper Breckquoy, Holm, Orkney, who writes that he was told by his father that No. VI. was a son of [Robert] Sinclair, Laird of Campston, that his name was over the old hall door, and a coat of arms over the gateway.

Hay, in his "Genealogie of the Sainteclaires of Rosslyn," has : "I think that the other charters relating to Pentland, and the Chapell of Roslin, may be found in Comeston's hands, or in Sir Alex. Gibson of Pentland's charter-chest, or els amongst my Lord Sinclair's papers."

THE SINCLAIRS OF DAMSAY.

I. HUGH SINCLAIR OF DAMSAY was a brother of Campston and Ness. He had lands scattered all over the Earldom. There are numerous notices of him.

He is apparently the Hew Sinclair, takman of Stromness for Wosterwoy in 1613, who will not compt. with the Takman of Sandwick for the roume of Newgair, etc., and may be the Hew Sinclair, merchant in Kirkwall, who with William Sinclair of Greinwall, sues Donald Stewart of Brugh 24th February, 1617, and who on the 7th January idem. had with other Sinclairs made suit against James Stewart of Gramsay and others. On 18th February, 1618, this Hew, the merchant, is on an Assise for 'ryot and bluidshed." On 9th November, 1618, Hew Sinclair, merchant in Kirkwall, brother-german to Campstoune, and Jonet Sventone, his spous, with Wm. Sinclair of Greinwall, are mentioned. On 2nd January, 1621, Hew was on the Assise to try John Learie for the "Thifteous stelling of ane quhyt yeik yow, of ane kaidie (pet) lamb, etc." ; and on the 5th idem, became security for Alex. Flett in How, Harra. On the 27th December same he produced a charter from Michael Balfour of Garth, with consent of Margaret Sinclair, his spous, of lands and houses of Swartmaill in Skeldwik, in Westra, etc. ; and on the 28th February, 1622, a charter of Alienation maid be The Right Honble. Hew Halcro of that Ilk to Hew and Jonet his spous and langest liver of them the houses and lands of Beanzeaquoy, in the parish of Firth. On 25th July, 1622, he is noted as owning Fealquoy (Evie) Kingshous and lands in Bimbuster, both in Harra, and many other properties all over the Earldom, acquired from Robert Monteith of Egilsa. On 4th November, 1623, and 25th January, 1624, Hew Sinclair of Kingshous is present as a Suitor at Court ; on 7th June, 1623, Hew Sinclair, merchand burgess of Kirkwall, in re lands of St. Ola, etc.; in 1627 he owns Cloike in Birsa, and on the 24th April same became cautioner for Robert Sinclair of Campstane, his brother-german. On 3rd May, 1631, amongst the suitors present are Hew Sinclair for his lands of Kingshous, Hew Sinclair of Damsay, etc., but these are evidently one and the same person. On the 8th June, 1632, on the Assise against Scollay, there are *inter alia*, Hew Sinclair of Damsay (Chancellour), John Sinclair (merchand in Kirkwall), Hew Sinclair of Yairphay, etc. In 1640 he is constituted bailie for Firth. On 15th April, 1614, a contract is completed at Rannibester between "Thomas Swentoun, Archdeane of Orknay, *and minister of God's Word at Kirkwall*," taking burden on him for his "dochter Jonet Swentoun," and Hew Sinclair of Damsay, sone of the late Robert Sinclair of Campstone. These young persons bound themselves to solemnise "ye bond of matrimonie in face of halie kirk with all solemnities due as effeirs," and Jonet had a tocher of six hundred merks. In 1642, Orphir, Smewgro, Cowbister, and Orokirk are now feued and in ye possession of Hew Sinclair of Damsay, also Ryssay in Walls, and North Witfirth in St. Olla. Damsay appears as a Suitor in 1638 and 1640, and on 19th January, 1641, for his lands thair, and in Over Brugh in Harra. June 23rd, 1645, he assigns a toft in Skabra in Sandwick to his son-in-law Andro Linklettir. January 31st, 1648, he exchanges Fealquoy, Cloike, etc., with David McClellane of Wodwick, Chamberlain of Orknay for Kirbuster in Orphir. On 16th January, 1649, George, sone to William Sinclair of Damsay, witnessed a deed between Jas. Louttit of Mirbuster and Johne Louttit of Corrigill. In 1651 Damsay, with others, is sued by Edward Sinclair of Gyre. He appears in the Valuation of 1653 as owning lands in all parts of the Earldom—Stromness, St. Andrew's, St. Olla, Orphir, Sandwick, Harra, Birsa, Firth, Walls, Ronsa, etc. On the 19th May, 1658, he sued Patrick Sinclair, his eldest sone, and others. Soon after this he died. In the "County Families of the Zetland Isles" it is noted that Katherine Mouat of the Garth family was married to Hew Sinclair of Damsay, but this does not receive support from any of the foregoing notices. He was married to Jonet Swinton, daughter of Thomas Swinton, Archdeacon of Orkney, and left issue—

1. PATRICK, who succeeded him. 2. THOMAS. 3. DAVID.
1. AGNES, who married Andro Linklater, of Benziecht, which is mentioned 26th April, 1677, as having been sometime life-rented to her.

II. PATRICK SINCLAIR, SECOND OF DAMSAY, appears *ats* of his father Hew in 1658 ; on 16th September, 1661, of his brothers Thomas and David, sones to the umqle. Hew

Sinclair of Damsay, for their interest, etc.; and on 6th January, 1664, Patrick most ungallantly sues Jean Ballenden, his spous, while on the same day Patrick Craigie, ex-Provost of Kirkwall, sues Patrick Sinclair of Damsay, Edward Sinclair in Booabrek, in Quhome, and others.

THOMAS SINCLAIR OF SMOOGROW was perhaps a son of Hew of Damsay, who had held that place. On the 10th September, 1675, John Henry, minister of Orphir, sued Thos. Sinclair of Smoogrow, Sibilla, relict of Hew Sinclair, Robert Sinclair, his sone, etc. On the 26th April, 1677, Compt. James, onlie sone to ffrancis Gordone, Baillie of Stromness, as pror. for Barbara Gordone, spous to Thos. Sinclair of Smowgrow, holding charter of Lyferent maid be sd. Thos. to her of his houses and lands of Smowgrow, etc., in Orphir. On the 18th July following he is a witness, and on 19th August, 1687, the lands of Smowgrow and Cowbuster belong to Thos. Sinclair and his aforesaid spous. On the 10th July, 1706, William Halcro is designed of Cowbuster. His brother was

DAVID SINCLAIR OF RYSSAY, apparently third son of Hew of Damsay.

On 25th February, 1662, David was sued, *inter alia*, by Robert Jack, mercht. burgess of Edinburgh; on 10th August, 1665, he is sued by R. Graham, mercht. burgess of Edinburgh, for his bond of dait 17th August, 1664, for £818 scots, and inhibited. David Bellanden, brother of Stonehous, put this to the horn. On 9th November, 1668, compd. David Sinclair of Ryssay, heritable proprietor of lands near Stromness, and sells "sum faddoms" near the "Boatisnewst" to John Brown in Stromness and his spous Kath. Cromartie. On 27th July, 1669, Rev. James Henrie of Orphir produced charter of lands from David Sinclair of Ryssay. August 4th, 1675, produced Precept of Sasine made by Ryssay and Elisabeth Johnstoun, his spous, for infefting William Davisone, writer in Kirkwall, in certane parts of the lands of Ryssay, because they could not repay that cash which they had borrowed from him. On 13th May, 1676, he sued Thos. Wilsone of Hunclett for £3,122 scots, and on 9th April, 1677, Francis and John, sons to James Mudie of Melsetter. On 26th December, 1677, compt. Robert Tulloch, indweller in Cowbuster, as pror. for George, second sone to David Sinclair of Ryssay, haulding Dispositioune, etc., maid be said David to said George and his airis, whom failing to his assignees, whom all failing (as God forbid) to his awin neirest aires his lands of Old and New Ness, Stromness, saveand lyferent to said David, and Eliz. Johnstoun, his spous. On 24th September, 1696, Ryssay was sued for 100 merks scots by Patrik Traill, maraner in Leith, and inhibited thereon the 17th November following. On 12th May, 1697, James Gray in Foubister, and his spous Anna, brother's dochter to Jon Grott of Fleck, sued Ryssay, etc., and finally on 6th December, 1736, " Forasmuch as the now deceast David Sinclair of Ryssay and Eliz. Johnston, spouses, by their Bond of 17th June, 1675 (63 years previous) borrowed from the also deceast John Groat of Fleik 309 merks scots, to be repaid at Whitsunday thereafter with interest if not then paid, and to infeft the said John Groat in lands in Orakirk, Orphir, Redeemable however . . . . . William Halcro, younger of Coubister, has paid and got reversion and lands, etc., etc." He had issue—

1.   2. GEORGE.   3. JOHN.

THE SINCLAIRS OF CONYAR,
HARRA.

No special enquiry has as yet been made as to the origin of this branch of the lineage, from which the author of this work derives. It is, however, variously stated that they are cadets of the Sinclairs of Damsay and Kingshouse (Konungs-garth) ; of the Sinclairs of Craya, Stromness ; and of the Sinclairs of Beboran, Harra, from whom Conyar is held, the last statement—which does not necessarily contradict the others—being the most likely one.

JEROME SINCLAIR, shipmaster in Stromness, and Jas. Allen, his servitor, on 18th December, 1725, witness the Disposition by Edward Sinclair, last of Campston. In 1705 Jerome Sinclair was in Seatter, Stromness; he, or a successor, appears in various records in 1718, 1747, '48, '52, '58, '61 and '70.

CHARLES SINCLAIR, son of the preceding, is party to an instrument in 1758, and later on inherits Beboran in Harra, as only son in life to the said Jerome Sinclair.

ROBERT SINCLAIR, FIRST OF CONYAR (1), is probably identical with Robert Sinclair in Harra, 1747, and of Furse, there, 1753. In his time the Norse language continued to be spoken in Harra, notable as the only Orcadian parish untouched by the sea, and also on account of there being about 100 proprietors, "The Hundred Lairds of Harray," who for the most part hold the same lands their ancestors held centuries back, by prescriptive right as Odallers (*Proceres Orcadium*), a "Yeomanry nobility" dependent in no way on charter or deed as the root of title, and under no feudal superior, not even king or earl. Robert Sinclair of Conyar had issue two sons, whose relative seniority is undetermined.

    2. THOMAS.   3. WILLIAM.

THOMAS SINCLAIR, SECOND OF CONYAR (2) born *cir*. 1758; married *cir*. 1781 Marjory Kirkness, a connection of Kirkness of Kirkness, Sandwick. They had issue three daughters, who died unmarried in advanced years, and one son, viz.,

    4. ROBERT, next of Conyar, born in 1782.
    5. MARGARET. 6. MERCY. 7. ELSPETH, baptised 24th July, 1785.

WILLIAM SINCLAIR (3) born *cir*. 1760; married in 1789 Jean Tulloch of Moen in Harra. He resided in Conyar until November, 1805, when he and his family removed to "The House of Howe" in the district or township of Bimbuster, Harray. He died the same year, and his widow then removed to Teevath, in the same neighbourhood, where she reared her family. Upon the marriage in 1825 of her daughter Margaret to Magnus Johnston of Müce, Birsa, he had a house built for her, where she dwelt until her death in 1834. She was a connection of Scarth, first of Binscarth, and her daughter Margaret is found witnessing the baptism of a child born to Nicol Scarth. William Sinclair had issue in Conyar—

    8. JEAN, baptised 28th November, 1790; died young.
    9. MARGARET, baptised 11th July, 1793; died 10th July, 1874; married 17th December, 1825, as second wife, Magnus Johnston of the House of Müce in Sabiston, Birsa.
   10. WILLIAM, born 10th February, 1795, of whom presently.
   11. ROBERT, bap. 11th June, 1797; drowned in Shields harbour *cir*. 1820; unmarried.
   12. JEAN, bap. 19th May, 1799; died young.
   13. ANN, born 16th April, 1803 (St. Magnus' Day); died in Müce *cir*. 1861; married in 1831 Peter Merriman of Stromness, who died same year, leaving posthumous issue.
   14. JOHN, born 22nd March, 1805; lost at sea *cir*. 1826.

ROBERT SINCLAIR, THIRD OF CONYAR (4) born 1782; died 1861; married in 1822 Barbara Vorston of Howan, Sabiston, Birsa (who died in 1839), and had in Conyar—

   15. ROBERT, born 23rd December, 1824.
   16. BARBARA, born 20th October, 1826; res. Conyar; single.
   17. MARGARET, born 20th July, 1828; res. Conyar; single.
   18. JAMES, born 11th May, 1830; died in Melbourne, unmarried.
   19. THOMAS BLYTH, born 4th August, 1834.
   20. JOHN, born 28th December, 1838; is an elder of the Established Church; res. Conyar; single.

ORCADIAN SCIONS.

CAPTAIN WILLIAM SINCLAIR (10) Harbourmaster of Kirkwall, was born in Conyar, Harra, on the 10th February, 1795. He married in Harra about 1822 Elisabeth, fourth daughter of Magnus Flett of Garth, there, by his second wife Katherine Borwick, of whom she was the second daughter. The only surviving son of his widowed mother, William Sinclair went to sea at an early age. In 1835-36 he was chief officer on board of the "Lavinia" of Stromness, Captain James Leask, trading between Stromness and foreign parts—Liverpool, Limerick, Holland, Russia, etc. At that time Stromness was the port of call for the Hon. the Hudson Bay Co.'s ships, and was a place of rising importance with a local company owning several trading vessels. William Sinclair was for some time captain of a trading schooner called the "Victory," of Stromness, in which he held some shares. In 1841, or earlier, he was captain of the schooner "Sir Joseph Banks," owned in Kirkwall, and trading between that port and Leith since 1800* The town crier of those days used to extol her as a "fast sailing clipper packet"—thirty-four hours was a smart passage. He changed his residence in 1842-43, removing from the north end of Stromness to the Broad St., Kirkwall, where about 1846 he began business as a produce merchant. The potato disease that so severely afflicted Ireland visited Orkney soon after, and for four or five years the crop was a failure. Captain Sinclair became a great benefactor to the townsfolk, by bringing over food supplies from Aberdeen, by steamer arriving every Saturday, when his premises were crowded by people anxiously awaiting and afraid to miss their turn. He became Harbourmaster of the port of Kirkwall in or about 1850, which position he held till his death. At first, while trade was small, he could manage to conduct his own business as well, but in a few years the post needed his full attention and that of one or two clerks also. He was a very popular man, thoroughly trusted by all who had any dealings with him, and literally respected by all who knew him. A good and diligent man of business, he was a kind friend to many who sought his ad-vice. He and his

wife acquired on 8th August, 1850, by Disposition from Robert Louttit, sometime Collector of Customs at Kirkwall, a house or tenement of land fronting the Broad Street, Kirkwall, for which Instrument of Sasine issued 13th May, 1854. He was admitted Burgess and Guild Brother of Kirkwall 6th November, 1851. The ticket is on vellum, the seal of the Burgh† is on red wax, encased in a tin round and attached to the parchment by means of a ribbon of royal blue colour. He executed a Disposition and Deed of Settlement 15th August, 1868, appointing as his trustees Thomas Traill of Holland; Andrew Gold, Chamberlain for the Earl of Zetland, residing at Grainbank; James Scarth Spence, banker in Kirkwall; Robert Tulloch, merchant in Kirkwall; and Peter Sinclair

---

* Barry's History.   † See illustration on page 95.

Heddle, writer there. At the time of his death Captain Sinclair was the most eminent of his name in the Isles. He was nearly related to the late Robert Scarth of Binscarth, the Rev. Dr. Logie of St. Magnus' Cathedral Kirk, and Provost Baue of Kirkwall. His wife (born 17th August, 1797) had died on the 13th September, 1861, and he followed her to the grave 25th July, 1874. Both lie buried in the kirkyard of St. Magnus' Cathedral, where a tombstone preserves them to memory. Children born in Stromness :

21. WILLIAM, born 20th November, 1823; went to sea in 1840, fell from the main-gaff of the brig "Useful" early in 1841, and stove in his side. The wound appeared to be healed, and, unconscious of his impending fate, his constant and cheerful letters to his mother always ended, "Yours until death." In May, 1842, the wound became serious, and he returned home, dying in Stromness on St. Clair's Eve, 16th July, 1842. He was buried in Harray, where a tombstone marks the spot.
22. JAMES LEASK, born 15th April, 1828 (St. Magnus' Eve).
23. JANE FLETT, born 7th October, 1834; died unmarried at Edinburgh 30th November, 1880, where she had been subjected to curative treatment, as in 1856 she became mentally weak. Letters written by her before that date appear those of a thoroughly practical and normal person.
24. JOHN BEATTON, born 15th January, 1837; died in 1845, and was buried in Kirkwall.

ROBERT SINCLAIR, FOURTH OF CONYAR (15) was born there on the 23rd December, 1824. He married Margaret, daughter of Thomas Sinclair of Beboran. Issue :

25. A daughter resident in Conyar.

THOMAS BLYTH SINCLAIR (19) born in Conyar 4th August, 1834; is married and has a large family of sons and daughters. In early life he went to South Africa. He resides at 38 Canning St., in Liverpool, where he carries on business as "Sinclair & Ellwood," shipchandlers and provision merchants, 41 South Castle St.; warehouse, 3 & 5 King St. (Glasgow agents, Jas. Porteous & Son, 5 Dixon St.)

JAMES LEASK SINCLAIR (22)—second son and eventually (1880) sole surviving issue of the late William Sinclair (see No. 10), sometime merchant and Harbourmaster of the Port of Kirkwall—was born at Stromness, Orkney, on the 15th April, 1828 (St. Magnus' Eve). He was named after a brother of the late Henry Leask of Boardhouse—the Capt. James Leask who had charge of the "Lavinia," when William Sinclair was next in command. He went first to school in May, 1836. When about ten years of age his mother remarked in jest that a new jacket she was finishing was for him to go to Russia with on his father's ship. He made good her words by going down that same afternoon to the vessel, on which he stowed safely away, nor did he show himself until too far from port to put back with him. So he got his trip to Russia after all, returning safely after an absence of several months, to be the hero of his school-mates for having at so early an age travelled over the "Viking Path." His school course was ended in about his fifteenth year, when he became a junior clerk in the warehouse of Messrs. R. Brotchie and Co., tea merchants in Leith, with whom he remained for about five years, rising from a junior to a senior clerkship. While in Leith he attended the classes in Edinburgh at the Watt Institution, and otherwise endeavoured to increase his knowledge by every possible means, commencing his studies at half-past three every morning in summer. As a consequence he made the most marked improvement, and letters written by him at the age of eighteen show the finished composition that is usually attained by persons of literary gifts only in their thirties or forties, and a beautifully clear and characteristic penmanship that we only expect to see from an accountant with a standing of years. Leaving Leith, he secured a clerical position with Messrs. Harrison & Crossfields, of

3 Great Tower St., London, E.C. But he had imbibed a love of travel, and so left and went to America. He was a short time in New York City, and had he made up his mind to stay could have done very well. At one time he was boating on the Mississippi, at another in Cincinnati, seldom staying long in any one place, as he preferred to travel as much as possible. About two years were thus spent, when he had an attack of fever and ague, ailments general to persons travelling through, but not permanent in, those parts. In 1851 or 1852 he returned to Kirkwall to recruit his health, where, staying with his parents, he pursued his studies at pleasure, occasionally, for his personal delectation, contributing local news to the *John o' Groats* or the *Scotsman*, and afterwards to the *Orcadian*, a local paper which he was instrumental in establishing. He married at Kirkwall 29th January, 1857, Mary, only child of John Mowat, of Rarewick, Taukerness, in the Earldom of Orkney, by Mary Muir, his wife. Shortly after this event he re-entered the service of Messrs. Harrison & Crossfields, but the excessive heat of the

MARY MOWAT SINCLAIR.

following summer impaired his health, and he was compelled to return to Kirkwall where he took over his father's business, but meeting with poor encouragement, he removed to Stromness in August, 1862, and tried there in the same line of business, but without success. Then he went to Scotland and took up a book agency for the Rev. Charles Rogers, and removed his wife and four children to Stirling, where a very trying winter was experienced. The next year, accompanied by his wife and children, he took passage to New Zealand by the "King of Italy," arriving at Auckland on the 6th September, 1865, after a voyage of ninety-three days from Gravesend, the second son William dying on board ship, 8thJuly, 1865. By virtue of being a passenger he was entitled to a Crown grant of 180 acres of land, which he selected at Hokianga, and subsequently he received an additional grant of 60 acres from the Auckland Provincial Government for arrears of salary. A few weeks after his arrival he received an appointment from the Auckland Board of Education, but upon that institution suspending payment he took to journalism and private tuition He held Board appointments at Kaurihohore, Auckland, in 1871-72; Taita, Wellington, 1873-75, Board of Education Office, Auckland, 1876; and at Ardmore, Auckland, 1884-85, when he came in for a small inheritance, which enabled him to retire from arduous duties. Early in 1893 he settled at Otahuhu, a suburb distant some eight miles from Auckland City, where he interested himself in the progress of the local Mutual Improvement Society He left his residence in his accustomed health on the evening of the 11th November, 1895, to attend an entertainment on the occasion of the breaking up of the Society, on returning home from which he was seized with an apoplectic or paralytic attack, and must have lain on the roadside all that night—the stormiest of the season—unmissed by the members of his household, who had retired, and untended save by a faithful house dog, "Spot" Mr Sinclair was found early the next morning, and at once conveyed home and medical attendance procured There appeared some glimmerings of pleased consciousness in response to expressions of affection from his family, but he was gradually sinking, and expired late at night on the 12th November, 1895 The *New Zealand Herald* has this reference to him —

"His familiar figure will be greatly missed in Otahuhu. He was a kind, genial man, well read, and full of information His grasp of the general character and methods of science—particularly what is called natural history science—his knowledge of literature and all literary subjects, combined with great kindness of manner, were invaluable in a community like Otahuhu Up to the very last he kept up a correspondence with the leading literary and scientific men in England and America It may be truly said of him that he tried ' to learn what is true, in order to do what is right ' "

"BOARD OF EDUCATION —The late Mr J L Sinclair At the Board of Education on November 19th, 1895, a well deserved tribute of respect was paid to the memory of Mr J L Sinclair, an old servant of the Board, and one who had done service in the office and in the schools, on the motion of the senior member of the Board, Mr S Luke, who moved that a letter of condolence be sent to the widow and children of the deceased gentleman, and in speaking in support of it he said the deceased gentleman was an estimable man, and a personal friend of his own Since his retirement from the Board's services he had taken much interest in educational matters Three of his daughters were now in the service of the Board, and another, who had to resign on account of ill-health, graduated from their own University College, and had taken her degree as a Master of Arts, with honours in Latin and English Under the circumstances it seemed to him (Mr Luke) only right that the services of such an old teacher should be recognised The motion was seconded by the Rev Canon Bates, and supported by several other members of the Board, who referred to Mr Sinclair's faithful services in the cause of education It is needless to say that Mr Luke's kindly motion was carried unanimously "

At the twenty-third session of the Otahuhu Mutual Improvement Association on 1st May, 1896, the attendance was very large. After the minutes had been read, a vote of condolence and sympathy with the widow and family of an old member, the late Mr. J. L Sinclair, was passed When the motion was put the whole audience rose from their seats and remained standing.

Mr. and Mrs. Sinclair conjointly produced "Orcadian Rhymes," a volume of poems which they published at Kelso in 1864, and each have from time to time written fugitive verses Mr Sinclair wrote an excellent Ode on the occasion of the Skakspetian Tercentenary, and won a prize of five guineas for forty lines in verse appropriate to the opening of the Opera House in Auckland in 1882 the five guineas went forthwith to the fund then in course of collection for the distressed Jews in Russia. He identified himself with politics when in Orkney, and continued to do so until the last. He has left a vast amount of epistolary literature extending over many years from persons eminent in Great Britain, the United States, and elsewhere. In these the signatures of Sir John Lubbock, Oliver Wendell Holmes, John Bright, etc , frequently come under notice. He left some 3,000 volumes, which by testamentary disposition 25th March, 1886, were bequeathed to the Auckland University College, and from which number that institution has selected 580 volumes. James Leask Sinclair, heritor of Kirkwall, Orcadian verse-writer, and New Zealand colonist, is survived by his wife, by whom he had issue—

26. ELISABETH, born at Kirkwall 13th February, 1859 ; res. Pollok, New Zealand.
27. JANE FLETT, born at Kirkwall 2nd January, 1861 ; res. Hautapu, New Zealand.
28. ROWLAND WILLIAMS, born at Kirkwall 9th July, 1862.
29. WILLIAM, born at Stromness 9th Mar., 1864 ; died 8th July, 1865, on board "King of Italy."
30. JOHN WILLIAM COLENSO, born Takapuna, N.Z., 10th April, 1866 ; died Auckland, 2nd January, 1867.
31. MARY MUIR, born Onehunga 2nd June, 1868 ; grad. M.A., 1889, N.Z. Univ.; res. Otahuhu.
32. JAMES LEASK, born Auckland City 18th April, 1870, and died same day.
33. JOHN JAMES, born Kaurihohore 23rd January, 1872 ; died Taita, 29th December, 1873.
34. WILLIAM HENRY, born Taita, 29th December, 1873 ; died Taita, 31st October, 1874.
35. ELLEN EVANGELINE, born Taita 21st December, 1875 ; res. Otahuhu.
36. CLARE, born and dead Auckland, 13th September, 1878.
37. OLIVER WENDELL HOLMES, seventh son, born at Auckland 17th March, 1880 ; collegiate ; res. Otahuhu ; is Secretary of the Mutual Improvement Society there.

ROLAND WILLIAM ST. CLAIR (28) came to New Zealand with his parents in 1865. At the age of six he was in the highest class in the Newton Academy, an Auckland primary school ; at twelve he passed highest of all scholars in the State schools of the Wellington Province, N.Z., and was *proxime accessit* for the College Scholarship of that year—1874 ; he passed the Junior Civil Service Examination in 1883. In July, 1876, he entered the office of the Wellington agency for McMeckan, Blackwood & Co.'s line of steamers in the Melbourne-New Zealand trade, and during his fifteenth and sixteenth years he occasionally went as acting purser on the steamers "Tui" and "Huia." In 1879 he transferred to Messrs. W. & G. Turnbull & Co., who had taken the agency of the "Tui" and "Huia," and remained in the service of that firm for seven years, retiring on the 31st May, 1886, to rejoin his relatives in Auckland. On the 9th July, 1886, he varied his name by public announcement to the form he at present uses, and joined the staff of Messrs. T. H. Hall & Co., wholesale merchants in Auckland, on the 1st August, 1887, in whose employ he continues to hold the position of accountant. Mr. St. Clair has been ardently interested in rowing and swimming, more especially the latter pastime. He was Deputy-Captain of the Wellington Rowing Club in 1886, and has since 1888 been a prominent official of the Auckland Swimming Club, of which he has been a director and is a gold-medallist life member. Mr. St. Clair was on the Committee of Management for the Jubilee Celebration at Auckland, and secured the inclusion of a Swimming Carnival on the 30th January, 1890. It was held in the Calliope Dock.* Over 10,000 persons paid for admission. The proceeds formed the nucleus of the fund towards endowing the Jubilee Institute for the Blind. He was first to apply the racing usage of numbering athletic competitors, a practice now general throughout New Zealand and elsewhere ; and inaugurated the celebration of the 1st October in each year as "Natation Day," when Australasian clubs and associations assemble in re-union and exchange intercolonial courtesies by electric telegraph. Mr. St. Clair founded the New Zealand Amateur Swimming Association in 1890, and edited the Annuals published by that institution, with which he has, however, ceased to be identified. The numerous rules codified by him in the 1894-95 Annual have been adopted by the swimming centres throughout

---

See illustration "Swimming," Badminton Library 1893.

Australasia, and utilised by other athletic bodies in adapted form. The New Zealand Government ordered 500 copies of that issue for distribution amongst the primary schools. In compliment to him the ST. CLAIR CROSS* was introduced into the design for the registered die, and to him is due in no small degree the decision of the New Zealand Government to reward bravery and merit in the saving of life by the presentation of gold, silver, and bronze medals.†

Reference to the author's ancestry discloses how essentially Orcadian is his origin. The northland names of Sinclair, Mowat, Flett, Tulloch, Borwick, Peace, Foubister, etc., marshall themselves in the list of his predecessors; and last century several of his ancestors spoke the Norse language. Mr. St. Clair accounts himself absolutely Norse by race.

Mr. St. Clair met with an accident in 1892 that compelled him to use crutches for nine months. During the evenings at home of that period this book was evolved and completed in the summer of 1893; the years intervening between then and now have been occupied in finishing off the work and collecting replies to outstanding queries.

---
* See Vignette in Chapter V.   † Press Association telegram, 29th January, 1896.

ROLAND WILLIAM ST. CLAIR,
Author of "The St. Clairs of the Isles."

THE ST. CLAIRS OF THE ISLES.

ZETLAND SCIONS.*

THE SINCLAIRS OF BRUGH, NESTING.

THE earliest notice of this family is to be found in the "Genealogie of the Sainteclaires of Rosslyn," on page 57, in these words: "The reversal concerning Orknay not being found sufficient by King Haquin, the embassadors sent by the Earle of Orknay were allowed to continue in the city of Tesberge, in Norway, till his Majestie was satisfied. In the meantime there was a marriage concluded, as is said, betwixt JOHN SAINTCLAIR, brother to the Earle, and Ingeberg, natural daughter to Waldemarus, King of Danemark, by Jova Litle, who was a daughter of Sir John Litle, Commissioner of Rugen. It is alleged that his sone WILLIAM serv'd the Emperor Henry in the Holy Warres; that in following times HENRY SAINTCLAIR, a *second* son of that House of Brook, and Laird of Stomue, left a sone named HEUGH, who became Laird of Brock, and espoused Grisall Stewart, daughter to Robert, Earle of Orknay, upon whom he begot LAURENCE, Laird of Brock, who had by Margaret, daughter to James Saintclair of Salaway, in Shetland, HEUGH Saintclair, present Laird of Brock in Orknay; yet I scarcely listen to what is vulgarly reported of the pedigree of Brock or Brusck. Few evidences may clear that genealogy."†

I. EDWARD SINCLAIR OF STROM was art and part in the slaughter of John St. Clair, Earl of Caithness, in 1529. About the year 1530 he acquired the lands of Brugh from Margaret Reid, heretrix of one Gilbert Cant. Eduerd Synclar of Stroym was Fold of Zetland in 1536, on the 24th June, in which year he conveys the merk lying in Russater in Fetlair to Adam of Still.‡ On the 19th September, 1539, he obtained a respite for his complicity in the slaughter of the Earl of Caithness,§ and on the 28th October, 1544, is found an attesting witness to the erection of certain offices in the Cathedral Church of Orkney.|| In 1549 Margaret Dischington, his wife, is noticed as under the special protection of Bishop Reid.¶ Strome is in the parish of Whiteness.

II. HENRY SINCLAIR OF STROM AND BRUGH was probably his [second] son. On the 9th December, 1561, Mr. Alex. Dick, Provost of the Cathedral Church of Orkney, and two chaplains there, found caution to underly the law on 15th April following, for convocation and gathering of our sovereign lady's lieges, to the number of four score persons, in September last, and searching for Henry Sinclair of Strom and Mr. William Mudy, with intent to slaughter them.* He died in 1575, having married Catherine Kennedy, and had issue—

NOTE.—At the loch of Strom are the remains of a castle, once the residence of the Earls of Orkney, of whom a descendant is said to have been slain by his father's orders, at the standing stone of Tingwall. (Peace's Handbook.)

* "Zetland County Families," by Grant. † Hay. ‡ Researches by Gilbert Goudie.
§ Barry's App. ‖ Peterkin's Rentals App. ¶ Craven.

1. HUGH, his heir.   1. JANET.
2. CAPTAIN WILLIAM, born 1547, was a witness to the attempt of Cultmalindie to murder Arthur Sinclair of Aith at Scalloway in 1575.
3. EDWARD OF MARRASETTER, in Whalsay, served heir to his brother Oliver, 18th August, 1618, and died 14th September, 1622. He married Margaret, daughter of Andrew Gifford of Weathersta, and had issue—
    1. ANDREW of Marrasetter.   2. HENRY.   3. DONSIE.
4. OLIVER OF EASTHOUSE, father of—
    1. HUGH of Easthouse, who married Lilias Sinclair, and
    1. MARTHA, who married William Adamson.

III. HUGH SINCLAIR OF BRUGH got a charter under the Great Seal on 7th November, 1587—under the declaration that the lands were to descend according to the custom in Scotland, and not to be divided among his children as was usual in udal holdings—of the lands called the canonical lands of the Cathedral of Orkney, and lying in the parishes of Dunrossness, Burra, Goldberryvik, Quhyteness, Weisdaill, Sandsting, Delting, Yell, Fetlair, and Unst. The Vicarage of Nesting, Quhalsa, and Lunnasting was at this time set in tack to the "guidman of Burghe," and "the Channonis landis set in few be Sir James Hay to Hew Sinclar off Burghe and payis yeirlie to his Majestie £20 13s. 4d." Colbein Ormesone of Symbuster conveys certain lands on the 20th November, 1581, to "Ane honorabill man and my guid freind Hew Sinclair of Burt," with obligation, in the event of himself or heirs requiring to dispose of any portion of his lands in Symbuster, to offer the same first to the said Hew, and if he or they should do so otherwise in ignorance, the same to be null and of none effect, because "the said land is lineallie discendit of the house and stock of Burt." The deed was dated at Burt, that is, Brugh.* On 7th October, 1590, Robert, Earl of Orkney, was bound in 5,000 merks not to harm Hew Sinclair of Brugh. He also got a charter from Robert, Earl of Orkney, to him and "to the airis lawfully gotten betwixt him and umquhill Grissell Stewart, our dochter naturall, ilk ane efter utheris successivlie without any divisioune of landis," of the lands of Howsbie and the Isle of Auskerry in Orkney, on 21st April, 1591. On 30th June, 1597, he is ordained by the Privy Council to find caution to the extent of 5,000 marks. On 23rd December, 1597, he amongst others preferred a complaint against the Balfours of Montquhanny, Stratherne, and Garth. He died about 1605, having married (first) the said Grissell Stewart, and (second) Jean, d. of Alex. Bruce of Cultmalindie, and had issue—

1. ROBERT, his heir.   2. LAURENCE, aftermentioned (No. V.)
3. HENRY, m. Margaret Umphray (d. 4th March, 1645), and had—
    1. HEW.   2. PATRICK.   1. HELEN.   2. JEAN.
4. ALEXANDER.
1. MARGARET, m. Malcolm Sinclair of Quendale.
2. CHRISTINA, m. Jas. Sinclair of Goat, and served heir portioner of her brother Robert, on 14th March, 1626.

IV. ROBERT SINCLAIR OF BRUGH was served heir to his father and grandfather on 8th October, 1605, in the Barony of Brugh, consisting of 182 merks of land in Nesting, 23¾ in Weisdale, 7 in Whiteness, 16 in Sandsting and Aithsting, 43½ in Walls, 9 in Northmaven, 37 in Bressay, 15 in Delting, 5 in Burra, and 9 in Unst, amounting in all to 347¼ merks. The inventory of his plate and household goods shows that he was possessed of 82 horses, 38 mares, 60 oxen, 118 cows, 3,060 sheep, 165 barrels of oats,

212 barrels of bear, and 3 chalders of bear. He died before 31st July, 1607, apparently unmarried, and was succeeded by his brother

V. LAURENCE SINCLAIR, FIFTH OF BRUGH, who on that date (31st July, 1607) was served heir to his father Hugh in the Barony of Brugh. He was a witness at the trial of Patrick, Earl of Orkney, before the Privy Council, in 1610, and was appointed on 10th August, 1614, a commissioner to apprehend any of the rebels of Orkney who may proceed to Shetland. He died in December, 1659, having married Margaret d. of James Sinclair of Scalloway, and had issue—

1 HUGH, his heir
1. JEAN, married to David Stewart in Sandwick

VI. HUGH SINCLAIR, LAST OF BRUGH, only son, served heir to his father on 6th June, 1671, and again on 11th June, 1706; was a Commissioner of Supply for Zetland in 1678 and 1704. He granted a wadset for 500 merks to James Mitchell of Girlesta over his 9 merks land in Stensland, in the parish of Walls, 3 merks in Tresta in Aithsting, and the island of Linga, lying in Whalsay Sound, on the 26th January, 1697. He married a daughter of Murray of Clauden. The estate of Brugh became the property of the Bruces of Symbister, in whose possession it still remains.

An incident known as "The Skerry Fight" has reference to this family (*voce* Hibbert). Some fishermen on the Busta estate erected a booth in pursuance of an old custom since legalised. Re-occupying it the following summer, and armed in expectation of dispute, they were besieged by the Sinclairs, headed by their lady. After a discharge of firearms on each side, Magnus Flaws, one of the Sinclair party, on attempting to break in through the roof, was shot dead by the Giffords, upon which the Sinclairs at once retired, leaving their chieftainess in the hands of the enemy. Gifford of Busta was at that time (after 1706) steward of the Islands, but did not think it necessary to take official cognizance of the misdeeds of the family dependents. Till within the last twenty years or so the remains of the chapel of the Sinclairs, Barons of Brugh or Burgh, delineated in Hibbert, were standing not far from the head of Catfirth Voe, but, stones being scarce in Shetland, they were pulled down to build a dyke round the burial ground of Garth.* On the south side of the bay of Nesting are the ruins of the mansion-house of the Barons of Brugh, the Scottish family named Sinclair, established in Shetland by James VI in 1587, on condition that they should hold their land by feudal tenure, and not according to the ancient law of *Udal succession*, the king at that time being desirous of obliterating all traces of Norwegian rule. In the same vicinage are the ruins of an ancient chapel, of which tradition vouchsafes no history.†

The arms of the Brugh family appear in the Armoury

THE SINCLAIRS OF HOUSS, AITH, AND SCALLOWAY, BURRA, ETC

I WILLIAM SINCLAIR OF HOUSS must have been born about 1460. He fought at Summerdale on 18th May, 1529, for which he was respited on the 19th September, 1539. He died in 1539, and is said to have married Elizabeth, d. of Alex Sinclair of Dunbeath in Caithness, but the dates do not admit of such a supposition. He had issue—

1. MAGNUS, his heir   2 LAWRENCE (perhaps of Norbister)
1. JEAN, b. *cir* 1485, married Henry Sinclair of Havera   2 ELIZABETH

II MAGNUS SINCLAIR OF HOUSS may be the Magnus Sinclare respited for having also fought at Summerdale in 1529. "Mawnyss Sinclar, ane worschipfull man," appends his seal as witness to a conveyance executed at Tygwall in Schetland the 27th October, 1525. Mawnis Sinclair of Howss affixes seal as witness to grant by Iggabrocht Kotrinsdocther in favour of Gylbert Kant of Brocht made at St Lorence Kyrk of Burray 11th March, 1547.† He married Janet, d. of Wm Keith, and died in 1557

* Tudor   † Peace's Handbook   , Goudie.

III. LORENCE SINCLAIR OF NORBISTER, attested execution of the deed by Ingaborg on the 11th March, 1547. He married Marion Katell, and had issue—

1. JAMES SINCLAIR of Norbister, who had issue—
    1. MARGARET, married Robert Tulloch, in Warbister, Burra, and died March, 1623, leaving issue
    2. CATHERINE, mother of Andrew Thomason
        Margaret and Catherine, as heirs portioners of their father, on 25th October, 1609, disponed their four merks land in the Isle of Halvery to Laurence Sinclair of Houss.

Lorence Sinclair of Norbister (with consent of his son and lawful heir James Sinclair, and of Marion Katell his wife, mother of the said James) disponed on 3rd July, 1560, to his brother

IV. LAWRANSS SINCLAR OF SANDES, Burgess of Kirkwall, the lands of Houss in Burra. How the two Laurences were brothers does not appear, but the documents are explicit in so describing them. He witnesses a deed at Scalloway 27th July, 1567 * Laurence of Sandes married Janet Strang, who survived him, and had issue—

1. ARTHUR, his heir
2. EDWARD of Scalloway, who on 21st August, 1580, granted a charter of 3 merks in Houss with consent of Barbara Mowat, his spouse, to his brother-german Arthur Sinclair of Aith
3. DAVID of Hunton, in Orkney, which lands he acquired 1588 (Reg G. Seal), father of
    JOHN and of
    CHRISTIAN, who married Jas Strang of Voesgarth, who thus acquired the 18 merks of land in Melby known as "The Sinclair's Last"
    Hunton was one of those complaining against the Balfours 23rd December, 1597. A David Sinclair is Foud of Burra in 1603
4. JAMES of Mail (died 23rd May, 1622), married Margaret Harcus, and had issue—
    1. JAMES, who disponed the lands of Mail (26th June, 1622) to his brother Hew
    2. HEW of Mail, who, on 14th August, 1620, granted a charter to Laurence Sinclair of Houss of lands in the island of West Burra
    3. MICHAEL, perhaps father of Margaret, married to Gilbert Gifford of Uphouse
    4. EDWARD   5. THOMAS   1 JANET   2 POLL.
5. WILLIAM of Ustaness, "ane honorabill man," whose signet Colbein Ormeson "procures with great instance," 20th November, 1581 On 30th June, 1597, he was ordained by the Privy Council to find caution for 2,000 merks, to maintain good order within his land On 23rd December, 1597, he is one of the complainants against the Balfours He died December, 1610, having married Elizabeth Sinclair (perhaps daughter of Alex Sinclair of Dunbeath), and had issue—
    1. LAURENCE of Ustaness, found guilty 16th August, 1602, of being art and part in the murder of Mathew Sinclair of Ness, and on 1st October, 1611, charged along with others before the Privy Council with having, as a servant of Patrick, Earl of Orkney, committed all kinds of wickedness and iniquity As he failed to appear he was denounced rebel He had issue—
        1. CAPTAIN WILLIAM, his eldest son, a witness along with his father to a charter by Nichol Rattray in Collasetter, to Patrick Cheyne of Vaila, on 17th June, 1637, probably identical with Colonel William Sinclair, in charge of Fort Charlotte, Lerwick, 1665, and with Colonel William Sinclair, who was a Commissioner of Supply for Zetland in 1667, and
        2. ROBERT
6. OLAVE of Norbie, called father's brother to Laurence Sinclair of Ustaness in a charter by the latter to him on 24th September, 1622, of the four merks land of Watsness and Sweuester, in Walls He died April, 1632, leaving issue—
    1. LAURENCE in Suthaliouse, who with his brother Henry was a witness to the sasine

* Goudie

ZETLAND SCIONS.

of his father in the lands of Watsness, 8th October, 1622 He was probably grandfather of

LAURENCE SINCLAIR, portioner of Norbie, who disponed 4 merks of land in Norbie to Jas Mitchell of Girlesta on 27th Sept, 1716, with consent of his spouse Ingagerth Walter's daughter, and

WALTER SINCLAIR, his eldest son

2 HENRY of Swenester, who had a son

JOHN, father of

HENRY, whose only surviving daughter

ELIZABETH married Thos Robertson in Crawton, in Sandness, and disponed her 4 merks of Swenester to John Scott of Melby, 20th November, 1802

3 ARTHUR.   4 ROBERT   5 DANIEL   6 JEROME

1 ORSELLA, who along with her five brothers, disponed their 21 merks land in Hellywick in Burra to their brother Arthur Sinclair of Aith on 16th August, 1587 She will be the Ursilla Sinclair married to the Rev Jas Pitcairn, Vicar of Northmaven in 1578, to which he was then presented by King James VI.

2 JANET, married James Sinclair of Brew

V ARTHUR SINCLAIR OF AITH was Sheriff of Shetland in 1572 He presented the Bill of Complaint against Laurence Bruce of Cultmalindie in 1576, in which he states that "he (A S) and his forbears hes had the tak and rowme of the land lyand in the parochin of Dunrossness, extending to xxxii. merk land, with auchtein merk land in Ayth." He further declares that he possesses the heritable title to St Ninian's Isle in Dunrossness. Various acquisitions of land by him are enumerated, extending from 1572 to 1617 On one occasion he pays as much as £2,000 scots, while on another he dispones a small allotment of 16ft. x 40ft "within the boundis of Scalloway" for a certain sum paid to him in his "urgent necessitie" This was in 1592, only one year after he had acquired the "toun of Scalloway." On 30th June, 1597, he was ordained by the Privy Council to find caution for good rule within his lands to the extent of 2,000 merks On 23rd December, 1597, he is one of those who prefer the complaint against the Balfours. His territorial designation of Aith was not perpetuated, and thus he has ceased to be remembered He is, however, entitled in the history of the Islands to be regarded as the foremost of native patriots * He held in tack the Vicarage of Unst. He received a charter from Adam Sinclair of Brew on 1st August, 1617, and died soon after, having married Margaret Colville, and had issue—

1 LAURENCE, his heir.   2 JAMES of Scalloway (see No VIII)

3 WILLIAM, witness to a charter by Nicoll Thomeson in Blowstay, to his father, of lands in Isle of Trondra, 19th April, 1615, probably identical with Wm of Reawick, who married Mary Bruce

1 MARGARET, m Magnus Henderson of Buness   2 JANET.

VI LAURENCE SINCLAIR OF HOUSS had a disposition from Robert, Earl of Orkney, on 15th August, 1588, of the lands of St Ninian's Isle in Dunrossness. The Wemyss, Lawrence Sinclair, fiar of Aith, etc., lodge a complaint against the bailies of Dysart, 17th February, 1607, which was disallowed; and on the 31st March following the bailies lodge a counter complaint. On 21st January, 1612, he and his brother James, with some forty retainers, are charged before the Privy Council with assaulting Robert Bruce, son of William Bruce of Symbister He was served heir to his father, 17th August, 1632, married Elizabeth Sinclair, who died in February, 1634, and had issue—

1 ARTHUR, his heir   2 JOHN   3 GEORGE   4 LAURENCE

1 GRIZEL   2 MARGARET   3 BARBARA   4 ELIZABETH   5 HELEN   6 ANNA

* Goudie

VII. ARTHUR SINCLAIR OF HOUSS served heir to his grandfather, 17th October, 1634. The estate, as specified in the deed, is very extensive, comprehending Houss and other places in the Isles of Burra, and numerous lands in Dunrossness, Tingwall, Whiteness, Weisdale, and Bressay. The Dunrossness property is described as "five lie lasts of the lands of Brow," *i.e.*, 90 merks in all. He died 15th November, 1667, having married Barbara, daughter of Arthur Barclay of Boghills, and had issue—

    1. ARTHUR, died young   1. GRIZEL, married her cousin Arthur Sinclair, son of

VIII. JAMES SINCLAIR OF SCALLOWAY, second son of Arthur Sinclair of Aith, who had received charter from his brother Laurence of the Kirkland of Scalloway, which had been disponed by the deceased Patrick Cheyne to Robert ——, and by him to umquhile Arthur Sinclair, their father, on 6th December, 1619. He was a Commissioner of Supply for Zetland in 1661 and 1667. He married (first) Margaret, daughter of James Sinclair of Brew, and (second) Margaret, daughter of George Smelholme, merchant in Leith, and had issue—

    1. GEORGE, died young   2. JOHN, died young   3. ARTHUR, his heir
    1. MARGARET (died 28th April, 1646), m. Laurence Sinclair of Brugh
    2. ELIZABETH, in 1646 Wm. Bruce of Sumburgh and *d s p*

IX. ARTHUR SINCLAIR OF SCALLOWAY succeeded his father therein, and by his marriage with his cousin, GRIZEL SINCLAIR OF HOUSS, he also acquired that property. He was a Commissioner of Supply for Zetland in 1678. He had issue—

    1. ARTHUR, his heir   2. CHARLES (see No. XII.)
    3. LAURENCE of Sandsound, father of—
        JOHN and CATHERINE
    1. MARGARET, m. Andrew Bruce, tutor of Muness, who d. 1696

X. ARTHUR SINCLAIR OF SCALLOWAY, married, 1692, Katherine, daughter of Laurence Bruce of Symbister, and had issue—

    1. ARTHUR, his heir   1. BARBARA, m. James Mitchell of Girlesta.

XI. ARTHUR SINCLAIR OF SCALLOWAY, bound apprentice to Alexander Guthrie, W.S., in June, 1704, died 30th December, 1705. On 29th November, 1692, this Arthur was served heir to his grand-uncle, James Smelholme. He was succeeded by his uncle

XII. CHARLES SINCLAIR OF SCALLOWAY, to whom, in 1706, his mother Grizel Sinclair disponed the lands of Houss. He died at Edinburgh 3rd July, 1710, having married Katherine, daughter of Robert Bruce of Sumburgh, and had issue—

    1. ARTHUR, next of Scalloway   2. ROBERT, his heir   3. LAURENCE

XIII. ARTHUR SINCLAIR OF SCALLOWAY was drowned going to college at Aberdeen in 1716.

XIV. ROBERT SINCLAIR OF SCALLOWAY, born 1702, was served heir to his father on 9th July, 1728, and died 3rd January, 1741. He married (first), in 1721, Philadelphia, daughter of Sir John Dalmahay, Bart., of that Ilk, and had issue one son and two daughters—

    1. JAMES, his heir
    1. ANNE, born 1722, died 1757 married (contract dated 19th January, 1748) John Scott of Melby
    2. KATHERINE, died 27th August, 1772, married in 1750 James Scott, merchant, afterwards of Scalloway

Robert Sinclair married (second) Barbara, daughter of John Montgomery of Wrae, but had no issue. His widow re-married Robert Sinclair of Quendale. An epitaph in Latin and an elegy were composed on the occasion of his death by the Rev. John

Skinner, Episcopal clergyman, at one time tutor in the family. They appear in the collected edition (Aberdeen, 1809), of the works of the author who was father of Bishop Skinner, well-known as composer of the "Reel of Tullochgorum."*

XV. JAMES SINCLAIR, LAST OF SCALLOWAY AND HOUSS, born 16th August, 1726, died August, 1762, unmarried. In a deed of 1760 he is designed "great grandson and only heir of the deceased Arthur Sinclair of Houss, heritor and udaller." He was succeeded by his sister Katherine and his niece Philadelphia, daughter of John Scott of Melby, by whom the estate was disponed on 30th April, 1771, to James Scott, merchant in Scalloway, husband of the said Katherine Sinclair.

Trondra and the Burra Isles were long owned by the Sinclairs of Houss, an ancient family descended from the Orkney Earls.† Houss is in the Isle of Burra; Aith in Aithsting or Cunningsburgh; and Scalloway in Tingwall. Carrick Pursuivant perused no less than 595 deeds in connection with this family alone. One of the instruments is a Commission by Christian IV. of Denmark to Magnus Sinclair, captain of the "Leoparden," bearing date 21st April, 1627, at the Palace of Copenhagen. Mogens Sinclair is written over a previously deleted name, which appears to be Mogens Davidszen.*

ARMS, see the St. Clair Armoury.

THE SINCLAIRS OF BREW,
DUNROSSNESS.

I. HENRY SINCLAIR OF HAVERA is noticed in the conveyance at Tyngwall 27th October, 1525, when the granter, Thomas Olosone of Wrasettyr, states, "In witness of the qubilk thyng becauss I had no propir saill present I haiff procurit one and haiff gyffyne my full powir to Nicoll Hawcro of Tygwall to procure the signet of ane worschipfull man Henry Sincleir of Hawere."* He died in the year 1545, leaving by his wife Jean, daughter of Wm. Sinclair of Houss, a son,

II. OLAVE SINCLAIR OF HAVERA, who fought on the side of the Islesmen at Summerdale in 1529, obtaining a respite on 19th September, 1539, for same. He held a scuin session at Howeff on the 10th December, 1546, at which he presided "ane honorabill man Olave Sinclayr of Havoray, heyd Fold of Zetland," whose seyll Thorald Sudyrland of Brucht, having none of his own, procuryt with greyt instance.* He subsequently held the office of Great Fowde of Zetland; and on 17th July, 1567, having failed to account to the Crown for the mails and rents of the Islands, he is ordered by the Privy Council to be put to the horn if he does not do so within twenty days. A MS. in the Advocates' Library states that in the reign of Queen Mary, his part of the country was several times invaded by Hutcheon Macleod of the Lewis, to avenge the death of his brother William, who, it is asserted, had been treacherously slain at the instigation of Oliver. During one of these raids no less than 60 persons were slain near Quendale, and Oliver himself only escaped by leaping over Sumburghhead, and landing on a piece of grass in the cleft in the rock, he received no further injury than the loss of an eye. On one of these occasions the Laird of Brew is stated to have defeated the Lewis-men on the Links of Sumburgh, between the Pool of Virkie and Grutness Voe, when they were slain to a man.‡ The scenes of conflict are still pointed out at the sandy shore at Scousburgh, where are the "Lewis Scords." It was this Laird of Brew who entertained James Hepburn, Earl of Bothwell, when he fled to Shetland in 1567, after the defeat of Queen

Goudie. † Peace's Almanac, 1886. * Hibbert.

THE ST. CLAIRS OF THE ISLES.

Mary at Carberry Hill. Bothwell, Duke of Orkney, on arriving at Shetland, entered into a contract with Geert Hemelingk of Bremen, dated at Schvineborchovett, *i.e.*, Sumburghhead, the 15th August, A.D. 1567, for the hire of his ship, the "Pelican," and for another ship of a Hanseatic merchant then on the coast. Both ships were taken in command by Bothwell, along with the two smaller vessels in which he and his party had escaped from Scotland. Olaf Sinclair of Bru, designed as "Kemener und overste principall van Hidtland," gave a testimonial to Hemelingk's character as an honourable merchant in Shetland. Bothwell was at dinner with Olafe Sinclair when Kirkcaldy of Grange and the other pursuers arrived. Bothwell with the "Pelican" and his other ships, after a battle fought with his pursuers off the Shetland coast, was seized in Norway and detained a prisoner, and Hemelingk craved the intervention of the Bremen authorities for the restitution of his ship, and the payment of charter money due by Bothwell. The testimonial from Olaf Sinclair of Bru, the petition from Hemelingk, and the letter thereupon from the authorities at Bremen to Frederick II. of Denmark are preserved in the Danish Royal Archives.* Olave Sinclair, by his will dated 18th February, 1570, divided his whole lands among his three sons, James, Mathew, and William. He died before 1579. By his wife Margaret, daughter of Alexander Baird, he had—

1. JAMES, his heir.
2. MATHEW of Ness. At Holyroodhouse, on 25th April, 1573, the Aberdeen magistrates were ordered to search for and secure James (called Captn.) Halkerston, Mathow Sinclair, and their complices, notorious pirattis, who took a ship in Burntisland and harried the Shetlands, seizing the King's proper rents and carried them to Aberdeen. He was murdered on 27th June, 1602, by Francis Sinclair of Uyea and his brother, Robert Sinclair, both his nephews; John Bruce, servitor to Adam Sinclair of Brew; John, son to Laurence Sinclair of Goat; Laurence, son to Wm. Sinclair of Ustaness; and John Lindsay, servitor to Robert Sinclair, who were all found guilty of the crime before the Lawting Court at Scalloway on 16th August, 1602, and being fugitive therefor, their whole goods, gear, and lands were forfeited. Garth Hemlein, the Bremen trader, was also suspected of complicity. He had a son—
   EDWARD, who succeeded him in Ness, and married Isabel Gordon.
3. WILLIAM of Underhoull, for whom caution is required 3rd June, 1573—in which year a Wm. Sinclair is Fowd of Zetland. He had on 5th March, 1571, a charter under the Great Seal, as one of the heirs of his father, of 57½ merks land, including Busta and Weathersta, in the parish of Delting, 32 in Nesting, 21 in Whalsay, 44¼ in Yell, 24½¾ including Underhoull and Uyea, in Unst, 5¾ in Fetlar, 2 in Bressay, 3 in Aithsting, 6 in Burra, 37 in Whiteness, 48 in Sandsting, and 6 in Dunrossness; in all 504¾ merks. As deputy of Cultmalindie he is charged, together with his nephew, Robert (Edward ?) of Ness, in 1575, with oppressing the inhabitants of the Isles of Unst and Yell; and on 15th February of that year he was ordained to find caution and lawburrows to the parishioners of Unst. On 7th February, 1579, he granted a charter to his eldest son Francis, of the lands which belonged to his deceased father, Olave Sinclair of Brew. In 1579 he assigned certain lands to *Sir* James Hay, Vicar of Unst, as security for money lent. The deed contains an endorsement acknowledging the final repayment on 18th July, 1580. He married Margaret, daughter of John Stewart, Prior of Coldingham (a natural son of King James V., and consequently half-brother of Queen Mary), who after his death married Wm. Bruce of Sumburgh, (and after her death the latter married (2nd) 14th February, 1595, Isabella, daughter of Sir Jas. Spence of Wormiston, and sister to Sir James Spens, in 1622 created Baron Spens of Orreholmen, in Vestergotland). On the outlawry of his stepson Sumburgh obtained possession of the property of his marital predecessor, Underhoull. Underhoull had issue—

* Goudie.

1. FRANCIS of Uyea, found guilty of being art and part in the murder of his uncle, Mathew of the Ness, in 1602. On 30th June, 1597, he is ordained to find caution by the Privy Council to the amount of 500 merks to maintain good rule within his lands. He disponed 12 merks of his lands in Underhoull to James, son of the deceased Arthur Sinclair of Aith, by a charter dated at Edinburgh 4th February, 1617; and on 9th August, 1634, he witnesses a charter by Erasmus Manson in Southsetter, in favour of Laurence Sinclair of Houss.
2. ROBERT. This is probably the Robert Sinclar, "ensenzie" (ensign) to Captn. Lawrence Sinkler, whom Jerhome Paintland, lieutenant, is cautioned, 27th April, 1605, in £500, not to harm while he remains in Scotland. He was also found guilty of the murder of his uncle Mathew. Outlawed as above-mentioned, Francis and Robert Sinclair, following their own courses, fell into evil habits and bad company in Scotland, resulting in poverty, discord, and litigation. This appears from a process at later date by Jas. Sinclair of Scalloway against Andrew Bruce of Muness.*
3. JAMES.   1. KATHERINE.   2. MARGARET.
1. BARBARA, married Adam Neven of Scousburgh.
2. ———, married Richard Leask, who was slain at the door of Sandwick Church by a servant of Henry Sinclair of Sandwick.

III. JAMES SINCLAIR OF BREW is probably the *sir* James Sinclair, notary public at Scalloway, who affixes his seal to a conveyance dated 27th July, 1567. He granted a discharge in 1588 to Laurence Bruce of Cultmalindie for the sum of £200 scots, being part of a sum of £1,100 of tocher of the latter's daughter. He married Janet, d. of Laurence Sinclair of Sandes, and had issue—
1. ADAM, his heir.   2. MALCOLM [of Quendal].   3. LAURENCE [of Goat].
4. JAMES [of Bullister].   1. MARGARET, married James Sinclair of Scalloway.   2. JEAN.

IV. ADAM SINCLAIR OF BREW was also charged with the murder of his uncle, Mathew Sinclair of Ness, and by a separate action at the instance of Robert Sinclair of Campston and Edwd. Scollay of Strynes, on 23rd August, 1602, he was found guilty by the Assize who "decernis the said Adam's hail moveabilities guidis and gere with his hail heritabil landis and possessionis to be escheit, and himself beneist the countrie within the space of 15 daies, and gif he beis apprehendit thairefter to be tane to the heiding-hill of Scalloway Bankis, and thair his heid to be tane and strickin frae his bodie in exempill of utheris." Four days previous he had sustained a criminal process for wrongous and violent intromission with goods of a broken Dutch ship, without leave of the owner, or any commission from my Lord his deputes or the Foud of the parish; "the Assize taking this to consideration, and trying him to have committit great wrang and oppressioun thairinto, thai all in ane vote decernis the said Adam, with his haill moveabill guids and gere, in my Lordis will thairfoir, in exampill of utheris, reserving place to satisfy the partie." Neither sentence was carried out, and he appears to have continued to possess his lands. On 6th June, 1597, he is ordained by the Privy Council to find caution to the extent of £1,000 for good rule within the same. Further, on 1st October, 1611, he is charged with others before the said Council with having as a servant of the Earl of Orkney committed all kinds of iniquity and wickedness, and was denounced a rebel. He died in 1627, having married (first) in 1588 Helen, daughter of Laurence Bruce of Cultmalindie, and had issue—
1. LAURENCE, his heir.   2. JAMES, afterwards of Brew.   3. MALCOLM.
1. JANE, married Jas. Kelman, an officer in the army of Montrose, and had issue.
2. BARBARA, married (1628) John Sinclair of Quendale.   3. HELEN.

* Goudie.

V. LAURENCE SINCLAIR OF BREW disponed in 1639 to his eldest son William, five score 14 merks 6 pennies the merk in Brew, 10 merks in Whilygairth adjacent, 47 merks in the said town and among the lands of Brew adjacent thereto belonging to the Kirk and the King, and the Lordis of Norroway, all in the parish of Dunrossness. He appears to have been succeeded by his brother,

VI. JAMES SINCLAIR OF BREW, who died 8th August, 1645, having married (first) Grizel Halcro, and (second) Elizabeth, d. of Patrick Cheyne of Esselmont, and had issue—

    1 ADAM, his heir   2 MALCOLM   3 LAURENCE   4. ARTHUR
    1. URSILLA, married Wm Bruce   2 JANET

VII. ADAM SINCLAIR OF BREW, died 1686, having married Jean, daughter of Captain Andrew Dick of Fracafield, and had issue—

    1 CHARLES, his heir   2 LAURENCE   3 JAMES   4 ARTHUR
    1 MARGARET, married James Mowat   2 BARBARA.

VIII CHARLES SINCLAIR OF BREW, died 1734, married Elizabeth, daughter of Robert Robertson of Gossaburgh, and had issue—

    1 ALEXANDER, his heir   2 ARTHUR   4 ADAM.
    3 ROBERT, married 3rd February, 1734, Charlotte, daughter of Sir John Mitchell, Bart
    1 JEAN, married 2nd December, 1740, John McIntosh, merchant
    2 MARION, married 4th February, 1742, Charles Leslie
    3 JANET, married James Craigie   4 ELIZABETH

IX ALEXANDER SINCLAIR OF BREW succeeded his father in the estate, which had by this time become to a large extent overblown with sand, the rental of the whole being then only £206 scots. He died 20th November, 1759, having married Elizabeth, daughter of Sir John Mitchell, Bart., of Westshore, and had issue—

    1 JOHN CHARLES, baptised 29th January, 1727
    2 OLA, born 13th July, 1746   3 ARTHUR, his heir
    1 ANN, baptised 26th March, 1730   2 ELIZABETH, baptised 9th April 1731, died young
    3 ANDRINA, baptised 14th May, 1732   4 JEAN, baptised 19th May, 1734
    5 JANET, baptised 10th December, 1735
    6 ELIZABETH, bapt 5th January, 1738, married 10th January, 1769, Wm Henderson in Papa
    7 PHILADELPHIA, born 2nd May, 1739   8 GILFORD, born 18th November, 1740
    9. CRAIGIE, born 7th February, 1743, alive in 1832
    10 MARGARET, married Alex. Fraser in Scalloway
    11 BARBARA, married Andrew Craigie

X ARTHUR SINCLAIR, LAST OF BREW, succeeded to a heavily encumbered estate, which, on 24th January, 1770, was adjudged from him by Sir John Mitchell, last of Westshore. He married Janet, daughter of Laurence Tarrel, merchant, Lerwick, and had issue—

    1 JAMES
    1 ELIZABETH MITCHELL, married 21st April, 1795, Wm Thos Craigie, merchant of Leith, second son of Jas Craigie of Stebbiegrind
    2 JANET

THE SINCLAIRS OF QUENDALE,
DUNROSSNESS.

Hay in his "Genealogie of the Saintclaires of Roslin," quoting a Danish writer called Van Bassan, says —

JAMES SINCLAIR of Stive [Brew?] was father of
   MALCOLM SINCLAIR of Quendale, who had a brother
      LAURENCE, reader at Dunrossness 1576 to 1580; at Crocekirk, Fair Isle, 1576: at Sandwick (Z.), 1586, resumed prior to 1593, continued 1608; Vicar and titular Dunrossness, 1610.

 I. MALCOLM SINCLAIR, FIRST OF QUENDALE, was lay vicar and reader of Dunrossness, to which he was presented on 20th December, 1565 [1575], and continued in 1601. His brother Laurence is probably to be identified as the reader of that name, successor to Malcolm. He held in tack the Vicarage of Dunrossness from Lawrence Sinclair, Vicar thereof; the Vicarage of Waais from the late Alex. Kincaid; and the Stowk called the Croce land from his Majesty for payment of £20 few mails and disponed to Jas. Sinclair, apparait of Quendale, for his lifetime. It was he who received at Quendale the men of the Spanish Armada wrecked at the Fair Isle in 1588. Quendale was ordained by the Privy Council to find security for £1,000 scots, on 6th June, 1597, and on 23rd December same he is one of those preferring complaint against the Balfours. He was appointed a Commissioner of Peace 28th November, 1609, and to apprehend rebels who may proceed to Zetland, on 10th August, 1614. He died on 6th January, 1618, and was buried in the old churchyard of Cross, at the head of Quendale Bay. By his wife Margaret, daughter of Hugh Sinclair of Brugh, he had a large family.

  1. JAMES, his heir. 2. WILLIAM. 3. GEORGE, of Craigends and Rapness, in Orkney.
  4. MALCOLM. 5. MICHAEL.
  1. ELIZABETH, married Patrick Forbes.
  2. MARGARET, married 1593 Michael Balfour of Garth, Orkney.
  3. ISABEL, married 1600 Andrew Bruce of Muness (who died in 1625);
    and 2nd Duncan Scollay of Hermansgarth, Orkney.
  4. HELEN, married Mr. Robert Swinton, minister of Walls.
  5. JANET, married John Neven of Scousburgh.

 II. JAMES SINCLAIR OF QUENDALE was a witness against the Earl of Orkney at his trial before the Privy Council in 1610, and was appointed a Commissioner of Peace 15th March, 1614. He was served heir to his father on 6th September, 1631, and died 21st September 1647. By his marriage with Barbara, daughter of James Stewart of Graemsay, who survived him, he had issue—

  1. JOHN, his heir. 2. LAURENCE. 3. HARRIE. 4. ROBERT.
  1. MARGARET, married 1st, Edward Sinclair of Gyre, Orkney, and
    2nd, James Mouat of Garth..
  2. HELEN, married Patrick Umphrey of Sand.
  3. JEAN, married Laurence Gifford of Weathersta.

 III. JOHN SINCLAIR OF QUENDALE was a Commissioner of Supply for Zetland, 1661 and 1667. He married in 1628, Barbara, daughter of Adam Sinclair of Brew, and had—

  1. LAURENCE, his heir. 2. JOHN. 3. ROBERT. 4. GEORGE.
  1. BARBARA, married 24th May, 1662, Hector Bruce of Muness, and died 22nd May, 1675.
  2. HELEN, died 1706; married 14th December, 1692, Ninian Neven of Scousburgh.
  3. MARGARET, married 1656 William Bruce of Sumburgh. 4. JEAN.

 IV. LAURENCE SINCLAIR OF QUENDALE was a Commissioner of Supply under Acts of Parliament 1675, 1689, 1696, and 1704. He married Jean, daughter of Laurence Stewart of Bigtown, and had issue—

  1. ROBERT, his heir. 2. ANDREW.
  1. LILIAS, married James Mitchell of Girlesta.
  2. MARGARET, married, 1st, Andrew Bruce of Muness; and
    2nd, Robert Baikie of Tankerness, Orkney.

V. ROBERT SINCLAIR OF QUENDALE, a Commissioner of Supply, 1705, succeeded his father in the estates, which at that time comprised 1,311 merks land in Dunrossness, 309 merks land in Dunrossness, 309 in Sandwick, and 368 in Aith, Cunningsburgh, with the Island of Mousa. He was Cashier of Excise, and from a report by George Drummond, the Accountant-General, afterwards Lord Provost of Edinburgh, dated 16th June, 1713, it is found he had embezzled a sum of £847 2s. 9½d. to his own uses He was a Jacobite in politics and an Episcopalian in religion. In 1750 his estate was sequestrated He died in 1767. He married (first) Barbara, daughter of John Montgomery of Wrae, and relict of Robert Sinclair of Scalloway, and had issue—

    JOHN, his heir

He married (second) at Fair Isle, 17th July, 1740, Mrs Jacobina Mackenzie

VI JOHN SINCLAIR OF QUENDALE was served heir to his mother in 1743, and was married to a daughter of William Greig, first of Vassay. The estate was sold on 26th February, 1770, and was purchased principally by John Bruce of Sumburgh, and Mr [James] Grierson

THE SINCLAIRS OF GOAT,
DUNROSSNESS.

I LAURENCE SINCLAIR, FIRST OF GOAT—probably a son of James Sinclair of Breue—was one of the complainants against the Balfours, 23rd December, 1597 ; and was one of the persons charged in 1602 with the murder of Matthew Sinclair of Ness, and ordered to find caution to appear and stand his trial therefor. The charge against him was, however, departed from. He is said to have married (first) Mary Stewart, one of numerous natural children of Robert, Earl of Orkney, and (second) in 1609 Margaret, d of Laurence Leask of Scatness, who is called his relict in 1626. They had issue—

    1 JAMES, his heir   2 MALCOLM   3 LAURENCE   4 WILLIAM, mentioned 1601
    1 ELIZABETH, married Andrew Shewan   2 JEAN

II JAMES SINCLAIR OF GOAT was found guilty of the murder of Mathew Sinclair of Ness on 16th August, 1602, and forfeited On 1st November, 1624, he disponed to Mr Thos Hendrie, minister of Walls, ten merks of land in that parish He married Christian, daughter of Hugh Sinclair of Brugh, and had issue—

    1. LAURENCE, his heir   2 JOHN
    1 GRIZEL, m in 1622 John Stewart of Bigton   2 BARBARA, m Gilbert Gifford

III. LAURENCE SINCLAIR OF GOAT, died in 1675. He was twice married (first), in 1629 to Margaret, daughter of Michael Balfour of Garth, and had issue—

    1. JAMES, his heir   2. WILLIAM (see No. VI).   3 PATRICK of Scotland.
    1 BARBARA, married, 1st, about 1683, John Umphray of Asta, and
                    2nd, Erasmus Mense of Whiteness
    2 MARGARET, married in 1709 Laurence Halcro

Laurence Sinclair of Goat married (second) Margaret, daughter of James Halcro of Ledigarth, and had issue—

    4 JOHN   3 ELIZABETH, married David Henderson

IV. JAMES SINCLAIR OF GOAT, died 17th May, 1689, married (first) 1672 Martha, daughter of Malcolm Sinclair of Rapness in Orkney ; and (second) Martha, daughter of Laurence Stewart of Bigton. He had issue—

    1 LAURENCE, his heir   1 MARTHA, married Laurence Strong, merchant in Dunrossness

V. LAURENCE SINCLAIR OF GOAT was born in 1686, and was father of Patrick, who predeceased him. He was succeeded by his uncle,

VI. WILLIAM SINCLAIR OF GOAT, who disponed his 26 merks land in Dunrossness, and 7 merks in Fair Isle, to John Scott of Scottshall in 1717; died 1724, having married, 1685, Elizabeth, daughter of Laurence Craigie, and had issue—

    1. LAURENCE, his heir.   2. WILLIAM.
    1. SARAH, m Rev. Robt. Donning, Lerwick.   2. MARGARET, m. Laurence Strong.   3. JEAN.

VII. LAURENCE SINCLAIR OF GOAT served heir to his granduncle James, 18th July, 1752; died 1756; married Ursilla, daughter of Wm. Dick of Fracafield, and had two daughters,

    1. MARGARET.   2. ELIZABETH.

THE SINCLAIRS OF BULLISTER AND SWINING.
NESTING.

I. JAMES SINCLAIR OF BULLISTER (perhaps a son of James Sinclair of Brew) lived in the reign of King James VI., and died 1600. He had issue—

    1. EDWARD, his heir.   2. GILBERT.   4. HENRY.   5. JAMES.
    3. ANDREW of Kirkhouse and Southerhouse, whose son
        EDWARD succeeded him in those lands.
    1. ELIZABETH, m. James Ross of Swarraster.   2. BARBARA.

II. EDWARD SINCLAIR OF BULLISTER. There is preserved a document in the Norse language in which Andrew Mouat of Hugoland, Shetland, and his dear spouse the worthy and honourable lady Else Trondsdaughter of Erisfiordt, acknowledge their indebtedness to the honourable and discreet man Effuart Sincklar, residing in Hietlandt at Bollesetter, for a friendly loan of 300 Rix dollars, and convey as security various lands in Shetland, being the just Odal inheritance of Lady Else. Sealed at Gieresvig in Norway the 20th June, 1597.* On 3rd July, 1602, he and William Sinclair of Ustaness promised to compt. and rakin among themselves before 1st August thereafter, and upon 26th August same, take certain acts of Court. He granted a charter on 1st August, 1623, with consent of James Sinclair, his eldest son, to their loving friend Thos. Cheyne, of

---

    Lady Else was one of several daughters of Christopher Throndson *Rustung*, a Norwegian, who after an adventurous career attained the position of Admiral to the King of Denmark and Norway. His seven daughters were—Else, Maren, Magdala, Margaret, Anna, Dorothy, and Christina, of whom Anna was married or betrothed to James Hepburn, Earl of Bothwell; Dorothy married, it is said, John Stewart, a Shetlander; and Else married (1st) John Haar of Gjeresvig in Norway, (2nd) Axel Fredrikson, Lawman at Bergen—1569-1585, and (3rd) Andrew Mouat of Hugoland, and had issue Axel, Christopher, and Karen. Axel is frequently mentioned (1630—1641) as a naval officer of high rank, latterly as Vice-Admiral of the Fleet, and much employed by the King. He died 29th January, 1661, aged 68, the owner of large estates in Norway. His sister Karen, who died in 1675, was married to Ludwig Rosenkrands of Rosendal, who collected all the property of the Mouat family (partly in Hardanger), which was made a Barony, under the name of Rosendal. Within seventy years thereafter most of this property, once belonging to Axel Mouat, was lost by the Rosenkrands family, which in 1723 became extinct in the male line, when the Barony reverted to the Crown. Admiral Mouat had a natural son Anders Axelson, living as late as 1690, whose descendants remain in Norway to the present day.—*
    Goudie.

certain lands which had been disponed to them by the deceased Andrew Wishart and Annabel Leslie, his spouse. He died 17th March, 1630, having married Janet Sutherland, who died 1623, and had issue—

    1 HENRY.   2 JAMES, his heir   3 ANDREW of Swining

III. JAMES SINCLAIR OF BULLISTER married Margaret, daughter of James Edmondston of Hascosay, and had issue—

    1 HENRY, his heir   2 HUGH   3 JAMES   4 ANDREW   5 JOHN
    1 ELIZABETH, married James Oliphant of Ure, a descendant of Oliphant of Gask
    2 JEAN, married Hugh Tarrel of Laxvoe.   3 MARTHA

IV. HENRY SINCLAIR OF BULLISTER, died 25th November, 1714, having married Christian, daughter of Robert Pitcairn

V ANDREW SINCLAIR OF SWINING (see above) died after 1684, having married in 1648 Elizabeth, daughter of James Buchanan, and had issue—

    1 HENRY, his heir   2 ROBERT, mentioned 1678   3 EDWARD   4 GILBERT
    1 LILIAS, married Hugh Sinclair of Skelberrie, Lunnasting
    2 BARBARA, married David Mouat   3 MARY

VI HENRY SINCLAIR OF SWINING died 16th December, 1718, married Martha, daughter of Gilbert Neven of Scousburgh, and had issue—

    1 GILBERT, his heir   3 ANDREW   4 [HENRY]
    2 HENRY of Still, who in 1767 conveyed the Island of Uyea and parts of Chivocast to Hunter of Lunna He had issue—
        DAVID of Still, whose daughter Martha married Thos Fea of Chivocast
        KATHERINE, m Wm Gauden of Overland and Swinister, and d 17th October, 1839
    1 MARY, married Hugh Tarrel of Laxvoe   2 MARTHA, married John Wallace   3 JANET

VII GILBERT SINCLAIR OF SWINING died 1720, having married (first) Katherine, daughter of William Tarrell of Laxvoe, and (second) Prudence McDougal, who after his death married Mr Thos Hay, minister of Yell, and died 26th June, 1730, aged 45 He had issue—

    1 HENRY, his heir   2 GILBERT
    1 MARTHA, married Arthur Edmondston of Hascosay   2 MARGARET   3 JEAN

VIII HENRY SINCLAIR, LAST OF SWINING, left Shetland and settled at Musselburgh, of which burgh he was Town Clerk He died 14th April, 1753, having married Susan, daughter of James Drummond of Mugdrum, and had issue—

    1 A daughter married Alex Orme, Clerk of Session
    2 A daughter married John Maclaurin

THE SINCLAIRS OF SANDWICK AND MOUSA.

HENRY SINCLAIR OF SANDWICK lived in the reign of James VI. From a MS.* description of Dunrossness it is learned that in revenge for some insult to his servant in the house of Brew, he, on the instigation of his wife, caused the man to kill Richard Leask, son-in-law to Oliver Sinclair of Brew, when he was about to enter Sandwick Church Upon hearing of the murder, Leask's son-in-law, Henry Dillidasse, proceeded from Orkney, where he was living, to Caithness, and having gathered together some of his friends, passed on with them to Zetland. They fell upon Henry Sinclair and his men upon a moor between Laxfirth and Lerwick, and in the mêlée which ensued Dillidasse

---

*Rev Jas Kay.

shot the murderer with a pistol. Several men fell in the encounter, Henry Sinclair escaping with difficulty, while one man, Sinclair of Burra, swam over to the Island of Trondra. To this family the Island of Mousa once belonged.

In 1716 HENRY SINCLAIR, *then* in SANDWICK, and his spouse disponed to Robert Sinclair of Quendale 23½ merks land in Nether Levenwick and North and South Voe. Quendale appears as owner of Mousa in 1705.

MOUSA TOWER.—A Pictish Erection.

THE SINCLAIRS OF TOFT,
DELTING.

I. EDWARD SINCLAIR, FIRST OF TOFT, was succeeded in these lands by his nephew,

II. EDWARD SINCLAIR, died 1681 ; m. Christian, d. of Robt. Fea, and had issue—
   1. JAMES, his heir.   2. WILLIAM (see No. 4).   3. Andrew.   4. HENRY.
   1. MARGARET, married Mr. Robt. Gray, minister of Nesting, and had with other issue—
      BARBARA, married James Greig of Vassay ; and
      CHRISTIAN, married, 1st, Edward Sinclair of Toft ; and, 2nd, Thos. Auchenleck.
   2. BARBARA, married Wm. Greig of Vassay.   3. JANET.

III. JAMES SINCLAIR OF TOFT wadsetted his lands to his brother-in-law, Mr. Robt. Gray, who thereafter brought a criminal suit against him, in consequence of which he fled to Holland, but returned after a few years. He did not obtain repossession of the estate, and died *s.p.* 1712, having married in 1700 Marion, d. of Jas. Murray of Clairden.

IV. WILLIAM SINCLAIR OF TOFT succeeded his brother ; granted a disposition dated 1st December, 1754, of 2½ merks land in Crookster to his daughter Margaret and her husband. He had issue—
   1. EDWARD, his heir.   1. MARGARET, married John Omond, wright in Toft.

V. EDWARD SINCLAIR OF TOFT, died before 1748, married his cousin Christian, daughter of Rev. Robt. Gray, minister of Nesting, and had issue—
   1. WILLIAM, his heir.   2. ANDREW (see No. VII.).   3. ROBERT, married Janet Chappie.
   1. BARBARA, married her cousin, Robert Simpson.

On the death of Edward Sinclair, his widow married Thos. Auchenleck, and had issue a daughter Margaret, married in 1773 John Angus, and had a daughter Andrina Christina, who married James Bain, Lerwick.

VI. WILLIAM SINCLAIR OF TOFT, designed in a factory granted by him in 1767, in favour of Thomas Auchenleck, as "of the Parish of St. John, Wapping, in the County of Middlesex, South Britain, mariner." Died 15th September, 1786, unmarried.

VII. ANDREW SINCLAIR, mariner in London, served heir to his granduncle, James Sinclair of Toft, 26th December, 1788; married Sarah Manuel, and had issue several children, who died young. He sold his property in Toft to his nephew, Gilbert Angus, merchant, Lerwick, on 7th February, 1808.

Amongst other Shetlanders preferring complaint against the Balfours, 23rd December, 1597, are Henrie Sinclair of Wolsettir, Wm. Sinclair of Sindburgh, and James Sinclair in Housbie.

THE EARLDOM OF CAITHNESS.

ILLUSTRATION OF THE SUCCESSION FROM 871 TO THE PRESENT TIME.

ORDER.	EARLS.	TITLE TO EARLDOM.	FLOURISHED. From	To	REMARKS.
		THE HOUSE OF ODIN, OR NORSE LINE.			
1	Thorstein *the Red*	Conquest	871	..	Slain in Caithness
* 2	Sigurd *the Sea-king*		871	882	,,
* 3	Guthorm	Son of Sigurd	882	883	Died issueless
* 4	Duncan	*Jure uxoris*	..	..	Mar. Groa, d. of Thorstein
* 5	Thorfinn *the Skullsplitter*	M. Grelod, dau. of Groa	910	963	G. nephew of Sigurd
* 6	Arnfinn	Son of Thorfinn	963	967	Murdered at Murkle, C.
* 7	Havard *the Happy*	,,	963	970	Slain at Stennis, O.
* 8	Ljot	,,	963	976	Slain in Caithness
* 9	Skuli	,,	963	974	Fell in Caithness
* 10	Hlödver	,,	963	980	Natural death
* 11	Sigurd II., *the Stout*	Son of Hlödver	980	1014	Fell at Clontarf
* 12	Thorfinn II., *the Great*	Son of Sigurd II.	1014	1064	Died natural death
* 13	Paul } *the Exiles*	Sons of Thorfinn II.	1064	1103	D. in exile at { Bergen, Nidaros
* 14	Erlend }				
* 15	Hakon *the Imperious*	Son of Paul	1103	1122	Died natural death
* 16	Harald *the Orator*	} Sons of Hakon	1122	1127	Poisoned
* 17	Paul II., *the Silent*		1122	1136	Deposed and spirited away
* 18	Erlend II., *the Younger*	Son of Harald	1127	1156	Slain in Damsay, O.
19	Mac William	Scottish Creation	1129	1160	See Dunfermline records
* 20	St. Rögnvald *the Crusader*	Son of Gunnhild, d. of 14	1136	1158	Slain in Caithness
* 22	Harald III., *the Younger*	Son of Ingigerd, d. of 20	1176	1198	Fell at Clairdon, C.
		THE HOUSE OF ATHOL, OR ROYAL SCOTTISH LINE.			
* 21	Harald II., *the Wicked*	Son of Margaret, d. of 15	1139	1206	Died natural death
* 23	David	} Sons of Harald II.	1206	1214	
* 24	John		1206	1231	Murdered at Thurso
		THE ANGUS LINE.			
* 25	Magnus *of Angus*	Kinsman of John	1231	1239	Sutherland now detached
26	Gilbride	Brother of Magnus I.	1239	..	
* 27	Gilbride II.	Son of Gilbride I.	..	1256	Had a daughter Matilda
* 28	Magnus II.	Son of Gilbride II.	1256	1273	..
29	Magnus III.	Son of Magnus II.	1273	1284	..
* 30	John II.	,,	1284	1310	..
* 31	Magnus IV.	Son of John II.	1310	1321	..
	Henry de St. Clair	*Ballivus*	..	1321	..

THE CAITHNESS SUCCESSION.—Continued.

Order.	Earls.	Title.	Flourished. From	Flourished. To	Remarks.
		THE STRATHERNE LINE.			
*†32	Malise I., *Earl of Stratherne*	Heir-at-law to Magn. IV.	1321	1333	Fell at Halidon Hill
*†33	Malise II. ,,	Son of Malise I.	1333	1344	Died *s.p. male*
34	Alexander *de la Arde*	S. of Matilda, eld. d. of 33	..	1375	Surrendered the dignity
	Isabella *de Stratherne*	2nd dau. of Malise II.	..	1405	Survived No. 34
		ALIEN EARLS.			
†35	David II., *Stuart*	*Scottish creation*	1375	.	Earl Palatine of Stratherne
36	Walter	,,	1424	1437	Earl of Athol
37	Alan	,,	1424	1431	Son of Earl Walter
38	George I., *Crichton*	,,	1450	1455	Lord High Adm. of Scotland
		THE SAINT-CLAIR LINE.			
	William de St. Clair	M. Isabel de Stratherne	..	c1363	Anc. St. Clairs of the Isles
*	Henry I., Earl of Orkney	Son of Isabella	..	1404	Slain in Orkney *vita matris*
*	Henry II. ,,	Son of Henry I.	..	1420	Earl *de jure* of Caithness
*39	William I. ,,	Son of Henry II.	1420	1476	Rec. C'thness 1455 abd. 1476
	William, Lord St. Clair	Disinherited	1481	1487	Buried at Dunfermline
40	William II.	Second son of William I.	1476	1514	Fell at Flodden
41	John III.	Son of William II.	1514	1529	Slain in Orkney
42	George II.	Son of John III.	1529	1582	Anc.Olrig, Dunbeath II.,&c.
43	George III., *the Wicked*	Grandson of George II.	1582	1643	Ancestor of Keiss
44	George IV.	Great gr'dson of Geo. III.	1643	1676	..
45	George V., of *Keiss*	Grandson of George III.	1676	1698	Died issueless
46	John IV., of *Murkle*	Descendant of Geo. II.	1698	1705	..
47	Alexander II.	Son of John IV.	1705	1765	Died *s.p. male*
48	William III., of *Rattar*	Descendant of Geo. II.	1765	1779	..
49	John V.	Son of William III.	1779	1789	..
50	James I., of *Mey*	Descendant of Geo. II.	1789	1823	..
51	Alexander III.	Son of James I.	1823	1855	..
52	James II.	Son of Alex. III.	1855	1881	..
53	George VI.	Son of James II.	1881	1889	..
54	James III., of *Durran*	Descendant of Geo. II.	1889	1891	..
55	John VI.	Son of James III.	1891	..	The present Earl

* Also Earls of Orkney and of † Stratherne.

*₊*Caithness, which included Sutherland till the death of the 24th Earl in 1231, is indisputably the oldest comitial dignity in Britain, having existed for more than a millennium. The present Earl is heir-male of line of both Thorstein and Sigurd who acquired the Earldom in 871 by joint conquest from Constantine, King of the Scots.

CHAPTER V

THE EARLDOM OF CAITHNESS

871—1476

THE transactions relating to the earlier history of this Earldom have been embraced in the articles dealing with the Sea-kings of Orkney, *reguli* of ancient Orcadia, which term will be found convenient to define the territories under their rule.

The Orcadian Jarldom consisted of two principal parts—Insular and Scottish. The former comprehended the twin archipelagoes of Orkney and Hjaltland, bestowed on Rognvald 'Riki' of Moeri Jarl, by King Harald Fairhair of Norway, about the year 871 of the Christian era. Insular Orcadia was generally referred to as the Earldom of Orkney, of which the Lordship of Shetland was an appanage or secundogeniture—lost in 1196 by Earl Harald II, 'the Wicked,' not to be recovered till the occasion of the accession of Earl Henry I, first of the House of Saint-Clair. The Isles have also been described as The Countries of Orkney and Zetland.

THE NORSE LINE.

Scottish Orcadia, or Caithness, was acquired by joint conquest in 871, by two celebrated warriors—Thorstein the Red, Prince of Dublin (son of Olaf the White, King of that city, hereafter the Irish metropolis), and Sigurd the Sea-King, brother of Rognvald, Earl of Moeri, from whom he had already received Insular Orcadia in free gift. Sigurd had been flag-captain to King Harald Fairhair in his western cruise of conquest and colonisation, and was descended from the deified hero Thor, first-born son of Odin. Thorstein and Sigurd, although effecting a conquest of Caithness so permanent as to transmit their honours for over a millenium to their direct heir-male of line—John VI, 55th Earl, 17th of the sirname of Sinclair—both yielded up their lives in battle with the Scot. The valour of Thorstein has been gloriously celebrated in verse by the poet Motherwell in "The Sword-Chant of Thorstein the Red." After his death his rights to the conquered country passed to his daughter Groa, married to Earl Duncan; Sigurd being succeeded by his son, Earl Guttorm, who dying without issue, his dominions in Caithness seem to have lapsed; while those in the Isles went in succession to his kinsmen Hallad, Einar, Arnfinn, Erlend, and Thorfinn *Hausakliuf*, 'Splitter of Skulls.' Thorfinn, 8th Earl of Insular Orcadia, by marriage with Grelod, or Grelauga, heiress of Groa and Earl Duncan, became 5th Earl of Caithness, uniting it to his Island dominions.

By Grelauga Earl Thorfinn had five sons, his successors—Arnfinn, Havard, Ljot, Skuli, and Hlodver (Ludovic). Arnfinn, 6th Earl, espoused Ragnhild, daughter of Eric Bloodaxe, ex-King of Norway and of Northumbria. After the death of Arnfinn, which event it was supposed had been achieved by Ragnhild, his brother Havard hazarded an alliance with her; and incredible as it may seem, although she was suspected of complicity in connection with the death of Havard, his brother Ljot had the hardihood to marry her also Skuli now laid claim to a portion of Orcadia, and received substantial assistance from the then (974) King of Scots (Kenneth III.), who created him a belted Earl and furnished him with a strong army, beside which he had the support of a Scottish chief, Magbiod This creation is the first instance of Scottish interposition in Caithness affairs. Ljot and Skuli engaged in battle, Skuli falling and Ljot being mortally wounded. To them succeeded the surviving brother Hlodver, uniting in his person the Caithness claims of both Grelauga and Thorfinn

Hlodver, 8th Earl, like his father was a great warrior, and while roving in the West became enamoured of Audna, daughter of an Irish royalet, Carroll, King of Dublin (Kiarval, King of the Ivar) The antiquity of the Earldom of Caithness can best be realised by pointing out that the foregoing Earls were contemporaries of those Scottish sceptred shades—Constantine II., Aodh, Eocha, Grig, Donald IV., Constantine III , Malcolm I , Indulf, Duff, Culen, Kenneth III , Constantine IV , Malcolm II , etc. ; but there is no record of the writs of these royalties running through Caithness, which was practically independent, the Jarls thereof having Ross and Moray under their sphere of influence , laying the Hebudes under tribute, governors being appointed in those regions for the collection of taxes ; and exercising not only in Caithness, but also in Insular Orcadia, all *jura regalia*, subject only with regard to the latter to occasional interpositions of the monarchs of Norway

Earl Hlodver had—with a daughter Hvarflod, married to Earl Gilli of the Suderies— one only son, Sigurd II , the Stout, 11th Earl, who married secondly Anleta, a daughter of King Malcolm II. of Scotland , and falling at Clontarf in 1014, was succeeded by Thorfinn II , son of that marriage, then in minority. Thorfinn was the greatest of all the Earls of Orcadia, and his alliance it was with 'the peerless Macbeth ' which helped to elevate that Prince to the Scottish throne By Ingibiorg,* daughter of Earl Finn Arnason, Thorfinn the Great left two sons, the exiled Earls Paul and Erlend, both of whom died in captivity in Norway in 1103, being succeeded in Caithness by Hakon, 15th Earl, son of Paul (by a daughter of the Norwegian Earl, Hakon Ivarsson and Ragnhild, daughter of King Magnus the Good), who dying in 1122 left two sons—Harald the Orator, poisoned in accident (1127) by his mother Helga , and Paul II , the Silent, abducted to Athol (1136) by Sweyn, a noted Orcadian Viking. Hakon left also two daughters—Margaret, married to Madach, Earl of Athol, a member of the Royal Celtic Line of Scotland, and nephew of King Malcolm III ; and Ingibjorg, married to Olaf, King of the Hebudes and Man On the death in 1156 of the 18th Earl, Erlend II , the Younger, son of Harald the Orator, the *male* line of the family of Sigurd the Sea-King came to an end.

A few instances of interpolated succession now occur From a Dunfermline record it appears that a Scottish noble, Mac William, had the title of Earl of Caithness, 1129- 1160 , and on the deposition of Paul the Second, Rognvald, a son of Gunnhild, daughter of Erlend the Exile, effected an occupancy of the Isles, and presently, by arrangement with the guardians of young Harald of Athol (son of Margaret of Orkney), he acquired the Caithness possessions also All Orcadia was to be held jointly by Rognvald and Harald, but under the sole rulership of Rognvald Rognvald the Rhymer, 20th Earl, was a celebrated Crusader and pilgrim-poet. His verses are still extant in the library at Opslo † He fell in 1158, a victim to the private vengeance of one of his turbulent subjects,

---

She married (2nd) King Malcolm Canmore.   † i e., Christiania

and the veneration of posterity has enrolled him in the calendar of saints. He left an only daughter, Ingigerd, married to Eric Stagbrellir, whose son, Harald III., 22nd Earl, in 1196 succeeded in obtaining the half of Caithness from King William the Lion. This title Harald II. of Athol was in no way inclined to allow, and a battle ensued at Clairdon in Caithness, where young Harald, after distinguishing himself by his valiant actions, found an early grave (1196).

THE ATHOL LINE.

Harald II. *the Wicked* was now in undisputed possession of Orcadia, which then comprised Orkney, Shetland, Caithness, Sutherland, and Strathnaver. He was twice married, first to Afrecca, daughter of the Earl of Fife, by whom he had a son Henry, reputed Earl of Ross by the contemporary Saga annalists; and Hakon, who perished in battle with the Irish. By his second wife Gormlath, a daughter of Earl Malcolm MacHeth of Moray (ex-Bishop Wimund), the pretender to the Scottish throne, he had numerous issue, the surviving sons being his successors—David, 23rd Earl, died 1214; and John, 24th Earl, killed in 1231, whose son Harald, the Master of Orcadia, had predeceased him, being lost at sea some years antecedently.

THE ANGUS LINE.

The Orcadian Earldoms now pass to one Magnus, who is assumed to be the second son of the Earl of Angus; but as the Earldom of Angus goes immediately to an heiress, it is difficult to reconcile that fact with the Orcadian and Caithness succession. It may be that Magnus, Earl of Orkney and Caithness, married twice, having issue by the first marriage his successor, and marrying secondly the heiress of Angus, thus becoming Earl of Angus *jure uxoris*, and accounting for his appearance in 1232 as Magnus, Earl of Angus and Kataness. By the second marriage with the heiress of Angus, Earl Magnus may have had the one daughter, Matilda, Countess of Angus in her own right, who married first John Comyn (†1242), and secondly Gilbert de Umfraville, in which latter family the Earldom of Angus continued for some length of time. The foregoing is, however, only speculative, and the accepted version is that Magnus, second son of the Earl of Angus, became 25th Earl of Caithness as heir-at-law to his predecessor, Earl John. To Magnus succeeded Gilbride I. and Gilbride II., whose son, Earl Magnus II., was the 28th in succession. He was with King Hakon at Largs, and entered into a contract of privileges with Magnus VI. of Norway. His son, Magnus III., received the title by investiture at Tunsberg in 1276, and was one of the seven earls of Scotland who, in 1283, agreed to recognise Margaret, "the Maiden of Norway," as next successor to the Scottish realm. Dying in 1284 without issue, the Earldom passed to his brother, John II., 30th Earl. In 1291 Earl John had a safe-conduct from King Edward I. of England to report the circumstances of the death of the Princess Margaret on the Orcadian Coast. In 1297 he recognised Edward I. as Paramount of Scotland. The seal he used on that occasion was a ship with a tressure of flower-de-luce around it. In 1299 he was betrothed to Ingibiorg, Princess of Norway (daughter of King Eric by Isabel Bruce, daughter of Robert Bruce, Earl of Carrick), but the betrothal does not seem to have resulted in marriage. He died before 1312, as his son, Magnus IV., appears then on record as Earl In Magnus' time, and presumably in his favour, the King of Norway restricted the use of the comitial title to the king's sons and the Earl of Orkney. He was present at the Treaty of Inverness, 1312, between Robert I of Scotland and Hakon V., and in 1320 subscribed the famous letter to the Pope Next year (1321) Henry de St. Clair appears as *Ballivus* in Caithness, which is the first notice of the Roslins in those parts. In 1329 Katherine, Countess of Caithness and Orkney, executes deeds *in viduitate*, and the Caithness possessions of Earl Magnus are found inherited by the Earl of Stratherne and Simon Fraser, reputed ancestor of the Lovats

THE STRATHERNE LINE

It is surmised that Malise III. of Stratherne, when in apparency only, married Matilda, daughter of Earl Gilbride II of Orkney and Caithness, and had issue Matilda contracted at the age of nineteen, in 1293, to Robert de Thony, and Malise IV., seventh Earl of Stratherne, born about 1272. Malise IV. of Stratherne succeeded, on the death of Earl Magnus IV , to the Earldoms of Orkney and Caithness, thus uniting in his person three important Earldoms at a time, when there were only about twelve in existence in Scotland. He appears in 1331 as possessed of the fourth part of Caithness Falling at Halidon, in 1333, he left issue a daughter, Joanna, and his successor Malise, II. of Orkney and Caithness, V. of Stratherne This puissant prince married, first, Johanna de Menteith, by whom he had a daughter Matilda, married to one Weyland de Ard , and secondly, the Lady Marjory of Ross, by whom he had, with other issue Annot *(d s p)*, married to Erengisle Suneson, and Isabella, ancestress of the St Clairs hereafter Earls. Dying in 1344 or 1345, an interval of confused succession occurs. His Earldom of Stratherne being (semble) a male fief, reverted to the Scottish Crown, and was granted in 1345 to [his cousin] Maurice Moray (d. 1346), who had married Joanna, Countess-Dowager of Athol, styled also Countess of Stratherne, Warrenne, and Surrey, and reported variously to be mother, stepmother, sister, wife, widow, and daughter of the last Earl Malise It then passed to Robert the Steward (brother-in-law to Malise), who afterwards, on becoming King of Scotland, bestowed it on his brother David. The Earldom of Orkney was, in 1353, conferred on Erengisle Suneson, a Swedish noble, *jure uxoris* Annot de Stratherne, but she died before 1357, in which year Erengisle suffered forfeiture Earl Malise had executed an instrument at Inverness on the 28th May, 1344, securing the Earldom of Caithness to his daughter Isabella, under the protection of her uncle, William, Earl of Ross Isabella presently married Sir William St Clair of Roslin The said charter was confirmed at Scone by King David II 12th May, 1362, and in 1367 it is noted that there remain in the hands of Sir William Keith £10 annual rent charge on the Earldom of Caithness by reason of ward of the heir of William St Clair Notwithstanding the incontestable rights of Isabella, Lady St. Clair, to the Earldom, as instructed by these charters, through Court intrigue and covetousness the possession was assumed to have devolved upon Alexander de Ard, son of Matilda de Stratherne, the eldest co-heiress of Earl Malise II Alexander de Ard, as heir-general, should have inherited the Earldom of Stratherne, but that fief was apparently limited to heirs-male, and a new creation had probably before birth of de Ard been given in 1345 to Sir Maurice Moray, who, dying without issue in 1346, the Earldom was granted anew to Robert Stewart, who, in 1370, became King of

Scotland. Reluctant to relinquish the revenues of the Earldom, and yet desirous to compensate de Ard, who had been superseded in Orkney first by Erengisle Sunesson, next by the St. Clairs, and finally by the Norwegian Crown, the Scottish sovereign permitted him to acquire possession of Caithness at the expense of Lady St. Clair and her children, then in minority. In 1375 Alexander de Ard resigned to King Robert II. his rights to Caithness, Stratherne, and all other lands in Scotland, and eventually died without issue.

INTERVAL OF ALIEN EARLS.
1375—1431.   1450—1455.

King Robert II. thereupon created his brother David Earl Palatine of Stratherne and Caithness, but the latter dying without issue male, the Earldom of Caithness returned to the Crown, and was bestowed on Walter Stewart, Earl of Athol, in 1424, who forthwith assigned it to his son Alan, on whose death, at Inverlochy, in 1431, it continued with his father till his execution in 1437, when reverting to the Crown it remained in commission for some years. In 1450 it was granted to George Crichton, Lord High Admiral of Scotland. He died without male issue in 1455, in which year *the Earldom was restored to the direct line* in the person of William Saint-Clair, 44th Earl of Orkney, and has ever since continued in his house.

EARLS OF CAITHNESS.

THE HOUSE OF SAINT-CLAIR
1345—1897.

It has been seen that there was a special destination of Caithness on the 28th May, 1344, to Isabella de Stratherne, who presently became Lady St. Clair of Roslin, that the charter was confirmed 12th May, 1362; and that in 1367 the Earldom was subject to a rent-charge by reason of the ward of the heir of Wm. St. Clair, and that the Scottish sovereign wrongfully recognised Alex. de la Ard as heir to the Earldom, on whose resignation in 1375 the rights of those in remainder were again ignored. Several similar instances occur in Scottish history, the most striking being that of the Earldom of Buchan and of the Barony of Sinclair, which see. It is not known when Alex de Ard died, but at his death his aunt Isabella de Stratherne, Lady of Roslin, was next in succession, and we are told by the Diploma that she outlived all her brothers and sisters and their issue, as also her son, Earl Henry I of Orkney, who died 1404, transmitting her claim to Caithness to her grandson, Henry II of Orkney, Earl *de jure* of Caithness (†1420), who does not seem to have secured a recognition of his right, and *during the minority of his son William* the Earldom was in 1424 a second time granted to the alien House of Stewart, and again in 1450 to that of Crichton Her great-grandson, Wm. St. Clair, Earl of Orkney, was, however, successful enough to recover it in 1455, when he became 39th Earl, in successional sequence, though first of his house by patent from the Scottish Crown.

WILLIAM I, 39TH EARL
1455—1476.

The 39th Earl, who died about 1481, surrendered the title and jurisdiction of Orkney in 1471, and five years later—1476—abdicated his remaining Earldom of Caithness in favour of his second son of the name of William, who was second son of his second marriage, thus passing over the claims of his eldest son William of the first marriage, who was ancestor of the Lords Sinclair of Ravenscraig, now reputed extinct in the male line, and of the Sinclairs of Warsetter, of Tohop, Saba and Grottsetter, as also the claims of his second son, Sir Oliver St Clair of Roslin, eldest son of the second marriage, ancestor of the St Clairs of Roslin, the Sinclairs of Pitcairns, Ethay, etc

WILLIAM II., 40TH EARL
1476—1513

This Earl, on the resignation of his father, obtained a charter of the Earldom, including the patronage of the Hospital of St. Magnus at Spittal, which was followed in

1480 by a charter of the jurisdiction. In 1478 he or his father was decerned by Parliament to refund to the borough of Innerkeithen the pettie customis of the brugh of Dysart, intromitted with for the space of 17 years.*

He joined the confederacy of nobles who hanged Cochran, and the other favourites of James II., at the bridge of Lauder, in 1481 ; and on the second rebellion of the barons in 1488, headed by the king's own son, he appears to have allied himself to the royal cause, as well as Huntly, Crawford, and many others who had leagued for the destruction of the favourites. Huntly and Crawford fought at Sauchieburn on the king's side, but Caithness appears not to have arrived in time for the battle, although Abercrombie and Holinshed distinctly state that he and others were on their way to the assistance of King James.†

This Earl is a party to two ancient charters, one of lands in Caithness, and the other in Hjaltland. The former was executed at Girnigoe Castle, 14th March, 1496, being a charter from William de St. Claro, Earl of Caithness, to John Groat, son to Hugh Groat, of one penny land in Duncansby, paying therfor yearly *tres modios Brasii* at Martinmas.† The Shetland charter was dated at Edinburgh, the 3rd December, 1498, where Earl William, with the consent of his brothers and sisters, disponed the lands of Swinburgh, in the lordship of Zetland. Nisbet, who states he saw this charter, adds : " to which *all* their seals were appended entire, with their proper differences, . . . that of the Earl being a seal *couchy*, and quartered first and fourth a ship under sail, second and third a lion rampant, and over all, dividing the quarters, a cross ingrailed ; the shield was timbred with a helmet, enseigned with a flower-de-luce for crest ; supported on the dexter by a griffin, and on the sinister by a lion, and the legend around the seal *Sig. Willielmi Comitis Cathaniae.*"‡ This instrument, if still extant, might clear up the question of seniority between Earl William and his brother Sir Oliver of Roslin, and might perhaps inform us of other relationships.

In 1503 Parliament passed an act saying : " Because there has been great lack and fault of justice in the north parts, as Caithness and Ross, for fault of the want of division of the sheriffdom of Inverness, to our regret, and these parts are so far distant from the burgh of Inverness, through which people cannot come speedily there by reason of the great expense, labour, and travel, and therefore great enormities and trespasses have grown, in default of officers within those parts who have power to put good rule among the people, etc., etc." On these grounds there was to be a sheriff of Ross and one of Caithness, the latter sitting at Dornoch or Wick as convenient. It is said that this act, though passed, was inoperative till ratified for Caithness in 1641 and Ross in 1649.§ At the Parliament in Edinburgh on 8th June, 1504, the Earl witnessed a document by the Earl of Athole promising to underlie the law for treason.

There is a remission cited as made by Geo. Hepburn (uncle of the first Earl of Bothwell), who was Apostle or Bishop of the Isles from 1510 to 1513, in favour of this Earl, " for all murders and crimes committed by him from the year 1501 to 1510." " Murders and crimes" must mean incidents of disputed administration, feuds, and property quarrels, according to the language of the period, not personal felony. In the sasine or possessory document following his son John's retour in 1513, there is this reference to the remission, " Wherein the murder of the Bishop is thought to be comprehended, of date 1510." This ecclesiastical remission was a pre-requisite to that on Flodden Field§ from the Scottish

---

* Hay.   † Calder.   ‡ Nisbet.   § Caithness Events.

sovereign, who had apprised Canisbay, etc., from him for a debt of £400. This Earl William, the second of the Sinclairs, who held the Earldom of Caithness, resided at Castle Girnigoe, situated on a projecting rock or precipice near Noss Head, on the east side of Sinclair Bay. From the ruins of this castle still standing, it was not only a mansion of great strength, but also, for those days, of considerable architectural elegance. Girnigo was built for strength, and Castle Sinclair for beauty. The old saying runs :—

> "Girnigo was Girnigo ere Sinclair's first stane was laid,
> And Girnigo will be Girnigo when that Sinclair is dead."

He was married to the Lady Mary Keith, daughter to the Laird of Inverugie, Aberdeenshire, afterwards Earl-Marischal of Scotland. The latter was possessed of lands in Caithness, and resided frequently at Ackergill Tower, a very strong keep at the most

Reproduced by permission of G. W. Wilson & Co., Aberdeen.
CASTLES SINCLAIR AND GIRNIGO.

inland part of Sinclair Bay, about a couple of miles west of Castle Girnigoe. He was possessed of property throughout the whole North of Scotland, and it is said that when he occasionally came from his chief seat of Dunottar Castle, in the Mearns, to visit his estate in Caithness, he could, during the course of his journey, rest every night in a house of his own.*

"Having quarrelled with with his son-in-law, the Earl of Caithness, he took an opportunity, on a New Year's Day morning, when Caithness and some attendants had been out coursing with greyhounds, and were returning on horseback within

---

* Kennedy M.S.

WILLIAM II., 40TH EARL.

bowshot of the battlements of Ackergill Tower, to wound him with an arrow, which stuck firm in the back of his neck. Finding himself wounded, the Earl did not attempt to withdraw the arrow, but, having clapped spurs to his horse, arrived at his own house of Castle Girnigoe. His lady enquiring what sport he had met with, he replied, 'Not much; only in passing by Ackergill Tower, your father sent home a New Year's gift for you, which you may find fixed in the back of my neck.' "*

In 1505, the Earl sat in the Scottish Parliament.† He began the erection of a large building at Knock Einar, in Caithness, but being called South to join in the Scottish invasion of England, the building was never finished.‡ He took a prominent part in the Battle of Flodden, being in the right wing, led by the Earl of Huntly, who defeated the English left, but on returning from pursuit found the rest of the Scottish army in sad straits. Of the leaders of the Scottish right, the Earls of Huntly and Sutherland saved themselves by flight, but Gordon of Gight and the Earl of Caithness stood their ground, and at the head of their men gallantly yielded up their lives. Andrew Stewart, Bishop of Caithness, and Lord Treasurer of Scotland, also fell on this unhappy occasion. A French contemporary gazette, in enumerating the killed, has *inter alia*: " L'Evesque de Katnes ; Le Conte de Katnes."†

Earl William II. married Mary, daughter of Sir William Keith, of Inverugie, by whom he had

1. JOHN III., his successor, and
2. ALEXANDER of Stemster and Dunbeath, ancestor of the first family of that designation.

He had also a natural son—

WILLIAM, legitimised in 1543, of whose descendants, if any, no account has been discovered.§

JOHN III., 41ST EARL,
1513—1529.

Soon after fatal Flodden, Adam, Earl of Sutherland, in anticipation of threatened dangers in the North, made overtures to Earl John, and entered into bonds of friendship and alliance with him for mutual protection and support. The better to secure the goodwill and assistance of the Earl of Caithness, Earl Adam made a grant of some lands on the east side of the water of Ully ; but the Earl of Caithness, although he kept possession of the lands, joined the foes of his ally and friend.‖ The Earl of Sutherland had also established a league of amity with Y-Roy-Mackay the same year, but he presently dying, a contest ensued for the succession to Strathnaver between his brother Neil and his two bastard sons John and Donald. John took possession, but Neil laid claim and applied to the Earl of Caithness for assistance to recover them. After many entreaties the Earl put a force under Neil and his two sons, and they promptly dispossessed John, but were surprised by Donald, who slew his cousins, and, being rejoined by John, captured Neil —who, being abandoned by the Earl of Caithness, had cast himself on their generosity— and regardless of mercy and the ties of blood, ordered him to be beheaded in their presence by the hands of Claff-na-Gep, his own foster-brother. ¶

---

*Kennedy MS. † Calder. ‡ Pope. § Henderson (Caithness Family History).
‖ Gordon, an historian of known bias to the House of Sinclair. ¶ Keltie (citing Gordon).

The Earls of Caithness and Sutherland were continually in opposition, and at last the latter brought an action before the Lords of Council and Session to recover the lands of Strathully on the grounds of non-fulfilment of the consideration, viz., to assist the Earl of Sutherland against his enemies. There were other minor points of dispute between the Earls, to get all which determined they both repaired to Edinburgh. Instead, however, of abiding the issue of a trial at law before the judges, both parties, by the advice of mutual friends, referred the decision of all the points in dispute on either side to Gavin Dunbar, Bishop of Aberdeen, who pronounced his award at Edinburgh on the 11th March, 1524, his judgment appearing to have satisfied both parties, as the Earls lived in peace with one another ever after *

In 1528 he was one amongst others to whom King James addressed a mandate urging the extirpation of the "Kin of Clanquhattane," but nothing severe seems to have been done to that then troublesome clan * The letter reads . "to our louittis cousingis Adam Erle of Suthirland, John Erle of Cathnes," &c

Earl John's next appearance is his last Under 1528 Tytler, quoting Lesley, has There now ensued a formidable but abortive attempt to separate the Orkneys from the dominion of the Crown. The author of the rebellion, whose ambition soared to the height of an independent prince, was the Earl of Caithness ; but his career was brief and unfortunate the majority of the islanders were steady in their loyalty, and in a battle James Sinclair, the Governor of Orkney, encountered the insurgents, defeated and slew their leader with five hundred men, and making captives of the rest, reduced these remote parts to a state of peace.

The Groat Inventories contain a Precept of Sasine by Jo. Sinclair, Earl of Caithness, for infefting John Groat in ane penny land in Dungsby Dated at Nose, 5th October, 1515. The Sasine thereanent, issues on 12th October following, and another of even date to William Groat in a farthing land, also in Duncansbay On the 28th September, 1521, a Precept of Sasine issues from Earl John for infefting Walter, son and air of umquhile William Grot in the said lands ; and he dates another at Girnigoe, 22nd October, 1523, infefting John Groat in one penny land in Dungsby conform to a charter granted yr anent.† Earl John granted to Alex Brisbane of Ekirnoss, dated Girnigoe Castle, 28th March, 1520, ‡ and there is another dated Wick, 19th October, 1523, one of donation to Trinity Convent, Aberdeen, for the soul of his father, of himself, and the souls of his friends and successors, 264 masses to be sung yearly in all § By his Countess Elizabeth, daughter of Sir William Sutherland of Duffus, he had

1 WILLIAM, Master of Caithness, who died without issue in 1527, *vita patris.*
2 GEORGE, his successor

He had also a natural son—

DAVID, Bailie to the Bishop of Caithness In 1556 Earl George obtained a remission for imprisoning David in Girnigoe Castle ‖

Some authorities state that Earl John married secondly, after the death or divorce of Elizabeth Sutherland, the fifth sister of Adam Gordon, Earl of Sutherland, but this seems exceedingly doubtful It arises perhaps from confusing Sir William Sinclair of Warsetter, Orkney, who married Helene. fifth daughter of George, Earl of Huntly, with his contemporary and kinsman, the Earl of Caithness.

* Keltie.   † Petrie Papers.   ‡ Bruce—Caithness MS   § Bain's Merchant Guilds of Aberdeen
‖ Henderson

GEORGE II., 42ND EARL.
1529—1582.

This Earl, with John, Earl of Sutherland, met Queen Mary at Inverness on the occasion of her arrival there in the month of July, 1555, to settle the disorders then prevailing in those parts. Although Earl George was requested to bring his countrymen along with him to the Court, he either neglected or declined to do so, and was therefore committed to prison at Inverness, Aberdeen, and Edinburgh successively, nor was he restored to liberty till he paid a considerable sum of money.*

Earl George took an active part in the intrigues in connection with the marriages of Mary, Queen of Scots. In 1560 he attended the secret convention of the Catholic party which entrusted Lesley, official of Aberdeen (afterwards Bishop of Ross), with a commission to repair to the French Court and present to their sovereign their offers of service and expressions of devoted attachment.* The next year (1561) William and Angus Sutherland of Berriedale, countenanced it is believed by the Earl of Sutherland, committed some gross outrages in Caithness, and killed several inhabitants of the county named Clyne, against whom they had a grudge. For these acts the Earl of Caithness banished them, and confiscated their castle of Berriedale. This incited them to resume their depredations, and through the influence of the Earl of Sutherland a pardon was obtained for them from Queen Mary. Earl George was greatly exasperated at the interference of the Earl of Sutherland, and to this incident we trace the foundation of that hatred which the two rival Houses of Caithness and Sutherland bore each other for so long a period.† He attended the convention of the Scottish nobility held at Stirling 15th May, 1565, to deliberate on the marriage of Queen Mary. On receiving the announcement of her intention to wed Darnley, all approved thereof.‡ The Earl was appointed Justiciary of the North of Scotland, with jurisdiction to include the whole of Sutherland and Caithness, on the 17th April, 1566. The commission included a power to banish and kill, and to pardon any crime except treason.† It was ratified by the Scottish Parliament the 19th April, 1567. The Justiciaryship had been vested in his predecessors, and was but the renewal of an heritable right. The Earl's crest was a Gallic cock, which accounts for the expression "Cock of the North" as applicable to him. He is stated to have joined the conspiracy of 1567 to destroy Darnley. He was chancellor of the jury that acquitted Bothwell, and in pronouncing judgment the Earl, on behalf of the jury, protested "that no crime should be imputed to them on that account, as no accuser had appeared, nor was proof brought of the indictment." After this nominal trial the Earls of Caithness and Sutherland, along with the other lords present, subscribed the bond acquitting Bothwell of the crime with which he had been charged, and recommending him as a fit husband for the Queen. Both Earls were members of the Privy Council, and friendly to Bothwell. Immediately after the murder of Darnley, they further signed the letter written by the Privy Council in 1567 to the Queen-mother of France, in which is given a delusive account of this shocking tragedy.†

On the night of the murder of Rizzio, Caithness was with the party which attempted the rescue of the Queen, but being outnumbered, retired from the contest for that

---
* Keltie. † Calder. ‡ Tytler.

night. Two days afterwards the Queen and Darnley, then reconciled, contrived to escape to Dunbar Castle, and were there joined by several of their friends, amongst whom was the Earl of Caithness and his followers.*

An incident now occurred which illustrates the wickedness of the times. The Earl, Countess, and Master of Sutherland, while staying at a hunting-lodge near Helmsdale, had poison administered to them by Isabel Sinclair, wife of Gilbert Gordon of Gartay, and sister of William Sinclair of Dunbeath. The Earl and Countess died from the effect of the poison, but the Master attended a little later and was warned by the Earl to avoid supper. The Earl of Caithness has been accused of procuring the crime, but, as on the death of the Master of Sutherland, Gilbert Gordon of Gartay would have been next in succession to the Earldom, it is clear that his wife had sufficient motive without any incentive from Caithness. Isabel was sent to Edinburgh for trial, where, being duly condemned, she died on the execution morn. By a singular retribution the poisoned draught was administered in mistake to her own son John Gordon with fatal results. These events happened in July, 1567.†

Y-Mackay of Far, an ally of the Earl of Caithness, now invaded Sutherland, being assisted in his enterprise by the Laird of Duffus. The Earl of Caithness prevailed upon Robert Stuart, Bishop of the county, to address a letter to the governor of Skibo Castle, in which the young Earl of Sutherland then resided, to deliver up the castle to him, a request with which the governor complied. Caithness carried the young Earl off to Girnigoe, and, although he was only fifteen, got him married to his daughter Lady Barbara Sinclair, aged thirty-two, between whom and Y-Mackay of Far there existed an undue intimacy, which was subsequently made the ground of a divorce. The Earl of Caithness then occupied Dunrobin Castle with his ward, and is stated to have burnt all the Sutherland archives, and to have formed the design of marrying his second son William Sinclair of Mey to Lady Margaret Gordon, the eldest sister of the Earl of Sutherland, whom he would then cut off, and his own son would thus become Earl. This design was frustrated by the escape of the young Earl in 1569.

About this time began the controversies between Laurence, Lord Oliphant, and Lord Caithness. The former makes complaint 12th October, 1569, of an attack on him and his men by George, Earl of Caithness, in which divers were mutilated and John Sutherland slain. The latter was the son of Alexander Sutherland of Clyne, son of Kathrine, daughter of John Sinclair, Bishop of Caithness. On 22nd of November following, Caithness has to appoint deputies to investigate the matter, and on 8th March, 1874, the Acts of the Justice Court held at Thurso, 30th August and 31st October, 1569, are required to be produced.

Conflicts now took place between the Murrays and the Sutherlands of Duffus, the latter receiving the support of Earl George, who sent John, Master of Caithness, with a large force to attack the Murrays in Dornoch. He fired the Cathedral, attacked the castle, and reduced the town, receiving the submission of the Murrays on terms, for the fulfilment of which hostages were taken (1570). The Earl, however, refused to ratify the terms of capitulation, and beheaded the hostages. This highly incensed both the Master of Caithness and Mackay, and from that time the Earl and the Master were at variance with each other, the latter retiring to Strathnaver, where he resided with Mackay.†

* Calder.   † Calder ; Keltie.

GEORGE II, 42ND EARL.

Rumours presently reached the Earl that Mackay and the Master were conspiring against him. He therefore resolved to inveigle them to Girnigoe, and get possession of their persons, to accomplish which purpose he professed the most earnest desire for a reconciliation with his son, and sent repeated invitations for them both to visit him in his stronghold. They eventually resolved to hazard the visit, and set out unattended. On passing the drawbridge Mackay observed an unusual number of armed men. Suspecting treachery, he immediately turned, spurred his horse across the bridge, which was still down, and escaped. The Master, however, was less fortunate Him they seized, though not without a desperate struggle as he was a man of vast bodily strength, and he was fettered heavily and immured for some years in a dark and noisome dungeon to die of thirst and starvation under great torture in 1576

Y-Mackay after escaping to Strathnaver, died within four months of grief and remorse for the many bad actions of his life During the minority of his son Houcheon, John Mor-Mackay, the cousin, and John Beg-Mackay, the bastard son of Y-Mackay, took charge of the estate, but the Earl of Caithness considering John Mor a favourite of the Earl of Sutherland, speedily relieved him of his charge, caused him to be apprehended and carried into Caithness, where he was detained in prison till his death

During this time John Robson, the chief of the clan Gunn in Caithness and Strathnaver, became a dependent on the Earl of Sutherland, acting as his factor in collecting the rents and duties of the Bishop's lands in Caithness belonging to the Earl This connection was exceedingly disagreeable to Earl George, who, to gratify his spleen against John Robson, instigated Houcheon Mackay to lay waste the lands of the clan Gunn, in the Brea-Moir, in Caithness, without the knowledge of John Beg-Mackay, his brother As the clan Gunn had always been friendly to the family of Mackay, John Beg was greatly exasperated at the conduct of the Earl in enticing the young chief to commit such an outrage, but he had it not in his power to make any reparation to the injured clan. John Robson, the chief, however, assisted by Alexander, Earl of Sutherland, invaded Strathnaver, and made ample retaliation, returning with a large booty and killing many of Houcheon Mackay's retainers The Earl of Caithness having resolved to avenge himself on John Beg-Mackay for the displeasure shown by him at the conduct of Houcheon, and also on the clan Gunn, prevailed upon Neil Mac-Iain Mac-William, chief of the Sliochd-Iain-Abaraich and James Mac-Rory, chief of the Sliochd-Iain-Mhoir, to attack them Accordingly, in the month of September, 1579, these two chiefs, with their followers, made a night attack, in which they slew John Beg-Mackay and William Mac-Iain Mac-Rob, the brother of John Robson, and some of their people *

On the 17th June, 1578, the Earl of Caithness, with others, protests against an ambassador being sent to England to treat of a further league, and in 1581 he was one of the principal leaders of the confederacy against Morton † He frequently appears as a member of the Privy Council

George II., 42nd Earl of Caithness, died at Edinburgh on the 9th September, 1582, and was buried in Roslin Chapel, where there is a monument to his memory, with the following Latin inscription "*Hic jacet nobilis ac potens Dominus, Georgius quondam Comes Cathanensis, Dominus Sinclair, Justiciarius hereditarius, Diocesis Cathanensis, qui obit Edinburgi, 9 die mensis Septembris, anno Domini, 1582*" His heart, which was extracted and encased in a leaden casket, was, by his dying request, sent to Caithness and deposited in

---
* Keltie. † Calder

the church at Wick. He had been Earl for fifty-four years, during which period he had amassed much wealth, and greatly enlarged his hereditary property. The whole of his money he bequeathed to his youngest son, George Sinclair of Mey.*

By his Countess, the Lady Elizabeth, daughter of William, Earl of Montrose, he had issue—†

1. JOHN, Master of Caithness, d. *vita patris* 1576.
2. WILLIAM, d. *s.p.l.*, ancestor of Ulbster.
3. GEORGE of Mey, Chancellor of Caithness.
1. BARBARA, m. Alex., Earl of Sutherland, div. 1573.
2. ELIZABETH, m., 1st, Alex. Sutherland of Duffus.
   2nd, Hutcheon McKay of Far, ancestor of the Lords Reay.
3.   m. Alex. Innes of Innes.
4. JANET, m. Robert Munro of Foulis.

The Earl was succeeded by his grandson George, eldest son of the Master of Caithness, who had died during the life-time of his father.

On Barrogill Castle there is an ancient carving of the arms of this Earl, displaying Caithness and Montrose, a vignette of which adorns the title-page of Caithness Family History, by John Henderson, W.S.

JOHN, MASTER OF CAITHNESS,

D.V.P. 1567.

On the 2nd October, 1545, the Master of Caithness obtained a charter from Queen Mary, by which the Earldom became a *male fee* to him and his heirs male. At Edinburgh, on the 1st December, 1565, he protested that his father should not be required to answer citation obtained by William Sutherland (Hectorsoun) in Berydaill, etc. Protests admitted, and their renewed complaints on 31st January thereafter were refused. In 1567 he stormed Dornoch, and his father's mal-treatment of the hostages then taken—in violation of the terms of surrender—was the foundation of the hatred between sire and son, which ended in the Master's death.

---

* Calder.   † Henderson.

Upon his imprisonment in Girnigo Castle there were three keepers appointed over him, namely, Murdoch Roy, and two brothers, Ingram and David Sinclair. Roy was the one who regularly attended him and performed all the menial services connected with the office. The other two, who were kinsmen of the Earl, and are stated to have had a bend sinister in their escutcheon, might be said to be inspectors or head gaolers. Roy, it would appear, was not altogether a hardened miscreant, steeled against the ordinary feelings of humanity. His heart was touched with pity for the unfortunate nobleman, and at the earnest and oft-repeated solicitations of the latter, he agreed to endeavour to set him at liberty. Unfortunately the scheme was discovered by John's brother William, who bore him no goodwill, and at once informed his father of the meditated escape. The Earl forthwith ordered Roy to be executed, and the poor wretch was immediately brought out and hanged on the common gibbet of the castle, without a moment being allowed him to prepare for his final account.* Soon after, William Sinclair of Mey visited the cell, and the brothers had an angry altercation. Embittered by the bad usage and long confinement he had endured, the Master, a man of powerful physique, and therefore called *Garrow* or the Strong, though heavily fettered, sprang upon his brother and actually crushed out his life in an iron embrace.† This deepened the father's antipathy to his unhappy son. He had now been nearly six years in duress, and it is stated that his keepers, the two Sinclairs, instigated by the Earl, deliberately compassed the death of the poor captive, and that by a most inhuman method. They first withheld food from him for a few days, and then supplied him abundantly with salt beef, of which, in his famished state, he ate voraciously. A raging thirst came upon him, but his brutal keepers denied him water, and left him to die in writhing agony. The accounts of his death differ as to details, but all agree that he was barbarously murdered. His remains were interred in the "Sinclair Aisle" in the churchyard of Wick, which his father had built some years before. The inscription on the stone over his grave is most legible. It reads: "Here lies entombed ane noble and worthie man, John, Master of Caithness, who departed this life the 15th day of March, 1576."†

He married Jean, Lady Morhame, daughter of Patrick Hepburn, Earl of Bothwell, who makes supplication in April, 1581, on behalf of her lawful son, Francis Stuart, Earl of Bothwell. By her he was father of—‡

1. GEORGE, 43rd Earl of Caithness.
2. JAMES, first of Murkle.
3. SIR JOHN, first of Greenland and Ratter.
1. AGNES.

The Master had also two natural sons—

1. DAVID, acquired Stirkoke 1587, legitimated 1588, died *ante* 1595, leaving a son
   JOHN, slain at Thurso in 1612, and a natural son
   COLONEL GEORGE, ambushed in Norway the same year.‡
2. HENRY, married Janet Sutherland, and had a son
   JOHN, probably ancestor of the Sinclairs, Wadsetters of Lybster till 1670. Henry received a conveyance from his brother, Earl George, of part of the lands of Borrowstown and Lybster, with "the miln and fishings." In a reversion by him in favour of the Earl, dated 3rd September, 1606, he is designed as his brother naturall. He accompanied Earl George III. in the expedition of 1614 to Orkney, and it is related by Gordon that, while besieging the Castle of Kirkwall, he "went to bed at night in health, but before the morning he was benumbed in all his sences, and remained so until his death."‡ A Henri Sinclair, servant to the Earl of Caithness, appears 5th January, 1615, in the jury empannelled to try Robert Stewart, base sone of Patrick. lait Erle of Orknay.§

---
*Calder.   †Calder: Scenes and Stories.   ‡Henderson.   §Pitcairn's Crim. Trials.

GEORGE III., 43RD EARL, *THE WICKED* *
1582—1643

This Earl is remembered in the traditional history of Caithness as the "Wicked Earl George," though perhaps the sobriquet might more fairly be awarded to the 42nd Earl. He signalised his accession to the Earldom by deliberately killing, in broad day, Ingram and David Sinclair, the two principal keepers of his late father. David lived at Keiss, and Ingram at Wester. Ingram was Laird of Blingery, and a large landed proprietor of over 3,000 acres. Ingram's daughter was to be married, and a large party, including his lordship, was invited to the wedding. On the forenoon of the appointed day, as the Earl was taking an airing on horseback, he met David on the Links of Keiss, on his way to Wester, and ran him through with his sword. Immediately on doing so he galloped over to Wester, and calling aside Ingram, who was at the time amusing himself with some friends at football, he drew out a pistol and shot him dead on the spot. He then coolly turned his horse's head towards Girnigoe, and rode off with as little concern as if he had merely killed a brace of moor fowl. Being a great nobleman, possessed of ample power of "pit and gallows," he escaped with impunity. Tradition adds that during the alarm and confusion caused by this shocking affair the wedding guests dispersed, and the ring was lost. Not many years since a finger ring of a curious construction—supposed to be the identical wedding-ring—was found at Wester. It was of pure gold, twisted so as to represent a serpent coiled with tail in mouth, as emblematical of eternity †

King James VI., at Holyrood House, Edinburgh, of date 19th March, 1585, gave letters of remission for the deeds to George, Earl of Caithness, James Sinclair, the Master of Caithness, his brother, David, their brother, Mathew, son of the deceased David Sinclair of Dunn; Archibald, Thomas, James, George, and Alex Hepburn; George Manson; William Manson or Rorison, Donald Groat, Donald Sutherland, son of Angus Hectorson, James Paxton, servant of the Master of Caithness; James and George Mullikin, Thomas Manson, son of the deceased William Manson in Field, John Hay, John Waterston; William Taylor, Malcolm Alexanderson, Edward Jameson, servants of the Earl, and others, their comrades. The letters were to last for their lifetime, and freed them from, among other things, "art and part of the slaughters of Ingram and David Sinclair, brothers, in the month of February, 1584." The readiness with which the remission was issued indicates the fatality as the result of a chance encounter, for Ingram was too important a person to be otherwise disposed of. Besides being Laird of Blingery, now containing 261 acres arable and 2,560 acres pasture, he had tacks of the vicarages or tithes of Bower and Watten, held a wadset from Knappo barony, Wick, and had been master of the household or chamberlain at Girnigoe Castle. Both Ingram and David Sinclair witnessed the charter of Canisbay, etc., given to William Sinclair of Mey, dated 1st March, 1572, at Girnigoe Castle, Ingram being described as "of Blingery." In a contract, of date Kirkcaldy and Girnigoe, 24th July and 30th December, 1595, to which Earl George was a party, not only is the "deceased Ingram Sinclair of Blingery" mentioned, but also his heirs, Earl George promising to respect their rights as given by his uncle, George Sinclair of Mey †

---
* Calder, and Keltic.   † Caithness Events

GEORGE III., 43RD EARL

This Earl being a minor at the time of his succession, the opportunity was considered by those interested a favourable one to detach the Justiciary from the dignity. A supplication was made on the 27th December, 1582-83, by George, Earl Marischal, Lord Keith, Laurence, Lord Oliphant, and the Abbot of Deer against the renewal of a Commission of Justiciary in favour of the present Earl, a minor; their supplication was successful. This was followed a few years after by revived differences between Lord Oliphant and the Earl. The former made complaint 21st November, 1587, that David Sinclair, brother natural to the Earl, in July, 1583, at the Earl's instance, and under silence of night, forcibly ejected William Oliphant of Newton (uncle of Lord Oliphant) from Thrumbustar, and further, that James, Master of Caithness, brother of the Earl, John Sinclair, another brother, and David Sinclair, with some 70 persons, came to the tour and fortalice of Tubister, and intromitted with live stock and other goods. On the 8th January thereafter, the said Earl, James, Master of Caithness, and David Sinclair, natural brother of the Earl, were denounced for the same. On the 16th March, 1587-88, Francis Stuart, Earl of Bothwell, Great Admiral of Scotland, became caution in 5,000 merks that his brother-uterine, George Sinclair, Earl of Caithness, shall answer upon 15th May next the complaint of Lord Oliphant, and a suspension of the letters raised against the Earl was then obtained until the 10th June. On the 11th June, 1589, Hector Monro of Kildermorie was put under caution of £1,000 not to harm Lord Caithness, who on 6th March, 1589-90, is found appointed Commissioner for Caithness re Acts against Jesuits. In July, 1587, Caithness is enumerated as having broken men on his lands, for which on 16th December, 1590, he had to find caution in £20,000. George, Earl of Huntly, became caution in £5,000 on 20th September, 1591, that Caithness would not harm Lord Oliphant, and when the case came up on 10th November, 1591, the Earl asserted that, having obtained Huntly as security, letters of horning, etc., should be suspended. The Lords stated it was not meet that Huntly or any of his degree or rank should be cautioners, and required others.

To strengthen and extend his influence in the North, Earl George married Lady Jane Gordon, sister of the Earl of Huntly. He and the Earl of Sutherland were almost constantly at war. The first opportunity occurred in 1585, when a quarrel arose between Neil Houcheonson and the Laird of Assynt. Houcheon Mackay assisted Assynt, who had married his sister, and Earl George supported them with men. The Earl of Sutherland, on the other hand, stood by Neil, who was commander of Assynt, and a follower of his. A temporary reconciliation was patched up in 1586 between the two potentates of Caithness and Sutherland, and they united to exterminate the clan Gunn. The latter, however, got timely notice of the plot, and prepared for resistance. Being joined by a party of the Strathnaver Mackays, they attacked the Caithness men before the latter effected a junction with their allies at Auldgown, on the borders of Sutherland, and completely routed them. The leader, Henry Sinclair, brother of the Laird of Dunn, and "cousin" to the Earl of Caithness, and about 140 men, were left dead on the field. The Earl was so enraged when he heard of this affair that he immediately hanged John Gunn, a leading man among the clan, whom he had some time before got hold of, and who was then a prisoner in Girnigoe.

The hollow friendship between the two Earls lasted for about a year, when a series of contests arose from what in legal phrase would be termed a piece of "malicious mischief." George Gordon, bastard of Gartay, waylaid the servants of the Earl, and, cutting off the horses' tails, bade them tell their master he had done so. Resenting the indignity, the Earl, knowing the futility of seeking redress from the Earl of Sutherland, whose follower Gordon was, resolved to himself punish the offender. For this purpose he set out with a picked body of men to Helmsdale, near to which Gordon lived, and, arriving in the night time, surrounded his house with the party. Gordon, after a desperate resistance, took to flight, pursued by Sinclair of Mey and some half-dozen followers. He then flung himself into the river of Helmsdale, hard by, and tried to make his escape by swimming across, but a shower of arrows was discharged upon him, and he was slain in the water. The Earl of Sutherland, although he disliked the conduct of George Gordon, who was also guilty of an improper intimacy with Sutherland's sister, resolved to request satisfaction from the Earl of Caithness. The latter replied by assembling his forces, and being joined by Mackay and the Strathnaver men, together with John, Master of Orkney, and the Earl of Carrick, brother of Patrick, Earl of Orkney, with a contingent of Orcadians, marched to Helmsdale to meet the Earl of Sutherland. Neither party cared to risk an engagement, and by the mediation of mutual friends the two Earls agreed to a temporary truce on the 9th of March, 1587, from the benefits of which Mackay of Strathnaver was carefully excluded. The latter, however, came to an amicable understanding with the Earl of Sutherland, at Elgin, in the month of November, 1588. On the expiration of the truce, Lord Sutherland, supported by his allies Mackay, Macintosh, Assynt, Foulis, and Rasay, entered Caithness with all his forces in the beginning of 1588, having obtained a commission from the Privy Council against Earl George for killing the Bastard of Gartay. His great object was to secure the person of the Earl of Caithness, but that nobleman prudently withdrew within the iron walls of Castle Girnigoe, a fortress strongly fortified, and prepared to withstand a siege. Foiled in his attempt, Sutherland ravaged Latheron, returning home with a large booty in cattle, which was divided among his followers. This foray was known as "Creach Iarn"—that is, the "harship" or harrying of Latheron. The town of Wick was pillaged and burnt, but the church was preserved. In it was found the heart of the late Earl of Caithness encased in a leaden casket, which was opened by John Mac-Gille-Calum of Rasay, and the ashes were scattered to the winds. Such was the singular fate which befell the heart of that proud and cruel nobleman. After twelve days the Earl of Sutherland raised the siege of Girnigoe, and ravaged the county as far as Duncansbay, killing several of the peasantry and returning with great spoil. This affair was called "La na creachmore" or "the great spoil."

Another truce ensued, but it was of brief duration, for the Earl of Caithness, burning to be revenged for the injuries done to the county, retaliated by a succession of inroads into Sutherland. Lord Caithness despatched a party of his men to Diri-Chatt, in Sutherland, under the command of Kenneth and Farquhar Buy, chieftains of the Siol-Mhic-Imheair, in Caithness. Lord Sutherland responded by sending 300 men into Caithness at Whitsunday, 1589, under Alex. Gordon of Kilcalmekill. In retaliation James Sinclair of Murkle, brother of the Earl of Caithness, collected an army of 3,000 men, with which he marched into Strathully in June, 1589, but after a long warm contest was forced to retire by Strathnaver and Kilcolmkil, who were in command of inferior forces. The Earl of Sutherland followed up this advantage and advanced as far as Corriechoich, in Braemore, where he encamped. The Earl of Caithness had convened his forces at Spittal, where he resolved to wait the approach of the enemy. The Earl of Huntly, the relation of both of the contestants, on hearing of the warlike preparations of the two hostile Earls, sent his uncle, Sir Patrick Gordon of Auchindun, to mediate between them, by whose friendly interference an armistice was concluded, and in November, 1589, the contending parties met at Elgin, where they subscribed a deed, by which they appointed Huntly and his successors hereditary judges and arbitrators of all disputes and differences that might henceforth arise between their two houses. This written agreement was valuable only as waste paper, for scarce a few weeks elapsed till the Earls were again at war.

The severest battle which was fought during this campaign was at Clyne, in Sutherland, and occurred about October, 1590. The Murrays and the Gordons disputed for the command of the vanguard of the Sutherland army, and as the Gordons insisted on their claims to the position, the Murrays withdrew and looked on throughout the engagement. The Caithness army had 1,500 archers in the van, mostly from the Western Isles, and under the command of Donald Balloch Mackay of Scourie. The combat raged with great fury, and was long sustained without advantage to either side. Thrice were the Caithness archers driven back, throwing their rear into disorder, and thrice did they return to the fray cheered on by their leader, but, though superior in numbers, they were unable to withstand the intrepidity of the men of Sutherland, and on the approach of night withdrew from the field of battle. The loss in wounded and slain was about equal, and few principal men were killed. The two Earls were once more reconciled by the mediation of the Earl of Huntly at Strathbogie in March, 1591.

The same year the Earl of Caithness received a visit from his brother-uterine, Francis Stewart, Earl of Bothwell, who had, by his exceptionally factious and turbulent conduct, rendered himself peculiarly obnoxious to James VI of Scotland. Bothwell had last distinguished himself by audaciously entering Holyrood with a party of armed men for the purpose of securing the person of the King. His scheme failing, he fled North to his half-brother; but a dispute arising, Earl George meditated delivering him up to the King. In this critical situation Bothwell owed his safety to James Sinclair of Murkle, who informed him of the design, on which Bothwell made his escape abroad. The Earl of Caithness was so offended with Murkle that it is said he banished him for some time from the county. On the 11th February, 1594-95, Sir Jas Scott of Balweary revealed the existence of a band between William, sumtyme Earl of Angus, George, sumetime Earl of Huntly, Francis, sumtime Earl of Bothwell, Francis, sumtime Earl of Errol, George Earl of Caithness, and umquhile Sir Patrick Gordon of Auchindoun, to capture the King and crown the Prince, Huntly, Errol, and Angus being regents. On the 7th February, 1598-99, assurances were required from Caithness and Orkney.

After the battle of Clyne the two rival houses remained quiet for some time. Alexander, Earl of Sutherland, died on the 6th December, 1594, and was succeeded by his son John. While the latter was absent on the Continent in 1600, the Earl of Caithness massed his forces with the apparent intention of entering Sutherland or Strathnaver, but did not carry his purpose into effect. The question of precedence between the Earls of Caithness and Sutherland was raised on 19th February, 1601, and as Caithness still continued to threaten an invasion, the Earl of Sutherland assembled an army to oppose him in July, 1601, being supported by Mackay, Assynt, and the Monroes. Meanwhile the Earl of Caithness advanced towards Sutherland with his army. The two armies encamped some three miles asunder, near the hill of Bengrime. A prophetic tradition had long been current that a battle would take place at that spot, which would result in the complete overthrow of the Caithness men, but at the sacrifice of many lives on the side of the Sutherland and Strathnaver men. The latter were, notwithstanding, eager to score their assured victory, but the Earl of Caithness, aware of the prophecy, proceeded to temporise, and sent messengers to the Earl of Sutherland to effect an amicable settlement of their differences. A pacific course was adopted, and in reply Sutherland intimated the willingness of his council to allow Caithness to retire, which he accordingly did. Eventually they agreed to a mutual disarmament, the Earl of Sutherland sending George Gray of Cuttle to see the army of Caithness disbanded, and the Earl of Caithness in his turn despatched Alexander Bane, chief of the Caithness Banes, to witness the dismissal of the Sutherland men.

The next disturbance happened in 1605, on the occasion of a visit of Alister-Mac-Uilleam-Mhoir, a retainer of Mackay. The Earl of Caithness, hearing of his presence in the county, despatched his bastard brother, Henry Sinclair, with a party of men to kill him. He was seized under cover of friendship, and brought prisoner to the Earl, who caused him to be beheaded in his own presence the following day; his fault being unwavering fidelity to Mackay, his chief, during the disputes between the two Earls. Mackay entered a legal prosecution at Edinburgh against Earl George, but by the mediation of the Marquis of Huntly the suit was quashed.

The Earl of Caithness, tired of his enforced state of quietude, made another attempt in the month of July, 1607, to hunt in Bengrime, but was prevented from doing so by the sudden appearance in Strathully of the Earl of Sutherland with his friend Mackay. The Earls then went through the usual formality of having the matter settled by their heritable arbiter, the Marquis of Huntly, at Elgin.

The next appearance of Earl George is a splendid illustration of his restless and capricious disposition, and the immunity of great nobles from the consequences of lawless acts in parts where they themselves held heritable jurisdictions. It happened that in 1608, a boat with some of the Earl of Orkney's servants on board, being overtaken with a severe gale while crossing the Petland Firth, ran for refuge to Sinclair's Bay. As soon as they landed, the Earl, who had a pique at Earl Patrick Stewart, a man very similar in disposition to himself, ordered the servants to be brought to Girnigoe. After plying them with a lot of liquor he then caused the one side of their heads and the one side of their beards to be shaved, and in this condition forced them to take boat and go to sea before the storm had abated. They fortunately reached Orkney in safety, and told their master how they had been treated. The Earl very naturally resented the barbarous usage which his domestics had received at the hands of the Earl of Caithness, and complained thereof to the king. His Majesty ordered the Privy Council to summon the two Earls before them and investigate the matter. Both attended at Edinburgh, but through the interposition of friends the case was not brought before the Council, an agreement being arrived at. The historian of Sutherland quaintly remarks :—"Only one example of this crime I do remember. The servants of David, King of Israel, were so entreated by Hannum, King of the children of Ammon. The Earl of Caithness thus far exceeded Hannum, that not satisfied with what himself had done, he forced the Earl of Orkney his servants to take the sea in such a tempest, and exposed them to the extremity of the raging waves; whereas Hannum suffered King David his servants to depart home quietly after he had abused them."

In 1610 Earl George and Mackay had a difference on account of the latter giving protection to his nephew, John Sutherland of Berridale, who having been outlawed, retaliated by depredations in Caithness. The Earl on one of these occasions sent a party of the Siol-Mhic-Imheair in pursuit, but they were surprised by Sutherland and defeated with a loss of several killed. This disaster exasperated the Earl who promptly served both Mackay and his son with a notice to appear before the Privy Council for giving protection to an outlaw. The affair was, however, withdrawn and adjusted by friends, it being arranged that the Earl should forgive John Sutherland and restore his possessions, that John and his brother Donald should in turn be kept prisoners by him, and that Donald Mac-Thomais-Mhoir, a follower of John's, should be surrendered to be dealt with by the Earl as he should think meet. Donald was hanged forthwith, and the Sutherlands performed the conditions required of them, and were presently released by Earl George at the intercession of the Mackays, whom the Earl was desirous of detaching from their adhesion to Sutherland. Mackay spent the following Christmas at Girnigo Castle, but the Earl was unsuccessful in his design.

The Earl kept round him at Girnigo a body of stout retainers ready for all emergencies. Among others there was one named William MacAngus Gunn from Strathnaver, a fellow of a resolute spirit, and possessed of extraordinary muscular power and agility. Gunn was in many respects a most useful person to the Earl, but was in the habit of annexing from the neighbouring peasantry whatever properties he fancied. This habit he presently applied to property belonging to the Earl, and fearing detection, fled. The Earl discovering the situation sent a *posse* in pursuit, but the fugitive had too good a start to be overtaken. Some few weeks later he was apprehended for cattle-stealing in Ross-shire and imprisoned in the Castle of Foulis. Not relishing confinement in this fortress he jumped from the tower, but broke a leg in the fall and was again taken into custody. The Sheriff of Tain, Sir Wm. Sinclair of Mey, had him forthwith conveyed under guard to Caithness to be lodged in the Castle of Girnigo and dealt with according to the pleasure of the Earl. On reaching that stronghold he was duly secured and consigned to the prisoner's cell; but his limb having by this time become whole he managed to free himself from his fetters, leaped from the castle into the sea, swam ashore and fled into Strathnaver (1612). The Earl sent his son Wm, Lord Berridale, in pursuit. Missing the fugitive, Lord Berridale in revenge apprehended a retainer of Mackay's, called Angus Henriach, without any authority from His Majesty, and carried him to Castle Sinclair where he was put in fetters and closely imprisoned on the pretence of having assisted William MacAngus to escape. Mackay brought the matter before the Privy Council, and the Earl was required to appear with his prisoner at Edinburgh in June next (1612) which he accordingly did, and MacAngus being found innocent by the lords was delivered over to Sir Robert Gordon, who then acted for Mackay.

The Earl of Caithness at this time possessed an extensive and valuable landed property in the county, including nearly the whole of the parish of Wick. By his reckless and extravagant habits, however, he had become deeply involved in debt, and was obliged to mortgage several portions of his estate to satisfy his creditors. To recruit his exhausted finances he fell, it is alleged, on a desperate expedient, and employed an ingenious vagabond of the name of Arthur Smith to coin money for him. Smith was originally a blacksmith in Banff, but being detected counterfeiting the coin of the realm, he and an assistant fled into Sutherland where they were apprehended in 1599 by the

Countess of Sutherland and were forwarded to Edinburgh for trial They were duly tried and condemned Smith's assistant was executed, being guilty of crimes of a deeper dye, but he himself was reserved for further trial, during which period he devised a lock of rare and curious workmanship, which took the fancy of the king and resulted in his procuring a release He then went North and offered his services to the Earl of Caithness, who accommodated him with a workshop in a retired apartment of Castle Sinclair which the Earl had lately built close by the castle of Girnigo The workshop was under the rock of Castle Sinclair, in a quiet retired place called the "Gote," to which there was a secret passage from the Earl's bedchamber There Smith diligently plied his vocation for seven or eight years, at length removing to Thurso, where he ostensibly prosecuted his calling as a blacksmith. In the meantime Orkney, Caithness, Sutherland and Ross were inundated with counterfeit coin, which was first detected by Sir Robert Gordon in 1611, and he on returning to England made the King acquainted therewith. A commission was thereon granted to Sir Robert, John Gordon, younger of Embo, and Donald Mackay to arrest Smith—whom all suspected of the offence—and bring him once more to Edinburgh for trial Mackay and Gordon proceeded to Thurso where they secured Smith and found in his house a quantity of base money, with all the necessary coining apparatus The citizens, although satisfied of Smith's guilt, were yet, from recollections of the past, distrustful of the Sutherland authorities, and regarded the commission very much in the light of a hostile invasion So the alarm-bell was rung to assemble the inhabitants, who accordingly rushed to the street, and presently John Sinclair younger of Stirkoke, James Sinclair of Durran, James Sinclair, brother of Dun, and other relatives of Lord Caithness who happened to be in town on a visit to Lady Berridale, made their appearance. The commissioners produced the royal authority for the arrest, but Sinclair of Stirkoke transported with rage, swore he would not allow any man whatever his commission to carry away his uncle's servant in his uncle's absence Swords were drawn, but the Thursoese, who were not so well armed as their opponents, finally gave way and retreated to their houses. Sinclair of Stirkoke was slain, James Sinclair of Dunn severely wounded, and James Sinclair of Durran saved himself by flight. None of the men of Sutherland were killed, but many were badly wounded. Sir John Sinclair of Greenland, who then lived at Ormlie Castle, and Sinclair, Laird of Dunn arrived when the fray was ended Dunn proposed to renew the attack, but Sir John considering what had already happened, would not agree to any such hazardous attempt. The men of Strathnaver slew Smith to prevent his rescue, and they and their Sutherland friends returned home with their wounded

The Earl of Caithness, who was then at Edinburgh, upon being apprised of the occurrences at Thurso instituted a criminal prosecution against the Earl of Sutherland and the commissioners for the slaughter of his "nephew" Stirkoke, while they, on the other hand, raised a similar process against the Earl of Caithness, Lord Berridale, and their coadjutors, for various matters, and in particular for resisting the royal authority to arrest Smith and attaching Angus Henriach without a commission, which was declared treason by the laws. On the day appointed for their appearance at Edinburgh the parties, with the exception of the Earl of Sutherland, met, attended by their respective friends The Earl of Caithness and his son, Lord Berridale, were accompanied by the Lord Gray, the Laird of Roslin, the Laird of Cowdenknowes, a son of the sister of the Earl of Caithness, James Sinclair of Murkle, Sir John Sinclair of Greenland, his brothers, along with a large retinue of subordinate attendants Sir Robert Gordon was attended by the Earls of Winton, Eglinton and Linlithgow, Lords Elphinstone and Forbes, Munro of Foulis, and the Laird of Duffus. The absence of the Earl of Sutherland and Mackay mortified the Earl of Caithness, who could not conceal his displeasure at being so much overmatched in the respectability and number of attendants by seconds and children, as he was pleased to call his adversaries The Council spent three days in hearing parties and deliberating upon the matters before them, but, arriving at no decision, adjourned the proceedings until the King's pleasure should be known The King recommended arbitration, and the parties signed a submission to that effect Arbiters were therefore appointed, but as neither party would yield a single point, they declined to act further, and remitted the whole case back to the Privy Council The arbiters were all members of the Council, and very much occupied with affairs of state. Those nominated by the Earl of Caithness were the Archbishop of Glasgow, Sir John Preston, Lord President of the Council, Lord Blantyre, and Sir William Oliphant, Lord Advocate, while Sir Robert Gordon appointed the Earl of Kinghorn, the Master of Elphinston, the Earl of Haddington (afterwards Lord Privy Seal of Scotland), and Sir Alexander Drummond of Meidhop. The Earl of Dunfermline, Lord Chancellor, was chosen oversman and umpire by both parties. The arbiters, being very busy, induced both parties to sign a deed of submission giving authority to the Marquis of Huntly, the near relation of both, to settle their differences, but he, finding them both obstinate, remitted the whole affair back to the Council, and it appears to have been left unsettled One of the counter charges of the Earl of Caithness against Sir Robert was that he had procured the commission solely with the intention of ruining him and his house, and that, previous to the affair at Thurso, he had on one occasion lain in wait to kill him at the Little Ferry. Sir Robert, of course, indignantly repelled the charge There was undoubtedly little love lost between these two, and Sir Robert, in his history of Sutherland, has never missed an opportunity of attributing unworthy motives to the Earl, many of which are capable of being completely controverted At an early stage of these Edinburgh proceedings Lord Gordon, son of the Earl of Huntly, was due from London, and Sir Robert, being exceedingly anxious to prepossess him in favour of the Sutherland side of the story, before his relative the Earl of Caithness could have access to him, hastened to meet him at the Borders, and accomplished his purpose. The Earl was so offended at this that he declined to visit Lord Gordon after his arrival at Edinburgh

At this time the High Street of Edinburgh was the principal promenade of the Scottish aristocracy, and it was fashionable—if not absolutely necessary by the then lawless state of society—for gentlemen to wear defensive armour. An evening or two after Lord Gordon's return, he and the Earl of Caithness, each with a retinue of friends, chanced to meet between the Tron Church and the Cross, when they began rudely to jostle and push one another into the strand. High words arose, swords were drawn, and a general scuffle ensued In the meantime Sir Robert Gordon and Mackay, with their followers, arrived on the scene, and the Earl finding himself outnumbered retreated from the scene of combat to his residence in one of the adjoining closes Lord Gordon and his party followed them, and tried to provoke his uncle to sally out, but Earl George prudently remained inside. This mêlée created considerable stir in the city, and the next day the two lords were called before the Council and reconciled to each other

As the Privy Council showed no disposition to decide the questions at issue, the Earl of Caithness sent his brother, Sir John Sinclair of Greenland, to Edinburgh to complain of the delay and to intimate that if he did not obtain satisfaction from them he would take redress at his own hands. He hoped this threat might influence a favourable decision, and in October, 1613, made a demonstration against Sutherland and Strathnaver by massing forces at a certain point, and bringing thither some pieces of ordnance from Castle Sinclair. The Earl of Sutherland upon hearing this movement assembled his countrymen and took post near the height of Strathully, where they waited the approach of the Earl of Caithness; but that nobleman, by advice of his brother Sir John, returned home and disbanded his forces. To prevent further tampering of the Earl of Caithness with the Privy Council, Sir Robert Gordon obtained a remission from the King in December, 1613, for all concerned in the slaughter of Sinclair of Stirkoke. This pardon Sir Gideon Murray, Deputy Treasurer for Scotland, prevented from passing through the seals till the beginning of 1616.

Caithness, baffled in his designs against the Earl of Sutherland, now fell upon a device which promised to succeed. The laws of Scotland were then very severe against Catholics, and so he represented to the Archbishop of St. Andrew's and the Scottish clergy that the Earl of Sutherland was at heart a Catholic, and prevailed upon the bishops to acquaint the King thereof. His Majesty thereon issued a warrant for the arrest of Sutherland, who was imprisoned in St. Andrew's, the high commission of Scotland having refused his application for a month's delay till the 15th February, 1614. His brother Sir Alexander communicated with their brother Sir Robert, then in London, who obtained from His Majesty a warrant for his liberation till August following, on the expiration of which time he returned to St. Andrew's, from which he was removed on his own application to the abbey of Holyrood House, where he remained till March, 1615, having in some measure satisfied the church concerning his religion.

The Earl of Caithness, thus again defeated in his views, tried as a *dernier resort* to disjoin the families of Sutherland and Mackay. Sometimes he attempted to prevail upon the Marquis of Huntly to persuade the Earl of Sutherland and his brothers to come to an arrangement altogether independent of Mackay, and at other times he endeavoured to persuade Mackay, by holding out certain inducements to him, to compromise their differences without including the Earl of Sutherland in the arrangement; but he completely failed in these attempts.

Earl George was now offered an opportunity of military exercise outside his own county. Robert Stewart, natural son of Patrick, Earl of Orkney, then in confinement, had taken illegal possession of Birsa Palace, Kirkwall Castle, the Palace of the Yards, and other places of strength in the Islands, which he fortified as strongly as he could. This was in 1614. The Earl of Caithness, then in Edinburgh, offered to proceed to Orkney and vindicate the authority of the law, provided he were furnished with sufficient troops for the purpose. Government agreed to give him a requisite force, and in August he set sail from Leith with sixty soldiers and two pieces of cannon from Edinburgh Castle. On arriving on the Caithness Coast, the vessel brought up in Sinclair's Bay; and having procured some additional men from his own property, the Earl, accompanied by his natural brother Henry Sinclair, sailed directly for Orkney, and disembarked his troops in the neighbourhood of Kirkwall. He then opened the campaign in true military style. He besieged and took in succession the different posts occupied by the insurgents. The last was the Castle of Kirkwall, which Robert Stewart, with only sixteen men, bravely defended for the space of three weeks. The King's cannon made little impression on the iron walls of the citadel, and it was taken at last only through the treachery of Patrick Halcro, one of the besieged. The prisoners, with the exception of Halcro, were all brought South and executed; and very soon after Earl Patrick himself was beheaded for high treason at the Market Cross of Edinburgh. Before leaving Orkney the Earl of Caithness delivered up the Castle of Kirkwall to Sir James Stewart of Kilsyth, afterwards Lord Ochiltree, on whom in the capacity of farmer-general the King had conferred a new grant of the county; and a few months after the siege the government ordered the Castle of Kirkwall to be demolished.

Early in January, 1615, the Earl of Caithness went to London to receive some reward from the King for his services in Orkney. His faithful adversary, Sir Robert Gordon, hearing of his advent hastened to first obtain audience and prejudice the King against the Earl; but in spite of all that the malice of the baronet could urge, the King granted the Earl a full remission of all by-past offences, with an annuity for his services in Orkney, and also appointed him one of his Scottish Privy Council. But all these royal favours and honours were subsequently forfeited by his imprudent and violent conduct.

In November, 1615, Earl George seems to have participated in an act of incendiarism with the intention of making the Lord Forbes "weary of his lands in Caithness." The circumstances leading up to this act require illustration. The Earl had harassed Wm. Sinclair of Dunbeath in a variety of ways, till he at last retired into Moray, where he died in exile, being succeeded by his grandson George, who married a sister of Lord Forbes. George Sinclair of Dunbeath being without likelihood of issue, the Earl obtained a deed entailing his lands on him, and is then stated to have devised means to make away with Dunbeath's life, which coming to the knowledge of the latter he left Caithness and resided with Lord Forbes, who reprobated the conduct of his sister, she having been privy to the Earl's designs. Dunbeath now recalled the deed of entail in favour of the Earl, and executed a new one, by which he conveyed his whole estate to Lord Forbes, and dying soon after without issue his lands of Downreay and Dunbeath were taken possession of by that nobleman. Disappointed in his plans to acquire Dunbeath's property, the Earl, under cover of discharging his duty as sheriff, took frequent occasion to harass and annoy Forbes' servants, complaints of which were made from time to time to the Privy Council, thus affording partial redress; but the more effectually to protect his tenants, Lord Forbes took up a temporary residence in Caithness. The Earl being thus foiled in any direct attack, opened the subject of harassing him to John and Alex. Gunn, and their cousin-german Alexander, whose father he had hanged in 1586. John was chief of the clan Gunn. By invitation they repaired to Castle Sinclair, where the matter was discussed, and he suggested the burning of the corn of Wm. Innes of Sanset, a tenant of Lord Forbes'. Alex. Gunn, the cousin, while willing to assassinate Innes, declined to do anything so paltry or dishonourable as burn a quantity of corn. The Earl then approached the two brothers, who eventually yielded to his entreaties, and fired all the cornstacks of Innes, which were in consequence consumed. This was in November, 1615. Sir Robert Gordon took the matter in hand, resolved to probe it to the bottom. Alex. Gunn, the cousin, fled from Caithness, to the concern of the Earl, and revealed the nature of the Earl's proposals to Sir Robert. The Earl, anticipating such a state of affairs, circulated a report that Sir Robert and his friends had caused the fire so as to bring him under suspicion. Lord Forbes cited the three Gunns to appear before the Lords Justiciary at

Edinburgh on the 2nd April, 1616, to stand trial for the incendiarism, and the Earl of Caithness as sheriff of the county was also summoned to deliver them up. With things this way, the Earl wrote to the Marquis of Huntly for his support, but he responded by sending the account of the affair as supplied by Sir Robert. At trial the Earl of Caithness was absent, but his son, Lord Berridale, put in an appearance. The lords of the Council required Lord Berridale and his father to present the three culprits before the court on the 10th June next. Lord Berridale, whose character was the reverse of that of his father, now offered Lord Forbes satisfaction in his father's name if he would stop the prosecution; but Forbes would only do so on conditions which Lord Berridale considered too hard, and therefore rejected. The Gunns then confessed before the Lords of Council the part the Earl had taken in the crime, and as neither the Earl nor Lord Berridale had surrendered Alex. Gunn and his acomplices, they were both outlawed and declared rebels, and again summoned to appear at Edinburgh in July following. A final agreement was arrived at in July, 1616, when the Earl of Caithness accepted the terms imposed, which were gallingly stringent.

In the January of 1616 the Earl had induced William, son of Kenneth Buidhe, to banish himself into Strathnaver, and take the first favourable chance of injuring the Strathnaver people. So, on the first absence of Mackay in Sutherland, Wm. MacKenneth started operations, and was making his way to Caithness with a great booty, but being observed by the clan Gunn, a fight ensued, resulting in the recapture of the booty and the surrender of William and all his party, except Iain-Garbh-Mac-Chonald-Mac-Mhurchidh-Mhoir, who, being a very resolute man, refused to surrender, and was in consequence killed. In consequence of the settlement of July, 1616, William and John, the two sons of Kenneth Buy, were delivered to Lord Berridale, who gave security for their keeping the peace.

Matters being thus settled, Lord Berridale presented himself for trial at Edinburgh, but no one appearing against him the trial was postponed. The Earl failing to appear, the diet against him was continued till the 28th of August following. The King was well pleased to have peace restored in the North, but could not overlook such a flagrant act, and commanded the Privy Council to prosecute with due severity all who had been principals or accessories to the offence. Lord Berridale was thereupon arrested on suspicion and committed to Edinburgh Castle, while his father, again declining to appear, was again outlawed, and declared a rebel as the guilty author. In this extremity Lord Berridale had recourse to Sir Robert Gordon, entreating that as all controversies were now settled, he would, in place of an enemy, become a faithful friend, and reminding him how free he was of the present crime, and how little he had to do with the past dissensions. The King could not, without a verdict against Berridale, proceed against the family of Caithness by forfeiture, as his lordship had many years before been infeft in his father's estate, and knowing him to be innocent, could not expect such a verdict, so on the earnest entreaty of the then Bishop of Ross, Sir Robert Gordon, and Sir James Spence of Wormistoun, he was pleased to forgive and remit the crime on the following conditions :—1st. That the Earl and Lord Berridale should satisfy their numerous creditors. 2nd. That they should renounce the heritable sheriffship and justiciary of Caithness. 3rd. They should deliver the three criminals who burnt the corn. 4th. That the Earl, with consent of Lord Berridale, should give up and resign *in perpetuum* to the Bishop of Caithness, the House of Scrabster, with feu lands, of the annual value of 2,000 merks scots, etc., etc. Commissioners were sent from London to Caithness in October, 1616, to see these conditions complied with. The second and last were forthwith implemented, but on the release of Lord Berridale he was immediately rearrested at the instance of Sir James Home of Cowdenknowes, his cousin-german, who had become surety for him and his father to their creditors for large sums of money. The Earl narrowly escaped the fate of his son by retiring into Caithness, but his creditors had sufficient interest to prevent his remission from passing till they should be satisfied

Deperate as were the Earl's fortunes, he presently (1618) had overtures made for an alliance by Sir Donald Mackay, who had become dissatisfied with the Sutherlands. The Earl and Mackay met at Dunreay, in Reay, in Caithness, during night-time, attended by only three men each, and, continuing their conferences for several days, they finally arranged to destroy the clan Gunn, particularly John Gunn and his cousin Alexander, and that John Mackay, the only brother of Sir Donald, should marry the Earl's niece, a daughter of James Sinclair of Murkle, the mortal enemy of all the clan Gunn

Sir Donald proceeded to Edinburgh to get a commission against the Gunns, but was foiled by the opposition of Sir Robert Gordon, and returned home to Strathnaver disappointed. In April, 1618, he went to Braill, in Caithness, where he met the Earl, with whom he continued three nights. On this occasion they agreed to despatch Alexander Gunn, the burner of the corn, lest Lord Forbes should request his delivery. Before parting the Earl delivered to Mackay some old writs of certain lands in Strathnaver and other places within the diocese of Caithness, which belonged to Sir Donald's predecessors, expecting that Sir Donald would bring an action against the Earl of Sutherland for the warrandice of Strathnaver, and thus free himself from the superiority of that Earl. Sir Donald did not succeed in securing the Gunns; and although the Earl of Caithness, who sought every occasion to quarrel with the House of Sutherland, tried to pick a quarrel with Sir Alexander Gordon about some sheilings which he alleged the latter's servants had erected beyond the marches between Torrish in Strathully and the lands of Berridale, the dispute came to nothing. The Earl advised the Marquis of Huntly of Mackay's intention to disturb Sutherland, and Huntly informed Sir Robert Gordon, tutor to the young Earl of Sutherland, who had succeeded in 1615, when only six years of age. Mackay seeing how little reliance he could place in the Earl of Caithness, renewed his friendship with the Sutherlands.

The resignation of the feu-lands of the bishopric was an event which preyed on the Earl of Caithness' mind and made him vindictive towards the bishop's servants and tenants. More especially was his hatred directed against Robert Monroe of Aldie, Commissary of Caithness, who acted as chamberlain to the bishop, whom he took every opportunity to molest. One of the first steps taken by Monroe was to remove James Sinclair of Durran from the lands which he occupied, of which he granted a lease to his own brother-uterine, Thomas Lyndsay. Sinclair adopted the Irish method of revenge, and meeting with Lyndsay soon after in Thurso ran him through with the sword. It was generally believed that the Earl had instigated the crime. Durran then fled the country, first going to Edinburgh and thence to London where he hastened to meet his kinsman, Sir Andrew Sinclair, third son of Henry Lord Sinclair, envoy from the King of Denmark, who interceded with the King for a pardon for him, but being refused, Durran then fled to Denmark for better security. Monroe now raised a criminal suit against the Earl of Caithness and Durran for the murder of his brother, and they were summoned to attend the Court of Justiciary at Edinburgh ; but as neither appeared they were both outlawed and denounced rebels. Hearing Durran was in London, Monroe hastened thither and His Majesty wrote a letter dated at Windsor, 25th May, 1621, directing the Privy Council to commission Sir Robert Gordon to arrest the Earl, reduce his places of strength, and require the county gentlemen to give sureties for their keeping the peace in time to come. Sir Robert being undesirous of the office proposed to Lord Berridale that he should undertake it, but that unfortunate nobleman was unable to procure from his creditors a parole release. The Earl, hearing of the steps being taken against him, wrote to the Privy Council in assertion of his innocence of the slaughter of Lyndsay, and attributing his non-attendance at trial to the fear of being arrested at suit of his creditors, and promising if His Majesty would grant him a safe-conduct, to find security to abide trial. On receipt of this letter the Lords of Council granted him a protection, and in August his brothers James Sinclair of Murkle, and Sir John Sinclair of Greenland, became sureties for his appearing at Edinburgh at the time prescribed. The execution of the commission was thus delayed.

Lord Gordon in the meantime had obtained permission from Lord Berridale's creditors to consent to his liberation on his personal guarantee. Berridale returned to Caithness in 1621, after a confinement of five years, but was unable to apprehend his father or reduce the family estates into possession. Some of the Earl's creditors went North to see him in April, 1622, but only received fair promises. About this time a reconciliation took place between the Earl and Lord Berridale ; but it was only of short duration, and upon the occasion of the new disagreement he lost the favour and friendship not only of his brothers Murkle and Greenland, but also of his best friends in Caithness. Berridale retired from Caithness to reside with Lord Gordon, who wrote to his friends at Court for a new commission against the Earl. As the King was daily troubled with complaints from the Earl's creditors he readily consented, and in December, 1622, instructed the Scottish Privy Council to issue such a commission to Lord Gordon. Its execution was delayed, however, by Gordon being required to proceed to France on affairs of state in 1623, and on his departure the Earl applied for a new protection, promising to appear at Edinburgh on the 10th of August of this year and satisfy his creditors, but he again made default and was re-denounced and proclaimed rebel, while a new commission was granted to Sir Robert Gordon to proceed against him and his abettors with fire and sword. Proclamations were at the same time issued, interdicting all and sundry from having any communication with the Earl, and a ship-of-war was ordered to proceed to Sinclair's Bay to prevent his escape by sea, and to batter down his castles in case he should attempt to withstand a siege.

The Earl of Caithness, seeing now no longer any chance of evading the authority of the laws, prepared to face the rising storm by fortifying his castles and strongholds. Sir Robert Gordon arrived in Sutherland in August, 1623, and was immediately joined by Lord Berridale, who was sent to Caithness to ascertain the intentions of the Earl and the disposition of the Caithnessians before taking further concerted action. Berridale reported that his father had resolved to stand out to the last extremity, that he had fortified the strong castle of Ackergill, which he had supplied with men, ammunition, and provisions, and upon the holding out of which he placed his last and only hope.

Lord Berridale also reported that many of the inhabitants stood well affected to the Earl.* Becoming apprehensive of the consequences, the Earl despatched a messenger to Sir Robert, soliciting an amicable arrangement, but the latter was not prepared to parley further, and required an unconditional submission to the royal mercy. He followed up his request by assembling his troops, all picked men and well-armed, at Dunrobin, on the 3rd September, 1623, whence they marched to the appointed rendezvous, Killiernan in Strathully, and next morning crossed the Helmsdale and advanced to Berridale, where he was met by Lord Berridale and James Sinclair of Murkle, one of the commissioners. Encamping at Brea-Na-Henglish they were advised of the arrival of the war-ship in Scrabster Roads and that the Earl of Caithness had abandoned the country, sailing by night to the Orkneys with the intention of passing on to Norway or Denmark. At Latheron, Sinclair of Murkle, Sheriff of Caithness, Sir William Sinclair of Mey, Sinclair of Rattar and others tendered their submission and services, and the party was joined by about 300 Caithness men consisting of the Calders and others who had favoured Lord Berridale. They were commanded by James Sinclair, fiar of Murkle, and were always kept a mile or two in advance of the army till they reached Castle Sinclair, a very strong place and the chief residence of the Earl. The keys of this fortress were surrendered to Sir Robert who then proceeded to Ackergill Tower and the Castle of Keiss and took possession of them also without any resistance being offered. The Countess of Caithness, who was then in residence near Keiss, entreated Sir Robert—her cousin-german—to use his interest to get the Earl restored to royal favour, which he promised to do if the Earl would attend to his advice. From Keiss Sir Robert returned to Castle Sinclair where according to directions received from the Privy Council he delivered the keys of all these castles and forts to Lord Berridale, to be kept by him till the further pleasure of His Majesty should be known. The commissioners drew up a set of instructions at Wick, leaving Lord Berridale in charge, and an annuity was allowed to the Earl during good behaviour.*

The only incident of importance during Berridale's administration was a series of depredations by William MacIver, chieftain of the Siol-Mhic-Imheair in Caithness, whom the former had removed from the lands and possessions held by him in Caithness. MacIver thereon retired to Argyle assuming the name of Campbell, as being originally an Argyle man, and sought the favour and protection of Lord Lorn, who unsuccessfully endeavoured by writing to the Earl of Sutherland, Berridale and others to effect a reconciliation. Seeing no hope of an accommodation MacIver collected a party of rebels and outlaws to the number of about twenty, and for four or five years made frequent incursions in Caithness, to end which Berridale got him denounced rebel and at last was successful in apprehending MacIver and his son whom he hanged, and the race of the Siol-Mhic-Imheair was almost extinguished. This event occurred about the year 1633. MacIver's son-in-law Gillie-Calum-Mac-Shomhairle with some outlaws of the clan Mhic-Iain-Dhuinn, continued the predatory incursions into Caithness and they finally met the same fate at the hands of the Earl of Sutherland.†

George "the wicked" Earl of Caithness died in February, 1643, at the advanced age of 79. By his tyrannical conduct he procured himself many enemies, and probably his faults may have been thereby much exaggerated. Some of the crimes, at least, with which he was charged were never fully proved against him; and it is clear, from the

* Calder and Keltie.   † Keltie.

whole course of his history that he had a very bitter enemy in Sir Robert Gordon, almost the only authority for the events of that period. "The quietness and moderation," says Mackay, "with which he appears to have conducted himself during the last twenty years of his life plead strongly in his favour."*

He married Jean Gordon, daughter of George, fifth Earl of Huntly, by whom he had†
1. WILLIAM, LORD BERRIDALE, married Mary, daughter of Henry Lord Sinclair. He died *v.p.*, leaving a son
    JOHN, Master of Berridale.
2. FRANCIS, of Northfield, married Elizabeth, daughter of Lord Fraser and had—
    1. GEORGE SINCLAIR of Keiss who succeeded as 45th Earl.
    1. JEAN, LADY MEY, married Sir James Sinclair of Mey and died 1716; and a natural daughter
        MARGARET married in 1653 to John, son of Alex. Sutherland of Lybster.
1. ELIZABETH married George, Lord Lindsay, afterwards Earl of Crawford, and died *s.p.*

Earl George had also two natural sons—
1. FRANCIS, first of Stirkoke, who about 1621 fought a duel with his relative Sir William Sinclair of Mey.
2. JOHN, who attained the rank of Lieutenant-Colonel in the German Wars.

JOHN, MASTER OF BERRIDALE.

† 1639.

The Master filed complaint on 11th August, 1587, for attack by McKenzie of Gairloch and others on him and his servant James Paxtoun in March last while they were " in peaceable and quiet manner " in the Chanonry of Ross. McKenzie was denounced rebel. On the 16th September thereafter Colin McKenzie of Kintail was also denounced for non-appearance of Gairloch for whom he was responsible, and on 5th March, 1587-8, had to find caution in 500 merks, to produce if required such men as " asseigit " James, Master of Caithness.

The Master of Berridale was a strong opponent to the introduction of Episcopacy in Scotland, and after the meeting of the famous General Assembly at Glasgow in 1638, he took the National Covenant and persuaded many county friends to do the same. He was subsequently one of five commissioners appointed to get the bond subscribed throughout the entire kingdom,* and was present with the army of the Covenanters north the Spey under the banner of his father-in-law the Earl of Seaforth.‡ Attacked by fever in the autumn of 1639 he died at Holyrood House. His early death was very much regretted by all ranks in Caithness.*

He married Jean, daughter of the Earl of Seaforth, and died in 1639. He had three sons—
1. GEORGE, 44th Earl.   2. JOHN; and 3. WILLIAM, who died *vita patris*.†

His relict afterwards married Sir Alex. Sutherland of Duffus, created Lord Duffus in 1651.*

GEORGE IV., 44TH EARL.*

1643—1676.

This Earl occupied a much less important position than his predecessor. He married at Roseneath 22nd September, 1657, Mary, daughter of the Marquis of Argyle,

---
* Calder.   † Henderson.   ‡ Keltie.

and died at Thurso Castle in 1676 without issue. Having no male heir to succeed him, and being greatly embarrassed in circumstances—his debts were said to exceed a million merks—he sold his estates and title to his principal creditor John Campbell of Glenorchy. Writing at Thurso Castle, 25th August, 1661, he fully explains the effect of the civil wars on his mansions: "I can give account of £200,000 scots of loss I sustained by Generals Middleton and Morgan, besides the burning of my houses, which put me in such a condition that I had not a place to settle myself in till I laid out a thousand pounds to repair the house I live in."* There were two dispositions, as they are termed, in favour of Glenorchy, the first dated 10th June, 1661, and the second 8th October, 1672, conveying all and sundry, the lands, &c. The latter bears that in case of non-redemption, Glenorchy and his heirs shall be holden and obliged to assume, wear, and use the surname of Sinclair and arms of the House of Caithness. There can be no doubt that this clause was inserted at the desire of Glenorchy, to be used as a pretext for the assumption of the titles at a subsequent period. After this transaction the Earl's chief means of support were derived from an annuity of 2,000 merks, which Glenorchy had bound himself to pay him.

After the Stuart Restoration the Earl became a decided royalist, and manifested great zeal in suppressing conventicles, as appears from a minute in the Presbytery records of Caithness, dated Thurso, 4th November, 1674. He was a member of the Privy Council, and Lord Lieutenant of his county. At the time of his death he was an elder in the church of Thurso, which has the following minuted 3rd May, 1676:—"Mr. Andrew Munro, minister of Thurso, did represent that the Earl of Caithness, being visited with heavie sickness, did earnestlie desire that all the Brethren of the Presbie. should remember him in their publick and private prayers to God, which desire was cordially entertained."

The Countess of Caithness soon married her kinsman Glenorchy, who was created Earl of Caithness by patent, but his right to the title was challenged by George Sinclair of Keiss, of whom presently as 45th Earl.

This Earl was committed prisoner to Edinburgh Castle for the slaughter of a soldier sent to quarter for deficiency of cess and excise.

GEORGE V., 45TH EARL.†

1676—1698.

On the death of George IV., Glenorchy assumed the title, his deed of conveyance having been confirmed by Royal Charter under the Great Seal. In order to secure county support he appointed Sir John Sinclair of Murkle, Sheriff and Justiciary-Depute of Caithness, as well as bailie of all the baronies on the Caithness estate. In the meantime George Sinclair of Keiss, son of Francis Sinclair of Northfield, disputed Glenorchy's right to the title, and more especially to the lands of Northfield and Tister, which he inherited from his father. The claims of both were submitted to the four most eminent advocates of Scotland, namely, Sir George Mackenzie, Sir Robert Sinclair of Longformacus, Sir George Lockhart, and Sir John Cunningham. Their decision was favourable to Glenorchy, and the king thereupon wrote to the Privy Council instructing them to issue

---

Lauderdale MSS. Brit. Museum.   † Calder and Keltie.

a proclamation prohibiting Keiss from assuming the title of Earl, etc., etc. Keiss paid no attention to the interdict, and not only retained possession of the lands, which he claimed as his inheritance, but annoyed Glenorchy's chamberlains so much that they found it exceedingly difficult to collect his rents. The county gentry all espoused Keiss' cause, the warmest supporters being David Sinclair of Broynach and William Sinclair of Thura, who even went so far as to assist him to demolish the castle of Thurso East, of which his rival had taken possession. The common people also were everywhere friendly to Keiss, and Glenorchy was generally regarded as an usurper who had taken advantage of the necessities of the late Earl to trick him of his title and estates.

At length the Privy Council, on 11th November, 1679, passed an act charging the "haill kin, friends, and followers of John, Earl of Caithness, to concur and assist" in recovering the contested lands. To carry this into effect, in the summer of 1680 Glenorchy invaded Caithness with a large force of 700 or 1,100 men, including the followers of the immediate descendants of his family, namely, Glenlyon, Glenfalloch, Glendochart, and Achallader, as also those of his brother-in-law, the Laird of Macnab. He was also attended by a detachment of the King's troops under General Dalzell, and they all marched North from the Tay. Keiss resolved to give battle in open field, and hastily collected 800 or 1,500 followers, mostly destitute of military tactics, and his only officer of experience was Major Sinclair of Thura, who had served in the German wars. The hostile parties met near Stirkoke, but the day being far spent, and the Highlanders fatigued with a march of nearly 30 miles, Glenorchy declined battle, withdrawing to the hills of Yarrow. The place whence they retired was long known by the name of "Torran na Gael," or the Highlanders' Hill. The Sinclairs marched into Wick, and celebrated their supposed advantage in a deep carousal, being liberally supplied, it is said, with drink by a secret agent of the Campbells. Pennant says, "Glenorchy thought proper to add stratagem to force. He knew that in those days whisky was the nectar of Caithness, and in consequence ordered a ship laden with that precious liquor to pass round and wilfully strand itself on the shore. The Caithnessians made a prize of the vessel, and in indulging themselves too freely became an easy prey to the Earl." Glenorchy appointed a strict watch, and took every necessary precaution against a sudden surprisal. The men not on guard wrapped themselves in their plaids, and lay down to sleep on the bare heath.

About eight o'clock next morning (13th July) Glenorchy quitted his bivouac, and crossed the river of Wick below Sibster, nearly opposite Stirkoke Mains, which his men are stated to have leaped across. The news spreading to Wick excited much alarm. The Sinclairs, mustering hastily, hurried up the riverside to engage the enemy, and Glenorchy ranged 500 of his men on the haugh adjacent to the burn of Altimarlach. This water-course in summer is quite dry, and may then be described as a huge gully, with steep banks on each side. It lies about two miles to the west of Wick. Nothing could be better adapted for an ambuscade, of which Glenorchy with great tact availed himself. He accordingly ordered the remainder of his men to lie down and conceal themselves in this deep gorge, nor stir from the spot until their officers should give them the word to rise. As the Sinclairs advanced they made a detour to the right, at some little distance from the head of the ravine, and of course did not see the ambuscade prepared for them. Their object in this movement was to have the advantage of the higher ground, and thus to place the enemy between them and the river. In the meantime, Glenorchy encouraged his men with the following short address, originally delivered in Gaelic: "We are this day in an enemy's country. He that stands this day by me, I'll stand by him, my son by his son, and my grandson by his grandson; but if this day goes against us, he will be a lucky man that ever gets home, for long is the cry to Lochawe, and far is the help from Cruachan." When the two hostile bodies were within a few yards of each other Glenorchy gave the signal for attack, and the deadly strife commenced. The onset of the Campbells was so furious that the Sinclairs, unfitted by their carousal of the previous evening, instantly gave way and fled with precipitation in the direction of the burn of Altimarlach. At this moment the reserve corps of the Highlanders, starting up from their ambush with a savage shout, met the fugitives in the face, and being thus pressed in front and rear, and at the same time outflanked on the left, the Sinclairs in desperation made a rush for the river. The Campbells chased them into the water as they attempted to escape to the other side, and committed such dreadful havoc that it is said they passed dry-shod over the fallen dead. Not a few of the Sinclairs who endeavoured to save their lives by running for the open plain were hewed down by the murderous battle-axe and broadsword of the infuriated victors. Sinclair of Keiss himself, Sinclair of Thura, and the other leaders of his party, owed their safety to the fleetness of their chargers. The engagement lasted but a few minutes, and was as bloody as it was brief, no less than 200 of the Caithness men being reported to have fallen in action. Such was the issue of the famous battle of Altimarlach, so disastrous to the county, and so humiliating to the pride of the Sinclairs. Originating in a family quarrel, it has a special interest as being the last instance of private war being waged in Scotland.

Glenorchy quartered a part of his troops in Caithness for some time, levying rents and taxes as in a conquered country, and subjecting the people to the most grievous oppression. The remainder of his men he sent home in detached companies immediately after the battle.

Nothing daunted by the reverse at Altimarlach, George Sinclair of Keiss continued his opposition, and finally laid siege to Castle Sinclair, which he took after a feeble resistance of the garrison. The reduction was effected with the aid of firearms and or artillery. For this affair he and his three friends who assisted him, Sinclair of Broynach, Sinclair of Thura, and Mackay of Strathnaver, fell under the ban of Government, and were declared rebels. At length, through the influence of the Duke of York, afterwards James II., Keiss finally secured his claim to the title of Earl of Caithness, and also obtained full possession of his patrimonial property, while Glenorchy was compensated for his loss by being created Earl of Breadalbane and Baron of Wick (15th July, 1681). The men of Caithness, detesting him for his cruelties at Altimarlach, lost no chance of "making him weary of his lands in the county," the most of which he sold to the Ulbster family in 1719.

George Sinclair, 45th Earl of Caithness, died without issue at Keiss in 1698, and was succeeded in the Earldom by his second cousin, Sir John Sinclair of Murkle.

JOHN IV, 46TH EARL.*

1698—1705.

This Earl was the eldest son of Sir James Sinclair of Murkle, knight, by his second wife Jean, daughter of William Stewart of Burray, in the Earldom of Orkney. He married Jean Carmichael, stated to be of the Hyndford family, by whom he had—

    1 Alexander, his successor
    2 John, Lord Murkle, Senator of the College of Justice, married Jean, daughter of the 1st Earl of Cromarty, and died s p 1755
    3. Francis of Milton of Lieurary, married Janet Morrison, and died s p 1762
    4 Archibald, died s p
    1 Janet, married in 1714 David Sinclair of Southdun, and had issue

Dying in 1705, Earl John was succeeded by his eldest son

ALEXANDER II, 47TH EARL.*

1705—1765.

He was present at the last Scots Parliament in 1707, when the Treaty of Union was discussed, but declined voting.† His principal place of residence was Haimer Castle, a square tower or fortalice which, after his death, fell into disrepair, and now no vestige of it remains In 1719 the Earl sought to have the transactions between the 45th Earl and Breadalbane set aside on the ground of alleged imbecility, but without success. During the '45 rising he stood firmly by the Government.

In 1761 the Earl had executed an entail of his estate of Murkle and other lands, by which they passed on his decease to Sir John Sinclair of Stevenson, a descendant of the Sinclairs, Barons of Longformacus, cadets of Herdmanston He was succeeded in the title by William Sinclair of Rattar, to whom he thus alludes in a letter to George Sinclair, Lord Woodhall —"Rattar is next, though very remote. Though he lives within four miles of me he never comes to see me, from which it seems he is disobliged because I did not give him all I had, and depend for subsistence on his generosity He cannot be very wise, for he could not have taken a more effectual way to disappoint his expectations "

By his Countess Margaret Primrose, daughter of the Earl of Rosebery, he had one only daughter,

    DOROTHEA, who married James, Earl of Fife, and died s p 1819

He had also issue natural :

    GEORGE in Geise, died s p
    PETER, father of
        JAMES, died s p
        One daughter, died s p
        Six daughters, married, and had issue

            Henderson   † Calder.

WILLIAM III., 48TH EARL.
1765—1779.

On the death of Earl Alexander a contest arose as to the succession, the dignity being claimed by James Sinclair in Reiss and William Sinclair of Rattar. David Sinclair of Broynach, only brother of the 46th Earl, John IV., by a second marriage—which was afterwards pronounced irregular by the highest legal authorities in Scotland—had two sons, David and Donald. The latter had a son dead *ante* 1767, and the elder son David had two sons, James in Reiss (the claimant) and John, living in 1767. Rattar claimed as heir-male of Sir John Sinclair of Greenland and Rattar. In conjoined claims to be served heir before the Macers, after proof by both parties, the jury, on 28th November, 1768, pronounced a verdict by a majority in favour of Rattar, which, after various proceedings before the Court of Session, was confirmed. In 1772 the Committee of Privileges adjudged him the title. In 1786 James Sinclair threatened to renew the claim, but dying in 1788 the matter was apparently ended, as no male descendant of Broynach was known then to be alive.

William III. married Barbara, daughter of John Sinclair of Scotscalder, and died at Edinburgh 29th November, 1779. By her he had—

1. JOHN, 49th Earl.
2. WILLIAM, lieutenant in the American war; died *s.p.* at New York.
3. JAMES.   4. ALEXANDER.   5. DAVID.   These three died young unmarried.
1. ISABELLA, died unmarried.
2. JANET, married James Traill of Rattar, and dying in 1805 was buried in Roslin Chapel.

JOHN V., 49TH EARL.
1779—1789.

Entered the army as Ensign of the 17th Foot in 1772, and became Major in the 76th Foot in 1777. He served for some years in America, and was wounded at Charlestown while reconnoitering. In 1783 he became a Lieut.-Colonel, and died unmarried at London on the 8th April, 1789, at the early age of thirty-three. The succession then opened to the Sinclairs of Mey.

JAMES I., 50TH EARL.
1789—1823.

Sir James Sinclair, Baronet of Mey, was in May, 1790, served as nearest lawful heir-male of William Saint-Clair, second of his name, Earl of Caithness, and his claim to the peerage was sustained by the House of Lords. His lordship, who was Lord-Lieutenant of Caithness and Postmaster-General of Scotland in 1811, married 2nd January, 1784, Jane, second daughter of General Alex. Campbell of Barcaldine (by his wife Helen, daughter of George Sinclair of Ulbster), and by her (who d. 2nd April, 1853) had issue—

1. JOHN, Master of Caithness, Lord Berriedale, born 1780, died unmd. in 1802.
2. ALEXANDER, 51st Earl.
3. JAMES, Lieut.-Colonel in the army, born 24th October, 1797; married in 1819 Elizabeth, youngest daughter of George Tritton, and died *s.p.* 18th January, 1856.

4. PATRICK-CAMPBELL, born in 1800, married Isabella, daughter of Major-General McGregor; and died 13th March, 1834.
5. ERIC GEORGE, R.N., born 1801; died 26th September, 1829.
6. JOHN, an officer in the army; born 1808; married 22nd October, 1833, Maria Petronella, youngest daughter of John Church, and died 8th January, 1861.
1. JANET, married 1805, Jas. Buchanan of Craigend Castle.   2. HELEN, died unmarried.
3. CHARLOTTE ANN, married in 1810 Major-General Alex. Murray McGregor, and died 7th April, 1854.

Dying in 1823 his Lordship was succeeded by his eldest surviving son,

ALEXANDER III., 51ST EARL.
1823—1855.

This Earl was born on the 24th July, 1790; and married on the 22nd November, 1813, Frances Harriett, daughter and co-heir of the Very Rev. William Leigh, of Rushall Hall, county Stafford, dean of Hereford, and by her he had—

1. JAMES, his successor, born 16th December, 1821.
2. ALEX. ERIC GEORGE, of 91st Foot; born 20th May, 1827; died 21st August, 1857.

Earl Alexander died 24th December, 1855.

JAMES II., 52ND EARL.
1855—1881.

Was born in 1824, educated at the University of Edinburgh, and succeeded his father in the title and estates in 1855. He was soon afterwards appointed Lord-Lieutenant, Vice-Admiral, and High-Sheriff of Caithness. He was a Lord-in-waiting to Her Majesty under Lord Palmerston's Administration, 1856-58, and again in 1859. For several years he was Governor of the British Fishery Society.

His Lordship was elected one of the representative peers for Scotland in June, 1858, in room of the Earl of Morton, and again in 1865. On May 1st, 1866, on the recommendation of Earl Russell, he was created a Peer of the United Kingdom by the title of Baron of Barrogill Castle, in the county of Caithness, the patent being to himself and the heirs-male of his body lawfully begotten.

Lord Caithness was well known in scientific circles, and for many years was a Fellow of the Royal Society. In early life he developed a strong taste for mechanics and other scientific pursuits. So strongly was his mind bent on engineering that he wrought for nearly a year at works in Manchester in order to get a practical insight into the subject, walking to his work a mile and a half in order to begin at six o'clock, summer and winter.

He became the patentee of a great many useful and ingenious inventions. One of these was a tape-loom, which enabled a weaver to stop one of the shuttles without stopping the whole, as had to be done previously. For this invention he received £500, but always said had he been a business man he would have made a fortune by it, as it had been so universally adopted, and such an immense saving had been obtained by its use. Another of his inventions was the Caithness Gravitating Compass, which is one of the steadiest known to navigators, and is used by many of the largest shipping companies. He was very proud of this compass, and thought more of it than of all his other inventions combined. He also invented a road locomotive with carriage, in which he travelled from Inverness to Barrogill Castle, attaining a speed of sixteen miles an hour on level roads. As road locomotives were then quite new, his journey created no little sensation in that district. Another ingenious invention by his Lordship was a machine for washing railway carriages.

He was for several years a most active director of the London North Western Railway, and a member of the Committee on Rolling Stock—the only stock, he used to say, of which he had any knowledge. Amongst his own people and his tenantry he was especially popular, and he will long be remembered as the most genial and warm-hearted of those noblemen who have ruled at Barrogill. Considering the size of his estates, few if any of the proprietors did more for the improvement of their property than he. He was the first in the North of Scotland to use the steam plough. Although not a literary man, Lord Caithness was in frequent request as a lecturer on sanitary subjects, and in 1877 he published a series of five of these lectures.

He was married in 1847 to Louisa Georgina, youngest of the three daughters of Sir George Philips, Bart., of Weston House, Warwickshire, and formerly M.P. for Poole, by whom he had one daughter and one son—

LADY FANNY GEORGINA, born in 1854, died in 1883.
GEORGE PHILIPS ALEXANDER, Lord Berriedale, born 30th November, 1858.

Louisa, Countess of Caithness, died in 1870, and his lordship married secondly at Edinburgh on 6th March, 1872, Marie, only surviving daughter of the late Señor Don José de Mariategui, and widow of His Excellency Condé de Medina Pomar, by whom there was no issue.

Lord Caithness died at the Fifth Avenue Hotel, New York, on the 28th March, 1881. He was on the point of starting on an extended tour in America with his son and daughter when his death took place. His remains were embalmed, and sent back to Scotland for interment. He was buried on the 19th April, 1881, in the Chapel Royal, Holyrood, where are also interred the remains of his first Countess, and of his father, mother, and grandmother.

GEORGE VI., 53RD EARL.
1881—1889.

George Philips Alexander, Earl of Caithness, succeeded his father in 1881. In the same year he was appointed Lord-Lieutenant of Caithness.

His sister Lady Fanny died at Barrogill Castle after a very short illness on the 11th October, 1883, greatly lamented. She was interred in the churchyard of Canisbay on the 17th of the same month.

Lord Caithness died suddenly at the Palace Hotel, Edinburgh, on the 25th May, 1889. He was buried at Holyrood on the 29th of that month. He was the last male of the senior branch of the Sinclairs of Mey, whose representation now passed to James Augustus Sinclair, of the Durran branch. The Barony of Barrogill, in the peerage of the United Kingdom, became extinct. On his death Barrogill Castle and the estates of the Mey family became estranged from the dignity.

JAMES III., 54TH EARL.

1889—1891.

This peer, the eldest surviving son of Lieut.-Colonel John Sutherland Sinclair of the Royal Artillery, was born 31st May, 1827, at Naples; educated at the Edinburgh Academy and the Edinburgh University He practised for many years as a chartered accountant, and was agent at Aberdeen for the Bank of Scotland He was a clerk of and Justice of the Peace for Aberdeenshire, and was a Fellow of the Scottish Society of Antiquarians

On the death of George, Earl of Caithness, in May, 1889, Mr. Sinclair was adjudged to be heir-male to the said Earl.

He was married on 26th April, 1855, to Janet, only daughter of the late Roderick Macleod, M D., of London (son of Roderick Macleod, Principal of King's College, Old Aberdeen), and had issue—

1 JOHN SUTHERLAND, present Earl, born 17th September, 1857
2 NORMAN MACLEOD, The Hon, Master of Caithness, born 4th April, 1862, educated at Uppingham School, and at Trinity College, Cambridge (B A 1884); admitted solicitor 1887, married 1893, Lilian, daughter of Higford Higford of 23, Eaton Place, S W, and has issue—
   A daughter, born in 1894
   Residence —1 Brunswick Gardens, Kensington, W   *Chambers* —38, Bedford Row, W C, 19, Parliament Street, S W.
3 CHARLES AUGUSTUS, Rev The Hon, born 11th May, 1865; educated at Aberdeen University (M A 1885), and at Trinity College, Oxford (B A 1889, M A 1892), is curate of Hornsey North   *Residence* —4, Church Lane, Hornsey North
4 GEORGE ARTHUR, The Hon, born 28th April, 1874, educated at Trinity College, Glenalmond

1. LADY MARGARET HELEN.   2 LADY EUPHEMIA WILHELMINA
3 LADY MEREDITH ISABEL   4 JANET (dead)   5 LADY MARY JESSIE.

James Augustus, Earl of Caithness, died on the 21st January, 1891, in London, and was interred in the Saint Machar churchyard, Old Aberdeen Lord Caithness was a man of considerable antiquarian research, and was the author of unpublished MS. on Scottish family histories, dealing more particularly with the Orkney and Caithness families.

Lady Caithness resides at 152, Gloucester Terrace, Hyde Park, W.

JOHN VI., 55TH EARL.

1891

John Sutherland Sinclair, present Earl, is also a Baronet. He was educated at Loretto School, and at the University of Aberdeen He is domiciled in the United States of North America, where he is proprietor of the Berriedale Farm at Lakota, in North Dakota.

Residence in Britain —152, Gloucester Terrace, Hyde Park, London, W.

JOHN VI., 55TH EARL OF CAITHNESS.

JOHN SUTHERLAND SINCLAIR,
The Right Honourable the Earl of Caithness.

CHAPTER VI.

CAITHNESS CADETS.*

THE SINCLAIRS OF STEMSTER AND DUNBEATH.*

THE first of this family was ALEXANDER, second son of William II., 40th Earl of Caithness, by his wife Mary, daughter of Sir William Keith of Inverugie. In 1507 Alexander Sinclair obtained a Crown charter of Stemster. He married Elizabeth Innes, evidently from what follows, of the family of Innes of Innes, whose chief had possession of Dunbeath in 1507, but on the resignation of Alexander Innes in 1529 a Crown charter was granted in favour of Alexander Sinclair of Stemster erecting Dunbeath, Reay and Sandside into a barony. The charter contains the following clause of some antiquarian interest :—" *Cum mulierum merchetis cum furca, fossa, sok, sak, thole, thieme, infangtheif, outfangthief, pit, et gallous.*" The "*mercheta mulierum*" was *(semble)* the right of levying a fine from a serf, or villain, on the marriage of his daughter.

I. ALEXANDER SINCLAIR had two sons and a daughter—
  1. WILLIAM, his successor.
  2. OLIVER, frequently mentioned as brother-german to William Sinclair of Dunbeath. He was probably named after his grand-uncle, Sir Oliver of Roslyn, and in The Maister of Elphinstoun's letter† he occurs as Oliephare Syncklare, brother to William Syncklare of Dunbeytht.
  1. ISABEL, married Gilbert Gordon of Gartay, uncle to John, 5th Earl of Sutherland. In 1567 she poisoned the Earl and Countess of Sutherland for the purpose of opening the way for her own son's succession.

Alex. Sinclair, first of Dunbeath, died before 1541, and his widow Elizabeth Innes apparently before 1557, in which year her son William got a grant of the non-entry dues of Dunbeath and the barony, of which lands his father and mother had been joint fiars. This Dunbeath was a benefactor to Trinity Convent, Aberdeen.‡

II. WILLIAM SINCLAIR, SECOND OF DUNBEATH, was apparently a minor and unmarried when his father died, for, in 1541, Oliver Sinclair of Pitcarnie, styled also of Solway Moss, obtained a grant of his casualty of marriage, nor was he infeft as heir to his father till 1557. In 1547 Dunbeath obtained from William Gordon, Treasurer of Caithness, and Rector and Parson of St. Magnus' Hospital at Spittal, a charter of Mybster and Spittal, confirmed by Queen Mary in 1565. In 1562 and 1564 he got from Adam, Bishop of Orkney, charters of Downreay, Brubster, Thura, and other lands, for which a Crown charter of confirmation issued in 1557 (*sic*).

Dunbeath was twice married, first to Beatrix Gordon, daughter of either Alexander, Master of Sutherland, or his son, Earl John, and secondly to Margaret, sole heiress of Alex. Innes of Innes and his wife Elizabeth, daughter of John, Lord Forbes. By these marriages William Sinclair had five sons, William, Richard and George usually stated as of the first marriage with Lady Beatrix Gordon, and Henry and David by Margaret Innes. It is, however, certain that William was a son of the latter. In 1540 Margaret

---

* Henderson. † Forbes' "Family of Innes." ‡ "Caithness Events," p. 38.

Innes had got from her natural brother, James Innes of Elrick, the lands of Over and Nether Monbeens; and in 1575 a precept was granted by her and her husband for infefting therein "William Sinclair of Stemster." Forbes in noticing this precept mentions him as the eldest son and heir of Dunbeath and Margaret Innes. Whether any of the other sons were certainly of the first marriage is uncertain. William Sinclair of Dunbeath, who led a long and active life, was much harassed in his old age by his relation the Earl of Caithness. Among other acts of violence the Earl "wasted Dunbeath by fire and sword, and besieged him in his house at Downreay," until he at length retired to Morayshire, among his wife's friends, and there died in 1608. In the register of Confirmed Testaments, 1606–13, there is an entry of the "Testament Testamentar, latter will and legacie and inventar of ye gudes and gear of umqle. an honle. man, William Sinclair of Dunbeath." In the Register of the Privy Council there is a sederunt at Holyrood of date 27th May, 1574, dealing with the attempt of Beatrix Gordon to recover her estates as she repudiated her marriage with Dunbeath. She describes the possession for "seven years by-past" of all her property by William Sinclair, which has put her to "such utter wrack" that if she "were not supported she had been able to perish, being put to such miserable case." The rents of Fisherne were appointed to her by the Lords of Council till the marriage cause should be settled by the head Commissariet, that of Edinburgh. She had been previously married to Alex. Innes of Cromarty.* His sons were—

1. WILLIAM of Stemster, heir to Dunbeath.
2. HENRY of Brubster and Brims, who in 1586 received a Crown charter of Ormlie and died *s.p.* about 1610.
3. DAVID of Thura, died *s.p. ante* 1620.
4. RICHARD, designed of Brims, 1610, received from his father in 1589 a charter of Mybster, Acalipster, and a twopenny land of Spittal. In 1569 he appears as *son* of William in contradistinction to the sons of Margaret Innes, who were minors in 1588. He is styled *lawful son* and put after Henry and David in 1598 when he is designed of Mybster. In 1620 he was served heir to his brothers Henry and David, and is "of Brims." He seems not to have died before 1625. He had two sons and a daughter—
    1. ALEXANDER of Brims, married (1619) Anna, daughter of Hugh Mackay of Scourie and Farr by Lady Jane Sutherland, and, dying *vita patris*, had—
        1. JOHN, served heir in Brims to his father Alexander and grandfather Richard. He married Anna Mackay, and had a daughter Elizabeth, "Mistress of Strathy," who married her cousin John McKay, 2nd of Strathy. In 1647 John Sinclair and Hugh McKay of Dirlot and Strathy executed a mutual entail. They were cousins-german. To this deed one of the witnesses was "James Sinclair of Gallowhill, brother-in-law to Brims, and keeper of a copy." In 1660 John Sinclair sold Brims to John Sinclair of Tannach. St. Clair of Brims was with Montrose at the defeat near Tain in 1650, and has been wrongly accused of having betrayed that gallant nobleman, the real traitor being Macleod of Assynt. This Brims lived at Ribigil, in Sutherland, and was the last of the Dunbeath family who resided at Brims Castle. In the Inquistions-General a son John heirs his mother Christina Mein, spouse of John Sinclair of Ribigil, on 28th February, 1691, but this was in Strathnaver, under their relatives the Reays.†
        2. WILLIAM, of whom no particulars have been learned.
    2. OLIVER, who in 1630 received from his nephew John of Brims a life-rent tack of Spittal. In 1631 he granted a bond for 500 merks as part of his sister's tocher.

---
* Notes by T. Sinclair. † Thos. Sinclair's Notes to Calder.

CAITHNESS CADETS.

    1. A daughter, who married Alexander Bane of Clyth, son of Henry Bayne in Mybster, and a man of some mark in his time.

  5. GEORGE, in Downreay and Durran, who is not much noticed. In 1643 he renounced a bond over Brims in favour of his grandnephew John of Brims. He had issue—

    1. JOHN, perhaps hereafter of Brims and Ribigil.
    1. BARBARA, married in 1640 David Sinclair of Lybster, in Reay.

    It is conjectured that James Sinclair of Borlum and latterly of Toftkemp, who held Brubster and many of the Dunbeath family's lands, may possibly have been a son of this George Sinclair.

  III. WILLIAM SINCLAIR OF STEMSTER is supposed to have married the Lady Janet, eldest daughter of George II., 42nd Earl of Caithness, and dying *vita patris* was succeeded by his son

  IV. GEORGE SINCLAIR OF DUNBEATH, who married Margaret, daughter of John, 8th Lord Forbes, by whom he had an only child Margaret, who apparently predeceased him unmarried. On the resignation of his grandfather in 1590 George Sinclair had received the estates of the Dunbeath barony, and in May, 1591, obtained a Crown charter of confirmation. He was either facile or a spendthrift, for in 1602 he put himself under "Interdiction." In 1610 he resigned the barony in favour of his brother-in-law Arthur, Lord Forbes, in supersession of a deed by which he had entailed the estates on his kinsman the Earl of Caithness.* He then withdrew from Caithness owing to the harassing conduct of the Earl, who is even accused of having contemplated his death, and resided with Lord Forbes. Dying in 1624, Alexander, Master of Forbes, sold Dunbeath to John Sinclair of Geanies, son of George Sinclair of Mey. The remainder of the barony and the lands of Spittal and Mybster were acquired by Sir Donald Mackay, first Lord Reay, who, in 1624, was infeft on a charter by the Bishop of Orkney, in Thura, Borlum, Downreay, and Brubster; and about the same time Sandside was purchased from Lord Forbes by William Innes, ancestor of the family of Innes of Sandside.

THE SINCLAIRS OF MURKLE.†

  I. JAMES SINCLAIR, FIRST OF MURKLE, was the second son of John, Master of Caithness, and grandson of George II., 42nd Earl. He held in feu certain bishopric lands in Orkney, and is frequently enumerated as a Suitor of Court. He married Elizabeth Stuart, daughter of Robert, Earl of Strathearn and Orkney, a natural son of King James V., and had—

    1. SIR JAMES, his successor.
    2. FRANCIS, officer in the German wars; married 19th July, 1621, Janet, daughter of Alex. Sutherland of Forse, and had—
      JAMES, died *s.p.*
    1. AGNES, married John Mackay of Dirlot and Strathy.

Murkle had also a natural son—

    JOHN SINCLAIR, first of Assery, which see.

  II. SIR JAMES SINCLAIR, KNIGHT, SECOND OF MURKLE, appears to have been twice married. In Janurary, 1633, a disposition was granted by him, with consent of Dame Margaret Dundas, his spouse, of part of the lands of Ormlie; and in October, 1634, there is a contract of marriage between him and Jean, daughter of William Stewart of Burray, Orkney, who is therein designed of 'Manur.' By Jean Stewart he had two sons and five daughters—

---

* Keltie.   † Henderson.

1. JEAN, named as eldest in maternal disposition 18th May, 1692.
2. MARY, married, 1st, George Sinclair of Forss; 2nd, Wm. Sutherland of Geise.
3. ANNE, "Mistress of Stemster," married Alex. Sinclair of Stemster, son of Alex. Sinclair of Latheron.
4. BARBARA, "Mistress of Geise," married James Cunningham of Geise and Reaster.
5. KATHERINE, married Walter Innes of Skaill.
1. JOHN, successor to Murkle.
2. DAVID of Broynach, who died between 1713-1716. By his first marriage, with a daughter of Wm. Sinclair of Dun, he had—
   1. JAMES, died *s.p.*, about 1754.
      1. ELIZABETH, married James Whyte in Meikle Clyth, afterwards in Thurso, and had—
         1. HENRIETTA, m. Wm. Miller, and had a son James and a daughter Isabella.
         2. JEAN, married Donald Oagg, and had two sons, James and Donald, and two daughters, Janet and Anne.

         On the death of Dorothea, Lady Fife, heiress of Alexander II., 47th Earl of Caithness, Jas. and Isabella Miller, and Donald and Anne Oagg, claimed and obtained a share of her executry as great-grandchildren of Broynach, her granduncle.

By a second marriage (performed by an unauthorised person, and declared to be invalid), with one Janet Ewen, Broynach had—
   1. DAVID, married Margaret More or Mackay, by whom he had—
      1. JAMES in Reiss, Capt. H.E.I.C.S., Claimant of the Earldom of Caithness, died *s.p.* 1788.
      2. JOHN, living 1767; died before 1788.
   2. DONALD, married and had a son and five daughters, all dead in 1767 except—
      ANNE, married Alex. Millis, merchant in Banff.

III. JOHN SINCLAIR, THIRD OF MURKLE, succeeded to the Earldom of Caithness in 1698, which see for fuller account.

THE SARCLET SINCLAIRS.*

I. The account of this family begins with DAVID SINCLAIR OF BROYNACH, only brother of John Sinclair, first of the Murkle branch to become Earl of Caithness, and 46th in successional sequence. By his first marriage with a daughter of William Sinclair of Dun, Broynach had a son James who died *s.p. circiter* 1754, and a daughter Elizabeth whose grandchildren (*voce* article on Sinclairs of Murkle) on the death of Broynach's grandniece Dorothea, Lady Fife, claimed and obtained a share of her executry. Broynach's first wife died in 1697 when he secured the services as housekeeper of Janet, daughter of Donald Ewing, laird of Bernice, in Argyll, from whom the wealthy baronetical family of Ardencaple Castle derive their descent. An intimacy arose between Broynach and his housekeeper resulting in the birth of a son in 1699, and the kirk-session of Olrig at once engaged about the necessary discipline, which both Broynach and she refused to undergo. They were therefore summoned to appear before the presbytery at Thurso on the 11th November, 1699. For the next few years both were frequently cited by the ecclesiastics (in some of which citations she is styled "his wife") and Broynach found himself and his wife-elect in a most unenviable position. Sincerely attached to Miss Ewing and desirous of marrying her, he had to contend with a county conspiracy to frustrate him in attaining his object. One or two illustrations will suffice to show his love and determination to do her honour. Not being in wedlock at the time of their first-

* Caithness Events.

born, she was sentenced by so-called Christian ministers to be drummed through the streets of Thurso bearing a paper crown, inscribed with the assigned reason, and an official was appointed to finish her punishment by so many lashes on her uncovered shoulders. A mob led by two ministers began carrying out the sentence, but when the point was reached where the scourging had to take place, Broynach could no longer repress himself, and with primed pistol and drawn sword attacked the procession, the "men of God" being first to flee. Wrapping a plaid around her uncovered back he conveyed her to their home. He had previously "treated" the official, in the hope of her having only to undergo a nominal infliction of the lash. Entreating the Rev. William Innes of Thurso and others to marry them, but without success, this ill-plighted pair started for Orkney to try to get the ceremony performed there, but they had only arrived at Scarfskerry to cross the Petland Firth, when they were seized and brought back by a detachment Earl John had sent for that purpose. Eventually Broynach ran the *extreme* risk of getting married by an "outed" episcopal clergyman. The witnesses and married pair were liable to fine and imprisonment, while the disestablished performer subjected himself to banishment to the American plantations, and death if he returned. The marriage was performed by the Rev. Arthur Anderson, who had been episcopal minister at Kilmany, Fife, in Cairnsburn House, near Barrogill, early in June, 1700, as he humanely said "to put them out of the necessity of sinning." There are numerous references on record with regard to this event which involves the Caithness succession. The marriage does not appear to be in dispute but on account of being performed by an unauthorised person has been treated as invalid, an attitude which the present author* is unable to understand in the face of the Scottish law which recognises a public declaration on the part of the man to be sufficient, and surely apart from the many minor notices in support of the true relationship of Broynach and Miss Ewing, no clearer or more public declaration could be wanted than evidence of a marriage ceremony whether by an unauthorised celebrant or otherwise. John Sinclair, vith of Forss, was married in the April preceding by the same clergyman to Elizabeth (or Barbara) daughter of John Sinclair of Rattar, but without in any way affecting the succession of his son of that marriage, John, viiith of Forss. Broynach died in 1714, when his second wife and family were provided for, in a way, by her stepson James into his house, on a small freehold sowing not more than 2½ bolls, which had been given him by one of the Murkle earls. Mrs Janet Sinclair lived till between 1730 and 1738 and had burial under the seat of the Hon. Francis Sinclair in the aisle of James Sinclair of Durran. There was issue of this second marriage—

    1. A SON, born in 1699, died in infancy.
    2. DAVID, born in February, 1701, of whom hereafter.   3. DONALD.
    1. MARGARET, born about 1703.   2. JANET.

II. DAVID SINCLAIR, second son of Broynach by his second marriage, was baptised in Claredon Hall about 1705. Many incidents are preserved in connection with his life. The Rev. Wm. Innes, on application of the water when christening him, at the age of four, was met with the startling reproof, "May the devil take you for wetting me." In early life he went to sea, but soon returned to Murkle. He next took to kelp-burning in Strathnaver, where he met with serious illness, receiving monetary help from Mackay of Clashinach; afterwards he worked as a day labourer with Charles Oliphant, a servant of

---

* Author "St. Clairs of the Isles."

THE SARCLET SINCLAIRS.

Ulbster; and he was also man-servant to the Rev. James Gilchrist, who was minister of Thurso from 1738 to 1751. He enlisted with John Milne in Thurso "for behoof of a recruiting officer in the Dutch service." When he returned from the Netherlands, he and his wife and their eldest son James went to what was then called the Moray side, being the southern shore of the firth of that name. There they stayed for three years, returning to Thurso, he being in a very bad state of health. He married, contract dated 21st October, 1744, Margaret More, *i.e.*, Mackay, and died about 1760, his funeral expenses being paid by the Hon. Francis Sinclair of Westfield, who had from time to time assisted him, and by others of the Caithness House. His remains lie in Thurso churchyard.

David Sinclair, son of Broynach, had issue—
    1. JAMES in Reiss.   2. JOHN, living 1767, dead before 1788.

III. JAMES SINCLAIR IN REISS, son of the foregoing, married Catharine Rosie, contract at Reiss 17th December, 1763. She was born at Brims in 1747, and her father having found treasure in a field at Oust, backed the young pair in fighting their rights before the court of session and parliament.

At the meeting of the peers of Scotland at Holyrood House to elect a representative peer for the House of Lords, he answered to the title of Earl of Caithness on the calling of the roll, and claimed his place and vote at the election, but was objected to till he proved his right. At an election of two representative peers 1st October, 1767, Lord Borthwick produced his proxy signed "James, Earl of Caithness," but it was not permitted. At another election in Holyrood House on 21st December, 1768, he personally answered to the title, and on the Lord Clerk Register objecting officially, gave in a protest signed "Caithness." He attended courts, commissions for evidence, the court of session, and at last the House of Lords, till his defeat in 1772 by Wm. Sinclair of Ratter on the one and cardinal point of not being able to prove Broynach's marriage to Miss Ewing. He sailed for Calcutta on the "Anson" in February, 1772, a cadet of the East India Company; distinguished himself in affairs under Warren Hastings, and returned in June, 1786, with the title of Captain and a handsome fortune. He then discovered in Caithness the ecclesiastical proofs of his grandparents' marriage, and immediately entered upon a process of reduction against the second Rattar Earl. Capt. Sinclair's printed case is dated 25th July, 1787, and the reply of the Earl in possession 28th same. On the eve of winning the contest, which should never have been entered upon, he died on 11th January, 1788, in Whitcombe Street, Pall Mall, London, at the age of 41. His wills in Somerset House, dated 1785 and 1787, make reference to his maternal aunt Janet More, and the grandchildren of his paternal aunt Mrs Whyte.

IV. DONALD SINCLAIR, the third son of Janet Ewing and Broynach, is stated to be identical with Donald Sinclair, captain of a vessel trading from Sarclet near Wick to Avoch in the Black Isle, Ross-shire, on both sides of the Moray Firth, and with other places, Banff in particular. On 25th October, 1736, this Donald Sinclair contracted with Catherine, daughter of John Sinclair in Thrumster, the marriage taking place on the 30th November following. They had issue—

    1. CHRISTINA, born 27th March, 1737.   2. JANET.   3. CATHERINE.
    4. DANIEL ANNE (daughter), companion to Lady Dorothy Sinclair, Countess of Fife, and legatee of Earl Alexander and of Lord Murkle; married Alex. Millis, merchant in Banff.
    5. JAMES, bapt. 14th May, 1744.   6. FRANCIS.   7. JOHN.
    8. ROBERT, merchant in Wick.   9. HENRY.
    10. ELIZABETH, schoolmistress.   11. DONALD.

A Gaelic stanza having reference to him was composed by Wm. Bain Nimmo more than 75 years ago. It runs thus :—

"Seumas Sinclair am Mordun,
 Ogh coir Dho'ill a Mhairich,
 Is icrogh Fhir Bhroidhnich,
 Roimh so an Gall thaobh."

"James Sinclair in Moredun,
 The worthy grandson of Donald of the Sea,
 And the great grandson of the laird of Broynach,
 Who was before now in Caithness."

This has been contributed by his grandson, the Rev. John Sinclair of Kinloch-Rannoch Manse, Perth. His grandfather, James in Moredun Farm, was a farmer and distiller, and son of Wm. Sinclair in the neighbourhood of Avoch, apparently a son of Capt. Donald Sinclair, who died in Sarclet in 1768.

THOMAS SINCLAIR, M.A.,
Author of "The Sinclairs of England," "Caithness Events," &c., &c.

V. JAMES SINCLAIR, eldest son of the preceding, traded in salt, following similar routes to his father, and is identifiable with James Sinclair, chamberlain at Thrumster House. He contracted marriage on 27th April, 1764, with Anne Robertson, by whom he had—

1. ALEXANDER, baptized 17th January, 1768.   1. MARGARET.   2. CATHERINE.

His wife died in 1770, and he married secondly Elizabeth Sinclair in Clyth, on 9th February, 1771, by whom he had—

2. FRANCIS, born 1772, lieutenant in R.N., died *s.p.*
3. DAVID, born 1777, married Catherine Mackay, and died *s.p.*
4. JOHN, baptized 1780, died 1857, married 1806 Barbara Cormack. Issue thirteen sons and daughters, of whom—
    ALEXANDER, born 1810.

THE SARCLET SINCLAIRS.

  DAVID, born 1812; resident at Geelong, Victoria, 1891; married Catherine Sinclair of the Freswick family, and had with other issue—
    PETER SINCLAIR of Christchurch, N.Z. (1891), who has sons.
  GEORGE DUNBAR SINCLAIR of Reay, born 1814, died 1891; married 1840 Helen Swanson, and had with other issue—
    JOHN SINCLAIR.
    THOMAS SINCLAIR, M.A., Edin., born 1843; author of "The Sinclairs of England," "Caithness Events," etc. *Residence*, Belgrave Lodge, Torquay.
  JAMES, born 1815. Resident at Geelong, 1891.
 3. CHRISTINA.

 VI. ALEXANDER SINCLAIR, eldest son of the preceding, and his eldest son James, were farmers of Torranrevach in Clyth. By Latheron parish register he was married on 2nd January, 1789, to Elizabeth Sutherland. He had with other issue—

 VII. JAMES SINCLAIR, born in 1790, drowned at the shore of Clyth in August, 1845. He is registered as married on 7th December, 1832, to Catherine Sutherland. Their eldest son

 VIII. JAMES SUTHERLAND LAING SINCLAIR, was born 27th May, 1838; and died 3rd March, 1893. He married in 1863, Margaret Grant, a niece of Lieut. Hugh Grant, 79th regiment. His eldest son is

 IX. JAMES SINCLAIR, born 14th October, 1866.

THE SINCLAIRS OF ASSERY.*

 James Sinclair, first of Murkle, had a son named John, who in a charter granted by his father in 1615, to which he is an instrumentary witness, is designed "*filio naturali dicti Jacobi Sinclair de Murkel*," and who, in a bond dated 28th January, 1619, also by his father, and in which he was cautioner, is mentioned as "John Sinclair, son natural" of the granter.

 I. JOHN SINCLAIR obtained in 1628 from William Sinclair, Lord Berriedale, a charter of the lands of Assery, to himself in liferent, and to his eldest son James in fee. In 1631 he got a charter of Brawlbin; and in 1633 a wadset of Forsie; and from him are descended the Sinclairs of Assery, of Lybster, of Geise, and of Scotscalder. He was twice married, and had by his first wife—
  1. JAMES, his successor.
  2. LT.-COL. FRANCIS SINCLAIR married in 1659 Anna, daughter of Francis Sinclair of Stirkoke.
    MARGARET, their daughter married in 1680 David Henderson of Gersay.
By his second wife Margaret Davidson, Assery had—
  3. JOHN, first of Lybster.
  4. WILLIAM, who in 1670 held the wadset of Forsie and was afterwards in Ulgrimbeg and Ulgrimore. He married Jean, daughter of William Sinclair of Dun, and had—
    1. MARY, married 1705 to Donald Gunn in Achalibster. 2. ELIZABETH.
  5. GEORGE, mentioned in 1652 and 1660.
  1. GRIZZEL, married John Doull, wadsetter of Thurster, near Wick.
  2. ISABEL, married 1st, Arthur Forbes, merchant, Edinburgh; 2nd, William Sinclair of Dun.
 &emsse;3. JANET, married in 1616 George Munro, Sheriff-clerk of Caithness.

* Henderson.

II. JAMES SINCLAIR, SECOND OF ASSERY, married first, Elizabeth Balfour, and second, Margaret, daughter of David Munro, Commissary of Caithness. He had several sons and daughters—

    1 GEORGE, eldest son of his first marriage } Brothers german
    2. JOHN, in Ulgrimbeg married Bess Craigie
    3 JAMES, merchant in Thurso, died 1713, had several sons, of whom—
        DANIEL, grad M A , Edin , 1705, was minister in Longformacus , died 1734 , married Elizabeth, daughter of Robert Hamilton of Airdrie
        WILLIAM, merchant in Thurso, was father of
            ARTHUR ST CLAIR, American General
        ALEXANDER, notary-public in Thurso, married Jean, daughter of James Sinclair of Wester-Brims
    1 KATHARINE, eldest daughter, married Alex. Gibson, Dean of Bower from 1668-1662

III. GEORGE SINCLAIR, THIRD OF ASSERY, was twice married. His second wife was Isabel, daughter of Patrick Sinclair of Ulbster. He had issue—

    1 JAMES, apparent in 1700   2 JOHN, called eldest lawful son in 1691.   3 PATRICK
    4 GEORGE, eldest son of Isabel Sinclair   5 FRANCIS, also son of the second marriage
    1 ELIZABETH, the only daughter, married Richard Sinclair of Thura

The creditors of James, second of Assery, had led apprisings against the estates, which were acquired by Ulbster and Sir William Dunbar. In 1675 Ulbster assigned his rights to John Sinclair (iv), while in 1682 Sir William Dunbar conveyed his rights to George Sinclair (iii), then of Assery, and his sons John and Patrick

IV. JOHN SINCLAIR, FOURTH OF ASSERY, succeeded his father George He married first in 1698 Elizabeth Innes, relict of Laurence Calder of Lynegar, and had—

    1 JOHN, his successor

He married secondly Barbara, daughter of Patrick Murray of Pennyland, by whom he had an only child

    ISABELLA, who married John Sinclair of Scotscalder

V. JOHN SINCLAIR, FIFTH OF ASSERY, was in 1728 served heir-in-general to his father, and in 1765 was infeft as eldest lawful son. He married Katharine, eldest daughter of Robert Sinclair of Geise, and had—

    1 ROBERT, his successor.   2 JOHN   3 CHARLES   4 JAMES
    1 ISABELLA married Robert Manson Sinclair of Brigend   2 KATHARINE
    3 JEAN, married Sir Benjamin Sinclair of Stemster

VI. CAPTAIN ROBERT SINCLAIR, SIXTH OF ASSERY, was served heir to his father *cum beneficio inventarii*, in 1772 He married Katharine Sinclair and had no issue.

The estate was brought to judicial sale by the creditors, and Captain Sinclair having died during the proceedings, they were continued against his brother John ; and in 1784 Assery and Brawlbin were purchased by Ulbster.

THE SINCLAIRS OF LYBSTER.*

I. JOHN SINCLAIR, FIRST OF LYBSTER, was eldest son of John Sinclair, first of Assery, and his second wife, Margaret Davidson In 1647 he was appointed "Baillie of Latheron" by the Earl of Caithness, who in 1655 gave him Lybster in wadset. He married Beatrix Sinclair, supposed to have been of the Thura family, and had—

    1. JAMES, his successor
    2. GEORGE, whose only daughter Beatrix married Alexander Sinclair of Sixpennyland.
    1. ELIZABETH married Alexander Boynd in Thurso

* Henderson

THE SINCLAIRS OF LYBSTER.

II. JAMES SINCLAIR, SECOND OF LYBSTER In 1692 he obtained the right of reversion to the wadset. He married Katharine, daughter of Patrick Sinclair of Ulbster, and had five sons and two daughters.

1. JOHN, third of Lybster.
2. PATRICK, in Northfield in 1702, who had issue—
    1. ALEXANDER, afterwards fourth of Lybster
3. WILLIAM of Hoy and Scotscalder
4. ROBERT of Geise, Advocate   5 GEORGE (1731)
1. BEATRIX, married in 1707 James Sutherland in Ausdale
2. ELIZABETH, married John Mackay in Kirtomy, third son of John of Strathy and Dirlot

III. JOHN SINCLAIR, THIRD OF LYBSTER, styled "Fiar" in 1694, and "of Lybster" in 1709 succeeded to the estate, and died *sans issue*.

IV ALEXANDER SINCLAIR, FOURTH OF LYBSTER, was the son of Patrick in Northfield. In 1710 he was served heir to his uncle, and to his grandfather James He married Æmilia, daughter of Alexander Sinclair of Sixpenny, and had—

1. PATRICK, his successor
1. KATHARINE, third wife of James Sinclair of Harpsdale
2. MARGARET, died unmarried   3 ÆMILIA, died unmarried

V LIEUT.-GENERAL PATRICK SINCLAIR, FIFTH OF LYBSTER, married Catharine Stewart, and had—

1. TEMPLE FREDERICK, successor to Lybster
2. JEFFREY, Surgeon-General in the Bombay Army, who left two daughters
3. THOMAS AUBREY, Stipendiary Magistrate at Granada, died unmarried
4. PATRICK, died unmarried
1. SUSAN, married David Laing, Surgeon in Thurso, and died in 1865.

VI. TEMPLE FREDERICK SINCLAIR, SIXTH AND LAST OF LYBSTER, was a captain in the Army, and died unmarried. In 1868 the estate was sold by his trustees to the Duke of Portland for £24,000

THE SINCLAIRS OF SCOTSCALDER.[1]

I. WILLIAM SINCLAIR, third son of James Sinclair of Lybster, had the lands of Hoy and Geise, which he exchanged in 1729 with James Murray, son of Patrick of Pennyland, for the estate of Scotscalder In 1713 William Sinclair adjudged Ulgrimbeg and Ulgrimore from the Sinclairs of Assery He had issue—

1. ALEXANDER, thought to be Alex Sinclair of Sixpenny   2 JOHN, second of Scotscalder.
3. ROBERT, referred to by his brother John in a letter of 1734
1. JANET, m John Mackay, 3rd of Strathy, and had a tocher of 6,000 merks   2. BARBARA.

II JOHN SINCLAIR, SECOND OF SCOTSCALDER, married in 1731 Isabella, only daughter of John Sinclair, fourth of Assery On his marriage his father conveyed to him, with consent of his eldest son Alexander, the lands of Scotscalder, Ulgrimbeg and Ulgrimore He had issue—

1. WILLIAM   2 ROBERT, who succeeded
1. ISABELLA, second wife of Captain Thos Dunbar of Westfield She died in 1829
2. BARBARA, married Wm Sinclair of Rattar, 48th Earl of Caithness   3 MARGARET, and
4. KATHARINE, one of whom was second wife of James Sinclair of Holbornhead

III ROBERT SINCLAIR, THIRD AND LAST OF SCOTSCALDER, had issue—
1 LIEUT COLONEL JAMES SINCLAIR of the Royal Artillery
1 A daughter, married Mr Aitken.   2 A daughter, married Mr Steel, officer of Excise

About 1812 Robert Sinclair sold the estate. He died on the 15th May, 1815.

SINCLAIR OF GEISE *

ROBERT SINCLAIR OF GEISE, Advocate 1711, was fourth son of James Sinclair of Lybster, and brother of Wm Sinclair of Hoy and Scotscalder. He married Katharine Ross, daughter of Wm Ross of Kindeace, and had a son† and four daughters—

1 KATHARINE, married John Sinclair of Assery
2 JEAN, married James Sinclair of Holbornhead and Forss
3 BARBARA, married Dr Wm Sinclair, physician in Thurso.
4. MARY, married Patrick Doull of Oldfield, merchant in Thurso

Robert Sinclair died in 1742, and his wife about 1757, She had been previously married to George Mackay of Bighouse, and retained the name of "Lady Bighouse" till her death, which occurred at Tiantlemore, Sutherland, where she latterly resided

THE SINCLAIRS OF GREENLAND AND RATTAR. *

I. SIR JOHN SINCLAIR, Knight, the first of this family, was third son of John, Master of Caithness, and was styled of Greenland, but his descendants have been designed of Rattar. From his brother George, 43rd Earl of Caithness, he obtained in 1609 the feu farm of the lands of Rattar, &c , by charter, to himself in liferent, and to his son William in fee ; and in 1613 he got a disposition from the Earl, of the lands of Rattar, Corsbach, Lieurary, Reaster, Murrsay, and Hailand, pertinents of the Barony of Achergill In 1612 he occupied the castle of Ormlie, near Thurso He married Janet Sutherland, and, dying in 1622, left five sons and a daughter—

1 WILLIAM, died *vita patris* before 1618
2 ALEXANDER, who in 1618 obtained from his uncle, Earl George, a precept of *clare* as heir to William. Of him Sir Robert Gordon writes :—"This year of God, 1620, the eldest son of Sir John Sinclair of Greenland perished in the water of Risgill, as he was riding that river in a great speat and storm of weather He was a young man of good expectation " He died without issue
3 JOHN, who had in 1623 precept of *clare* to Alexander, and died *s p*
4 JAMES of Reaster, who obtained a precept on 15th December, 1634, and was afterwards of Rattar
5 FRANCIS, died *s p*   6 THOMAS, living, 1630
1 ELISABETH, married John Cunningham of Geise and Brownhill.

Sir John had also a natural son—

GEORGE, mentioned in a sasine of 1619

II JAMES SINCLAIR, of Reastar and Rattar, married Janet, daughter of William Bruce of Stanstill, and had two sons and three daughters—

1. WILLIAM, his successor   2 JOHN, who died without issue
1 JANET, married Walter Bruce of Ham
2 MARGARET, married in 1655 John, son of William Smith, minister of Dunnett
3. ELSIBETH, married about 1652 William Bruce of Stanstill

* Henderson   † Henderson does not give name of son

THE SINCLAIRS OF GREENLAND AND RATTAR.

III. WILLIAM SINCLAIR, THIRD OF RATTAR, married, first, in 1642, when in apparency only, Elizabeth, daughter of John Sinclair, first of Ulbster, by whom he had—
  1. JOHN, his successor in Rattar

In 1661 Rattar acquired from Mowat of Balquhollie the lands of Freswick. He married, secondly, in 1647, Jean, daughter of John Cunningham of Geise and Brownhill, long locally remembered as "Jeanag of Rattar" By her he had three sons and two daughters—
  1. JAMES, 2 ROBERT, and 3 DAVID, successively of Freswick, *quod vide*.
  1 JANET, married John Sinclair of Ulbster
  2 ANNE, married first Robert Sinclair of Durran, secondly John Campbell of Castlehill, Commissary and Sheriff-clerk of Caithness

IV JOHN SINCLAIR, FOURTH OF RATTAR, married Elizabeth, daughter of Sir William Sinclair of Mey, and had—
  1 JOHN, his successor   2 WILLIAM, who in 1712 succeeded to Freswick
  1 BARBARA, married John Sinclair of Forss
  2 FRANCES, married James Sinclair of Latheron
  3 MARGARET, married (1) Alexander Sinclair of Brabster, (2) Alexander Gibson, Minister of Canisbay
  4 KATHARINE, married George Manson of Brigend

V. JOHN SINCLAIR, FIFTH OF RATTAR, married Janet, daughter of Patrick Sinclair of Southdun, and died in 1733. He had two sons—
  1 JOHN, died unmarried in minority   2 WILLIAM, who succeeded

VI WILLIAM SINCLAIR, SIXTH OF RATTAR, was a minor at his father's death, and the estate was taken charge of by his uncle, William of Freswick. His mother also claimed the management, and, pending the dispute, "lodged in the garrett, while Freswick occupied the other parts of the house of Rattar" In 1772 his claim to the dignity of Earl of Caithness was sustained by the Committee of Privileges, but the preceding Earl, Alexander II, had devised all his estates to the Sinclairs of Stevenson, one of his objections to Rattar being that the latter had not received the education of a gentleman   Further particulars *re* Rattar appear in the articles on the Earls of Caithness.

THE SINCLAIRS OF FRESWICK *

I WILLIAM SINCLAIR, third of Rattar, grandson of Sir John of Greenland, was the first Sinclair of Freswick   He acquired Freswick in 1661 from the Mowats of Balquholly   By his second marriage with Jean Cunningham he had three sons, successively of Freswick—James, Robert, and David.

II. JAMES SINCLAIR, SECOND OF FRESWICK, got a Crown charter on 30th April, 1672, in favour of his mother in liferent, and himself and his brothers in succession in fee. He is said to have died in France, having been taken prisoner when on his way to Edinburgh to be married, but in "Chamber's Domestic Annals" it is stated that having made his case known to the Scottish Privy Council, he was released in exchange for Mr. David Fairfoul, a priest detained in prison at Inverness   His arms are recorded in the Lyon Register   He died issueless before 1696.

III. ROBERT SINCLAIR succeeded his brother James, and dying unmarried was in turn succeeded by his brother—

IV. DAVID SINCLAIR OF FRESWICK, who was twice married — 1st, to Barbara, daughter of Sir Wm. Sinclair of Mey, 9th April, 1695 , 2nd, to Sophia, daughter of Sir Wm. Stewart of Burray, Orkney, 25th June, 1702 He had no issue by either marriage, and in April, 1712, executed an entail in favour of William, second son of his half-brother, John Sinclair of Rattar, who thus acquired Freswick to the exclusion of David's sisters Janet and Anne

V. WILLIAM SINCLAIR OF FRESWICK, second son of John of Rattar, added largely to the family estate In 1751 he purchased Dunbeath. He it was who built the House of Freswick. He was very influential in the county, and of a dignified and imposing appearance. He married Katharine, daughter of Geo Sutherland of Forse, and died in 1769. His had issue—

1 JOHN, his successor
1 ELIZABETH, married George Beau, a Writer in Inverness
2 JEAN, married Alex Sinclair of Barrock, grandfather of the late Sir John

VI JOHN SINCLAIR OF FRESWICK, Advocate 1749, Sheriff of Caithness, married, 1st, Margaret, daughter of Sir John Dalrymple of Cousland, a lady to whom he was greatly attached, but his father for some unknown reason opposed the marriage. By her he had a son and a daughter—

1 WILLIAM, in 1778, Lieutenant in the 78th Regiment. He predeceased his father without issue
1 KITTY, died *vita patris* in her fifteenth year

By his second wife, Margaret, daughter of James Moray of Abercairney, who survived him, Freswick had no issue He died 26th June, 1784, and was buried at Bath Referring in 1782 to the settlement of the Freswick estates, he wrote to his second cousin, Dr. Wm Sinclair of Lochend, afterwards of Freswick " I look on my grandfather (John Sinclair of Rattar) as the head of my family , from his descendants I never will give away what my father left me, but of these I will choose him I think most worthy. A cousin or a nephew are equal with me in the scale. Whoever merits most will be preferable." Accordingly, on 30th May, 1775, he executed a strict entail of the estates, by which they passed to the descendants of his paternal grand-aunt, Barbara of Rattar, who married John Sinclair of Forss.

VII. ROBERT SINCLAIR OF FRESWICK, eldest son of James Sinclair of Holburnhead, and afterwards of Forss, succeeded in 1784, and died at Dunbeath Castle without issue in November, 1794 He married Esther Bland, reputed an actress, and sister or near relative of the celebrated Mrs Jordan.

VIII WILLIAM SINCLAIR OF LOCHEND, which estate he acquired by purchase in 1778, was grandson of John Sinclair of Forss, and succeeded his cousin-german, Robert Sinclair of Freswick, in 1794. He was an M D., and before succeeding to the estates practised many years in Thurso and the county. He purchased Thura in 1801 He was twice married, and died on the 15th March, 1838, aged 90 By his first wife, Isabella, daughter of Alex. Calder, last of Lynegar, he had—

1 JOHN, died unmarried in 1832, aged 21
1 BARBARA MADELINA GORDON, twin-sister of John
2 ISABELLA, married Thomas Cochrane Hume of Halifax, North America

In 1816 Wm. Sinclair married, 2nd, his cousin Jean, daughter of John Sinclair of Barrock, and had—

1. WILLIAM JAMES JOHN ALEXANDER, who succeeded.
1. WILLIAMINA, died young.
2. JANET SINCLAIR TRAILL, died at Torquay, unmarried, in June, 1870.
3. JANE, married Major-General Augustus Halifax Ferryman, and died in 1851.

IX. WILLIAM JAMES JOHN ALEXANDER SINCLAIR succeeded his father in 1838, while yet in minority. He served a short time in the army, and died unmarried on the 20th February, 1855, aged 31, and was succeeded by his half-sister—

X. BARBARA M. G. SINCLAIR, who married William Thomson, Deputy Commissary-General of the Forces.

THE SINCLAIRS OF MEY.*

I. WILLIAM SINCLAIR, second son of George II., 42nd Earl of Caithness, obtained from his father in March, 1572, a charter of the lands of Mey, and was thus the first laird thereof. He died unmarried.

II. GEORGE SINCLAIR, SECOND OF MEY, succeeded his brother William, and in 1573 got a precept of *clare constat* from Robert, Bishop of Caithness. In 1585 and 1592 he obtained Crown charters. In 1572 the Bishop appointed him Chancellor of the Diocese of Caithness. He was a man of ability, who lost no opportunity of promoting his family interests, and considerable additions to the family estates were made by him. Before 1583 he married Margaret, daughter of William, seventh Lord Forbes, and died in 1616, having had issue—

1. SIR WILLIAM, his heir.
2. SIR JOHN of Geanies and Dunbeath.
3. JAMES, who died young.
4. ALEXANDER of Latheron, ancestor of the Barrock family.
1. JANET, married Walter Innes of Inverbrakie.
2. MARGARET, married in 1608 Alexander Sinclair of Forss.
3. BARBARA, married in 1610 Alexander Keith of Pittendrum.
4. ELIZABETH, married William Dunbar, first of Hempriggs in Morayshire, and grandfather of Sir William Dunbar of Hempriggs, &c., in Caithness.
5. ANNE.

III. SIR WILLIAM SINCLAIR, KNIGHT OF MEY, was usually styled Sir William of Cadboll. In 1595 a mutiny broke out among the scholars and gentlemen's sons attending the High School of Edinburgh, arising from a dispute with the magistrates as to their vacation. They laid in provisions in the schoolroom, manned the same, and took in arms with powder and bullets, and refused all entrance to masters or magistrates until their claims were conceded. After a day passed in this manner, the Council resolved on strong measures, and a posse of officers, headed by Bailie John Macmoran, proceeded to the school, and failing to persuade the scholars to surrender, attempted to prize open the doors. The scholars finding no attention paid to their threats, to "put a pair of bullets through the best of their cheeks," unless they desisted, "one Sinclair, the Chancellor of Caithness' son, presented a gun from a window, direct opposite the bailies' faces, boasting them and calling them *buttery carles*. Off goeth the charged gun, pierced John Macmoran through his head, and presently killed him, so that he fell backward straight to the ground without speech at all." The culprit was William, afterwards Sir Sir William Sinclair of Mey ; but in the end he and seven other youths implicated got

* Henderson.

clear off. Mey was visited in 1628 by William Lithgow, the celebrated Scottish traveller, and he took advantage of the occasion to compose some verses giving honourable mention to "fruitful Mey," which he dedicated to Earl George of Caithness, with his honourable cousin and first accadent of his house, the right worshipful Sir William Sinclair of Catboll, Knight, Laird of Maji. The lines appear further on in this work. Sir William married in 1600 Katharine, second daughter of George Ross of Balnagown, by whom he had—

 1. SIR JAMES SINCLAIR of Canisbay, baronet. See Baronetical Branches, Chapter vii.

THE SINCLAIRS OF DURRAN.

A James Sinclair of Durran appears in the conflict at Thurso in 1612. In 1621, being ejected by the Bishop's Chamberlain from lands which he occupied as tenant under the Earl of Caithness, he killed the Chamberlain's brother-uterine, one Thomas Lyndsay, to whom the lands had been given. He then fled to his "kinsman" in London, Sir Andrew Sinclair (third son of Henry, Lord Sinclair, and whose sister Mary was married to William Sinclair, Lord Berriedale), envoy for the King of Denmark, whose intervention he sought to obtain the royal pardon, but in this was unsuccessful and fled to Denmark. It is not known of what family he was.

I. ROBERT SINCLAIR, FIRST of DURRAN, was third son of Sir James Sinclair of Canisbay, Baronet of Mey. The Durran estate was held in wadset from the Earl of Caithness. Robert Sinclair married in 1678 Anne, youngest daughter of William Sinclair of Rattar, afterwards styled "Lady Harland," and had—

 1. JOHN, his successor.
  1. ANNE, married first as third wife James Sutherland of Langwell, and secondly John Sinclair of Barrock.
  2. JANET.

II. JOHN SINCLAIR OF DURRAN married Elizabeth, daughter of George Sinclair of Barrock. In 1717 Lord Glenorchy granted him a disposition of Durran, &c. He died in 1728, having had issue—

 1. ROBERT, died 1725.   2. JOHN, died 1727.   3. JAMES, afterwards of Durran.
 4. GEORGE, Major in the 65th Regiment, who died without issue.
  1. JEAN, married her cousin-german James Sutherland of Swinzie.

III. JAMES SINCLAIR OF DURRAN married twice. By his first marriage with Elizabeth, daughter of Sir Patrick Dunbar of Northfield. He had—

 1. PATRICK, his successor.
 2. GEORGE, Writer to the Signet, married 19th September, 1775, Elizabeth, daughter of John Sutherland of Forse, and, dying 6th December, 1779, had—
  1. JOHN SUTHERLAND, Lieut.-Colonel in the Royal Artillery, who died in 1841. By his first marriage to Marianne Gamble, Colonel Sinclair had—
   1. GEORGE, (W. Signet), died 16th January, 1834; 2. JOHN, Lieut. R.A., died 1828; 3. FRANCIS; and (4.) a daughter ELIZABETH; all of whom died unmarried.
  By his second marriage to Frances Ramsay he had (5-7) three daughters, and by his third marriage to Euphemia, daughter of Thomas Buchan of Auchmacoy, he had several children, of whom—
   8. JAMES AUGUSTUS, 54TH EARL OF CAITHNESS, died 1891.

THE SINCLAIRS OF DURRAN.

9. THOMAS BUCHAN, died *s.p.* 1838.
10. CHARLES HOME, born 1837; formerly Principal Clerk in Exchequer and Audit Department, Somerset House; married 1868, Mary Louisa, daughter of Colonel John Paton of Grandholm, and has issue living—
    1. EUPHEMIA HELEN.   2. MARY ESME.
    Residence—Durran Lodge, East Sheen, Surrey.   *Club*—Union.
11. EUPHEMIA, and   12. NICOLA, who died young.
3. MAJOR ROBERT, who died at Bombay, in 1793, unmarried.
1. MARGARET, married Patrick Honeyman of Graemsay, Orkney.
2. KATHARINE, married Alex. [William], son of James Robertson of Bishopmiln.
3. ELIZABETH, married William Robertson of Auchinroath.

James Sinclair married, secondly, Dorothea Bruce, by whom he had—
4. JOHN, who seems to have died young before 1789.

IV. PATRICK SINCLAIR OF DURRAN, Captain in the Royal Navy, died at St. Domingo in 1794, in command of the frigate "Iphigenia." He married Anne, daughter of James Sinclair-Sutherland of Swinzie, and had—

1. PATRICK, died young and unmarried.   2. JAMES.   1. KATHARINE.

V. JAMES SINCLAIR OF DURRAN was a lieutenant of Marines. He was killed in action in 1801 at cutting out the French corvette "La Chevérite," and was succeeded by his sister Katharine, who married Captain John Worth of Oakley, R.N., and died in 1849, leaving a daughter

MARY CATHERINE SINCLAIR-WORTH, who married Admiral Sir Baldwin Walker, Bart., K.C.B.

THE SINCLAIRS OF OLRIG.

I. GEORGE, fourth son of Sir James Sinclair of Canisbay, was the first of this family. He married Elizabeth, daughter of Alexander Sinclair of Latheron, and had a son Alexander, his successor. John, Master of Berriedale, granted a wadset of Olrig to Sir William Sinclair of Mey and his son Sir James for 8,000 merks, which the latter assigned as a provision to his son George.

II. ALEXANDER SINCLAIR, SECOND OF OLRIG, bought the property from Lord Glenorchy in 1708 for 12,900 merks (£650 sterling), "reserving the swans and swans' nests on the Loch of Durran." He married Katharine, daughter of Donald Budge of Toftingall, and was killed in a duel in 1710 by William Innes of Sandside. He had issue

1. DONALD, his successor.   3. ALEXANDER.   4. WILLIAM.
2. JAMES, in Duncansbay and Warse, 1739—1747, and also a merchant in Freswick.
1. ELIZABETH, married Chas. Sinclair of Bilbster.
2. ESTHER, married John Sinclair of Forss.
3. KATHARINE, married William Budge of Toftingall.

III. DONALD SINCLAIR OF OLRIG AND BILBSTER married Fenella, heiress of Charles Sinclair of Bilbster, and had—

1. CHARLES, his successor.
2. HENRIETTA, married Capt. Benjamin Moodie of Melsetter, Orkney.

IV. CHAS. SINCLAIR OF OLRIG married Elizabeth, daughter of Eric, Lord Duffus, and had—

1. DONALD, his successor.   1. FENELLA.   2. ELIZABETH.   3. JANET.

V. DONALD SINCLAIR OF OLRIG died without issue, and was succeeded by his sister Fenella, who married Archibald Cullen, barrister-at-law, and had issue. The lands of Olrig and Bilbster were sold by Mrs. Cullen. The heir-male (if any) of George Sinclair, first of Olrig, is next in succession to the Earldom of Caithness after the present line of Durran.

THE SINCLAIRS OF LATHERON, ETC.*

I. ALEXANDER SINCLAIR, FIRST OF LATHERON, was fourth son of George Sinclair of Mey, Chancellor of Caithness. He was wadsetter of Latheron, of which he got a charter in 1635, but his descendants acquired the reversion and held the lands in fee, and he seems also to have had some right over Stemster. He married in 1632 Jean, daughter of John Cunningham of Brownhill, and in 1647 was dead. He left three sons and four daughters—

1. WILLIAM, his heir.
2. JOHN of Brabster-myre, ancestor of the Brabsters.
3. ALEXANDER of Stemster, married Anna, daughter of Sir Jas. Sinclair of Murkle, and d. s.p.
4. GEORGE of Barrock, ancestor of that family.
1. ELIZABETH, married in 1657 Walter Bruce of Ham, and was afterwards Lady Olrig as wife of George Sinclair of Olrig.
2. JEAN, married in 1651 Magnus Mowat of Balquholly.
3. MARGARET, married Sir William Dunbar of Hempriggs.

II. SIR WILLIAM SINCLAIR OF LATHERON, DUNBEATH, AND GEANIES was a gentleman of considerable estate and position, and, in addition to his landed property, held large apprisings affecting the Earldom, although before his death he appears to have had considerable debts. In 1661 he was one of the County Commissioners in the Scottish Parliament. He married in 1656 his cousin Elizabeth, daughter of Sir James Sinclair of Mey, who survived him, and died in 1722. He died in 1690, having issue—

1. ALEXANDER, younger of Dunbeath, a Commissioner of Supply in 1685, died s.p.
2. JOHN, heir to his father.
3. WILLIAM of Stemster, to which he succeeded on the death of his uncle Alex. He married Helen Munro, and died sans issue 1699.
4. SIR JAMES, who was created in 1704 Baronet of Dunbeath, q.v.
5. DAVID, who died without issue.
1. ANNE.   5. MARGARET.
2. ELIZABETH, married in 1698 James Sutherland of Langwell, and died s.p.
3. JANET, married Andrew Bruce of Muness Castle, Shetland, and died s.p.
4. JEAN, married in 1682 Sir George Sinclair of Clyth, M.P.
6. KATHARINE, Lady Bowermadden, who married Sir Patrick Dunbar.

III. JOHN SINCLAIR, as eldest surviving son, took up on the death of his brother the succession to the estates of Dunbeath, Latheron, and Geanies, which latter he sold in 1703 to Æneas Macleod of Cadboll. He is said to have been a weak man, and to have made a marriage so displeasing to his father that "he conceived a mortal hatred to him." Certain it is that in addition to his wife's liferent of Dunbeath, and his own debts, his father burdened him with large provisions to his other children, besides reserving the apprisings against the Earldom, amounting to 14,000 merks. Latheron married Isabella, daughter of McKenzie of Ardloch, and had—

1. JAMES, his successor in Latheron.
2. WILLIAM, Colonel in the Bavarian service, who left no issue.
1. BARBARA, who died unmarried.
2. A daughter, married Mr. Tyrie of Edinburgh, and had a son David Tyrie, who on 27th September, 1790, was served heir-general of his uncle James.

IV. JAMES SINCLAIR OF LATHERON, and heir-apparent of Dunbeath, never got possession of the latter estate through the machinations of his uncle Sir James. In 1728 he married Frances, daughter of John Sinclair of Rattar, by whom he had an only child, his successor James. He supported the Rising of 1745, and although considered "a weak and timid man," he collected 100 men and attended a muster at Spittal Hill. He also fought a duel with Wm. Sinclair of Bridgend, son of George of Barrock. In 1751 and 1753, with consent of his son, he sold his claim to Dunbeath to his brother-in-law, Wm. Sinclair of Freswick. He died in 1775.

V. JAMES SINCLAIR, LAST OF LATHERON, died unmarried in 1788.

THE SINCLAIRS OF BRABSTER OR BRABSTER-MYRE.*

I. JOHN SINCLAIR, first of this family, was second son of Alex. Sinclair of Latheron. On 2nd December, 1650, his uncle, Sir John Sinclair of Geanies and Dunbeath, disponed him the lands of Brabster-Myre, acquired from the Mowats. He appears to have become involved in the political troubles of the time, for in 1658 John Murray, writer in Edinburgh (son of Murray of Pennyland), writes to Walter Bruce of Ham, who had married Brabster's sister: "If your brother-in-law, John Sinclair, be come home, he would doe weill to keep himself quiet, for this day Ortoun shews me who has been in Dalkeith, yet the General has sent ane ordere to Capt. Pantimane to apprehend him when he comes into the country." Brabster m. Elizabeth, d. of Patrick Sinclair of Ulbster, and had—
1. ALEXANDER, his successor.
1. JEAN, married Harry Innes of Borlum, ancestor of the latter Sandsides.

From an annuity bond dated 6th December, 1683, we ascertain that Brabster had a second wife, for in this deed he provides an annuity of 500 merks to his "beloved bedfellow and spouse" Sibella Halcrow, who may have been of the Orcadian family of Halcro of that Ilk.

II. ALEXANDER SINCLAIR, SECOND OF BRABSTER, married Margaret, daughter of John Sinclair of Rattar, and had—
1. GEORGE, his successor. 2. PATRICK.

III. GEORGE SINCLAIR, THIRD OF BRABSTER, married Janet, second daughter of James Sutherland of Langwell. "Lady Brabster" lived to an advanced age, and was a shrewd active woman in her eighty-first year. In 1787 she purchased West Canisbay. Brabster had issue:—
1. CAPTAIN ALEXANDER, who died in 1756. 2. JAMES, drowned at Elgin.
1. ANNE, his successor.

Mrs. Anne Sinclair of Brabster married in 1762 her cousin Robert Sutherland of Langwell, and had issue, George Sinclair Sutherland, who succeeded, and a daughter Alexandrina, married to James Macbeath.

* Henderson.

THE SINCLAIRS OF BARROCK.*

I. GEORGE SINCLAIR, FIRST OF BARROCK, was the fourth son of Alex. Sinclair of Latheron, son of the Chancellor of Caithness. He acquired the lands of Barrock, held in wadset from the family of Rattar, from a provision of 6,000 merks received from his uncle Sir John Sinclair of Geanies and Dunbeath. Although in 1673 John Sinclair of Rattar redeemed the wadset, and the lands now belong to Mr. Traill, the family designation continues to be "Sinclair of Barrock." Between 1681 and 1697 he purchased one-third of Lyth, part of Hastigrow, Fitches, and Sortopt (all of which, except Hastigrow, still form part of the family estate); and in 1698 he acquired from the Mowats the estate of Swinzie, now called Lochend. George Sinclair was thrice married, and died in 1724, aged 90 years. By his first wife Anne, daughter of John Dunbar of Hempriggs, he had:

    1. JOHN, his successor.
    1. JEAN, married John Sinclair of Stirkoke.
    2. KATHARINE, married Chas. Sinclair of Bilbster, "Earl of Hell."
    3. MARGARET, married James Murray of Clairden.

He married, secondly, Elizabeth, daughter of David Murray of Clairden, and had—

    1. ALEXANDER, ancestor of the Sinclair-Sutherlands of Swinzie.
    2. WILLIAM, ancestor of the Manson-Sinclairs of Bridgend.   3. DAVID.
    1. ELIZABETH, married John Sinclair of Durran.   2. ANNE, died unmarried.

He married, thirdly, Elizabeth, daughter of William Cumming, last Episcopal minister of Halkirk, by whom he was father of—

    1. JAMES, who died abroad.   2. GEORGE.   3. ROBERT.
    4. BENJAMIN, sometime in Duncansbay. None of these sons left issue.
    1. JANET, who died unmarried in 1772.

II. JOHN SINCLAIR, SECOND OF BARROCK, acquired many estates. He was twice married, and died in 1743. By his first wife Anne, daughter of Robert Sinclair of Durran, he had—

    1. ALEXANDER, who succeeded, born in 1706.
    1. JEAN, married George Murray of Clairden.
    2. MARGARET, married Sir James Sinclair of Mey.   3. ELIZABETH.

He married, secondly, his cousin Janet, daughter of Sir Jas. Dunbar of Hempriggs, and had—

    1. GEORGE, an army officer, died of a wound in Antigua in 1759, while he was still a minor.
    2. JAMES, who died young.
    3. JOHN, who succeeded to Sibster. He married Helen, daughter of George Sinclair of Stirkoke, and had—
        1. BENJAMIN.
    The estate was judicially sold and John Sinclair and his son left Caithness.

III. ALEXANDER SINCLAIR married Jean, second daughter of William Sinclair of Freswick, and had—

    1. JOHN, his successor.   2. WILLIAM (W. S.), died 7th July, 1799, unmarried.
    3. GEORGE, bond of provision dated in 1764.
    1. KATHARINE; and 2. ANNE; both died unmarried.
    3. MARGARET, married Colonel Borthwick, and died *s.p.*
    4. JEAN, married William Chas. Reoch, and died *s.p.*

* Henderson.

THE SINCLAIRS OF BARROCK.

IV. JOHN SINCLAIR married, first, Ann Longmire of Penrith, and had—
    1. ALEXANDER, who died young.   2. JOHN, his successor.
    1. MARIA, died unmarried, 9th March, 1876, aged 87.
    2. JANE, married William Sinclair of Freswick.
    3. ANNE, married William Smith, minister of Bower.
    4. MARGARET, married Mr. Paton.
    5. ELIZABETH, married Lieutenant Allan Robertson, Sheriff-clerk of Caithness.

Barrock married, secondly, Janet Miller, and had by her—
    1. WILLIAM, who died young.   2. DONALD, M.D., who died in 1873, and left issue.
    1. ISABELLA, married the Rev. Peter Jolly of Dunnet.
    2. JESSIE, married Scarth of Binscarth, Orkney.   3. CATHERINE, married Mr. Sine.

V. JOHN SINCLAIR, FIFTH OF BARROCK, succeeded his father, and on the death of General Sir John Sinclair in 1842 succeeded to the BARONETCY OF DUNBEATH, which see.

THE SINCLAIR-SUTHERLANDS OF RISGILL OR SWINZIE.*

I. ALEXANDER SINCLAIR, the founder of this family, was the second son of George Sinclair, first of Barrock. He had acquired the property of Swinzie, now called Lochend, from his father. In 1717 he married Anne Sutherland, second daughter of James Sutherland of Langwell, on whose death in 1708 she had succeeded to the estate of Risgill, which after her marriage was called Swinzie. Alex. Sutherland (*né* Sinclair) died in 1738, leaving a son James.

II. JAMES SUTHERLAND OF SWINZIE is mentioned as being "a very facetious, entertaining man, who loved to pass his jokes." In 1739 his mother disponed the estate to him, and in 1743 he married his cousin-german Jean, daughter of John Sinclair of Durran. She was known as "Lady Swinzie," and resided during the latter part of her life at Thurso, where she died, a very old woman, in 1819. Swinzie had a son and three daughters—
    1. JOHN, who succeeded.   2. JANET.
    1. ANNE, who married Patrick Sinclair of Durran, Capt. R.N.
    3. ELIZABETH, married Benj. Henderson, tacksman of Clyth.

III. JOHN SUTHERLAND OF SWINZIE was served heir to his father in 1777. He married Margaret, daughter of Donald Williamson of Banniskirk, and died without issue in 1789, when his brother-in-law, Capt. Patrick Sinclair of Durran was served heir.

THE MANSON SINCLAIRS OF BRIDGEND.*

I. WILLIAM SINCLAIR, third son of George Sinclair, first of Barrock, married Sidney, heiress of Geo. Manson of Bridgend, and had—
    1. ROBERT MANSON SINCLAIR, who succeeded.   1. A daughter, who married Mr. Bogie.

II. ROBERT MANSON SINCLAIR, SECOND OF BRIDGEND, married Isabel, daughter of John Sinclair of Assery. She died in 1779, and he about 1790. He was of very convivial habits, and "Brigend's Bowl," famed in his own time as ever in need of sugar, whisky, or water, thereby calling for constant additions, is still locally a "Bowl of renown." The estate was judicially sold in 1788. In 1772 he had issue alive three sons and five daughters—

* Henderson.

1. WILLIAM. 2. GEORGE, Lieut. in the army, who in 1782 was served heir *cum beneficio*.
3. ROBERT, who was a Writer in Edinburgh. 1. CATHARINE, died unmarried.
2. ELIZABETH, married John Rose, Sheriff-Substitute of Caithness and Collector of Customs at Thurso (marriage contract, October, 1772). There is no information as to the other daughters.

THE SINCLAIRS OF DUN.*

There is difficulty in determining with certainty the origin of the Sinclairs of Dun, but they are believed to be cadets of the Caithness family.

In Calder's "History of Caithness" there is an unsupported statement that the Duns settled in the County in 1379, but there is no evidence of the Sinclairs appearing in connection with lands in Caithness till 1455, unless we can accept the charter of *Henricus de Sancto Claro comes Orchadiae* to the founder of the Budges of Toftingall, of tenements in Wick, as establishing such a fact. It is certain that in 1508 Dun was possessed by the Caldells or Calders, and the first trace of a "Sinclair of Dun" is in 1540, when John Sinclair of Dun attests the *Precept of Clare Constat* granted by George II., 42nd Earl of Caithness, to John Groat of Duncansbay. In 1541 "David Sinclair of Dunn" was cautioner in a tack of teinds to the Earl of Caithness. The same year David Sinclair, natural son of John, Earl of Caithness, and who was Bailie to the Bishop of Caithness, also appears in a tack of the teind sheaves of Canisbay. About 1557-58 a marriage was arranged by Earl George between Y-Mackay of Farr and Christian Sinclair, whom Gordon designs "daughter to the laird of Dun, and *cousin to the Earl*." McKay, referring to this marriage, states that Christian Sinclair was the daughter of "Wm. Sinclair, laird of Dun," and that she was the Earl's cousin. In a charter of January, 1560, granted by John, Earl of Sutherland, to David Sinclair, then of Dun, the Earl and his Countess Eleanor style Dun "*noster consanguineus-germanus.*" The "Genealogie of the St. Clairs of Rosslyn" has it that "St. Clair of Doun is a great-grandchild of John, Lord Berridall. The first of this surname was one David, who married one Marie, heretrix of Doun, daughter to Wm. Calder, and begot John, who espoused Agatha, daughter of Hugh Grott of Soutdun." Sinclair of Freswick, in a MS. written about 1770, has it that the progenitor of the family of Dun, to which he himself belonged, was David, second son of William II. St. Clair, Earl of Caithness. The late Capt. Kennedy of Wick, in a MS., informs us that George, 4th St. Clair, Earl of Caithness, had a son called David, who begat John Sinclair of Dun and Wm. Sinclair of Forss-Milns. The Sutherland charter of 1560 is to David Sinclair of Dun in liferent, and to "*his sons*" William, Alexander, and Henry in succession, and to the "*heirs-male of their bodies lawfully begotten,*" in fee, the lands of Forss and Baillie. In 1586 a Henry Sinclair, who was unquestionably the brother of Christian, the laird of Dunn's daughter, was killed in a fight with the Clan Gunn, then under command of Hutcheon McKay, Christian's son and Henry's nephew. As no other Henry Sinclair is mentioned about this period, it may be that Christian Sinclair's brother was the same Henry named in the charter, and thus that she was a daughter of *David* Sinclair of Dun. If so, as she was "cousin to the Earl of Caithness," so must her father also have been connected with that family. There is a summons extant dated 12th March, 1562, issued at the instance of John Sinclair, "*eldest son and heir of the deceased David Sinclair of Dun,*" with consent of his curators,

* Henderson.

THE SINCLAIRS OF DUN.

the Earl of Caithness and John Grote, against Wm. Sinclair of Forss as an intromitter with the writs and evidents of David Sinclair, immediately after his decease in March, 1560. In this action Forss is required to produce acquittances given to David Sinclair of Dun in connection with the lands of the Caithness bishopric. From this circumstance it is reasonable to assume that David Sinclair, first of Dun, was identical with David Sinclair, Bailie of the Bishopric and natural son of Earl John. The summons makes no reference to any relationship between David Sinclair of Dun and William of Forss; and thus while it is certain that Forss was a son of the David Sinclair of Dun in the charter of January, 1560, and that John Sinclair was son of the David of Dun who died in March, 1560, it is not clear that the two Davids were identical, nor that Wm. Sinclair of Forss and John Sinclair of Dun were brothers. It is difficult to reconcile the fact of John Sinclair, eldest son and heir, suing with curators in 1562 (thus apparently in minority) with his being brother to Wm. Sinclair, who in 1561 had been admitted as vassal in Forss, had granted deeds as owner in possession of those lands, had witnessed the execution of important deeds, and otherwise conducted himself as a man of full age. David Sinclair may have had an elder son David, who after succeeding to Dun died young, leaving his son and heir John a minor, and this seems the most likely explanation.

I. With the exception of the incidental reference to John of Dun in 1540, while conflicting as to the paternity, all accounts point to a DAVID SINCLAIR as first of Dun. From Hay's "Genealogie" we have learnt that he was a son of John, Lord Berridall, afterwards Earl of Caithness; and that marrying Marie, heretrix of Dun, daughter to Wm. Calder, he acquired those lands, and had by her—

II. JOHN SINCLAIR, SECOND OF DUN, his eldest son and heir, who succeeded him. In 1591 he was infeft by charter from the Earl of Caithness, and in 1592 had a Crown charter of confirmation. By his first wife, whose name is unknown, he had—

    1. DAVID, successor to Dun.   2. JAMES, wounded in a skirmish at Thurso in 1612.
    3. GEORGE, designed in 1616 as son of "Umquhile John Sinclair of Dun."

His second wife was Agatha, daughter of Hugh Grote of Southdun. She was life-rented in Dun, with which her name occurs from 1628 to 1642. By her Dun had a son—

    4. WILLIAM, ancestor of the Southdun branch of the family.

III. DAVID SINCLAIR, THIRD OF DUN, was twice married. By his first wife, Elizabeth, daughter of John Sinclair of Ulbster, he had issue—

    1. FRANCIS, fourth of Dun.   2. WILLIAM, fifth of Dun.   3. JAMES.
    1. JEAN, who married in 1695, George Sinclair of Forss.

IV. FRANCIS SINCLAIR, FOURTH OF DUN, was served heir in 1650. He married Jean, daughter of John Sinclair of Ulbster, by whom he had—

    KATHARINE.

V. WILLIAM SINCLAIR, FIFTH OF DUN, was served heir of provision to his brother Francis, and in 1663 he got a charter from the Archdean of Caithness, of Scarmclett, Larrel, Galshfield, Clayock, and Campster. He was thrice married, first in 1643, to Elizabeth, daughter of Alex. Sutherland of Forse; secondly, to Isabel, daughter of John Sinclair of Assery; and thirdly, to Katharine Sinclair, "Lady Dun," daughter of Alex. Sinclair of Telstane. He had—

    1. ALEXANDER, next of Dun.   2. DAVID.
    1. JEAN, m. in 1670, William, son of John Sinclair of Assery, brother to her father's second wife.
    2. ——, who married David Sinclair of Broynach.

VI. ALEXANDER SINCLAIR, SIXTH OF DUN, received a disposition from his father in 1680. The name of his first wife has not been ascertained, but by her he was father of four sons and two daughters—

1. WILLIAM, mentioned in 1731 as younger of Dun
2. HENRY, who resided in Achravole in 1769, and who is mentioned as eldest son.
3. RICHARD, merchant in Thurso, who was drowned in crossing the river at Thurso in 1755 He married Elizabeth, sister of John McKay of Strathy, and left two daughters
4. DAVID, youngest son, who had a provision of 3,500 merks
1. ELIZABETH, who in 1737 received paternal bond of provision, and is in 1755 designed as widow of Patrick Forbes
2. KATHARINE, who had a provision of 3,000 merks.

Alex Sinclair married, secondly, in 1751, Barbara, youngest daughter of Alex Henderson in Gerston, but by her had no issue The family estate becoming involved in debt, what remained of it was sold in 1751 to David Sinclair of Southdun. Dun died in 1754

Richard Sinclair, third son of the last Dun, has given his name to "Sinclair's Pool" in Thurso river, and also to a curious tale of "second sight," which it may be of interest to relate At the time of the accident there was no bridge across the river, and it was crossed at a ford, or by ferry boat lower down Mr. Sinclair had crossed to the east side by the ford in the morning and gone to the country on business His wife had some women friends with her in the evening, which was dark and rainy, and having occasion to leave the room where her guests were, she observed, as she believed, her husband pass upstairs to his room, and she desired the servant to carry up some fire, as he appeared to be very wet. The servant not finding her master in the room, a search was made, with the result that he was not to be found within the house. The appearance seen by Mrs. Sinclair was held to portend coming evil, and accordingly her husband was found drowned in the pool which still bears his name, man and horse having been carried off by a sudden spate in the water.

The last Dun acted as second to Innes of Sandside in the fatal duel of 1710 between the latter and Sinclair of Olrig, and thereafter Dun fled the country. Calder relates that the possessor of Dun in 1745 shot himself, because prevented by his mother from keeping an engagement to join the Stewart party This is certainly incorrect as referring to Alex Sinclair, then of Dun, but may apply to his eldest son and apparent heir in 1731— William There is in the Lyon Register a record of the arms of Laurence Sinclair, descended from the family of Dun in Caithness, but of him there is no trace in the county annals

THE SINCLAIRS OF SOUTHDUN.*

I. WILLIAM SINCLAIR, FIRST OF SOUTHDUN, was the son of John Sinclair, second of Dun, by his second marriage with Agatha, daughter of Hugh Grote, perhaps of Brabsterdorran William Sinclair is occasionally styled *of* Dun and *in* Dun He married Marjory, daughter of Saul Bruce of Lyth, and had two sons and a daughter—

1. DAVID, second of Southdun, and first so styled
2. FRANCIS, portioner of Brabsterdorran, in 1657 styled "lawful brother of David Sinclair of Southdun He married an Elizabeth Sinclair and was ancestor of the Brabsterdorrans
3. ISOBEL, who married in 1652, Thomas, son of Malcolm Grote in Warse

Henderson

THE SINCLAIRS OF SOUTHDUN.

II. DAVID SINCLAIR, SECOND OF SOUTHDUN, is repeatedly mentioned in writings by Agatha Grote as her "Oy," or grandchild. He married Jean, daughter of John Sinclair of Ulbster, and had—

1. PATRICK, next of Southdun.
2. JAMES of Lyth, who in 1707 acquired Alterwall and part of Brabsterdorran.
3. DAVID in Brabsterdorran, who fought on the Stewart side at Sheriffmuir in 1715. He married and had a son—
    DAVID, who married Jean, daughter of George Sinclair, second son of Brabsterdorran, and had a son—
        ALEXANDER,* who in 1780 sold his interest in Brabsterdorran.
4. ALEXANDER.
1. MARGARET, married William Bruce of Stanstill.
2. ELIZABETH, married Donald Budge of Toftingall in 1672.
3. ISOBELL, married Lawrence Calder of Lynegar in 1653.

III. PATRICK SINCLAIR, THIRD OF SOUTHDUN, married Janet, daughter of Jas. Murray of Pennyland, and had—
1. JAMES.   2. DAVID.   3. PATRICK.
1. MARJORY, married William Calder of Lynegar.   2. JEAN.
3. JANET, married John Sinclair of Rattar.   4. ELIZABETH, married Henry Budge.

IV. JAMES SINCLAIR, died in minority, and was succeeded by his brother

V. DAVID SINCLAIR. He executed an entail of the estate in 1747. He was three times married: First, in 1714, to Lady Janet Sinclair, daughter of John, Earl of Caithness, who died 1720. By her he had—
1. PATRICK, who died about 1724.   1. JEAN, who died young.
2. JEAN II., married Sir William Dunbar of Hempriggs, and died s.p
3. JANET, married Dr. Stuart Threipland of Fingask.

He married, secondly, in 1748, Marjory, daughter of Sir Robert Dunbar of Northfield, and had—
1. MARJORY, married first, John, son of Sir Patrick Dunbar of Northfield, her cousin-german, and had no issue; secondly, James Sinclair of Harpsdale and had with other issue died unmarried—
    1. HENRIETTA of Southdun.   2. JANET, married Colonel Williamson of Banniskirk.
2. KATHARINE, died unmarried.

He married, thirdly, Margaret, daughter of James Murray of Clairden, and had—
1. MARGARET, died unmarried at Lyons in 1774.

David Sinclair was succeeded in Southdun by his granddaughter HENRIETTA SINCLAIR of Harpsdale, who married Colonel Wemyss, and had an only child

WILLIAM SINCLAIR WEMYSS, late of Southdun, who married Henrietta, daughter of Sir Benjamin Dunbar, Lord Duffus, and died in 1831 leaving issue.

THE SINCLAIRS OF BRABSTERDORRAN.†

I. FRANCIS SINCLAIR, first of this family, was second son of William Sinclair, first of Southdun, by his wife Marjory Bruce. Francis held a portion of Brabsterdorran in 1683. He married Elizabeth Sinclair (family uncertain), and had—
1. PATRICK, who succeeded.
2. GEORGE, who m. Elizabeth, d. of Alexander Gibson, dean of Bower, and had an only child—
    JEAN, married her cousin David Sinclair in Whitegar, and had issue—
        ALEXANDER SINCLAIR of Brabsterdorran.

---
* See Sinclairs of Brabsterdorran.   † Henderson.

II. PATRICK SINCLAIR, a portioner of Brabsterdorran, married in 1703 Barbara, second daughter of William Cumming, minister of Halkirk, and his wife Katharine, daughter of John Murray of Pennyland. Patrick is said to have had two sons—

1 WILLIAM, nicknamed "La Mode," a midshipman in the navy, and thereafter in the Customs at Thurso He m. Rachel, d of Mr. Cumming of Craigmiln in Morayshire, and among other children had—
 KATHARINE, married Alex Cumming, tacksman of Rattar
2 JAMES, who was tide-waiter in the Customs at Thurso

In 1670 Henry Dundas, then one of the portioners of Brabsterdorran, granted a wadset to John Sinclair in Brabsterdorran, and Margaret his wife, and William their eldest son. In 1693 Margaret Sinclair, then relict of John, assigned the wadset to her son Alexander. Whether these Sinclairs were connected with the Brabsterdorran, or Dun and Southdun families, has not been ascertained

III *ALEXANDER SINCLAIR OF BRABSTERDORRAN, portioner thereof in right of his mother, was born at Rattar House, retoured heir to his great-grandfather, Francis Sinclair, 2nd April, 1772. He married in 1768 Margaret, daughter of John Christie, bleacher at Ormiston. She died at Edinburgh 6th April, 1837, aged 87 He sold his interest in Brabsterdorran in 1780 to Miss Sinclair of Southdun, and dying shortly thereafter was buried in the Kirk of Bower He had six children—

1 WILLIAM, born in 1771, died in West Indies, unmarried
2 DAVID, born 1772, married Ann Dilworth, who died 13th November, 1818, aged 42. He died 1st April, 1840, and had issue—
 1 DAVID. 2 WILLIAM 3 ALEXANDER. 4 JAMES
 5 MARGARET 6 GEORGINA
3 MARY, born 1774, married, 1799, Wm Griffith, who died 30th June, 1820, aged 56, She died 24th December, 1856, aged 84, and had issue—
4 CATHERINE, born 1777, married, 1810, Geo Thomson, solicitor
5 JOHN, aftermentioned
6 DOUBLEDAY, born 1780, married, 1803, Thos Tait, and had issue—

IV JOHN SINCLAIR, born 4th February, 1777, was killed in a railway collision near Edinburgh 7th December, 1854. He married in 1799 Elisabeth, daughter of James Grant of Corrimony, advocate She died 12th December, 1840, aged 70, and had issue—

1 MARY ANNE, died young 2 ALEXANDER, died young
3 MARGARET, born 1805, died 18th January, 1832 4 JOHN, born 1807, died 23rd May, 1847
5 JANE, married 23rd May, 1840, Dr John Park, R N , and died 15th Aug , 1870, and had issue—
 LUCY ANN, born 2nd December, 1841, died 19th August, 1860
 MAITLAND, born 12th May, 1844, married at Brisbane, Margaret Maclean Kennedy
6 ANNE, died 28th April, 1862, unmarried
7 VEITCH, M D , born 28th October, 1810, died at London 22nd May, 1892, married 1st June, 1842, Harriet, daughter of Thos Tweedie of Quarter, Peeblesshire, and had issue—
 1 THOMAS VEITCH, died 16th November, 1846 2. ALEXANDER, died young
 3 HARRIET ELISABETH
 4 ALEXANDER JAMES, M D , born September, 1848, died 23rd February, 1889, m 7th June, 1881, Louisa, daughter of Geo Stewart, and had issue
 5 HENRY TWEEDIE JAMES, L R C.P S , married 22nd February, 1887, Mary Louisa, daughter of J J Macswiney, London, and has issue a daughter
 6. ARTHUR VEITCH AUGUSTINE, M D , born 12th July, 1856, married Matilda Donaldson, and has issue
 7. ADELAIDE JANE, born 27th December, 1858, died 14th February, 1859

---

* The subsequent information as to this branch was supplied by Francis J. Grant, "Carrick Pursuivant."

8 MARY, died young   9 ELIZA, died young
10 WILLIAM, died 16th March, 1868; married, 1838, Jane, daughter of David R Andrews, Dundee, and had issue—
    WILLIAM, married 16th March, 1868, Sophia, daughter of Robert Paton, W S
    And several others who died young
11 LUCY, born 29th September, 1820, died 31st May, 1879, married 1st October, 1839, Anthony Clapham, Newcastle-on-Tyne, and had issue—
    1 LUCY, born 11th July, 1840, married 10th July, 1861, her mother's cousin, John Grant, Marchmont Herald, and had issue—
        CALVERT JOHN   LUCY ANTONIA   EDITH MARGARET
        FRANCIS JAMES GRANT, W S, "Carrick Pursuivant," *author of "Zetland County Families," ' Grants of Corrimony," &c, &c*
    2 REGINALD, b 20th February, 1848, d 3rd January, 1889, and had issue 5 children
    3 MARY JANE   4 MARIA ANNE   5 ANTHONY CALVERT, b 18th December, 1856
12 JAMES, born 1822, died at Cape of Good Hope, June, 1874

THE SINCLAIRS OF FORSS *

Previous to 1567 the lands of Forss and Baillie belonged to the Bishopric, but in that year they were feued out to John, Earl of Sutherland, and Eleanor his wife; and in January, 1569, they were granted in feu to David Sinclair of Dun (*quod vide*) in liferent, and to his three sons, William, Alexander, and Henry, and to the heirs-male of their bodies lawfully begotten, in succession, in fee

I. DAVID SINCLAIR OF DUN, and FIRST SINCLAIR OF FORSS, was probably of the Caithness family, and died in March, 1560 He had five sons—
    1 WILLIAM, fiar of Forss   2 ALEXANDER, mentioned in 1560, *vide supra*.
    3 HENRY, conceived to be the Henry Sinclair slain in 1586
    4 GEORGE, who with his brother William witnesses a contract of marriage at Girnigo Castle 22nd November, 1563
    5. MATHEW, mentioned in 1584

If Henry Sinclair, slain in 1586, was the son of David Sinclair of Dun, then the latter had also a daughter—
    1. CHRISTIAN SINCLAIR, the cousin of the Earl of Caithness, who married about 1557-58 Y-McKay of Farr

II WILLIAM SINCLAIR "OF FORSS" is so styled in 1561-62-63 and subsequent years, and in 1567 he was a witness, along with *John* Sinclair of Dun, to a notarial instrument in favour of Alexander, Earl of Sutherland In May, 1561, he was admitted vassal in Forss by the Earl of Sutherland, from which we may safely infer that his father was then dead In the same year he gave a liferent right in Forss to one Mary Stirling He married Janet Urquhart, held to be of the ancient knightly family of Urquhart of Cromarty, and had issue two sons—
    1 DAVID, married Janet, daughter of Murray of Pulrossie, and or Spanziedale, both in Sutherland He died in apparency, and without issue
    2 ALEXANDER, successor to his father

III. ALEXANDER SINCLAIR OF FORSS married in 1608 Margaret daughter of George Sinclair of Mey. She is mentioned as "Gude Wyff of Forss" They had two sons and a daughter—
    1 DAVID, and 2 GEORGE, successively of Forss
    1 KATHARINE, married George Innes of Oust

IV. DAVID SINCLAIR died without issue, and was succeeded by his brother

V. GEORGE SINCLAIR OF FORSS, who married twice. By his first wife Jean, daughter of David Sinclair of Dun, he had—

    1 MARGARET, married Malcolm Grote of Warse.

By his second wife Mary, daughter of Sir Jas. Sinclair of Murkle, he had—

    1 JOHN, his successor

VI. JOHN SINCLAIR OF FORSS was married three times. First, to Janet, daughter of William Sutherland of Geise, by whom he had—

    1 GEORGE, who succeeded

Secondly, to Barbara, daughter of John Sinclair of Rattar, by whom he had—

    1 JOHN, afterwards of Forss   2 JAMES of Holbornhead, and afterwards of Forss.
    3 WILLIAM, physician in Thurso, who married in 1742, Barbara, daughter of Robert Sinclair of Geise, and died in 1767. He had—
        1. DR. WILLIAM SINCLAIR, afterwards of Freswick.
        1 JANET, married James Mackie, an officer of Excise
    1 ELIZABETH

Thirdly, Elizabeth, daughter of Richard Murry of Pennyland, by whom he had—

    1 MARY, married James Campbell of Lochend } Joint Sheriff-clerks of Caithness
    2 JEAN, married Hugo Campbell
    3 MARGARET, died unmarried in 1771

VII. GEORGE SINCLAIR OF FORSS seems to have led a reckless life, and in 1728 was strongly recommended by his brother John to renew his addresses to a young lady with money, "and never to give over till you have obtained your wishes," and thus to pay his debts, "which you'll never pay but by marrying a person with money." The Laird disregarded his brother's advice and died unmarried.

VIII. JOHN SINCLAIR OF FORSS, half-brother of George, was minister of Watten in 1733, and died in 1753. He married Esther, daughter of Alex Sinclair of Olrig, and had a son Alexander

IX. ALEX. SINCLAIR OF FORSS was somewhat eccentric in his habits. He died unmarried and was succeeded by his uncle,

X. JAMES SINCLAIR OF FORSS AND HOLBORNHEAD, who married in 1737, Jean, daughter of Robert Sinclair of Geise, advocate, and had by her—

    1 ROBERT, Captain in the Army, afterwards of Freswick
    2 WILLIAM, surgeon in the Army, died unmarried at St. Domingo in 1794.
    3 JAMES, next of Forss
    1 CATHARINE, Mrs Campbell
    2 ELIZABETH, married John Bane, Tacksman of Dale, in 1782

Holbornhead married, secondly, apparently after 1775, a daughter of John Sinclair of Scotscalder, of which marriage there was no issue. The social habits of Caithness in 1737 are well illustrated in a letter given by a gentleman present at Holbornhead's marriage. "We had a rantin bridal and a brave jolly company of ladies and gentlemen; your sisters and the ladies of the familie, Freswick, Brabster, Scotscalder, Assery, Thura, Lybster, Mass John Sinclair (Rev John Sinclair, minister of Watten), the Frenchman, Mr. Harry Innes, John of Bower, Toftkemp, etc. We danced four days out, and drank heartily, and thereafter went home with the young wife, where we renewed our mirth to a height."

THE SINCLAIRS OF FORSS

XI. JAMES SINCLAIR OF FORSS was a lieutenant in the Army. He married Johanna, daughter of George McKay of Bighouse, and had—

1 JAMES
2 GEORGE LEWIS, W S , of Dalveoch, married 11th February, 1830, Frances Ann, second daughter of John Boazman of Acornbank, Westmoreland , died *sans issue* on 22nd October, 1878, aged 75
3 WILLIAM, Captain in the Army , died unmarried
4 HUGH, died unmarried in Australia
1 JEAN, died unmarried 2 ÆNEASINA, married Mr. Stevenson.
3. LOUISA, married Captain Hector Macneill 4 ELIZABETH 5 JANET

Forss was succeeded by his eldest son

XII. JAMES SINCLAIR OF FORSS, Twelfth Laird, advocate 1827, died at Forss, 1st March, 1876, aged 73. He married 26th June, 1828, his cousin Jessie, daughter of Wm. Sinclair Wemyss of Southdun, and had issue thirteen sons and four daughters, of whom eight sons and three daughters survived him. They were—

1 JAMES, Lieut -Colonel, R A , died unmarried in 1873 2 HENRY, d in India, unmarried.
3 GEORGE WILLIAM, married Janet, daughter of Wm Young of Korsit, Victoria, and had—
   1. CHAS WEMYSS, now of Forss 2 GEORGE WM. YOUNG, born 1867.
4 ROBERT 5 CHARLES 6 RAMSAY, died *s p* 7 EDWARD
8 GARDEN OCTAVIUS, died 1883, and left a son 9 WILLIAM, died *s p* 1878
10 ALBERT, died young 11 JOHN, died unmarried 1876
12 FREDERICK, died unmarried, 1879 13 WELLESLEY, died young
1 JOANNA 2 JANET, died young 3 HENRIETTA 4 LOUISA, died 1883

THE SINCLAIRS OF STIRKOKE.

I In 1587 DAVID SINCLAIR obtained a Crown charter of Stirkoke and Alterwall, in which he is designed "*filio naturali quond. Joannis Magistri Cathanensis*," and in 1588 he received letters of legitimation He died *cir* 1595, leaving a son John, as also a natural son, Colonel George Sinclair, who was slain in an expedition to Norway in 1612.

II. JOHN SINCLAIR OF STIRKOKE fell in fight at Thurso in 1612 It is uncertain whether he had any issue

III. FRANCIS SINCLAIR, LAIRD OF STIRKOKE in 1624, was a natural son of George III., 43rd Earl of Caithness by *(semble)* Barbara Mearns Stirkoke married Margaret Williamson, by whom he had—

1 FRANCIS, his successor 2 JOHN 3 GUSTAVUS
1 MARJORY, fifth wife of Donald, first Lord Reay
2. ANNE, married Colonel Francis Sinclair of Scrabster, son of the first Assery

In about 1621 he fought a duel with his relative Sir Wm Sinclair of Mey

IV. FRANCIS SINCLAIR OF STIRKOKE married in 1658, Anne, eldest daughter of Patrick Sinclair of Ulbster His mother and his 'uncle,' Francis Sinclair of Northfield, were parties to the marriage contract. Francis Sinclair had four sons and a daughter—

1 PATRICK, eldest son in 1676 2 JOHN, who succeeded.
3 GEORGE, called the second son, who in 1673-5 had a charter to Sibster-Wick
4 CHARLES of Bilbster, who had the unenviable *sobriquet* of "Earl of Hell " He married, first, Katharine, daughter of George Sinclair of Barrock , and secondly, Mary Dunbar He had issue—
   FENELLA, married to Donald Sinclair of Olrig
1 JEAN, married John Gibson, minister of Evie Orkney.

V. JOHN SINCLAIR was served heir to his father in 1681, and died about 1706. He married Margaret, daughter of Sir Jas. Sinclair of Mey, and had two sons—

    1. FRANCIS.   2. GEORGE, successively of Stirkoke.

VI. FRANCIS SINCLAIR had several daughters, of whom—

    FRANCES, married Bernard Clunes, merchant in Cromarty, and had issue.

Having no sons, Francis Sinclair disponed the estate to his brother George in 1610. Some litigation ensued between the daughter Frances Clunes and her uncle with regard to the lands, but under a submission they were awarded to him as heir-male.

VII. GEORGE SINCLAIR OF STIRKOKE married Isabella Strahan, and died in 1744, leaving three sons and two daughters—

1. CHARLES, apparent in 1768.	2. FRANCIS, shipmaster in Wick.
1. ELIZABETH, m. Geo. Smith in Dunnett.	2. HELEN, m. John Sinclair of Sibster.

VIII. CHARLES SINCLAIR OF STIRKOKE married Elizabeth, daughter of Alexander Sinclair of Olrig, and had an only daughter—

    KATHARINE SINCLAIR OF STIRKOKE, who resided and died at Scorraclett, unmarried.

THE SINCLAIRS OF ULBSTER.*

The ancestor of this family was William Sinclair, first Laird of Mey, second son of George II., 42nd Earl of Caithness. His elder brother John having with his connivance been imprisoned by his father in Castle Girnigo, he was, on the occasion of a visit to the dungeon of the Master, laid hold of by him and crushed to death in an iron embrace. The event occurred in 1572 or 1573, and prevented him from legitimatising by subsequent marriage either of his two natural sons Patrick and John. The mother of the former was Margaret, daughter of James Mowat of Balquhollie, and of the latter was Lucy, daughter of Gordon of Gight. Letters of legitimation passed the Great Seal on 20th June, 1567, for "*Patricio et Magistro Joanni Sinclair filiis naturalibus quondam Willelmi Sinclair de Mey.*"

I. PATRICK SINCLAIR, FIRST OF ULBSTER, got a disposition of these lands in 1596 from his "cousin" George, 43rd Earl of Caithness, and dying without issue, was succeeded by his brother

II. JOHN SINCLAIR OF ULBSTER, who was a man of education and ability. His name is invariably prefixed by "Mr." or "Maister," a term usually applied to pedagogues, preachers, notaries, and the like. In 1601 the General Assembly planted ministers in the families of the Catholic nobles, and Lord Gordon, eldest son of the Marquis of Huntly, and the Master of Caithness were allotted to the care of two pedagogues, one being John Sinclair, who was compelled to declare himself an adherent of the reformed faith. That John Sinclair the pedagogue was afterwards Mr. John Sinclair of Ulbster is clear, for in a letter from him to his "uncle" George Sinclair of Mey, in 1604, we find that he and the Master of Caithness lived in the family of the Marquis of Huntly at Bogg Gight ; and in regard to the Master he writes : "always the Mr. is verie weill, God be praysit, and commends him heartily to you." John Sinclair was twice married : first, to Jean Chisholm, daughter to the Laird of Straglass, and

---

* Henderson.

secondly, to Katharine Stewart. By his first marriage he had two sons and a daughter—
- 1 PATRICK, his successor
- 2 GEORGE, a merchant in Leith
- 1. HENRIETTA, married the Rev Wm. Abernethy (son of John, Bishop of Caithness) of Halkirk 1627, and of Thurso in 1636.

By his second wife Ulbster had a son and two daughters—
- 1 JOHN of Tannach and Brims, who served in the German wars, and in 1660 bought Brims from the heirs of the first Sinclairs of Dunbeath He married Ann Goldman, and had—
  - 1. JOHN, afterwards of Ulbster
  - 2. WILLIAM of Thrumster, married Margaret, daughter of Jas Innes of Thursater His wife had Oust in liferent He had a son—
    - 1 WILLIAM, who in 1719 disponed Oust to John Sinclair of Brims He m Jean, natural d of Sir George Sinclair of Bilbster and Clyth [Bart]
  - 3. CHARLES.
- 1 JEAN, married, first, Francis Sinclair of Dun, and secondly, David Sinclair of Southdun
- 2 ELIZABETH, married Wm Sinclair of Rattar.

John Sinclair of Tannach had two natural sons, one of whom was James, probably James Sinclair "in Lythmore," and the same James Sinclair who in 1702 obtained from his "brother," John of Ulbster and Brims, a wadset of Holbornhead, Uttersquoy, and Sandiquoy

III PATRICK SINCLAIR OF ULBSTER was served heir to his father John in 1640, and in 1647 married Elizabeth, daughter of John McKay of Strathy and Dirlot. He had two sons and seven daughters—
- 1 JOHN, who succeeded
- 2 SIR GEORGE SINCLAIR of Bilbster and Clyth [Bart], married Jean, daughter of Wm Sinclair of Dunbeath, and had no issue He had three natural daughters—
  - 1 JEAN, m. Wm Sinclair, yr of Thrumster   2. MARY.   3 ANNE
- 1 ANNE, married Francis Sinclair of Stirkoke
- 2 ELIZABETH, married in 1660 John Sinclair of Brabster
- 3 MARY, married in 1675 Sir Robert Dunbar of Northfield
- 4 ISABEL, married in 1673 George, eldest son of James Sinclair of Assery.
- 5 MARGARET, married in 1679 her cousin-german Hugh McKay of Cairnsloch, son of John McKay of Skerray   6 JEAN, married Angus McKay, apparent of B.ghouse
- 7 KATHARINE, married James Sinclair of Lybster

In 1660 Ulbster and his son John acquired various lands by purchase from the Earl of Caithness, and others from Lord Glenorchy in 1676

IV. JOHN SINCLAIR OF ULBSTER married Janet, daughter of Wm Sinclair of Rattar Having no family he settled the estates in 1709 by an entail, the first substitute being John of Brims, eldest son of John Sinclair of Tannach and Brims.

V. JOHN SINCLAIR OF BRIMS AND ULBSTER was twice married, first to Jean, daughter of Munro of Culrain; and secondly, to Jean Cores. By his first marriage he had issue—
- 1 JOHN, his successor.
- 2 PATRICK of Brims Tradition ascribes to him an intrigue with a daughter of James Sinclair of Uttersquoy (probably natural brother of his father) She disappeared mysteriously, and was supposed to have been spirited away by Brims, and her body concealed in the castle, which consequently had the reputation of being haunted Patrick left the country, and is said to have enlisted in the Guards
- 3 JAMES of Holbornhead This property, which was disponed to him by his father, he sold to Robert Sinclair of Geise.   4 GUSTAVUS, a merchant in Leith
- 1 SIDNEY, eldest daughter   2 JEAN or JANET, m first, Benj Dunbar, yr of Hempriggs
- 3. ELIZABETH, married John McKay, second of Strathy

VI. JOHN SINCLAIR OF ULBSTER, sometime younger of Brims, married Henrietta, daughter of Geo Brodie of Brodie, and died in 1736 He had—

1 GEORGE, his successor
2. JAMES of Harpsdale He m first, Marjory, d of David Sinclair of Southdun, secondly, Mally Sutherland of Spinningdale, and thirdly, Katharine, daughter of Alex Sinclair of Lybster, and died *s p* m   3 CAPT JOHN, married Elizabeth, widow of John Wilmer.
1 ÆMILIA, married John Sutherland of Forse

VII GEORGE SINCLAIR OF ULBSTER married Janet, daughter of Lord Strathnaver. He died in 1776, having had—

1 JOHN, who succeeded
1. HELEN, married Alex. Campbell of Barcaldine, whose daughter Jane married James, Earl of Caithness in 1784   2 MARY, married James Homerigg of Gamalshiels.
3. JANET, married Wm Baillie, Lord Polkemmet of the Court of Session

VIII. SIR JOHN SINCLAIR OF ULBSTER was born in 1754, and in 1788 was created a baronet, with remainder in default of male issue to the male issue of his daughters.

THE SINCLAIRS OF KIRK AND MYRELANDHORN *

I. HENRY SINCLAIR IN CANISBAY in 1592 got a charter from the Earl of Caithness of part of Kirk and Myrelandhorn In 1582 there is mention in the Earl of Caithness' testament of Henry Sinclair, his servitor, who may have been the Henry Sinclair of 1592. Henry Sinclair of Kirk had two sons—

1 JAMES   2 DAVID in Olrig

II. JAMES SINCLAIR got a charter from his father in 1627, and was succeeded by his brother

III. DAVID SINCLAIR, only lawful brother, got a precept of *clare constat* in 1667, and was succeeded by his son John

IV JOHN SINCLAIR got a disposition from his father in 1669, and a charter of *novo-damus* from the Bishop in 1680. John Sinclair was "servitor to Sir Wm. Sharp, Keeper of the Signet," and he afterwards appears to have been a merchant in Edinburgh

In 1643 Wm Sinclair, elder, merchant in Thurso, got a wadset from James Sinclair; and had a son Thomas, who again had a son William. They adjudged Kirk and Myreland, and in 1680 Wm Sinclair disponed these lands to John Sinclair, who sold them to John Sinclair of Barrock Nisbet mentions the arms of "Thomas, lawful son to Wm Sinclair, merchant in Thurso, of the family of Caithness" These may have been the same Sinclairs who apprised Kirk and Myreland, and who may have been connected with the Sinclairs descended from Henry Sinclair in Canisbay, who got the lands from the Earl of Caithness.

THE SINCLAIRS OF LYBSTER, REAY *

Before the rise of the Sinclairs of Lybster in Latheron, there were Sinclairs of Lybster in Reay, dating from at least 1636 Their origin is uncertain, but it is conjectured that they may have been the descendants of Henry Sinclair, who died about 1614, a natural son of John, Master of Caithness, and who got from his brother, the Earl of Caithness, a

---

* Henderson

THE SINCLAIRS OF LYBSTER, REAY

wadset of Downreay and part of Lybster. Or possibly this family may have been of the Sinclairs of Dunbeath, who held Downreay and other lands in Reay.

In 1636 there is mention of David Sinclair of Lybster, and in 1638 of Wm. Sinclair of Lybster, who then appears as witness to a deed by Oliver Sinclair of Spittal, son of Richard of Brims, and grandson of Wm. Sinclair of Dunbeath. David and William were probably brothers, each inheriting a portion of Lybster. William had a daughter Margaret, who as heir to her father executed a renunciation in 1648, in favour of her cousin, James Sinclair of Lybster.

DAVID SINCLAIR OF LYBSTER had two lawful sons—

1. JAMES, fiar of Lybster in 1637, who died between 1648 and 1661. He married Margaret Macleod, and had—
    1. DAVID, who is mentioned down to 1670.
        1. BARBARA, married Donald Campbell, Elder in Thurso
2 ROBERT, who with consent of his brother James, in 1640, married Barbara, daughter of George Sinclair in Downreay, the brother of Richard Sinclair of Brims, and son of Wm Sinclair of Dunbeath

THE SINCLAIRS OF ACHINGALE AND NEWTON.*

I WILLIAM SINCLAIR, first of Achingale and Newton, was the son of Alex. Sinclair of Sixpenny, who is thought to be identical with Alex, eldest son of Wm. Sinclair of Hoy, of whom there is otherwise no particular account. Alex. Sinclair married in 1697 Beatrice, only daughter of Geo Sinclair, second son of Jas Sinclair, first of Lybster, and she and her husband, on the supposition that the latter was son of Wm. of Hoy, stood in the relation of cousins. By this marriage Alex. Sinclair had several sons and daughters, among whom were—

1. WILLIAM, mentioned in 1733 as second son.   2. FRANCIS.   3 SIDNEY
1 MARGARET, eldest daughter, married in 1722 Alex. Calder of Achingale

II. WILLIAM SINCLAIR OF ACHINGALE married in 1738 Elizabeth, daughter of Sir James Sinclair of Dunbeath. Sir James had acquired the right of reversion of the wadsets of Achingale held by the Calders; and about 1738 or 1740 he had redeemed the lands, which he thereafter sold to Wm Sinclair, by whom a Crown charter was expede in 1752. Wm. Sinclair had a son and two daughters—

1 ALEXANDER   1 JANET   2. MARGARET

III. ALEXANDER SINCLAIR OF ACHINGALE, who was a merchant in Jamaica, succeeded his father, and was infeft in 1768. He died without issue

IV JANET SINCLAIR succeeded her brother, and died unmarried in 1783

V. MARGARET SINCLAIR succeeded her sister, and married in 1798 Alex. Sinclair, a son of Alex. Sinclair, tenant in Houstry, Halkirk, who had been for some time in Jamaica. In 1804 they sold the lands to Wm Sinclair of Freswick for £7,000. There was no issue of the marriage, and the family of Sinclair of Achingale is presumably extinct

THE SINCLAIRS OF HOY AND OLDFIELD.*

I. John, Master of Berriedale, granted in 1630 a wadset of Hoy to one WILLIAM SINCLAIR, who held also the lands of Cairdscroft, Oldfield, and Hallowtoft, near Thurso

This William Sinclair is a different person from William Sinclair of Hoy and Scotscalder, and is probably "William Sinclair in Thurso East" who is mentioned in the proceedings against the Earl of Caithness and others for the forcible abduction in 1668 of William McKay of Scourie. By his wife Katharine Anguson William Sinclair had two sons—

    1 JAMES   2 WILLIAM

II. JAMES, the eldest son, was *fiar* of Hoy in 1676, and *in* Hoy in 1700. He married Elizabeth Sinclair, who in 1730 is described as relict of James Sinclair of Oldfield. James Sinclair of Hoy and his wife disponed the wadset of these lands to Sir George Sinclair of Clyth, through whom it came into the hands of his nephew William Sinclair of Hoy and Scotscalder.

III. The second son of William Sinclair of Hoy and Oldfield was WILLIAM SINCLAIR, Commissary of Caithness, who married Elizabeth, eldest daughter of James Innes of Sandside. He had two sons—

    1 WILLIAM, who got from his grandfather in 1690 a disposition to Oldfield, Cairdscroft, and Hallowtoft, which he disponed to his brother in 1729.
    2 ROBERT, Rector of Bulfen, in Essex, who in 1731 disponed Oldfield, Cairdscroft, and Hallowtoft to William Innes of Sandside.

THE SINCLAIRS OF BORLUM, TOFTKEMP, AND THURA *

There is in the South or "Murkle Aisle" of the parish church of Thurso a mural inscription on the north-west wall in the following terms :—"This is the burial place of James Sinclair of Borlum, and here lyes James Sinclair, his eldest son, and his spouse Elizabeth Innes, who left behind them the Rev. Mr John Sinclair, who was Rector of [James] interred in Leckpatrick, nigh Strabane in Ireland, 1665." "Here lyes Isabel Sinclair, who was married to the Rev Geo Anderson, Minister of Halkirk; and Elizabeth Sinclair, married to John Farquhi, Bailze of Thurso, and Margaret Sinclair, spouse to Geo Sinclair in Ulgrimbeg."

Who James Sinclair of Borlum was, is very uncertain. He may have been a grandson of William Sinclair of Dunbeath, to whom Brubster, Brims, Toftkemp, and Thura belonged, Borlum's name occurs in common with all these places in the county records from 1624 to 1646, or he may have been a son of James Sinclair, first of Murkle, and brother of John Sinclair, first of Assery. There are numerous incidents connecting the descendants of Assery and Borlum. If of the Dunbeath family, he was probably a son of George Sinclair of Downreay, and it is known that there were transactions between James Sinclair and the descendants of William Sinclair of Dunbeath in relation to lands which belonged to the family. In particular, there is mention of a renunciation of rights held by Borlum over Spittal, granted by him in 1649 to John Sinclair of Brims, grandson of Dunbeath, which instrument, if extant, would perhaps throw light on his history.

I. JAMES SINCLAIR, FIRST OF BORLUM, who was killed by Neil McKay between 1648–59, had four sons and a daughter Jean.

    1 JAMES of Wester-Brims.
    2 CAPTAIN ALEXANDER, First of Bowertower, and afterwards of Telstane, married Isabel, daughter of John Cunningham of Brownhill, and had—
        1 JOHN (1683)   2 JAMES

* Henderson

THE SINCLAIRS OF BORLUM, TOFTKEMP, AND THURA.

    1. KATHARINE, Lady Dun, wife first, of William Sinclair of Dun, and thereafter of Alex. Sutherland of Ausdale.
    2. ———, married John Fullerton.
    In 1666 there is on record an inhibition at the instance of John, Alex., George, Elizabeth, and Margaret Sinclair as "lawful heirs" of Alex. Sinclair of Telstane, but without illustration of the relationship.
3. MAJOR WILLIAM had paternal disposition of Thura in 1651. He served in the German wars and fought for the Sinclairs at Altimarlach. He married Margaret, daughter of John Doull of Thurster, and had—
    1. JOHN of Thura, who disponed the estate in 1702 to his brother.
    2. RICHARD of Thura, who married Elizabeth, daughter of George Sinclair of Assery, and had a son—
        1. CAPTAIN JOHN SINCLAIR, who in 1754 sold Thura.
    3. JAMES, of whom there is no further account.   1. JEAN.
4. ROBERT, had a daughter Elizabeth, who married Donald Henderson in Sibster.
1. JEAN, married in 1658 Alex. Steill, who is designed as "servitor to the Earl of Caithness." Her brothers, Captain Alexander and Major William, were parties to the contract of marriage, and her tocher was 1,000 merks.

II. JAMES SINCLAIR OF WESTER-BRIMS married Elspeth or Elizabeth Innes, probably of the Inneses of Thursater and Wester-Brims. He died before 1659, leaving a son—
    1. JOHN, minister of Leckpatrick in Ireland, and several daughters, of whom—
    1. ISABEL, married the Rev. Geo. Anderson of Halkirk.
    2. JEAN, married Alex. Sinclair, notary public in Thurso.
    3. ———, married, first, Alex. Abernethy in Swordale; and, secondly, Alex. Mulliken in Papigo, chamberlain to the Earl of Caithness.

CHAPTER VII

BARONETICAL BRANCHES

MEY

I. SIR JAMES SINCLAIR OF MEY, during his father's lifetime was styled of Canisbay, and so appears in charters of 1635 and 1636 On the 2nd June, 1631, he was created a baronet, with remainder, "*haeredibus suis masculis et assignatis quibuscunque*" In 1645 he granted John, his second son, a bond over Stangergill He married Elizabeth, daughter of Patrick, Lord Lindores, and died in 1662. He had five sons and two daughters—

    1 SIR WILLIAM of Canisbay and Mey, his successor
    2 JOHN of Stangergill, who died without issue
    3 ROBERT of Durran, ancestor to the present Earl of Caithness
    4 GEORGE of Olrig
    1 ANNE, married George, first Earl of Cromarty
    2 ELIZABETH, married her cousin, William Sinclair of Dunbeath.

II SIR WILLIAM SINCLAIR, BARONET, OF CANISBAY AND MEY, was infeft in Mey in 1662 as heir to his father, on a precept of *clare constat* by the Bishop of Caithness He married Margaret, second daughter of George, second Earl of Seaforth, and had—

    1 SIR JAMES, his heir   2 GEORGE
    1. ELIZABETH, married John Sinclair of Rattar
    2 BARBARA, married David Sinclair of Freswick   3 MARY

The estate was so involved in debt by Sir William, that after his death it was judicially sold by his creditors in 1694

III SIR JAMES SINCLAIR, BARONET, OF MEY, married first, it is said, Frances, daughter of Sir John Towers of that Ilk and of Innerleith; and secondly, Jean, daughter of Francis Sinclair of Northfield. By the first marriage Sir James had a son and a daughter—

    1 SIR JAMES, his heir
    1 BARBARA, who married Francis Sinclair of Stirkoke.

Sir James had also a natural son—
    JOHN, to whom he conveyed a wadset of Hollandmake

The Mey estates had been bought by his cousin Viscount Tarbet, afterwards Earl of Cromarty, who in 1698 reconveyed them to the family by a disposition and deed of entail "*animo donandi*" in favour of James, eldest son of Sir James, and other heirs.

IV SIR JAMES SINCLAIR OF MEY married Mary, daughter of James, Lord Duffus, and had—

    1. SIR JAMES   2 WILLIAM   3 KENNETH
    1 MARGARET

V SIR JAMES SINCLAIR OF MEY obtained a Crown charter in 1740 He married Margaret, daughter of John Sinclair of Barrock, and had—

1. SIR JOHN.
2. WILLIAM, married Elizabeth, daughter of Richard Sinclair, merchant in Thurso, second son of Alexander Sinclair, last of Dun. He had—
    1. JOHN, Captain in the 79th Foot, fell at Waterloo, 1815.
    1. WILLIAMINA, died unmarried.

VI. SIR JOHN SINCLAIR OF MEY was served heir of taillie and provision in 1763. He married Charlotte, second daughter of Eric, Lord Duffus, and had issue—
  1. SIR JAMES, his successor.
  1. MARGARET, who married the Rev. William Leslie of Darkland.

VII. SIR JAMES SINCLAIR, seventh baronet and eighth in descent from George of Mey, Chancellor of Caithness, was served heir to his father in 1785; and on the death of John V., 49th Earl of Caithness, was served in May, 1790, as nearest and lawful heir-male of William St. Clair, second Earl of Caithness of the line of St. Clair, and thereafter took the dignity of Earl of Caithness.

DUNBEATH.*

I. THIS baronetcy was created by letters patent dated 12th October, 1704, in favour of JAMES SINCLAIR, fourth son of William Sinclair, second of Latheron, etc.: "ejusque haeredes masculos in perpetuum." On his father's death James Sinclair got from his mother a renunciation of her liferent of Dunbeath, at that time worth £200 per annum, and then he ejected her from possession, a step which led to a complaint at her instance to the Privy Council. Next he bought up her family provisions and the debts due by his brother; and finally, in 1720, he adjudged Dunbeath for £48,000 scots, and was infeft in 1722. In the same year his mother's liferent ceased by her death, and he entered into possession of Dunbeath. In 1704 he was created a baronet, and he died in the Abbey in 1742.

Sir James was violent and unscrupulous in character. In 1734, as Baron of Dunbeath, he held a Criminal Court, and adjudged one William Sinclair to death for the crime of theft; but the proceedings were quashed, and Sinclair having raised an action against Sir James, obtained large damages. In 1739 one George Sutherland raised an action for wrongous imprisonment against Sir James, in which the latter was subjected to fine and damages, and declared incapable of public trust in time coming. He was twice married, first, to Isabel, daughter of Sir Archibald Muir of Thornton, Provost of Edinburgh, by whom he had—
  1. SIR WILLIAM, second Bart.
  2. ALEXANDER, to whom his brother Benjamin was served heir.
  3. SIR BENJAMIN, fourth Bart.   4. ARCHIBALD, died in Jamaica, unmarried.
  1. MARGARET, married William Sinclair of Achingale and Newton.

He married, secondly, and shortly before his death, Isabel, daughter of John Lumsden, shipmaster in Aberdeen, and had—
  1. JEAN, married Robert Campbell (linen draper), Abbeyhill, Edinburgh. As wife of Lieut. Robert Campbell, —— Regt., she was served heir in Keiss, etc., to her mother, Dame Isabel Lumsden, wife of Sir Jas. Sinclair, 19th December, 1777.

In 1721 Murdoch Campbell in Brubster married Janet, a daughter of Sir James, probably a natural child, as she is not mentioned in the family pedigree.

* Hendrson and Burke.

II. SIR WILLIAM SINCLAIR, second Bart. of Dunbeath and Keiss, succeeded his father. Keiss was acquired by the Dunbeath family through a transaction with Lord Breadalbane, embracing the discharge of the apprisings against the Earldom. As heir-apparent to Dunbeath, Sir William sold his interest therein in 1752 to William Sinclair of Freswick, and in 1753-54 he made up a title. Having fallen into pecuniary difficulties, he sold Keiss to "Ulbster" for £7,000 sterling. He married Charlotte, second daughter of Sir James and Dame Elizabeth Dunbar of Hempriggs, and had two sons and a daughter—

1. CAPTAIN ALEXANDER SINCLAIR, died *vita patris*.
2. KENNEDY MUIR SINCLAIR, of whom there are no particulars, but it is presumed he died without issue.

CAPTAIN ALEXANDER SINCLAIR married Elizabeth, daughter of Eric Sutherland, eldest son of Kenneth, third Lord Duffus, and died before his father, leaving an only son, who succeeded his grandfather, as

III. SIR ALEXANDER SINCLAIR, third Bart. He went to the West Indies, where he perished at sea on his passage from Jamaica to Halifax in 1786. He is not known to have left any issue.

IV. SIR BENJAMIN SINCLAIR OF STEMSTER, third son of Sir James, took up the title on the death of his grandnephew Sir Alexander. He had been served heir to his brother Alexander, and in 1740 received a paternal disposition to Stemster, but all his life he was in reduced circumstances. He married Jean, youngest daughter of John Sinclair of Assery, and had—

1. SIR JOHN, fifth Bart.   1. ISABELLA, died unmarried.
2. HELEN, married Dr. Watson, head of the Medical Board at Madras.

V. SIR JOHN SINCLAIR, fifth Bart., took up the style of "Sinclair of Dunbeath." After serving as lieutenant in the Sutherland Fencibles, he went to India where he attained the rank of Major-General. Returning to England he died there in 1842. He married, first, Miss Notley at Madras in 1803. She died in 1806 and had—

1. JOHN NOTLEY, who died young.
1. JANE, married in 1822 Patrick Wallace of the H.E.I. Co.'s Naval Service.

Sir John married, secondly, Sarah Charlotte Carter, who died in 1867 without issue, at the age of 65.

The fifth baronet was the last heir-male of Sir James Sinclair in the direct line, and on his death the succession opened to collaterals, the nearest being John Sinclair, fifth of Barrock, representative of George Sinclair, first thereof, uncle to the first baronet.

VI. SIR JOHN SINCLAIR OF BARROCK married in July, 1821, Margaret, youngest daughter of John Learmonth of Edinburgh, and had—

1. JOHN, Captain 39th Madras N.I., killed while gallantly defending the left wing 3rd Regiment Hyderabad Contingent at the capture of Jhansie, 5th April, 1858, and was unmarried.
2. ALEXANDER YOUNG, Lieut.-Colonel in the Bombay Army; died at Jeypore, Bombay, 3rd February, 1871. In 1861 he married Margaret Crichton, daughter of James Alston, and left two sons and three daughters—
    1. JOHN ROSE GEORGE, present baronet, born 10th August, 1864.
    2. NORMAN ALEXANDER, born 29th July, 1869.
    1. MARGARET, married 4th November, 1884, George F. S. Sinclair, second son of Sir J. G. Tollemache Sinclair, third Bart. of Ulbster.

2. EDITH GRACE, died 1869.   3. MAUDE, died 1869.
Mrs. Sinclair resides at 11, St. George's Road, S.W.

3. GEORGE, born 1826, retired Captain in the Bengal Army. Married in 1859 Agnes (†1876), daughter of John Learmonth of the Dean, Edinburgh, and died 23rd March, 1871, leaving by her—

1. JOHN, born 1860; educated at Edinburgh Academy, at Wellington College, and at Royal Military College, Sandhurst; formerly Captain 5th Lancers; served with the Soudan Expedition, 1885 (medal with clasp); was assistant private secretary to the Secretary of State for War (Right Hon. H. E. Campbell-Bannerman), August, 1892, to June, 1895; unsuccessfully contested Ayr District, 1886; sat as M.P. for Dumbartonshire (L.) 1892-95, when he sustained an electional reverse. Captain Sinclair represented East Finsbury on the first County Council, and at the commencement of 1897 was elected M.P. for Forfarshire. He was aide-de-camp to the Earl of Aberdeen when Lord-Lieutenant of Ireland, and recently was attached to the staff of His Excellency the Viceroy of Canada.
Residence—101, Mount St., W.   *Clubs*—Brook's, Army and Navy.
2. CHARLES GEORGE, born 1862.   3. GEORGE HENRY, born 1866.

Sir John died 21st April, 1873, and was buried at Holyrood. His three sons were gentlemen of high character and promise, and their death in the prime of life occasioned much general regret. He was succeeded by his grandson

VII. SIR JOHN ROSE GEORGE SINCLAIR, formerly lieutenant 4th Battalion Cheshire Regiment; is Vice-Lieutenant for Caithness, and Lieut.-Colonel 1st Caithness Artillery Volunteers; married 7th June, 1885, Elizabeth, daughter of Lieut.-Colonel William Matthew Dunbar, one of H.M. gentlemen-at-arms.

Seat—Barrock House, Wick.   *Town Residence*—11, St. George's Road, S.W.   *Club*—Scottish.
Arms : See Armoury.

ULBSTER.*

I. JOHN SINCLAIR, who succeeded to Ulbster in 1776, was the only son of George Sinclair, heritable sheriff of Caithness, by Janet, daughter of William, Lord Strathnaver, and sister of William, Master of Strathnaver, the 17th Earl of Sutherland. John Sinclair, the celebrated statistician of Scotland, on 14th February, 1786, was created a baronet with remainder in default of his own male issue, to the male issue of his daughters respectively. A more complete notice of Sir John appears later on. He married, first, 26th March, 1776, Sarah, daughter of Alex. Maitland of Stoke Newington, by whom he had one surviving daughter—

1. JANET, married to Sir James Colquhoun, Bart.

He married, secondly, 6th March, 1788, Diana, daughter of Alexander, first Lord Macdonald, by whom (who died 22nd April, 1845) he had—

2. GEORGE, next baronet.
3. ALEXANDER, born 17th June, 1794; died unmarried 9th Aug., 1877; formerly in H.E.I.C.S.
4. JOHN, born 20th August, 1797; died 22nd May, 1875; M.A., in holy orders; Archdeacon of Middlesex, and Vicar of Kensington.
5. ARCHIBALD, born 20th September, 1801; died 1st June, 1859; captain R.N., an officer of high repute, and much and very generally esteemed. Captain Sinclair founded the Naval and Military Club in Scotland, and was the author of a popular volume of naval reminiscences.

* Burke, Debrett, etc.

BARONETICAL BRANCHES.

6. WILLIAM MACDONALD, born 4th September, 1804; died 1878; in holy orders, Rector of Pulborough, Sussex; married, first, December 28th, 1837, Helen (died 1842), daughter of William Ellice, and by her he had issue—
    1. ALEXANDER EDWARD, born in 1839.
    2. WALTER, born 15th April, 1841; died 1887; married 4th February, 1874, Kathleen, daughter of Henry Dickenson of Ashton Keynes, and had issue—
        GLADYS MURIEL.

The Rev. W. M. Sinclair married, second, in 1846, Sophia, daughter of the Rev. James Tripp, Rector of Spofforth, and by her he had—

  3. WILLIAM MACDONALD, The Ven., born 1850; educated at Balliol College, Oxford (M.A., 1874; B.D., 1888; D.D., 1892); is Archdeacon of London, Canon of St. Paul's, Chaplain-in-ordinary to H.M. the Queen, and Examining Chaplain to the Bishop of London. *Residence*—Chapter House, St. Paul's Cathedral, E.C. *Club*—Athenæum.
  4. JAMES.
  5. JOHN STEWART, The Rev., born 1853; educated at Oriel College, Oxford (M.A., 1878); is Vicar of St. Dionis', Fulham, and a J.P.; married, 1893, Clara Sophia, daughter of J. Dearman Birchall, J.P., of Bowden Hall, Gloucestershire, and has issue living—
        RONALD SUTHERLAND BROOK, born 1894.
        Residence—Arundel House, Fulham, S.W. *Club*—Oxford and Cambridge.
  6. HUGH MONTGOMERIE, born 1855; is Major R.E.; was D.A.A.G., N.E. District, 1892-95. *Clubs*—Junior United Service, Wellington.
  7. HELEN SOPHIA, married, 1880, the Rev. George Edmund Hasell, Rector of Aikton. *Residence*—Aikton Hall, Wigton, Cumberland.
  8. JANET MARY.

7. JAMES, H.E.I.C.S., born 18th November, 1805; died 20th June, 1826.
8. GODFREY, born in 1812; died at his residence in Edinburgh in June, 1890. Accidentally lamed in infancy, in spite of vast personal strength, he was never able to take an active part in life.
9. ELIZABETH DIANA, died 30th May, 1863.
10. MARGARET, died 5th August, 1879.
11. JULIA, married 13th November, 1824, to George, 4th Earl of Glasgow.
12. CATHERINE, distinguished as an authoress; died 6th August, 1864.
13. HELEN, married 10th August, 1826, Stair Stewart of Glasserton and Whysgill, N.B., and died 25th April, 1845.

The Right Hon. Sir John Sinclair, P.C., who was Cashier of the Excise of Scotland, died 21st December, 1835. He was offered a peerage, which he refused.

II. SIR GEORGE SINCLAIR OF ULBSTER, M.P., was born on the 23rd August, 1790. He married, 1st May, 1816, Lady Catherine Camilla, sister of Lionel, 6th Earl of Dysart, and had—

1. DUDLEY, died unmarried at Auckland, New Zealand, in 1844.
2. JOHN GEORGE TOLLEMACHE, present baronet, born 8th November, 1825.
3. GRANVILLE, died in 1833.
4. EMILIA MAGDALEN LOUISA, married, first, on 12th August, 1837, Henry Tollemache, which marriage was dissolved by the Court of Session in Scotland in 1841, and since also by the Court for Divorce in London; and second, to Major John Power, son of the late P. Power, of Bellevue, County Waterford.
5. ADELAIDE MARY WENTWORTH, married in August, 1845, George, second son of John James Hope Johnston, of Annandale, M.P.
6. OLIVIA SOPHIA, died recently [1895].

SIR GEORGE, died on the 9th October, 1868.

III. SIR JOHN GEORGE TOLLEMACHE SINCLAIR, second son of the preceding, succeeded his father. He was formerly a Page of Honour to Queen Adelaide, and

Lieutenant Scots Fusileer Guards; is Vice-Lieutenant and a D.L. for Caithness; sat as M.P. for same (L.) 1869-85. Married 22nd November, 1853, Emma Isabella Harriet (whom he divorced 4th July, 1878), daughter of the late William Standish Standish, of Duxbury Park, Lancashire, and Cocken Hall, Durham. Issue—

1. CLARENCE GRANVILLE, born 3rd April, 1858; died 1895; D.L. for Caithness, late Lieutenant Scots Guards, and Major 2nd Volunteer Battalion Seaforth Highlanders. He married in 1889 Mabel (died 1890), daughter of the late Mahlon Sands, of New York. Issue ARCHIBALD HENRY MACDONALD, born in 1890.
2. GEORGE FELIX STANDISH, born 1861; formerly Lieutenant 3rd Battalion Black Watch (Royal Highlanders); formerly Captain 2nd Volunteer Battalion Seaforth Highlanders (Ross-shire Buffs, the Duke of Albany's). Married, 1884, Margaret, only sister of Sir John Sinclair, VIIth Bart. of Dunbeath. Issue—
    1. ALGERNON RONALD TOLLEMACHE, born in 1886.
    2. DOROTHY EMMA OLIVIA, born in 1885.
    3. OLIVE MARY CAMILLA, born 1892.
    Residence—Thurso Castle. *Club*—Bachelors'.
3. AMY CAMILLA, married 8th July, 1874, John Henry Fullerton Udny, of Udny Castle, Aberdeen.
4. NINA MARY ADELAIDE, married 22nd July, 1881, Major-General Owen Lewis Cope Williams, of Temple House, Bucks, M.P. for Great Marlow.
5. CONSTANCE, died in 1861.

Seat—Thurso Castle. *Town Residence*—14, King Street, St. James', S.W. *Club*—Travellers'. Five generations of this family have represented the Earldom of Caithness in the Imperial Parliament.

ARMS—See Armoury.

CHAPTER VIII.

THE LONGFORMACUS LINE.

LORDS OF LONGFORMACUS.*

LONGFORMACUS is situate in Berwickshire, and the Longformacus Line of Sinclairs has been thought to begin with one GREGORIE ST. CLAIR, who is enumerated amongst the gentry of the shire as swearing allegiance at Berwick to Edward I. of England, 28th August, 1296. He is thought to have been a son of the first Roslin on record, and upon account of his appearing with the gentry of Berwick, in which county the lands of Longformacus lie, he is taken to be brother to Henry St. Clair, second of Roslin, and the relationship of this line with the Roslins is presently acknowledged by Henry St. Clair, Lord of Roslin, Earl of Orkney. The seal of Gregorie de St. Clair was appended to his declaration of homage. There are further references to Berwickshire St. Clairs about the same period : John de St. Clair renders homage under seal in 1296 ; August 25-28, same finds him one of the jurors on an Inquisition at Berwick, and on the 3rd September, same, a writ issues to the Sheriff at Berwick to restore his lands to John de St. Clair. On 22nd August, 1301, John de St. Clair receives at Glasgow 100s. for the Earl of Dunbar ; and William de St. Clair, Esq., of Berwick, renders homage in 1312.†

I. JAMES ST. CLAIR is the first on record of Longformacus (charter 7th June, 1384-93)‡. He is probably identical with the James de St. Clair, brother-uterine of Margaret, Countess of Mar and Angus, who witnesses a charter by that lady dated 12th August, 1381. Nisbet states: "When and how they had those lands I cannot be positive; but for certain they had them in the reign of Robert II. from the Earl of March. I notice a charter from King Robert III. in the fourth year of his reign confirming a charter of George Dunbar, Earl of March, granted to James St. Clair of Longformacus of the same lands lying within the Earldom of March and Sheriffdom of Berwick. I have also seen a charter wherein *Henricus de Sancto Claro comes Orcadiae et dominus de Roslyn*, firmly and faithfully obliges himself to his well-beloved cousin—*carissimo consanguineo suo, Jacobo de Sancto Claro, Domino de Longformacus*—to infeft him in a twenty merk land." The obligation is dated at Roslin the 22nd June, 1384. He and his son John were made prisoners in 1402 at the Battle of Homildon Hill.§ His son

II. JAMES ST. CLAIR got from Henry II., Earl of Orkney, *Dominus de Sancto Claro, et de Vallis de Nyth*, an annuity of twenty merks, to be uplifted out of the lands of Lenny, dated the 20th February, 1418. Douglas cites a charter of January, 1418, as also having reference to this Longformacus.

III. DAVID SINCLAIR (charter 8th April, 1448‡) is found thus referred to in the Ex. Rolls, 1455 : " Luchirmacus in ward by reason of the death of David Sinclair," and 1456 : " And the £15 from the lands of Luchirmacus in ward as above." He was evidently succeeded by a son similarly named.

---
* Nisbet, etc. † Bain's Calendar of Documents. ‡ Douglas' Peerage. § Hay.

IV. DAVID St CLAIR (charters 7th February, 1463, and 6th February, 1477*) He married Elizabeth Murray She is probably identical with Elizabeth Sinclare, spouse of the late Patrick Dunbar, who in 1459 receives £20 On 9th July, 1460, King James gives "til oure louede cosingnace Elyzabet Syngclare" £20 life annuity from Haddington customs In 1460–62 Elizabeth Sinclare is paid £40 for charge of the Princess Mary, and in 1480 the payment of her pension terminates Upon his resignation his eldest son and apparent heir

V. JAMES SINCLAIR obtained a new charter of the barony of Longformacus from Alex Duke of Albany, Earl of March, Lord of Annandale and the Isle of Man, dated at the Castle of Dunbar 12th October, 1472. He married (charter 21st May, 1491*) Isabel Howieson

VI. ALEXANDER SINCLAIR (charter 11th October, 1502*) is named in 1503 as son to Lochormacus. By Mariote Forman, his spouse, he had a son and heir

VII. JAMES SINCLARE, who obtained a charter of confirmation 4th January, 1505–6

VIII JOHN SINCLAIR of Longformacus was cited on 23rd August, 1567, to appear on the 31st idem

IX MATHEW SINCLAIR (charters 2nd September, 1558 , 8th February, 1574*) of Longformacus is stated to have been served heir to his father JAMES in 1553 On 12th February, 1571, at Jedburgh, he subscribed a band for pursuing Fauneyhirst On the 17th May, 1588, he became caution in 1,000 merks for Katharine Lauder, Lady of Swinton. He married Elizabeth, daughter of Sir John Swinton of that Ilk, and had four sons—†

    1 SIR ROBERT, next of Longformacus
    2. GEORGE (charter 1604*), reputed progenitor of the Stevensons
    3 JAMES, mentioned 11th August, 1603, as third brother of the Laird of Longformacus He married Elizabeth Home (charter 2nd January, 1609*), and was father of
        SIR JAMES SINCLAIR of Kinnaird, Fifeshire, who being cited (23–25th February, 1680) for absence from King's host in June last, pled sickness, which defence was found relevant He is probably identical with Sir John Sinclair, designated of Lochend, who, 14th July, 1683, pursues Bailie Kelly in Dunbar for oppression of the hedges in not permitting their own men to ship corn. He heired his uncle Thomas, and was, 27th January, 1686, at suit of Sir Robert St Clair of Stevenson for payment of a jointure to Anna Foulis, Bilbster's widow
    4 THOMAS SINCLAIR of Bilpster, Caithness, Master of the Horse to George, 43rd Earl of Caithness, Lord Sinclair of Berriedale He is buried in the Sinclair Aisle, Wick Churchyard, where is an inscription recording parentalia, offices, arms, etc , and the phrases "Remember death " "Regard! Good service will get good reward! A B M R M " He married Anna Foulis, and died 26th October, 1607, aged 42

X. SIR ROBERT SINCLAIR (charter 14th May, 1609*) of Longformacus prefers a complaint 23rd April, 1607. He is probably the Robert Sinclair, writer, 18th August, 1587, appearing as proc for George Gordon of Candidyen On 13th December, 1589, caution is taken for Robert Sinclair, writer to the Privy Council, that he shall deliver the House of Blanse, and who on 28th January next thereafter recites that he has liferent in gift from the King on 1st August preceding, of all lands belonging to David Sinclair of Blanse. By Margaret, sister of Sir Archibald Douglas of Whittinghame, he had issue—

    1. JAMES, next of Longformacus
    2. REV JOHN, in Muirtown, minister of Spott (A M St Andrew's, 27th July, 1616), married Marion Stewart, and had a son—
        JAMES

* Douglas Peerage   † History of Caithness, Notes by T Sinclair

XI. JAMES SINCLAIR of Longformacus granted a wadset of Muirtown to his brother the Rev John Sinclair Issue—
>ROBERT, next of Longformacus, created a baronet

BARONETS OF LONGFORMACUS *

I. ROBERT SINCLAIR, advocate before the Court of Session, son of James Sinclair, eleventh of Longformacus, was created a baronet of Nova Scotia, 10th December, 1664, with remainder to his heirs-male whatsoever He married, first, Elizabeth, daughter and heiress of Douglas of Blackerstone in the Merse, by whom he had—

1. SIR JOHN, who succeeded
2. GEORGE, married Jean, daughter of George Purves of Ewford. Issue—
    1 ROBERT, married Lilias Anderson Issue—
        SIR JOHN, sixth Bart.
    2 GEORGE, died *s p*   3 EUPHEME, died *s p*
3. SIR ARCHIBALD, knight, died *s p* He was M P for Kirkwall, Orkney, in the Scottish Parliament from 1690-1702, and was author of "Some Thoughts upon the Present State of Affairs," 1703, 4to He was Procurator in defence for the Rev James Lyon, of Kirkwall, 12th June, 1710
4. MARGARET, married William Home of Linthill.
5. A daughter, married Sir Jas Cockburn of Ryslor
6. A daughter, married Captain Urquhart.
7. A daughter, married Francis Montgomery of Giffen.

Sir Robert married, secondly, Margaret, daughter of William Alexander, Viscount Canada, eldest son to the Earl of Stirling, and had by her—

8 JEAN, married John, Master of Bargeny   9 ANNE, married John Swinton of that Ilk

Sir Robert died in 1678, and was succeeded by his eldest son

II. SIR JOHN SINCLAIR, who married Jean, daughter and heiress of Sir John Towers of Innerleith, and dying about 1689, was succeeded by his only son

III SIR ROBERT SINCLAIR, who died in 1725 or 1726. This gentleman married Christian, daughter of the Right Hon Adam Cockburn of Ormistoun, Lord Justice-clerk, by whom he had—

1 SIR JOHN, his successor   2 SIR HARRY, fifth baronet
3 SUSAN, died unmarried   4 JEAN, married Chas Gilmour of Craigmillar.
5 ANNE, died unmarried   6 CHRISTIAN, married John Inglis

IV. SIR JOHN SINCLAIR, married Sidney, daughter of Robert Johnston of Hilton, but dying without issue in 1764, was succeeded by his brother

V SIR HARRY SINCLAIR, at whose decease without issue in 1768 the succession opened to his second cousin

VI SIR JOHN SINCLAIR, grandson of George Sinclair, second son of the first baronet This gentleman married Elizabeth, daughter of Charles Allan. He was a writer in reduced circumstances, resident in the Canongate, Edinburgh, where he died 7th January, 1798, and is said to have been succeeded by

VII SIR JOHN SINCLAIR, of whom there is no further account

Arms—See Armoury

---

* Burke , Douglas, etc

BARONETS OF STEVENSON.*

I. JOHN SINCLAIR, whose paternal grandmother was of the family of Longformacus, and who is himself said to belong paternally to that family as son of George (charter 1604), second son of Mathew Sinclair of Longformacus, amassed a considerable fortune as a merchant at Edinburgh, of which metropolis he was Lord Provost, and purchased the lands and barony of Stevenson, in the counties of Edinburgh and Haddington, in 1624. He founded a Sinclair Society about 1620. A Scottish song entitled "The Clouting of the Cauldron," was made about this baronet He was created a *Baronet of Nova Scotia* 18th January, 1636 By his wife Marion, daughter of McMath of Newbyres, he had (besides younger issue)—

    JOHN, who died *vita patris* 1643, leaving issue by Isabel, daughter of Robert, sixth Lord Boyd
      1 SIR JOHN, second baronet   2 SIR ROBERT, third baronet
    ELIZABETH, married Sir John St Clair of Herdmanstown, ancestor of the present St Clairs of Herdmanston, Lords Sinclair

Sir John died in 1648, and was succeeded by his grandson

II SIR JOHN SINCLAIR, at whose decease, unmarried, about 1652, he was succeeded by his brother

III. SIR ROBERT SINCLAIR, Lord Stevenson, who was appointed by King William II in December, 1689, sheriff of Haddington, a Privy Councillor in the May following, and one of the Barons of the Exchequer In 1689 he was Lord Justice-Clerk He was representative in Parliament for Haddingtonshire 1689-1702. On 29th July, 1680, he was pannelled for factiously opposing Act of Privy Council, levying 5,500 militia; on the 13th and 14th March, 1683, assoilzied from damages claimed by Sir John Seton of Garmilton, but on the 30th same the Chancellor caused the Lords to alter above and make Stevenson liable, though damage was from a cause *ab extra* On the 2nd August next thereafter Sir Robert was imprisoned in castle for declining purge *re* Test Act, but was presently released. In 1663 he had his lands erected into a barony Sir Robert married, first, Helen, daughter of John, 14th Earl of Crawford and Earl of Lindsay, and secondly, Anne daughter of Sir William Scott of Ardross, *s p* He died July, 1713, and had issue—

    1. SIR JOHN, his successor   2 CHARLES, died unmarried
    3. ROBERT, married Anne, daughter of John Balfour, third Lord Burleigh.
    4. WILLIAM, died *s p*   5 DR PETER, died *s p*.
    6 DR ARCHIBALD, married Helen Strachan, died *s p*.
    7. MARGARET, married Robert Dundas of Arniston
    8. ELIZABETH, married Thos Menzies of Letham   9 A daughter, died unmarried.

He was succeeded by the eldest son of the first marriage,

IV SIR JOHN SINCLAIR, who represented Lanark in Parliament 1703-7. He married in 1698 Martha, widow of Cromwell Lockhart of Lee, County Lanark, and daughter of Sir John Lockhart of Castlehill, a Lord of Session, sole heir on her brother's death to a large estate, by whom he had eight sons and five daughters—

    1. ROBERT, Sir, successor to his father
    2 JOHN, assumed the surname of Lockhart, married Charlotte, daughter of Jas Bogle, W S, and left three daughters.

THE LONGFORMACUS LINE

    3 GEORGE, assumed the name of Lockhart on succeeding to the Castlehill estate, became one of the senators of the College of Justice by the title of Lord Woodhall, and died *s p*
    4 JAMES   5 CHARLES.   6 WILLIAM   7 THOMAS   8 PATRICK. All died *s p*
    9 ANNE, married George Bogle, of Daldowie
   10 KATHARINE   11 HELEN   12 MARTHA   13 MARGARET. All died single

Sir John died in 1726, and was succeeded by his eldest son

V. SIR ROBERT SINCLAIR This gentleman married in 1732 Isabella, only daughter of Colonel James Kerr, of the 3rd Regiment Foot Guards, by whom he had four sons and four daughters—

    1 JOHN, Sir, successor to his father
    2 JAMES, assumed the surname of Lockhart on succeeding his uncle, Lord Woodhall of Castlehill His son or grandson
       1. ROBERT LOCKHART born 17—; died 1850, married, first, 1804, Eliza (died 1816), daughter of Richard Newman Newman, M D , of Thornbury Park, Gloucester, secondly, in 1817, Charlotte Simpson (died 1869), daughter of Captain William Mercer of Potterhill, N B Issue by first marriage—
          1. JAMES SINCLAIR, his heir, J P and D L, born 11th September, 1808, died *s p* 1873
          2 ROBERT ALEXANDER, Major 80th Regiment
          3 JOHN HAMILTON, born 24th November, 1814, deceased
          4 MARY EMILIA
          5 ELIZA ANNE, married, 1825, John Percy Henderson of Foswell Bank, Perth.
          6 SUSAN   7 ANNE NISBET
       Issue of second marriage—
          8 WILLIAM MERCER, born 1818, drowned 1849
          9 GRAEME ALEXANDER LOCKHART of Castlehill, C B., born 1820, entered Army 1837, became Captain 1850, Major 1858, Lieut -Colonel 1859, Colonel 1866, Major-General 1867, served with 78th Highlanders in Persian War, 1857 (medal with clasp), and in Indian Mutiny campaign 1857-8 (medal with clasp), J P and D L for County Lanark, married in 1861, Emily Udny, daughter of James Brebner of Aberdeen, advocate
         10 GEORGE DUNCAN LOCKHART, born 1821, died 18—, married 18—, and has issue—
              ROBERT DUNCAN LOCKHART
         11 CHARLOTTE   12 FRANCES CHARLOTTE MERCER
         13 LOUISA   14 ELENORA JANE
         15 MARGARET DOUGLAS   16. ROBERTA EMILIA
         17 BARBARA FORBES, married, 1859, Alex Whitelaw
    3 ROBERT, advocate 1762, died *s p* 9th September, 1802   4. WILLIAM, died *s p*
    5 ELIZABETH, married William Hay of Spot
    6 MARTHA   7 AGNES   8 ANNE, died single

Sir Robert died in 1754, and was succeeded by his eldest son

VI. SIR JOHN SINCLAIR, who succeeded 19th August, 1766, to Alex Sinclair, Earl of Caithness, in Murkle and other lands under an entail He married Mary, youngest daughter of Blair of that Ilk, by whom he had—

    1 SIR ROBERT, his successor   2. KATHARINE

He was succeeded at his decease in 1789 by his eldest son

VII. SIR ROBERT SINCLAIR of Stevenson and Murkle, Lieut.-Governor of Fort St George in Scotland. This gentleman married, 3rd April, 1789, Madalina, second daughter of Alex., fourth Duke of Gordon. Dying 4th August, 1795, he was succeeded by his heir

BARONETS OF STEVENSON.

VIII. SIR JOHN GORDON SINCLAIR, a distinguished seaman, 63 years in the Royal Navy. Born 31st July, 1790, and served when a mere youth in the "Victory" flagship under Lord Nelson. His own gallant conduct while commanding the "Redwing" in the Mediterranean at Morjean and Cassis was officially commended and won much public approbation. He became captain in 1814, and an admiral in 1861. He married 15th June, 1812, Anne, only daughter of Admiral the Hon. Michael de Courcy, and had issue

1. ROBERT CHARLES, Sir, ninth baronet.
2. JOHN MICHAEL DE COURCY, born 22nd November, 1823, an officer in the Madras Artillery, died at Secunderabad 15th June, 1862.
3. GORDON CORNWALLIS, lieutenant R.N., born 13th August, 1835; died 21st March, 1866.
1. ANNE ELIZABETH, died 14th June, 1860.
2. MADALINA, married 15th August, 1839, Captain the Hon. Dudley Pelham, R.N., son of the first Earl of Yarborough.
3. GEORGIANA, died 2nd January, 1870.   4. MARY, died 26th October, 1856.
5. SUSAN HAY, married 12th June, 1867, Major-General Sir Wilbraham Oates Lennox, R.E., K.C.B., U.C., fourth son of Lord John George Lennox.

IX. SIR ROBERT CHARLES SINCLAIR of Stevenson, County Haddington, and Murkle, County Caithness, Deputy-Lieutenant for Haddington; J.P. and D.L. for Counties Haddington and Caithness, and Inverness; late Captain 38th Regiment; Hon. Colonel 1st Caithness Artillery Volunteers (V.D.); born 25th August, 1820; married, first, in 1851, Charlotte Anne, daughter of Lieutenant John Coote, 71st Regiment, and secondly, 5th December, 1876, Louisa, eldest daughter of Roderick Hugonin, Esq., of Kinmylies House. *Seats*—Murkle, Caithness; Stevenson, Haddington.   *Residence*—Achvarasdal Lodge, Reay, Thurso.   *Clubs*—Arthur's New (Edinburgh).

Sir Robert is patron of one living—Ripple Rectory, Kent.

Arms—See Armoury.

CHAPTER IX

THE LORDS OF ROSSLYN.

GENEALOGIE OF THE SAINTECLAIRES OF ROSSLYN.

(FEUDAL PERIOD)

BY J. VAN BASSAN.

[A REPRINT.]*

MALCOLM KEANMOORE having recovered, by the support of Edward, King of England, his realm, which Machabeus did possess, was crowned at Scone not long theraftar, upon the fifth of Aprile, in the year 1061; and holding a parliament att Forfar in Angus, he created severall Earles, Lords, Barons, etc., in compensation of their service and loyalty. The Normande Conquerour in his days maistered England, I call so William, Duke of Normandie, notwithstanding that I have seen severall Judges reprehending gentlemen att the Barre that casually gave him that title; for though he killed Harald the Usurper, and rooted his armie, yet he pretended a right to the kingdome, and was admitted by compact, and did take ane oath to observe the laws and customs of the realme Edgar, who was righteous heir, resolves to pass again to Hungaria with his mother and sisters; but being tossed a while att sea, is carried att length safe to a place on the River of Forthe, named Queensferry, from Margaret, whom the King espoused in 1067 Many gentlemen came about that time to Scotland, part with the Queen, as Chrichton, Fodringhame, Giffard, Maulis, Borthik, Lesly, etc., all Hungariens; part from England to shun the Usurper, as Lindesay, Vans, Ramsay, Lowall, Towrs, Bodwell, Monteith, Preston, Sandilands, Bissart, Fowlis, Wardlaw, Maxwell, Ross, etc; part from France, as Forfar, Boswell, Montgomery, Bodwell, Montith, Boys, Campbell, Betoun, Murray, Warwin, Telfer

Amougst the last was one SIR WILLIAM SINCLARE, second sone to Woldonius, or Wildernus, in France, whose mother was daughter to Duke Richard, a man well proportioned in all his members, of midle stature, faire of face, yellow hair'd, surnamed the Seemly, whom King Malcolm made cupbearer to his Queen The gentleman haveing serv'd sometime att Court, desired liberty to visit his parents, which was granted, and after sometime spent with them, returns loadned with presents, which he presented to the King and Queen The gifts were well accepted of, and he, by his liberality, winning preferment, married Dorothe, as some say Agnas Dunbar, daughter to Patrick, first Earle of Marche, or as some writters have, fifth Earle of Marche, and obtained the Barony of Rosline, so called because it represents ane peninsule, being

---

* Omitting portions which appear elsewhere throughout this work.

environ'd almost on all sides with water. After this he was made Wardin of the Southern Marches, in defending whereof he was kill'd. He begat upon his Lady a sone named HENRY, who lived in the Conqueror's days, and in whose time Malcolme the third was killed by Percy This Henry got of the King and Queen, Rosline in free heritage, with the Barony of Pithland. He married Rosabell, or as some say, Kathrine, daughter to Forteith, Earle of Strathern he was of a free nature and candid in his thoughts and words, very wise, and more given to studie warre than peace, for which rare qualities he was intrusted with the militarie commands He was dubbed knight by King Malcolme, and left to succeed him a sonne named also HENRY, who is supposed to have foughten the battle of Allertowne, where the English army was rooted under the reign of Saint David He outlived King Malcolme, and died under King William, by whom he was sent embassador towards Henry, King of England, to redemand Northumberland in the name of the Scots He receaved from David the first the lands of Carden and the command of 8,000 men a-foot, as likewise the honour of knighthood. Att first our Kings bestowed upon their subjects lands as a reward of their service, but after their liberality, finding no such way of gratification towards those who behaved themselves manfully, they fell upon ane easier way, which was in giveing them place amongst the nobility of their realm, and ranking them above the most common sort, either in creating them knights, which was performed by girding them with a belt, or in makeing them Earles, which was done by other ceremonies This Sir Henry married Margaret Grathenay, daughter to the Earle of Marre, upon whom he begot a sone named William, to whom he resigned his lands, and shortly after chang'd his inconstant habitation for a perpetuall one herafter.

"THE HISTORY OF THE SAINTCLAIRS" says that Malcolme Keanmoore made some earles, some barons, and some knights, att Forfar, in 1057, or, as Buchanan says, in 1061. Malcolmus Scotorum, Rex 86, Scone coronatus, anno 1061, inde Forfarum generale indixit concilium, volens ut Primores, quod antea non fuerat, aliarum more gentium, a praediis suis cognomina caperent, quosdam vero etiam Comites, vulgo Earles, quosdam Barones, vulgo Lords, alios Milites aut Equites auratos, vulgo Martiall Knights, creavit. Mak-Duffum Fifæ Thanum, Fifæ Comitem; Patricium Dumbarum Marchiarum Comitem, aliosque viros praestantes, Monthetiæ, Atholiæ, Marriæ, Cathanesiæ, Rossiæ, Angusiæ dixit Comites,—Johannem Sowls, Davidem Dardier ab Abernethia, Symonem a Tweddell, Gullielmum a Douglas, Gillespium Cameron, Davidem Briechen, Hugonem a Culdella, Barones, cum diversis aliis,—Equites auratos perplures, pauci vero Thani relicti Many new surnames were given to the families of the Scots, as Mar, Calder, Lockhart, Meldrum, Gordon, Seaton, Liberton, Lawder, Shaw, Leirmont, Strachane, Dundas, Lesly, Cockburn, Abercrombie, etc Many were named from the lands they had in possession, some from their office, as Stewart, Dorward, Bannerman, Forman, etc. Some from the proper names of valiant men, as Kenneth, Gray, Keth, etc This worthy Prince, according to the same history, made a law whereby all Barons might give judgment upon murtherers within their own bounds About which time William Duke of Normandie, comeing with a great armie to England, vanquished Harald and conquered the kingdome. (Edward) Edgar Etheling, the righteous heir, takeing his mother and his two sisters, Margaret and Christien, went to sea, designing to pass to Hungary, but being tossed with cross winds for a time, arrived att length att a haven called Queensferry, in the Firth, where King Malcolm met them, and conducted them to Dumfermeling, there he married Margaret, daughter to Agatha, with great solemnity, after Easter in 1067. William the Conqueror haveing got knowledge therof, fearing least some evill might ensue therby, banished all friends of (Edward) Edgar, wherof severalls came to Scotland, and got lands from King Malcolme, as Ross, Lindesay, Ramsay, Lowell, Towrs, Preston, Sandilands, Bissart, Fowls, Wardlaw, Maxwell, and others There came also some from Hungaria with Margaret, as Chrichton, Forthingham, Giffart, Mauld, Borthwick; some also from France, as Frazer, Bodwell, Montgomery, Monteith, Boas, Campbell, Vervin, Telfer, Boswell, amongst whom came also WILLIAM SAINTCLAIR, second sone to Wildernus, Earle of Saintclair in France, whose mother was daughter to Duke Richard of Normandie, father to William the Conqueror. He was sent by his father to Scotland, to take a view of the people's good behaviour. He was able for every game, agreeable to all company, and stiled "The Seemly Saintclair." The report of his qualifications came to the Queen's ears, who desired him of her husband, because of his wisdome The King made him her cupbearer, in which station he purchased to himself great favour and love of both Princes. But when he had served a long time, he desired liberty to visit his father and friends. The Queen yeelded therto, upon condition he should return again to Scotland, which he promised. His father was not willing he should return, yet perceaving he was earnest to fulfill his word, bestowed upon him jewells, gold, cloathing, horses, and other gifts, to present to the King and Queen, with which he returned back, and was welcomed by the courtiers and servants, to whom he was very beneficiall. He married Dorothea Dunbar, daughter to the Earle of Marche, upon whom he begot Sir Henry Saintclair. He got also of the King and Queen the barony of Rosline in liferent; after which, being desirous to try his fortune in warres, he obtained a company of men, underwent many dangers in resisting the Southern forces, and was appointed to defend the borders. William the Conqueror, offended att King Malcolm because he would not deliver in his hands (Edward) Edgar Etheling, sent about this time the Duke of Gloucestre, with a great army, to invade the Scots King Malcolm hearing therof sent the Earles of Marche and Monteith with a company of men of warre, to aid and assist the Sinclair's forces, wherupon Sir William Sinclair rushed forward, with a design to put the enimie out of ordre, but being enclosed by the contrary party, he was slain by the multitude of his enimies, wherof he made fall many in heaps flat down before his feet The news of his death comeing to the two other chaiftains, Marche and Monteith, they fell so boldly upon the enimie, that they scarce left any alive. The King and Queen lamented his misfortune, and vow'd to be revenged of the Southerns' cruelty.

He left three childring, two daughters, who died infants, and one sone, SIR HENRY SAINTCLAIR, who succeeded his father, and was entirely beloved of the King and Queen, who gave him Roslin in free heretadge, and made him Knight He was not inferior to his father He was made governor and captain of 600 men, past to Northumberland and Cumberland with the King, to be avenged upon the Southerns for his father's death, when William the Conqueror rencountered him with great force, but he being vehimently stirred up to anger by remembring the cruell slaughter of his father, went amongst his enimies like a lyon, so that in a short time he put them to flight The King beholding this was overjoyed, and rewarded him with the barony of Penthland. Not long after King Malcolme was slain att the siege of Anwick, in Northumberland; for when those who were within the Castle were almost starved, and readie to yield, one of their company came riding in armes on horseback, with a speare in his hand, and the keys of the Castle upon the point of the spear, as the Scots thought upon purpose to deliver them to the King, but with the point of the spear, he peerced the King att the left eye, and escaped by flight This companion after this was called Percie, which name his successors retained. The King died of his wounds A little before Saintclair married Rosabell Forteith, daughter to the Earle of Strathern, who bore to him Henry Saintclair, to whom he resigned all his lands, desireing the King to make him new charters, the others being lost.

Not long after he died, and left to succeed him his sone SIR HENRY SAINTCLAIR, whom King David made Knight This Prince, remembring the good service done to his father by Sir William and Sir Henry Saintclair, made this Sir Henry a Privy Councellor, with the Earles of Marche, Monteith, Fife, and Angus. His dwelling was at Roslin, which is thought to have been founded by Asterius, whose daughter Panthioria, a Pictish Lady, married Donald the First. Roslin was att that time a great Forrest, as also Pentland Hills, and a great part of the countrey about, so that there did abound in those parts great number of harts, hynds, deer and roe, with other wild beasts. This Sir Henry married Elizabeth Gartnay, daughter to the Earle of Marre, and begot William Saintclair, Henry Saintclair, and three daughters, Marie, Margaret, and one who died young. About this time Stephen, King of England, sent the Duke of Gloucestre to Northumberland to waste it with fire and sword, because King David refused to doe him hommage for Northumberland, Cumberland, and Huntingdonshire. King David heareing this, made Sir Henry Saintclair captain of 8,000 men affoot, collected out of the north parts of Scotland. The Earles of Marche and Angus were appointed to command the companies collect out of the south parts, viz., Lothian, Merse, Teviotdale, Galloway, etc. Those armies meeting, att length joyned in battle It was uncertain for a long time to whose side the victory should incline Att length the strongest wing of the English army being disordered by the Earle of Marche with a company of horsemen, Sir Henry Saintclair forced the English to fly, none being able to abide his blows. In this battle, which was given att Allertoun, many English were slain, many were taken prisoners, amongst whom the Duke himself, and other nobles were. scarce the tenth part got away. King David, after this victory, returned home, and rewarded largely his nobles. He gave to Sir Henry Saintclair Cardain, which from him, was called Cardain Saintclair, and haveing concluded a peace, he deceased in the 29th year of his reign, 1153 Malcolm, surnamed the Maiden, because he was never married, nor knew woman, succeeded his grandfather. About the beginning of his reign there was a plague and famin through all Scotland Somerled, Thane of Argyle, beholding this, and contemning the King's adge, who was but about 13 years of adge, came into the countrey, robing and killing all that resisted him. The King, sieing this, sent Gilchrist, Earle of Angus, against him they killed two thousand of his men Somerled fled to Ireland. King Malcolme reigned 12 years, and dieing att Edinburgh, was buried at Dumfermeling. Next to him succeeded his brother William surnamed Lyon, who sent Sir Henry Saintclair ambassador toward Henry King of England, about the beginning of his reign, to redemand Northumberland. King Henry appeared willing to doe him justice, after which Saintclair, returning home, died, leaving behind him two sones, William and Henry, and two daughters, Marie and Margaret.

His sone SIR WILLIAM succeeded. he was Baron of Roslin, Pentland, Pentland Moore, in free forestrie, Shirriff of Lothian, Baron of Cousland, Cardaine Saintclair, and

Great Master Hunter of Scotland. King William deceasing in the 29 year of his reign, the 74 year of his adge, and of our Lord 1214, Alexander the Second, a valiant prince, his sone, succeeded He loved Sir William Saintclair, whose excellent beauty and delicat proportion of body he mutch esteemed , he made him Knight, Shirriff of Lothian, and bestowed upon him considerable gifts att which time the Commons of England, not being willing to endure King John's tyranny, sent to Scotland and France for succor. King Alexander entered England, and shortly after Lewis, Dauphin of France, came to London without any impediment. King Alexander informed thereof, gathered 30,000 men, with a design to joyn him. For that effect he sent Sir William Saintclair with 5,000 light horsemen before, to observe the passages , and finding no impediment he came to London, where haveing met with Lewis the Dauphin, they conferred about the presente state of the countrey. Afterwards they sailed over into France to King Philip, to renew the ancient friendship betwixt France and Scotland, takeing only ten ships with them, leaveing the rest of the armys to be governed by Sir William Saintclair and the Earle of Marche. Their bonds of friendship being renewed, they returned to London Att that time King John, through displeasure, died. They sieing this, and takeing away all occasion of warre, by their counsell, returned to their countreys King Alexander, after his return, did reward his nobles, amongst whom he gave to Sir William Saintclair the Barony of Cousland in heretadge, as charters yet extant do record He made him also new charters of his lands of Rosline, for it would appear his old charters had been burnt, or destroyed some way or ane other in King William's time, because of the great trouble that was then in the country He gave him also the Baxter lands of Innerleith.

Not long after King Alexander died, in the 35 year of his reign, and of our Lord 1249 Next to him succeeded King Alexander the Third, who raised ane armie of 40,000 men against King Acho of Norway, who did invade the Isles, and subjected them to his dominion, the which armie was divided into three bodies In the one was Sir Alexander Stewart of Dundonald, with the Earles of Monteith and Lennox, who governed the men of Argyle, Athole, Lennox, and Galloway ; in the other was Sir William Sinclare of Roslin, with the Earle of Marche, who governed the men of the Merse, Teviotdale, Lothian, Berwick, Fife, and Stirlingshire , and in the middle was King Alexander, with all the power of Scotland So the armies joyning, the Scots became victorious with no great difficulty, and slew of the Danes 24,000, so that King Acho was compelled to fly to the castle of Aire, and from thence to Orkney, where he ended his life The same day was borne to Alexander a sone named Alexander, wherat the Scots had double cause of joy After this, by the persuasion of one Symon Strong, some of the nobility of England rose up against Henry their king, who sought for help from Scotland, to whom was sent Sir William Saintclair and John Cummyn, with 5,000 men, who soon pacified the matter and returned home. Not long after King Alexander, rideing a hunting upon a fierce horse att Kinghorne, by chance, att the west end of the rock, towards the sea side, fell and broke his neck, in the 37 year of his reign, and of our Lord 1286 Stories record that the day before the King's death, one Thomas Leirmont said to the Earle of Marche, that before the afternoon of the next day there should blow sutch a winde as should bring great calamity to Scotland, which was fulfilled by the King's death, which ensued before the afternoone of the next day. After the death of King Alexander, in respect he had no posterity, there was appointed governors. In the meantime, one Robert Bruce, Earl of Carrick, and one John Balliol, Earl of

FEUDAL PERIOD (GENEALOGIE). 271

Galloway, did strive who should be king ; the which difference they thought meet to be taken away by the judgment of Edward the First, King of England, who made John Balliol King, although it did of right belong to Robert Bruce, but on this condition, that he should have it as holden of him, and so should be att his command, which he condescended unto. At the same time King Edward sending for help from John Balliol against the French, and not being obeyed, he sends a navie to Berwick against him. His company sieing the number of their enimies, yet nothing dismayed, discomfited eighteen of their ships King Edward, greatly offended att this, sent a greater number, who, for all that, could not prevaill, the city was so well defended, but were compelled to use deceit First, they feigned flight, afterwards made standards like to the Scots, and sent them who were fled to them for feare to the city to make open way for John Balliol. The citizens, sieing the Scots' banner, opened the ports to their enimies. They haveing got entrance to the city, spared neither men, women, nor childring ; and sundry Knights were taken, among whom some of the most valiant fled to the Castle, as Sir William Saintclair, the Earle of Monteith, and others, who for want of provisions were compelled to yeeld John Balliol was also delivered by John Cummin in the hands of Edward, to whom he resigned his title of the kingdom of Scotland, who was subject to the Southernes' cruelty, and had been altogither undone had not God raised up a young man named Sir William Wallace, sone to Sir Edward Wallace of Craigie, who, by his insuperable and victorious hand, relieved his countrey and was made governor of it. He was not long governor, when he began to be hated of his countreymen, which he perceiving, by the flight of the Cummins at Falkirk, would be no longer governor, and therfor John Cummyn, Earle of Buchan, was made governor, who, with his two colleagues, Sir William Saintclair of Roslin, and Symon Frazer of Bigger, proved valliant att Roslin Moore. King Edward sent to Scotland 30,000 chosen men, under the government of one Rodolph Comfrene, thinking therby to make a whole conquest therof, without let or stay This Rodolph divided his men into three armies, appointing to every one of them 10,000, and ordained them all to meet at Roslin Moore, and from thence to pass through the rest of the countrey, with slaughter and burning This comeing to the governor s ears, who haveing but eight thousand in his company, and two other captains, to witt, Sir William Saintclair and the Frazer, yet for all that resolved to hazard himself, and comeing to the place is rencountered with ten thousand men, att a place in the moore named Bilsdone burne, where he with the other two, after encouragement of the company, proved so valiant, that in a short time they became victors, slew Rodolph their Generall the death of whom, after it came to the ears of a lady in England, who intirely loved him, she made be sett up in remembrance of his death into that part, a crosse of stone, which att that time was all gilded over. But to our purpose

The victory being gained, the spoile gathered, and unsuspicion of any danger to ensue, att once they behold marching against them 10,000 men. Att the sight therof, all amazed, made the prisoners be slaine, least they should raise again, and att the counsell of Sir William Saintclair, who knew all those bounds, passed over Draidon Burne, where there was rood for them to escape in if they were put to flight. Their enimies, thinking to be revenged on the slaughter before committed, came to that part where when the battle was joyned, their fortune was so bad that they became companions to the former company. This victory scarce was obtained, when, behold, a new company of ten thousand men is readie to joyne in battle with them, which the Scots beholding became all dismayed, yet, through the persuasive exhortations of their captains, their courage became fresh; and anone the three captains went through all the companys where the wounded and slain were, and slew all the English that were alive, and to every Scot liveing they gave a weapon, to the end they might kill the English that came upon them, and after that they went to prayer, desireing God to remove their offences, and to consider how just their cause was. The English thinking because they were with heads uncovered, and knees bended, that they craved mercie of them; and so, without thought of any resistance to be made, they came over Draidon Burne, where, contraire to their expectations of friends, they found foes, of men overcome, men redie to be victors. Yea, within short time, put them to flight, although the battle continued for a space with uncertain victory. This victorie, to speake by the way, gained as great praise to our countrey as any they ever obtained. But to our purpose.

After this great victory was obtained, every one of the three cheftains radie to receave part of the spoile, they went to consultation what way it should be divided, and to Sir William Saintclair, because his dwelling was in that part of the countrey, they gave the ground wheron the battle was fought, the first of them at Bilsdon Burne, besides Draidone, the which, to this day, is called the Shinne Bones, some bones and swords being therin found to this day, the other two betwixt Draidon and Hathornden, which place is called the graves. The other two cheftains divided the rest of the spoil betwixt them. Sir William Saintclair, after his good success in this battle, returned to his dwelling not farre from that place, and carried with him one English prisoner, a man of no small estimation in England, whom he entertained so well, that whilst he remained with him, all things that might anyway turn to the best he gave him counsel in, as amongst the rest, because he saw the Castle of Rosline not to be strong enough, he advised him to build it on the rock where it now standeth, which councell he embraced, and builded the Wall Tower with other buildings, and there he dwelt . He had two sones, Henry and William, of whom hereafter.

After the battle, this countrey was greatly vexet by the tyranny of Edward Longshanks; neither ever did any Scot live att ease, except those who yeelded to him, untill the time that Robert Bruce was made King, who when, after great trouble, he had established his realme under his own government, then did he reward those who were partakers of the paines he took in relieving the countrey from tyranny; amongst whom, by all the rest, he rewarded ritchly that valiant champion, Sir James Dowglasse and Sir William Saintclair, that worthy warriour, which two he preferred above all the rest in respect of their fidelity, which appeared after that att the battle of Bannockburne, fought upon Saint John's Day, 1314, wheratt they two proved most valiant. But also the two sones of Sir William Saintclair proved so well, that all men admired their valour, the report therof comeing to the King's ears, he receaved the eldest, to wit, Henry, into his service, and made William, Bishop of Dunkeld .

When King Robert the Bruce was returned from Ireland with his countrey free from King Edward's tyranny, he began to take pleasure in pastimes, as hunting and hawking . . . It was at one of these functions that Sir William Saintclair of Roslin is stated to have staked his head that his two hounds, Help and Hold, would kill a certain white faunch deer before she could cross the Marcheburne. They caught her in mid-stream. (The incident is recounted more fully in *Cameos of the Gens*.) In his need he had sought assistance of Saint Katharine, and in gratitude built the church of St Kathrine in the Hopes.   Sir William, after this, proved valiant in Northumberland, togither with his companion, the doughty Dowglas, and after the death of King Robert, they, togither with Sir Robert Logan, tooke Bruce his heart enclosed in a coffer of gold, and delicately spiced, to Hierusalem, where, royally, they buried it, and then joyned themselves with their company, to Christians, where they valiantly subdue their enimies, and returning home by force of winde, was driven upon the coast of Spain, where they found the King of Arragon warring against the Sarrazens of that countrey, and joyned themselves to his forces, so, through their good fortune in fight, they became careless, not esteeming of their enimies, till att length, through deceit of Sarazens, they were slain. So ended those valiant Knights, in defence of the right, whose vertues are as examples to allure men to doe the like A modern poet hath made the following verses on Sir William Saintclair and Sir Robert Logan, two honourable and hardy Knights, famous for their fortitude in the warres of the Bruce,—for their expedition to the Holy Land with his heart,—for many knightly deads in the Holy Warres, where they were slain, the year of Christ 1330 —

> The constant courage, and the loyall love,
> The hardie hearts, the readiness of hands,
> While that the strong King stiff and stoutly strove,
> By force and flight, to free, half lost, his lands,
> That in thir two, tried in his worthie warres,
> Makes them now glister like two golden starres

> The oppositions and alterations oft,
> That to imped their Prince his piece appear'd,
> Made nought, ther gallants leave him, while aloft
> On honour's rock his royal sege was rearde,
> No, nor when deade, but both to after death,
> Thir Knights, weel kithed, to leave their Lord was loath

> For with that hardie Counte that had his heart,
> To be inhumed att the Holy Grave,
> This pare, therwith, to pass prepar'd departe,
> To do 't, the honour last that it should have,
> Which duely done, as the deceast deserved,
> 'Gainst Saracens, whill they were slain, they served

After the death of Sir William Sinclair succeeded to him his eldest sone Henry . . when John Cummin the governor, after the captivity of John Raiddell (Randolph) Earle of Murray and Governor before him, began to tyrannize over all favourers of King David Bruce, he with his confederats raised ane army, and in open battle slew him (1338); in whose place was constituted Andrew Murray as Governor of Scotland, wherat the Cummins, mightily offended, came and destroyed all parts in the North, where they came with fire and sword, wherfor the Governor sent for help of the Prince of Orkney, who comeing with his forces vanquisht the Cummins, with all the assistants and favourers of Balliol, in open battle, and then returning to his country of Orknay, by the way he met a navie sent by King Edward to destroy Orknay, whom he rencountred so bravely, that with his small number, he slew two thousand, and put all the rest to flight, and so went home. Soon after this died Andrew Murray, in the year of our Lord 1338, and within three years after came King David Bruce to Scotland, who, rememb'ring the injurys done to him by the Southerns, sent ane army under the government of the Prince of Orknay, and John Raiddell into England, who returned with great spoile. King David, not contented therwith, made the Prince of Orknay bring a thousand chosen men out of Orknay, the which adding to his army of 19,000 men, he sent them to England under the command of the Prince of Orknay, and the Earle of Marche, who burnt and slew in all parts where they came, and returned with a ritch prey; wherfor the King rewarded them, for he made Henry Saintclair, Lord Saintclaire and Lord Chief Justice of Scotland. After this King David was taken att Durham (1346) where he had sent an army in help of the King of France, and sundry of his nobles were slain through the flight of Robert Stewart Prince of Scotland, and the Earle of Marche, through which shortly after his return to his country he died, and was buried at Holyrood-house, in the 39th year of his reign, in the year of our Lord 1370 . Next to Prince Henry Saintclair succeeded his eldest sone Henry, second of the name, Prince of Orknay, etc . who left behind him one sone named William and one daughter who was married to the Earle of Marche. .*

The history of Southerland derives the Saintclairs from Walderin or Woldonius in France, whose sone, Guillelmus de Sancto Claro, did, as they alledge, marie Agnas Dunbar, daughter to Patrick, first Earle of Marche They say that Kathrin, daughter to Forteeth, the Earle of Strathern, married Sir Henry Saintclair, whose sone Henry, married Margaret, daughter to Gratney, the Earle of Marre. This Henry's sone, Sir William, pass'd into Spaine with good Sir William Douglas, who carried the Bruce's heart to Hierusalem, he was married to Elizabeth Sparie, daughter to the Earle of Orknay and Shetland, and so by her became first Earl of Orknay of the Saintclairs. His name was Julius Sparre. He is also reputed Earle of Stratherne and Cathnes. The second Earle was Henry Saintclair Prince of Orknay and Shetland, Duke of Holdembourg, Knight of the Golden Fleece, etc, who married Florentina, daughter to the King of Danemarke. The third Earle was his sone, Henry Saintclair, Prince of Orknay and Shetland, Duke of Holdembourg, Lord Saintclair, Knight of the Cockle, and of the Ordre of Saint George in England, etc. It is to be noted, nevertheless, that his name is not inroll'd or registrat amongst the Knights att Windsor. He married Giles Dowglass daughter to William Dowglas, Lord Nithsdale, called the Black Dowglas, and Giles Stewart, daughter of King Robert the Second The fourth Earle was Sir William Saintclair, called Prodigus, Knight of the Cockle and Golden Fleece, Prince of Orknay and Shetland, etc . . . This William married Elizabeth Dowglass, daughter to Archibald *Tineman* first Duke of Turaine, and after her death he married Margaret Southerland, daughter to Alexander of Southerland, eldest sone of John Earle of Southerland, second of the name, by whom he had Oliver, Laird of Roslin, etc, and William. The last obtained the Earledome of Cathness in the latter end of King James the Second's reign, and was slain att Flowdon, 1513. (In Nisbet's Heraldry there is a similar account of the Saintclairs.)

All what is above recorded by the Genealogists doth not agree with the Evidences, Historys, Registers and other privat Memoirs I have found in Gentlemen's hands It's certain that the Saintclairs came originally from France, where there are as yet severall places of that name In Normandy there is a place named Saintclair, upon the river of Epte, where the Emperor Othon was beat by the Normans in 949, whilst Lewis the Third

---

*The preceding is evidently by Van Bassan, and what follows by Hay

was King of France. There is also a village called Saintclair two leagues distant from Moncontour, where Gaspard de Coligny, Admiral of France, incamped the 30th of Septembre, 1569, but whilst he was decamping he was met by the army of the Catholicks, and lost 200 foot souldiers and 120 horse. It is probable that the Saintclairs tooke their surname from some place or other so called in France. They came over to England with William, Duke of Normandy. I find in the annals of Clifteaux, written by Angelus Manriquez, p 436, ad annum 1167 "Hugonem de Santo Claro, cum Roberto de Lacy, Jocelino de Balliolo, Thoma filio Bernardi, excommunicatum a Sancto Thoma Cantuariensi, quod in possessiones et bona Ecclesiae Cantuariensis manus extenderat, ut eis abuteretur, et eorum usus impediverat, quorum necessitatibus erant deputata." This proves that they were established very early in England. In the History of the Earles of Drewx in France, I find Eleoner, daughter to Robert the Second, Earle of Drewx, and Joland of Coucy, married first to Hugo Lord of Chateauneuf, and afterwards to Robert de Saintclair. This Eleonor's nephew, Robert the fourth Earle of Drewx, who died in 1282, begot upon Beatrix, only daughter to John, Earle of Montfort, Joleta, first married to Alexander the Third, King of Scotland, in 1286, and afterwards to Arthur, the second Duke of Brittany, Earle of Richmond and Montfort, which proves the Saintclairs to have been considerable men in those parts. As for Scotland, I find none of them named amongst us before King William's time. The first I find recorded is Alane Saintclair, to whom Roland, Earle of Galloway, grants the lands of Hermaneston, bounded as att present. As for Roslin, it was not in the Saintclairs' hands till that King's time att soonest, for in the beginning of his reigne I find Thomas de Roslyn witness to a charter, granted by Robert de Monteforti, in the Chartulare of Aberbrothe, and Roger of Roslin is witness to severall charters of William of Lysuris, Laird of Gorton. Henry of Roskelyn resigns his lands to Alexander the Third, which are disponed in favour of William Saintclair in 1280. Whether this Henry was of the same surname or not I cannot determine till further enquiry.

The further observations of Father Hay will be found under the different sections of this work. The Editor of his MS. refers to him in these words —

"Of Father Hay, some account will be found prefixed to the 'Genealogie of the Hayes of Tweeddale.' His mother, Jean Spotswood, having, upon the death of her first husband, George Hay, youngest son of Sir George Hay, Lord Register, married James Saintclair of Rosslyn, this connection naturally afforded the stepson access to the muniments in the Rosslyn charter-chest, and from these writings he was enabled principally to compile this genealogy of the family. It is to be regretted that the reverend gentleman was so careless in making his transcripts, as in many instances various evident mistakes have crept in, which the absence of the original documents renders it sometimes difficult to correct. Fortunately these inaccuracies, generally speaking, are of no very great moment; and it will be always remembered that Father Hay was no more faulty than the other Scottish antiquaries and genealogists of the period, who attached no importance to that extreme accuracy which in modern times is so properly deemed essential to the transcription and publication of ancient writings. Much, therefore, as we may desiderate the too frequent occurrence of error, we must be thankful that copies of deeds of such value were taken, as no traces of the original charters and other papers can now be found."

Since Maidment wrote the foregoing, one document at least has been discovered in private ownership, "The Testament of Alexander Sutherland of Dunbeath, in Caithness," and a comparison with Hay's transcript shows that they agree in every way. The History of the Saintclairs was written by one James van Bassan, a Dane who lived long at Roslin Castle, and whom Nisbet terms 'a very confident genealogist.' The mediæval St. Clairs of Rosslyn bore the names of William and Henry in alternation, and this has occasioned a transposition of many historical references, some being antedated by one or two generations, and others being postdated similarly.

SCOTTISH-NORMAN ALLIANCES

Illustrating the Kinship of the St. Clairs with the Celtic Royal Line

SCOTLAND	DE COUCY.	DREUX	SAINT-CLAIR
			WM. DE ST CLAIR. (living 1139.) Endows Priory of Villers-Fossard.
HENRY, PRINCE of SCOTLAND. (S of David I by Matilda, d of Waltheof, E. of N'thumb'land), d, *v.p.* 1152, m , 1139, Ada, d of Wm Count of Warrene, and 2nd E. of Surrey	**RAOUL, SIRE DE COUCY.** m 1st, Agnes de Hamault 2nd, Agnes, d of Robert II de Dreux	**ROBERT I, COUNT DE DREUX** (5th son of K. Louis VI of France) m 3rd, Agnes de Baudemont, Dame de Braine He died in 1188, and left by her—	**AMORI DE S. CLER.** Warrior in the xiiith Crusade
	2nd wife 1st wife.		
WILLIAM THE LION. (1165–1213) M, 1186, Ermengarde, dau of Richard, Viscount Bellomont	**ENGUERRAND III. JOLANDE.** = 2 (*Le Brun*) m (3rd) Marie, d of Jean Seigneur de Montmirel et d'Oisy, and Helvide de Dampierre	**ROBERT II**, Count of Dreux of Braine and Nevers († 1218 or 1219)	**ROBERT DE SAINTCLAIR.** A Robert de St Clair appears in Scotland *temp* Alex II and Alex III , 1261, 1264, etc., attesting royal instruments.
ALEXANDER II, 2 = 1 **MARIE**,		**ROBERT III.** 1 **JOHN I** 2 **ELEANOR**, 2 = (d 1233) (d 1248) m, 1st, Hugh, m Eleanor, only d m Marie de Lord of of Thomas Sieurde Bourbon Chateauneuf St Valeri by Adela of Ponthieu	**SIR WM. DE ST. CLAIR**, Knt, *Vice comes* of Haddington and Linlithgow in 1264, Guardian of the Prince of Scotland, 1279-81, Grantee of Roslin, 1280, Ambassador to France, 1284, Justiciary of Galloway, 1288-89, Seneschal of Edinburgh, 1292
asc 1213 † 1249 Queen of Scotland She M, 1st, Joan, dau of King died John of England She died 2nd, Jean de Brienne. *s p* 1238		**ROBERT IV Earl of Dreux.** (d 1282), m Beatrix, only child of John I, Count of Monfort, l'Amauri by Jean du Chateau du Loir or Chateaudun	
ALEXANDER III., m 2nd (and d), 2 = 1 **JOLANDE** 2 = 2 **ARTHUR II , DUKE OF BRITTANY** 1285, b 1241, m 1st Margaret of († 1322) (son of John II of Brittany, and England Beatrix, d of Henry III of Eng'and), Count of Richmond and Montfort			**SIR HENRY DE ST. CLAIR,** Knt, Lord of Rosslin, *Baltheus* of Caithness, Panetarius Scotiæ
ALEXANDER, PRINCE OF SCOTLND, m Margaret, dau of Guy, Count of Flanders, and died *s p,* 1284		**JOHN DE MONTFORT** Claimant of Bretagne	

THE LORDS OF ROSSLYN.

FEUDAL PERIOD.

SAINT CLAIR is the principal town in the canton of that name in the arrondissement of St. Lô in Normandy The site of the castle was to be seen when M. de Gerville wrote his valuable work on the castles in La Manche * The Lord of St Clair accompanied the Norman invaders of England, and is duly recorded in the Battle Abbey Roll, as also in the other lists of the conquerors by Wace, Duchesne, and Leland. The former in his description of the great battle has :—

> " Dunct puist Hue de Mortemer
> Od li sire d'Auviler,
> Cil d'Onebac e de Saint Cler
> Englez firent mult enverser "

Hugh de Mortimer, with three other knights, the sires of Auviler, Onebac, and St Cler, charged a body of the Angles who had fallen back on a rising ground, and overthrew many. A Richard de *Sencler* is entered in Domesday, from whom the British Sinclairs are assumed to descend.* Almost immediately after conquering England they appear in high positions, not only in that kingdom, but also in the principality of Wales and the neighbouring kingdom of Scotland, wherein two families of the name —between whom no connection can now be traced—were settled at an early period, the one at Herdmanston, and the other at Rosslyn The first on record of the Herdmanston Line was Henry St Clair, who received (circa 1160) a charter of Langild from William de Moreville, Constable of Scotland, which charter was afterwards confirmed by Roland fitzUthred (successor to Wm de Moreville) thereafter Earl of Galloway, to Alan de St Clair and Matilda of Windsor, his spouse † Robert de St Clair attests at Windsor, 20th September, 1261, an Inspeximus by the King, Henry III., of a charter of Alexander, son of the King of Scots , and again there is an inquisition before him 18th October, 1264 Robert de Sancto Claro attests a charter executed at Alicht by Alexander II to the burgh of Aberdeen 27th February (1213-49). After him there is an hiatus until the war of the Scottish Succession, consequent upon the premature death of the Maiden of Norway (1290), when, beside William and John St Clair of Herdmanston, William St Clair, presently of Roslin, his heir Henry, his second son William, the warrior-priest of Dunkeld, and Gregory St Clair [of Longformacus], assumed to be his son, come on the scene.

SIR WILLIAM ST CLAIR, 1st LORD OF ROSLIN,

is constantly *en evidence* amongst the foremost patriots of the period, and is found high in favour at the Scottish Court Burke‡ has it that he was appointed *vicecomes* (sheriff) of the County of Edinburgh for life in 1271 ; but the " Memorial of the ancient family of St Clair of Roslin "§ sets forth that " He executed the office of high-sheriff of the shire of Edinburgh in the 30th year of Alexander III. *anno* 1278 " There are several notices

---

Planch   ⟨ Hay   ‡ Art E of Caithness   § Nisbet

SIR WILLIAM ST. CLAIR, 1st LORD.

of Sir William in the Exchequer Rolls of Scotland, where he figures as sheriff of various shires from 1264 to 1290, viz.: Haddington, 1264-66; Linlithgow, 1264; Edinburgh, 1266; Dumfries, 1288; Edinburgh, 1288-90; and Linlithgow, 1290. In 1288 he was allowed 18s. 4d. for wages to a gardener at Haddington and outlay on garden, but notified that he must in future keep the garden at his own cost. He was Justiciarius Galwythie 1288-89, and in 1288 returned his *lucra* for one year as £9 1s. 8d. He figures as Guardian of the Prince of Scotland 1279-81. This is shown by the following letters from Prince Alexander of Scotland to his uncle Edward I. of England :—Alexander his nephew, and firstborn son of Alex. King of Scotland, to his most hearty uncle the King, expresses the warmest affection for himself, the Queen and their children, and wishes to hear of them more frequently. He prays him to grant the petition which Sir Ingram de

Umfraville is about to make for the lands of his late father Sir Robert de Umfraville on whose behalf his lord father has also written. He believes the King will be glad to hear good news of himself and kindred, and having no seal of his own he appends that of Sir Wm. de St. Clair his guardian (c. 29th March, 1279). Again, c. 1281. Alex. his consanguineous, first-born of Alex., King of Scotland, to his uncle the King, as he is greatly delighted to hear of his health begs him to send accounts of it oftener and assures him of his own well-being, having no seal of his own he appends that of Sir Wm. de St. Clair his guardian.

With regard to his ancestry, the History of the St. Clairs,* while doubtless recording many incidents based on facts, is considerably at variance with contemporary annals. The best theory seems to be that this Sir William was second son to the Robert de Saintclair in Normandy who married Eleoner, relict of Hugh, Lord of Chateaunef, daughter to Robert, the second Earl of Dreux in France, by Joland of Coucy.† Crossing to Scotland, he became a great favourite with King Alexander, who bestowed on him the baxter lands of Innerleith on the 8th April, 1280; while on the 14th September following, on the resignation of Henry of Roskelyn, he acquired from King Alexander a further charter of the lands and barony of Rosslyn, to be held for half a knight's service.* Father Hay thinks that Sir William obtained with the lands of Innerleith the appointment or office of Panetarius. Although the office was also held by his successor Sir Henry, it does not seem to have been hereditary, as in 1348 it had gone to John Comyn, Earl of Menteith, and thereafter upon his forfeiture to the Moray family.‡ Monsieur Baron, in his Art of Heraldry, gives us the arms of the Comte de Cosse, Grand Paneter of France, who as the badge of that office carries (says he) below his shield, on the dexter side thereof, a cup, and on the sinister a standish with pen and ink.‡ The foregoing digression is inserted to account for the confusion in the Genealogie in applying incidents such as the office of cupbearer to a Sir William St. Clair of the time of Malcolm Canmore, being evidently an antedating of the Sir William, Pantler du Roi of the time of Alexander III. The charter of 1280 is the earliest record of the connection of the St. Clairs with Roslin, unless the previous owners were also of the same surname, which is not clear. A Thomas *de Roslyn* attests a charter granted by Robert de Monteforte (vide Chartulare of Aberbrothe), and Roger of Roselyn attests severall charters of Wm. of Lysuris, Laird of Gourton.† About the same time Sir Wm. St. Clair acquired the Temple lands of Gourton from

---

* Van Bassan, fabulist.   † Hay.   ‡ Nisbet.

Walter fitz Stephen de Melville, which lands are further referred to in a charter from Thomas Modok to (his son) John, and in the attestation thereto are *Dominus Willielmus de Sancto Claro, miles*, and *Henricus de Sancto Claro*.[*] Sir William sat in the Scottish Parliament at Scone, 5th February, 1283-4, when the succession to the crown of Scotland was settled in the event of the demise of King Alexander III.[‡] In 1284 one William de Saint Clair is joined with William de Hamilton as keeper of the Bishopric of Winchester in England, which had become void by the death of Nicholas de Ely.[*] The association with a name hereafter so essentially Scottish as Hamilton supports the inference that the Wm St Clair whom King Edward designates *custos nostros Episcopatus Wintoniensis tunc vacantis*, was from north of the Tweed. The next year, 1285, Sir William was one of the Scottish embassy to France to escort back the Queen-elect, Joleta of Dreux, daughter of Robert, fourth Earl of Dreux, and Beatrix, only daughter of John, Earl of Montfort. The other members of the embassy were Thomas Charteris, Chancellor of Scotland; Sir Patrick Graham, and Sir John Soulis.[§] It will be observed that if Sir William was, as is assumed, the son of Robert de St Clair, who married Eleanor de Dreux, the relict of Hugh, Lord of Chateaunef, then was he nearly related to both Alexander III and Joleta of Dreux, for Marie de Coucy, Queen of Scotland and mother of Alexander III., was niece to Joland of Coucy, wife of Robert II, Earl of Dreux, who had issue Eleanor aforesaid, espoused by Robert de St Clair. In brief, Robert de St. Clair married Eleanor de Dreux, cousin to Alexander III. of Scotland, which sufficiently explains the visit of Sir William 'the Seemly' to that country, his appointment as (Cup-bearer) Panitarius, his favour with King and Queen, to both of whom he was so closely allied; his return to France on the embassy mentioned, and his acquisition of lands and honours. The "History of the Saint Clairs"—written in Saga form—assigns these incidents to a period contemporary with William, Conqueror of England, instead of the later temporary Conqueror of Scotland—Edward I. The mistake has been perpetuated by subsequent genealogists. In the Innerleith and Roslin grants of 1280 there is no territorial designation given to Sir William, which supports the inference of his being first of his line to settle on Scottish soil. In the celebrated letter to Edward I from the community of Scotland, dated at Bergham, 1289, amongst the barons is *Guillam de Seincler*. Sir William was appointed to take fealties in Galloway in 1291, and on 12th January, 1292, Edward I of England issued an order to William de St Clair and William de Boyville to take the fealty of the Bishop of Whithern, and thereafter with the Bishop those of all Galloway. (Amongst those enumerated in the Submission and Fealty sworn by the generality of the Scots Nation to King Edward I of England, in 1292, 1296, 1297, etc., is a Willielmus de Sancto Claro. His seal thereto displays the Merse cognisance of the three boars' heads. Nisbet remarks on this person that he takes this gentleman to be of a branch of the Sinclairs, but neither the families of Roslin or Hermiston.) Soon after the meeting of the Estates of Scotland at Brigham, Edward I of England secured to his interests two of the Scottish Regents. By this measure he trusted that he could over-rule their deliberations, and grown confident in his power, he intimated to the Estates "that certain rumours of dangers and perils to the Kingdom of Scotland having reached his ears, he judged it right that all castles and places of strength in that kingdom should be delivered up to him. This demand effectually roused the

---

[*] Hay   [†] Nisbet, p 65   [‡] Burke, Art Earl of Caithness See sketch on p 277   [§] Hay, Balfour's Annals, etc

Scots, and Sir William Sinclair, Sir Patrick Grahame, and Sir John Soulis, three knights who had been high in the confidence of Alexander III., with the other Captains of the Scottish castles, peremptorily refused in the name of the community of Scotland to deliver its fortresses to anyone but their Queen and her intended husband, for whose behoof they were ready to bind themselves by oath to keep and defend them. With this firm reply Edward had to be satisfied ; and, sensible that he had over-rated his influence, he patiently awaited the arrival of the young Queen. Edward's scheme for the subjugation of Scotland was not yet completed ; but all had hitherto succeeded according to his wishes. He had procured the acknowledgment of a claim of superiority over that kingdom, which if Baliol should refuse to become the creature of his ambition, gave him a special title to compel obedience as Lord Paramount. By holding out the prospect of a crown to the various competitors, and by many rich grants of estates and salaries to the prelates and the nobility, he had succeeded in securing them to his interest ; and if any feelings of indignation, any spirit of ancient freedom and resistance remained, the apparent hopelessness of fighting for a country which seemed to have deserted itself, and against a prince of so great a genius as Edward, effectually stifled it for the present. His various grants receive illustration from the 'Rotuli Scotiae,' vol i , p 24 *et passim*. He gave the Bishop of Glasgow an obligation to bestow on him lands to the annual value of £100, to James the Steward, lands of the same annual value ; to Patrick, Earl of Dunbar, lands of £100 annual value

To John de Soulis, lands of 100 marks annual value
William Sinclair ,, 100 ,, ,,
Patrick de Graham ,, 100 ,, ,,
Wm. de Soulis ,, £100 ,,

All these persons were to have lands of the aforesaid value, 'Si contingat Regnum Regi et haeredibus suis remanere.' Edward afterwards changed his plan, and gave these barons and prelates gratifications in money or other value. But to John Comyn the King of England gave the large sum of £1,563 14s 6½d ('Rotuli Scotiae,' vol 1, p 17, 6th January, 1292). He took care, however, to reimburse himself by keeping the wards, marriages, and other items of revenue which had fallen to the Scottish Crown during the interregnum, as may be seen from many places in the 'Rotuli Scotiae' '"*

Sir William next appears as a witness to a charter from John, Abbot of Newbottle, in favour of William Bissett, granted at Berwick-on-Tweed on St. John the Baptist's Eve *i e.* 23rd June, 1292 Sir William is therein described as *Dominus Willielmus de Sancto Claro, tunc vice-comite de Edinburgh, miles* † There is another William de St Clair on p. 51 of Hay's Chartular of Newbottle.† Sir William was one of the nominees on the part of Balliol in the competition for the crown of Scotland ‡ Sir William was present att Newcastle-upon-Tyne when John Balliol swore fealty to King Edward, 20th November, 1292,* and in the Letters Patent by John Balliol, giving a general release to Edward I, besides his own seal the King of Scots has caused the seals of Wm. de St Clair and others to be appended ; and on the 10th same William de St Clair attests his homage. The last appearance of the Lord of Rosslyn was at the siege of Dunbar, in 1296, of which Tytler says —"The castle of Dunbar was at this time one of the strongest and by its situation the most important in Scotland Its lord, Patrick, Earl of Dunbar, served in the army of Edward ; but his wife, who held the castle and hated the English, entered into

* Tytler. † Hay. ‡ Burke (Earl of Caithness)

a secret negotiation with the Scottish leaders for its delivery into the hands of her countrymen. The Earls of Ross, Athole, and Menteith, the Barons John Comyn, WILLIAM SINCLAIR, Richard Seward, and John de Mowbray, with 31 knights and a strong force threw themselves into the place on St Martin's Day and, assisted by the Countess, easily expelled the few soldiers who remained faithful to England. Edward determined to recover it at all hazards, and despatched the Earl of Surrey with 10,000 foot and 10,000 heavy-armed horse to regain it. When summoned by Warrenne the garrison agreed to surrender unless relieved in three days, and the Scots, axious to retain so strong a place, led on the whole of their army and possessed themselves of a strong and excellent position in the high ground above Dunbar, 40,000 foot and 1,500 horse encamped on the heights near Spot; and confident of rescue, the garrison of the castle insulted the English from the walls as if already beaten. Surrey advanced, and some confusion being observable in his ranks was mistaken by the Scots for flight, in their temerity they left their point of vantage only to meet a compact army under perfect discipline, and having in vain endeavoured to regain their ranks, after a short resistance were utterly routed. Surrey's victory was complete, and for the time decided the fate of Scotland. 10,000(?) men fell in the field or in the pursuit. Sir Patrick Graham, one of the noblest and wisest of the Scottish barons, disdained to ask for quarter, and was slain under circumstances which extorted the praise of the enemy. A great multitude, including the principal of the Scottish nobility, were taken prisoners, and next day the King of England coming in person with the rest of his army before Dunbar, the castle surrendered at discretion. The Earls of Athole, Ross and Menteith, with four barons, seventy knights, and many other brave men submitted to the mercy of the conqueror. All the prisoners of rank were immediately sent in chains to England, where they were for the present committed to close confinement in different Welsh and English castles. After some time the King compelled them to attend him in his wars in France, but even this partial liberty was not allowed them till their sons were delivered into his hands as hostages." In Rotuli Scotiae, vol 1., sub Ed. I., c. xxv. p 44, a great many of the names of the prisoners will be found, among them being Sir Wm. de St Clair who is sent to the Tower, Sir Henry St Clair to St Briavel's Castle, Alex. de St. Clair, Esq., to Windsor, and Reginald de St. Clair, Esq., to Kenilworth Castle (16th May, 1296). The "History of the St Clairs"* makes him one of the victorious leaders in the triple battle of Roslin, 1302. Little more is known of him except that he may have been "the Seemly St Clair," who married Agnes, daughter of Patrick Dunbar (1st or 5th) Earl of Marche. Edward I issued a two years' protection for Amicia, widow of William de St Clair, dwelling by the King's leave in the county of Edinburgh, 7th April, 1299. He left two sons and a daughter—

    1 SIR HENRY, his successor.   2 WILLIAM, Bishop of Dunkeld—the King's Bishop
    3 ANNABEL, married to Sir David Wemyss †

SIR HENRY ST CLAIR, 2ND BARON OF ROSLIN.

It has already been seen that Sir Henry swore fealty to King Edward, circiter 1292, as appears by the Ragman Roll. His father had been in the first place a supporter of Balliol, but Sir Henry was one of the patriot warriors who rallied round Bruce. He

---

* Van Bassan   † Nisbet (Art Earls of Wemyss).

attested a charter by King Robert the Bruce at Dundee 21st October, 1314 In Nisbet's "Memorial of the Sinclairs of Roslin" we are informed that Sir Henry made a very illustrious figure in the war occasioned by the competition for the crown betwixt the Bruce and the Balliol, and being a faithful adherent of the former, King Robert, in the eleventh year of his reign (1317), erected the muir of Pentland and several other lands into a free hunting, as they were in the reign of King Alexander, for the payment of a tenth part of a soldier The same year he received from Edward de Gourton a parcel of Gourton* tenanted by Roger de Harewood, a William de St. Clair being one of the witnesses, and on St. Magdalen's Eve, 1328, in the presence of William de St Clair, *Dei Gratia, Episcopi Dunkeldensis, apud Roselin*, Gilbert de Gardano conveyed a further parcel of Gourton.* In 1320 Henry St Clair is one of the signatories to the ever-memorable letter of the Barons of Scotland to the Pope in assertion of the independence of Scotland. In this document, which was executed at Aberbrothe on the 6th April of that year, he is ranked as Panetarius Scotiae This important office did not, however, remain long with the Roslins, for soon after John Comyn, Earl of Monteith, who was forfaulted in 1348, is designed *Panetarius*, after whom John and Thomas Murray, sons to Sir Andrew Murray, Governor of Scotland, are found in a charter designed *Panetarii Scotiae*.† The office was one of the Royal Household, and was in those days of great importance. The other offices were Steward of Scotland, Butler of Scotland, Great Constable, and Marshal The Steward was, it seems, Mayor of the Palace, the Butler was cup-bearer to the King, and controlled the cellar, while the Panetarius occupied a similar position with regard to the supervision of other stores for the Royal household, an office of State best understood by reference to the Pharaohs, Kings of Egypt ; he was governor of the kingdom's corn-trade.‡ The badge of office was a cup and a standish with pen and ink In the letter to the Pope, after the eight Earls, the Steward and Butler follow, and five further down the Grate Constable and Marischall, and then, with an interval of one, is Henry de St. Clair, *Panetarius* of Scotland, after whom are some sixteen other barons The next year, 1321, Sir Henry was evidently up in Caithness, for in a document dated at Cullen, 4th August, 1321, addressed by King Robert Bruce to the "ballivi" of the King of Norway in Orkney, he complains that Alexander Brun, "the King's enemy," convicted of *lese majestatis*, had been received into Orkney, and had been refused to be given up, though instantly demanded by our "ballivus in Caithness, Henry St Clair."§

"Bain's Documents" has him indexed thus Sir Henry de St. Clair, 16th May, 1296, prisoner in England, 7th April, 1299, to be exchanged for Sir William FitzWarin, 16th July, 1299, to be taken from Gloucester to York ; his expenses, 3rd August, 1299, and 12th September ; sends the king passing by Pentland a falcon gentil (August 1303–4) ; Sheriff of Lanark (15th September, 1305), mainprise by him (and others) for the Bishop of St. Andrew's, 22nd June, 1306, ordered to aid against Bruce (September, 1307) ; asked to obey the Earl of Richmond as warder ; intercedes for Sir Patrick de Graham in prison (1308) ; receives wine (September 1309) ; discharged (autumn, 1309) of mainprise for Malise, Earl of Strathern ; he and Alicia, his wife, forfeit a third of the barony of Rosselyn, 13th October, 1335–6.

There is this notice of him in the Exch. Rolls ‖ "Three pensions to members of the Saint Clair family appear first in the rolls immediately after King Robert's death. Sir

---
*Hay †Nisbet ‡Sinclairs of England ¾Ork Saga intro Vol I p 77, Preface

Henry Saint Clair of Roslin, one of the heads of the national party, had a charter dated 27th December, 1328*, a pension of 20 marks granted to himself and his heirs till provided with lands to that value." He is said to have married a daughter of Ramsay of Dalhousie † The christian name of his wife was Alicia ; she survived him, and as his widow her dower in Rosslyn, etc , was forfeited and given to Geoffrey Moubray, 10th September, 1336,‡ and it is noted that the baronies of Cousland, Rosselyn, and Pentland, belonging to *John* de St Clair, are given in custody to Geoffry de Moubray, 28th January, 1335-36 Sir Henry had issue—

 1 SIR WILLIAM OF SAINT CLAIR, his eldest son, one of the knights chosen to accompany Sir James Douglas on his expedition to Palestine with the heart of Bruce in charge , and it is known to all readers of Scottish history how, in an encounter with the Saracens on the Plains of Andalusia, Douglas lost his life in a fruitless effort to save his friend and comrade One of Bruce's latest acts was to settle, in 1329, on Sir William of St Clair a pension of £40⅔ in anticipation of the service he was about to do him This had been immediately preceded by one of 'ane annual '§ In the Lord Chamberlain's account for 1329 he is credited with the payments to Sir Henry St Clair of £13 6s 8d, Sir William St Clair £20, and John St Clair £10 , and in 1330 the full payments are noted of £27 13s 4d , £40, and £20 , and again of £13 6s 8d , £20, and £10 respectively at St Martin's term In 1331 Sir Henry received £13 6s 8d and £27 13s 4d , while those of the late Sir William St Clair, knight, and of the late John St Clair are received by the heir to whom John St Clair was uncle ‖ 14th December, 1331 Sir William de St Clair apparently left issue—

  1 WILLIAM DE ST CLAIR, next of Rosslyn
  2 THOMAS DE ST CLAIR, ballivus of Orkney, 1364 Both he and his son ALEXANDER DE ST CLAIR attest an instrument at Kirkwall in that year, and on the 1st November, 1371, Alexander, son of the quondam Thos de St Clair, receives from King David confirmation of a charter of the lands of Estirtyry, Aberdeen, from Hugh Ross of Philorth, and confirmation of another from William Earl of Ross of the lands of Bray, with pertinents in the *maresium de ffornewyr in vic de Inverness.*
  3 JOHN SINCLER, witness to an Orcadian instrument in 1367
  4 MARGARET, ¶ wife, first, in 1353, of Thomas, Earl of Angus, and, secondly, of Sir William St Clair of Herdmanston This is the first connection that can be traced between the two distinct branches of the Norman race of De Sancto Claro.

 2 JOHN OF ST CLAIR formed one of the expedition with his brother, and was slain at the same time The brothers were survived for a short time by their father, who died between 14th December, 1331, and 28th January, 1335-6

WILLIAM DE ST. CLAIR, 3RD LORD OF ROSSLYN,

who succeeded Sir Henry, was clearly a grandson to that knight, and in minority at the death of his father and grandfather, which is made manifest, by an entry in the Rolls 8th August, 1348, stating that Ardekelly is in ward by reason of William de St. Clair The annuity of forty marks granted to Sir Henry was confirmed to William St Clair by King David at Perth, on the 17th September, 1358. The recital terms him "our worthy and faithful William de St Clair, heir of the late Lord Henry de St Clair, Knight "[1] He further received from King David a charter of the lands of Merton and Merchamyston, bearing date at Edinburgh, the 11th February, 1358[1] (confirmed in 1363), and the same year proceeded to the Continent in gallant array.

---

* Genealogie, p 52   † Burke   ‡ Bain's Documents.   § Robertson's Index   ‖ Exch Rolls
          ¶ Burke, Ex Peerage   [1] Hay.

Under 1358 Tytler has —"At this period the Scottish kingdom was beset with designs against its independence, so dangerous in their nature and so artfully pursued that it was unfortunate that a spirit of military adventure carried many of its best soldiers to the continental wars. Sir Thomas Bisset, and Sir Walter Moigne, with Norman and Walter Leslie, previous to King David's return had left the country on an expedition to Prussia, in all probability to join the Teutonic knights who were engaged in a species of crusade against the infidel Prussians. Not long after Sir William Keith, Marshal of Scotland, SIR WILLIAM SINCLAIR, Lord of Roslin, Sir Alex. de Lindesay, Sir Robert Gifford, and Sir Alex Montgomery, each with a train of sixty horse and a strong body of foot soldiers, passed through England for the continent eager for distinction in foreign wars, with which they had no concern, and foolishly deserting their country when it most required their services (Rotuli Scotiae, vol. i., 32 Ed. III, p. 380.) Yet this conduct was more pardonable than that of the Earl of Mar, who entered into the service of England, and with a retinue of 24 knights and their squires, passed over to France in company with the English monarch and his army. The example was infectious, and the love of enterprise, the renown of fighting under so illustrious a leader, and the hopes of plunder, induced other soldiers to imitate his example." If William St Clair of Roslin is the same as Willielmus de Sancto Claro, Dominus de Pentland, who attests a charter granted by Patrick de Graham, Lord of Kinpont, and David de Graham, Lord of Dundaff, in the King's presence at Edinburgh, 1362,* then that must be accepted as evidence of his safe return from the Continent; and indeed there is a record of William de St. Clair, Lord of Dyserth, attesting a royal charter at Dundee, 20th November, 1364, while in the sheriffship accounts for Inverness in January, 1367, there is noted in the hands of Sir William Keith, Knight, " *Wardam hed. Willi de Sco. Claro, | p excambin t c de Anno Redd Coilat 'catanie £10* "

This William St Clair married† Isabella, second daughter, and eventually sole heiress, of Malise, II of Orkney and Caithness, and V of Stratherne, and had issue—

    1 HENRY, his successor   2 DAVID ‡

It is thought that William St. Clair died leaving his sons in minority, for though it is stated* that his son Henry was sent Ambassador to Denmark in 1363, it is certain that Henry was not Earl till 1379, and presumably younger than his cousin Alex de Ard, who, a minor in 1367, was Governor and Commissioner of Orcadia in 1375. The minority of Wm. St. Clair's son explains the appointment in 1364 of Thos. de St Clair as *ballivus regis Norvagie*, by virtue of his guardianship of Henry St. Clair the Earl prospective.

The next three Lords of Rosslin were —
   IV HENRY I, the Holy, 42nd Earl of Orkney,
   V HENRY II. 43rd Earl of Orkney, Lord St. Clair, and
   VI WILLIAM, 44th Earl of Orkney and the Earl of Caithness, 2nd Lord St. Clair

---

    * Hay.   † Diploma of Succession   ‡ Ork Saga intro

FEUDAL-TRANSITION PERIOD

LINEAGE *

VII SIR OLIVER ST. CLAIR, Knight, was 7th Lord of Rosslyn. It has been seen that Earl William of Orkney and Caithness had a son, William of Newburgh, by his first marriage. For reasons not to be discovered at this distance of time, he thought fit to pass by Sir William St Clair, his eldest son, in the succession to the gross of the estate, and gave him only the barony of Newburgh, in Aberdeenshire, while betwixt two sons of his second wife, Marjory, daughter of Alexander Sutherland, of Duffus, he divided his great estate. To SIR OLIVER ST CLAIR, his eldest son of that marriage, he disponed (9th September, 1476) the baronies of Roslin, Pentland, and Pentland Muir, the barony of Herbertshire, the lands of Cousland, the barony of Ravenscraig, Dubbo, Carberry, Dysart, etc , being the whole of the Earl's estate be-south Tay. This deed is confirmed by a charter under the Great Seal of King James III., the 10th September, in *anno* 1476, still extant in the rolls Sir Oliver has two appearances on the 3rd July, 1480 In one he is found instituting a suit—most probably a friendly one—as son to *umquhile* William Earl of Caithness, against Johnne Sinklar (his brother), Chanon of Glasgow, for wrongly taking land and tenement in Blackfriar's Wynde The decree which followed was adverse to the Canon until he should adduce evidence to substantiate his case † The other instance was that of a bond of even date, received from George, Lord Seton, for the peaceable "brookeing and joiseing" of his lands of Roslin, Pentland, Pentland More, Morton and Mortonhall, Harbarshire, Cosland, Dysart, and Ravenscrage, etc Amongst the witnesses to this instrument are John St Cler and Edward of St. Clair, probably of the Dryden family. He is noted as a Baron of Parliament 9th May, 1485, 1st October, 1487, the 11th January next thereafter, and lastly on the 3rd February, 1505 In 1481, having it seems in his own conscience a thorough conviction of the injustice his father had done to the eldest brother, he freely (voluntarily) conveyed to his elder brother, William of Newburgh, the lands of Cousland, of Dysert, and Ravynscraig, with the Castellis, etc , in Fyffe, and in the same instrument William and his apparent heir Henry renounced all claim to Roslin, and later on—in 1493—Henry, then Lord Sinclair, ratified the contract His other appearances are in 1491, when he gives over to George Saintclair his sone, Roslin and Herbertshire , in 1498, as a party to the Charter of Swinburgh, with his other brothers and sisters, to their brother Sir David Synclar, of Swinburgh , in 1504 he and his son George execute an agreement with William, Lord Borthwick, amongst the witnesses being [his brothers] Robert and Arthur Sinclair ; in 1511 he grants Lord Fleming some lands in Herbertshire; and in 1512 grants (it is stated) his son, Henry Saintclair, the lands of Braidle. Sir Oliver began a quarrel with Lord Borthwick, which lasted several years betwixt the two families. Roslin, having his ward, caused throw one of them

---

* Hay, Nisbet, Exch Rolls, etc   † Acta Domini Concilii

over the drawbridge of Roslin after dinner. This action was hotly pursued by Borthwick, as were the nonentries and wards by Roslin, which is evident by various charters.

Sir Oliver finished the Chapel of Roslin, as appears by his scutcheon in the vault, whereon there appears only a ragged cross, as also on the left hand of the window of the sacristie underground. He was thrice married First, to Christian Haldane,* secondly, to Elizabeth, daughter of William, third Lord Borthwick, and thirdly, to Isabella Livingstone He had several children, of whom were—

1. GEORGE, fiar of Roslin, married Agnes, daughter of Robert Crichton, Lord Sanquhar. On the 5th January, 1491-2, on his father's resignation, a charter of confirmation passed the Great Seal to George Sinclare, son and apparent heir of our cousin Sir Oliver Sinclair of Roslin, and again on the 9th May, 1506, he and Agnes Crichton, his spouse, are confirmed in the barony of Herbertshire, while on the 11th April, 1510, he is cited as dead, his widow as married to Andrew Ker of Cessford, and William Sinclair, his brother, as his heir
2. SIR WILLIAM, next of Rosslyn
3. HENRY, Bishop of Ross, &c
4. OLIVER of Pitcairns and Whitekirk } See Historiettes
5. JOHN, Bishop of Brechin, &c
6. ALEXANDER, who received from James V a charter of the lands, lordship, and barony of Cokbrandspeth, with tour, fortalice, &c, 5th April, 1541, it issues to "his familiar" servant Alexander, brother-german of Sir William Sinclair of Roslin He was made captive at Solway in 1542, and is rated by the English in lands per annum £100 scots=£25 and goods the like He did not long retain Colbrandspeth, for on 24th July, 1547, Sir George Douglas of Pettindrecht, knight, produced from him a charter of alienation followed by infeftment An Alex Sinclair, notary public, is named 24th February, 1538, and is noted as attesting a document 15th August, 1546
7. ARTHUR, who obtains 8th March, 1539, a charter of Lessuadin, &c, from Andrew, Abbot of Melrose, and on 30th August, 1546, confirmation passes the Great Seal of a charter by "our familiar" M John Sinclair to his brother-german Arthur, of the lands of Kirkhill, Linlithgow, for his aid during the English siege of 1544
8. JAMES, who on 5th December, 1537, obtains confirmation of a charter by Mr Henry Sinclare, son of Sir Oliver Sinclare of Roslin to his brother-german, James Sinclare (the king's familiar), of the lands of Stevenson with tower, fortalice, &c Witness John Sinclair, prebendario de Corstorphine There had previously been a charter to Jas Sinclair (de Stevenston) of Todrig in Berwick, 18th November, 1516, and of Todriklaidis et Fulschotlaw on 6th May, 1517, while on 28th August, 1536, there is a confirmation of sale by M Henrico Sinclair of lands of Stevinstoun in Berwick, to which John Sinclare de Gosfurde and Jac. Sinclare make attestation James Sinclair was made prisoner at Solway in 1542, and is rated by the English in lands per annum £100 scots=£25 and goods the like
1. MARGARET, married Sir Thos Kirkpatrick of Closeburn, who fought at Solway in 1542 He was a hostage for her brother Oliver Sinclair of Pitcairns

Sir Oliver St Clair must have died before 1523, when his eldest son in life

VIII. SIR WILLIAM SAINT CLAIR, of Roslin, is found in possession, for in that year he mortifies some parcels of ground for the use of the Prebendars of the College of Roslin. In the enumeration in this document reference is made to William, formerly Earl of Orkney and Caithness, and Lord de St. Clair, Chancellor and Great Justiciary of the Scots, Marjory Sutherland, his spouse, Oliver Sinclair, quondam of Roslin, Knight, and his spouse Elizabeth Borthwick, Alexander Stewart,† Commendator of the Monastery of Scone ; Sir William himself; his wife, Allisone Hume ; his sons, William and Gilbert ;

Stirling Protocol Book
† Cousin to Sir William, being son of his aunt Katharine Sinclair and the Duke of Albany.

and his brothers, Oliver and Alexander. The seal was red upon white wax, a ragged cross. On the 27th November, 1526, a confirmation passed to Sir William Sinclair, of Roslin, and Alison Hume, his spouse; and in 1527 he received a charter from King James V. confirming him in Roslin Castle, the barony and burgh of Roslin, Otislee, Lee, Dryden, Westercaikmure, Netleflat, Coubrehill, Catounne, *Baxterland de Inverleith, 20 merks annually from the lands of Lanv*, Halderston, Easter Ravinsnuke, Wester Ravinsnuke and Cairnhill, the right of patronage to the Collegiate Chapel of Roslin and the Chapel of St. Mathew there, the lands of the Barony of Herbertshire, etc. In 1531 he gave his son, Alexander St. Clair, a charter of the lands of Cuthiltoun and Little Deny, which is attested, amongst others, by James Sinclair in Lee. King James V. gave him, in 1533, a charter renewing some older ones of Roslin to his ancestor Henry Earl of Orkney; and in 1542 he executed an entail of Roslin and Herbertshire to his sons Wm., Gilbert, Patrick, Alexander, John, Oliver, Mathew, and Edward successively, whom failing to his brothers Oliver, Alexander, Arthur, and James. The next year, 1543, William, Lord Borthwick's retour is made *coram honorabilibus viris, Alexandro Heburne et Magistro Johanne Sinclar, vicecomitibus deputatis de Edinburgh*, . . . *per istos honorabiles viros subscriptos, viz., Edwardum Sinclar de Drydane, etc., etc.* Seasine to Catune is granted in 1544, by Sir William, in the presence of, amongst others, Edward Sinclair. Sir William received an annual pension of 300 merks from the Queen-Dowager, Marie of Guise, in 1546, for his allegiance to the crowne of Scotland. He lastly appears in an obligation of John Lord Borthwick, 23rd June, 1551, two of the attesting parties being Oliver and Thomas Saintclair.

Sir William was in a high degree of favour with King James V., who by his special writ of summons called him frequently to sit in Parliament, as appears from the Registers thereof. He married Alison Hume, daughter of George Lord Home, by whom he had issue—

    1. SIR WILLIAM, his successor, retoured in 1554.   2. GILBERT.   3. PATRICK.
    4. ALEXANDER, of Cuthilton and Little Denny, who had a son
        HERCULES, perhaps the reverend iconoclast of Shetland.
    5. JOHN.   6. OLIVER [of Westravensneuk].   7. SIR MATHEW.
    8. EDWARD SINCLAIR, of Dryden and of Ethay, in Orkney (*vide* Charter 28th October, 1583), *à quo* the Sinclairs of The Isle of Ethay.

Dying before 1554, Sir William was succeeded by his eldest son

IX. SIR WILLIAM SAINTCLAIR OF ROSLIN, who in that year was retoured to the barony, Oliver Sinclair of Pitcairns, Edward Sinclair of Dryden, and John Sinclair of Blans, being present. He redeemed the lands of Cuthiltoun from his brother Sir Mathew in 1558, and the next year, 1559, was appointed by Marie, Queen-Dowager of Scotland, Justiciary of the Lothians. He sided with Mary, Queen of Scots, at Langside, in 1568, for which he obtained a remission in 1574. In 1570 he was confirmed in his office of Justiciary. On the 1st September, 1567, the King, with advice and consent of the Regent and the Lords of Secret Council, required *inter alia* William Sinclair of Rosling to deliver his house of Roslin within twenty-four hours. On the 26th April, 1569, Sir William Sinclair, of Rosling, Knyght; James Forester, of Corstorphin; Maister Johnne Marjoribanks; and George Ramsay, of Dalhousie, became sonertie that Roslin sall presently rander and deliver to George Sinclair in Ley, samekill of his gudis as is presentlie undisponit, intromettit with be the said Williame or ony at his command, als gude as the samyn wes the tyme of the intromissioun thairwith; and for onything that

FEUDAL-TRANSITION PERIOD.

wantis, the saidis persons ar becum souertie for randering and restitutioun thairof, or the avale of the same, betwix and the xxix. day of Maii nixtocum, and the said Williame obleist him to releve   And the said Geo. Sinclair renunceit the summondis and actioun of spulye that he may haif aganis the said Williame for the gudis spulyeit or intromettit with be him, or ony at his command, perteining to the said George. The quhilk day the said Rosling and George Crauford of Lesnoreis assurit ilkane of thame for thame and all utheris that thai may lett, quhill my Lord R Grace gif his decreit and decln. upon the blank subscribed be the said parties. Sic subscribitur William Sinclair of Rosling, Knycht,—Geo. Ramsay of Dalhousie—Corstorphin—Mr. Johne Marjoribanks.

He appends his seal to the charter of *Dominus Johannes Robeson, praepositus de Rosling*, 26th February, 1571, which is also subscribed by *Henricus Sinclar prebendarius*   On the 28th April, 1571, with his consent, Dominus Johannes Dickson, praepositus of Roslin, executed a charter concerning Roslin lands, to which William Sinclair, brother-german of Sir William Sinclair, of Herminston, Knight, is a witness   On the 6th July, 1573, he was charged to produce certain gold buttons belonging to the King's modir, of which he denied receipt ; on the 18th August, same, he was charged to enter his pledge re David Bell, of which obligation he was relieved on the 31st idem   In 1574, he and John Sinclair in Gosfuird, obtained a remission for their being present at Langside in 1568, and the same year he resigned his lands in favour of his eldest son Edward   On 12th October, 1590, there was Registration of Caution that Roslin will not harm John Crichton of Brunstoun, and on the 19th idem Crichton entered into Caution to the like effect with reference to Roslin.   Roslin was denounced as rebel 2nd August, 1591, for having failed to appear, and on the 16th idem Caution for him was subscribed before Oliver Sinclair, of Ravens-neuk, and Henry Sinclair, of Quhitekirk , while on the 10th August, 1604, Roslin had to enter Caution not to harm Ravensneuke

Sir William gathered a great many manuscripts, which had been taken by the rabble out of our monasteries in the time of the Reformation, whereupon we find as yet his name written thus : " Sir William Sinclar, of Roslin, Knight , he delivered once an Egyptian from the gibbet in the Burrow Moore, ready to be strangled, returning from Edinburgh to Roslin. upon which accompt the whole body of gypsies, were, of old, accustomed to gather in the stanks of Roslin every year, where they acted severall plays, dureing the moneth of May and June   There are two towers which were allowed them for their residence, the one called Robin Hood, the other Little John ''

Sir William gave a charter to William Lord Borthwick in 1578, to which an Oliver Saintcler is a party, and the seasine following thereon in 1581 issues from Oliver Sinclare of Westerravensneuk, by virtue of letters from William Saintclaire   Sir William inhibits James Lord Borthwick and other tenants in Catoun Milne the 8th January, 1582 , and on the 1st November following he required Lord James, his vassal and ward, to compleat and solemnise the bond of matrimony with either his eldest daughter Elspeth or his third daughter **Helen Saintclair**   Among the witnesses to this instrument were Edward Sinclair of Dryden, his brother, and Oliver Sinclair of Westerravensneuk.   On the 22nd December, 1582, he disponed to his son William the lands of Catoune. From various incidents in connection with the Roslin-Borthwick litigation it would seem that Sir William was alive as late as the 1st June, 1602.

It is stated in Nisbet's Heraldry that he married Elizabeth or Isabel, daughter of Sir Walter Ker of Cessford, while Hay has it that he married .   Lindesay, daughter to the Laird of Egle, brother-german to the Earl of Crawford, by whom he had with three daughters (Elspeth, Isobell, and Helen) two sons—

1. EDWARD, married to Christian, daughter of George Douglas of Parkhead, Governor of Edinburgh Castle, by whom he had no issue. He had obtained a charter of Roslin on the resignation of his father in 1574. Before his marriage he had chosen curators, and thereafter when he was over twenty-one years, being childless, in 1582 he resigned the barony in favour of his brother-german William, a witness to the Deed of Resignation eing Henry Sinclair of Whitekirk. Upon this, litigation ensued, for at Edinburgh, 4th May, 1583, entry is found for Caution in £400 by Sir Wm. Sinclair of Roslin and William his second sone as principals, Manis Sinclair of the Leyis and Mr. John Henrysone of Drydane as sureties that Christiane Douglas, daughter of Geo. Douglas of Parkhead, her tenants and servants of the lands of Herbertshire, said to belong to her in conjunct fee, shall be skaithless. On the 15th same she prefers complaint that her husband, Edward Sinclair, fiar of Roslin, had been abducted and kept captive in Roslin to his own prejudice, and also to that of her dower, etc. On the 23rd September following there is caution for Edward Sinclair that Christian Douglas his spouse shall have peaceable access to him at Roslin.

2. WILLIAM, next of Roslin.

Sir William was succeeded in the representation by his second son

X. WILLIAM, the first Hereditary Grandmaster of the Scottish Order of Freemasons, so constituted by charter, which see. In 1582 his brother Edward had conveyed to him the Baronies of Roslin and Herbertshire, *coram* Henry Saintcler of Qwhitkirk. This Roslin built the vaults and great turnpike of Roslin. Upon the last his name and arms, with the arms of his lady, are as yet seen (1700). He builded one of the arches of the Drawbridge, a fine house near the Milne, and the Tower of the Dungeon, where the clock was kept. The initiall lettres of his name are graven on a stone, above the dyall, with the following, 1596, which designs the year wherin that worke was finished. He gets a Charter in 1601 from Henry Saintcler, Provost of Roslin, of the Church lands. He resigns his lands *lying within the Earledome of Cathnes* in 1612. In his time Alexander Saintcler infeft Hercules Saintcler his sone in Cuthiltoun and Little Denny.

He married Jean or Janet Edmonstone, daughter of the Laird of that Ilk in the Merse, by whom he had a son, Sir William Sinclar of Pentland, knight, his successor. On the 25th March, 1617, Wm. Sinclair and his son Sir William resigned the Baronies of Roslin and Pentland, and a new infeftment issued to Dame Anna Spotswood, spouse to the said Sir William, in liferent, of all and haill the lands and toune of Pentland, and sichlike of the lands of Otislie, and the part of Roslin then occupied by Robert Park, and also for new infeftment to be made to the said Sir William and to his heirs-male; which failing to Robert Sinclair of Loucharmagus, etc.; which failing to the said Sir William's nearest heirs, bearing the surname and armes of Saintcler, of the Baronies of Roslin, Pentland, Morton, and Mortonhall. Seasine followed on the 1st February, 1619, in the presence of Oliver Saintcler, brother-german of Henry Sinclair of Qwhitkirk. Hay writes of him: "Sir William Sinclair was a leud man. He kept a miller's daughter, with whom, it is alleged, he went to Ireland; yet I think the cause of his retreat was rather occasioned by the Presbyterians, who vexed him sadly because of his religion being Roman Catholic."

XI. SIR WILLIAM SAINTCLAIR, designed *of Pentland*, succeeded his father. His contract of marriage with Dame Anna Spotswood, daughter to John Spotswood, then Archbishop of Glasgow, thereafter Archbishop of St. Andrew's, and Chancellor of Scotland, is dated at Leith 20th November, 1609, and registered in the books of Counsell

7th August, 1610, at which time Pentland was wadset to Archibald Douglas of Tostis in liferent, and to his sone in fie under reversion, to which Sir William was made sessioner. He had numerous issue, viz —

    1 WILLIAM, died in France He had two natural daughters—
        1 MARGARET (by a niece of Scougall of Whitekirk), married to James Carruthers, tutor of Annandale   2 ELIZABETH, unmarried
    2 JOHN, commonly called "the Prince," next of Roslin.   3 JAMES, hereafter of Roslin.
    4 LEWIS, Capt of Horse in General Duncan's Regiment, killed at the siege of Hallingsted in the county of Hall   5 HENRY.   6 PATRICK
    7 CHARLES, who was possessed by a spirit He died abroad.
    8 ROBERT.   9 GEORGE, died young   10. ARCHIBALD, who died unmarried
    1 RACHAEL, m. to Hume, Laird of Foord
    2 RACHAEL *(sic)*, died unmarried   3 MARGARET, died young
    4 HELEN, married, 1st, to Sir John Rollo of Bannockburne ; 2nd, to Stirling of Herbertshire ; and 3rd, to Colin McKenzie, brother to the Earl of Seaforth

This Sir William also received a charter of the Hereditary Protectorate from the Scottish Freemasons in 1630, and in 1635, upon the appointment of Sir Anthonie Alexander to the office of Master of Work for Scotland, preferred an objection as being in prejudice to his hereditary charge of the Masons of the Kingdom. He died during the Civil War, and was interred in Roslin Chapel, the very same day that the battle of Dunbar was fought, 3rd September, 1650

XII. JOHN SAINTCLAIR, second son to Sir William, succeeded his father His estate being in burthen was wodset to Sir John Saintclair of Herdmanston, who in 1663, with consent of his son John, disponed irredeemably of the lands of Cattune to John, Lord Borthwick In November, 1666, Roslin raised letters of lawborrowes against Herdmanston, and inhibited him in 1667, and the next year, 1668, received back the lands of Roslin from Sir Robert Sinclair of Longformacus, who had acquired Herdmanston's interest for 10,000 merks scots On his father's death in 1650 John Saintclair, commonly called "the Prince," kept out the house of Roslin against General Monk after the battle of Dunbar, and after the surrender of the castle was sent prisoner by Cromwell to Tinemouth, where he remained during the troubles He only surrendered after one side was battered down by General Monk's superior force. John Saintcler of Roslin died in 1690, and was buried at the charge of Mrs James Saintclaire, the third of Marche, in which year, the last Friday of Februarie, 1690, by her industrie, was found att night in Roslin the best burning coal in Scotland

XIII JAMES SAINTCLAIRE, who succeeded his brother, had redeemed the estate several years before, to which end his wife, who was also nearly related to him, did much contribute Hay records· "He was in his youth bound apprentice in London, thereafter he went to France, where he spent some years with Mr Monteith, author of 'The Troubles of Great Britain,' who was settled in the beginning with M. de la Porte, Great Prieur of France and Knight of Malta, as I have heard of the present Duke of Mazarine, his nephew, sone to the Marechal de la Mailleraye After the Great Prieur's death, he entered into the service of the Cardinall de Rets, Coadjutor of Paris, then Archbishop of Corinth, to whom Roslin dedicat his Booke of the 'Troubles of Brittany,' being left his heir After Mr Monteith's death he applyed himself to my Lord Rutherford, Viscount of Teviott; he stayed some years with him as his Secretarie att Dunkirk, whilst the fortifications were perfiting, and att Tangiers in Africa Thereafter he was made

Commissar of Shetland, and after my father's death he espoused my mother, Mrs. Jean, daughter to Sir Henry Spotswood (Sheriff of Dublin), who bore to him—

1. JAMES, born 8th March, 1671, who was Page of Honour to Queen Marie and Cornett of her Guards in Parker's Company. He was killed att the Boyne, fighting for King James in Ireland. His death gave rise to the quatrain in an ' Orange Song ' :—

" . . . St. Clair is dead,
And all his men are from the battle fled ;
As he rode down the hill he met his fall,
He died a victim to a cannon-ball."

2. ALEXANDER, next of Roslin, born 30th November, 1672.
3. THOMAS, born 4th March, 1676 ; married Elizabeth, daughter of Capt. Wachope. Issue—
    1. JAMES, in French army, married a daughter of Commissioner Wedderburn.
    2. FRANCIS, a General in the Neapolitan service.
    3. A daughter, married to Bower of Methie and Kincaldrum. 4. A daughter.
1. HELEN, born 15th March, 1670 ; married Henry Kerr of Gredane in the Mers.
2. ANNA, born 20th February, 1674 ; died at the age of nine, by the negligence of Mr. Davidson, a seminary priest.

"Roslin, their father was a very civil and discreat man. He dealt with us that were childering of the first marriage, begotten by Mr. George Hay, very kindly, notwithstanding that he scattered us far off after his marriage, sending the one to France, ane other to England, and a third to sea. He was much taken up with building, and addicted to the Priests ; those two inclinations spoiled his fortune. He died in a good adge, and with the reputation of ane honest man ; yet I have perceived in examineing his papers after his death, that he was too easie, and that his correspondents at Rowen, Mr. Alexander att Paris, Lady Magdalene Creichton, one of the heirs of Francis Irwine, and the Scots Mission of Seminarie Priests, have imposed on him, which goodness of his brought, after his death, some trouble to my mother. He acquired a brae att Gortoun, with a design to imparke the wood ; he built a well about the Colledge and the garden towards the Lynne ; he builded also the fore part of the Castle on the left hand entring the drawbridge, upon which his arms and name are seen conjunctly with my mother's ingraven on a stone. He builded likewise the legions of the bridge on the Water of Esk, under the Castle, with a gate to stop the passengers, with severall other parcells of walls about the parks and other buildings. He was made Burges of Edinburgh by Provest Currie, notwithstanding that he was Roman Catholick. It was by his means that one Bruse, who had married a Flemender, was imployed to bring in water to the severall fountains of Edinburgh. The same brought in water in lead pipes to the inner court of the Castle of Roslin, and to the lower vaults. My mother, after his death, sent James and Alexander, her childering, to Paris, under the government of Mr. Davidsone. They stayed sometime in a French Pension near to the Colledge of Lysieux ; therafter they were confined to the Scots Colledge by the Missionaries advice. Whilst they were there the Dutches of Yorke was willing to accept of both of them for her pages. Mr. Innes, then principall, as I think, being unwilling to let them both return home att once, hindered their fortune. He detained Alexander, next Laird of Roslin, with him att Paris, and allowed the other to returne to Scotland. He was made page att his comeing to the country, and his brother remaining abroad, the other place designed for him was filled up by ane other.

"When my goodfather was buried, his corps seemed to be intire att the opening of the cave, but when they came to touch his body it fell into dust ; he was laying in his armour, with a red velvet cap on his head on a flat stone ; nothing was spoild except a piece of

FEUDAL-TRANSITION PERIOD

the white furring that went round the cap, and answered to the hinder part of the head. All his predecessors were buried after the same manner in their armour. Late Roslin, my goodfather, was the first that was buried in a coffin, against the sentiments of King James the Seventh, who was then in Scotland, and severall other persons well versed in antiquity, to whom my mother would not hearken, thinking it beggarly to be buried after that manner. The great expenses she was att in burieing her husband occasioned the sumptuarie acts which were made in the following Parliaments."

Lady Rosline petitioned James the Seventh and his Queen for some compensation for the great losses sustained by the Rosslyns during their loyal adhesion to the royal cause, such as would enable her to make needful reparations to the Chapell and Castle of Roslin. The petitions made recital of the injury done to Roslin Castle when defending it against the artillery of General Monk, and that by adhering to King James the Fifth's dowager and his daughter, Mary Queen of Scots, the then Roslin had been obliged to sell the lands of Herbertshire, Pentland, Mortoun, and Mortounhall. These petitions were of little use, and all she succeeded in getting was a commission for her son as Cornet of the Guards. Her second son succeeded to Roslin, viz,

XIV. ALEXANDER ST CLAIR, who married Jean, daughter of Robert, seventh Lord Semple. This laird was of considerable poetical ability, his poems in MSS are preserved in the Advocates' Library. He had issue—

1 WILLIAM, his successor.

Two sons and three daughters, who died young.

He was succeeded by his son

XV. WILLIAM ST CLAIR, last of Roslin, who married Cordelia, daughter of Sir George Wishart of Cliftonhall, by whom he had three sons and five daughters, who all died young except his daughter Sarah.

He was a man of magnificent physique, and in all the manly sports which require strength and dexterity was unrivalled; his particular delight being archery. A fuller account of him will appear in Historiettes.

The line of Roslin is generally assumed by peerage and other writers to be extinct, but it seems scarcely credible that there are no male descendants extant of the eight sons of Sir Oliver, the eight sons of the first Sir William, or the ten sons of Sir William of Pentland. They are perhaps to be found in the Isles, where Hercules, son of Alexander Saintcler of Cuthiltoun and Little Deny, is discovered acquiring notoriety as an iconoclast; and Edward Sinclair of Dryden, the "Gudeman of Ethay," left issue several sons. It is stated in the "Genealogie" that Henry, third sone to Sir Oliver Saintclere of Roslin, by Isabella Levingston, was governor of the Castle of Bergen in Norway, where his arms are seen upon that part of the Castle that was built in his time, and in the Holy Cross Church of Bergen his name is written. He married Gurena Guldelove, by whom he had severall childering, settled in Norway, whose posterity remain there to this day. This may be the Henry to whom Sir Oliver assigned the lands of Braidle in 1512, but it is generally understood that the only Henry, son of Sir Oliver, was the Bishop of Ross, who could not have been identical with the Governor of Bergen Castle, nor was the stone Bergen Castle then erected.

THE SINCLAIRS OF PITCAIRN AND WHYTKIRK *

I. OLIVER SINCLAIR OF PITCAIRN AND WHYTKIRK was the fourth son of Sir Oliver St Clair of Roslyn. A charter of Pitcairn in Perth, issued to him and his spouse Katherine Bellenden on the 13th January, 1537. On the 13th January, 1538-9, Letters of Legitimation were issued to James Sinclair, natural son of "our familiar" Oliver Sinclair de Pitcairn, he and his wife are mentioned 15th February, 1541-2. Taken prisoner at Solway in 1542, the English rate him as having lands value 500 merks scots per annum = 125 merks sterling; goods £1,000 scots = £125 sterling. On the 13th December, 1543, there are several entries referring to a suit instituted by the Queen-Dowager against Oliver. On the 1st September, 1567, Oliver Sinclair of Quhitkirk was required to enter his person in ward within the castell of Down of Menteith within three days, remaining there at his own expense until relieved. On 18th November, 1567, he was required to compeire under pane of rebellion and horne to answer the complaint of Andro Lamb against Petcarne and others, his accomplices, for invading and pursuing, etc., him and his for occupying the lands of Polmore. On the 24th August, 1568, Oliver Sinclair of Whytkirk, was desired to appear in presence of my Lord Regent and the three estates of Parliament. "To p'cure to p'test as effeirit for the laird of Roslin, his chief and kinsman." He had issue—

1. HENRY SINCLAIR of Whytekirk
2. OLIVER SINCLAIR, his brother-german, perhaps of Ravensneuk, witness 1st November, 1582.
1. ISABELLA, natural and legitimate daughter of Oliver Sinclair and Katherine Bellentyne, most probably legitimised by marriage subsequent to birth
   JAMES, natural son, Letters of Legitimation 13th January, 1538-9

II. HENRY SINCLAIR OF WHYTKIRK and Oliver Sinclair of Ravensneuk are caution for Roslin 16th August, 1591, and in 1582 he had witnessed the conveyance by Edward Sinclair, fiar of Roslin, to his brother William. On the 11th August, 1590, Oliver Sinclair in Ravensneuke is one of those cited as a troubler of ministers and for being suspected of ecclesiastical offences. Mr. Henry Sinclair, Provost of Roslin, appeared 28th January, 1601, for Oliver, brother of Henry Sinclair of Whytekirk. On 9th January, 1602, Oliver Sinclair of Ravensneuke became surety for the appearance of Henry Sinclair of Whitekirk touching the ravishing of Margaret Carkettle, on the 28th same, he was committed to ward, but horning was suspended. In defence he denied the abduction. On the 26th August, 1606, he was accused of invading the house of Margaret Murray, Lady Ford.

THE SINCLAIRS OF DRYDEN, SPOTTS, WOODHOUSLEE, ETC.*

I. An EDWARD SAINTCLAIR OF DRAIDON is referred to by Hay as witnessing a migratory procession of rats from Roslin Castle four days before the feast day of St. Leonard, 1447, and one of the witnesses to the instrument of infeftment of Herbertshire, dated 26th November, 1447, and in favour of the Countess of Orkney is *Edwardus de Sancto Claro, Armiger.* Later on John St Cler and Edward of St. Clair witness a bond by George, Lord Seton, to Sir Oliver St. Clair of Roslin, the 3rd July, 1480, and in 1502 an Edward Sinclair defeats in the Orkneys an English incursion under Sir John Elder.

---

* Exch Rolls, Reg Privy Seal, &c.

On the 12th April, 1481, David Sinclair has to restore to Edward Sinclair a brown horse he had taken from him. He had issue—

1. SIR JOHN SINCLAIR, knight, next of Dryden
2. WILLIAM, brother-german to Sir John, apparently identical with William Sinclair, "*ostiarius*"-usher of the outer door of the king's chamber,—who in 1490 receives his fee of £13 6s 8d , and gives a receipt for George Sinclair of Hefeld ; in 1492 William Sinclare is tenant of the Mill of Culwen (Galloway) , 1499 William Sincler *hostiarius camere exteriorus*, on 21st March, 1499/1500, the hostiarius receives for good services land and a house in Edinburgh, in 1503, there is this enumeration—"And Andrew, Lord Avondale, first usher of the chamber to our lord King , Patrick Crichton, *panitarius*, Peter Crichton, *in gardiroba*, knights , Walter Leslie, John Stewart, Thomas French, John Inglis, and James Mercer, mariscallis , Williame Sinclair, *ostiarius camere exteriorus* , who are nine persons in number " In 1508 and 1509 there is William Sinclair, noted as usher of the Queen's chamber, and lastly a similar notice in 1514
3. GEORGE, brother-german of Sir John, probably George Sinclair of Hefeld, who is frequently noticed —In 1489 he receives payment on behalf of the Earl of Bothwell for expenses of the Duke of Ross, and various other payments , in 1490 he has a lease of Slewindaw, in Galloway, with building obligation, in 1493 he is stewart-depute of Kirkcudbright , on the 13th May, 1503, he has a lease of the merkland of Kilbride, Galloway , on the 25th February, 1505, he affixes his seal to a conveyance of the bordland of Lagan , on the 1st April, 1506, he is fined by the Baillary Court at Dirleton, held at Dirleton Castle, he being present, for not entering suit for Hefeld , and he is lastly mentioned in 1513 in the charter by his brother-natural, Patrick Sinclair of Spottis
4. M. WILLIAM, brother-german to the preceding, perhaps identifiable as Master William Sinclair, tenant of the Bankis of Row, 11th April, 1502, acquired by John Sinclair [of Dryden] the king's armiger, 11th May, 1491. In 1503 the grassums of the quondam William Sinclair were remitted, and in 1505 Bankis of Row were assigned with consent of the relict of William Sinclair, but in 1508 Master William Sinclair is still noted as tenant and feuar of that property He was alive in 1513

Edward Sinclair of Dryden had also two natural sons—

1. PATRICK SINCLAIR of Spottis, and
2. HECTOR SINCLAIR, his brother-german

Patrick Sinclair has a separate notice in the Historiettes He was in great favour with the Scottish Court On 23rd March, 1502, a charter issues Tenementum terre infra burgum de Linlithgow to Patrick Sinclair, our familiar , on the 21st February, 1506-7, he is granted the lands of Spottis ; on the 30th October, 1507, he is assigned £27 from Lessualt and Monybrig , the same year he receives other sums , in 1508 there issues from King James IV a charter and precept to "our loved familiar for good and faithful services " of an annuity of £27 from the fee-duty of Lessualt and Monybrig, in Galloway, which is accounted for in due course in 1509 and 1510 , and in 1512 Patrick Sinclair of Spottis receives a lease of Mote of Ur and Grange of Spottis, alleged to be feued to him.

On the 20th July, 1513, there is Confirmation to Patrick Sinclere of Spottis of the lands of Spottis, with mill, in Kirkcudbright remainder to the legitimate heirs of his body whom failing to (1) Hector Sinclair, his brother-german , (2) Sir John Sinclair of Dryden, knight , (3) William Sinclair, brother-german of Sir John , (4) George Sinclair, also brother-german ; (5) M. William Sinclair, also brother-german ; whom all failing to the lawful and nearest heirs of the said Sir John Sinclair. *Insuper ex* special grace concede Patrick and Hector, brothers, bastard sons of the late Edward Sinclair de Dridane, the right to make disposition In 1515 Patrick Sinclair and the Lady of Coldonknowis, his wife, are to be cited (Brechin and Nevaire) ; in 1517 Patrick Sinclair is sheriff of Roxburgh—*senescallus in hac parte*, in 1522 he is noted as of Lesswalt and Monybrig, and in 1524 is named as of Spottis re the Mote of Ur On the 29th September, 1529, a charter issues to Robert, Lord Maxwell, of Spottis, which Patrick Sinclair resigned, and the 11th October thereafter he is noted as witnessing a document. A charter issued to him on the 25th March, 1530, of the lands of Castellaw, Est-Raw, Myltoun, and Woodhouselee, Edinburgh, and on the 29th January, 1545, he gave a charter as Patrick Sinclair of Woodhouselee to his natural son John Sinclare, and Isobelle Hamilton, his spouse, of the lands of Castellaw, Eistraw, Shakentyhole, Mylntoun, etc., with the exception of Woodhouselee This is his last appearance

II SIR JOHN SINCLAIR OF DRYDEN, knight, has a separate notice in the Historiettes The numerous entries in the records indicate that the Roslins and Drydens were at this period held in a special degree of favour by the royal household On the 11th May, 1491, the King's letters issued to John Sinclare, 'armigero suo,' and his successors, granting to him the lands of Westir Row, Bankis of Row, Ovir Argathe, Lundylug, Estir-Argathe, Argath-Corntoune, Lundyskeuch, Lundy Arthur, Lundy Makcane, Eglisdisdane, et Ballechragane in Menteith. In 1492 he has the dominical lands of Houston, with mill and cottages, assigned to him, to which reference is again made in 1496, 1497, 1498, and in 1502 when he is styled Sir John of Dryden, knight, in 1507, when they are assigned to him for life, in 1512, 1513, and finally in 1514

It is not clear that subsequent notices of Sinclairs of Dryden are of his descendants

III EDWARD SINCLAIR OF DRYDEN was the eighth son of Sir William Sinclair of Roslin He appears so styled on several occasions. From a charter of date 28th October, 1583, he is identified as Edward Sinclair of the Isle of Ethay, in Orkney

IV. JAMES SINCLAIR OF DRYDEN, 25th October, 1587, finds caution for James Giffard, younger, of Shereffhall

V. JOHN SINCLAIR OF DRYDEN, presently mentioned, was, by Katharine Crichton, father of

VI. JOHN SINCLAIR, to whom, on 15th July, 1595, an order issued as son of the late (v.) JOHN SINCLAIR OF DRYDEN and Katharine Crichton, his mother, and all other keepers of the manor place of Lessuade to deliver the same to officers within three hours under pain of treason On the 5th June, 1600, John Sinclair, sometime of Dryden, is charged with having assaulted his servant upon the latter's going to the said John's dwelling-house at Dalkeith. John Sinclair of Dryden gave a charter of Lasswade 21st May, 1591, to John Nicolson, advocate, father of Sir John Nicolson of Lasswade, Baronet.

CHAPTER X

BARONS OF RAVENSCRAIG.*

I. HENRY II., EARL OF ORKNEY, is the first of his line to whom the title of Lord Sinclair is found allotted in public documents By his Countess, the Lady Egidia Douglas, he had an only son

II. WILLIAM ST. CLAIR, Lord Sinclair, Earl of Orkney and Caithness. He was twice married first, to Elizabeth Douglas, Countess-Dowager of Buchan and the Garioch, by whom he had—

    1 WILLIAM, the disinherited Master of Orkney and Caithness

and secondly, to Marjory, daughter of Alexander Sutherland of Duffus, by whom he had with other issue—

    1 2 {SIR OLIVER of Roslyn
           {WILLIAM II , Earl of Caithness

Earl William had resigned the Earldom of Orkney in 1471, and obtained in exchange the Castle of Ravenscraig and the lands of Wilton, Carberry, and Dubbo in Fife. In 1476, in supersession of his eldest son, he assigned Roslin, Pentland, Pentland Moor, Mortoun, Mortonhall, and Harbertshire to his son Sir Oliver, ancestor of the subsequent line of Roslins; and in the same year resigned the Earldom of Caithness to the Crown, upon which a new charter issued to his son William of the second marriage in derogation of the rights of the elder William, son of the first marriage Various reasons have been assigned for the disinherison Hay informs us that Earl William and his first countess were separated on account of consanguinity and affinity, but the issue of this marriage could hardly have been considered as unlawful, for we are told that the Earl, not contented with this separation, sent to the Pope, who dispensed therwith, and so he married her anew again into St Mathieu's Church, where they were separated The Earl may have taken a deep dislike to his son on account of his mother being a Douglas, as after his wife's death to be identified with that family meant being a mark for attack from the Crown, and we find the Earl on the side opposed to the Douglases The most likely reason, however, is to be found in the action of the Master of Orkney himself, who, by his imprisonment in 1466 of William Tulloch, Bishop of Orkney, was the primary cause of the loss of that Earldom But it seems questionable whether the Master was disinherited at all, for we find him possessed of Newburgh (which had formerly belonged to David St Clair, brother of Earl Henry I.), and there is no doubt that he had also numerous lands in the Isles The Earl's devise was probably an equitable one, in keeping with his life. He died about the year 1480, and was survived by his eldest son

III. WILLIAM ST CLAIR OF NEWBURGH, *de jure* third Lord Sinclair He first appears in records in 1456, when on behalf of the Earl of Orkney, Wm. Sinclare forcibly takes the price of the tierce of Mar from Wm Seton of Echt; and on 13th February, 1463, *apud* Carten-Sinclare a charter issued by William, Master of Orkney and Caithness

---

* Exch Rolls , Reg. Privy Seal , Burke , Hay, etc

and Lord of Carten-Sinclare (Menteith) et Yemy (Lennox) to Malm MacClery (confirmed 17th August, 1465) In 1466 he imprisoned the Bishop of Orkney. On 15th April, 1478, there is confirmation of a sale of fishing-rights in Ithane by Wm. de St Clair, Lord of the Barony of Newburgh, with consent of Christian his spouse, to Sir James Ogilvy of Deskford, knight. In 1480 he had sasine to Cousland and Dysart On 17th June, 1486, Nicholas Ramsay was confirmed in Wilstoun and Carberry, which William Sinclare resigned ; and on 20th July, 1487, there is confirmation of a sale by Wm de St Clair, Baron de Newburgh, with consent of Christian Leslie his spouse, of the lands of Archadlie in Newburg *cum subscriptione manuali* Williame Lord Synclare, at Stirling Peerage writers inform us that his life was spent in a struggle with the more favoured brothers for a share of the paternal inheritance

William, Earl of Orkney and Caithness, having also infeft Sir Oliver of Roslyn, his son of a second marriage, in all his baronies lying within the sheriffdoms of Edinburgh, Fife, and Stirling, to the prejudice of William Sinclair of Newburgh, his eldest son of the first marriage It was sustained by Newburgh, post excessum patris, that the disposition made by his deceased father was null, 1 mo. in respect he was the only child that had undoubted title to those lands by the common law, as being heir to the deceased Earl, and so could not be prejudged by any private deed made in behalf of the younger children, since the collector of our Regiam Majestatem, lib 2 cap 27 art 2 de successione filii ad patrem, expresses himself thus Si pater fuerit miles, tunc eo casu, ejus filius primogenitus succedit in totum ita quod nullus fratrum suorum partem inde, de jure, petere potest 2 do That in the greatest rigour, and even stretching the law, his father was only allowed by the 2nd chap art. 2 to give filiis postnatis, id est, post primogenitum natis, partem rationabilem de hæreditate sua, cum consensu hæredis Whereas he had granted to Sir Oliver the bulk of his estate lying as said is in Fife, and towards the South of Forth, without his consent: and by that means he had deprived him of his right to the succession Which was his third exception Which right could no more have been abstracted from the heir than the roundness from a bowl or sphere ; according to the 20th chap art 1, Non licet filium ex hæredare After some replies and duplies made by the advocates, the lands in debate were divided by the agreement of both parties, under form of instrument, whereby Sir Oliver and his heirs resigned and gave over to William Lord Saintclair of Newburgh, his elder brother and his heirs all and haill, the lands of Cowsland, with their pertinents, lying within the sheriffdom, Edin , and his lands of Dysart within the barony of Samin ; with lands of Ravenscraig and castle of same , the lands of Dubbo, Carberry and Wilston, lying in Fife , patronages of kirks and chaplainries, office of bailery, etc., to remain heritably with the said William and his heirs perpetually [and shall give William all charters, sure evidents, infeftments, and obligations yet he hes, or may give of the saidis lands, or of ony lands yat may be profitable to the said William and not skaithless to himself in other lands, nor to his younger brother William] And on the other hand, William of Newburgh, designed, Primogenitus et Haeres Magnifici et Potentis Domini, Domini Willielmi Comitis Orcadiæ et Cathaniæ ; and his son Henry likewise called Primogenitus et hæres apparens dicti Willielmi, Domini de Newbrugh ; renounce their interest to the baronies of Roslin, the castle of the same, and patronage of the college, or provostry, to the lands of Pentland, Pentlandmure, Morton and Mortonhall, and to the barony of Herbertshire. And both of them bind themselves to stand by one another, under the penalty of £5,000, whereof £3,000 were payable to the King, and £2,000 to the Archbishop of St Andrew's *nomine poenæ* within 40 days; as also under the penalty of infamy and inhability, and of being mensworn men, they having sworn on the Holy Evangils the performance of the foresaid articles. And it is thereby declared that Sir Oliver shall worship and honour the said William as effeirs, and accords him to do to his eldest brother. And if there happen any plea or contestation betwixt the said William of Newburgh and William his younger brother for the Earldom of Caithness, the said Sir Oliver shall stand neuter between them, as he should do betwixt his brethren, and take no part with either of them during the quarrel. The agreement is dated 9th February, 1481. Witnesses William, Archbishop of St. Andrew's, Andrew Stuart, Lord Avondale, Chancellor Scotland, Colin, Earl of Argylle, John, Earl of Athole, William, Bishop of Ross, Andrew Stuart, Provost of Lincluden, Mr George Carmichael, Treasurer of Glasgow, Alex. Lumsden, rector of Flisk; and Alex. Borthwick, clerk of St. Andrew's. And sealed with the seals of the Archbishop of St Andrew's, the Lord Chancellor, and the Earl of Argyle, and subscribed by the public notaries. This agreement is ratified 18th February, 1481.*

William of Newburgh, third Lord Sinclair, is generally called "William the Waster." He died in 1487, and was interred at Dunfermline,† leaving by his wife Lady Christian Leslie, daughter of George, first Earl of Rothes—

1 HENRY, Master of Sinclair, next Baron
2 SIR WILLIAM of Warsetter, Orknay, *a quo* they of Warsetter, Saba, etc
1 ELIZABETH, married as second wife to John Glendonwyn († 1503)

IV. HENRY II ST CLAIR was an active personality. Immediately after the death of his father the Scottish Parliament passed in his favour an Act recognising him as "Chief of yat blude" and willing "yarfor that he be callit Lord Saintclair in tyme to cum," 26th January, 1488-89. This Act did not constitute a new creation, but was only a recognition of the Barony of St Clair existing in the person of his ancestor Henry II, Earl of Orkney. He sat as a Baron of Parliament on the 14th January, 1488, and on the 4th December, same, Confirmation issued to Henry, Lord of St Clair, and Margaret, his spouse, for the lands of Cousland, house and fortalice, and Ravenscraig, and adjacent lands, viz., Woolston, Carberry, and Dubbo.

Notices of this Baron in connection with the Orcadian dominions are of frequent occurrence. On the 6th August, 1485, he granted an annuity to the Bishop of Orknay, he being then Tacksman of those Isles, and it was probably by his influence that an Act of the Scottish Parliament in 1503 to annul all foreign laws within the realm was so altered as to spare the native laws of Orknay and Zetland ‡ There are in existence copies of several of his Rentals of Orknay, extending over a period of from 1492 to 1502, the earliest, prepared in 1492, being known as "My Lord Sinclair's Rental that deit at Flodden." On the 28th May, 1489, three grants were issued to him. A 13 years' lease of Orkney and Zetland, the custody of Kirkwall Castle and the fortalices; and the Justiciary, Folderie, and Balliatus for 13 years. On the same day, three precisely similar instruments issued to his brothers-in-law, Patrick, Earl of Bothwell, and John, Prior of St Andrew's. There are continuous notices of his intromissions for the farms of Orknay and Shetland, viz:—On the 21st June, 1484, per Peter Hakket and Alexander Lask, for the farms of Sanday, in 1488 as Henry Sinclair for Orknay and Zetland, in 1489 do as dom de Sancto Claro, in 1491 he is arrendatarius; in 1494 do., and on the

*Scottish Antiquities † Sir Jas Balfour's Catalogue , Balfour's Memorial

22nd February, 1494, in the Grant of Burray to St. Magnus, he is referred to as " dilecto consanguineo nostro Henrico Domino Sinclar "; in his 1495 accounts there is a payment to John Sinclair; in 1497 his Island accounts are rendered per Alexander Lask; in those of 1498 Gilbert Kemp and Edward Spittal are named. There is also a note below of a letter from King James to the Comptrollar and auditouris in which he charges them " to make thankful allowance to our loved cousin Henry, Lord Sinclar ": Edinburgh, 10th July, in the 3rd year of our reign. He got a regrant of the Isles on 1st May, 1501, for a period of 19 years, and his accounts for same are duly noted in 1502, 1503, 1506, and 1507. He conveyed Cousland to William, Lord Ruthven, and Isobel, his spouse, confirmation of which is dated 1st July, 1493. In 1502 he had sasine to Newburg and Ythane, and in 1509, as Newburgh had fallen into the King's hands by recognition, he received a new grant, with a license to infeft vassals.

RAVENSCRAIG CASTLE.

He was created on 13th March, 1510, Master of the Artillery, with a fee of £100 a year, which he was allowed to deduct from his Orknay accounts. His chief residence, Castle Ravenscraig, is one of the best specimens of sixteenth century architecture, and the administration of Orknay and Shetland was probably done by deputies. His account for these lands is one of the simplest of the Rolls, consisting merely of debiting himself with the stipulated rent, and taking credit for rental of the Isle of Burray, which King James created into a Regality in favour of the See of Orknay, and for a few payments in the King's account, chiefly the price of hawks sent from the islands for the royal

WILLIAM III, 5TH LORD SINCLAIR. 301

sport The present accounts contain the warrant, dated 15th March, 1513, appointing Lord Sinclair "Master of all our Machines and Artyllerie," with a fee of £100 a year. He was to have meat and drink for himself and eight persons in the King's Hall, and "all other privileges the Masters of Artyllerie had enjoyed in the past"

Lord Henry seems to have been generally on ill-terms with the inhabitants of Dysart,* as is shown in 1509 by the complaint of Johne of Wynde, burgess of Dysart In 1512 he was captain of the "Great Michael," the Scottish flagship He was a literary nobleman, and it was at his request that his relative, Gavin Douglas, Bishop of Dunkeld, undertook his celebrated translation of the Æneid into Scottish verse In the proem to this admirable version, he says that he "tuke" to translate "this maist excellent buke"

> " At the request of ane lorde of renowne,
> Of ancestry maist nobill, and illustir baroun,
> Fadir of bukis, protector to science and lair,
> My special gude lord, Henry lord Sinclare.
> Quhilk with great instance, diverse tymes, sere
> Prayit me translate Virgil or Homere,
> Quhais plesure soithlie, as I undirstude,
> As near conjoint to his lordship in blude," etc

Henry, 4th Lord Sinclair, married Margaret, daughter of Adam Hepburn, Lord Hailes, and sister of the first Earl of Bothwell, by whom he had—

1. WILLIAM, his heir
1 CATHERINE, married 1511, Sir David Wemyss of Wemyss, ancestor to the Earls of Wemyss She is mentioned 28th August, 1512 (Ex Rolls)
2 HELEN, married to James, 4th Lord Ogilvie of Airlie
3 JEAN, wife of Alexander Lindsay, Master of Crawford, son of the eighth Earl
4 AGNES, wife of Patrick Hepburn, third Earl of Bothwell Issue—
  JAMES, fourth Earl of Bothwell, Duke of Orkney. He married, first, Anna, daughter of Christopher Throndson, Norwegian Admiral, secondly, Jean, daughter of George, fourth Earl of Huntly, thirdly, Mary, Queen of Scots He had no lawful issue, but there is mention of William Hepburne, a natural son, 26th December, 1571.
  JEAN, married, first, John Stewart, Prior of Coldingham (a natural son of James V), by whom she had—
    FRANCIS STUART, Earl of Bothwell, Admiral of Scotland
    MARGARET, married, first, William Sinclair of Underhoull, Zetland, secondly, William Bruce of Sumburgh, Zetland
  She married, secondly, John Sinclair, Master of Caithness Issue—
    GEORGE, 43rd Earl of Caithness   JAMES of Murkle
    SIR JOHN of Greenland and Rattar

He had also a natural son
  M WILLIAM SINCLARE, legitimated 20th February, 1539-40, who, down to 1564, was Chaplain, Rector of Olrig, and latterly Vicar of Latheron Died before 1585 Issue—
    JOHN, mentioned 1585   JANET, married, 1558, William Sutherland of Forse

V WILLIAM SINCLAIR On the death of Lord Henry St Clair his widow, Dame Margaret Hepburn, held the Crown lands in Orkney by successive tacks for nearly thirty years, without interruption but not without disturbance † Her husband had, about 1489, found means to be appointed one of the commissioners for collecting the King's rents in Orkney and Shetland, and some years later (1501) advanced a step towards regaining the Isles by obtaining a lease of the Earldom for a period of nineteen years.‡ Early in 1514 Lord Sinclair is noted as

---

* Acta Dominorum Concilii   † Balfour   ‡ Barry

having sold to James IV., eight of the machines called serpentynis, and their price, £100, was paid to his dowager in the same year after his death at Flodden. A notice in 1514 refers to the late Henry Lord Sinclair killed under the King's standard in the fields of Northumberland. It also mentions his fee "pro officio suo artilyearie," and the serpentynis he had sold to the King. In the same year Lady Margaret as Custumar accounts for the customs of Dysart. In the second year of Lady Sinclair's widowhood, 1515, the Orcadians elected James Sinclair (natural son of Sir William Sinclair of Wassatter, Sanday) as their leader and virtual Governor, the possessor, though illegitimate, of most of the wealth of his family, and the inheritor—as a born and bred Orkneyan—of all its popularity. On the plea of a general devastation by the English fleet in Orkney, they withheld Lady Margaret's Rents for three years (1523–25), and forced her son Lord William to surrender her castle of Kirkwall and escape into Caithness.* On 17th April, 1524, Confirmation issued to William Lord Sinclair, and Elizabeth Keith his spouse, of Newburgh and the fishing of Eythan. He next appears as one of the Council of Nobles convened by James V on the escape of that monarch from the Douglases in 1528.† Perhaps in return for his support he obtained from King James the Letter of Four Forms sanctioning the invasion of Orkney in the following year to force James Sinclair to surrender the usurped governorship. Forming an alliance with his near kinsman John, Earl of Caithness, they collected a considerable military force, and embarked for Orkney sanguine of victory, but sustained a crushing defeat at Summerdale, the Earl and 500 of his followers being slain, while Lord William of Ravenscraig and others were made prisoners. It appears from a complaint of Lord Sinclair that James Sinclair had been guilty of excessive cruelty. Previous to the fight at Summerdale he slew several of his lordship's friends and attendants in the Castle of Kirkwall, and a week or two after the battle, among other atrocities, he put to death in cold blood thirty men who had fled for sanctuary to the Cathedral of St. Magnus and other places of worship in the country. It is stated in the complaint that he dragged them by force out of the church, stript them naked, and then cruelly killed them "in his contemption of God and halikirk, and breaking of the privilege of the Girth."‡ King James demonstrated his authority by renewing Lady Sinclair's rights till 1540, and in 1543, on the occasion of the suit instituted by the Queen-Dowager against Oliver Sinclair of Pitcairns, William Lord Sinclair is found interposing a protest that whatever Oliver Sinclair had done should not prejudice his right to tack and assedation.

William, Lord "Sanchar," is one of the principal Scots nobility who agree in 1544 to support the authority of the Queen-Mother as regent of Scotland against the Earl of Arran, and declare him to be deprived of that office.§ This Lord Sinclair married, first, in 1515, Lady Elizabeth Keith, relict of Colin, Master of Oliphant, daughter of William, third Earl Marischall, by whom he had issue—

    1 HENRY, next lord.   2. MAGNUS [of Kinninmonth], Charter 6th December, 1561
    1 MARGARET

He married, secondly, Agnes, or Mariota Bruce. He died in 1570, and was succeeded by his eldest son.

VI. HENRY SINCLAIR. This Lord has many appearances in the national records, the first being on 1st August, 1560, when he is found a Baron of Parliament, though then only Master of Sinclair. At Edinburgh, on the 13th January, 1564-5, Andro, Earl

---

Balfour.   †*Tytler.*   ‡*Calder.*   §*State Papers.*

of Rothes, consentit that Patrick, Lord Lindesay, etc, and the Master of Sinclair be exempt from the jurisdiction until proun. of the decreit arbitrall betwixt Rothes and Lindsay. On 15th May and 1st August 1565 [Willelmus], Magister de Sinclair is enumerated under the heading of Extraordinarii Ratione Conventus, on 12th September, same, he, with other the gentry of Fife, signs at St. Andrew's a bond to the King and Queen to take part against and pursue all rebels into England . . . and on the 19th October thereafter of those appointed as Keepers of Havens, the Master of Sinclair is recorded for Dysart and Ravenscraig He is found mixed up with certain transactions relating to the Sinclairs of Auchinfranco These begin with a notice on the 19th June, 1568 :—My Lord Regentis Grace, with avise of the Lordis of Secreit Counsale, ordains cautioun to be ressavit for Auchinfranko and Wauchop, ilk ane under the pane of ane thousand merkis, and of ilkane of the uther four quhilkis wer takin yesterday, under the pane of iiic. markis, that thai sall compeir befoir my Lord Regent and Counsale in Edinburgh the first day of June. The samyn day the Maister of Sinclair became cautioun and souertie for William Sinclair of Auchinfranko, and Alexander Sinclair, his brother, to the effect above written. That is to say, the said William, under the pane of jm markis, and the said Alexander, his brother, under the pane of iiic. merkis, and Johne Maxwell of the Hills actit to relief him Having duly appeared on the appointed day, Auchinfranco asked for and obtained on the 1st July next thereafter, instruments relieving their sureties, including [William] Maister of Sinclair Henry, Master of Sinclair was one of the Lords of Convention at Perth, 27th July, 1569, and on 29th, same, recorded his vote against the Queen's divorce On the 26th December, 1571, he becomes caution at Leith for Agnes Sinclair, relict of uniq. Patrick, Erle Bothuille, not to intercommune with William Hepburne, bastard sone to James, sometime Erle of Bothwell, and Ormistoun, sometime of that Ilk, and other rebels

He succeeded his father in 1570 On the 15th August, 1573, Henry, Lord Sinclair, admitted that he had let Andro Littill and Johne Scott to libertie upon band and promise, and on the same day he gives surety to present certain Borderers ; he had on the 3rd June previous become a surety. The 4th July, 1577, finds an entry by him of obligation of relief to sureties He makes complaint 22nd October, 1579, that his house of Knockhall, in Aberdeenshire, has been sacked, of which he suspects William Forbes of Spayside, a broken man An order issued requiring the occupiers to surrender house. On the 6th January, 1590–91, caution was taken for £1,000 each from Henry, Lord Sinclair, and James, Master of Sinclair, that they will not harm William Sinclair of Leyis or Oliver Sinclair of Ravensneuk, his tutor testamentary, for his interests. On the 24th April, 1594, there was registration of a band releasing caution entered into for Henry, Lord Sinclair, and his sons Patrick in Dysart and William. On the 2nd December, 1596, Lord Sinclair was ordered to free William Bonar of Rossie, whom he had imprisoned at Ravenscraig. There are many appearances of this lord as a Baron of Parliament

There is in the Bodleian Library a collection of MS poems by various authors— it is described as "*liber Henrici dni Sinclar*" The MS contains 231 folios, and has various writings and signatures scattered throughout, of which are "Mawnis Synclar," "Be me Laurence Sincla . . ," "Elezabeth synclar within . . ," "Villam Lord (?)," "be me patrik schiner," "Jeff [or Jess] Sinclair," and one looking like "Maluin Sin. . " (perhaps Malcolm). There is a blazon of the arms of Orkney on folio 118, considered to be the earliest specimen extant of Scottish heraldic art on vellum or paper. One of the poems in Lord Sinclair's album is "The Kingis Quhair," the authorship of which has been ascribed erroneously to King James I.*

This Lord was one of the party of nobles that rallied round James VI. on his escape from the custody of the Ruthvens.† This lord was chivalrous and high-spirited to a degree. On the death of Mary Queen of Scots at Fotheringay Castle, 8th February, 1567, King James had desired his courtiers to appear before him in mourning, and that noble came in a complete suit of armour, upon which the King looked angrily at him, asking if he had not heard of the general order. "Yes!" replied Lord Sinclair, making his coat of mail ring through the court, "*This* is the proper mourning for the Queen of Scotland.'‡'

In February, 1591-92, the Earl of Huntly, after killing the ex-Regent Moray, took momentary refuge in the Castle of Ravenscraig, belonging to Lord Sinclair, who told him, with a mixture of Scottish caution and Scottish hospitality, that he was welcome to come in, but would have been twice as welcome to have passed by.§

There is an opinion of the Scottish nobility in 1592, which refers to Lord Henry thus: Sinkler, Lord Sinkler, of 65 years. His mother, Oliphant (?); his wife, the Lord Forbes' daughter. Seat, Ravens-Crage. This would make him born 12 years after his father's marriage.

He was twice married: First, to Janet, daughter of Patrick, Lord Lindesay, of the Byres, by whom he had—

1. JAMES, Master of Sinclair, who died *v p* in 1592. He gave caution for £1,000, 4th March, 1589-90, in favour of Grissell Gaw or Allardice, Lady Skadney. He married the Lady Isabella, daughter of Andrew Leslie, fourth Earl of Rothes, by whom he had—
    1 HENRY, 2 JAMES, 3 PATRICK, all successive Lords Sinclair
    1. CATHARINE
    2 MARGARET, wife of William Lord Berriedale, eldest son of George III, 43rd Earl of Caithness

There is a notice in 1601 as to the recapture of ecclesiastical offenders by Issobell Leslie, Mistress of Sinclair, and John (?) and John Sinclair, her servants, Gilbert Sinclair in Dysart, etc
2. PATRICK of Balgreggie. He married Catherine, daughter of James Boswell of Balmuto, by whom he was ancestor of a line of Sinclairs of Balgreggie, which did not fail in the male line till 1710, in the person of
    JOHN SINCLAIR of Balgreggie, who, as he survived the last Lord Sinclair in the male line for 34 years, was during that long period head of the House of Sinclair, and if the title were limited to heirs-male would have had an undoubted right to it. His family is now represented in the female line by Aytoun of Inchdairnie
3 SIR ANDREW, member, in 1617, of the Danish Rigsraad—Council of the Realm. He married Kirstine Kaas, a noble Danish lady, by whom he had at least four children, a daughter and three sons. Of these—
    1 CHRISTIAN (b. 1607 † 1645), m Elizabeth Below and had two children, who d young
    2. JAMES, married and left several children, but his family seems to have become extinct in the next generation 3 ROBERT
    Sir Andrew died in 1625, a distinguished member of the Danish aristocracy.
4. MAGNUS 1 HELEN, wife of Andrew Kinninmont of Kinninmont

Lord Henry married, secondly, Elizabeth, daughter of William, 7th Lord Forbes, by whom he had—

[HENRY] 1 LAURENCE 2 WILLIAM 2 JANE
1 ELIZABETH, m Sir Duncan Campbell of Glenorchy, ancestor to the Earl of Breadalbane

* "Authorship of the Kingis Quhair, a New Criticism," by J T T Brown † Balfour's Annals
‡ Catherine Sinclair § Tales of a Grandfather

The "Genealogical Descendance" of the Swedish Sinclairs begins their pedigree with Henry, eldest son of Henry, sixth Lord Sinclair, by his second wife, the Lady Elizabeth Forbes

Henry Lord Sinclair died in 1601, and was succeeded by his grandson

VII. HENRY SINCLAIR, who died the year following, 1602 There is notice of a precognition, 3rd May, 1604, obtained against this Lord Sinclair and Robert Sinclair.

VIII. JAMES SINCLAIR, his brother, then succeeded Dying in 1607, he was succeeded by the third brother

IX. PATRICK, as 9th Lord Sinclair. He married Margaret, daughter of Sir John Cockburn of Ormiston, Lord Chief Justice-Clerk of Scotland, by whom he had issue—
    1 JOHN, his heir.   2. HENRY, died unmarried, 1670

Dying in 1617 he was succeeded by his son

X. JOHN, 10th Lord Sinclair. This Lord was an active royalist, taken prisoner in 1651, and detained in prison till 1660. He constantly figures in important passages of State Balfour in his Annals has many references to this baron —

1633, June 19 —He is enumerated as one of the Lords in the order and soleme ryding of the Parliament haldin by King Charles at Edinbrughe

1639, March 22 —Some of the cheiffe covenanters, viz , the Earles of Rothes, Home, Louthean, with the Lords Zester, St Claire, and Balmerinoche, went to Dalkeith, and with them a 1,000 commandit musqueteires tooke the regalia from Dalkeith to Edinburghe

March 30 —Sir James Arnott of Ferney, and some gentlemen with him, and 60 musqueteirs, commandit by one St Claire, marched from Couper, in Fyffe, to Darsey

1639, April 19 —He is one of the Lords Covenanters who subscribe to a letter addressed to the Earl of Essex The letter is given in full

August 31 —He is one of the Lords present at the last Parliament held in the ancient form

1641 —He attends the Parliament at Edinburgh May 25, July 15, August 17, November 17

Sept 24 —One of a committee to examine Sir Donald Mackdonald

Nov 13 —Made one of the Counselors to His Majesty

1644, June 5 —The Housse appoynts a Committee of 4 of eache (of the three) estates anent the commissione of Lieutenant-Generall to be given to the Earle of Callendar, and expeditione of this present armey towardes England under his command The four nobles were the Earls of Argyle and Louthean, Lords St Clair and Kircubright

June 11 —He is one of the nobles on the Committee for considering quhat may concerne the armey in Irland.

June 19 —He is named one of the three nobles on the Committee appointed to wait on the Earl of Calendar, Lord Lieut -General

June 21 —The House enacts that the Commissary, William Thomsone, shall pay to the Lord St. Claire 20,000 merkes, and to take his discharge on the same

1645, Jan 7.—In the Parliament at Edinburgh, Lord St Clair being present, the Lord Borthwicke protested that the calling of the Lords Zester and St Clair should not preiudge him of hes place of precedency

Feb 21 —Johne Fletcher, in his depositions, attached the Lordes Carnegey, St Claire, and Kircubright

1646, Jan 22 —The Lord St Clair being examined, was by the Housse exonered and discharged of that charge against him, for trincatting at Hereford with the enemy.

1648, April to April, 1649 —Reference is made to levies of horse and foot under the Lords St Claire, etc

1650, May 18 —He is one of those named in the Act passed anent excluding divers persons from entring within the kingdome, from beyond the seas, with his Maiestie, untill they give satisfactione to the church and stait

May 30.—A great maney of the letters found in the Hall's frigatt read in the Housse this day, amongest wich ther was one directed to his Excellence, James, Marques of Montrois, from Amsterdam, wrettin all with the Lord St. Clair's auen hand of the dait 13 February, 1650,

T

quherin he wretts to him that he was his humble servant, and vold with all earnestnesse prosecutie thesse ends proposed by his Excellency to install the King in his throne, etc., quhom the rebells had detruded ; and as for himselve (he wretts) he did evidently see that ther was no other way to effectuat the same, bot by the suord. And that the Scotts trettey with the King was bot a trape to catche him in ; with maney other opprobious speaches against the kingdome. The Housse ordains this letter of the Lord St. Clair's to be marked, produced in Parliament, and to be vssed against him as a prouffe for drawing vpe a process of forfaultrie against him.

1650, June 1.—Bill exhibit to the Housse by the Laird of Lawers that he may have the Lord St. Clair's fyne, formerlie assigned to him by the Committee of Estaites for payment to him of 58 thousand pound Scotts, with the annualls thereto restand unpayed.

June 4.—The Housse, by ther acte, assinges the Lord St. Claire's fyne to Dr. Sharpe's wyffe, the Laird of Lawers, and Mr. James Campbell, provest of Dumbartan ; quhat they want of that, to have it out of the first and reddiest of the fynnes of Orknay and Cathnes men, nixt after the payment of the Lord of Assin, and the officers. John, Lord St. Claire, is named in the Acte against classed delinquents, 4 June, 1650, and on the same day it is ordered that 800 bolls meal, and 200 bolls malt, and a 1000 lades of colles, out of the Lord St. Clair's coleheuch be layd vpe with all expedition in Edinbrughe Castle.

1650, June 28.—Lord St. Claire is one of maney mentioned in a list of those to be removed from the King ; with certificatione, if that they depairt not, as said is, that they wich are strangers, shall be without protection.

Oct. 26.—He is one of the signatories to "The Northerne Band and Othe of Engagement" sent by Mideltone to L. Generall David Lesley.

Lord John married in 1631 the Lady Mary, eldest daughter of John, first Earl of Wemyss, by whom he had an only daughter—

CATHARINE, Mistress of Sinclair, who married on the 15th April, 1659, John, eldest son of Sir John St. Clair of Herdmanston, by whom she had with two children who d. unmarried—
HENRY, next Lord Sinclair.

The Mistress of Sinclair died *v.p.* in 1666, and was followed to the grave by her husband, while her son was in minority.

John, 10th Lord Sinclair, died in 1676, and was succeeded in (titles and) estates by his daughter's son, Henry St. Clair, heir-male of Herdmanston and heir-general of Rosslyn and Orkney, thus uniting in his person the two great Norman lines of de Sancto Claro.*

* Burke.

CHAPTER XI

THE LORDS SINCLAIR.—HERDMANSTON LINE *

XI. HENRY ST CLAIR OF HERDMANSTON, 11th Lord Sinclair, with a view to favour his father's family, obtained from King Charles II., on 1st June, 1677, a new patent of the Sinclair peerage, with a remainder to the heirs-male of his father in default of the male issue of his own body, thereby bringing a totally different family into the succession, to the prejudice of the heirs-of-line of his own body. The new patent conferred all the honours, dignities, and precedency in Parliaments and General Assemblies of the States, as fully and freely as the said title was enjoyed by John, 10th Lord, or any of his predecessors.† Henry St. Clair did not, however, on obtaining this new patent resign the old Sinclair peerage to the Crown, which accordingly is presumed to still exist unaffected by the remainder in the new patent, and the claim to which is, according to Burke, vested in the heir-of-line of the 11th Lord, on the ground that the Barony of Sinclair was a lesser dignity enjoyed by the Earl of Orkney and Caithness, and the succession to which would follow that of the higher titles, and that the Caithness succession was to heirs-general. In this view Burke is clearly wrong in taking the Caithness dignity as the basis of his reasoning, for the Barony of Sinclair would follow the Orcadian succession, and a reference to the Installation documents of Henry I, Earl of Orkney, will show implied provision for heirs-male, but not for heirs-general, and the instrument of 1391 executed by Elisabeth Lady Drummond indicates the intention to limit succession to males. This is still further supported by the records of the Privy Council 15th July, 1681. "On that date a Committee having been named to order and adjust the differences in riding the ensuing Parliament, the Lord Sinclair put in his clame for precedency before many old lords (and particularly my Lord Semple, who by the decreet of ranking *apud me*‡ in 1606 is placed before him). He was opposed as only being descended of the last Lord's daughter, and though the patent bore hæredibus in general, yet that in the old feudal construction signified only airs male, and so he could not clame their place, but only came in as a lord of a new creation. Some advised him to forbear riding at this time, however, the Council declared they would continue him in his possession till in a declarator he was postponed to these other competitors, and accordingly he took precedency in the Parliament, and voted before them : but as Sinclar rode up first, so Semple rode down the way first, and Sinclar was more at this time a follower of York's than Semple was."

This Baron obtained a State pardon on the 2nd March, 1685, and in 1689 was the only member of the British Peerage who dared to make an energetic protest against William, Prince of Orange, coming to the throne of the Stuarts § He married, in 1680, Grizel, d of Sir Jas Cockburn, baronet of Cockburn, and died in 1723, leaving issue—

1 JOHN, Master of Sinclair   2 JAMES, *de jure*, 12th Lord
3. MAJOR WILLIAM, died in London unm   4 DAVID, died *v p*, unm, at Aix-la-Chapelle

---

* Douglas ; Burke, Debrett, etc   † See case for Chas Saintclair, Esq , claiming the title of Lord Sinclair, 1782, folio   ‡ Sir John Lauder of Fountainhall   § Sinclairs of England

THE LORDS SINCLAIR.

5 HENRY, died January, 1766, unmarried   6. MATTHEW, died April, 1747, unmarried

1 GRIZEL, married John Paterson of Prestonhall, eldest son of the last Archbishop of Glasgow, and had—

    COLONEL JAMES PATERSON, who succeeded to the Dysart and Roslyn estates, assumed the suffix surname of St Clair, and died unmarried at Dysart, 14th May, 1789

    MARGARET, married John Thomson of Charleton, County Fife and had—

        GRIZEL MARIA THOMSON, married Colonel John Anstruther, whose grandson, John Anstruther-Thomson, Esq , is representative and heir-of-line of the 11th Lord

2 CATHARINE, married Sir Wm Erskine, Bart of Alva, and had issue—

    SIR HENRY ERSKINE, married Janet, sister to Alex Wedderburn, Lord Chancellor, Lord Loughborough, and Earl of Rosslyn, to which title Sir Henry's son Sir James succeeded, and also by a special destination to the estates of Dysart and Roslyn, on the death of his father's cousin, Colonel Jas Paterson St Clair of Sinclair and Dysart He thereupon assumed the prefix surname of St Clair, and is ancestor of the St Clair-Erskines, Earls of Rosslyn

3 MARGARET, married Sir Wm Baird, Bart of Newbythe Her son died *s p*

4 ELIZABETH, married David, 3rd Earl of Wemyss and had issue two daughters—

    1 ELIZABETH, Countess of Sutherland   2 Mary, Countess of Moray

5 ANNE

JOHN, MASTER OF SINCLAIR, was engaged in the "Rising" of 1715, for which he was attainted, and though he outlived his father never assumed the title of Lord Sinclair He married, first, Lady Margaret, daughter of James Stewart, 5th Earl of Galloway ; and secondly, Amelia, daughter of Lord George Murray and sister to the 3rd Duke of Athol He had no issue by either wife, but has been affiliated by C. F Baron de St Clair as father of Charles Gideon Baron de St Clair, Colonel commanding the Royal Swedish Regiment, who after having consecrated his life to the service of the kings of France, was sacrificed at Dijon 29th January, 1793, the victim of his devotion for Louis XVI. The Baron was celebrated in Sweden as a military tactician, where he died *s p* , but Charles Ferdinand, Baron de St Clair, *colonel de cavalerie,* who figured remarkably about the assassination of the Duc de Berri, claims the Swede as sire He warned the authorities of the conspiracy in time, but was rewarded with imprisonment His papers are published in book form, and illustrate a military career of twenty-three years' service, in which he received eighteen wounds and won innumerable decorations, his field of action comprehending the Rhine, the Condé, the Antilles, England, Holland, Egypt, Italy, Spain, Portugal, Russia, and Germany.* The Master of Sinclair died in 1750

XII THE HON JAMES ST CLAIR, *de jure* 12th Lord Sinclair, never assumed the title He was a General in the army and a distinguished diplomatist In 1735 he or his brother purchased the ancient ancestral Castle of Rosslyn from the last heir of that cadet branch, and added it to the other baronial estates of the family,—of Ravenscraig, Dysart, etc., which were settled by deed of entail 31st October, 1735, failing issue of the body of the granter, upon the heirs-male of his sisters. Dying without issue in 1762, General St. Clair was succeeded in the estates and representation of the Sinclair family by his nephew, Colonel James Patterson St. Clair ; while the claim to the title of Lord Sinclair devolved, according to the remainder in the new patent of 1677, granted by King Charles II to Henry, 11th Lord Sinclair, on the son of Mathew Sinclair (youngest paternal uncle of that Baron), viz —

* Sinclairs of England

CHARLES ST. CLAIR OF HERDMANSTON

XIII. CHARLES ST. CLAIR OF HERDMANSTON, *de jure* 13th Lord He married Elizabeth, daughter of Sir Andrew Hume of Kimmerghem, a Lord of Session Dying in 1773, he was succeeded in his claim by his son

XIV. ANDREW ST. CLAIR OF HERDMANSTON, *de jure* 14th Lord. He married Elizabeth, daughter of John Rutherfurd, jr of Edgerton and grand-daughter of Sir John Rutherfurd of Edgerton, and had issue—
    1 CHARLES, Lord Sinclair, b 30th July, 1768   2 MATHEW, Com R N., lost at sea in 1800
    1 ELEANOR, died unmarried in 1786

XV CHARLES ST CLAIR OF HERDMANSTON, *de jure* 15th Lord, had his claim to this peerage confirmed on the 25th April, 1782 He married, first, on 13th February, 1802, Mary Agnes, only daughter of Jas Chisholme of Chisholme, by whom he had issue
    1 JAMES, late Peer, born 3rd July, 1803
    2 MATHEW, born 2nd April, 1808 , died 11th August, 1827.
    3 CHARLES ST CLAIR of St Ella's Lodge, Eyemouth, County Berwick, born 8th June, 1811, Commander R N , married 1st September, 1840, Isabella Jane (died 1852), fourth daughter of W. Foreman Home of Paxton, County Berwick, and by her had—
        1. WM. HOME CHISHOLME, born 9th September, 1841, Captain R.N , 1880, married 1st July, 1869, Emma Searle, daughter of Julian Slight, and has issue—
            1 CHAS HOME DOUGLAS, born 3rd June, 1873
            2 FREDK CATHCART GUY, born 29th May, 1878 *Club*—U S
        2 CHAS JAS CHISHOLME, R N., born 19th January, 1844 , died 4th August, 1861.
        3 MATHEW JOHN, born 30th May, 1845, married 23rd April, 1869, Charlotte Fraser, daughter of the Rev D M Sinclair of Warwick, Queensland, and has issue—
            MAY, born 1870 , married 1889, Russell Hughes   ELLA, born 1871
            EVA, born 1873   A daughter born 1883
    4 ADOLPHUS FREDERICK, Commander R N , born 27th December, 1847
    5 JAMES ANDREW, born 31st December, 1851, is married and has issue living
        1 MARY JANE, born 1846, married 4th April, 1877, to the Rev Fredk Geo Stapleton
        2 ISABELLA HOME, b 1849 , married 2nd August, 1883, Watkin Williams Jones, M D
He married secondly, 1st July, 1854, Anne Crawford, fourth daughter of Sir John Pringle, 5th Baronet, and died 8th February, 1863, having by her had—
    1 JOHN PRINGLE, born 1862   1 SUSAN EVA, born 1859
    1 SUSAN, married 6th August, 1829, to F. D Massy Dawson, cousin of Lord Massy
His Lordship married, secondly, 18th September, 1816, Isabella Mary, youngest daughter of Alex. Chatto of Mainhouse, County Roxburgh, and by her had—
    1 JOHN, born 12th July, 1820, died 31st March, 1842
    1 The HON ELEANOR, born 1818. *Residence*—Pilmuir, Paynton Road, Torquay
    2 The HON JANE ELIZABETH, born 1822, married 6th September, 1853, Rev Wm Leyland Feilden, Rector of Rolleston and Hon Canon of Liverpool

Lord Sinclair was one of the Scottish representative Peers. He entered the British Army in 1784, and was Lieut -Colonel of the 15th Foot He retired at the peace of 1802, and was afterwards appointed Lieut.-Colonel of the Berwickshire Militia He died on the 30th September, 1863, and was succeeded by his eldest son

XVI. JAMES, LORD SINCLAIR, a Scottish representative peer, and captain of the Grenadier Guards He married 14th September, 1830, Jane, eldest daughter of Archibald Little, of Shabden Park, Surrey, and had issue—
    1 CHARLES WILLIAM, present peer, born 8th September, 1831.
    2. ARCHIBALD, Commander R N , born 2nd October, 1833, died 2nd March, 1872
    3. HON. JAMES CHISHOLME, born 21st November, 1837, served in Madras C.S., 1857-82. *Residence*—24, Ryder-street, St James', S W *Clubs*—Conservative, East End U S., New (Edinburgh).

THE LORDS SINCLAIR.

4. Hon. LOCKHART MATHEW, born 25th July, 1855; educated at Wellington College and at Cooper's Hill; is an Executive Engineer in Public Works Department of India; sometime Engineer to Nepaul Government; married 30th July, 1881, Ellen Mary Margaret, daughter of Surgeon-General William Roche Rice, C.S.I., M.D. Issue—

    1. JAMES CHISHOLME RICE, born 22nd March, 1882; died 11th August, 1883.
    2. WILLIAM LOCKHART, born 1883.   3. GEORGE JAMES PAUL, born 1885.

Clubs—Junior Carlton, New (Edinburgh).

1. THE HON. MARY AGNES, born 1840.   2. HELEN, died 19th August, 1849.

His lordship died 24th October, 1880.

THE RIGHT HON. LORD SINCLAIR
(CHARLES WILLIAM SAINT-CLAIR).

XVII. CHARLES WILLIAM SAINT CLAIR, 31st Lord of Herdmanston, 17th Baron St. Clair or Sinclair in the peerage of Scotland, and a Representative Peer, born 8th September, 1831; succeeded, 1880; educated at Royal Military College, Sandhurst; entered the Army in 1848, and retired as Colonel, having served with 57th Foot in the Crimean Campaign of 1854-55, and as A.A.G. to the Forces on the Bosphorus 1855-6 (medal with three clasps and Sardinian and Turkish medals), and in New Zealand War, 1861-62, as Acting Assistant Military Secretary and A.D.C. to Sir Duncan Cameron (medal); D.S.O., 1896; is a J.P. and a D.L. for County Berwick. It will be observed that while St. Clair is the family surname, the title has succumbed to the levelling process of the ages, and become assimilated to the corrupt Scots vernacular, and in conformity thereto the present Baron appends to all State and other documents the signature "Sinclair." Lord Sinclair married, 6th October, 1870, Margaret Jane, youngest daughter of James Murray, of 16, Bryanstone Square, W., and has issue as undernoted—

    1. THE HON. ARCHIBALD JAMES MURRAY, Master of Sinclair, born 16th February, 1875; is Lieutenant 3rd Battalion King's Own Scottish Borderers.
    2. THE HON. CHARLES HENRY MURRAY, born 19th December, 1878.
    1. THE HON ADA JANE, born 1871.   2. THE HON. MARGARET HELEN, born 1873.
    3. THE HON. GEORGINA VIOLET, born 1877.

CHAPTER XII

THE LORDS OF HERDMANSTON*

FEUDAL AND TRANSITION PERIODS

THE St Clairs of Herdmanston can illustrate a more ancient establishment in Scotland than the St Clairs of Roslyn, Earls of Orkney, but no common origin can be traced. The Herdmanstons derive from

I HENRY DE ST. CLAIR, *vice-comes* of Richard de Moreville, Constable of Scotland, from whom he received, in 1162—for certain military services—a charter of the lands of "*Hermanestum cum tota terra quam Ricardus Camerarius tenuit de Hugone patre meo, de Morevilla et de me,*" which lands have ever since continued in the family, thus in point of ancient descent the first in East Lothian. Very few, if any, of the great Scottish families possess ancestral estates granted at so early a period. What adds to the singularity in the present instance is the fact that Herdmanston is not a large estate, and on that account must have been greatly exposed to the rapacity of the more opulent and powerful neighbouring nobles. Anderson† has engraved a curious charter, in quitclaim of certain "*nativi,*" by which Richard de Moreville conveys to Henry Sainteclair "*Edmundum filium Bonde et Gillimichel fratrem ejus, et filios et filias suas, et totam progeniem ab eis descendentem.*" In the Acts of the Scottish Parliament, Henry de St Clair appears as a witness in the year 1180. From the close association with the de Morevilles, it may be inferred that this Henry de St Clair was of the same family as Hugh de St. Clair, co-excommunicate with Balliol and de Moreville after their opposition to the tyranny of Becket, the English Archbishop. In the "Haigs of Bemerside," Petrus de Haga is stated to have married, *cir* 1203, Ada, daughter of Sir Henry de St Clair of Carfrae. In succession to him is

II ALAN DE ST. CLAIR, who, with his spouse, Matilda of Windsor, received a charter from William de Morevill, Constable of Scotland, on whose death in 1196 a charter of confirmation issued from Roland Fitz-Uthred, Earl of Galloway, who had married the Constable's sister, and succeeding him in his estate and office, was bound to confirm the former gift. About 1244 Alan de Saynclair, or Sçincler, as it is also spelled, takes oath with others that he did not send people to waste the land of the Kings of England. Alan's wife was evidently English.

III JOHN OF HIRDEMANSTUNE, who was with the Scottish King and army in Argyle in 1248, may be considered as the successor to Alan. This John was succeeded by

IV JOHN DE SEINCLER, Dominus de Hirmanstane, who swore allegiance and fealty to King Edward of England at Montrose, 10th July, 1296. The seal affixed by him to

---

* Exch Rolls, Reg Privy Seal, Bain's Documents, Genealogie of the St Clairs Report of Hist MSS Commission—Athol and Home, etc, Nisbet, etc   † Diplomata Scotiæ, fol 76

this document is lost   He will be the J. de St Clair noted as receiving at Glasgow, 22nd August, 1301, 100 shillings for the Earl of Dunbar   After the Battle of Bannockburn, amongst the prelates, nobles, and barons assembled by the victorious Bruce at Cambuskenneth, 6th November, 1314, is *Johannis de Sancto Claro*. His successor was

V SIR WILLIAM ST CLAIR, who, like his predecessor, and his contemporary namesake of Roslyn, was the companion-in-arms of King Robert Bruce, who, on account of his heroically valiant services at the famous and decisive Battle of Bannockburn, presented him with a sword, on the broad side of which were engraved the words—" Le Roi me donne, St Cler me porte." Sir William obtained in 1325 a charter from King Robert I of the Barony of Cesswith or Cessford *faciendo servitium quatuor architenertum in exercitu regis*   Under reference to the Herdmanstons, Hay has—" *Wilhelmus Saintclair occiditur in obsidione Berwici facta per Robertum Senescallum, David Rege captivo* " This siege occurred in 1355

VI SIR WILLIAM ST. CLAIR, NEXT OF HERDMANSTON, allied in marriage with the other ancient, but far more powerful, family of the St Clairs of Roslyn, who, in truth, exceeded most other families in the kingdom for grandeur and wealth   His lady was Margaret [daughter of William St. Clair of Roslin], afterwards Countess-Dowager of Angus. Being within the fourth degree of relationship, she had obtained in 1353 a papal dispensation to marry Thomas Stewart Earl of Angus, Chamberlain of Scotland, in 1357. The Earl died in Dumbarton Castle about, and not later than, 1362—when an entry appears in the Rolls for his funeral expenses—leaving issue by Margaret St Clair a daughter Margaret, in her own right Countess of Angus, on whose resignation, in 1389, her natural son George—by William, Earl of Douglas—obtained a charter of that Earldom   King David had, in 1342, assigned to John de St. Clair the thanage of Cowie (Colby) in place of a pension of £20, and in the 34th year of his reign—13th April, 1364 —King David granted a charter to Margaret de Santo Claro, Countess of Angus, for £20 sterling annually from the same thanage of Colby   By this noble lady Sir William had three sons—
  1 JOHN, next of Herdmanston   2 JAMES, probably first of Longformacus
  2 SIR WALTER, Baron of Cessford, whose heiress—
    CHRISTIAN, married Sir William Cockburn, who disputed about the Barony of Cessford in 1416

VII SIR JOHN ST CLAIR, OF HERDMANSTON, was brother-uterine to Margaret, Countess of Angus and Mar—the former in her own right and the latter by marriage   The relation is recited in a charter executed by the Countess in 1389, amongst the witnesses to which is *Joannes de Sancto Claro de Hermiston frater noster*. This Lord of Hirdmanston witnessed a charter at Perth, 13th January, 1367 ; and a John St Clair is noted as a witness on 23rd February, 1369, and in 1371. In 1376 he resigned Cessford to Sir Walter St Clair, and Robert the Second issued a charter on the 8th March, same, at Perth, to " our faithful Walter de St Clair all the Barony of Cesswith, with the mill and pertinents. on resignation of John de St Clair "   A charter, dated 12th August, 1381, by Margaret, Countess of Mar and Angus, has as witnesses her brothers John and James of St. Clair. Polwarth was bestowed upon Sir John in 1377 by reason of his marriage to Elizabeth, the daughter and sole heir of Sir Patrick de Polwarth of Polwarth. He had issue—
  SIR WILLIAM ST CLAIR, next of Herdmanston

VIII. SIR WILLIAM ST. CLAIR, EIGHTH OF HERDMANSTON, was made prisoner at Homildon in 1402. A Sir William St. Clair had safe-conduct to England and back (September, 1405), and was hostage for the Earl of Douglas (September 1405). Sir William St Clair, Lord of Herdmonston, has safe-conduct till Pentecost (March, 1407); the Lord of Hyrdmaston, hostage for the Earl of Douglas, safe conduct till Midsummer (May, 1407).

XI. SIR JOHN ST CLAIR, next on record, obtained in 1434 a notarial transumpt of the charter to his predecessor, Henry de St. Clair, of the lands of Carfrae formerly mentioned, which transumpt is attested by a Thomas St. Clair, and in 1444 Sir John had an investiture of the Barony of Polwarth. In 1446 he was allowed £13 6s 8d for his expenses at the siege of Edinburgh Castle. There is a reference in the Exchequer Rolls of 1359 to the rent of Polmase-St Clair, and in 1455 Polmass-Sinclair and Polmass-Weland, Stirling, are each found assessed at 10s annual rent. In the latter year there is also an entry as to the Castle ward of the ville de Polwarde, which in 1456 is remitted on account of the waste condition of the lands. On the 8th December, 1440, Sir John de St. Clair, Knight, Lord of Lethrig, and John de St Clair, *dom de Hirdmanston*, appear as witnesses, also Jno. de St. Clair de Polwarth, 24th July, 1444, and J de St. Clair of Herdmanston, armiger, on 28th March, 1450, attests confirmation of charter by Sir George Seton of Langnudre, Knight, to Lady Katherine Seton, relict of quond. John, Lord of Seton, his grandfather. He appears again as a witness 11th April, 1450, also on 17th October, 1463, and 12th October, 1464, finds him one of a jury. He had issue—

1. JOHN, *d v p*, married Katharine, daughter of Sir Thomas Hume of that Ilk, by whom he had two daughters
    1. MARION, the eldest, was married to Sir George Hume of Wedderburn. She got sasine of Polwarth 10th November, 1475.
    2. MARGARET, married Sir Patrick Hume, brother of Wedderburn, and ancestor of the Earls of Marchmont. Margaret Sinclair was retoured in 1476 as one of the heirs of her grandfather, and another retour on 7th May, 1504, apprises us that Margaret Sinclair, mother of Alexander Hume, died, seized of Kimmerghem Berwick.

    From these double marriages the families of Hume quarter the coats of St. Clair with their paternal bearings
2. SIR WILLIAM ST. CLAIR, next of Herdmanston   3. ALEXANDER   4. JAMES

JOHN ST CLAIR, FIAR OF HERDMANSTON, died in apparency, for on the 2nd May, 1472, a charter was transumed as requested by Katherine Home, relict of the late John Sinclair, son and apparent heir of Hyrdmanstoun. Dying without issue male, there arose a dispute and a question in law anent the right of succession to the estate betwixt his two daughters, the heirs of line and at law, and his brother Sir William St. Clair, his heir-male (Registers of Parliament). At length, by the mediation of their mutual friends, the matter was settled and composed, the heir-male got the ancient family estate of Herdmanston, and the heirs-female got the estates of Polwarth and Kimmerghem.

XII. SIR WILLIAM ST. CLAIR, succeeding his brother, continued the line of the family. He may be the William St. Clair, Lord Conservator of the truce, 14th August, 1451. His successor

XIII. JOHN SINCLAR had sasine to Herdmanston in 1481, and is named in the Acta Domini Concilii of 1484. As superior he received on 21st February, 1501-2, the resignation by George Ker, of Samuelston, and Marion Sinclair, his spouse, of the lands of Friarness, Berwick. On the 3rd March, 1504-5, upon resigning his patrimonial lands, a charter of confirmation issued to John Sinclair of Herdmanston, and his heirs, of all and singular, the lands of Herdmanston with castle, fortalice, and mill, and the patronage of the chapel of St John the Evangelist near the castle, lands of Carfra with mill in bailie of Lauderdale, near Berwick, and lands and Barony of Wester Pencaitland, with the mill, which latter were fallen in the King's hands by the non-entry of John, Lord Maxwell

XIV. SIR WILLIAM SINCLAR, FOURTEENTH OF HYRDMINSTON, had sasine in 1513 He is noticed in a complaint of 25th May, 1519, preferred against him by Dame Nicholas Ker, Lady of Samnelston, *re* the lands of Friarness, in Lauderdale, belonging to her in heritage, and held by her from him in chief In sequence to the foregoing, on the 9th June, 1519, a writ stopping execution was sent to the Castle of Herdmanston requiring Sir William Sinclair *of that Ilk* to give copy of process led against Nicholas Ker On the 30th July, 1522, confirmation issued to William Sinclair de Herdmanston and Beatrix Rantoun, his spouse, for Herdmanston, Milton, and Wester Pencaitland, and Myddyll in Berwick On the 2nd January, 1530-31, William Sinclar of Herdmauston issued a Charter of Frierness, in Carfra, to Elizabeth Home, Lady Hamilton, which formerly belonged to her grandfather, George Ker of Samuelston, and was adjudged to William Sinclair in the time of Nicolas, daughter of George Ker Witnesses. Alexander and James, brothers of granter. Signed, "Willyam Sinclar of Herdmanstoun" Seal attached Shield couché bearing a cross engrailed. Crest A griffin's head and neck Legend "S WYLLMI SINCLAR DE HYRDMINSTON."

XV JOHN SINCLAIR DE HERDMANSTON, and Margaret Sinclair, his spouse, got confirmation 27th June, 1545, and on 10th July, 1546, as Lord of Herdmanston, he issued a Precept of Sasine in favour of George, Lord Home, for the lands of Friarness, which he held in chief for ward and relief On the 5th May, 1552, he infefts Alexander, Lord Home. In 1542 he is witness to a resignation made of the Baronies of Roslin and Pentland He died before 7th September, 1567, when the Regent and Lords of Secret Council charge Margaret *Sinclair*, relict of John Sinclair of Herdmanstou—now the spouse of James Ormistoun of that Ilk—the said James, and others, their servants, and all others, possessors, keepers, holders, and detainers of the tower, fortalice, and house of Herdmanston, to render and deliver same to the officers executors hereof under pain of rebellion and horne.

XVI SIR WILLIAM SINCLAIR OF HIRDMESTOUN, and James Ormistoun of that Ilk, appear apud Edinburgh, when Herdmanston claims the teinds of Pencaitland Ker of Cesfurde and Fadounsyde make complaint 13th August, 1586, that Francis, Earl of Bothwell, obtained a commission to arrest Fawdonside's brother for that he allegit intromettit and awaytuke from Sir William Sinclair of Herdmauston certain cattle. They state that the commission was most inconsiderately and inadvisedly granted. John (Adam ?) Robsoun, in Thorbrands-heuch, entered caution 17th March, 1586-87, to underlie the law for crimes which Herdmanston and his tenants have to lay to his charge. Caution was taken on 10th January, 1588-89, that John Cockburn of Wodheid shall relieve Sir William Sinclair of Herdmauston of his part of the first barons' tax of £40,000 for his lands of Wodheid, if found that he should do so, and on the 19th February following caution was given by Patrick Livingstone of Saltcoats for the second term of barons' tax for his lands of Kelhop, lying within the barony of Carfra and bailiary of Lauderdaill, besides 20s. already consigned by him in the hands of the Clerk of the Council. Again, there is caution 14th July, 1590, for 5,000 merks from Patrick Murray of Falahill in favour of Herdmanston. The latter became caution in 1,000 merks 27th November, 1591, for James Sinclair of Ewingston that he should not harm Alexander Aicheson of Gosfurd, William Sinclair of Roslin being cautioner in relief. Again, on 8th December, 1591, there is caution by Sir William Sinclair of Herdmanston as principal, and Sir William Sinclair of Rosling as surety, Robert Sinclair, writer, being proc. for the parties, and amongst other witnesses is Oliver Sinclair of Ravensnuke. On the 2nd November, 1592, Herdmanston has a dispute about some lands, and this is his last notice in the records. He is noted on 23rd August, 1582, as one of the signatories to the Secret Band, in which the Ruthven raid originated. On 24th May, 1587, Archibald Turnbull, in Hova, made complaint that Herdmanstone has kept captive his son Gawine for alleged theft of sheep. The Lords ordain Gawin to be still kept pending satisfaction.

In the Chartular of Roslin there is an entry in 1571 of *William St. Clair, brother-german* to Sir William St. Clair of Herdmanston, knight, appearing as witness to an infeftment. Nevertheless, to cite Hay, the story runs thus :—

XVII. SIR JOHN SINCLAIR OF HIRDMANESTON, as is said, married Janet Hume, upon whom he begot

XVIII. HENRY, who succeeded to the estate. His son

XIX. SIR WILLIAM, espoused Sibilla, daughter to Sir John Cockburne of Ormestouue, Secretarie of Scotland, upon whom he begot

XX. SIR JOHN, who was Commissioner for Haddingtonshire in 1644. He married Margaret, daughter to James Richardson, Laird of Smitoun, by whom he had

XXI. SIR JOHN, who held Roslin in wodset. In 1666 John St. Clair of Roslin raised letters of lawborrowes against Sir John St. Clair of Herdmanston and Dame Helen his wife.

XXII. SIR JOHN married Elizabeth, daughter of Sir John Sinclair, Bart, of Stevenson, by whom he had issue—

    1. JOHN, next of Herdmanston   2. ROBERT, who had no male issue
    3. GEORGE, whose issue failed   4. MATHEW, of whom hereafter

XXIII. JOHN ST. CLAIR, married in 1659 Katherine Sinclair, Mistress of Sinclair, only daughter of John, 10th Lord Sinclair of Ravenscraig. The only surviving issue of this marriage was a son Henry, who succeeded his father in Herdmanston, and to his maternal grandfather as Lord Sinclair.

XXIV. HENRY ST. CLAIR OF HERDMANSTON, LORD SINCLAIR. In 1677 he got a new patent of the Sinclair peerage, with remainder in default of the male issue of his own body to the heirs-male of his father. By his lady, Grizel, daughter of Sir James Cockburn, Bart., of Closeburn, he had with other unmarried male issue two sons—

    1. JOHN, Master of Sinclair.   2. THE HON. JAMES ST. CLAIR.

Dying in 1723, Lord Sinclair was succeeded in the Sinclair estates by his eldest son

XXV. JOHN, MASTER OF SINCLAIR, who, having participated in the Rising of 1715, was attainted, and never assumed the title. He died without issue in 1750, and was succeeded by his brother

XXVI. THE HON. JAMES ST. CLAIR, *de jure*, 12th Lord Sinclair, who never assumed the title. He was a general in the army and a distinguished diplomatist. He died without issue in 1762, when the representation of the Herdmanstons opened to the descendants of his granduncle,

DR. MATHEW ST. CLAIR, fourth son of Sir John St. Clair of Herdmanston, who married Elizabeth, daughter of Sir Thomas Ker of Cavers. He had issue—
 1. CHARLES, *de jure* Lord Sinclair.
 1. A daughter, married to Mr. Molleson.
He died in 1728, and was succeeded by his son

XXVII. CHARLES ST. CLAIR OF HERDMANSTON, Advocate, 1722, who, on the death of General the Hon. James St. Clair of Dysart, inherited a claim to the Sinclair peerage in virtue of the remainder contained in the new patents of 1677. He married Elizabeth, daughter of the Hon. Sir Andrew Hume of Kimmerghem, a Lord of Session in Scotland; and dying on 4th January, 1775, he was succeeded by his son

XXVIII. ANDREW ST. CLAIR OF HERDMANSTON. He married Elizabeth, daughter of John Rutherford, younger of Edgerton, and granddaughter of Sir John Rutherford of Edgerton, and had issue—
 1. CHARLES of Herdmanston. 2. MATHEW, Commander R.N., lost at sea in 1800.
 1. ELEANOR, died unmarried 1786.
Andrew St. Clair died in 1776. His eldest son

XXIX. CHARLES ST. CLAIR OF HERDMANSTON succeeded him, and in 1782 preferred his claim to the dormant barony of Sinclair, which he got acknowledged after an investigation in the House of Lords. He thus became Lord Sinclair, and was the first of his line to hold that title without descent from the Earls of Orkney, Lords Sinclair. The original Sinclair Barony was not resigned to the Crown when the new patent—in virtue of which the family of Herdmanston now enjoy the title—was granted by King Charles II. in 1677.

CHAPTER XIII

NOBLES IN SWEDEN AND ALSACE.*

HENRY, LORD SINCLAIR, who fell at Flodden in 1513, left issue by Margaret, his wife, daughter of Patrick Hepburn, Earl of Bothwell

WILLIAM, LORD SINCLAIR, who married in 1515 Elizabeth, daughter of William Keith, Earl Marischal, and, dying about the year 1550, left by her two sons—
    1. HENRY, his successor, Lord Sinclair, and
    2. MAGNUS [Master of Kinninmonth, in the Earldom of Fife]

HENRY, LORD SINCLAIR, married, first, Janet, daughter of Lord Lindesay of the Byres, by whom he had, with other issue, a son—
    1 JAMES, Master of Sinclair, ancestor of subsequent lords

He married, secondly, Elizabeth, daughter of the seventh Lord Forbes, and had by her—
    1 HENRY (pedigree of Swedish family attested by Sir John Sinclair of Ulbster)
    2 WILLIAM   3 LAURENCE
    1. ELISABETH   2 JEANNE   3 BARBE

HENRY SINCLAIR, eldest son of the second marriage, married Margaret Sutherland, daughter of the Lord Duffus, and had three sons—
    1 JOHN, of whom immediately   2 DAVID, and   3 WILLIAM

JOHN SINCLAIR, married Margaret Ballantyne, daughter of the Lord Stenhouse, and had a son

JOHN SINCLAIR, MASTER OF SEBA AND BROBSTER, who married Marie, daughter of the Lord B   ng   [Blantyre], and had sons—
    1 HENRY, slain in Denmark   2 JOHN, of whom immediately
    3 WILLIAM, next of Seba and Brobster, of whom presently
    4 JAMES SINCLAIR, Baron of Randel, of whom hereafter

From this John Sinclair of Seba and Brobster all the Swedish families are derived

JOHN SINCLAIR, son of the preceding, had issue

FRANCIS SINCLAIR, born in Scotland, went to Sweden and attained the grade of colonel He was made Swedish nobleman (No 444) in 1649, and died in 1666 By his lady, Margerit Williams, he left to succeed him

JAMES SINCLAIR, Colonel, married to Elisabeth Clerck, and had by her

JAMES SINCLAIR, Captain, married to the Baroness Brita Lagerfelt, and died $s\,p$ in 1683

WILLIAM SINCLAIR, MASTER OF SEBA AND BROBSTER, married Barbe, daughter of Sir Hugh Halcro, by whom he had two sons—
    1 JOHN, ancestor of the noble Alsatian family
    2 DAVID, ancestor of the Barons of Finnekumla

John and David Sinclair went to Sweden in 1641

---

*Genealogical Descendance penes me Lambahof archives Royal Archivist of Sweden, etc

JOHN SINCLAIR, the elder son, established himself in Sweden, where he was Colonel of an infantry regiment He fell at the siege of Thorn in Poland in 1656 He may be identical with the John Sinclair, Major in the Green Brigade of Sir James Hepburn, serving under Gustavus Adolphus in 1631, etc. Major John Sinclair was present at the siege of Frankfort and the battle of Leipsig, and as Lieut.-Colonel Sinclair covered the retreat at Neustadt in 1632 He was killed at Neumosk.

His issue established themselves in Germany, where the male descendants became extinct in the person of his grandson—

> LOUIS SINCLAIR, who died at Strasbourg, in Alsace, in 1733, leaving *an only daughter* married to Adam, Count de Lewenhaupt, Marechal du Camp in the French service

BARONS SINCLAIR OF FINNEKUMLA.

DAVID SINCLAIR, second son of Seba by Barbe Halcro, also established himself in Sweden, where he was naturalised and admitted into the College of Nobles under the number 626, in the year 1655. He was Colonel of a Regiment of Cavalry, and married Katherine, daughter of John Maclean, Seigneur de Gasvadholm and Hagby This David Sinclair was slain at the battle of Warsaw, in Poland, in 1656, leaving

> 1 WILLIAM SINCLAIR, his heir and
> 1 ANNE DE SINCLAIR, married to Colonel the Baron de Kruse

After Colonel Sinclair's death his relict married Major-General Hamilton

WILLIAM SINCLAIR, [second] son of the preceding, inherited the possession of Finnekumla, in Westergothland. He was twice married, first to Katharine Hamilton, by whom he had—

> 1 DAVID, died in infancy   2 MALCOLM, his successor, and
> 1 KATHERINE, married Lieut.-Colonel de Schantz

He married, secondly, Marie Moucheron, and had—

> 1 DAVID, who died without issue   2 HENRY, third Baron, and
> 1 ANNE MARIE, who married the Baron de Leyonhielm, a Captain of Cavalry

This William Sinclair was created Baron by Charles XII. He was Major-General and Chief of an infantry regiment, Commandment at Malmoe Dying in 1715, he was succeeded by his eldest surviving son

MALCOLM SINCLAIR, SECOND BARON, assassinated in 1739 by Russian emissaries. (See Historiettes) Having no issue, the title passed to his half-brother

HENRY SINCLAIR, THIRD BARON, a Knight of the Swedish Order of the Sword, and Chevalier of the Order of Military Merit in France. He married Katherine de Grape, and died at Strasbourg in Alsace 1776, leaving as his successor an only son.

CHARLES GIDEON SINCLAIR, FOURTH AND LAST BARON, a military celebrity, of whom a fuller notice appears in the Historiettes He was Lieut.-General of the Swedish Army, General-in-Chief of the Royal Artillery ; Colonel in the French Regiment Royal Swedish ; Commander Grand Cross of the Order of the Sword ; Chevalier of the Order of Military Merit in France and of the White Falcon in Saxony He married a noble and illustrious lady, Louise Henrietta Eikbrecht, daughter of the powerful noble, Lord Christian Eikbrecht de Durkheim, Count of the Holy Roman Empire and Lord of the Provostry of Schomeck, in Alsace. By her he had no issue. Born in Stralsund in 1730, he died in 1803, when the line of Sinclairs, Barons Finnekumla, came to a termination.

COUNTS SINCLAIR OF LAMBAHOF.

JAMES SINCLAIR, BARON OF RANDEL, one of the sons of John Sinclair of Seba and Brobster, had a son

JOHN SINCLAIR, married to Mary Bruis of Onovitz [Muness], by whom he had a son

ANDREW SINCLAIR, who went to Sweden in 1635, and attained the rank of Colonel. He was Governor in Thorn, where he rejected the storm of the enemy eight times successively. He was made Swedish nobleman (No. 965) in 1680, and died in 1689, leaving by his wife, Anna Amendsson, a son, his successor

CHARLES ANDREW SINCLAIR, Colonel in a Regiment of Foot; Major-General, who died in 1753. By his wife, Barbara Christina v. Schwartzenhoff, he had issue

FREDERIC CHARLES SINCLAIR, of Lambahof, Ostergötland, born 17th October, 1723; Lieut.-Colonel of the Infantry of Ostergötland; Colonel of the Army; Daily-in-waiting to the Crown Prince Gustavus, afterwards Gustavus III.; Baron (No. 270) in 1762; Knight Grand Cross of the Order of the Sword; Senator in 1769; Count (No. 95) in 1771; Governor - General in Pomerania; Chancellor of the Academy of Griefswald in 1772; Knight of the Order of the Seraphim in 1774; when he kept the old motto of the family arms " Via crucis, via lucis"; dead in 1776. He participated in the campaigns of Finland in 1740; was licensed in 1745 to enter the French Army, where he was taken prisoner by the Austrian troops, but soon got an opportunity of saving himself from imprisonment. The very same year he took part in the French campaign at the Rhine, and in 1746 at the Maas, and the siege of Namur; was commanded in 1757 to the war of Pomerania, when he led the siege at Pensmünde; got five severe wounds at Löckewitz; attended several Diets and contributed to the revolution of 1772. In 1749 he married Sophie Reuter of Skälboö (b. 1713 † 1769), by whom he had—

RIKSRADET GREFVE,
FREDRIK CARL SINCLAIR.

FREDERIC, SECOND COUNT SINCLAIR, Major in the Cavalry, and Chamberlain of the Queen. He married Britte Madelaine Fock, and dying in 1816, was succeeded by his son

FREDERIC, THIRD COUNT SINCLAIR, Captain in the Army and Chamberlain. He died in 1835, leaving issue by his Countess, the Baroness Britte Eleonor Lagerfelt—
1. ISRAEL WILHELM MALCOLM, fourth Count.
2. COUNT CHARLES FREDERIC ADOLPH, of Rosenkœlla, Knight of the North Star, married the Baroness Henriette Lagerfelt, and died in 1888.
3. COUNT JAMES HENRY of Lambahof, formerly Officer in the Horse Guards, married to Amelie v. Holst.

ISRAEL WILHELM MALCOLM, FOURTH COUNT SINCLAIR, married the Countess Althild Spens. He died in 1885, and left issue—
1. CHARLES GUSTAF, fifth Count, and   1. COUNT FREDERIC, unmarried.

CHARLES GUSTAF SINCLAIR, FIFTH AND PRESENT COUNT SINCLAIR, is a Captain in the Swedish Infantry and a Knight of the Sword, now in his 48th year, and married to a Swedish lady, Elly Smedberg.

ELLY SMEDBERG, SIR CHARLES GUSTAF SINCLAIR,
COUNTESS SINCLAIR OF LAMBAHOF. COUNT SINCLAIR OF LAMBAHOF.

INCIDENTAL SCANDINAVIAN NOTICES.

There are a few other scattered notices of the Sinclairs in Norway, Sweden, and Denmark, which it will be most convenient to submit in annal form :—

1416—David Sinclar is named as a civil officer of high rank at Bergen.
1461—Anders Sinclar, chief command in Bohuus Castle till 1464.
   Aaseline, daughter of Henry Sinclar of Sanneberg, married Anders van Bergen of Onerheim Farm, in Sóndhordlehn, who, at the close of the fifteenth century, was a Norwegian Councillor of State.*
1513 (circ.)—Henry St. Clair, third son of Sir Oliver Sinclair of Roslin, is stated to have been Governor of the Castle of Bergen, in Norway, and to have married Gurena Guldlove, by whom he had several children there settled.
1611—Michael Sinclair of Dalsholt, in the county of Halland, fell when captain at the siege of Calmar, 1611. Halland, now Swedish, was then a Danish province. His pedigree is thus outlined :—

* Samlinger til det Norske Folk-prog og Historie," vol. iii. p. 576.

INCIDENTAL NOTICES.

Arthur Sinclair married Dorothea Dumbar.

David Sinclair married Rutilia Mouatt.

Michael Sinclair married Anna Maanskjold.

Boel Rutilia Sinclair married Carsten v. Bassen.

1645—Captain Sinclar is named.

1669, Aug. 2—David Sinclar is appointed by King Frederic III. Bailie of Eger or Lier. This David Sinclar held the farm of Sem, in Eger, as tenant under the Crown.

1688—Gregers Sinclair, undoubtedly related to the preceding, lived in 1688 at Vestfossen in Eger, where in that year at the farm of Hals, he caused to be erected copper works, with a smelting house and stamping mill, but which, after working unsuccessfully for four years, he was obliged to abandon.

1578—John Sinckeler obtained burghership of Bergen, and after him are noticed others of the name, ending with

1643—Daniel Sinckler (Johnsson) in 1643. From these citizens of Bergen, the family which lived in Norway until the first half of the 18th century, is supposed to descend, and of them a good account is given in Personalhistorisk Tidskrift (3rd series, 2nd vol.).

Even at the end of the last century persons of the name resided in Norway. (Kraft's "Norges Beskr," part ii., pp. 406, 407; Ström's "Eger's Beskr," p. 56; and documents in the State Archives, and those of the Municipality of Christiania.)

CHAPTER XIV.

IRISH SCIONS.

THE SINCLAIRS OF HOLYHILL.*

I. JOHN SINCLAIR, Rector of Leckpatrick at the time of the siege of Derry, was the first of the Holyhill family. The tradition of the family was that he was a son of a *Sir* James Sinclair of Caithness, from which we may infer that his known father, James Sinclair of Wester-Brims, was perhaps a clerk in holy orders. From the mural inscription referred to in the notice of "The Sinclairs of Borlum," and a deed of 1660, his paternity is clear. He was succeeded by his son

II. JOHN, father of

III JOHN, whose son

IV. WILLIAM SINCLAIR died *vita patris* He married Isabella, daughter of Thomas Young of Lough Eske, County Donegal, and had issue—

    1 JAMES of Holyhill.
    2. THOMAS, married Alicia, daughter of Thomas Young of Lough Eske, and died 1808
    1 REBECCA (died 1845), married John de Cluzenn

V JAMES SINCLAIR OF HOLYHILL, D L, born 1772, married, 1805, Dorothea, daughter and heiress of Rev. Samuel Law, and died, having issue—

    1. WILLIAM, now of Holyhill
    2. JAMES, married, June, '62, Katharine, daughter of Rev Robert Alexander of Augnachoy, County Derry, and has issue—
        1 ALEXANDER MONTGOMERY   MARY   DOROTHEA   MARION
        REBECCA, married 1847 Lieut.-Colonel Sinclair, H E I C S (who died May, 1861), and has issue—
            A daughter
        ANN   ISABELLA, died May, 1864.   CAROLINE ELIZABETH.

Mr Sinclair died February, 1865.

VI. WILLIAM SINCLAIR OF HOLYHILL, County Tyrone, and of Drumbeg, County Donegal, J.P. and D L, County Donegal; High Sheriff, 1854, and J P, County Tyrone, Barrister-at-law, born 17th April, 1710, married December, 1839, Sarah, daughter of James Cranbourne Strode, and has issue—

    1 JAMES MONTGOMERY of Bonnyglen, Inver, County Donegal, B A, J P; born November 22nd, 1841, married January 29th, 1868, Mary Everina, youngest daughter of Lieut.-Colonel Hugh Barton (late 2nd Life Guards) of The Waterfoot, County Fermanagh, and has issue
        1 WILLIAM HUGH MONTGOMERY, born December, 1868
        2 EVERINA MARY CAROLINA, born 31st May, 1870.
        3 ROSABEL, born November, 1883
    2 WILLIAM FREDERICK, born May, 1843, died August, 1843
    3 WILLIAM FREDERICK (II), of the Bombay C S   4 DONALD BROOKE
    5 ALFRED LAW, Captain Bombay Staff Corps
    1 JEMIMA SARAH   2 DOROTHEA MARY

---

* Burke and Henderson.

THE SINCLAIRS OF HOLYHILL

There are one or two further references to this family, viz. —1. Early in the 18th century Robert Lowry, grandfather of the first Lord Belmore, married Miss Sinclair, daughter of the Rev. James Sinclair of Holyhill, County Down, and granddaughter of sir James Sinclair of Caithness.*

2. ROBERT SINCLAIR, recorder of York, who married, in 1811, Elizabeth Sothern, daughter of Sothern of Darrington Hall, Yorkshire, was of this line.† John Sinclair of Freswick writes in 1782 from Knaresboro'. "At York ther'se a very respectable sensible man, Councillor Robert Sinclair, of the Holyhill family, in Ireland. He has a property there of £400 a year, is marry't here to a lady of good family, by whom he will get £10,000. The late Mr. Pope of Reay knew to what family in Caithness they were connected. He wants to know his descent, when they emigrate, or when came of the Caithness family."*

THE SINCLAIRES OF BELFAST.

This branch of the family has been located in the town of Belfast since the closing years of the seventeenth century.

I WILLIAM SINCLAIRE was born in the neighbourhood of Newtonards, County Down, in 1679, and became one of the leading merchants in Belfast. He died in 1759, leaving several sons and daughters

II. THOMAS SINCLAIRE, eldest son of the preceding (born 1719, died 1798), succeeded his father in business, and was for many years one of the largest shippers to America of linen cloth. He married, in 1753, Esther Eccles, daughter of Thomas Pottinger of Belfast (by his wife, Lady Grisetta, daughter of the sixth Earl of Dundonald), and by her had a large family.

III. THOMAS SINCLAIRE, the eldest son, died without leaving male issue

IV JOHN SINCLAIRE, the second son (born in Belfast, 1764, died 1857), married, in 1792, Margaret, daughter of Surgeon John Clarke of Belfast, and had nine children, of whom—

 1. THOMAS, born in Belfast   2. WILLIAM, married and had issue, died in New York
 3. JOHN, unmarried, died in early manhood.
 4. RICHARD SINCLAIRE, of Upper Falls, Belfast, the youngest son of John Sinclaire, is now the senior representative branch of the family at present resident in Ireland. He was born in 1811, and married Isabel McKee, who died in 1881, by whom he has issue—
     1 MARGARET, married W Allardice   2 ISABEL, married Mr. Neill
     3 RICHARD KER, resident at Auckland City, New Zealand, born 1857, married 1889, Ellen Stevenson   Issue—
         1 ISABEL   2 VIOLET GWENDOLINE   3 RICHARD STANLEY
         4 ALBERT WILLIAM   5. ELLEN.
     4 GEORGE HUTCHINSON, resident in Hawke's Bay, New Zealand
     5 WILLIAM RITCHIE   6 HENRY   7. CLARA.
     8 CATHERINE   9 MABEL   10 ALBERT, deceased

V. THOMAS SINCLAIRE, eldest son of John Sinclaire; born in Belfast, 1796, died 1860; married, in 1830, Augusta, daughter of Conway Montgomery, barrister-at-law. Issue—

 1. AUGUSTA,   2 THOMAS,   3 MARY,   4 CONWAY, (all dead.)
 5 JOHN, of whom as VI   6 EMILY, married William Miller, Merchant, and died *s p*

---

* Henderson   † Sinclairs of England

VI. JOHN SINCLAIRE, of Richmond Road, Auckland City, New Zealand, was born at Cushenhall, County Antrim, Ireland. He married Mary Carson. Issue—
    1 JOHN, born 1863   2 AUGUSTA   3 THOMAS
    4 EMILY, married in 1896 to W J Blair, of Karangahake, New Zealand
    5-6. Twins HENRIETTA, dead ; MARY, married in 1897; C C Ferguson, of Auckland
    7. CONWAY   8. AMY.
    9 FREDERICK, collegiate, Auckland College and Grammar School

The Sinclairs of Holyhill, County Tyrone, and this Belfast family have been considered as descended from two brothers who came from Scotland at the time of the Plantation of Ulster early in the seventeenth century. It is to be observed that the members of this branch have, since the earliest times, used a final "e" in spelling the surname—the family tombstones show it since 1759.

THE SINCLAIRS OF BALLYMENA.*

I. GEORGE SINCLAIR, from Scotland, settled in County Armagh, and held until his death the agency for the estate of Viscount Gosford. He is described in deeds as "Esquire and Gentleman," and his descendants account him to be a nephew of John St Clair, the attainted Master of St. Clair. He died on the 10th October, 1787, aged 67 years. Issue—
    1 ABRAHAM   2. ROBERT, died in Jamaica, 1st April, 1784, aged 32
    3 ALEXANDER, died 10th April, 1804, aged 37
    4 ARCHIBALD ACHISON, died 4th May, 1843, aged 69. Issue—
        1 GEORGE, died 7th January, 1811, aged 27

II. ABRAHAM SINCLAIR, born in 1749, predeceased his father, dying 26th June, 1787. He married Elisabeth Johnston of White Hall, a connection of the Peels of Cumberland. She took her children to England for their education, returning to Market Hill when her son became of age. She died on the 16th April, 1824, aged 68. Issue—
    1 JAMES, died 24th January, 1779, aged 16 months
    2 GEORGE, died 16th November, 1825, aged 44 years
    3 ELISABETH, died 27th February, 1814, aged 30 years   4 ARCHIBALD

III. ARCHIBALD SINCLAIR, born 1786; died 28th January, 1827, aged 41; married Frances, daughter of Compton of College Hall, County Armagh, and Mary, his wife, daughter of Arthur Richardson of Rich Hill Castle, County Armagh. Mrs Sinclair died 15th March, 1833, aged 30. Issue—
    1 ABRAHAM, unmarried   2 GEORGE, married
    3. MARY JANE, married Dr William Gray of Market Hill, and died in 1843, aged 24, predeceased by her husband and son
    4 ELISABETH, died unmarried in 1850, aged 29
    5 ANNE, married Robert Greene (+ 1852), and died in 1885, aged 69. Issue—
        GEORGE GREENE, resident at Cape of Good Hope
        FANNY HARPER GREEN, residing at Ballymena

James St Clair, son of George Sinclair, senior, went to America, and was never afterwards heard of.

ROBERT SINKLER, of Comber, County Down, was born in 1595; married, *circ*, 1619, Giels Gordon, who died in 1673, aged 74 years. Issue—
    JOHN SINKLER, born 1620, died 1681

---

*Contributed in 1891 by Abraham Sinclair to the Hon C H St Clair, of Morgan City, La. See tombstones in Mullaback churchyard.

THE SINCLAIRS OF BALLYMENA.

WILLIAM SINCLAIR, born in Drumbloo, Down, in 1676, went to New England in 1729, settled in 1735 in Spencer, Mass., U.S.A., where he died 4th July, 1753. His wife, Mary, died 9th August, 1765, aged 79. Issue—

1. ANNA, married John Cunningham. 2. MARY, married 5th May, 1738, Jonas Mayes.
3. AGNES, married 11th December, 1746, William Breckinridge of Palmer, Mass.
4. ELIZABETH, married John Dunn of Northbridge, Mass.

SIR EDWARD BURROWES SINCLAIR (son of the Rev. Richard Sinclair, Vicar of Cashel, Longford), born 1824; married, 1849, Louisa, daughter of John Munn, M.D.; knighted 16th December, 1880; B.A., Trinity College, Dublin, 1847; M.A., 1859; M.D., 1861; King's Professor of Midwifery in School of Physics, Trinity College, Dublin; Physician to Sir P. Dun's Hospital at Dublin; and Secretary of the Vaccine Department, Local Government Board, Ireland.

Residence—Upper Sackville-street, Dublin.

MR. T. SINCLAIR of Hopefield, Belfast, one of the new Privy Councillors for Ireland, is a prominent and popular Ulster Unionist. He has helped to organise a number of great meetings in the province to protest against Home Rule. He is a magistrate of Belfast City, and also of County Antrim, of which he is a Deputy-Lieutenant. He has more than once refused to become a candidate for Parliament.—*Graphic*, 11th January, 1896.

CHAPTER XV.

THE ST. CLARES OF ENGLAND.*

SAINT CLAIR is the principal town in the canton of that name in the arrondissement of St Lô in Normandy. The remains of the old baronial castle—the Schloss Stamm—were still visible when M de Gerville wrote his valuable work on the castles of La Manche † There are also places named St Clair in the arrondissements of Havre and Yvetot

The Saga History of the Scottish St Clairs commences with one Walderne, Earl of St. Clair, in France, whose mother was a daughter of Duke Richard of Normandy. In another work it is stated that Agnes, the daughter of Waldron, Earl of St Clare, was married to Philip Bruce, the grandson and heir of William, Lord of Breos, Normandy, and of Bramber, Sussex.‡ In the roll of the Church of Dives, Richard de St. Clair is mentioned as one of the companions of the Conqueror in 1066, and Wace in his "Roman de Rou" tells us that "Hue de Mortemer with three other knights, the sires of Auvilier, Onebec, and St Cler, charged a body of the Angles who had fallen back on a rising ground, and overthrew many" Richard appears in Domesday Book under Suffolk "*Hertesmara H Wortha len & Richard de Sencler de R.*" Richard de St Clair holds Wortham from the King In Norwich he is entered as "*i house, Ricard de sencler,*" and again, "*Et Richard de Sentebor (pottus Sentcles) i dom*" In Blomfield's *History of Norfolk,* quoting the *Register* of the monks of Castleacre, he has it that "Richard de Sancto, or St Cleer, gave the said monks his right in the church in free alms for ever, for the health of his own and his wife's soul, his heirs' and ancestors' souls, with all the liberties thereto belonging " Britel de St Clair held lands in the hundred of Bolestane, Somersetshire, *vide* Exon Domesday Book "And from the half hide which Britel de St. Clair holds the king has no tax," and Britel attests the foundation charter of the priorate of Montacute Many other lands are held in the south-western counties by a Britel, but without further designation

After the conquest the notices of the St. Clairs in England are numerous, while those in Normandy receive but scant attention in historic pages. When King Stephen granted a charter of the Earldom of Essex to Geoffrey Mandeville it was witnessed by a William de St. Clare (1135). There is preserved in the public record office, Fetter Lane, London, a beautiful transcript from Basse-Normandie and Gascony rolls, of the charter given by William de St. Clair to Savigny Abbey. "Charte de Mathilde de Glocester et Guille de St Clair No. 18 Mathilde comtesse de Glocester et Guille de St Clair donnent a l'abbaye de Savigny toute leur terre de Villers et de Than title qu'ils la tenoient du tems de Henri Ier roi d'Angleterre Cette charte était scellie en cire janue et en double queue, mais il ne reste plus que le sceau de Guilli. de St Clair " His seal alone survives. It is as large as a penny Round the edge, in quaint and somewhat irregular capitals, runs " SIGILLVM WLELMO DE SCO CLARO," the beginning

---
* The Sinclairs of England † Planchi ‡ Collins' Peerage

and end of the inscription separated by a cross for a full stop. The centre is occupied by a crusader on an armoured horse, the warrior armed *cap-a-pie*, with spear, from which depends a pennon "*en treble queue*," with sword to his side and an oval shield, having a central device on his left shoulder. The peculiar saddling, the size of the stirrups and spurs, and the long, thin, loose look of the knight's boots towards toes and heels are characteristic of the time. Over the horse's head and neck are ribbed plates of shining steel. In 1139 the priory of Villers-Fossard was founded by a person of the same name.* In the Magnum Rotulum Scaccarii of 1131 or 1140, under "Nova Placentia et Novae Conventiones Dorseta," this occurs "In pdon. br. Willo de Sco Claro," twice, as paying taxes in that county. In de Joinville's Memoirs of the Eighth Crusade, by Louis IX. of France (St. Louis), in the list of knights of the King's Household who accompanied Louis to Tunis is Messire Amori de St. Cler, A.D 1245–50.

The Norman castle of St. Clair was taken by Henry I in 1116 † In 1414, during the regency war between the Dukes of Orleans and Burgundy, it is mentioned that the king, Charles the Sixth, warred against the latter, and so serious was the war expected to be that he went first to the monastery of St Denis to take with all ceremonies the oriflamme, the standard raised when France was in danger, to lead his army. To "Messire de Bruneau de Saint Clair" and to the "Sire d'Aumont" it was given for defence, as the bravest men of all the French. In that time of faction Bruneau was made provost of Paris. The castle was occupied by the English in 1417, when Henry V. invaded France It had been burnt by William Mandeville, Earl of Essex, in Henry the Second's reign, of which king it was a favourite residence, who planted trees there with his own hands

Robert de Saintclair in Normandy married, *circ.* 1260, Eleanor, daughter of Robert, second Earl of Dreux (by Jolande de Coucy), and relict of Hugh, Lord of Chateaunef ‡ This Robert is assumed to be the ancestor of the House of Roslin A John de St. Clair, Knight-bachelor of France, appears in historic lists of Crusaders An account of the French family of Sinclaire will be found in Lehr's "L'Alsace noble"

There can be no doubt of the Norman origin of all the British St. Clairs, who first appear as companions of the Conqueror, and soon afterwards are scattered throughout various English counties. One of the *gens* built the Castle of St Clare in Wales anterior to 1189 In records the Welsh town and its pertinents occur as the "Barony of St. Clare There was of old a chapel of St Clare at Rye, in Kent In the following notices of the English St. Clairs an attempt has been made to group together those that are apparently connected with each other

THE CASTELLANS OF COLCHESTER

Eudo Fitz Hubert, Dapifer, erected the Castle of Colchester, and founded Colchester Abbey, which he endowed with numerous manorial and other lands An unknown herald, circiter 1640, gives illustration of his lineage in the Harleian MSS , No 154. in British Museum, which begins the pedigree with Hubert de Sancto Claro, and displays arms on a shield with a thick upright cross of gold dividing the quarters, three of which are *gules* or red

A Hamon de St Clare attests King Stephen's second charter to the English in 1136. The town of Colchester was held in fee-farm by Hamo during the reigns of

---

*Planché †Dict Nat Biog ‡Genealogie §Thierry's Nor Conquest, page 367

King Stephen and Henry II His running accounts with the treasury were of this nature · "Hamo de St Clair renders an account of the fee-farm of the town of Colchester; in the treasury, £38 16s 7d, and he owes £23 0s. 10d. There are frequent entries of such kind as this, "Et idem Hamo de Sco Claro, r. c de xx. l. de auxilio Civitatis Colecestriæ. In thesauro xiij l ij s and iiij d." And the same Hamo de St Clair concerning the aid from the town of Colchester In the treasury £13 2s. 4d. The Ruber Liber Scaccarii has Hamo de Sco. Claro as one of its familiar names There are several entries relating to him in the Roll of the Pipe, 1131. Another entry runs thus. "Muriel, the daughter of Ralph of Sainineio, renders an account of £18 6s. 8d. that she has to pay for land free from all claim from Hamo de St Clair In the treasury ten marks silver, and she owes £11 13s 4d." Hamo de Sco. Claro gifted Stokes Manor to the church of St John of Colchester, founded 1097-1104 by Eudo Dapifer. He was succeeded by Hubert de St. Clere, the hero of Bridgenorth, who was also a benefactor to St. John's, to which he gave Greenstead Manor and Lexden Mill A William de Sancto Claro was also a donor to that church. The Harleian collection in Bloomsbury preserves a charter of Hubert's "Carta Huberti de Sco Claro ecclesiæ S. Trinitatis de Norwicæ de ecclesiæ de Chaucra et in eodem manerio terr et ann. redd" "Charter of Hubert de St. Clair to the church of Holy Trinity of Norwich, about the church of Chalke, and land, and an annual return in the same manor" Hubert fell at Bridgenorth in 1165, having heroically sacrificed his life for his sovereign, Henry II., by receiving an arrow intended for him. When dying he commended his daughter to the care of Henry, who married her to William de Longueville.

THE AESLINGHAM GROUP

When Thomas à Beckett fled to France in 1163, he began to excommunicate all those who had thwarted his plans. First to fall under his fulminations were John of Oxford, Richard of Ilchester, Jocelin of Baliol, Ranulph of Broc, Thomas Fitz Bernard, and Hugo de Sancto Claro. He gives particulars as to the crimes of the last two. "Excommunicavimus etiam Hugonem de Sancto Claro et Thomam filium Bernardi, qui ejusdem ecclesiæ Cantuariæ bona et possessiones absque connivencia nostra occupaverunt" "We have also excommunicated Hugh de St. Clair and Thomas Fitz Bernard, who have taken possession of the goods and properties of the same church of Canterbury without our permission" Hugh and his fellow-excommunicates had been guilty of taking lands which the Archbishop had probably gripped from them. In the Red Book of the Treasury of Henry II., with reference to Normandy, there is noted under this heading—"Hi sunt qui nec venerunt nec miserunt nec aliquid discerunt" These are they who neither came nor sent nor said anything—Hugo de Sancto Claro, who is specially mentioned as holding lands in Algia or Auge or Ou In the Report of the Historical MSS. Commission he appears in Normandy as witness— "Hugo de Sancto Claro"—together with the chief men in Henry the Second's Court, to the endowment of a religious house there by a Norman noble In the *Textus Rossensis* there is a double entry of a charter to the Lord of Aeslingham, as it calls Hugo The Bishop of Rochester grants a free chapel to Hugo within his manor of Æslingham as recompense for the many benefits by him and members of his family to St. Andrew's, Rochester To this valuable charter the signatures are: Hugo de Sancto Claro (himself), Philip Gruer de Sancto Claro, Robert de Clovilla, William Richard de Clovilla, another

Hugo de Sancto Claro, Robert de Sancto Claro, Roger de Sancto Claro, and some others. Roger is mentioned as his brother. Hugo is given by Ralph of Ingulstadt as one of the signatories to King Stephen's charter in 1136, but Hamo—as others have it—is more likely to be correct, the date being early for Hugh. (The Hugh and Philip Gruer above were monks of Rochester.)

In the time of Henry II Robert de Sancto Claro held two knights' fees from Walter de Meduana (Medway), and John St Clair another two, while William de Clovilla held three and Ralph of Cloville half a fee. Hugh seems to have left descendants in Essex, where, in 1196, a William de St. Clair pays of the second shield-money for Richard I, and in 1202 pays 30s. of third scutage. The manor of St. Clere in Danbury was owned by the *gens*. Following William is one John, as Palgrave's *Rolls from the King's Court* show, as holding a fee from William Munchesni in Kent, while Dunleia in the county was also his, as is proved by the *Rotuli Chartarum*, 9 and 10 John (1208-9). There is among these rolls a charter of confirmation to Henry of Cobham of a whole tenement at Dunleia in gift and grant from John St. Clair. Sylvester St Clair appears as the brother of John in signing a document of the *Textus Rossensis*, but of his lands or doings nothing more has been found. A Robert signs an undated charter of Henry of Cobham to Rochester Church, and later, on to a charter of lands given to a Cobham in 30 Henry III (1246), *Dominus* William de Sencler is a signatory. William de St. Clare was governor of Rochester Castle, and successfully defended it against Simon de Montfort till relieved by the arrival of King Henry [1264] He died the same year. In the official guide the following is to be found: "Henry the Third entrusted William St. Clare with the custody of this castle, whose ancient seat was at Woodlands in Kingsdown parish, in this county." His son was *(semble)* the William de Sancto Claro indicted at Chelmsford in 1255 for having knight's fees and not being knighted. For siding with de Montfort he lost his lands, as appears from the Curia Scaccarii of 51 Henry III., 1267, two years after the battle of Evesham. "Willielmus de Sancto Claro Extenta terrarum suarum quas occasione transgressionum, sibi impositarum rex dederat Baldewino de Akeny"—"William de St. Clare· The extent of his lands which by reason of transgressions charged against him the king had given to Baldwin of Hackney." The Great Rolls of Henry III give further information. The sheriffs took possession of his lands in East Tilbury soon after the battle of Evesham at the instance of the Earl of Gloucester, but he made a settlement with the Earl, by which he retained his lands. This is confirmed by the Patent Rolls in the Tower of London, 1267 "The King has restored to Wm. de St Clare all his inheritance." He died the same year, and the *Calendar of Inquisitions after Death* gives the list of his inheritance under the heads of Estilberry, Danigsbury, and the lands and liberties of the castle of Rochester. He was succeeded by another William, who is enumerated in the *Quo Warranto* of 2 Ed I, 1274, as holding from William Mountchesney in the hundred of Shamele, Kent, half a knight's fee in Merston and another half in Higham. In 1266 he had acquired from Cicely St Clair, wife of Ralph of Osyth, Chichridell and other manors near St Osyth, Essex, and also some property of hers at East Tilbury. In 1279 he was sheriff of Essex and Hereford. He died, 11 Ed. I., 1283, possessed of Danehoberry Park alone, in Essex. He had married, in 1270, Felicia, daughter and one of the co-heiresses of Nicolas le Boteler, with whom he got many lands. North Walsham he got as himself heir to the half of Sir Richard Butler's lands there (Blomfield's History of Norfolk), and in 1273 conveyed it by fine to William the younger of Heveningham, "to be held of him and his heirs by the service of a sparrowhawk." He is twice referred to in the *Inq ad q* d , of 18 Ed I , 1290 : "Johannes filius Simonis executor testamenti Willielmi de Sancto Claro pro capella de Danigbury," and again, " Willielmus de Sancto Claro pro cantaria facienda Danigsberry terr. Essex "

William de St Clare was apparently succeeded by Robert de S. Claro or St Clere. He appears in the Placita de Quo Warranto of 21 Edward I (1293), com " Kanc " as Robert de Sancto Claro, *miles*, and, again, as Sir Robert de Seynt Cler he is engaged in connection with an enquiry on the manor of East Chalk, Kent. Morant has it that in 1301 he possessed the manor of St. Clere's in East Tilberry. To him also came the manor of St. Clere's, Danbury Both Robert de Seincler and Nicholas St Clair of Ore appear in support of Ralph Fitz Bernard's title to Kingsdene, Otterdene. The latest notice of Robert St Clare has to do with Essex in 3 Ed. II., 1310, when the Abbot of St. Ann's, Colchester, has to get the concurrence of the whole convent before some land transaction can be completed. There was a St Clere's manor near Colchester in his possession Of Nicolas some further reliable items have survived. Hasted states that in 1279 William de St Clare held Great and Little Okeley, and that soon after these estates were possessed by different branches of this family Great Okeley, he says, descended to Nicolas, and after some little time Little Okeley also became his. In 1347 Little Okeley was possessed by John St Clare, who paid aid for making the Black Prince a knight in that year In *Magna Britannia* (by the Rev Thos. Cox, the antiquary) it is stated that this John held them united, and that he also held Merston manor, and a quarter of a knight's fee in the same district as from Swanscombe Castle of the Mont-chesnies They had other properties like Oare in Kent; but John came also into possession of the Essex properties, being holder of them in 1334 He married Elizabeth, daughter of Sir Anthony Colepepper of Bedgeberry, and died *s p* There is a John St. Clare of Hardaness, Kent, mentioned frequently in the *Report of the Hist. MSS. Commission* especially in connection with the endowment of a chapel of St. Clare on the Hardaness property, and also a William, of whom only one scanty note survives in the Bodleian Library, Oxford, among the *codices manuscripti* of Roger Dodsworth, vol. xxx.: "Carta inter Will de Sancta Clara & Jo Sutton militem de jure advoc Ecclesiæ de Tendring facta apud Colcestr."—2 Ed III. (1329). William and John must be of near kin to the John of 1334 Passing from him to a namesake, John de St Clare is found coroner of Kent *ante* 1272 He is in succession to Thomas of Aeslingham manor. In the *Textus Rossensis* there is a charter of the prior and convent of Rochester, to which Thomas de St. Clare is a witness Nicholas of Ore, the brother of Sir Robert of Estilberry and Merston (contiguous to Aeslingham) also signed this document. To the chapel for which Hugo got the notification and grants of privilege from the Bishop of Rochester, Hugo left a charter, which is confirmed by Thomas in 1289. The church of Frindsbury or Aeslingham must have been this same chapel He granted Nelefield, Kent, to it. Hasted has it that John, the second Bishop of Rochester, dedicated St Peter's Church, Aeslingham, as part of other favours, to Hugo St Clare, who paid liberally in return *Dominus* John de Seint Cler, *Coronator*, is frequently noticed in the Quo Warranto Rolls and Hundred Rolls In 25 Ed. I , 1297, he appears as *Magister* Johannes de Sancto Claro, and signs Letters of Protection of the Clergy with the King at Langley On 11th October, 2 Ed I , the King challenged the coroner of Kent—

Dominus Johannes de Sancto Claro   He married Nicolaia, daughter of Dominus William de Camville of Clifton.   He appears as one of the signatories to the returns from the Bishop of Rochester's feu at Dartford.

His nearest successor is difficult to discover, but next to him was Thos de St. Clair, noticed as holding the Essex properties in 1384, of whom there is an earlier notice as acquiring the manor of Frothewick with the pertinents in Chicheridell, St. Osyth, Crustwich, Chiche, Comitis, and Chichesrethwick in 1364. Some account of the younger descendants of the Coroner may be given before returning to his direct line   In the Easter *Issue Rolls* of 30th June, 1450, it is noted that disbursements were made to Alex Eden, sheriff of Kent, and others, by *inter alia* John Seyncler, and on 8th June, 1456, there is, in the acts of the Privy Council, note of a letter from King Henry the Sixth himself to "John Saintcler, squier," and other knights and squires of Kent calling on them to meet at Maidstone and see that the King's justice be done in reckoning with rebels   In the digested report of the recent Historical Commission the list of pardoned *re* this same John Mortimer, or John Cade, begins with John Sencler, lord of Feversham, Kent   Another of the name occupied a lower position   "Hic jacet Rogerus Sentcler quondam serviens Abbati et Conventui de Lesnes qui obiit primo die mensis Januarii, 1425, Cujus anime .   " and the Issue Rolls of the Privy Purse tell of a court doctor, Rauffe Sentcler, and give the interesting information that the royal medical fee was then (Henry VII.'s reign), at the palace of Sheen, the sum of £1.

Hasted in his History of Kent, under "Woodland," has most difficult account of no fewer than four of the surname holding it, the last of whom was Thomas, whose descendants passed it away at the end of Henry the Seventh's reign. In 9 Ed III. (1336), John, son to John St Clere, enjoyed Woodland, and was succeeded by a Thomas, who died 4 Henry IV, 1403   The wife of a Philip St Clare, Margaret, is also recorded as its holder, 1 Henry IV (1423).   In the Calendar of Inq. after Death, 1476, there is "Thomas Seinclere, armiger, 15 Ed IV , null tenuit terr' neque ten' in comitat' Essex." A Robert de St Clair had properties near Dover, and especially the manor of Hastingleigh in the neighbourhood of Ashford   In 1331 he was married to a Joan, and he had four sons, Robert, William, Richard, and Thomas.   Jeake's Charters, page 49, show that a Guy St Clere held the then perhaps most coveted position in the kingdom, Constable of Dover Castle, and Warden of the Cinque Ports.   He held them separately and together, and may have been of this Hastingleigh family

At the funeral ceremonies of King Edward the Fourth in 1483, first at Westminster Abbey, and then at Windsor, Sir Thomas St Claire took a leading position

To the Essex properties John Seyntclere added the manor of Coldhall, Great Bromley, in the Tendring hundred   Till his death on the 26th August, 1493, he resided at Hedingham Castle, and the chief possessions were its pertinents, with Chichridill, St. Cleres, Frodewick, Fenhouse, Danbury, and Cold-Hall   To him succeeded his son, noted in 1512 as "John Seyntclere of St Osith's, alias Chicheridill, sheriff of Essex and Hertford."   In 1513 he had by king's appointment the same sheriffship, which he demitted on 23rd January, 1515   He was a Commissioner of Peace for Essex, and in Brewer's Letters and Papers of the Reign of Henry the Eighth he appears knight of the body in the royal household as early as 1516.   In 1523 and 1524 he is a subsidy commissioner in Essex, and in 1525-26 and 30 has fresh grants of commission of the peace in that county. About these years he had returns from his lands of Newington in Kent   In the Harleian charters of the British Museum is preserved an "Indenture between Sir John Seyntcler, knt., and George Harper and Thomas Colepepper, son and heir to Sir Alexander Colepepper, declaring void a bond for 200 marks" *Cum Sig*, 34 Hen. VIII He took part in the suppression of the monasteries (see his letter to the lord privy seal *re* an interview with the Abbot of Colchester), and was one of the commission of enquiry into the nunnery of Polesworth From being knight of the household he became master or controller, and died on the 25th November, 1546 His son John succeeded him, and in 1554 he passed St. Clere's Hall to Thos., Lord Danbury, by fine Of John Seynt Clere, last of Danbury, there is no further account Almost contemporary with him, however, was a John Sencler, vice-chamberlain and appreciator-general to Cardinal Wolsey On 28th May, 1544, John Seint Clere, esquire, took an inventory of the first Duke of Norfolk's valuables in the castle of Framyngham in Suffolk. In sequence to this valuation, the next Duke (better known as the Earl of Surrey) wrote on 12th July, 1526, "My sister will deliver the goods . the coming of Master Synclere shall be nothing displeasant to her " The Dean of Ipswich College, writing to the Cardinal in 1528, acknowledges receipt of nine *bukks*, "oon from Mr Sentclere, your grace's servaunt " On the 1st November, 1529, Ralph Sadler, the Scottish ambassador, notes that "divers of my lord's servants, Mr Sayntclere, etc , are sworn the king's servants " But after Wolsey's fall Sayntclere remained friendly, and they had business together about ships on the Thames, Sayntclere then living twelve miles from Oxford, the date of the commission being April, 1530 There may have been a permanent Oxford family of the name, for in the list of the gentry of Oxfordshire drawn up by Henry the Sixth's commissioners in 1433 a Johannis Chantclere occurs As early as the fifth year of this reign, 1514, there is notice of a John Seinteler, *armiger*, of Kebworth, who bore arms, "The sun in its glory, or ", and the visitation of 1574 found the St Clare arms in Stafford manor-house, Cornbury Park.

In July, 1524, the vice-chamberlain got a lease of the manor of Lammerslie in Essex, and was in 1525 granted the keepership of Tytemanger, Hertfordshire, with so much *per diem* On 1st June, 1528, Wolsey gave John Sencler the office of keeper of the woods of Brumeham, and a dozen places besides belonging to the monastery of St. Alban's For this he had a salary

Capitaine John Seinctclier was in command of "The Jhesus of Lubick," 600 tons burden, and carrying 300 men She was the second ship in the vanward of the three divisions of the English fleet which had orders to sail in search of the French, 10th August, 1545

In leaden coffins in the chapel at Danbury, five miles from Chelmsford, were buried several knightly St Clares who had followed the standard of the cross in crusades to the Holy Land. "The hill of Danbury, Essex, by the Thames, beneath London, is a landmark and a tower to this lineage, as it had been for ages to the world's greatest city, and its chapel will always stand fixed to memory as something notable that has been " Another says of them "All that was highest in marriage, lands, or office, they had in England for nearly a century after the Conquest, and the glow of their fame, and their physical and intellectual powers kept them high for centuries afterwards in a way rare to any one particular lineage "

THE BRADFIELD ST. CLARES.

The lands of Marlingford, Norfolk, are mentioned in the Great Roll of the Pipe, 1189–90, as being in possession of Richard de Sancto Claro. In 1196 they are sold by Gerebert de Sco Claro The latter appears frequently in Palgrave's Ancient Calendars and Inventories, 1195–99, his name being spelt with considerable variation He was attorney for one Adam of Hilleg, sheriff of Norfolk, whom he afterwards succeeded in that office. "Gilebt de Sco Claro, Vic de Norf & Suff" is one of 150 witnesses, 1217. In the reign of Henry II, *ante* 1180, Gibert de Sancto Claro holds one *miles*, or knight's fee from the abbey of St. Edmondsbury In a letter to the sheriff of Essex from Henry III., 1217, is noted "Eod. mo scribitur Vic. Essex p Jam. de Seincler," and the same year, "Eodem mo scribitur Vic. Suff. p. Rob de Seinclow" In 1218 Gerebert gave lands in Stone and Bishopstone, Bucks, to a Hugo de Seincler, and in 1227 gave large additions there. John de Sancto Claro succeeded Hugh as heir in 1237. There are numerous transactions of Gereberd's with Jews about monies, and it would appear that he died about 1251 In a record of 36 Hen. III (1252) is an entry, *De servitiis regi debitis Gereberdus alias Gerebaldus de Seint Cler et Johannes de Seint Cler defuncti* by which it appears that Gereberd and his successor John were both dead at this date, and their properties awaiting possession by the new heir They must have died within a year of each other: from the Cal of Inq. after death of 36 Hen III., number 22 deals with Gerebert as quondam proprietor of Topesfield of the honour of Bolonia in Essex; and number 48 of 36 Hen. III, John de Sancto Clauro for the same place In 37 Hen. III., John is again mentioned as formerly of "Bradfeud maner, Suffolc."

In the Patent Rolls of the Tower of London, 40 Hen III, John is mentioned as "*nuper defunctus*" in connection with 80 acres and one *messuagium* which he held for the third part of a knight's fee, and also occurs "Idem tenuit duo feod' mil' in Bradfield et Watlesfield de Abbate Sancti Eddi" (Edmondsbury), in which was formerly Alesia, Countess Warrenne. In the *Testa de Nevill*, the book of the fees in the court of the treasury, he appears under 'Norfolk" as holding half a fee of Elvedon from the *feoda* of the Count Warrenne.

On the death of John in 1252 the family branched into two, in the persons of John, his successor, and Robert This second John had Bradfield St Clare as the head of his barony, and of him considerable account has survived He "kept court" at Bradfield from 41 Hen. III. On his father's death a mandate was sent with regard to the Essex lands. "The king commanded the abbott of [Pershore] Gloucester that without delay he must take into the hand of the king the manor of Topefield, which was that of John de St Claro, who held *in capite* from the king the honour of Boulogne, and that he keep that safely till the king has given further order With the king witness, at Woodstock, 16th August [1252]" The Inq p m. being held shortly thereafter, this is the result in Essex, where Topefield was the head property "Johannes filius Johannis de Sancto Claro propinquior hæres ejus est et est de ætate novendecem annorum" The following year, by an exactly similar process, he was declared heir to the Suffolk lands In the State Rolls of 51 Henry III., 1257, there is a presentation by Richard de Bosco against John de Sencler, Robert de Mundeville, *milites*, Edmund de Seincler, Peter de Sencler, parson of Weathersfield, summetar John de Sencler, and others, sent by Robert Enel, or Howel (the head of the Montfort malcontents in the Isle of Ely), who had come with horses and arms to his house in Walberwickam and removed cups, dresses, gold rings, weapons of war, and other valuables. Morant says John occurs in 52 Hen. III. (1268) as a lord, his possessions compelling him to the full duties of a baron of the kingdom. The *Rotuli Hundredorum* was drawn up by commission subscribed under the Great Seal, 11th October, 2 Ed. I (1283) There were ten men appointed for the St. Edmondsbury district, and there John de Sco Claro appears as one of the four of best rank,—*milites*. As late as 1302 a John de St. Cleer pays his feudal respect to the abbot of St Edmondsbury for some possessions connected with the manor of Bradfield St Clare.

Guy St Clair, escheator to the king, was probably of the Bradfield connection He is noticed in 1335 as, with his wife Marjory, holding Wyrun Hall, Norfolk. In 1349 he was made King's *vice-comes*, or sheriff, of the united counties of Cambridge and Huntingdon, in both of which he had lands and held office till 1354. In 1356 he became escheator for Norfolk and Suffolk, in 1357 was sheriff of same, and in 1358 had re-appointment. The last of his sheriffships traced was in 1359, but he was often escheator at other periods, and there is preserved in the British Museum a parchment *carta*, an order by him as *vice-comes* of Norfolk in 1357. His son Pain, or Paganus de St Clare must have died without male issue, for in 1376 he pre-leases to Edwd. de St. John and Joan his wife and her heirs all his right in the manor of Grimston.

Contemporary with Gerebert, Robert St. Clair appears as signing a mandate for the viscount of Lincoln, from the king, 2 Hen III , " Eod mo. scribitur Vic Suff p Rob de Seinclow." They may have been brothers. As the pious gravestone has it, 'In their death they were not divided. One of the open rolls of the tower, 36 Hen III., the year of Gereberd's death also, gives account of Robert and his son Robert " Concerning homage taken The king took homage of Robert Sayncler, son and heir of the late Robert Sayncler, for all the lands and tenements which the aforesaid Robert, his father, held from the king *in capite* in the day on which he died, and he restores to him those lands and tenements And it was ordered to Master Wm Clifford, escheator for this side of the Trent, that having accepted security from the aforesaid Robert about his reasonable tax to be rendered to the king at the treasury of the king, he make him heir, without delay, with full possession, to the same Robert with regard to all his lands and aforesaid tenements, and in respect to which the aforesaid Robert, his father, was possessed in his own demesne as of a fief in the day on which he died, and what by reason of the death of that Robert was taken into the king's hand . with the king witness, at Saint Edmundsbury, 14th Feb., 1252." Robert, junior, had Edmund for successor, probably he of 1266, who raided R. de Bois In 1294 Edm. de Sco Claro and others attest a gift of Suffolk lands, and again two of the same place in 1339. To another of the same lands in 1351 Edm Synclowe is a witness, and again in 1360.

It has been noticed that Gereberd gave Stone in Bucks to a Hugo, who had also Essex properties. Hugo dying in 1227, the seat reverted to John FitzGerebert, who died in 1252. A connection got it again at a later period He appears as Robert de Seyncler of Stone at an enquiry in which he took part, and in 1274 William de Sco. Claro, a proprietor of large substance, appears as of Stanes, Bucks. At this same time there were Stephen St. Clare in the hundred of Balberg, Suffolk; Gerard St. Clare in that of Periton, Ox , and a Geffrey St. Clare in Upthorp, Hunts Thirty years later a John held Calendon in Beds. In Leicestershire, 41 Ed. III., John Seincoler had Lobenham, and in 46 Ed. III. (1373) his son John is put in possession of the same manor Still another

THE BRADFIELD ST CLARES. 335

John, with his wife Alicia, held it 3 Ric. II. Adam St. Clere, who was born out of wedlock, had 11 Henry IV., Warton, Stippershall, and divers messuages and lands as from the castle of Tamworth. These properties were in Warwickshire. A Peter held Chaddesden 11 Ed. III., and in 36 Ed. III. a Margaret St. Clare died possessed of Boyleston manor as of the honour of Tuttebury Castle in Derbyshire. By the Inq. p m., 1387, Maria, the wife of Sir Roger Bellers, "prius nupta John Seynt Clere," possessed Grymston, Cryche, etc., in Leicester and Derby. In 19 Ric. III (1396) Rowland Sentclire had land from the fief of William de la Zouche, *miles* of Haryngworth in Northamptonshire. In the Roll of the Hundreds, 1274, Philip de Sco. Claro appears frequently as a prominent proprietor in Cambridgeshire. In 1280 he is one of a jury sworn by Sir William Muschet. A Robert de Sco. Claro is also noted in this roll record Philip was succeeded by Nicolas de Sco Claro.

THE ST CLARES OF ALDHAM, IGTHAM, BURSTOW, ETC

John St Clare of Igtham (who died in 1327) married about 1300 Joan de Aldenham, by which marriage his son became heir to his cousin Francis of Aldham, which then, circ. 1322, began to be called Aldham St Clere. John, the son, died in 1335, leaving lands in Kent, Sussex, Hants, and North Hants He was succeeded by his son, John III , of whose age proof was taken in 1351 The former apparently had married Isolda Aldham, relict of William Inge, Chief Justice of the King's Bench, who died in 1316. In 1347 King Edward confirmed the grant of Queen Philippa to John Seintcler, chevalier, of her manor of Maresfield, together with the king's park in the same place, the town of Grinsted, etc , during her life On the Queen's death in 1369 there is note of a confirmation of an Essex gift to Marie de Seint Cleir of the lands and tenements of Markdiche, Havering-at-Bowre. In 1377 Sir John became sheriff of Sussex and Surrey. He appears as custodian of the lands which belonged to Letitia, relict of William Seintcler of Kingswood, who had for predecessor Thos. Seintcler of Kingswood, who, in right of his wife Juliana, held lands in Gloucester, 1365. Sir John married Mary (who re-married Sir Roger Bellers), and dying in 1389, left a son Sir Philip St. Clere, the elder of Igtham. Among the Harleian charters is one given by Sir John under seal at Penshurst, "mon seal à Penshurst," 44 Ed. III (1371). The writing runs "Johan de Seyntcler susrendu à M. Nichol de Louvayne chev. tout l'estat que j avoi de son lees en tous les manoirs fies et advowsons " They are both called *armigeri* in the document, which is a parchment 2½ x 11 inches, folded double and three, of six and one-third lines well written but dim old French, the seal being yet attached, and hardly imperfect since " .EINTCLER " remains, and nearly the whole of the shield with "the sun in its glory " blazoning its entire field.

Sir Philip St Clere, who was M P for Sussex in 1377, married Joan de Audley. Their eldest son was probably Thomas Sencler, one of the five *armigeri* who officered with the Earls of Arundel and Surrey, etc , a contingent consisting mostly of archers at Agincourt Thomas St Clere married Margaret, daughter of Sir John Philpott, Lord Mayor of London, and died in 1416, leaving a son and heir Philip, to whom he left a manor in Wold, North Hants. This Philip apparently died without issue, and the line is found continued by his uncle Sir Philip St Clere of Burstow. The latter married in 1371 Margaret, daughter and eventual heiress of Sir Nicholas de Louvaine. In 1397 he contributed two messuages called the Coldharbour in the parish of All Saints' at Fenn, in Roperia, London, for enlarging the church and making a cemetery. In 1405 he was sheriff of Sussex. In 1406 he and his wife received a quittance from one Elizabeth Mortayne. He died in 1408, and his wife in 1409, leaving extensive possessions in Somerset, Cambridge, Suffolk, Oxford, Surrey, Sussex, Leicester, and Kent, the bulk of which was put under guardianship for their sons, John and Thomas, the elder of whom was only twelve at his father's decease. Sir John Pelham obtained their wardship, and married John St Clere to his daughter Joan Pelham, but he died in 1419 at the early age of twenty-three, when he was succeeded by his brother Thomas, who had also by 1422 succeeded to his cousin-german Philip of Igtham, being then mentioned in the escheats as of Igtham and Parva Preston. Among the *Probat' ætatis* records he appears in 2 Hen VI (1424) as "Thomas Seintcler frater et hæres Johannis filii Philippi Seintcler chevalier." In 1426 a Thomas Seyncler is fined 100 marks for breach of the peace. As lord of the manor of Stene he presented Simon Smyth to the incumbency, 18th February, 1427. He died on the 6th May, 1435, aged only 34, leaving by Margaret, daughter of Lord Hoo and Hastings, three co-heiresses to his extensive possessions—

1. ELIZABETH, married to (1) William Lovel, (2) Richard Lewknor
2. ALIANOR, married Sir John Gage, ancestor of the Viscounts Gage, who quarter the St Clere arms and still retain ancient court rolls of Heighton St Clare
3. EDITH, married Sir Richard Harcourt

THE SOMERSET ST CLARES

"A little to the north-west of Ash is Stapleton, which for a number of successions belonged to the family of St Clare." The earliest notice of this family is in the reign of Richard the First. In 1195-96 Ralph de Seincler owes 40 marks for having recognisance of 5½ knights' fees, of which his father was possessed in the days when he took the garb of religion, by the pledges of Herbert Fitz-Herbert and Henry de Alneto. Among what are called new promises by Hubert, Archbishop of Canterbury, is the pipe roll extract dated 7 Ric I. William de Seincler accounts for 20 marks for having plenary seizen of his land of Stapleton, and he has delivered them in to the treasury, and is quit. Again in An 3° Johann, A D 1202 · Rotuli de Oblatis Sum'set. Walter of Esselegham (Aeslingham?) gives to his lord the king 60 marks silver as his peace offering because he arraigned Ralph de Sco Claro, and because he remanded him, and that he did not use, as regards the rest, except what Walter had of his right of office. In 6 Hen. III. (1222) Robert de St Clare held of the king in chief ten pounds a year of land in Stapleton, by the service of finding an armed servant with a horse in the king's army for forty days at his own cost. He was succeeded by his son Robert, who, 7 Hen III. (1223), paid ten marks for his relief of the land which he held here of the king by serjeanty. This Robert died 2 Ed. II., being then certified to hold the manor of Stapleton of the crown *in capite* by the service of holding a towel before the queen at the feasts of Easter, Whitsuntide, and Christmas, and likewise at the king's coronation. Robert de St. Clare, his grandson, succeeded to the manor of Stapleton, of which he died seized, 10 Ed. III., leaving issue another Robert, his son and heir, who held only a moiety of this manor, of which he died seized 33 Ed III , and was succeeded by Richard, his son and heir. The other moiety was held, 42 Ed III., by Ralph Seyncler, who died without issue, as did also the said Richard, and Margaret his wife, upon which the manor reverted to Robert de St Clare, a cousin of the above-mentioned lords, who died 46 Ed III., and Sibill, his wife, had an assignment of the third of this manor for her dower, remainder to Sir William Bonville and his heirs, 9 Hen. IV Sir William held a moiety of the manor of Stapleton and one carucate of land in Martock, called Sayes Place, from the Earl of Somerset. At this time there was a chapel in Stapleton, which seems to have been built by one of the St. Clares. It was subservient to the church of Martock, and has long since been destroyed, and nothing further appears memorable of it or the place. In Sir William Bonville's will, executed 13th August, 1407, amongst other bequests is one to "Raulyn Sayncler, to purchase a corrody for his life, £20"

On 18th October, 1264, Robert de Sancto Claro was escheator for the county of Somerset, and in the same year Richard de Sco. Claro died possessed of Mertock, Stapleton, and other lands. He is noticed in the Rotuli in Curia Scaccarii of Hen III., Ed I., and Ed II , under Somerset. Richard Seincler and Margaret, his wife, give ten pounds for license to acquire two parts to the two, of the divisions of the manor of Stapleton with its followings In the Treasury Rolls there is a dateless entry "The king, for five marks which Thos. Warrenne paid, granted to Robert Seintcler that he may give two parts of the manor of Stapleton, with the pertinents, etc., to Thomas the aforesaid, to be held for his whole life as fee-farm" Again, in the *Hundred Rolls*—when Edward I. challenged the English landholders generally—in the hundred of Martock, Somerset, the *jurati* have their statement thus: "Dicunt et quod Robs de Sencler Rict' de Bolougne, etc., pcipuunt et retinuit avia de astraura set nesciunt quo waro" In the *Hundred Forinsec de Sum'ton* he occurs again · "And Robert de St. Clare has taken possession of a part of the hundred for twelve years past, which part his predecessors were accustomed to pay for, and this section was possessed in the time of Thomas de Perham, fee-farmer of the manor and hundred of Somerton.' In the *Quo Warranto* records, the sequel to the *Hundred Rolls*, he appears several times, and especially about disputed parts of his manor of Somerton He was summoned to answer as to his rights in a court in Somersetshire, and again by William of Chiselham, the king's commissioner, to Exeter, to state his rights to parts of the properties which he held The piece at Somerton in particular had to be fought for "Robert St. Clare came," says the record, "and said that Richard le Bure, his grandfather, had it with certain tenements as gift from Ralph de Huse, or Hussey." (In 1199–1200 Hugo de St. Clare and Hugo de Bures are arbiters about lands in Tilbury, Essex, belonging to Sibilla, aunt of John of Wirrefield in that county)

Robert St Clare died in 1309, and was succeeded by his grandson Robert, who died in 1337, being possessed of Stapleton manor, Andredseye, Saltmore, Bergham, and indefinite moor and pasture lands Before continuing, mention must be made of an Everard St. Clare, who in the hundred of Stone, Somerset, was challenged as to some payments and possession of tenements said to be subtracted from the hundred and added to his lands in Allberry. He was a side member Robert died possessed of Stapleton, Somerton, etc., and also of Budelege manor. This is another of the same to Buddleigh in Devonshire. In 18 Ed. III , 1345, Elizabeth St Clare had at her death Stapleton and its pertinents. In 1352 a Robert holds these manors, who died in 1360, leaving two sons, Richard and Ralph, between whom there was a division of the lands. Richard married a Margaret, but died without issue, as also died Ralph in 1369, the properties being left to their cousin Robert, showing that there were several branches in the county. The

v

Treasury Rolls have account of Richard being put in possession of part of Stapleton :—
"Somersetshire : It was commanded to John of Bekington, escheator of the king in Somerset, that, having received security from Richard, son of the late Robert Seyntcler, of a reasonable sum, he may make full possession to Richard of two parts of the manor of Stapleton near Martock, which he holds of the king *in capite* by the service of half one knight's fee." Of the last mentioned Robert, the cousin, there is a charter preserved in the British Museum, dated 29 Edwd. III., 1356, having devices on a shield on the still attached seal. He is *Robertus Saincler de Somerton et de Stapleton*, and his parchment conveys a gift of land to the famous abbey of Glastonbury in Somersetshire. He died in 1372. His manors were Stapleton, Botecle, Coker, Somerton, etc. His wife, Sibilla Sentcler, died the following year, and she had the third part of Stapleton, Milton, Fauconberge, part of Lymington manor, Todenham manor, Somerton manor, Compton manor, Dowden, etc. There are a few further notices of the name in the county. Sir John St. Clare of the Aldhams was custodian of Estham for the heir of the wife of William St. Clare of Kyngswoode in Edward the Third's time and the beginning of that of Richard II., Lætitia dying in 1377. Besides Estham she had part of the manor of Castlecary, with the advowson of the chapel on it. In 20 Ric. II., 1397, William Seyntclere held Ashbrutell manor, and at the same time Robert held Andredseye manor. There is mention of a William Seint Cler in the Treasury Rolls of Hen. III., Ed. I. and II., and also of a Nicholas, his brother, as of Somerset. They had a cause at Westminster about some land, and Ivo of Ashelond was their fellow-defendant. John of Legyh and Isabella, wife of Nicholas de Helmunden, recovered some lands from the three in Croukhern. The notices end with Nicholas Seyntcler, *miles*, who had Alicia as wife as the Cal. of Inq. p.m. of 19 Ed. IV., 1480, state. He had the properties of Pokeston, Cammelerton and Churchill.

THE DEVONSHIRE HOUSE.

The *ecclesia de Sancto Claro* is mentioned in 1245 as giving more than double the returns of seven others in Devon. In the *Inq. ad Quod Damnum*, No. 128, 1321, appears: "*Will'us Seintcleer : Baunton balliva et hund' parcell' maner' de Baunton : Devon.*" William St. Clare held a portion of the manor of Baunton.

John de St. Clere by marriage with Joan, heiress of William Tidewell, acquired the propertie of Tudwell, to which seven of the name of St. Clere succeeded each other, ending with Gabriel St. Clere. Richard Seint Clare of Todewill acquired Clisthidon by marriage with Isabel, daughter of William Hidon ; it was sold by the said Gabriel. Kynawersy of "the Knights" Hidon, also came unto Seintcleer by the heir, and Egidia, one of the three co-heiresses of William Carew, becoming wife of William St. Clere, brought a third part of Torrington Parva to him. Johanna, daughter of Richard St. Cleere of Ashburton, armiger, married John Hull, armiger, and the Hulls of Larkebeare, therefore, quarter the St. Cleere arms, per pale. or and az. the sun in his beams counterchanged. After the dissolution the manor of Polsloe, to which Budleigh is subservient, was sold to St. Clere of Tidwell. Budleigh had been previously owned by the Somerset St. Clares. Gabriel St. Clere sold it to Thomas Ford of Bagster. John St. Clere, son and heir of Gilbert St. Clere of Budleigh, married Joan Ford, and his sister Joan married George Ford. Gilbert St. Clere of Toodwell, Devon, married Joan, daughter of

John Strawbridge of Collyton, and had Agnes, wife of John, son and heir of Thos Carew of Bykeley, Devon [son of Edmund, Lord Carew]; Joan, wife of George Ford, George, William, Thomas, and Phillipa St Cleer, the daughter. At Wilton, of the great nunnery, in Wiltshire, in a church there, a 10-inch monumental pictorial brass exists to John Coffer and his wife Philippa St. Cleer, this daughter John is in the kneeling attitude. The date is 1585 Above the female effigy is the shield of her husband, an armiger or squire, and one quarter has the St. Cleer arms Per pale or and azure a sun counterchanged. Gabriel St. Clere was last in possession of Tidewell It is recorded of him that "he was a man well qualified, but that by prodigality having consumed his estate, whereof being ashamed, he did (*a malo ad pejus*) counterfeit lunacy, and in that humour pulled down his house and sold timber and stones, affirming that none of his posterity could prosper so long as that house, where so much sin had been committed, stood, and it was credibly reported that a dead man, booted and spurred, was found in one of his fish ponds, and also the bones of divers children " The *Proceedings of Chancery in the reign of Elizabeth* refer to his case, S s 19 No. 61 · "Elizabeth, wife of Gabriel Saintclere, plaintiff: Thos Ford and Robert Mylls, defendants Object of suit, premises . For relief of the plaintiff and her children, charging the defendant Thomas Ford with keeping away her husband from her and family, and by fraudulent means procuring a conveyance of the capital messuage, barton, and demesne of Tudwell, on which the plaintiff had a settlement as jointure, and also his manor of Budleigh, and lands in Budleigh and Ashburton, and by fraudulent practices and promise of payment to plaintiff of a rent charge of £10, procured her to levy a fine with her husband of all his estates, to the utter ruin of the plaintiff and her family, the defendant not allowing her access to her husband County Devon."

Arscot, a younger brother of Arscott of Annery, married Gabriel's daughter and rebuilt Tidwell Joan Ford was the wife and widow of a Gabriel, perhaps predecessor to the last of Tidwell, and a Mark St. Clare married a lady named Bois in Devon In the *Chancery Proceedings*, Elizabeth, No 10, is another entry of interest "Hugh Pomerye, esq , plaintiff · Gawen St Clere, Sampson Letheby, Barbara (his wife), John Keymer, and Thos Jones, defendants Object of suit to quit plaintiff's possession premises—the manor of Engesdon, otherwise called the manor of Over Engesdon, in the parish of Ilsington, and divers lands in Ilsington, the inheritance of plaintiff: Devon county " In the *Valor Ecclesiasticus* of Henry VII., a George St Clere is noted as rector of a Devonshire chapel In Braybrook, Rothwell hundred, Northampton, there is a mural monument, with the arms, a sun in its glory, and having two side inscriptions in Latin which translate thus "The woman reverencing her lord shall be praised," and "Gracefulness is fleeting and beauty is hollow," while the chief inscription runs "To Mary, risen from the Devonshire family of the ancient and honoured nobility of the Sinclers, his very faithful and good wife dead by too bitter fate at Braybrook Thos Valence, her surviving husband, has placed this therefore with the highest love and eternal devotion She died in the hope of the resurrection on the fourth day of September, in the year of human salvation 1571. Tears will remain her monument."

INCIDENTAL NOTICES

There was a Willo de Sco Claro referred to as in 1140 paying taxes for Dorset lands In the neighbouring county of Hampshire a Gaufi de Sco Claro is on record in

1216. It was then commanded the sheriff of Winchester and Dorset that he give to Philip Brito the land which belonged to John de Boneville and Geffrey de St. Clare, held in his bailiwicks or provinces of jurisdiction, to be held as long as the lord the king shall please: At Reading, 7th April, 1216. Geffrey held lands near Southampton from "the counts of the Island in 1222." In Cornwall is a parish so named, noted in 1288-91. There was a St. Cleer chapel also there, with a holy well close by connected with an ancient nunnery. The baptistery of St. Cleer and the wayside cross are remnants of days gone by. In the Great Rolls of the Pipe, 1158, is an entry, "The same sheriff accounted for 20 marks silver for Roger the fisher of Moneth, Cornwall, paid Hugoni de Sco. Claro." Later on, in the fourth parliament at Westminster, *an* 2 and 3, Philip and Mary, 1555, the member for West Loe, County Cornwall, was John Seyntclere, or St. Clere, esquire.

Master John de Sancto Claro is indexed in the Calendar of Papal Registers as clerk of the diocese of Canterbury, 1291 (10 Kal. Mar.), as rector of Fulcham, or Folcham, therein (4 Non Mar. same), and presently thereafter as Canon of London, and the hostility towards him by the Archbishop of Canterbury was silenced by Papal Mandate. Nicholas III. issued a dispensation on account of the illegitimacy of the said John de St. Clair.

"St. John's Hospitalle (Northampton) was originally founded by one William Sancte Clere, archdeacon of Northampton, and brother to one of the Simon Saintcleres, as sum of St. John's name them; but as I have redd alway they were caulid Saincteliz (*Sylvanect ensis*) and not S. Clere": Thus Leland. The similarity in sound may well explain his doubt. The St. Liz family held the Earldoms of Huntingdon and Northampton. There is a charter of date 19 Hen. III., "Simon de Seyntclere et Anna uxor ejus; Seyton boscus quiet' de vasto et regard' forestæ, &c.; Rotel," which tends to show that these St. Cleeres and St. Liz were all of one stock. The name also assimilates with St. Hilary. An Aelard de Seynteler was son of James de St. Hillary, and his (Aelard's) sister Maud became Countess of Clare and Hertford. In a *carta* of William of Albini (circ. 1127) appears the name of Aelardus de Saincler, who promises to furnish for his lands two knights' fees in case of war, but the "c" gets faint through interchange with Seynt Liz, the alternate name, and is lost gradually. Seynteler grew to be Seynt Eler or Seynt Elerio, and by aspiration ended in the "St. Hilary" of later records. In the reign of Henry III. another Alard was in possession of properties in Leicestershire, etc., and was ancestor of the subsequent St. Hillaries. He was a benefactor to the convent of St. Albans.

THE ST. CLAIRS OF STAVERTON COURT.*

This is a branch attributed to the Scottish family.

I. DAVID ST. CLAIR, ESQ., by his wife Louisa Wemyss of Dysart House, County Fife, was father of

II. WILLIAM ST. CLAIR, who, by Mary his wife, was father of

III. WILLIAM ST. CLAIR, Colonel 25th Regiment, who married, in 1772, Augusta, daughter of Gerard Tinling, Esq., and had issue—

1. JAMES PATTISON (Colonel R.A.) of Felcourt Lodge, Surrey, born 1780; married, first, in 1809, Charlotte, daughter of Michael Head, of Halifax, Nova Scotia, by whom he had—

---

* Burke's Landed Gentry.

THE ST. CLAIRS OF STAVERTON COURT.

1. WILLIAM AUGUSTUS, of The Beacon, East Grinsted, J.P., Sussex, Captain late Bombay Artillery, and Colonel Royal Sussex Artillery Militia ; born 1810 ; married, 1846, Emma, daughter of George Crawshay, of Colney Hatch, Herts, and died 8th January, 1879.
2. JAMES LOUIS, of Staverton Court.
3. DAVID JOHN, Captain Bombay Infantry, married 1845, and died s.p. 4th June, 1866.
1. CHARLOTTE MYERS, married 1839, Andrew Peterson, of Wakefield, County York.

He married, secondly, in 1830, Susannah, daughter of Sir Thos. Turton, Bart., and had by her a daughter

1. ROSABELLE MARY ELIZABETH.

James Pattison St. Clair died 3rd January, 1867.

2. DAVID LATIMER.
3. WILLIAM, Captain 25th Regiment, killed in action in 1809 at Martinique.
4. THOS. STAUNTON, Major-General, C.B., received nine medals, died 1848.
1. LOUISA MATILDA. 2. AUGUSTA.

The second son

IV. DAVID LATIMER ST. CLAIR, first of Staverton Court, Captain R.N., Knight of the Sword, J.P. and D.L., born 8th May, 1784 ; married, 13th April, 1819, a daughter of John Farhill, of Chichester, but had no issue. He died 24th November, 1861, and was succeeded by his nephew

V. JAMES LOUIS ST. CLAIR, of Staverton Court, County Gloucester, J.P., late Captain H.E.I.C.S., born 10th September, 1816 ; married, 28th June, 1848, Juliet, daughter of George Crawshay, of Colney Hatch, Middlesex, and by her (who is deceased) had issue—

1. JAMES LATIMER CRAWSHAY, Major Argyle and Sutherland Highlanders, born 16th October, 1850.
2. DAVID FARHILL, born 18th August, 1852.
3. WILLIAM AUGUSTUS EDMUND, Captain R.E., born 18th August, 1854.
1. CHARLOTTE ELIZABETH LOUISE. 2. JULIET MATILDA.

CHAPTER XVI

THE ST. CLAIRS AND SINCLAIRS OF NORTH AMERICA.

NEW HAMPSHIRE SCIONS *

FIRST AND SECOND GENERATIONS

JOHN SINKLER (1), Britisher, an American colonist, appeared in Exeter, N H, as early as 1658, for on the 6th January, 1659, he purchased ten acres of land, and is mentioned in the deed, which is extant, as of Exeter On 10th October, 1664, the town of Exeter, at a public meeting, granted him "fifteen acres" lying in old Salesbury way, beyond James Wall's land On the 27th April, 1667, he and Mary, his wife, conveyed fifteen acres to a fellow citizen He is mentioned in a boundary agreement between two neighbours on the 11th February, 1672, against one of whom he made suit on 8th October following for trespass There is no record of the result, but there is a reference to the matter in an enactment of the Selectmen of Exeter, dated 8th June, 1682 On 30th November, 1677, he "took oath of allegiance to His Majestie and fidelity to the country." He applied for a grant of land 6th April, 1678, and on the 6th December thereafter purchased twenty acres of upland in Exeter, which town granted him a like acreage 23rd January, 1680. The Province Rate of 9th May, 1682, assesses "ffor the town of Exeter, John Sinclere £0 19s 4d " (Province Rate made in Exeter, 13th April, 1682, to be pay'd in boards at 30/- p m. and white oke p p staves at 3/- pr thousand, wheat at 5/- pr bushel, pease at 4/-, millet at 3/6, Indian corn 3/- @ bushel)

His name appears on a petition to the Government 20th February, 1689–90, against the Governor, one Edward Cranfield, and praying for protection from the Indians, and that the military officers of the train soldiers should be chosen by the soldiers of the respective towns There is a doubt as to the signature being a genuine autograph He dwelt on the banks of Wheelwright's creek Only the Christian names of his wives have been preserved, that of the first being Mary, and that of the second Deborah, who made with him a business contract before their marriage In 1698 (September 11th), upon the formation of the first Congregational Church, thirteen persons were "dismissed in order to their being incorporated into a church state in Exeter " Among them was Mrs. Deborah Sinkler

John Sinkler, on 7th January, 1699–1700, "being sick of body but of sound and perfect minde and memory," for which he expressed devout thankfulness, made his last will and testament, which was admitted to probate 14th September, 1700. There is no signature appended to the instrument, but in place thereof is a circle, known in common parlance as the "Round Robin." Children born at Exeter, N.H

2 JAMES, born 27th July, 1660, resident Exeter, N H.

---

* Prepared by permission from "History of the Sinclair Family" by the Hon Leonard A Morrison, of Windham, N H

FIRST AND SECOND GENERATIONS.

3 MARY, born 27th June, 1663, she married a Mr Wheeler
4 SARAH, born 15th September, 1664, this will be the daughter that married Mr Jones, whose sons John and Benjamin are named in John Sinkler's will
5 MARIA, born about 1666, married Mr Bedell
6 JOHN, born about 1668, resident Exeter, N H

ROBERT SINKLER of Wells, Me, was probably also a son

SECOND AND THIRD GENERATIONS.

JAMES SINKLER (2), husbandman, dwelt near "Wheal Right's creek." At the early age of sixteen he rendered military service in "King Philip's War" in Captain John Holbrook's company. He took the oath of State allegiance 30th November, 1677. In 1682 (April 13) his province rate in Exeter was 1s. 6d He signed the protest against Governor Cranfield, and joined his father and brother in petitioning the "Bay Government,' 20th February, 1689–90, for protection against the Indians. He was constable of Exeter in 1694 and in 1697; juryman at the Superior Court in Portsmouth, N H, 10th August, 1703; and was selectman of Exeter in 1695, 1700, 1706, and 1721

From 1702 to April 11, 1713, "Queen Anne's War" kept the New Hampshire colony in constant unrest and fear James Sinkler was a soldier, and his account of personal services at Newbury blockhouses in 1704 was £2 18s. 6d He will be the Sergeant Sinkler of 1610 in charge of a scouting party. He was again a juryman 12th August, 1712; on the grand jury 9th February, 1719–20, and was one of the 215 proprietors of Gilmantown 20th May, 1727. His wife was Mary, youngest child of Richard and Prudence Scammon She was born 31st May 1763 From her parents she received all the 'salt medde" between Quoboag road and Moore's creek His will was executed on 23rd July, 1731, within four days of his seventy-first birthday, and probate was granted 15th February, 1732–33. Birthdates of his children can only be approximately stated Children born Exeter, N H

7 JOHN, born about 1690
8 JOSEPH, born about 1692
9 SAMUEL, born about 1694
10 JONATHAN, born about 1700
11 RICHARD, born about 1705
12 EBENEZER, born after 1710
13 BENJAMIN, born about 1712
14 MERCY; she married Ralph, son of Kingsley Hall, of Exeter
15 MARTHA, married Jeremiah (?) Bean
16 DAVID, born about 1717, living 23rd July, 1731
17 KESIAH, born about 1718, living 23rd July, 1731.
18. MARY, born about 1719; living 23rd July, 1731.

JOHN SINKLER, JUNR. (6), was born in Exeter about 1668. He was a signatory of the petition to the Government of Massachusetts 20th February, 1689–90, but there is a doubt as to the genuineness of the petition. In 1709 his name again appears on a petition to the Government. He was a constable of Exeter June 5th, 1711–12, and served as juror February 14th, 1715–16, and at the court which was in session August 27th, 1717, and was on the grand jury February 9th, 1719–20 On the 9th February, 1726, he purchased house and lands in Exeter, and on 20th June, 1729, deeded one-half of his lands and estate to his "beloved son John Sinkler of sd Exeter." His wife, who survived him, was Elisabeth, daughter of John Bean, senr., of Exeter, where she was born on 24th September, 1678. His will bears date 28th December, 1730, and was admitted to probate 16th November, 1731 His wife was sole executrix. She was directed to return appraisal of the estate at the Probate Court 16th February, 1732–33 Children born Exeter, N.H..

19 JOHN.
20 SAMUEL
21 ABIGAIL, born c 1710
22 MARGARET, born c 1712
23 ELISABETH, born c 1713

THIRD AND FOURTH GENERATIONS

CAPTAIN JOHN SINKLER (7) was born in Exeter about 1690, and presumably the eldest child, being first mentioned in his father's will, which provided for only a slight legacy to him, indicating that his portion had been advanced during the lifetime of his father. He was early a settler on the "Squamscott Patent," a tract incorporated into a a town called Stratham, 14th March, 1715-16, where he and his wife deeded land the following year. He was one of a committee chosen to secure a "learned Authordox Minister," and to "set off" the pews of a meeting-house in Stratham, for the erection of which the act of incorporation provided. He served as selectman in 1720-24 and 1728, '29, '31, '32. Though elected constable in 1726, he declined to act. In 1729 he was on the committee to seat the meeting-house, and on 13th July, 1730, helped to give his brother Richard place "in the great congregation." At a town meeting 18th January, 1733, he was chosen one of a committee to take down the broken bell of the meeting-house and to send it to 'Lundon to be New Cast Again.'" He was a large dealer in real estate. On 17th June, 1727, he bought land in Bow, near what is now Pembroke. In 1736, '37, '39, '40, and '42 he served as assessor. In 1739 he is called Lef'n John Sinkler; is styled John Sinkler, *Gentleman*, 13th April, 1743, and eventually Captain John Sinkler. He died in Stratham 16th September, 1745. His house was on the "King's Road," where the Sinkler barn is still standing, but the other buildings have disappeared. He married Anne Chase, widow of Bradstreet Wiggin, she was living 24th February, 1753. Children born Stratham, N.H.

24 ANNA, born 15th April, 1711.
25 RACHAEL, born 6th August, 1713; married Thos Moore of Stratham; issue.
26 MERCY, born 5th April, 1717.
27 HANNAH, born 25th April, 1719; married John Purmont, and had issue.

JOSEPH SINKLER (8) was born in Exeter, N.H., about 1692, as he was of age and doing business on 23rd March, 1714. He was an original proprietor of Gilmantown, and by paternal devise inherited forty acres in Epping, which he sold 10th January, 1743-44, a James Sinkler attesting the conveyance. His name is on a Newmarket election petition dated 5th June, 1745. He was called "Yeoman," and dwelt in South Newmarket, N H., till 12th September, 1751, when he and his wife sold their home of forty-two acres. He acquired, 14th January, 1755, fifty-nine acres, lot No 1, Buckstreet Lotts Division, in the town of Pembroke, which was acknowledged 29th October, 1765. He sold the property to his son John 15th April, 1761, and last appears 3rd September, 1767, as one of sixty-four petitioners for the appointment of John Bryant as a J P. He married Elisabeth, daughter of Thos Lyford of Exeter, N.H. Children born South Newmarket, N H.

28. THOMAS.   29 JOSEPH, JUNR   30 JOHN   31. JAMES

SAMUEL SINKLER (9), "laborer," resident of Exeter, N H. He sold on 28th August, 1734, for £150, all his right in a fifty acre grant " to my Honored father James Sinkler, dec'd by the town of Exeter on the 31st day of January, 1680, and given to me by my father's will." On 21st November, 1746, he, his brother Joseph, and nephew Thomas, petition for a bridge at Newfields, now South Newmarket. Anna, his wife, on 7th February, 1748-49, relinquished her right of administration of his estate.

JONATHAN SINKLER (10) was born in Exeter, N H., about 1700. He received only twenty shillings by his father's will, indicating previous provision. A resident of Wells,

Me, that town granted him fifty acres of upland and ten of meadow, which his father by his authority sold on 6th November, 1729.

RICHARD SINKLER (11) was born in Exeter, N.H., about 1705, and on 20th May, 1727, was one of 215 original proprietors of Gilmantown, N.H. Forty acres of the town commons was laid out to him in 1725. His parents, for "love and affection to their beloved son Richard Sinkler of Exeter," deeded him land in Stratham, which remained in the possession of his family for several generations. The site of his home is still known as the "Sinclair Place." "The Sinkler Path," the tortuous winding of which can still be traced leading through the woods to his home, and the "Sinkler's Reach" is a straight on Squamscott River noted on the map of Stratham in 1793. His name occurs often in the Stratham records. The seat in the meeting-house assigned him 13th July, 1730, was "in the horrid long front seat below on the men's side." He was tything man in 1741, surveyor in 1748. On 5th April, 1748, he and his wife sold to her brother David for £100 "all right to the estate of our Honored Father Nathaniel Stevens, deceased, within the township of Bow, in the Province abovesaid, and the four acres of land that lies upon Rail-timber hill." Mr. Sinkler died on the 9th July, 1751, having on the 25th June same made his will, which obtained probate on the 27th August of the same year. His executors had an allowance from the estate for two sheep killed by wolves; total value of estate, £2,889 10s. He married, 27th June, 1728, Catherine, daughter of Nathaniel and Sarah Folsom Stevens, by whom he was survived for many years. The administration of her estate was granted to her son Richard. Children born Stratham, N.H.:

  32. NATHANIEL 39 RICHARD 40 JOHN
  33 MARY, married Theodore Hilton of Newmarket, N H, issue.
  34 SARAH, married Nathan Preston, shipwright, Newmarket
  35 CATHERINE 36 RHODA 38 ANN, mentioned in father's will
  37 ABIGAIL, probably married Ephraim Green before 19th April, 1758.

EBENEZER SINKLER (12) was born in Exeter after 1710, and was under age at his father's death. By the will he received "the one halfe part of my Right or propriety in Gilman Town. Also all my Land where in Exeter near Wheel Right's Creek with the hous barn and orchard and all my stock utensils for work be they of what kind soever." This old homestead of twenty-three acres, with buildings, was sold by him 4th August, 1741. A farmer, resident in Exeter, he was a soldier in Captain John Light's Company, Colonel Moore's Regiment, 20th November, 1745, and was at the capture of Louisburg. He married Abigail, daughter of Jonathan and Anna Ladd Folsom. He died 1754, and she before 3rd April, 1761. Children born Exeter, N H.:

  41. JAMES 42. RICHARD
  43 ABIGAIL, born about 1743, married William Hackett about 1765

BENJAMIN SINKLER (13) born Exeter about 1712, in minority 1731, sold his inherited land in Gilmanton 18th May, 1736. He lived with his brother Ebenezer until he was twenty-one, and always resided in his native town, where he was last taxed in 1757. Adversity then came upon him, and he received public aid. His death occurred before 26th March, 1759. Nathan Taylor of Exeter dug his grave and tolled the bell of the meeting-house at his funeral. His wife Elisabeth died 1766 or 1767.

JOHN SINKLER (19) was born in Exeter before 20th June, 1708, as on the same day, 1729, he received a deed of one-half of his real estate in Exeter, inclusive of "Sinkler's Point." By various sales he had disposed of most, if not all, of this tract by the 11th

December, 1733. He retained his residence in Exeter, and in public documents was called yeoman and husbandman. He was also a seafarer, and is called *coaster*. He died before 28th September, 1747. Nicholas Perryman was administrator. The appraisal was taken December 28th, 1747, and consisted of thirty acres.

SAMUEL SINKLER (20) was born previous to 1709, and was to inherit after his mother's decease one-half of the homestead on Wheelright's creek. This was sold by his mother as executrix, and himself as legatee, on 4th December, 1734. He was one of the 215 original proprietors of Gilmanton 20th May, 1727. He sold this land on 3rd December, 1731, being then "of Newmarket in Exeter," and the sale was signed by Sarah, his wife. On June 6th, 1733, they relinquished to her brother Richard all right to the estate of their honored father, Richard Mattoon of Exeter, deceased. He deeded to Edward Sinkler, 3rd March, 1747-48, ten acres in Newmarket, Exeter, and acknowledged by him 27th February, 1758. He married Sarah, daughter of Richard and Jane Hilton Mattoon. Children born Exeter, N.H.:

  44 EDWARD, a Revolutionary soldier, born as early as 3rd March, 1726
  45 RICHARD, born before 3rd December, 1731
  46 EBENEZER, Revolutionary soldier

Nos 44 and 46 appear to be sons of No 20, and the probabilities are so strong that they have been so arranged.

FOURTH AND FIFTH GENERATIONS

THOMAS SINKLER (28), born 1721, was apparently named after his mother's father. His signature is attached to several petitions—at Newmarket, 21st November, 1746; Pembroke, 1758, and 13th July, 1764; and at Sanbornton, 8th January, 1768. He bought a farm in "Ellonstown," 21st September, 1764, to which he moved. This he sold 25th December, same year, and settled down at Sanbornton, where he was surveyor of highways in 1772, '82, '87, and tything man from 1773-76, and signed the Association test in the latter year. He enlisted 22nd July, 1777, and his company marched from Sanbornton to Charleston, N H. He was discharged 27th September, 1777. Elected Constable of Sanbornton 30th March, 1784, he paid his fine in preference to accepting office. He sold his 90-acre farm on Steele's Hill to his son John, 28th January, 1785, and lived at Sanbornton from 1st February, 1768, to February, 1793 = 25 years. He finally moved to Hardwick, Vt., where the town record apprises us. "Died, December 7th, 1796, Thomas Sinclair, when under the care of James Sinclair, age 75." Children

  47 BENJAMIN 48 THOMAS
  49 SARAH, married her cousin James, son of Joseph Sinkler of Sanbornton
  50 BATHSHEBA, married Simeon Walton, residence, Vt
  51 JAMES 52 ZEBULON 53 CONSTANTINE

JOSEPH SINKLER (29), born in South Newmarket before 27th May, 1736, as a boy went to Pembroke, N H, then called Buckstreet. He bought 60 acres in Allanstown, 27th May, 1757, subject to certain conditions subsequent. He is probably the Joseph Sinkler of the French and Indian war, who was in the same company as Richard, afterwards Colonel Sinkler of Barnstead, N.H., who enlisted in Captain J. Marston's company, 20th April, 1760, and was in the service at least as late as 6th July, 1760. Soon after he was resident in Holderness, N H., where, before its incorporation, he was made fence-viewer 10th June, 1769. He lived on South Hill on Lot No 62 of 100 acres,

FOURTH AND FIFTH GENERATIONS

which he and Martha, his wife, sold 23rd July, 1771 On December 16th, 1776, then of Sanbornton, he enlisted for the war, and was paid 31st December, 1779, for "36 months' and 27 days' service." He was in Whitcomb's Rangers, side by side with his nephew, James Sinkler († Barre, N Y) The Depreciation Rolls of 1780 have him in the Third N.H., while on 1st March, 1784, he was again in Whitcomb's Rangers. After the war he resided and died in Sanbornton. The administration of his estate was granted 4th July, 1792, to James Sinkler, and according to the best obtainable information he appears to have had two sons—

54 JOSEPH, jun , Soldier of Revolution, Richardson's Company, Bedell's Regiment, service, 11 months 26 days

55. JAMES, who perhaps bought land in Henniker, N H , 1st July, 1789 He married his cousin Sarah, daughter of Thomas Sinkler, and is believed to have settled in Vermont or Canada

JOHN SINKLER (30), born in South Newmarket, 1738 , removed to Pembroke, 1751 , signed petition 1st November, 1759 ; purchased his father's home farm 15th April, 1761, of which he disposed 9th November, 1768 He made numerous purchases of land at Wolfborough, N H , the first being one of 86 acres on 30th August, 1769 The annual town meetings were frequently held at his house, viz., in 1771, '73, '74, '75, and '76. He was Selectman in 1771, Clerk in 1773, Moderator in 1778, '80, and '82, Constable in '79, Surveyor in '76, '79, and '82, and frequently Collector of Taxes, Auditor in '74, and Deer-keeper in '81 and '82. On the 20th February, 1776, all the training soldiers of Wolfborough met at his inn, and he was re-elected Captain This was one of the "Train Bands " He was mustered into service as a soldier in Chandler's Company, Wyman's Regiment, 10th August, 1776 On 29th January, 1778, he sold to Peter Hodgdon of Kensington, N H , the land he had bought 30th August, 1765, and 9th December, 1769 He last appeared publicly in Wolfborough on 3rd June, 1782, when he presided at a special town meeting On public records he is written "Captain" and "Gentleman." He was in Fairlee, Vt., 1st December, 1783, and in Moretown, Vt , 24th September, 1784, when he and Mary, his wife, sold land in Sanbornton. He was resident in Essex, Vt., 1st July, 1791, where he died 19th July, 1803, aged 65 His wife, who was born in 1740, had preceded him on 13th April, 1799, aged 59 They are both interred in the burial-ground at Essex Center, as are many of their descendants and kindred. On his tombstone he is called John Sinclair Children

56 JEREMIAH   57 SAMUEL

58 JOHN, jun , born probably in Wolfborough, about 1770, resident in Essex, Vt , took Freeman's oath 6th September, 1808, farmer and lumberman A soldier in the war of 1812-15, he rallied with the company from Essex, and fought in the Battle of Plattsburgh, N Y, some thirty miles from his home, yet the severity of the cannonade shook his crockery His first wife was named Mary, and it is probable he married secondly an Elisabeth

59 JAMES   60 JOSEPH

61 JONATHAN, probably born in Wolfborough, supposed to be a son of No 30 and brother of 56/60 He took the Freeman's oath in Essex, Vt , 2nd September, 1794

JAMES SINKLER (31) was born in South Newmarket about 1730 , he was a housewright and farmer, and a soldier in the Indian war. His great-grandson, Professor Benjamin Davis, of Concord, possesses a unique powder-horn, beautifully embellished with artistic designs in illustration of a battle-scene and incidents of the chase, inscribed "James Sincler, his Horn, mad at fort edward, November 17th, 1758."

On 31st August, 1754, the town of Epping laid out a highway through the Sinkler farm, a small holding of about 40 acres. The site can still be identified even to a depression in the soil, where was the Sinkler cellar Children born Epping, N H.·

 62. JACOB   63 BARNABAS, possibly son of 31   64 NOAH
 65 ELISABETH, born about 1757, married Nathaniel Martin
 66 SARAH, born about 1759, probably his daughter, married Winthrop Colbroth.

NATHANIEL SINKLER (32) was born in Stratham before 1737, signed petition for bridge at Newfields in 1755, soldier in Hart's Company in Crown Point expedition (in the French war) previous to 18th March, 1757. On 19th April, 1758, then of Stratham, he and his wife Deborah deeded real estate in Epping. Signer of a petition, 21st November, 1765; he petitioned Government and obtained permission 19th March, 1777, "to export 303 bushels corn from Portsmouth to Machias." He and his wife Deborah were residents of Hampton Falls as early as February, 1762, and dwelt there for several years. He may have married secondly, as Sarah Allen, of Portsmouth, in July, 1782, married Nathaniel Sinkler, of Stratham, and no other is known of at that date.

RICHARD SINKLER, JUNR, (39) born in Stratham, 1740, inherited his father's homestead, known in 1890 as the "old Sinclair place," and there spent his life Juror in 1786; tything man in 1791; member of Baptist Society 1786; and owner of considerable real estate. He deeded the homestead to his second son in life, Richard, and died there 31st May, 1814, aged 74. His wife, Elisabeth Morn of Stratham, died 8th January, 1820, aged 70 Children born Stratham, N.H.

 67 RICHARD, born December 1st, 1771, died December 28th, 1772   68 JOHN.
 70 RACHEL, born about 1779, married Joseph French of Stratham   69 RICHARD
 71 RHODA, born 10th July, 1785, (married Jos Wiggin), resident Portsmouth, died 1870
 72 ELISABETH, born 4th July, 178-, resident Portsmouth, died February, 1860, single

JOHN SINKLER (40) was born in Stratham 1747, where he lived and died. Farmer and blacksmith, he was in 1786 a member of the Baptist society He dealt considerably in real estate His home was sold in 1822 He died 3rd July, 1821, and his wife, Elisabeth Pickering of Greenland, N H, survived him until the 3rd October, 1822 They are both buried in the cemetery near the Congregational church in Stratham Children born Stratham, N.H ·

 73 MICAJAH   75 SAMUEL.   77 JAMES
 74 MEHITABLE, born about 1794, lived and died single in South Carolina.
 76 MARTHA, born about 1797, lived and died single in Stratham
 78 DANIEL, born April, 1800, carpenter, resident in Bangor, Me, Roxburgh, and Boston, Mass Late in life returned to Stratham, where he died single 18th December, 1879, leaving several thousand dollars in trust for the benefit of the sick and destitute of his town

CAPTAIN JAMES SINKLER (41) was born in Exeter 14th February, 1737, O.S. By trade a housewright, he was a citizen of Exeter until after 3rd April, 1761, removing to the adjacent township of Brentwood before 15th June, 1764. He sold, 4th November, 1765, his original right or proprietor's share of land "granted me in the town of Sandwich." He purchased from his brother Richard his right in land at "Wall's Cove" in Exeter This James Sinkler was second lieutenant of the 30th Company enlisted in N.H to replace the recalcitrant troops from Connecticut 6th December, 1775, and he is noted as captain in Waldron's Regiment 6th March, 1776, which title he retained till his death. His will is dated 25th February, 1802, and the appraisement was sworn to on 6th

FOURTH AND FIFTH GENERATIONS.

September, 1811. He had ninety acres of land with buildings, which, with personal property, were valued at $3,252·40. He married, first, 20th March, 1760, Rachel, daughter of Benjamin and Rachel Folsom of Exeter. She died 20th May, 1764, leaving two children. He married, secondly, Abigail Veasey, 16th May, 1765. She died, and he married, thirdly, Elizabeth Blake, who survived him, and died 28th December, 1827. Children born at Brentwood, N.H. ·

    79 BENJAMIN FOLSOM.   80 JAMES, JR   84 JONATHAN   87 DAVID
    81 HENRY, born 9th February, 1766, died March 7th, 1766.
    82 ABIGAIL, born February 13th, 1767, married Joshua Beede, res and died Danville, Vt
    83 RACHEL, born May 9th, 1769, married Timothy Harris, resident Danville.
    85 MARY, born 15th May, 1775, married Jonathan Danforth, resident Danville
    86 DEBORAH, born 9th June, 1777, married John Clifford, resident Brentwood
    88 EBENEZER   89 ELISABETH, born 7th June, 1782, died 25th February, 1802

    RICHARD SINKLER (42) was born in Exeter about 1740 A minor when his father died in 1754, General Nath Folsom was his guardian By trade he was a hatter and a farmer He and his brother James (No 41) each secured a seventy-second share of the town of Sandwich, laid out 25th October, 1763, and soon after 15th October, 1765, settled there, living first in a log cabin some twenty rods distant from the large two-storied house he afterwards erected, and which still stands He signed the Association Test in 1776, joined the Northern Continental Army in 1777, serving 2 months 8 days—July 22nd to September 29th, 1777 He re-enlisted the next day, and marched to join the Continental Army under Gates at Saratoga, and after Burgoyne's surrender marched with the guard as far as Northampton, Mass, and was there discharged He was collector of taxes for Sandwich in 1781 and '90. On 19th October, 1784, he bought fifty acres in Moultonborough, N.H, and for over forty years owned and lived on this farm, situate on the old Toppan road, until he sold it with other lands 5th October, 1807, to his son Jonathan, and presently removed to Haverhill, N.H. He and his wife died and were buried in Haverhill, N H Children ·

    90 RICHARD, JUNR   91 JONATHAN   92. EBENEZER.   93 SAMUEL
    94 ABIGAIL, married John Hackett, resident and died Sandwich, N H
    95 SARAH, married Amos Hill, resident and died Sandwich
    96 ELISABETH, married Andrew Bean, resident and died Sandwich
    97. HANNAH, married Mr Brown, resident Haverhill, N H.

    EDWARD SINKLER (44) born about 1726 Received on 3rd March, 1747-48, ten acres from Samuel Sinkler, and was then of Newmarket, where he is again noticed as signing a petition for the bridge at Newfields in 1755. On 14th November, 1770, then of Holderness, N H, he bought land there In 1775 he is one of twelve volunteers resident in Gilmantown, and enlisted 8th May, 1775, serving until August 1st—3 months 1 day. He was in the battle of Bunker's Hill, after which he is lost to sight, but circumstances point to his settling in Maine and being ancestor to the Sinklers of Blue Hill, there.

    COLONEL RICHARD SINKLER (45) was born in Newmarket about 1730; was carpenter and wheelwright by trade, and resident of Nottingham, N H, in 1752, when he is found selling 40 acres in Epping As resident of Newmarket 15th January, 1757, he bought one-fourth part of lot No 4, Summer-street, Nottingham At that period he dealt considerably in real estate, owned mills, and cut and sawed lumber, which was the main business of his life He enlisted 28th March, 1760, in Marston's Company, Goffe's Regiment, for invading Canada He bought land in Canterbury, 27th April, 1764, and in November of same became a pioneer in Gilmantown, living for two years on lot No 1, in the first range of the lower 100-acre lots. He signed the call convening the first town meeting in Gilmanton, which was held 31st July, 1766, and in the latter part of the year became a resident of Barnstead On the 2nd June, 1767, he bought 100 acres, being "the lot said Richard Sinkler now lives on, and is lot No. 64 in second division in Barnstead." On the same date he sold one-fourth part of a sawmill standing on Bear Pond stream In the War of Independence he is first found holding a captain's commission in the 10th Regiment He was a captain in active service in Colonel Waldron's Regiment stationed at Temple's farm, in Sullivan's Brigade in the Continental Army 6th March, 1776. In 1780 he commanded a company in Bartlett's Regiment, raised June, 1780, for defending the fortress at West Point The regiment was disbanded 27th October, 1780, and he returned to Barnstead It was during this term of service that Arnold unsuccessfully attempted to betray West Point to the British Captain Sinkler was made Second Major of the 10th N H. Regiment, 3rd November, 1780. He served as Moderator in his town at special meetings, and at the annual meetings of 1775, '76, '79, and '82, as Selectman, 1777, '78, and '80; and as Chairman of the Board in 1775, '82, '83, and '84, was a Surveyor of Highways and Auditor in 1792. On the 26th April, 1775, the town voted to "Captain Richard Sinkler, £1 11s. 6d., Lawful money for his and the men's expence for going Down below For the Defence of our Country." He served on the committee to hire money and soldiers for Barnstead, and on the committee of regulation in 1778. On the 14th December, 1784 the town resolved to rebuild a bridge over the Suncook River, and Richard Sinkler Esq, was made "overseer of the hol bridge" On the 25th October, 1785, he was made overseer of the work, receiving 5s per day for his services and the others 2s 6d He is first styled Colonel on the 25th March, 1788, when he is appointed one of a committee to locate a site for the erection of a meeting-house On 11th March, 1788, he deeded a 100-acre lot (No. 98, second division) with sawmill to his son John, "in consideration of love and goodwill that I bear to him", on 23rd March, 1790, he sold 65 acres to his son Richard, a part of lot 64, second division, in Barnstead, and the remainder, "about 100 acres, with all buildings standing on said premises, it being the same land and buildings where I, the said Richard Sincler now live," to Joseph Cilley, 15th April, 1791. Colonel Sinkler died in Barnstead 27th July, 1813 He married in 1752-53 Mary, daughter of Captain Joseph Cilley, of Hampton, N.H Both husband and wife were buried in an orchard, near the homestead which no longer exists, but the site of the cellar is indicated by a depression of the soil, and thereon flourishes a stately elm more than a foot in a diameter Children

  98 BRADBURY.   99 RICHARD, jun
  100 MARY, born Nottingham, N H, 1758, married a Mr Weed
  101 JOSHUA   102 SAMUEL   103 JOHN
  104 ELSIE, born Gilmantown, N H, about 1764; died Vassalborough, Me, aged 18.
  105 JOSEPH   106 DAVID.

EBENEZER SINKLER (46) was probably a son of Samuel Sinkler (No. 20). By trade a joiner, he lived in different places, and was a soldier in the French and Indian war before 1764. He married Mary, daughter of Captain Jonathan Blunt, of Chester, N H., of which town he was resident before 5th July, 1771, when he and his wife sold the land set off to her from her father's estate. On 31st December, 1772, he was a resident of Weare, N H (Hail's Town), where they had inherited land from Captain Blunt, for they deeded to Samuel Blunt, of Chester, certain rights in land and building

" out of the estate of our honored father, Captain Jonathan Blunt, of Chester, deceased " He enlisted early in the revolutionary struggle, and served almost continuously, until at Saratoga he made the supreme sacrifice, that of life itself, for the American cause He was a private in Richard's Company, Stark's Regiment, from April 23rd to 1st August, 1775   At Bunker's Hill his station was with the other men from Weare, N H., "behind the rail fence," extending from the redoubt part of the way east to the Mystic River   On 22nd March, 1777, he enlisted (Merrill's Company, Cilley's Regiment), in the Continental Army for three years, and received a bounty of £22 5s 6d , for which he gave a receipt. At the Battle of Saratoga, N.Y , 7th October, 1777, a British detachment marched out of their position upon the left of the American forces   The English force consisted of the grenadiers and light infantry, and six field pieces   They placed themselves upon an elevated point in a cleared field, a fourth of a mile distant from the American forces   The three N H Regiments were ordered to attack them, which they did in splendid style. The fight lasted for half-an-hour, when the enemy were driven from their position with the loss of their cannon and some prisoners. The Americans pressed forward, attacked the German troops, capturing military stores and provisions   It was during these famous exploits that Ebenezer Sinkler, the brave soldier, was killed.   His family being left in destitute circumstances, his widow applied to the State for assistance, which was not granted, though she received help from the town.   His property consisted of 150 acres of wild land in Wentworth, N H. Children :

> He had three children, the eldest under 14 years of age , Nos 107, 108, 109, names not known

EBENEZER SINKLER, of Charleston, N.H , was probably a son of No. 46. On 6th April, 1795, he bought from Joshua Gove, in Weare, all the right he had in John Page, junr 's, land in Wentworth   Mary Sinkler was witness to the deed   On 1st September, 1795, then living in Wentworth, he sold the same.   An Ebenezer Sinclair, apparently the same, was resident of Barre, Vt , previous to 1804, and was residing there on 24th December, 1808, when he disappears from the records.   He was frequently at law with his neighbours, and his name often appears in the Court records at Chelsea, Vt.

JOHN ST. CLAIR, of Strafford, Vt., was probably another son of No 46

FIFTH AND SIXTH GENERATIONS.

BENJAMIN SINCLAIR (47) was born in Newmarket, N.H., about 1750 An early settler of Meredith, N H (2nd November, 1772), he bought from his brother Thos , 28th November, 1772, part of Lot 19. div 2 ; and from the same brother and others on 19th October, 1774, he bought 100 acres in Meredith, which he sold 20th February, 1775   A Revolutionary soldier, he was a member of Moody's Company, Baldwin's Regiment, raised in N.H. in September, 1776, to reinforce the Continental Army at New York, The regiment participated in the battle of White Plains, 28th October, 1776, and was discharged in the December following, when Mr Sinclair was allowed £8 13s. 4d. for 320 miles travel   He lived in Meredith in 1780, and on 18th August sold part of his homestead   Removing about 1790 to Greensborough, Vt., he settled on a fifty acre farm. In old age he moved to Hardwick, where he died about 1810. He married Hannah Sanborn. Children

> 110 RUAMIE, born 3rd July, 1779 died 8th December, 1845, married Benj Philbrook , issue
> 111 NATHANIEL.   114 BENJAMIN   115. JEKEMIAH   117 ENOCH.   118 ASA

112. HANNAH, married Stephen Adams in Greensborough, Vt
113 SARAH, married Amos Smith   She died in Greensborough
116 DOLLY, married Levi Stevens   They died in Greensborough

THOMAS SINCLAIR (48) was born in Newmarket, N H., 14th April, 1751, and settled in Meredith before 13th November, 1772, when he conveyed land to his brother Benjamin. The land of Constantine Sinclair adjoined theirs. Farmer; Baptist. Married, first, 9th August, 1774, Mary Meed, secondly, 9th January, 1791, Nancy Pike   Children born Meredith, N H ·

119 JOHN MEED   120 JAMES.   121 THOMAS   123 WILLIAM.   124 JOSEPH
122 MARY, born 12th April, 1781, married Hezekiah Smith
125 SARAH, born 27th March, 1787, died 27th Sept, 1834, married Jonathan Cram, issue
126 SUSAN, born 15th May, 1789, died 6th March, 1824, married James Foss

JAMES ST. CLAIR (51) was born in Newmarket in 1757, resident Meredith 1776; enlisted 5th December, 1776, in Whitcomb's Rangers, and served till 31st December, 1779 Though a Meredith resident, he went as a soldier for Sanbornton, and received a bounty. On 7th January, 1779, he bought 65 acres in Sandwich, N H, and re-enlisted the same year in Whitcomb's Rangers, and then for a time in Rowell's Company. He was made corporal 1st November, 1780, and afterwards became a sergeant, his service ending with honourable discharge at West Point, N Y, signed by Washington, and receiving at the same time a "Badge of Merit"   It was well won.   In a lineage noted for its numerous soldiers, and their attested devotion to country by valiant and repeated services, Mr St. Clair had by continuity and length of time surpassed them all.   He was subsequently pensioned by the Government. After the war he resided temporarily at Sandwich, N H., and then, his father, Thos Sinkler, being old, he bought from him the homestead in Sanbornton, N H, to which they moved. Living there till 17th March, 1792, he sold his 90 acres, and with his aged father, in February, 1793, settled in Hardwick, Vt., where in 1796 he was one of a committee to arrange for the settlement there of the Rev. Mr. Tuttle   A dealer in real estate in 1801, he moved to Wolcott, Vt., where he was selectman in 1802-3 and '4, and moderator of the annual meeting in 1804   About 1808 he, with the Northrops and other friends, removed to Russelltown, Canada, till the outbreak of the 1812-15 war, when, abandoning all possessions, he and his family fled by night across the frontier into the United States   They lived in Peru, Union Springs, and Palmyra, N.Y., and in 1816 he removed his family to Vermont.   He joined his son in Barre, N Y, and visited General Arthur St. Clair, then living on Chestnut Ridge in the Ligonier Valley, Penn, in the neighbourhood of the large estate he had owned at the commencement of the Revolution   At that time General St. Clair was farming   Help being short, his visitor, James St Clair, lent an assisting hand, and helped him secure his crop of corn   He stayed with the General some three months. The incidents of this visit and the assistance he rendered the General were often related to his family, and afforded him pleasure and delight   The subject of their relationship was discussed by them, and he stated on his return that they were relatives, "cousins"; the degree of cousinship was not stated   He returned to Barre, N Y., where he lived with his family until death, 27th January, 1836.   A notice contemporary to that event states "He was at the battles of Monmouth and Brandywine : was at Valley Forge, and at the taking of Burgoyne   He was at West Point at the time of Arnold's treason, and in the unsuccessful attack on Quebec, and in several other actions of less importance "   He spelled his name Sinclair or Sinclear until late in life, when he changed to St Clair.

FIFTH AND SIXTH GENERATIONS.

He signed James Sinclear, application for pension 12th June, 1818, and James St Clair 4th September, 1820, affidavit asking for the transfer of the payment of his pension from one agency to another St Clair is the form used by his family and descendants He married Sarah, daughter of Philip Hunt of Haverhill and Sanbornton, N.H. Children.

127 MARY, born Sandwich, N H, 2nd October, 1784, died in infancy.
128 JOSEPH   129 MARY, born 11th November, 1787, died 6th March, 1812, married Hezekiah Whitney, issue   130 JAMES
131 SARAH, born 10th March, 1791, married, first, John Myers, secondly, Nehemiah Randall
132 ELISABETH, born 18th October, 1792, married 28th March, 1810, Jadutham Sherman
133 MIRIAM, born 3rd October, 1794, married 7th September, 1817, George McKinstry
134 NANCY, born 22nd November, 1796, married Dr James Brown, of Mechanicsburgh, Ill
135 RACHEL TUCKER, born 15th June, 1798, married William Culver, residence, E. Beekmanton, N Y   136 LEVI HUNT
137 ELECTA JANE, born Wolcott, Vt, 13th November, 1802, died Barre, N Y, 25th May, 1825 Teacher   138 PHILIP, born and died Wolcott, Vt, 1804

ZEBULON SINCLAIR (52), born in Newmarket, N H, resident of Sanbornton, whence he enlisted in Clough's Company (Poor's Regiment, Sullivan's Brigade), serving one year—31st December, 1775, to 31st December, 1776 Entering the Continental service for the war, he served till 1st April, 1778—1 year and 3 months—when he procured a substitute and returned home During this period he was in Smith's Company, which, on the alarm of 7th July, 1777, marched to the relief of the garrison at Ticonderoga He was one of the soldiers under General Stark of N.H, who, on 16th August, 1777, defeated a detachment sent by Burgoyne to seize stores at Bennington, Vt, and he continued with the forces which pressed on and joined the American army, which, at Saratoga and Stillwater, defeated Burgoyne, and caused his surrender to Gates on 7th October. He was for a time in Addridge's Company of Rangers under Whitcomb, and was also in several skirmishes with the Indians After the war he lived first in Sandwich, where he sold 27 acres, 2nd February, 1790, then in Meredith, where he sold 165 acres and buildings, 1st September, 1801, and then in Holderness, where he sold land, 16th April, 1810 He had a Government pension for military services He married 1st March, 1779, Annie Conant, probably of Newmarket, N H., and died 11th June, 1840. Children

139 ANNA, born and died 4th November, 1781   140 JOSEPH, born 1782, died 1784
141 ANNA, born 1786, married Mr Jewell, and lived in Tamworth Both dead
142 CATHERINE, born 4th August, 1789, married Mark Jewell, of Tamworth, N H Both dead
143 JOSEPH   144 SARAH PEAS, born 26th February, 1793, married Samuel Tilton, of Tamworth, issue   145 ZEBULON
146 POLLY MEAD, born at Meredith 12th February, 1801, died 19th June, 1801

CONSTANTINE SINCLAIR (53), farmer, evidently lived on the boundary between Meredith and New Hampton, as in official documents he is domiciled in both As early as 2nd November, 1772, he owned and probably lived upon lot 19, division 2, in Meredith He bought land in New Hampton 1st March, 1781. Administration of his estate was granted 3rd September, 1783, inventory taken 27th November, 1783, Huldah, his widow's, third, set off 8th December, 1783; and license granted to sell the real estate 23rd July, 1784 Dr Beniah Sanborn attended him Benjamin Pease, of Meredith, was administrator No mention of children.

JEREMIAH SINCLAIR (56) was born in Pembroke, N H., 1765; passed his youth in Wolfborough, N.H, enlisted 21st September, 1781, in Smith's Company of Rangers, raised for the defence of the northern frontiers, New Hampshire, and received discharge

6th November of same year. Resident at Wolfborough, 23rd December, 1783, a document of that date has his signature, the surname spelled Sincler. After the war he resided in Eaton, N.H., and bought 19th October, 1799, 150 acres from Eli Glines for $300, "the land he now lives on," situate one mile from Eaton Centre and near Glines' Hill. Later on he removed to Essex, Vt., bought a farm, erected buildings, and there spent the remainder of his life. He was a soldier of two wars—the Revolution, and the last with Great Britain, 1812-15. He was with the company from Essex, Vt., and with them participated in the fight at Plattsburg, N.Y. A powerful man, in his youth he was fond of athletic sports, and noted for his successful feats in lifting, jumping, and wrestling, the games then in vogue at public fairs and gatherings. Farmer by occupation. He married Abigail, sister of Colonel Eli Glines, of Eaton, N.H. They were members of the Freewill Baptist Church. Mr. Sincler died in Essex, 19th November, 1822. Children:

    147. NOAH.   148. ABIGAIL, married John Keeler; residence, Essex, Vt., and died there 7th November, 1870.   149. THOMAS.   150. ELI.   151. JOHN.
    152. MARY, married Joseph Barney Weed; resident and died in Essex, Vt., in 1870.
    153. MERCY, married Jonathan Moses; residence, Huntingdon, Vt. Two daughters.
    154. LEANDER DUDLEY.   155. DAVID.

SAMUEL SINCLAIR (57), born Pembroke, N.H., 1768; passed his youth at Wolfborough, N.H., and Essex, Vt.; baptised Dover, N.H., 10th March, 1770; after 1784 his life was largely spent in Essex; took Freeman's oath 3rd September, 1793; farmer, owning highly productive and valuable intervale farm on Onion River; also engaged in the lumber business. He married Nancy Calkins, and dying in Essex 27th July, 1833, in his 65th year, is buried at Essex Centre, beside his father and others of his race. Children born Essex, Vt.:

    156. MICHAEL.   157. SAMUEL CONNOR.   158. CHESTER HENDERSON.
    159. GEORGE W.   160. ELIZA, born 1810, died 1812.
    161. SUSAN, married Alonzo Stevens; residence, Essex; both deceased; issue.
    162. CHARLOTTE, married Eli Chittendon, of Williston, Vt.; daughter.
    163. HOSEA B.   164. WARNER, born February, died 1st November, 1800.
    165. LUCY, born 1802; died 19th February, 1830, aged 28; married Elijah Cockle.
    166. A son, born 17th April, 1818; died 18th July, 1818.

JAMES SINCLAIR (59) had a small farm in Essex, Vt. Deaf and dumb from early years; lamed by an accident; married, but lived alone during his latter years. His wife's name is not known, nor is there record of children.

CAPTAIN JOSEPH SINCLER (60), born 16th March, 1779; lived in Essex, Vt., on a farm near the bridge spanning Brown's River, and was a farmer and lumberman. He owned and operated a sawmill at Jericho Corner, two miles from his home. During the war of 1812-15 he was Captain of the Essex Company, which participated in the victorious Battle of Plattsburg, N.Y. He took the Freeman's oath early in life, 6th September, 1803. An energetic and successful business man, he died in Essex, Vt., 2nd December, 1857. He married Mary Thompson, of Essex. Children born Essex, Vt.:

    167. FANNIE, born 3rd June, 1800; married Carlos Stevens, of Essex; no children.
    168. FREEMAN A.
    169. SARAH, born 19th June, 1806; died 6th June, 1882; married Joel Bellows, of Essex.
    170. GEORGE H., born 24th April, 1814; died 28th Sept., 1817.   171. GEO. BROUGHTON.

LIEUTENANT JACOB ST. CLAIR (62) was born in Epping, N.H., 27th December, 1752. He enlisted in a New Hampshire Company 23rd April, 1775; fought at Bunker's

FIFTH AND SIXTH GENERATIONS 355

Hill 17th June, 1775, at Trenton, N.J., 26th December, 1776, and at Princeton, N.J., on 3rd January, 1777   His military service of 22 months ended February, 1777, when he received a discharge, being therein called lieutenant, and his pension of $8 per month began 5th March, 1819   He married, 16th June, 1777, Rachel Clifford, of Epping, N.H , and on 24th March, 1778, rented a farm there till 1790, when, on the 22nd February, "[James] Jacob Sinclear, of Epping, Gentleman," for £100, bought a farm of 50 acres, with buildings, in that part of Moultonborough called the "Gore," now in New Hampton   Starting with his team and goods on the 2nd March, 1790, he arrived on the 5th, and dwelt there ever after   Nine years after he erected a large and commodious house, making and himself burning the 20,000 bricks required for the chimney.   He presently doubled the area of his territory by purchasing the farm of his neighbour Dow, and 50 acres from Deacon Rand.   To his farming he added tailoring   He died 5th September, 1830, aged 77 years, 8 months, 9 days.   Children

    172 ELIZABETH, born 10th February, 1778, died 10th March, 1858; married, first Joshua Roberts, secondly, Noah Robinson
    173. MARY, born 21st December, 1780, accidentally killed at age of five by the falling of a bough   174 BENJAMIN.
    175 MARY, born 15th February, 1789, died 10th June, 1863, married Washington Smith, of Laconia, N H   176 IRA

BARNABAS SINKLER (63), resident of Unity, N H , at time of Revolution ; member of Wetherbee's Company ; sent to join Northern army 20th August, 1776, receiving £9 18s. 10d. advance wages and bounty.   On 5th November, 1776, was at Mt Independence, and surviving the war, lived many years at Unity.   Signed petitions against the division of that town in 1790, and on 23rd May, 1794 ; his name is not in the records of that town after 1795.   He is considered a son of No 31.

NOAH SINCLAIR (64) was born at Epping, N H , 20th February, 1755, or 17th February, 1756   Of Epsom, 1775, he enlisted 2nd May for eight months as drummer in Dearborn's Company (Stark's Regiment, N.H. line), and fought at Bunker's Hill on June 17th   He re-enlisted for one year, commencing 31st December, 1775, in Morrill's Company (Stark's Regiment), and while at St John's, in Canada, 14th June, 1776, was severely wounded by being shot through the wrist of his left arm with two musket balls, which fractured both bones, " by which he lost the use of his hand." For this he was pensioned by the State and nation   He took part in the Battles of Bennington and Saratoga ; was present at Burgoyne's surrender ; harassed the British rear in New Jersey 1778, and fought at Monmouth 28th June.   Was with the 3rd N.H in the Indian Campaign of 1779, and fought them with success at Newtown (now Elmira, N.Y), 29th August, 1779   He had been promoted to be drum-major 28th May, 1779, and received his discharge 25th January, 1780   At one time a Pembroke resident, after the war he settled in Canterbury, N.H., where, on 25th May, 1781, he bought 80 acres   He became an extensive landholder, and is called in records Yeoman and Gentleman.   A good mechanic, he made all his ploughs and farm requisites, was an excellent athlete, and a respected deacon of the church   His wife was Lovina Gault, of Canterbury, N H   Children, surnamed St Clair, born Canterbury, N H

    177 ELISABETH, born 9th January, 1782, died young
    178 JAMES born 2nd April, 1784   went to sea, never returned   179 WILLIAM
    180 SARAH born 1st March, 1788, died 3rd May, 1872, in Concord, N H
    181 JOHN   182 MARY born 22nd July, 1792, died sin in Canterbury 13th June, 1848

183 NOAH   184 ABIGAIL, born 10th March, 1797, married Israel Davis, of Loudoun, N H
185 NANCY, born 2nd October, 1799, married 26th March, 1822, John Fletcher, of Canterbury, N H   186 WINTHROP

JOHN SINCLAIR (68), born Stratham, N H, 28th January, 1775; owned property there, in Exeter, and a farm in Nottingham, N H   He was a farmer resident in Exeter, where he died August, 1815.   He married, first, Rhoda Flint, and secondly, Abigail Marston, by whom he was survived.   Children

187 MARY F, born 16th November, 1800, m Aaron Sawyer, and resided in Methuen, Mass
188 SUSANNAH, born 27th February, 1803, married Parker Manson of Portsmouth, N H
189 RHODA, died young   191 GEORGE MARSTON
190 CATHERINE, married Amos Bangs; removed to Gardiner, Me, and died there

RICHARD SINCLAIR (69), was born in Stratham 11th October, 1777   A farmer, resident in his native town on the home farm, he conveyed it to Joseph, his eldest son, and in old age lived with his son-in-law James Chase, dying on 20th August, 1856   He married 21st April, 1801, Susan Wiggin.   Children born Stratham, N.H

192 MARTHA, born 8th August, 1807, m 22nd July, 1842, Lewis B. Hawkins, resident Boston.
193 JOSEPH F   194 JOHN T   195. WILLIAM R
196 SUSAN E, b 11th March, 1822, m 1st December, 1842, James Chase of Stratham, issue

MICAJAH SINCLAIR (73), born in Stratham about 1793, carpenter, married, first, Nancy Hoyt of Northwood, N H, and secondly, Abigail —, afterwards Mrs Ayer, who survived his death in Stratham, May, 1847   Children born Stratham, N H .

197 CHARLES, born about 1824, resident in Newmarket, N H, and died single about 1884
198 LUCRETIA, born about 1825, married Mr Willis, died about 1855
199 LYDIA ANN, born about 1827, died about 1880, married Benj Clough of Pittsfield, N H
200 ELISABETH, born about 1830, married Mr Miles of Epping, N H, is dead.
201 JOHN WILLIAM, born about 1832, resident San Francisco, married and had issue
202 MARTHA born 1843, died February, 1867, m Asa G Dame of Durham, N H., child

SAMUEL SINCLAIR (75), born Stratham 2nd March, 1795; factory machinist for many years, residing in Dover, N H, in Exeter, and in Newmarket; he then purchased a farm in his native town, on which he died 20th June, 1867   He married Elizabeth, daughter of Jas Lane of Stratham   Children

204 WM HENRY, born Newmarket, 21st April, 1828, died 18th August, 1847, student Bowdoin College, Me   203 SAMUEL JAMES
205 ELIZABETH DEBORAH, born 28th September, 1830, died 4th July, 1853, married 1852 George Stickney of Exeter
206 MARY JANE, b 29th Sept, 1832, m first, 1858, Wm Oliver Brooks of Eliot, Me, issue, secondly, Wm Hill of Eliot, Me
207 CAROLINE NEWMAN, born 10th March 1842, married, 1871, Rev Benj D Conkling

JAMES SINCLAIR (77), born Stratham 20th September, 1799, carpenter, resident Bangor, Me, and vicinage, Roxbury, Mass., eventually dying at Stratham, 1st January, 1877.   He married, first, 5th October, 1828, Mary Leavitt; and secondly, 16th September, 1855, Mrs. Caroline Robinson of South Newmarket   Children

208 SARAH ELIZABETH, born 16th October, 1829, m Jas H Diman of Stratham, children.
210 MARY L, born 2nd July, 1832, died 19th June, 1857, resident Stratham
211 CAROLINE, born 18th February, 1834, m, first, George Stoddard, secondly, Mr Woodward
212 MARTHA, born 5th April, 1835, died 22nd December, 1875, married John M Geer of Stratham and Concord   209 JAMES
213 ABBY W, born 21st January, 1839, died 16th June, 1853
214 LUCY ANN, born 28th July, 1841, died 19th June, 1864   219 IDA MAY
215 JOHN I., born 3rd July, 1843, died for the Union at Fort Wagner, 18th July, 1863

FIFTH AND SIXTH GENERATIONS

216 CORINNA ALICE, born 22nd August, 1845, married Josiah Kelly of Stratham
217 ELLEN MARIA, born 26th June, 1847, m Horace Ellison, d in Newmarket, N H, issue
218 ABBIE FRANCES, married Clinton Norton of Northwood, N H

BENJAMIN FOLSOM SINCLAIR (79), was born in Brentwood, N H, 16th November, 1761 He accompanied his father in the War of Independence, and was his awaiter for him when at Bunker's Hill He settled in Waterborough, York Co, Me, where he purchased some 200 uncleared acres Farmer and miller; Baptist. He married, first, 13th April, 1784, Mary Peavey, and secondly, 19th December, 1797, Dorothy Stevens He died in Waterborough, 9th April, 1851. Children born Waterborough, Me

220 JAMES, b. 11th November, 1786, d single 9th July, 1869, soldier in British war of 1812-15
221. SAMUEL.   222 JOHN.   226 DAVID.   228 HENRY.   229 JOHN LEWIS
223 BENJAMIN, b 18th September, 1793, died single 26th April, 1865, permanent invalid at 23
224 MARY PEAVEY, born 4th December, 1795, married Joshua Sawyer of Limington, Me
225 SARAH, born 5th September, 1797, married Wm Stimson of Limerick, Me
227 JOANNA, born 4th December, 1800, resident East Waterborough, Me.

JAMES SINCLAIR (80), tanner, was born in Brentwood, N H, 23rd April, 1764, where he continued to reside, democrat, Baptist He married Mary Nay Children born Brentwood, N H ·

230 SAMUEL   232 HENRY.   235 BENJAMIN.
231 RACHEL, born 31st August, 1789, married Sam C Shaw of Brentwood in 1806
233 ABIGAIL, married Eliphalet Robinson of Brentwood
234 MARY, married James Marston of Brentwood

JONATHAN SINCLAIR (84), sailor, born at Brentwood 13th June, 1773; went early to Maine, and settled in Palmyra He died in Canaan, Me, having married Eunice Porter Children born Palmyra, Me

236 HIRAM PORTER   240 JAMES, born 2nd October, 1818, died 5th July, 1819
237 CLARISSA ANN, born 2nd January, 1811, died 6th June, 1848, married Rev Sullivan A Maxim, Baptist   238 HARRIET, born 9th June, 1813, died single, 8th September, 1830.
239 MARIA, born 20th September, 1816, died single, 2nd March, 1835

DAVID SINCLAIR (87) was born in Brentwood, N H, 7th May, 1779, and settled in Palmyra, Me He was a soldier in the 1812-15 war, and died at Plattsburg, N Y, 20th May, 1813 He married Cynthia Porter, who, as his widow, received a pension from the Government Children

241 DAVID PORTER   242 JOHN TURNER
244 CYNTHIA, born 1814, married, first, James [Richard] Hawley, secondly, Henry W. Purdy, children   243 EBENEZER NAY, went West early, no issue
245 DIANTHA JANE, married 31st March, 1831, William Libby, died 24th January, 1888
246 LOUISA ANN, married 18th June, 1834, Isaac Newton Colby, resident Danville, Vt

EBENEZER SINCLAIR (88), farmer, was born in Brentwood 7th May, 1780, went early to Maine, and settled in Monmouth He cultivated his broad acres till death, 15th June, 1843 He married Mary Seaborn. Children

247 ABIGAIL, born 2nd April, 1803, deceased, married John Coombs of Readfield, Me, issue.
248 ANN, born 12th June, 1805, lived and died single in Monmouth, Me
249 ELIZABETH, born 24th July, 1807, deceased, married Daniel McDuffie
250 HENRY BLAKE, born October, 1809, married, no issue, resident on homestead
251 JAMES MADISON   254 JOSEPH DALTON
252 HARRIET, born 18th January, 1815, deceased, married Dr Addison Brawn, child
253 CYNTHIA, b 14th January, 1821, single, resident on homestead

RICHARD SINCLAIR (90), carpenter and wheelwright, was born in Sandwich, N H, in January, 1766. He occupied part of his father's original farm, his house being some

20 rods from his father's He sold most of his property to his father 14th November, 1803, after his removal to Falmouth, Me , and carried on business in what is now Portland, Me. Returning to Sandwich, he there lived and died on a portion of the old homestead 28th May, 1848. He was a member of the Congregational Church, and very attentive to religious observances. He married, about 1790, Rebecca Gilman of Gilmanton Children born Sandwich, N H

    255 JONATHAN   260 EBENEZER
    256 JUDITH GILMAN, born 20th September, 1793, married Mich Gilman of Gilmanton , issue
    257 ELIZABETH, born 1st October, 1795 , died 15th December, 1877, married, 1821, Meshech Robinson, junr
    258 JOSEPH GILMAN, born 24th November, 1797, left Sandwich when young, and never returned , lived for some time in Boston, Mass , when he disappeared
    259 CLARISSA, born 31st August, 1799 , married, first, Mr Tilson, secondly, Isaac Mitchell , children

JONATHAN SINCLAIR (91), blacksmith, was born in Sandwich, N.H , about 1768 He carried on business for many years at Moultonborough Corner. He was there on 3rd July, 1803, and was called "Gentleman" in deeds He acquired the paternal farm in Sandwich, and considerable real estate Before 30th March, 1809, he had removed to Haverhill, N H., and on 26th September, 1810, he makes acknowledgment of the conveyance of his house and shop in Moultonborough He was a leading spirit in Haverhill His blacksmith business was managed successfully, as also was his country store He also owned and managed an hotel For a number of years he was deputy sheriff and captain in the militia He married, 24th July, 1800, Abigail Frieze Late in life they removed to Newton, Mass , died there, and are buried in Mt Auburn Child

    261 AUGUSTA, born Moultonborough, married Ezra Hutchins of Newton

EBENEZER SINCLAIR (92), farmer, born in Exeter, N H , was baptised 29th August, 1762 His farm was near the Red Hill of Exeter. He married 11th April, 1786, Mercy Hoag, of Sandwich They were both members of the Society of Friends. His death was occasioned by falling from a loaded team in the field, and took place 29th September, 1815 Enoch Hoag administered the estate, of which inventory was taken 16th October, 1815 His wife survived him. Children born Sandwich, N H.

    262 ASA   Blacksmith , settled in Haverhill, N H
    263 JUDITH, married, May, 1813, Josiah Ambrose, of Moultonborough
    264 ELIZABETH, married 27th April, 1809, John Johnson, of Sandwich
    265 JOHN   266 LYDIA, married Joseph Smith, of Moultonborough
    267 SARAH HILL, born 10th January, 1795 , married John Cook, of Sandwich
    268. MOSES HOAG   269 WILLIAM M   270 ISAIAH GOULD
    271 MARY, born 8th November, 1806, died 14th November, 1827.

SAMUEL SINCLAIR (93) owned a small part of the original homestead of his father, and his house stood near that of his brother Richard He sold it to his brother Jonathan, who took the buildings down Samuel carried on a blacksmith's business near his brother Jonathan's, but sold the premises on 18th April, 1800 In 1803 he resided in Sandwich, but soon moved to the north part of Haverhill , received a life lease of land there, built a block house, and there lived, died, and was buried His life was not a successful one, and was marred by some moral blemishes He married, 17th November, 1791, Sarah Moulton, of Sandwich Children born Sandwich, N H.

    272 JAMES, who went to sea absent and silent for some 20 years, when he returned, and died at Haverhill, N H   273 JOHN   274 SAMUEL
    275 HANNAH, married Simeon Hildreth resident Haverhill

FIFTH AND SIXTH GENERATIONS

276. MYRA, married, first, Mr Davenport, secondly, Levi Hamblett, issue
277 STEPHEN BADGER

BRADBURY SINKLER (98) was born in Newmarket, N.H , 8th March, 1754, and resided in Barnstead, N H. He was early a soldier in the Revolutionary war, and by repeated enlistments was in the service the greater part of his life till his death. He was a corporal in Badger's Company 29th August, 1776, and succumbed to the privations of the Valley Forge winter, dying in camp 5th March, 1778. He had married, 26th June, 1777, Sarah Bunker, who married again.

LIEUTENANT RICHARD SINKLER (99) was born in Newmarket, N II , 6th October, 1756, and lived in Barnstead, N H. He first entered military service on the 23rd July, 1776, as a member of Badger's Company (Badger's Regiment) On 29th August he was re-mustered into the same company for Canadian service He was then drummer The American army having retreated from Canada, the company finally joined the Northern army in New York. His pension papers show that the company marched to Ticonderoga, was stationed awhile at Mount Independence, and that he served six months in that campaign He enlisted 23rd April, 1777, for one year in Scammell's Company, 3rd Battalion N H , which term he served, re-enlisting 23rd April, 1779, for a similar period. He again enlisted, this time as ensign in his father's company (Bartlett's N.H. Regiment), 29th June, 1780, and went to the fortress of West Point. During this period, Arnold, commander of West Point, turned traitor, and arranged its betrayal to the British. Major Andre, a British spy, visited the treacherous Arnold 21st September, 1780, only to be arrested, tried, and executed most properly *as a spy* on the 2nd October next thereafter. Arnold escaped. On the 27th October the company of Captain Richard Sinkler was disbanded, father and son returning to Barnstead, when the military career of Lieutenant Sinkler ended, enabling him to attend to his duties as civilian He was Selectman in 1781, '82 , Surveyor of Highways in 1785, '86, '87, '88, and '91 ; and Collector of Taxes in 1783, '84, and '85. He signed a petition for appointing Captain Charles Hodgdon a J.P , 23rd December, 1788, and was Moderator of special town meetings, 2nd February, 1789, and 13th January, 1801 He was chosen one of the town's committee, 3rd November, 1789, to settle the boundary lines between Barnstead and Barrington Soon after he and others petitioned for a higher tax to enable the Suncook River to be bridged Juror, 3rd May, 1794; and member of an important town committee, 31st March, 1795 His cousin, the Hon Bradbury Cilley, bought from him land in Barnstead 10th June, 1802 For $1,000, on July 1st, 1802, he sold Charles Hodgdon "all my land and real estate in the town of Barnstead, together with two pews in the Northerly Meeting House in Barnstead, adjoining the Minister's pew so called, and the other write over it in the gallery, also all my buildings and outhouses to me belonging " About 1809 he left Barnstead to join his brother John, located near French Creek, Penn. With him he henceforth lived In 1820 he set out on a visit to Cincinnati, but fell ill by the way, and died in Ohio He was married to Elizabeth, daughter of Charles Hodgdon, 27th October, 1784 Children born Barnstead, N H

278 NANCY, born 1786, died 2nd June, 1856, married, 1810, Obadiah Fastman
279 MARY CILLEY, born 2nd May, 1789 , married, 2nd July, 1807, Abraham R Bunker.
280 CHARLES GRANDISON
281 ELIZA S born 1800, married 28th November 1825 Wm Jenkins of Barnstead, N H.

JOSHUA SINCLER (101) was born in Nottingham, N H , 16th April, 1760 At four his father removed to Gilmantown, and he was resident in Barnstead in 1767. He enlisted in company of Badger, junr (10th N H), mustered 23rd July, 1776, and on 29th August following was fifer of the same. His pension papers disclose that he was attached to the person of his uncle, Colonel Joseph Cilley. His bounty as Continental soldier from Barnstead was £27 13s 6d. He enlisted in the 1st N H (Morrill's Company), serving from 20th June, 1777, till discharged, 20th June, 1780   He shared in the two fights at the taking of Burgoyne, in October, 1777 , suffered in Valley Forge, 1777 ; and fought in the victory of Monmouth, 28th June, 1778   He shared in Sullivan's campaign against the Five Nations, and was in the engagement at Elmira, N.Y., 29th August, 1779. A carpenter by trade, his boyhood was passed in Barnstead. He then joined his brothers, Samuel and John, in getting out ship timber, and in operating sawmills at Vassalboro' on the Kennebec   This was his home for some years   He married Abigail Pattee of that town   Their home was afterwards in Unity, Me. In 1834 he offered to educate his nephew, now the Hon John G Sinclair   In 1847 he went westwards to join his son, Dr. William St Clair, and died two years later in November, 1849, at Maumee City, Ohio   Children

  282 GEO. WASHINGTON 284 WM ST CLAIR. 285 THOS JEFFERSON. 287 JOSHUA
  283. ABIGAIL, born Vassalboro' 26th March, 1798 , died 1829 , m. 1818, Thos Bagley , issue
  286 MARY, born Unity, 2nd April, 1803 , died 1841 , married, 1832, Alden Chandler
  288 JANE, born Unity, 19th February, 1807 , died single at 21.
  289. ELIZABETH LOVEJOY, born Unity, 23rd August, 1809 , married Alpheus W Boynton
  290 DANIEL LOVEJOY, born 1811 , died 1816
  291 DORCAS BURNHAM born Unity, 6th March, 1813 , was second wife to Alden Chandler.

MAJOR SAMUEL SINCLEAR (102) born in Nottingham, N H., 10th May, 1762, spent his early life there, in Gilmantown, and in Barnstead   When too young to enlist, for a year he acted as attendant to his uncle, Colonel Joseph Cilley ; he then enlisted 20th June, 1777, and was mustered on the 1st July, being then fifteen years of age   His regiment evacuated from Fort Ticonderoga, 6th July, 1777; fought with distinction at Stillwater, 19th September, 1777 ; and rendered even more valiant service at Saratoga, 7th October, 1777, where his position was in the centre of the company, in the front rank   This was one of the most desperate encounters of the war. Ten days later the enemy surrendered at Saratoga, and the 1st N.H moved slowly southward, joining Washington's army 21st November, and on 13th December took up its winter quarters at Valley Forge, where great privations were endured. Mr Sinclear's brother Ebenezer had fallen in contributing to the victory at Saratoga, and now another, Bradbury, succumbed 5th March, 1778, to the fearful exposure of Valley Forge   His regiment contributed to the defeat of the British at Monmouth, 28th June, 1778, and took part in Sullivan's victorious campaign against the Indians, who were engaged at Newtown, near Elmira, 29th August, 1778, where the celebrated chief Brandt was posted with 1,000 or more The power of the Indians was broken, and their country laid waste. The regiment was disbanded 6th April, 1780   Mr Sinclear was only eighteen at the time of his discharge, and had had remarkable experience for so young a soldier. After the war he spent some time in Barnstead and Gilmantown, N.H., was resident at Vassalborough, Me., in 1784, and on 16th April, 1788, bought land there, erecting sawmills, before 1795 had settled at Utica, where he worked on the long bridge over the Mohawk ; then spent a year at Cherry Valley, N Y ; and in 1796 settled at Eaton, Madison Co., N Y , as on 11th April

FIFTH AND SIXTH GENERATIONS

same he received a commission as Captain in the militia, and a little later he was promoted to be First Major of Militia, by which title he was known ever after. While in Eaton he was a farmer. In 1805 he bought 55 acres in Madison for $1,000, and in 1807, for $1,400, 57 more, which he cleared and erected thereon a tavern. In 1808 he bought land at French Creek, Penn., which he sold in 1809, and then purchased from the Holland Land Company, for £1,530, 1,530 acres, comprising lot 41 (now Sinclairville), 360 acres, lot 28 (now Charlotte), and lot 63, and portions of lots 64 and 65, in Gerry, all in Chatauqua County, N.Y. 1809 was occupied in moving, 1810 and 1811 in clearing and building two houses, a sawmill, and a gristmill. Major Sinclair had brought with him $6,000 or $7,000 dollars, then a large sum, and some ten hired hands, and pushed on matters with expedition. In his lifetime the locality was called the "Major's," or "Major Sinclair's," but after his death, 8th February, 1827, it began by common consent to be called Sinclairville. He had been Master of the Sylvan Lodge of Freemasons in Sinclairville, formed in 1823, and the exercises at his death were conducted according to the Masonic ritual. His funeral was attended by almost the entire population, for the town had lost its most respected citizen. In the charming village of Sinclairville, on an elevated plateau, is the Evergreen Cemetery, ground donated by himself to the public. In that cemetery rest the remains of Major Samuel Sinclair, until the great awakening. He married, first, 8th February, 1785, Sarah Perkins, and secondly, 14th March, 1805, Fanny Bigalow, relict of Obed Edson, who survived him. Children :

    292 MARY, born 19th April, 1786, married Elijah Haswell   293 JOHN
    294. SOLOMON, born 6th August, 1789, died 1799
    295 SARAH, born 5th May, 1791, died 6th October, 1792
    296 SOPHY, born 30th March, 1793, died Iowa 1866, married Mr Ward
    297 SAMUEL, born 15th July, and died 6th August, 1794
    298 SARAH, born 20th December, 1795, died 10th November, 1887, married Wm Barrows
    299 RICHARD, born 21st May, 1799, died 17th January, 1802
    300 SAMUEL   301 AGNES, born 3rd September, and died 1803   303 DAVID BIGALOW
    302. NANCY, born 24th January, 1806, died 6th September, 1855, married Mr Putnam
    304 JOSEPH, born 15th March, 1809, died Fort Wayne, Ind., 7th September, 1854
    306 ORLINDA, born 10th May, 1813, died 28th July, 1846, married Dr Chas Parker
    307 VIRTUE ELVIRA, born 3rd February, 1816, married, 6th May, 1835, Chester Cole
    308. HIRAM, born 29th August, 1817, died 15th March, 1818   305 GEO WASHINGTON

JOHN SINKLER (103), shipbuilder and millwright, was born in Gilmantown, N.H., 13th January, 1763. He went with his parents to Barnstead at the age of four, and in 1788 received from his father 100 acres and a sawmill. In October, 1791, he sold one-eighth part of Sinclair's sawmill in Barnstead, where he dwelt in 1792. He married Abigail Clark, 13th May, 1785. He located in Danville, Vt., in 1793, where he lived till about 1799, when he was at Black River, N Y. In 1803 he was at Harbor Creek, Penn., in 1805 at Rockdale, Penn., and then in Perry, Ohio, whence he went West, dying on 4th November, 1845, at Frederick, Ill. Children

    309 SARAH, born 22nd June, 1786, married Calvin Snell
    310 BRADBURY, born 2nd July, 1788, died July, 1857
    311 JOHN JR, born 2nd December, 1790, died 5th January, 1822, soldier in 1812 war
    312 DAVID, born 19th October, 1792   Soldier 1812-15 war
    313 LEONARD, born 20th January, 1793, died 29th December, 1876, married Sarah St John
    314 ABIGAIL, born 25th October, 1796, married Mr Casper
    315 SAMUEL, born 17th February, 1801, drowned 28th May, 1804   316 JOSHUA

317 PRUDENCE, born 29th December, 1805, married, first, Mr Kibbie, secondly, Mr Lord
318 JOSEPH, b 22nd October, 1807, d 16th April, 1867   319 DANIEL, b 28th March, 1811.
320 MARY, born 3rd April, 1813, married, first, Jefferson Rice, secondly, Col Wilcox

JOSEPH SINKLER (105), farmer, was born in Gilmanton, N H, 9th April, 1766; lived there till 1794, when he moved to Danville, Vt He owned a large, highly-productive farm, on which was a large two-storied house, his home until 1826, when he went to Peacham, Vt, and two years later returned to Perry, Lake Co, Ohio, where he lived on a farm on the North Ridge, which he deeded to his son Milton, at whose place he died in his 80th year, 12th May, 1845, and was buried at Perry in the village cemetery, that beautiful "City of the Dead" He married Olive Colbath Children

321 JOSEPH   324. GREENLEAF CILLEY   328 MILTON
322 SARAH, born 11th August, and died 1st September, 1791
323 ELIZABETH, born 19th June, 1792, died 31st December, 1810
325 ELIZABETH, born 1795, died about 1812
326 STATIRA, born 22nd December, 1796, died 7th March, 1832, married Mr McDowell.
327 ROXANNA, born 13th December, 1798, married Asa Glines
329 SARAH, born 10th March, 1802, married Stephen B Glines
330 OLIVE, born 5th January, 1804, married, 15th September, 1833, Amherst Call
331 ARIT, born 5th April, 1806, died single 23rd January, 1736 Farmer, Perry, Ohio
332 ELIZABETH B, born 19th March, 1811, married Carlos Norris

DAVID SINKLER (106) was born at Barnstead 3rd January, 1770. Resident Danville, Vt, 4th March, 1796 to 1816, Leroy, N.Y., 1816; and Perry, Ohio, 1818-53, where he kept an hotel and owned a large farm He was a fine marksman, a great hunter, kept hounds, and many were the deer that he successfully hunted When over eighty he would follow a fox all day, and generally with success He died on the 20th May, 1853 His wife was Sarah Batchelder, and they had children

333 PRENTICE   336 CALVIN   342 DAVID
334 EUNICE, born 16th July, 1797, died 4th June, 1803
335 MARY, born 26th July, 1799, died 22nd August, 1802
337. SARAH, born 22nd May, 1804, died 30th April, 1807
338 ELIZABETH, born 3rd June, 1806, married, 27th February, 1827, Elisha Coltran
339 NANCY, born 14th November, 1808, married, 18th October, 1826, Freeman Tisdell, issue
340 DOLLY, b 10th February, 1811, d 17th July, 1887, m 27th February, 1845, Daniel Parmly
341 SARAH, born 3rd February, 1813 died 5th January, 1845, married Samuel Wortman.
343 MARY, born 17th October, 1817, married Benj Wolverton
344 EUNICE born 21st March, 1820, married, 20th April, 1852, Lyman Durand, child

SIXTH AND SEVENTH GENERATIONS

NATHANIEL SINCLAIR (111), farmer, was born in Meredith, N.H., 19th September, 1773 He married Sarah Pease, 2nd March, 1795 He lived in Greensborough, Vt, and the adjoining town of Hardwick in 1793. Was in Greensborough 1801, and on 3rd June, 1805, he and his wife deeded all their right to the Meredith homestead of her father Benjamin to Simeon Pease. In Stanstead, Con, 1808, in Danville, Vt, 1813; in Hardwick (where he leased a farm 24th August, 1813) until 1829. He died in Woodstock, Vt, 2nd July, 1843, aged 69 years 9 months, 13 days Children

345 ANNA, born 27th December, 1796, married Allen Gardner   346 SIMEON PEASE
347 HANNAH, born 6th May, 1799, married Mr Bugbee.   348 NATHANIEL
349 BENJAMIN, born 15th October, 1802, died 21st April, 1812 350 STEPHEN A
351 SOPHRONIA, born 27th March, 1805 married, 7th February, 1836, Luther Ayer, issue

SIXTH AND SEVENTH GENERATIONS 363

352 ROBERT, born 2nd December, 1807, died 25th April, 1808   353 AMOS S
354 RICHARD M, born 13th August, 1810; he married, and died in Lowell, Mass, 4 weeks after, 30th October, 1835
355. WILLIAM C B, born 7th February, 1812, died single 20th May, 1835

BENJAMIN SINCLAIR (114), farmer, was born in Meredith, N H., 28th January, 1778, and died 15th May, 1840. He was resident at Hampton Falls, N H., at Monmouth, Me., and lastly at Levant, in the same State. He married, 5th September, 1805, Mary Cram. Children

356 JONATHAN CRAM.   357 JOSEPH PORTER, born 28th October, 1811, died *s p* 20th May, 1874, married, first, Belinda Drew, secondly, Emily Hodgdon
358 CAROLINE TILTON, born 8th January, 1813, married William Higgins
359 MARY ANN TRUE, born 4th January, 1817, died single in Lowell, Mass
360 RHODA CRAM, born 8th March, 1821, married Royal W Clark
361 BENJAMIN WOODBURY, born 4th August, 1826; married, and had children
362 ELBRIDGE AUGUSTUS, born 10th December, 1828, married, and left children

JEREMIAH SINCLAIR (115) lived in Greensborough, Vt, and erected the present Calderwood House, which was then his residence. He lived for a while in Canada, where his first wife died. He married, secondly, Rhoda Fay. Two of his children were buried on the Calderwood Farm. He sold his farm in 1825, was for a while in Hardwick, and finally moved to Pt. Kent, Black Rock, or some other place in New York. He had at least two children (363-4) as before mentioned

ENOCH ST CLAIR (117), farmer, etc., was born in Meredith, N H., 1st September, 1790, and died at Hampton, Iowa, 3rd April, 1873. He married Huldah Townsend, 9th December, 1816. Their children were all born at Concord, N Y

365 ROXALENA, born 1st November, 1818, died 13th August, 1822
366 LOUISE LETITIA, born 10th April, 1821, married Ephr R Bennett, 22nd Nov, 1847
367 ELIZABETH, born 24th July, 1823, died 1889. Married, first, Rev P M. Huffman, secondly, Alonzo D Hendrickson   369 JOHN, born 29th Jan., died 3rd Feb, 1829
368 BENJAMIN, born 26th April, and died 26th July, 1825   374 AUGUSTINE DUROC
370 LOIS JOSEPHINE, born 18th July, 1830, married, 4th Nov, 1849, Lewis Milton Stevenson
371 ROXA CLEMENTINE, born 25th June, 1833, married Jacob Tobey
372 LAURA ELVIRA, born 22nd May, 1835, teacher, resides Hampton, Iowa
373 MARY JANE, born 28th April, 1837, married Thomas Wayman Jones

ASA ST CLAIR (118), farmer, was born in Hardwick, Vt, 7th November, 1795. He resided in Concord and Barre, N Y.; Petersburg, Mich; and Rollin, Mich, where he purchased a farm, on which he lived till his death, 18th March, 1848. He married, first, Rebecca Page, and secondly, Mary Bragg. Children

375 Child not named, died young   376 Child not named, died young
377 WILLIAM, born 19th April, 1819, died 3rd April, 1856   378 PERRY
379 LAURA, born 24th May, 1822, married Thomas Patrick   382 ASA
380 ELIZA, born 28th November, 1824, married Nathaniel J Hodges
381 MARY, born 16th July, 1825, died 1846   386 SARAH, born 11th Nov, 1841, unmarried
383 MARY, born 17th October, 1836, married, 1855, George W Hodges
387 REBECCA, born 7th October, 1843, married, 1863, Frank Coleman
388 GEORGE, born 3rd October, 1845, farmer, Union soldier, died unmarried in hospital 23rd April, 1863   384 BENJAMIN   385 AARON

JOHN MEED SINCLAIR (119,), farmer, was born in Meredith, 11th February, 1776; died in Freedom, Me, 30th October, 1826. He was elected assessor for Freedom in 1812, and several successive years. He married Sarah Levett. Children born Freedom, Me;
389 JAMES, killed it about age of ten by fall of tree

390 ELIZABETH, died in Thornsville, Me 391. MARY, died in Freedom, 18th August, 1826.
392 ORVILLE, married Mary Wheeler, farmer, Windsor, Me, no children
393 CAROLINE, born 3rd August, 1815, married, 31st December, 1840, Stephen Thorn.

JAMES ST CLAIR (120), farmer, etc, was born in Meredith, 9th May, 1777; and died in South Thomaston, Me., 25th June, 1858, in which latter place he settled in 1803. "The St. Clair path," over the hill, still marks the way he and Sarah Wiggin, his wife, trod in going to worship. Children

394 LAVINIA, born 22nd October, 1801; married Benj Burgess of Matinicus, Id, Me
395 MARY SMITH, born 15th February, 1804, married, 1823, Sion Payson
396. GEO WASHINGTON   399 JAMES MADISON   400 ERASTUS.
397 MAHALA, born 2nd June, 1808, m, first, 1828, Jonathan Hall, secondly, Hugh Kelsey
398 THIRZA, born 2nd June, 1808, married, 1829, Capt Isaac Tolman
401 SARAH, b 5th September, 1816, died 1849, m Samuel Crie   404 GUILFORD DUDLEY
402 LUCY LOVEJOY, born 16th November, 1818, married Abijah F Metcalf
403 ABIGAIL BURGESS, born 27th June, 1822, married, 1846, Saml Hastings.

THOMAS SINCLAIR (121), farmer, was born in Meredith, 27th December, 1778; he died in Dover, Me, 3rd July, 1844. He was resident in Beaver Hill Plantation (afterwards Freedom) from 1806 to 1824, when he acquired a farm at Dover He married his cousin, Mary Robinson, a daughter of his mother's sister. Four of their children became cripples as they arrived at maturity Children

405 HANNAH, born 9th August, 1806, invalid, died 28th September, 1857   406 AHIRA
407 ALVAH   408 GIDEON ROBINSON   409 CHAS PERRY   412. THOMAS RILA
410 WILLIAM MARTIN, born 20th June, 1816, died, Cal., 7th May, 1854, single
411 URIAH R, born 1st August, 1818, died, Dover, 25th September, 1876, single, invalid
413 MARY J, born 20th November, 1829, single, resident Dover, Me

WILLIAM SINCLAIR (123), shoemaker, was born in Meredith, 18th September, 1782, lived on part of the paternal homestead, and died suddenly 15th April, 1815. His wife, Nancy Dow, was appointed administratrix 19th June, 1815. Child·

414 THOMAS

JOSEPH SINCLAIR (124), farmer, was born in Meredith, 17th Sept., 1785, lived on the paternal homestead, where he died 2nd March, 1847. He was a very religious man He married, 27th March, 1805, Isabel Dockman, who was so deft with her fingers that by her weaving alone she paid for nearly 50 acres of woodland She lived to be over 97 Their children were

415 BELINDA, born 18th February, 1806, married John Cotton   417 JOHN LANGDON
416 THOMAS JEFFERSON, born 3rd May, and died 4th May, 1808   418 NOAH
419 MARY JANE, born 16th July, 1816, died 13th June, 1872, married Daniel Howe
420 WILLIAM PLUMMER, born 23rd July, 1818, died 1st August, 1819
421 NAOMI CHENEY, born 16th July, 1820, died 23rd November, 1847

JOSEPH ST CLAIR (128), farmer, was born in Sanbornton, N H., 17th January, 1786; lived in Eagle Harbor, N Y.; removed to Rochester, Ill.; and died 8th May, 1839. He married, 20th November, 1815, Lucy Brown Children·

422 AUGUSTA FLAVILLA, born 24th August, 1816, married James Musick
423 JULIA ANN, b 9th October, 1818, d 29th August, 1873, m, 1838, Andrew F Hollenbeck
424 ORANGE PARDEZ, born 11th January, 1821, dead, his widow lives in Newton, Kan
425 JOSEPH NORMAN

JAMES ST. CLAIR (130), farmer, was born in Sanbornton, 6th September, 1789; accompanied his people to Hardwick and Wolcott, Vt., and to Russelltown, Canada. While in the Dominion he became engaged to Patience Matilda Northrop, of New

Milford, Conn., and as marriages in Canada were illegal unless solemnised by an Anglican clergyman, he and his fiancée made up a party of sixteen horse, rode over the dividing line into New York State, and were duly married by the Episcopal service and clergyman in Chateaugay, Franklin Co. For a while they lived in Peru and in Palmyra, N Y Eventually he bought land at Barre (now Albion), N.Y, and in the spring of 1816 brought his family to the new home The Erie canal, constructed a few years later, flows through nearly the entire length of the farm His death occurred in Barre 1st April, 1874 He was a twelfth child, and so was his wife Children

  426 CHAS NORTHROP 428 CALEB NORTHROP 430 JAS JULIUS II
  427 HENRY ARTHUR, born 12th April, 1816, died 12th July, 1818
  429 JAS. JULIUS, born 13th August, 1820, died 26th November, 1820
  431 ANGELINE SOPHIA, born 21st December, 1823, resident Albion, N Y, educated Phipps Union Sem, Albion Authoress of "Senora Ines, or the American Volunteers," and many fugitive magazine contributions
  431A OSCAR FITZALAN WARES ST CLAIR, born 1826, died in U S service, Bangkok, Siam; adopted son, nephew of Mrs St Clair

LEVI HUNT ST CLAIR (136) was born in Wolcott, Vt, 6th May, 1800, and died at Rochester, Ill., 14th April, 1866 He was Quartermaster of the 40th Brigade of Infantry 6th October, 1828, and Paymaster of the 54th Regiment Ill State Militia 6th April, 1840. He superintended a woollen factory at Essex, N Y, farmed for two years, 1830–31, at E Cleveland, Ohio; and in 1832 located at Rochester, Ill., where he died. He married, first, 1823, Lorinda Spaulding, secondly, 1854, Priscilla Church, and thirdly, Eliza M. Rayne Children

  432 HANNIBAL CICERO 433 LORRACE OSCAR 438 LEVI MORTIMER II
  434 LORINDA HELEN, born 24th September, 1826, married, 1850, Geo Lucian Ormsby
  435 MARION JEANNETTE, born 18th September, 1828, married, 1852, S D Fisher, Secretary Ill Board of Agriculture, etc
  436 MARY TAYLOR, born 11th October, 1829, married, 1850, Francis J Taylor
  437 LEVI MORTIMER, born 2nd May, 1834, died 9th February, 1835
  439 AMELIA ELIZA, born 8th April, 1843, married, 1866, Calvin C Johnson

JOSEPH SINCLAIR (143), farmer, born 28th November, 1791, resident in Holderness, and at St. Charles, Minnesota On 3rd June, 1820, he had unpleasant litigation with Elijah Hawkins of Vershire, Vt He married Annie Connor and had issue

  440 ALEXANDER SINCLAIR, farmer, resident St. Charles, Minn

ZEBULON SINCLAIR (145), farmer, was born 25th February, 1798, died in Holderness, N H, 28th March, 1782 He married Mary Seavey, and had

  441 THOMAS, born about 1826, died 28th March, 1866, m, March, 1866, Abigail Moulton
  442 ELIZA ANN, born about 1830, died in Holderness, 21st September, 1864
  443 JOHN TAYLOR GILMAN
  444 WILLIAM, born 11th September, 1840, farmer, lives in Holderness, single

NOAH SINCLAIR (147), farmer and merchant, was born in Essex, Vt, 24th April, 1792. There he lived, and took the Freeman's oath 1st September, 1812. He fought at Plattsburg, 11th September, 1814, was injured then, for which he afterwards received a pension After the war he resided in Bartlett. He married, first, Lucinda (or Elizabeth) Carleton, and secondly, her cousin, Elizabeth Carleton He died 13th March, 1872 Children

  445 ELVIRA, married Mr Wheelock, resident Port Henry. N Y.
  446 DAVIS, deceased, resident Montpelier, Vt 447 HENRY, died, aged 9 months
  448 LYDIA FRANCES, born 8th November, 1820, married Joshua Larkin Wentworth
  449 HENRY WHITE 450 EDWARD CARLETON

THOMAS SINCLAIR (149), a resident of Essex, Vt , was a soldier in the 1812–15 war, and was stationed once at Swanton, Vt He was lamed for life in the Battle of Lundy's Lane, for which he was pensioned. For many years he resided at Berkshire, Vt , and then removed to Bartlett, N H., in 1834 , dying in Conway, N.H , 11th September, 1865, aged 75 He married, 22nd August, 1813, Mary Austin Children
 451 POWELL AUSTIN 452 GEORGE HOWE. 454 ORISON THAYER.
 453 MINERVA, deceased , married Daniel Lord, of Eliot, Me 455 CURTIS
 456 LUCETTA, born 22nd May, 1832 , married John Hoyt, of Jackson, N H
 457 EDWARD, married Nancy Chaplin, resident Morning Sun, Iowa
 458 SARAH E , born 17th May, 1835 , married Warren C Wentworth

ELI SINCLAIR (150) lived in Essex, Vt , was lame, and invalid for many years Married Almira Miller, of Richeford, Vt , in which place he died, when she re-married.

JOHN SINCLAIR (151), farmer, spent most of his life in Essex, Vt Then he removed to Grafton, Mass , where he died 4th January, 1862. He married Lucretia Wheelock. Children .
 459 JOHN ELBRIDGE 460 FRANKLIN J
 461 PERSIS LUCRETIA, born March, 1837 married, May, 1862, James W Plimpton

THE HON LEANDER DUDLEY SINCLAIR (154) was born in Essex, Vt , 19th August, 1804 , died in Ossipee, N.H , 28th October, 1889 He had an excellent staging business, which he conducted successfully for 45 years, when railroad extension curtailed it He then took a farm, and actively interested himself in the affairs of his town, of which he was postmaster for 17 years. He was a Republican member of the legislature for two years (1844–45) He married, first, in 1832, Olive W. Kimball, and secondly, 1867, Addie W. Tasker, relict of Nathaniel Spencer. Children :
 462 PRUDENCE ABBEY, born 16th October, 1832 , married Spencer M. Kallock
 463 JEREMIAH 465 ELIZABETH C , born 15th October, 1837, died 1st February, 1864
 464 MARY ODELL, born 3rd December, 1855, married John T Pitman
 466 JOHN KEELER, born 4th July, 1839 , married Rachael Murdock 467 MOSES CANNEY
 468 OLIVE ANN, born 25th February, 1844 , married Miner C. Baldwin
 470 CHARLES HENRY, born May, 1849, married Alvesta Goodwin merchant, Beverly, Mass
 471 GEORGE M , born 20th April, 1851 , died 22nd May, 1855 469 LEANDER DUDLEY
 472 WILLIAM C , born 3rd February, 1854 , is station agent at Ossipee, N H
 473 CARRIE ESTELLA, born 7th June, 1857, at Ossipee , book-keeper there

DAVID SINCLAIR (155), resident and died in Essex, Vt , married first, [N.N] ; secondly, Mercy Tiffany. Children :
 474 One child by first wife 475 CLARISSA, married Mr Robinson
 476 ROSWELL M , died in Lowell, Vt

MICHAEL SINCLAIR (156), carpenter, lumberman, and farmer, was born in Essex, Vt., 29th July, 1793 The last years of his life he spent at Hubbell's Falls and Burlington, Vt , where his remains rest in the Green Mountain cemetery. He married Annis White Children
 477 ELIZA, born 14th November, 1813, died 12th October, 1815 478 ORVILLE
 479 LOUISA, born 13th June, 1817 , died 20th March, 1819
 480 MINERVA BUTLER, born 5th March, 1819 , married Horace W Barrett , dead
 481 MARY MARILLA, born 13th Sept , 1822 , married Henry Timans , died 21st Dec., 1843
 482 CHARLOTTE, born 3rd Dec , 1826, died 6th January, 1876 , married Jonathan Newell
 483 ANGELINE, died at Winooski, Vt.

SAMUEL CONNOR SINCLAIR (157), millwright, was born in Essex, Vt , 12th July, 1795. In 1835 he moved to Lyndonville, N Y   He married, first, Samantha Barney ;

SIXTH AND SEVENTH GENERATIONS. 367

and secondly, Sarah Remington, and died at Lyndonville, N Y, 18th November, 1838 Children:
    484 HEMAN BARNEY.   485 HENRY MALCOLM   487 SAMUEL CONNOR
    486 ELIZA GOODWIN, born 22nd October, 1822, married, 1884, Warren E Sawyer.
    488 HELEN MALONE, born 28th June, 1827, married William Hutchinson
    489 LUCIUS AUGUSTUS   490 SIDNEY FRANKLIN
    491 MARY SAMANTHA, born 16th January, 1835, married William Gray.

CHESTER HENDERSON SINCLAIR (158), farmer, was born at Essex, Vt, 19th July, 1806; and died at Moira, N.Y, 4th June, 1887 He resided at Essex, and Charlotte, Vt, and Moira, N Y He married, first, 1826, Laura W. Austin; and secondly, 1857, Sarah J. Hoyt Children
    492 ELLEN FRANCES, born 25th January, 1830, married, 1849, Lucius Saxton
    493 LURA LUCINDA, born 15th June, 1832, married, 1852, Enoch B Harris.

GEORGE W SINCLAIR (159) was born in Essex, Vt; took Freeman's oath there 1st September, 1829, moved in 1842 or '43 to Moira, and then to Lyndonville, both N Y, and about 1849 to Schoolcraft, Mich He married, first, Jane McLean, secondly, Electa Cady; and thirdly, a lady in Michigan By tradition his family is as follows —
    494 MARY JANE, died, aged 6,   495 GEORGE FRANKLIN, both born at Essex, Vt
    496 MERCY LETITIA, born Essex, Vt, married Dr Seeley, of Schoolcraft
    497 LAURA MARILLA, born Moira, N Y   498 MARY JANE   499 NANCY.

HOSEA B SINCLAIR (163) took Freeman's oath in Essex 6th September, 1825. Married Lucinda Barney. Child
    500 CORNELIA

FREEMAN A SINCLAIR (169), farmer, was born in Essex 28th May, 1802, lived in Essex, then Jericho, and died in Cambridge, Vt, 26th February, 1871 He married, first, Eunice Griffin; and secondly, Olive Hutchings (Mrs. Ransom). Children
    501 CHARLOTTE, born 29th July, 1823, married, 1850, Josephus Thatcher
    502 FANNIE JANE, born 1827, died 3rd June, 1882, married John Bliss
    503 LUCINDA M, born 1st December, 1837, married Andrew Lavigne   504 FREDERICK T
    505 MARY ANN, born 18th January, 1842, married, 1858, Dwight Williams

GEO BREIGHTON SINCLAIR (171) was born in Essex 23rd March, 1822, where he died on his farm 21st July, 1888. He married, 26th December, 1847, Elizabeth Keeler Children
    506 JAMES WAYLAND, born 19th August, 1848, died 22nd December, 1858
    507 EDWARD FRANK, born 28th July, 1850, died 21st December, 1858
    508 GEORGE ARTHUR, born 28th December, 1851, architect   512 WILLIE SPENCER
    509 JOHN KEELER, born 20th October, 1853, died 20th December, 1858
    510. EDMUND SHATTUCK, born 2nd October, 1855; married, 18th May, 1892, Ruth A Clark, millwright   511 CLINTON JEWELL, born 10th March, 1857, clerk, Bristol, N H
    513 ABBIE ELIZABETH, born 11th July, 1861, artiste, resident Essex, Vt.
    514 HAMMOND WHITTOCK, born 23rd May, 1866, m, 1892, Kittie Hanley, resident Essex

BENJAMIN ST CLAIR (174) was born 11th November, 1782; died 5th October, 1872 He succeeded to his father's homestead, to which he added greatly by various purchases He was commissioned Lieutenant of Militia (5th Company, 29th Regiment) 17th June, 1811, and was subsequently promoted to a Captaincy. He married, 5th June, 1805, Nancy Pease Children
    515 JOHN MOONEY   517 BENJAMIN FRANKLIN   518 CHARLES PINCKNEY
    516 ELIZABETH MARTIN, born 11th May, 1811, married Thomas J Hilton

IRA ST. CLAIR (176), lawyer, was born on the family homestead at New Hampton, N H, and died without issue at Deerfield Parade, N H 25th April 1875 He commenced practice in 1824; in 1848 was appointed Judge of Probate for Rockingham County, and held the position until 1858. His reputation was very high. Judge St. Clair married, first, 1827, Anna S. Jenness, and, secondly, 1846, Eliza, daughter of Judge Creighton.

JOHN ST CLAIR (181) was born 1st June, 1790. Corporal of 9th Regiment; was in seven battles of 1812-15 war. Shot by an Indian while on picket, 1815. Single.

WINTHROP ST. CLAIR (186) was born in Canterbury, N H., 7th May, 1802, succeeded to his father's homestead, Colonel in the 3rd Regiment of Militia. Selling his farm in 1839, he removed to London, N H., Springfield, East Concord, and finally settled in Richmond, N H., where he died 15th June, 1874. He married, 1st September, 1834, Martha Maxfield. Children

    519 JOHN MURRAY, born 14th October, 1838, drowned in the Merrimac, 14th June, 1848
    520. CATHERINE DAVIS, born 28th February, 1841, married, 1863, Charles F Hastings
    521 CHARLES   522 FRANK P

GEORGE MARSTON SINCLAIR (191) was born in Exeter, N H., 12th April, 1808; died Boston, Mass, 10th June, 1871. He married, 1837, Charlotte Jennings. Children.

    523 JOHN, born 25th January, 1839, died single, 6th November, 1871
    524 CHARLOTTE, born 10th September, 1840, resident East Boston, Mass
    525 GEORGE, born 5th August, 1846, died, unmarried, 4th April, 1884

JOSEPH F. SINCLAIR (193), born Stratham 27th June, 1809; died Chicago in 1874. Real estate owner, lost heavily by Chicago fire. Married Lucy Larabee. Children

    526 LUCY ANN, married Geo Ellis of Boston   527 SUSAN WIGGIN, single

JOHN T. SINCLAIR (194) born Stratham 24th April, 1817; died Exeter, 4th May, 1889, married Minerva Severy. Children:

    528. JOHN ALBERT   529 EMMA, married, 11th January, 1870, George A Janvrin
    530 IDA, married, 23rd January, 1880, Dana B Cram

WILLIAM R SINCLAIR (195), born Stratham 25th January, 1819; lived and died in Newton, Mass, twice married. Child

    531 WILLIAM GERRY, born 1844, died 4th November, 1887

SAMUEL JAMES SINCLAIR (203), born Dover, N H., 21st December, 1824, lives on the farm his father owned. He married, first, 1847, Annie D. Thompson, and secondly, 1855, Frances Deborah Jewett. Child.

    532 WILLIAM HENRY, born 23rd October, 1850, died 9th September, 1855

JAMES SINCLAIR (209) was born 21st December, 1830; resident Newmarket, N H. He married Addie ——, and has three children (533-5)

SAMUEL L SINCLAIR (221), cabinetmaker and manufacturer, was born in Waterborough, Me, 21st January, 1789, resided in Portland, Me., and died at his birthplace in 1848. He married Eunice Foss. Children

    536 MARY ELIZA, born 26th August, 1814, married Shirley Libbey
    537 SAMUEL, died at Yarmouth, Me., aged about 21 years

JOHN SINCLAIR (222), farmer, was born in Waterborough, Me, 1st March, 1791; occupied a portion of the homestead; and died there 19th September, 1826. His wife was Joanna Lyman. Children

    538 MARY, born 1st February, 1818, died December, 1845, single   540 NATHANIEL G
    539 HANNAH, born 20th July, 1820, married Joseph C Roberts
    541 ELIZABETH born 22nd September, 1824 died August, 1846, single

SIXTH AND SEVENTH GENERATIONS.

DAVID SINCLAIR (226), farmer, born Waterborough, Me , 1st April, 1799; resident there many years, removed to Biddeford, Me., and there died   Married, 20th March, 1828, Mary Hastie   Child

    542 ABBIE A , highly educated , married Dr G M Baker of Standish, Me

HENRY S SINCLAIR (228), machinist, was born at Waterborough, 30th August, 1802 , removed to Minneapolis , acquired wealth and died there. He married Rachael Boston   They had nine children

    543 DAVID BOSTON   544 SARAH, married Isaac Gilpatrick   545 MARY, m Mr Fisk
    546 DOROTHY, married   547 MELVINA, married Monroe Boynton   548 LUCY, single
    549 JAMES HENRY.   550 EMMA, married Henry O'Brien   551 ROXANNA.

JOHN LEWIS SINCLAIR (229), farmer, born Waterborough, 27th April, 1804; married, first, 1833, Joanna Chadbourne , secondly, 1847, Nancy Hill   Children

    552 IVORY ROBERTS, born 13th December, 1834 , died 19th April, 1865   553 JOHN

SAMUEL SINCLAIR (230), farmer of Brentwood, N H , died 29th December, 1820   He married Hannah Clifford   Child

    554 HANNAH, died 24th May, 1830

HENRY SINCLAIR (232) was born in Brentwood, 13th March, 1792, where he resided till a few years before his death, when he removed to Exeter, where he died 25th September, 1841. He married, first, 1812, Mary Marston , secondly, 1826, Eliza Blake , and thirdly, 1833, Eliza Ann Robinson   Children

    555 SARAH TUCKER, born 13th September, 1813 , married, 25th December, 1834, Robert Rowe
    556 MARY FOWLER, born 14th September, 1815 , married Eliphalet B Wood
    558 NARCISSA, born 3rd Nov , 1821 , married Stephen Fellows   557 JONATHAN MARSTON
    559 SAMUEL, born 13th July, 1823 , died 17th October, 1825   563 JOHN ELBRIDGE
    560 RACHEL, born 16th November, 1824 , died 20th October, 1825
    561 JAMES RUSSELL, born 18th April, 1829   died, cr , 1850
    562 CHARLES HENRY, born 10th October, 1830 , died, cr , 1851

BENJAMIN SINCLAIR (235), farmer, was born 13th April, 1800, in Brentwood, N H , where he always resided   He was a lieutenant in the militia , an active business man , and a zealous Baptist   He died 2nd March, 1847   He married, 15th December, 1826, Abigail Clark   Issue

    564 MARY ELIZABETH, born 2nd February, 1828 , married, 16th October 1850, Orin Swain
    565 RACHEL ANN, born 1829 , died 1852

Twins, born 4th May, 1832

    566 (HOLLIS JACKSON, invalid, died 1887
    567 (LEWIS WASHINGTON, soldier, 15th New Hampshire Volunteers, married, October, 1862, Sarah M Kimball , died 25th July, 1863
    568 EMMA HOWARD, born 9th October, 1841 , resides on homestead

HIRAM PORTER SINCLAIR (236), farmer, was born at Palmyra, Me , 11th December, 1804, where he always resided, dying there 13th September 1855   He married, 1st January, 1829, Lydia Tuttle, and had issue

    569 JAMES SULLIVAN   570 LEWIS EDWIN.   571 NICHOLAS TUTTLE
    573 LYDIA ANN, born 19th June, 1842, married, 13th November 1867, Benjamin Franklin
    574 WILLIAM PORTER, born 27th May, 1844 , farmer , enlisted, 1862, in Company " K," 22nd Me Volunteers, discharged 1863 , married, 11th August, 1877, Maria A McCrillis, relict of J S Collmore   572 HIRAM CALVIN
    575 HARRIET AUGUSTA, born 17th May 1846, m , 25th Nov 1871 Melvin M Buzzell
    576 MARTIN A , born 22nd February, 1850 farmer , single resident Palmyra, Me

DAVID PORTER SINCLAIR (241) lived in Ormstown, Canada, where he died, cr. 1870. Married twice, and said to have had seven children, but the following is all that has been ascertained —

 577 DAVID, once resident Hamilton, Can 578 WILLIAM, resident Ormstown, Canada
 579 SOPHIA, resident Ormstown 580–582 Three sisters, resident with 577

JOHN TURNER SINCLAIR (242) lived in St Johnsbury, Vt, then resided eight years in Milwaukie, Wis, and died in Sacramento, Cal, in 1852. He married Louisa C. Noyes Children

 583 CHARLES HENRY. 589 WILLIAM P, born 3rd January, 1847
 584 JOHN EDWIN, born 7th September, 1836, m, 1862, Maggie Kenyon, died Chicago, 1867
 585 GEO GRESHAM, b 2nd May, 1838, m, 1862, Frances Anderson, d, 1885, Little Rock, Ark
 586 ALBERT CARLTON, b 20th March, 1840, m, 1861, Julia H Clark, resident Chicago, Ill.
 587 AUGUSTA LOUISE, born 26th July, 1842, married, 1864, William A Stanton
 588 MARY PUTNAM, born 17th May, 1845, married, 1864, Oscar L Chatterton
 590 JAS WALLACE, born 10th January, 1850; married, 1874, Harriet Hallen Veck

JAMES MADISON SINCLAIR (251), farmer, born Brentwood, 25th March, 1812, resident many years in Monmouth, Me.; then removed to Weeks' Mills, China, Me; subsequently settled in Durham, that State, and is now on a farm in Augusta, Me. He married Hannah Slade Children

 591 HARTSON DALTON, born 26th February, 1843, grad in commercial college at Boston, and was clerk in provost-marshal's office there, enlisted in 2nd Mass cavalry, and died at hospital in Maryland, May, 1865
 592 HENRY MADISON, born 1st March, 1848, married, 26th October, 1877, Abbie P Norton, resident Salem, Mass
 593 CHARLES ROSCOE, born 17th August, 1849, died September, 1865 594 JAS ELLERY

JOSEPH DALTON SINCLAIR (254), born 7th October, 1825; resident Monmouth, Me; married Elizabeth Stimpson Child ·

 595 FRANK H

EBENEZER SINCLAIR (260), carpenter, born Sandwich, N H, 15th February, 1801, removed to Boston, Mass, where he died He married Mary White. Child

 596 EMILY, born and resides in Boston Mass

JOHN SINCLAIR (263), blacksmith, settled in Haverhill, N H, married three sisters, Nancy, Elizabeth, and Mary Page, the last was in 1814 No information as to children

MOSES HOAG SINCLAIR (268), shoe manufacturer, was born in Sandwich, N.H., 5th March, 1797, removed to the Corner, Haverhill, where he died 22nd February, 1844 For 21 years he kept the gaol of Grafton County He served as moderator of town meetings, and was known as Major Sinclair He married Mary Wells Children .

 597 ASA CROSBY, born 17th December, 1824; died 14th August, 1871, married, 24th May, 1849, Zeruah Eggleston
 598 HENRY MERRILL 599 GEORGE HUTCHINS 600 NELSON BURNHAM

WILLIAM M SINCLAIR (269), farmer, born Sandwich, published to Lucy A Smith, 20th August, 1833; died Parishville, N Y., 9th May, 1879. Children

 601 SARAH JANE, born 25th Sept, 1835, married Elias G Mosher 602 JAMES HENRY
 603 JOHN HARVEY 604 HELEN AMELIA, born 4th July, 1848, died 23rd April, 1855

ISAIAH GOULD SINCLAIR (270), farmer, born Sandwich 10th March, 1799; died there 23rd December, 1856 Married, first, 20th November, 1823, Mary B. Lee, secondly, 23rd September, 1830, Louisa Cox and thirdly, 23rd December, 1844, her sister, Mary Abbie Cox   Mr Sinclair succeeded his father on the farm near the Red Hill. Child

 605 MARY LOUISE, born 24th August, 1843 , married, 1st May, 1867, the Rev Geo E Lovejoy

JOHN SINCLAIR (273) born Sandwich, settled Haverhill, where his life was largely passed on his father's farm   He married Jane Hamblett. Children

 606. FRANK, died, aged 12 607 JONATHAN, married Miss Titus, and lived in Lowell, Mass
 608 MYRA, married, as second wife, Mr. Bancroft, of Haverhill, *d s p*
 609 JANE, died young
 610 STEPHEN BADGER, born, cr , 1835 , pub to Lydia J Fitz, 14th Sept , 1857, children

SAMUEL SINCLAIR (274) was born 14th December, 1800 ; resident Haverhill ; died 20th January, 1871 ; married Eliza Hamblett   Children

 611 SARAH, married her cousin, Ephraim Hildreth 612 MARY, married Rufus Keyes
 613 SOPHIA, married George W Woods 615 PHŒBE, married Charles Robinson
 614 ALBERT, is deceased, leaving a family in Clinton, N H 618 EDWARD CHAPMAN
 616 CHARLOTTE, married Henry T Swan. 617 LUCY ANN, married James Wilson.
 619 ADALINE DAVENPORT, born 22nd August, 1850 , married James F Sleeper

STEPHEN BADGER SINCLAIR (277) born in Sandwich, lived in Haverhill, died in Moultonborough, all in N H. He was published to Sarah Nute 17th January, 1831   Children

 620 EDWIN DAVENPORT 621 WILLIAM HENRY HARRISON, born 1838 , lived in Sandwich , enlisted, 1862, in Company "K," 14th New Hampshire Volunteers, and died in the service, 1865, at Savannah, Ga

CHAS GRANDISON SINCLAIR (280) was born in Barnstead, N H , 4th May, 1793. He took part in the U S -British war of 1812-15. Enlisting at Portsmouth 5th July, 1814, in Lovering s company, 21st Regiment, he was made corporal. From February 28th to May 15th he was sergeant in Marston's company   He was in a detachment of troops under Lieutenant Jas Pratt of the 21st Regiment which crossed from Buffalo to Fort Erie and joined the American army under General Jacob Brown. He there acted as clerk for General Ripley, and a member of Captain Bradford's company, participated 17th September, 1815, in the desperate fight with the British called the " Sortie," where he was severely wounded in the right shoulder by a musket ball, and was taken from field to hospital   Upon partially recovering he was transferred to Marston's company, in which he continued till disbanded at the close of the war   For his wounds and service he received a Government pension, which commenced 23rd February, 1830. After the war he became a trader at Barnstead Parade   He was an expert accountant, and considered an authority among his townsmen in drafting contract and other legal papers , and, notwithstanding his wound, he excelled in subduing unmanageable horses   He married, 20th January, 1825, Martha G Norris, and dying 18th July, 1834, left her in legacy two unfortunate suits at law, in which, though finally successful, the bankruptcy of the defendants left Mrs. Sinclair with only seventy dollars and her furniture   Child ·

 622 JOHN GRANDISON

GEO WASHINGTON SINCLAIR (282), farmer, was born in Vassalborough, Me., 14th November, 1796. In early life he moved to Unity, where he married, 14th January, 1819, Elizabeth Murch. He enlisted in 1812, and served throughout the war, after which he settled in Unity, where he died 28th October, 1830   Children :

 623 ROBERT STRONG born 9th November 1819 sailor and trader , died, unmarried, 18th September 1851 at Shafta Cal 625 JOSHUA CILITY

624 ABBIE, born 20th December, 1822, resident Brooklyn, N Y, has contributed greatly to the information herein given   626 NAPOLEON BONAPARTE
627 ALBERT, born 14th February, 1830, resident Midland, Cal

DR WM ST. CLAIR (284), physician, was born 3rd May, 1799, in Vassalborough, Me   He resided in Fremont, Ohio, ten years, in Maumee City, Ohio, for twenty years; and for ten years in Kansas City, Mo, and died there November, 1877   He married, first, Laura Barney; secondly, Ann E. Lovejoy; and thirdly, N. M. Colby.   Child

628 MADISON W ST CLAIR, born 13th January, 1826, married, 19th October, 1859, Ellen L Bostwick, resident Kansas City, Mo, banker

THOS JEFFERSON SINCLAIR (285) was born in Unity, Me, 13th June, 1801; married Celinda Bakeman, went to Milwaukee, Wis., in 1845, and died there 1855   Children:

629 JEFFERSON; probably resides in St Louis, Mo
630 ARABELLA WINGATE, born 22nd February, 1834, married Dr Bailey of Buffalo, N Y.
631 HELEN MARR, married Geo F Wheeler   632 MARIA, married Mr Williams

JOSHUA SINCLAIR (287) lumberman, was born in Unity, 12th July, 1805, married, 17th November, 1829, Seville Jackson, lived in Maine and Wisconsin; died at Racine, Wis, 17th October, 1848   Children

633 GILMAN JACKSON, born 1831, died 1833   634 CALVIN DWINAL
635 JUDITH PARKHURST, born 17th February, 1835, resident Racine, Wis

JOHN SINCLAIR (293) was born in Vassalborough, Me, 6th January, 1788   In the fall of 1809 he went to Sinclairville, and assisted in erecting the first house in that village. He located there in March, 1810.   He was a millwright, carpenter, and farmer, and assisted in building the first sawmill in Sinclairville.   He enlisted for the 1812-15 war in Seizer's Co, from Eaton, N Y, in which place and Gerry, same State, he resided after the war, dying at Gerry 27th April, 1864   He married Elizabeth Lee   Children

636 ABERDEEN   639 FRANKLIN
637 HEPZIBAH, born 8th October, 1811, married, 1831, Mr Bennett
638 ELIZA, born 10th November, 1813, married Benj Graham
640 NANCY, born 30th September, 1819, married Jas Albert Clark
641 ANN BURLINGAME, born 30th March, 1822, married Orsamus Alex White

LIEUT -COLONEL SAMUEL SINCLAIR (300) was born in Eaton, N Y., 14th Aug, 1801   Located for good in Gerry in 1810, and lived there ever after   He was a Lieut.-Colonel of the 212th Regiment   He was very athletic, and a skilful marksman and hunter   A farmer, carpenter, and millwright, he erected the first framed barn ever built in Gerry, and became widely known for his skill in constructing sawmills, building a large number in his own locality, in Pennsylvania, and in Canada.   While attending to business at Kinzua, Penn, he was taken ill, and died 22nd October, 1848   He married Martha Bucklen 19th October, 1819   Children

642 SOPHIA, born 6th September, 1820, married Chas P Ward   643 SAMUEL
644 SARAH, born 2nd Sept, 1824, died 19th June, 1829   646 MAJOR   647 ELISHA WARD
645 NANCY, born 22nd October, 1828, married, 2nd May, 1847, Isaiah Cobb
648 MARTHA MELISSA, born 16th November, 1836, married Theodore Barrett Cobb

DAVID BIGELOW SINCLAIR (303) was born in Madison, 10th March, 1807, and died at Sinclairville, 8th October, 1879   A millwright by trade, he had remarkable powers in that line, and was the inventor of an improved waterwheel.   He possessed great physical strength, and was a noted marksman and hunter   He is buried in the Evergreen cemetery at Sinclairville, N Y   He married in early life Sophronia Elliott.   Children

SIXTH AND SEVENTH GENERATIONS 373

649 CALVIN, born 6th December, 1832, died 3rd December, 1841
650 MARY, born 1st November, 1836, died 17th February, 1837

THE HON JOSEPH SINCLAIR (304) was born in Madison, N Y, 15th March, 1809, and was brought by his parents to Sinclairville in 1810 He received a good education In early life was apprenticed dry goods clerk in Sinclairville, and later on was a merchant. Between 1830-40 he went to Fort Wayne, Ind, and is mentioned as one of the early attorneys of that State Elected clerk of Allen Co, there, during Polk's administration he was appointed Indian Agent, and superintended the removal of the Miami Indians of Indiana and Michigan to their reservations west of the Mississippi He was a member of the Indiana Senate from 1841 to 1844 He died of cholera at Fort Wayne 7th September, 1854 He married, 7th April, 1837, Susan S Edsall. Children

651 FRANCES C, born 12th March, 1838, teacher, resident Fort Wayne.
653 JOHN M, born 10th February, 1843, died 6th August, 1845   652 SAMUEL EDSALL
654 ORLINDA P, born 14th June, 1847, teacher, died Fort Wayne 8th January, 1885
655 ISABELLA J born 4th April, 1849, died 10th September, 1851
656 SUSAN S, born 20th December, 1853, teacher, resident Fort Wayne, Ind

GEO. WASHINGTON SINCLAIR (305) was born in Sinclairville, 4th July, 1811. He has passed a large part of his life in operating different milling establishments, but on account of failing health some thirty years ago bought a farm in Gerry, N.Y., on which he has since lived Athlete, marksman, hunter, in his old age he still goes almost yearly to the forests of Michigan for a few days of this sport. He married, first, Diana Ferguson, and secondly, Charlotte Sylvester Children

657 DIANA, died 3rd October, 1836, aged 5 months   658 GEORGE
659 MARY ANN, born 20th August, 1849, married Geo S Wheeler

JOSHUA ST CLAIR (316) was born at Harbour Creek, Erie Co, Penn, 26th February, 1802 Farmer, cooper, and carpenter by occupation, at various times he lived at Hamburg, Ohio, Waterloo, Crow Fish R, Cottage Grove, Hatchville, Lodi, Newport, Summit, and Seven Mile Creek, all in Wisconsin, where he died 21st April, 1885 He married Rhoda Moore, relict of Chas McClellan. Children:

660 ENOCH, died young   661 FRANKLIN   664 CHAS LA FAYETTE
662 OLIVIA CORDELIA, born 1st August 1827, married John Coleman
663 PHYLANDER VICTOR, born 10th April, 1829, fisherman, resident at White Fish Bay, perished on Lake Michigan 17th March, 1855, body found by Indians and interred in Michigan City   666 JOHN WESLEY
665 MELINDA FLORILLA, born 26th August, 1835, married Geo R Curtis
667 SUSAN MELISSA, born 10th March, 1838, died single 26th April, 1888

JOSEPH SINCLAIR (321) millwright, was born in Barnstead, N H., 15th October, 1789, resident in Danville, Vt, and probably in Perry, Ohio He married Sarah Dane of Danville, Vt She died and he married again. No children by second marriage He died in Sioux City, Iowa Children

668 JOHN   669 JOSEPH W
670 HORATIO, married Miss Bullen in Chicago, died in California

GREENLEAF CILLEY SINCLAIR (324), carpenter and farmer, was born in Danville, Vt, 22nd December, 1798, when of age lived at or near Danville Green He died in Perry, Ohio, 19th September, 1876 He married Susan T Batchelder. Children

671 SUSAN ALMIRA, born 20th January, 1823, married, 30th August, 1841, Orrin Harper.
672 RICHARD BAXTER   673 DAVID BATCHELDER   675 JOSEPH FRANKLIN.
674 ELIZA MILLICENT, born 11th October 1830, died 4th November, 1882 m Theodore Wire

MILTON SINCLAIR (328) was born at Danville, Vt , 11th July, 1811 ; lived there till 1831, when he located in Derby, Vt , where he owned a farm and hotel, which he managed for five years, removing to Perry, Ohio, 2nd February, 1836 He went in sleighs with goods and family, and was twenty-two days on the journey He erected the Sinclair hotel in Perry in 1848, and managed it till his death, 6th October, 1852. He married Mary Kelsey. Children

676 MARY ANN, born 31st July, 1823 , married, 20th September, 1849, Samuel Wire
677 HARRIET, born 30th August, 1824 , married, 27th February, 1862, John Perry
678 LUCIUS CHARLES   679 MILTON HUGH.   683 WM WALLACE II
680 WM WALLACE, born 1833 , died, aged 2 months
681 ELIZA JANE, born 1st September, 1834 , died 16th May, 1871
682 CORILLA, born 11th August, 1837 , married Lucius Greene

PRENTICE SINCLAIR (333), farmer, was born in Danville 24th March, 1796 ; accompanied his parents when young to Perry, O., which was ever after his home. Soldier in the 1812–15 war He died at Perry, Ohio, 6th February, 1845 He married Sarah Jennings Children

684 NANCY, married Rollins Ballard   686 THIRZA, married Joseph Richardson.
685 EURANA, married Alonzo Wellman , died 22nd February, 1849

CALVIN SINCLAIR (336) was born in Danville 13th April, 1802 , settled in Perry, Ohio, when nine years of age He donated the land to the Church of the Disciples on which to erect their house of worship He died 21st March, 1852. He married, 24th May, 1837, Nancy Gray. Children

688 CHARLES, born 1841 , died 1862   690 EMILY L , born 1847 , died 1849
689 MARY JANE, born 2nd January, 1845 , married Samuel L Lapham   687 HENRY
691 EMMA E , born 28th February, 1851 , married, 9th December, 1868, Burgess Herrick

DAVID SINCLAIR (342) was born 4th June, 1815, in Danville, Vt. He lived in Perry till 1853, when he removed to Warren, Ill, and from there in 1873 to Kingston, Neb. He married, first, Mrs. Mary Pike Wooley, who died s p in Perry , and secondly, his cousin, Martha M Barrows Children :

692 FREMONT B   695 ALANSON   696 SARAH, born 12th October, 1866
693 ALBERT W , born 22nd October 1861, single , resident Kingston, Neb
694 MARY A , born 24th August, 1864 , married, 1882, William H Coltrin
697 DAVID W P , born 25th December, 1869 , resident Hanover, Neb

SEVENTH AND EIGHTH GENERATIONS.

SIMEON PEASE SINCLAIR (346) was born at Hardwick, Vt , December 17, 1797, where he resided till his death, 8th December, 1874 He held numerous public positions, and commanded the respect and esteem of his townsmen He married, 3rd June, 1824, Sarah Bugbee. Children

698 MARION BRUIDFOOT, born 1825 , died 1872   700 CELIA ANNA BUTLER, born 1828
699 ARVILLA ELLEN, born 23rd August, 1826 , m Chas S Dana   701 LUCY M , born 1831
702 MARTHA L , born 1834 , married, 1860, John Goss
703 FLORENCE JOSEPHINE, born 1842 , died 1861
704 HARRIET ESTHER, born 24th November, 1843 , married, 1866, Dean D Patterson, of St Johnsbury, Vt

NATHANIEL SINCLAIR (348) born Greenborough, Vt , 10th May, 1801 , died Springfield, Mass., 12th February, 1885 , married, Hardwick, Vt , 21st June, 1824, Laura Hager. Children

SEVENTH AND EIGHTH GENERATIONS

705 ALLEN G.   706 ADAMS O.   707. SARAH E , born 1827 , married Alonzo Johnson
708 LAURA ANN, born 1831   709 EUNICE M , born and died 1837
710 CHARLES J N , born 1839 , died 1842

STEPHEN A. SINCLAIR (350) born at Greensborough, Vt , 8th January, 1804 , resident Littleton, N H., in 1833, and at Taunton, Mass , 1840, where he died 28th April, 1868. He married, 19th June, 1836, Celia P Bragg.   Children .

711 MARCELLA M , born 1839 , married, 1860, James A Deane
712 ELIZA E A., born 1845 , married, 1866, Nathaniel H Wood

AMOS S SINCLAIR (353), born Stanstead, Canada, February 14, 1809 , was railroad employé the last year of his life , died in Scituate, R I., February, 1857 , he married in 1827, Joanna Faunt   Children :

713 SARAH LOUISE, born 1832, married, 1851, Thaddeus S. Eldridge.
714 ELLEN MELISSA, born 1836, married, 1854, Geo S Harvey

JONATHAN CRAM SINCLAIR (356), born cr., 1807, Hampton Falls, N H ; died in California ; married Mary Stockbridge of Corinth, Me.   Two children (715 and 716).

AUGUSTINE DUROC ST CLAIR (374) was born at Concord, N Y , 31st July, 1839 In 1863 he settled at Hampton, Franklin County, Iowa, since his home   He has filled public offices in his county, but his 400 acre farm receives his almost undivided attention. He married, 28th January, 1872, Florence J Jakway.   He was at one time a teacher. Children

717 WINNIE CELIA, born 1873 , student Univ Des Moines, Iowa
718 EDSON DE WITT, born 1874   719 FRANK EARL, born 1876
720. FLORENCE AMELIA, born 1883   721 HOWARD AUGUSTINE, born 1888

PERRY SINCLAIR (378), born Barre, N Y , 15th November, 1823 , married, 12th March, 1855, Miss Whaley , farmer , resident Dundee, Michigan, where he died 21st October, 1865   Child

722 IDA, born 26th February, 1856, married, 25th January, 1874, Hardin Marsh

ASA SINCLAIR (382), born Barre, N Y , 18th October, 1833 , married, 9th November, 1859, Louisa Lamb   Enlisted in 1st Michigan Regiment, 23rd December, 1863   He was made prisoner by Forrest's cavalry 15th December, 1864, marched 700 miles to Andersonville prison, 18th February, 1865, where he remained till 18th March , was then paroled, sent to Black River, Miss , and exchanged, went into hospital at Vicksburg, Miss ; transferred to Jefferson Barracks, near St. Louis, Mo , and discharged 4th August, 1865   Weighed when captured 150 lbs , when discharged, 75lbs   A farmer, for the last 29 years he has resided in Bushnell, Montcalm County , Mich.   Children

723 WILLIS DUANE, born 1860 , married, 1879, Dora Scott, farmer, resident Bushnell
724. GEO BOSWELL, born 1862   725 FREDERICK ALBERTUS, born 1864.
726. ULYSSES GRANT, born 1869   727 EUGENE JEROME, born 1872

BENJAMIN SINCLAIR (384), born in Petersburg, Mich , 3rd August, 1835 ; married, 4th July, 1863, Anna Sloan , occupied milling in Pioneer, Ohio. He resided for some time in Ranson, Mich , removing in 1871 to Springfield, same State, where he resides on his own clearance of 80 acres   Has served as Town Treasurer and on the School Board Children

728 WALTER ADELBERT, born 1864 , married, 1887, Carrie Place , resident Fife Lake, Mich
729 MARY E , born 1866, married, 1885, Henry Lanks   730 FRANK B , b 11th July, 1868.
731 CARRIE A , born 1871.   734 GEO ARTHUR, born 6th May, 1882
732-33 { DORRIS R   { born 27th December, 1876   { died 22nd March 1877
        { MORRIS JAY   { died 20th February 1878

AARON J SINCLAIR (385) born Petersburg, Mich , 23rd November, 1838 ; married 26th March, 1859, Eliza Edgar Is in the insurance business, and resides at Grand Rapids, Mich Children

 735 EDITH, born 1860, married, 1888, Chas P. Jacobson
 736 CHAS H , born 1865, died 1869 737 EMMANUEL, born 1866, died 1869

GEO. WASHINGTON ST CLAIR (396) was born in Warren, Me , 22nd April, 1806 · carpenter and farmer He was employed many years in the ship yards at Thomaston, Rocklands, and Warren, Me Married, first, 1834, Sabra Hall; secondly, 1853, Mrs Eliza Smith Brewster He died in the insane asylum at Augusta, Me , of softening of the brain Children

 738 EMFRY J 739 MARY H 740 GILBERT M 741 GEO WASHINGTON

JAMES MADISON ST. CLAIR (399), farmer and ship carpenter, was born in Union, Me , 11th November, 1811 ; was for several years in the ship yards at Rocklands, Me , and lived in Camden He then removed to South Hope, and purchased a farm, which he worked for 25 years In 1885 he returned to Rocklands, Me , where he lives with his son Aubert He married, 25th December, 1838, Orinda B. Payson Children

 742 THOS JEFFERSON 744 ASA PAYSON 745 MADAN KING
 743 LEONORA ADALAIDE, born 1843, m , 1862, William Henry Maxcy, resident Warren, Me 746 AUBERT A

ERASTUS ST CLAIR (400), born Union, Me , 14th February, 1814 , resident on the homestead, and the farm is still owned by the family. He married, 1836, Sarah E Bowley He died 24th February, 1873 Children

 747 WM BOWLEY 748 GILMAN, born 1840, died 1841 754 SAMUEL BOWLEY
 749 JOHN LERMOND, born 1842 , soldier , died 1864 from effects of army life
 750 ELIZA EMALINE, born 1847, single 753 MARTHA ELLA, born Nov 1855, died 1866
 751 HENRY FRANKLIN, born 1850, died 1882
 752 CAROLINE SARAH, born 1852, died 1876 , married Nathan A Hewett
 755 CHARLES RILEY, born 1861 , single , resident Rocklands, Me

GUILDFORD DUDLEY ST CLAIR (404), ship carpenter and farmer , born Union, Me , 30th September, 1824 ; married, 25th December, 1845, Leonora Helen, daughter of Colonel Asa Payson He was actively occupied in constructing ships, 1845–77 In 1870 he purchased the "Mt Pleasant Farm," in Camden, Me Children

 756 ASHLEY 757 GEO FRANCIS, born 1849 , died 1850 758 LAURISTON FENNO
 759. EDA FRANCES, born 1852, married, first, 1872, Abner R Mitchell , secondly, 1881, Franklin A Oxton 760 EVA LEONORA, born 1854, m , 1877, Edwd I Cleveland
 761 GRACE LILLIAN, born 1863 , married, 1885, Rockland Jones
 762 ELMER CARROLL, born 1847, farmer, resident on "Mt Pleasant Farm "

AHIRA SINCLAIR (406), farmer, was born at Beaver Hill Plantation, Me., 27th October, 1807 The most of his life was spent in Dover, Me He removed to Midland, Mich , in 1869, where he resided in 1888 He married, 1st June, 1836, Harriet Bartlett Children

 763 MARY ELIZABETH, born 1837 , married, 1859, Samuel Sias 767 DAVID LOWRIE
 764 ANNA MARIA, born 1838 , married, 1859, Orrin P Dorr 771 ALBION AURELIUS
 765 ELIZA BARTLETT, born 1839, married, 1859, Joel A Dorr 766 CHAS WILLIAM
 768 THOS WILSON, born 1847 , died 1848 769 ALVAH WILLIS, born 1849, died 1862
 770 GIDEON ORMAN, born 1851 , died 1863 772 HATTIE THOMPSON, born 1859, died 1863
 773 AMY BARTLETT, born 1862 , married, 1881, Alfred Moore Burd

ALVAH SINCLAIR (407) was born at Freedom, Me , 20th April, 1810. His early life was spent in Dover, Me , where his farm adjoined that of his father and that of his

SEVENTH AND EIGHTH GENERATIONS

brother Ahira He was an exemplary Christian, for more than forty years deacon in the Baptist church For many years he was selectman of the town, and was a member of the Farmer's Grange, of which he was Grand Master. He died 26th March, 1888 On 23rd June following, memorial services were held in his honour, and his grave was decked with the sweetest flowers of all the field. He married, 17th September, 1834, Hannah Baxter Children

  774 CELISSA BROWN, born 1839 , married, 1864, George H Williams, of Dover, Me
  775 MARTHA ELLEN, born 1842 , died 1888 , married, 1867, Charles Speed
  776 HOLMAN DEXTER   777 DELIA AUGUSTA, born 1847 , died 1848
  778 FRED KEATING, born 1851 , married, 1878, Alice Isabel Rand , resident Dover, Me

GIDEON ROBINSON SINCLAIR (408) was born in Freedom, Me , 6th August, 1812 , married, first Emeline Coburn ; and secondly, 14th October, 1847, Lucinda Jackson Carpenter and farmer, he resided at different places in Me , N H , N Y , and Va About 1850 he went to California, and was in the mining business , returned East in 1856 , removed to Dixon, Ill , where he remained till 6th March, 1876, when he settled in Carroll County, Iowa, and died at Jasper Top, 1st December, 1886 Children :

  779 GEO PICKERING, born 1852, resident Glidden, Carroll County, Iowa , farmer, has been
    clerk and assessor for Glidden   780. FRANK HAMILTON

REV. CHARLES PERRY SINCLAIR (409), born Freedom, Me , 3rd October, 1814 , prepared for college; became Baptist clergyman, and preached till health failed , died 14th August, 1886 He married Susan Bradman

  781 One child, died in infancy

THOMAS RILA SINCLAIR (412), born Freedom, Me , 14th October, 1829 , married, 16th September, 1856, Mrs. Charlotte Doore (birthname Brann) He was a teacher in Ellsworth, Me., and died 29th August, 1876 Children

  782 WALTER ERNEST, born 1857 , died 1862   784 JOHN, born 1862 , died 1863
  783 ELMER EUGENE, born 1860, teacher , resident Pomona, Los Angelos County, Cal

THOMAS SINCLAIR (414) was born in Meredith, N H , in August, 1808 ; married Caroline Abbie Tracy ; died 17th March, 1883 A farmer, and traded in live stock He lived in North Beacon Street, Brighton, now Boston, where he had a valuable farm He had also farm property in the West Children

  785 WM TRACY   786 ALBERT THOMAS
  787 LOUISE CARRUTH, born 1849 , married Jeremiah A Marston, of Boston, merchant

REV JOHN LANGDON SINCLAIR (417) was born in Meredith, N H , 10th July, 1809 ; educated academically, was first a teacher, then a preacher, receiving license to preach 18th April, 1832 As a financier the Rev Mr. Sinclair had few equals He saved to give, and loved to give He aided students preparing for the ministry , gave $1,000 to the Freewill Baptist Church at Concord, N H , $500 to the society at Lake Village ; to Storer College he gave $10,000 , $1,000 to the Sinclair Orphanage in Balasore, Bengal, India, and educated at his private expense a Hindoo youth, who took his benefactor's name, and who now, with his wife, is a teacher at the English Bible school at Midnapoar, Bengal, India He married Olive E Haynes, 19th August, 1837, and died 16th August, 1888 Child

  788 JOSEPH HAYNES, born 1838 , grad N H'ton Academy July, 1858, died 25th July, 1858

NOAH SINCLAIR (418) was born in Meredith, N H , on Sunday, 2nd January, 1814 ; and died there 10th January, 1843 He married, 7th May, 1837, Hannah Cotton, who married, secondly, Joseph Hart , thirdly Daniel Smith Children

  789 THOS JEFFERSON   790 MARINDA JANE born 1841, died 1877   791 NOAH LEROY.

NEW HAMPSHIRE SCIONS.

JOSEPH NORMAN ST CLAIR (425), born 23rd August, 1823, resident Mechanicsville, Ill.; died in Kansas 14th August, 1879. Children

  792 JOSEPH NORMAN, born 24th August, 1851.   794 EMMET F, born 1854
  793 ALICE A, born 1853, married Mr Craig, resident Lake Park, 6th Street, Des Moines
  795 AUGUSTA J, born 1856, resident Wichita, Kan   796 ANDREW F, born 1861
  797 ZELPHA, born 1864   798 CHAS LEVI, born 1866   799 WILLIE CLARENCE, b 1871

CAPT. CHARLES NORTHROP ST. CLAIR (426) was born in Russelltown, Quebec, 9th June, 1812 When an infant of five months his parents settled in Barre, N.Y., which was ever after his home. The St. Clair homestead is in that portion of Barre which when divided became and is now Albion There Mr. St. Clair grew up, was educated, and aided his father in clearing the lands At twenty he was a good musician, for he had much musical talent, becoming an excellent performer on several instruments, and was a composer and writer of music. His mechanical skill was exhibited in the manufacture with his own hands of violins, guitars, and violoncellos of a high order At twenty he was captain of the Orleans Grays, one of the finest military companies in that section of the country. By that title he has ever since been known At one period of his life he owned and commanded boats on the Erie canal, running from Buffalo to New York City, but presently chose farming for his business, and to that devoted his life.

He married, 10th June, 1833, Elmina Baldwin, daughter of Joel and Elizabeth Turrell of Pleasant Valley, Dutchess County, N Y. The young couple built for themselves a house on a portion of the St. Clair estate. At different times Mr. St Clair left the farm and engaged in business Mr. St. Clair and his wife were members of the Episcopal Church, in which all their sons were baptized They celebrated their golden wedding in 1883 He died in Albion of paralysis 29th October, 1893; and his wife died there also on 6th October, 1896. Both are buried in the Mount Albion cemetery. Children

  800 ALPHONZO TURRELL.   801 CHARLES HENRY   802 ARTHUR KNOWLES
  803. FRANCIS OSMOND   804 JOEL FULLER TURRELL
  805 JAMES JULIUS, born 29th September, 1846, single, resident on homestead
    HELEN LOUISA ST CLAIR, an adopted daughter, born 23rd July, 1849, adopted December,
    1849 Her parents, named Wiggins, died when she was young She married Moses
    C Weaver, and lives in Savannah, Ga

CAPT. CALEB NORTHROP ST. CLAIR (428) was born in Albion, N Y, 23rd March, 1818. He engaged in steam-boating on the Mississippi and its tributaries, with headquarters at St Louis or New Orleans When war was declared with Mexico, he volunteered from New Orleans and went to Mexico, serving under General Zachary Taylor and other commanders He fought in the battles of Cerre Gordo, 18th April, 1847; Contreras and Cherubusco, 20th August; El Molinos del Rey, September 8, and on September 13th, he was in the victory at Chepultepec, which opened the gates of the Mexican capital to the U S forces He was desperately wounded in the storming of Chepultepec, and was a long time in the city of Mexico before he recovered While in Mexico City he met, loved, and married a beautiful and wealthy lady of Spanish blood, Marie Lucie Avilla. She died at the close of the first year of their married life, and he then returned to New Orleans, resuming his former business, with an occasional visit to Cuba. He married, secondly, 25th March, 1850, Anna Maria Morris, of N.O, who died 7th September, 1853, when he married, thirdly, 5th April, 1861, Isabel Bickerton, relict of a Mr. Murray, of N O

Captain St Clair was an active supporter of the Confederate cause during the U S Civil War, and died of paralysis at his post, as first officer, upon the Confederate transport steamer Frolic, in the Red River, at Alexandria, 10th January, 1863 He was buried in the Pineville Cemetery, where his nephew, the Hon. C. H St Clair, has erected a monument to his memory. He left no issue His relict married, thirdly, Robert Hay, who soon died , she resides in New Orleans, La

DR. JAMES JULIUS ST. CLAIR (430), born in Barre, N Y, 5th October, 1821, educated at Albion Academy, graduated at Oberlin College, Ohio, and practised the profession of medicine at Royalton. In 1851 he became agent of the Cleveland Iron Mining Co. at Marquette, Mich , where he had hardly been a year before he almost entirely recovered from the consumptive tendencies that had occasioned his removal from Cleveland, where he had been in business with his uncle, Judge Benjamin Northrop He resumed the practice of his profession In 1855–56 he purchased mining property, which proved very valuable He was supervisor of the Marquette Company for four years, registrar of the U S Land Office in 1859, '61, '62, and editor and proprietor of the Marquette Mining Journal He died in Marquette of pneumonia 16th May, 1882 He married, 17th June, 1846, Rachel Ann Griffith Issue .

  806   EUGENE GRIFFITH   807   GEORGE ARTHUR
  808   JAMES OSCAR.   809   JULIUS NORTHROP

ANGELINE SOPHIA ST. CLAIR (431) was born in Albion, N.Y , 21st December, 1823. Educated at the Phipps Union Seminary at Albion, she is an interesting writer, her articles have appeared in many papers and magazines. One of her books, "Senora Ines, or the American Volunteers," is very interesting It is through her thoughtfulness, love of kindred, great care and painstaking, that much of the information of her branch of the St Clair family has been preserved.

THE HON. HANNIBAL CICERO ST CLAIR (432), born in Essex, N Y , 18th July, 1825; went to E. Cleveland, Ohio, with his parents, and in 1832, to Rochester, Ill He received a primary education, was brought up on a farm, and was made acquainted with mill or factory work. In 1846 a mercantile apprentice at Mt. Pulaski, Ill ; in 1849 he crossed the plains to California with an ox team While there he was a merchant in Sacramento · was engaged in boating on the Sacramento River ; mining ; and a contract builder in Nevada City, where he made and lost a fortune In 1851 he returned to Illinois, via Mexico, Central America, Cuba, and New Orleans, locating as merchant in Mt. Pulaski

Mr. St Clair rendered valuable services in the cause of the Union during the Civil War Enlisting in Company "G," 35th Regiment, Illinois Infantry, 1st March, 1862, he was promoted to be First Lieutenant, and detailed as Brigade Quartermaster ; subsequently was appointed " A A Divn Qr.-mr., 3rd Div , 4th Army Corps, Army of the Cumberland," and held that position till the close of his term of service. He participated in several battles at Corinth, May 28th and 29th, 1862 , at one period was in command of Georgetown, Ky ; skirmished continually during the memorable march to Atlanta, Ga., which town he was one of the first to enter ; while on General T J Wood's staff, during the battle of Nashville, Tenn , he was one of the first to scale the intrenchments ; the explosion of a caisson in this battle caused him the loss of the use of one ear. His last fight was in the battle of Franklin, and soon after he was discharged

After the war he resided at Mount Pulaski, then at Decatur, and in 1871 removed to Belle Plaine, Sumner County, Kansas, and pre-empted 160 acres of land, and fenced it with hedge fences; had valuable orchards and a fine park His farm was a model, and his time was devoted to raising fine stock, fruit, and vegetables His public record has been one of honour, and of which any man might be proud He was once coroner of Logan County, Ill ; and in 1875 was elected to the State Senate of Kansas, from the 25th district, comprising 13 counties, by a majority of over 6,000 For eleven years he was member of the State Board of Agriculture, and Vice-President of the Board in 1880, 1882 and 1883 For several years he was a member of the State Horticultural Society, and took a decided and intelligent interest in the development of all those special industries and fruits beneficial to agriculturalists For twelve years he was statistical and crop reporter for the national and State governments, was appointed by the Governor as agent to the Philadelphia and New Orleans expositions; and twice appointed as a member of the Farmers' Congress Attended as delegate the National Republican Convention at Chicago, and the National Encampment of the Grand Army of the Republic at San Francisco, Cal , St Louis, Mo , and Columbus, Ohio As an active advocate and helper in the building of school-houses, churches, and the founding of colleges, he has benefited the public. He has been active in Illinois and in Kansas in the locating and building of railroads, and for years was a director in some important ones He has for many years been identified with the Masonic fraternity, and with the M E Church.

Mr. St Clair's life has been one of great activity. He is strong and vigorous. At the age of 71 his usefulness is not at an end, and to use his own words, he stands ready "to assist in developing another State, to wit, Oklahoma " In the summer of 1889 he struck again for the frontier, and located at King Fisher, Ok , where he now resides He married, 6th November, 1851, Eliza Ellen Neal, who died 27th September, 1854. leaving one child He married, secondly, 7th October, 1858, Catherine Ring. Issue

 810 MARY ANN, born 3rd November 1853, at Mt Pulaski , resident Rochester. Ill

LORRACE OSCAR ST. CLAIR (433), born E. Cleveland, Ohio, 1st January, 1832 : married, 10th February, 1853, Nancy E Neal, born 1830 He died in Mt Pulaski, Ill , 15th October, 1853. She lives in Rochester, Ill Child .

 811 OSCAR CICERO, born 6th May, 1854 , resident Chicago, is in dry goods business there

LEVI MORTIMER II ST CLAIR (438), born in Rochester, Ill , 17th October, 1840 , married, first, 2nd April, 1865, Elizabeth Louise Kimball ; and secondly, 2nd September, 1880, Mary Virginia Stettler. He resided in his birthplace till 1871, when he removed to Belle Plaine, Kan., since his home ; farmer, once a merchant Issue ·

 812. MARGUERITE LOUISE 813 LEVI KIMBALL 814 LAMAN JOSEPH
 815. JOHN STEITLER 816 HELEN AGNES

JOHN TAYLOR GILMAN SINCLAIR (443), farmer, born 7th May, 1834 , resides on the homestead in Holderness, N.H He married, first, 1854, Tabitha Moulton , secondly, 28th February, 1866, Etta M Hilliard Issue

 817 AI, born 1855 , died 1857 818 EMMA BELLA, born 1858 , married, 1876, Frank Dow,
 819 ALICE EMMA, born 1864 , m , 1887, Frank Marsh 820 JENNIE MARTHA, born 1867

HENRY WHITE SINCLAIR (449), farmer, born Bartlett, N H , 24th November, 1824 , resides in Hingham, Mass , and has lived in that town and vicinage for over forty years Married, first, Cordelia Morse , secondly, Charlotte Philips. Issue :

 821 AMANDA, married Orin Poole 822 EDWARD FISHER
 823 FRANKLIN 824 DELIA, married Clarence Nute

SEVENTH AND EIGHTH GENERATIONS

EDWARD CARLETON SINCLAIR (450) was born in Bartlett, N H , 10th September, 1826 When 21, removed to Weymouth, Mass , where he farmed for 23 years; then resided 2 years in Boston, when he returned to Bartlett, locating on a farm Democrat. Has been Collector of Taxes for several years He married, 3rd September, 1858, Frances Elizabeth Pitman Issue

    825 ELLA FRANCES, born 1859, married, 1880, Geo E Gale   826 EVON ERNEST

POWELL AUSTIN SINCLAIR (451), farmer, born Berkshire, Vt , 29th July, 1814 : lived there till he approached his majority, when he settled in Bartlett, N H , where he has ever since resided. Married, first, 29th November, 1837, Eliza Emery , and secondly, 25th December, 1880, Sarah Burbank (Mrs Chandler) Issue

    827 GEO HARRIS   828 LUCINA GAINES, born 1840 , married David Clough
    829 LUCY ANN, born 1842 , married, first, Mark W Pierce, secondly, Geo Lane
    830 JEREMIAH POWELL   831 ELIZA JANE, born 1846 , married Edward J Downing
    832 SUSAN MARIA, born 1848 , single , died Conway, N H   834 LAOMI B. D
    833 GRATIA WELLS, born 1853 , married, 1877, Burleigh B Hackett

GEO HOWE SINCLAIR (452), born Berkshire, Vt , 19th October, 1817 ; removed to Toronto, Canada , married, 1st September, 1839, Matilda Hazeltine Issue

    835 WILLIAM   836 WOLFORD, died 1846   837 JOHN   838 GEO HOWE
    839 EDWIN   840 LEANDER D , born 1852 , married Jane Ingalls, farmer in Berkshire.
    841 ELLA F , born 1853 , married Eugene Miller, farmer, in Berkshire

REV ORISON THAYER SINCLAIR (454), born Berkshire 7th June, 1820 , was a self-made man Self-educated, he entered the ministry of the M E Church, and preached in Salisbury and Hooksett, N H Finally, he withdrew from the conference, and purchased a farm in Bartlett, N H , upon which he spent the remainder of his life He died 11th June, 1878 He married, 8th July, 1842, Fannie F Carlton (Mrs. Goodhall)

    Adopted child—SUSAN A. SINCLAIR, born 1835 , died 1848

CURTIS SINCLAIR (455), born Berkshire, Vt , 25th July, 1831 , went, when young, to Bartlett N H , with his parents Has resided in these towns in Maine Hiram, Brownfield, and Fryeburg, and for the last 22 years has lived in Conway, N.H ; carpenter and farmer He married, 3rd December, 1848, Mehitable Davis Children

    842 GEORGE HENRY   845 FANNIE NETTIE   846 EMMA CLARA
    843 MARY ABBIE, born 1857 ; m , 1879, Otis B Merrill, of Conway
    844 NELLIE HOWELL, born 1859 , married, 1887, Franklin P Davis, of Conway
    847 ORION WILMONT   848 ORISON THAYER

JOHN ELBRIDGE SINCLAIR (459), farmer, born Essex, Vt , 2nd February, 1824 , resides in North Grafton, Mass , married, 1st May, 1858, Fannie Janet Plimpton Issue.

    849 ELBRIDGE HERBERT   850 JENNIE MARIA, died 1864
    851 NELLIE JANET, born 1866

FRANKLIN J SINCLAIR (460), born Essex, Vt , 28th April, 1825 , resident Johnson, Vt., carpenter and farmer He married, 22nd December, 1846, Adelia E Knowles Issue ·

    852. ABBIE E , born 1850 , married, 1871 George Smith, of Johnson Vt   854 JULIUS F
    853 FLORENCE A , born 1852 , married, 1872, Hollis A Mudgett, of Johnson, Vt
    855 JOHN HARMON   857 JESSIE P , born 1862 resident Johnson, Vt
    856 MINNIE L , born 1858 , married, 1885, Leroy G Scribner, of Johnson, Vt

JEREMIAH SINCLAIR (463) was born at Conway, N.H 13th April, 1834 He was connected with the railway mail service for nearly a score of years, and the latter part of his life was mail agent, running from Boston, Mass , to Bangor, Me He was murdered in the mail car in June, 1888. He married Susie E. Gilman Issue

    858 HARRY H , born August, 1869, at Ossipee, N H , where he resides
    859 EMILY WINGATE, born November, 1870

MOSES CANNEY SINCLAIR (467), farmer ; born Ossipee, N H , 26th November, 1841, where he now resides , married Achsah Wentworth. Issue :

    860 FRANK   861 CHESTER WENTWORTH

LEANDER DUDLEY SINCLAIR (469), born Ossipee, N.H (cr. 1845-48) ; has resided some years in San Francisco, Cal., where he is superintendent of gas business He married Hattie Sweeter. Issue

    862 LEON, is deceased   863 CHARLES

ORVILLE SINCLAIR (478), born in Essex, Vt , 13th February, 1816 , resident Burlington, Vt , was a carpenter and lumber manufacturer, owning and operating a mill on the Orion River , late in life farmed at Colchester, Vt. , Methodist ; democrat, was an alderman for several years while living in Burlington, Vt , at which place he died 14th April, 1878 He married, 10th February, 1852, Amantha Augusta Brown Issue :

    864 ORVILLE GATES, born 1852 , died 1861   866 HORATIO HAWKINS, born 1856 , died 1857
    865 HENRY TIMANS, born 1854 , successful ranch owner and cattle raiser in Wagon Mound, New Mexico, married, 1886, Eva Eastman, of Eastman, Ontario
    867 SUSIE AUGUSTA, born and died 5th February, 1858
    868 MICHAEL, born 14th January, and died 28th July, 1859
    869 FRANK OSCAR   870 FRED BROWN, born 1862 , died 1863
    871 SAMUEL THAYER, born 28th March, 1865 , grad at bus college, Poughkeepsie, N Y , in 1884 , civil engineer, resident Marietta, Ga
    872 GEORGE SWIFT, born 22nd October, 1871 , resident Burlington, Vt

HEMAN BARNEY SINCLAIR (484), born in Essex, Vt , 22nd August, 1816 , moved to Lyndonville, N Y , in 1833 , married there, 19th September, 1844, Tabitha Mudgett , died Chicago 8th November, 1888. A mechanic, his powers as an inventor were of a high order, and he invented several machines of great utility, the last a laundry machine of much merit and extensively used Issue

    873 SCOTT H , born 1847 , died 1890   874 CHARLES M , born 1855, died at Chicago

HENRY MALCOLM SINCLAIR (485), born Essex, Vt , 3rd July, 1819 , married, 2nd April, 1843, Hannah Maria Denning , resident some years at Lyndonville, N Y. , merchant in 1889 , resident Cleveland, Ohio Issue .

    875 CORNELIA, born 1847 , married, 1867, Henry Moore, of Bellevue, Ohio
    876 JESSIE H , born 1850, married, 1868, Alfred Williams, of Bellevue

SAMUEL CONNOR SINCLAIR (487), born Essex, Vt., 19th September, 1825 , mechanic and landlord , resident Lyndonville, N Y., where he died 23rd September, 1872. He married Anna Manahan 15th November, 1851 Issue (all died young)

    877 ELIZA, born 1853 , died 1856   878 CLARA, born 1857, died 1863
    879 WILBUR CONNOR, born 1866 , died 1871

LUCIUS AUGUSTUS SINCLAIR (489), born Essex, Vt., 7th November, 1829 , left Essex at age of three , lived in Lyndonville for 30 years, when he moved to Bellevue, Ohio, where, after 24 years' residence, he died 18th January, 1886. His business was that of miller and wheelwright. He married, first, Frances Van Brocklin , and secondly, on 16th November, 1859, Clara M. Heath. Issue :

    880 HENRY L , born 1860 , died 1862

SEVENTH AND EIGHTH GENERATIONS.

881. ALICE D , born 1863 , married Chas McKeloey , they reside Paxton, Ill
882. ERNEST H , born 1864 , railway clerk, Bellevue, Ohio.
883. WARREN B , born 1868 , engineer, resident Bellevue
884. KATIE B , born and died 1870 885 MARY C , born 1875 , resident Bellevue

LIEUT SIDNEY FRANKLIN SINCLAIR (490), born Essex, Vt , 28th June, 1831 ; lived at Lyndonville, N.Y , with his parents , subsequently located at Bellevue, Ohio Lieutenant in Union army, and served during the war. He died 2nd April, 1865, at Murfresborough, Tenn He married, 6th April, 1854, Maria Catherine Grover Issue :

886 FRANCES MARY, born 1855 , married, 1874, to Herbert Klein
887 CHARLES, 888 HELEN, 889 ERVIN, 890 HENRY, all died young
891 EVA BELL, born 1861 , married, 1880, Orrin Wm. Crooks
892 AGNES AGONATHA, born 1863
893. MAUD FLORENCE, born 1864 , married, 1881, Fred Sultzbaugh.

FREDERICK T. SINCLAIR (504), farmer, born 14th February, 1839 , resident in Cambridge, Vt ; married Louise Locklin of Jericho, Vt. Issue

894 ALLEN B

WILLIE SPENCER SINCLAIR (512), born Essex, Vt , 4th August, 1859 ; died 2nd October, 1882, at Sweatland, Cal.; married, 4th June, 1882, Katie Kyle, who resided Sacramento, Cal. Issue

895 MARY, born 22nd May, 1883

JOHN MOONEY ST. CLAIR (515), born New Hampton, N H , 20th February, 1806 , moved, 20th November, 1826, to Cambridgeport, Mass , where he carried on a large and lucrative business, and was the owner of considerable real estate. He married, 1st January, 1832, Eliza Newton, and died 3rd April, 1883 Issue

896 CHARLES FRANCIS, born 23rd November, 1835 , died 29th November, 1839
897 NANCY ELIZABETH, born 23rd November, 1835 , married, 4th January, 1855, Joseph Whittemore

BENJAMIN FRANKLIN ST. CLAIR (517), born New Hampton, N H , 14th August, 1813 ; in September, 1835, engaged in a prosperous mercantile business at Bangor, Me , where he died 11th June, 1856. He married Nancy True on 5th February, 1839 Issue

898 JOSEPH FRANKLIN, born Bangor in 1840 , is in business and resident there , he married, first, 1867, Emma L. Hallowell, and secondly, Mary A Bean
899 ELIZABETH ANN , and 900 MARY CAROLINE , both died young

CHAS PINCKNEY ST. CLAIR (518), born New Hampton, N H , 8th November, 1823 ; lived on the original homestead there He greatly enlarged it, and had in all some 500 acres. He died 25th January, 1890. He married Julia Ann Woodman Issue

901 BENJAMIN FRANKLIN 902 LIZZIE LINCOLN, born 1859, m , 1879, Lester Plaisted
903 NANCY JULIA, born 1861 ; married, 1878, Victor R Bixby , is divorced and assumes her maiden name 904 Infant son, born and died 1863
905 SARAH ADDIE, born 1865 , married, 1887, Benjamin F Robertson
906 CHARLES GRANT, born 1866 907 IRA MARTIN, born 1871
908 Infant daughter, born and died 1872 909 JOHN EVERETT, born 1874

CHARLES ST CLAIR (521), born Contoocookville, N.H , 4th November, 1846 ; married, 1875, Abbie S Whitney ; resident in Boston, Mass Issue .

910. CHERRIE WHITNEY, born 1876 911. SAMUEL WINTHROP, born 1878

FRANK P ST CLAIR (522), born E. Concord, N.H., 30th June, 1849 ; married, 1872, Clara G. Tupper ; coal merchant ; resident in St Louis, Mo. Issue

912 MABLE LOUISE , and 913 EVA , both died young.

JOHN ALBERT SINCLAIR (528), carpenter, resident Exeter, N H He married, 27th December, 1869, Parmelia C Page, of Exeter Issue ·

 914. EFFIE G 915 CHARLES A 916 LUCY A 917 JOSEPH F
 918 SUSAN M. 919. MATTIE S

HON. NATHANIEL G SINCLAIR (540), farmer, born Waterborough, Me , 12th August, 1822. He was repeatedly elected to offices in his native town, and was a member of the Maine House of Representatives one or more times. He died in Waterborough, 31st December, 1870. He married, 30th August, 1859, Roxy G Guptill Issue

 920 JOHN HENRY 921 CHARLES M

JOHN SINCLAIR (553), farmer born Waterborough, Me , 3rd December, 1837 , resident Hollis, Me , moved to Boston, Mass , in 1885, resident at No 95, F Street, S Boston. He married, 13th December, 1865, Sarah Katherine Clough Issue

 922 JENNIE NANCY, born 1869, marr, 1888, Ab Lincoln Sprague of 114 F Street, S Boston

JONATHAN MARSTON SINCLAIR (557) was born in Brentwood, N H , 2nd January, 1818 He spent a short period of his life in Exeter, the remainder was passed in Brentwood, where he was engaged in the lumber business and in trade The various town offices, from selectman to representative, were filled with acceptance by him During the Civil War he was chairman of the Board of Selectmen, and had charge of raising the town's quota of men He died at Brentwood 12th January, 1870 He married Hannah Robinson, 10th December, 1839 Issue

 923 MARY ELIZABETH, born 1842, married, 1866, Geo W Weeks, merchant, Laconia, N H

PROFESSOR JOHN ELBRIDGE SINCLAIR (563), born Brentwood 28th March, 1838 ; graduated from Chandler department of Dartmouth College in 1858, and receiving an assistant professorship there in 1863, was made full professor 1866, which position he retained till 1869 During this period he spent one winter in England and France In the summer of 1869 he was elected Professor of Mathematics in the Worcester Polytechnic Institute, and still lives in that city Washington University conferred on him in 1863 the degree of A M Dartmouth College also conferred the A M degree on him, and on the 25th anniversary of his graduation, in 1883, gave him the Ph D. degree. He married, first, 24th December, 1864, Isabella Aiken, daughter of the Hon John Ware Noyes : and secondly, on 21st November, 1870, Marietta Surivetta Fletcher. Issue

 924 ANNIE NOYES 925 ISABELLA AIKEN 926 HARRY 927 LOUISE GRANT
 928 ALICE 929 MARY EMILY 930 HELEN MELORA

JAMES SULLIVAN SINCLAIR (569), born Palmyra, Me , 2nd November, 1834 , farmer there, where he died 17th June, 1866 He married, 2nd November, 1862, Martha Maria Hackett. Issue

 931 ADA ETHEL, born 1864, married, 1887, Geo Farnham Webber, resident Hartland, Me

LEWIS EDWIN SINCLAIR (570), farmer , resident Palmyra, Me , where he was born 1st October, 1836 , married, 24th May, 1866, Lois Ellen Towle Issue

 932. MYRTLE ELIZABETH, born 2nd May, 1878

NICHOLAS TUTTLE ST. CLAIR (571), farmer and miller , resident Palmyra, Me , where he was born 8th July, 1838 Married, 31st December, 1874, Marietta Jane Roberts Issue

 933 ALICE JANE, born 11th June 1878

SEVENTH AND EIGHTH GENERATIONS. 385

HIRAM CALVIN SINCLAIR (572), born Palmyra, Me , 19th May, 1840, went to Winthrop, Me , in 1859, and is a carpet printer there. He married, 26th February, 1872, Bethia Alice Smith Issue

    934 HELEN MAY, born and died 1874   935 FRED WINTHROP, born 1876
    936 MARY CARR, born 1882

CHARLES HENRY SINCLAIR (583), born 12th July, 1834, married, 1861, Maria Celest Shotovin , residence, 834, 19th Street, San Francisco. Issue

    937 CHARLES AUGUSTUS, born Brooklyn, N Y , 1864, marr , 3rd Nov, 1888, Nellie R Brown

JAMES ELLERY SINCLAIR (594), born Monmouth, Me., 1st February, 1857, educated at the academy there was in 1888 employed in a wholesale provision store, 221-223, Washington-street, Salem, Mass He married, 1877, Emma Whitney Issue

    938 FLORENCE

HENRY MERRILL SINCLAIR (598), born Haverhill, N H , 30th March, 1827; a printer, was in that business in Haverhill and Concord, where he continues He married, 25th September, 1853, Emily Augusta Hodgdon Issue

    939 CHARLES HENRY   940 FRANK BURNHAM
    941 MABEL SHERMAN ⎫ Twins, born 31st October, 1867, resident Concord N H
    942 ALICE MERRILL ⎭

GEORGE HUTCHINS SINCLAIR (599), printer, born Haverhill, N.H., April 17th, 1829, engaged in business in Haverhill, N H., Concord, N H , and in Chicago He died in Concord He married, 28th November, 1850, Ruhamah Brainard. Issue

    943 MARY GRACE, died, aged 19 years

NELSON BURNHAM SINCLAIR (600), born Haverhill, N H , 19th June, 1836 , lived there till 1854, and then moved to Concord, where he learned the silverplating business, and was engaged in it for ten years, when he learned the watchmaker's and jewellery business, in which he is still engaged He married Mary Ann Horner, and resides in Concord Issue

    944 HATTIE NEWELL, born 1859, died 1861   946 CARRIE MARSTON, born 6th Aug , 1872
    945 ADDIE GREENLEAF, born 1862 , married, 1883, Merrill A Randall

JAMES HENRY SINCLAIR (602), farmer, born Keesville, N Y , 12th September, 1836 , resident Parishville, N Y , married, 26th October, 1857, Betsey F L Graver Issue

    947 ELSIE AMELIA, born 1867, m Edgar Northup   948 MARTHA LOUISE, born 1875

JOHN HARVEY SINCLAIR (603), born Parishville, N Y , 2nd January, 1844 ; farmer and cooper , resident in his native town ; married, 1st September, 1864, Candace O Hart Issue

    949 ETTA ADELIA, born 25th January, 1867

EDWARD CHAPMAN SINCLAIR (618), born 31st December, 1845, at Haverhill, N H , where he resides , married, 19th March, 1870, Bessie Adalaide Corliss Issue

    950 JOHN HENRY, born 1875   951 FRANK B , born 1879

EDWIN DAVENPORT SINCLAIR (620), born Haverhill, N.H., 9th June, 1831 ; married, 5th May, 1860, Sarah Augusta Cram. Farmer, he resided in Sandwich, in Moultonborough, and now lives in Meredith Village, N H Soldier in the Civil War, enlisting 14th August, 1862, in Comp. K 14th Regt N H. Volunteers , he was discharged 9th August, 1864 Issue

    952 OSCAR HARRISON , died 18th August, 1865

Hon. John Grandison Sinclair (622), born in Barnstead, N.H., 25th March, 1826; married, first, 29th October, 1847, Tamar Merrill, daughter of Col. Daniel Clark of Llandaff, N.H.; and secondly, 10th July, 1874, Mary Elizabeth Pierce of Bethlehem, N.H., relict of Willard A. Blandin. He entered into mercantile employ at Llandaff when thirteen, and after abandoning the idea of a collegiate course, for which he had been making preparation, he engaged in business, first in Manchester, N.H., then in Lawrence, Mass.: and having accumulated some means he located in Bethlehem, N.H., as proprietor of a country store and a manufacturer of starch. He represented Bethlehem in the legislature in 1852, '53, '54, '55, '62, '63, '76, '77, '78, and was a member of the

THE HON. JOHN GRANDISON SINCLAIR,
ORLANDO, FLA.

convention chosen to revise the Constitution of the State. In 1873, while a resident of the adjoining town of Littleton, he was elected to represent that town in the legislature. In 1858 and 1859 he was a member of the N.H. Senate. There were some brilliant episodes in his career during his long and active legislative history. He was acknowledged to be one of the most daring, most aggressive, and clear-headed leaders of the Democratic party in N.H.; one of its keenest, most pungent, and brilliant speakers. In 1866, '67, and '68 he was the Democratic candidate for Governor, and in the latter year was chairman of the N.H. delegation in the National Democratic Convention. During Governor Baker's administration he was appointed bank commissioner; he was candidate of the

Democrats for Speakership of the House, and was nominee of his party in the legislature in 1876 for U S Senator. In 1879 he removed to Orlando, Orange County, Florida, where he has organised a large and lucrative real estate business Issue

 953 CHARLES ARTHUR
 954 EMMA PEAVY, born 1851, married, 1874, Rev Charles Fowler of Bristol, N H
 955 MARTHA AROLINE, born 1855, married, 1885, John W Weeks, resident Boston, Mass

JOSHUA CILLEY SINCLAIR (625), was born in Unity, Me , 9th August, 1825 At 16 he went to sea, continuing on the ocean till nearly 40 The last two years he commanded a government transport for carrying supplies to U.S forts in the South during the Civil War At the close of the war he settled in Brooklyn, N Y., where he now resides ; occupation, ship's clerk. He married, first, October, 1862, Mertie A. Newell ; and secondly, 29th December, 1873, C Frederika Tompkins Issue

 956 CHARLES ALBERT, and 957 CLARENCE EDWIN, both died young
 958 CARLOTTA WEST, born 9th May, 1875

NAPOLEON BONAPARTE SINCLAIR (626), born in Unity, Me , 27th November, 1827 , went to sea at 14, was chief officer, and by death of captain became master of a ship at the early age of 21, in which position he continued till 1857, when he started in business as a stevedore at Brooklyn, which he still continues with success He married, first, 3rd July, 1851, Ann Elizabeth Harbinson ; and secondly, 20th August, 1863, Elizabeth Turner Hall Issue

 959 ROBERT STRONG   960 ELIZABETH, born 1856   961 HENRY HARBINSON
 962 ARTHUR, died 1861   963 CORNELIA ANDERSON, born 1866, m , 1888, Chas A Peck
 964 ISIDORA, born 1868   965 MAUD ADELAIDE, born 1871
 966 NAPOLEON BONAPARTE, died 1877   967 JENNIE STUYVESANT, born 1878

CALVIN DWINAL SINCLAIR (634), born in Unity, Me , 11th December, 1832 , married, 27th Sept , 1866, Martha A Mitchell Mr Sinclair is a waggon manufacturer, and has resided in Racine, Wis , since 1846 Previous to then his life had been spent in Maine Issue

 968 MATTIE M , born 1870.   969 LUCY E , born 1875

ABERDEEN SINCLAIR (636), born Champion, Jefferson County, N Y , September 12th, 1808; resides Stockton, Chatauqua County, N.Y He married, 27th December, 1829, Sylvia Ann Holmes Issue

 970 FRANKLIN BENJAMIN.   971 JOHN HENRY, born 1837
 972 WILLIAM WALLACE, died 1843
 973 HELEN MAR, born 1845, died 1872, married Hamilton Hudson

FRANKLIN SINCLAIR (639), farmer, born 19th January, 1818, at Sinclairville, N Y , where most of his life has been spent He lived in Eaton, N Y ; Nelson, Canada , near Elgin, Ill ; Cookville, Wis ; and then in Sinclairville, where he resided in 1888 He married, 15th May, 1844, Rachel Diantha Ellis Issue

 974 ELIZABETH, born 1845, married, 1863, George Tackley , resident Pomfret, N.Y
 975 MELVINA, born 1847, married, 1868, John Langworthy , resident Ellicott, N Y
 976 ADELAIDE, born 1856, married, 1877, Chas E Edmunds, of Charlotte, N Y
 977 ANNIE ISABEL, born 1858, died 1882   979 JOHN FREEMAN, born 1865
 978. FRANKIE, born 1861, mar , 1880, Sam Spear , resident Gerry   980 LILLIAN, born 1867.

SAMUEL SINCLAIR (643) was born at Gerry, N Y , 9th May, 1822 In September, 1841, he got a position in the business department of the New York *Tribune*, where he remained till 1872, having filled successively the positions of book-keeper, cashier, and publisher, which latter office he filled for thirteen years previous to 1873 To a large extent he was instrumental in building the enormous circulation as well as the large advertising business of that great journal, and to him are the readers of the *Tribune* indebted for the broad columns and large type on which that newspaper is printed. For several years Mr Sinclair was the largest owner of the *Tribune*. He lived in New York City from September, 1841, to January, 1873, and has since resided at Croton-on-Hudson, on a farm he bought in 1864. He married, 23rd October, 1848, Charlotte Ann Perry, a cousin of Horace Greeley, the great U S journalist. Issue

    981 SAMUEL ERIC, born 1849, married, 1871, Miss Towle
    982 KATE ELOISE, born 1851, married, 1875, Wm Forse Scott, lawyer, died 1881.
    983 MARY FRANKLIN, born 1857, musician, N Y City

MAJOR SINCLAIR (646), born 6th October, 1831, in Gerry, N Y, where he lives on the homestead, and is a successful farmer and dairyman. Has served his town as collector of taxes and road commissioner. He married, 1st January, 1850, Amanda Garrett. Issue:

    984 MARTHA NANCY, born 1854   985 Infant daughter, born and died, 1859

ELISHA WARD SINCLAIR (647), born Gerry 19th April, 1833, resident Poulteney, Vt. A popular and successful photographer and artist, he accompanied the Union army in the Southern States during the Civil War, and took many views. After the war he was for several years in the office of the N Y *Tribune*, and was then appointed Inspector of Customs in the N Y Custom House. He then farmed in Ionia and Sedalia, Mo, but failing health necessitated removal to Colorado, and in 1889 he resided in Longmont, Col. He married, first, 25th September, 1851, Anna A Pattee, and secondly, Mattie Geary. Issue

    986 IDA, born 1852   987 EDNA, born 1854, m Mr Richards, resident Poulteney, Vt
    988 ORLINDA I, died young   989 ORLINDA II, resident with parents

HON. SAMUEL EDSALL SINCLAIR (652) was born in Fort Wayne, Ind, July 11th, 1840. He studied law with his uncle, the Hon Obed Edson, at Sinclairville, and graduated with the highest honours at the law school at Albany, N Y, and was admitted to practice in the Supreme Court of N.Y. Returning to his native city, he there practised his profession. In 1868 he was Deputy State's Attorney, and in 1872 he was nominated and elected Judge of the Court of Common Pleas of Allen and Huntington Counties. In 1882 he was elected a member of the legislature, and was a candidate for Mayor of his city in 1885. He died 23rd March, 1887.

GEORGE SINCLAIR (658), born June 2nd, 1841, in Sinclairville, lived there and in the neighbouring town of Gerry. He served during the Civil War in the 112th Regiment N Y. Volunteers, fighting in some of the most desperate actions and charges, viz., at Cold Harbor, both attacks on Fort Fisher, and front of Petersburg, Va. After the war he settled down to farming at Luddington, Mich, where he still lives. He married, in 1862, Roxa Wright. Issue

    990 LEROY, born 1866   991 MAUD E, born 1868, married, 1886, Thos Southwell
    992 LOTTIE, born 1874   993 WALTER, born 1877   994 ALICE, born 1883

FRANKLIN ST CLAIR (661), born in Ohio, 15th April, 1824; married Sarah Ann Caspar; employed on a canal, died at Seven Mile Creek, Wis, 21st April, 1877. Issue

    995 GEO HENRY, farmer, Wonewoc, Wis   996 ALBERT MONROE, farmer, Elroy, Wis
    997 FRANKLIN, farmer, Wonewoc   998 ELLEN ANGELINE, and 999 MARY ANN, are dead
    1000 AMANDA, is dead   1001 IRENA JANE, marr Edwd Beeker, resident Wausau, Wis.
    1002 RHODA ANN, married 4th July, 1861, Dennis Curtis, farmer

SEVENTH AND EIGHTH GENERATIONS 389

CHARLES LA FAYETTE ST CLAIR (664), born at Rockdale, Penn, 1st April, 1833; married, 25th December, 1860, Caroline Matilda Dana; resident at Seven Mile Creek, Wis   Issue.

  1003 ORLANDO ADELPHUR, born 1st September, 1862, merchant, married, 1886 Ida May
  1004 FLORA BELL, born 1864, married, 1884, Samuel Casper, died 1866
  1005 IDA MAY, born 1866, married, 1886, Herbert Marvin Coleman
  1006 CARRIE EMMA, born 1868, married, Frank Leslie Coleman
  1007 SARAH MARGARET, born 1872   1008 WELLMAN ARTHUR, born and died 1874
  1009-10 Twins, born 21st February, 1876, MERTIE EVA and GERTIE EFFIE
  1011 RITMOND CHARLES, born 1880   1012 EDNA LAURA, born 1883

JOHN WESLEY ST CLAIR (666), born Rockdale, Penn, 17th May, 1837, married 4th April, 1865, Mary Ann Judd, carpenter, resident at Seven Mile Creek, Wis, where he died 1st September, 1882   Issue

  1013 MILTON, born 1867   1014 LESLIE, born 1869
  1015 EDELLIE, born 1871, married, 1887, Amberry Coleman, farmer
  1016 LENNIE, born 1874, and 1017 LOTTIE, born 1876, reside Reedsburgh, Wis

JOHN SINCLAIR (668), stage driver and millwright, resident Geneva, Ohio; married, first (N N), secondly, Delia Scranton (Mrs Dane)   Issue by first marriage

  1018 CHARLES, resides Geneva, single

JOSEPH W SINCLAIR (669), farmer, born May, 1820; lived in Madison City, Ohio, where he died 8th August, 1876   He married, first, 1st April, 1858, his cousin, Lydia Dane, who left one child, and secondly, Harriet A Waterman, who, then resident at Lebanon, N H, on 8th August, 1878, was appointed guardian of her children, by the Probate Court of Grafton County   Issue

  1019 JENNIE (by first marriage), died young   1020 JENNIE A, over 14 on 8th August, 1878
  1021 LYDIA M,   1022 JOSEPH W, and 1023. THOMAS S, all under 14 at that date

RICHARD BAXTER SINCLAIR (672), was born at Danville, Vt, May 24th, 1824, removed to Perry, where he was in business as a produce dealer, the firm being Thompson and Sinclair   He died February 8th, 1870   He married Celestia Brown   Issue·

  1024 GEORGE   1025 EVA IDA, born 1853, married, 1874, Garrett E Lockwood, of Perry
  1026 LAVINA, born 1860, died young   1027 ALMA, born 1863, m, 1884, Joseph Hommel
  1028 SUSAN MARY, born 1865, married Edwd Tucker, resident Huntsburg, Ohio

DAVID BATCHELDER SINCLAIR (673), born Danville, Vt, December 16th, 1827, was moved to Perry in 1832; a carpenter and builder, he was for several years a general produce dealer in a large way. He was a Sergeant in the 14th Ohio Battery Mustered into service 20th August, 1861, for the term of three years, he was in the battle of Shiloh, and several skirmishes   Invalided in the service he was discharged 12th September, 1862. He married, 23rd February, 1868, Sarah Frances Wyman, and resides at Perry, Ohio. Issue

  1029 MARY WYMAN, born 30th November, 1868.

JOSEPH FRANKLIN SINCLAIR (675), born in Perry, Ohio, 5th April, 1837, has always resided there   A member of the 14th Battery, Ohio Volunteer Light Artillery, he was mustered into the U S service 10th September, 1861, and discharged 20th August, 1865. He was in many battles, among them Shiloh, Corinth, Miss., Resaca, Ga., Dallas, Ga, Burnet Hickory, Ga   Athens, Ala : and in the fight before Atlanta, Ga., July 22nd, 1864, when nearly one-half of the men in his portion of the army were lost, he was also in the fight at Nashville, Tenn. After disbanding he returned to Perry, where he now lives farming. He married, 28th December, 1867, Stella Owen. No children.

LUCIEN CHARLES SINCLAIR (678), born Danville, Vt., September 22nd, 1827, has travelled extensively in the Southern States, farmer and nurseryman, residing at Perry, Ohio. He married, as third husband, 18th March, 1878, his cousin, Olive Downing Glines, relict of (1) Jahial P. Cook, and (2) Hiram Owens. No children.

MILTON HUGH SINCLAIR (679), born Danville, Vt., 14th December, 1831, went to Perry, Ohio, where he farmed till 1888, when he moved to Roscommon City, Mich., and is largely engaged in manufacturing lumber. He married Susan Race. Issue

    1030 HATTIE, married William Eaton, carpenter, resides Geneva, Ohio
    1031 EDWIN   1032 GRANT, blind since 12, resides Geneva
    1033 MARY, resides Austenburg, Ohio   1034 EMMA, resides Geneva

WM. WALLACE SINCLAIR (683), born Perry, Ohio, in 1840, resident Geneva, married Mary Scranton. Issue

    1035 GEORGE, and 1038 LUCIUS, single, are in railroad employ, Geneva
    1036 JENNIE, married Nathaniel Beard of Collingwood, Ohio
    1037 EFFIE, married Byron Pierce of Geneva, rail employe

HENRY SINCLAIR (687), born Perry, 3rd April, 1838; farmer, in occupation of the homestead in his birthplace. A corporal in the 171st Regiment National Guards of Ohio, he served 100 days in 1864. He married, 5th August, 1868, Mira Bell Owen. Issue

    1039 FANNIE, born 1873   1040 CHARLES A., born 1876
    1041 ALICE EMMA, born 1878   1042 HENRY, born 1888

FREMONT B. SINCLAIR (692), born Warren, Ill., 27th September, 1856; farmer; resident Ainsworth, Neb. He married, January, 1882, Sophia Liebolt. Issue

    1043 MARY, born 1882   1044 ELLEN, born 1884   1045 GERTRUDE, born 1887

EIGHTH AND NINTH GENERATIONS.

ALLEN G. SINCLAIR (705), born Hardwick, Vt., 25th March, 1825, married, 1st January, 1849, Mary A. Hosmer. Issue, born Springfield, Mass.

    1046 ADA M., born 1852, died 1888   1047 HENRY A., born 1856, married 1882

ADAMS O. SINCLAIR (706), born Hardwick, Vt., 13th August, 1826, married at Canton, Mass., 2nd January, 1849, Harriet L. Pettengill. Issue

    1048 FREDERICK O., born Canton, Mass.

EMERY J. SINCLAIR (738), born 1835, married Caroline S. Long. He was a carpenter, and resident at Owl's Head, Thomaston, Me. He was employed on a vessel belonging to his brother-in-law, Captain Sam Maddocks, which sailed from Portland, Me., and was lost at sea. Issue

    1049 AUSTIN, born 1864   1050 LENA, born 1866, died 1885.

GILBERT M. ST. CLAIR (740), born East Union, 1st December, 1839; joiner, married Louisa Warren; resident Wellesley Hills, Mass. Issue

    1051 ALBERT W., born 22nd October, 1873   1052 WM. PORTER, born 11th July, 1878

GEORGE WASHINGTON ST. CLAIR (741), born 31st July, 1860; farmer; resident Owl's Head, Me.; married, 1881, Mary J. Kinney. Issue

    1053 GEORGE F., born 7th February, 1822   1054 ANNE M., born 5th October, 1883
    1055 ROBERT R., born 3rd February, 1885   1056 FLORENCE C., born 16th May, 1888

EIGHTH AND NINTH GENERATIONS

THOS JEFFERSON ST CLAIR (742), born Hope, Me., 22nd September, 1839, shoemaker. Has resided at Vinal Haven, Me, and in 1889 at Rockland, Me He married, first, 4th July, 1869, Etta Ames Sellers (Mrs Tobin), and secondly, February 14th, 1880, Arabel Eolia Hatch Issue.

    1057 ARTHUR WASHBURN, born Rockland, Me, 18th August, 1881

ASA PAYSON ST. CLAIR (744), born Camden, Me, 3rd September, 1847. Has lived in South Hope, where he was a trader, and in 1889 resident in Rockland, Me, where he is a wholesale confectioner He married, 14th February, 1874, Erville Emma Leach Issue born Hope, Me.

    1058 GEO LEACH, born 25th November, 1874   1059 ETTA, born 3rd December, 1876

MADAN KING ST. CLAIR (745), born Hope, Me, 10th July, 1851; blind manufacturer, resident Camden, Me, married, 2nd October, 1876, Ida Frances Payson Issue

    1060 FLORENCE E, born Hope, 16th May, 1879
    1061 CHARLOTTE M, born Camden, 1885, died 1886

AUBERT A ST CLAIR (746), born Hope, Me, 17th December, 1852, wholesale confectioner, resident Rockland, Me, married, 26th December, 1876, Clara Frances Leach Issue, born Hope, Me.

    1062 EMMA ERVILLA, born 8th Jan, 1879   1063 GEO AUSTIN, born 12th Feb, 1883

WM BOWLEY ST. CLAIR (747), born Union, Me, 18th March, 1837; enlisted for nine months in Comp B 24th Maine Volunteers, 10th September, 1862 Was at the surrender of Port Hudson, La, in 1863, and was sunstruck in the service, and has never fully recovered from the wear and tear of army life in that malarial region of the South He has always resided in Union He married 15th March, 1872, Addie Chapman Issue, born Union, Me.

    1064 BERTON EDGAR, born 22nd Feb, 1873   1065 ZETTA ELLA, born 19th June, 1874

SAMUEL BOWLEY ST CLAIR (754), born Union, Me, 1858, resident Rockland, Me, married Elizabeth Long. Issue

    1066 EFFIE ARLETTA

ASHLEY ST. CLAIR (756), born Camden, Me, 22nd March, 1847: enlisted in Comp. E 2nd Maine Cavalry for three years on 10th November, 1863, and served till the close of the war, being mustered out in December, 1865 He was educated at the Normal School, Farmington, Me., and has been a teacher in Calais, Me, for eighteen years, but has now entered the legal profession, and is practising as an attorney at Calais, Me, firm name Hanson & St Clair He married, 7th September, 1871, Sarah Evelyne Tarbox. Issue

    1067 LOUISA EVELYNE, born 3rd June, 1872   1068 EDA ESTELLE, born 18th Aug, 1874
    1069 ALICE WINNIFRED, born 27th September, 1883, died 12th August, 1885

LAURISTON FENNO ST CLAIR (758), born Rockland, Me, 13th April, 1851, blacksmith by trade; resident Camden, Me, is now in the dyeing department of a worsted mill at Camden He married, 3rd May, 1874, Belle Conway Issue

    1070 EUGENE MILLS, born 1875, died 1877   1071 ARTHUR PAYSON, born and died 1877
    1072 LENA, born Rockland Me, 10th July, 1881

CHARLES WILLIAM SINCLAIR (766), born 31st March, 1843, at Dover, Me., married, August 7th, 1866, Josephine M Keith, resident Midland, Mich Issue

    1073 LIZZIE   } Twins, died young   1076 NORA BLANCHE, born 1873
    1074 ALICE MAY }   1078 WILLIE KEITH, born 1877
    1075 SUSIE BITTE, born 15th July, 1871   1079 HATTIE MARD, born 1880
    1077 MABEL EDITH, born 1875   1080 MILTON ELIZA, born 1882

DAVID LOWRIE SINCLAIR (767), born Dover, Me., 5th July, 1845, married, 27th August, 1881, Harriet McRea ; resident Midland, Mich.   Issue

    1081 ALICE MAY, born 1882   1082 ANNIE MARIA, born 1884
    1083 BLANCHE ETHLYN, born 1888

ALBION AURELIUS SINCLAIR (771), born Dover, Me., 20th October, 1856, married, 1st June, 1882, Edna M Hart, resident Midland, Mich.   Issue

    1084 RALPH, born Midland, 8th May, 1883

HOLMAN DEXTER SINCLAIR (776), born South Dover, Me., 11th November, 1845, married, 1st May, 1878, Ida May Curtis, employed in a woollen mill, resident Dover, Me.   Issue

    1085 HARRY ALVAH, born Dover, Me., 6th June, 1882

FRANK HAMILTON SINCLAIR (780), born 13th December, 1857, in Dixon, Lee County, Ill., where he received a high school education ; teacher and farmer ; resident Glidden, Iowa.   He married, 25th October, 1882, Libby Shiner Seburn   Issue

    1086 EARL MORTON, born 1884   1087 LEE SEBURN, born 1886

WM TRACY SINCLAIR (785), born Brighton, Mass., September, 1841, lives in Iowa, is an extensive farmer and stock raiser   He married Elizabeth Carter   Issue

    1088 JOSEPH DOANE   1089 THOS ALBERT
    1090 LOUISE CAROLINE   1091 ROSE HENRIETTA

THOS JEFFERSON SINCLAIR (789), born Meredith, N H, 3rd April, 1838. His father died when he was five, and on his mother's second marriage in 1846 he went to live on the farm in Meredith with his step-father, Joseph S Hart, and succeeded him on the place, where he resided   He married, 17th October, 1858, Elizabeth Melissa Doe, and had issue in Meredith

    1092 LAURA ETTA, born 28th July, 1861, m Edmund P Anthony, resident Concord, N Y
    1093 NOAH LEROY   1094 MYRTLE BEATRICE, born 21st June, 1872

NOAH LEROY SINCLAIR (791), farmer, born Meredith, N.H, 2nd November, 1842 ; resident at birth town.   He married, 16th November, 1867, Henrietta Laurence   Issue

    1095 MINNIE IVA, born 21st January, 1873

ALPHONSO TURRELL ST CLAIR (800), born in Barre, now Albion, N Y, 2nd January, 1835 ; lived in Barre ; carpenter and farmer, while lumbering in the woods was killed by a falling tree, 22nd February, 1865   He married, 5th November, 1857, Savilla Lummis Thurston   Issue, born in Barre

    1096 FRANCIS ALPHONSO

THE HON CHAS HENRY ST CLAIR (801) was born at Albion, Orleans County, N Y., 8th August, 1836, and completed his education at the Albion Academy when eighteen years of age   After spending two years in Union Springs, N Y, Bloomington, and Rochester, Ill, he went to New Orleans, La., in 1858, and he entered the medical college, and subsequently engaged in the business of steam-boating on the Mississippi River. He secured his license as a pilot of the first-class when the war broke out in 1861   He made a daring escape from the Confederates, and became pilot of and aboard of the U.S. ship *Harriet Lane*, under Commander Wainwright, of Admiral Farragut's fleet   Was before Vicksburg, Grand Gulf, and Port Hudson   When Farragut's fleet left the Mississippi River, he piloted the entire mortar fleet over the S W. Pass bar and out to sea   The fleet consisted of 13 schooners, each carrying an 11-inch mortar. With high testimonials from his commander, he was ordered to join the Mississippi squadron under Admiral D. D. Porter, at Cairo, Ill., and was assigned to duty on the steamship *General Price*, and served on the lower river till the close of the war. He had many vivid experiences and hair-breadth escapes. He was selected as pilot for exposed wooden steamers, transports, and despatch boats. With an open transport steamer he, as pilot, towed the great ironclad *Essex* and others into position before Vicksburg, Port Hudson, and other places, and in the exposed pilot house of the ram *General Price* he *rammed* an opening through the obstructions in the Red River, cleared away the torpedoes, and towed many of the ironclads through the channel. Often during these times the leaden hail fell thick and fast about him, and the sailors used to say "it rained lamp-posts," for the 18-inch conical rifle shells were continually whizzing around. After the war, Mr. St. Clair resumed the business of steam-boating on the Mississippi and other rivers. On 30th October, 1866, he was married in Trinity, La., to Mary Alice, only daughter of Captain Isaac Johnson, of New Albany, Ind. During their wedding tour, while he was in New Orleans, the steamer was blown up, and all save two of her officers were killed. At the earnest solicitation of Mrs. St. Clair he gave up that avocation, and went into business in New Orleans, La., where he remained till 1872, when he removed to Morgan City, that State. He was elected city treasurer in 1873, elected mayor in 1874, and served for eight years. Was elected a member of the General Assembly in 1879, for the parish of St. Mary, and served on many important committees till 1884. Then he was re-elected, but, being a Republican, was denied his seat. He is in business in Morgan City, La., where he resides, and has for many years held places of trust and honour in different orders and societies. A writer, Nathan W. Goodale, says of him: "Always honoured, respected, and beloved, his courage and tireless labour during the awful yellow fever epidemic of 1878-79 for his people has endeared him to them more than words can express, and will

THE HON. CHAS. HENRY ST. CLAIR.
MORGAN CITY, LA.

for a generation to come cause his name to be spoken of with heart-felt blessings by those who knew him personally and by reputation." Issue :

1097. CHARLES ARTHUR.

DR. ARTHUR KNOWLES ST. CLAIR (802), born in Barre, N.Y., 27th June, 1838; received his early education in Albion Academy, and graduated at the College of Physicians and Surgeons of New York City, heading his class of nearly 200, and winning the celebrated "Dr. Valentine Mott Prize." He commenced practice at Marquette, Mich., in partnership with his uncle, Dr. Jas. Julius St. Clair. Entering the army as 2nd assist. surgeon 1st Michigan Cavalry, he was soon made chief operator of the brigade, then assist surgeon 5th Michigan Cavalry, and later on surgeon of same with rank of Major, while during the last year of the war he was surgeon-in-chief of the brigade under General Stagg Notice of his remarkable surgical operations while in the army are recorded in the "Medical and Surgical History of the War of the Rebellion," by Charles Smart, Major and Surgeon U S Army He participated in at least fourteen battles, and volunteered to solicit from the Confederates the body of General Wadsworth In this matter he was successful, but though starting with a flag of truce only reached the enemy's line after being subjected to a heavy fire He returned with the body.

After the war he resumed practice at Marquette, where he married, 22nd October, 1867, Henrietta A. Smith, the sister of his business partner, Dr A. K. Smith. Their married life was short, as he died 20th April, 1868, from the effects of army exposure Dr. St Clair had no children.

DR FRANCIS OSMOND ST CLAIR (803) was born in Barre, N Y , 10th December, 1839, and was educated at Albion Academy, and at the Georgetown Medical College While there the Civil War broke out, and he joined the 17th Pennsylvania Cavalry Detailed as hospital steward, he served in the medical department of the army till the close of the war, when he resumed his medical studies at Washington D C , graduating from the Georgetown College 2nd March, 1869 He was appointed clerk in the State Department, with which he has ever since been connected, though practising his profession to some extent outside his official duties On the 1st November, 1881, he was appointed permanent chief of Consular Bureau, and served till recently in that capacity In 1881 the U S Government sent him on a tour of inspection of the consulates of Canada , in 1882 on the same service to the West Indies In July, 1890, he was sent by the Government to preside over a Convention of U S Consuls, to be held in August, 1890. It was a position of honour, trust, and responsibility, which his long service in the State Departments admirably qualified him to fill He was the accredited agent of the United States to present in Bristol, England, in the name of the President, a gold watch and chain to a brave British seaman, who had rescued the crew of an American schooner During Dr St. Clair's stay in Edinburgh, Scotland, a Masonic Lodge meeting was called, attended by many dignitaries, at which he was present, and was the recipient of honours, as other St Clairs had been in the past It is said that he is able to give without hesitation the name of U S representatives in any port of the world He married, 1st November, 1866, Lelia Cecelia, daughter of Colonel John Dent He has prepared an attractive home in Maryland, near Washington, where he hopes to pass the closing days of a busy life. Issueless.

JOEL FULLER TURRELL ST CLAIR (804) was born 14th September, 1841, in Barre, N.Y , and was educated at the academy there At the commencement of the war he left his farming work and enlisted as private in the 151st Regiment, N Y Infantry Sharpshooters, and became a sergeant. In the battle of Mile Run, Va , he was desperately wounded After falling upon the field, his knapsack and canteen were literally shot to pieces, no less than eight minie balls having passed through them and his clothes He was carried to the hospital at Alexandria, Va., and the minie ball, which entered his leg at the knee, passed upward and lodged in the hip, was not extracted till nine days after he was wounded, nor was the wound dressed until a week had elapsed His life was probably preserved by the skill and attention of his brother Arthur After a time he was furloughed, and returned home to Albion After some

EIGHTH AND NINTH GENERATIONS

months of pain, he recovered sufficiently to return to his regiment, and served till the war was ended

For a time he was in the U.S Custom House at New Orleans, La., later as assistant pilot on the Mississippi with his brother Charles. He married, first, 20th August, 1867, Mary H. Baird, and a few years later he and his family removed to New York, where he lived on the old homestead as a farmer Mrs St Clair died there, 1st August, 1874, when he left his children with friends, and went West to seek his fortune, and located at Denver, Col He married, secondly, 26th November, 1879, Maggie J. Stuckell, and thirdly, February 28th, 1888, Emma L Stoapes He is engaged in mining, and resides in Gold Hill, Boulder County, Col Issue .

    1098 ISABELLA ELMINA born and died 1868
    1099 MARY ISABELLA, born 1869
    1100 HELEN ELMINA, born 1871
    Adopted names 1099 HIGGINSON
    Twins { 1101 CHAS FRANCIS, b and d 1873
           { 1102 LILIIE ROSE, b 9th May, 1873.
    1103 CLARA ELIZABETH, born 1882
    1100 OSBORNE 1102 NORTHROP

HON EUGENE GRIFFITH ST CLAIR (806) was born at Strongville, Ohio, April 5th, 1847. For ten years he was cashier and book-keeper for the Washington Iron Co., at Humboldt, Michigan He is secretary and treasurer of a mining company, and a banker. He was a member of the Legislature. He married, 16th October, 1878, Flora Dell, daughter of John Quincy Howe, M D. He resides Ishpeming, Mich Issue

    1104. FLORENCE AMELIA, born 1880   1105 ARTHUR HOWE, born 1881
    1106 HAROLD GRIFFITH, born 1885

GEO ARTHUR ST CLAIR (807), born Strongville, Ohio, 9th September, 1848, has been a mine operator, owner, and superintendent, merchant and banker; resides Ishpeming, Mich. He married, 26th June, 1872, Rosetta Amelia, daughter of Dr John Q Howe Issue ·

    1107 GEO HOWE, born 1874   1108 FRANK EUGENE, born 1876, died 1878
    1109 LILIAN RACHEL, born 1878   1110 GRACE AMELIA, born 1883
    1111 RACHEL, born 1886   1112 RALPH GRIFFITH, born 1889.

JAMES OSCAR ST CLAIR (808), born Strongville, 19th October 1851, educated at Albion Academy, N Y, and at the college at Ypsilanti, Mich He spent six years in Albion, New York, and one in European travel He has been many years in mercantile and banking business, was a superintendent of iron mines, and resides at Republic, Marquette County, Mich He married, 10th June, 1875, Kate Thorpe Issue:

    1113 JAMES THORPE, born Negaunee, Mich, 23rd May, 1876

JULIUS NORTHROP ST CLAIR (809), born Marquette City, Mich, 23rd December, 1853, educated at Albion College, graduating at Ypsilanti; has been engaged in iron mines with his brothers, and is now Secretary of the Deer Lake Lumber Co He married, 10th July, 1877, Sophie Gordon Rood, and has issue born Ishpeming, Mich.

    1114 SOPHIE ROOD, born 1878   1115 WILLIAM ROOD, born 1880
    1116 GORDON GRIFFITH, born 1882   1117 GUY NORTHROP, born 1884

LEVI KIMBALL ST CLAIR (813), born Rochester, Ill, 4th October, 1868; married, 18th April, 1888, Levina M Courtney, farmer; resident Norfolk, Madison County, Neb. Issue .

    1118-19 Twins, born January, 1889 JOSEPH COLLINS and ZILPHA LOUISE

EVON ERNEST SINCLAIR (826), born Bartlett, N H, 3rd October, 1865, married Cora Harden Child ·

    1120 JOHN ANDREW, born 24th April, 1887

GEORGE HARRIS SINCLAIR (827), born 6th August, 1838, at Bartlett, N H., where he farms. Married, first, Abigail B. Deering; secondly, Addie F Billings. Issue.
 1121 SALINA A, adopted by her grandfather, John B Deering
 1122 WHITTEN T   1123 CHARLES F   1124 GEO HARRIS, died young
 1125 CLARA, died, aged 6   1126 LILLA, lives in Bartlett, N H

JEREMIAH POWELL SINCLAIR (830), born Bartlett, 10th July, 1844, farmer and mechanic, resident in Bartlett. He married, first, 9th November, 1862, Abbie Caroline Sanborn; secondly, October 19th, 1870, Harriet D. Hill, who died 15th June, 1873; and thirdly, Mary Susan Burbank. Issue
 1127 WILLIE   1128 LUCINA.   1129 FREDDIE L

LAOMI B. D SINCLAIR (834), born Bartlett, 12th April, 1864, farmer at Bartlett; married, November 1st, 1855, Emma A Drown. Issue
 1130 ARCHIE B, born 6th August, 1886   1131 LIZZIE A, born 11th September, 1887

WILLIAM SINCLAIR (835), born 10th October, 1841; married, 1st March, 1870, Jane Berdick, tanner: resident in South Troy, Vt. Issue
 1132 EDA BELL, born 1870   1133 BERNIE, born 1877   1134 HARVEY D, born 1881

JOHN SINCLAIR (837), born 1st March, 1846; married, 26th July, 1866, Mary Jewett; farmer, resident Montgomery, Vt Issue
 1135 LOREN, born 1867   1136 CHARLES L, born 1874
 1137 IDA MAY, born 1877   1138 ADDIE E, born 1878

GEORGE HOWE SINCLAIR (838), born 26th March, 1848, married, 31st August, 1876, Sarah Ann Loveling, farmer, resident Berkshire, Vt. Issue.
 1139 CARLOS A, born 1880   1140 RUTH J, born 1883   1141 ANNIE A, born 1886

EDWIN SINCLAIR (839), born 18th June, 1850, married, 29th November, 1884, Carrie E Gross, farmer, resident Berkshire, Vt Issue
 1142 LEE, born 14th September, 1885   1143 BELVAH G, born 18th April, 1888

GEORGE HENRY SINCLAIR (842), born Conway Centre, N H, 24th May, 1851, farmer, lived in Conway and Stowe, Me He married, 5th September, 1874, Susie Leighton, and died in Fryeburg, Me, 11th December, 1884 Issue
 1144 COLON CURTIS, born 20th October, 1875   1145 MYLO MARTIN, born 13th July, 1879

ELBRIDGE HERBERT SINCLAIR (849), farmer, born 9th October, 1859, married, 26th November, 1885, Eva Lillian Pratt, of Grafton, Mass, where they reside Issue:
 1146 ELBRIDGE NORMAN, born 3rd August, 1891

JULIUS F SINCLAIR (854), born 15th May, 1855; farmer; married, 2nd January, 1886, Carrie E Scribner, of Johnson, Vt Issue
 1147 CLARENCE SCRIBNER

JOHN HARMON SINCLAIR (855), born 11th November, 1856. Is a farmer, and resides in Johnson, Vt He married, 14th November, 1877, Mary Etta Crowell. Issue
 1148 WM FRANKLIN, born 1878   1149 PERCIVAL CREIGHTON, born 1881
 1150 BENJAMIN GRAVES, born 1883

FRANK OSCAR SINCLAIR (869), born Burlington, Vt., 7th September, 1860; graduated at University of Vt, in Burlington, in 1882; is civil engineer on railroads. He married, 15th August, 1882, Kate Anna, daughter of Rev Joseph Enwright. Issue.
 1151 ORVILLE ENWRIGHT, born and died 1883   1152 JESSIE HAWKINS, born 1887

ALLEN B SINCLAIR (894), born 1st April, 1861, married Hattie Warner, of Cambridge, Vt, where he is a farmer Issue
 1153 HENRY WARNER, born 6th July, 1883

EIGHTH AND NINTH GENERATIONS.

BENJAMIN FRANKLIN ST CLAIR (901), born New Hampton, N.H , 20th October, 1855 , married, 24th November, 1877, Kate E. Elliot ; merchant, resident in Plymouth, N H. Issue

1154 ANNIE ELIZA, born 25th May, 1879   1155 EARLE JASON, born 24th February, 1884

JOHN HENRY SINCLAIR (920), born Waterborough, Me., 23rd June, 1860 ; received education at primary schools ; in business Hanover Street, Boston, Mass ; married, 1st January, 1855, Annie E Chadbourne   Issue ·

1156 ETHEL MAY, born 12th February, 1887

CHARLES M. SINCLAIR (921), born Waterborough, Me., 8th March, 1862 , is in business with his brother in Hanover Street, Boston, Mass., married, 20th August, 1881, Bella Smith   Issue

1157 WALTER S , born 16th April, 1882   1158 JOSIE R , born 10th November, 1883

CHARLES HENRY SINCLAIR (939), born 21st January, 1859, Concord, N.H., where he is an engraver and jeweller ; married, 2nd January, 1884, Cora Mabel Nelson

FRANK BURNHAM SINCLAIR (940), born 8th February, 1822, at Concord, N.H., where he is clerk in freight office of the Concord railroad , married, 21st November, 1883, Carrie A Hazeltine   Issue ·

1159 BERTHA, born 9th April, 1885

COLONEL THE HON. CHARLES ARTHUR SINCLAIR (953) was born at Bethlehem, N H , 21st August, 1848   His boyhood and youth were passed in his native town   His education was received in the primary schools of Bethlehem, at the seminary at what is now Tilton, N H , at the academy at Newbury, Vt , and at Phillips' Academy at Exeter, N.H.   He entered Dartmouth College, but did not graduate   His tastes led him into a more active field   He withdrew from college and entered into business   For a year and a-half he was in Lexington, Mich.   He returned to N.H , and soon established a wholesale and retail flour and feed store in Littleton   While a resident of that town he was elected a representative to the Legislature.   Governor Jas A Weston made him a colonel on his staff   Subsequently he moved to Portsmouth, N H., and became a partner with the Hon Frank Jones in his large and extensive business   this partnership has continued to the present   His business office is 17 State Street, Boston, Mass

In business and railroad circles he is one of the most active and prominent men in N H.   He is a large owner in the Boston and Maine railroad, and was a director in that great corporation for several years   Much stock of the Worcester, Nashua, and Rochester railroad is his, and he was president of that road for several years   He, with others, built the Hereford railroad, the Upper Coos railroad, and the Upper Coos Extension railroad, making in all about 110 miles of road   Of the Manchester and Lawrence railroad he is a large owner, and for several years successively has been annually chosen its president

He is the founder of the Morley Button Manufacturing Co , the largest industry of its kind in the United States   The Portsmouth Shoe Co was founded by him, of which he is the largest owner.   It is the largest shoe manufactory of its kind in the world, and employs about 1,200 hands, with an annual pay roll of over $500,000   He is a director in several banks and trust companies   A newspaper has engaged his attention.   Of the *Portsmouth Daily Times*, published in Portsmouth, N H , he is the owner and publisher

He was a member of the N.H. Senate from 1888–1892, and was one of its readiest speakers and most influential members, and no other young man of his party has been so prominent. He was elected M.H.R. for N.H. from 1892-94, and in 1893 was for the third time elected State Senator for the term from 1894-96, an office he still holds. He has been twice selected by the Democrats as their candidate for U.S. Senator against the Republican nominee, and in all these contests has received the full support of his party.

He married in November, 1873, Emma Isabel, the niece and adopted daughter of the Hon. Frank Jones, and resides in Portsmouth, N.H. Children born Portsmouth, N.H.:

1160. GRACE JONES, born 23rd August, 1874; married, 1st January, 1896, Parker Williams Whittemore, who graduated at Harvard University in 1895.
1161. MARTHA SOPHY, born 11th Aug., 1876.   1162. MARY LOUISE, born 23rd Jan., 1879.
1163. ELLEN MARIA, born 17th April, 1886.

COL. THE HON. CHAS. A. SINCLAIR,
PORTSMOUTH, N.H.

ROBERT STRONG SINCLAIR (959), born New York City 1st January, 1853; married, 5th April, 1882, Eliza Ann Aitken Morton. Business address: Sinclair & Babson, 18 Exchange Place, New York City, importers of Portland cement. Resides South Orange, N.J., and Brooklyn, N.Y. Issue:

1164. WALLACE MORTON, born 17th July, 1883.   1165. EDITH, born 4th October, 1885.
1166. HAROLD, born 24th August, 1888.

EIGHTH AND NINTH GENERATIONS

HENRY HARBINSON SINCLAIR (961), born Brooklyn, N Y , 22nd December, 1858, was educated in Brooklyn primary schools and at the Military Academy at Bethlehem, Penn At 17 he shipped on a sailing vessel and made several voyages He abandoned sea-faring and entered Cornell College at Ithaca, N Y , and nearly completed his course, when an accident prevented his graduating For five years he was in business with his father in New York City He then studied law, but failing health obliged him to seek another and milder climate He purchased a fruit farm, mostly oranges, in Lugonia, Southern California, where he located in 1887, and where he now lives in excellent health This place has been united with Redlands as a city , and, a Republican in politics, he is one of the five trustees with a term of four years in the city government He is director of the Water Company, and director and manager of the Fruit Growers' Association, and is thoroughly identified with the growth and development of that section He married, 4th January, 1882, Agnes Munson Rowley Issue

1167 MARJORIE ROWLEY, born 5th Aug , 1883   1168 ARTHUR ROWLEY, b 15th Sept , 1885

FRANKLIN BENJAMIN SINCLAIR (970), born Sullivan, N Y., 25th September, 1833, married ; died Warren County, Penn , 10th May, 1870. Issue

1169 One child

GEORGE SINCLAIR (1024), born Perry, Ohio, 18th April, 1851, married, 6th February, 1873, Jennie Forrest He is owner and operator of a lumber manufactory at Hudsonville, Mich Issue

1170 THEODORE, born Jefferson, Ohio

NINTH AND TENTH GENERATIONS

FREDERICK O SINCLAIR (1048), born Canton, Mass , in June, 1856, resides 14, Orleans-street, Springfield, Mass. He married, first, at New Haven, Conn , 16th April, 1875, Hattie E Baldwin, born there 1856 , and secondly, at Springfield, Mass , 3rd May, 1888, Minnie W Decker Issue

1171 HATTIE MAY SINCLAIR, born New Haven, Conn , 31st July, 1876

NOAH LEROY SINCLAIR (1093), born Meredith, N H , 6th December, 1863 , copper plater , settled in Concord, N H , in 1886 He married, 21st September, 1884, Georgianna Cotton, adopted daughter of John Beatty, of Holderness, N H Issue :

1172 OMAR FAY SINCLAIR, born Concord, N H , 23rd June, 1887

DR FRANCIS ALPHONSO ST. CLAIR (1096), born Barre, N Y , 21st July, 1861 Graduated as Valedictorian at the National College of Pharmacy, Washington, D.C., 10th June, 1886 He studied medicine, and became a practising physician He married Mary Emma Keyes , resident Washington, D C. Issue

1173 ALBERT THURSTON ST CLAIR, born Washington, D C , 7th January, 1891

CHARLES ARTHUR ST CLAIR (1097), born Morgan City, La , 11th December, 1873 ; married, 1896, Maime Marie, daughter of Judge A. A Bourgeois, of La Issue

1174 ANGELINA ELMINA ST CLAIR, born 1897

THE SINCLAIRS OF MAINE.

ROBERT SINKLER (1175), probably a son of John Sinkler of Exeter (1), was resident in Wells, Me , early in the eighteenth century, for that town in a public meeting on 12th March, 1712-14, voted him a grant of 100 acres and 10 acres meadow. Elizabeth, his wife, married, secondly, Peter Rich of Wells, 28th April, 1718, and several times she and her husband relinquished in deeds power of thirds and right of dower in Robert Sinkler's land. Issue

JOHN SINKLER (1176), cordwainer, born as early as 1713, probably in Wells, Me , as he deeded the 10 acres of meadow land 20th May, 1734, and must have been of age On 10th December, 1734, he alludes to his father Robert as "late of Wells, deceased," and on the 23rd same deeded away land which had belonged to his father. He bought land and two-thirds of a sawmill 1st February, 1738 ; sold his dwelling house, land and fences to John Storer, 17th March, 1741, resident Arundell, Me , 5th September, 1744, and at Boston, Mass , where, on 19th August, 1748, he sold land in Arundell He volunteered from Wells under Captain John Storer, and was in the expedition which captured Louisburg on 28th June, 1745 Again resident at Arundell, " for not frequenting the public worship of God on the Lord's day for six months, from January 1st, 1749," he was brought before the court and fined He lived in Arundell till about 1770, when he removed or died He married, 19th April, 1739, Mary Wakefield Issue

    1177 ADONIRAM   1178 MARY, married, 12th November, 1766, to Mark Fisk

ADONIRAM SINKLER (1177) located in Lisbon, Me , 1760, clearing the land on which he settled, and transforming it into a highly productive and beautiful farm. It was situated in the north part of the town, six miles from Lisbon Falls, and is still known as the Sinclair homestead He was not a religious man until a few years before his death, which event took place when he was about ninety years of age. He married Elizabeth Joy Both died and are buried in Lisbon Issue

    1179 JOHN   1180 THOMAS   1185 ADONIRAM   1186 MOSES
    1181 JOSEPH, born 1775, at sea for 14 years , returned home, where he died
    1182 MARY, born 6th September, 1779 , married Ezekiel Rich , resident Otisfield, Me
    1183 NATHANIEL
    1184 EBENEZER , married, family resident Litchfield, Me } Twins, born 28th Sept , 1782

JOHN SINCLAIR (1179), farmer, born Lisbon, Me , 17th December, 1769 , died 22nd June, 1845 , resident on homestead, a fine farm of 150 acres. He married Mary Hyde, Mrs Harmon. Issue

    1187. NATHANIEL   1190 MOSES
    1188 ELIZA JOY, born 1802 , married Major Edmund Hinkley , resident Lewiston, Me
    1189 ABIGAIL, born 1804 , married, 1830, Jas Lambert Trufant , resident Auburn, Me
    1191 LUCINDA, born 1809 , died 1877 , married Captain Wm Webber
    1192 ARBA HYDE, born 1812 , died, unmarried, 1841 , carpenter and builder , erected the house now standing on the Sinclair homestead

THOMAS SINCLAIR (1180), born Lisbon, Me , 4th February, 1772 , resident Litchfield, Me., married Abigail Hyde, sister to his brother's wife. Issue

    1193 JOSEPH   1194 EZEKIEL   1195 MARY   1197 REBECCA, res Monmouth, Me
    1196 MEHITABEL, married Owen Lawrence, and resident Wayne, Me

NATHANIEL SINCLAIR (1183), born 28th September, 1782, in Lisbon, Me , where he resided , killed, 10th June, 1816, by a load of wood falling on him in Brunswick, Me By Eleaner, his wife, he had issue in Lisbon

THE SINCLAIRS OF MAINE

1198. WILLIAM, born 1803 1199 ENEAS, born 1804, resident Brewer, Me
1200 SOLON, born 1807, res Bangor, Me 1201 CYRUS BOURKE, born 1810, res Bangor
1202 ELEANER, born 26th April, 1814 1203. NATHANIEL, born 20th June, 1816

ADONIRAM SINCLAIR (1185), born Lisbon, Me, 4th March, 1786, resided in Clinton and Waterville, Me Issue.

1204 DUDLEY. 1205 HENRY 1206 ELIZABETH, and perhaps other children

MOSES SINCLAIR (1186), born Lisbon, Me, 15th April, 1787; enlisted as U S. soldier in 1812–15 war with Great Britain, and is thought to have died in the service Resident Phippsburg, Me, and had issue by Elizabeth, his wife

1207-9 Three children.

NATHANIEL SINCLAIR (1187), born Lisbon, Me, 29th December, 1799; resident at Bath and Gardiner, Me, and was drowned while rafting logs on the Kennebec river at Gardiner, Me, 18th August, 1831. He married Dollie Greenleaf Issue

    1210. JOHN GREENLEAF, born Bath, Me, January, 1826, carpenter, started for Philadelphia in 1855, and has never been heard from
    1211 MARY HYDE, born 1827, married, 1851, Edwd M York, resident Hammond, Minn
    1212 LYDIA ANN, born 1829, married Wm. R Pomeroy, resident 354, 11th St, San Francisco

MOSES SINCLAIR (1190), born Lisbon, Me, 15th March, 1807, after lumbering at Lisbon Falls till 1852, and storekeeping at East Auburn, Me, 1852-55, bought a farm in his native town, where he lived till his death, 28th September, 1883 He married, 5th June, 1846, Lucretia Totman Higgins Issue

    1213 ANGELINE ROENA, born 1847, married, 1867, William Herbert Faunce
    1214 EVERETT MOSES 1215 WILLIS WEBBER 1217 SILAS TRUFANT
    1216. TRUFANT, born and died 1854 1218 CHAS TRUFANT, born 1859, died 1864
    1219 JENNIE WEBBER, b. 1863, grad Lisb Falls High School, 1882, res E Rochester, N H

EVERETT MOSES SINCLAIR (1214), born Lisbon, Me, Aug 16, 1848, in 1863 entered the Androscoggin mills, Lewiston, Me, as picker boy, from which position he has worked his way steadily up, and in 1884 was elected superintendent of the Cocheco mills at East Rochester, N H., which position he still holds He has served the town some time as a member of the Board of Education, having the supervision of the public schools; and has written many articles upon mechanical and local historical subjects. He married, first, January 30th, 1870, Eleanor Perry Hill; and secondly, May 23rd, 1880, Carrie Mary Manson. Issue

    1220 ANGIE MAY, born Bridgeton, Me, 20th April, 1871.
    1221 JOHN EVERETT, born East Rochester, N H, 24th December, 1873

WILLIS WEBBER SINCLAIR (1215), born Lisbon, Me, 23rd July, 1852, in 1886 commenced business as trader in East Rochester, N.H, of which place he was appointed postmaster, 19th March, 1888 He married, first, August 30th, 1878, Kate Veaza Jaquith; and secondly, May 2nd, 1883, Lucy Maria Wyman. No children.

SILAS TRUFANT SINCLAIR (1217), born Lisbon, Me., 8th January, 1857; graduated High School, Lisbon Falls, in 1875, in 1881 promoted to be overseer of the mill of the Cocheco Woollen Manufacturing Company at East Rochester, N.H., which post he still holds. He married, 1st December, 1878, Grace Ann Boocock. Issue

    1222 ETHEL SINCLAIR, born East Rochester, N H, 28th December, 1879

THE SINCLAIRS OF COLUMBIA, ME

THOMAS SINCLAIR (1223), farmer, said to have been born in N.H , was probably an offshoot of the Vermont branch of the N.H family About 1800 he settled in Robinston, Me., where several of his children were born. He removed to Columbia, Me , and was killed there about 1830 while stoning up a well He married Dolly, or Martha, daughter of Gideon Allen, who died in that town They attended the Baptist Church. It is said he was a soldier in the war of 1812-15 Issue

    1224 DANIEL   1225 ISAAC, lived in Columbia, Me., married Rebecca Foss , died *s p.*
    1226 MARTHA, married Jas Hinkley , resident Jonesport, Me
    1227 ANNA, married Alex Tenney , resident Columbia, Me
    1228 SUSAN, died young   1230 WILLIAM
    1229 JUDITH, married Pierpont Smith, of Indian River, or Addison, Me
    1231 HANNAH, married William or Amaziah Bracey, of Cherryfield, Me
    1232 HULDAH, married David Floyd , resident Centreville, Me

DANIEL SINCLAIR (1224), farmer, born Robinston, Me , June, 1803 ; resident Columbia Falls, Me , and died there in September, 1887 He married Lovicy Leighton. Issue

    1233 THOS JEFFERSON   1234 ANNA JERUSHA, born 1839 , resident Sandwich, Mass.
    1235 AMANDA HATHAWAY, born 1843 , resident 24 Central Street, Salem, Mass
    1236 ALMOND ROWELL, born cr 1845 , drowned Columbia Falls, cr 1869
    1237 GEORGE LEMUEL, born 1848 , resident 24 Central Street, Salem
    1238 ISORA THELMA, born 1841 , resident 7 Central Street, Salem

WILLIAM SINCLAIR (1230), farmer, born in Columbia, Me , and resident there the greater part of his life, but is now residing in Harrington, Me. He was a member of the 1st Maine Heavy Artillery He married Mary Phillips, now deceased Issue .

    1239 MARY, married, and 1240 JOSEPH , both resident Harrington, Me
    1241 GEORGE, resident Columbia, Me   1242 ARVILLA   1243 WILLIAM.   1244. ADELA.

THOS JEFFERSON SINCLAIR (1233), farmer, born 24th April, 1838, Columbia Falls, Me where he resides , married, 25th March, 1860, Margaret A Cummings Issue born Columbia, Me

    1245 BREMEN ELIOT, born 2nd July, 1861 , teacher, educated at Bates' College, Lewiston, Me.
    1246 WM LANDER, born 22nd May, 1864 , resident Columbia Falls, Me
    1247 KATE LOVICY, born 7th Nov , 1865 , grad Norm School, Salem, Mass , res Col Falls
    1248 IRVING LESLIE, born 11th February, 1868 , at home
    1249. AMANDA HATHAWAY, born 9th June, 1871 , resident Columbia Falls
    1250 THOS JEFFERSON, born 29th June, 1873 , resident Columbia Falls
    1251 GUY VINCENT, born 10th April, 1878 , at home
    1252 MAGGIE A , b 7th April, 1880, and 1253 ROY LEIGHTON, b 15th June, 1882, at home

---

JOHN ST. CLAIR, of Strafford, Vt (1254), was without question an offshoot of the N H family There is strong reason for supposing that he was a son of Ebenezer Sinkler (46), the martyr soldier of the War of Independence, though there is no positive evidence He had land deeded to him in Strafford by Asael Chamberlain His date of birth was 18th January, 1778, and he died in Burlington, Vt., 4th July, 1817 He married, 18th September, 1797, Rhoda Merrill, of Claremont, N H Issue ·

    1255 JOHN MERRILL   1257 EBENEZER   1258 THOS JEFFERSON   1259 HOLLIS
    1256 CYNTHIA, born 1804, married Dana Rogers, wheelwright
    1260 ORILLA, born 22nd November, 1812 , died 9th June, 1830

THE SINCLAIRS OF COLUMBIA, ME. 403

JOHN MERRILL ST. CLAIR (1255), born 13th January, 1800, at Strafford, Vt., where he died, 26th September, 1835. He married, 3rd December, 1822, Catharine Rogers Issue.

    1261. ROXANNA MARY SYLVANA, born 1823, died 1851, married Colonel John Pressey.
    1262. HARRIET, born 30th March, 1825, married Abel Goodrich Pearson.
    1264 LORUHAMAH, born 1830, married William H Pearson, resident Lowell, Mass
    1263 ANNETTE, born 1827, died 1835   1265 WILBUR FISK, born 1834, died 1835

EBENEZER ST. CLAIR (1257), born Strafford, Vt, 5th May, 1806 First a farmer, later on he was agent of the Copperas Hill Mining Works, and filled the place acceptably for many years. In 1836 he went to New York City, and was connected with the establishment of the Croton Water Works. He returned to his native town, and in 1840 became owner and manager of an hotel at South Strafford, where he died 27th June, 1853 He married, 1st September, 1833, Eleanor West Issue

    1266 ELLEN LOUISA, born 1834, died 1860
    1267. MARY FRANCES, born 1836, married, 1860, Calvin Aug Jones, res Manchester, N H
    1268 WM MONROE, born 1838, died 1863, Union soldier, member 15th Regt Vt Volunteers
    1269 ADELAIDE, born 1840, resident Kalamazoo, Mich
    1270 HENRIETTA, born 1841, married, 1871, Hale Page Kauffer

THOS JEFFERSON ST CLAIR (1258), born Strafford, Vt., 8th March, 1808; resident in Plainfield, or Marshfield, Vt, where he died 24th January, 1872. He married, 7th May, 1833, Finette Roby. Issue

    1271 ROYAL   1272 ORILLA, married Mr Smith, and lives in Marshfield, Vt

HOLLIS ST. CLAIR (1259), born Strafford, Vt., 13th June, 1810, and lived on a farm till he was 16, after which he was employed for nine years in the Copperas Mining Works, during which period he attended the primary school, and had two terms in the academy at Thetford, Vt He taught country schools for three winters. In 1835 he went to Jewell's Island, in Casco Bay, Me., and had charge of the copperas and alum works, where he remained six years. In 1840 he purchased a farm in Cumberland, Me He has been a J.P. and quorum for the State for forty-seven years. In 1844-45 he was commissary for parties engaged in establishing the north-eastern boundary between Canada and the United States He was inspector of customs in the custom-house at Portland, Me, during the four years of President Jas. Buchanan's administration He married, first, 15th October, 1840, Jane Sturtevant, and secondly, 2nd November, 1882, Jane Sturtevant Merrill Issue

    1273 FRANCES GERTRUDE, born Portland, Me, 18th March, 1842.
    1274 HERBERT, born 5th February, 1860, Cumberland, Me, farmer there

JOHN SINCLAIR (1275) was *first called Peter* His mother died when he was quite young His father's Christian name is not known; married again, and they had one daughter Peter Sinclair was bound out when young, but, being unkindly treated, ran away, and to escape detection changed his name to John, by which he was ever after known. He was a soldier in the war of 1812 Tradition says he was born in N H, that his father's name was John, and came with a brother from Scotland, and lived in N.H., and that his father served in or through the War of Independence. Appearances (but not proof) indicate that he was a descendant of John Sinkler, of Exeter, N H, and it is not improbable that he was an offshoot of one of those N H. Sinclairs that migrated to Essex, Vt., and vicinity, of some of whose sons we have no account Mr. Sinclair was a farmer, lived in Allegheny County, N Y , and in Seneca County, and other places, and died in Allegheny County He married Phebe, daughter of Major Quigley, of the Revolutionary army, and had nineteen children Issue

 1276 THOMAS 1277 CATHERINE, mar Marquis Hatch 1279 DANIEL. 1283 JOHN
 1278 POLLY, mar , first, Samuel, and secondly, Daniel, Sisson 1287 PETER. 1288 ELISHA.
 1280. ANNA, mar Mr Harris 1281 JANE, m Mr Perry 1282 BETSEY, m Mr Perry
 1284 AMANDA, m Mr Burlingame. 1285 RHODA ANN, m Mr Hill 1289 CORNELIUS
 1286 SALLY, married Mr Mackay 1290. BENONI, married, had children.
 1291 LORENZO 1292 FLORA 1293 ISAAC. 1294 PHEBE. 1295. TOCA 1296 MARY.

THOMAS SINCLAIR (1276), married, and had three children .
 1297 MARIA 1298 and 1299 Two other children

DANIEL SINCLAIR (1279), farmer, born near Seneca Lake, N Y , May 10, 1801 ; died in Waverley, Ohio, June, 1871. He married Harriet R. Fowler, in Rochester, N Y , 4th July, 1835 Issue
 1300 DANIEL M 1301. HARRIET A , born 1837, married, 1858, Truman Allen

JOHN SINCLAIR (1283), married, and had a son
 1302. THOMAS

PETER SINCLAIR (1287), married. Issue .
 1303 GEORGE 1304 BENONI 1305 WILLIAM 1306 WARREN 1307 MARY

ELISHA SINCLAIR (1288), married Issue
 1308 PHEBE 1309 MARIA 1310 MARION

CORNELIUS SINCLAIR (1289), born Seneca County, N Y , 25th January, 1822 ; married, 30th November, 1845, Emily Nye Mr Sinclair lived in Branch County, Mich , 14 years, and for 36 years in Calhoun County, Mich , in the town of Partello He is a farmer, and was a soldier in the late war Issue
 1311 MARY ETTIE, born 1847 , married, 1868, Edway Page, resident Muskegon, Mich
 1312 EDGAR LAFAYETTE, born 1851 , married, 1874, Gertie Ketchledge , res Shepherd, Mich.
 1313 MARIA AVASIA, born 1854, married, 1875, E Clark, farmer, Calhoun County , Mich
 1314 MAZILLA, born 1859, died 1863 1316 ROLLIE OWEN, born 23rd October, 1869
 1315 EMMA MAY, born 1866, married, 1868, Ellsworth Collins, farmer, Partello

DANIEL MERRITT SINCLAIR (1300) The Rev. D M Sinclair was born in Rochester, N.Y , April 5th, 1836 , educated at the academy in Clarkson, N.Y., and at the seminary in Brockport, N Y He is an M E clergyman ; licensed local preacher in 1857, has been itinerant since 1858 He has filled appointments in various states, and at different times served as presiding elder, 13 years in all, and is a member of the West Wisconsin Conference He married, 17th April, 1860, Mary Ellen Swazey Issue
 1317. BENJAMIN R , born 1861, died 1862 1318 WILLIAM B , born 3rd August, 1864 , resident Ledgerwood, N Dak , is station agent , he mar , 11th April, 1889, Eva Stair
 1319 CHARLES S , born 26th December, 1866 , druggist, resident Dundee, Ill , he married, 2nd July, 1890, Estella L Morgan
 1320. ELLEN M , born 20th February, 1872 , resident Boscobel, Wis

---

GEORGE SINKLER (1321) There are indications that this person was of the Exeter family, probably a son of James Sinkler (2), or John Sinkler (6). Born as early as 1707, he was in business in 1728 He first appears on the records of Exeter, N H , September 17th, 1728, receiving from Aaron Morrill of Salisbury, Mass., 10 acres in Nottingham, N H , in consideration of his settling on Morrill's land there. On January

8th, 1733-34, as resident there, he sold 40 acres. He had lots Nos 38 and 40 in King Street. On May 8th, 1734, "now of Exeter," he bought land there from John McCrelis. He resided Haverhill, Mass., 21st July, 1743, when he bought one-third of 200 acres in Nottingham from Aaron Morrill. He was of Kingston, N H , November 28th, 1761, when he bought land in Hampstead, N H., where he resided till his death, which occurred between 10th April (date of will) and 27th May, 1867, when probate was granted. By trade he was called "Tayler." He was survived by Hannah, his wife. Issue

 1322 SARAH, unmarried at death of father, and was to inherit one-half of his dwelling house at her mother's decease
 1323 HANNAH, married 31st March, 1767, in Hampstead, Moses Poor, of Plaistow
 1324 SUSANNAH, probable daughter, married in Hampstead, 2nd December, 1784, John Clark

WILLIAM SINCLAIR (1325) of Blue Hill, Me , married October, 1789, Polly Carleton of Bradford, Mass. He is thought to have been a son of Edward Sinclair (44).

EDWARD SINCLAIR (1326) resided at Blue Hill, Me. By Elizabeth, his wife, he had issue there:

 1327 EDWARD DUDLEY, born 1st August, 1826, died December 6th, 1833
 1328 FREDERICK AUGUSTUS, born March 9th, 1828; died in California 30th August, 1858
 1329 ELIZABETH, born 1st October, 1829, married Mr Carter
 1330 MARY C , born 9th September, 1830, married John Burnham, resident Sherman, Me
 1331 ROBERT HASKELL, born Aug 6th, 1833, m Lorana D Bradbury, res Sargentville, Me
 1332. EDWARD, born June 14th, 1835 1333 FRANCIS, born 3rd April, 1838
 1334 ANDREW E H , born Nov 1st, 1840, married Clara L Sleeker, resident Sargentville

INCIDENTAL NOTICES

CHARLES SINKLER is enumerated in the roll of N H. soldiers under Colonel Shadrach Walton. "The account is for 60 men from July 21st to November 8th, and for 10 men from that time to November 14. The year was not mentioned, but it was probably 1710, on the expedition against Port Royal, which resulted in the capture of that place.

GEORGE SINCLAIR enlisted at Philadelphia, 18th September, 1777, as seaman on frigate *Washington*; then enlisted for one year on *Hell Cat*, which vessel was burned on Mud Island. Was then steward on ship *Repulse*, burned by the Americans. He enlisted May, 1778, in Ridding's Company, 2nd Regiment, commanded by Colonel Shreve, and served till March 1st, 1783; then drafted into Wyman's Company, Colonel Ogden's (the 1st) Regiment, and was discharged 3rd June, 1783. He was in the battles of Monmouth and Springfield, N J., and was at the capture of Lord Cornwallis and the British army, 19th October, 1781. He was a resident of Hanover, Butler County, Ohio, 17th July, 1820, and was 66 years of age. It is thought that his descendants are still in that place.

CAPTAIN JOHN SINCLAIR had in the 1812-15 war with Great Britain been an under-officer or seaman of Captain Thomas Shaw, who commanded the privateer *Portsmouth*, "the Dandy of the Seas." This craft sailed from Portsmouth, N H , and made great havoc on the British merchant ships on the high seas. Mr. Sinclair had been with

Captain Shaw throughout all the cruises of the ship, aided in capturing its prizes, and shared in the glories of those conflicts and successes He succeeded to the command in November, 1814, and on that day put out to sea from Portsmouth harbour. On 13th November, when near Cape Sable, he recaptured the schooner *Nancy* of Newburyport, Mass On the 28th he captured the British *Ocean* with timber for Glasgow; they took out provisions and burned her. On same day he captured the brig *Langton* from Richebucto, N.S., with timber for Scotland. He parolled the crews of the two vessels, and gave up the latter one, after obtaining £700 sterling as ransom He had a variety of adventures till 14th December, which is the last notice of him.

GEORGE ST. CLAIR, born at New York City about 1761; enlisted September 28th, 1812, in Captain George McGlassin's Company, 15th Regiment U.S Infantry, was wounded in the battle of Little York, Upper Canada, 1813, discharged May 28th. 1815

SAMUEL SINCLAIR was a private in Captain Joseph Smith's Company, 4th Regiment Detached Militia, enlisted September 14th, 1814, served eighteen days. Regiment was stationed at the Rope-walk in Portsmouth, N H, near the Arsenal.

UNITED STATES ARMY AND NAVY
1776—1887.

ARMY OFFICERS —General Arthur St Clair, Daniel St. Clair, James B. Sinclair, William Sinclair

NAVY OFFICERS —Arthur Sinclair, Charles Sinclair, George F. Sinclair, John S. Sinclair, William B. Sinclair, Arthur Sinclair, Charles H Sinclair Henry Sinclair, Malcolm Sinclair, Arthur Sinclair, Daniel Sinclair, James D. Sinclair, William Sinclair, Charles Sinkler.

EARLY ARRIVALS

1651—SALAMON SINCLARE, passenger in the *John and Sara* from London for America
1658—JOHN SINKLER, was in Exeter, N H
1677—ROBERT SINCLAIR, emigrant, came to N.Y "He was son of James Sinclair, a lineal descendant of the Earls of Orkney and Caithness."
1680—ALEX. SINKLAIRE, resident St Michaels, Barbados, and had 10 acres land.
1710—CHAS. SINKLER, was in the military service of New Hampshire.
1714—ROBERT SINKLER, resident of Wells, Me.
1717—DAVID SINCLAIR, died in Boston, Mass, November 9th, 1717
1729—WILLIAM SINCLAIR, came to New England, he was born in Drumbloo, Down, Ireland, in 1676, in 1735 he settled in Spencer, Mass
1746—DUNCAN SINCLAIR, of Boston, married Agnes McQueston, 21st August, 1746.
1747—JOHN SINCLAIR, political exile from Scotland, located in Virginia
1757—ARTHUR ST CLAIR, arrived as British officer, became United States general. William St Clair, a relative, arrived later on
1760—CAPTAIN JOHN SINCLAIR, and Sir John Sinclair, were British officers in French and Indian War
1768—THOMAS SINCLAIR, of Boston, Mass, married, 28th August, 1768, Constantia Condon

THE SINCLAIRS OF VIRGINIA.

JOHN SINCLAIR (1), the founder of this branch of the lineage, was Scottish. He came to the American colonies in 1747 with the families of Douglass, McDonald, Shepherd, and others, they were political exiles. He located as a planter near Leesburg, Va., on the Potomac river. The name of his wife is not known. His family was large, and he died upon his estate about the year 1800. His descendants in Va. are Baptists, while those in Ill. are members of the M E church. Issue:

 2. AMOS, farmer, resident about ten miles from Leesburg, Va.   3 JOHN.
 4 SAMUEL. 5. GEORGE. 6 SALLY, married Mr Craven, res near her brother Amos
 7 JEMIMA, married Mr. Hawlings, died 1883, near Leesburg
 8 JANE, married Mr Smith, resident near Waterford, Va

JOHN SINCLAIR (3), born Va; removed first to Tenn, then to Ky., and later to Jacksonville, Ill., in 1835. He married Rachel Steer. Issue

 9 JOHN, Methodist clergyman in early conference of Ill., died s p 1858
 10. WILLIAM   11 WATSON   12 SAMUEL   15 AMOS
 13 MARY M, married Mr Thompson, resident Georgetown, Ky
 14 ELIZABETH, married Mr Boise, resident near Jacksonville, died cr. 1879

GEORGE SINCLAIR (5) was born near Leesburg, Va. He became a planter, owning some 600 acres. He married Margaret Craven, and resided near Leesburg. Issue

 16 ELEANOR, born November 18th, 1801, married Chas Guillette, and lives in the stone house on the old Sinclair homestead, near the Chanocacy Aqueduct, on the Potomac river. This farm has for over a century been the home of these Sinclairs
 17 GEORGE. 18 SAMUEL

WATSON SINCLAIR (11), farmer, married, first, Miss Morrison, secondly, Miss Maddox; thirdly, Mrs Kuns. Died 1879-80. Issue:

 19 ROBERT, dead   20 JULIA, resident Missouri
 21. ANNA, married Mr. Mason, res Mo   22 KNOTTY, mar Miss Stout, res Virginia, Ill
 23 LOW. 24 NEWTON 25 MYRA. 26. ADDIE

SAMUEL SINCLAIR (12), farmer, born Tenn, 17th July, 1808, died 8th May, 1868. Issue all resident Ashland, Ill.:

 27. SALLY, married John Beggs   28. ELIZABETH, married Mr Carrell
 29 MARY, married Levi Letherman   30 SAMUEL WATSON 31 WILLIAM

GEORGE SINCLAIR (17), born near Leesburg, 18th May, 1806, and resident in London County until after marriage to Ruth Ann Belt, when he removed to Charlottesville, Albemarle County, where he died 31st December, 1851. Issue:

 32 GEO ALFRED   33 JOHN CAMPBELL, farmer, Charlottesville
 34 SAMUEL JAMES, born 1833, died 1858
 35 CHARLOTTE ELLEN, born 28th October, 1836, married Rev. Dr. John A Broades
 36 VIRGINIA LUCRETIA, born 7th March, 1843, married Dr Wm. A Hawes, New York City
 37 CHAS GUILLETTE, born 23rd July, 1845, farmer, Charlottesville
 38 CEPHAS HEMPTON, born 4th December, 1847, married Julia Farish, is in U S Coast Survey, and resident Sacramento, Cal

SAMUEL SINCLAIR (18), born near Leesburg, Va., 8th June, 1808, married, first, 28th October, 1834, Euphemia Craven, and secondly, October 21st, 1863, Dolly Beggs, he died in Springfield, Ill, where he had lived for five years. He had formerly resided for 19 years near Ashland, and for 28 years near Sinclair, both in Illinois. He was a farmer and stock raiser. Issue

 39 GEORGE   40 SAMUEL JAMES, born 1837, died Sinclair, Ill, 1858

41 ELLEN CRAVEN, born 1839, died 1881, married, 1870, Samuel L Hamilton, merchant
42 PETER AKERS   43 VIRGINIA FRANCES, b 1842, m , 1862, Howard M Atkins, attorney.
44 HENRY CLAY, born 1844, married, 1872, Lucy E Beggs, died, 1888, at Royalton, Minn
45 AMANDA CRAWFORD, born 1846, died 1847   47 JAMES SAMUEL
46 MARY ELIZABETH, born 1848, married, 1872, Dr N M Gailey, resident Ashland
48 RUTH ANN, born 1850, married, 1883, Samuel L Hamilton, of Ashland
49 JOHN, born 1853, married, 1881, Virginia Bowers, fruit farmer, San Diego, Cal.
50 EMMA LOUISE, born 1865, and 51 MARGARET, born 1869, resident W Springfield, Ill

GEORGE ALFRED SINCLAIR (32), brick and lumber dealer, resident Charlottesville, Va , born near Leesburg, 17th December, 1831 ; married, 24th March, 1868, Glenna Frances Dillard   Issue, resident Charlottesville, Va.

52 GEO BURNLY, born 1869   53 RUTH, born 1870   54 PEARL VIRGINIA, born 1872
55 MARY CUSTIS, born 1874   56 ALFRED BELT, born 1876, died 1877
57 JOHN A BROADUS, born 1879   58 GLENNA FRANCES, born 1889   61 PERCY
59 BESSIE BELLE, born 1884   60 CHAS SAMUEL, born 1885   62 OLIVER.

GEORGE SINCLAIR (39), born Sinclair, Ill , August 20th, 1835, married, February 16th, 1859, Sarah Gaines, farmer, resident Princeton, Minn , where he died, December, 1874. Union soldier during Civil War   Issue

63 LOVICY   64 MAGGIE   65 CHARLES

PETER AKERS SINCLAIR (42), born Sinclair, Ill., September 26th, 1840, married, 16th April, 1865, Emma Tyron, Union soldier in Civil War , farmer, resident Ashland, Ill   Issue

66 SAMUEL   67 LYLE   68 ALICE   69 VERNE   70 ROSCOE.

JAMES SAMUEL SINCLAIR (47), born Sinclair Ill.. September 15th, 1848 ; married, October, 1880, Tella Scott, Union soldier in Civil War , farmer, resident Seattle, near Washington   Issue

71 CHARLES   72 SCOTT   73 SADIE

THE SINCLAIRS OF NORTHUMBERLAND COUNTY, PENN

DUNCAN SINCLAIR (3), weaver had three brothers, Neale (4), John (5), and Archibald (6), and one sister, Margaret (7). They were all born in Scotland. Their father (1) had but one brother (2)   They fled from Scotland to the north of Ireland to escape religious or political persecution   They went there about 1762, and lived some twelve years, when the two eldest sons, Duncan and Neale, went to America in 1772, just previous to the War of Independence   John, Archibald, and the sister Margaret— who, it is believed, was then married to a Mr Robert Johnson, a teacher—came later   Mr Johnson, who was born in Scotland, settled in Washingtonville, Penn., teacher and farmer. He died about 1801   He had a son and two daughters, of whom the younger married her cousin, Robert Templeton Sinclair

DUNCAN SINCLAIR (3) was born in Scotland in 1753   He served three years as volunteer under General Green in the United States army.   He married Hannah Templeton, and died in Geneseo, New York, 5th January, 1833   Issue
    8 ROBERT TEMPLETON, born Derry, Penn , in 1797.

NEALE SINCLAIR (4) had issue
    9. JOHN SINCLAIR, who a few years ago lived near Milton, Penn

ROBERT TEMPLETON SINCLAIR (8) went with his parents in 1799 to Geneseo, N.Y., which was his home till his death   farmer. He owned the homestead near Lakeville, in

THE SINCLAIRS OF NORTHUMBERLAND CO., PENN

Geneseo, overlooking Conesus lake. He married, 10th May, 1821, his cousin, Margaret Johnson, born Washingtonville, 1799   Issue, born Geneseo

   10 JAMES, born 1822, died 1882, married, 1851, Emma Corwin, clergyman
   11 NANCY, born 1824, married, first, 1843, Jas Haynes, secondly, 1859, Revilo Bigelow
   12 JOHN HENRY, born 1826, married Fannie Corwin, clergyman, died 31st October, 1883
   13. ROBERT TEMPLETON, born 1828, married Elizabeth Haynes, farmer, resident Geneseo
   14 MARY, born 1830, died 1849   17 EDWARD PAYSON, born 1841, res New York City
   15 ELIZABETH FINNEY, born 1836, mar, 1855, Zerah Blakely, missionary, Scotland, S Dak
   16 MARGARET HANNAH, born 1838, teacher, Geneseo, died there, 1866

THE SINCLAIRS FROM PENNYCUICK, SCOTLAND

JAMES SINCLAIR (1) was born in the parish of Pennycuick, Scotland, and there he spent his life. In 1798 he married Martha Hartley   Issue

   2. ALFRED, born and died 1799   3 THOMAS   4 KATHERINE, born 1802
   5 JAMES, born 1804, died 1806   6 JAMES, born 1807
   7-8 Twins HANNAH (died young) and JEREMIAH, born 11th April, 1809
   9 ROBERT, born 1810, m Anne Robertson   10 MARTHA, born 1812, m. David Hunter
   11. MARY, born 1814, m John Richardson   12 ISABEL, born cr 1816, m John Forsyth

THOMAS SINCLAIR (3), born Pennycuick, 6th October, 1800, married, first, 13th May, 1825, Margaret Robertson, who died 1844, and secondly, Janet Cornell.   Issue

   13 ANNE, born 1826, died 1828   14 JAMES
   15 ANNE, born 1829, married Frank Mackin, resident Cleveland, Ohio
   16 THOMAS, born 1830, married Elizabeth Thompson, both deceased
   17 JEREMIAH, born 1831, died 1894   19 HUGH, born 1834, married Christiana Flucer
   18 MARGARET, born 1833, married Thos Dickson, both dead
   20 JOHN, born 1835, married Mary Baine, both dead   21 ALEXANDER BROWN.
   22 MARTHA, born 1838, married Geo Leighton, she is dead   23 ELIZABETH, born 1840
   24 DAVID, born 1841, is dead   25 CHRISTIANA, born 1842, died 1845
   26 ALISON, born 1848   27 ROBERT, born 1850   28 ISABEL, born 1852   29 HENRY, b 1854

JAMES SINCLAIR (14), born Pennycuick, July 11th, 1827; married, first, Eliza Lindsley, who died in Scotland, and secondly, Margaret Brown   He went to the United States about 1855, finally locating in New Haven, Conn   In 1858-59 he was in the employ of Joseph Parker, one of the oldest blotting paper manufacturers in the States   He did much to make it a success, and was a member of the firm at his death in 1876.   No children.

ALEXANDER BROWN SINCLAIR (21), born Pennycuick, September 5th, 1837, went to the United States in 1857   Since the war he and some of his family were engaged in the paper business   He married Augusta Clark, 20th January, 1861, and resides New Haven, Conn   Issue

   30 ISABEL ARLINDA, born 1861, married John Henry Cannon, resident New Haven
   31 THOMAS, born 16th March, 1863   32 WILLIAM, born and died 1865
   33 JAMES, born 18th May, 1866, resident Westville, New Haven   34 ALEX B, born 1872

THE SINCLAIRS FROM TIREE, ARGYLESHIRE.

DONALD SINCLAIR (1) lived in Caithness, removed to the island of Tiree, where he was factor for Mac Lean of Kingerloch who owned the island   He had a son

DONALD SINCLAIR (2), also of Tiree, whose son

PETER SINCLAIR (3), farmer, was born at Tiree in 1758, where he died *cr.* 1834. By Margaret Campbell, his wife, he had a son

REV JOHN CAMPBELL SINCLAIR (4), born in Tiree, August 15th, 1797, studied in the universities of Edinburgh and Glasgow, at which latter place he graduated. In 1838 he and his family emigrated to Picton, Nova Scotia, and he became a minister of the Presbyterian Church. His fluency as a Gaelic scholar and preacher made him very attractive to thousands of his Scottish countrymen and their descendants. In 1858 he moved to North Carolina, and after the Civil War laboured among the Freedmen until 1869, when his voice suddenly failed, the result of his open-air addresses. After 1870 he lived with his son, the Rev Alex Sinclair, and his son-in-law, the Rev. Dr. D. A Cunningham, at whose residence in Wheeling, West Va., he died, 23rd April, 1878

Mr. Sinclair married at Scalastil House, in the island of Mull, Argyleshire, in 1822, Mary Julia, daughter of John McLean, by Margaret McLean, his wife She was an orphan, and lived at Scalastil House with her cousins on her father's side. Sir Archibald McLean and Sir Hector McLean, major-generals in the British army, were her cousins She died in Pittsburg, Penn., 24th May. 1854, and is buried in the Allegheny cemetery. Issue

REV. JAMES SINCLAIR (5), born Tiree, Scotland, came to America with his parents, entered Western Theological Seminary at Allegheny City, Penn., in 1854, graduating in 1857, in which year he was called as pastor to the Presbyterian Church, Smyrna, N C In 1851 he was made chaplain of the 5th N C Infantry by Jefferson Davis He commanded half of the Regiment at Bull Run, and in December, 1861, was made Colonel of the 35th Regiment, N C After the battle of Newberne, N C, he became disgusted with the manner in which the war was conducted, resigned his position, and retired to his home He became an ardent Republican after the collapse of the rebellion, was elected to the Legislature of N C, and was appointed U.S. assessor in the district of Cape Fear by President Grant He married, first, in Prince Edward Island, in 1846, Mary, daughter of Samuel McPherson; she died in September, 1859. He married, secondly, in 1860, Mary E, daughter of Dr Edward McQueen, of Lumberton, N C, and had two children. He died at Monroe, N C, 5th August, 1877, and is buried at Lumberton, N C Issue

6 JAMES JOHN 7 JULIA, married Samuel T Neill, attorney at Titusville, Penn
8 ALEXANDER 11 EDWARD 12 CUNNINGHAM
9 MARY ELLEN } Twins, born 1857 in Sharpsburg, Penn
10 SARAH ELIZABETH
13 ANNIE, married, 24th August, 1858, Rev D A Cunningham, D D, of Wooster, Ohio
14. MARGARET, married John Q McDougald, of Fayetteville, N C
15 REV ALEX SINCLAIR

THE REV. ALEX SINCLAIR (15) was born in Mull, Scotland, 14th March, 1834 He entered the Western Theological Seminary at Allegheny. Penn, in January, 1854, graduated in 1856, and was ordained pastor of the Presbyterian Church in Sharpsburg, Penn. In 1857 he was called to the First Presbyterian Church in Charlotte, N.C., and was installed in the fall of that year. He died in Salisbury, Md., 22nd February, 1885. He married, first, Nellie Plummer, of Newburyport, Mass., who died *s p*, and secondly, Mary Laura, daughter of Adam Brevard Davidson, of Charlotte, N C. Issue.

16 BREVARD DAVIDSON 17. MARY DUART, born 28th July, 1861

18. John Campbell, born 1863, died 1864
20. Alex Peter, born 27th November, 1867
22. Richard Springs, born and died 1873
19. Alex. McLean, born and died 1866
21. Laura Virginia, born 20th Aug, 1870
23. Annie Harley, born 3rd Feb, 1875

The Rev. Brevard Davidson Sinclair (16), born at Charlotte, N C, October 31st, 1859; became a lawyer, then studied for the ministry, and lived in Newburyport, Mass., in 1892 The information of this branch of the Sinclair lineage is prepared from "An Historical Account of the Genealogy of the Children and Grandchildren of Rev. John Campbell Sinclair," written by the Rev B D. Sinclair He married, October 26th, 1887, Tabulah Rice Bair Issue :

24 Brevard Davidson, born 30th July, 1888
25 Alex Malcolm, born 5th October, 1889, at Newburyport, Mass.
26 Robert Augustus, born 27th May, 1891, at Newburyport

GENERAL ST CLAIR AND HIS DESCENDANTS.

General Arthur St. Clair (1), born in Thurso, Caithness, 23rd March, 1736, was the son of William Sinclair, merchant there He received a commission bearing date May 13th, 1757, in the 60th Regiment of Foot, and went to America with Admiral Boscawen's fleet. He served under General Amherst at the capture of Louisburg, July 26th, 1758; under Wolfe at Quebec, September 30th, 1758, and again in the victorious battle on the Plains of Abraham, September 13th, 1759 He was made a lieutenant 17th April, 1759, which position he resigned 16th April, 1762.

After the siege of Quebec he obtained a furlough, and repaired to Boston, Mass. He had formed an attachment to Miss Phœbe, daughter of Balthazar Bayard and his wife Mary Bowdoin, a half-sister of Governor James Bowdoin, and grand-daughter of Jas. Bowdoin, a wealthy citizen. The marriage was solemnized 14th May, 1760, in the Trinity Church, Boston, by the Rev William Hooper, rector. By this marriage St Clair received £14,000 from his wife's grandfather, Jas. Bowdoin He lived for a time in Boston and its vicinity, and on 20th May, 1760, bought land and buildings in Hollis St, in that city. Soon after he was a resident of Braintree, Mass, where on August 16th, 1763, he sold 19 acres of land on Boston Neck, and all interest in the Old George tavern Resigning his British commission in 1764, he and his young wife removed to Bedford, Penn., and later to a fine landed estate in the picturesque Ligonier Valley of Western Pennsylvania, where several Scottish families of consequence had already settled Here he had a great tract of land of 10,881 acres, 8,270 lying in Westmoreland County. On May 21st, 1766, he and his wife were living in St Mary's County, Md They returned to Pennsylvania, and he filled various offices On April 5th, 1770, he was appointed surveyor for district of Cumberland, and a member of the Governor's Council the same year. After 1779 he lived at Plattstown, Penn., for several years The account of his military career is relegated to the Historiettes section of this work. He died at Chestnut Ridge, Penn, August 31st, 1818. Issue

2 John Murray.   3. Daniel   4 Arthur
5 Elizabeth, born at Ft Ligonier, Penn, 1768, married, first, Captain John Lawrence, and secondly, Colonel Vance, a lawyer Her descendants have all been persons of prominent positions
6 Louisa, born in 1772, mar., 1795, Saml Robb, in Ligonier Valley, she died May 27, 1840
7 Jane, born 1774, married, cr, 1800, Samuel Jervis she died at Chestnut Ridge, Penn
8 Margaret, born 1776, died in girlhood or young womanhood

JOHN MURRAY ST. CLAIR (2), born 1762; married Jane Parker, of Allegheny County, Penn., cr. 1783   He was a farmer, residing at Chestnut Ridge, where he died March 29th, 1844, and is buried in the Ligonier cemetery   Son:

   9 ARTHUR ST. CLAIR, single, died in 1862 in Atchinson, Kansas

DANIEL ST. CLAIR (3)   Captain St Clair was born in 1764, and married in 1789 Rachel, daughter of Dr Robert Shannon, of Penn Square, Penn, where Captain St. Clair resided. Dying there in January, 1833, he was buried at Evansburg, Penn.   He was a J P., a lawyer, and a captain in the War of Independence   He was a generous man and liberally aided his less fortunate relatives   In June, 1828, he resided in Norristown, Montgomery County, Penn.   He was a lieutenant and then a captain in the 2nd Regt. Penn Line   He served from 1777 to the end of the war   In the fall of 1807 he lost his commission as captain, with other valuable papers, which were in a chest or trunk, by sudden freshet of the Ohio river   He was pensioned by the Government, and on the 17th April, 1818, he was allowed $20 a month, the pension certificate being signed by John C Calhoun, Secretary of War.   His form of signature was D S Clair   He and his sister Louisa were administrators of his father's estate   On the 30th August, 1818, he received from the Treasurer of Pennsylvania $350 pension money due his father [at the time of his death] from the State of Pennsylvania, and $400 more on November 24th, 1818, from Richard M Crain, Treasurer   Some members of the family state that the surname of his wife was not Shannon, but Knight.   Issue

   10 ARTHUR, farmer, born 16th December, 1791, at Penn Square, where he resided and died 1875, married Sarah Pugh [or Mary Fitzwater]
   11 SARAH, born May 28th, 1793, died young   13 SARAH, born Nov 25th, 1795, died young
   12 PHŒBE, born August 15th, 1794; married March, 1823, David Boyd, resident Philadelphia, where she died 1887
   14 ROBERT, born August 8th, 1798, lawyer, resident Penn Square, where he died in 1834
   15 WILLIAM, born May 4th, 1800, died young
   16 SARAH, born 15th June, 1801, died at Ligonier in 1843
   17 MARGARET BALFOUR, born 17th July, 1803, m Richd Edey, d, 1870, at Bunker Hill, Ill
   18 JAMES, born April 25th, 1805, married, 1835, Julia Edey; res. Penn Square, died 1841
   19 MARY ANN, born Dec 26th, 1807, and 20. RACHEL, born May 10th, 1810, both died young
   21 LOUISA, born 23rd December, 1811, married, first, Mr Kneit, secondly, Mr Ferguson, died, 1870, at McRug's Ft
   22. DANIEL, born August 13th, 1813, and 23 DANIEL, born June 3rd, 1815, both died young

ARTHUR ST CLAIR (4), lawyer, born 1766, married Frances Lytle or Stall   Issue.

   24 ARTHUR, married Mary, sister of Senator Lane, died s p   25 JOHN
   26 MARGARET BALFOUR, married George W Tabscott, is deceased
   27 FRANCES M, married Mr Mayo   28 LAURA, and 29 ELIZA, both single

JAMES ST. CLAIR (18) was born April 25th, 1805, married, 1835, Julia, daughter of Richard L A Edey, of Barbados, West Indies   Mr St Clair was a gentleman farmer, resident at Penn Square, where he died August 11th, 1841   Issue

   30 RACHEL, born 1837, married, first, July 26th, 1860, William A Jacoby, and secondly, 12th August, 1893, Jas A Miller, issue
   31 JULIA EDEY, born 1840, married, 14th June, 1864, Rev Jno W Geadenham, died 9th June, 1865

JOHN ST CLAIR (25), born March 2nd, 1806; married, August 26th, 1827, Ann Crooker, of Madilla, N Y   Issue.

   32 MARY, died aged 11 years   33 WILLIAM H

WILLIAM H. ST CLAIR (33) was born in Cincinnati, Ohio, May 23rd, 1828. He married, August 11th, 1857, Eliza Ann Jackson, who is deceased. He is a physician, resident at Effingham, Illinois. Issue:

    34 ARTHUR, and 35 JOHN, both are dead.
    36 WILLIAM, married to Winnie Marie Seely   37 CHARLES
    38 MAY, and 39 LAURA. One of these is Mrs Torrence, Wichita, Kansas
    40 CARRIE, married to B. T. Napier, Glenwood Springs, Col
    41 BALFOUR ("Birdie"), married Elias E Dorsey, Del Norte, Col

SCIONS FROM FRANCE

M. SINCLAIR (1), a teacher of music, resided in France, at Nantes near Paris. He had issue

    2. LEWIS GEORGE   3 CASIMIR
    4 HELEN, and 5 SIDDONIA, both of whom remained in France.

LEWIS GEORGE SINCLAIR (2) was born at Nantes in 1800. In early life he followed the sea. He went to the United States in 1816; married at New Haven, Connecticut, Jane Talmadge, a lady of the same family as De Witt Talmadge, the widely-known oratorical preacher. Mr. Sinclair died in 1860, and is still survived by his widow, who is now 88 years of age. Issue

    6. GEORGE F SINCLAIR

CASIMIR SINCLAIR (3) accompanied his brother to America and settled at Charleston, South Carolina, but owing to some misunderstanding communication between these brothers was not kept up

GEORGE F SINCLAIR (6) resides at Grand Rapids, Michigan, where he is secretary and treasurer of the Grand Rapids Brass Company

VARIOUS

PETER J. SINCLAIR (1), born in Scotland, went to the United States with his parents. He married, first, in Pittsburg, Penn, Ellen, daughter of John L. Arthur, of that city, where she died in 1873. He married, secondly, in September, 1874, Margaret Carson, of Pleasant Gardens, Marion County, N C. A lawyer by profession, he was a major in the Southern Army. After the war he resumed the practice of law. Issue of first marriage:

    2 JOHN C SINCLAIR
Issue of second marriage:
    3 MAGGIE CARSON   4. JAMES ALEXANDER

ALEXANDER SINCLAIR (1), painter by trade, was born in Paris, France, resident in Albion, New York, some 30 years ago; died about 1872 in Lockport, N Y. He married, first, Helen Kirkpatrick of Bristol, England, who died in Albion in April, 1861, and secondly, Amanda Melissa Davis, who died in Lockport, 1873. He had eight children, of whom

    2 HENRY LEON ST. CLAIR, born in Syracuse, N Y, resident in Harvard, Ill.

GEORGE ... hness, was

married to a Sutherland. He is stated to have been of the Lybster branch of Sinclairs. Issue:

ALEXANDER SINCLAIR (2), of Braemore, a glen at the foot of the Scarrabhein, in Berriedale, Caithness. He married Margaret Doull, and had issue

DR ALEX DOULL SINCLAIR (3), born Braemore, September 15th, 1828, went to United States in June, 1848, fitted for Cambridge University for the Sophomore year, then in the Lawrence Scientific School, then became a student of medicine in the medical school, and graduated in medical school, Harvard, in March, 1857, afterwards attending the medical school in Edinburgh University, 1857-58. He located in Boston, Mass, 5th November, 1858, and has been in practice since, residing at 35 Newbury Street. He married, October 4th, 1880, Ingeborg, daughter of the late Judge George Juergensen of Kiel, Schleswig-Holstein. Issue

    4 INGEBORG MARGARET, born Boston, November 1st, 1882
    5 EDITH ELLA, born Boston, July 31st, 1884

THE SINCKLERS OF BARBADOS.

POWELL SINKLER, who lived in Barbados, died in 1747. His name in his will is written thus: "Powell (his X mark) Sinkler." A crest is affixed to the will, which is said to resemble the arms of the Sinclair family of Stirkoke, Caithness. Children

    1 THOMAS SINKLER
    2 WOODROFFE SINCKLER, married a Miss Howard, and died in 1807

This family is extinct

THE SINCKLERS OF BARBADOS,

WEST INDIES

JAMES SINCKLER (1), born 1735, died 23rd August, 1788, aged 53 years, planter (i e, manager of a sugar plantation) of the parish of St George. By Mary, his wife, he had issue:

    2 JAMES   3 WILLIAM   4 ELIZABETH

JAMES SINCKLER (2), scrivener, proprietor of St George, died 31st July, 1807; married, 27th May, 1785, Jane, daughter of Edward Hall. Issue:

    5 MARY ELIZABETH, baptised 8th October, 1786, married, 26th October, 1805, John Mapp, and has issue resident in America
    6 JAMES WILLIAM   7 GEORGE EDWARD

JAMES WILLIAM SINCKLER (6), born 26th December, 1789, died 21st August, 1853, married, 30th August, 1810, Mary Elizabeth Arthur. He was medical practitioner in physic and surgery; Captain 1st or Royal Regiment of Barbadian Militia, Master Mason, Albion Lodge, No. 196, E R Barbados. Issue

    8 ELIZABETH JANE, born 13th July, 1811, married John Walcott, M D, both died in England, where they left issue sons and daughters
    9. JAMES WILLIAM.   11 JOHN GEORGE   12 FREDERICK AUGUSTUS
    10 ANNE, bapt 11th November, 1815, died *s p*, 1889, in America, m., 1838, Anthony Archer.
    13 EDWARD GRIFFITH
    14 MARY WALCOTT, born 13th February, 1828, died in America, 1884, married, 1853, Robert McAlpine, and has issue sons and daughters resident in America.

THE SINCKLERS OF BARABDOS

GEORGE EDWARD SINCKLER (7), born 28th September, 1797; married, 13th April, 1819, Margaret Ann Harding (who died 18th July, 1854, aged 61 years) and had issue

    15 GEORGE EDWARD, *d s p*   16 MARGARET ELIZABETH bap 23rd March, 1822, *d s p*
    17 THOMAS EDWARD.   18 CAROLINE JANE, born 4th March, 1826

JAMES WILLIAM SINCKLER, M D. (9), born 21st November, 1813, died in England, medical officer, police, Barbados, Master Mason, Albion Lodge, No 196, E R. He married three times: first, Lee, daughter of David Martindale, of Barbados (issue one son), secondly, Jane Paterson, Englishwoman, died *s.p*, and thirdly, Susan Glover, an Englishwoman, by whom he had two daughters, viz. .

    19 JAMES WILLIAM SINCKLER, died without issue
    20 GERTRUDE, and 21 ALICE, are resident in England

JOHN GEORGE SINCKLER (11), planter in British Guiana, was baptised February 17th, 1818 He married Elizabeth Wilson; both are dead   Issue ·

    22 LEE, married, first, Mr McCray, secondly, Mr Cuckoo, had three daughters
    23 ANNIL, born 1850, died 1892, married, 1878, John Green, an American lawyer, issue
    24 AUGUSTA, born 1853, died unmarried in America, 11th April, 1857
    25 JOHN, planter in British Guiana, accounted dead

FREDERICK AUGUSTUS SINCKLER (12), accountant, born 17th March, 1820 deceased; married, first, Ann Farr (Englishwoman), secondly, Mrs Jones (W^o o Texas, U.S A), who died *s p* Issue by first wife, two daughters

    26 FARR, and 27 ANNA, both resident in America

EDWARD GRIFFITH SINCKLER (13), clerk in Holy Orders, born 16th February, 1823; died 17th October, 1881; married, 6th October, 1853, to Henrietta Briggs (born 27th July, 1825), daughter of W. M Howard, J P, of " River " Plantation, Barbados, (member of Colonial Parliament, Master Mason, Albion Lodge), by Elizabeth Briggs, aunt to the late Sir T G Briggs, baronet   The Rev E G Sinckler was born at Wakefield House, Pinfold Street Bridgetown, then the property of his father   He received his early education at a private school in Bridgetown, and his classical education from the Rev G Duncan Gittens   In 1844 he became a student at Codrington College, where he matriculated, in 1846 he was ordained deacon, in 1847, priest   His first curacy was at Barrouallie, in the beautiful island of St Vincent, where he remained from 1846 to 1847 In the latter year he was transferred to the island of St Lucia, where he resided till the year 1851   Here he made many friends, who welcomed him back and showed him much attention when he revisited the island in 1876   In these islands he worked very hard, and succeeded in greatly improving the Cures committed to his trust. And this was no easy matter, for the means of getting from one place to another was, at that time, chiefly done by means of piroges, and it often happened—as it does now to the traveller when the currents run high—that every one in the canoe got thoroughly drenched with sea-water   On leaving St. Lucia he was presented with an address and a purse by his parishioners   In 1851 he returned to Barbados and became Curate of St Lucy's, which curacy he held till the year 1854   It was here that he became introduced to and after-wards married his wife. It was customary in those days for the officiating clergyman to wear the surplice during the reading of the prayers, etc, but always to preach in a black gown. Mr Sinckler, some time after he became curate, put away this black gown and commenced to preach in the surplice   This innovation raised a perfect *furore* of indignation amongst some of his parishioners, the controversy eventually finding its way into the newspapers, where it raged furiously for some time. In these days, when every clergyman preaches in his surplice, it seems absurd to think that the doffing of this "black gown" should have created such a commotion. While Mr. Sinckler was at St Lucy's the awful plague of cholera broke out, and that, as every one knows, was a trying time for the clergy and medical men. Such was the reign of terror in St. Lucy's, that he sometimes had to assist in putting the corpses in the coffins when the terrified relations and friends of the deceased persons had run away from the houses in the hope (perhaps after all a vain one) of escaping the plague. In 1854 he was appointed Curate of St. Michael's Cathedral Here he came in contact with the present Dean Clarke, who afterwards on several occasions proved a true friend. In 1855 he was appointed to the curacy of St Leonard's, which he held till his death in 1881 Here he worked hard for his church and his people, endeavouring to make the church beautiful in every respect and its services more attractive; and establishing, with the help of the gentry of the district, a soup kitchen (which still exists), and friendly societies and other charitable and benevolent institutions. During his time St Leonard's had the best organists and one of the finest choirs in the West Indies Just before his death he went to the United States of America for the benefit of his health, and Bishop Mitchinson did his work for him during his absence He died 17th October, 1881, and was laid to rest beneath the shadow of the church he loved so well He had been offered two rectories, but refused them On his death his congregation added an aisle to the church in his memory. The following is the inscription "St Leonard's Church, 21st September, 1882 The Feast of St. Matthew, Apostle, Evangelist and Martyr To the Greater Glory of God and in pious remembrance of Reverend E G. Sinckler The corner stone was laid by the Right Reverend Herbert Bree, D D, the first year of his Episcopate, assisted by His Excellency Governor William Robinson, C.M G" Issue

  28 EDWARD MURRELL, born 30th May, 1854, died 3rd June, 1854
  29 HENRIETTA BEATRICE, born 12th August, 1855, died in London, 9th May, 1861
  30 EDWARD GOULBURN, born 19th November, 1856
  31 WILLIAM MURRELL HOWARD, born 17th April, 1859
  32. LEONARD FRANCIS, born 29th January, 1863, in United States of America
  33 HENRIETTA ALEXANDRIA BEATRICE MARY, born 14th April and died 6th December, 1864
  34 CYRIL PACE, born 12th January, 1866, is in Colonial Secretary's Department, Barbados

THOMAS EDWARD SINCKLER (17), baptised 2nd February, 1824, married Susan Philipps; both are deceased Issue

  35 FABIAN THOMAS, died without issue
  36 SUSAN ADELINE, born 22nd November, 1805, married, 4th June, 1887, George Whitfield Smith, and has issue resident in Grenada, West Indies
  37 REYNOLD RUSSELL, born 4th October, 1857, married, 15th December, 1887, Mary Willoughby Clarke, is manager of the Telephone Co, Barbados
  38 EDITH EMINA, born 22nd December, 1859

EDWARD GOULBURN SINCKLER (30), J.P. (Court of Appeal, Barbados), born 19th November, 1856; entered the Colonial Secretary's office, Barbados, in November, 1874, acted as clerk to Lieut.-Governor, 1878, second clerk, correspondence branch, Colonial Secretary's office, 1879; acting assistant clerk to His Excellency Governor W Robinson, 1880; first clerk, record branch, Colonial Secretary's office, and clerk, court of ordinary and error, January, 1883; acting chief clerk, 1886, commissioner of census, 1891; chief clerk to judges, 1892, J P., October, 1892, acting registrar friendly societies, June, 1893, acting senior police magistrate, Bridgetown and District "A," August to October, 1893; acting police magistrate and judge, District "F," Barbados, 1896. Married, December

THE SINCKLERS OF BARBADOS.

12th, 1883, Eva Douglas (born March 1st, 1858), daughter of J. C. Richards, J.P. (deceased), of "Holder's" Plantation, Barbados (member of Colonial Parliament; high position among the Freemasons—a Knight Templar), by Mary Elizabeth (deceased), grand-daughter of James Douglas,* of the "Bath" Plantation and of London, who married a Miss Lessingham. Issue :

39. EVA BEATRICE, born 13th September, 1885.

---

*CREST on all the old family silver and buttons : Heart with wings.

HIS EXCELLENCY MAJOR-GENERAL ARTHUR ST. CLAIR,
GOVERNOR NORTH-WEST TERRITORY, U.S.A.

CHAPTER XVII.

GUILLERMUS,

GODFATHER OF THE GENS.*

"S. CLARUS, sive Guillermus, patria Scotus, in Gallia eremiticam egit vitam, et ibi tandem martyrio coronatur Scripsit Divini Officii Formulas, lib i Claruit anno circiter DC. Colitur 17 Julii Memoria ejus conservatur in villa Neustria ejus nominis, in publico ad Rotomagum itinere " St Clair, or Guillermus, was Scottish by country. He wrote the "Ritual of Divine Duty" (1 vol), and lived the life of a hermit close to a well to which those whose sight is affected still make pilgrimages He flourished about 600 A D , and is worshipped on the 17th of July † His memory is preserved in the town of St Clair-sur-Epte—noted also as being the place where Rollo the Northman acquired Neustria by cession from Charles the Simple—and thus originates the surname of the Orcadian "St Clairs of the Isles," their ancestor Walter, Count of St Clair, being designated from his territorial possessions

The French town is situated near and north-east of Vernon, and is two hours' ride from Paris The site of the hermit's abode is one mile distant from the railway station at St Clair. It is situated on a rich and fertile plain among tall trees on the bank of the river Epte Passing through the unlocked gate, one soon reaches the "Holy Well" of St Clair, which is surrounded by an iron railing, and is some four feet in length, three in width, and four in depth, with a brick or cemented bottom Its clear and limpid waters are reached by three stone steps. At one end is a half-circular piece of stone masonry, six feet or more in height, surmounted by a ball of stone, and this by a stone cross Inside of this structure, in a niche two feet from the floor, is a statue of St. Clair, made of the soft stone of the country. In his hands he bears his dissevered head, for he was executed by direction of a cruel woman whose crimes he had sharply rebuked.

Passing through another gateway, in a high faced stone wall, his hermitage is reached This wall surrounds a plot of ground some fifteen rods in length by eight rods in width. Another wall divides this from a cultivated garden, filled with fruit trees and with vines The wall separates the land devoted to cultivation from that dedicated especially to the honour of St. Clair. The latter is some seven rods in length by five rods in width. At regular intervals there are niches in the walls filled with statues of different individuals. In a recess, with a roof rising from the top of the wall, is the hermitage Its floor is of stone, rising six inches from the ground. Within is a stone altar two feet or more in height, on which is a representation of the Crucifixion and Christ's descent from the cross, while near at hand are His devoted female followers. This is surrounded upon the wall by flying angels bearing a scroll or robe On the right of this scene is a statue of St Clair with his neck protruding from his clothes, while within his hands is

---

*This notice is prepared from "Sinclair Family " by Morrison † Sinclairs of England

his ghastly head with face upturned towards the heavens. In this shrine of the hermit there is another altar some three feet high, where often many candles are kept burning. On the outer wall are various figures, while upon its front are these words:

> "ICY EST LE VERITABLE HERMIT
> AGE, OU LE BIEN HEUREUX ST.
> CLAIR AVES, CU, ET AETED ECOL'E,
> ET MARTYR ISE. EN L'AN, 884."

The chapel faces the hermitage. It is a one-storey building constructed of light stone, and its four roofs come to a point at the top, above which is a bell, surmounted by a roof of slate about two feet square, and this is capped by a weather vane,—a cock. The roof of the chapel is of tile. The entrance is surmounted by a ball of stone and a stone cross. Each corner is capped by a ball of stone at least eight inches in diameter. The two Norman windows and door are of equal height, and the coloured glass is protected by iron bars. Inside the chapel there is room for some thirty people. Facing the entrance is a stained glass window, and also one window on each side. At the end of the chapel, facing the entrance, is an upraised altar, upon which are the crucifix, the holy candles, and the vases of flowers. On either side, in niches in the wall, are statues, in front of which are often kept candles burning. In the church there is the chapel of St. Clair. Upon a pedestal is placed a statue of the holy man, while his head is plastered upon the front of the upraised platform which holds his statue.

The Dict. of Christian Biography, vol i. (London, 1877), contains notices of nine saints named CLARUS. The account there given states that the Clarus from whom St. Clair-sur-Epte is named was a personage of the ixth century, a native of Rochester, who settled in Vexin, in the diocese of Rouen.

CHAPTER XVIII

ORCADIAN FAMILIES*

AN OUTLINE

BAIKIE —This name has long been identified with the Orcadian mainland, and is considered to be the diminutive of *beck*—a stream The earliest notice of the surname is to be found in the Rental of Merwick (*pro Rege*) 1595, where Henry Baky is noted as having excambed land in Ysbustar, Marwick, for *ob terre* in Tronston In 1623 James Baikie purchased the first part of the estate of Tankerness In 1686 James Baikie of Tankerness received a Grant of Arms, and in 1780 Robert Baikie of Tankerness was elected to represent Orknay and Zetland as an M P for the United Kingdom, but was unseated on petition A fuller account appears in Burke's "Landed Gentry," which see

BALFOUR.—The Balfours were hereditary sheriffs of Fife, and the name is derived from Balfour Castle, in the vale or Strath of Or, a tributary of the Leven The first ancestor on record is one Siward, in the reign of Duncan I (1033) The Orcadian line was founded by Sir Gilbert Balfour, Master of the Household to Mary, Queen of Scots He married Margaret Bothwell, stepdaughter of Oliver Sinclair of Pitcairns, and sister of Adam, Bishop of Orknay and Zetland, who granted a charter 30th June, 1560, to Gilbert Balfour and Margaret Bothwell, his wife, of lands in Westray. This was followed by grants of other church lands in Westray, Sanday, Stronsay, and S. Ronaldsa Mrs Brunton, the novelist, author of "Self Control" and "Discipline," was a daughter of this family, which has on three occasions represented the Earldom in the Parliament of the United Kingdom, and has ever been identified with movements tending to advance Orcadian interests David Balfour, late of Balfour and Trenaby, prepared the "Memorial for Orkney"—a lucid exposition of its "Odal Rights and Feudal Wrongs" For further particulars of this family the reader is referred to Burke's "Landed Gentry"

BEATTOUN —This family is stated to derive originally from France, where the spelling is "de Bethune" David de Betune is mentioned as a Scottish baron in 1289 The Scottish scions acquired importance through the eminence of the Cardinals so named It is not clear whether the Orcadian Beattons are indigenous, or Scottish offshoots. As early as 1503 Symon or Sigmund Beatoun is noticed in the Stromness Rental, and Jas. and John Beatoun are in that of Orphir The lineage continues numerous in the same locality.

BELLENDEN —Oliver Sinclair of Pitcairns held the Isles in tack 1540-48, and was married to Katherine Bellenden, relict of Francis Bothwell, Provost of Edinburgh,— one of the fifteen original Senators of the College of Justice, founded in 1532 The intermarriages of the Bellendens with the Bothwell-Sinclair connection account for

---
* Peterkin's Rentals etc

Sir Ludovic Bellenden obtaining a similar grant later on [1587] His widow married Earl Patrick of Orkney, who thus acquired a large jointure. For some time after this the Bellendens appear as holders of lands in Stenhouse and Evie In 1595 Sir Patrick Bellenden holds various Orkney lands in feu. There is a peerage dormant in this family. In 1565 Patrick Bellenden was Provost of Kirkwall

BORWICK —Perhaps the Scottish baronial family may be traced to one of the places in Orkney thus named The Borthwicks always appear in close connection with the St. Clair Earls In 1514 Alexander Borthwick attests the decree of Tohop and he is doubtless the legatee of that name in Sir David Synclar's will in 1506.

CLOUSTON.—On the 22nd March, 1503, it is noted Earl William of Orkney had bought from Evot, spouse of umquhile John Cloustane, a penny land in Garmistane, Sandwick Clouston is a sixpenny land in the same parish. The word is also spelled Cloustaith, and William Cloustaith attesting to the above fact will doubtless be the William Clouthcath, Rothman, present at the adjudication of Tohop in 1514 The family is very numerous in the neighbourhood of Stromness

CORRIGALL of that Ilk —The town of Corrigall (anciently Corgill) is a twopenny land in Harra, where are also the Kame, the Dale, and the Burn of Corrigall. The members of this family are noticed as "of that Ilk" in Orcadian records, where their names appear frequently, and occasionally throughout this work.

CRAIGIE —James af Cragy, laird of Hupe [Westray], is mentioned in 1422 as having married Margaret, daughter of Earl Henry I. of Orkney, by [son of] Elisabeth, daughter of the late reverend and venerable Malise, Earl of Orkney. Johannes de Krage is mentioned in the Complaint of 1426, and in or about 1446 Joan Cragy, "my armig," attests the Diploma of Succession prepared by Bishop Thomas Tulloch In 1504 John Cragy is *legifer*, while James of Cragy, his wyff, and Sir Thos Cragy are also on record In 1514 Hendrie, Thomas, and Nicoll, brether-german to umqle. John of Cragy, affirm the conveyance of Tohop In 1529 James Cragy of Brogh, Gilbert Cragy, William Cragy, and John Cragy of Banks fought at Summerdale, and were respited in 1539, while in 1544 James of Brugh attested the Deed of Erection for the Cathedral Chapter of Orkney. At various times Craigies have represented the Earldom in Parliament The family seat was at Gairsay, and the arms, according to Nisbet, are Ermine, a boar's head, couped *gules*, armed and langued *or* Crest a boar passant *argent*, armed and langued *azure* Motto Timor omnis abest The ruins of their mansion-house, supposed to have been built at the end of the 17th century, are to be seen on the south shore of Gairsay At that period the Craigies were a distinguished family, and the loop-holes in the building show that they were in a position to defend themselves from intruders Just outside the mansion there are the ruins of an old chapel Hugh Craigie was M.P for Orkney and Zetland in the Scottish Parliament, 1661-63, Sir William Craigie of Gairsay, 1681-82, 1689, 1689-1702; David Craigie of Over-Sanday, M.P for Kirkwall, 1681-82, 1685-86, and Robert Craigie of Glendoig, Lord Advocate, M P for the Tain Burghs (including Kirkwall) in the Imperial Parliament, 1742-47 Patrick Craigie was Provost of Kirkwall in 1660, and Hugh Craigie in 1691 William Craigie of Gairsay is mentioned 8th November, 1640 On 25th May, 1670, David Craigie of Over-Sanday desired at a Sederunt (the Lord Bishop being present) "in respect his umquhile brother, Hugh Craigie of Gairsay, left in legacie to the church £5 sterling, which himself had delivered to the church thesaurer (as was well knawn to the members of the session), that the burial place, quhich is beside the sixt and sevent pillar from the west church dore on the south syde, where his father, mother, and foresaid brother lyis all interred, may be appropriated to ther familie, and that no other persone have privilege to bury the died ther, which desire my Lord Bishope and session thought reasonable, and hes appropriate the said ground to their familie, with this provision, that they hold up the glasse window above the said burial-place." The name is also spelled "Croy"

CROMARTY.—This is a family of numerical strength in the South Isles, especially in South Ronaldsa In 1502 Magnus Cromertie has Arneip viz. Burvik, and Quyscharpis, which latter is possessed by John Crommarty of Cara in 1595. Johnne and Magnus Cromarte fought at Summerdale 1529, and received remission 1539. In 1640 John Cromartie, younger, was bailie for South Ronaldsa. Adam Cromarty, tacksman of South Ronaldsa, held Paplay there in 1595.

CURSETTER of that Ilk —Cursetter is a threepenny land in Firth. Magnus Cursetter in that Ilk is confirmed by Lord Robert Stewart, 3rd May, 1581, in his lands of Wasdale, Setter, Bingascart, and Rossmyre, of which he and his predecessors "have been in peacable possession past memorie of man"

DISCHINGTON —William de Dischington received from King Robert Bruce the lands of Balglassie, Aberlemno, and others in Forfar Prior to the year 1330 he married Elisabeth, the king's younger sister Of his two sons, John, the younger, obtained the lands of Langhermiston. William, the elder, was, by David II, his cousin, knighted and appointed steward of the palace In 1368 he received a royal charter of a third part of the barony of Ardross, Fife, in succession to his relative John Burnard, and also the same year a charter of the lands of Kynbrachmont A skilful architect, he constructed the castle of Ardross, and the church of St. Monan's, which latter was erected at the cost of David II to denote his gratitude to God for being preserved from a storm which overtook him and his queen, Margaret de Logie, when crossing the firth to visit William de Dischington at Ardross The Dischingtons continued in Fife till 1673 In 1549 Margaret Dischington is noted as wife of Edward Sinclair of Strome, and as being under the special protection of Bishop Reid In 1583 John Dischington, a younger son of the Laird of Ardross, passed to Orkney, and was acknowledged as a relative by Earl Patrick Stewart, who appointed him Sheriff and Commissary of Orkney and Zetland. Several of his descendants figure as officers in the royal navy and as ministers of the church.

FEA.—This is the name of several places in Orkney It is pronounced in two syllables, with stress on the first as indicated by diæresised e Two hundred years ago it was one of the mediatised families in the Isles On the old house of Stove—their mansion in the Isle of Sanday—was this inscription "Soli Deo gloria Septem proavi hæc nobis reliquerunt J F (Jacobus Fea) B T (Barbara Traill), 1671." "These *septem proavi* were all direct ascendants, all of the same name, James Fea, and holders of the same property and title, 'Clestron'" Over the door of the house of Whitehall stood the initials "P F" and "B.T" and the date 1671. The latter was the family residence in the Isle of Stronsay. James Fea, of Stowe and Clestran, gave evidence on oath before Bishop Graham, 25th June, 1627, Oliver and Robert Fia had been sworn in like manner at Stronsay the day preceding. Oliver and Malcolm Feas were bailies for Stronsa in 1640 In 1711 James Fea had a chaplain in his family upon whom also devolved the education of the children, and in 1714 he erected near his mansion house of Stove a handsome little Gothic chapel with nave and chancel, and vaulted roofs, supported on fourteen pillars, the Fea burial place being in the chancel. This gentleman first introduced into Orkney the manufacture of kelp. His son James Fea, a Jacobite, captured Gow the Pirate in 1725, and is said to have been ruined by the vexatious suits brought against him for his share of the prize money *

FLETT.—Harald Flett, Danish by family, had a son Swend, who became a great viking and champion. He was a very clever man, and of high birth in his own country. He was fostered by Thorer of Steige, and was very dear to King Hakon of Norway, on whose death (in 1093) he led an army against his successor. Winning one or two engagements, he was eventually defeated and fled to Denmark, and remained there; and at last came into great favour with King Eystein, the son of King Magnus, who took so great a liking to Swend that he made him his dish-bearer, and held him in great respect. The dish bearer was an office of dignity, equivalent to the chamberlain in modern courts—the *dapifer*. Guttorm, son of Harald Flittr, was a king's officer at Konghelle [1135]. About 1136 Thorkell Flett, a violent and powerful man, lived in Westray. Thorkell contributed a ship, which he commanded in person in the naval engagement between Earl Paul and Olvir Rosta. He received from Paul the lands in Stroma, which had been owned by Valthiof Olaf-Rolfsson, a fatal gift, for Valthiof's kinsmen attacked and burnt him in the house there. His son Haflidi was commander of a ship under Earl Rognvald. Wilhelm Flett is referred to in the complaint of 1426, and Kolbein Flæt appends his seal to same. In the rentals of 1503 Johne Flet has Hundskarth (Harray), and Cloustaith (Stanehous), and Sir Robert Flett is noted as having "of lait (1503) bocht fra ane uthalman iij d terre in Lyrland als Leyland" (St. Cross, Sanday). In 1506 Sir David Sinclair leaves "to William Flete and his bruder Criste Flete my littil schipe, wyth al geir, and all my landis in Orknaye with my iunes in Kyrkwall excep Setter and Vactesquyr." In 1514 Johnne Flett of Harray is one of the Council of Lawmen at Kirkwall. In 1525 Robert Flett attests probate of Sir David Sinclair's will. Arms —*Argent*, a chev between three trefoils, sa.

FOTHERINGHAME.—In the Seals in the British Museum there is one, of date 1170, of Sir Hugh de Fotheringay, or Fotheringham, and one of similar arms in use in 1459 by David de Fotheringham of Powrie in Forfarshire, ancestor of the family so designated. In 1440 Richard Fodringame, Lawrik man at Kirkwall, appends his seal to the Diploma; in 1502 William Fotheringhame is noted as of Hermausgarth, in St Colm's, Sanday; and in 1640 Jerome Fothringhame is a bailie for that Isle.

FOUBISTER of that Ilk.—In 1502 the fourpenny land of Fowbustare was in the parish of St. Andrews. Hendrie Fowbuster is a Rothman of Orkney at Kirkwall, June, 1514. John Fowbister is of that Ilk, 1613, and Malcolm Foubister of that Ilk is noticed 1617–61.

GARRIOCK.—This family apparently commences with a South country immigrant, or the name may derive from Garek, as in Gareksay, or Gairsay. Henry Garoch is named in the Complaint of 1426. In 1502 Henry Gareoch is assessed for the lands of Brugh and Terland in Ronaldsa. Magnus Gariacht fought at Summerdale 1529. In 1640 Magnus Gareoch in Braquoy is a bailie for Holm.

GORDON.—This family has sustained two or three changes of name. Originally surnamed Winton, by marrying the heiress of the Setons the latter name was assumed,

* Craven

and some generations later, upon marrying the heiress of the Gordons, a similar change was made. The Huntly and Sutherland Gordons are all of the Winton stock. After the storming of Dornoch in 1570, Hugh Gordon of Drummoy retired to Orkney, where he married one Ursula Tulloch. He was a cadet of the Sutherland Gordons, and is probably ancestor of the family of Gordons who a little later are found permanently connected with the lands of Cairston, Stromness.

GRÆME.—Donald Greme held Nether Knarstane in 1502. The principal Græmes in Orkney were, however, descendants of Bishop Geo. Graham (a cadet of Braco, in Perth), who gave origin to two families—the Græmes of Græmeshall, and those of Breckness, the latter being now represented by Watt of Breckness and Skaill. Harie Graham of Breckness was M.P. for Orkney in the Scots Parliament (1686-89). Admiral Patrick Græme was of the Græmshalls. A fuller account of the family, their arms, etc., is to be found in the article Sutherland-Græme in Burke's "Landed Gentry."

GROAT.—This family comes from Caithness (Scottish Orcadia), where Hugh Grot is noticed as early as 1496, and a very clear succession is illustrated from old inventories down to 1741. Malcolm Groat of Tankerness, 1570, appears in the Rentals of 1595. In 1627 William Grott is of Tankerness, and Johnne Grott of Traistads, Sanday. The Groats held a good position in Orkney until recent times.

HALCRO of that Ilk.—This family commences with Andrew Halcro of Halcro (then pronounced Hawcro), mentioned in 1544 as dead. The first appearances of the name in earldom records are these—1519, *sir* Hugh Halcro and sir Nicol Halcro, priests in Orkney; 1525, Nicoll Hawcro of Tygwall, Shetland; 1530, sir Nicoll Halcro, rector of Orphir, Mr. Malcum Hawcro, Archdean of Zetland and Canon of St Magnus; 1539 schir Nycholl Halkraye is parson of Orfer, in Orknaye and on the 20th Janr., 1544, *apud* Halcro, the sons and heirs of the quondam Andrew Halcro *de eodem*, viz., Hugh Halcro, Canon of the Eccles. Chapter of Orknay, and Mr Malcolm Halcro, Provost of the said church, and Archdeacon of Zetland, with consent of Elizabeth Halcro, their sister, spouse of Gilbert Moody, issue a charter of lands, various, of Halcro, alias Holland, etc., in Rannaldsay, to their cousin Hugh Halcro—remainder to Ninian Halcro, his brother, Edward Halcro, his brother-german, Henry, son of quondam Magnus Halcro—James, brother of Henry, Magnus, son of the quondam Andrew Halcro, and William, son of quondam John Halcro, without division between brothers and sisters, but according to the custom in Scotland. The instrument establishing the Cathedral Chapter of Orkney, 28th October, 1544, enumerates Mr Malm. Halcro Bachelor in Sacred Letters, Prebend in St. Trinity, and Vicar of Rannaldsay, with sustentation of the Church of Barwick, also Archdeacon of Zetland, *dominus* Nicholas Halcro, Prebend of Orphar and Vicar of Stanhous; and *dominus* Hugh Halcro, Prebend of St Magnus': the two first attest execution of the deed. In 1548 Patrick Mowat of Balquholly entered into a contract with Malcolm Halcro of that Ilk for the marriage of their son and daughter. A charter about this time from Balquholly to Halcro mentions several carnal sons of the latter, some being in holy orders. Magnus Halcro married Margaret, heiress of Sir James Sinclair of Sanday and the Lady Barbara Stewart, and for the next two or three generations the Halcros are found matching with the more powerful families in the Isles, the Sinclairs, Stewarts, Moodies, Mowats, Bellendens, etc. In St. Mary's Kirk, S Ronaldsa are the chalice, cross, and arms of *sir* Hugh Halcro of Halcro, who died 20th August, 1545. In 1581 a grant of Cava issued to William Halcro of Aikeris, now represented by John Halcro of Hogarth, in Rendall, who is also "af Halcro," the senior branch of the family having become extinct towards the close of the xviiith century. A certain knight, Sir Hauq'n, is a witness at Kirkwall, 23rd April, 1391. The earlier history of this family is difficult to unravel. Perhaps the solution may lie in the Vatican Library. Unmentioned in the national documents of Orkney until 1519, they presently appear in full canonicals, possessing offices, power, wealth, houses, and lands. They are not noted in the Rental of 1503, nor in the Respite of 1539, yet in 1544 the charter discloses several families of the name. It may be that they received their name from the picturesque headland so styled in S. Ronaldsa, but even that is not clear, for the lands were also called Holland. A Certificate of Character was given to Margaret, lawful daughter of the late Hugh Halcro, in the Isle of Weir, and Margaret Stewart, his spouse, which has, "As also, that she is descended of her father, of the house of Halcro, which is a very ancient and honourable family in the Orkneys." Kirk of Evie, 27th May, 1606. This clearly implies an Orcadian establishment of more than two generations, or only sixty years.

HARCUS.—In early Scottish records Alan de Harcarres and William de Harkars are noted 1250-1350. Robert Harechas was Sheriff of Perth in 1305. The arms of Harcarse of that Ilk, Berwick, are cited in the Catalogue of Seals, British Museum. Members of the Orkney family first come before us in the Respite of 1539 for complicity in connection with the Battle of Summerdale, 1529. That parchment includes the names of Robert, Johnne, and George Hercas, being three out of thirty-one names enumerated, a very fair percentage, indicative of the relative importance of the family at that time. The name sometimes appears written as Arcus.

HEDDLE of Haddale in the parish of Firth. Wilhelm de Hedal is referred to in the Complaint of 1426. In the Rental of Stanehouse, 1503, John Haddale has lands in Garmistane there, and William Haddale bears witness to a conveyance of Garmistane lands. Harrie Haddell, of that Ilk, is reported as absent from the Sederunt of the *Curia Vicecomitatus*, 4th November, 1617, held in the Palace of the Yairds in Kirkwall, and on 14th January, 1640, Harie Haddell of Haddell is noted as similarly absent. James Haddell, indweller in Shapinsa, is one of the Islesmen whose advice is sought as to the estate of that Isle, 24th June, 1627. He is the James Haddell of Elwick who gave similar information upon oath on the 13th June, same, relative to Shapinsa. James Haddell and Walter Haddell in Lintoun are appointed with others as bailies for the Isle of Shapinsa, 4th November, 1640. See Burke's "Landed Gentry" for later account of this name.

HOURSTON is a sixpenny land in North Sandwick. It is spelled in 1503 as Thurstacht. In 1544 Peter Hourstoun is Rector of Hoy and Vicar of Walls. In 1640 Hew and Magnus Hourstoun were appointed bailies or superintendents for Sandwick and Evie respectively.

IRVING.—William de Irwin was secretary and armour-bearer to Robert Bruce, and subsequently Master of the Rolls. Bruce gave him in free barony the lands of Drum, 1324. He had two sons, Sir Thomas, successor to Drum, and William de Erwin, an inhabitant of Kirkwall in 1369. The complaint of 1426 mentions Wilhelm Yrving "John off Eiwyne" is mentioned 1438 (Wilson's Prehist. Annals), and in the Rental for Hurray Brugh in 1503 it is noted that Earl William St. Clair (1420–71) exchanged with Elizabeth Urving the lands of Garth and Midgarth in Harray for three merks land in "Claistrand apud Orphair" James Irwine "Lawman," or Chief Judge (*Legifer*) of the Orkneys in 1560, was father of Magnus of 1608, the first Shapinsha Irving, ancestor of the celebrated Washington Irving, from whose "Life and Letters" this notice is in great part extracted The Irvings of Sabay were also a principal family of this name.

ISBISTER of that Ilk.—The place is noted in 1503 as Eisterbuster, ninepenny udal land, and in 1595 as Ysbustar At the latter date a Robert Isbuster is resident in Birsay Be-South. Henceforward various Isbusters pass under review.

JOHNSTON.—This name, more properly John's son, is, of course, a general one, and it is thus difficult to identify the various families as being derived from a common ancestor In 1369 Hakon Jonsson was Norwegian prefect of Orkney. Erengisle, Earl of Orkney, 1353, was the son of Sune Johnson, and in 1360 one William Johnsson was Archdeacon of Hjaltland, and he is supposed to be identical with Bishop William V, 1382-94. There is, however, no known connection with the Annandale Johnstons, and the rarity in Orkney prior to 1550 of the personal name John renders it probable that most of the families now so named are not only indigenous Orcadians, but of the same stock. The Complaint of 1426 notes Malcolm, John, and Nicol Johnsson, and the Rental of Deirness, 1502, finds Andro Johnstoun in Sanday there, while in North Sandvik, 1503, Christie Johnesoun has Hammerclet in Scalbrycht (Scabra)

JOHNSTON of Coubister.—James Johnston of Outbrecks, in Stromness, was succeeded by a younger brother Richard, a Stromness merchant, about 1690. Their father had come from Birsay and bought that property. Richard's only son, John, born in 1690, also a merchant in Stromness, acquired considerable property throughout the Islands, including one-third of Stromness His son Joshua, a lawyer in Stromness, married Margaret Halcro, heiress of Coubister, Cava, and Gyre Their son. John Johnston of Coubister, sold all the Johnston property. A sister of Joshua Johnston married Adam Irvine, and they settled in Canada Among their descendants may be mentioned the late Colonel Irvine, A.D.C. to the Governor-General, and his sons, the late Colonel Acheson Irvine, the Hon. George Irvine, at present a judge, and the late Commissary-General Bell Irvine Joshua's brother John also settled in Canada, and is now represented by Lady Meredith, widow of the late Chief Justice of Quebec A sister of the late James Johnston of Coubister (son of John Johnston of Coubister) married Commander John Nugent, R N. (son of Count Nugent of Balinacorr), with whom Mr Johnston served as a midshipman during the war of 1812-1814. Mr Johnston's son, the present laird of Coubister, is best known from the interest he takes in farming in Orkney, having revived and successfully carried on the Orkney Agricultural Society Mr Johnston and his brothers, and their sons, are the only male representatives of this family of Johnston in Orkney, tracing at least as far back as 1560. The tradition in their family is that their ancestor was a son of the laird of Annandale, who, as the result of a border feud, had to go into exile, and fled to Orkney, where he lived in hiding among the Birsay folk as one of themselves, and where his family afterwards remained *

KIRKNESS of Kirkness, in Sandwick —Sir Thomas of Kirkness is a witness at Kirkwall, 13th April, 1391, to a conveyance executed by Henry I., Earl of Orkney, to his brother David St Clair On 6th March, 1503, in noting the lands of Over Garsend, in North Sandwick, there is a reference to a Sir Stevenissonn and Johne of Kirknes sone,

---

* Contributed by Alfred W Johnston youngest son of the late James Johnston of Coubister

ORCADIAN FAMILIES.

as subject to rent charge. In 1611 letters were issued against William Kirkness for assisting Robert Stewart, Bastard of Orkney

KNARSTON of that Ilk in Harra —In 1503 Nerstaith was a fourpence halfpenny udal land William Knarston is noted in 1595 and Gilbert Knarston of Knarston 1617-40, when the latter is bailie for Harra.

LAING of Strynzie —In the list of voters for Kirkwall, 1800, Robert Laing, Esq (of Strynzie), last Provost, Gilbert Laing, merchant, and Malcolm Laing, Esq , advocate, are enumerated. The latter, who was born at Strynzie in 1762, was the celebrated historian of Scotland He represented Orkney and Shetland in the Parliament of the United Kingdom, 1807-12. Later on Samuel Laing of Crook has at various times been returned for the Northern electorates, 1852-85, and has been secretary to the Treasurer and Finance Minister for India. Samuel Laing the elder was the translator of the "Heimskringla." The Weirs of Damsay registered arms in 1801 quartering Laing thus 2nd and 3rd *Ar* three piles in point *sa* in middle chief a martlet *or*

LEASK of that Ilk —Leask is located in Buchan Thomas de Laysk is a witness at Kirkwall 23rd April, 1391 James Leask appends his seal to the Diploma at Kirkwall, *circiter* 1446. On June 21st, 1484, Alex. Lesk is mentioned *re* the farms of Sanday, and in 1497, Lord St Clair's accounts for Orkney are rendered pr. Alex Lask In 1506 Sir David Sinclair appoints Richard Lesk co-executor of his will, and leaves him " 20 merkis landis in Cwndistay and my Inglis schipe with all geir." The arms of this family are *Sa* A fesse between three mullets in chief and as many mascles in base Crest . A crescent *ar* Motto Virtute cresco.

LINKLATER of that Ilk, North Sandwick —In 1505 Lynkclet was a threepenny land. The Complaint of 1426 enumerates amongst other nobles Christian de Ellingeklat Andro Linclett is one of the Council of Lawmen in 1515 John Linkleter is mentioned in 1595. In 1621 Andro Linklatter is of that Ilk, and in 1640 three are appointed bailies James for Harra, Henrie for Rendell, and Alexander Linkletter of Linklatter for Sandwik There is a place similarly named in South Ronaldsa.

LOUTTIT.—Maurice Lowtefute appears in the Exchequer Rolls of 1456 as collector of the ferms of Stratherne. In 1426 Paris Lutzit, a dependent of Thomas Sinclair, mandatary for Earl William, complained of having been imprisoned by David Menzies In 1502 Olay Loutfut has Sandisand and Gloupquoy in Dourness ; 1503, Dowskarth, Stennis is noted as pertening to the heirs of the Lutfuttis ; James Loutfut has Netherlyking in South Sandwik ; and Peiris Loutfut has then Howth in Orphir, the last is a Rothman at Kirkwall, June, 1514 Johne Louttit fought at Summerdale 1528 Magnus Louttit of Lyking has notices 1595-1653, and many others appear during and after that period

MONCRIEFF.—John Moncrieffe of Rapness (said to be a son of Sir John Moncrieff of Moncrieff by Beatrix Forman) was father of David of Rapness, who married, first, Barbara Baikie of Tankerness, and secondly, Mary Nisbet of Swannie By the first marriage he had Thomas, clerk of the exchequer and treasury, who was created a baronet of Nova Scotia, 1685, and dying *s p* , was succeeded by his nephew, Thomas of Rapness. For fuller account see Baronetage works James Moncrieffe was M P for Kirkwall in the Scottish Parliament, 1669-74

MOODIE.—This family has generally been considered as indigenous to Orkney, and even attributed to Harald Mudadson, whose male issue, Buchanan informs us, were all carefully emasculated by William the Lion. The Moodies are more likely Scottish. In 1455 William Mudy, Bishop of Caithness, gave church lands to his nephew Gilbert, and also the castles of Scrabster and Skibo; confirmation issued in 1478. Sir Thos. Moody witnesses a deed by William Tulloch, Bishop of Moray, in 1481. Lands in Hoy in 1503 are held "*In manibus Magistri Willielmi Mudy*, while in 1506 Sir David Sinclair leaves " to Jhone Mude xx. merkis the quhilk I bocht fra him in Scatness and the ful payment tharof." In 1567 *Magister* William Mudie of Breckness, and Katharine Sinclair, his wife, received a grant of lands in the Utter Town of Stromness. The Moodies of Melsetter were an important family in Orkney. James Moodie, younger of Melsetter, was M P. in the U K Parliament for Orkney and Zetland in 1715-22. Nisbet (1700) states, "it is an old family in Orknay, upwards of 400 years standing, who have possessed several lands in Caithness since 1470. Captain James Moodie, late commander of H.M ship "Prince George," for his merit and great services done to Her Majesty Queen Anne, and in particular for relieving the town and castle of Denia in Spain, when besieged by the French in 1707 and 1708, was honoured by Queen Anne with a coat of augmentation to his arms " The ancient coat of Mudie of Melsetter was . *Az*. a chevron ermine between three pheons, *or* in a chief a hunting horn Motto . " God with us."

MOWAT.—The Norman form of this name was Monhault, invariably Latinised into Monte Alto—the high mount Like the Sinclairs, before reaching Scotland and Orcadia they passed through England, and were Welsh Lord Marchers. Sir William of Montealt obtained from King William the Lion (1165-1214) the lordship of Ferne in Forfarshire of which county Eustace de Montealto was sheriff in 1263, while in 1241 Richardo de Montealto, Justiciario Scotiæ, witnesses a confirmation of Alexander II Contemporary to Richard is Sir Robert de M-A to a charter by whom Laurentio de M-A is a witness Bernardus de Mohane was one of the Scots Nobles parties to the treaty with Wales about 1259, and later on he witnessed the grant of Roslin in 1280 In 1281 Sir Bernard Mouat, knight, was one of the Norwegian Embassy, and was drowned on the return voyage Nisbet notices a Michael de Monte Alto in 1252 in connection with the perambulation of Cleish, in Fifeshire In 1275 William de Monte Alto witnessed an agreement between Archibald, Bishop of Caithness, and William, Earl of Sutherland In 1289 Guillam de Muhaut subscribes to the Scottish letter of Brigham, and he will be the Willielmus de Monte Alto, *miles*, who submitted to Edward I in 1296 This is the earliest Scottish surname associated with the Island history. In 1312 Patrick of Mowat, a Scot, was seized by the Orcadians and held to ransom Robert Bruce granted (1306-30) a charter of Freswick in Caithness to a Mowat of the principal family of Balquholly, in Aberdeen In 1377 Richard de Montealto, Chancellor of the Church of Brechin, received grants of the baronies of Fferne and Kynblachmond, Forfar. The Duke of Albany, between 1406-13, confirmed a wadset of Freswick and Aukengill, granted by William Mowatt of Loscraggy to his son John, who, in 1419, was killed in the chapel at Tain Further notices of the Mowats are to be found in "Caithness Family History" and "Zetland County Families " They are apparently all of the Balquholly stock In 1545 Alexander Mowatt witnesses a charter of *Sir* Hugh Halcro, and the same year Patrick of Balquholly attests the erection of the Cath Chapter in Orkney, while in 1548 the latter contracted with Malcolm Halcro of that Ilk in Orkney for the marriage of his son (Mowat) to Halcro's daughter. In the Provostry Rental of 1584 Magnus in

Hoxa, Magnus in Stowis, and Ingoram Mowat in Mersettir are named. Patrick Mowat of Swinzie (1638), married Elizabeth Leask, and was succeeded by Alexander of Swinzie, who married Jean, daughter of Hugh Halcro of that Ilk. "In the churchyard of Flotta is a tombstone with the inscription 'Heir is the Buriall—Place of the Antient—Names of the Mouats—In Feira, William—Mouat and Marjorie D—Sutherland and his Gran—Mother.' These Mouats were a branch of the noble Mouats of Hoy, the baronetcy of which family has been allowed to drop." Sir George Mowat of Inglistoun was created a baronet of Nova Scotia by letters patent, 2nd June, 1664, with remainder to heirs male of his body. He was succeeded by Sir Roger as second Baronet, to whom his brother, Sir William, was served heir in February, 1683, while Nisbet (circ 1700) refers to Sir Alexander Mowat of Ingliston, Baronet, descended of Balquhollie, as then having arms—*Argent*, a lion rampant *sable* armed *gules*, within a bordure of the second, Crest, an oak tree growing out of a rock, ppr, motto, *Monte Alto*.

MUIR.—This family has been located in Sanday since 1502, when William of Mure and his brother are recorded by Henry, Lord St Clair. William, who is designed as of Clat, there, held also the bull (mansion house) of Brugh, Lemsgarth, and Brusgarth. Sir Nicholas Muir, Canon of Orkney, is named in 1426.

REDLAND of Redland, Stromness.—William Redland is named in 1595 and 1614. John Redland of that Ilk, and his second son, Magnus, have an appearance in 1622. Several are enumerated in the Valuation of 1653, and other earldom records. This family owned the Palace of Brittabreck.

RENDALL of Rendall.—Henrie Rendale, as Lawman of Orkney (1426), appends his seal to the Diploma. In the Rental of 1503 Sir Hew of Randale is noted as having been sent to Norway for his lifetime by Earl William. Johnne Rendale fought at Summerdale 1528, and was respited in 1539, and as Johanne Randaile *de eodem* attests the Cathedral Erection of 1544. In 1640 John Rendell is a bailie or superintendent Westray.

SINCLAIR.—Notices of this lineage appear elsewhere throughout this work.

STEWART.—There have been several families derived from legitimated and natural issue of the Orkney Earls so named. Some of the members of these have represented the Islands in Parliament.

SUTHERLAND.—Alexander de Suderland named in the Complaint of 1426 is probably identical with Alexander Sutherland, who having married Mariota de Ross, received from her brother Alexander, Earl of Ross, a charter of the lands of Dunbeath in Caithness, sasine issuing 24th October, 1429. By his testament, made in 1456, it is clear that he was a person of great importance. His daughter Marjory married William St. Clair, Earl of Orkney. Dunbeath's sons were Alexander, Archdean of Caithness, Robert, Nicholas, Edward, and John. Contemporary with these were Richard Sutherland of Forse, and William Sutherland of Berriedale, son and apparent heir of Alexander Sutherland of Duffus, an account of the descendants of whom is given in "Caithness Family History." The Rentals of 1503 disclose Sir Robert Sutherland as owning Sandisend in Grimsey, Ovirquhame and Bowbrek in Stromness, and Ovir Garsand and Mobisyord in North Sandwick, and it is recited that he has withheld the king's scatts for twenty-two years. In 1546 Thorrald Sudyrland and his sister Margaret Reid are cited as heirs of Katrin, daughter of Thorrald of Broycht, a great estate in Shetland. The name is very numerous in the South Isles.

TRAILL.—Nisbet derives this family from the Tyrol, of which the name is a corruption. There was one Hugh Trail who, at a tournament in Berwick (temp. Robert III), defeated an English champion, John Morlo. Walter Traill, Archbishop of St. Andrew's, purchased the lands of Blebo in Fife (Robert III) which he gave to his nephew. The Orkney Traills derive from those of Blebo. They have represented the Earldom in Parliament.

TULLOCH.—Tulloch is a place-name in Aberdeen, and there is also a Tulloch Castle, Inverness. The family has been erroneously derived from an apocryphal Earl of Orkney, Harald the Holy *(la helig)*. Thomas Tulloch was Bishop of Orkney, 1422–55, and to him is attributed the erection of Noltland Castle ; in 1438 he granted Kynclune to his brother David de Tullach, and in 1445 Walter de Tulach receives from the Orcadian bishop a pension of £5. In 1446 Nicolas Tulloch attests the Diploma. In 1456 the Test of Alexander Sutherland of Dumbethe enumerates several of the name. In 1455 William Tulloch became Bishop of Orkney. In 1481 Sir Martin Tulloch witnesses a charter by Bishop William. In the rental of 1503 Nicol Tulloch is named, and Tullo of Ness in the adjudication of 1514. In 1544 Thomas Tulloch is of Fleuris, and in 1567 Hieronimus Tulloch grants Breckness to Mudie. They have been Members of Parliament for the Earldom. See Burke's "Colonial Gentry" for amplified notice.

YULE.—Sir Robert Yule is noted in the Rental of 1503, and to the Rev. Yule of later times Orcadians are indebted for the measures taken to preserve St. Magnus' Cathedral.

VARIOUS.—The "afs" are in *italics*, and similar place-names are astericised.

ADIE, Aikers,* Aim, Annal, Aith * BANKS,* Benston, Berstane* (1503, '14, '39), Bews, Bichan (Buchan, 1369), Bigland,* Brass, Breck,* Brock* or Brough,* Broun, Budge, Burgar.* CAITHNESS, Corsie, Corston,* *Coubister, Cumloquoy* DEERNESS,* Delday, Dinnison, Drever. FIRTH,* *Folster, Flaws* GARMISTANE,* Garsand (1426), or Garson,* Gray, Grieve, Groundwater * HARRALD, Harray,* Hay, Hestwall,* Housgarth,* *Hunto* or Hunter, Hurie INKSGAIR, Inkster,* *Instabillie* KELDIE, Kirkbrek * LANG-SKAILL*, Larquoy,* Laughton, Linay* (Altars of Linay). MAINLAND, Male, Manson, Marsetter,* Marwick,* Matches (Mathew's), Meason of Whytquay (Holm 1617), Meil, Moar, Midhouse,* Miller of Redland (1716) NORQUOY,* Norn, Nestegard,* Newgar * ODDIE, Omand, Orkney PAPLAY* (1369, 1539), Peace (1310), Petrie ROUSAY* (now Rosie, Rosey, and Rossey), Ritch, Rusland * SABISTON,* Scarth* (1514), Sclatter, Scollay, Seatter,* Shearer, Shurie, Skae, Skethaway,* Skaill,* Spence, Stanger,* Stove, Stockan,* Swanney, Stainsgar * TAIT, Towrie or Tyrie, Turfeus, Twatt.* VELZIAN, Vedder, Voy WALLS,* Work, Wick. YORSTON, and other less frequent names.

---

* Craven

BOOK II.

HISTORIETTES.

THE EARLS OF ATHOL.—ROYAL CELTIC LINE.*
(1115—1215)

ATHOL was one of the ancient comitial divisions of Celtic Scotland. In early times it was written in a variety of ways, first as Athfothla (Fotla's ford), then Atheodle, and lastly, after a few further variations, settling down as Atholl. The first Earls of Athol were descended from KING DUNCAN THE FIRST, who had issue, by the miller of Forteviot's daughter, an illegitimate son who succeeded to the Scottish crown as Malcolm Canmore, and two lawful sons, Donald Bane and MELMARE OF ATHOLL. The latter is found in the Book of Deer witnessing one of the charters as Malmori d'Athotla, and in the Orkneyinga Saga is a reference to his son and successor, Moddad, Jarl af Atjoklum, son of (Melmari) Melmare, brother of King (Melkolm) Malcolm, father of David, then King of Scots. Thus the first Earl on record is

I. MADACH *Comes* (1115—1153),

who in 1115 witnesses the foundation charter of Scone by King Alexander I and Sibylla his queen. As "Maddoc" and "Madeth Comes" he also witnesses charters of King David I. Torfæus, the Danish historiographer, writing of this Earl of Athol, states he was the noblest prince of Scotland. "Omnium Scotiae principum facile nobilissimus patruelis quippe Davidis regis Scotiae in praesens regnantis." From a charter of King Malcolm the Maiden, granting aid for the restoration of the Abbey of Scone, we learn that the style of the Earls of Athole was "Comes de Ethoel," the Atjokl of the Saga.

Earl Madach was twice married. By his first wife, whose name is unknown, he had issue Malcolm, his successor to Athol. He married, secondly, Margaret, eventually sole heiress of Earl Hakon of Orkney, soon after which event a noted Orcadian viking—Sweyn Asliefsson—succeeded in abducting Earl Paul the Silent, who then ruled Orcadia, and conveying him to Athol, delivered him into the custody of his sister Margaret, Countess of Athol, and Earl Maddad, who at this time seems to have occupied the *rath* or fortress of Logierait, mentioned in one of the Scone charters as being in the twelfth century the capital of the Earldom.† A fairly ample account of the reception of poor Paul is given in the Saga, which tells us that he never returned to his dominions. It was generally considered that he had been put to death by the Countess and Earl of Athol in order to secure the Orcadian succession to their infant son then (1139) three years of age, viz.:

> HARALD, who, in right of his mother, eventually became sole EARL OF ORCADIA, then an extensive region comprising Orkney, Shetland, Caithness, Strathnaver, and Sutherland. A fuller account of this powerful Earl is given elsewhere. Like his Athol ancestors he had

---
* Burke, Ork Saga, Nisbet, and Skene.   † Ork Saga.

THE EARLS OF ATHOL.

a partiality for the Abbey of Scone, to the monks of which it is recorded (circa A D 1165) Harald, Earl of Orkney, Hetland, and Cataness, granted a mark of silver, to be paid annually by himself, his son Turphin, and their heirs By his first marriage with Afrecca sister of Duncan, Earl of Fife, he had with daughters

1 HENRY, reputed Earl of Ross, of whom there is no further account

2 HAKON, fell in ambush at Dublin

By his second marriage with Gormlath, daughter of Malcolm McHeth, Earl of Moray, he had with daughters

1. THORFINN, died in Roxburgh Castle, 1201

2 DAVID, Earl of Orcadia, died *s p m*, 1214

3 JOHN, Earl of Orcadia, who on the death of Earl Henry of Athol (in 1215) became heir-male of Athol He had a son

HARALD, Master of Orcadia, who perished at sea in 1226 *vita patris*

Earl John was murdered in 1231, and left no male issue

Earl Madach died about the year 1153, and was succeeded by his son of the first marriage Madach is the Gaelic equivalent of "Ulf"

II. MALCOLM (1153—1180)

This Earl appears in connection with several religious grants and endowments He was a donator to the Abbey of Scone, for by his deed and grant he made over to the Abbot and convent perpetually the church of Login Muchbed with four chapels thereunto belonging for the safety of his soul . He was also a benefactor to the monks of Dunfermline, for to that convent he gave in pure and perpetual alms the patronage and tithes of the church of Moulin "pro salute animae suae, et anima sponsae suae et pro animabus regum Scotiae, predecessorum suorum, ibidem requiescentium", and that when it shall please Almighty God to call him and the countess his wife to His mercy, that they shall be interred in the abbey church there This deed is attested by King William and the Bishops of Glasgow, Aberdeen, Dunkeld, and Brechin Earl Malcolm also granted to the Abbey of Cupar (1178–1180) timber for its construction from his forest of Athole In the Acts of Parliament (*temp* William the Lyon) a charter is cited in which Earl Malcolm refers to his spouse E   and his son H   In 1164 he is a witness. This Earl of Athol married Hextilda, a granddaughter of King Duncan, after the death, in 1189, of her first husband, Richard Cumin In first marriage she had received from King David some of his possessions in North Tynedale, viz., Thornton, Staincroft, Walwick, and Hethingeshatch, and as Countess of Athol she bestowed some of these lands on the monks of Durham In the Chartulary of Cupar Abbey three sons are named

1 HENRY, his heir   2 MALCOLM.   3 DUNCAN

III HENRY, THE LAST EARL OF HIS LINE,

ratified and confirmed to the Abbot and convent of Dunfermline the grants his father had made to them for the health and welfare of himself and relations, whether dead or alive. In 1211 he went north to Ross in pursuit of Gothred MacWilliam, a claimant to the Scottish throne, whom he secured * He was one of the seven Earls of Scotland present at the coronation of Alexander II

The last Earl of Athol was not succeeded by either his son or grandson, both of whom may have predeceased him. On his death the representation devolved on his cousin, Earl John of Orcadia, as heir-male, while the Athol dignity and lands were transmitted, in accordance with Celtic usage, to his two daughters, whose husbands in their right were severally, and apparently contemporaneously, designed Earls of Athol. The name of his dowager was Maria [or Margaret] He had issue a son and two daughters

1 CUMMING, who granted the monks of Cupar the privilege of his woods at Glenherthry and Tolikyne (It is elsewhere stated that Conan [Cumming], son of Henry, Earl of Athol, received from his father *temp* Alexander II the lands of Glenerochy, now Strowan, and was succeeded by his son Ewen Fils Conan of Glenerochy, who married Maria, one of the daughters and co-heiresses of Convalt, lord of Tullibardine, in Stratherne, by whom he obtained a large accession of territory)

    EWEN, or Eugenius, confirmed the grant of his father Cumming to the monks of Cupar

1 ISABELLA, married, first, Thomas of Galloway, Earl of Athol, who died in 1231 Their son PATRICK, Earl of Athol, was murdered in 1242, *s p*

And, secondly (in 1231), Alan Durward, Earl of Athol, High Justiciary of Scotland, b whom she had a daughter—

    LORA, Countess of Athol (+1269), who married Malcolm de Insulis, thus Earl of Athol Her son was the

        JOHN, Earl of Athol, who married Isabel, sister to King Robert Bruce, and flourishing till about 1298, then ended his days in France *s p*

2 FORFLISSA, Ferelith or Fernelithe, married Sir David de Hastings, *jure uxoris*, Earl of Athol, and had an only daughter—

    ADA, who, marrying John de Strathbolgie (grandson of Malcolm, Earl of Fife) that baron was *cinctus gladio Comitatus Atholie* In the year 1253 they confirmed a grant made by Ferelith to the Monastery of Cupar for the soul of her husband, Sir David de Hastings The Countess Ada had a son—

        DAVID, Earl of Athol, who married Isabel de Chilham, he was forfeited in 1268, and went to Palestine in the course of the following year He had a son—

            JOHN, designed de Strathbolgie, also son and heir of Earl David, until restored by Robert Bruce in 1306.

On the death of the heir-male, John of Athol, Earl of Orcadia, in 1231, he was succeeded by Magnus, second son of ——, Earl of Angus, as his heir-at-law.

MAORMORS OF ANGUS *

ANGUS, the older name of the County of Forfar, was the territory of one of the great Pictish tribes or sub-kingdoms, and was governed by a succession of Celtic maormors. The Pictish Chronicle furnishes us with the names of three, viz .

INDRECHTAIG, who flourished about the year 900 His son

DUBUCAN, died about 935, and had a son named

MAELBRIGDI, perhaps the Maelbrigdi of the Saga; after him the next record of a ruler of Angus is

DUFUGAN *Comes*, one of the seven Earls of Scotland appearing in the reign of Alexander I The similarity of the name to that of the second maormor justifies the allocation of this Earl to the Angus line After him comes a succession of five Earls from father to son, first of whom is

GILLEBRIDE, who fought at the battle of the Standard in 1138, and about 1160 witnessed a charter of Malcolm IV. to the Monastery of Dunfermline In 1164 he and

---

* Skene's Celtic Alban , Burke s Peerage , Nisbet's Heraldry

Adam his son attest a national document. Gilbert, son of this Earl, acquired the lands of Ogilvie, and is reputed ancestor of the Ogilvies, Earls of Airlie, Findlater, Seafield, and Lords Banff. Earl Gillebride was succeeded by his eldest son

GILCHRIST, who first appears opposing Somerled, Thane of Argyle and the Isles. That ambitious chief had made war against the authority of Malcolm IV. After various conflicts Somerled was repulsed, though not subdued, by Earl Gilchrist, and the peace concluded with this powerful chieftain in 1153 was considered of such importance as to form an epoch in the dating of Scottish charters * A still more formidable insurrection broke out in Moray under Gildominick, on account of the attempt to intrude in that county the Anglo-Norman jurisdiction of the Lowlands on their Celtic customs, and the settling of Anglo-Belgic colonists among them. These insurgents laid waste the neighbouring counties, and so regardless were they of the royal authority, that they actually hanged the heralds sent to summon them to lay down their arms. King Malcolm despatched the gallant Earl Gilchrist with an army to subdue them, but he was defeated and forced to recross the Grampians (circa 1160) † Gilchrist was one of the hostages for King William the Lion in 1174. His seal appended to a charter of his to the monastery of Dunfermline shows on the helmet a flourishing branch of a palm tree, which is the earliest instance in Scotland of a shield being timbred with helmet and crest † He is stated to have married Mauld, a natural daughter of King Malcolm and sister of Duncan. To him succeeded

GILLEBRIDE, who about 1180 witnessed a charter of King William the Lion to the Abbey of Aberbrothock. His son William appears *ante* 1200 in the Arbroath Chartulary, and another son Angus 23rd September, 1219, in the Acts of Parliament. He is stated to have married, first, a daughter of Patrick, Dunbar Earl of March, and secondly, the heiress of John, 30th Earl of Orkney and Caithness. He had issue

1. DUNCAN, next Earl 2. MAGNUS, 31st Earl of Orkney and Caithness
3. GILBRIDE, 32nd Earl of Orkney and Caithness 4. WILLIAM 5. ANGUS.

DUNCAN, will be the Earl of Angus at the coronation of Alexander II. in 1214. His successor was

MALCOLM (1225-1242?), the last Earl of this Celtic line. A fac-simile of his seal appears in Laing's Catalogue (No 420) A charter of King Alexander II to the Chapel of St Nicholas at Spey, dated 2nd October, 1232, is witnessed by M   , Earl of Angus and Kataness. Magnus, son of the Earl of Angus (second son of Earl Gilbride), who was present at the perambulation of the Aberbrothock Abbey boundaries, 16th January, 1222, is taken to be the first of the Angus line Earls of Orkney. Earl Malcolm married a daughter of Sir Humfrey Barclay,† and died circa 1237, leaving a daughter

MATILDA, Countess of Angus in her own right, who married, first, John Comyn, *jure uxoris* Earl of Angus. Dying in France in 1242, he left an infant son, BERTRALDE, Master of Angus, who followed his father to the grave the same year. In 1243 the Countess Matilda married Sir Gilbert Umfraville, thereupon designated Earl of Angus, and by him (who died 1245) had

GILBERT UMFRAVILLE, Earl of Angus, noted as in ward 1264, and a year or two later as of age. He was a prominent person in the wars of the Scottish succession, and, in 1291, commanded the important Castles of Dundee and Forfar,

*Keltie's Clans   Nisbet

which he declined to surrender to Edward I. of England until he received a formal letter of indemnity from the Estates of Scotland.* After the forfeiture of the Umfravilles, the Earldom was conferred on John Stewart of Bonkill, whose granddaughter Margaret resigned the Earldom in 1389 in favour of her natural son George, by William, first Earl of Douglas and Mar, who thus became founder of the Douglas line and ancestor of all subsequent Earls of Angus, Marquises and Dukes of Douglas, and Dukes of Hamilton, etc., etc. The descendants of the Umfravilles are the representatives of Matilda, Countess of Angus, while the representation of the male line devolved on Malise, Earl of Stratherne, who, about 1321, succeeded Magnus of Angus, last of his line, Earl of Orkney.

In Balfour's Annals Prince David, Earl of Huntington, is described as also Earl of Angus from 1170 to 1205.

THE EARLS PALATINE OF STRATHERNE †

THE EARLDOM OF STRATHERNE was certainly one of the most ancient dignities of the Scottish realm, for we find the Earls made mention of as far back as 1115. In earlier times it formed a division of the Kingdom of Alban, and was known under the name of Fortrenn, but after the battle of Nectansmere (685) Alban became termed the Kingdom of the Picts. Fortrenn, or ancient Stratherne, originally comprehended the district of Menteith, which was erected into a separate Earldom in the reign of Malcolm IV., and it also contained the thanages of Struan and Duning held under the Earls, and that of Forteviot and the abthanerie of Maddeity in the Crown. In Irish annals Stratherne is invariably referred to as Fortrenn. Collateral to the Earls was a line of Seneschals termed *de Stratherne*, one at least of whom bore a name in hereditary use with the line of these Earls, viz., *Malise*, and this has been a source of much confusion to historians generally. The old Earls carried for arms *or* two chevrons *gules*. The first on record is

I. MALISE, who appears as one of the seven Earls of Scotland witnessing the foundation charter of the Priory of Scone by Alexander III in 1115. He is there designed *Mallus Comes Stradarniæ*. He signalised himself eminently at the battle of the Standard, 22nd August, 1138. Before the battle numerous dissensions arose regarding the right to occupy the van, which King David was allotting to the Norman men-at-arms, in derogation of the claims of the men of Galloway to that honourable position. Thereon Malise, Earl of Stratherne, exclaimed indignantly to the King, "Whence arises this mighty confidence in these Normans? I wear no armour, yet they who do will not advance beyond me this day." Malise is a witness to two charters by King David—one in the early part of his reign to the Monastery of Dunfermline, and one later in which David grants to Dunfermline the whole "shire" of Kirkcaldy. His son and successor was

II. FERETH, 2nd *Comes Stradern*. Soon after the accession of Malcolm IV Fereth appears as witness to a charter of confirmation by that monarch to the Monastery of Dunfermline, being the first charter noted in Malcolm's reign. Malcolm, Earl of Athol, and the *Comes de Angus* were also present on that occasion. This Earl headed the revolt of six of the seven Earls of Scotland against Malcolm IV in 1160. Various motives have been attributed for this disaffection of the nobles. One authority ascribes the conspiracy to the too great familiarity of Malcolm with Henry, the English King, and his dislike of Louis, the French King. Another imputes the intention to depose Malcolm, and establish on the throne William the Atheling, "the Boy of Egremont," grandson of Duncan. Fordun, quoting the Chronicle of Melrose, says:—"Six Earls, Ferchard, Earl of Stratherne, to wit, and five other Earls, being stirred up against the King—not to compass any selfish end or through treason, but rather to guard the common weal—sought to take him, and laid siege to the keepe of that town (Perth). God so ordering it, however, their undertaking was brought to nought for the nonce, and after not many days had rolled by he was, by the advice of the clergy, brought back to a good understanding with his nobles." In the same year Fereth witnesses a grant by Malcolm to the Monastery of Scone. Dying in 1171, he left two sons Gilbert, next Earl; and Malise, designed brother of Gilbert in the foundation charter of Inchaffray, and to whom King William the Lion gave Kincardine, to be holden of Earl Robert. *The History of the Saint Clairs* assigns to Fereth a daughter, Rosabelle (or Katharine), who became lady to Sir William St. Clair.

III. GILBERT, 3rd Earl, succeeded in 1171 on the demise of Fereth, his father. Three years later (1174) he is one of the hostages for the ransom of William the Lion, and presently (1178-80) he appears receiving a charter from that monarch, which is followed by another at an interval of a few years, anterior, however, to 1189. In 1198 he founded the Monastery of Inchaffray, *Insula Missarum* (the Isle of Masses), in Stratherne, and endowed it largely for canons regular. In July, 1210, he divided his Earldom into three equal portions: one he gave to the Bishopric of Dumblane, another to the Monastery of St. John the Evangelist and monks of Inchaffray, and the third portion he reserved to himself and his heirs. He is one of the seven Earls of Scotland at the coronation of Alexander II. in 1214. Contemporary with this Earl was Gilleness, *Seneschal de Stratherne*, who left two sons, Malise, *Seneschal de Stratherne*, and Anechol, thane of Duning. Earl Gilbert died in 1223. By Matilda, daughter of William d'Aubigny, Earl of Albemarle, he had issue

1 GILCHRIST, 2 WILLIAM, and 3 FERQUHARD, died *v p*
4 ROBERT, 4th Earl   5 FERGUS, living circ 1200
1. CHRISTIAN, married Sir Walter Oliphant.   2 MARY, married William Hamilton

IV. ROBERT, 4th Earl, witnessed a charter of Alexander II. of the Earldom of Fife in the eleventh year of that sovereign's reign, 1224-5. On the 3rd April, 1231, Alexander II., by charter under the Great Seal, ratifies and confirms a former deed and grant by Earl Robert to Congal, son of Duncan, son of Malcolm, of the lands of Tullibardine. Muriel, daughter and heiress of Congall, married Malise, *Seneschal of Stratherne*. When the differences between Alexander II. and Henry II. were accommodated by the Cardinal Legate at York in 1237, Robert was one of the witnesses to the treaty, and was bound by oath to maintain the agreement. He died before 1244, having, besides Malise, his son and heir, Annabella, married to Sir David Graham of Dundaff (ancestor of the Dukes of Montrose), who got with her the barony of Kincardine, and Amatilda, married to Malcolm, Earl of Fife. (Elsewhere it is stated the widow of Malcolm, Earl of Fife, married the heir of the Earl of Mar.) In another work he is reported to have had a daughter, Lucia, married to Sir William St Clair. Isabel, Countess of Strathern, mentioned as second wife of Sir Walter Comyn, Earl of Menteith, was probably relict of this Earl

V. MALISE II, 5th Earl, succeeded his father in fortune and dignity. When Alexander II. and Henry III, *anno* 1244, entered into a similar treaty to that between Alexander and Henry II, this Malise was one of the guarantees. In 1249 he assisted at the coronation of Alexander III. He married, about 1243, Marjory (aged 24 in 1249, and dead in 1254), the second of the three daughters and co-heiresses of Robert de Muschamp, Baron of Wooler, and had issue two daughters and co-heiresses

1 MURIELLA, born in 1244, married the Earl of Mar, and died 1291-2 *s p*
2 MARJORY or MARY, born in 1248, married Nicholas de Graham (died *ante* 1306), and was mother of John de Graham, aged 28 in 1306

It is also stated* that Issenda, sister of Sir Gilbert Gask, was Countess of Stratherne. She would be contemporaneous with this Earl. According to Douglas, he married the lady Egidia Comyn (she married, secondly, Philip Meldrum), daughter of Alexander, second Earl of Buchan, but Nisbet has it that he married Mary, daughter of Sir John Comyn, Lord of Badenoch, by whom he had Malise, his heir. Balfour, in his Annals, has under 1272 "This same zeire, also, deyed that gallant and generous noblemane, Malisse, Earle of Stratherne, in France, quhosse corpse wer enbalmed and brought home to Scotland and solemly interred at Dumblaine"

VI. MALISE III, 6th Earl, succeeded on his father's demise. He may have firstly married the Lady Matilda of Orkney, daughter of Gilbride II of Orkney, she being contemporary with him. He certainly married Maria, daughter of Alexander, Lord of Argyle, and Dowager-Queen of Man, whose husband, Reginald, King of Man, had died in 1269. Malise was one of the guarantees of the marriage treaty of the Princess Margaret of Scotland with Eric, King of Norway, in 1281. He sat in the Parliament of Scone, 1283-4, when the Scottish nobles became bound to acknowledge Margaret of Norway as their sovereign in the event of the demise of Alexander III. At Duffaly, on All Saints' Eve, 1284, Henry, son of the quondam Malise, *Seneschal* of Stratherne, confirms the charter of his mother, Muriel, daughter of Congal, to William de Moravia (son of Malcolm de Moravia) and his wife Adda (daughter to Muriel and sister to Henry) of the lands of Tullibardine. This Muriel, lady to Malise, *Seneschal* of Stratherne, has been erroneously mentioned as Countess of Stratherne, and Sir George Mackenzie, in his Science of Heraldry, gives us as an uncouth specimen, and in illustration of the antiquity of using supporters, the shield of arms of Muriel [Countess of Stratherne] supported on the left side by a falcon standing upon the neck of a duck, lying under the base point of a formal shield, and all placed within a lozenge, which he dates from the year 1284, and which is 'the oldest and ancientest that ever I met with'" In 1286 he grants a charter of the lands of Cairntulloch to Malcolm, Lord of Logie, son of the quondam Malise, *Lord Seneschal of Stratherne*. This deed is witnessed by Alexander, Earl of Buchan, Justiciary of Scotland, and Sir Malcolm Moray, who married the daughter and heiress of Sir Gilbert Gask, and whose son William married Adda, daughter of Malise, *Seneschal* of Stratherne, by Muriel, daughter of Congal Fitz-Duncan. Malise, Earl of Stratherne, appears together with Maria, *Regina de Man* and *Comitissa de Stratherne*, in July, 1292, swearing fealty to Edward I of England. In 1292 Maria, *Comitissa de Stratherne*, who was wife of Hugh de Abernethy, was summoned to Parliament to show cause why she should not restore to Alexander, son of the said Hugh, certain properties. From this it would seem that Alexander de Abernethy was nearing, or had attained, his majority, hence the claim. That this Maria was not the Queen-Dowager of Man is made manifest by them both appearing in a list of widows in 1296. It is most consistent with chronology to suppose the re-marriage of Maria Comyn, relict of Malise II., who died in 1271-2, with Hugh Abernethy soon after the Earl's death, and thus Alexander, the issue of the second marriage, would be attaining his majority and claiming the paternal estates. In 1293 Malise had a daughter, Matilda, contracted to Robert de Thony, being not yet in her twentieth year.* Malise was one of the Scottish nobles summoned to attend Edward I. into Gascony, 1st September, 1294. In 1296 he was in the Scottish army that invaded England, for which, it appears, his estates were sequestered. He, however, again rendered fealty to Edward on the 13th July, 1296, when the English monarch issued an order to repone Maria (*quae uxor* Malise, Earl de S.) in her possessions. As Maria, Countess of Stratherne, who was wife of Hugh de Abernethy, also appears in a list of widows that year (1296), Skene presumes that Malise was then dead, thus accounting for her widowhood, and, going back to her previous appearance as Countess of S. in February, 1292, considers it established that Malise III had died before that date, and that his son and successor, Malise IV, held the dignity for the brief interval between February, 1292, and 1296, and was the husband of Maria, Countess de Stratherne, who was the wife of Hugh de Abernethy, and that by 1296 Malise IV had died. This is all highly speculative and improbable, and it is more likely that Malise III did not die till after 1310, as Malise IV—presumably of almost even age with his sister Matilda—would have been born about 1272, and could scarcely have had a son old enough to appear in the siege of Perth in 1310. Malise IV joined John Comyn, Lord of Badenoch, in an expedition to England in 1297, where they besieged Carlyle, but had to raise the siege and return to Scotland. Presently they re-assembled, and took Dunbar, but the English made a vigorous effort and succeeded in recovering it. Nisbet, with uncertain authority, places the death of "the loyal Earl Malise, last of his race," in 1300. The Earl was with the English garrison in Perth, besieged by Bruce in 1310, under whose banners his son Malise fought and made him prisoner. It is likely both sire and son fought for Bruce at Bannockburn. Gordon, in his "History of Bruce," when describing that battle, makes King Edward rush into the throng with the 'characteristic bravery of his race,' killing the Earl of Stratherne and his son, and other knights whose names are unrecorded

> "Their angry King
> Most bravely from his troops doth forth advance,
>   *   *   *   *
> And there were killed by his princely hand
> Seven valiant Knights whose names hath Time forgot
>   *   *   *   *
> Stratherne's old Earl there dy'd beneath his Brand
> Whose Son with Sorrow prick'd, with Fury hot
> Did fiercely him assail, but all in vain,
> Death made him soon forget his Father's pain"

The Earl died between 1310 and 1320, leaving, beside his son and successor, Malise IV, a daughter Mary, married to Sir John Murray of Abercairney, who had issue Sir Maurice Moray, who married his cousin, Johanna de Stratherne, Countess-Dowager of Athole, in 1339, created Earl of Stratherne in 1345; and fell at Durham in 1346; and another daughter, Matilda, in 1293, contracted to Robert de Thony, who died *s p* 1311.

---

* Ork. Saga introd.

THE EARLS PALATINE OF STRATHERNE

VII MALISE IV., 7th Earl, was born about 1272, and we have already seen him figure at the siege of Perth in 1310. He was married *vita patris**, as appears by a charter of King Robert (1306-29) of the lands of Kingkell, Brechin, to Maria de Stratherne, wife of Malise de Stratherne, being then in apparency only, as the title is not accorded him, yet this same Maria figures as Countess of Stratherne when involved in the Brechin-Soulis conspiracy of 1320, so his father, Malise III. must have died before that year. Soon after 1319 he confirms the grant of his father, Malise III, to Sir John Murray and Mary, daughter of Malise III. In 1320 he signs the celebrated ltre. to the Pope. In 1331 he possesses the fourth part of Caithness, and falls at Halidon Hill on 11th July, 1333. The Orcadian Diploma records that Malise II of Orkney, and V. of Stratherne, married, first, Johanna, daughter of the Earl of Menteith, but it seems certain that Malise IV also married, secondly, a daughter of Sir John Menteith, by whom he had a daughter, Johanna, married, first, to John Campbell, Earl of Athol, died 1333, secondly, John de Warrenne, Earl of Warren, Surrey, and Stratherne, and, thirdly (during life of her second husband), to her cousin, Sir Maurice de Moray (died 1346), whom she survived. Malise seems also to have married the heiress of Orkney (probably a daughter of John II by his countess, a daughter of Graham of Lovat), for he acquired the possessions and dignities of the Earldoms of Orkney and Caithness, and these, as well as those of Stratherne, he transmitted to his son and successor.

VIII MALISE V., 8th Earl. From Dean Gule's translation of the Orcadian Diploma we ascertain that King Magnus of Norway had directed the Lawman and Commons of Orkney to deliver to Earl Malise all charters, evidents, and letters of privilege pertaining to him concerning the Earldom of Orkney. Very little is known of this Earl. In 1334 he had endeavoured to recover Stratherne, which Earldom King Edward III of England had bestowed on Earl John de Warrenne, brother-in-law of Malise. He is supposed to have visited Norway about the same year, and in 1344 failing heirs-male, makes a special estimation of the Earldom of Caithness to his daughter Isabella, who presently married Sir William St Clair of Roslin, and, surviving all other issue of her father, died post 1404, transmitting her claim to that Earldom to her son Earl Henry II of Orkney, who allowed it to remain dormant, but the claim was successfully revived in the person of his son, Earl William, who thus became first of his line Earl of Caithness, *anno* 1455. The Diploma states that Earl Malise married, first, Joanna, daughter of the Earl of Menteith (perhaps his cousin), by whom he had—

1. MATILDA, married Weyland de Ard, and had an only child—
    ALEXANDER DE ARD, EARL OF CAITHNESS (1375) *s p*

And secondly, Marjory, daughter of Hugh, Earl of Ross, by whom he had—

1. ISABELLA, married to Sir William St Clair of Roslin, and had, with other issue—
    HENRY ST CLAIR, EARL OF ORKNEY, 1379
2. ANNOT (or MFRETTA), married Erengisle Suneson, *jure uxoris*, Earl of Orkney, 1353-57, *s p*
3. Daughter, married Gothorm Spar, and had
    SIR MALISE SPAR, CLAIMANT OF ORKNEY, slain *s p*.
4. EUPHEMIA, died without issue

The Earldom of Stratherne was apparently a male fief. Earl Malise is presumed to have died before 1345, in which year [his brother-in-law and cousin], Sir Maurice Moray, was created Earl of Stratherne, who falling at Durham the following year, the Earldom was given to Robert Stuart,† first of his line King of Scotland, who, later on when he ascended the throne, assigned it to his brother David.

Burke. The Steward was also brother-in-law to Earl Malise V

THE ORCADIAN EPISCOPATE *

1050 c. THOROLF was consecrated Bishop of Orkney in the middle of the xith century by Adalbert, Archbishop of Hamburg, in response to a requisition from the Orcadians.

—— ADALBERT is mentioned as his successor in the see.

1070 c RALPH was consecrated at York by Thomas, Archbishop of York (1070—1100), assisted by Wulstan, Bishop of Worcester, and Peter, Bishop of Chester. It appears from a letter that Ralph, an Orcadian cleric, had been sent by Earl Paul to Lanfranc, Archbishop of Canterbury, to be consecrated Bishop of his realm. Ralph will be the bishop who assisted the Archbishop of York in 1109 to consecrate Turgot as Bishop of St Andrew's. Anselm, Archbishop of Canterbury (1092—1107), wrote to Earl Hakon Paulson exhorting him and his people to obey the Bishop, "whom now by the grace of God they had."

1100 c. ROGER was consecrated by Gerard, Archbishop of York (1100—1108).

1138 c RALPH, presbyter of York, said to have been elected by the Orcadians, was consecrated by Archbishop Thomas, successor to Gerard. He figures in the accounts of the battle of Northallerton, 1138. Papal letters were addressed in his favour to the Norwegian kings Sigurd and Eystein, in one of which it is expressly stated that another bishop had been intruded in his place.

The preceding appointments appear to have been only titular, in exercise of primatial contention by York that Scotland and the Isles lay within the jurisdiction, and by Hamburg that as successors to St Anschar, Hamburg was metropolitan for all Scandinavian churches. Meantime the Norwegians made their own bishops, and conveyed possession of the see, which disposed effectually of the pretensions of prelates with titular consecrations.

1102 I WILLIAM I., the Old, occupied the see for 66 years from consecration in 1102 till death in 1168. His remains were discovered in 1848 in St Magnus' Cathedral in a leaden cist inscribed "Hic Requiescit Willialmus Senex, Felicis Memoriæ, Primus Episcopus." The see was first at Birsay, where was Thorfinn's cathedral erection of Christ's Kirk, but when St Magnus' was built in 1137 the see was translated. Anastasius made Trondheim metropolitan in 1154, and declared Bishop William one of its suffragans.

1168 II WILLIAM II. died in 1188.

1188 III BJARNI *Skald* was the son of Kolbein Hruga. He was a famous poet, and to him is ascribed the *Jomsvikingadrapa*—Lay of the Jomsburg Vikings. Innocent III. addressed to him a bull, 27th May, 1198, in connection with the refusal of John, Bishop of Caithness, to collect in the latter diocese an annual tribute granted by Earl Harald II. He conveyed to the monastery of Munkalif, Bergen, the land called *Holand*, near the Dalsfiord, north of Bergen, "for the souls of his father, mother, brother, relations and friends." He died in 1223.

* Dr Anderson's introduction to Orkn Saga

THE ORCADIAN EPISCOPATE.

1223 IV. JOFREYR, Dean of Tunsberg, was consecrated in 1223. Gregory IX, by bull at Viterbo, 11th May, 1237, enjoined Sigurd, Archbishop of Drontheim, to either remove him or provide him with an assistant, as he had been paralytic for many years Jofreyr, however, retained the see till his death in 1247 In his time Honorius III. issued a Brief dated 3rd November, 1226, to Nicolas, Archdeacon of Jhatland, directing him to disburse the twentieth of all ecclesiastical revenues to Jarl Skule, then arming for a crusade

1247 V. HENRY, Canon of Orkney, received dispensation 9th December, 1247, from Innocent IV. for defect of birth He accompanied King Hakon in 1263, and died in 1269.

1270. VI PETER was consecrated in 1270, and died in 1284 A Brief of his at Tunsberg, 3rd September, 1278, grants forty days' indulgence to those in his diocese contributing to restore St Swithin's Cathedral at Stavanger, which had been destroyed by fire

1286. VII DOLGFINN, consecrated in 1286, died in 1309.

1310. VIII. WILLIAM III was consecrated in 1310 At the Provincial Council held at Bergen in 1320, Eilif, the Archbishop, preferred several complaints against Bishop William. Eilif had sent Kormak, Archdeacon of the Sudreys, and Grim Ormson, prebendary of Drontheim, on a visitation to the Orcadian diocese These clerics reported that the Bishop had squandered the property of the see, had bestowed the offices on foreigners and apostates, had compromised his dignity by participation in the boisterous pastime of hunting and other unseemly diversions, had imprisoned Ingilbert Lyning, a canon of Orkney, and had refused to permit removal of the corpse of an Orcadienne, although her will directed interment in the Trondheim Cathedral

1328. IX. WILLIAM IV succeeded sometime after the year 1328. He is noticed in an important record of 1369, and was slain in 1382.

1390 X WILLIAM V occurs in a Scottish instrument *temp* Robert III

1394 XI HENRY II. Torfæus cites an appearance in this year

1397. XII. JOHN is a party to the Union Treaty of Calmar.

—— XIII PATRICK appears in an attestation by the Lawman of Orkney, two canons of St. Magnus', and four *burgesses* of Kirkwall, as to the descent and good name of James of Cragy, laird of Hupe. The instrument alludes to many losses, injuries, and disquietudes endured by this bishop at the hands of his adversaries

1416. XIV. ALEXANDER Vause, *sii*, the elected Bishop of Caithness is now Bishop-elect of Orkney.

1418. XV. THOMAS de Tulloch first appears in existing records in 1418. He seems to have been previously Bishop of Ross The chief events of his episcopal rule have been already referred to

1461. XVI WILLIAM VI., de Tulloch, was the last bishop during Norwegian domination in the Orkneys. In his time Sixtus IV. by bull, 17th August, 1472, transferred the Orcadian see from the Norwegian to the Scottish metropolitan. In succession to him were

1477 XVII ANDREW·[1501 ANDREW], 1511. XVIII EDWARD Stewart [THOMAS], 1525 XIX ROBERT Maxwell 154. XX. ROBERT II., Reid, 1555. XXI ADAM Bothwell to 1580; 1606 XXII JAMES Law; 1615 XXIII. GEORGE Graham; [1639. ROBERT Baron]; 1662 XXIV THOMAS St. Serf, 1664. XXV. ANDREW III, Honyman, 1676 XXVI MURDOCH Mackenzie [1688. ANDREW Bruce]

Abolition of episcopacy.

THE CAITHNESS EPISCOPATE.*

Before the death of Earl Rognvald in 1158 there was a monastery at Dornoch, for King David (1124-53) addressed a missive to Rognvald, Earl of Orkney, and to the Earl of Caithness (Harald Maddadsson), and to all good men in Caithness and Orkney, requesting them to protect the monks living at Durnach in Caithness, their servants and their effects, and to see that they sustained no loss or injury. The diocese was seemingly co-extensive with the older Earldom, comprehending Caithness and Sutherland as far south as the Kyle of Sutherland. The see was first at Halkirk, near Thurso, the *Há Kirkiu*, or High Kirk of the Saga; in later times the Cathedral Church was at Dornoch

1153 I ANDREW, the first bishop on record, was a learned man, much about the court of David I. He is said to have been author of the curious treatise "De Situ Albaniæ," attributed to Giraldus Cambrensis In 1153 he received from David I. grant of the lands of Hector Conon, and gave one of the Church of the Holy Trinity of Dunkeld to the monks of Dunfermline, in 1165 he and Murethac, his clerk, witness a charter confirming the said gift, by Gregory, Bishop of Dunkeld, about 1181 he witnesses the grant of Earl Harald to the see of Rome of a penny annually from every inhabited house in Caithness, he is also a witness to a document engrossed in the Book of Deer, by which King David I. declares the clerics of Deer to be free from all lay interference and undue exaction, "as it is written in their book, and as they pleaded at Banff and swore at Aberdeen." He died at Dunfermline, 30th December, 1185.

1198 II JOHN, refusing to collect the grant to Rome, Innocent III in a bull, 27th May, 1198, enjoined Bishops Bjarni of Orkney and Reginald of Ross to compel Bishop John to cease opposing the collection on pain of the censure of the Church When Earl Harald recovered Caithness in 1202 he was so exasperated with the Bishop as to authorise or allow the soldiery to mutilate him Bishop John survived till 1213

1214 III ADAM, Abbot of Melrose, was consecrated in 1214 by Malvoisin, Bishop of St Andrew's In 1218 he went on a pilgrimage to Rome with the Bishops of Glasgow and Moray Exasperating the Caithnessians by excessive exactions, they burnt him in his own kitchen at Halkirk in 1222. In consequence of apparent comitial complicity or approval of this crime, Alexander II deprived Earl John of Sutherland, and tortured 80 of the ringleaders Honorius III., in January, 1222, addressed a letter to the Scottish bishops commending the promptitude and zeal shown by the Scottish king. His body (or ashes) received interment in the church at Skinnet, and was afterwards, it is said, removed to Dornoch in 1239.

1223. IV. GILBERT de Moravia, Archdeacon of Moray, was consecrated in 1223 He built the Cathedral at Dornoch, and his charter of constitution is still extant in the archives at Dunrobin. The churches assigned to the prebends were those of Clyne,

---

* Dr Anderson's introduction to Orkn Saga

THE CAITHNESS EPISCOPATE

Dornoch, Creich, Rogart, Lairg, Farr, Kildonan, and Durness, in Sutherland; and Bower, Watten, Skinnet, Olrig, Dunnet, and Canisbay, in Caithness. Golspie and Loth, Reay, Thurso, Wick, and Latheron were reserved to the bishop. He named the Abbot of Scone as one of his canons. The abbey of Scone was proprietor of the church of Kildonan, which, with its chapels and lands, was confirmed to the canons of Scone by Honorius III in 1226. This prelate built the "Bishop's Castle" at Scrabster, and was made keeper of the king's castles in the north. He found a gold mine in his lands in Durness, and is traditional builder of Kildrummy Castle in Mar. He was Lord Chancellor of Scotland. Dying at Scrabster in 1244 or 1245, he was afterwards canonised. His relics were preserved in Dornoch Cathedral and long held in reverence. A record of 1545 apprises us that the parties then compearing before John, Earl of Sutherland, in the chapter-house, Dornoch, made oath by touching the relics of the blessed Saint Gilbert.

1250. V. WILLIAM appears with other Scottish bishops in an address of 1259 to Alexander III. He died in 1261 or 1262.

1263. VI. WALTER de Baltrodin, canon of Caithness, was chosen his successor. Urban IV in a letter of 1263 announces that in consideration of the election being unanimous, etc., etc., he is satisfied to accept it, although not in canonical form. He died before 1274. On his death, Nicolas, Abbot of Scone, was chosen to succeed him, but rejected by the Pope, when

1275. VII. ARCHIBALD, Archdeacon of Moray, was chosen. The Pope's letter of confirmation mentions as his nominees, R., the Dean, Patrick, the treasurer, and Roger de Castello, canon of Caithness. In his time Boyamund de Vitia was commissioned by Gregory X to collect moneys in aid of the crusade, the accounts for 1274 and 1275 furnish the names of various churches and their contributions. Dying before 1279 the chapter elected R., the dean, and constituted Magister Henry of Nottingham, a canon of Caithness, to procure confirmation, but the latter confessing in the Papal presence that the dean had a son, thirty years of age, and was senile, the Bishops of St. Andrew's and Aberdeen were enjoined to use their influence to oblige him to resign.

1290. VIII. ALAN de St. Edmund, an Englishman, was elected by the influence of Edward I., with whom he was a great favourite. He signed the letter of 1290 to that king proposing marriage between the Maid of Norway and Prince Edward of Wales. He was made Chancellor of Scotland in 1291 by King Edward, who in that year directed Alexander Comyn, keeper of the royal forest of Ternway in Moray, to supply Bishop Alan with forty oaks suitable for the fabric of the Cathedral Church of Caithness, which the king had granted for the souls of Alexander, King of Scots, and Margaret, his queen, the sister of the donor. Alan died the same year, when the chapter elected as his successor I. (oannes?) their archdeacon, but the election not being in canonical form H is Holiness preferred to the vacant diocese.

1296. IX. ADAM II., precentor of Ross, who died at Sienna shortly after the papal letter in his favour, 1296.

1297. X. ANDREW II., Abbot of Cupar, was thereupon preferred to the vacancy, and the Bishops of Aberdeen, Glasgow, and Ross were instructed to consecrate him.

1310. XI. FERQUHARD Beleraumbe acknowledged Bruce in 1310; in 1312 attested payment of the Annual of Norway by Robert the Bruce; and is noted 10th July, 1321, in a Scottish record (Reg. Great Seal). He was dead and the see vacant in 1328. After him are these:

XII. NICHOLAS, bishop-elect in 1332. XIII. DAVID, dead before 1340. XIV ALAN II., Archdeacon of Aberdeen, confirmed in 1341, dead in 1342. XV. THOMAS de Fingask, confirmed November, 1342; attests writs by William, Earl of Ross, in 1355, declaring the abbey of Ferne exempt from all the king's taxes; in 1359 he witnessed a deed with Ingelram of Caithness, Archdeacon of Dunkeld   Dying at Elgin in 1360 he was buried under the Bishop's seat in our Lady's aisle of the chanonry church there XVI. MALCOLM confirmed 21st February, 1369   Gregory XI in March, 1376, confirms to Dr. William of Spynie, the chanonry and prebendary of the church of Orkney, rendered vacant by the preferment of Malcolm to the Caithness see. XVII. ALEXANDER is bishop in 1389, when he is found adjusting a dispute between the Earl and Bishop of Moray. Sir Alex Vause is in 1416 the elected Bishop of Caithness and Bishop-elect of Orkney   He is noticed in the Exch. Rolls then, and in 1420; and in 1426 John of Vause gives discharge to the Bishop of Caithness for £3 6s 8d, and the Bishop of Orkney for £5   XVIII ROBERT Strathbrock, 1434—1444   XIX JOHN Innes, dean of Ross, died 1448   XX. WILLIAM Moody, 1448—1469   XXI PROSPER, elected, but resigned in favour of XXII., JOHN Sinclair, canon of Glasgow, 1481, bishop-nominate for 24 years, during which time it is stated that the dean, Adam Gordon, third son of the Earl of Huntly, discharged the official duties. XXIII. ANDREW Stewart (1490), Abbot of Fearn, Rosshire, Lord Treasurer of Scotland. XXIV ANDREW Stewart (1518), son of the Earl of Athol, translated from Dunkeld   XXV ROBERT Stewart, 1542, Earl of Lennox, died 1586, when the see was vacant for fourteen years   XXVI GEORGE Gledstanes, 1600, minister of St. Andrew's, translated to St Andrew's   XXVII. ALEXANDER Forbes, 1606, rector of Fettercairn, translated to Aberdeen, 1615. XXVIII. JOHN Abernethy, 1624, parson of Jedburgh; deprived by the assembly of Glasgow, 1638   XXIX PATRICK Forbes, 1662.   XXX. ANDREW Wood, translated from the Isles; ejected soon after the Revolution in 1688, and died at Dunbar 1695.

ORCADIAN ARGONAUTS,

OR

VOYAGES OF THE ZENI *

1374—1404

THE World's Fair, recently held in Chicago (1892) in commemoration of the discovery of America by Columbus in 1492—four centuries ago—will doubtless cause considerable interest to attach to authenticated accounts of previous discoveries by navigators of equal enterprise and daring, in whose wake he sailed, and more especially will interest be concentrated on the expedition of discovery immediately preceding that of Columbus, of which he must have heard when he visited Iceland, and the knowledge of which, in all human probability, demonstrated to him the certain existence of land towards the western confines of the Atlantic

Almost a century before Columbus commenced his baffling search for a patron among the sovereigns of Europe, Henry I., 42nd Earl of the ancient, autonomous maritime principality of the Orkneys (which comprehended the Lordship of Zetland), and Premier Magnate of the Norwegian realm, had commissioned his Admiral, Antonio Zeno, a Venetian navigator, scion of the renowned Ducal family of that name, to retrace the footsteps of the Scandinavian discoverers of the Western World † The narration of the voyages and discoveries was published at Venice in 1558 by Nicolo Zeno, member of the Council of Ten, a descendant of Antonio, and, recently, under the auspices of the Hakluyt Society, a British translation has been printed, edited by the late R H Major, a distinguished member of the Society and Secretary of the Royal Geographical Society. His able exposition of what had been previously considered irreconcilable inconsistencies, and his copious elucidations, have completely established the genuineness of the discovery.

Major states The first to do himself honour by vindicating the truth of the Zeno story was the distinguished companion of Captain Cook (the circumnavigator), Johann Reinhold Forster, in a work published in 1784 and 1786. Amongst others who uphold the narrative we have the following brilliant array of savants —Eggers, Cardinal Zurla, Zach, Malte Brun, Walckenaer, de la Roquette, the Polish geographer Joachim Lelewel, and the Danish antiquary Bredsdorff, also the illustrious and far-seeing Humboldt, who, with his usual large-mindedness, although he perceived the difficulties attaching to the narrative of the Zeni, said, "On y trouve de la candeur et des descriptions détaillées d'objets, dont rien en l'Europe ne pouvoit leur avoir donné l'idée " Briefly the story is as follows :—

Toward the end of 1389, Nicolo Zeno, a member of one of the noblest and most ancient families of Venice, went, at his own expense, on a voyage, rather of curiosity than discovery, to the Northern seas. After passing through the Straits of Gibraltar he steered north, and presently encountered a terrible storm, which bore the vessel helplessly on, wrecking him on the Faroe Islands. This was in the year 1390. Most of the goods were saved, and he and his companions were rescued from the wreckers who beset them by Henry Saint-Clair, the Orcadian Earl, who happened to be near the place

---

* Prepared from Major's work by permission of the Hakluyt Society.   † Balfour

with an armed retinue. Accosting them in Latin, he assured the Venetians of his protection and took them into his service. St Clair was a great lord, and possessed certain islands lying not far from the Faroes to the south, being the richest and most populous of all those parts, and besides the said small islands he was Duke of So Rano [So Ronaldsa?], lying over against Scotland. St Clair then, such as is described, was a war-like, valiant man, and specially famous in naval exploits. Having the year before (1389) gained a victory over the representative of the King of Norway (this relates to the conflict in 1389 between Henry St Clair and Sir Malise Spar, his cousin), who was lord of the island, he, being anxious to win renown by deed of arms, had come with his men to attempt the conquest of the Faroes, which are somewhat larger than the Shetlands, so the first exploit in which Nicolo participated was the reduction of that group. (When Hjaltland was separated from Orkney in 1195 it was united to the Faroes. They had the same Foud and Lawman, who resided at Scalloway.) This was accomplished with a fleet of thirteen vessels, whereof two only were rowed with oars, the rest were small barks and one ship. As Nicolo greatly contributed towards the skilful navigation of the fleet through the dangerous channels between the various islands, the Earl in recognition of his services conferred on him the honour of knighthood.

Sir Nicolo then wrote to his brother Antonio, relating his adventurous experiences, and asking him to join him and bring a vessel with him. Antonio did as desired, and, after a long voyage, in which he encountered many perils, at length joined Sir Nicolo, not only his brother by blood, but also in courage. Both brothers won much favour with Earl Henry, and to gratify Sir Nicolo, and also because he knew full well his value, he made him Commander of his Navy (Armada).

In that capacity Sir Nicolo, with his brother, accompanied the Earl to Hjaltland and established order in that group. The Earl, after effecting the pacification of Hjaltland, built a fort in Bressay, where he left Sir Nicolo with some small vessels and men and stores, and then, thinking he had done enough for the present, returned with the rest of the squadron to the capital of his Archipelagian dominions.

Being left behind in Bressay, Sir Nicolo determined the next season to make an excursion with the view of discovering land. Accordingly, in the month of July, he fitted out three small barks, and, sailing towards the North, arrived in Greenland of the "glittering plains and snowy mountains." There he found a monastery of the order of the Friars Preachers, and a church dedicated to St Olaus, hard by a hill which belched forth fire like Vesuvius and Etna. To this monastery resort friars from Norway, Sweden, and other countries, but the greater part come from Iceland. Sir Nicolo gives a detailed account of the manners and customs of the friars, and of the inhabitants, as also of the trade of that district with other places. He discovered a river, which is shown on the map of Greenland, drawn by the Nicolo of later times from a mutilated chart belonging to Antonio. At length Sir Nicolo, not being accustomed to such severe cold, fell ill, and a little while after he returned to Grislanda (Hross-ey or Gross-ey

NOTE.—It seems from information received since preparing this article that Major's case is weakened by the discovery of the Carta Marina of Olaus Magnus. There is, however, no doubt in my mind but that voyages took place as represented in unknown latitudes in the Northern seas. Frobisher and other almost contemporary navigators adopted the narration without question. See map of 1570 in "Saga Time" by Sigurd Stephans, Rector of Skalholt.

becomes Gross-Islanda to the Venetians), where he died, a victim to the rigorous climate of those northern regions. The text sets forth that Nicolo was wrecked on the Faroes in 1390, soon after which he was joined by Antonio, who, at the time of Nicolo's death, had been with him four years. Nicolo sailed for Greenland in July, and died shortly after his return, which event would probably have occurred before the end of the year, and, as he had been a little more than four years in the service of the Earl, we are enabled to place his death as towards the end of 1394.

Antonio succeeded him in his wealth and honour, but, although he strove hard in various ways, and begged and prayed most earnestly, he could never obtain permission to return to his own country. For the Earl, being a man of great enterprise and daring, had determined to make himself master of the sea. Accordingly he proposed to avail himself of the services of Antonio by sending him out with a few small vessels to the westward, because in that direction one of his fishermen subjects had reported the existence of certain very rich and populous lands.

Six-and-twenty years before then (about 1374) four Orcadian fishing boats put out to sea, and, meeting a heavy storm, were driven over the ocean in utter helplessness for many days; when at length, the tempest abating, they discovered an island called Estotiland (probably Newfoundland, but unquestionably in North America), lying to the westward about 1,000 miles from (Grislanda = Hrossey) the Orcades. One of the boats was wrecked, and six men in it were taken by the inhabitants to the ruler of the place, but none understood the language of the Orcadians, except one that spoke Latin, and had also been cast by chance upon the island. The original castaway, on behalf of the king [chief], asked them who they were and whence they came; and when he reported their answer, the king desired that they should remain in the country. Accordingly, as they could do no otherwise, they obeyed his commandment, and remained five years on the island and learned the language. One of them in particular visited different parts of the island, and reports that it is a very rich country, abounding in all good things. It is a little smaller than Iceland, but more fertile; in the middle of it is a very high mountain, in which rise four rivers, that water the whole country.

The inhabitants are very intelligent people, and possess all the arts like ourselves; and it is believed that in time past they have had intercourse with our people, for he said that he saw Latin books in the library of the ruler which they at this present time do not understand. They have their own language and letters. They have all kinds of metals, but especially they abound with gold. Their foreign intercourse is with Greenland, whence they import furs, brimstone, and pitch. Here it will be well to make allusion to earlier Scandinavian discoveries in North America. In 1001 one of the first achievements of Greenland colonists was the discovery by Leif, son of Eric the Red. The tracts of land then discovered were Helluland (i.e., Slate land), supposed to be Newfoundland; Markland (i.e., Woodland), supposed to be Nova Scotia, and Vinland or Vineland. While there is much uncertainty about the situation of the former, the site of Vineland is less problematical. An old writer says "On the shortest day in Vinland the sun was above the horizon from (Dagmaal) 7 30 a.m to (Eikt) 4 p m," from which it follows that the length of the day was nine hours, which gives the latitude of forty-one degrees. This deduction is confirmed by a curious coincidence. Adam of Bremen, writing in the eleventh century states on the authority of Svein Estridsen, King of Denmark, a nephew of Knut the Great, that Vinland got its name from the vine growing wild there, and for the same reason the English re-discoverers gave the name of Martha's Vineyard to the large island close off the coast, in latitude 41 degrees 23 min. The old documents also mention a country called Huitramannaland, or Whiteman's Land, otherwise Irland it Mikla, or Great Ireland, supposed to include North and South Carolina, Georgia, and Florida. Hrafn, a Limerick trader, reported this land to Thorfinn the Great, Earl of Orkney.* There is a tradition among the Shawnoe Indians, who emigrated some years ago from Florida and settled in Ohio, that Florida was inhabited by white people who used iron instruments. It is further recorded in the ancient MSS that the Greenland Bishop, Eric, went over to Vinland in the year 1211, and that in 1266 a voyage of discovery to the Arctic regions of America was made under the auspices of some of the clergymen of the Greenland Bishopric. The next recorded discovery was made by Adelbrand and Thorvald Helgason, two Icelandic clergymen, in the year 1285, the country found being supposed to be Newfoundland. The last record preserved in the old Icelandic manuscripts relates a voyage from Greenland to Markland, performed by a crew of seventeen men in 1347. The account written by a contemporary nine years after the event, speaks of Markland as a country still known and visited in those days, and it was, until now, the latest document that spoke of the intercourse between Greenland and America. In the Zeno document we have, however, the very latest evidence known in literature of the continued existence of that intercourse down to the close of the fourteenth century, a hundred years anterior to the time of Columbus. The foregoing digression has been made to account for the comparatively civilised condition of Estotiland.

Resuming the narrative of the Orcadian fisher:—Towards the south [of Estotiland] there is a great and populous country, very rich in gold. They sow corn and make beer, which is a kind of drink that northern people take as we do wine. They have woods of immense extent. They make their buildings with walls, and there are many towns and villages. They make small boats and sail them, but have not the loadstone, nor do they know the north by the compass. For this reason these Orcadian fishermen were held in great estimation, insomuch that the king sent them with twelve boats to the southwards to a country which they call Drogio (evidently a native name for an extensive tract on the North American coast); but in their voyages they had such contrary weather that they were in fear for their lives. Although, however, they escaped the one cruel death, they fell into another of the cruellest, for they were taken into the country, and the greater number of them were eaten by the savages, who are cannibals, and consider human flesh very savoury meat.

But, as that fisherman and his remaining companions were able to show them the way of taking fish with nets, their lives were saved. Every day he would go fishing in the sea and in the fresh waters, and take a great abundance of fish, which he gave to the chiefs, and thereby grew into such favour that he was very much liked, and held in great consideration by everybody.

As the Orcadian's fame spread through the surrounding tribes, there was a neighbouring chief who was very anxious to have him, and to see how he practised his wonderful art of catching fish. With this object in view he made war on the other chief with whom the Orcadian then was, and being more powerful, and a better warrior,

---

* Heimskringla

he at length overcame him, and so the fisherman was sent over to him with his compatriots During the space of thirteen years that he dwelt in those parts, he says that he was sent in this manner to more than five and twenty chiefs, for they were continually fighting among themselves, this chief with that, and solely with the purpose of having the fisherman to dwell with them ; so that wandering up and down the country without any fixed abode in one place, he became acquainted with almost all those parts He says that it is a very great country, and, as it were, a new world ; the people are very rude and uncultivated, for they all go naked and suffer cruelly from the cold, nor have they the sense to clothe themselves with the skins of the animals which they take in hunting They have no kind of metal They live by hunting, and carry lances of wood sharpened at the points They have bows, the strings of which are made of beasts' skins They are very fierce and have deadly fights amongst each other, and eat one another's flesh They have chieftains and certain laws amongst themselves, but differing in the different tribes. The farther you go south westwards, however, the more refinement you meet with, because the climate is more temperate, and accordingly there they have cities and temples dedicated to their idols, in which they sacrifice men and afterwards eat them. In those parts they have some knowledge and use of gold and silver (This appears to have been, for the close of the fourteenth century, a pretty good description of the state of things in America as far down as Mexico.)

Now this Orcadian, after having dwelt so many years in these parts, made up his mind, if possible, to return home to his fatherland—the land of the Runic Rhyme—but his fellow-islesmen despairing of ever seeing it again, gave him "God's speed," and remained themselves where they were Accordingly he bade them farewell, and made his escape through the woods in the direction of Drogio, where he was welcomed and very kindly received by the chief of the place, who knew him, and was a great enemy of the neighbouring chieftain , and so, passing from one chief to another, being the same with whom he had been before, after a long time and with much trouble, he at length reached Drogio, where he spent three years Here, by good luck, he heard from the natives that some boats had arrived off the coast, and full of hope of being able to carry out his intention, he went down to the seaside, and to his great delight found that they had come from Estotiland He forthwith requested that they would take him with them, which they did very willingly, and as he knew the language of the country, which none of them could speak, they employed him as their interpreter

He afterwards traded in their company to such good purpose that he became very rich, and fitting out a vessel of his own, returned to the Orkneys [Grislanda], and gave an account of the wealth of those distant countries to his lord and earl, Henry St Clair The sailors, from having had much experience in strange novelties, give full credence to his statements. Antonio Zeno wrote his brother—the famous Carlo Zeno, who in 1382 saved the Venetian Republic—saying that St. Clair was resolved to equip a fleet and send him forth towards those parts on a voyage of discovery and conquest , and he continues, "there are so many that desire to join in the expedition that I think we shall be very strongly appointed without any public expense at all." Antonio set sail with a considerable number of vessels and men, but had not the chief command, as he hoped for the Earl went in person

In a subsequent letter to Sir Carlo describing the enterprise, he relates Our great preparations for the voyage to Estotiland were begun in an unlucky hour for exactly three days before our departure the fisherman who was to have been our guide died; nevertheless, St Clair would not give up the enterprise, but in lieu of the deceased fisherman, took some sailors who had come out with him to the island. Steering westwards, we sighted some of the Faroes, and passing certain shoals, came to Lille Dimon, where we stayed seven days to refresh ourselves and to furnish the fleet with necessaries. Departing thence, we arrived on the first of July at the island of Skuoe, and, as the wind was full in our favour, we pushed on; but not long after, when we were on the open sea, there arose so great a storm that for eight days we were continuously kept in toil, and driven we knew not where, and a considerable number of the boats were lost. At length, when the storm abated, we gathered together the scattered boats, and sailing with a prosperous wind, we discovered land on its western side. Steering straight for it, we reached a quiet and safe harbour, in which we saw an infinite number of armed people, who came running down furiously to the water side, prepared to defend the island. St. Clair now caused his men to make signs of peace to them, and they sent ten men to us, who could speak ten languages, but we could speak to none of them, except one that was from Shetland. He was brought before our prince, who, asking the name of the island, received answer Kerry, and was told that the people refused intercourse altogether and would oppose his landing. To this our prince made no reply beyond enquiring where there was a good harbour, and making signs that he intended to depart. Accordingly, sailing round about the island, he put in with his fleet in full sail into a harbour which he found on the eastern side.

The mariners went on shore to take in wood and water, which they did as quickly as they could, lest they might be attacked by the islanders; and not without reason, for the inhabitants made signals to their neighbours with fire and smoke, and taking to their arms, the others coming to their aid, they all came running down to the seaside upon our men with bows and arrows, so that many were slain and several wounded. Although we made signs of peace to them, it was of no use, for their rage increased more and more, as though they were fighting for their own very existence. Being thus compelled to depart, we sailed along in a great circuit about the island, being always followed on the hill tops and along the sea coasts by an infinite number of armed men. At length doubling the northern cape of the island, we came upon many shoals, amongst which we were for ten days in continual danger of losing our whole fleet, but fortunately all that while the weather was very fine. All the way till we came to the east cape we saw the inhabitants still on the hill tops and by the sea coast, keeping with us, howling and shouting at us from a distance to show their animosity towards us. We therefore resolved to put into some safe harbour, and see if we might once again speak with the Shetlander, but we failed in our object, for the people, more like wild beasts than men, stood constantly prepared to resist us should we attempt to land. Wherefore St Clair, seeing that he could do nothing and that if he were to persevere in his attempt the fleet would fall short of provisions, took his departure with a fair wind and sailed six days to the westwards; but the wind afterwards shifting to the south-west and the sea becoming rough, we sailed four days with the wind aft, and at length discovering land, as the sea ran high and we did not know what country it was, we were afraid to approach it, but by God's blessing the wind lulled, and then there came on a great calm. Some of the crew then pulled ashore, and soon returned to our great joy with news that they had found an excellent country and a still better harbour. Upon this we brought our barks and our boats to land, and on entering an excellent harbour we saw in the distance a great mountain that poured forth smoke, which gave us good hope that we should find some inhabitants in the island ; neither would St. Clair rest, although it was a great way off, without sending a hundred soldiers to explore the country and bring an account of what sort of people the inhabitants were Meanwhile they took in a store of wood and water, and caught a considerable quantity of fish and sea-fowl They also found such an abundance of birds' eggs that our men, who were half famished, ate of them to repletion.

"Whilst we were at anchor here the month of June (August) came in, and the air in the island was mild and pleasant beyond description , but as we saw nobody we began to suspect that this pleasant place was uninhabited To the harbour we gave the name of Trin, and the headland [Cape Farewell] which stretched out into the sea, we called Capo de Trin. After eight days the hundred soldiers returned and brought word that they had been through the island and up to the mountain, and that the smoke was a natural thing proceeding from a great fire in the bottom of a hill, and that there was a spring from which issued a certain matter like pitch, which ran into the sea , and that thereabouts dwelt great multitudes of people half wild and living in caves. They were of small stature and very timid, for as soon as they saw our people they fled into their holes They reported also that there was a large river and a very good and safe harbour When the Earl heard this, and noticed that the place had a wholesome and pure atmosphere, a fertile soil, good rivers, and so many other conveniences, he conceived the idea of fixing his abode there and founding a city But his people having passed through a voyage so full of fatigues, began to murmur, and to say that they wished to return to their own homes, for that the winter was not far off, and if they allowed it once to set in, they would not be able to get away before the following summer He therefore retained only the rowboats and such of the people as were willing to stay with him, and sent all the rest away in ships, appointing me against my will to be their captain. Having no choice, therefore I departed, and sailed twenty days to the eastwards without sight of any land, then turning my course towards the south-east, in five days I lighted on land, and found myself on the island of Neome (sic), and, knowing the country, I perceived I was past Iceland, and as the inhabitants were subject to the Earl, I took in fresh stores, and sailed in a fair wind in three days to Orkney [Grislanda], where the people, who thought they had lost their prince in consequence of his long absence on the voyage we had made, received us with a hearty welcome."

Nicolo Zeno, the younger, writes " What happened subsequently to the foregoing I know not, beyond what I gather by conjecture from a piece of another letter, which is to the effect that St Clair settled down in the harbour of his newly-discovered island, and explored the whole of the country with great diligence, as well as the coasts on both sides of Greenland, because I find this particularly described in the sea-chart, but the description is lost " The beginning of the letter runs thus —

"Concerning those things that you desire to know of me as to the people and their habits, the animals, and the countries adjoining, I have written about it all in a separate book, which, please God, I shall bring with me In it I have described the country, the monstrous fishes, the customs and laws of Grislanda, of Iceland and Shetland the Kingdoms of Norway, Estotiland, and Drogio , and lastly, I have written the life of my brother, the Chevalier Messire Nicolo with the discovery which he made and all about Greenland I have also written the life and exploits of St Clair, a prince as worthy of immortal memory as any that ever lived for his great bravery and remarkable goodness. In it I have described the discovery of Greenland on both sides, and the city that he founded. (The combination of these two expressions in one sentence leads to the inference that the discovery of Greenland on both sides was due to the Earl.) But of this I will say no more in this letter, and hope to be with you very shortly, and to satisfy your curiosity by word of mouth."

It is known that Antonio died in Venice before 1406, and as he remained ten years in the service of the Earl after the death of Sir Nicolo in 1394, it is probable he returned in 1404, thus coinciding with the death of Earl Henry, an event which would operate to release him. The last-mentioned letter seems to have been written almost immediately prior to Antonio's return, and as in it he states he has written the *life* and exploits of St Clair, the expression would almost justify the deduction that the Earl was then dead. History informs us that the Earl was slain in the Orcades while defending his dominions against an invasion of the Southrons.

Nicolo Zeno, the younger, ends by saying "All these letters were written by Messire Antonio to Sir Carlo the Chevalier, his brother, the Venetian admiral (Saviour of Venice in 1382), and I am grieved that the book and many other writings on these subjects have, I don't know how, come to ruin, for being but a child when they fell into my hands, I, not knowing what they were, tore them in pieces as children will do, and sent them all to ruin, a circumstance which I cannot now recall without the greatest sorrow. Nevertheless, in order that such an important memorial should not be lost, I have put the whole in order as well as I could in the above narrative, so that the present age may, more than its predecessors have done in some measure derive pleasure from the great discoveries made in those parts where they were least expected, for it is an age that takes a great interest in new narratives and in the discoveries which have been made in countries hitherto unknown, by the high courage and energy of our ancestors."

Mr Major concludes "Now the question may be asked. *Cui bono* all this toil of analysis and research? The facts may answer for themselves —

1 If the realities which have been here laid bare had been detected any time during the last three centuries and a quarter, so that the site of the lost east colony of Greenland had been proved to demonstration instead of being a matter of opinion, the kings of Denmark would have been spared the necessity of sending out a great number of unsuccessful expeditions, and

2 A number of learned disquisitions by some of the most illustrious literati in Europe would have been rendered superfluous

3 The Zeno document is now shown to be the *latest* in existence, as far as we know, giving details respecting the important lost east colony of Greenland, which has been so anxiously sought for

4 It is the *latest* document in existence, as far as we know, giving details respecting the Scandinavian settlers in North America—although a century before Columbus' great voyage across the Atlantic—and showing that at that period they still survived

5 The honour of a distinguished man, whose only faults as regards this ancient story, fruitful in confusion as they have been, were, that he did not possess the geographical knowledge of to-day, and that he indulged in the glowing fancies and diction of his sunny country, has been vindicated

The foregoing incorporates R H Major's notes, with the text of the narrative as edited by him in "The Voyages of the Zeni," printed in London in 1873 for the Hakluyt Society. In one or two places Grislanda has been substituted for Frislanda, and Iceland for Shetland, the sense seeming to so require it. No *gentes* have been more distinguished in the annals of their respective countries than the Zeno *gens* and the *gens de Sancto Claro*. The heroic achievements of the Zeno family, given in detail in Mr. Major's work suitably illustrate the eminence of the voyagers who so adored the Orcadian Earl for those valiant exploits in which they shared

"And gray stones voiced their praise in the bays of far isles"

FOLD OF HJALTLAND

JOHN ST. CLAIR (fl. 1411-18)

This personage was the son of Earl Henry the Holy. His first appearance is in 1411, when Earl Henry II appoints him procurator to redeem lands in the Mearns. It is also recited that he got from his brother, lands in Lothian, namely, Kirkton Loganhouse, Earncraig, East and West Summerhopes. There are many references of passports into England, 1392—1421, in favour of a Sir John St Clair, but these may relate to a contemporary namesake. In 1418 he became client for Hjaltland, swearing fealty to Eric, King of Denmark. It is stated that he married Ingeborg, a natural daughter of Waldemar, King of Denmark, by Tova Litle (daughter of the Commissioner of Rugen), whom legends still invest with a romantic interest. Gurre, which Waldemar imparadised, was the scene of the lovers' wooing. William St Clair, his son, served, it is said, under the German Emperor in the Holy Wars, and from him derive (*remolable*) the Sinclairs barons of Brugh in Hjaltland.

CHAMBERLAIN OF ROSS

SIR DAVID SYNCLAR OF SWINBURGH, KNIGHT (1498—1507)

Sir David Sinclair was a son of William, Earl of Orkney, by Marjory Sutherland. He acquired the lands of Swinburgh in 1498, and in 1502 there occurs in the Orkney accounts a payment to him of 200 merks at the time of his passage to Denmark, and in the Reg Great Seal, 3rd September, 1502, is a memo of a grant to him of 50 merks yearly from the king's coffers "pro servicio impendendo." The Norwegians at that time had risen against the rule of Denmark, and Sir David evidently accompanied the fleet of vessels equipped with soldiers sent by the King of Scots to co-operate with the Danish king to reduce the insurgent Norse. He was Governor of the Palace Guard at Bergen, and Foud of Hjaltland. He renders accounts, 1505-7, as Chamberlain of the Earldom of Ross, and he is noted as keeper of Dingwall Castle and the Red Castle, to which offices emoluments were attached. He executed his Last Will and Testament in 1506, and 14th July, 1507, then at Stirling, grants receipt for all goods contained in an indenture between James, Archbishop of St Andrew's, and his chamberlain. He died in July or August, 1507, leaving issue sons and daughters. Many lands of his are referred to in the Complaint of 1576 by Arthur Sinclair of Aith, and others. His will affords a most complete glimpse into those remote times. Honoured in the three kingdoms of Denmark, Norway, and Scotland, his possessions were large, his bequests geographically wide, and his benefactions great.

HEREDITARY PROTECTORATE
OF
THE SCOTTISH MASONIC CRAFT *

Scottish Masonry is an old institution, and seems to have originated in trades-union organisations amongst the masons in Scotland contemporaneously with the erection of the Abbeys of Holyrood, Kelso, Melrose, and Kilwinning, the Cathedral of Glasgow, and other ecclesiastical fabrics of the twelfth and thirteenth centuries.

Legislative enactments were made in Parliament at Perth in March, 1424, instituting the office of "Deakon or Maister-man" for the protection of the community against the frauds of craftsmen. The power of the Deacons was, however, restricted by an Act of September, 1426, and Wardens chosen from each craft were authorised to be appointed by the town councils to regulate the wages of masons and wrights. It was further ordained that in sheriffdoms "ilk Barronne sall garr prise in their barronnies and punish the trespassoures, as the Wardene dois in the burrowes". It seems the Deacons continued holding assemblies in subversion of the powers of the Wardenry Courts, which brought about a statute in July, 1427, prohibiting the office of Deacon altogether. In 1493 James IV came into collision with the trade combinations of his time. The masons and wrights had through their conventions ordained that "they should have fee as well for the holiday as for the work-day," and that "where any begins a man's work an other shall not finish it". Public tumult arose through the resistance of the community to these demands. The Legislature therefore interposed, and in 1493 passed an Act in which the "makers and users" of the statutes in question were ordered to be punished as "oppressors of the king's lieges". The Act also restricted the powers of Deacons to a testing of the quality of the work done by their respective crafts. Again in March, 1540, Parliament overrode the Masonic statutes and authorised the employment of unfreemen equally with burgesses, and anew armed magistrates with power to enforce obedience.

Sixteen years afterwards, while Queen Mary was yet under age, Parliament again found it necessary to interpose and repress the extortionate charges of tradesmen made at the instigation of deacons, and this hitherto irresponsible class of trade officials was attempted to be got rid of. The private conventions of craftsmen and statutes other than those approved of by town councils were rendered illegal, while "Visitors" were appointed in lieu of the former Wardens. On attaining her majority Queen Mary, so far from homologating the Act of the Regency suppressing the Deaconry of Craft, repealed it as injurious to the common weal, and in remedy thereof granted letters under the Great Seal restoring the office of Deacon and confirming the trades in the privilege of self-government, the observance of the customs that were peculiar to each, and the unrestricted exercise of all other rights which they had enjoyed under former monarchs.

The next reign furnishes the first authentic evidence of the sovereign's direct control over the Masonic Craft. The Privy Seal Book of Scotland contains a record of the ratification by James VI of Patrick Copland of Undaught's election in 1590 to the office of "Wardane and Justice" over the Masons within the counties of Aberdeen, Banff,

* Murray Lyon's "Freemasonry of Scotland"

and Kincardine This royal missive sets forth that the newly-appointed Warden's predecessors had been ancient possessors of the office, but that in the present instance the king in anew granting right to the fees and privileges of the office, had given effect to the choice of a majority of the Master Masons of the district in which the Warden was to minister justice in connection with matters affecting the art and craft of Masonry It is apparent that this was a strictly civil appointment, similar to that of the Barons to the Wardenrie of the Crafts in 1427

Emerging from chaos to the period of Masonic twilight, we find the Deacons, Masters, and freemen of the Masons within the realm of Scotland granting a charter (1600-1601) to William St Clair of Roslin, submitting themselves to the hereditary jurisdiction of the lairds of Roslin The lodges of Edinburgh, St Andrew's, Haddington, Acheson's Haven, and Dunfermline were parties to this document, which recites that the lairds of Roslin have from age to age been observed among the Masons as the patrons and protectors whom their predecessors have obeyed and acknowledged The term "lodge" signifies a separate assembly of Masons, and is apparently derived from the term applied to a shed or other temporary structure for shelter or during meal hours Hence the general application of the word in its Masonic usage. It first appears in the Burgh Records of Edinburgh in a "Statute anent the government of the Maister Masonn of the College Kirk of St Giles, 1491" The word again appears in the "Indenture betwix Dunde and its Masonn," A D 1536, as given in the "Registrum Episcopus Brechinensis," and is interesting as containing the earliest authentic instance of a Scottish lodge following the name of a saint, viz, "Our Ladye (i e, St Mary's) Luge of Dunde"

The recital of the Masonic charter to (Sir) William Saint Clair of Roslin is explicit, and implies in distinct terms that the position of patron had existed for some generations. The earliest notice of the Roslins having any special connection with the craft is in the account of the erection of the Collegiate Church at Roslin, *circa* 1446, when many masons were employed, and treated with great liberality Henry St. Clair, son of Sir Oliver, first of Roslin, was in 1541 Commendator of the Abbey of Kilwinning, a fact perhaps not without significance, as from that place comes the Mother Lodge of Scotland.

The charter of 1600 was followed by another in 1628 from the "Maissones and hammermen" of Scotland to Sir William Sinclar of Rosling, son of the previous grantee. The recital of this charter also refers to the Lairds of Roslin being patrons and protectors of the craft from age to age, and further informs us "whereof they had letters of protection and other rights granted by His Majesty s most noble progenitors of worthy memory, which with sundry other of the Laird of Rosling's writs being consumed and burnt in a flame of fire within the castle of Roslin in an   the consummation and burning whereof being clearly known to us and our predecessors" . . . "In the which office privilege and jurisdiction over us and our said vocation the said William Sinclar of Rosling ever continued to his going to Ireland, where he presently remains"

 . The date of the second charter is allotted to April, 1628, a conclusion borne out by an unfinished minute in the records of the Lodge of Edinburgh "At rosling the first of May, 1628 The quhilk day Sir Williame Sinklar —" It is thought that this fragmentary item has reference to a meeting that had been convened at Roslin for the purpose of presenting to Sir William the deed that had been executed in his favour

THE FIRST GRAND MASTER*

WILLIAM, ST. CLAIR, LAST OF ROSSLYN.†
(† 1778)

To the success attendant upon the erection of an English Grand Lodge is attributed the movement for a Scottish Grand Lodge; and the minutes of Canongate Kilwinning furnish the earliest record of the election of a Grand Master having formed the subject of consideration by a Scottish lodge. They also contain data in illustration of "the last Rosslyn's" Masonic career. On 29th September, 1735, the duty of "framing proposals to be laid before the several lodges, in order to the chusing of a Grand Master for Scotland," was remitted to a committee of the brethren, who were again (October 15th) instructed to "take under consideration proposals for a Grand Master." In the interval between this and the next mention of the Grand Mastership, William St. Clair was (May 18th, 1736), on payment of the usual fee, made a "brother of the Antient and Honourable Fraternity of Free and Accepted Masons," and on the 2nd of the following month was "advanced to the degree of fellow craft," he paying into the box as usual. On the 4th of August, 1736, John Douglas, surgeon, a member of the Lodge of Kircaldy, was, in consideration of "proofs done and to be done," affiliated into the Canongate Kilwinning, and was at the same sederunt appointed "Secretary for the time, with power to appoint his own deputy, in order to his making out a scheme for bringing about a Grand Master for Scotland." On the 20th of the next month the Lodge was visited by brethren "from the Lodge kept at William Gray's Edinburgh (Kilwinning Scots' Arms), who made some proposals anent a Grand Master for Scotland." Again, the Lodge having (October 6th, 1736) met in "order to the concerting proper measures for electing a Grand Master for Scotland, being duly formed, heard proposals for that purpose, which were agreed to, and gave it as an instruction to their representatives, at the first meeting of the four lodges in and about Edinburgh, in the first place to insist that a proper Secretary should be appointed to the meetings of the said lodges, who should be invested with the powers mentioned in said proposals, or such as then should be agreed on, which Secretary was then named." Eight days previous to the Grand Election, St Clair was advanced to "the degree of Master Mason." Two days afterwards he signed the document that was to facilitate the election of a Grand Master, which was written and attested by three of the more prominent of the brethren belonging to St Clair's mother, or, to use the phraseology of the time, "original" lodge—a circumstance which adds to the presumptive evidence upon which it is considered that Canongate Kilwinning was the originator of the scheme for his advancement to the Grand Orient.

The delegates from the four lodges—Mary's Chapel, Canongate Kil., Kil Scots' Arms, and Leith Kil.,—met at Edinburgh on the 15th of October, 1736, when certain regulations were framed for the "good and prosperity of Masonrie in general," and provision made for the election of a Grand Master. The methods and regulations arrived at unanimously by these four lodges were to be printed, and copies transmitted to all known regular lodges in Scotland, accompanied with a letter explaining the object of the proposals submitted by the convening lodges. St Mary's Chapel thereon nominated the

---
* Murray Lyon. † Maidment's Notes, Sir Walter Scott, &c.

Earl of Home but Canongate Kilwinning had three weeks earlier issued its deliverance upon the "Method and Regulations anent the Election of Grand Master," and was unanimously of opinion that Br William Sinclair of Rosline was the most worthy person, and recommended to the Brotherhood his interest in a very earnest manner ; and likewise were of opinion that in case Br Sinclair should not succeed in the election of Grand Master, that the following persons (all of Canongate Kilwinning) were proper officers to be named for the Grand Lodge, and hereby recommend their interest to the several brethren, viz . Mr Hew Murray, S W ; John Douglas, J W., Thos Trotter, Treasurer, Da Maule, Secretary " The lodge "thereafter appointed a committee to meet on the 15th of the month (November, 1736) in order to their concerting any further matters anent the said election of Grand Master "

After several meetings of the convening lodges, it was on 25th November, 1736, appointed that the election of Grand Master should take place in St Mary's Chapel on Tuesday, 30th of November, at half-past two p.m According to this arrangement, then, the first General Assembly of Scottish Symbolical Masons was convened at Edinburgh 30th November, 1736 On completing the sederunt 33 of the 100 or so lodges that had been invited were found to be represented, each by a Master and two Wardens ; and to prevent jealousies in the matter of precedency, always a rallying point for Masonic asperities, each lodge was placed on the roll in the order of its entrance to the hall Upon the final adjustment of the roll, and no amendments having been offered to the form of procedure, or to the draft of the constitution of Grand Lodge that had been submitted to the several lodges, the document known as the "Deed of Resignation" was tendered by the Laird of Roslin and read to the meeting By this celebrated instrument he resigns the Hereditary Protectorate of the Craft which had been vested in his ancestors since 1600 or earlier He renounces all right, jurisdiction, etc., which may be vested in him, "in virtue of any deed or deeds made and granted by the said Massons, or of any grant or charter made by any of the Kings of Scotland to and in favour of the said William and Sir William St Clairs of Rossline, OR ANY OTHERS OF MY PREDECESSORS, etc " Edinburgh, 24th November, 1736

Though some of the representatives present had been instructed to vote for another than Mr. St. Clair, so fascinated do the brethren seem to have been with the apparent magnanimity, disinterestedness and zeal for the Order, displayed in his "Resignation," that the success of the scheme for his election was complete, the Deed was accepted, and with a unanimity that must have been grateful to the lodge at whose instance it had been drawn, the abdication of an obsolete office in Operative Masonry was made the ground of St Clair's being chosen to fill the post of first Grand Master in the Scottish Grand Lodge of Speculative Masons

A report by the Master of the proceedings of the Grand Lodge was presented to St. Mary's Chapel at its communication on St John's Day, 1736, "of which proceedings the Brethren of the Lodge unanimously approved " The recommendation by Mary's Chapel of the Earl of Home for the Grand Mastership, and its subsequent approval of the conduct of its representatives in unanimously supporting the nomination of St Clair, would seem to imply that up to the time of election that Lodge had been ignorant of the grounds upon which the latter gentleman's claims to the honour were to be urged, a circumstance which affords presumptive proof that the leading Scottish Masons of the time were entirely oblivious of any constituted authority in trade matters apart from

Lodges and Incorporations St Clair was a member of neither when the question of a Grand Mastership was first propounded, nor in his subsequent admission and advancement as an Accepted Mason was he introduced to the brethren in any other character than that of a private gentleman

The whole facts seem to show that the Lodge Canongate Kilwinning took the initiative in the agitation for a Grand Lodge for Scotland, and the circumstances connected with the affiliation of Dr Douglas render it probable that he had been introduced for the purpose of perfecting a previously concerted plan whereby the election of a Grand Master might be made to contribute to the aggrandisement of the Lodge receiving him. His subsequent advancement and frequent re-election to the chair of Substitute Grand Master would indicate the possession of high Masonic qualifications, and to these the Craft may have been indebted for the resuscitation of the St Clair charters and the dramatic effect which their identification with the successful aspirant to the Grand Mastership gave to the institution of the Grand Lodge of Scotland. Whatever may have been the immediate motive of the originators of the scheme, the setting up a Grand Lodge ostensibly upon the ruins of an institution that had ceased to be of practical benefit, but which in former times had been closely allied to the guild of the mason craft, gave to the new organisation an air of antiquity as the lineal representative of the ancient courts of Operative Masonry, while the so-called resignation of St Clair was, if not too closely criticised, calculated to give to the whole affair a sort of legal aspect that was wanting at the institution of the Grand Lodge of England. In December of the same year (1736) he made a grand visitation to Canongate Kilwinning, accompanied by Lord Kintore, the Acting Junior Grand Warden.

Although he only filled the Grand Throne during the first year of Grand Lodge's existence, he continued to take an active interest in its affairs, and through his influence with the nobility and gentry of Scotland, secured as his successors in the Throne craftsmen of high repute. Forty-two years elapsed between his retirement from the chair and his death During that long period he was almost always present at the annual festival of St. Andrew, and was at the one immediately preceding his death, which occurred on 4th January, 1778, in the 78th year of his age. A solemn Funeral Grand Lodge was held in honour of his memory "On this occasion the masters, officers, and brethren of all the lodges in Edinburgh, to the number of near 400 appeared in deep mourning The lodge was opened by Sir William Forbes, Baronet, Grand Master Mason of Scotland, with a funeral oration, after which the Resurrection Hymn, the Hallelujah, and other select pieces of solemn vocal music were performed with great taste and execution by gentlemen, brethren of the Order. The whole ceremony was conducted with a degree of solemnity and propriety highly suitable to the occasion, and which exhibited in a very striking point of view the true spirit and principles of Masonry."*

The following elegy, composed for the event, was sung to the tune of *Rosslyn Castle*

Frail man, how like the meteor s blaze !	Where e'er our various journies tend
How evanescent are thy days !	To this we soon or late descend
Protracted to its longest date,	Thither from mortal eye retired,
How short the time indulged by Fate !	Though oft beheld and still admired,
Nor force Death s potent arm can brave,	St Clair to dust its claim resigns,
Nor Wisdom's self elude the grave	And in sublimer regions shines

---

* Maidment s Notes

THE FIRST GRAND MASTER.

Let us, whom ties fraternal bind, | Like St. Clair live, like St. Clair die,
Beyond the rest of human kind, | Then join the Eternal Lodge on high.*

An Edinburgh lodge has been named St. Clair in commemoration of the first Grand Master, and the prominence of the Rosslyns in connection with the craft doubtless explains the popular perpetuation of St. Clair as a Christian name in so many families unrelated to the *gens*.

"The last Rosslyn," says Sir Walter Scott "(for he was uniformly known by his patrimonial designation, and would probably have deemed it an insult in any who might have termed him Mr. Sinclair) was a man considerably above six feet, with dark grey locks, a form upright, but gracefully so, thin-flanked and broad shouldered, built, it would seem, for the business of the war or chase, a noble eye of chastened pride and undoubted au- thority, and features handsome and strik- ing in their general effect, though some- what harsh and ex- aggerated when con- sidered in detail. His complexion was dark and grizzled, and as we schoolboys, who crowded to see him perform feats of strength and skill in the old Scottish games of golf and archery, used to think and say amongst our- selves, the whole figure resembled the famous founder of the Douglas race, pointed out, it is pre- tended, to the Scottish monarch on a con- quered field of battle, as the man whose arm had achieved the victory by the ex- pressive words, *Sholto Dhuglass*,—'behold the dark grey man.' In all the manly sports which require strength and dexter- ity Roslin was un- rivalled : but his par- ticular delight was in archery." He was proprietor and occu- pant of a house near the bottom of Liber- ton Wynd, Edin- burgh. It was a small self-contained edifice, adjoining the east side of the alley, and having a southerly exposure to the Cowgate, from which street the front was visible. He

WILLIAM ST. CLAIR OF ROSLIN, ESQ.,
GOLFER, ARCHER, GRANDMASTER MASON.

married Cordelia, daughter of Sir George Wishart of Cliftonhall, by whom he had three sons and five daughters, who all died young except his daughter Sarah. He sold what remained of the family estates to General Saint Clair, second son of Henry Lord Sinclair, the heir-of-line of William St. Clair, last Earl of Orkney, and they were until recently in possession of the Erskines, Earls of Rosslyn. The representation of the family is claimed by the Chevalier Enrico Ciccopieri, a major in the Italian service, who has been served by the Sheriff of Chancery as heir-of-line to Colonel James St. Clair, who died in 1807.

The last Rosslyn was captain of the Honourable Company of Gentlemen Golfers These enthusiasts resolved, on 11th March, 1771, "to have the picture of their present captain (William St Clair) in full length in his golfing dress in their large room," and "requested him to sit for the same, which, he having agreed to, Sir George Chalmers is appointed to paint the same, which is to be done at the Golfers' expense as soon as conveniently the same can be done." The linkmen of Leith becoming embarrassed pecuniarily, their effects were exposed for sale in 1831, when this portrait passed into the possession of the Royal Company of Archers, of which incorporation the last Rosslin had been President of Council during the years 1768-1778 It now hangs on the walls of their hall at Edinburgh Rosslyn is in the costume of a golfer, with a round blue Scottish bonnet, and a very fine scarlet swallow-tail coat, and stands in the act of driving a ball from the *tee* There is another portrait in the possession of Canongate Kilwinning, where he was initiated a Mason, the genuineness of which is disputed It is known to have been in the lodge from about 1793 (only fifteen years after his death), and the artist is thought to be Allan Ramsay, a son of the poet In it St Clair is in Masonic costume, in his hand a scroll, and bears the level suspended from his sash, it being the badge at that time general among the craft *

THE KING'S BISHOP
WILLIAM ST CLAIR, BISHOP OF DUNKELD †
1312—1332.

This militant prelate was a son of Sir William St Clair of Roslin He was elected Bishop of Dunkeld in the seventh pontifical year of Clemens V, *apud* Vienne 1312 (vii *Idus Mau*) On the 10th July, 1321, he attests a national document (No 84) In a certain semi-historical work, I have also come across the notice, referring to William Sinclair, 'The Bishop of Dunkeld, who had fought against the enemies of the Cross on the plains of Hungary, and was as brave a soldier as ever drew a sword," etc Henry the Minstrel refers to him thus :—

A prelate next unto Ardchattan came
Who of his lordship nought had but the name
He worthy was, both prudent, grave and sage,
Of Sinclair blood, *not forty years of age*
The pope, to save poor sinful souls from hell,
Did him create lord bishop of Dunkell
But English men, through greed and avarice,
Deprived him basely of his benefice
Not knowing then to whom to make his suit,
To save his life dwelt three full years in Bute
During which space he was kept safe and sound,
And under the Lord Stewart shelter found
Till Wallace who won Scotland back with pain,
Restored him to his livings all again

Good Bishop Sinclair, without longer stay
Met him on Glammis, and travelled on the way
To Brechin, where they lodged all that night,
         .   and unto Perth repaired,
There Bishop Sinc'air met him in a trice,
And wisely gave to Wallace his advice

Good Bishop Sinclair is in Bute also,
Who, when he hears the news, will not be slow
To come and take his fate with cheerful heart,
He never yet did fail to act his part

Where Bishop Sinclair came to him on sight,
With clever lads from Bute, all young and tight (¹)

The southron bishop that fled from Dunkel',
To London rode, and told all that befell

Thus in defence the Hero ends his days,
Of Scotland's right, to his immortal praise,
Whose valiant acts were all recorded fair,
Written in Latin by the famous Blair,
Who at that time the champion did attend,
Was an eye-witness and his chaplain then,
And after that, as history does tell,
Confirmed by Sinclair, Bishop of Dunkel'

*Laws and Constitutions Scot Con 1845   His Chartulary Tytler Hist Tales of Scottish Wars

There are two episodes in Scottish history in which he occupies an honourable prominence

During the absence of King Robert Bruce in Ireland to assist his brother Edward in the conquest of that country, the English, who made several attempts to disturb the tranquillity of Scotland, appeared with an armament in the Frith of Forth, and anchored off Inverkeithing The panic created by the English was so great that the Earl of Fife and Sheriff of the County with difficulty assembled 500 cavalry with which to oppose the landing These, intimidated by the superior numbers of the English, were afraid to encounter them, and consulted their safety by flight Fortunately, however, the spirited Bishop of Dunkeld, who had in him more of the warrior than the ecclesiastic, received timely notice of the desertion Putting himself at the head of 60 of his servants, and with nothing clerical about him except a linen frock or rochet cast over his armour, he threw himself on horseback, and succeeded in rallying the fugitives, telling their leaders that they were recreant knights, and deserved to have their gilt spurs hacked off "Turn," said he, seizing a spear from the nearest soldier, "turn, for shame, and let all who love Scotland follow me." With this, he furiously charged the English, who were driven back to their ships with the loss of 500 men, besides many who were drowned by the swamping of one of the vessels On his return from Ireland, Bruce highly commended his intrepidity, declaring that St Clair should be his own bishop, and by the name of the King's Bishop this martial prelate, who is described as "right hardy, meikle, and stark," was long remembered in Scotland

When Edward Balliol won Scotland by the disastrous battle of Dupplin in 1332, secure from all opposition, he repaired to Scone, and in the presence of many of the gentry from Fife, Gowrie, and Stratherne, was crowned King of Scotland by his two prisoners, "Duncane, Earl of Fyffe, and William St Claire, the stoute Bishop of Dunkelden" "The King's Bishop" was the founder of the old Cathedral of Dunkeld. He is gracefully introduced by Lithgow in alluding to the motto of the Earls of Caithness

> "Commit thy work to God,
> O sacred motto! Bishop Sinclair's strain
> Who turned Fyfe's lord on Scotland's foes again"

THE GREAT MINION *

OLIVER SINCLAIR OF PITCAIRN AND WHITEKIRK.
1523—1585

This historical personage was fourth son of Sir Oliver St Clair of Roslyn, the favourite son of William St Clair, Earl of Orkney and Caithness, last Lord of the Isles His name figures frequently in Orcadian, Scottish, and English national records A staunch Romanist, he was a favourite with James the Fifth, over whom he had a great influence For these reasons he and his brothers incurred the special displeasure of the reformer Knox, who tells us that "many of King James' minzeons war pensionaris to preastis, amangis whome, Oliver Synclare, yitt remaning ennemye to God, was the principale" He was Governor of Tantallon Castle in 1540, when Sadler, the English ambassador, narrowly escaped seizure by him, and on 20th April, 1541, on rescission of Lady Sinclair's grant of Orkney, the Isles were committed to him as Donatary of the Tack

The most eventful incident with which the Minion is associated is the Scottish surrender at Solway Moss on the 23rd November 1542 The account of this so-called battle has usually been related to his

---

Knox's Memorial Hay's Chartulary Tales of a Grandfather, &c.

disparagement, and it is fitting that his memory should now be vindicated, although it may be a tardy removal of an unfair verdict. It had long been the wish of the Scottish Catholics to involve James V in war with his English uncle. Assembling an army, he advanced to Berwick and wished to enter England, but the nobility refused to follow him. Mortified by their action, he resolved to re-muster forces for an expedition to be known as his own raid. On approaching the river Esk the halt was sounded, and Oliver Sinclair was elevated on the "shield of war" to read the royal commission proclaiming him commander-in-chief. The disloyally affected nobles seized the appointment as a pretext for again thwarting their sovereign, and allowed themselves to be captured by a small party of English cavalry. The effect on King James was electrical, crushed in spirit, he died within a few days after the event. The captured nobles on their return formed a political faction with English interests, known as the "Assured Lords."

On the restoration of the Earl of Arran's government in 1584 Oliver Sinclair of "Solway Moss" made his historical exit in an object lesson to that bastard upstart. One day when the favourite was bustling into the Court of Justice, at the head of his numerous retinue, an old man, indifferently dressed, chanced to stand in his way. As Arran pushed rudely past him, the man, stopping him, said, "Look at me, my lord,—I am Oliver Sinclair." Oliver, as favourite of James V, had exercised during his reign as absolute a sway in Scotland as Arran now enjoyed under his grandson James VI. In presenting himself before the present favourite in his neglected condition, he gave Arran an example of the changeful character of court favour. The lesson was a striking one, but Arran did not profit by it.

HENRY, BISHOP OF ROSS *
†1565

Henry, third son of Sir Oliver St Clair of Roslin, was born in 1508, studied at St Andrews, and was incorporated in St Leonard's College in 1521, in 1537 was appointed Lord of Session, and admitted 13th November, same, as Rector of Glasgow, in 1541 became Commendator of the Abbey of Kilwinning, exchanged in 1550 for the Deanery of Glasgow. While Dean of Glasgow he went as ambassador to England in 1550, and thence to Flanders and concluded a peace with the Emperor. On his return from France in 1555 many legal reforms were introduced at his instance. He was a boundary Commissioner in May, 1557, became Lord President of the Court of Session 2nd December, 1558, and in 1560 was nominated to the see of Ross, special means being taken to expedite his appointment. A prelate present at the Convention of 22nd December, 1561, the Bishop of Ross was selected as one of twelve Privy Councillors, his high qualifications outweighing the then unpopularity of his cloth. Queen Mary asking his counsel, 20th May, 1563, as to the acts in limitation of Romanism, he affirmed "that she must see her laws kept or else she would get no obedience," and when she held her ninth parliament in June, 1563, in which the "Act of Oblivion" was ratified, the privilege of those worthy to enjoy it was entrusted chiefly to his decision. He disconcerted the Queen in December, 1563, by speaking in favour of Knox, then arraigned before Queen and Council. Queen Mary applied to Elizabeth of England, 20th February, 1563-4, for a safe conduct "unto our traist Counsalour Henry, Bischop of Ross." He died at Paris 2nd January, 1564-5, after undergoing a painful surgical operation. His name written upon various books and MSS preserved in the Advocates' Library, and in other collections, evince his great love of literature.

JOHN, BISHOP OF BRECHIN †
†1566

This prelate, fifth son of Sir Oliver St Clair of Roslin, was admitted Lord of Council and Session under the title of Rector of Snaw, 27th April, 1540, and in 1549 sat in the Provincial Council at Edinburgh as Dean of Restalrig. On 18th September, 1564, Queen Mary applied for a safe conduct for his return from the parts of France. He solemnised the marriage of Henrie, King, and Marie, Queen of Scots, at 6 a.m. Sunday, 29th July, 1565, in the Chapel of Holyroodhouse. In 1565 the Dean was promoted to the see of Brechin, and on 13th November, same, succeeded his brother as President of the Court of Session. He died of fever in April, 1566, at the house of James Mossman, Forrester's Wynd, Edinburgh, having then in his possession the materials collected by his brother Henry for writing a history of Scotland.

---

* Memorials of Knox. Tytler. Balfour's Annals. † Memorials of Knox.

SCOTTISH COURTIERS

'THE QUEEN'S KNIGHT'*
1490—1513

SIR JOHN SINCLAIR of Dryden, the subject of this sketch, was one of King James the Fourth's attendants or courtiers, and may have been of descent from the Edward Saintclair of Draidon of 1447. Sir John's name occurs in the Treasurer's Accounts as early as 1490, and it frequently appears down to 1512-13. In 1503 he was furnished with clothes preparatory to the king's marriage, and was one of his attendants. He probably afterwards became the "Queen's knicht," as the poet Dunbar styles him. The king and he frequently played at "rowbowlis" and "the cartis." November 3, 1506, he had a gratuity of £28 by the king's command. His wife received £10 as a New Year's gift, 1511-12, and a similar sum next January. Dr West, the English ambassador, writing 13th April, 1513, to King Henry, describes an interview with James V, and states when he went to see Queen Margaret at Linlithgow Palace he was "fetched by Sir John Sinclair on Sunday."† Sir John may have fallen at Flodden, as notices of him cease about that date. Dunbar refers to him thus in the first verse of his poem "Of a Dance in the Queen's Chalmer":

> Sir John Sinclair begouth to dance,
> For he was new come out of France,
> For ony thing that he do micht,
> The ane foot gaed aye unricht,
> And to the tother wald not gree
> Quoth ane, Tak up the Queen's knicht
> A merrier dance micht na man see

QUEEN MARGARET'S "PET."‡
1520-1528

On the exit of Sir John Sinclair of Dryden a PATRICK SINCLAIR enters on the scene. Margaret Tudor, Queen-Dowager of Scotland, in a letter of 1520 refers to her "man of law," PET SYNGLAR, and for the next few years he figures in connection with her English correspondence and embassies. In the State Papers of Henry the Eighth there are many letters written to, by, and about him, the notices being quite voluminous. Scotland was then disturbed by the contentions of two factions which had developed after the battle of Flodden, a French party headed by Alexander, Duke of Albany, and an English party which rallied round the Queen Dowager. Surrey writes Wolsey from the Borders, "Sinclair says that Albany must invade England or send the Frenchmen (6,000 upwards) home, for Scotland cannot support them." During the absence of the Regent Albany in France, Queen Margaret effected a *coup-d'état* by which her son King James, then in his thirteenth year, was declared of age, and proclamations were instantly issued in his name, while the Lords of Scotland in Council recognised him by a Profession of Obedience at Edinburgh, 31st July, 1524. The letter written to Henry in the name of the young king, informing him of his assumption of the government, was sent by Patrick Sinclair, whom Cardinal Wolsey denominates a right trusty servant of James, and at the same time describes as a spy of Dr. Magnus—the English ambassador—and a constant friend of England.

Queen Margaret in one of her letters to Patrick, commends herself heartily to him, and signs her strange literature, "Yours ze vyt,"—"Yours ye know." Patrick Sinclair, as she writes her brother, was her "trusty and true servant, and ever hath been to the king my husband." In 1526 (1528?) he was ambassador to England, and many letters testify to his kind reception. The one by Cardinal Wolsey is especially remarkable, recommending Patrick Sinclair as "right trusty" to Henry, then at Winchester, and reciting long and faithful services to his sister's party. Bishop Clerk's letter thence telling of the king's imperturbable silence as to what passed privately between himself and Patrick is a study as to secular wisdom baulking clerical curiosity.

---
* Dunbar's Poems † Sinclairs of England ‡ Sinclairs of England Tudor State Papers

Dr Magnus, the English ambassador at the Northern court, writes Wolsey that Patrick is one of the six nobles then wholly devoted as "right good Englishmen." He is never tired of praising him as "an honest gentleman," "our good friend and special lover," and as "very forward" in the cause. "Patrick Sinclair and Mr John Chisholm are nightly with us," writes the ambassador. Queen Margaret's letter in favour of Patrick to her brother of England is a highly historical document, part of which runs "Wherefore I beseech your grace kindly to be his good prince for my sake, and that you shall give commandment to the Earl of Surrey and the Lord Dacres, that he may be received and well treated in your said realm, if he has need. And this you will do at my request." Later on he was eclipsed by Henry Stuart, second son of the Earl of Avondale, and whose sister Barbara was married to Sir James Sinclair of Sanday, Orkney. His eclipse is well illustrated in a letter from the Duke of Norfolk in reply to a query from Wolsey. The Duke writes the Cardinal that Patrick Sinclair and Henry Stuart, who was becoming the favourite, were at variance, and he could not write letters by Patrick as bearer, because Patrick "cannot please her now." Henry Stuart, he informs the Cardinal, is made lieutenant to Lord Maxwell of some 200 men of special dignity, and "he doth put in and out at his pleasure, which Patrick Synclere did before." He says for final, "To please Henry Stuart she quarrelled with Patrick Synclere for not bringing a letter from me." By and bye Patrick regained his position. On the escape of James V from the custody of the Earl of Angus (a warm partisan of the English) in 1528, he despatched Patrick Sinclair to the English court with a message to Henry, informing him of the change which had taken place, and the assumption of the supreme power by the young monarch, and one of the charges against Angus was that he had used the royal authority against those border barons who declined to enter into bonds of maurent with him, "so that the king would not be able to have domination above him and his lieges"—MS Caligula, b 11, 224. Articles and Credence to be shewn to Patrick Sinclair, July 13th 1528. Signed by James the Fifth

Patrick was a natural son of Edward Sinclair of Dryden

THE KEEPER OF THE PRIVY SEAL *
1567

The abdication of Mary Queen of Scots in 1567 was obtained by violent means. Lord Lindsay being admitted to audience, his stern demeanour at once terrified her into compliance. He laid the instrument before her, and with eyes filled with tears and a trembling hand, she took the pen and signed the papers without even reading their contents. It was necessary, however, that they should pass the Privy Seal, and here a new outrage was committed. The keeper, THOMAS SINCLAIR, remonstrated, and declared that the Queen being in ward, her resignation was ineffectual. Lindsay attacked his house, tore the seal from his hands, and compelled him by threats and violence to affix the seal to the resignation †

COUNCILLOR OF THE DANISH REALM ‡
SIR ANDREW SINCLAIR
†1625.

Sir Andrew§ was third son of Henry III, sixth Lord Sinclair. Passing to Denmark at the close of the xvi th century, in 1611 he appears as Governor of the castle and town of Calmar, in 1617 as member of the "Rigsraad," and in 1621 as ambassador to England. In 1606 he accompanied King Christiern and acted as mediator between that king and Lady Nottingham, wife of the aged Armada hero, who had misconstrued an action of the royal Dane. A great friendship existed between Sir Andrew and the Lady Arabella Stuart, which letters still extant testify. The queen's jeweller received £320 for a diamond bought by His British Majesty to bestow on his "trusty and well-beloved servant, Sir Andrew Sinclere, knight." He died in 1625. In 1607 he received from King James a pension of £1,000, and in 1610 urged Robert, Earl of Salisbury, to send him his pension, and also to obtain a loan from King James as he had bought lands [Saintclersholme] in Denmark of the value of 40,000 crowns, part of

---

* Tytler † Blackwood's Magazine, October, 1817
‡ Scot's Expedition of 1612, Strickland's Queen, Sinclairs of England, Arabella Stuart, Danish Royal Archivist § See p 304

which he still owed. He also asked Lord Salisbury to be godfather and give his Christian name to a son born in that year. Many of his letters to Lord Salisbury written between 1610–1627 are in the Record Office, London. The Lyon Register of Genealogies has it that Sir Andrew of St Clair, Lord thereof, Councillor of Denmark, and Lord of Ghadsey, married a daughter of Stewart of Grandtully, and had a daughter Isobel, who married Andrew Bruce of Muness.

ACADEMICAL CELEBRITIES

DAVID ST CLAIR, PROFESSOR OF MATHEMATICS, UNIV. DE PARIS
(fl. 1603–1622.)

This professor was a man eminent in his time. There are extant some Latin tracts of his, one of them forming sixteen quarto pages of hexameters, celebrating the coming of James the Sixth to the English throne in 1603, and finishing appropriately with an astronomical diagram of the king's horoscope. There also survive thirteen Latin pages of his criticism of Euclid and Archimedes. His skill in drawing procures for him from one of his admirers the title of *eruditissimus Apelles*, while *Le Sieur de Philalethe, Disciple de Monsieur de Sainct Clair, Conseiller et Professeur du Roy es sciences mathematiques* attempts under his auspices the squaring of the circle. In 1607 David addresses Latin verses to the Queen of France, Margaret of Valois, on political grounds. Two lines of the poem by 'A M.' in his own praise may complete notice of this distingué.

> " Ergo te (Sanclare) manent tua debita landis
> Praemia, et ingenio debita palma tuo.' *

His works are: 1. *De Inauguratione Jacobi I*, Paris, 1603, 4to; 2. *Pro Archimede et Euclide Δικαιολογία*, 1622, fol.; 3. *Direction Cyclometrique, par le Sr. de Philathe*, 1622, fol. †

JOHN SINCLAIR, A.M., ‡
REGENT IN ST LEONARD'S COLLEGE, ST ANDREW'S,

was presented to the church and parish of Ormiston in East Lothian in 1646, and admitted 1647, member of Assembly 1648, visitor to Edinburgh University 1649. An adherent of the Protestors, in 1654 the Protector named him for visiting universities, &c. His sister Catherine is cited 8th and 9th October, 1679, for hounding and sending people to the rebellion. In December, 1682, he was deposed by public order of the Bishop of Edinburgh, when he removed to Holland and started an academy to prepare compatriots sojourning there for the university. Elected to the congregation at Delft in 1683, his admission was delayed till 1684, the Scottish Government having raised process against him for treasonable practices, ending in his forfeiture September, 1684. He died in 1687, aged about 69 years. His son John, minister of Kirkpatrick Irongray in 1690, died in 1623, much given to mathematical studies, but unfortunately disposed to melancholy; by Jean Maxwell, his wife, he had a daughter Sarah.

GEORGE SINCLARE, PROFESSOR AT GLASGOW UNIVERSITY ‡
1654–1696.

GEORGE SINCLAIR or SINCLARE, brother of the Rev. John Sinclar, Regent of St Andrews, elected Professor of Philosophy in the University of Glasgow 1654, and ejected in 1662 for refusing to comply with the episcopal form of church government, was restored in 1688, and retained his professorship (to which in 1691 that of mathematics was added) until his death in 1696. There is also a record of the Town Council of Edinburgh paying £10 sterling in 1672 as salary for one year to George Sinclair, one of the Regents, for acting in the capacity of Tutor of Mathematics § In 1665 a George Sinclair was Regent of Philosophy at the University of Edinburgh. The Regents of Philosophy taught in rotation the four classes in the Curriculum of Arts, the "Bajans," the "semi-Bajans," the

---
* Sinclairs of England. † ‖‖ ‡ Satiru's Invisible World Discovered, Preface. § Edinburgh University.

"Bachelors," and the "Magistrands," as the students of the first, second, third, and fourth years were respectively styled. Each Regent therefore taught every subject in the curriculum—the Regent of Humanity (Latin) being subordinate to the Regent of Philosophy, and being employed as a tutor in Classics to unmatriculated students. This system continued till 1708, when separate Professors were substituted for the Regents in the various chairs of the Faculty of Arts *

Chambers' Domestic Annals inform us that the almost sole active cultivator of physics in Scotland during that age was the celebrated George Sinclair, Professor of Philosophy in the University of Glasgow. He took a considerable interest in the operation of diving bells in connection with wreck recovery, and in a work entitled "Hydrostatical Experiments" describes an invention of his own—a kind of diving-bell which he called an ark. Referring in another work, "Ars Nova et Magna Gravitatus et Levitatus," to the recovery of some ordnance from the sunken wreckage of the *Florida*, he says the salvors were surprised to find that the bullets employed for the guns were stone instead of metal. The work by which he is most remembered, however, is "Satan's Invisible World Discovered." This curious book in defence of the belief in witchcraft was endowed by the Lords of the Privy Council with a copyright of eleven years. Notices of Professor Sinclair will be found in Wodrow's "Life of David Dickson," Hutton's Dictionary, Chambers' and Thomson's Biography, Dictionary of Eminent Scots, ed 1855, N 263 †

ANDREW ST CLAIR, PROFESSOR OF MEDICINE, UNIVERSITY OF EDINBURGH *
(fl 1720—1747)

ANDREW ST CLAIR, born c 1693, graduated in Arts 6th July, 1720, and Medicine 10th July, 1720, in the University of Angers, in France. He occupied one of the chairs in the Faculty of Medicine at the University of Edinburgh, and when a re-arrangement was made in 1726, by which the four professors then (9th February) appointed divided the teaching among themselves, the Chair of the Institutes of Medicine was allotted to him. In lecturing he took for his text book the "Institutiones Medicae of Boerhaave," and did not go beyond what was therein contained. His lectures were delivered in Latin, as indeed all those of the Medical Faculty then were, with the exception of those in Anatomy. Sinclair's Latin was considered remarkably elegant. On February 4, 1733, Dr St Clair was appointed by George III "our first physician within that part of Great Britain called Scotland" at an annual salary of £100. He wrote on the "Histories of Fever," &c Ed Med Ess, 1733 † His health failing, he withdrew from the professorial position, it is said in 1747, but from papers in the possession of Lord Sinclair it appears that he died before 28th September, 1742, when the widow of Dr St Clair is referred to.

*₊*Another of the *gens*, PATRICK SINCLAIR, occupied the Chair of Hebrew and Oriental Languages in the Faculty of Divinity at Edinburgh University in 1692. He is doubtless the "Patricius Sinclarus" whose Encomium of "Satan's Invisible World" and its author appears included in that work

THE MASTER OF SINCLAIR ‡
† 1750

John St Clair, Master of Sinclair, born 5th December, 1683, was the eldest son of Henry, Lord Sinclair, first baron of the Herdmanston line. He served as lieutenant in Marlborough's army with good reputation, but in vindication of his honour slew two officers, brothers to Sir John Shaw, of Greenock. Tried by court-martial, 17th October, 1708, he was sentenced to death, but in consideration of the great provocation given, recommended to the royal mercy, and meantime, with the connivance of Marlborough, escaped into Prussia. On the advent of the Tory administration in 1714 a pardon was accorded him.

In 1715 he reluctantly espoused the Jacobite cause. A vessel loaded at Leith with firelocks and other weapons intended for Sutherland got windbound at Burntisland. The Master being apprised of the circumstance, "suggested the seizure of these arms by a scheme which argued talent and activity, and was the first symptom the loyalists had given of either one or the other. This gallant young

---
Edinburgh University   Allibone   ‡ Sir Walter Scott

nobleman with about fourscore troopers, and carrying with him a number of baggage horses, left Perth about nightfall on the 2nd October, and to baffle observation took a circuitous road to Burntisland. His arrival in that little seaport town had all the effect of a complete surprise, and though the bark had hauled out of the harbour into the roadstead, he boarded her by means of boats, and secured possession of all the arms, amounting to 300 stand." At Sheriffmuir the Master led the Fifeshire squadron and two squadrons of Huntly's cavalry, forming the advance of the whole army, but remained inactive on the field, being, it seems, held in check by the dragoons of Argyle's second line. After the defeat the Master proceeded north to Strathbogie, and thence to Orkney, where, after viewing the ruins of the ancestral stronghold of Kirkwall, and moralising thereupon, he seized a vessel and escaped with some of his companions in misfortune to the Continent, where he remained until 1726, in which year he received a pardon for life. He then returned to Scotland, and resided at Dysart till his death, 20th November, 1750. He seldom ventured to Edinburgh, and always travelled armed and well attended, prepared for attack by the Schaws or other enemies. He married, first, Lady Margaret Stewart, daughter of James, fifth Earl of Galloway, and secondly, Emilia, daughter of Lord George Murray, and sister of the third Duke of Athol, but had no issue by either wife. In 1735 he had bought the Rosslyn estate, and was succeeded by his brother, General James St. Clair.

A DISTINGUISHED DIPLOMATIST.

The Hon. James St. Clair, *de jure* Lord Sinclair, was brother of the Master of Sinclair. He was a General in the British Army and a distinguished diplomatist. Hume, the celebrated historian, was at one time a member of his staff. The estate of Ravenscraig had, about 1715, been settled by Henry, Lord Sinclair, on the General and his brother, Major William, nominally in supersession of the Master of Sinclair, but virtually in conservation of his interests, as they were to account for the income to trustees appointed on his behalf. General St. Clair died without issue in 1762, when the estates became alienated from the St. Clair lineage and passed into possession of the Erskines.

AN UNFORTUNATE ENVOY.

MALCOLM, BARON SINCLAIR, SVENSK MAJOR *
(b. 1691 † 1739.)

Few events created a greater sensation in Sweden than the tragic fate of Major Malcolm Sinclair in 1739. He had previously been captured by the Muscovites at the decisive battle of Pultowa in 1709 and sent to Siberia for thirteen years. One of the most favourite officers of King Frederic, he was basely assassinated by Russian emissaries on his way to Constantinople bearing important despatches with reference to a treaty between Sweden and the Porte. The infamous Russian Court, having examined the despatches, coolly sent them, *via* Hamburg, to that of Sweden. Then the excitement became great. At Stockholm the population rose and wrecked the houses of Catherine's ambassador, crying out "that they were inspired by the soul of Sinclair." The remains of the latter were placed in a magnificent tomb, inscribed thus, by order of King Frederic. "Here lies Major Malcolm Sinclair, a good and faithful subject of the kingdom of Sweden, born in 1691, son of the worthy Major-General Sinclair and Madame Hamilton. Prisoner of war in Siberia from 1709 to 1722. Charged with affairs of State, he was assassinated at Naumberg, in Silesia, 17th June, 1739. Reader! drop some tears upon this tomb, and consider with thyself how incomprehensible are the destinies of poor mortals."†

His fate is feelingly alluded to in verse by Anders Odel, a noted poet, in the well-known lines of "Malcolm Sinclair's Visa."

SENATORS OF THE COLLEGE OF JUSTICE.

Several Sinclairs have been Senators of the College of Justice. Mention has already been made of Henry St. Clair of the Roslin family, who in 1537 was appointed a Lord of Session, and in 1558 became Lord President. On his death in 1565 his brother John St. Clair, then Dean of Restalrig, was advanced

---

* Scottish Soldiers of Fortune.

to the Presidentship, having been previously admitted as a Lord of Council and Session under the title of Rector of Snaw, 27th April, 1540. Both these brothers were learned in the law, and held in the highest estimation for their judicial qualities. At an interval of two centuries the *gens* again supplied two contemporary Lords of Session in the persons of John Sinclair, Lord Murkle, and George Sinclair, Lord Woodhall.

JOHN, LORD MURKLE
(*d.s.p.* 1755.)

was the second son of John Sinclair, 46th Earl of Caithness. He married Jean, daughter of the first Earl of Cromarty, by Anne, his wife, daughter of Sir James Sinclair of Mey. He died in 1755 without issue. He was appointed Solicitor-General on 18th January, 1721.

GEORGE, LORD WOODHALL.
(† 1761-5.)

George Lockhart Sinclair was the second son of Sir John Sinclair of Stevenson, Bart., by Martha, daughter of Sir John Lockhart of Castlehill. He became one of the Senators of the College of Justice by the title of Lord Woodhall. Alexander Sinclair, Earl of Caithness (brother to Lord Murkle), in 1761 executed an entail of Murkle and his other lands in favour of Lord Woodhall and his heirs-male of line. On the Earl's death in 1765, under this destination, the succession was taken up by Sir John Sinclair of Stevenson, nephew of Lord Woodhall, the latter having died without issue.

THE PASTOR OF KEISS.
SIR WILLIAM SINCLAIR OF DUNBEATH, BART.
† 1767.

Sir William Sinclair of Keiss was the eldest son of Sir James Sinclair, first baronet of Dunbeath, by Isabel, daughter of Sir Archibald Muir of Thornton, Provost of Edinburgh.

Keiss was founder of the Baptists in Caithness, who cherish his memory with affectionate regard. On embracing Baptist views Sir William went to London, where he was formally baptised, and admitted a member of his adopted church. He commenced preaching in Caithness about the year 1750, and continued to do so with great zeal for the space of fourteen years. In 1750 he formed the church at Keiss—the earliest Baptist church in Scotland—over which he regularly presided as pastor. In 1765 he removed to Edinburgh, where he died in 1767. His hymnal—containing some sixty songs of his own composition—was published in his lifetime, and is still in occasional use in his Keiss church. It is styled "A Collection of Hymns and Spiritual Songs," by Sir William Sinclair, Minister of the Gospel of God and servant of Jesus Christ." In his younger days it is stated that he was a short time in the army, where he learned to become an expert swordsman. He rendered a service to the Earldom by capturing a noted highwayman, one Marshall, the "Robber of Backlas," who had long levied blackmail on all and sundry, and terrorised the neighbourhood, having twice broken into the castle of Keiss and once into that of Dunbeath.

COMRADE OF WASHINGTON.†
MAJOR-GENERAL ARTHUR ST. CLAIR, U.S.A.,
1736–1818.

Arthur St. Clair, son of William Sinclair, merchant in Thurso, was born there, 22nd March, 1736. He studied at the University of Edinburgh in preparation for a professional life, and was indentured to the famous physician William Hunter, of London, but at the age of twenty-one abandoned medicine for an ensigncy in the army, 13th May, 1757. Under Amherst at Louisberg his gallantry won him promotion to the rank of lieutenant (17th April, 1759), and in the fatal struggle on the Plains of Abraham (1760), seizing the colours that had fallen from the hands of a dying soldier, he bore them

* Allibone.   † St. Clair Papers.

until the field was won by the British. Resigning his commission in 1762, in 1764 he settled on a fine landed estate in the Ligonier Valley, where he filled a number of prominent positions and took an active part in adjusting the boundary disputes between Pennsylvania and Virginia; but as the spirit of resistance towards British aggression gained growth, he in December, 1775, resigned his civil offices, took leave of wife, children, and as the event proved of fortune, repairing to Philadelphia on a summons from President Hancock. In January, 1776, he raised a regiment, and in May reached Quebec at a critical time and covered the retreat of the imperilled army. Through the disastrous days which followed Colonel St. Clair rendered efficient service until the wearied, weakened, plague-stricken and demoralised forces were brought into camp on the banks of Lake Champlain. On the 9th of August, 1776, St. Clair was made a Brigadier-General by Congress, and later in the year was ordered to leave the Northern Department and join Washington in the Jerseys. During the trials and hardships of the dark winter which followed, when the genius of Washington shone out so brightly at last, St. Clair was one of the faithful and trusted advisers of the Commander-in-chief. To his counsel are attributed the victories of Trenton and Princeton. It was in recognition of his distinguished services in this campaign that he was commissioned a Major General in February and assigned once more to command in the North. On the 12th of June, 1776, he took command of Ticonderoga, and was subjected to much cruel censure for abandoning that post twenty-four days later, where his works were commanded by guns of an enemy nearly 8,000 strong, against less than half that number of his own ill-equipped and worse-armed troops. His skilful retreat and generalship in evacuating preserved his troops to the Republic, resulting in the surrender of Burgoyne at Saratoga and the triumph of the American cause. He was court-martialled for the evacuation, but *unanimously* acquitted of all charges and WITH THE HIGHEST HONOUR. Suspended for a time from command he became a member of Washington's military family. He participated in the battle of Brandywine, shared the sufferings of Valley Forge, was a member of the court-martial which tried Andre, and the closing days of the war found him marching to the support of Greene in South Carolina.

Equally efficient in civil and military life, he was elected President of the last Continental Congress, 1787, and Governor of the North Western Territory, 1787, a post which he held for fourteen years, and under his administrative control the broad foundations of coming States were securely laid and established in the freedom and education guaranteed by the great charter. He was removed in 1802 by President Madison, and returned to Pennsylvania in his old age, to find his fortunes wasted, while the Government which he had served pleaded the statute of limitations to escape re-imbursing him for money advanced to prevent Washington's army from melting away. While administering Indian affairs he had become responsible for certain supplies, and this amount was also refused at first on the ground of an informality in his accounts, and when this was rectified the statute was pleaded once more. His property, a valuable one for those times, was finally forced to a sale and the old soldier and his family were reduced to want. In a log house on a bleak ridge by the side of the old State road from Bedford to Pittsburg, almost in sight of the broad acres which once were his, the closing days of the venerable patriot were ended selling "supplies" to waggoners. One day in August, 1818, he was found lying insensible on the road, the wheel of his waggon having come off in a rut, the faithful pony standing near waiting the word of command. He never rallied from the shock, and died on the last day of summer (31st August, 1818).

The General was President for Pennsylvania for the Society of the Cincinnati. His portrait is in a public building at Washington, below is an autograph signature graced with a beautiful whipcord flourish. Lake St. Clair and other American places are named in his honour. Numerous letters exist sent to His Excellency from military and diplomatic celebrities, amongst others Washington, La Fayette, Visct. Malartic, Generals Butler, Wayne, Gates, Greene, Knox, Paul Jones etc. His treaties with the Wyandottes and the Six Nations are very curious documents.

THE ABLE ULBSTERS.

SCOTLAND'S PROTO-STATISTICIAN.

THE RIGHT HON. SIR JOHN SINCLAIR OF ULBSTER, BART., 1754-1835.

Sir John Sinclair, only son of George Sinclair of Ulbster and Lady Janet, daughter of William, Lord Strathnaver, of the House of Sutherland, was born at Thurso Castle on the 10th of May, 1754. He succeeded to the estates at the age of sixteen. Educated first under the tutorship of John Logan, the poet-divine, he passed through the universities of Edinburgh and Glasgow, completing at Trinity College, Oxford. In 1780 he was returned M.P. for Caithness, which he represented until 1811, when he vacated his seat. No less than 367 publications are said to have emanated from his pen, traversing all manner of topics, but chiefly in the nature of industrial, agricultural, or political advancement. Some of these have been of incalculable benefit to the empire. Most notable among them may be cited "The History of the Revenue of the British Empire, 1784," "The Statistical Account of Scotland, 1798," "The Code of Health and Longevity," and the "Code of Agriculture." By his exertions the Board of Agriculture was formed in 1793, of which he was president for thirteen years. He made a European tour in 1786, visiting the courts of France, Holland, Prussia, Denmark, Russia, Sweden, etc., collecting much valuable information. In conversation at Warsaw with Stanislaus, King of Poland, the latter mentioned that the name of *Sinclair* was well known to him, especially in its Swedish connection, and King Gustavus remarked that in about sixty of the Scoto-Swedish nobility there were no less than three noble families of the name of Sinclair. Major Sternsward of Engelholm, in Scanie, writes him in the same connection, 8th January, 1808 : "I hope the name of Sinclair, by valour eternised in Schweden, gives to this, its second native country, a proof of its wish, that the happiness of mankind may increase." Sir John was knighted in 1786, and in 1788 was created a baronet with remainder in default of male issue to the issue of his daughters. He had, in 1784, applied to Pitt for a baronetage, by virtue of being heir and representative of Sir George Sinclair of Clyth ; and being then

THE RIGHT HON. SIR JOHN SINCLAIR OF ULBSTER, BART.

a widower with two daughters, he requested that the title should be descendible to them. As some reward for his public services, he was appointed Cashier of Excise, with an income of £2,000 a year He died at Edinburgh on the 24th December, 1835, in the 81st year of his age, and was buried in the Chapel Royal of Holyrood. In Caithness, which was a desert till his active spirit improved it, hundreds owe their success in life to his assistance at the outset. His sterling characteristics have been transmitted to his descendants, several of whom have attained meritorious eminence, viz.: Sir George Sinclair, M.P., 2nd Bart., author, died 1868; Catherine Sinclair, authoress, died 1864; The Ven. John Sinclair, Archdeacon of Middlesex, died 1875; The Ven. William Macdonald Sinclair, Archdeacon of London, born 1850.

SWEDISH SOLDIERS OF FORTUNE.

CHARLES GIDEON, BARON SINCLAIR,
MILITARY TACTICIAN (†1803.)

Charles Gideon, Baron Sinclair of Finnekumla, born at Stralsund, 12th November, 1730, was captain of the German Infantry Regiment, la Dauphine in France; Knight of the French order, "Pour la Mérite Militaire"; Knight of the Saxon order, and Second Chief of the French Colonel in the Swedish service; Gustavus III.; Colonel and Chief Master of the Ordnance; Knight Sword; General in 1799. In Louise Henrietta Eikbrecht de Roman Empire, by whom he With him expired the line of although from the notice next this Baron Sinclair was claimed St. Clair, a French soldier of dis- Descendance" attested by Sir attributes to this line a direct Ravenscraig, but the earlier A copy certified correct by the possession of the author of this connects with the Barons Finne- James Sinclair, Baron of Randel, line of Sinclairs, Counts of

BARON C. G. SINCLAIR.

Colonel of the said Regiment; "The White Falcon"; Colonel Regiment, Royal Suèdois; First Aide-de-Camp with King of the Swedish Artillery; General- Grand Cross of the Order of the 1773 he married at Strasburg, Durkheim, Countess of the Holy had no issue. He died in 1803. Sinclairs, Barons Finnekumla, hereafter it would appear that as sire by Charles Ferdinand de tinction. The "Genealogical John Sinclair, first of Ulbster, descent from the Barons of generations require examination. Royal Archivist of Sweden is in work. The same document kumla in the earlier generations from whom derives the present Lambahof. They thus now

represent the senior line of Finnekumla, and it may be also the Barons of Ravenscraig. They appear to be cadets of the Orcadian Sinclairs of Saba.

CHARLES FERDINAND, BARON DE ST. CLAIR,
KNIGHT OF THE LEGION OF HONOUR,

occupied a very foremost position in the Napoleonic Wars. In 1820, Charles Ferdinand, Baron de St. Clair, *colonel de cavalerie*, figured remarkably about the assassination of the Duc de Berry. "*Je suis assassiné.*" He protested to the chamber that he had warned the highest authorities, police and other, of the conspiracy, but that these, being themselves involved in it, had arrested and imprisoned him for his loyalty to the Bourbon prince. His papers are published in book form, and there are many references to his extraordinary military career, *aux bords du Rhin, dans l'armée de Condé, en Angleterre, aux Antilles, en Hollande, en Egypte, en Italie, en Espagne, en Portugal, en Russie, et en Allemagne*. He had seen twenty-three years' service, got eighteen wounds, and gained innumerable decorations. His enemy, M. Decazes, Minister of Police, afterwards Count, put him into great difficulty, because he accepted the cross of the Legion of Honour which one of the Bourbons offered him, through the Prince of Condé, two years later. He twenty-five years' of service formally needed were expired. The book is of historic interest as to a curiously unsafe time. The baron does not scruple to tell M. Decazes his mind, "N'etait point un parvenu comme lui, mais bien un descendant des ducs de Normandie (du côté maternal) et des comtes des Orcades et Oemodes ; un descendant de Jean comte de Saint Clair qui en 1649 préféra être depouillé de l'existence la plus brillante que de reconnaitre Cromwell ; un descendant de Henri comte de Saint Clair qui en 1689, fut le seul membre des parlement Britannique qui osait faire un protestation energique contre l'avenement de Guillaume prince d'Orange au trône des Stuarts ; le petit-fils de Jean, sire de Saint Clair qui en 1715 sacrifia des biens immenses, et fut obligé de s'expatrier par son energique devouement à la même cause : le fils de Charles Gédéon,* baron de St. Clair, colonel commandant le regiment royal Suédois, qui àpres avoir consacré sa vie au service des rois de France, fut sacrifié à Dijon le 29 Janvier, 1793 ; victime de son dévouement pour Louis XVI."

EMINENT ANTIPODEANS.

THE HON. ANDREW SINCLAIR, M.D.† (†26TH MARCH, 1861).

Andrew Sinclair, sometime Colonial Secretary of New Zealand, paid a visit to that Colony in the first instance for scientific purposes, landing at Wellington in 1840. He was appointed Colonial Secretary in succession to Lieutenant Shortland, on the 6th January, 1844, by His Excellency Governor Fitzroy, Captain R.N. The position was more than the equivalent of the Premiership of the present day, as in the absence of the Governor it then devolved upon the Colonial Secretary to fulfil his duties and act as Administrator, a function now assigned to His Honor the Chief Justice. This important office he continued to hold until the complete introduction into the colony of responsible government in May, 1856. He had in early life served as a surgeon in the Royal Navy. He is remembered as the first collector of specimens of New Zealand natural history, botany, conchology, and entomology. Indeed, so many specimens did he send Home by almost every mail to the Kew Gardens and the British Museum, that Dr. Grey, of the latter institution, was induced to commence the first scientifically arranged catalogue, which appears in Dieffenbach's work on New Zealand. Subsequently he accompanied Dr. (afterwards Sir Julius von) Haast in his first expedition to explore the sources of the rivers Rangitata and Ashburton. He attached himself to this party mainly with the intention of assisting in the proposed botanical researches in the mountain ranges, and whilst so engaged he met with his death in an attempt to wade across one of the main branches of the Rangitata. His companions buried him in a lonely grave at the foot of the glaciers, amongst the native shrubs and other natural objects which had formed the subject of his ill-fated researches,

THE HON. A. SINCLAIR, M.D.

26th March, 1861. Sinclair Head, in Cook Straits ; Mt. Sinclair in the Province of Nelson ; and various New Zealand flora are named after him.

The *Lyttelton Times* of 3rd April, 1861, refers to him thus : "Of all accidental deaths since the foundation of the settlement, none can be found so lamentable as that which it is our painful duty now to register. . . . Dr. Sinclair has left a name and a character behind him to which we regret we must fail to do justice. . . . The loss of one of his attainments and character is a public calamity. . . . The passion for science by no means closed the heart of Dr. Sinclair to human sympathies. If he earned reputation at a distance as a natural historian, he was better known in his immediate neighbourhood as a true philanthropist. In 1843, '44, and '45 Auckland underwent severe privations and distress, such as the settlers in our parts have never known. Many an industrious and honest man received then at Dr. Sinclair's hands the assistance necessary to tide him over the crisis ; and not a few prosperous men of the present day have reason in recalling that time, to name him as the man who enabled them to be what they are."

* This must be another than the Swedish tactician, as he died *s.p.*
† Mennell's Dictionary of Australasian Biography.

FOUNDERS OF BLENHEIM, N.Z.

JAMES SINCLAIR of Nybster, Wick, Caithness, had issue there, by Christina Campbell his wife, on 1st November, 1817, a son also named James, the subject of this notice. The latter was married by the Rev. John Mackay of Lybster on the 14th May, 1850, to Christina (born 25th December, 1827), daughter of John Sutherland, merchant, of Hillhead of Lybster, and Jane Harriet Gordon Sutherland, his wife. Acting under medical advice, Mr. Sinclair resolved to emigrate to New Zealand, and took passages for self, wife, eldest son, and nurse (afterwards well-known in Wairau as Mrs. Charles Brindell) in the ship *Agra*, which left London in November, 1851, and arrived in Wellington 3rd March, 1852. The May following he removed to Nelson, where he started business with a stock of goods which he had brought out with him from Manchester. Hearing favourable reports of the Wairau, Mr. Sinclair went there in October, 1852, and so greatly was he impressed with the capabilities of the district, he determined to establish himself at Blenheim there, although the Wairau massacre was still fresh in the minds of all.

CHRISTINA SUTHERLAND SINCLAIR,
Foundress of Blenheim.

JAMES SINCLAIR, M.P.C.
Founder of Blenheim.

Prospering greatly, he put himself in the forefront of every movement to send the district ahead. Gifted by nature with commanding abilities, he commenced an agitation which culminated in the separation of the Wairau from Nelson and the creation of the Province of Marlborough. Mr. Sinclair was one of the first members of the new Provincial Council, and continued to hold his seat until the Abolition of 1876. Though repeatedly pressed, he declined the office of Superintendent, but his great popularity and political influence made him a power to be reckoned with. With the assistance of Messrs. W. H. Eyes and Henry Dodson, he succeeded in deposing Picton as the provincial capital in favour of Blenheim, but although he tried very hard, he was unable to get the latter city made the Colonial seat of Government. After abolition of the provinces Mr. Sinclair gave his attention more to questions of river conservation and matters municipal. A staunch Presbyterian, while unostentatious in his religious professions, Mr. Sinclair was a liberal supporter of the Kirk both in money contributions and in land. No friend ever asked his help in vain, so long as he possessed the means of assistance, and in the early days his hospitality was proverbial, while his succour in times of distress and floods will long be remembered. He died at Blenheim on the 9th August, 1897, his remains received Christian burial on the 11th same, the pall-bearers consisting of the Mayor, the Town Clerk, and other leading citizens of Blenheim, desirous to thus attest their respectful estimation.

Mrs Sinclair predeceased her husband. They built the first house in Blenheim. An affectionate and devoted wife, she braved the dangers of her environs, and speedily won from the natives respect and friendly regard. Brought up in an affluent and genial home, hospitality and kindness were natural to Mrs Sinclair, whose sweet and amiable nature endeared her to all of her friends and acquaintances. She died at Blenheim on the 23rd December, 1895. The memory of these two estimable colonists will long be preserved in Marlborough. Issue

1. JAMES JOHN SINCLAIR, born 2nd September, 1851, married at Rangiora 12th June, 1883, to Jane (eldest daughter of the late William Atkinson of Rangiora, sheepfarmer, and his late wife Dorothea Henrietta Christiana), relict of William Blick, of Blenheim. Mr Sinclair is resident at Christchurch, N Z, where he is trustee for several important estates. While a burgess of Blenheim the interests of Mr J. J Sinclair and that city were one and indivisible. If the father had been founder of the capital, superintendent-maker and provincial patriarch, no less was the son in line with the parental policy. An assiduous councillor of Blenheim for six years, that city has been greatly a gainer by his energising influence, especially in the matter of extensive building improvements. These he commenced to enterprise in 1883, now recalled by citizens as the "Sinclair Era," when the click of the hammer resounded from Grove Road to the further extremity of the town belt. His most notable erection was the Criterion Hotel, a palatial building of 75 rooms, of which the furniture alone cost £4,200. The present fine appearance of Blenheim is largely attributable to his initiative ventures. Defective municipal appliances and the prohibitory insurance rate of £4 per cent rendered it impossible to make adequate provision against fire, a contingency that occurred some years later, and occasioned a series of reverses that suggested removal to Christchurch, where the facilities of artesian water minimise such hazards. Issue

   ALBERT TREVOR, born in Blenheim, 16th April, 1884
   JAMES RUSSELL, born in Blenheim, 20th March, 1890

2. JOHN SINCLAIR, born 2nd July, 1853, builder by occupation, at sea, reported last from Antwerp, 15th July, 1894, when he was on the ship *Record*, owned by Andrew Gibson of Liverpool

3. WILLIAM SINCLAIR, born 6th March, 1855, Crown Solicitor at Blenheim for the Judicial District of Marlborough from 1879 to 1893, when he resigned in order to contest a seat in the House of Representatives for the Wairau electorate, but was not successful. A Liberal in politics, Mr Sinclair's entry into political life is desired by many of our leading politicians, when elected, it will not be long before he occupies a portfolio. For many years he has held office as Councillor of Blenheim, and as a member of the Education Board of Marlborough, he is one of the leading barristers in New Zealand. Mr Sinclair married, 19th November, 1878, Sarah McRae, third daughter of the late Alexander Mowat, of "Altimarlock," Awatere. Issue

   KATE LILIAN, born 9th Sept, 1879 ETHEL MURIEL, born 31st Dec, 1880
   AMY MILDRED ALICE, b June 28, 1882 WILLIAM ROBERT, born 3rd Dec, 1883
   ALEXANDER MOWAT, died 6th September, 1886, aged 6 months
   GERALD ERNEST MOWAT, born 11th January, 1888
   ELSIE EDITH VIOLET EVELYN, died 10th July, 1894, aged three and a-half years
   SIBYL GERALDINE, died 11th April, 1897, aged 1 year and 1 month

4. SON, born and died 10th September, 1856 5 SON, born and died 30th March, 1858
6. JANE HARRIET GORDON, born 15th April, 1859, resides Blenheim, married at Wakefield, Nelson, 9th August, 1878, to her cousin, Sutherland John Macalister, who died at Blenheim, 3rd December, 1897
7. DAVID SINCLAIR, born 5th October, 1860, died 30th December, 1862
8. PATRICK SUTHERLAND SINCLAIR, born 16th May, 1862, died 19th January, 1868
9. DAVID PATRICK SINCLAIR, born Dec. 23, 1868, barrister and solicitor, resident at Blenheim.

MAYOR OF INVERCARGILL.

JOHN SINCLAIR,
Mayor of Invercargill, New Zealand.

John Sinclair was born in Latheron, Caithness, on the 19th October, 1857. His parents emigrated to New Zealand in 1859, and took up land on the Taieri, some twenty-eight miles from Dunedin, where they and some of the children still reside. John Sinclair, the eldest son, has achieved civic distinction in the Province of Southland, having in 1895 been elected Mayor of Invercargill, the southernmost borough of the British Empire. His career has been one of constant effort. Up to the age of 21 he worked on the homestead, and acquired a high local reputation for skill in agricultural matters, gaining numerous prizes for ploughing, which at that time, when only the single furrow plough was in use, required a steady hand and true eye. He next occupied himself striking the forehammer in a station blacksmith's shop on the Waitaki, transition from which to the agricultural work required on the station was easy, and, as was to be expected of one who threw his whole energy into his work, his employers were so well satisfied that, opportunity arising, they recommended him for the position of manager of an estate of 20,000 acres in the McKenzie country, where he remained until 1879, when, tired of a comparatively isolated existence, he returned home. After a short interval, he assumed management of a property near Waihola, owned by Mr. A. Lee Smith, who presently entrusted him with that of a more important estate at Toi Toi, Mataura, consisting of four properties known as Birchwood, Thornhill, Ocean View, and Springfield, and comprising in all about 9,000 acres, then in a somewhat neglected condition. In four years' time improvements were brought about, and the proprietors availed themselves of a favourable opportunity to realise. At this stage Mr. Sinclair turned his attention to business of an entirely different character. Taking up his residence in Invercargill, he became connected with the firm of Carswell and Co., stock and station agents. From this starting point he became auctioneer for the J. G. Ward Company, and remained in that capacity until 1893, and was recognised as one of the best wool salesmen in the colony. Nelson Bros., Limited, having bought the Ocean Beach Freezing Works, Mr. Sinclair was selected as chief buyer, and remained in that situation until 1896, when for personal reasons he severed the connection.

John Sinclair, Mayor of Invercargill, N.Z.

From the time of his arrival in Invercargill, Mr. Sinclair took a lively interest in municipal and political affairs. A councillor in 1892, he was returned for his ward for a second term unopposed, and in 1895 was elected Mayor by a large majority. He stood in Liberal interests for Invercargill at the General Election of 1896, and polled 1,659 votes against 2,237 and 646 registered in favour of the other candidates. While managing at Waihola, Mr. Sinclair married Miss Jessie McIntyre, who was born in Argyle, Scotland. They have issue four daughters and three sons.

BOOK III

CAMEOS AND SAGAS

ST CLAIR

A PRAYER, BY R W ST CLAIR.

I

THOU, *the godfather of a lofty race*,
  In daily prayer kneeling within thy cell,
Lived in humility beside a well—
  Which since relieves afflictions of the face
And ever, when the suff'rer wends to dip
  Into its crystal depths, his sight revives,
He blesses thee, who art his *Hope*—his "Ship
Of Promise"—he but trusts in thee and thrives

II

Thou, who did write in the far years long past
  "THE RITUAL OF DIVINE DUTY" (for all
Of future ages, who in doubt should fall)—
  A golden deed, the meed whereof shall last
It guides the Christian in his darkest hour—
  It comforts him when dolour o'er him hangs,
In time of tribulation 'tis a tower,
Shelters him from the Serpent and his fangs.

III

Thou, who when tried thyself, withstood all ill,
  And dared the Tempter—though in woman's guise
He plied thee with the cunningest device—
  Tried to pollute thy fountain at the rill—
Albeit triumphant, still thy life thou lost
Relentless foes slew thee when stricken down,
  Despatching thee to join the Heavenly Host,
Winning for thee for aye the Martyr's Crown

IV

Thine ashes peaceful were not let to rest—
  Scattered by pagan Norsemen o'er La France,
In many burials came to earth, perchance
  O'er all a hallowed fane each spot doth test
Guard thou thy *Name*, o'er it keep watch and ward!
Protect thy *gens*, shield them from every taint!
  This is the prayer of those who serve thy Lord—
Evangelist and Hermit! Martyr! Saint!

ORCADIA

LAND OF THE ENGRAILED CROSS
(DAVID VEDDER)

Land of the whirlpool—torrent—foam,
  Where oceans meet in maddening shock,
The beetling cliff—the shelving holm—
  The dark, insidious rock
Land of the bleak, the treeless moor—
  The sterile mountain, sered and riven,
The shapeless cairn, the ruined tower,
  Scathed by the bolts of heaven
The yawning gulf—the treacherous sand—
I love thee still, my native land

Land of the dark—the Runic rhyme—
  The mystic ring—the cavern hoar,
The Scandinavian seer—sublime
  In legendary lore
Land of a thousand Sea-kings' graves—
  Those tameless spirits of the past,
Fierce as their subject Arctic waves,
  Or hyperborean blast
Though polar billows round thee foam,
I love thee! Thou wert once my home

With glowing heart, and island lyre,
  Ah! would some native bard arise
To sing with all a poet's fire
  Thy stern sublimities,
The roaring flood—the rushing stream
  The promontory wild and bare,
The pyramids where sea-birds scream
  Aloft in middle air,
The Druid temple on the heath,
Old, even beyond tradition's breath

Though I have roamed through verdant glades,
  In cloudless climes, 'neath azure skies,
Or plucked from beauteous orient meads
  Flowers of celestial dyes
Though I have laved in limpid streams,
  That murmur over golden sands,
Or basked amid the fulgid beams
  That flame o'er fairer lands,
Or stretched me in the sparry grot,—
My country! Thou wert ne'er forgot

THE SWORD CHANT OF THORSTEIN THE RED
(WILLIAM MOTHERWELL)

Thorstein the Red was a son of Olaf the White, King of Dublin. Uniting his forces with those of Earl Sigurd of Orkney, they conquered Caithness, Strathnaver, and Sutherland from the Scots (875). On the death of Guttorm, son of Sigurd, the conquered territories appear to have passed to Earl Duncan (*a quo* Duncansbay), a Scottish noble who had married the Lady Groa, daughter of Thorstein, and heiress of his Scottish conquests. Their daughter Grelauga married Earl Thorfinn of the Orkneys, whose fame has been recorded as the "Cleaver of Helmets," and from these two is lineally descended the present Earl of Caithness, and all the St Clairs of the Isles. Thorstein's warlike spirit is graphically presented to us in the following animated stanzas:—

'Tis not the gray hawk's flight o'er mountain and mere,
'Tis not the fleet hound's course, tracking the deer,
'Tis not the light hoof-print of black steed or gray,
Though sweltering it gallop a long summer's day,
Which mete forth the lordships I challenge as mine,
    Ha! ha! 'tis the good brand
    I clutch in my strong hand,
That can their broad marches and numbers define
    LAND GIVER! I kiss thee

Dull builders of houses, base tillers of earth,
Gaping, ask me what lordships I owned at my birth,
But the pale fools wax mute when I point with my sword
East, west, north, and south, shouting "There am I lord!"
Wold and waste, town and tower, hill, valley and stream,
    Trembling, bow to my sway
    In the fierce battle fray,
When the star that rules fate is this falchion's red gleam
    MIGHT GIVER! I kiss thee

I've heard great harps sounding in brave bower and hall,
I've drunk the sweet music that bright lips let fall,
I've hunted in greenwood, and heard small birds sing,
But away with this idle and cold jargoning!
The music I love is the shout of the brave,
    The yell of the dying
    The scream of the flying,
When this arm wields death's sickle and garners the grave
    JOY GIVER! I kiss thee

Far isles of the ocean thy lightning hath known,
And wide o'er the mainland thy horrors have shone
Great sword of my father, stern joy of his hand,
Thou hast carved his name deep on the stranger's red strand,
And won him the glory of undying song
    Keen cleaver of gay crests,
    Sharp piercer of broad breasts,
Grim slayer of heroes, and scourge of the strong!
    FAME GIVER! I kiss thee

In a love more abiding than that the heart knows,
For maiden more lovely than summer's first rose,
My heart's knit to thine, and lives but for thee
In dreamings of gladness thou'rt dancing with me,
Brave measures of madness, in some battle-field,
    Where armour is ringing,
    And noble blood springing,
And cloven, yawn helmet, stout hauberk, and shield
    DEATH GIVER! I kiss thee

The smile of a maiden's eye soon may depart,
And light is the faith of fair woman's heart,
Changeful as light clouds, and wayward as wind,
Be the passions that govern weak woman's mind
But *thy* metal's as true as its polish is bright:
    When ills wax in number,
    Thy love will not slumber,
But, starlike, burns fiercer the darker the night
    HEART GLADDENER! I kiss thee

My kindred have perished by war or by wave,
Now, childless and sireless, I long for the grave
When the path of our glory is shadowed in death,
With me thou wilt slumber below the brown heath,
Thou wilt rest on my bosom, and with it decay,
    While harps shall be ringing,
    And Scalds shall be singing
The deeds we have done in our bright fearless day
    SONG GIVER! I kiss thee

THE VISIT OF EARL THORFINN

(SIR EDMUND HEAD)*

"The history of the event touched upon here is to be found in the *Orkneyinga Saga*. Earl Thorfinn, who was the fourth son of Sigurd, died in 1064. He was only five winters old when he was made an earl by Malcolm, King of Scots, his mother's father; and he held the title for seventy years. This fierce and warlike man not only slew his nephew, Earl Rognvald, the son of Brusi, but he also put to death in cold blood those adherents of King Magnus who had sided with Rognvald. It is to that massacre the ballad alludes. After his death his deeds of bravery were celebrated in verse, which may be seen in the Saga above referred to. One of the closing stanzas is given as a specimen of the Scandinavian poetry of that wild period :—

> 'The bright sun swarthy shall become, in the black sea the earth shall sink,
> Austri's labour shall be ended, and the wild sea hide the mountains,
> Ere there be in those fair islands born a chief to rule the people—
> May our God both help and keep them! Greater than the lost Earl Thorfinn.'

Such a glimpse into the beginning of the eleventh century reveals the condition of North Britain under the ruthless Jarls. The traveller from the South may now pass through all those places without having his sensibilities shocked by any cold-blooded massacre. The eternal sea whispers not of such scenes as her waves ripple at your feet; and the rocky caverns only moan a requiem over all such melancholy incidents."†

> The sea still ebbs and flows the same as then,
> The same stars peep from out the midnight sky,
> But in those isles and bays are other men
> Than those who lived and died in days gone by—
> Those days that are so far beyond our ken.

King Magnus sat at his mid-day meal,
  Where his fleet at anchor rode,
When a stranger crossed the royal deck,
  And straight to the table strode.

He greeted the king, he took the loaf
  That lay upon the board,
And broke, and ate, as if of right,
  Whilst neither spoke a word.

King Magnus gaz'd, as he wiped his beard,
  "Wilt thou not drink?" he said,
And passed the cup. The stranger drank,
  And bowed in thanks his head.

"Thy name?" "My name is Thorfinn, sir."
  'Earl Thorfinn! Can it be?'
He smiled. "Well, yes, men call me thus
  Beyond the western sea."

"And is it so?" the king replied
  "I had resolved me well
That if we two met—what pass'd when we met
  Thou should'st not live to tell.

"Together now we've broken bread,
  And thus my hand is stayed;
But think thou not the score is quit,
  Though vengeance be delayed."

It chanced as friends they drank one day—
  On the deck a Norman stood,
"Lord Earl," he said, "from thee I claim
  The price of a brother's blood.

"When Kirkwall street was drench'd in gore,
  And the King's men slaughter'd lay,
By thy command that brother died—
  Wilt thou his man-bote pay?'"

Loud laughed the Earl. "What ho! thou fool,
  Thou must oft have heard it said,
How Thorfinn scores of men hath slain,
  But man-bote never paid."

"All this, lord Earl, is nought to me;
  'Tis nought if our king sits by,
Nor cares to avenge those men of his
  Led out like sheep to die."

---

* Fraser's Magazine of January, 1868.   † "Rambles in the Far North," by R. M. Ferguson.

Then Thorfinn looked again, and swore
 "By the rood ! I know thee well ,
Why, I gave thee thy life in Kirkwall town,
 When all thy comrades fell

"My chance is hard—I have oft been blamed
 Too many that I slew ,
And now this coil hath come about
 Because I've slain too few "

The king's brow flushed with wrath—"Forsooth'
 It seemeth to vex thee sore
That in thwarting my rights and slaying my men,
 Thou hast not done still more "

* * * *

But now a fair breeze fills each sail,
 And pennons are floating free,
As the long warships, with their dragon heads,
 Go cleaving the dark blue sea

And aye to the west of the Norway fleet,
 Earl Thorfinn steers his bark ,
Men saw her holding her course with them
 One night when the sky grew dark

But when morning broke that bark was gone
 Far, far o'er the western foam,
Where Orkney breasts the waves, and where
Earl Thorfinn sits in Kirkwall fair,
 Sole lord of his island home.

THE ROYAL HUNT OF ROSLIN.*

King Robert the Bruce, when he was returned from Ireland, and his countrey free from King Edward's tyranny, began to take pleasure in pastimes, as hunting and hawking So upon a time he appointed a great hunting upon Pentland Hills, which was then the king's forrest, and when his nobles were all assembled, and had made two or three days' pastime, he declared to them how he had oft hunted a white faunch deer, neither ever could his hounds prevaill, and desired them if they had any to try them They hearing the king's speech, denied that they had any could kill the deer Sir William Saintclair, haveing two red fellow hounds, named Help and Hold, says, not thinking that any should charge his words, that he would wager his head that they should kill the deer before ever she came over the marche burne , but the words no sooner evanished in the aire, but it was declared to the king, who takeing indignation that his hounds should be speediest, would have him abide att his word, and laid against his head all Pentland Hills and Pentland Moor, with the Forest, and immediately he caused make proclamation that all should bind up their hounds, and be quiet, least they should affray the deer, except a few horsemen with ratches to search her forth Sir William Saintclair, greatly astonished at that, went with his hounds to the best hounding part he could find, and, according to the custome of that time, he prayed to Christ, the blessed Virgin Marie, and Sainte Kathrine, as mediators, to save him from danger His prayer was no sooner ended, but the deer, by clamour of the people being raised, came off the back hills to that part where he was, who hunting his hound called Hold first, then Help, and followed speedily himself, being mounted upon a gallant steed, till he saw the hinde passe to the middle of the burne, wherat he fell on his face, beseaching Christ to have mercie on him, but the hound called Hold came to the deer, and made her stay in the burne, and then Help came and made her goe to the same side where Sir William was, and there slew her The king sieing this, came and embraced Sir William, and gave him those lands in free forestrie, which contained the Kirktone, Loganhouse, Earncraig, Whitehaugh, Easter and Wester Summerhopes, Back and For Spittles, Midlethird and Skipperfields After this Sir William Saintclair, in remembrance of this, in the place where he made his last devotion, builded the church of St Kathrine in the Hopes, which now remains to this day Know, reader, that the hill on which King Robert stayed till the deer was hunted, to this day is called the King's Hill, and the place where Sir William hunted is called the Knight's field It is reported that Sir William Saintclair sent a priest to the grave of that holy woman Saint Kathrine, in which there is a precious oyle, that issueth from her bones, to bring him therof, that he might carry it to his new-builded chapell The priest goeing, and returning with the oyle, he became so weary that he was forced by the way to rest him att a place a mile distant from Libertoune Church, where falling asleep upon a rush bush near by, lost his oyle The news wherof comeing to Sir William Saintclair, he made workemen to digge the place where the oyle was spilt, and presentlie up sprung a fountaine, which to this day hath like a black oyle swimming upon it He then bethought himself of the great robberie committed about Sainte Kathrines in the Hopes, considering that Saint Kathrine would not permit the baulme of her bones to be brought to sutch a prophane place, least they who came to worship there should, without all relligious reverence, be rigorously robbed *

EFFIGY,
SIR WM. ST. CLAIR.

Sir William was slain by the Moors in Spain while escorting the Heart of Bruce to the Holy Land in 1330. The effigy on his tombstone on the floor of Roslin Chapel depicts him standing upon the dead stag, in the attitude of adoration and gratitude. The figures of his two hounds, Help and Hold, are near the top of the stone at either side of the knight's head. Sir William erected a chapel at Pentland endowed with ground in the neighbourhood; the Reformation levelled this chapel to the ground, but the churchyard is still in good repair, and there are two stones lying flat upon the ground, the crusading cross and sword on each of them, with the inscription nearly obliterated, which, in all probability, are connected with the knight and his history. A stone of the identical pattern was lately (1848) found at Roslin, with "Sir William St. Clair" upon it, but no date or other inscription. The knight, likewise erected upon the same estate another monastery, dedicated to St. Katherine, the tutelary saint of the family, which was also demolished at the Reformation. Lady St. Clair, the heiress of Orkney, built and endowed near the Meadows, at Edinburgh, on the same Pentland estate, a splendid monastery for Dominican nuns, and dedicated to St. Katherine of Sienna. At the Reformation, too, the magistrates of Edinburgh seized upon the revenues of this convent, and the poor gentlewomen who had been educated as nuns, and spent their lives in devotion within its sacred walls, were turned out upon the wide world; nor would the magistrates, until compelled by Queen Mary, allow the nuns a subsistence out of the funds with which Lady St. Clair had endowed the convent.

Early in the present century the chapel built upon the spot where the stag was killed was in fair preservation; but stone enclosures being in progress of erection on the farm on which it stood, the farmer, with a feeling worthy only of a Gothic age, took its stones to build the dykes. Beneath the altar the workmen came upon an urn. The barbarians, impatient to see what it contained, broke it to shivers, and, to their joy, it was found to contain gold and silver coin, no doubt deposited by the heroic huntsman when laying the foundation of the chapel. This quasi-sacrilegious act was followed by a visitation termed by the pious as

THE VENGEANCE OF HEAVEN,

for the labourers employed to pull down the chapel and who broke the urn, being employed a few days after in a stone quarry, a mass of earth fell upon them, killing all but one man, who was made lame for life, and wandered in poverty as a living monument of sacrilegious profanity.* And again, by a curious coincidence, when the proprietor of the place whereon was situated the Dominican nunnery founded by Lady St. Clair employed masons to pull down the sacred walls of that chapel, the scaffolding gave way and the tradesmen were killed. This being viewed as a judgment of heaven for demolishing the house of God, no entreaties nor bribes have been able to prevail upon tradesmen to accomplish its entire demolition.†

HELP AND HOLD.

A LEGEND OF THE HOUSE OF ST. CLAIR.
(BY G. J. WHYTE-MELVILLE.)

"Now fie! now fie!" quoth Robert the king—
  And the red blood flew to his brow, [ring—
And the weight of his hand bade the beakers
  "I am shamed this day, I trow!

"In stable and hall I have steeds and men,
  I have hounds both staunch and free;
But the white faunch deer of the hawthorn glen
  Makes light of my woodcraft and me!

And I vow to St. Hubert as I sit here,
  To St. Andrew, St. Rule, and St. Bride, [deer,
Till I've sounded '*the mort*' o'er the white faunch
  No more in the woodland to ride!"

Then up and spake the bold St. Clair,
  Was drinking the red wine free,
"The lands of thy vassal are scant and bare,
  My liege, as they should not be.

---

* Royal Hunt of Roslin (Jackson)   † Arnot's Edinburgh.

"But had I the space by wood and wold,
    To breathe them a summer's day,
I'd ask but my two hounds, Help and Hold,
    While I brought the white deer to bay!"

"Ye are stout," quoth the King—"ye are stout,
    As behoves a St Clair to be,   [my lord,
But there's many a brag at the evening board
    Winna stand in the morn on the lea

The lands of the Strath, both far and near,
    Shall be yours if her flight ye can turn,
And bring me to grips with the white faunch deer,
    Ere she win through the black march burn

But a man dare not take if he dare not lose,
    And the venture is yet to be said   [choose,
Should your good hounds fail, then ye shall not
    My lord, but to forfeit your head"

"A wager! a wager!" cried bold St Clair.
    "See, bring me both hound and horn,
Go saddle the bonny black Barbary mare,
    The fleetest that feeds on corn

A wager! a wager! on Help and Hold!
    Was never a lord of my line
But wou'd wager his life against lands and gold,
    My liege, the broad Strath shall be mine!"
          *   *   *   *   *
They saddled their steeds at mirk o' night,
    They mounted when dawn was near,   [light,
And they slipped the good hounds with the dim grey
    On the track of the white faunch deer

The white faunch deer like an arrow flew,
    The good hounds followed fast,
I trow they drove her from slot to view,
    Ere noon was fairly past

Still first in the chase rode bold St Clair,
    The Bruce spurred hard in his track,

And the foam stood white on the Barbary mare,
    And the King's bonny bay grew slack

"She fails," quoth St Clair, "and the good
    St Katherine speed their flight! [hounds gain,
Now cote her! and turn her across the plain,
    For the black march burn is in sight!"

The black march burn falls steep at the bank,
    To the pitch of a horseman's chin,
But Hold's grey muzzle is hot on her flank,
    And the white faunch deer leaps in

Light down! light down! thou St. Clair bold!
    Or never go hunting more,
Now have at her, Help! now hang to her, Hold!
    And they turn her back to the shore

The King's bonny bay a good bow-shot mark
    Stopped short of the Barbary mare,
And the hounds stood grim and the deer lay stark
    At the feet of bold St Clair

"My liege! my liege! will ye take the knife?"
    The St Clair bent his knee
"By St Katherine's aid, both lands and life
    Have my good hounds won for me

And I vow to St Katherine I'll build a shrine
    In 'the Hopes' by the western wave,
And I vow to St Hubert these hounds of mine
    Shall be carven in stone on my grave!"

The bold St Clair he sleeps in Spain,
    For with good Lord James he had part,
When they hewed a red path through a host of
    To follow the Bruce's heart   [slain,

But Help and Hold, as I've been told,
    May be seen in St. Katherine's chapelle,
And scion and heir of the house of St. Clair
    Still love a good hound well

THE HEART OF THE BRUCE *

When on his deathbed King Robert the Bruce assembled around him the nobles and counsellors whom he had most trusted, whom he informed that it had been his intention had he lived to have gone to Jerusalem to make war upon the Saracens who held the Holy Land, as some expiation for the evil deeds of his life, more particularly for the murder of the Red Comyn But as he was about to die, he wished his heart to be taken to Palestine, and entrusted the sacred office to Sir James "the Good" Douglas, who, accompanied by Sir William St Clair of Roslin, Sir Robert Logan, and many other Scottish barons, started on the journey, but were fated never to reach the intended destination Hearing that Alonzo, King of Castile and Leon, was fighting against Osmyn, the Moorish Governor of Grenada, the Scots, having regard to the religious nature of their mission and the vows they had taken before leaving Scotland, viewed the cause of Alonzo as a holy warfare, and before proceeding to Jerusalem determined to first visit Spain, and signalise their prowess against the Saracens. They met

Tytler Tales of Grandfather

in action near Theba, on the Andalusian borders, when the Moorish cavalry suffered defeat, but the Scottish warriors, advancing too eagerly in the pursuit, were surrounded by a strong division of the Moors, which had rallied on seeing them so far from the main body of the Spanish army. Sir William St Clair of Roslin had been foremost in the chase of war, as in the chase of the hunting field. His perilous position was manifest. "Yonder worthy knight will be slain," Douglas said, "unless he have instant help." With that he galloped to his rescue, but in attempting it became inextricably involved with the enemy and perished in company with his comrades, Sir William St Clair, Sir Robert Logan, and divers others (on the 8th September, 1330*). It will be sufficient for the purposes of this work to submit the closing verses of Aytoun's well known poem :—

THE HEART OF BRUCE
(W. E. AYTOUN.)

* * * * * * *

The trumpets blew, the cross-bolts flew,
    The arrows flashed like flame,
As spur in side and spear in rest.
    Against the foe we came.

And many a bearded Saracen
    Went down, both horse and man ;
For through their ranks we rode like corn,
    So furiously we ran !

But in behind our path they closed,
    Though fain to let us through,
For they were forty thousand men,
    And we were wondrous few.

We might not see a lance's length,
    So dense was their array ;
But the long fell sweep of the Scottish blade
    Still held them hard at bay.

"Make in ! make in !" Lord Douglas cried,
    "Make in, my brethren dear !
Sir William of Saint Clair is down ;
    We may not leave him here !"

But thicker, thicker, grew the swarm,
    And sharper shot the rain,
And the horses reared amid the press,
    But they would not charge again.

"Now Jesu help thee," said Lord James,
    "Thou kind and true Saint Clair !

An' if I may not bring thee off,
    I'll die beside thee there !"

Then in his stirrups up he stood,
    So lion-like and bold,
And held the precious heart aloft
    All in its case of gold.

He flung it from him, far ahead,
    And never spake he more,
But—"Pass thee first, thou dauntless heart,
    As thou wert wont of yore !"

The roar of fight rose fiercer yet,
    And heavier still the stour,
Till the spears of Spain came shivering in,
    And swept away the Moor.

* * * *

"O Bothwell banks ! that bloom so bright
    Beneath the sun of May,
The heaviest cloud that ever blew
    Is bound for you this day.

And, Scotland, thou may'st veil thy head
    In sorrow and in pain ;
The sorest stroke upon thy brow
    Hath fallen this day in Spain !

We'll bear them back unto our ship,
    We'll bear them o'er the sea,
And lay them in the hallowed earth,
    Within our own countrie."

THE DEATH OF HACO.†

Irritated by the ravages of Farquard Kiarnach Machonas, Earl of Ross, on the Western Isles, then subject to the Norwegian crown, King Haco of Norway fitted out a magnificent fleet containing over 100 galleys, with which he sailed west to make reprisals on the Scots. He called at Hjaltland, and passed thence to Orkney, where most of the summer was occupied in completing his preparations. There he obtained the support of Earl Magnus of Orkney and finally steered through the Petland Firth, plundering Caithness, subjugating the islands, and carrying all before him, till he anchored near the mouth of the Clyde, and landed on the Scottish coast near Largs. The young King, Alexander III.,

---

Balfour's Annals. Clouston's Guide to Orkney.

CAMEOS AND SAGAS.

THE NAVE, ST. MAGNUS.

hesitated to meet in battle such a formidable host; but as the autumnal equinox was at hand, the Scottish generals wisely delayed, expecting help from the elements. Nor were they disappointed, for a violent storm arising, dashed many of the ships against each other, and greatly injured the fleet. A battle ensued, in which 16,000 of the Norsemen fell, though, after all, the victory was doubtful. Haco, however, retired, having first burned the damaged ships, and buried the slain on the field of battle. He came to Kirkwall with the shattered remains of his grand fleet, and the stormy weather having now set in, they were compelled to remain in Kirkwall for the winter. Haco occupied the upper flat of the Bishop's Palace, while his men were quartered throughout the island. In a short time, however, the brave old monarch sickened, and soon he died, it is believed of a broken heart, for the loss of his ships and his brave followers. The body lay in state in the upper chamber of the palace, after which it was coffined and placed before the shrine of St. Magnus, where his warriors watched it by turns during the winter. In spring the body was conveyed to Bergen, and buried in the royal sepulchre of Norway.

There is a full account of these occurrences in the " Edinburgh Magazine " for 1787 (translated from an Icelandic Chronicle), which is so fine and graphic that one would be tempted to reproduce it but for the fact of almost literal illustration in the lines that follow.

THE DEATH OF HACO.
(JOHN STUART BLACKIE.)

The summer is gone, Haco, Haco,
    The yellow year is fled,
And the winter is come, Haco,
    That numbers thee with the dead !
When the year was young, Haco, Haco,
    And the skies were blue and bright,
Thou didst sweep the seas then, Haco,
    Like a bird with wings of might.
With thine oaken galley proudly,
    And thy gilded dragon-prow,
O'er the bounding billows, Haco,
    Like a sea-god thou didst go.
With thy barons gaily, gaily,
    All in proof of burnished mail,
In the voes of Orkney, Haco,
    Thou didst spread thy prideful sail ;
And the sturdy men of Caithness,
    And the land of the Mackay,
And the men of stony Parf, Haco,
    Knew that Norway's king was nigh.
And the men of outmost Lewis, Haco,
    And Skye with winding kyles,
And Macdougall's country, Haco,
    Knew the monarch of the Isles.
And the granite peaks of Arnsy
    And the rocks that fence the Clyde

Saw thy daring Norsemen, Haco,
    Ramping o'er the Scottish tide.
But scaith befell thee, Haco, Haco!
    Thou wert faithful, thou wert brave ;
Yet truth might not shield thee, Haco,
    From a false and shuffling knave.
The crafty King of Scots, Haco,
    Who might not bar thy way,
Beguiled thee, honest Haco,
    With lies that bred delay.
And hasty winter, Haco, Haco,
    Came and tripped the summer's heels,
And rent the sails of Haco,
    And swamped his conquering keels.
Woe is me for Haco, Haco !
    On Lorn, and Mull, and Skye
The hundred ships of Haco
    In a thousand fragments lie !
And thine oaken galley, Haco,
    That sailed with kingly pride,
Came shorn and shattered, Haco,
    Through the foaming Pechtland tide.
And thy heart sank, Haco, Haco,
    And thou felt that thou must die,
When the bay of Kirkwall Haco
    Thou held with drooping eye.

And they led thee, Haco, Haco,
  To the bishop's lordly hall,
Where thy woe-struck barons, Haco,
  Stood to see the mighty fall ;
And the purple churchmen, Haco,
  Stood to hold thy royal head,
And good words of hope to Haco
  From the Holy Book they read
Then outspake the dying Haco,
  "Dear are God's dear words to me,
But read the book to Haco,
  Of the kings that ruled the sea "
Then they read to dying Haco
  From the ancient Saga hoar,
Of Haldan and of Harald,
  When his fathers worshipped Thor
And they shrove the dying Haco,
  And they prayed his bed beside ,
And with holy unction Haco
  Drooped his kingly head and died
And in parade of death, Haco,
  They stretched thee on thy bed,
With a purple vest for Haco
  And a garland for his head
And around thee, Haco, Haco,
  Were tapers burning bright,

And masses were sung for Haco,
  By day and eke by night
And they bore thee, Haco, Haco,
  To holy Magnus' shrine,
And beside his sainted bones, Haco,
  They chastely coffined thine
And above thee, Haco, Haco,
  To deck thy dreamless bed,
All crisp with gold for Haco,
  A purple pall they spread
And around thee, Haco, Haco,
  Where the iron sleep thou slept,
Thro' the long dark winter, Haco,
  A solemn watch they kept,
And at early burst of spring-time,
  When the birds sang out with glee.
They took the body of Haco
  In a ship across the sea—
Across the sea to Norway,
  Where thy sires make moan for thee,
That the last of his race was Haco,
  Who ruled the Western sea
And they laid thee, Haco Haco,
  With thy sires on the Norway shore,
And far from the isles of the sea, Haco,
  That know thy name no more

THE HERO OF BRIDGENORTH.

HUBERT DE ST CLARE, CASTELLAN OF COLCHESTER CASTLE
(† 1165)

The heroism of Hubert St. Clair has been a favourite theme with English annalists Lord Lyttelton Stowe, Camden, Speed, Sir William Pole, Polwhele, &c , all notice the noble self-sacrifice of his life Hubert was the son of Hamo de St Clare, whom Henry I had appointed Constable of Colchester, and in course of time succeeded his father in that office Lord Lyttelton's account of his fate, appearing in his *Life of Henry the Second*, gives us a vivid presentment of the scene —

"Mortimer, though abandoned by his friends, would not lay down his arms Henry, incensed at his obstinacy, led a great army against him, with which, having divided it into three bodies, he at once assaulted the three castles of Clebury, Wigmore, and Bridgenorth , and though it was expected that each of them would stand a long siege, they were all surrendered to him in a short time. Before that of Bridgenorth, which was defended by Mortimer, he commanded in person, and exposed himself to so much danger, that he would there have been slain, if a faithful vassal had not preferred his life to his own For while he was busied in giving orders too near the wall, Hubert de St Clare, constable, or governor of Colchester Castle, who stood by his side, seeing an arrow aimed at him by one of Mortimer's archers, stepped before him, and received it in his own breast The wound was mortal he expired in the arms of his master, recommending his daughter (Adelaide), an only child, and an infant, to the care of that prince It is hard to say which most deserves admiration, a subject who died to save his king, or a king whose personal virtues could render his safety so dear to a subject, whom he had not obliged by any extraordinary favours ! The daughter of Hubert was educated by Henry, with all the affection that he owed to the memory of her father, and when she had attained to maturity, was honourably married to William de Longueville, a nobleman of great distinction "

In Knight's " History of England " an illustration of the event is given

Speed ("History of Great Britain, 1611") has " It bound Tiberius most of all to Sejanus, when a part of the banqueting cave in which they were, suddenly falling, Sejanus was found to have borne the ruins from the emperor, with the peril of his life; but Sejanus survived that adventure, which our Senclere did not, save only in the better renown thereof, which deserves to be immortal being an act of piety worthy of a statue with Colrus, Curtius, Manlius, or whosoever else have willingly sacrificed themselves." The incident is also recorded by Ralph Niger, a contemporary chronicler under the year 1165, who further tells us that William Longville acquired with Hubert's heiress her paternal heirship, and had by her a son, whom he called by his own name and surname.

ROSLIN CHAPEL.*

By WILLIAM WORDSWORTH, D.L.

The wind is now thy organist—a clank
(We know not whence) ministers for a bell
To mark some change of service. As the swell
Of music reached its height, and even when sank
The notes in prelude, ROSLIN! to a blank
Of silence, how it thrilled thy sumptuous roof,
Pillars and arches,—not in vain time-proof,
Though Christian rites be wanting! From what bank

Came those live herbs? By what hand were they sown
Where dew falls not, where rain-drops seem un-
Yet in the temple they a friendly niche [known?
Share with their sculptured fellows, that, green-
grown,
Copy their beauty more and more, and preach,
Though mute, of all things blending into one.

*Composed therein during a storm.

The beautiful chapel of Roslin is still in tolerable preservation. It was founded about 1446 by William Saint Clair, the princely Earl of Orkney, Zetland, and Caithness, etc., etc. The architecture is Gothic in its most rich and florid style. Among the profuse carving on the pillars and buttresses,

THE UNDER CHAPEL, ROSSLINN.

the rose is frequently introduced, in allusion to the name, with which, however, the flower has no connection; the etymology being Rosslinnhe, the promontory of the linn, or waterfall. The chapel is said to appear on fire previous to the death of any of his descendants. This superstition, alluded to in the text, is probably of Norwegian derivation, and may have been imported by the Earls of Orkney into their Lothian dominions. The tomb-fires of the North are mentioned in most of the Sagas. The Barons of Roslin were buried in armour in a vault beneath the chapel floor.

Sir Walter Scott has from these incidents evolved the beautiful ballad in the "Lay of the Last Minstrel," in which Harald, the Earl's bard, tells us of the hapless fate of the dutiful Rosabelle. The earlier Earls of Orkney undoubtedly had scalds on their staff, so it is in perfect keeping with historical traditions to allot one to their successors, the St. Clairs. The name of Rosabelle only occurs once in connection with the family, and it is doubtful if the name was ever in general use. The Lords Marchers had met at Branxholme, and were passing time listening to the popular minstrelsy of the day. Albert Graeme had treated the nobles to a favourite Border ballad, "For Love will still be Lord of all" the Saxon Fitztraver attuned his harp to the praises of "Surrey and Geraldine"; and then from his seat with lofty air, rose

HARALD, BARD OF BRAVE ST CLAIR *

St Clair, who feasting high at Home,
Had with that lord to battle come
Harald was born where restless seas
Race round the storm-swept Orcades,
Where erst St Clairs held princely sway
O'er isle and islet, strait and bay,—
Still nods their palace to its fall,
Thy pride and sorrow, fair Kirkwall!—
Thence oft he marked fierce Petland rave,
As if grim Odin rode her wave,
And watched the whilst with visage pale,
And throbbing heart, the struggling sail,
For all of wonderful and wild
Had rapture for that lonely childe
  * * * * *

And much of wild and wonderful
In these rude isles might fancy cull,
For thither came, in times afar,
Stern Lochlin's sons of roving war,
The Norsemen, trained to spoil and blood
Skilled to prepare the raven's food,
Kings of the main their leaders brave,
Their barks the dragons of the wave

And there in many a stormy vale,
The Scald had told his wondrous tale,
And many a Runic column high
Had witnessed grim idolatry
And thus had Harald, in his youth,
Learned many a Saga's rime uncouth,—
Of that Sea-Snake, tremendous curled,
Whose monstrous circle girds the world,
Of those dread Maids, whose hideous yell
Maddens the battle's bloody swell,
Of Chiefs, who, guided through the gloom
By the pale death-lights of the tomb,
Ransacked the graves of warriors old,
Their falchions wrenched from corpses' hold,
Waked the deaf tomb with war's alarms,
And bade the dead arise to arms!
With war and wonder all on flame,
To Roslin's bowers young Harald came,
Where, by sweet glen and greenwood tree,
He learned a milder minstrelsy,
Yet something of the Northern spell
Mixed with the softer numbers well

THE DIRGE OF ROSABELLE *

O listen! listen ladies gay!
No haughty feat of arms I tell,
Soft is the note, and sad the lay,
That mourns the lovely Rosabelle

" Moor, moor the barge ye gallant crew!
And, gentle ladye, deign to stay!
Rest thee in Castle Ravensheuch,
Nor tempt the stormy firth to-day

" The blackening wave is edged with white
To inch and rock the sea-mews fly,
The fishers have heard the Water-Sprite,
Whose screams forbode that wreck is nigh

' Last night the gifted Seer did view
A wet shroud swathed round ladye gay,
Then stay thee, Fair, in Ravensheuch,
Why cross the gloomy firth to-day?"

" 'Tis not because Lord Lindesay's heir
To-night at Roslin leads the ball,
But that my ladye-mother there
Sits lonely in her castle-hall.

" 'Tis not because the ring they ride,
And Lindesay at the ring rides well,
But that my sire the wine will chide
If 'tis not filled by Rosabelle "

O'er Roslin all that dreary night
A wondrous blaze was seen to gleam,

'Twas broader than the watch fire's light,
And redder than the bright moon-beam

It glared on Roslin's castled rock,
It ruddied all the copse-wood glen,
'Twas seen from Dryden's groves of oak,
And seen from caverned Hawthornden

Seemed all on fire that chapel proud,
Where Roslin s chiefs uncoffined lie,
Each baron, for a sable shroud,
Sheathed in his iron panoply

Seemed all on fire within, around,
Deep sacristy and altar's pale,
Shone every pillar foliage-bound,
And glimmered all the dead men's mail

Blazed battlement and pinnet high,
Blazed every rose-carved buttress fair—
So still they blaze, when fate is nigh
The lordly line of high St Clair

There are twenty of Roslin's barons bold
Lie buried within that proud chapelle,
Each one the holy vault doth hold—
But the sea holds lovely Rosabelle!

And each Saint Clair was buried there,
With candle, with book, and with knell,
But the sea-caves rung, and the wild winds sung
The dirge of lovely Rosabelle

---

* Scott.

THE DRUM-HEAD CHARTER *

A TALE OF FLODDEN FIELD †
1513

One of the peers slain at Flodden was William St Clair, Earl of Caithness This nobleman had been forfeited by James III, and the sentence still remained in force, yet his rank was acknowledged and he joined the army with his retainers When the English were pressing hard on James at Flodden, he perceived a knight and his followers advancing in gallant order, all clad in green He asked those beside him who they were They replied that they thought they were the men of Caithness, and that the Earl himself was at their head The king mused a little, and then said, "If that be William Sinclair, I will pardon him" The knight was William Sinclair, the name of the Earl of Caithness There being no parchment in the camp, King James ordered the deed of removal of forfeiture to be extended on a drum-head When the pardon had received the royal signature, it was cut out and delivered to the Earl, who forthwith despatched one of his men with it to Caithness, strictly enjoining him to deliver the valuable document to his lady, that in the event of his death in battle the family might be secured in his restored honours and estates The bearer—one of the Clan Gunn—was the only one of the Caithness corps that ever returned, the rest having been slain in the engagement Such was the impression which their fate made in the remote district of their birth, that, as he and his followers had passed the Ord of Caithness on a Monday to join the royal army, the Sinclairs had a mortal aversion to pass that promontory on Mondays, or to wear any dress of a green colour

What youth, of graceful form and mien,
   Foremost leads the spectred brave,
While o'er his mantle's fold of *green*
   His amber locks redundant wave ?
When slow returns the fated *day*,
That viewed their chieftain's long array

Wild to the harp's deep, plaintive string,
   The virgins raise the funeral strain,
From *Ord's* black mountain to the northern main,
And mourn the *emerald* line which paints the vest of spring ‡

It has been said that this deed, granted to the Earl of Caithness on the field of Flodden, was preserved by his descendants, Earls of Caithness, until the death of Earl Alexander in 1766, when it was secured by his son-in-law and executor, the Earl of Fife, with whose family it still remains. The author is advised by the Duke of Fife that there is no record of such an instrument ([1]) ever having been in the Fife archives

THE HOUSE OF SINCLAIR

A GENEALOGICAL POEM, BY WILLIAM LITHGOW

"Travels through Europe, Asia, and Africa" Lithgow, under date 1628, writes thus "And now being arrived at Majj (Mey) to embark for Orkney, sight, time, and duty command me to celebrate these following lines, to gratify the kindness of that noble lord, George, Earl of Caithness, with his honourable cousin and first accadent of his house, the right worshipful Sir William Sinclair of Catboll, knight, laird of Majj :—

Sir ! sighting now thyself and palace fair,
I find a novelty, and that most rare,
The time though cold and stormy, sharper sun
And far to summer, scarce the spring begun,
Yet with good luck, in Februar, Saturn's prey,
Have I not sought and found out fruitful May,
Plank'd with the marine coast, prospective stands,
Right opposite to the Orcade isles and lands,
Where I for flowers, ingorg'd strong grapes of Spain
And liquor'd French, both red and white amain

Which palace doth contain two four-squar'd courts
Graft with brave works, where th'art drawn pencil sports
On walls, high chambers, galleries, office bowers,
Cells, rooms, and turrets, platforms, stately towers,
Where green fac'd gardens, set at Flora's feet,
Make nature's beauty quick Apelles greet,
Nay, not by blood, as she herself can do,
But by her pattern, feeding younglings too,
For which this patron's crescent stands so stay,
That neither spate nor tempest can shake May,

Whose scutcheons cleave so fast to top and side,
Portends to me his arms shall ever bide
So Murckle's arms are so, except the rose
Spread on the cross, which Bothwell's arms disclose,
Whose uterine blood he is, and present brother
To Caithness' Lord, all three sprung from one mother,
Bothwell's prime heretrix, plight to Hepburn's race,
From whom religious Murckle's rose I trace,
This country's instant shrieve, whose virtue raised
His honoured worth, his godly life more praised
But now to rouse their roots and how they sprung,
See how antiquity time's triumph sung,
This scallet, worth them blanched, for endeavour
And service done to England's conqueror,
With whom from France they first to Britain came,
Sprung from a town, St Clair, now turn'd their name,
Whose predecessor, by their val'rous hand,
Won endless fame, twice in the Holy Land,
Where in that Christian war, their blood been lost
They loath'd of Gaul, and sought our Albion coast,
Themselves to Scotland came in Canmoire's reign
With good Queen Maig'ret and her English train.
The ship from Orkney sail'd, now rul'd by Charles,
Whereof they Sinclairs long time had been earls,
Whose lord, then William, was, by Scotland's king
(Called Robert Second, First whence Stewarts spring)
Sent with his second son to France, called James,
Who eighteen years lived captivate at Thames
This prisoner last turned king, called *James the First*,
Who Sinclair's credit kept in honour's thirst
The galley was the badge of Caithness lords,
As Malcolm Canmoire's reign at length records,
Which was to Magnus given for service done
Against Macbeath, usurper of his crown,
All which survey'd, at last the midmost gate
Designed to me the arms of that great 'state,
The Earls of Caithness, to whose praise imbaged
Thy muse must mount, and here's my pen incadg'd,
First then their arms, a cross did me produce
Limb'd like a scallet, traced with flour du luce,
The lion, red and rag'd, two times divided
From coin to coin as heralds have decided,
The third join'd stance denotes to me a galley,
That on their sea-wrapt foes dare make a sally,

The fourth a gallant ship, puft with taunt sail
'Gainst them their ocean dare, or coast assail
On whose bent crest a pelican doth sit—
An emblem for like love, drawn wondrous fit
Who as she feeds her young with her heart's blood
Denotes these lords, to theirs, like kind, like good
Whose best supporters guard both sea and land
Two stern-drawn griffins, in their strength do stand
Their dictum bears this verdict, for heaven's ode
Ascrib'd this clause, *Commit thy work to God*
O sacred motto! Bishop Sinclair's strain
Who turned Fyfe's lord on Scotland's foes again
Lo! here's the arms of Caithness, here's the stock!
On which branched boughs rely as on a rock
But further in I found like arms more patent,
To kind Sir William and his line as latent,
The premier accade of that noble race,
Who for his virtue may reclaim the place,
Whose arms, with tongue and buckle, now they
Fast cross sign ty'd, for a fair Lesly's sake [make
The lion hunts o'er land, the ship, the sea,
The ragged cross can scale high walls, we see
The wing-laid galley with her factious oars,
Both heavens and floods command, and circling shores,
The feathered griffin flies, O grim-limb'd beast!
That winging sea and land, upholds thy crest,
But for the pelican's life-sprung kind story
Makes honour sing, *Virtute et amore* *
The lion came, by an heretrix to pass.
By marriage, whose sire was sirnamed *Douglas*
Where, after him, the Sinclair now record
Was Sheriff of Dumfries and Nithdale's lord,
Whose wife was niece to good King James the Thrid
Who for exchange 'twixt Wick and Southern Nidde,
Did lands excambiate, whence this Caithness soil
Stands fast for them, the rest their friends recoil
Then circle-bounded Caithness, Sinclair's ground,
Which Pentland Firth environs, Orkney's sound
Whose top is Dunkane's bay, the root the Ord
Long may it long stand fast for their true lord
And as long too heavens grant what I require,
The race of Maji may in that stock aspire,
Till any age may last, time's glass be run,
For earth's last dark eclipse, of no more sun

TRADITIONS OF SUMMERDALE †
(1528)

Several curious traditions have been handed down about this battle, which present a striking picture of the superstition and savage barbarity of the northern people at that period —

"When the Earl of Caithness and his men landed at Orphir in Orkney, a witch preceded them on their march, unwinding two balls of thread as she walked before them One was blue and the other

---

* Sir William Sinclair's motto   † Elder

red, and the thread of the latter having become exhausted, the witch assured the Earl that the side on which blood was first drawn would certainly be defeated. Placing implicit faith on this prognostication, the Earl resolved to slay the first Orcadian that crossed his path, and so insure victory to himself and his followers in the coming conflict. Soon afterwards a boy was descried herding cattle, so thinking that if it was Orkney blood, it was no great matter whether man or boy, the Earl and his men, with eager haste, caught the boy, and mercilessly slew him without a moment's warning. But they had reckoned without their host, for the boy was then recognised by some of them to be a native of Caithness, who had for some time been a fugitive in Orkney, and it speedily occurred to them that if the words of the witch were worth anything, they had, by the cruel murder of a helpless boy, now lying a bleeding corpse at their feet, rendered certain their own discomfiture. Prone to superstition as the Earl and his men seem to have been, this untoward circumstance must have had a strong tendency to depress their spirits and unnerve their arm, and this is probably the key to the subsequent battle of Summerdale, where they were met and completely routed by the Orcadians.

"The battle," says the tradition, "was fought on a piece of smooth grass, where no stones were to be seen previous to the morning of the encounter, but they were then found in such abundance that the Orcadians threw down the pitchforks with which they were armed, and plied their Caithness foes so effectually with stones that they were unable to get near enough to use their weapons. The incessant and murderous showers of these primitive missiles soon told with effect on the ranks of the Caithness men, who were at last compelled to betake themselves to an ignominious flight. Throwing their arms into the Loch of Kisbister, they fled pell-mell over the broken ground towards their landing-place, but they were closely pursued, and in a short time only a few survived to continue the hopeless race for life. Amongst these was the Earl of Caithness, who reached the farm of Oback in Orphir, and dashing through the 'close' between the dwelling house and the offices, in the hope of escaping the merciless pursuers, who were close at his heels, rushed unwittingly into the arms of another party of his foes, who slew him on the spot. Not one of the Caithness men escaped to carry home the tale of their discomfiture. The Earl was among the last that fell, and his head, sent back in proud defiance, was the sole relique that reached the shores of Caithness of the fated band.

Notable events are seldom limited to one tradition, and another informs us that "the Earl in his flight from the field outran his pursuers, and entered a farm house to solicit refuge. There was nobody in but an old woman sitting before the fire and spinning from a distaff. The Norse tongue was then the language of the peasantry, but the Earl, by means of signs and the magic power of a few pieces of money, contrived to make her comprehend the purpose of his visit. She rose from her seat, led him to the far end of the byre, which was quite dark, signed to him to lie down, covered him with straw, and then returned to her work. A little after a party of ten entered, and asked the old woman if he was in the house. She replied, 'He is not here,' but while she said so pointed with her finger to the spot where he lay concealed. Thither they accordingly went. Finding that he was betrayed, the Earl started up, and with his drawn sword defended himself for some time with unshrinking courage. At length, however, he was overpowered and slain, but not until four of his assailants had fallen down before him mortally wounded. He was buried in a field not far distant from the cottage, and a slab was erected over his grave, which was afterwards broken and carried away for some domestic purpose."

"Only one Orcadian fell on that day, which proved so fatal to their adversaries, and his death was a tragic one. He had dressed himself in the clothes of one of the slaughtered Caithnessians, and was coming towards his own house in the evening, when he was met by his mother, who, not recognising him, but believing him to be one of the enemy that had escaped the general carnage, struck him a fatal blow on the forehead with a stone which she had put into the foot of one of his own stockings, and was carrying in her hand."

"The motive which led to the Earl's hostile visit to Orkney is involved in obscurity; but the relentless spirit of the contending parties, as displayed in the murder of the boy, in the complete slaughter of the invaders, and in the fiendish thirst for vengeance exhibited by the woman, who, in the blindness of her fury, murdered her own son, sufficiently proves that a bitter animosity existed between the inhabitants of Orkney and Caithness, which it has taken upwards of three centuries to extinguish."

A MERRIE JEST *

"The History of Sutherland," written by Sir Robert Gordon, the avowed adversary of the Caithness Sinclairs, gives us an extraordinary instance of the spirit of wanton cruelty and mischief in which hostilities were carried on three centuries ago. Since the defeat of Summerdale, Caithness and Orkney had ceased to hold amicable intercourse, and a rooted hatred which had frequently broken out into open strife, had long existed between the Earls of those countries.

In the year 1608 some of the Earl of Orkney's servants had been forced to land in the county of Caithness "by a contrarie wind and vehement storme of weather. First, *the Earl of Catteynes* maid them drunk ; then, in a mocking iest, he cause sheave the one syd of their beards and one syd of their heads ; last of all, he constrayned them to tak their weshell and to goe to sea in that stormie tempest ! The poor men, feareing his farther crueltie, did choyse rather to committ themselves to the mercie of the senseless elements and rageing waves of the sea, then abyd his furie. So they entered the stormie seas of *Pentlay Firth* (a fearfull and dangerous arme of sea between *Catteynes* and *Orkney*), whence they escaped the furie thereof, by the providence and assistance of God, who had compassion on them in this lamentable and desperat case, and directed their course, so that they landed saiflie in *Orknay*. This affront and indignitie wes highly taken by *the Earle of Orknay*, who complained therof to THE KING and his *Counsell*. His MAIESTIE did write to the *Councell of Scotland* to punish the *Earle of Catteynes* severlie, after dew tryall, as haveing committed a fact against his authoritie. But when both *the Earles of Catteynes* and *Orknay* came to Edinburghe, readie to informe one against another, they aggreid all their privatt quarrells, by the mediation of friends, *least they should reveile too much of either's doings*! So this controversie was past over with silence, and some acknawledgement was maid by *the Earle of Catteynes* to *the Earle of Orknay*, as a satisfaction for abusing his servants," etc.

The historian of Sutherland quaintly remarks "Only one example of this crime I do remember. The servants of David, King of Israel, were so entreated by Hanun, King of the Children of Ammon. The Earl of Caithness thus far exceeded Hanun, that not satisfied with what himself had done, he forced the Earl of Orkney his servants to take the sea in such a tempest, and exposed them to the extremity of the raging waves ; whereas Hanun suffered King David his servants to depart home quietly after he had abused them."

The Earl of Caithness at length brought ruin upon himself and family, by endeavouring "to mak the Lord Forbes wearie of his landis in Catteynes." This benevolent purpose he tried to effect by constant oppression of his tenants and servants, in virtue of his office of Sheriffship, which he had obtained from the Earl of Huntlie on his marriage with Lady Jean Gordon, his sister. He secretly caused incendiaries burn all the corn standing in the corn yard of Sansett in November, 1615 ; and to remove suspicion from himself, industriously rumoured abroad that the fire-raising had been done by Mackay's tenants, with whom the Forbes were then at feud.

A LEGEND OF STROMA.†

"There is an amusing legend in an old topographical work on Scotland, which says that a dispute once arose between the Earls of Orkney and Caithness as to which county Stroma belonged. Instead of deciding the quarrel by the arbitrament of the sword, the chiefs on both sides agreed to refer the decision of the matter to an experiment in natural history. Some venomous animals—of what kind we are not told—lived in Stroma. A certain number of them were shipped at the same time as colonists to Orkney and Caithness. Those that were brought to Caithness took kindly to the soil as to a congenial habitat ; while those that were sent to Orkney, from the unfavourable effects of the climate on their constitution, sickened and died. By this singular fact Stroma was adjudged to Caithness."

During the Norse period Stroma—the Straumsey of the Sagas—was important as an Orcadian outpost, and had a governor appointed to reside in it. The Sinclairs soon after their accession to the Earldom of Caithness, obtained by royal grant the property of the island. In 1574 George Sinclair of Mey was served heir of entail to his brother William, of various lands, *inter alia* Stroma. The island was noted for its non-putrefying properties. In a vault of the Kennedies of Carmunks the remains of the dead were converted into mummies by the continual saltish air caused by the rapid tides of the Pentland. Murdo Kennedy used to beat the drum on his father's body, and seating it at table, by pressing the foot, "made the figure move." Numbers of other bodies were suspended by nails on the walls, etc.

* Scottish Wars   † Calder

ROSLIN CASTLE.

This air is identical with one known as "The House of Glams," though which title has the better right to the air is not manifest. The air of "Roslin Castle" was used for the Masonic elegy on the death in 1778 of William St. Clair, "the last Rosslyn." Hewitt has written some lines of a rural nature which generally are attached to the air, viz.:

> 'Twas in that season of the year,
> When all things gay and sweet appear,
> That Colin, with the morning ray,
> Arose and sung his rural lay :
> Of Nannie's charms the shepherd sung,
> The hills and dales with Nannie rung ;
> While ROSLIN CASTLE heard the swain,
> And echoed back the cheerful strain.
>
> And other three verses.

FAIR ISLE.

AN INCIDENT OF THE SPANISH ARMADA.*

> ". . . . . A lonely isle
> 'Twixt Hetland and the Orkneys there looms forth,
> Uprearing high to Heaven its bold, proud head.
> The Fair Isle—to Shetland appertaining,
> And of like origin, and by like race
> Inhabited at first. A mere insect
> It seemeth, from a thick swarm disjoined,
> And here alone into the wave cast down.
>
> Scarce to one hundred count the souls who dwell
> Upon the south side of this desert spot,
> Like earth's last habitants, or like to men
> Forgotten by the world, strange to the age,
> Unmoved to other change than the raindrops
> Of birth and death which variation make,
> And grave themselves into their life's hard soil."
> —"Fair Isle," from the German of Jensen.

Fair Isle, the *Fridarey* of the *Saga*, belonged to the Sinclairs of Quendale till somewhere about the middle of last century, when one of them, according to tradition, lost it at cards to the then Stewart of Brugh. The great historical incident connected with Fair Isle, and which furnished the theme for Jensen's poem, was the wreck in Sivars Geo, of one of the ships of the Spanish Armada, *El Gran Grifon*, the flagship of Don Juan Gomez de Medina, who was in command of the eighth division, consisting of 23 transports, hulks, and storeships, and which was termed the "Armada de Vrcas." The event occurred on the 17th September, 1588. One of his officers, a Captain Patricio, is buried in St. Magnus' Cathedral. The shipwrecked Spaniards paid the Islanders for all supplies, but the latter, at last fearing a famine, began to conceal their stock. So a boat was sent to Shetland to Andrew Umphray of Berry, then tacksman of the Island, requesting assistance. Umphray responded by despatching a small vessel he possessed to bring the survivors to Dunrossness, where they were landed at Quendale. Here they were hospitably treated whilst waiting till Umphray got a vessel ready to convey them to Dunkirk. On landing at Quendale, Don Gomez (imagining the people did admire him) made his interpreter ask Malcolm Sinclair whether he had ever seen a finer man? To which Malcolm replyed, "Farcie in that face, I have seen many prettier men hanging in the Burrow-moor." "From Zetland Andrew Umphray carried them in his shallop to Dunkirk, for which the Don rewarded him with 3,000 merks."†

FAIR ISLE.

A silver cup with heraldic shields, given by Don Gomez to Malcolm Sinclair, is now in the possession of Mr. Balfour, of Balfour and Trenabie, into whose family it came through a marriage of one of the Sinclairs to a Balfour.

Tudor.   Monteith.

THE KRINGELEN AMBUSH.*

Misfortunes never come singly. The Sinclairs of Caithness have bitter experience of the truth of this adage. Reference has already been made to the losses suffered at Flodden (1513) and Summerdale (1528), and now the third and heaviest wave of adversity was to break over them. It was the depopulation of Caithness from these three disasters that weakened the Sinclairs in their family feud with the Sutherlands. Their third misfortune was the massacre of Kringellen, in which a whole regiment was blotted out. There are several accounts of this tragical incident, and recently (1886) Michell has written a "History of the Scottish Expedition to Norway in 1612." Epitomised the story reads thus :

Colonel George Sinclair was a natural son of David Sinclair of Stirkoke, and "nephew" of the Earl of Caithness. A soldier of fortune, he had been early in the army of "The Bulwark of the North." Before embarking for Norway he had been engaged in a somewhat desperate affair, the arrest of John Maxwell, Lord Nithsdale, whose pathetic "Good Night" is printed amongst the Ballads in the Border Minstrelsy, and when the hand of fate overtook Colonel Sinclair, it was deemed but a just retribution by the whole Maxwell clan. The Colonel's action in apprehending Lord Nithsdale for the murder of Sir Jas. Johnstone was, however, an ordinary unavoidable executive duty as justiciary for his uncle the Earl.

Gustavus Adolphus, King of Sweden, dispatched officers to Scotland in 1612, for the purpose of raising troops to assist him in a war with the Danes and Norwegians. As King James of Scotland was brother-in-law to the Danish king, Christian IV., troops were levied in a clandestine manner, and the Privy Council as a deterrent threatened to put the leaders "to the horn," *i.e.*, to declare them outlaws after three blasts of the horn at the cross of Edinburgh. Among those who volunteered their services from Scotland was Colonel George Sinclair, son of Stirkoke, in his native county, Caithness, raised a regiment of 900 men, almost all of them of his own clan and name. Landing at Vibelungsnaest, on the Romsdal coast, he discovered that owing to the Swedish shore from Nyborg to Calmar being in temporary possession of the Danes, and Stockholm invested by their fleet, his only way of reaching Sweden was by an overland march across the Norwegian Alps. He therefore determined upon that hazardous experiment, which had recently been managed by Colonel Munckhoven. As soon as the news of the arrival of the Scottish invaders reached Lars Hage, the Lehnsman of the Dovre, he hurried to the parish church, where service was being held. Striding into the building, he struck thrice upon the floor, and cried, "Listen ! the foeman is in the land." The congregation upon this immediately broke up, and it was finally agreed to lay an ambush at Kringelen, which from the precipitous nature of the ground overhanging the road, was well adapted for the purpose. Signal fires were lighted on every commanding height, and the *budstick* (message-rod or fiery cross) transmitted to all for a general muster. Some 500 peasants assembled, armed with rifles and axes, under the leadership of Berdon Segelstadt of Ringeboe, and, unable to meet the Sinclairs in open field, had recourse to stratagem. One of the Norwegians offered to guide the regiment, his intention being to lure them to their destruction, whilst on the opposite side of the river rode a peasant on a white horse, whose orders were to keep alongside of the advancing enemy. A peasant girl was stationed on a hill over the water, with her cow-horn, with which to signal as soon as the Scots had fallen into the snare. These precautions were necessary, as from their ambuscade the peasants were unable to see below. In the march Colonel Sinclair was accompanied by Fru (or Lady) Sinclair. She was a young and beautiful woman, unwilling to part from her husband, to whom she had been but recently united. Disguising herself in male attire, she succeeded in getting on board ; nor did she reveal herself until the corps had landed in Norway. The title of Fru implies that she was his wife, and she is still affectionately remembered by the Norwegians. A mermaid appeared to Colonel Sinclair by night, and warned him of death if he advanced ; but he replied "that when he returned in triumph from the conquest of the kingdom, he would punish her as she deserved." The mermaid's name was Ellen, and some allege that she was *Fru* Sinclair in disguise. An insolent speech of the Colonel's is still repeated by the Norwegians with great indignation : "I'll recast the old Norway lion, and turn him into a mole that will not venture out of his burrow !"

On marched the Sinclairs through the fatal Pass of Kringelen, the "defile of death." The air which their pipes played is still remembered in Norway, and it was certainly their own "dead march."

*Calder Vedder ; Scottish Soldiers of Fortune ; An Oxonian in Norway.

Presently the strange and melancholy tones of an Alpine horn resounded from a distant height. At the same instant down thundered a mass of half hewn trees and loosened rocks, urged over by levers, that swept away whole sections and hurled them into the mountain torrent that foamed below. Sinclair himself fell as a Scotsman should always fall—in the foremost rank, when gallantly essaying to storm the rocks, claymore in hand. He was shot by Berdon Seilstadt, who had bitten one of his silver buttons into the shape of a bullet, so as to be sure of Sinclair, who was supposed to bear a charmed life. Taking aim, he hit him on the left temple, and death was instantaneous. Among those hurled into the stream was the *Fru*, "but, being supported by her ample robes, she was able to carry her infant son safe across in her arm." All perished in the pass save sixty and the adjutant. These were at first distributed among the inhabitants; but the latter grew tired of supporting them, and, marching them into a meadow, murdered nearly all in cold blood, excepting the *Fru* and two others. One of these escaped through the instrumentality of a robust female peasant, whom he afterwards married. Their descendants are numerous, and their origin is well-known in the district. Another Sinclair, a prisoner, when about to be killed, rushed up to a Norwegian horseman, exclaiming, "Protect me! I am not prepared to die!" The Norwegian was more merciful than his compatriots, and Sinclair afterwards sent his salvor in Norway a stained glass window representing an angel protecting a suppliant. The window has been preserved, and is highly valued by the people. The *Fru* Sinclair apparently remained in the place, and when the child died, adopted a young Norwegian. The bodies of the slain were barbarously left unburied, a prey to the wolf and the vulture. But some respect was paid to the remains of the leader, which were decently interred. The Norwegians are proud of pointing out to strangers the spot where he is buried. It lies in a remote solitude near the fatal pass, and over the graves is a wooden cross with a tablet, on which is the following inscription in the Norse language:—"Here lies Colonel Jorgen Zinclair, who with 900 Scots, were dashed to pieces, like earthen pots, by the boors of Lessoe, Vaage, and Froen. Bergen Segelstadt, of Ringeboe, was their leader." There is a fairly long Norwegian ballad on the event, entitled, "Herr Sinclair's Vise af Storm," that is literally, "Lord Sinclair's Song" by Storm, in which the prowess of the peasants is highly extolled. It is sung everywhere

COLONEL SINCLAIR'S GRAVE.

throughout "Gamel Norge," and constitutes one of the great national airs. There are several translations of this ballad. Calder has one in his "History of Caithness"; Vedder, the Orcadian poet, has one in his collection; but perhaps the best is that given in the "Scottish Soldiers of Fortune," by Grant, who calls it a translation from Oehlenschalager, the Danish national poet. The opening lines by Vedder run thus:

 Childe Sinclair and his menyie steered
  Across the salt sea waves;
 But at Kringellen's mountain gorge
  They filled untimely graves.

 They crossed the stormy waves so blue,
  For Swedish gold to fight;
 May burning curses on them fall
  That strike not for the right!

 The horned moon is gleaming red,
  The waves are rolling deep;
 A mermaid trolled her demon lay—
  Childe Sinclair woke from sleep.

 "Turn round, turn round, thou Scottish youth,
  Or loud thy sire shall mourn;
 For if thou touchest Norway's strand,
  Thou never shalt return.

   *   *   *   *

In Storm's ballad the Sinclairs are untruly accused of burning and plundering all in their line of march. Their best vindication is the official report of Envold Kruse, a local stadtholder: "We have also ascertained that those Scots who were defeated and captured on their march through this country have absolutely neither burnt, murdered, nor destroyed anything."

THE MASSACRE OF KRINGELLEN

(A translation of Oehlenschalager, taken from "Scottish Soldiers of Fortune")

Childe Sinclair sailed from Scottish land,
  Far Noroway to brave,
But he sleeps in Gulbrand's rocky strand,
  Low in a bloody grave
Childe Sinclair sailed the stormy sea,
  To fight for Swedish gold,
"God speed thy warrior hearts and thee,
  And quell the Norseman bold!"

"He sailed a day, and two, and three,
  He and his gallant band,
The fourth sun saw him quit the sea,
  And touch old Norway's strand
On Romsdal's shore his soul was fain
  To triumph or to fall,
He and his twice seven hundred men,
  The gallant and the tall

"O stern and haughty was their wrath,
  Cruel with sword and spear,
Nor hoary age could check their path,
  Nor widowed mother's tear
With bitter death, young babes they slew,
  Though to the breast they clung,
And woful tidings, sad, but true,
  Echoed from every tongue

"On hill and rock the beacons glared,
  To tell of danger nigh,
The Norseman's sword was boldly bared—
  The Scots must yield or die!
The warriors of the land are far,
  They and their kingly lord,

Yet shame on him who shuns the war,
  Or fears the foreign horde!

"They march—they meet—the Norwayan host,
  Have hearts both stern and free,
They gather on Bredalbigh's coast—
  The Scots must yield or flee
The Lauge flows in Leydeland,
  Where Kringen's shadows fall,
Thither they march, that fated band,
  A tomb to find for all

"In the onslaught first, Childe Sinclair died,
  And ceased his haughty breath,
Stern sport for Scottish hearts to bide,
  God shield them from the death!
Come forth, come forth, ye Norsemen true,
  Light be your hearts to-day!
Fain would the Scots the ocean blue
  Between the slaughter lay!

"Their ranks yield to the leaden storm,
  On high the ravens sail—
Ah me! for every mangled form
  A Scottish maid shall wail!
They came a host with life and breath,
  But one returned to say,
How fares the invader in the strife
  He wars with Old Norway?

"There is a mound by Lauge's tide,
  The Norseman lingers near,
His eye is bright—but not with pride—
  It glistens with a tear!"

MALCOLM SINCLAIR'S VISA.

(ANDERS ODEL †1773)

Malcom Sinclairs albekanta, fordom öfver hela landet sjunga visa har ofta blifvit tryckt under följande titel, "Hjeltarnes samtal med den tappre och omistelige, men pa sin hemresa fran Constantinopel i nejden af Breslau d 19 Juni 1739, förrädeligen mordade Svenska Majoren vid Uplands regemente, den välborne Herren, Herr Malcom Sinclair, uppa de ljufva eliseiska fälten i de dödas rike berättadt af herden Celadon, som af en gammal obekant gubbe blifvit oförmodligen dit och dadan förd"

*   *   *   *   *   *

26

Strax lättes blanka dörren opp,
En svensker karl framträdde
Med skjuten, sargad hjelte-kropp,
Dock miner inte rädde,
Hans ansigt var med blod beskoljdt,
Nedsabladt, trampadt, slaget,
Och bröstet, som hans hjerta doljt,
Had' grofva skott intaget

26

Clang! wide the open doors disclose
A Swedish knight to view,
Although bescarred with numerous blows,
Yet is his courage true
His face with blood is crimson red,
Covered with wounds and hacks,
The frame whose spirit scarce has fled,
Is bruised with spear and axe

27
Hans hjerna satt i haret klent,
Jag ryser det att namma,
Men glädes, att ej är för sent
För himlen sadant hämma,
Han hade spänd pistol i hand,
Liksom han ville skjuta,
Men dödens hardt atsnörda band
Befallte'n förr att sluta.

27
Clotted his hair is, cloven his brain,—
Matters I loathe to mention—
May vengeance swift th' assassins gain
By Jesus Christ's subvention.
His pistol cocked is held in hand,
As if for firing ready;
But clay-cold winds from Charon's strand
Have slackened sinews steady.

MALCOLM SINCLAIR.

28
Han helsade pa svenskt maner,
Da kongen nadigt svara,
Och sad', "Vi känne inte Er,
Hvem skulle I väl vara?"
"Jag är" sad' han, "en svensk major
Mitt namm är Malcom Sinclair,
Min sjal un nylig 'af mig för
Fran hjertats vrar och vinklar.

28
He greeted them most courteously,
In Swedish way and manner.
Questions the King, "Do we know thee?
Foughtest thou for our banner?"
"I was," said he, "of major's rank
And Malcolm Sinclair called:
I from beyond the Stygian bank
Arrive here unappalled."

29

"Hur," sade kungen, "blef du död?
Du tappre krigs-buss store !
Du äst I blod sa färgad röd,
Liksom du slagtad vore."
"Jo," sade han, "Hans Majestät !
En ofórskämd Bellona
Har sa betalt de trogna fjät,
Jag gatt för Sverges krona."

29

"How," said the King, "becam'st thou dead,
Warrior renowned and skilled ?
And why with blood so smeared and red,
Like deer unkindly killed ?"
"Sire," said the Swedish warrior bold,
"Bellona, Dame capricious,
Rewards at times, so I am told,
With presents thus malicious."

SINCLAIR'S CHAINS.

There are three different accounts as to the origin of this lock puzzle, "bojor," and all unite in ascribing it to Malcolm Sinclair, the murdered ambassador. It consists of a bolt, which has to be disconnected from seven rings. (1) It is said that when captive in Siberia, he was promised to be set at liberty if he could open this lock with which his prison door was closed. (2) That while there imprisoned, by way of amusement or mental occupation, he invented the lock. (3) That his despatch-box when *en route* for Constantinople was so fastened. This toy is in general circulation in the three northern kingdoms — Norway, Sweden, and Denmark — where the solution of the "bojor" is a favourite pastime—exercise.

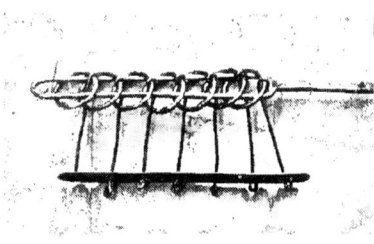

SINCLAIR'S "BOJOR."

ROSLIN'S DAUGHTER,
OR
CAPTAIN WEDDERBURN'S COURTSHIP.*

[This popular and amusing ballad is reprinted from Mr. Jamieson's text, with a few variations supplied by Mr. Kinloch to previous editors. * Legendary Ballads of Scotland.]

The Laird o' Roslin's daughter,
  Walked thro' the wood her lane ;
And by cam Captain Wedderburn,
  A servant to the king,
He said unto his serving man,
  "Were't not against the law,
I wad tak her to my ain bed,
  And lay her neist the wa'."

"I am walking here alane," she says,
  "Amang my father's trees ;
And you must let me walk alane,
  Kind sir, now, if you please ;
The supper bell it will be rung,
  And I'll be mist awa:
Sae I winna lie in your bed,
  Either at stock or wa'."

He says, "My pretty lady,
  I pray, lend me your hand,
And ye'll hae drums and trumpets
  Always at your command ;

And fifty men to guard you wi',
  That well their swords can draw ;
Sae we'se baith lie in ae bed,
  And ye'se lie neist the wa'."

"Haud awa frae me," she said,
  "And pray let gae my hand ;
The supper bell it will be rung,
  I can nae langer stand ;
My father he will angry be,
  Gin I be mist awa ;
Sae I'll nae lie in your bed,
  Either at stock or wa'."

Then said the pretty lady,
  "I pray tell me your name ?"
"My name is Captain Wedderburn,
  A servant to the king :
Though thy father and his men were here,
  O' them I'd have nae awe ;
But wad tak you to my ain bed,
  And lay you neist the wa'."

He lichtit aff his berry brown steed,
 And set this lady on,
And held her by the milk-white hand,
 Even as they rade alang
He held her by the middle jimp,
 For fear that she should fa',
To tak her to his ain bed,
 And lay her neist the wa'"

He took her to his lodging-house,
 His landlady lookit ben,
Says, "Mony a pretty lady,
 In Edinbruch I've seen,
But sic a lovely face as thine
 In it I never saw,
Gae mak her down a down-bed,
 And lay her at the wa'"

"O haud awa frae me," she says,
 "I pray you let me be,
I winna gang into your bed,
 Till ye dress me dishes three
Dishes three ye maun dress me,
 Gin I should eat them a',
Afore I lie in your bed,
 Either at stock or wa'."

"It's ye maun get to my supper
 A cherry without a stane,
And ye maun get to my supper
 A chicken without a bane,
And ye maun get to my supper
 A bird without a ga',
Or I winna lie in your bed,
 Either at stock or wa'."

"Its when the cherry is in the blume,
 I'm sure it has nae stane,
And when the chicken's in the egg,
 I wat it has nae bane,
And, sin' the flood o' Noah,
 The doo she has nae ga',
Sae we'll baith lie in ae bed,
 And ye'se lie neist the wa'"

"O haud thy tongue, young man," she says,
 Nor that gate me perplex,
For ye maun tell me questions yet,
 And that is questions six
Questions six ye'll tell to me,
 And that is three times twa,
Afore I lie in your bed,
 Either at stock or wa'."

"What's greener than the greenest grass?
 What's higher than the trees?
What's waur nor an ill woman's wish?
 What's deeper than the seas?

What bird sings first? and whereupon
 First doth the dew down fa'?
Ye sall tell afore I lay me down
 Between you and the wa'."

"Vergris is greener than the grass,
 Heaven's higher than the trees,
The deil's waur nor a woman's wish,
 Hell's deeper than the seas,
The cock craws first, on cedar tap
 The dew down first doth fa',
Sae we'll both lie in ae bed,
 And ye'se lie neist the wa'"

"O haud your tongue, young man," she says,
 "And gie your fleechin ower
Unless ye find me ferlies,
 And that is ferlies four,
Ferlies four ye maun find me,
 And that is twa and twa,
Or I'll never lie in your bed,
 Either at stock or wa'"

"It's ye maun get to me a plum,
 That in December grew,
And ye maun get a silk mantel,
 That waft was ne'er ca'd through,
A sparrow's horn, a priest unborn,
 This night to join us twa,
Or I'll nae lie in your bed,
 Either at stock or wa'"

"My father he has winter fruit,
 That in December grew,
My mother has an Indian gown,
 That waft was ne'er ca'd through,
A sparrow's horn is quickly found,
 There's ane on every claw,
And twa upon the neb o' him,
 And ye shall get them a'

The priest, he's standing at the door,
 Just ready to come in,
Nae man can say that he was born,
 Nae man, unless he sin,
A wild boar tore his mother's side,
 He out of it did fa',
So we'll baith lie in ae bed,
 And ye'll lie neist the wa'"

Little kenn'd Girzie Sinclair,
 That morning when she raise,
That it wad be the lattermost
 O' a' her maiden days
But now there's no within the realm,
 I think, a blyther twa,
And they baith lie in ae bed,
 And she lies neist the wa'

THE STANDING STONES OF STENNIS.*

The Standing Stones of Stennis are in several groups, of which the most remarkable are those termed the Circle of Stennis, and the Ring of Brogar. The former of these is on the south side of the Bridge of Brogar, near the edge of the Loch of Stennis, and at a short distance from the public road. A great portion of the circle is destroyed, but it appears to have been about 235 feet in diameter, measuring from the outer edge of the embankment. The original number of the stones composing the Circle was probably twelve, although only two now remain standing the tallest of which is 18 feet in height, 4 feet 7 inches in breadth at the base, much broader at the top, and about 11 inches thick. The other stone is 15¾ feet high, and much thicker and broader than its neighbour. Another very large block of stone, 18 feet long, and calculated to weigh upwards of 10 tons, lies on the ground, having been thrown down in 1815. The circle, when complete, must have had a very imposing appearance. The remains of a cromlech are still visible within the circle. It is not in the centre, but towards one side, and the remains of the flat top stone still rest partially on two of the upright stones, which have latterly been pushed outwards from beneath it. The perforated Stone of Odin stood to the northward, near the Bridge of Brogar, and at the south end of the bridge the immense "Watch Stone" raises its

THE STANDING STONES OF STENNIS.

hoary head. The hole that was cut through the upper part of this Stone of Odin was for the purpose, it is supposed, of tying the sacrificial victim; but in after years it was used in quite another way. When young people fell in love, they resorted to the Stone of Odin, and joining hands through it, plighted their troths. "When the parties had agreed to marry, they repaired to the temple of the Moon, where the woman, in the presence of the man, fell down on her knees and prayed to the god Woden (for such was the name of the god whom they addressed on this occasion) that he would enable her to perform all the promises and obligations she had made, and was to make, to the young man present; after which they both went to the temple of the Sun, where the man prayed in like manner before the woman. Then they went to the Stone of Odin; and the man being on the one side, and the woman on the other, they took hold of each other's right hand through the hole in it, and there swore to be constant and faithful to each other."† When the couple wished to annul this vow, they simply repaired to the Church of Stennis—the one passing out at the north door, the other at the south

---

* Anderson's Guide to the Orkney Islands.
† This betrothal ceremony was known as the "Promise of Odin."

—and the thing was done. It is said that the people used to leave offerings at the stone; and there was a prevalent belief to the effect that a child who was passed through the Stone of Odin would never shake with the palsy. The large circle of Standing Stones is on a slope on the north side of the bridge, and is 366 feet in diameter, measuring from the inner edge of the ditch which surrounds the circle of stones. The ditch or trench is about 29 feet wide, 6 feet of average depth, and incloses a space containing nearly 2½ acres. The number of stones in this ring was probably sixty originally, but thirteen only are now standing, and ten are lying on the ground, besides several stumps. The highest standing stone is 13 feet 3 inches, and the lowest 4½ feet, but the latter has evidently been broken. The ground within the circle has never been levelled.

THE LEGEND OF LOUISA ST. CLAIR *

The proposed Indian treaty at Duncan Falls, in 1788, being postponed and adjourned to Fort Harmar, the Indians prepared for peace or war, and were hostile to holding a convention to adjust peace measures under the guns of Harmar and Campus Martius. Young Brant, son of the famous chief of that name, came down the Tuscarawas and Muskingum trail with 200 warriors, camped at Duncan Falls, nine miles below Zanesville, and informed Governor St. Clair, by runner, that they desired the treaty preliminaries to be fixed there.

The Governor suspected a plot to get him to the Falls and abduct him, yet nothing had transpired of that import. He sent Brant's runner back with word that he would soon answer by a ranger. Hamilton Kerr was dispatched to Duncan's Falls to reconnoitre and deliver St. Clair's letter. A short distance above Waterford, Kerr saw tracks, and, keeping the river in sight, crept on a bluff and raised to his feet, when hearing the laugh of a woman, he came down to the trail, and saw Louisa St. Clair on a pony, dressed Indian style, with a short rifle slung to her body. Stupefied with amazement, the ranger lost his speech, well knowing Louisa, who was the bravest and boldest girl of all at the fort. She had left without knowledge of anyone, and calling "Ham"—as he was known by that name—to his senses, told him she was going to Duncan's Falls to see Brant. Expostulation on his part only made her laugh the louder, and she twitted him on his comical dress—head turbaned with red handkerchief, hunting shirt, but no trousers, the breech-clout taking their place. Taking her pony by the head, he led it up to the trail, and at night they suppered on dried meat from Ham's pouch. The pony was tied, and Louisa sat against a tree and slept, rifle in hand, while Ham watched her. Next morning they pursued their way, and finally came in sight of the Indian camp. She then took her father's letter from the ranger, and telling him to hide and await her return, dashed off on her pony, and was soon a prisoner. She asked for Brant, who appeared in war panoply, but was abashed at her gaze. She handed him the letter, remarking that they had met before, he as a student on a visit from college to Philadelphia, and she as the daughter of General St. Clair, at school. He bowed, being educated, read the letter, and became excited. Louisa perceiving this, said she had risked her life to see him, and asked for a guard back to Marietta. Brant told her *he* guarded the brave, and would accompany her home. In the evening of the third day they arrived with Ham Kerr at the fort, where she introduced Brant to her father, relating the incident. After some hours he was escorted out of the lines, returned to the Falls, and went up the valley with his warriors, without a treaty, but in love with Louisa St. Clair. In January, 1789, he returned, took no part in the Fort Harmar treaty, was at the feast, and asked St. Clair in vain for the hand of his daughter.

In the fall of 1791, Brant led the Chippewas for a time during the battle of Miami, where St. Clair was defeated, and told the warriors to shoot the general's horses, but not him. St. Clair had four horses killed, and as many bullet holes in his clothes, but escaped unhurt. Had St. Clair given his daughter to young Brant, would the alliance have averted war?

LEGEND OF "THE POLWARTH THORN." †

Polwarth is one of those poetical localities which so frequently arrest the traveller's attention on the frontiers, and exert such pleasing or impressive influence on the fancy—the effect of past association

---

* The St. Clair Papers, pp. 179-180.
† Scotland Illustrated by Wm. Beattie. London, Geo. Virtue & Co. 1838, pp. 2-8.

rather than the force of existing circumstances or scenery The legend of the Polwarth Thorn is founded on the following circumstances connected with the ancient family of Sinclair, to whom this estate originally belonged In the fifteenth century, it is said, the direct male line having failed, the inheritance devolved upon two daughters, co-heiresses of the family, whose favour became an object of no small ambition Of their many suitors, preference was conceded to the sons of their powerful neighbour, Home of Wedderburn, and it so happened that the younger sister was beloved by the elder Home—George, while the elder placed her affections on the younger—Patrick After death of their father the young ladies passed into ward of an uncle, who, anxious to prevent their marriage that he himself might become their heir, immured them in his castle, somewhere in the Lothians In this dilemma the fair prisoners contrived to transmit a letter to their suitors by means of a mendicant woman, and they were soon gratified with the sight of the two Homes accompanied by a band of men of the Merse The uncle made vain resistance and remonstrance, his nieces were forcibly taken from him, and carried off in triumph

On their arrival at Polwarth the two marriages were celebrated in due form, and the merry rural dances which succeeded under "the thorn" were the first to commemorate an event propitious alike to the houses of Wedderburn and Polwarth. From that date the custom was introduced of holding all marriage festivals at 'Polwarth on the Green," which gave rise to a dance tune so named, to which songs have been successfully adapted The trunk of this celebrated "nuptial tree" is still preserved in Marchmont House

THE ORCADIAN HOMELAND

(Mrs J L Sinclair)

Written on receiving a newspaper from the Northland Isles The expression "gownsmen" is in allusion to the progress made in education, so many Orcadians appear to be gaining University honours

In the land of the rocks and the heather,
  The Northern Lights and the snow,
When the Islesmen assemble together,
  I should like to be present, I know
I should like to attend their meetings
  A-near the cathedral chime,
As I cannot, I send kind greetings
  To the "Land of the Runic Rhyme"

By mountain, by field, or by river,
  Where duty impels to go forth,
Our hearts, like the needle, turn ever
  To the dear island home in the North
For our sires in the old time were sea-kings,
  Who sailed o'er the waves alway,
Thus our pulses are stirred like a viking's
  At the sight of the salt sea spray

To the land of the cross *engré'ee*,
  The land of the midnight sun,
My thoughts revert thitherward daily,
  Ere ever the day is done
And when darkness comes with the night-time,
  As I put aside my work,
Once more I hear the bright-chime
  Of the old cathedral kirk

A message from o'er the Pacific
  Has come to the Maoriland shore,
It acts as a magic specific,
  Reviving the memories of yore
Oftentimes I peruse in press pages
  The name of some schoolmate or friend,
Who has passed thro' this life's serried stages,
  Enduring, in hope, to the end

Here's "Good Luck" to our old fellow towns-
  And women, so tender and true— [men—
Of whom many have since become gownsmen,
  And many more likely to do
And success to dear "Ultima Thule"
  In all that is brightest and best !
May her children act wisely and truly,
  Until they are called to their rest

In the land of the rocks and the heather,
  The Northern Lights and the snow,
When my countrymen gather together,
  I should like to be present, I know,
Once more to hear at their meetings
  Tales of the northland clime,
As I cannot, accept these greetings
  For the sake of the olden time

Reproduced by permission of Valentine & Sons, Ltd., Dundee.
ROSLIN CHAPEL.

BOOK IV

APPENDICES.

A—CHARTERS OF HERDMANSTON*

I—THE ORIGINAL GRANT OF CARFRÆ

WM. DE MOREVILLE TO HENRY DE ST CLAIR
(CIRCA 1160)

WILLIELMUS DE MOREVILLE, Constabularius Regis Scotiæ Omnibus amicis et probis hominibus suis presentibus et futuris salutem Sciatis, me concessisse, et hac mea charta confirmasse, HENRICO DE SANCTO CLARO, Carfra, per suas rectas divisas, scilicet, sicut Langilde se jungit ad Mosburne, et illinc descendit usque ad Ledre, et ex superiori parte, sicut Mosburn ascendit usque ad Venneshende, et de Venneshende usque ad Sumunindnight, illinc per descentum usque ad viam de Glengelt et illinc usque Ledre, tenendam de me et hæredibus meis, illi et hæredibus suis, in feodo et hereditate, in terris et aquis, in pratis, et pascuis, et bosco et plano, et extra forrestam, libere et quiete, per servitium unius militis Concessi etiam illi ut in feodo suo, Molendinum suum habeat sine multura. Concessi et ut nemo utetur terra sua vel pastura, vel bosco suo, nisi per eum excepto, et simul utemur communi pastura de dominiis nostris His testibus, Comite Duncano, Rollando filio Uthredi, Hugone Giffarde, Alexandro de Sancto Martino, Herberto Decano, Stephano filio Richardi, Alano de Culstene, Roberto Samuelis filio, Godfredo de Ros, Petro del Haya, Edulfo filio Uthredi, Gilberto de Lane, Richardo filio Gilberti, Adam Patre, Adamo filio Edulfi, Herberto filio Roberti, Willielmo Clerico.

II—CHARTER OF CONFIRMATION

ROLAND FITZ UTHRED TO ALAN DE ST CLAIR
(CIRCA 1196)

Rolandus filius Uthredi, Constabularius Regis Scotiæ, omnibus hominibus et amicis suis, præsentibus et futuris, salutem Sciatis me dedisse et concessisse, et præsenti charta mea confirmasse, ALANO DE SANCTO CLARO, et Mathildæ de Windsoure sponsæ suæ, et hæredibus eorum, qui ex iis exierint, illam terram quam Willielmus de Morevill iis dedit, tenendam de me et hæredibus meis in marriagium, scilicet sicut Mosburn descendit in Langild, et Langild in ascendendo usque ad caput de Langild, et de capite de Langild usque ad divisas de Laodonia versus Lamberlawe His Testibus Herberto Decano de Glesco, Alexandro filio Cospat, Gilberto de Umfravilla, Alano de Clesan, Thoma Anglico, Willielmo filio Rogeri, Jacobo de Rosse, Alexandro de Cheon, Waltero et Ethelredo, Clericis meis

The seal thereunto appended was of white wax, representing on the one side ane armed man, with ane naked sword in his hand, a horseback, the horse covered also with armour, haveing chevrons on the pans, sutch we have seen att the carousels

It is to be observed that William of Morevill died in 1196, without heirs of his body, and that Roland, Earle of Galloway, who had married his sister, succeeded him in his estate, and, consequently, was bound to confirme the former gift, wherof we have ane instrument taken by John Saintclair of Herminston in 1434, as follows —

Roslyn Chartulary

III.—INSTRUMENT IN RENEWAL OF THE CHARTER OF WM. DE MOREVILLE, 1434, A.D.

IN DEI NOMINE, AMEN. Per hoc presens publicum instrumentum, cunctis pateat evidenter, quod, anno a nativitate ejusdem MCCCCXXXIV. indictione XII., ac mensis Maii die XIII. Pontificatus sanctissimi in Christo patris, ac Domini nostri, Domini Eugenii, divina providentia, Papæ IV., anno IV. In mei notarii publici, et testium subscriptorum presentia, personaliter constitutus, prudens vir JOHANNES DE SANCTO CLARO, dominus de Herdmanston mihi notario publico, quandam litteram in pergamento scriptam, cum suo sigillo in cera alba antiquo more sigillatam, non rasam, non cancellatam, non abolitam, nec aliquo more suspectam, tradidit, perlegendam, et in formam publicam redigendam, cujus tenor sequitur in hæc verba. (Here follows a recital in Latin of the charter from William de Moreville.) Super quibus omnibus et singulis, in prædicta littera, sive in prædicta charta contentis præfatus JOHANNES DE SANCTO CLARO sibi presens publicum petiit fieri instrumentum. Acta fuerunt hæc apud CASTRUM DE HERDMANSTON, hora quasi decima ante meridiam, sub anno, indictione, die, mense, et pontificatu, quibus supra. Præsentibus providis ibidem viris THOMA DE SANCTO CLARO, Patricio Dickson, et Edwardo Stenson, cum multis aliis testibus ad præmisso vocatis specialiter et rogatis.

Et Ego, Guilielmus Harpar, Clericus Glasguensis Diocæsis Publicus, imperiali authoritate, Notarius, præfatam litteram sive chartam vidi, tenui, et legi, ac de verbo in verbum fideliter copiavi, præsensque instrumentum inde confectum, meaque propria manu scriptum, meis signo solito et subscriptione signavi, rogatus et requisitus, coram his testibus prædictis, in fidem et testimonium omnium et singulorem præmissorum.

B.—GRANT OF INNERLEITH*
IN 1280 TO
SIR WILLIAM DE ST CLAIR, FIRST OF ROSLYN

ALEXANDER, &c. Cum Nicholaus *pistor* quondam serviens noster, nobis resignaverit, per fustim et baculum, terram de Innerleith, cum pertinentiis suis, quam idem Nicholaus de antecessoribus nostris et nobis quondam tenuit, per chartam bonæ memoriæ Willielmi Regis Scotorum illustris. Noveritis, nos, eandem terram de Innyreth, dedisse, concessisse, et hac præsenti charta me confirmasse, WILLIELMO DE SANCTO CLARO, militi, et heredibus suis. Tenendam et habendam, sibi et heredibus suis, de nobis et heredibus nostris, cum omnibus justis pertinentiis. Concessimus etiam eidem Willielmo, et heredibus suis, ut bladum suum de domo sua propria molant ad molendinum nostrum, libere, absque multura aliqua inde danda, sed homines sui multuram dent. Testibus Willielmo de Soulys Justiciario Loadoniæ, Hugone de Perisby, Thoma Randulph, Simone Fraser, Nicholao de Haya, et Nicholao de Vetere Ponte. Apud Hadington, octavo die Aprilis, anno regni nostri tricesimo primo.

The seal is white wax, the tak, parchement, the King a horseback, the horse covered with a cloath, upon which is seen a lyon rampant in a double tressure floure and contre floure, the reverse, the King in a seat of justice.

In the reign of King William the Lion (1165-1214) these lands were held of the crown by "Reginaldus janitor Castelli de Edinburgh," after whom they were granted by King William to "Ailifo, pistori meo, per servitium sui corporis" (vide Charta apud Castellum Puellarum, Roslyn Chart.) This was followed later on by a charter from the same king to "Nicholao filio Ailif, Pistori meo," confirming him in the lands of Innerleith formerly held by Reginald and by Ailif, and on the resignation of Nicholas in 1280 a charter issued as above to SIR WILLIAM DE ST CLAIR, which is the first record of the Roslyn family acquiring Scottish lands. Innerleith was afterwards given to the family of Towres, with reservation of the superiority, whereupon there is yet a charter of inquisition, and a retour (1525) of Innerleith in Roslin's charter-chest, justifying what is above mentioned.

It is thought that the office of Panetarius accompanied these lands.

Roslyn Chartulary

C—CHARTA ALEXANDRI REGIS,
1280

TERRARUM DE ROSKELYN ET DE CATEKON*
TO
WILLIAM DE ST CLAIR

ALEXANDER, &c., Cum Henricus de Roskelyn tenens noster de terris de Roskelyn, et de Catekon, resignavit per fustim et baculum in manu nostra, et quietum clamaverit pro se, et heredibus suis, prædictas terras de Roskelyn et de Catekou Tenendas et Habendas prædicto WILLIELMO DE SANCTO CLARO, et heredibus suis, de nobis et heredibus nostris, in feodo et hereditate, cum socco et sacca, et furca et fossa, cum Thol et Them, et infangantheif, in boscis et planis, pratis et pascuis, molendinis et stagnis, et omnibus aliis libertatibus, et aysiamentis ad prædictas terras pertinentibus, adeo libere et quiete, integre et pacifice, sicut predictus Henricus de Roskelyn, terras illas, liberius, quietius aut melius, aliquo tempore tenuit aut possedit Faciendo inde nobis, et heredibus nostris servitium dimidii militis Testibus, Roberto Episcopo Glasguensi, Willielmo Fraser Cancellario nostro, Gilberto Comite de Anegus, Willielmo Comyn de Kilbryde, Symone Fraser, Bernardo de Monte Alto, Willielmo Byseth, Patricio de Graham et multis aliis Apud Trevequayr, decimo quarto die Septembris anno regni nostri tricesimo primo.

D—DIPLOMA OF THE ORCADIAN SUCCESSION†
(870 TO 1420)

DIPLOMA OR DEDUCTION CONCERNING THE GENEALOGIES OF THE ANCIENT JARLS OF ORKNEY, FROM THEIR FIRST CREATION TO THE FIFTEENTH CENTURY DRAWN UP FROM THE MOST AUTHENTIC RECORDS BY THOMAS BISHOP OF ORKNEY, WITH THE ASSISTANCE OF HIS CLERGY AND OTHERS, IN CONSEQUENCE OF AN ORDER FROM ERIC, KING OF DENMARK, TO INVESTIGATE THE RIGHT OF WILLIAM LORD SAINT CLAIR TO THE JARLDOM.

Quoniam inter ceteras hujus fluctuantis seculi curas & solicitudines, pensata temporum, morum ac hominum in hac lacrimarum valle, labilitate & brevitate, testante venerabili illo cronographo Martino, Domini nostri pape Penetentiario & Capellano, necesse videtur de congruo extrahere progenitorum, regum, principum & aliorum preclarorum genealogias per quos mundus iste transitorius regitur, Reges regnant & principes gubernant signantq, in deduccionem & agniccionem veritatis, quo ad eorundem successionem verisimiliter evenire speratur Illustri ergo & excellentissimo Domino nostro, principi supremo, Norwegie regi, suisq successoribus, satrapis, patriciis, consulibus & proceribus dicti regni, Thomas, Dei & Apostolice sedis gracia Episcopus Orcadie & Zetlandie, Canonici Ecclesie Cathedralis sancti Magni Martyris gloriosissimi, legifer, ceteriq, proceres, nobiles, populus ac communitas ejusdem, gracia, pax, caritas, gaudium, longanimitas, misericordia a Deo Patre omnipotente, & a Jesu Christo in Spiritu Sancto In omnibus vobis per quem reges regnant & in cujus manu corda sunt regum cum omni subjectione, humilitate & obediencia prompti & parati, vestram in Jesu Christi visceribus zelantes & facientes salutem in caritate non ficta Requirentes ut in dicendis in nostra simplicitate vestra suppleat regia sublimitas, & quia scimus firmiter & longi temporis spacio, efficax rerum magistra nos experienta docuit, quod in dubium non revocamus qualiter erga Comites Orcadie, regalis ipsa sublimitas zelum semper exuberantem exercuit Quamobrem firmam spem gerimus, plenamq, fiduciam obtinemus quod illa regia majestas verba nostra benique recipiat, diligenter intelligat & effective prosequatur, ut infra pectoris claustrum solicite considerare convenit ipsa regia sinceritas & diligenter attendere, quod adulatorium vestre serenitati aliquid non scribimus, quod secundum Petrum Blessensem in suo prologo canentem, Olei venditores esse non intendimus, sed patefactores veritatis

Ergo arbitramur pium esse & meritorium, testimonium, perhibere veritati re veritas occultetur, presertim illa per quam innocenti possit prejudicium generari, & cum uterq, reus est qui veritatem occultat & mendacium dicit, quia ille non prodesse iste nocere desiderat, quod a nobis Deus avertat, potissime cum in dicendis per quondam recolende memorie Erici vestri predecessoris regis nostri

---

* Roslyn Chartulary †Wallace's Description

admoniti patentes literas fuissemus testimonium perhibere veritati prout latius in sequentibus patebit Hinc est quod nos Thomas Episcopus, Capitulum, Canonici, Legifer, ceteriq; proceres, nobiles, populus, communitas sive plebei antedicti, coram Deo in fide ac fidelitate quibus vestre regie Majestati tenemur astricti, fideliter attestamur & ad perpetuam rei memoriam deducimus fidemq, facimus vobis & omnibus presentibus & futuris Jesu Christi fidelibus, sancte matris ecclesie filiis, in forma & effectu subsequentibus Coram nobis congregatus comparens magnificus & prepotens Dominus, Dominus Willielmus de Sancto Claro, Comes Orcadie, Dominus le Sinclar in ecclesia sancti Magni Martyris in Orcadia proposuit in hunc modum, supposuit enim quod nobis bene & ad plenum cognita res fuisset, quo modo magnis retroactis temporibus antecessores sui & progenitores ac ipsi Orcadie comites juste ac juridice, inconcusse, linialiter & gradatim jure hereditario comitatum Orcadie superdicto successerant, ac illam per tempora magna & longeva nulla aliena generatione interveniente, quietissime possederant Et qualiter diverse carte, evidencie, instrumenta, libri censuales & alia diversa probacionum genera fuerant igne consumpta, deperdita & alienata, hostilitatis tempore & guerrarum emulorum inimicorumq, nonnullorum, defectu & carentia firmissime domus seu municionis inexpugnabilis ubi hujusmodi collocarentur, subjunxit idem Dominus Comes quod habuit literas quondam supremi Domini nostri Regis Erici illustris, patentes, quas nobis ostendit & perlegi fecit, precepta continentes subsequencia, scilicet quod si quis nostrum habuerit vel qui habuerint aliquas cartas, evidencias, cirographa, instrumenta, munimenta, codicillos, acta vel privilegiorum literas ad progenitores, antecessores, vel ad se spectantes, dictumq, suum comitatum concernentes, quod indilate & sine mora aut contradictione seu obstaculo, quibuscunq, eidem Domino comiti deliberaret vel deliberarent, secundum quod ipsius Domini nostri Regis evitare velimus indignacionem Virtute quarum literarum sicut eadem comitis continebat propositio nos requisivit ut si de hujusmodi antedictis munimentis, aliqua habuissemus in nostris scriniis, apothecariis, thecis, cistis, archivis seu cartophilaciis, quod ipsa sibi deliberaremus, & in casu quo non habuerimus, sed sciremus ab aliis ea haberi quod sibi intimaremus & revelaremus Et si nec unum nec reliquum sciremus, tunc nos requisivit earundem literarum autoritate, quatenus nos Deum, justitiam, & equitatem pre oculis habentes in declaracionem veritatis, velimus sagaciter & studiose mature digestis iterum iterum ac tertio perscrutari scripturas, cronicas autenticas & approbatas que faciunt fidem illas perlegere, diligenter inspicere, sane concipere & intelligere, ac naturas infeodacionis & ecclesiarum fundaciones perspicue intendere, quibus sic mature rimatis & ad plenum discussis velimus supremo Domino nostro manifestare per genealogias ac cronicas autenticas, per quos & a quibus linealiter & gradatim idem Willielmus Comes processit & per quanta tempora, legitime, juste, bene & inconcusse predecessores sui & ipse gavisi sunt dicto comitatu cum universis & singulis suis insulis, commoditatibus & justis suis pertinenciis, ne hujusmodi successio ultra debitam procelaretur hominum memoriam His omnibus sic propositis, avisatis, discussis, digestis mature & ad plenum conceptis & intellectis, habitis prius diversis & singulis hinc inde tractatibus, ad honorem Dei omnipotentis, manifestationem veritatis & obedienciam & reverenciam supremi Domini nostri Regis, tanquam filii obediencie, precep arii, mandatarii prout decet in his quæ audivimus a senioribus nostris, deinde que legibus intelleximus & concepimus & ad plenum sano effectu digessimus per libros scripturas, cronicas regnorum utrorumq, Scocie et Norwegie & progenitorum eorundem, sic quod singulariter singuli & universaliter universi, uno animo, una fide, unico consensu & assensu respondemus fidem ut prefertur & testimonium veritatis facientes univers s superscriptis Quod universa genera munimentorum, cartarum, evidenciarum et aliarum probacionum species que apud nos erant ob reverentiam supremi Domini nostri dicto Domino Comiti deliberavimus & exhibuimus ante dictum comitatum concernencia Sed verum est, et in veritate attestamur ex relatione fidedignorum antecessorum & progenitorum nostrorum quod principulus & precipuus mansus sive manerium Dominorum Comitum Orcadie fuit diversis temporibus igne combustus & ad nihilum redactus & funditus destructus, et patria tota depredata & vastata per emulos nostros & inimicos, per quas depredaciones, consumpciones & destrucciones firmiter credimus quod principales evidencie, carte & alie patentes, diverse litere fuerunt & sunt alienate & consumpte spectantes et concernentes ad antecessores & progenitores dicti Domini Comitis, defectu unius castri in quo tutissime ipse evidencie, & carte, & alia patrie jocalia firmissime poterant collocare Ast quantum ad linealem progressum & gradum successionis dicti Domini Comitis & suorum antecessorum seu progenitorum Comitum Orcadie, nos prenominati superius expressatis, juxta nostrum ingenium, sensum et intellectum perscrutati sumus & mature avisati lucidissime per diversa linguarum genera, scripturas autenticas et approbatas cronicas, scilicet in lingua Latina & Norwegica per quas reperimus infeodaciones ecclesiarum nostrarum genealogias nostras & antecessorum nostrorum, cartis & evidenciis ipsorum & nostrorum manifestantibus & claro stili eloquio testimonium perhibentibus ad fidem facientibus, in quibusdam cronicis, libris, cartis ac aliis autenticis scripturis reperimus nomina diversorum comitum Orcadie, tempora infeudacionum ipsorum juxta modum et formam sequentem sed de eorum strenuis & notabilibus operacionibus, gestis, nominibus filiorum filiarumq, suarum, de modo migrandi ab hac luce, de divisione seu unione hereditatis ipsorum, de incremento vel decremento possessionum suarum pro presenti brevitatis causa pretermittimus, & nos ad antiquas cronicas & genealogias autenticas & approbatas referimus

Reperimus itaq, imprimis quod tempore Haraldi Comati primi Regis Norwegie qui gavisus est per totum Regnum suum, hæc terra sive insularum patria Orcadie fuit inhabitata & culta duabus nacionibus scilicet Peti & Pape, que due genera naciones fuerant destructe radicitus ac penitus per Norwegenses de stirpe sive de tribu strenuissimi principis Rognaldi, qui sic sunt ipsas naciones aggressi quod posteritas ipsarum nacionum Peti & Pape non remansit Sed verum est quod tunc non d nominabatur Orcadia sed terra Petorum sicut clare verificatur hodie adhuc cronica attestante, per mare dividens Scociam et Orcadiam, quod usque, ad hodiernum diem mare Petlandicum appellatur & sicut pulchre subjungitur in iisdem cronicis Rex iste Haraldus Comatus primo applicuit in Zetlandiam cum classe sua & consequenter in Orcadia & contulit illam Orcadiam & Zetlandiam antedicto principi Rognaldo robusto ex cujus stirpe ut prefertur prefate due naciones, fuerant everse & destructe sicut cronice nostre clare demonstrant, a quo quidem Rognaldo processerunt linealiter & gradatim omnes Comites Orcadie & possederunt temporibus suis dictum Comitatum libere sine quacunq, exactione quocunq, canone seu sensu, excepto obsequio prestando regibus Norwegie tributi ratione, sicut in clausula sequenti latius patebit que in cronica de verbo in verbum continetur Revera enim usq, hodie illorum posteritatis dominio subjacent excepto quod jure tributario Norwegie regibus deserviunt Qui quidem princeps Rognaldus strenuissimus hujusmodi comitatum libere & pure donavit cuidam fratri suo Swardo nomine, qui Comes Swardus procreavit quendam filium Gothormum nomine, qui comes Gothormus possedebat dictum Comitatum per unum annum & decessit sine herede legittimo, et sic reversus est iterato dictus Comitatus dicto principi Rognaldo, qui pure & libere illam contulit cuidam filio suo Eynar nomine qui postea cognominabatur Turffeinar, qui quidem per longa tempora possedebat dictum Comitatum & habundavit opibus & plenus fuit diviciis Cui successit filius ejus Thurwider Hedclevar, cui successit filius ejus Hlauderver, cui successit filius ejus Comes Swardus robustus ac corpulentus, magnus & strenuissimus bellifer Adhuc tamen non fuit regeneratus sacri baptismatis lavacro neq, alii Comites prenominati In cujus quidem Comitis Swardi diebus supervenit Olaus Thurgonis filius Rex illustrissimus de occidentalium partium guerris, cujus inductione comes ille Swardus una cum gente Orchadie devenerunt Christiani, gentilitatis relinquentes errorem. Cui Comiti Swardo successit filius ejus comes Thurfinus, procreatus ex filia quondam excellentissimi Principis Malcomi Regis Scotorum illustris Qui quidem Rex contulit dicto Thurfino terras de Cathnes & Suthirland sub unica denominatione comitatus in Scocia, & illis gavisus est una cum comitatu Orchadie Zetlaudie & pluribus aliis dominiis in Scocie Regno jacentibus, & vixerat diu, & strenuissimus erat in campis Post cujus quidem Comitis Thurfini obitum successit sibi ejus filius Comes Erlinus primus, & iste Erlinus primus genuit Comitem Paulum & Erlinum Secundum, qui Paulus Comes genuit Comitem Haco Comes Erlinus Secundus procreavit Comitem Magnum, gloriosissimum Martyrem, patronum Orcadie, qui sanctissime abijt ab hac luce virgo & martyr Post cujus quidem Magni Martiris decessum, & post obitum Comitis Hacon successit Comes Rolandus, qui primo fundavit Ecclesiam Sancti Magni Martiris, illamq, magnis possessionibus diviciis & redditibus dotavit, predictus virq, sapiencia & virtute pollebat per plura bona pietatis opera famabatur venerabaturq, & reputabatur pro sancto viro. Post cujus quidem obitum successit ejus frater Ericus comitatui, Cui successit Comes Haraldus, Cui successit comes Johannes filius ejus, Cui Johanni successit comes Magnus secundus, a quo Alexander Scotorum Rex cepit comitatum de Sutherland Cui Magno comiti secundo successit comes Gilbertus primus, cui successit Comes Gilbertus secundus ejus filius, qui gavisus est comitatibus Orchadie & Cathnes in Scocia Qui quidem Gilbertus secundus procreavit Magnum tertium & quandam filiam Matildam nomine Iste Comes Magnus filius Gilberti secundi genuit Comitem Magnum quartum, & quendam Johannem, & ille Magnus comes quartus ab hac luce abijt sine prole, cui successit Johannes ejus frater in antedictis comitatibus Orchadie & Cathnes Joannes iste genuit quendam Magnum Comitem quintum Cui Magno quinto jure Successionis linealiter successit Dominus Malisius comes de Stratherne in Scocia tanquam heres legittimus jure hereditario ad utrosq, comitatus Orchadie et Cathnes sicut clarissime manifestant munimenta, evidencie & carte utrorumq, regnorum Scocie et Norwegie confirmacionis desuper confecte Qui qui-

APPENDICES.

dem Comes Malisius revera primo desponsavit filiam Comitis de Menteith in Scocia & ex ea genuit filiam Matildam nomine, post cujus quidem prime uxoris obitum desponsavit filiam quandam quondam Hugonis Comitis de Ross, & ex ea procreavit quatuor filias & decessit sine masculis, sicq, ejus dominia terræ & possessiones fuerunt divise inter illas Filiam vero antiquiorem ex prima uxore procreatam, Matildam scilicet duxit in uxorem Welandus de Ard, qui ex ea procreavit quendam filium Alexandrum de Ard, qui Alexander jure Regni Scoc e & consuetudine hereditarie successit Comiti Malisio de Strathern in principali manerio sive manso ratione sue matris Comitatus de Cathania & possedebat jure & appellacione Comitis & eadem ratione & eodem jure gavisus est certa perticata sive quantitate terrarum Orchadie & gerebat se pro Balivo & Capitaneo gentis Orchadie, Norwegie Regis ex parte, Idemq; Alexander de Ard tempore suo vendidit & alienavit quondam recolende memorie Domino Roberto Stewart primo Scotorum Regi dictum comitatum de Cathnes mansum sive manerium principale & omnia alia jura spectantia seu concernencia ad se ratione matris ejus tanquam ad antiquiorem sororem jure & consuetudine regni Scocie cum denominacione comitatus sive Comitis Iste vero Alexander finaliter decessit sine herede de sua corpore quocunq, legittimo procreato Nunc vero vertamus stylum ad quatuor filias ex secunda uxore procreatas, quarum una desponsata era cum Domino Willelmo de Sancto Claro, Domino le Synclar, qui Dominus Willelmus ex ea genuit Dominum Henricum de Sancto Claro, qui Dominus Henricus desponsavit Jonetam filiam Domini Walteri de Haliburtoun, Domini de Dirletoun, & ex ea procreavit Dominum Henricum de Sancto Claro secundum, qui ultimo decessit comes Orcadie indubitatus, qui in uxorem habuit venerabilem Dominam Dominam Egidiam filiam filiae antedicti quondam Domini Roberti Scotorum regis illustris filiamq, quondam strenuissimi Domini Willelmi de Douglas Domini de Nydysdale, & ex ea procreavit presentem Dominum Willelmum de Sancto Claro comitem Orcadie, Dominum le Synclare Quedam alia filia secunde uxoris desponsata fuit cum quodam milite denominato Here Ginsill de Swethrick partibus oriundo, qui vero miles in Orcadie partibus venit ex ratione sue uxoris gavisus est quadam parte terrarum Orchadie, que quidem uxor ab hac luce sine herede migravit leggittimo ex suo corpore procreato Tertia vero filia secunde uxoris fuit nupta cum quodam Gothredo nomine Gothormo le Spere qui ex ea procreavit quendam filium Dominum Mahsium le Spere militem, qui tandem decessit sine herede legittimo de suo corpore genito, similiter & quarta filia decessit sine herede ex suo corpore legittime procreato Verum iste Dominus Henricus, primus Dominus le Sinclare, ejus matre, Alexandro de Ard & domino Malesio Spere adhuc viventibus ad Dominum nostrum supremum regem Norwegie adivit Hacon nomine, cum quo rege certas iniit pactiones, condiciones et appunctuamenta per quas reversus est ad Orchadie partes illisq; gavisus est usq, ad extremum vite sne, comesq, Orcadie obijt & pro defensione patrie inibi crudeliter ab inimicis peremptus est Et post decessum istius Henrici comitis primi in Orcadie partibus, supervenit dicti Comitis Henrici primi mater, filia Domini Malesij Comitis prenominati, & ibi fixe remansit usq, post obitum filij ejus Henrici Comitis primi, & supervixerat post obitum omnium sororum suarum, filiorum filiarumq, suorum, sic quod ipsius antedicti quondam Comitis Henrici primi mater successit omnibus sororibus ejus eorundemq, filijs et filiabus tanquam unica & legittima heres comitatus Orcadie & terrarum de Cathnes sibi tanquam uni sorori debitarum, parte duntaxat & porcione exceptis sororis sue antiquioris de terris de Cathnes sub denominacione & appellacione comitatus sive Comitis, quam partem ut superius dictum est alienavit & vendidit ipse quondam Alexander de Ard regi Scocie prenominato Hujusq, rei testes sunt adhuc viventes fidedigni qui ipsam matrem Henrici primi oculis viderunt labijsq, sunt locuti cum ea communicantes ad plenum, Cui successit ejus nepos Henricus Secundus filius primi Henrici, cui Henrico secundo successit presens & superstes Dominus Wilelmus comes modernus Dominus le Sinclar

Excellentissime Princeps ut premissimus in principio ita fine protestamur quod vestra serenissima regia sublimitas ac ipsius benignissima majestas juxta ingenij nostri modulum & sensuum capacitatem nos linguamque naturam incultam nebulis ignorancie multipliciter obfuscatam velut rudes indoctos a Rhetorica sciencia alienos in fecunda facundia ignaros habere excusatos quamvis barbarico more non poetice locutionis, modo grosso loquamur, quia Insulares sumus, a literarum sciencia penitus alieni, imo quod condecenti rethorice locutionis stilo sive scriptura non referimus vestre regie majestatis ea & nos submittimus correctioni Sed verum est ut attestamur quod more nostro barbarico omnia que superius vestre majestati scribimus vera sunt, quia ex antiquis libris, scripturis autenticis, cronicis approbatis & relacionibus fidedignorum antecessorum nostrorum, ac infeodacionibus nostris ecclesiarum nostrarum ista extruximus & compilavimus Et si opus esset plura quam in pre-enti epistola vestre celsitudini latius manifestare sciremus ipsamq, in premissis informare, sed quia longa solent sperni, hec pauca sufficiunt pro presenti Et ut hec nostra epistola taliter qualiter compilata vestre regie majestati ac dominis vestri consistorij & palatij circa latera vestra existentibus majorem fidem ac roboris firmitatem faciat, animos vestros ad plenum informet, ac inter archana pectorum vestrorum radicem emittat veritatis firmam, & ceteros Christi fideles sancte matris Ecclesie filios instruat ad Deum, et sacrosancta dei evangelja per nos corporaliter tacta juramus quod premissa modo quo super relata deponimus ad Dei honorem vestreq, celsitudinis, predecessoris mandatum & non alias nec prece nec precio, odio, amore vel favore vel sub spe cujuscunq, muneris presentis vel futuri sed pro veritate duntaxat dicenda In quorum omnium & singulorum fidem & testimonium premissorum sigilla Thomi Episcopi, Canonicorum & Capituli antedictorum, totiusq, populi & communitatis patrie nostre Orcadie, quod dicitur sigillum commune & mei Henrici Randale legiferi in nostra publica & generali sessione non sine magna maturitate & plena digestione presentibus sunt appensa apud Kirkwaw mensis Maij die quarto Anno Domini millesimo quadringentesimo tertio

There is a translation, apparently from another copy, in Barry's History, made in 1554 by Dean Thos Gwle, munk, at the request of ane honorable man WILZEM SINCLAIR, barroun of Roslin, Pechtland, and Herberschire "To the faytht and witnessing of all and singulare thir premissis oure salis, that is to mene the saill of Bischop Thomas, and of the chanonis of the chaptre foresaids, and of all the pepill and commonite of the cuntrie of Orchadie, quhilk is callit the commune saill, the saill of myn, Henrie Rendale, law-man, of Nichohe Tullach myn, of Joan Cragy my armig, of Richard Fodringame Lawrik-men myn, of Alexander Sinclare myn, of Joane Tod myn of James Lask myn, of Alexander Brown myn, and of Angus Mangson myn, with certane sawlis of others faythfull parsonis of the cuntrie, till thair presents ar to hangit at Kirkwaw in Orchadie, the first day of the monetht at Junii, the zer of oure Lord ane thousand 4 hundrecht and 40 sex "

E —INSTALLATION DOCUMENTS OF EARL HENRY I
(2nd Aug., 1379)

1 —THE COMITIAL OBLIGATION *

"To all who shall see or hear the present letters, Henry, Jarl of the Orkneys, Lord of Roslin, wishes salvation in the Lord Because the very serene Prince in Christ, my most clement lord Hakon, by the grace of God, the king of the kingdoms of Norway and Sweden, has set us by his favour over the Orcadian lands and islands, and has raised us into the rank of jarl over the beforesaid lands and islands, and since this is required by the dignity, we make well known to all, as well to posterity as to contemporaries, that we have made homage of fidelity to our Lord the king himself, at the kiss of his hand and mouth, and have given to him a true and due oath of fidelity, as far as counsels and aids to our same lord the king, his heirs, and successors, and to his kingdom of Norway must be observed And so, let it be open to all that we and our friends, whose names are expressed lower, have firmly promised in faith and with our honour to our same lord the king, and to his men and councillors, that we must faithfully fulfil all agreements, conditions, promises, and articles which are contained in the present letters to our beforesaid lord the king, his heirs, and successors, and to his kingdom of Norway.

"In the first place, therefore, we firmly oblige us to serve our lord the king outside of the lands and islands of the Orkneys with 100 good men or more, equipped in complete arms, for the conveniences and use of our same lord the king, whenever we shall have been sufficiently requisitioned by his messengers or his letters, and forewarned within Orkney three months But when the men shall have arrived in the presence of our lord the king, from that time he will provide about victuals for us and ours

"Again, if any may wish to attack or hostilely invade, in manner whatsoever, the lands and islands of the Orkneys, or the land of Hjaltland, then we promise and oblige us to defend the lands named, with men whom we may be able to collect in good condition for this solely, from the lands and islands themselves, yea, with all the force of relatives, friends, and servants

"Also, if it shall be necessary that our lord the king attack any lands or any kingdoms, by right or from any other reason or necessity, then we shall be to him in help and service with all our force

---

* Translated by Thos Sinclair, M A author of "Caithness Events," from the Latin in Torfœus "Orcades"

"Moreover, we promise in good faith that we must not build or construct castles or any fortifications within the lands and islands beforesaid, unless we shall have obtained the favour, good-pleasure, and consent of our same lord the king

"We also shall be bound to hold and to cherish the said lands and islands of the Orkneys, and all their inhabitants, clergymen and laity, rich and poor, in their rights

"Further, we promise in good faith that we must not at any time sell or alienate that beforesaid earldom and that lordship, whether lands or islands, belonging to the earldom, or our right which we obtain now to the earldom, the lands, and islands, by the grace of God and of the king our lord, from our lord the king himself, or his heirs, and successors, or from the kingdom, nor to deliver these or any of these for surety and for pledge to any one, or to expose them otherwise, against the will and good-pleasure of him and his successors

"In addition, if it happen that our lord the king, his heirs, or successors, wish to approach those lands and islands for their defence, or from other reasonable cause, or to direct thither his councillors or men, then we shall be held to be for help to our same lord the king, and his heirs, to his councillors and men, with all our force, and to minister to our lord the king, and his heirs, his men and councillors, those things of which they may be in need for their due expenses, and as necessity then requires, at least to ordain so from the lands and islands

"Moreover, we promise that we must not begin or rouse any war, law suit, or dissension with any strangers or natives, by reason of which war, law suit, or dissension the king my lord, his heirs, or successors, or their kingdom of Norway, or the beforesaid lands and islands, may receive any damage

"Again, if it happen, but may this be absent, that we notably and unjustly do wrong against any within the beforesaid lands and islands, or inflict some notable injury upon any one, as the loss of life, or mutilation of limbs, or depredation of goods, then we shall answer to the pursuer of a cause of that kind in the presence of our lord the king himself and his counsellors, and satisfy for the wrongs according to the laws of the kingdom.

"Also, whensoever our lord the king shall have summoned us, on account of any causes, to his presence, when and where he shall have wished to hold his general assembly, then we are bound to go to him, to give him advice and assistance

"Further, we promise that we shall not break the truces and security of our same lord the king, nor his peace, which he shall have made or confirmed with foreigners or natives, or with whomsoever others, in any manner whatever, to violate them, nay, defend them all as far as our strength, and hold those as federated to us whom the king of Norway himself, our lord, may wish to treat as his favourers and friends

"We promise also that we must make no league with the Orcadian bishop, nor enter into or establish any friendship with him, unless from the good-pleasure and consent of our lord the king himself, but we must be for help to him against that bishop, until he shall have done to him what is of right, or shall be bound to do so for that special reason, upon those things in which my lord the king may wish or be able reasonably to accuse that bishop.

"Besides, when God may have willed to call us from life, then that earldom and that lordship, with the lands and islands, and with all the jurisdiction, must return to our lord the king, his heirs and successors freely, and if we shall have children after us, procreated from our body, male, one or more, then he of them who shall claim the above said earldom and lordship must demand, with regard to this, the favour, good pleasure, and consent of our lord the king himself, his heirs, and successors

"Further, we promise in good faith that we shall be bound to pay to our abovesaid lord the king, or to his official at Tunsberg, on the next festival of St. Martin the bishop and confessor, a thousand golden pieces, which are called nobles, of English money, in which we acknowledge us to be bound to him by just payment

"Also, we promise, because we have been now promoted to the earldom and lordship oftensaid by our lord the king himself, that our cousin Malise Sparre must cease from his claim and dismiss altogether his right, if it be discernible that he has any, to those lands and islands, so that my lord the king, his heirs, and successors shall sustain no vexation or trouble from him or from his heirs

"Again, if we have made any agreement or any understanding with our cousin Alexander Ard, or have wished to enter into any treaty with him in that case we will do similarly on our part and on the part of the king my lord to whatever was done in precaution about Malise Sparre

508   APPENDICES

"Further, we, Henry, earl abovesaid, and our friends and relatives, namely, Simon Rodde, William Daniels, knights, Malise Sparre, William Crichton, David Crichton, Adam ByLeton, Thomas Bennine, and Andrew Haldaniston, armsbearers, conjunctly promise in good faith to our oftensaid lord the king, Hakon, and to his first-born lord the king, Olaf, and to his councillors and men within-written, namely, to the lords Sigurd Haffthorsen, Ogmund Findersen, Eric Ketelsen, Narvo Ingualdisen, John Oddosen, Ulpho Johnsen, Ginther de Vedhonsen, John Danisen, Hakon Evidassen, knights of the same lord the king; Hakon Jonssen, Alver Hardissen, Hantho Ericsen, Erlend Phillippsen, and Otho Remer, armsbearers, and for this, under preservation of our honour, we bind ourselves and each of us, in a body to the aforesaid lords, that we must truly and firmly fulfil all the agreements and conditions and articles which are expressed above to our lord the king, within the above-written feast of St Martin, the bishop and confessor, so far as one particular business was declared by itself above

"That all these things now promised may have the greater strength for this, and may be fulfilled the sooner, we, the aforesaid Henry, Earl of the Orkneys, place and leave behind us our cousins and friends Lord William Daniels, knight, Malise Sperre, David Crichton, and the lawful son of the said Simon, by name Lord Alexander, here in the kingdom hostages Upon their faith they oblige and promise themselves to this, that from our lord the king of Norway, or from that place in which he shall have wished to have them within his kingdom of Norway, they in nowise may go away, publicly or secretly, before all the abovesaid things be totally fulfilled with entire integrity to our lord the king, and particularly and specially, the conditions and articles for whose observation the within-written reverend fathers, bishops, and prelates of the churches of the kingdom of Scotland, and the other nobles within-written of the same kingdom, Lord William, Bishop of St Andrews, Lord Walter, Bishop of Glasgow, Lord William, Earl of Douglas, Lord George, Earl of March, Lord Patrick Hepburn, Lord Alexander Haliburton, Lord George Abernethy, Lord William Ramsay, knights, must promise in good faith, and upon this remit their open letters to our same king the lord, with their true seals, in the before-noted time, as in our other letters written upon this is declared more fully.

"Also, we promise in good faith that we must assume in no direction to us the lands of our lord the king, or any other rights of his which his progenitors and the king our lord are known to have reserved to themselves, and concerning those lands or jurisdictions not to intromit in any manner whatsoever They have reserved those laws, indeed, and those pleas within the Orcadian earldom, as is before said, and the lands and pleas of that kind will remain in all cases safe for them, but if, upon this, we shall have his special letters, then we ought to be specially bound thereafter to our same lord the king

"Besides, but may it be absent, if all those abovesaid things shall not have been brought to conclusion, and totally fulfilled to the same my lord the king as it has been expressed above, or if we should have attempted anything in the contrary of any of the premises, then the promotion and favour which we have experienced from the king our lord, and of his grace, ought to be of no strength, yea, the promotion and favour of that kind done to us must be broken down altogether, and in their forces be totally empty and inane, so that we and our heirs for the rest shall have no right of speaking for the beforesaid earldom or for the lands or beforesaid islands, or we of acting about those lands and islands in any way whatsoever, that it may be manifest to all that the promotion and grace of this kind was given by no force of law or justice

"And so we append our seal, together with the seals of our said friends, to our present letters, in testimony and the firmer evidence of all the premises

"These things were done at Marstrand, in the year of the Lord 1379, the 2nd day of August."

2 —BOND EXECUTED BY SCOTTISH SURETIES *

"Henry de St Clair, Earl of Orkney, Lord of Roslin in Scotland, salvation in the Saviour of all We make well known to your entirety, by the presents, that we have promised in good faith, and by the tenor of the presents we promise with all fidelity, to our most excellent prince and lord the lord Hakon, the illustrious King of Norway and Sweden, that we will on no account alienate, pledge, or deliver as surety the lands or islands of the earldom of Orkney, or the crown possessions of the kingdom itself, from our beforesaid lord the king, his successors, or from the kingdom, without the consent of our lord the king abovesaid, his heirs, or successors, and that we shall observe faithfully all the premises

* Caithness Events

"The venerable lords and fathers in Christ, Lords William and Walter, Bishops of St Andrews and Glasgow, William and George, Earls of Douglas and March, William Ramsay, Walter Haliburton George Abernethy, Patrick Hepburn, John Edmonston, Alexander Haliburton, John Thumbce, Robert Dalzeil, barons and knights, also have promised.

"In testimony of all which things our seal was appended, and we have procured to be appended to the presents the seals of the said bishops, counts, barons, and knights

"Given at St Andrews on the first day of the month of September, 1379"

F — AMENDS OF MALISE SPARRE *
1387

To all to whose knowledge the present letters shall have arrived Malise Sper, Lord of Skuldale, salvation in the Saviour of all Let your entirety know that I have made, in the presence of a magnificent lord, James, Earl of Douglas, firm friendship with Henry St Clair, Earl of Orkney and Lord of Roslin, and have condoned and remitted finally all actions of injuries and offences, by him, his men, or whomsoever in his name, to my men, lands, and possessions whatsoever, and as to his universal goods, acquired by him or his. Further, I firmly promise to restore, pay, and satisfy, with my men whomsoever, concerning all injuries, offences, and things acquired as to the beforesaid Lord Earl, or whomsoever in his name, up to the present day, with lands and possessions excepted, if there are any to which my men have the right of claiming according to the laws of the country In testimony of this transaction, my seal was appended to the presents at Edinburgh, 18th November, 1387"

G — CHARGES OF THE ORCADIAN COMMONS*

AGAINST DAVID MENZIES OF WEMYSS, PRÆSES OF THE ISLANDS, LAID BEFORE KING ERIC THE POMERANIAN (1425)

I Although years adverse to the crops distressed the country, and in public council, with the consent of David himself also, it had been decreed that no corn should be exported, but sold to the inhabitants at a reasonable price, nevertheless the president himself carried away with him corn to Scotland in four vessels, and before this decree had been made, sent off elsewhere five or six ships laden with produce, to the very great hurt of the islanders

II Besides, he brought in foreigners who had violently pushed themselves on the whole of the people, even on those who administered the courts, burdensome very much to hospitality by the great losses and troubles to the citizens

III He took away the public seal of the country against the will of the supreme prefect of the law, and contrary to the laws and customs adhibited it for signing what he pleased, and when a certain notable, by name Christian Ellingefiet, expostulated that the seal of the people was drawn into abuse preposterously, he made a great fine of money When also the earl came and asked that he would produce and bring the same, to seal the evidence by which his right over the Orkneys was conveyed from his ancestors to himself by order of succession, and at the same that certain of the more important of the inhabitants would be permitted to pass over the sea with him to the most serene king and his senate, to declare the public condition and to bear authentic testimony concerning his right, he neither obtained the seal nor any companions except Thomas Sincler and the Archdeacon of Hjaltland and two native servants

IV — In the next year from that in which the earl had stayed in Denmark with the most serene king, when the beforesaid David had been about to set out thither, he solicited the whole assembled inhabitants of the islands for a testimonial to the life passed among them, and he obtained that by writs to the most clement king and by letters given to him with this condition, that twenty-four men of the first rank should follow him to the king, who, if they had arrived thither, the citizens nowise doubted would inform the king as well about the king's interests as also about the administration of David But they remained at home, prohibited by David from the journey He set out alone, carried the people's seal with him, nobody of the notables accompanying him

Translation by Thomas Sinclair M A

V. He lessened the value of the royal money to such a degree that he ordered one Scotch coin to be equal to two royal coins, and this until he had all but emptied the whole region of money When, however, Thomas Sincler had returned last time out of Denmark, it was restored to the same value which it possessed in Norway, and that was promulgated publicly, which also it holds to-day.

VI His rigid exactions of the fines due to the king and the earl, beyond the rules of laws, privileges, or renewals, wronged the inhabitants not a little.

VII The wife and relatives of the supreme judge of the islands, whom they call the lawman, have charged that, twice apprehended, he had been cast into the tower prison for such causes as these. The first was that John Baddi, servant and relative of the lawman, had fetched back his horse from Michael Magi, a relative of David, who, going somewhere, had taken him against his will, for which reason he shut up the lawman in the tower, who was apprehended while walking in the Place of Kirkwall Again, after he had dismissed the Caithness foreigners thrust into his house, he made the strong-room to be broken open, and whatever things were contained there to be carried forth, and all the articles great and small which were in the house to be destroyed, without even an exception He threw the lawman, seized afresh, into the tower, only because he had refused to deliver to him the seal of the country to sign whatever he wished, and there he detained him till he had submitted himself to him, and his wife had placed the seal and code of laws on the altar of St Magnus From that time David took the seal and code into his own custody, and appointed another lawman, who had assumed that office with difficulty

VIII During the period in which he had shut the supreme judge in the tower, he also thrust into prison at the same time another native notable, against the laws and without a reason

IX John Loggi accused him that he also was confined in the same prison because he refused to him the seal demanded unless it had been entrusted for keeping

X Thomas Sincler, mandatary for the earl, expostulated with David because out of the earl's annual dues, since the death of his father and the year which preceded, he took eight pounds English, besides other things This the earl resolved to implead before the most clement king

XI Thomas Sincler complained also himself in his own name particularly, because after he had been fortified with royal letters, in which the king had received under his regal protection him, his servants, goods, ship, and whatever things were his, nevertheless his household servant, David Smid, was apprehended, beaten within his house as far as to blood, thrust down into the depths of the tower, and there, with fetters put on, detained till his own return out of Scotland Himself as soon as he came back into the Orkneys, with good men warning him, went immediately to his house with his people, and there remained till the close of the day, where then John Kroge and his sister's son came and advised that he should take refuge in the cathedral or elsewhere, unless he and his preferred to perish by fire When he had betaken himself thither he appealed without effect to the rights of the cathedral and to the letters of royal protection which at the same time he exhibited In the end he slipt away secretly His friends and those of the most clement king assembled, he demanded that under the king's favour they would vindicate themselves from oppression, and claimed again and again the guardianship of the laws for them and theirs Accompanied by these, when he had returned to the cathedral, and sent his servants thence, his sister's son had been slain Then the lawman with other principal men interposing themselves, that dispute was settled thus, that securities given by each side, they would commit the whole case to be decided by the court of the king or the earl Thomas gave caution by twelve securities, David none Also, when the former had returned into Scotland, the earl died This known, David extorted from those twelve securities thirty-six pounds English, and refused all delay so as together they might be forthcoming in the court of the king and the senate These things so ordained, he fined those who had adhered to Thomas Sincler at the sacred house, in upholding the king's letters of protection, eighty pounds English and fifty shillings These, indeed, were they who had heard the words of David and Thomas when Thomas appealed for sentence of law and judge, to wit, Nicholas Myre, Master Laurence, Master John the canon, William Hedal, Alexander Suderland, John Kroge, William Irving, William Flet, Adam Nestegaard, Christian Ellingeklat, and many others of that country, good men, both clerical and lay

XII He also bound with fetters William Bress without any judicial process, much less convicted of any crime, merely because he had gone into Scotland for an interview with the earl.

XIII When the commons of Rognvaldzo complained to the president of their province concerning those who are called the savages of the Scots, because of their threatening and swaggerings towards them and other annoyances in serious repetition, having declared they would rather die than be tormented ever and anon by such great injuries, David replied that they were not to die all in one and the same day, but some on each of the days as long as he ruled over them

XIV David Meyner took two English half pounds from Henry Garoch because he adhered to the beforesaid Thomas in vindicating the authority of the royal diploma

XV He took from John Simonson on the same day eleven shillings English

XVI Malcolm Jonson also complained that he spoiled him of a ship and other goods, to the sum of two hundred nobles, without action of law

XVII The beforesaid David commanded John Johnson to be apprehended, and threw him into the tower bruised to blueness and blood, and cheated from him one boat of six oar-rests to the sum of two English pounds, with more other goods without reason

XVIII Shipmaster Thomas Brun complained that he was cast into the tower by David because he had not come at the first messenger

XIX Also when David had last returned from Denmark, he seized a ship of the beforesaid Thomas which was laden with goods, and sent it against his will into Scotland, and there spoiled him of fine flour to the value of twenty-four nobles, and detained him the greatest part of the winter, at the end of which, when the ship had sailed home, it made a loss of some of the goods and sailors

XX John Loggi complained that out of the cargo of the beforesaid ship he was stripped by David in ten casks called tuns with barley, eight filled with fine flour, eight butts with pitch bound by one iron, eleven measures which they call stones of wax, twenty-six great and small caldrons, two balances, two worked washhand basins, one hundred and eight pounds of hemp, six pewter tankards, eleven decades of white and red pots, which together in sum rose to twenty-six pounds English

XXI The beforesaid David took of Andrew Jonson from the same vessel six caldrons, to the value of six nobles

XXII The beforesaid David made Nicholas Jonson be spoiled of forty shillings English, in gold and silver, because he had joined Thomas Sincler, and obeyed the diploma of the most clement king in that he appealed to the laws, but in vain

XXIII He took two cows and one ox from Patrick Thyrgelson for the same reason

XXIV John Fif, thrown into the tower, he bound cruelly with iron fetters, and fined him twenty nobles, only because he said that the earl was more powerful by right than he in the Orcadian country, and that himself was related by blood to the earl

XXV He seized by night from John Blatt fifty marks English, because he had united with Thomas Sincler in vindicating the mandates of the king and also implored for the laws and a trial, but without success

XXVI William Graa complained that he was forced by him to send over his ship to an island far distant in the sea, called Suleskerry, under threats of banishment, and when he had placed his two younger brothers and eight other natives on the ship all perished with it, the ship with its tackle and goods estimated at fifteen English merks

XXVII Samson Williamson deplored that he was violently snatched from the cathedral, bound after the manner of the condemned, destined by David to the loss of his head forthwith, unless the canons with his own wife had interceded and, besides, fifty-one shillings English were wrung from him without process of law, only because he had charged himself that he had wounded his servant, and was not allowed, though he wished it, to purge himself of the crime by the laws

XXVIII Paris Lutzit had declared that he also was shut up in the tower, forced into fetters of iron, three whole days and nights, then obtained his freedom by payment of ten minted merks, convicted of no crime inadvertently, only because, a dependant of Thomas Sincler, he studied to run the king's mandates

XXIX. The beforesaid mandate, while being read to Paris, was snatched by David, who remarked that he could buy such letters, translated into a foreign language, for eighteen English pence in Denmark He retained it then, and retains it to day, when this complaint has been initiated

XXX He seized from Thomas Bimson twenty-one merks English, the case unheard

XXXI The case also unheard, without trial, against the laws, he took from Magnus Jenneland twelve casks full of barley to the value of twenty-four shillings English

XXXII He put William Geredson and his horses into the tower, without legitimate process, only because he supported the rights of Thomas and of the royal mandate compelled to buy his liberation with thirteen merks English

XXXIII.—For the same reason he spoiled by night Sander Brun of twenty-seven English merks.

XXXIV.—The servant also of the beforesaid Sander he spoiled of eleven merks English on the pretext of the same charged offence.

XXXV. Sir Nicholas Myre and Sir Laurence, canons, complained because he had taken out the seal of the chapter, which stood in a box in the inmost part of the cathedral, and had detained it beyond half a year, and ordained that anything to be written he would make to be sealed for himself, not for them.

There are many more things which could and were necessary to be written about the deeds of David Meyner and the losses brought on the Orcadian people by him, but the heap and long series of his crimes they are unable to declare at present; only in testimony of these heads more strongly, and in the greater security, these letters were signed by the seal of their country and people, confirmed also by the seals of a revered and worthy man, William Thurgilson, lawman of the region, Kolbein Flæt, John Magnusson, and William Irving.

H.—THE TESTAMENT OF SIR DAVID SINCLAR OF SWYNBROCHT, KNYCHT,*
1506.

IN THE NAME OF GOD, AMEN.

Be it kend til al men and be knawin that I, DAVID SINCLER OF SWYNBROCHT, KNYCHT, seik in my bodye nevir the less hail in my mynd, makis my Testament in maner and forme as efter ffollowes. Item. In the fyrst I lief and commendis my saule to God Almychte in quhaiis protectione and defense I incal the blyssit Virgen Mare and all the Sanctis in hevin. Item, I lief my bodye to be erdit in Sanct Magnus Kyrk of Tyngwell. Item, to proteir and defend my Testament I chuis and humblie praiss oure maist Soverane Prince, Kyng James, trought the grace of God Kyng of Scottis: In the quhilkis releuatione of labouris I ordene discreit men, that is to saye, Richard Lesk and Thorrald of Brucht, veray executoris of this Testament, the quhilkis sal dispose my geir baytht vrettin and onevrettin as thai will answer befor God. Item, the penchione of Dingvell and the Red Castell paiis thar dittis this zeir. Item, I lave na thing to my Lorde Sincler bot the penchione of Zetland for the zeir present, to the quhilk Lorde I geive and leissis all the landis that I possessit efter my Fader deide in Zetland, and my best siluer stope wyth twelsse stoppis inclussit in the samen wyth my schipe callit the Carvell wyth hir pertinentis, and twa sadillis. Item, I leiffe to my Ladye Sincler my myd stope of silver wyth twelsse stoppis inclusit in the samen. Item, I leife to the sone and aire of Henre Lord Synclar my best siluer stope with sex stoppis inclusit in the samen and wyth all the moveabill beistis that ar contenit in the landis afor assignit to my Lord his fader. Item, I leife to my bruder Sir William Sincler, Erle of Caithtness, my innes in Edinbrucht wyth the pertinentis. Item, I leife to Sir William Sincler, the Knycht [of Warsettir?] my doublet of kletht of gold and my gray satein goune wyth thre ostreche fedderiss. Item, I leiff to Allan Aitsone my blak govne of dammess wyth silver bouttouneis, my graye scarlet hoiiss and my doubled of doune cramesse. Item, I geive and leiffss to Gertrude my great siluer belte and ane pece of kletht of gold the lyntht of ane Flanderiks Ellin. I leif to William Flete and his bruder Criste Flete my litill schipe wyth al geir, and all my landis in Orknaye wyth my innes in Kyrkwall: excep. Setter and Vachtesequyr wyth housis and uder pertinensis, the quhilk I leite to Alexander Borthvick, togedder wyth twa kye in Kyrkwall; and al the moveabill gudis in Schalpandsaye. Item, I leife to James Sincler, capitane for the tym in Dingvell, al my geir that is in Ross, that is to saye, my harness, gooneiss, kletht in gold, siluer, bestis, corne, and generaly al that ever I have thare except my red cote of weluote, the quhilk I leife to the hie Alter of the Cathedrall Kyrk of Orknaye. Item, I leif to ilk Sone I have fyive scoir merkis land, and to ilk Dochter fyfte; and I mycht schaw it now as this time, but gif I cannot schaw it I command my executoris to schaw it. Item, I leife to Thorrald of Brucht and to his wife and his airis ten merkis land in Glaitness and xv. merkis land in Linggo with all gudis thar contenit, and xxij merkis in Pappale, ten merkis in Brucht. Item, I leif to Richart Lesk twenty merkis landis in Cwndistay and my Inglis schipe with all geir. Item, I geive to William Spens all my landis in Gloppa and xv. merkis in Baltone. Item, I leife to Alexander Smeythtone xii. merkis in Eistrud wyth all bestis that is thare. Item, I leife to Jhone Mude xx. merkis the quhilk I bocht fra him in Scatness, and the ful payment thar of. Item, I leife to

---

* Bannatyne Miscellany, iii., p. 103.

APPENDICES

Sanct Magnus Kyrk in Tynguell the twa part of my blak welwoss cote, and the third parte I leife to the corss Kyrk in Dynrosness. Item, the chelleris of Sanct Magnus in Tyngvell is in Dyngwell, the quhilk I command to be deliverit. Item, I leife to Magnus Sincler my blew doublet, the brest set wyth precious staneis, and my hude set with precious staneis, and my golden chenze, the quhilk I wear daill. Item, I leife to Jhone Aundour twenty licht florens Item, I leife to Peter Merchell my blak doublet of wellouss and my redd hoiss and my schort red cote of weliouss wythout sclewis Item, I geve and leius to my Sister dwelland in Orknaye al my gudis that ar in Pappay and Housbe Item, I leife to Doctor Jhone Oke twelfe ellis of yper blak and twa roiss nobillis and my sadell wyth the pertinenss, the tane half of   and ane schort blak cote of welouss Item, I leife to Sir Magnus Harrode twa nobillis, and the Buk of Gud Maneris

Item, I leife to the Provest of Byrrone my signet Item, I leife to Thome Haa four merkis in Morra Nordammad Item, the geir that is nocht dispomit be efter the gift of my gud beneuolanss I ordinat to be deuidit betwixt my Soneis and Dochteris Item, gif ony of my Soneis or Dochteris of myne discessis wythout airis of thar awne body that part to be devidit amange the leife of Breder and Sisteriss Item, the puir folk that come out of Orknay wyth me I leife thame thar awne land or ellis also gude Item, I leife to Segreit in Rorik twa pak of wedmell and twa kye Item, I leife to the Halye Cross in Stanebruch twa nobillis of the roiss Item, I geive to Sanct Georgeis alter in Rosskyill my golden Chenze, the quhilk is callit ane collar, the quhilk chenze the Kyng of Denmark gave me Item, I leif to Thome Bosvell my best   , the quhilk came hame to me with my schipe out of Norrowaye Item, ten pundis of gold to be pait to Jhone of Veinde in Desert the quhilk Henre Spens resauit Item, xv merkis I ordane to be pait to the Inglisman that sauld me the schipe Item, I leife to Jhone Boide the best piece of ane lynnein robe, the quhilk I boucht fra the Flemyngis Item, I leife the fruitis of my landis of the zeiris crope to the puir folkis Item, I leife to Saude Sincler my bruder some sex ellis of grein claitht Item, I leif to Patre Cuke and James Baxstair ten ellis of grein claitht Item, I leife to Ingarecht in Cransetter twa kye Item, I leife to Henrie Sincler, my bruder son, all my brutell bestis that is in Oxvoo Item, I leife and commandis to geive to Jhone Glappayr ix merkis, the quhilkis I promit to hym in his spoussage

GIFFIN AT TYNGWELL the zeir of God I M fyfe hundreths and sex zeiris, the aucht day of the Vesitatione of our Ladye thir men be and presente—Sande Brothvik, Peter Merchell, Jhone Mude, Jhone Boide, Magnus Sincler, Peter Cuk, Alexander Smeithtone, wyth utheris mony sundri and divers

Ita fateor ego Doctor Johannes Oke de Gesteria me ascultasse et concordat de verbo ad verbum cum suo illeso originali quod fateor man propria, etc

Haec est vera hujus originalis copiata sive collationata de verbo in verbum, ac translata de latino in Anglicam linguam haud in ullo discrepans, sed per omnia concordano per me Dominum Jacobum Scuill, sacre millesimo quingentissimo xxv, die vero sexto mensis Augusti, hora quasi quinta post meridiem vel eo circa presentibus ibidem venerabilibus viris Roberto Flet, Domino Georgio Dufe, Alexandro Paulsone et Andrea Sanger cum diversis aliis formaliter, sicut stat omni meliori forma qua potui, et etiam roboravi, meis signo, nomine cognomine, et manuali subscriptione quibus utor

JACOBUS SCUILI, Notarius Publicus

I.—SPECIAL DESTINATION OF CAITHNESS,*
1344

David, by the grace of God, King of the Scots, to all true men of his whole kingdom, greeting Know ye that we have examined a certain charter of Males, Earl of Caithness, to this effect "To all the sons of Holy Mother Church who shall examine this present letter, Males, Earl of the earldoms of Stratherne, Caithness, and Orkney, greeting (health everlasting) in the name of our Lord Be it known unto your order that we, not moved thereto by force, fear nor fraud, but of our mere and unrestrained will and pleasure, have given and granted the right of marriage of our daughter Isabella, begotten of us and of our lawful spouse Marjory, to the noble William, Earl of Ross, to marry her when and at such time as shall seem to him good, conveniently with our true purpose herein The said Isabella we do hereby make, appoint and designate our heir and successor to all our earldom of Caithness, with its rightful appurtenances, if we shall not have had heir male and surviving by our

---
*Translation of the original Latin in the Dunrobin Charter-room

lawful spouse the said Marjory And the said William, Earl of Ross, has promised and faithfully undertaken to defend and maintain with all his power the said earldom of Caithness equally with the earldom of the said William of Ross In testimony whereof we have set our seal to these presents in the house of the preaching friars of Inverness on the 28th day of the month of May, A D 1344," which in all points, articles, conditions, etc , we hereby approve, etc Given at Scone the 12th May in the 32nd year of our reign, i e , 1362

J—ACT IN RECOGNITION OF HENRY, LORD ST CLAIR *
1489

Henry, Lord Saintclair (son to William, Lord Newburgh) in the first Parliament of King James IV , 1489, begun at Edinburgh Die Lunæ, sexto die mensis Octobris and continued, is declared chief of the blood, Lord Saintclair, and heir to the Earl of Orkney and Lord Newburgh, the 14th January The act is recorded in the Lower House folio, verso 113, in the following terms —

"Item, anent Sir Henry Saintclair, that our Soveraine Lorde, with advyce and delyverance of the estaitis of his Parliament, declares that sene the said Sir Henry's grandschire and faider, Lords Saintclair, for the tyme are decessit, and the said Sir Henry richwise heretor to thaim , that he is chef of that blude , and will therefor that he be callit Lord Saintclair in tyme to cum, with all dignities, emenents, privilegis, tenandiis, tenandriis belonging thairto, efter the forme of chartars and evidents made thairupon"

K—RESPITE
IN FAVOUR OF EDWARD SINCLARE AND OTHERS FOR THE SLAUGHTER OF THE EARL OF CAITHNESS
(From the Original Parchment)†

James, be the grace of God, King of Scottis To all and sundry our justices, wardanis, lieutenants, justice clerks, shreffs, stewartis, crounaris, yare deputis, provestis, auldermane, and baillies of burrowis, and all oyeris our officiaries pyt and to cum, and yare deputis, liegis, subditis, quham it efferis, quhaire knawlege yir our letteris sall cum, greting

Wit se we, of oure special grace, to have respitt, supersedeit, and delayit, and be yir or letteris in ye law speahe respittis, supersedes, and delayis, Edward Sinclare of Strome, Magnus Sinclare of Wersettir, Johnne Sinclare of Tollap, William Sinclare of Houne, Olive Sinclare of Hilwra, Magnus Sinclare, Lawrence Sinclare, James Sinclare, James Cragy of Brogh, Johnne Rendale, Adam Sclatter, Johnne Burness, Johnne Cromarte, Magnus Cromarte, Robert Hercas, Johnne Hercas, George Hercas, William Perisone, Johnne Jamezon William Kardy, Gilbert Cragy, William Zorstone, Walter Forester, Christe Jane, Magnus Midhouse, Johnne Loutit, Johnne Paplaye, Magnus Gariacht, Williame Cragy, John Cragy of Banks, and Edward Birstane, and generally all and sundry uyeris persones, kynismen, fryndis, assistaris, adherentis, partakoures and complices wt ye said Edward and persones above written, dwelland wtin ye ylis of Orknay and Zetland, being with them in company at the committing of any cryms and arts, and part wt thame yrintill in ony tyme bygane before ye day of ye date of yir pytis ffor art and part of the convocation and gadering of our lieges in arrayit battel agains umqll Johnne, Erle of Caithness, and for art and part of ye slaughter of the said umqll Erle and his friendis and partakours being with yame in company at that tyme, and for all uyeris slaughteris, mutilations, oppressiouns, ressis, forthot fellonies, tressonis, crymes, transgressiouns and offensis quhatsumever committit and done by yame, or any of yame, or in any uyir part or place wtin or realm, in ony tymes bygane, before ye day of ye dait hereof, treasoun in or owne proper person allenarlie exceptit, for ye space of 19 zeres next to cum eftir ye date of yir pyttis , to indure but any revocatioun, obstakle, impediment, or againcalling quhatsumever Attour we will, grantis, and ordains, yat yis oure speale respitt, supersedere, and delay, sall be of als grate strenth, avale, force, and effect to ye persones yatt are not namyt and comprehendit in the samen, being wt ve said Edward and his complices at ye committing of ye saidis cryms, and art and part wt yame yrintill, as and yare names and surnames were spealie and particularly, indinyt thereintill Quharefore we charge you straithe, and commandis zou all and sundry our justices, wardanis, lieutenants, justice clerks, shreffis, stewartis, crounaris, provestis, aulder-

---
Antiquities of Scotland, Edin 1830   † Barry's History

mene and baillies of burrowis, and all uyris our officiars pynt and to cum, and zor deputis, liegis and subditis forsaidis, yat nane of zou tak upon hand to call jornay, attacke, arrest, accuse, molest, truble, follow and persew ye saidis persones, yare kynnismen, freyndis, assistaris, adherentis, partakeris and complices, or any of yame wtin ye saidis boundis, for ye saidis crymis bygane, or to do or attempt ony thing incontrar violation or breking of yis our speale respitt, supersedere and delay, in ony wise, during all ye tyme and space above written, under all the hieast pane and charge yat aftir may follow Discharging you, and ilk ane of you of zor offices in yat part, in ye meyntyme, be yir oure leeris, given under oure Privie Sele, at Striveling, ye nineteen day of September, and of our reigne ve [25] zeres

Per signaturam manu, S D N ,
Regis Subscriptam

Upon the label to which the seal (which is broken off) had been affixed, is inscribed "Respectuatio Edwardi Sinclere de Strome et triginta aliorum"

Marked thus on the back "Ane nynteen zeris respitt to Edward Sincler and his complices, for ye slaughter of the Erle of Cathness, etc " The date was 19th September, 1539

L —DEED OF RESIGNATION*
OF
THE HEREDITARY PROTECTORATE OF THE SCOTTISH MASONIC CRAFT
BY
WILLIAM ST CLAIR OF ROSLIN

I, WILLIAM ST CLAIR OF ROSLIN, Esq , taking into my consideration that the Masons in Scotland did, by several deeds, constitute and appoint Wilham and Sir William St Clairs of Roslin, my ancestors, and their heirs, to be patrons, protectors, judges, or masters , and that my holding or claiming any such jurisdiction, right, or privilege, might be prejudicial to the craft and vocation of Masonry, whereof I am a member, and I being desirous to advance and promote the good and utility of the said craft of Masonry to the utmost of my power, DO THEREFORE HEREBY, for me and my heirs, renounce, quit-claim, overgive and discharge all right, claim or pretence that I, or my heirs, had, have, or anyways may have, pretend to or claim, to be patron, protector, judge, or master of the Masons in Scotland, in virtue of any deed or deeds made and granted by the said Masons, or of any grant or charter made by any of the Kings of Scotland to and in favour of the said William and Sir William St. Clairs of Roslin, my predecessors , or any other manner of way whatsoever, for now and ever , And I bind and oblige me and my heirs, to warrand this present renunciation and discharge at all hands And I consent to the registration hereof in the books of Council and Session, or any other Judge's books competent, therein to remain for preservation , and hereto I constitute my procurators, &c

IN WITNESS WHEREOF I have subscribed these Presents (written by David Maul, writer to the signet) at Edinburgh, the twenty-fourth day of November, one thousand seven hundred and thirty-six years, before these witnesses, George Fraser, deputy-auditor of the Excise in Scotland, master of the Canongate Lodge, and William Montgomery, merchant in Leith, master of the Leith Lodge

W ST CLAIR

Geo Fraser, Canongate Kilwinning, witness
Wm Montgomery, Leith Kilwinning witness

M —CALENDAR OF DOCUMENTS RELATING TO THE EARLIER HISTORY OF ORCADIA
TWELFTH CENTURY

(1150) The Old Metrekey, or *Clavis Rhythmica*, by Earl Rognvald and Hall Ragnasson	(In appendix of Heimskringla Egilson's edition
(1165) Charter by Earl Harald	Scone Chartulary
(1181) Grant of Peter s Pence by Earl Harald	Dip Norvegicum, vii , p 2
1196 Scottish-Caithness war, Acct of Roger de Hoveden	Rolls Edwd IV , pp 10, 12
1198 Bull of Pope Innocent III	Diplomaticum Norveg , vii , p 2
Mortification of Norwegian lands by Bishop Biarni	Chart of Munkalif

APPENDICES

THIRTEENTH CENTURY.

(1202)	Ltre. from Innocent III to Bishop Bjarni	Dip Norveg, vii, p 3
1222	Ltre of Pope Honorius III re murder of Bishop Adam of C	Theiner's Vet Mon, p 21
(1223) (1245)	Constitution of Cath Chapter of Caithness	(Records, Dunrobin Castle (Ban Miscellany, vol iii
1237	Bull of Pope Gregory IX re Bishop Jofreyr of Orkney	Dip Norveg, vii, p 18
1247	Dispensation by Innocent IV re Bishop Henry of Orkney	Torfæus, p 172
1266	Treaty of Perth between Scotland and Norway	
1263	Letters from King Hakon to Caithnessians	Compota Camer. Scotiæ 1, p 31
(1274)	Accts of Caithness churches, pr Boyamund de Vitia	Theiner's Vet Mon, pp 112-115
1275	Deed containing claim of then Bishop of Caithness	Ork Saga, p 107
1278	Brief of Peter, Bishop of Orkney	Torfæus, p 172
1290	Extract @ Wardrobe Rolls of King Edward I.	Ork Saga Intro, p 50
1297	Earl John of O and C swore fealty at Murkle, his seal	
1299	Norse document referring to Burra Firth	Dip Norveg, vol 1, p 81

FOURTEENTH CENTURY

1312	Treaty of Inverness, Norway and Scotland	Peterkin's Rentals, App
1320	Letter from Community of Scotland to the Pope	Scottish National MSS
1321	Letter from Robert Bruce to the "ballivi" of Orkney	Ork Saga Introd, Iv
1320	Archiepiscopal complaints against William, Bshp of Orkney	Diplom Norveg
1327	Mortgage of Shetland Bishopric dues	,,
1327	Letter—Bishop of Bergen to Bishop of Orkney	,,
1329	Charters (2) Katharina, Countess of Orkney and Caithness	,, ii, 146
1334	Letters (2) King Edward of England re Earl Malise	Rymer's Fœdera, Syll 1, p 272
1340	Reference to John More (?= Beg Sutherland) re Berridale	Scottish Chamb Rolls
1344	Contract of Marriage executed by Earl Malise	Dunrobin Charter-room
1364	Deed of Conveyance at Kirkwall to Hugh de Ross	Reg Aberdonense 1, 106
(1360)	Scot Ordinance adopting Pondus Cathaniæ as standard	King David II
1367	Scottish Royal Edict re harassing Orkney	
1369	Agreement at Kirkwall—Bishop Wm of Orkney and anr	Dip Norveg 1, 308
1375	Commission to Alex de Ard	,, ii, 337-339
1379	Deed of Investiture of Henry St Clair as Earl of Orkney	,, ii, 353-358
1387	Amnesty—Malise Sper to Henry, Earl of Orkney	Hay's Genealogie
1389	Enumeration of Orcadian nobles (and their seals) at Helsingborg	
1391	Grant of Newburgh and Auchdale	Dip Norveg ii, 401
1395	Quittance @ Sir John Drummond to Earl of Orkney	Perth Charter-chest
1397	Union Treaty at Calmar Eminent Orcadians present	

FIFTEENTH CENTURY

(1418)	Attestation of descent of James of Cragy	Misc Spald Club v, 257
1418	Fealty of John St Clair for Hjaltland	Dip Norveg ii, 482
1426	Complaints of Orcadian Commons	Balfour's Memorial, App
1433	Deed of Gift at Kirkwall	Deeds relating to Ork, p iii.
1437	Diploma of The Orcadian Succession	Barry's Orkney
1448	Patronage of St Duthac's	Hay's Genealogie
1451	Bond, Sutherland of Forse to Chaplain St Andrew's, Golspie	Caith. Fam Hist, p 153
1455	Charter of Caithness Earldom, also precept thereon	Hay's Genealogie
1455	Grant of Stambuster by Thomas, Bishop of Orkney	Ork Saga Introd, 79
1456	Testament of Alex Sutherland of Dunbeath	Hay's Genealogie
1468	Resignation of Orkney	,,
1471	Ratification of Ravenscraig	,,
1468	Acts re Impignoration of the Isles (to 1471)	
1472	Bull of Pope Sixtus re Orcadian See	
1476	Charter of Earldom of Caithness to William II St Clair	

APPENDICES

1481	Agreement between William, Master of Orkney, and his brother, Sir Oliver St Clair of Roslin	Charter-chest of Sir John Gibson
1484	Annuity to Bishop of Orkney, pr John Sinclare	O P S
1485	,, ,, Henry de Sancto Claro	,,
1485	Ancient Skatt Book of Zetland	Balfour's Memorial, Appendix
1485	Norwegian Decree re Shetland lands	Mackenzie's Grievances
1486	Charter of Kirkwall as a Royal Burgh	Kirkwall Records
1488	Scottish Act recognising Henry, Lord St Clair	
1490	Charter of Regality to Andrew, Bishop of Orkney	Peterkin's Rentals
1496	The Groat Inventories	Calder's Caithness
1498	Charter of Swinburgh in Shetland	Peterkin's Notes
1497	Rentals of Orkney	Peterkin

SIXTEENTH CENTURY

1500	Rentals of Orkney (to 1503)	Peterkin
1501	Confirmation of Charter of Regality, 1490	Peterkin's Rentals, Appendix
1503	Caithness Charter to A. Byrsbane	Calder's Caithness, Appendix
1506	Will of Sir David Sinclair	Bann Miscellany iii, p 103
1513	Drum-head Charter to Earl of Caithness	(Fife Charter chest?)
1514	Adjudication of Tohop in Orkney	Mackenzie's Grievances
(1519)	Decree of Orkney Lawman	Mackenzie's Grievances, p 6
1527	Charter of Murkle &c, to William, Master of Caithness	Caith Family Hist Intro, p 23
1527	Complaint of William, Lord Sinclair	Barry's History, p 236
1528	Mandate to John, Earl of Caithness, to King James	Keltie's Clans, p 94
1529	Jo Ben's Account of Orkney	Barry's History, Appendix
1529	Charter of Dunbeath to Alex Sinclair	Caithness Family History, p 19
1536	Charter re Burgh of Kirkwall	Glimpses of Kirkwall, p 5
1539	Respite to Orcadians re Summerdale	Barry's Appendix
1543	New Charter to John, Master of Caithness	Caithness Family History, p 6
1544	Erection of Cathedral Chapter, Orkney	Peterkin's Rentals, Appendix
1545	Confirmation of same	,,
1560	Balfour's Charters (3), 1565, 1566	Peterkin's Notes, Appendix
1564	Charter to Earl Robert Stuart	,,
1567	Mudie's Charter	,,
1567	Erection of "Dukery"	p 107
1574	Sederunt at Holyrood re William Sinclair of Dunbeath	Reg Priv Council
1575	Complaint of Islesmen	
1581	Confirmation to Earl Robert	Peterkin's Notes, Appendix p 16
1583	Opinions of Nobility	Bann Miscellany
1585	Cursetter Charter	Peterkin's Notes, p 125
1586	Agreement at Girnigo, Earls of Caithness and Sutherland	Calder's Caithness, p 326
1589	Erection of Wick into Burgh	,, P 344

Also, Norwegian, Danish, Scottish, English, French, and Vatican Records, &c, &c

N.—CHARTULARY OF ROSSLYN

CONTENTS

TWELFTH CENTURY

(1160)	Charter	Wm de Moreville	to Henry de St Clair
(1196)	,,	Roland fitz Uthred	to Alan de St Clair
	Grant of ...	... Wil... ...	... ... meo
			to ... ... Ailif

THIRTEENTH CENTURY

	Charter	Wm de Lysuris	to various
	,,	,,	to Stephen de Melville
	,,	,,	to Thomas de Melville
1280	Grant of Innerleith	King Alex III	to Sir Wm de St Clair
1280	Grant of Roslin	,,	,,
1292	Charter of Merton	John, Abbot of Newbottle	to Sir Wm Bysett

FOURTEENTH CENTURY

	Charter of Temple lands	Walter fitz Stephen de Melville	to Sir Wm de St Clair
	Charter of Gourton lands	Thomas Modok	to John de Hanewich
1317	,,	Edward de Gourton	to Sir Henry St Clair
1328	,,	Gilbert de Gardan	,,
1328	Pension	King Robert the Bruce	,,
1358	Confirmation of same	King David Bruce	to Wm de St Clair
1358	Grant of Merton	,,	,,
1367	Amnesty	Malise Sper	to Henry, Earl of Orkney
1389	Confirmation of Herbertshire	King Robert II	to Sir Wm de Douglas

FIFTEENTH CENTURY

1404	Charter re Castle Guard	King Robert III	to Henry, Earl of Orkney
1407	Conveyance of Herbertshire	Arch Earl of Douglas	to Hy II, Earl of Orkney
1407	Confirmation of same	The Regent Albany	,,
1411	Procuration	Henry II, Earl of Orkney	to Joan de St Clair
1413	Charter of Tullicultre	The Regent Albany	to Earl & C'tess of Buchan
1419	Indenture	Henry II of Orkney	to Adam of Dalkell
1434	Renewal of Charters	Wm Harper, Notary	to John de St Clair
1437	Grant of Garioch Revenues	King James	to Eliz, C of Orkney
1438	Complaints	Egidia, C of Orkney	to Lord Lieut of Scotland
1447	Instrument of Infeftment		to Eliz, C of Buchan and Orkney
1448	Patronage of St Duthac's	Bishop of Orkney	to Earl of Orkney
1455	Grant of Earldom of C'thness	King James II	to Wm, Earl of Orkney
1455	Precept of Infeftment thereon	,,	to Officials in Inverness [Sheriffship
1456	Erection of Roslin into a Burgh of Barony	,,	to Wm, Earl of Orkney
1456	Testament of Alex Sutherland of Dumbethe		
1471	Discharge for Orkney	King James III	to Wm, Earl of Cathness
1471	Ratification of Ravenscraig	,,	,,
1476	Charter of Roslin	William, Earl of Cathness	to Sir Oliver Sinclair
1476	Charter of Herbertshire	,,	,,
1480	Bond	George Lord Seton	,,

SIXTEENTH CENTURY

1504	Agreement	William, Lord Borthwick	to Sir Oliver Sinclair
1523	Mortification of Lands	Sir Wm Sinclair	to Roslin Eccles College
1527	Confirmation in Roslin, etc	King James	to Sir Wm Sinclair
1531	Ch of Cuthiltoun and Little Deny	Sir Wm Sinclair	to his son Alexander
1533	Renewal of Charters	King James	to Sir Wm Sinclair
1542	Entail of Roslin	Sir Wm Sinclair	
1543	Retour of Lord Borthwick		
1543	Seasine thereon	Sir Wm Sinclair	
1546	Bond	Marie, Queen-Dowager	to Sir Wm Sinclair
1551	Obligation	John, Lord Borthwick	to Sir Wm. Sinclair
1554	Retour		,,

APPENDICES

1558	Premonition	Wm Sinclair of Roslin	to Sir Mathew Sinclair
1559	C of Justiciary of Lothian	King Francis and Queen Mary	to Wm Sinclair of Roslin
1571	Charter	Provost of Roslin Chapel	
1571	,,	,,	
1572	Inquisition	Wm Lord Borthwick	
1574	Remission for Langside	King James VI	to Sir Wm Sinclair, etc
1574	Resignation of Roslin, etc	Sir Wm Sinclair	to Edward Sinclair
1574	Confirmation of same	King James VI	
1578	Charter	Sir Wm Sinclair	to Wm, Lord Borthwick
1581	Seasine thereon		,,
1582	Resignation of Roslin	Edward Sinclair	to Wm Sinclair
1582	Notice re Marriage	Wm Sinclair of Roslin	to James, Lord Borthwick
1584	,,	,	,,
		SEVENTEENTH CENTURY	
1602	Charter of Jurisdiction No 1	Scottish Masons	to Wm Sinclair of Roslin
1617	Resignation of Roslin, etc	Wm Sinclair	to Sir Wm Sinclair
1618	Seasine thereon		
1630	Charter of Jurisdiction No 2	Scottish Masons	to Sir Wm Sinclair
1647	Valuation of Rosling		
(——)	Petitions (two)	Lady Roslin	to Queen Mary d Este

O — THE NAME OF ST CLAIR

THE FOLLOWING ARE SOME OF ITS VARIANTS —

DE SANCTO CLARO —de Sancta Clara, de Santo Claro, de Sancto Clario, de Sancto Clauro, de Sanct-Clare, de Sancte Clair, de Sancto Cleer, de Sco Claro, de Sco Clero, de Saint Claro

ST CLAIR —St Claire, St Clara, St Clare, St Claro, St Clario, St Clauro, St Clayr, St Cler, St Clear, St Cleer, St Clere, St Cleere

SAINT CLAIR —Sainct Clair, Saincler, Saintclaire, Saintclayr, Saintclar, Saintclare, Saintclair, Saintclaire, Saint-Cler, Saintcler, Saintclere, Saint Clere, Sanct Clare, Sanctclare, Sancte Clere, Santcler, Sayntclere, Sayncler

SEINT-CLER —Seint-Clare, Seintcler, Seint-Cleir, Seint-Cleyr, Seint-Clere, Sentcler, Sentclere, Seintcleir, Seintcleer

SEYNTCLER —Seyntclere, Seyncle, Seyncler, Seynclere, Seynt Clere, Sentclire, Seynt-Clare, Seynt-Cler, Seynt Cleyr, Seynclowe

SAINCLER —Sainclar, Sauclar, Sanclair, Sanclayr

SENCLER —Seincler, Seincleyr, Seincoler, Seinclow, Seinclere, Sencleer Senincler

SINCLAIR —Sinclair, Sinclaire, Sinclare, Sinclaro, Sincleir, Sincler, Sinclere, Sincklar, Sinklar, Sinkler, Sintclare, Sinklair, Sinclayr, Sinclayre

SONCLERE —Sonncler, Sonnclere, Sonneclere

SYNCLAIR —Syncklare, Sy ncklayr, Synclowe, Synclare, Synglar, Synclere, Shingler)?), Chantclere

ZINCLAIR.—Zinclar, Zinchel, Zichmni

le Sinclare, von Sinclair, von Zinclair, Childe Sinclair, de St Clair, &c , &c , &c

P—EARLIER SCOTTISH EARLDOMS

A Comparative Table

		In Hereditary Succession		REMARKS
1	(CAITHNESS		870	Extant
2	(Orkney ..		870	Surrendered 1478
3	Buchan	p	1033	Mentioned in 6th century
4	Moray	c	1086	
5	Fife	p	1093	Previously in royal family
6	MAR	p	1107	Mentioned in 1014, extant
7	Dunbar or March	c	1070	
8	Athole	c	1115	Branch of royal line
9	Angus	c	1115	Mentioned in 10th century
10	Stratherne	c	1115	
11	Menteith	p	1153	Detached from Stratherne
12	Ross	p	1153	
13	Carrick	c	1186	
14	Lennox	c	1205	Cadets of Fife
15	SUTHERLAND		1228	Severed from Caithness
16	Galloway		—	
17	Mearns		—	Mentioned 1094

Of these, the earldoms of Caithness, Mar, and Sutherland are still extant, but have been transmitted through female succession. The Sinclairs thus hold the oldest comitial dignity in Britain, although the precedence only dates from [1455]. They also represent the earliest Earls of Athole, Angus, and Stratherne.

Q—SCOTTISH HISTORICAL FAMILIES

TABLE SHOWING DATES OF ENNOBLEMENT TO COMITIAL RANK

CENTURY						
XI	(1069) *Dunbar*					
XII.	(1153) *Ross*					
XIII	(1211) *Comyn*		1228	*Sutherland*		
	(1258) *Stewart* (d)		1271	*Bruce* (d)		
XIV	1357 *Douglas* (c)		1379	ST CLAIR (a)	1398	*Lindsay* (c)
XV.	1404 *Erskine* (a)		1411	*Macdonald*	1437	*Leslie* (c)
	1450 Seton (c)		1453	Hay (b)	1457	Campbell (c)
	1458 *Keith* (a)		1488	*Hepburn* (c)	1488	Cunningham
XVI	1503 Hamilton (c)		1505	Graham (c)	1508	*Montgomery*
	1509 Kennedy		(1582)	*Ruthven*		
XVII	1600 *Livingstone* (a)		1605	Drummond	1605	Home
	1606 *Lyon* (a)		1606	Murray (c)	1606	Kerr (c)
	1606 *Fleming*		1613	*Maxwell*	1619	*Scott*
	1623 *Mackenzie*		1624	Maitland	1633	Ramsay
	1633 Carnegie (a)		1633	Wemyss	1639	Ogilvie (a)
	1639 Dalzell		1643	*Johnston* (b)	1661	Boyd
	1669 Blair		1682	Gordon	1690	Melville
XVIII	1703 Boyle, Hope		1703	Dalrymple	1703	Primrose

The object of this table being to show at what period the leading Scottish houses became of *continuous historical consequence*, the dates given are those when extant earldoms were *permanently* acquired, and the table therefore omits those short-lived creations which expired without succession, nor does it include honours since 1703, being more British than Scottish. *Italicised* names indicate that the earlier dignity has left the family named by extinction, female succession, attainder or otherwise. Honours acquired since first elevation to earldom are indicated thus (a) earldoms, (b) a marquessate, (c) ducal, and (d) royal honours. The St Clair family has perpetuated the dignity of earl in unbroken and legitimate masculine succession for a longer period than any other family in geographical Scotland.

R.—THE ST CLAIR ARMOURY *

ARMS OF DOMINION

ORKNEY (Earldom of) —Az, a ship at anchor, oars in saltire and sails furled, within a double tressure flory counterflory, or

CAITHNESS (Earldom of) —Az, a ship under sail or, the sails ar

ARMS OF THE LINEAGE

ST. CLAIR (Rosslyn in XIII and XIV centuries) —Argent, a cross engrailed, sable

SI CLAIR (Henry II, Earl of Orkney, 1411) —Quarterly—1st and 4th, a ragued crosse for Roslin, 2nd and 3rd, Orkney, a galey of one maste, her sails up, cordages, and on her stern a head like to a goats contourne. No supporters

(Egidia, "Comitissa Orcadie, Domina Vallis de Nith et baronie de Harbartshire," 10th September, 1425).—Quarterly—1st, Orkney (3 masts), 2nd, Douglas, 3rd, Roslin, 4th, Nithsdale (the Lion of Galloway, facing towards the left)

(William, Earl of Orkney, 9th September, 1476) —Quarterly—1st and 4th, Orkney, 2nd and 3rd, Cathnes. Upon the tout a ragued cross, Roslin. Supporters, two grifons, about the scutcheon, Sigillum Will Comitis Orchadiæ et Cathaniæ Domini de Sancto Claro

SINCLAIR (The Lords Sinclair, Barons of Ravenscraig) —Quarterly—1st and 4th, Orkney, 2nd and 3rd, Caithness, over all an escutcheon ar. charged with a cross engrailed sa for Sinclair of Roslin. Crest—A swan with wings expanded ppr ar ducally gorged and chained or. Or sometimes they give for crest—A phœnix in a flame of fire. Supporters—Two gryphons ppi armed and beaked or. Motto—Feight. (Esplin gives for crest—A griffin's head)

(Balgreggie) —As Lord Sinclair, with a crescent for difference

(Sainteclersholme, in Denmark) —As the Lords Sinclair

(William II St Clair, Earl of Caithness, 1496) —On a seal couchy and quartered, 1st and 4th, Caithness, 2nd and 3rd, Nithsdale, and over all dividing the quarters Roslin, the shield was timbred with a helmet, ensigned with a flower-de-luce for crest, supported on the dexter by a griffin, on the sinister by a lion, and as legend around the seal, "Sig Willielmi, Comitis Cathaniæ"

Esplin, Marchmont Herald, assigns as sinister supporter, a mermaid combing her hair ppr, and for crest, a demi-bear issuing out of a coronet, with motto—Commit thy work to God

(George, Earl of Caithness, 1529–83) —Quarterly—1st, Orkney, 2nd and 3rd, Nithsdale, 4th, Caithness, Roslin over all dividing the quarters. Motto—Comitt yi vark to God. Supporters—ppr two griffons. Crest—A pelican feeding her young

(Murkle) —As the last, the cross differenced with a rose

(Freswick and Rattar) —As the Earl of Caithness, within a bordure chequy or and gu. Crest—A cross pattee within a circle of stars ar. Motto—Via crucis, via lucis. The Freswicks acquired Dunbeath and are sometimes so styled

(Dunbeath, Bart., 1704) —Quarterly, as Earl of Caithness, within a bordure indented gu. Crest—A man displaying a banner ppr. Motto—Te duce gloriamur

(Stemster) —As Dunbeath within a bordure invecked gu. Same crest and motto

(Barrock as recorded 1757, succeeded to Dunbeath baronetcy 1842) —Quarterly, as Earl of Caithness, within a bordure erm. Crest—A cock ppr. Motto—Fidelitas

(Dun) —Ar a cross engrailed sa within a bordure of the second charged with 8 plates. Crest—A man on horseback ppr. Motto—Promptus ad certauen

(Lawrence Sinclair, cadet of Dun, 1672) —Ar a cross engrailed sa within a bordure wavy of the second charged with six stars of the first. Crest—A demi-man, holding in one hand a sea-chart, in the other a pair of pencils all ppr. Motto—Sic rectius progredior

(Forss, cadet of Dun).—Arg., a cross engrailed sa. within a bordure of the second, charged with eight plates. Crest—A man on horseback ppr. Crest—Promptus ad certamen.

(Stirkoke).—Quarterly, as Earl of Caithness, within a bordure compony gu. and or. Crest—A naked arm issuing out of a cloud, grasping a small sword, with another lying by, all ppr. Motto—Ille [me] vincit ego mereo.

(Ulbster, Bart, 1786).—As recorded 1678—Quarterly, as Earl of Caithness, within a bordure compony sa. and ar. Crest—A star issuing out of a cloud ppr. Motto—Ad aspera virtus. As recorded 1778—Quarterly, as Earl of Caithness, with the engrailed cross quarterly ar. and sable all within a bordure quarterly or and gu., the last charged with three stars of the first. Crest—A star of six points waved ar. Supporters—Two red deer ppr. Mottoes—Ad astra virtus; and J'aime la meilleur.

(Harpsdale, cadet of Ulbster, 1750).—Ar. a cross engrailed on the outer side and invecked on the inner sa. within a bordure compony of the second and first. Crest—An arrow and a branch of palm in saltire ppr. Motto—Detur forti palma.

(Brims, successors to Ulbster).—Same arms, &c.

(Thos., son of William Sinclair, merchant in Thurso, descendant of Caithness, 1672).—Ar., a cross engrailed sa. between two mullets, az. Motto—Fear God and live.

(John Sinclair, writer in Edinburgh, descendant of Caithness, 1672).—Argent, a cross engrailed between two mascles in chief sa. Motto—Crux det salutem.

(Staverton Court, Gloucester).—Quarterly, 1st and 4th, Orkney; 2nd and 3rd, Caithness; over all an escutcheon ar. charged with Roslin. Crest—A phœnix in flames ppr.; over it the device, Renasce piu gloriosa. Motto—Fight.

(Sir James Sinclair of Oldbarr, baronet).—Ar., a cross engrailed quarterly sa. and gu. in the dexter canton, the badge of knight-baronet. Crest—(An otter issuing out of the wreath) a demi-otter issuant. Motto—Quocumque ferar.

(Sir William de Sco. Claro, c. 1296).—From a seal with shield on which is a cross engrailed in a centre of rounded tracery, and in each of the three compartments a boar's head couped with the legend, " S'. Willelmi de Scō. Claro Militis."

(Longformacus, Bart., 1664).—Ar. a cross engrailed gu. Crest—A cock with open bill and wings expanded ppr., having a broken chain or about his neck. Motto—Vincula tenuo. These arms were subsequently borne quarterly—1st and 4th, Longformacus; 2nd and 3rd, three stars of the first for Towers of Innerleith.

(Stevenston, descendants of Longformacus, Bart., 1636).—Originally—Ar. on a cross engrailed gu. five bezants, or. As recorded in 1767, in consequence of an entail by the Earl of Caithness to bear the name and arms of Sinclair of Murkle. Quarterly, as Earl of Caithness (the engrailed cross being blazoned quarterly ar. and sa.) with a crescent argent in the centre. Crest—A griffin's head erased ppr. Supporters—Two griffins per fess or and gu., armed and langued az. Motto—Candide sed caute.

(Roslin, post 1476).—MSS. of Sir David Lyndsay assign Roslin arms with a mullet for difference. Nisbet saw the seal of Sir Oliver St. Clair to a document of 1481, and it had only a cross engrailed. Hay (circ. 1700) assigns the Roslins, Ar. a cross engrailed sa. Supporters—Dexter Ane Mermaiden and ane Griffon on the Senistre; ane Helmet befitting his quality; above which is a Dove argent, becked and membred, gules. Motto—Credo. The Mermaiden hath ane combe in the right hand, and in the left a branch of some sea wrack. In a charter of 1523 Hay adds: Sir William St. Clair's seal was red upon white wax. A Ragued Cross, and again the like in 1571. As recorded 1672, Ar. a cross engrailed sa. Crest—A dove ppr. Motto—Credo.

(Deskford, 1420).—As Roslin.

(E. Sinclair, of Essinquoy. Carving from an oak pew in St. Magnus' Cathedral, circ. 1630).—1st and 4th, a galley; 2nd, three escallops; 3rd, a crown between three mullets, over all dividing the quarters, a cross engrailed.

(Sinclair of Rapness, Westray, 1676, from tombstone in choir of St. Mary's Kirk, Pierowall, Westray). —Quarterly—1st, Orkney; 2nd and 3rd, Nithsdale; 4th, Caithness; over all, dividing the quarters, a cross engrailed sable.

(Sinclair of Houss, Shetland) —Argent, on a cross engrailed sable a man's heart gules, and in the dexter chief a crescent   Crest—a winged heart

(Sinclair of Quendale, Shetland, as quartered on the tombstone of Rev John Gaudie, Archdeacon of Shetland) —Engrailed cross and galley of the Sinclairs with a mullet or star in the other quarters

(Sinclair of Brugh, Shetland) —Quarterly—1st and 4th, argent, a cross engrailed sable , 2nd and 3rd, a mullet between three inescutcheons   Mottoes—"Remember to die, and after that to live eternally", and "In earth nothing containeth, and man is but a shadow"

(Herdmanston, County Haddington) —Ar a cross engrailed az   Crest—An eagle's head ppr crowned or   Motto—Entends-toi

(The St. Clairs of Herdmanston, Lords Sinclair) —Quarterly—1st and 4th, Orkney, 2nd and 3rd, Caithness, over all an escutcheon ar charged with a cross engrailed sa. for Sinclair. Crest—A swan ar ducally gorged and chained or   Supporters—Two gryphons ppr armed and beaked or   Motto—Fight

(James St Clair, younger son of Lord Sinclair, as recorded 1735)   Quarterly—1st and 4th, a cross engrailed sa, in the dexter canton a cock gu, 2nd, Orkney, 3rd, Caithness   Crest—A swan ppr having a ducal collar and chain or   Motto—Fight and faith

(Blanse, Haddington, 16th century) —Quarterly—1st and 4th, Ar a cross engrailed az, 2nd and 3rd, or 3 martlets gu for Gourley

(Earlston) —Arms as Herdmanston

(Northrig and Morain) — Arms as the last

cf—Compare peerage works for arms of the present day

DENMARK

(Saintclersholme) —As the Lords Sinclair of Ravenscraig

SWEDEN

(No 444 in the House of Nobles, descended from Frans Sinclaire, colonel in the Swedish service and naturalised as Swedish nobleman in 1649   Family extinct 1683) —Quarterly—1st, Orkney, 2nd and 3rd, Nithsdale, 4th, Caithness   Crest—A cock

(No 626, descended from David Sinclair, came to Sweden 1651, and was naturalised as Swedish noble 1655, and fell as Colonel at Warszawa 1656   Family extinct 1803).—Quarterly—*a* and *d*, Nithsdale, *b*, Orkney, *c*, Caithness, the escutcheon divided by a cross "engrelve" with a white rose in the middle

(No 965, descended from Anders Sinclair, Swedish musketeer 1635, and later became colonel, naturalised as Swedish nobleman 1680, barons 1766, counts 1771) —Arms Quarterly—*a* and *d*., Orkney, *b* and *c*, springing hound   Crest—An armigerous arm

(Counts Sinclair—No 95 from grandson of the last) —Quarterly—*a*, Orkney, *b* and *c*, Nithsdale, *d*, Caithness   escutcheon of pretence with a cross "engrêlee"   Crest—A cock. Supporters—Two hounds   Motto—Via crucis via lucis

ENGLAND

1	St Clere [Suffolk]	or, a lion rampant gu
2	,,	,, or, a lion rampant, tail torked gu collared ar
3	,,	,, or, a lion rampant, tail forked and nowed gu, collared ar
4	,,	[Dorset] ar a lion rampant gu, in a border sa, crusally or
5	,,	,, or, a lion rampant gu, collared ar
6	,,	[Essex] gu, a fesse between three lions' heads erased or
7	Seyncle	,, gu, a fesse between three lions' heads erased or.
8	Seyncler	gu, a fesse between three lions' heads erased ar
9	St Clere [Corn and Essex]	on a canton gu, a lion pass. ar
10	,,	on a canton gu, a lion pass ar
11	,,	or, a lion rampant gu within a bordure sa
12	,,	or a lion rampant within a bordure sa charged with crosses crosslet of the field

13	St Clere [Corn.]	or, a lion rampant gu., tail forked collared of the field
14	St Cler	or, a lion ramp gu., within a bordure sa., charged with eight bezants
15	St Clere [Corn and Essex]	az., a sun in its glory, or
16	St Cleere	az., a sun in his glory
17	St Clere	az., a sun in its glory, or.
18	[Devon]	per pale or and az the sun in his beams counterchanged
19	[Sussex]	az., the sun in splendour, or
20	[Tidwell, Devon]	per pale or and az a sun counterchanged.
21	[Oxford]	az., the sun in splendour or Crest—A ram statant ar horned or
22		az., three suns, or, two and one
23		az., three suns within a bordure engrailed or
24		az., three suns within a bordure engrailed sa
25	St Clere	az., three suns, a border engrailed or
26		az., on a chev ar between three suns or, as many mullets pierced sa
27	Sonclere or St Clere [Devon]	per pale or and az., three suns counterchanged
28	Sonnclere	az., on a chev ar between 3 suns or, as many mullets pierced gu
29	Sonneclere	per pale az and or, three suns counterchanged
30	St Clere	ar., two bars gu Crest—A fox courant ppr
31		az., a star of sixteen points or
32		gu., a fesse between three boars' heads ar
33	St Clere or St Cleere	ar., a saltire sa
34	Sinclair	ar., on a cross sa three crescents in fesse or
35	St Clere	ar., a cross engrailed sa voided of the field
36	(Geo Sinclair, M.A., Notts 1775)	Caithness arms, impaling a chevron between three roses, gu., and on a chief as many mullets of the first.

MARCH.—The "Sinclair March" will be found in the "Scots' Expedition to Norway in 1612."

WAR CRY.—In 1335 the "cri de guerre" of Thomas of Rosslyn was "A Rosslyn."

BADGES.—Clover and whin.

TARTANS.—There are two. Of these the old green one is the true lineage tartan as worn at Flodden Field, and the red or full-dress is of modern origin, having been designed early this century by the then Countess of Caithness and Lady Sinclair of Ulbster. There should be a third tartan for the "St Clairs of the Isles."

SAINTS' DAYS.—St Clair 17th July, St Katherine, tutelary saint of the lineage, 25th November, St Magnus, 16th April, St Olaf, 29th July, St Rognvald, 20th August.

CADENCY DISTINCTIONS.—Arms are thus differenced. The eldest son during life of father carries on his shield a label or file. Other sons are distinguished thus: 2nd, a crescent, 3rd, a mullet, 4th, a martlet, 5th, an annulet, 6th, a fleur-de-lys, 7th, a rose, 8th, a cross-moline, 9th, an octofoil or double quatrefoil. Unaffiliated descendants could use a Thor's hammer for difference.

COLOURS.—Or=gold, argent (ar)=silver, azure (az)=blue, sable (sa)=black, gules (gu)=red, (erm)=ermine.

The sun in glory may be a punning allusion to sun-glare, which has almost the same sound (*idem sonans*), as St Clair, and the three boars' heads in the seal of 1292 may be similarly accounted for as sanglier=St Clair.

All persons descended from an *armigerous* ancestor are entitled to bear arms, but if there is no proof of descent from such, or from a Grantee, then the person desiring to acquire the right must become a Grantee himself. In Scotland it is necessary to matriculate, but as Orkney and Shetland are entitled to their own laws, registration has not been exacted in those parts until recent centuries. Arms paternal and hereditary are those transmitted from the first possessor to his heirs, the son being a gentleman of second coat-armour, the grandson a gentleman of blood, and the great grandson a gentleman of ancestry. Seize-quartiers require that the great great grandparentage should have been *armigerous*

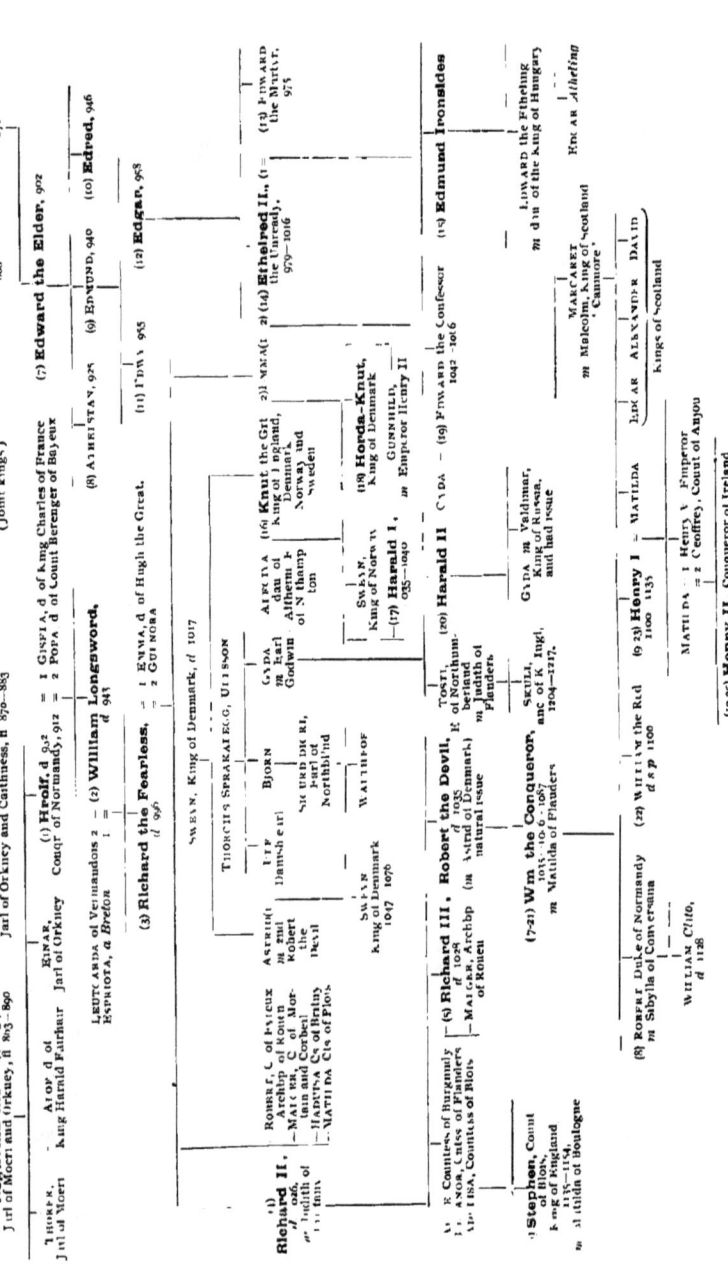

JARLS OF ORKNEY.

THE NORSE LINE, or HOUSE OF ROGNVALD, THE MIGHTY.

Fornjotr (*vide* Thor), mythical king and giant, flourished in the Odinic age. From him descended

Halfdan the Old, father of

Ivar, Jarl of the Uplands, fl. 790.

Eystein "Glumra," Jarl, fl. 830. (Augustine the Orator)		Olaf the White, King of Dublin, m. Aud, d. of Ketil Platnef, Hebridean chief.
		Thorsten the Red, fl. 900, m. Thurid, d. of Eyvind Easterling.

Hrolf Nefja, Norse chief.

Hilda = (1) **Rognvald**, Jarl of Moeri, d. 890, 1st Jarl of Orkney. | (2) **Sigurd**, Jarl of Orkney and Caithness. | (5) **Einar**, 885–910. | (3) Guttorm, fl. 883, d.s.p. | Groa. Earl Duncan.

Halfdan the Black, Norwegian royalet.

King Harald Fairhair, fl. 863–934. | Alof orled. | Ivar, d. 870. | Hrolf, d. 932, Conq. of Neustria, m. Gisela, dau. of K. Charles of France. Icelandic pioneer. | (4) Hallad, fl. 883. | Hrollaug. | (8) **Thorfinn**, fl. 950–963. | (13) Hlodver, d. 980. | King Kiarval of Dublin.

Eirik Blodox, King of Norway and Northumbria, m. Gunnhild. | Bergliot, m. Sigurd, Jarl of Hlade. | Thorer, Jarl of Moeri. | Daughter. = (6) Arnkell. (7) Erlend, fell in Northumbria, 941. | Einar Klining. | (12) Skuli, d. 974. | (14) **Sigurd II. the Stout**, fell at Clontarf, 1014. | Grelod. | Ethne. | King Malcolm II. of Scotland.

Hakon Jarl, Ruler of Norway. | Einar Harbktopt. | Ragnhild.

1 { (9) Arnfinn, d. 967
2 { (10) Havard, d. 970
3 { (11) Ljot, d. 976

Gilli, Jarl of the Suderies = Hvarflod …

Thorkell Krafa. | Hundi, d.s.p. (15) Somerled, d. 1015. (16) Einar II., d. 1026. | (17) Brusi, d. 1041. (18) **Thorfinn II.** The Great, d. 1064. | (20) **Paul.** (21) **Erlend.** Joint Earls of Orkney and Caithness. | [Ingibjorg] = K. Malcolm III. of Scotland "Canmore." | Duncan. Wm. Fitz Duncan.

(19) Rognvald II., slain 1046. | [Anleta.] | "The Boy of Egremont."

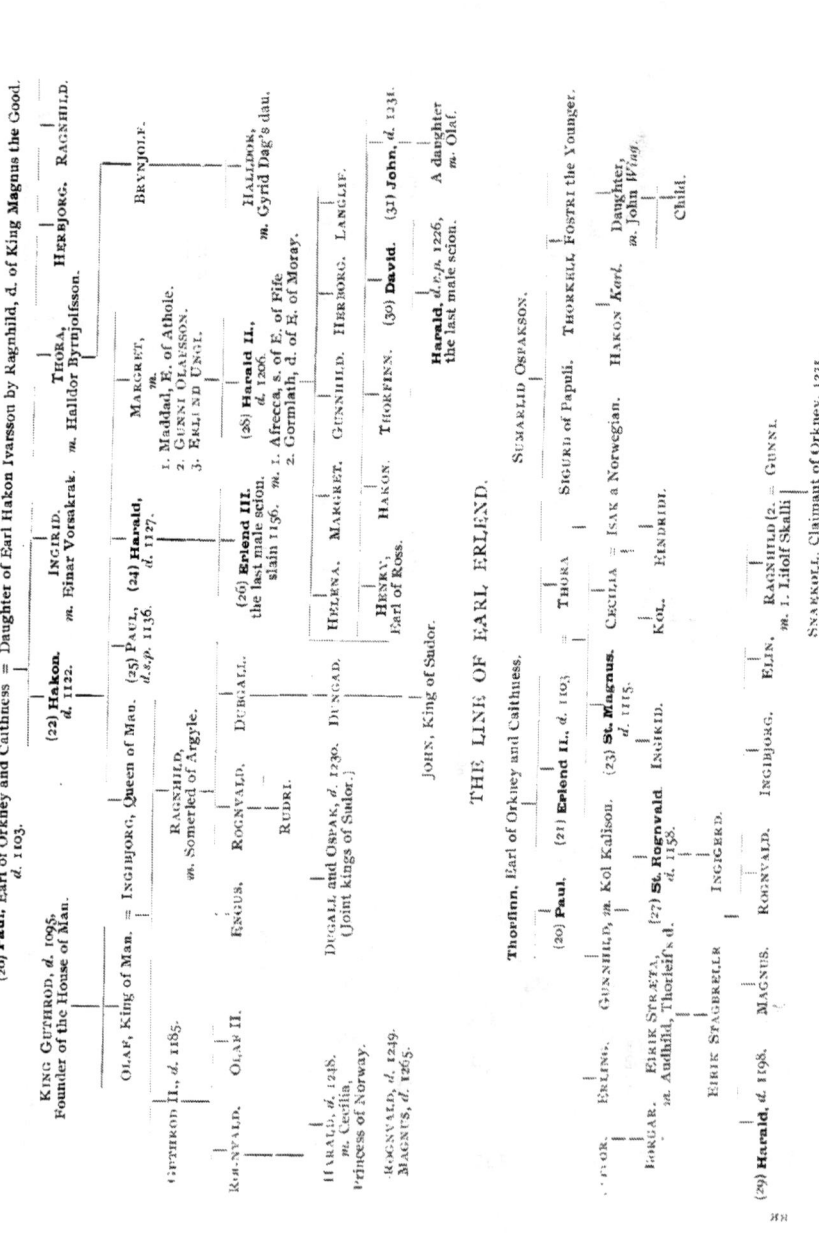

DESCENDANTS OF PAUL THE FIRST.
(AMPLIFIED TABLE.)

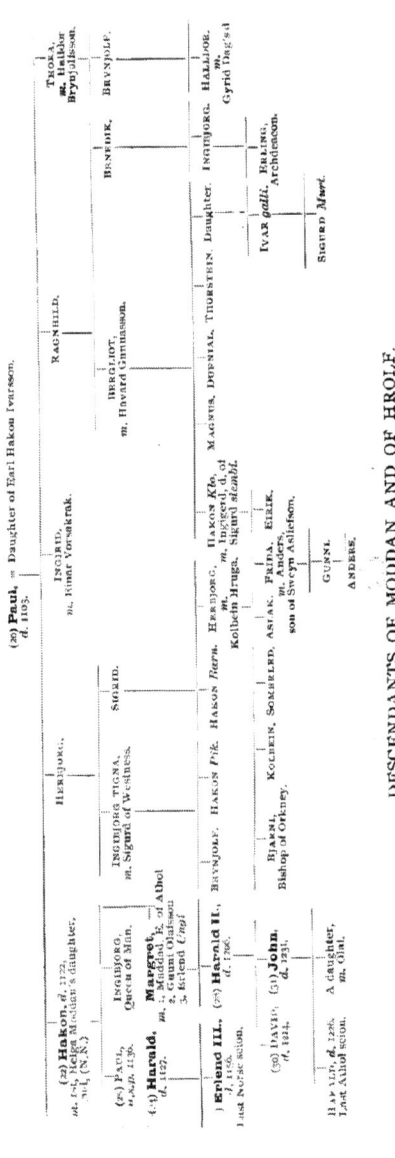

DESCENDANTS OF MOIDDAN AND OF HROLF.

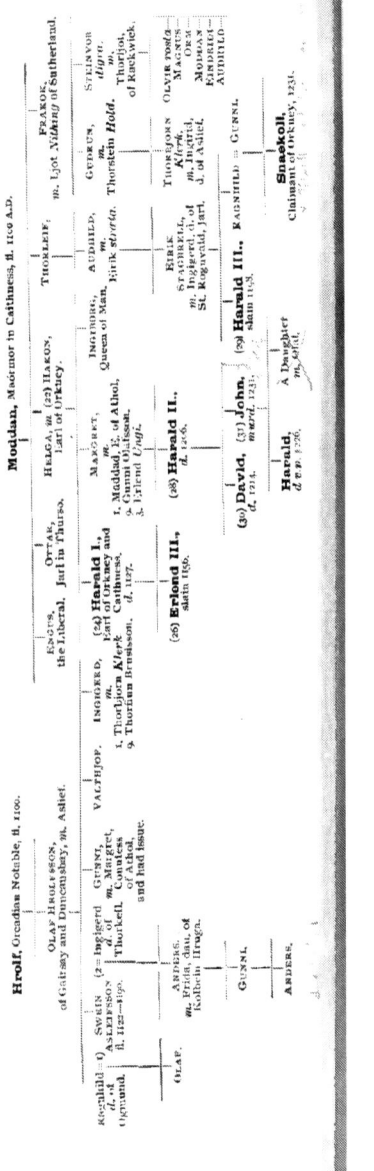

THE ANGUS AND STRATHERNE LINES.

ANGUS.

Gilbride, Earl of Angus.

Malcolm, Earl of Angus and Caithness, fl. 1225–1237.

Matilda, Countess of Angus
m. (1) **HUMBERT L' ASERVILLE**, Earl of Angus, m. 1243, d. 1243.
(2) **Gilbert Umfraville**, Earl of Angus, fl. 1264, 1301.
(3) **ROBERT COMYN**, d. 1244.

ORKNEY AND CAITHNESS.

Gilbride, Earl of Angus. [(1) m. **John of Atholl** (Haraldson), Earl of Orkney and Caithness, d. 1231.]

(3¹) **Gilbride I,** Earl of Orkney and Caithness.

(3²) **Magnus II,** Earl of Orkney and Caithness, d. 1239.

(3³) **Gilbride II,** d. 1256, Earl of Orkney and Caithness.

(3⁴) **Magnus III** Earl of Orkney and Caithness, d. 1273.

(3⁵) **Magnus IV,** Earl of Orkney and Caithness, d. 1284.

HUGH, Earl of Ross.

(3⁶) **John II,** Earl of Orkney and Caithness, fl. 1312.

(3⁷) **Magnus V,** Earl of Orkney and Caithness, 1321–1331, m. Katharina.

(3⁸) (3⁸) **Malise V,** Earl of Stratherne, Caithness and Orkney, d. 1368.

MARJORY
m. (1) **JOHN PILCHE**,
m. (2) **Robert Stewart,** 1 Earl of Stratherne, cr. 1371, = (3) **ROBERT II,** King of Scots, 1374.

ISABELLA
m. Sir Wm. St. Clair of Roslin.

AGNETTA
m. (4) **Erengisle**, Earl of Orkney, 1353–d. 1394.

(4¹) DAVID, Earl of Orkney and Caithness, 1379.

Daughter of Earl of Ment.ith.

DAVID ST. CLAIR, of Newburgh, 1394.

(40) **Henry St. Clair,** d. 1430, Lord St. Clair, Earl of Orkney.

DOUGLAS
Earl of Wm., Lord of Nithsdale, Duke of Sprue,

JOHN ST. CLAIR, Feud of Highland, 1418.

(4²) **William, Lord St. Clair**, Earl of Orkney and Caithness, d. 1480.

Daughter of Graham of Lovat.

JOANNA dau of Sir John Menteith.

Daughter m. Godburn Spar.

SIR MALISE SPAR, Lord of Skindale, slain 1379.

THOS. ST. CLAIR, Mandatory in Orkney, 1416.

STRATHERNE.

1. **Malius**, Earl of Stratherne, fl. 1115–1138.
2. **Fereth**, Earl of Stratherne, d. 1171.

(3) **Gilbert**, d. 1223. = **MATILDA**, dau. of William, Earl of Albemarle.

GILCHRIST WILLIAM FARQUHARD } d.s.p.

(4) **Robert**, d. 1244, m. Isabel, who m. 2nd, Sir Walter Comyn, E. of Menteith.

FERGUS, aetat. 1200.

MALISE of Kincardine,

MARY, m. Sir Walter Oliphant.

CHRISTIAN m. Sir William Hamilton.

(5) **Malise II**, d. in France, 1271, m. 1st, c. 1243, Marjory de Muschamp, d. 1254; m. 2nd, Egidia, d. of Wm. Comyn, Earl of Buchan (she m. 2nd, Sir Philip Meldrum.)

ANNABELLA m. Sir David Graham, of Duntarn.

AMATILDA, m. Malise, Earl of Fife.

(6) **Malise III**, fl. 1272–90.
= MARIA DE REGAINA, Queen Dowager of Man, Mary Comyn, d. of Sir John of Budenoch, who also m. Sir Hugh Abernethy.

MURIELLA, m. Earl of Mar.

MARJORY, m. Nicholas de Graham.

(7 or 9) **Malise IV,** d. 1331, Earl of Stratherne, Orkney & Caithness.

MATILDA, contracted 1293 to Robert de Thony, who d. s.p. 1311.

MARY = Sir John Murray of Aberrainney.

JOHANNA m. (1) John Campbell, Earl of Athol, d. 1334, (2) John de Warrenne, d. 1347, Earl of Surrey.

(8 or 9) Sir Maurice Moray, Earl of Stratherne, d. 1346.

MATILDA, m. Weyland de l'Ard.

EUPHEMIA, d. unmarried.

ALEX. DE L'ARD, Earl of Caithness, aft. 1375, Governor of Orkney, 1375.

MARJORIE, m. Sir David Menzies of Wemyss, Prefect of Orkney, 1422.

THE ST. CLAIR LINE.

(1) **Sir Wm. de St. Clair,** = AMICIA.
Gaulter of Roslin in 1280, prisoner 1296, dead 1297.

(2) **Sir Henry St. Clair,** = ALICIA DE FENTON. WILLIAM ST. CLAIR, fl. 1317–1337. GREGORY, = ANNABEL,
Panetarius Scotiæ, 1320, balivus of Orkney 1321. Bishop of Dunkeld. m. Sir David Wemyss.

(3) Sir **William St. Clair,** and fell in Spain, c.p., 1330. JOHN ST. CLAIR.

(3) **Sir Henry St. Clair,** = ISABELLA, d. of Malise, THOMAS, JOHN, Sir WILLIAM ST. CLAIR = 1) MARGARET (2 THOS. STEWART, THOMAS,
3rd Lord of Roslin, last Earl of Orkney, ballivus of 1367. of Herdmanstone. ST. CLAIR. Earl of Angus, Earl of
m. 1356, 1358, and 1363. Caithnes and Strathearne. Orkney, 1330. m. 1363, d. 1362. Angus.

(4) **Sir Henry St. Clair,** — JANET, dau. of DAVID ST. CLAIR, ALEXANDER, KATHARINE, SIR JAMES SIR JOHN MARGARET Countess GEO. DOUGLAS. BEATRIX = JAMES, 7th
4th Lord of Roslin, Walter Hali- of Newburgh, of Estirtyry m. ST. CLAIR, ST. CLAIR, of Angus, m. Earl of Earl of Angus, Earl of Douglas.
Earl of Orkney, 1379–1403. burton, Lord 1391. and Bray, Sir Wm. Seton, anc. of anc. of Mar, d. s.p. and had 1389.
 of Dirleton. 1364. Longformacus The Herd- natural issue by Wm.
 and Stevenson. manstons. Earl of Douglas & Mar.

[Bx. m.] STINA Princess of (5) **Henry St. Clair,** = EGIDIA, heiress of Sir Wm. — JOHN, Fond of Zetland, 1418. MARJORY, m. Sir David Menzies of Wemyss. WILLIAM 8th Earl.
Denmark; a d. of the K. 5th Lord of Roslin, Douglas, Lord of Nithsdale, — THOMAS, Mandatary in Orkney, 1420. — ELIZABETH, m. 1st, Sir John Drummond, JAMES, 9th Earl.
of Sweden; Elizabeth, 1st Lord St. Clair, [Duke of Spruce, and — WILLIAM. and, Sir John Edmonstone. ARCHD., Earl of Moray.
co-heiress of the Earl of Orkney, Prince of Dantzing.] MARGARET, m. John Craigie, Lord of Hope. HUGH, Earl of Ormond.
Earl of Strathearne. Admiral of Scotland. JEAN, m. Sir John Forrester of Corstorphine; and, it is stated, other daughters m. to JOHN, Lord Balvery.
Ramsay of Dalhousie; Sandilands of Calder; Hay, Earl of Erroll; HENRY, Bp. of Dunkeld.
melzier; Cockburn of Stirling; Heron of Merton; and Somerville of Carnwath.

ELIZABETH, d. of Arch. II., = 1) (7) **William St. Clair,** = MARJORIE, d. of
Earl of Douglas, 2nd Lord St. Clair, Alex. Sutherland,
Duke of Touraine. Earl of Orkney and Caithness, of Dunbeath.
 d. 1480.

KATHARINE, SIR OLIVER, WM. II. ST. CLAIR, — SIR DAVID OF Swinburgh, — ELEANOR, m. Sir John Stewart, E. of Athole.
m. Alex, ancestor of Earl of Caithness, Fond of Zetland, 1506. — ELIZABETH, m. Sir John Houston, of Houston.
Duke of Albany. the Roslins. 1476–1513. — JOHN, Bishop-nominate of — MARGT., m. Sir David Boswell of Balmuto.
 Caithness. EUPHEMIA.
 — ALEXANDER; GEORGE; MARJORIE, m. Andrew Leslie, Mr. of Rothes.
 — ROBERT; ARTHUR. MARIETTA.

(8) **William St. Clair**
of Newburgh,
ancestor of the Lords
Sinclair, &c., &c.

THE LORDS SINCLAIR.

Henry St. Clair, Lord of Roslin, Earl of Orkney (1379–1400), Admiral of Scotland, had issue

(1) **Henry Lord St. Clair**, Earl of Orkney (1400–1420), Admiral of Scotland, whose heir

(2) **William, Lord St. Clair**, Earl of Orkney and Caithness, Admiral of Scotland, died 1481, leaving issue

(3) **William St. Clair of Newburgh**, "the Waster," Master of Orkney and C'thness. Lord St. Clair, d. 1487, leaving issue by Christian Leslie, d. of Geo., 1st Earl of Rothes, two sons

Henry, 4th Lord. Capt.-General of Orkney, Admiral of Scotland, d. 1513.	= Margaret Hepburn, d. of Lord Hailes, Baroness-Regent of Orkney, 1513–1540.	**Sir Wm. Sinclair of Warsetter**, Orkney, acquired Tobup 1513.	= Helen, d. of George, 2nd Earl of Huntly, by Annabella, Princess of Scotl'd

Andrew Stewart, 2nd Lord Avandale (1489), Lord Chancellor.

Sir Jas. Sinclair, Governor of Kirkwall Castle, d. 1556.

Magnus Sinclair of Warsetter, ancestor of the family so designated.

John Sinclair of Tobup.

Magnus Sinclair of Tobup d 1560 they of Tobup and Salm probably extinct.

George, 4th Earl of Caithness.

Henry, Lord Methven, m. Margaret Tudor, Queen-Dowager.

Barbara (1 m. 2nd, The Bruce of Lewis.

Margaret = Magnus Halcro.

James, D. of Orkney, Admiral of Scotland, m. 1567, to Mary, Queen of Scots, Queen Dowr. of France.

Jean, m. 1st, John Stewart, of Coldingham, m. 2nd, John, Master of Caithness.

Francis Stuart, Earl of Bothwell, Lord High Admiral.

Margaret Stuart, m. 1. William Sinclair of Underhoull, 2. William Bruce of Sumburgh.

Elizabeth, m. Sir Duncan Campbell of Glenorchy.

Katherine.

Margaret = Wm. Sinclair, Lord Berridale.

John, Master of Berridale = Jean, daughter of the Earl of Seaforth. d. 1634.

George, 4th Earl of Caithness = Mary, daughter of Murr. of Argyll. d. 1678.

(3) **William, 5th Lord.** m. 1. Elisth, d. of Wm., 3rd Earl Marischal, and relict of Colin, Master of Oliphant. m. 2. Agnes Bruce.

| Agnes, m. Patrick, 3rd Earl of Bothwell. | Magnus | Margaret. |

Henry, 8th Lord (= Elizabeth, d. of William, 7th Lord Forbes.

Master of Sinclair d. ... m. Isabella, d. of ... Earl of Rothes

Patrick, anc. of the Balgregie branch, Andrew, anc. of the Danish line, Magnus

Helen, m. Andrew Kinninmont of that Ilk.

Henry, Lawrence, William, Jan.

(2) **Patrick**, d. 1607. = Margaret, dau. of Sir John Cockburn of Ormiston.

John Sinclair of Herdmanston

... (2) **Henry**, d. 1601.

(3) **James**, d. 1607.

Sir John Sinclair of Herdmanston

George, Matthew.

(1a) **John**, d. 1656.

= Mary, dau. of John, 1st Earl of Wemyss.

John St. Clair = Katharine, Mistress of Sinclair, d. 1666.

(2) **Patrick**, d. 1607.

(1) **Henry, 11th Lord Sinclair** = Grizel, dau. of Sir Jas. Cockburn. d. 1723.

Two other children, d. unmarried.

Charles St. Clair of Herdmanston, Lord Sinclair.

John, Master of Sinclair, d.s.p. 1750.

(12) **James, 12th, Lord Sinclair**, d.s.p. 1762.

Mrs. William, (13) Henry, d. 1766. Matthew, d. 1787.

1. Grizel, m. John Paterson of Preston Hall, anc. of Jno. Anst.-Thomson, heir-gen.
2. Katherine, m. Sir Wm. Erskine, Bart. of Alva, anc. of the Earls of Rosslyn.
3. Margaret, m. Sir Wm. Baird, Bart. of Newbythe, and had issue
4. Elizabeth, m. David, 3rd Earl of Wemyss.
5. Anne.

(14) **Andrew St. Clair**, d. 1775, 13th Lord Sinclair.

(15) **Charles St. Clair of Herdmanston**, who had his claim to the dignity of Lord Sinclair confirmed in 1782.

(NOTE.—Henry Lord Sinclair (d. 1513) had a natural son William, legitimised in 1580, Rector of Olrig, Caithness, 1561.)

THE ST. CLAIRS OF ROSLIN.

(8) **Sir Oliver St. Clair**, acquired Roslin by paternal disposition, 1476.
 = 1. CHRISTIAN HALDANE (Stirling Protocol Book, 1084).
 = 2. ELIZABETH, dau. of Lord Borthwick.
 = 3. ISABELLA LIVINGSTONE.
 and d. 1511–13.

(9) **Sir William St. Clair** of Roslin, d. c. 1554, Justiciary of the Lothians.
 = ALISON HUME of the Lord Hume's family.

3. HENRY, Bishop of Ross, d. 1565.
6. JOHN, Bishop of Brechin, d. 1566.
5. ALEX. of Cofhrandspeth, prisoner at Solway.
6. ARTHUR of Kirkhill.
7. JAMES in Lee and of Stevenson, pris. at Solway.

4. SIR OLIVER = KATHERINE of Pitcairns and Whyikirk, Gov. of Orkney, fl. 1539–84.
 BELLENDEN, unmarried, and had issue.

MARGARET, m. SIR THOS. KIRKPATRICK of Closeburn.

(10) **Sir William**, d. after 1602.
 2. GILBERT. 4. ALEX. of Cothiltoun
 3. PATRICK. and Little Demy.
 5. JOHN
 6. OLIVER.
 7. SIR MATTHEW.
 8. EDWARD of Ethay.

ELIZABETH, d. of Sir Walter Kerr of Cessford or f dau. of Lindsay of Edze.

(11) **William**, Patron and Protector of the Scot. Masons, fl. 1610.
 = JEAN, dau. of Edmonston of that Ilk.

1. ELSPETH. 2. ISOBEL. 3. HELEN.

REV. HERCULES, Minister of North maven in Shetland.

MARGARET = Rev. Robert Ramsay, only child. Minister of Yell.

Christian, d. of Geo. Douglas of Parkhead.

EDWARD, d. in France, 1674 82, had two natural daughters.

(12) **Sir William** of Pentland and Roslin, Patron and Protector of the Scottish Masonic Craft.
 = ANNA, dau. of John Spotswood, Archbp. of Glasgow & St. Andrews, Chancellor of Scotland.

WILLIAM, d. in France, had two natural daughters.

(13) **John** of Roslin, d.s.p. 1690.

(14) **James** of Roslin, Commissar. of Shetland, fl. 1690.
 = JEAN, dau. of Sir Henry Spotswood, Sheriff of Dublin.

4. LEWIS.
5. HENRY.
6. PATRICK.
7. CHARLES.

8. ROBERT, unmarried.
9. GEORGE, d. young.
10. ARCHIBALD.

THOMAS, born 1678.

1. RACHAEL, m. to Hume of Foord.
2. RACHAEL, d. young.
3. MARGARET, d. young.
4. HELEN, m. (1) Sir John Rollo, (2) Stirling, (3) Mackenzie.

ANNA, d. young, 1685.

JAMES, d. at the Boyne, 1690.

(15) **Alexander** of Roslin.
 = JEAN, dau. of Robert, 7th Lord Semple.

JAMES, in French Army, General in Neapolitan service.
 m. dau. of Commissioner Wedderburn.

HELEN, m. Henry Kerr of Gredane in the Merse.

FRANCIS, m. Bowet of Methie and Kincaldrun.

Daughter.

(16) **William St. Clair**, The last Roslin, d. 1778.
 = CORDELIA, dau. of Sir Geo. Wishart of Cliftonhall.

Three sons. Four daughters.
Died young.

Two sons, three daughters.
Died young.

SARAH.

EARLS OF CAITHNESS (ST. CLAIR LINE).

(1) **William, Lord St. Clair,**
Earl of Orkney, resigned Caithness in 1455, and died in 1484, leaving with other issue

```
William, Lord St. Clair,    Sir Wm. Sinclair    Katharine,      Sir Oliver of Roslin.    (2) William II, (1) Earl of Caithness,
                            of Warsetter.       Duchess of                                m. Mary, daughter of
                                                Albany.                                   Sir William Keith of Inverugie.
                                                                                          │
                                                                                          ├──────────────────────────┐
                                                                                          │                          Alexander,
                                                                                          │                          et qui they of
                                                                                          │                          Dunbeath (?).
(1) Wm., Lord St. Clair,  Magnus Sinclair,   John Sinclair,    Sir Wm. Sinclair   Edward Sinclair,
who had issue.            a quo they of      a quo those of    of Roslin,         "Gudeman of Rday,"
                          Warsetter.         Tobup and Saba.   who had issue.     a quo the Sinclairs of the
                                                                                  Isle of Ethay.

                                                                                              (3) John III, d. 1529,
                                                                                              m. Elizabeth, dau. of Sir William
                                                                                              Sutherland of Duffus.
                                                                                              │
                                                                                              William,
                                                                                              Master of Caithness,
                                                                                              d.v.p. 1527.

(3) William (3) of Mey,        Barbara,                    Elizabeth,                Agnes.        (4) George II.,
d.s.p.d.                       m. Alex., Earl of           m. 1. Alex. Sutherland of Duffus.                   m. Elizabeth dau. of
                               Sutherland.                 2. Hutcheon McKay of Farr.                          William, Earl of Montrose.
                                                                                                               │
                                                                                                               Daughter,
                                                                                                               m. Robert Munro of Foulis.

(3) Master of Caithness,       George of Mey,              John Sinclair,
d. 1576,                       ancestor of those of        ancestor they of Rattar,                            Janet,
m. Joan, daughter of           Mey (5th Earl) and          from whom 5th Earl.                                 m. Alex. Innes
Patrick, Earl of Bothwell.     Durran (6th Earl).                                                              of Innes.

(4) George III. (4) = Jean, dau. of George,    James Sinclair (?),
d. 1643.                Earl of Huntly.        ancestor Sinclairs of Murkle,
                                               from whom 4th Earl.

                                               Francis of Northfield (6)
William, Lord Berridale = Mary, daughter of Henry   m. Elizabeth, daughter of Lord Fraser.   m. Geo. Lindsay, Earl of Crawford.   Elizabeth,
                          Lord Sinclair.                                                                                          m. Sir James Sinclair of Mey.

John, Master of Berridale = Jean, daughter of the    (5) George V. (of Keiss),    Jean = Sir James Sinclair of Mey.
d. 1639.                    Earl of Seaforth.        d.s.p. 1698.

(6) George IV. = Mary, daughter of     John ; and William, d.s.p.
d. 1676.        Marquis of Argyle.
```

NATURAL SONS.—(1) William, legitimised 1545 ; (2) David, mentioned 1566 ; (3) David of Stirkoke, and Henry of Borrowston ; (4) Francis of Stirkoke, and John Sinclair, Lieut.-Colonel in German Wars ; (5) Patrick, and John Sinclair, ancestor of the Ulbsters ; (6) Margaret, married John Sutherland of Lybster ; (7) The Sinclairs of Assery, Lybster, Scotscalder, and Geise, derive in similar manner from James Sinclair, 6rst of Murkle.

SEIZE QUARTIERS.

JOHN V, XLIXTH EARL OF CAITHNESS, d 1789

AN ILLUSTRATION OF INTER-LINEAL MARRIAGES

{ John Sinclair of Rattar
{ Elizabeth Sinclair } John Sinclair of Rattar
{ Patrick Sinclair of Southdun
{ Janet Murray } Janet Sinclair
{ William Sinclair of Scotscalder
{ N N } John Sinclair of Scotscalder
{ John Sinclair of Assery
{ Barbara Murray } Barbara Sinclair

} William III, 48th Earl of Caithness, died 1772

} Barbara, Countess of Caithness

1. John Sinclair of Rattar
2. Elizabeth, daughter of John Sinclair of Ulbster
3. Sir William Sinclair of Mey
4. Margaret, daughter of George, fourth Earl of Seaforth
5. David Sinclair of Southdun
6. Jean, daughter of John Sinclair of Ulbster
7. Jas Murray of Pennyland
8. Elizabeth, daughter of Captain John Wemyss
9. James Sinclair of Lybster
10. Katherine, daughter of Patrick Sinclair of Ulbster
11. N N
12. N N
13. George Sinclair of Assery
14. Isabel, daughter of Patrick Sinclair of Ulbster
15. Patrick Murray of Pennyland
16. Daughter of Jas Cunningham of Getse

JOHN SINCLAIR OF TOLHUIP fl 1539

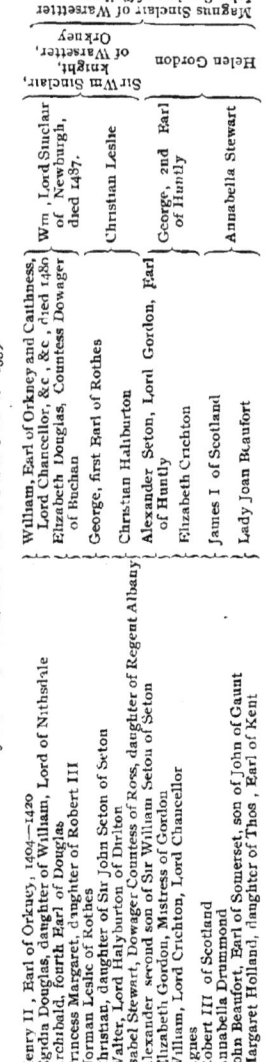

1. Henry II, Earl of Orkney, 1404—1420
2. Egidia Douglas, daughter of William, Lord of Nithsdale
3. Archibald, fourth Earl of Douglas
4. Princess Margaret, daughter of Robert III
5. Norman Leslie of Rothes
6. Christian, daughter of Sir John Seton of Seton
7. Walter, Lord Halyburton of Dirlton
8. Isabel Stewart, Dowager Countess of Ross, daughter of Regent Albany
9. Alexander second son of Sir William Seton of Seton
10. Elizabeth Gordon, Mistress of Gordon
11. William, Lord Crichton, Lord Chancellor
12. Agnes
13. Robert III of Scotland
14. Annabella Drummond
15. John Beaufort, Earl of Somerset, son of John of Gaunt
16. Margaret Holland, daughter of Thos, Earl of Kent

TOPOGRAPHY.*

There are several places in France named St. Clair. From one of these originates the lineage surname, the lord thereof being territorially designated St. Clair-sur-Epte is celebrated as the place where cession of Neustria was made to Hrolf the Northman. There is the Barony of St. Clare in Wales; Sinclair Bay and Sinclair Castle in Caithness; Sinclair town in Fife; Lake St. Clair in Tasmania; Sinclair Head, Mount Sinclair, and the favourite marine resort of St. Clair, in New Zealand.

Monuments to the St. Clairs in America, more enduring than any of the Old Country, and of necessity causing the name to be known and used by thousands of people, daily for all time:—

Lake St. Clair, in Michigan and Canada; St. Clair River, in Michigan and Canada; St. Clair County, in Missouri; St. Clair County, in Michigan; St. Clair County, in Illinois; St Clair County, in Alabama; Santa Clara County, in California.

TOWNS AND POST OFFICES.

Saint Clair, Lowndes County, Alabama; Saint Clair, Crittenden County, Arkansas; Santa Clara, Santa Clara County, California; Santa Clara, Huerfano County, Colorado; Saint Clair, Burke County, Georgia; Saint Clere, Pottawatomie County, Kansas; Cinclare, West Baton Rouge County, Louisiana; St. Clair Springs, St. Clair County, Michigan; Saint Clair, Blue Earth County, Minnesota; Saint Clair, Franklin County, Missouri; Saint Clair, Cascade County, Montana; St. Clair, Antelope County, Nebraska; St. Clair, Churchill County, Nevada; Sinclairville, Chautauqua County, New York; St. Clara, Franklin County, New York; St. Clairsville, Belmont County, Ohio; St. Clair, Columbiana County, Ohio; St. Clair, St. Clair County, Michigan; Upper St. Clair, Alleghany County, Pennsylvania; St. Clair, Alleghany County, Pennsylvania; St. Clairsville, Bedford County, Pennsylvania; Saint Clair, Schuylkill County, Pennsylvania; Sinclair, Lexington County, South Carolina; St. Clair, Hawkins County, Tennessee; Santa Clara, Washington County, Utah; St. Clair, Smyth County, Virginia; St. Clair, Doddridge County, West Virginia; Sinclair, Preston County, West Virginia; Santa Clara, Brown County, South Dakota.

Schools, squares, parks, hotels, and streets in cities all over the country also bear this name, given in honour of some member of this family.

BIBLIOGRAPHY.†

ST. CLAIR OF ROSLIN, Alexander.—MS. poems in Advocates' Library, Edinburgh.
— A. B.—Russian Imperial Freedom v. Turkish Constitutional Liberty. London, 1877, 8vo.
— ANDREW, M.D., Edin., 1733.—Histories of Fever, &c., Ed. Med. Ess.
— ANGELINE SOPHIA.—"Senora Ines, or the American Volunteers."
— ARTHUR, Maj.-Genl.—"Narrative of the manner in which the Campaign against the Indians in the year 1791 was conducted under the command of Major-Genl. St. Clair; with his observations on the statements of the Sec. of War." Phila., 1872, 8vo.
— ARTHUR, Lieut., U.S.—"Two years on the Alabama." Gay and Bird, 1896.
— A.—John L. M. Lawrence, Viceroy of India. London, 1887, cr. 8vo.
— CHAS. FERDINAND, Baron de.—See p. 471.
— DAVID, Paris, 1622.—See Historiette, p. 465.
— GEORGE.—1. Darwinism and Design; or Creation by Evolution. London, 1873, p. 8vo. 2. Evil, Physical and Moral ("Modern Handbooks of Religion") London, 1887, 12mo.
— HENRY, Bishop of Ross, died 1565.—Continuation of Boece's "History of Scotland."
— JOHN.—Appeal to Parents on the Education of their Children; 2nd. edn., Glasgow, 1874, 8vo.
— JOHN, Bishop of Brechin, died 1566.—Sinclair's "Practicks," a legal work contained in manuscript in the Advocates' Library.
— JOHN, Master of Sinclair, died 1750.—"Memoirs of the Rebellion of 1715," published by the Roxburghe Club, 1858.

---

* The American Notes were supplied by the Hon. C. H. St. Clair N.Y. Bar.
† Allibone's Dictionary; Dict. National Biography &c.

BIBLIOGRAPHY.

ST. CLAIR, LADY HARRIET.—Dainty Dishes, 3rd. edn. Edin. 1866, p. 8vo. Phila., 1867, 1mo.
——— MARY.—Somebody and Nobody; a Tale. London, 1871, p. 8vo.
——— ROBERT, M.D.—1. The Abyssinian Philosophy Considered and Refuted; or Telluris Theoria neither Sacred nor agreeable to Reason. London, 1697, 8vo.
   2. Eruptions of Fire in Italy, &c., Phil. Transactions; 1698.
——— ROLAND, WM.—"Annuals of the N.Z. Amateur Swimming Association," 1891-92 to 1894-5. "The St. Clairs of the Isles," Auckland, N.Z., 1898.
——— S. G. B. AND C. H. BROPHY.—Residence in Bulgaria. London, 1869, 8vo.
——— T. S.—Residence in the West Indies and America. London, 1834, 2 vols., 8vo.
SAINT CLAR, ROBERT.—The Metropolitan; or know thy neighbour. New York, 1865, cr. 8vo.
SAINTE CLAIRE, ARTHUR M. DE.—On the Causes of the Terminal differences affecting the Gender of French Nouns. Edin., 1878, 8vo.
SINCLARE, GEORGE, PROF.—See Historiette, p. 466.
SINCLAIR, SIR ARCH'D.—Some Thoughts upon the Present State of Affairs. 1703, 4to.
——— ALEX. (Ulbster).—Historical, Genealogical, and Miscellaneous Tracts, 8vo. N. D.
——— CAPTN. ARCH'D.—Reminiscences of the Discipline, Customs, and Usages of the Royal Navy, 1814 to 1831, sm. 8vo. N. D.
——— CATHERINE (1800-1864).—1. Modern Accomplishments, or the March of Intellect.   2. Shet-
——— CHEVALIER VON.—A notable German dramatist.
land and the Shetlanders.   3. Wales and the Welsh.   4. Scotland and the Scotch (republished in America, and translated into various languages).   5. Holiday House (once very popular with children), and some twenty other publications.
——— F. S., M.A.—Cambridge Natural History, vol. 5, Myriapods, 1896.
——— JOHN.—"Scenes and Stories of the North of Scotland," cr. 8vo. "Heather Bells," &c.
——— JAMES, 52ND EARL OF CAITHNESS (1821-1881).—Lectures on Popular and Scientific Subjects.   1877.   2nd. edn., 1879.
——— JAMES AUGUSTUS, 54TH EARL OF CAITHNESS.—MS. on the family history of the north of Scotland.
——— JOHN, vocalist (1791-1857).—Composer of "Come, sit ye doon," "The Bonnie Breast Knots," "The Mountain Maid," "Johnny Sands," &c., &c.
——— JAMES LEASK, died 1896} "Orcadian Rhymes," Kelso, 1864, and a considerable quantity of
——— MARY MOWAT   } fugitive verse.
——— MRS. FRANCIS.—"Hawaiian Flowers," 4to.
——— REV. JOHN, Archdeacon of Middlesex (1797-1875).—" Dissertations vindicating the Church of England," 1836; "Life and Times of Sir John Sinclair," 1837; "Vindication of the Apostolical Succession," 1861; Letters and Reports on National Education," 1861.
——— REV. WM. SINCLAIR (1804-1875).—1 "The Dying Soldier: A Tale Founded on Facts," 1838. 2. "Manual of Family and Occasional Prayers," 1854. 3. "The Sepoy Mutinies: their Origin and Cure," 1857. 4. "Charges of Archdeacon Sinclair of Middlesex," 1876.
——— SIR WM., Bart. of Dunbeath, 1751.—Composer of 60 Hymns. See Historiette, p. 468.
——— SIR GEO., Bart. of Ulbster, died 1868.—Various works.
——— SIR JOHN, Bart. of Ulbster, died, 1835.—See Historiette, p. 470.
——— THOS. M.A.—The Sinclairs of England; The Gunns; Caithness Events, 1894; Poems; The Messenger; The Mount; Love's Trilogy; Goddess Fortune, 3 vols.; Quest; Essays in Three Kinds; Travel Sketch; Humanities; Humanitatstudien.
——— THE HON. ANDREW, M.D., died 1861.—"Remarks on Physalia pelagica" (Tasmanian Journal of Natural Science, vol. 1, 1842), and a letter "On the Vegetation of Auckland," (Hooker's "Journal of Botany," vol. iii., 1851).

GLOSSARY.

GLOSSARY *

OF UNFAMILIAR WORDS AND EXPRESSIONS USED HEREINBEFORE,
WITH NOTES WHERE NECESSARY.

"The power thou dost covet
O'er tempest and wave,
Shall be thine, thou proud maiden,
By beach and by cave;—
By stack and by skerry, by noup and by voe,
By ayre, and by wick, and by helyer and gio,
And by every wild shore which the northern winds know
And the northern tides lave."—*Scott.*

ABBREVIATIONS.

C., Caithnessian.†	N., Norse.
Celt., **Celtic**.	O., Orcadian.
Fr., French.	Sco., Scottish.
Ice., Icelandic.	Sw., Swedish.
Z., Shetlandic.	

A, ay—an island, N.
aergin—a shieling, Celt.
aith—a tongue of land, O. and Z.
al-thing—a general assemblage of Free-men, N.
arff—heritage, succession, N., erffd.
ats—contraction for " at suit of."
ayr, aer—an open beach of sand and or shingle, O. and Z.

Banks—the cliffs where fowling is pursued, O. and Z.
bard—a bold headland, with top projecting beyond its base, O. and Z.
bear, bere—a species of barley with six rows of grains, Sco.
berg—a rock, O. and Z.
bœndi—a yeoman or Odaller, *plural* bœndr, N.
bracken—heathery, O. and Z.
bref, breve—an officer of authority, N.; cf. Bishop Thomas, breff af Orknoy (1418) and the Breve of Lewis.
broch, brough, or brugh—prehistoric towers reputed Pictish, see p. 177, also applied to a detached precipitous rocky islet, O. and Z.
brother-german—full brother, an expression used when either parent has been married more than once.
bru—a bridge, or in the neighbourhood of one, O. and Z.
bruike—to enjoy or possess, Sco.
bu, bull—the principal farm or manor house on an Odal estate, O. and Z.
but, bot—without, not burdened with, Sco.

Chemis-place—the manor house or baronial residence, Sco.; cf. *chesmez*, old Fr.
cheytrey—revenue arising from the Scottish casualty of Escheit, Sco.
commonty—a right of pasturage in common with others, Sco.

---

* Balfour's Memorial; Edmonston's Glossary; Jamieson's Dictionary; Dennison's Sketch-Book; Peterkin's Notes and Rentals; Tudor's Orkney.
† Many words glossed as O. and Z. are also current in Caithness.

GLOSSARY.

compeirit—appeared with, Sco
conqueist—acquired, purchased, Sco
coram—in presence of, Latin
corss—the signal in Norse times for clerical assemblies
cosingnace—feminine of cousin, Sco
cost—victual, two-thirds malt, one-third meal
cowsworth—part of a mark of land, one-third, one-fourth, or one-eighth
craig—the neck or throat, Sco
craigie—a long-necked bottle, Sco
cru—a small enclosure, generally a sheepfold, Z
cuttell—a measuring rod of the length of a Scottish ell, used in Shetland as the fundamental unit of length and valuation, N

Donatary—a grantee of the Crown Skatts, Males, and Duties, Sco
drong—a steep rock rising out of the sea, O and Z

Eirde-house—earth-house, Sco
excambion—exchange of land
ey—an island, N

Ferd—fared, travelled, N
fey—demented, witless, O and Z
ferry-louper—one from over-sea beyond Orcadian confines, O and Z
fiar, feuar—usually applied to the eldest son during life of father, Sco
fjell—a mountain range
flet—scolded
flesh—rent paid in cattle, generally estimated by weight
flow—a reach of the sea, N, cf Scapa Flow
fold—originally Collector of the King's scats, afterwards Chief Judge, and lastly Sheriff of the Foudrie of Shetland, N
foss, force—a waterfall, N
foy—a festival or convivial gathering, O and Z

Garth—an enclosed portion of the Odal heritage, N
geo—a cave, a rocky creek or inlet, a deep ravine which admits the sea, a fissure, O and Z
gill—a deep rut or ravine on the side of a hill, N
gloup—a sea cave with roof collapsed at landward end, O and Z
gœdingr, gofugr—terms applied in Sagas to Odallers of position, N
gudeman—gude-wyff—are self-explanatory, Sco
guid-folk—the elfin race
good neighbours—the good fairies
grencher—great-grandfather, O and Z
gutcher—grandfather, Sco
grind—a sea gate, in the Fuoes applied to a whale-drive, O and Z
guestquarters—occasional residence of the Jarl as guest of the Husbondi, whose bord-land was therefore exempt from skatt

Havers—fictitious gossip
haf—the deep sea, O and Z
hawk-hens—hens exacted by the royal falconer on visiting the Islands, O and Z
helyer—a tidal cavern, O and Z
herad—a district
heritor—a landowner
hoch—haug, or how, a mound or tumulus, O and Z
holm—a small island, uninhabited, used only for pasture, pronounced as *ham*
hope—a small bay, O and Z
horn—proclamation of outlawry by three blasts "at the King's Horn," Sco

GLOSSARY. 541

Ilk—the like, *de eodem*, Sco.
impignoration—a mortgage.
infangtheif—the right of trying a thief captured within the baronial jurisdiction.
infeft—enfeoffed.

Jarl—earl, N.

Kirk—church, N.

Laing—a narrow ridge of land, as distinguished from "skift," a broad ridge, O. and Z.
langersam—a longing for something, O. and Z.
last—as a measure = 12 barrels; as a weight = 24 meils, O. and Z.
law-book—the book of laws, N.
law-man—President of the Althing and Chief Judge, N.
lispund, or setteen—24 merks = 28lbs. av.

Male—rent, Sco.
manbote—compensation for manslaughter, N.
mart—cattle salted for winter provision, killed about St. Martin's Day (11th Nov.), Sco.
master—a title of address to the eldest son or heir apparent to a Scottish earldom or barony, affected of late by principals of English colleges; cf. Master of Balliol.
meil—a weight = 6 lispunds, N.
merchetis mulierum—a clause frequently found in charters, probably the right to a fine upon the marriage of a tenant's daughter.
mark—a weight = 24 lispunds; also a land-measure *ad valorem*, N.
merk—a Scottish coin, nominal value 13s. 4d.
moor—a heavy and dense fall of snow. A snowdrift was called a *wind moor*, a snowfall a *lift moor*, O. and Z.
moul, maol, or mull—a bold promontory or headland, N. or Celt.
muir—heath pasture, common to all Skathalds and Hrepps of a Herad, Ice.
muir-stane—the idol, afterwards the thing-stone, N.

Non-entry—a Scottish feudal casualty, the failure of heir to renew investiture with superior, on death of predecessor, Sco.
norn—old Norse language.
noss, ness—a promontory, O. and Z.
noup—a lofty headland, precipitous seaward, sloping landward, O. and Z.
noust—a boat hauling-place, O. and Z.

Odal—"a term applied to lands held by uninterrupted succession, without original charter, feudal service, or acknowledgment of any superior," N.
opgestry—conveyance of property, subject to maintenance of granter for life, O. and Z.
oy—a grandchild, O. and Z.
oyse—an inlet of the sea, O. and Z.

Pas—a step, precedence, Fr.
peerie—little, tiny, O. and Z.
pit and gallows—a baronial privilege conferred by charter allowing a *pit* for drowning women, and *gallows* to hang men convicted of theft, Sco.
planking—the process by which runridge lands are laid into severalty.
provost—the chief magistrate of a burgh, Sco.

Quern—a small handmill for grinding corn, N.
quhair throw—where through, through which, Sco.
quhyt—white, Sco.
quhilk—which, Sco.
quhill—while, Sco.

GLOSSARY.

quondam—the deceased, Latin.
quoy—a fenced enclosure, O. and Z.
quoyland—a possession enclosed from common, and not intermixed with town lands; it pays no scat, O. and Z.

Riding the hagrie—is when the parochial heritors ride the scattald marches, O. and Z.
rentals—records of the various burdens chargeable by the Donatary.
roost—a strong current, race or rush, occasioned by the meeting of rapid tides, O. and Z.
rancelman—the official appointed to ransack the parish for goods stolen, O. and Z.
ruurig—lands variously owned lying intermixed.

Saga—an ancient Northern composition, usually in verse, and dateless, N.
schind—an inquest of Thing-men upon matters of heritage, O. and Z.
scart—the cormorant or shag, O. and Z.
scord—a deep indentation in the top of a hill at right angles to its ridge, O. and Z.
scutage—shield-money.
set—an agreement, the letting of land, N.
setteen—a synonym for the lispund.
setter—the infield pasture of a town, N.
sixareen—a six-oared boat, O. and Z.
skat—tribute for Orcadian defence, payable to the Suzerain or his donatary, N.
skald—court bard to the King or Jarl, N.
skaw—a promontory, N., Ice.
skerries—rocky reefs, or insulated rocks, O. and Z.
skyld—tenant's rent as opposed to skat, odaller's tax, Danish.
span—a synonym for lispund or setteen.
stack, a precipitous insulated rock, O. and Z.
stem-bod—a symbol of citation, being a Staff for ordinary meetings, an Arrow for matters of urgency, an Axe for a Court of Justice, and a Cross for Ecclesiastical or Religious affairs, N.
stent—skat according to extent of land, N.
stoup—a flagon, Sco.
swa o' sea—the music of the sea-swell, O. and Z.

Tack—a lease, to tak possession, Sco.
tang—seaweed, O. and Z.
teind—tithes, Sco.
thing—an assembly of Free-men, N.
tocher—dower, Sco.
toft—land once tilled, but abandoned, N.
town—a collection of houses within a dyke, N.
trows—evil elves, such as Hill (*i.e.*, unseen), Kirk, and Water trows, N.
tumail—land enclosed from the common or hill, and tilled, Sco.
tutor—a term often applied to a relative as guardian of a noble in minority, Sco.

Urisland—an 18d. land, N.
umquhile—late, deceased, Sco.

Vatn—a loch or lake, N.
viking—pirates from wicks, "bay-boys," N.
voe—a long narrow bay, O. and Z.
vor—spring, O. and Z.

Ward—the turf or fuel prepared for beacon-fires on the ward-hill, N.
wick—an open bay, O. and Z.

Yon—yonder, Sco.
yule—the old pagan festival of the Norse at New Year, O. and Z.

NOTES AND QUERIES.

PAGE 33.—Dörrud: Torfæus interprets this as the name of the person who saw the vision, but in reality it signifies a *range of spears*, from *Daur* Hasta et *Raðir* Ordo. See note in Gray's poems.

PAGE 37.—The precise apportionment of Insular Orcadia into trithings is not clear.

PAGE 39.—Olaf the Holy was foster-brother to Rögnvald II. A prince or chief slain on his own estates was *heilag*, or holy. Thus Rögnvald II. qualified for the expression equally with his royal foster-brother.

PAGE 42.—Petland Firth: Scottish scribes have corrupted this word—always appearing as Pettland (*i.e.*, Pict-land) in the Sagas—to an assimilation with the Pentlands, a range of hills near Edinburgh, and conversely the latter are often found spelt Petland.

PAGE 62.—Harald "The Wicked": This soubriquet is of recent ascription, and appears to be unmerited. It is not made use of in the Sagas.

PAGE 72.—Bard: This is the equivalent of the Irish surname Barrett.

PAGE 73.—Gilla-odran is found attesting a charter of Malcolm IV. in 1161. See Cupar chartulary.

PAGE 83.—Langlif: A John Langlifsson is mentioned in the Haconian expedition of 1263.

PAGE 84.—Earl John II. appears to have married a daughter of Graham of Lovat. See History of "The Frasers of Lovat." Earl John was apparently dead in 1303, when "La lettre *Weyland de Stikelawe* tesmoignant sa venue a la pees le Roi d' *Engleterre* et aussint que le Roi li bailla la garde du corps *Munes* fuiz et heir le Counte de Cateneys, Ian. xxxi.," *i.e.*, Edwd. I. (Bishop Stapleton's Kalendar). Stickley is a Caithness place-name. There is an Orcadian family named Stickler, *cf.*, also the English Stukelys.

PAGE 85 *et seq.*—It is probable that only one of these Stratherne earls was Earl of Orkney, as notices 1320–1333 appear to refer to the last Earl Malise.

PAGE 91.—It is difficult to locate the de Ards. There was a Gascon family de Lart, or de Lard, one of whom settled in England, coming in the train of the Black Prince. The de la Ards were once owners of "the Aird," a district lying between Inverness and Beauly. In 1342, Godfrey del Arde, son of Alexander del Arde, forcibly retains the ward and marriage ot his heir and Isabel Fenton, wife of the latter. In 1368 Lord Fenton of Baky and Alexander de Chishelme, *jure uxoris*, are co-portioners of *the barony of Ard*. In 1403 Margaret de la Ard, *domina de Erchless*, and Thomas de Chishelme, her son and heir, on the one part, and William de Fenton of Baky, divide between them the lands of which they were heirs-portioners, and among these is *the Barony of Aird or Ard*. In 1513 *Wiland* de Chisholm obtains charter of the lands of Comer.

PAGE 91.—The Spar or Sperra family are Hjaltlanders. Ivar Sperra appears there in 1299 and 1307, and Malis Sperra in 1386 (Dipl. Norveg.). Sir Malise Spar held the lands of Holm and Quendale in Outer Westness, in Rousay (see Rental, 1503).

PAGE 100.—Alexander de Claphame, at Kirkwall, 1391. King Erik the Pomeranian at Lund, 15th April, 1412, grants to his trusty servant, Alexander van Klapam, all his lands in North Maven, in Shetland—"Alt vaart godz sem ligger uppa Hieltland for Nordan Mawed huiliket plæger att skyllda ok gifua tiu loduga marker til skat landskyld ok wesel," &c. (Dipl. Norveg.).

PAGE 101.—Van Bassan: See page 275 for estimate by Father Hay.

PAGE 109.—The indenture of 1419 between Earl Henry II. and Adam of Dalkell is in the Scots' vernacular, it requires payment when made to be "betweyn the ryseing of the sone and the down passing of the *ilk*." This Earl and his brother, William de St. Clair, died, says the Book of Cowper (1422), "of a deadly disease which the vulgar call *le quheu*," which would make them the earliest recorded victims of influenza in Scotland. This notice has been erroneously applied to Earl William on p. 125.

PAGE 126.—The last Earl of Orkney had by each of his two marriages a son named William. See page 167 for two brothers Sinclair, each named Laurence; and on page 295 there are two each named William. This confusing custom occurs in other Scottish families, but only with brothers-uterine.

PAGE 128.—Yat: The initial letter in this and other instances is not meant for *y*, but merely a contraction for *th*, and is to be pronounced accordingly.

PAGE 130.—Midhouse, Netherhouse, &c., all indicate relative position to the main house in the neighbourhood.

PAGE 131.—"Yellow Carvel": May the Orcadian fleet have provided a nucleus for the Scottish navy. The first admiral on record is Henry I. Sinclair, next after whom is his son Henry II. (1412)

and grandson William I. (1435). Henry, Lord St. Clair, commands in 1512 the flagship the "Great Michael," and thereafter the office passes heritably to the Hepburns of Bothwell, evidently because of their St. Clair connection and the minority of the fifth Lord.

PAGE 133.—"The Description of the Isles of Orkney," by John Bellenden the Benedictine, attributed to 1529, must have been written at a later period, for in referring to Earl John of Caithness, slain at Summerdale in 1529, he makes him grandfather to the Earl now living. The "Description" must thus have been written later than 1582. Bellenden is also inaccurate in dating the battle as in 1527, an error impossible to make if written two years after so important an event.

PAGE 134.—Even the *debris* of Kirkwall Castle is now removed, and a modern hotel has been erected on the Castle "Stance."

PAGE 156.—*Proceres Orcadium.* See Buchanan's "History of Scotland."

PAGE 165.—There are Sinclairs at Dunedin, New Zealand, claiming to derive from the Barons of Brugh.

PAGE 167.—Henderson of Buness, Unst.—This family derives from Hendrich Hendrichson, Great Foud, Lawman, and Chancellor of Hjaltland, whose commission, granted by King Christian I. of Denmark, in the year 1450, and written in the Danish language, is said to have been in the possession of James Henderson, last of Gardie, died 1799, and to have been presented by Thomas Mouat of Garth in 1792, along with all the old papers of the family to a Swedish knight.

PAGE 169, line 13.—For 595 deeds read 535.

PAGE 175.—Rustung: This sobriquet occurs in the Decree by the Lawman of Bergen in 1485 A.D., when Endrith Svenson-Rostungh is noted as a Council-man of [Bergen or] Shetland.

PAGE 186.—The Charter of Caithness, if extant, should be examined, to determine the relative seniority of the Roslin and Caithness cadets. It will be observed that the charter of Roslin secures succession first in remainder to William II., Earl of Caithness. Had he been senior to Sir Oliver, the remainder would have gone to the next younger brother. The titles (emoluments) of Carnoch and Innernavir attached to the earldom charter of 1455 refer to estates in the Caithness appanage or province of Strathnaver.

PAGE 187.—In the Swinburgh charter of 1498 the enumeration is first according to rank and then to seniority in this order: William, Earl of Caithness; Oliver St. Clair of Roslin, knight; Messrs. Alexander, George, Robert and Arthur Sinclare; Elenor Sinclare, Countess of Athol; Elizabeth Sinclare, Lady of Houston; Margaret Sinclare, Lady of Balmuto; Catherine, Euphamia, Marjorie and Marieta Sinclair. Thus the ex-Duchess of Albany yields precedence to her married sisters.

PAGE 194.—Barbara, Countess of Sutherland, will be the Barbareta Sinclar, wife of Alexander Urquhart, whose seal is appended 19th June, 1571, to his Procuratory of Resignation of lands of Helmsdale to Alexander, Earl of Sutherland.

PAGE 195 —Alliances with the Hepburns of Bothwell invariably resulted in unruly issue. Examine the career of the descendants of the Earls of Bothwell in the direct male line and in the descendants of Jean, Lady Morham, for which latter see the Caithness family, that of Sinclair of Underhoull, Shetland, Bruce of Sumburgh, and Stuart, Earl of Bothwell.

PAGE 195.—Agnes Sinclair, sister or daughter of John, Master of Caithness, married, first, Andrew, seventh Earl of Errol; second, Alexander Gordon of Strathdon.

PAGE 210.—Sir Thos. Urquhart applauds the prowess of Francis Sinclair, the valiant bastard of Caithness, who conquered a gallant nobleman of High Germany in the presence of the Emperor and all his court.

PAGE 215.—In the event of the Sarclet Sinclairs establishing legitimacy of descent from David Sinclair of Broynach, the comitial designation accorded to the 48th and subsequent earls will become void. Nos. 52 and 53 will then become Barons Barrogill, and No. 50 *et seq* baronets of Mey.

PAGE 217.—Marie, late Countess of Caithness, Duchesse de Pomar, died in 1895. She was authoress of "The Mystery of the Ages" and other Theosophical publications. At "Holyrood," her salon in Paris, celebrities of cosmopolitan note were accustomed to assemble.

PAGE 225.—For "Daniel Anne" read only "Anne." It is stated that the eldest son of Donald Sinclair (iv., article Sarclet) was William Sinclair, whom Alexander II., 47th Earl of Caithness, made tacksman of Isauld barony with its many subtenants. In 1760, while purchasing corn in Reay market, an affray arose in which he killed a Mackay in open fight, after which event he retired with his wife and two children to Muirends, near Avoch, in Ross-shire. His son James in Muirends was succeeded by his eldest son John in Muirends, whose son the Rev. John Sinclair, B.D., author, &c., is a minister in the Established Church at Kinloch-Rannoch, Perth. He is married to a sister of Hugh Ballingall, Lord Provost of Dundee, and by her has two sons, aged 11 and 8.

PAGE 240.—There is a remote likelihood of the Sinclairs of Dun being descended from Sir David Sinclair of Swinburgh.

PAGE 244.—Corrections: The issue of Veitch Sinclair, M.D., should read thus: 5, Henry Tweedie; 6, James, L.R.C.P.S., &c.; 7, Arthur Veitch; 8, Augustine, M.D., &c.

PAGE 249.—Sir George Sinclair of Clyth was an M.P. in 1706 and probably a baronet.

PAGES 266-274.—These are inserted partly as a curiosity, chiefly to illustrate how valueless are the numerous statements when tested by modern research.

PAGE 277.—The St. Clairs of Roslin seemingly came direct from Normandy in the reign of Alexander II., 1213—1249, as they do not identify armorially with any of the English St. Clares nor with the Herdmanston family.

PAGE 283.—Lady St. Clair is noted in the Dict. Nat. Biog. as Alicia de Fenton. John de Fenton, sheriff of Forfar, 1261, was father of Alicia and William (1292), married Cecilia Bisset, and had Isabella, married to Godfrey del Arde or his heir.

PAGE 287.—The lands of Stevenson were subsequently acquired by cadets of the Longformacus line.

PAGE 294.—Oliver Sinclair of Pitcairn is now represented by the Ramsays of Dalhousie.

PAGE 294.—Edward Sinclair of Dryden is seemingly a son of William, Earl of Orkney, by first marriage.

PAGE 298.—Surely this agreement between Lord St. Clair and Sir Oliver is still extant.

PAGE 307.—It is not clear whether Major William St. Clair and his brother David survived Lord James, but Henry, the fifth son did.

PAGE 311.—John of Hirdmanestune may not have been of the St. Clair lineage. Andrew Herdmonston was of Balnagowan in Ross, *circ.* 1368.

PAGE 313.—Polmase St. Clair and Polmase Weland: Can Polmase have been so divided on the occasion of the Stratherne heiresses marrying Weyland de Arde and William St. Clair?

PAGE 314.—Beatrix Rantoun, Lady Herdmanston, has several notices of an uncomplimentary nature in records.

PAGE 317.—The earlier generations for the Swedish families do not synchronise.

PAGES 319 and 320.—Lambahof is not attached to the dignity, which is personal, and should appear as Count Sinclair *pur et simple*.

PAGE 357.—Rachael Sinclair (231) was great grandmother of J. R. Shaw, a subscriber hereto.

PAGE 353.—Mary St. Clair (129) is grandmother of Henrietta Marie (May) Whitney (Mrs. Dr. Nathaniel Emerson), an authoress of note, organiser and secretary of the Society De Sancto Claro in America.

PAGE 352.—In recomitting to his relatives the history of his family, James St. Clair (51) said: "Our first ancestor in America was named John, he came to America from near Edinburgh, Scotland. His father's name was Henry; he was a farmer. We are related to General Arthur St. Clair, and I am going to pay him a visit." The visit was made in 1816, and on his return he stated they were "cousins." On these grounds the New Hampshire scions are affiliated to Henry Sinclair (see page 195), son of John, Master of Caithness (died 1567), and although the said Henry is explicitly described as brother-natural to the 43rd Earl, it is lately alleged that a charter has come to light establishing his legitimacy. It is not clear how James St. Clair of 1816 could have acquired the knowledge necessary to enable him to make the statements recorded as his with regard to his origin, and as evidence it appears to be quite insufficient. At the time John Sinkler, first of New Hampshire, emigrated, viz., 1658, there must have been many namesakes to whom affiliation could be claimed on precisely similar grounds

PAGE 424.—An examination of the Mowat-Halcro charters will throw light on the history of these families in their Orcadian connection.

PAGE 446.—Frobisher, the Elizabethan navigator, records sighting the coast of Friesland in 1576, 1577, and 1578, thus accepting the chart of the Zeni. His account of the condition of the Orcadians in 1577 does not indicate an advanced state of civilisation.

PAGE 453.—Examination of the succession to the Summerhopes should result in affiliating subsequent Sinclairs to Sir John St. Clair, Foud of Hjaltland; and a like perusal of the Complaint of 1576 should disclose descendants of Sir David Sinclair of Swinburgh.

PAGE 457.—In 1635 Sir William St. Clair of Roslin claimed hereditary charge of the Scottish Masonic Craft (see page 291).

PAGE 461.—The Dunkeld Register gives the death of Bishop Sinclair as 27th June, 1337.

PAGE 464.—Footnote ‡: For "Scot's" read "Scottish"; for "Queen" read "Queens."

PAGE 466.—"Satan's Invisible World Discovered": This title has recently been travestied by Stead of the *Review of Reviews* in his book styled "Satan's Invisible World Displayed."

PAGE 466.—The Master of Sinclair was, in 1708, chosen member of Parliament for the county of Fife.

PAGE 467.—The Hon. James St. Clair became Colonel in 1722, Major-General in 1741, and on 4th June, 1745, Lieut.-General with command of British forces in Flanders. In 1746 he was appointed to the command of a force of 6,000 men originally intended to act against Quebec, but eventually sent against Port L'Orient with an additional 2,000 men. Large reinforcements having been thrown into the town, he resolved to abandon the siege, and after destroying the forts in Quiberon Bay, reembarked for England on 17th October, 1746. The historian Hume was his secretary during this expedition. General St. Clair afterwards acted as ambassador to the courts of Vienna and Turin. On 10th March, 1761, he was promoted to the rank of General. He sat in the House of Commons for many years, being chosen for the Dysart burghs in 1722, 1727, and 1747; for the county of Sutherland in 1736 and 1741; and in 1761 for the county of Fife. He died at Dysart, 30th November, 1762, being then Governor of Cork, and Major-General on the staff in Ireland. By his wife, Janet, youngest daughter of Sir David Dalrymple of Hailes, and widow of Sir John Baird of Newbyth, he left no issue.

PAGE 468.—Reference to the entry of General Arthur St. Clair into army life should throw light on his parentage.

PAGE 472.—The Hon. Andrew Sinclair is represented by his nephew, Andrew Sinclair, of "Kuranui," Symonds Street, Auckland, N.Z.

PAGE 476.—The verses dedicated to St. Clair are merely a poetical exercise by the author upon the incidents narrated in paragraph 1, page 418, and do not involve religious belief.

PAGE 488.—The thread unwound by the witch represented the "clew of fate."

PAGE 510.—The text implies that Simon Rodde is the father of Alexander Ard.

PAGE 510.—Ogmund Findzson as the King's steward, adjudged on 8th October, 1386, to Herr John and Herr Sigurd Hafthorsson the estates left in Shetland by Fru Herdis Thorvaldsdaughter, and which Malis Sperra had unlawfully appropriated.

PAGE 127.—Jon de Baddi. The lands of Goirisness in Rendall were escheated prior to 1503 from one Baddi because he "drew bluid in the kirkyaird."

PAGE 515.—Bishop Arnthor of Bergen certifies on 11th August, 1512, that he has seen the Testament of Her David Syncklare demising half of Samphray to Dr. Hans Eek, who sold 12 marks land there by deed at Bergen 21st July, 1512, in which he is described as "Dr. Hans Eek aff Gestryalandh, vicarius j Skatzta högbwreen herres Jacob med gudz nad konunges aff Skotlandh kappelan." He is doubtless ancestor of the family of Hawick of Scatsta, Shetland.

PAGE 123.—There was nothing extraordinary in King Christian pawning Orkney. He had often placed Copenhagen in pledge.

PAGE 123.—In the treaty concluded between Denmark and England in 1667, this article was inserted: "That the suspension of the restitution of Orkney and Zetland should not have any effect to the prejudice of the King of Denmark and Norway, nor diminish his right to recover them, which is acknowledged to remain open, entire, and unviolated, and which he may prefer at a more convenient time."

PAGE 123.—Forty years after the Impignoration (1508) this curious entry occurs in the minutes of the Lords of the Articles: "Compeirit Jhone Skrimgeour Mastr. and askit Instrumentis that he advertist the Lordes forsaid how that the tyme of his being in Denmark he knawis that the discharge of Orknay and Scheteland myt have been had sovirly to the King's grace and that therefor the Lordes suld now laubor for the samyne." On 6th December, 1567, a Committee of the Scottish Parliament considered, "Quhidder Orknay and Zetland sall be subject to the comone law of this realme or gif thai sal bruk thair awne lawis." The Committee "finds thai aucht to be subject to thair awne lawis." In 1587 a commission was granted to certain persons, with "power to heir determyne and conclude in the matter of the answer to the Petitionis of the King of Denmark anent Orknay." A Scottish embassy to Denmark contracted with Christian IV., and his four Regents and Governors on 20th

August, 1589, when, in addition to the matrimonial contract between James VI. and Anne of Denmark, this was also read and exhibited before Christian and his Regents: "Togidder with the forme and tennor of the attestations seillit subscrivit and deliverit be thame to the saidis Regentis anent the Isles of Orknay proporting in effect a grant maid at their requisitioun be the foirsaidis King and Regentis that all further claim or repetitioun of the foirsaidis Ilis upon quhatsoever pretendit richt or interesse allegit thairto be that Crown sal be supersedit and continuit for thair partis unto the said elected Princes perfite aige. And the saidis Ambassadouris acceptatioun thairof in name foirsaid always but prejudice of quhatsoever richt or title acclamit thairto be ather of the Crownis as at mair lenth is contenit in the said attestationn Quhairof the authentiq subscrivit be the handis of the saidis haill four governors bearing the dait forsaid was likwayes exhibited and reid befoir his Hieness and Lordis foirsaidis." And it finds that the Ambassadors have conformed themselves in every point to their commissions and instructions. The proceedings of the embassy were ratified in 1592 by James VI.

PAGE 123.—Cottonian MS. British Museum (Titus. c. viii., art. 71. f. 134.) "Notes on King of Denmark's Demand of the Orcades." Orcades, 1587.

"Frederik, King of Denmark, told Daniell Rogers that the King of Scotts dallied with him, and that he had not answered him to make restitucion of the Orcades when he sewed for his daughter Anne to be his wife; neither kept promise in shewing such ltres. as he pretended to have from the King of Denmarke, by which it would appear that he weare released from the contract by which his predecessors were bound at all tymes to be ready uppon the receipt of one hundred thousand gildern, to restore the Orcades unto the kingdome of Denmark againe, which he must needs have agayne, for that the state of his kingdome had putt him in mynde of his oath, which he made when he was contracted."

In 1549 an assessment was levied in Norway by Christian III. for the purpose of paying off the sum for which Orkney and Shetland were pledged. In 1804, Napoleon Bonaparte in a proclamation addressd to the army assembled at Boulogne for the invasion of Britain, descanted on the claim of the Danish King of Norway to the Orkneys.

PAGE 123.—Section 35 of the Agreement, Promise or Hand-binding of Frederik the First to Norway in 1524 is as follows:—"Should we again be able to release or recover to Norway's Crown the Orkney and Shetland Islands which our dear Lord and Father Christian I. pawned or parted with without the will or consent of the Norwegian State Council, &c., &c."

PAGE 132.—The Orcadian Law-book was required to be produced in 1575, Nicol Randal v. Robert, Earl of Orkney, for dispossession of the Isle of Gairsay, the odal inheritance of plaintiff.

PAGE 132.—Provost Craigie of Kirkwall (circ. 1660) in a MS. under his own hand, writes, "That on pretence of distraining for a private debt, Earl Patrick Stewart seized upon the charter-chest of Kirkwall, and destroyed all the town's charters and records."

PAGE 143.—Monteth describing the defeat at Tain in 1650 says, "Montrose swam over the river accompanied by the gallant Sir Edward St. Clair and St. Clair of Brims, a gentleman of Caithness." The former was an Orcadian Major, and the latter Alexander Sinclair of Brims.

PAGE 142.—The band subscribed by the country people of Orkney in favour of adhereuce to Robert Stewart, bastard son of Earl Patrick, was produced at Edinburgh, at the trial of the latter in 1615. It should disclose important information.

PAGE 164.—About 1611 Captain Andreas Sinckler commands a company 600 strong. Aarsberetninger fra det Kongelige Geheimearchiv, vol. 6.

PAGE 214.—"Earl Alexander disinherited his daughter because he did not like his son-in-law [Lord Macduff, afterwards Earl of Fife], and the supposed heir having called [at Hemer Castle] and being kept waiting, his expressions of impatience were reported to Earl Alexander by the old Earl's servant, and *the Earl cut him off*. This alludes to an unfortunate man who could not obtain the title though it was afterwards proved he had the right. He gave his estates to his remotest relation of our surname *because one of them was at school with him!* The beneficiary was 30 degrees off." (Notes printed privately by Alexander Sinclair, of the Ulbster family.)

PAGE 98.—Henry Earl of Orkney and Malise Spar were both present at the Norwegian State Council Meeting at Helsingborg, in June, 1389, when Erik the Pomeranian was proclaimed heir to Norway. The transactions are recorded in two documents, the one in Swedish containing signatures and seals of 20 Councillors including the signature of Malise Spar, but it does not occur in the Latin copy which only contains 10 seals and signatures. Perhaps he was slain before he had time to sign the latter.

NOTES AND QUERIES.

PAGE 103.—Martin V. was elected Pope in 1417, by the five nations of Christendom. France then contended that England, Ireland, Scotland, etc., ought not to be counted one of the five, but the learned priests of Britain successfully argued at Rome the right to equality. Their chief argument, to quote Gibbon, was "that including England, Scotland, Wales, the four kingdoms of Ireland, and the Orkneys, the British islands are decorated with eight royal crowns."

PAGE 230.—Sir John Sinclair of Rattar, was justiciary and sheriff of Orkney in 1614.

PAGE 307.—A Scottish Peerage could, down to the Union, be resigned into the hands of the King to be re-granted to a new series of heirs, a transaction to which the heir *alioqui successurus* had no right to object, and which was completed by a Crown charter of resignation.

PAGE 214.—Prince Charles Edward Stuart when fugitive in the North of Scotland, assumed the name of "Sinclair."

PAGE 14.—Palgrave in enumerating the descendants of Richard I., of Normandy, Sans Peur, states, "Mauger who acquired much importance in French affairs was assuredly legitimate" . . . and again, "Mauger, much distinguished by his policy and valour, was invested with the extensive County of Mortaigne as an inheritance, while through marriage he acquired Corbeil."

PAGE 312.—The "Sword of Bruce" was stolen from the Herdmanston family early last century.

PAGE 102.—Commission of Bailliary by Lady Marjorie Menzies in 1418, to John, her son and heir, and nomination by Henry Earl of Orkney, wherein the Earl styles Sir David Menzies his brother-in-law.

PAGE 304.—Ross of Craigie (cadet of Innernethie), and Aytoun of Inchdairnie represent the Sinclairs of Balgreggie through heiresses.

PAGE 138.—Henry Sinclair was Provost of Kirkwall in 1549, and Edward Sinclair of Essinquoy, 1622 to 1635; Nicoll Sinclair, Dean of Guild, 1567, and a Baillie in 1595; Arthur Sinclair, Baillie in 1619 and Hew Sinclair of Damsay, Baillie 1623 to 1628, 1633 and 1642 to 1644.

PAGE 127.—In the complaint of 1575, one of the charges preferred against Robert Stewart, the Abbot Earl, was sending his Maister Household, Gawin Elphingstone, and Henry Sinclair, his chamberchyld, to the King of Denmark in order to offer Orkney and Zetland to him, and attributed this "to his fearing sometime God's judgment." It is alleged that Elphinstone got the Danish King's confirmation of Lord Robert's title, which came home in a strictly private way "enclosed in a bolt of Holland Clayth."

PAGE 127.—Patrick, Earl of Orkney, was Provost of Kirkwall in 1604. He set up a mint and coined money in Orkney.

PAGE 278.—These notices of Robert de St. Clair occur in Bain's "Documents," and would appear to have reference to attestation of the original Scottish charters in 1213 rather than the Inspeximus of 1261 and Inquisition of 1264.

PAGE 460.—The King's Bishop: Master [Dominus] Wm. de St. Clair and other Scottish prisoners taken in Dunbar Castle were committed to Gloucester Castle, 16th May, 1296. A writ issued 13th August, 1297, allowing money for expenses re same to Walter de Beauchamp the castellan, from 1st May, 1296, to 30th June, 1297. On 11th March, 1302-3 pardon issued to Beauchamp's heirs and executors for all action in connection with the escape of Master Wm. de St. Clair, a Scottish rebel.

In 1565 one Saint Cler was a French officer in America under Laudonniere.

PAGE 51.—This Ljot of Sutherland is considered ancestor of the Macleods. Strafleet is named after him.

PAGE 68.—Gunni Olafsson is accounted ancestor of the Clan Gunn.

PAGE 51.—From Helga is derived the place-name Helgarie, on the Helmsdale, near Kildonan, in Sutherland.

PAGE 442.—Adam I., Bishop of Caithness, is cited by Sir Robert Gordon as author of a History of Scotland in 3 vols.

PAGE 442.—St. Gilbert resided in Burnside Castle. He contributed to the defeat of the Danes at Embo. He translated the Psalms and the Gospels into the Gaelic language. He is worshipped on the 1st April.

PAGE 83.—The first survey of Orkney was made at command of Hakon IV. in 1263, who issued orders to divide the whole occupied lands of O. and Z. into Marklands containing eight Eyrislands or Urislands, each of which should find quarters and supplies for a Hofding and a fixed number of men, probably in proportion to the Skatts formerly paid.

NOTES AND QUERIES 549

PAGE 470.—In a letter to Sir John Sinclair of Ulbster, George Washington writes, "Certainly no good reason can be assigned why the hemp of New Zealand should not thrive with us, as that country lies in about the same southern latitude that our middle states do in the northern Phila, 10th Dec, 1796

PAGE 470.—A letter to Sir John from Robert Sinclair of Baltimore, Maryland, (30th November, 1819), contains an account of the latter's parentage and family

Patronymics have been in vogue in Shetland until this century In 1733, Patrick Gilbertson, aged about 90, reckoned himself the 22nd generation in lineal possession of Islesburgh (Gifford)

PAGE 441.—A Genealogical MSS written by Wm Tulloch, Bishop of Orkney was in Rosendal's house in Norway (Wallace)

PAGE 441.—Bishop Adam Bothwell crowned James VI in 1567 A full account of Orcadian Bishops will be found in Craven's "History of the Church in Orkney"

PAGE 263.—In 1633, John Sinclair was M P for Edinburgh

PAGE 339.—Captain David Sinclair, "an old officer of courage and honour," was prisoner for debt in the fleet in 1726

PAGE 339.—The poet Savage in 1727 ran a Mr James Sinclair through the body, when he was not in a posture of defence

PAGE 339.—Patrick Sinclair was rector of Norfolk livings (presented by Horace Walpole) 1700-1750 There is a monumental tablet to his wife "the good Mrs St Clair" who died in 1727, "the year terrible for fevers"

PAGE 339.—Geo Sinclair, M A , rector of Wilford, Notts, died there, 12th June, 1775, aged 46 years See Armoury

PAGE 445.—The "Carta Marina" of Olaus Magnus in 1539 has been discovered in Munich The most important paper on the Zeno voyages was read by the Prof , Dr Gustav Storm of Christiania, 17th December, 1890, and published in the annual volume of Det Norske Geograficke Selskabs Arbog II , 1890-91 Comparison of the Zeno map with the Carta Marina proves the Frislanda of the former to be the Faroe group, with the internal waterways omitted (An abstract of notes kindly supplied by C H Coote of the Map Department, British Museum) See also "Athenæum," 6th February, 1892, and 10th June, 1893

PAGE 532.—David Sinclair was succeeded by John de St Clair of Newburgh, in 1414 residing in the tower of Crail, when he took the balance of accounts from the bailies of that place

PAGE 532.—Richard de St Clair, ' Our worthy and faithful seutifer," was confirmed 31st July, 1367, in the lands of Finlettre, and again 5th June, 1382, to which is attached the Grieveschip of Culane with the pertinents These lands were put to the horn in 1391

PAGE 220.—Magnus Budge, custumar of Wick, is noted in the Exch Rolls in 1429 for hides custumed by him at Wick, and re-entered at Aberdeen

PAGE 127.—Si Alex McCulloch of Mirtone, knight, first (chief) falconer of the King going to Orkney for falcons, was married to Marjory Sinclair Charter, 17th February, 1499

PAGE 311.—Blans George Sinclair in 1455 received £13 6s 8d from the Customs of Haddington, and in 1461 had sasine , in 1473 Edward Sinclair is of Blans , in 1491 George de Sancto Claro , in 1513 John Sinclair, who is a witness in 1531 , 1575-1590 David Sinclair is of Blans , and on 16th April, 1605, there is caution in £1000 for Wm Sinclair of Blans

PAGE 311.—Gosfurd Thos Sinclair witness, 1463 , receives, 1464, repayment from Queen of £100 money lent, in 1465 receives fermes of the County of March , in 1474 has charter of Gosfurd and pertinents subject to 24 marks, annual rent, has confirmation 28th January, 1458-59, to him and his spouse Mirabelle Dalrymple In 1506 John Sinclair has sasine, and is in 1507-10 chamberlain of the lordship of Ballincrief and Gosfurd Ballincrief in 1471 was tenanted by William Sinclair, in 1508 by James Sinclar , in 1569, John, son to William Sinclair in Gosfuirde , in 1582, Alexander, son to the late William Sinclair of Gosfurd, and John, son to Alexander in Ballincrief are cited to appear

In 1513 William Sinclare in Morham is vice comes in hac parte, viz , Edinburgh infra Haddington, also for Roxburgh, Selkirk, Linlithgow, and Berwick

Adam Sinclar de Fynlark, 1438 , John Sinclere is de Finlarge, 1498, George de St Clair of Hume, 1439 , William Sinclare de Northrig, 1497 , quondam Archibald Sinclar de Westhall, 1503, Andrew Sincler (de Sco Claro), Vicar of Lagan and Notary Public 1500, in 1527 and 1529 is Canon of Ross , Mariote Sinclere notar, In oti pruatius Sethi, and David Carruthers her spouse, 1512 Dominus

Patrick Sinclare, Rector of Auldehamstokis, 1450, William Sinclair of Auchinfrankach, 1501, John Sinclare of Auchingilbert, 1515, William Sinclair of Fynlarg in Forfar, royal charter in 1529, charter to Edward Sinclair of Galvelmoir in Perth, 1528-29, confirmation to him and Elizabeth Lytill his spouse, 1544-45, charter to Jas Sinclair and Isabelle Inglis his spouse, of Murdocarny in Fife, 1529, *Dominus* Adam Sinclair, prebendary of Crichton 1543, D Thos Synclare, *capellanus* witness, 1449, D George Sinclare, rector de Polwarth, 1536, John Sinclair, rector of Comry, 1533, D Stephen Sinclare, vicar de Aberfule, 1543, the king confirms in 1495 the charter of William Sinclair, Lord of Auchingibbert, to his nephew Richard, with reservation of a third to Margaret Gladstainys, wife of granter, &c, &c &c

George Seintcler received safe conduct to England, 23rd March, 1424

Alexander Sinclere received passport to England, 25th February, 1425-26

Earlston This was bought in 1472 by a younger son of Sir John St Clair of Herdmanston from Sir Patrick Hepburn of Hailes In 1541 John Sinclair is of Erlistoun (Ex Rolls), he married Janet, daughter of John Gordon of Troquhain, and was succeeded by a son John, who married Catherine, daughter of John Glendinning of Drumrash, and had two daughters (1) Margaret, married, 1582, to John Gordon of Airds, whose issue succeeded, and (2) Rosina, married to John Stewart of Ardoch George Sinclair, son of, and brother of the late John Sinclair of Earlston, is noted in 1590 John Sinclair had a son accidentally drowned, and a natural son also named John, afterwards legitimated but excluded from the succession He was an officer in Lord Kenmure's troop of horse at Killiecrankie and from him lineally descended William Sinclair, who held farms on the Kenmure estate The devotion of Robert Sinclair to Viscount Kenmure is well known His mother, Annie Gordon, was of near kin to the Viscount Robert was grandfather of John Sinclair, farmer, who died at New Galloway in 1813 or 1814, leaving sons and daughters His grandsons, William and Robert, left only daughters, and his grandson, John Sinclair, had by his wife, Mary Jane Sadler, daughter of a Bristol merchant, John Sinclair, architect, in Western Australia , Robert Sinclair, auctioneer, Toowoomba ; and David Dalrymple Sinclair, law student in Western Australia About a hundred years ago a seal was found in the garden of Earlstoun bearing the arms of Sinclair and having this legend, "Sigillum Barones Baroniæ De Earlstoun"

The Sinclairs of Kellister and Snarness, a small estate on the shores of St Magnus Bay, Shetland, have a tradition that their forbears escaped from Castles Girnigo and Sinclair by cutting their way from the dungeon floor to the sea, and then fleeing to the Orkneys The old deed of land situated in Sinclair Bay was in their possession in 1854 (letter from Robert Sinclair of Gympie, Queensland, a member of this family)

ECCLESIÆ SCOTICANÆ.—These ministers have brief notices *Morton*, 1640—Adam Sinclair, A M , Edinburgh, died 1673, aged 71 *Lochrutton*, etc —Archibald Sinclair, 1572—1615 , his son Archibald died 19th June, 1620 *Langton*—Samuel Sinclair, A M , died 1653, aged about 74, left a son Robert *Boukle* and *Preston*—William Sinclair, 1574—1616 *Bolton*, 1692—John Sinclair, grad Edin , 1675, died 28th February, 1707, married Eupham Reid, issue, five sons, five daughters *Spott*—Robert Sinclair, A M , Edinburgh, 1656, died 1688, aged 52 , married, 1666, Jean Clelaine, nieces Maria and Jean served heirs *Kirkmahoe*—John Sinclair, 1576-79 *Whittingham*—Thos Sinclair, 1734 *Balfron*—Geo Sinclair, died 1759 , Jeane Baine, his widow, 1784 *Madderty*—Robert Sinclair, A M , Edinburgh, flourished 1578—1607 *Northmaven*, 1662—Hercules Sinclair, A M , St Andrews, 25th July, 1657

SCOTTISH MEN-AT-ARMS IN FRANCE —1469, Jas Cinclar the elder, and Jas Cinclar the younger, Thos Cinclar, Joe Cinclar , 1494-97, Adam Sainct Cler , 1496, James Saint Cler, 1498-99, Alexandre St Cler, 1505-7, James Sancler , 1507, Georges de Saint Cler, 1550, Jourdain Gresinclar, 1554, Jehan de St Clere , 1473—1504, Guill Singlar , 1485-94, Georges Singler , 1487-94, Robin Sinclar, 1509-11, James Sinclar, 1509-15, Patrix Sinklar , 1523, Guillaume de St Cler, to 1553, and Jehan to 1568 , 1527, Jacques St Clar, to 1557 , 1543 Robert de St Cler, to 1561 , 1587, James St Clair These were chiefly "Archiers de la garde du Roi"

The title of Oldenburg attached to the Danish royal family has by some means got transferred to the Sinclairs The error probably originates through Sir James Balfour misreading a reference in Latin to Henry I , Earl of Orkney, in this manner "He was created by Christian I of Denmark, Duke of Oldenburgh, Earl of Orkney," to mean that the Earl of Orkney was also created Duke of Oldenburg The error is of the die-hard species, and should easily be run to earth

PAGE 63 — Examine the account of the Haconian expedition for the possibility of Orcadian names

PAGE 325.—Captain John St Clair died at Mountmellick, Ireland, in 1784. His will was proved in Dublin the same year. He had been an officer in the 17th Light Dragoons, and had served with his regiment in the American War. He had a son James, who was a boy at the time of his father's death, and who subsequently became an officer in the 1st Royals, which, from the army lists of that period, would appear to have hardly ever been without one or more of the name amongst its officers (Notes and Queries, 8th Series).

PAGE 196.—The continual contention between the leading families in Scottish Orcadia is well exemplified in the still current couplet

"Sinclair and Sutherland, Keith and Clan Gunn,
There never was peace where these four were in"

The reference is to the Earls of Sutherland, and not to the family, which is found to be always at amity with the Sinclairs.

PAGE 101.—The right to coin money was never exercised by any of the Orcadian Earls, nor can any Orcadian coins be found in the numismatic collections of Scandinavia.

PAGE 50.—Taken in a geographical sense, St Magnus was the last Scottish saint.

Orkney and Shetland have supplied a larger number of occupants of professorial chairs in Scotland than any other county of the same size and population.

REGISTERS

ORKNEY *

	Births	Marriages	Deaths
Birsay	begins 1631	1631	—
Cross and Burness	1711	1711	—
Deerness	1753	1753	—
Evie	1725	1725	—
Evie and Rendall	1802	1802	1816
Firth and Stenness	1732	1732	1746
Harray	1784	—	—
Holme and Paplay	1654	1654	—
Hoy and Græmsay	1799	1799	—
Kirkwall and St Ola	1657	1657	—
Orphir	1711	1718	1817
Ronsay and Eagleshay	1733	1733	—
St Andrews	1657	1657	—
Sandwick	1728	1727	—
Shapinsay	1632	1631	1793
South Ronaldsay and Burray	1749	1764	—
Stromness	1695	1695	1763
Stronsay	1743	1801	1801
Westray	1733	1784	—
Eday and Lady made no return	—	—	—

SHETLAND *

Delting	1751	1751	—
Fetlar and Northyell	1754	—	—
Lerwick	1704	—	—
Sandsting and Aithsting	1733	—	—
Unst	1776	—	—
Yell	1723	1800	1740
Dunrossness	1746	1746	—

Delting, Nesting, and Northmaving, are not made clear   No returns made from Bressay, Burra, and Quarff, Tingwall, Whiteness, and Weesdale, or Walls

CAITHNESS *

Bower	—	—	—
Canisbay	1651	1706	—
Dunnett	—	—	—
Halkirk	1790	—	—
Latheron	1740	1755	—
Olrick	1700	—	—
Reay	1745	—	—
Thurso	1648	—	—
Watten	1701	1714	—
Wick	1701	1703	—

*Turnbull's Parochial Registers of Scotland, 1849

REGISTERS

PARTICULAR REGISTER OF SASINES—

CAITHNESS
I (1) 1646-1674, (2) 1658-1661 II 1675-1869

ORKNEY AND ZETLAND
I (1) Orkney 1617-1626,   (2) Zetland 1623-1672
    and 1634-1656
II (1) Orkney and Zetland combined, 1661-1752
   (2) Orkney, 1753-1869, gap from 21st November, 1765, to 1st September, 1767
   (3) Zetland, 1744-1869

GENERAL REGISTER OF SASINES—

    1869, Orkney, Shetland, and Caithness

TESTAMENTS
Caithness 1661, Orkney and Zetland 1611, and deeds 1644

Retours, or Inquisitiones post mortem commence in 1545 and continue to the present day. They are equivalent to service of heir to property of a deceased landowner.

AUTHORITIES AND AIDS

ANDERSON, Joseph, LL D , Keeper of the National Museum, Edinburgh — "Introduction to Orkneyinga Saga"

BALFOUR, David, of Balfour and Trenaby —"Odal Rights and Feudal Wrongs A Memorial for Orkney" Edinburgh, 1859

BARRY, The Rev George, D D —" History of the Orkney Islands" (Edinburgh, 1805) , with Notes by the Rev James Headrick Edinburgh, 1808, 4to 3rd edition, Kirkwall, 1867

BELLENDEN, John —" Descriptio Insularum Orchadiarum, per me, Jo Ben, Ibidem Colentem, in Anno, 1529" (Appendix to Barry's History)

BRAND, The Rev John — 'A Brief Description of Orkney, Zetland, Pightland Firth, and Caithness" Edinburgh, 1701, 8vo

BURKE C B , LL D , Sir Bernard — "A Genealogical and Heraldic Dictionary of the Peerage and Baronetage London. 1884

CALDER, James Trail —"Sketch of the Civil and Traditional History of Caithness from the Tenth Century" Second edition, Wick, 1887

CLOUSTON, M D , The Rev Charles —" Guide to the Orkney Islands " Edinburgh, 1862, 8vo

CRAVEN, The Rev J B —" History of the Episcopal Church in Orkney, 1688—1882, 1662—1688, and 1558—1662 " Kirkwall, 1883, 1893, and 1897

CURSITER, James W , F S A , Scot —List of Books and Pamphlets relating to Orkney and Shetland Kirkwall, 1894

DENNISON, Walter Traill —" The Orcadian Sketch book Being Traits of Old Orkney Life, written partly in the Orkney dialect" Kirkwall, 1880, 8vo

DICTIONARY OF NATIONAL BIOGRAPHY, vol lii Edited by Sidney Lee, London, 1897 Articles ' Sinclair "

EDMONDSTON, Thomas —" An Etymological Glossary of the Shetland and Orkney Dialect " Edinburgh, 1866, 8vo

GIFFORD, Thomas, of Busta —An Historical Description of the Zetland Islands in the year 1733" Edinburgh, 1879, 8vo

GORRIE, Daniel —" Summers and Winters in the Orkneys" London, 1868

GRANT, Francis J , W S (Carrick Pursuivant of Arms) —"Zetland County Families" Lerwick, 1893

HAY —Richard Augustin, Prior of St Pieremont —" Genealogie of the Sainteclaires of Rosslyn, including the Chartulary of Rosslyn" Edited by James Maidment Edinburgh, 1835

HENDERSON, JOHN, W S —" Caithness Family History " Edinburgh, 1884

HIBBERT, Samuel, M D —" A Description of the Shetland Isles " Edinburgh and London, 1862, 4to

JAMIESON, John —" An Etymological Dictionary of the Scottish Language," 2 vols Edinburgh, 1808, 4to Two Supplemental vols , 1825 Second edition, revised, &c , 4 vols Paisley, 1879-82, 4to

JOHNSON, The Rev A H , M A —"The Normans in Europe" (Epoch series) London, 1877

KELTIE, J S —" History of the Scottish Clans" Edinburgh, 1885

LAING the Elder, Samuel —" Sturleson s Heimskringla Translated from the Icelandic," 3 vols 1844, 8vo

LOW, George —" Tour through the Islands of Orkney and Shetland in 1774 " Kirkwall, 1879, 8vo

MACKENZIE, James —"The General Grievances and Oppressions of the Isles of Orkney and Shetland " Reprint Edinburgh, 1836, 8vo

MAXWELL, C H —" Historical Tales of the Wars of Scotland" cited as "Scotish Wars " Edinburgh, 1852

MICHELL, Thos , C B — ' History of the Scottish Expedition to Norway in 1612 " Christiania, 1886

MORRISON, The Hon Leonard Allison, A M —" History of the Sinclair Family in Europe and America for 1,100 Years " Boston, Mass , 1896

NISBET, Alexander —"A System of Heraldry, Speculative and Practical," 2 vols Edinburgh, 1722—1742, folio

ORKNEYINGA SAGA Translated from the Icelandic by Jon A Hjaltalin and Gilbert Goudie Edited by Dr Anderson Edinburgh, 1873, 8vo

AUTHORITIES AND AIDS.

ORKNEYINGA SAGA and Magnus Saga with Appendices. Edited by Gudbrand Vigfusson, M.A. Icelandic Text; Rolls edition. London, 1887.
ORKNEYINGERS' SAGA (Rolls edition). Translation of preceding by Sir G. W. Dasent, D.C.L. London, 1884.
PETERKIN, Alexander.—"Rentals of the Ancient Earldom and Bishopric of Orkney." Edinburgh, 1890.
PETERKIN, Alexander.—"Notes on Orkney and Zetland." Edinburgh, 1822, 8vo.
SCOTTISH ANTIQUARY, The.—A quarterly magazine, price 1s. Edinburgh.
SCOTT, The Rev. Hugh, D.D.—"Fasti Ecclesiæ Scoticanæ; or, the Succession of the Ministers in the Parish Churches of Scotland from 1560 to the Present Time." Edinburgh, 1870, 4to.
SIBBALD, Sir Robert, Knt., M.D.—"Description of the Islands of Orkney and Zetland, by Robert Monteith, of Egilsea and Gairsay, 1633." Edinburgh, 1845, 8vo.
SINCLAIR, Thos., M.A.—"Caithness Events." Wick, 1894.
SINCLAIR, Thomas, M.A.—"The Sinclairs of England." London, 1887.
SKENE, William Forbes.—"Celtic Scotland," 3 vols. Edinburgh, 1876-80, 8vo.
SMITH, William Henry.—"The St. Clair Papers: The Life and Public Services of Arthur St. Clair, Soldier of the Revolutionary War, President of the Continental Congress, and Governor of the North-Western Territory." Cincinnati, U.S.A., 1882.
TORFÆUS, Thormodeus.—"Ancient History of Orkney, Caithness, and the North." Translated by Alexander Pope, Minister of Reay. Wick, 1866, 12mo.
TUDOR, John R.—"The Orkneys and Shetland: their Past and Present State." London, 1883.
TYTLER, Patrick Fraser.—"History of Scotland," 4 vols. Edinburgh, 1864.
WALLACE, James, M.D., F.R.S.—"An Account of the Islands of Orkney." London, 1700, 8vo.
ZENO the Younger, Nicolo.—"The Discovery of the Islands of Frislanda, Eslanda, Engronelanda, Estotilanda, and Icaria, made by two brothers of the Zeno family: viz., Messire Nicolo, the Chevalier, and Messire Antonio." With a map of the said Islands. Venice, 1558. Translated, London, 1873, by R. H. Major, F.S.A., &c., for the Hakluyt Society.

CONCLUSION

'The Earldom of Orkney and Lordship of Shetland combined has come down through all the ages as a distinct and determinate *corpus*. It is otherwise with the Scottish Maormordoms and Thanages, which can now be recognised only as traditional and undeterminate, in respect both of their extent and their revenues. It is this living permanence, so indissolubly and so largely mixed up with the history of the islands, that gives to the Earldom its abiding interest, and renders the investigation of its records from age to age important in the study of Orkney and Shetland history.'*

"No family in Europe beneath the rank of royalty boasts a higher antiquity, a nobler illustration, or a more romantic interest than that of St Clair. Cradled in the baronial castle whose towers crown the brink of the most precipitous and wooded glen in the Lothians, and buried under the florid arches of the richly decorated chapel which crowns the adjacent bank, the Lords of Roslyn made Scotland ring with the renown of their deeds, which needed not to be enhanced by romance and poetry—for both are outdone by the vicissitudes of their fortunes."†

From the preceding citations it will be readily recognised that this work on the "Sea-Kings of Orkney" and the "St Clair Lineage" can only serve as a fore-runner to the many volumes required for the more complete elucidation of material available in so extensive a field of research. The documents in the Diplomatarium Norvegicum, in the Vatican Records, and in the Scottish, English, and French national repositories, relating to the earlier history of Orcadia, remain unpublished, and what is worse still, *uncalendared*, while no attempt has as yet been made to grapple with the enormous amount of information lying hidden in the Particular Register of Sasines, the Retours of Heirs, the Wills and Testaments, and the numerous Parochial Registers, and there are of course many other supplemental sources.

A Scottish Record Society has recently been formed, and in due course its operations will arrive at the Orcadian section. This might be greatly expedited by Orcadian support, nor should the interest be limited to those resident in North Britain, as there are now more Orcadians abroad than at Home. Many are to be found in Canada, in the United States, in Australia, and in New Zealand. The Sinclairs and St Clairs in New Zealand alone number about 1,000 out of a total population of some 650,000 Europeans and 50,000 *indigènes*.

The author will be glad to receive communications having reference to Orcadia or the St Clairs.

ROLAND S₁ CLAIR

Auckland, N Z,
16th April, 1898

---

* Goudie   † Burke

LIST OF SUBSCRIBERS

(Prior to Issue)

Allan, A A , (Pres O and S Society), Bay Street, Toronto
Auckland Swimming Club
Auckland Free Public Library
Auckland University College
Balfour, St Clair, Hamilton, Ontario
Beatton, James, P O. Augusta, South Australia
Christiania University, Library of, Norway
Clouston, Dr T S , M D Royal Edinburgh Asylum, Morningside, Scotland
Douglas & Foulis, No 9, Castle Street, Edinburgh
Douglas & Foulis, No 9, Castle Street, Edinburgh
Douglas & Foulis, No 9, Castle Street, Edinburgh
Drever, W B , Solicitor, Kirkwall, Orkney
Dulau & Co , 37 Soho Square, London
Edinburgh Public Library, Edinburgh
Flaws & Son, R , Manchester Buildings, Melinda Street, Toronto
Fotheringham, Rev T F , St John s, New Brunswick
Gellibrand, Thos , Auckland, N Z
Gordon & Gotch, Melbourne
Goudie, Gilbert, 37 Northumberland Street, Edinburgh
Gray, Wm , (Cook & Gray), Auckland
Hall, J W , Merchant, Auckland, N Z
Johnston, Alfred W , Imperial Institute, London, S W
Leask, Dr , Mount Farquhar, Sepoy Lines, Singapore
Mackenzie, W Dalgleish, of Farr, Inverness
Menzies & Co , John 12, Hanover St , Edinburgh, per Simpkin, Marshall, Hamilton, Kent & Co
Mitchell Library, The, 21 Miller Street, Glasgow
Mitchell Library, The, 21 Miller Street, Glasgow
Mowat, Daniel, 93 Stanford Hill London, N
Mowat, Daniel, 93 Stanford Hill, London N (2nd copy)
Myers, Leo M , Director Campbell-Fhrenfried Co , Auckland N Z
Nutt, David, 270 Strand, London
Ottawa Parliamentary Library, Ottawa, Canada
Peace, W G , Solicitor, Grantown, Strathspey, Scotland
Redkey, Mrs Nancy St Clair, Rainsboro, Highland Co , Ohio
Rendall, J H , Old Blythesdale, S & W R , W Queensland
Samson and Wallin, Booksellers, Stockholm, Sweden
Shaw, J R , Hunter Street, Stockton, Cal
Sievewright, Basil, Solicitor, Dunedin, N Z
Stout, Sir Robert, K C M G , Wellington, N Z
Stout, Sir Robert, K C M G , Wellington
Sutherland, Mrs , Kaneira, via Wycheproof, Victoria
Sydney Public Library, New South Wales
Toronto Public Library, Toronto, Canada
Trail, John Arbuthnott, LL B , W S , 17 Duke Street, Edinburgh
Viking Club The, 17 Grosvenor Road, Westminster
Warren, Rev C F S , Coventry, England
Wigg & Son, E S (Perth Library), Hay Street, Perth, W A
St Clair, Albert M , Leland, Miss U S A
St Clair, Ashley, Calais, Me , U S A
St Clair

LIST OF SUBSCRIBERS

St Clair, W Græme, Editor Free Press, Singapore
Sinckler, E G , J P , &c , Stirling, Belleville, St Michael's, Barbadoes, West Indies
Sinckler, E G , Barbadoes (2nd copy)
Sinclaire, Henry P , Corning, N Y , U S A
Sinclaire, Richard Ker, Auckland City , N Z
Sinclair, Andrew, "Kuranui," Symonds Street, Auckland, N Z
Sinclair, Count James Henry, Lambahof, Linkoping, Sweden
Sinclair, David, 353 Great Horton Road, Bradford, U K
Sinclair, David, Springlands, Blenheim
Sinclair, Dr James Edward, 1 Queen Anne's Gate, S W
Sinclair, D P , Solicitor, Blenheim
Sinclair, H Herr, Count, Mjolby, Sweden
Sinclair, Francis, of Honolulu, Berkeley, California
Sinclair, Geo F , G R Brass Co , Gran Rapids, Mich
Sinclair, Geo , No 161, Queen Street, Auckland, N Z
Sinclair, James, c/o Macrae and Robertson, solicitors, Kirkwall, Orkney
Sinclair, James, Senr , Dumbarton, Newcastle, W A
Sinclair, James Sutherland, The Right Hon the Earl of Caithness, Lakota, N Dak
Sinclair, James J , 115 Durham Street, Christchurch, N Z
Sinclair, James J , 115 Durham Street, Christchurch, N Z
Sinclair, Jessie, Miss, Esperance, W A
Sinclair, John Clyde Street, Invercargill
Sinclair John S , Rev , Arundel House, Fulham, London, S W
Sinclair, John R G , Sir, Barrock House, Wick, N B
Sinclair, John G Tollemache, Sir, Thurso Castle, N B
Sinclair, John G , The Hon , Orlando, Fla , U S A
Sinclair, J P , Swanson, N Z
Sinclair, Junr , Arthur, 366 Washington Street, Boston, Mass
Sinclair, Lord, The Rt Hon , 55 Onslow Square, London, S W
Sinclair, Mrs H A , West Lebanon, N H , U S A
Sinclair, Rev A Maclean, Belfast, Prince Edward Island
Sinclair, Robert, Lands Registry Office, Dunedin
Sinclair, Robert, Hilton Road, Gympie, Queensland
Sinclair, Robert, Toowoomba, Queensland
Sinclair, Robert, Waipawa, N Z
Sinclair, Russell, A M P Buildings, Brisbane
Sinclair, S G , 1 Sunnyside, Devonshire Road, Liverpool
Sinclair, S G , Prince Park, Liverpool
Sinclair, The Hon Norman, Master of Caithness, 38 Bedford Row, E C
Sinclair, The Hon Chas A , 17 State Street, Boston, Mass
Sinclair, Thos , M A , Belgrave Lodge, Torquay, England
Sinclair, Thos , Stockman's Lane, Upper Falls, Belfast, Ireland
Sinclair, W M , The Ven Arch , St Paul's Cathedral, London
Sinclair Wm , "Rosslyn," Lisburn, Antrim, Ireland
Sinclair, W J L , Coolgardie, West Australia
Sinclair, Wm , Solicitor, Blenheim

Printed in the USA
CPSIA information can be obtained
at www.ICGtesting.com
LVHW022252220923
758653LV00007B/199